The SAGE Handbook of Applied Social Psychology

REVIEWERS

John Berry, Queen's University, Canada
Mary Breheny, Massey University, New Zealand
Alexander Bridger, University of Huddersfield, United Kingdom
Peter Branney, University of Bradford, United Kingdom
Stuart Carr, Massey University, New Zealand
Donatienne Desmette, Université catholique de Louvain, Belgium
David Fryer, University of South Africa, South Africa
Allison Harell, Université du Québec à Montréal, Canada
Elsie Ho, The University of Auckland, New Zealand
Wendy Li, James Cook University, Australia
James liu, Massey University, New Zealand
Malcolm MacLachlan, Trinity College, Ireland
Jeanne Marecek, Swarthmore College, United States
Maritza Montero, Universidad Central de Venezuela, Venezuela
Mandy Morgan, Massey University, New Zealand
Deirdre O'Shea, University of Limerick, Ireland
Chris Sonn, Victoria University, Australia
Ottilie Stolte, University of Waikato, New Zealand
Thomas Teo, York University, Canada
Ellen van der Werff, University of Groningen, Netherlands

The SAGE Handbook of Applied Social Psychology

Edited by
Kieran C. O'Doherty and
Darrin Hodgetts

SAGE reference
Los Angeles | London | New Delhi | Singapore | Washington DC | Melbourne

SAGE

Los Angeles | London | New Delhi
Singapore | Washington DC | Melbourne

SAGE Publications Ltd
1 Oliver's Yard
55 City Road
London EC1Y 1SP

SAGE Publications Inc.
2455 Teller Road
Thousand Oaks, California 91320

SAGE Publications India Pvt Ltd
B 1/I 1 Mohan Cooperative Industrial Area
Mathura Road
New Delhi 110 044

SAGE Publications Asia-Pacific Pte Ltd
3 Church Street
#10-04 Samsung Hub
Singapore 049483

Editor: Becky Taylor
Editorial Assistant: Colette Wilson
Production Editor: Anwesha Roy
Copyeditor: Sunrise Setting Ltd.
Proofreader: David Hemsley
Indexer: Cathryn Pritchard
Marketing Manager: Lucia Sweet
Cover Design: Bhairvi Gudka
Typeset by: Cenveo Publisher Services
Printed in the UK

Library of Congress Control Number: 2018944682

British Library Cataloguing in Publication data

A catalogue record for this book is available from the British Library

ISBN 978-1-4739-6926-1

Contents

List of Figures, Tables and Boxes

FIGURES

TABLES

BOXES

Notes on the Editors and Contributors

THE EDITORS

Kieran C. O'Doherty is an Associate Professor in applied social psychology at the University of Guelph, and director of the Discourse, Science, Publics research group. His current research focuses on the use of deliberative methods on diverse social issues, health psychology, and investigation of the broader social, psychological, and ethical implications of science and technologies. O'Doherty has designed and implemented several deliberative public engagements on controversial areas of science and technology. He has also published widely on theory and practice of public deliberation as a mechanism to inform policy. Other contributions to the academic literature and practice include analyses of the meaning of genetic risk in genetic counselling sessions, ethical implications of involving children in biomedical research, and the development of theory and methodology to involve lay publics in the governance of biobanks. Current and previous funding sources include the Canadian Institutes of Health Research, The Office of the Privacy Commissioner of Canada, the Ontario Ministry of Research & Innovation, Genome Canada, and Genome British Columbia. O'Doherty is currently editor of the journal *Theory & Psychology*.

Darrin Hodgetts is Professor of Societal Psychology at Massey University New Zealand, where he teaches applied social and health psychology. Before taking up his current post, Darrin held positions in Community Medicine at Memorial University in Canada, Social Psychology and Media at the London School of Economics and Political Sciences in England, and Community Psychology at the University of Waikato in New Zealand. Darrin is a review editor for the *Journal of Community and Applied Social Psychology* and an Associate editor for *Sage Communication*. His recent books include the *Social Psychology of Everyday Life* and *Asia-Pacific Perspectives in Intercultural Psychology*. Darrin's primary areas of research are societal and health inequalities, urban poverty and homelessness. He has been involved in a range of projects designing services to address issues of urban poverty, food insecurity and homelessness. Darrin is also the co-initiator and coordinator for the Global Living Organisational Wage (GLOW) network in psychology which is a scholarly cooperative with hubs across four continents (http://www.massey.ac.nz/massey/learning/departments/school-of-psychology/research/project-glow/project-glow_home.cfm).

THE CONTRIBUTORS

Michael Adams (Uncle Mick to most) is a descendent of the Yadhiagana/Wuthathi peoples of Cape York Peninsula in Queensland and of the Gurindji people of Central Western Northern Territory. He is a Senior Research Fellow at the Australian Indigenous HealthInfoNet, Edith

Cowan University. He is nationally and internationally recognised for his active involvement in addressing issues associated with the health and wellbeing of Indigenous males.

Stefan Agrigoroaei is an Associate Professor in psychology and ageing at the Université catholique de Louvain (UCLouvain). He approaches his research with an interdisciplinary and lifespan perspective. His general research program is in the area of health and ageing, with a focus on the contribution of psychosocial (e.g., sources of disparities, control beliefs), behavioural (e.g., physical and cognitive activities) and stress-related factors (e.g., cortisol response) for optimising and maintaining good cognitive and physical health as people age. His projects involve a wide range of cognitive and physical health assessments, including biomedical indicators, in both surveys and laboratory settings.

Fabiana Alceste is a PhD student at John Jay College of Criminal Justice and the CUNY Graduate Center. Interested in the psychology of police interrogations and confessions, she has published research on the psychological state of police custody; the process by which accurate, non-public details contaminate false confessions; and a survey of opinions of confession experts all over the world. She is a member of the American Psychology-Law Society, is an active member of her student government, and a professor of undergraduate psychology. She has trained in the two most common specialised interview and interrogation techniques in the United States.

Louise R. Alexitch is an Associate Professor in the Department of Psychology at the University of Saskatchewan (Saskatchewan, Canada). She earned her doctorate in Applied Social Psychology at the University of Windsor (Ontario, Canada) and has published in the areas of achievement motivation, academic advising and help-seeking behaviours in post-secondary students. For the last 10 years, she has conducted research in the academic adjustment, persistence and sense of belonging of ethnic minority students. In addition, she has been involved in the development and evaluation of academic programmes designed to increase the success of Canadian Indigenous university students. Her work appears in such journals as the *Journal of College Student Development*, *Canadian Journal of Higher Education* and *Journal of American Indian Education.* She is currently the Coordinator of the Culture, Health and Human Development graduate programme and Chair of Undergraduate Programmes in the Department of Psychology.

Aria Amrom is a PhD student at John Jay College of Criminal Justice and the CUNY Graduate Center. Interested in the psychology of police interrogations and confessions, she has conducted research on the effect of confession evidence on character witnesses and juror decision-making. She has also examined the impact of video recording police interrogations on the behaviour of suspects. She is a member of the American Psychology-Law Society and a teaching assistant for undergraduate psychology courses.

Eleni Andreouli is Senior Lecturer in Psychology at the Open University, UK. She completed her doctoral and postdoctoral research at the London School of Economics. Her research interests are in the social psychology of citizenship, immigration, and identity in diverse societies. She has published widely in these subjects and is co-editor of *The Cambridge Handbook of Social Representations* (Cambridge University Press) and *The Social Psychology of Everyday Politics* (Routledge).

Alma Au works as Associate Professor at the Department of Applied Social Sciences and the Research Co-ordinator of the Institute of Active Ageing at the Hong Kong Polytechnic University. She is a Fellow of the Hong Kong Psychological Society. She has obtained a number of grants, both from both government and non-government organisations, and has published various papers on caregiving, developing sustainable models of health care, and productive ageing in the context of inter-generational relationships.

Paula C. Barata is an Associate Professor in the Department of Psychology (Applied Social Stream) at the University of Guelph. Her research is explicitly feminist, has largely focused on violence against women, and has always had an applied bend. She has examined women's experiences with the criminal justice system, minority women's definitions of abuse, housing discrimination against survivors, and housing programmes for women who have experienced abuse. More recently, she has collaborated on a successful multi-site randomised clinical trial evaluating the effectiveness of a sexual assault resistance programme, and she continues to work on the wider implementation of the programme. Currently, she is also working with a community partner on a programme for pre-schoolers who have witnessed violence against their mothers.

R. Thomas Beggs has a master's degree from the University of British Columbia and is completing his PhD at the University of Guelph. His research focuses on health and social psychology, including topics such as perceptions of social support in chronic pain patients and the use of yoga for non-specific low back pain. His thesis research investigates the association between the perceived descriptive and injunctive norms of various reference groups and vaccination hesitancy and intentions among first-time expecting parents. He is also interested in program evaluation and has completed several evaluations during the course of his degree.

Mary Breheny is a Senior Lecturer in Public Health at Massey University and member of the Health and Ageing Research Team. Her research focuses on the ways that inequalities throughout the lifespan accumulate in later life and constrain older people from ageing well. She is the co-author of *Healthy Ageing: A Capability Approach to Inclusive Policy and Practice* for the Routledge book series *Critical Approaches to Health* with Christine Stephens.

Alexander J. Bridger is a Senior Lecturer in Psychology at the University of Huddersfield. His teaching and research interests include psychogeography, critical social psychology, and qualitative approaches such as psychoanalysis and discourse analysis. He is also a co-organiser for the 4th annual World Congress of Psychogeography.

Stuart C. Carr is Professor of Psychology, Industrial/Organizational Psychology Programme, Massey University, NZ. He co-coordinates the End Poverty and Inequality Cluster (EPIC), which includes transitions from precarious labour to decent work and living wages. He coordinates Project G.L.O.W. (for Global Living Organizational Wage), a multi-country, multi-generational, interdisciplinary study of links between decent wages and sustainable livelihoods for the eradication of poverty – UN Sustainable Development Goal (SDG1). Stuart co-convened a *Global Task Force for Humanitarian Work Psychology*, promoting Decent Work aligned with local stakeholder needs, in partnership with global development agencies. He was a lead investigator on Project ADDUP, a multi-country DFID/ESRC-funded study of pay/remuneration diversity between national and international labour in low-income economies. Stuart is a

Fellow of the Royal Society of New Zealand, Society for Industrial and Organizational Psychology, New Zealand Psychological Society. He edits *International Perspectives in Psychology: Research, Practice, Consultation*, which supports the SDGs.

Kerry Chamberlain is a Professor of Social and Health Psychology at Massey University, New Zealand. He is the co-editor of *Qualitative Health Psychology: Theories and Methods* (Sage; with Michael Murray), co-editor of *Existential Meaning: Optimizing Human Development Across the Life Span* (Sage; with Gary Reker) and co-author of *Health Psychology: A Critical Introduction* (Cambridge; with Antonia Lyons), and co-editor (with Antonia Lyons) of the Routledge book series *Critical Approaches to Health*, and has published widely on health psychology and methodology in international peer-reviewed journals and in book chapters. His research interests focus on health in everyday life, with a particular interest in food, materiality, media, medications and minor illness, and the use of innovative qualitative methods. He is a founding member of the *International Society for Critical Health Psychology*.

Leigh Coombes is a Senior Lecturer in the School of Psychology, Massey University. Her research focuses on issues of gender and violence with special attention to the historical, social, and cultural conditions of gender and the effects of colonisation on particular communities. She uses innovative qualitative methodologies to ask new questions of wicked problems that enable understandings of lived experiences of gendered psychological wellbeing with a particular focus on how the systematic marginalisation of women informs interventions into domestic violence. Promoting knowledge of gender-related issues within community collaborations is prioritised so that the issues of service delivery can meet contemporary demands. She is a member of a collaboration that teaches applied social and community psychology with a focus on social justice.

Homero Gil de Zúñiga has a PhD in Politics from the Universidad Europea de Madrid and PhD in Mass Communication from the University of Wisconsin–Madison, holds the Medienwandel Professorship at University of Vienna, where he directs the Media Innovation Lab (MiLab). Prior to joining Vienna, he participated in the summer doctoral programme at the Oxford Internet Institute, after which he was appointed Nieman Journalism Lab Research Fellow at Harvard. He was formerly Associate Professor at University of Texas–Austin. Presently, he serves as Research Fellow at the Universidad Diego Portales and the Center for Information Technology Policy at Princeton University. His research addresses the influence of new technologies and digital media over people's daily lives and the impact of its use on the overall democratic process. He has published several books, book chapters, and over 60 articles in journals such as *Journal of Communication*, *Communication Research*, *Journal of Computer-Mediated Communication*, *Human Communication Research*, etc.

Stephanie Denne is a Lecturer in the School of Psychology, Massey University, working as part of a collaborative team invested in exploring issues of power, social justice, and ethical integrity within psychological research, teaching, and practice. She has been involved in the curriculum development and teaching of a range of courses in applied community and social psychology, including forensic psychology. Her research interests lie in the exploration of the complexities of lived experiences for those marginalised within our communities, particularly in relation to domestic and gendered violence.

Donatienne Desmette is a Professor of social and work psychology at the Université catholique de Louvain (UCLouvain), Belgium. Her research interests are concerned with ageism in the workplace, management of age diversity, older workers' wellbeing, and retirement. She has published in international journals in social and organisational psychology as well as in psychology of ageing (e.g., *Basic and Applied Social Psychology*; *European Journal of Work and Organizational Psychology*; *Work, Aging and Retirement*).

Trevor Diehl is a doctoral student and instructor at the Department of Communication at the University of Vienna, Austria. He previously worked as a research assistant at the Annette Strauss Institute for Civic Life in Austin, Texas. He currently teaches courses in research methods and communication theory. His research interests include the role of social media in politics and populist movements, journalism practice, and science communication.

Neil Drew is Director of the Australia Indigenous HealthInfoNet. Neil has over 30 years' experience working with a diverse range of Aboriginal and Torres Strait Islander communities and groups throughout Australia. He was the programme head and cofounder of the Wundargoodie Aboriginal Youth and Community Wellbeing Program in East Kimberley, established in 2006. The programme promotes wellness and suicide prevention with young people in East Kimberley Aboriginal communities.

Bianca Dreyer is a PhD student of community psychology and environmental justice at Wilfrid Laurier University. She works on building community–university partnerships, as part of the Community, Environment & Justice Research Group. She is also a research associate at the Center for Community Research Learning and Action where she mentors students in community-based research and conducts participatory program evaluations. Bianca completed an MA in Social Psychology and was the outreach lead for the David Suzuki Blue Dot Campaign in Kitchener-Waterloo. Bianca's PhD work aims to develop a framework for socially just sustainability work. She wants to explore how psychological theory and practice can contribute to social change as it pertains to issues of climate change communication, adaptation, mitigation, climate justice, and environmental activism. Her approach to research and action is shaped by her experiences of growing up in post-war Berlin and influenced by German philosophical traditions. Bianca is an SSHRC Vanier Scholar.

Sophia Emmanouil is an Architect and Independent Scholar. She is also a participatory arts facilitator and runs a range of projects in partnership with schools, community groups, and other voluntary and community collectives. Her research, which incorporates situationist approaches to space, place, and mapping, transgresses architecture, design, and education, and takes experimental approaches to sustainability and psychogeography. Sophia's work also considers art, design, and architecture from a public engagement perspective.

Lia Figgou is Associate Professor of Social Psychology at the Department of Psychology of the Aristotle University of Thessaloniki. She undertook her doctoral studies and completed her PhD at the University of Lancaster (UK). Her research interests lie in the field of immigration and citizenship. She has also studied the understandings of prejudice and racism in social scientific and lay discourse and the construction of social categorisation in political discourse. Her publications appear in international journals such as the *British Journal of Social Psychology*, *Journal of Community and Applied Social Psychology* and *Journal of Ethnic and Immigration Studies*.

David Fryer is Professor Extraordinarius at the Institute for Social and Health Sciences and Medical Research Council–University of South Africa Safety and Peace Promotion Research Unit, University of South Africa (2016–2019) and Honorary Research Associate Professor, School of Education, University of Queensland (2018–2021). He is an Associate Fellow of The Critical Institute, a Fellow of the British Psychological Society and a Fellow of the Society for Community Research and Action (Division 27 of the American Psychological Association). He has served as President of The European Community Psychology Association and co-editor of *Journal of Community and Applied Social Psychology*.

Anne Galletta is Professor at the College of Education and Human Services at Cleveland State University. As a social psychologist, her research interests include the nature of social and structural relations as they relate to equity in education. To address dimensions of human experience within schools and communities, she draws on critical social theory, attending to structural violence as well as liberatory impulses within public institutions. She employs qualitative research methods, with particular strengths in participatory action research, ethnography, and the case study approach. Guided by dialogic methodologies, Dr Galletta works with educators, youth, and community members in studying issues affecting neighbourhoods and schools and engaging in collective action.

Benjamin Giguère is an Associate Professor in the Department of Psychology at the University of Guelph. Broadly speaking he is interested in understanding the influence of socio-cultural groups on thoughts, emotions and behaviour in order to foster positive social changes. His work focuses on issues related to health and wellbeing, immigration and biculturalism, and, on occasion, collective actions. He is involved with projects that serve primarily traditional basic research objectives, as well as projects that serve primarily applied objectives, such as community informed interventions.

Ashley Jade Gillis is a doctoral student in social psychology at The Pennsylvania State University, with a specialisation in methodology, and a Graduate Research Fellow at Mt. Cuba Center. Ash is broadly interested in perceptions of the natural environment and pro-environmental behaviour. Ash's research focuses on (1) psychological processes involved in how people respond to changes in the natural environment, (2) spillover of pro-environmental behaviour, and (3) community-focused solutions to preventing and addressing environmental problems. Ash received a Bachelor's degree in psychology from University of South Florida and a Master's degree in general psychology from University of North Florida.

Shiloh Groot is of Te Arawa descent and is an interdisciplinary and Indigenous social scientist who works in the fields of Indigenous worldviews and communities, relational resilience, urban poverty, and social justice. Their research is located within a decolonising and intersectional framework to better conceptualise and address socio-cultural and economic concerns. This is reflected in their role as Co-Chair of the Māori Caucus to the New Zealand Coalition to End Homelessness (NZCEH), where they advise on the expansion of research strategies to inform the development of national policy and service provision. Shiloh is a Senior Lecturer in Social and Community Psychology at the University of Auckland (Aotearoa/New Zealand).

Allison Harell holds the UQAM Research Chair in the Political Psychology of Social Solidarity at the Université du Québec à Montréal. She is co-founder and co-director of the

Political Communication and Public Opinion Lab and regularly publishes research on the sources of citizens' attitudes towards public policies related to diversity and inequality.

Johanna Hellgren is a PhD student at John Jay College of Criminal Justice and the CUNY Graduate Center. Interested in the psychology of police interrogations and confessions and plea bargaining, she has conducted research examining the effect of confession evidence on alibis, the impact of video recording police interrogations on the behaviour of suspects, and the effects of collateral consequences on plea-bargaining decisions. She is a member of the American Psychology-Law Society and a teaching assistant for undergraduate psychology courses.

Hélène Henry is a PhD student in work psychology and teaching assistant at the Université catholique de Louvain (UCLouvain), Belgium. Her research interests involve age management, older workers' wellbeing, work–family balance, and retirement. She has published in international journals of psychology *(Carrer Development International; Frontiers in Psychology; Work, Aging and Retirement*).

Tessy Huss is a doctoral researcher at the Centre for Global Health, Trinity College Dublin. She holds an MSc in International Politics from Trinity College Dublin and a BA in Politics and Sociology from University College Dublin. Tessy has a particular interest in social inclusion. Her doctoral research focuses on challenges to the inclusiveness of the national disability policy in Timor-Leste. She previously worked with government and civil society representatives in Malaysia, Cambodia and Timor-Leste to make public policies more inclusive of vulnerable groups. She has also conducted research in the areas of child injury prevention and patient experience in Ireland.

Eric R. Igou received his PhD from University of Heidelberg in 2000 under the supervision of Herbert Bless. Since then, he has worked at the University of Mannheim, the New School University and New York University (postdoc fellowship 2002–2004), Tilburg University (tenured; 2004–2008) and now the University of Limerick (since 2008). He served as Head of Department (2010–2013), developed two master programmes, and served as director of various courses. His research centres on experimental existential psychology, person perception, and biases in judgement and decision making.

Katherine Johnson is Professor and research director of the Social and Global Studies Centre at RMIT, Australia. She works in the field of gender, sexuality and mental health drawing on critical and community psychology perspectives. She is author of *Sexuality: A Psychosocial Manifesto* (Polity, 2015) and Routledge series co-editor, *Transforming LGBTQ Lives.*

Saul M. Kassin is a Distinguished Professor of Psychology at John Jay College of Criminal Justice. He received his PhD at the University of Connecticut, after which he was awarded postdoctoral fellowships at the University of Kansas, the US Supreme Court, and Stanford University. Kassin is an author of several books – including *Social Psychology*, a textbook now in its tenth edition. In the 1980s, Kassin pioneered the scientific study of false confessions. He went on to write numerous books and articles and is senior author of the official 'White Paper' on false confessions. His work is cited all over the world – including by the US Supreme Court. He has received Distinguished Contribution Awards from the American Psychological Association (APA), the American Psychology-Law Society (AP-LS), and the European Association of Psychology and Law (EAPL). In addition to his extensive scholarly work,

Kassin has consulted on a number of high-profile cases and has served as an analyst on all major news networks and in several documentaries.

Andrea LaMarre is a Postdoctoral Fellow at the Propel Centre for Population Health Impact, University of Waterloo. She recently obtained her PhD in the Department of Family Relations and Applied Nutrition at the University of Guelph, where she used qualitative and arts-based approaches to explore the experiences of people in recovery from eating disorders and their supporters. Her research has been funded by the Vanier Canada Graduate Scholarship and the Ontario Women's Health Scholar programme through the Ministry of Health and Longterm Care.

Rebecca Lawthom is a Professor in Community Psychology at Manchester Metropolitan University. She uses community participatory methods and is interested in areas such as migration, disability, and community work.

Wendy Wen Li is a Senior Lecturer in Psychology in College of Healthcare Sciences at James Cook University, Australia. Dr Li has extensive research experience and has led projects in Australia, New Zealand, and China in the areas of ageing, mental health, intergroup relations and discrimination, migration and refugees, and problem gambling and substance abuse. Dr Li has been active in voluntary sectors for many years in Australia and New Zealand. She was the founding Chairperson of the Hamilton Chinese Golden Age Society of New Zealand. Dr Li is currently the President of the Townsville Chinese Club, a Committee Member of Townville Sisters Cities Program and a Member of the Inclusive Community Advisory Committee for the Townsville City Council.

James H. Liu (刘豁夫) is Professor of Psychology at Massey University in New Zealand, managing over 100 full-time staff. He completed a PhD at UCLA in 1992, followed by a post-doc at Florida Atlantic University. He previously taught at Victoria University of Wellington (as Professor and Co-Director of its Centre for Applied Cross-Cultural Research). His research is in cross-cultural, social, and political psychology with a specialisation in social representations of history and their relationship to identity, prejudice, and international relations. James has more than 195 refereed publications that have been cited over 8,000 times (H-index = 48 according to GoogleScholar). He calls the Asian Association of Social Psychology (http://asiansocialpsych.org) his organisational home, having served as President, Secretary General, Treasurer, and Editor-in-Chief of its flagship journal over 20 years of membership in the association. He self-identifies as a Chinese-American-New Zealander.

Antonia Lyons is Professor of Health Psychology at Victoria University of Wellington, New Zealand. Her research focuses on the social, cultural and mediated contexts of behaviours related to health. Antonia was the lead editor of *Youth Drinking Cultures in a Digital World: Alcohol, Social Media and Cultures of Intoxication* (Routledge, 2017 with Tim McCreanor, Ian Goodwin and Helen Moewaka Barnes), co-edited the text *Qualitative Research in Clinical and Health Psychology* (Palgrave 2015, with Poul Rohleder) and is co-author of *Health Psychology: A Critical Introduction* (Cambridge; with Kerry Chamberlain). She is currently co-editor for *Qualitative Research in Psychology*, Associate Editor for *Psychology and Health* and co-editor (with Kerry Chamberlain) of the book series *Critical Approaches to Health* (Routledge).

Malcolm MacLachlan is Professor of Psychology and Social Inclusion and Director of the recently established ALL (Assisting Living & Learning) Institute, at Maynooth University, Ireland. Previous appointments include holding a Personal Chair in Global Health at Trinity College Dublin, and Head of the Department of Psychology at the University of Malawi. He has also held visiting professorships at the universities of Stellenbosch, Olomouc and Harvard. He has worked as an academic, clinician, organisational consultant and policy advisor in Europe, Asia, Africa and South America; with government, civil society, corporates and United Nations agencies. Mac is currently Research & Innovation Lead for the World Health Organization's Global Collaboration on Assistive Technology (GATE) programme; and Knowledge Management Co-Lead for the United Nations Partnership to Promote the Rights of Persons with Disabilities (UNPRPD). He also serves as a Clinical Advisor to the Irish health service's National Disability Team.

Paul J. Maher is an Assistant Professor in the School of Psychology at University College Dublin. Prior to this appointment, Paul worked as Lecturer at the University of Limerick, where he also received his PhD. His research focuses on emotions, meaning-regulation, and political polarisation. Paul has recently published research on meaning-regulation, intergroup bias, and political ideology. He has presented his research at international conferences across Europe and in the United States. He has been awarded funding from the Irish Research Council.

Hasheem Mannan is an Associate Professor at the School of Nursing, Midwifery, and Health Systems, University College Dublin, Ireland. Hasheem completed his PhD on disability policy and family studies at the University of Kansas, US in 2005. Most recently, he was a Senior Research Fellow at the Nossal Institute for Global Health, University of Melbourne. Prior to that, he was a Senior Research Fellow at the Centre for Global Health, Trinity College Dublin. He also held a two-year Marie Curie Fellowship at the National Institute for Intellectual Disabilities, Trinity College Dublin. He has worked for the University of Kansas, the World Health Organization, the US National Center for Health Statistics and the National Disability Authority (Ireland). Hasheem's areas of expertise include content analysis of health policies; human resources for health and service delivery; disability measurement and statistics; and social inclusion.

Antar Martínez-Guzmán is Professor and Researcher in the Department of Psychology in the University of Colima, Mexico. He works in the field of non-normative gender and social expressions from the perspective of critical and social psychology. He is also interested in developing discursive, narrative and participatory methods.

Tracy A. McFarlane completed doctoral studies at the CUNY Graduate Center in Social and Personality Psychology, with a concentration in Health Psychology, and a postdoctoral Psychiatric Epidemiology Training fellowship at Columbia University Mailman School of Public Health. Dr McFarlane's research is mainly in the areas of social identity and its relationship to higher education, health, immigrant adjustment and stigma. She is currently a senior lecturer at the University of the West Indies, Mona. In addition, she works as an independent consultant with local and regional organisations and community groups to improve wellbeing, interpersonal/intergroup processes and psychosocial outcomes among their members.

Joanne McVeigh is a Post-Doctoral Researcher at the Department of Psychology, Maynooth University, Ireland. Joanne received a BA Joint Honours Sociology and Business (2007), Postgraduate Higher Diploma in Psychology (2010), Postgraduate Certificate in Statistics (2015), and PhD (Psychology) (2018) at Trinity College Dublin, Ireland. Her work is interdisciplinary, focusing on the interface between Psychology and Global Health. Supporting psychosocial wellbeing and social inclusion, particularly for occupational groups at high risk for stress and for marginalised populations, is a core focus of her work. Joanne has worked with senior corporate management, health service users and providers, and policy-makers, within multidisciplinary and international research teams. She has conducted research in the UK, Ireland and Philippines, with funders including the European Commission, Shell and the World Health Organization. Joanne has published articles in numerous leading healthcare journals and presented at several international conferences in relation to social inclusion and organisational justice.

Mandy Morgan is a Professor of feminist psychology in the School of Psychology at Massey University, Aotearoa/New Zealand. She has particular interests in theoretical debates concerning the relationships between feminism, poststructuralism, and psychology. As well as these theoretical interests, she works within a research collaboration conducting programmatic critical and discursive studies on issues of gender-based violence.

Tracy Morison's primary research focus is in the area of sexual and reproductive health and critical feminist theories, including Sexual and Reproductive Justice Theory. Her work draws on critical qualitative methodologies, including internet-based methods. Previously, she worked as a researcher in South Africa on projects dealing with sexuality and gender, such as gender-based violence, gender equity in education, and LGBT health service delivery. At present, she teaches Critical Health and Social Psychology at Massey University (Aotearoa/New Zealand) and is an Honorary Research Associate of the *Critical Studies in Sexualities and Reproduction* research group at Rhodes University (South Africa). She is the co-author of *Men's Pathways to Parenthood: Silence and Heterosexual Gendered Norms* (HSRC Press; with Catriona Macleod) and co-editor of the volume *Queer Kinship* (Unisa Press & Routledge; with Ingrid Lynch & Vasu Reddy).

Deirdre O'Shea is a Chartered Work and Organisational Psychologist and Senior Lecturer at the Kemmy Business School, University of Limerick, Ireland. She is the current Chair of the MSc in Work and Organisational Psychology. She received her PhD from Dublin City University in 2011. Deirdre's research interests include: psychological resource-based interventions, emotions and self-regulation, work motivation, proactive behaviour, occupational health psychology, the psychology of entrepreneurship, and voice and silence in the workplace. She has published in both national and international peer-reviewed journals and regularly presents at international conferences. She has received research funding from Erasmus+ (2016), the Irish Research Council (2014), Enterprise Ireland (2008, 2009) and European Association of Work and Organisational Psychology (2013), among others.

Amy F. Quayle is a Lecturer in psychology at Victoria University, Melbourne, Australia. Completing her PhD is community psychology in 2017, Amy's research interests are in the area of intergroup relations and the role of community arts for psychosocial transformation. Her research is informed by critical social theory, including critical race and whiteness studies, critical narrative inquiry, and liberation psychologies. She has co-authored several articles on these topics that are published in refereed journals such the *American Journal of Community Psychology* and the *Journal of Community and Applied Social Psychology* and book chapters.

Christopher Quinn-Nilas is a PhD candidate in the Department of Family Relations and Applied Nutrition at the University of Guelph. He studies factors associated with relationship and sexual satisfaction and how relationships develop over time. His research is supported by a SSHRC Doctoral Fellowship.

Melissa Rangiwananga is of Māori (Ngāti Ruanui, Kai Tahu) and Pākehā descent. She is a senior tutor at Massey University who works as part of a professional collaborative that understands the practice of psychology as an ethical commitment to social justice. She has been involved in the development and teaching of community psychology and forensic psychology, and her research interests lie in issues of marginalisation and exclusion within our social political relationships.

Manuel Riemer is an Associate Professor of community psychology and sustainability science at Wilfrid Laurier University. He received his PhD in Psychology from Peabody College at Vanderbilt University, where he also served as research director at the Centre for Evaluation and Program Improvement. At Laurier, he has served as the director of the Centre for Community, Research, Learning and Action (CCRLA) from 2012–2018 and the Community, Environment and Justice Research Group since 2009. Starting in 2018, Dr Riemer is leading the Viessmann Centre for Engagement and Research in Sustainability (VERiS), with a focus on human aspects of sustainability and fostering a culture of sustainability. Using community-engaged research and principles, Dr Riemer applies community and other psychology principles, theories, and tools to address issues related to sustainability, including global climate change mitigation and resiliency, with a special interest on engagement and in promoting a culture of sustainability in organisations and communities

Katrina Roen's research addresses questions about minoritised youth, emotional distress and embodiment. She has a particular focus on intersex children and their families, transgender youth, self-harm and psychological support. Katrina takes an interdisciplinary approach to investigating these areas, drawing from critical psychological approaches to discourse, empirical research on emotional wellbeing, and poststructuralist feminist and queer understandings of embodiment and subjectivity. Katrina is a Professor in Cultural and Community Psychology at the University of Oslo (Norway) and a Professor of Sociology at the University of Waikato (New Zealand).

Mohi R. Rua is a Senior Lecturer at the School of Psychology, The University of Waikato and the co-director of the Māori and Psychology Research Unit, the University of Waikato. Mohi's primary research interests include Māori psychology, Indigenous psychology, and community psychology. He is actively involved in indigenous service development.

Saba Safdar is an Iranian-born Canadian-educated Professor in the Psychology Department at the University of Guelph in Canada. She is Director of the Centre for Cross-Cultural Research at the University of Guelph. She conducts research examining the wide range of factors that are relevant in understanding the adaptation processes of newcomers, including immigrants, refugees and international students. Professor Safdar is an active member of the International Association for Cross-Cultural Psychology (IACCP) and Deputy Secretary General of the IACCP (2016–2020). Professor Safdar is a Fellow of the International Academy for Intercultural Research and a Fellow of the International Association of Applied Psychology. In addition, she is Associate Editor for the *International Journal of Intercultural Relations* (2017–presnt) and a member of the Editorial Board of the *Journal of Cross-Cultural Psychology* (since 2010). Professor Safdar has held academic appointments in Canada, USA, UK, France, Spain, India, Russia and Kazakhstan.

P. Wesley Schultz is Professor of Psychology at California State University, San Marcos. He is Fellow at the Association for Psychological Science, and the Society for Experimental Social Psychology, and has served as President of the Environmental Psychology Division of the International Association of Applied Psychology. His research interests are in applied social psychology, particularly in the area of sustainable behaviour. Relevant books in this area include *Social Marketing for Environmental Protection*, *Psychology of Sustainable Development* and *Attitudes and Opinions*. His current work focuses on social norms, and the importance of social norms in fostering sustainable behaviour. He has worked on projects for a variety of organisations, including the Environmental Protection Agency, Keep America Beautiful, the National Institute of Justice and the National Science Foundation

Colin Scott is a PhD candidate with the Centre for the Study of Democratic Citizenship at McGill University in Montreal, Canada. His research interests are at the intersection of social, political, and cross-cultural psychology, with a particular focus on accommodation, prejudice, and discrimination, along with their consequences for immigrant integration.

Charlene Y. Senn is a feminist social psychologist, Canada Research Chair in Sexual Violence (CIHR) and Professor of Psychology (Applied Social Track) and Women's & Gender Studies at the University of Windsor. Her research focuses on male violence against women and girls with an emphasis on developing, evaluating and implementing effective sexual violence interventions, particularly those developing women's capacity to resist sexual assault. She also explores the social factors and contexts necessary to support the effectiveness of evidence-based interventions to reduce sexual violence for students of all genders. She developed the feminist EAAA (aka Flip the Script) programme, which has been proven to substantially reduce the sexual violence women experienced (30–64%) for at least two years. With her colleagues on the Bystander Initiative team, she has worked since 2010 to institutionalise effective bystander sexual assault education and to study its short- and longer-term impact on campus culture.

Fuschia M. Sirois is a Reader in Health and Social Psychology at the University of Sheffield in the United Kingdom, and a former Canada Research Chair in Health and wellbeing. Her research investigates how the cognitive, affective and behavioural aspects of personality and self-perceptions influence motivation and self-regulation, and the implications of these intrapersonal processes for physical and psychological health of wellbeing. Specific applied topics include coping and adjustment to chronic illness such as arthritis, fibromyalgia and inflammatory bowel disease, and the role of time orientation and emotions as resources for effective regulation of health behaviours and disease management.

Olga Smoliak is an Associate Professor in Couple and Family Therapy at the University of Guelph, Canada. She has taken a social constructionist approach to psychotherapy and has explored the links between discourse and therapy. Olga has studied linguistic and interactional methods used by therapy participants to give and receive advice, collaborate, accomplish specific therapeutic tasks, and negotiate responsibility for blameworthy conduct. She is currently examining how therapists request in-session practical actions from clients and how the authority to direct clients' actions is interactionally implemented and negotiated.

Christopher C. Sonn is Associate Professor of community psychology. His research is in the area of sense of community, social identity, immigration and intergroup relations. His research is concerned with examining histories of colonialism and oppression and its continuities in various forms of structural violence and its effects on social identities and intergroup relations. Chris is also concerned with developing critical and culturally anchored approaches to research and praxis that can contribute to changing psychological and material realities. He holds a Visiting Professor position at University of the Witwatersrand. He is co-editor of *Creating Inclusive Knowledges* (with Alison Baker) and *Places of Privilege* (with Nicole Oke and Alison Baker). *Psychology and Liberation* (with Maritza Montero) and co-author of *Social Psychology and Everyday Life* and Associate Editor of the *American Journal of Community Psychology* and *Community Psychology in Global Perspective*.

Christine Stephens is a Professor of Social Science Research at Massey University in New Zealand. She teaches in critical health psychology and co-leads the Health and Ageing Research Team to conduct longitudinal and qualitative research on the health of older people. She has a particular interest in the contribution of social participation to wellbeing. She is the co-author of *Healthy Ageing: A Capability Approach to Inclusive Policy and Practice* for the Routledge book series *Critical Approaches to Health* with Mary Breheny.

Karla Stroud received her PhD in Applied Social Psychology from the University of Guelph. She is currently a programme evaluation consultant with five years of experience and has worked with a wide range of community based organisations, employing participatory designs that generate useful evidence that can inform action. She has led projects at the local and national level on topics relating to healthcare, ageing, poverty reduction, mental health and youth engagement.

Heather Barnes Truelove is an Associate Professor of Psychology at the University of North Florida. Her research interests centre on the social psychology of pro-environmental behaviour with focuses on pro-environmental behavioural spillover, climate change adaptation and factors that influence pro-environmental behaviour. Her work on spillover and adaptation has been supported by the National Science Foundation. She serves on the editorial board of the *Journal of Environmental Psychology*. She earned her PhD in experimental psychology from Washington State University and completed a postdoctoral fellowship at the Vanderbilt Institute for Energy and Environment and the Consortium for Risk Evaluation and Stakeholder Participation.

Eleftheria Tseliou is an Associate Professor of Research Methodology and Qualitative Methods at the University of Thessaly, Greece, and a systemic family psychotherapist. She teaches research methodology, qualitative methods and family psychology. Her research interests include the development of discursive research methodologies, like discursive psychology, and the study of psychotherapeutic and educational processes by discourse analysis methodology. She is author of articles in international journals (e.g., *Family Process*, *Journal of Marital Therapy*, *Journal of Family Therapy*) and book chapters on methodological aspects of discursive research methodologies and on family psychotherapy process studies. She is co-editor (with Maria Borcsa) of a special section on discursive methodologies for couple and family therapy research (*Journal of Marital and Family Therapy*).

Fons J. R. van de Vijver is Emeritus Professor of Cross-Cultural Psychology at Tilburg University, the Netherlands, and has honorary positions at the University of Queensland, Australia, and North-West University, South Africa. He has authored more than 50 publications, mainly in the domain of cross-cultural psychology. The main topics in his research involve bias and equivalence, psychological acculturation and multiculturalism, cognitive similarities and differences, response styles, translations, and adaptations. He is former President of the International Association for Cross-Cultural Psychology, a former editor of the *Journal of Cross-Cultural Psychology*. He has received several awards for his work, including the International Award of the American Psychological Association (for his contributions to international cooperation and to the advancement of knowledge of psychology) and the Fellows Award of the International Association of Applied Psychology (for contributions to applied psychology).

Introduction: Applied Social Psychology – An Evolving Tradition

Darrin Hodgetts and Kieran C. O'Doherty

As well as comprising a scientific sub-discipline, Applied Social Psychology is an artistic endeavour that involves putting research into practice, navigating the complexities of human relations and promoting social change in order to support human flourishing. For almost 100 years, applied social psychologists have grappled with the complexities of social issues, seeking to apply and reformulate our disciplinary understandings to inform efforts to address the problems faced by our fellow human beings. Some of our collective efforts have been progressive, other projects less so (Guthrie, 2004; Herman, 1995). As with any complex scholarly endeavour – and theorising, documenting and addressing social issues is inherently complex – there are considerable tensions in terms of theory, method and application. These require critical reflection, trial and error. They also make for a dynamic, heterogeneous and responsive disciplinary space.

Early, and somewhat persistent, tensions emerged between variants of social psychology focused primarily on the individual (McDougall, 1908) and the group (Ross, 1908) as the primary unit of analysis. These tensions have remained and are also evident today in tensions around the epistemic foundations of how we produce actionable knowledge. In the process, we have learnt that we need to understand personal and group thoughts and actions in the historical, societal and cultural contexts in which these social psychological phenomena take shape.

Today, Applied Social Psychology remains a diverse and evolving sub-disciplinary field. Despite apparent overlaps with 'social psychology' and 'applied psychology', we see Applied Social Psychology as a distinctive academic sub-discipline. The term 'Applied Social Psychology' has been in existence for some time, with several psychology departments internationally having graduate programmes dedicated to it and several journals incorporating the term in their titles. However, there is surprisingly little scholarly work that provides an overview of the field or that collects prominent research literature under a common banner. The purpose of this Handbook is to provide such an overview, with a particular focus on bridging epistemic divides between different academic communities associated with the label of Applied Social Psychology, and thus provide a strong impetus for invigorated applied scholarship in social psychology.

In setting the scene for the Handbook, this chapter provides a brief introduction to key developments and figures in Applied Social Psychology as a sub-disciplinary field. We then draw on the tensions between scholarship founded on the principles of the physical and the human sciences to offer a synthesis of key contemporary trends. In particular, we identify three broad types of epistemic approaches that seem to characterise research and practice in applied social psychology and are useful as organising categories for the structure of this book. At the risk of glossing over important distinction, we loosely term these categories social cognition approaches, critical approaches and community approaches. Each topic covered in the Handbook has chapters that illustrate research and practice from each of these three approaches. Although this Handbook, as a whole, will treat these three epistemic traditions separately, the rigidity of boundaries between them varies depending, in part, on the object of inquiry. We therefore include some thoughts about the value of working across these epistemic distinctions and incorporating elements of all three approaches within pragmatic efforts to address social issues.

APPLIED SOCIAL PSYCHOLOGY: BOUNDARY PUSHING IN AN EVOLVING TRADITION

Since the inception of the discipline of psychology, scholars have sought to engage with the issues of the day, including the rise of mass society that came with rapid industrialisation and urbanisation in the late 1800s and early 1900s. It was at this time that the contemporary discipline was taking shape, and psychologists began to research issues of poverty, crime, civil unrest, the environment, education, health, work and community development (Hodgetts et al., 2010). Historical events such as the great depression continued to have major impacts on the application of social psychological knowledge, sparking initiatives such as the development of the Society for the Psychological Study of Social Issues (SPSSI) in 1935 (Stagner, 1986). This organisation emerged, in part, from growing frustrations among politically progressive psychologists in the United States with the discipline's delayed reaction to the horrors of the great depression. The early SPSSI provided a focal point for many social psychologists working to overcome the distance between the academy and communities in need and to support efforts for progressive social change. Like today, societal level changes were seen as being necessary to ensure human flourishing.

Our discipline's orientation towards application was reinforced with developments during the Second World War, where psychologists proved themselves useful to the war effort in developing knowledge of effective leadership and transitioning civilians into comparable military occupations (Herman, 1995). Subsequently, considerable effort has been devoted to understanding the rise of totalitarian regimes and addressing associated issues of group conformity. The social change agenda returned to prominence again during the 1960s; a period of social turmoil in many countries, including the United States, which had the highest concentration of social psychologists (Hodgetts et al., 2010). We were far from united at the time on whether, or if so how, we should respond to events in society (Herman, 1995). Some psychologists promoted the preservation of the deeply sexist, racist and classist social structures of the time. Others sought to foster emancipation and progressive social reform. This situation contributed to the well documented crises in social psychology in the 1970s (Gergen, 1973; Lubek and Apfelbaum, 2000). Long held tensions surfaced around who defines and benefits from the activities of social psychologists, and how we should respond to historical and societal events that impact the lives of groups in society. This led to considerable disciplinary soul searching. As the discipline went global the need for a more diverse epistemological base and applied focus became even more apparent. Many scholars became aware that social psychology is fundamentally embedded within the very societal structures with which practitioners seek to engage. As a result, groups of applied social psychologists emerging especially in the 1970s in Latin America, Europe, and the Global South fostered the pluralising of theories, approaches and applications (Pe-Pua and Perfecto-Ramos, 2012; Staeuble, 2004; Stam, 2006).

There has been a vibrant proliferation of modes of understanding human phenomena and society, leading to the development of new theoretical frameworks, research and engagement strategies underlying social psychological inquiry. These include the emergence of participative approaches that seek to work with social groups to address the issues affecting their lives. Of considerable importance is the emergence of issues of diversity evident in scholarly practice in social cognitive, critical and community approaches included within this Handbook. Today, there is significant plurality in theory and ways of working in Applied Social Psychology. What binds these approaches into our sub-discipline is the will to action and a desire by many scholar practitioners to support human flourishing by addressing significant social issues. Contemporary scholarship embraces the need not only to understand social psychological issues (such as diversity, health, ageing, poverty, crime, work, the environment and education), but also to develop practical responses aimed at enhancing social life. Key terms central to the development of the field include engagement, immersion, participation, actionable knowledge, liberation, action research, intervention and evaluation. Of central interest are issues of praxis and the need to bridge theoretical and practical developments.

We have identified three key figures who exemplify tensions and diversity within the field of Applied Social Psychology and whose scholarship still speaks to present dilemmas and plurality in the field. Marie Jahoda, Francis Sumner and Kurt Lewin each exemplify aspects of diverse epistemic traditions in our discipline (social cognitive, critical, community). The work of these scholars draws attention to tensions in the development, focus and practice of Applied Social Psychology. It is ironic that Marie Jahoda and Francis Sumner have been written out of most textbook histories of social psychology, arguably because they complicate simplified accounts of the slow accumulation of impartial knowledge that are dominant in psychology today. Along with the more high profile Lewin, Jahoda and Sumner questioned our disciplinary orthodoxies, without totally dismissing useful insights, and pushed for a discipline that contributed to the promotion of healthier and more equitable societies. Their work showcases how social psychology has and continues to respond to economic crises, social upheavals, inequities and the mundanity of power and discrimination (Cartwright, 1979; Murphy, 1998).

Marie Jahoda was part of the founding generation of Applied Social Psychology and was elected the first woman president of the Society for the Psychological Study of Social Issues or SPSSI (Campbell, 1981). Jahoda's work does not fit neatly within a single epistemic tradition. Her contributions contain a focus on human thought and action (social cognition) as well as offering criticisms of disciplinary orthodoxies (critical) and lengthy engagements with groups in society (community). Jahoda took a pluralistic, politicised and theoretically informed approach that involved 'immersing' herself within the lives and social problems faced by the groups she sought to understand and help (Fryer, 1986; Rutherford et al., 2011). This work involved developing 'substantive knowledge' of unemployment, the meaning of work, factory life, organisational processes, prejudice, authoritarianism, mental health, women in leadership and youth issues (Fryer, 1986). Jahoda conducted research *with* rather than doing research *on* groups to avoid dissolving local people into statistical trends and so that actionable understandings relevant to the experiences of local people could be developed (Jahoda, 1992). In the early unemployment project, for example, Jahoda et al. (1933/1971) committed to not just documenting what was happening in the everyday lives of community members but also to activities that directly assisted the people around them. Briefly, Jahoda worked to understand people, their thoughts and actions within the context of broader socio-economic structures, which she also sought to deconstruct and change (see Fryer, Chapter 14, this collection). The unemployed community of Marienthal offered a case study for exploring how political, economic and social structures manifest in the changing culture of the village and lives of residents (Jahoda et al., 1933/1971).

Likewise, Francis Cecil Sumner was a scholar from the foundational generation of Applied Social Psychology who also pushed the boundaries of our discipline. Sumner is often referred to as the father of Black psychology in the United States, where he developed a broad understanding of psychological theory and research, having translated more than 3,000 articles from German, French and Spanish into English (Guthrie, 2004). Of particular importance was the emphasis Sumner also placed on the need to understand people and social issues in the context of social structures and broader intergroup relations. His scholarly endeavours remind us how our disciplinary understandings of social issues can change over time and often require critical reflection (Murphy, 1998). Sumner spent his career navigating the racial politics of the United States and psychology. In doing so, he promoted the relevance of intergroup, historical and cultural considerations for psychologists. He was an early critic of hereditary, biological, evolutionary and genetic determinism in psychology (Sumner, 1924; 1928). For example, Sumner challenged psychological theory and methods of measurement that were used to give 'scientific credibility' to racist assertions of the racial inferiority of people of African descent. He emphasised similarities between racial groups, rather than differences, and in doing so, brought into question the racist use of intelligence tests and comparisons based on Eurocentric assumptions of superiority (Guthrie, 2004). He encouraged wider consideration of historical relations, socio-economic structures and the resulting circumstances to which African American people were consigned as explanations for differences in intelligence and achievement. In doing so, Sumner changed measurement practices in Applied Social Psychology. Sumner also prepared many African American students for careers in psychology, several of whom made valuable contributions to the civil rights movement (Guthrie, 2004; Sawyer, 2000). His orientation to promoting the importance of culture, diverse perspectives, history and ideology in psychology foreshadows attempts to decolonise social psychology today (see Sonn, Rua and Quayle, Chapter 3, this collection; Roen and Groot, Chapter 5, this collection).

A humanitarian scholar practitioner of some note, Kurt Lewin was also a past president of the SPSSI and defined many of the characteristics of that organisation and our sub-discipline. Lewin had a wide range of interests, including child development, group processes, identity, democracy, leadership, organisational change, worker wellbeing, prejudice, discrimination, migration, rehabilitation, social justice, participative problem solving and social change (Marrow, 1969). He also emphasised the importance of historical and societal contexts for understanding social psychological phenomena, including local cognitions and behaviour. Lewin developed his field theory out of his concepts of 'social atmosphere', 'action wholes', 'life spaces' and 'psychological realities' in an attempt to locate individuals, groups and their experiences and behaviour within broader societal landscapes. The concept of a 'field' was taken to mean '…the totality of coexisting facts which are conceived of as mutually interdependent' (Lewin, 1951: 240). Central here was consideration of how personal actions can be better understood within the historical and social contexts within which people interact. Lewin's efforts to promote equality, intergroup cooperation and social change to address collective histories of colonialism and exploitation are associated with the development of action research (Adelman, 1993; Lewin, 1946). For Lewin, action research required the active participation of people facing social problems in the development of understandings of, and solutions for, these problems (Adelman, 1993). His application of a cognitive perspective is well documented (Adelman, 1993; Marrow,

1969), but it is also important to note that Lewin engaged in community action and critical reflection regarding applied developments in our discipline. He spent much of his career grappling with the societal factors that lead to social problems, as well as influences that prevent changes to address these problems (Marrow, 1969). Diversity in his theoretical and applied work has led some to propose philosophical contradictions between Lewin's early philosophical stance and later research practice (Billig, 2014). It is useful to remind ourselves that such contradictions are often inherent to theoretically informed applied work. Applied endeavours require scholars to learn through experience and to generate actionable knowledge that may not be as pure or coherent as some focused more on theoretical debates might desire.

Marie Jahoda, Francis Sumner and Kurt Lewin were all engaging teachers who demonstrated a generosity of spirit. Their students went on to become socially responsive and high profile applied social psychologists also engaged in the promotion of human flourishing. These historical figures continue to be valuable role models whose legacies of responding to events in society that adversely affect particular communities continue to shape our sub-disciplinary area today.

Whilst remaining highly positive about the work of such scholars and the contributions that applied social psychologists more broadly have made to enhance the human condition for some time, we also need to remain vigilant in our efforts to address complex social issues. This is particularly apparent in relation to topics such as poverty that are inherently structural or societal in nature, but which are approached by some social psychologists as simply the product of individual deficits (Hodgetts and Stolte, 2017). We must remind ourselves that seminal early social psychologists, including Jahoda, Sumner and Lewin, emphasised the need to explore human cognition and behaviour in relation to the broader contexts in which people are situated. These contexts are shaped by economic conditions, joblessness, colonial histories and ongoing inequalities in power and resources.

We need a range of theoretical and practical approaches to respond to the complexities of social issues faced by humanity today. This Handbook showcases many of these. The collection contains micro-focused accounts of socio-economic, institutional and cultural marginalisation as well as efforts to decolonise society that inform our understandings of local thoughts, action and discriminatory practices (McFarlane, Chapter 2, this collection; Sonn, Rua and Quayle, Chapter 3, this collection). Many practitioner scholars continue to grapple with the space between tightly defined constructs that can be evaluated through experimental manipulation and those more focused on the subtle richness of human experience (Stephens, 1998). This means that applied social psychologists seek to contribute to the development of laws of human behaviour for predicting human action as well as seeking richer understandings of human experiences and actions within particular cultural, historical, social and physical locales (Hill, 2006). In the present epoch of global change, movement, interconnection and the intensification of social issues within and across many societies, applied social psychologists need to continue evolving in response to increasing issues of diversity and the overlapping and unique needs of local and global communities. It is timely that we bring together these disparate and evolving approaches into an edited collection.

APPROACH AND STRUCTURE TO THE HANDBOOK

The production of a handbook at a time of transition is important because it constitutes an essential resource for those who are shaping the future of the discipline. Central to the Handbook is an international perspective of Applied Social Psychology with contributions situated in multiple national contexts. As we have indicated above, we observe three relatively distinct orientations within Applied Social Psychology. Each is characterised by different epistemological foundations, values and practices. These three orientations are separated to a large degree through communities of practice that often have little contact with each other. This is evident in conferences, journals and scholarly societies that cater exclusively to only one type of epistemic tradition in applied social psychology, though there are exceptions. Our typology of epistemic traditions is not intended to create artificial boundaries for the sake of structuring a handbook and, indeed, some of the domains we cover in the Handbook show a strong integration of two, or even three, of the epistemic traditions. The domain of gender and sexuality is notable in this regard (see Barata and Senn, Chapter 4; Roen and Groot, Chapter 5; Johnson and Martínez Guzmán, Chapter 6; all this volume). However, for the most part, each chapter in this Handbook illustrates strong affiliations with only one of the epistemic traditions. We see this in the types of studies that are conducted, the values (implicit or explicit) that underlie authors' commitments and the particular philosophy of science that supports the generation of knowledge. We have categorised these divergent epistemic traditions as (1) social cognition approaches, (2) critical psychological approaches and (3) community psychological approaches.

Social cognition approaches are characterised by a commitment to values reminiscent of those in the natural sciences: objectivity, accuracy and a focus on prediction. Methodologically, practitioners seek to define variables of interest, identify and test relationships between them and use this knowledge to design interventions that lead to a desired behavioural change in a population of interest. The analytical unit of interest tends to be the individual and applied social psychologists in this tradition draw on theories that focus on intra-psychic constructs and processes (e.g., cognitive dissonance, theory of planned behaviour). Accordingly, most research in this tradition is quantitative. Successful interventions use social psychological theories to link particular interventions to psychological change of individuals, which in turn, leads to some desired behavioural change (e.g., better academic performance, adoption of health promoting behaviour, pro-environmental behaviour). The strengths of social cognition approaches lie in their precision. A well designed and evaluated intervention can be designated as a success or failure and effect sizes quantified and compared to alternatives (Gruman et al., 2017).

Critical social psychological approaches, in contrast, tend to reject values typically associated with the natural sciences (neutrality, objectivity, etc.) based on observations that all human phenomena are inherently subjective and political. Thus, attempting to carve out aspects of human phenomena for experimental study without considering structural inequalities within which human phenomena manifest is seen as futile. Critical social psychologists tend to be sceptical of psychological approaches that see the cause and solution to social problems within the individual (Tuffin, 2005). Human subjectivity and action are conceptualised instead as emergent from the social conditions within which individuals exist. Critical social psychological approaches thus give priority to the study of social structures, cultural context, institutional setting and historical considerations. Moreover, these factors are seen as a rich and detailed source of data. Culture, for example, is not seen as a variable that can be plugged into a statistical analysis, but rather a dynamic fabric surrounding and imbuing individuals and groups with meaning. Accordingly, most critical research is qualitative. The epistemic foundation of critical psychological approaches tends to be social constructionist or critical realist. Although we treat critical psychological approaches as one category for the purposes of this Handbook, there are many distinctive scholarly traditions that are drawn on in conducting critical work, and there are both tensions and complementarities among them. Notable traditions underlying applied critical scholarship include liberation psychology, Foucauldian scholarship, feminism, German critical psychology, cultural psychology and discursive psychology. Applied critical social psychology involves the analysis of social phenomena with the aim of making visible the effects of institutional and social arrangements leading to oppression. The applied aspect of this work accordingly seeks to subvert such structural arrangements to promote social justice and human flourishing.

Community psychological approaches are most explicitly associated with a set of values. These include, among others, a commitment to social justice, collaboration with communities, a focus on wellness and prevention, respect for diversity and aiming towards community participation and liberation. A core aspect of community psychological approaches is that they do not involve conducting research *on* people but rather *with* people. Research participants are thus not conceived of as objects to be studied; they are related to as partners in the research process and can be involved in any number of ways, including research design, data collection, analysis and design, as well as write-up and dissemination of findings. Ultimately, community psychological research seeks change motivated by the needs and values of the community, not those of the researcher. Community members are also central to the design and implementation of strategies for addressing social problems (Nelson and Prilleltensky, 2010; Watkins and Shulman, 2008).

Quite obviously, not all social psychological research is applied, and there is some disagreement about precisely what should be considered applied research. Moreover, applied research from a social cognition perspective looks very different from applied critical research. In selecting suitable contributions to this Handbook that we characterised as *applied* social psychology, we required that research satisfy *at least one* of the following criteria:

- Proposes responses (interventions or policies) to issues based on empirical evidence and/or scholarly theoretical arguments;
- Engages critically with particular interventions or policies or practices based on empirical evidence and/or scholarly theoretical argument;
- Engages directly with particular communities for the purpose of social change using scholarly principles.

We considered work that draws on any tradition of social psychology and satisfies at least one of these criteria to be within the scope of 'applied social psychology' and eligible for inclusion in the Handbook. We excluded social psychological work that does not satisfy any of these criteria. For example, research on prejudice might be considered applied given the nature of the topic as socially relevant. However, it would not fit within the Handbook's criteria of applied social psychological research if it does not explicitly develop and test an intervention (social cognition approaches), or explicitly criticise existing interventions or policies in society (critical approaches), or directly engage with marginalised communities (community approaches). While non-applied scholarship may be important in informing more applied work, we see it as a possible precursor to Applied Social Psychological work, not an exemplar as such.

One of the consequences of the proliferation of disciplinary sub-cultures has been a fragmentation of academic communities that have an affinity with the label of Social Psychology. This fragmentation is evident in epistemological divides between positivist and social constructionist commitments, methodological divides between quantitative and qualitative approaches and separation of scholarly outputs into different journals based not on content of inquiry, but on the approach to research that is taken. Further, the very idea of applied work in social psychology sits on the precarious foundation of a Social Psychology that is, itself, fragmented and resists unification on theoretical and methodological grounds. Though many individual researchers are unlikely to work with, or across, multiple epistemological positons, we believe that to be truly 'applied' and problem focused, at the very least an understanding is required of the diversity of approaches within the field.

In this Handbook, we embrace the scholarly diversity evident in Applied Social Psychology. Our intent is not to develop elaborate theories of unification, but rather to showcase diverse approaches and studies that have an applied value for a given social issue or domain of action such as health and work. Our premise is that there is strength in diversity of sub-cultures, particularly when applied to real-world problems. Different approaches to a problem can yield different ways of thinking about, and responding to, the topic and the contexts within which an issue manifests. In showcasing different approaches to Applied Social Psychology, we are then not seeking to 'triangulate' to arrive at an optimal solution; rather, we are seeking to broaden horizons, enabling development and elaboration of creative mechanisms towards social change and justice. Our effort to bring distinct strands of social psychology into conversation is evident in the work of key figures in our sub-discipline and the very structure of this Handbook. Diversity of theoretical orientations, interests and approaches is a strength upon which we need to reflect and build. For seminal early figures in Applied Social Psychology, tensions in theory, research and application seemed to have been managed through a will to action.

Our approach to this Handbook is domain based. We identify ten key areas of application (domains) and, for each domain, present research that illustrates applied social psychological work across each of the three epistemic traditions listed above. That is, for each domain, we present applied social psychological work that illustrates social cognition, critical and community psychological approaches to the issue. In most cases, there are three chapters per domain, each covering one type of approach. In some domains (e.g., gender and sexuality), diverse epistemic traditions are better integrated than in others (e.g., work) where chapters do not fit as neatly into our categorisations of social cognition, critical and community Applied Social Psychology.

Clearly, there are areas of social life to which social psychology has been applied that are not represented in this Handbook. We had to make hard decisions about what to include and what to exclude. Reflecting, in part, the commitments of important pioneers of Applied Social Psychology, such as Lewin, Jahoda and Sumner, as well as our own values and interests, the ten domains we selected are heavily weighted towards social justice issues. In addition, many of the research programmes we collect in this volume under the banner of Applied Social Psychology are, in some instances, themselves each associated with other sub-disciplines or fields of psychology. We therefore also wanted to ensure that particular sub-disciplines that have an important place in relation to Applied Social Psychology were accommodated in the structure of the Handbook. For example, Chapter 1, which illustrates social cognition approaches to culture, is also illustrative of a branch of *cross-cultural psychology*; Chapter 3 illustrates community approaches to indigenous and *cultural psychology*; Chapter 13 examines social cognition in the workplace and is also illustrative of work in the field of *industrial/organisational psychology*; and Chapter 20, which illustrates critical approaches to communication, also provides an overview of the field of *discursive psychology*. As well as focusing on the local settings, contributing authors also situate their respective chapters in relation to international literature. Each chapter provides a brief history of the body of research and practice they draw on, key developments, particular practical initiatives and future theoretical and empirical work that is needed.

Overall, this structure provides a pragmatic means for approaching this project as it emphasises the importance of the particular epistemic tradition that informs applied work in social psychology. Below, we provide an overview of the content of the book and a summary of each chapter.

OVERVIEW OF THE TEN TOPIC DOMAINS AND CONTRIBUTING CHAPTERS

The Handbook is structured according to ten domains (topics). Our original intention was to include three chapters in each domain: one each dedicated to illustrating social cognition approaches, critical approaches and community approaches to Applied Social Psychology. In large part, the Handbook now reflects this intention. However, as will be recognisable to experienced applied social psychologists, even the best laid plans are subject to change. This has occurred to a minor degree in two of the thematic domains in this collection. For various reasons, we did not accept three chapters in these two domains and have progressed with two chapters on education and two chapters on criminal justice, law and crime. In each case, we have a chapter from the social cognition perspective and a chapter covering both critical and community perspectives. Below, we offer a brief overview of each thematic domain and an introduction to each contributing chapter.

Domain one focuses on **culture and indigeneity**, which are central to understanding intergroup relations, power, identities and the everyday social practices and needs of diverse groups in society. Issues of culture and ethnicity are increasingly recognised as being central to human experience in our increasingly interconnected world. Applied social psychologists often engage in intergroup comparisons but also develop diverse, culturally-based approaches to a range of social psychological issues. Chapter 1 presents a social cognition perspective on cross-cultural research and acculturation as a central concept for understanding processes of adjustment that occur when people move between different socio-cultural settings. Saba Safdar and Fons van de Vijver engage with some of the complexities around applying models of acculturation across different contexts. Foregrounding the use of the concept of ethnicity in social psychology, Chapter 2 offers a critical perspective focused on issues of racism and how this social psychological phenomenon relates to issues of power and exclusion between groups in society. In this chapter, Tracy McFarlane questions the dominant focus in social psychology on urban minority group struggles and intergroup conflicts. This author calls for more focus on intersectional relationships between ethnicity, class, gender, sexuality and age. This is important for extending our understandings of, and responses to, inequalities and discrimination. Embracing notions of praxis, Chapter 3 by Chris Sonn, Mohi Rua and Amy Quayle focuses on the importance of the concept of culture in extending disciplinary understandings of human functioning. Contributing to broader efforts to decolonise psychology, the authors adopt an emic or insider perspective associated with indigenous and cultural psychologies to illustrate how social psychologists can work with their own communities to address a range of applied issues. Combined, these chapters offer insights into the diverse perspectives that are driving applied scholarship in the area of ethnicity, culture and indigeneity in social psychology today.

Domain two explores issues of **gender and sexualities** that have become prominent in applied settings, and which intersect with issues of culture, ethnicity and difference in shaping power relations in society. Although this domain follows the overall structure of the Handbook in illustrating social cognition, critical and community approaches, research and practice in applied social psychology on the topic of gender and sexualities have developed in ways that are more integrated than work on other topics. Chapter 4 explores research and applications that draw primarily on the social cognitive approach to understanding gendered relations, attitudes and interventions aimed at promoting gender equity. In this chapter, Paula Barata and Charlene Senn focus specifically on how interventions to address violence against women have been enhanced through the application of theory and research from social psychology. Although writing primarily from a social cognition perspective, these authors demonstrate the interlinking of approaches to applied social psychology by drawing on, and adopting, an explicit feminist agenda and arguing for the incorporation of community and interdisciplinary feminist approaches to men's violence against women. In Chapter 5, Katrina Roen and Shiloh Groot showcase the rich vein of research and activism emerging around the lives of trans* or gender diverse (TGD) youth in this rapidly evolving area of research and practice in psychology. These authors also attend to the institutional violence that comes with the intersectional or multiple layering of minoritisation for many TGD youth. Roen and Groot identify particular concerns that applied social psychologists need to address. Completing domain two, Chapter 6 also focuses on trans* identities and issues of marginalisation; this time with more emphasis on a community perspective. Katherine Johnson and Antar Guzmán focus directly on issues of embodiment and social justice and provide reflections on two participative, action research projects. The first is with trans* youth in the UK and the second considers activist women in Mexico. Both exemplars showcase the importance of engaged, participatory scholarship when social psychologists work with marginalised groups who are struggling for social change.

Domain three focuses on **politics** and the long-standing engagements applied social psychologists have had with issues of civic, intergroup and community politics. Chapter 7 focuses on democratic citizenship and civic participation within pluralistic societies with a view to promoting positive social changes that lead to increased social inclusion across diverse groups in society. In this chapter, Colin Scott and Allison Harell adopt a social cognition perspective to address classic issues of prejudice and discrimination in applied settings, with a view to guiding policy makers in the implementation of policies that contribute to more equitable forms of civic participation. Chapter 8 focuses on politics from a critical social psychological perspective and, in doing so, considers a core tension in social psychology between approaches adopting an objective stance to the measurement of social phenomena and approaches that involve scholars working on behalf of marginalised groups in overtly political ways. In this chapter, Eleni Andreouli and Lia Figgou attend to links between everyday politics, personal experiences and socio-political contexts. Their approach is exemplified through an engagement with issues of citizenship and immigration. In Chapter 9, Malcolm MacLachlan, Joanne McVeigh, Tessy Huss and Hasheem Mannan present an argument for what they call Macropsychology, which is designed to promote structural changes that promotes a politics of inclusion. Their focus is on how to change social structures from the bottom up. These processes are illustrated through examples from the authors' collaborations with institutions within civil society as well as United Nations organisations. A core focus across all three chapters in this domain is on the politics of exclusion and efforts to foster increased social inclusion among members of marginalised groups.

Central to domain four is **health**. Social psychologists have engaged in research into a range of physical and mental health topics as well as developing a range of health promotion strategies. As is evident across the three chapters in this domain, social psychologists have developed rich understandings of how personal behaviour, societal ideologies, material living conditions and the relationships between groups in society shape peoples' health. In Chapter 10, Ben Giguère, Thomas Beggs and Fuschia Sirois outline how models of social cognition are deployed to enhance efforts to promote the physical and mental health of persons and communities. The focus here is on making positive changes to people's perceptions and health-related behaviour. Chapter 11 presents applications of a critical approach to health psychology. Adopting a classic communitarian approach to social psychology, Tracy Morison, Antonia Lyons and Kerry Chamberlain foreground the importance of linking the wellbeing of persons, communities and societies with broader social, cultural and global contexts or the social determinants of health.

Rather than orientating towards personal behaviour change, these authors emphasise the need to transform unhealthy societies so that the people who inhabit these have more chance of remaining healthy and responding effectively to illness. In Chapter 12, Neil Drew and Michael Adams outline the importance of community case-based initiatives and the importance of natural helpers in providing mental health care in the context of deinstitutionalisation and colonisation in Australia. In doing so, they outline the importance of principled practice in developing and conducting participative programmes with Indigenous Australians.

Social psychologists have long recognised the centrality of **work** to human existence and relationships. Applied scholarship in this domain has often focused on paid employment and has been extended to unpaid, familial and volunteer work as well as unemployment. In Chapter 13, Paul Maher, Deirdre O'Shea and Eric Igou consider the future of research and interventions in relation to the meaning of paid employment from a social cognition perspective. This focus is important because high meaning of work scores are heavily correlated with better health outcomes, slower age-related cognitive declines and reduced mortality. In Chapter 14, David Fryer offers personal and critical reflections on the role of social psychological research and interventions in the cultivation of labour-market subjects. Fryer's focus is on unemployment and extends from the classic scholarship of leading applied social psychologists in the 1930s to current scholarly activities. A key assertion in this chapter is that such research comprises part of the psy-complex. The result are subjectivities for people who are unemployed that meet the needs of neoliberal capitalism more than the people themselves. Finally, adopting the perspective of humanitarian work psychology, which draws insights from community and industrial psychologies, Chapter 15 considers the importance of sustainable livelihoods and decent work for poverty reduction. In this chapter, Stuart Carr presents the United Nations Sustainablity Goals as offering a global structure for increasing the efficacy of social psychological programmes to create jobs and improve the working conditions and remuneration of people experiencing poverty.

The average age of populations in many countries is increasing and social psychologists have responded with an explosion of applied research and interventions. As such, domain six provides an introduction to **ageing** as a growing area in applied social psychology. Chapter 16 opens the domain with a focus on ageism. Here, Donatienne Desmette, Hélène Henry and Stefan Agrigoroaei present the study of ageism and discrimination as a crucial orientation for extending present understandings of wellbeing in later life and for targeting interventions to promote the health of older people. Adopting a critical perspective, Chapter 17 considers links between new social identity formations among older people and ageing related policies. In this chapter, Mary Breheny and Christine Stephens question negative and stigmatising perspectives on ageing that dominate many social narratives and which promote notions of mental and physical decline. These authors showcase the importance of a more positive focus on helping people to age well. In the third chapter in this domain (Chapter 18), Wendy Li and Alma Au contemplate successful ageing in community settings. These authors emphasise ageing in place policies as important responses to the ageing of populations in most nation states and for ensuring 'successful ageing', which is associated with freedom of choice and empowerment in later life.

Applied social psychologists have paid particular attention to issues of human communication between individuals, groups and societies. Domain seven is concerned with issues of **communication**. Chapter 19 offers an introduction to the broad area of social cognition and communication as applied to cross-cultural research and technologies of digital influence. James Liu, Homero de Zúñiga and Trevor Diehl identify the classic focus in social psychology on the impacts of persuasion on attitudes before expanding the focus from individuals to social networks and both intra- and inter-individual processes. As both critical social psychologists and Liu and colleagues argue, attitudes are not just the property of individuals. Attitudes are also evident in the public meaning systems that have been theorised by social psychologists as social representations and discourses. In Chapter 20, Eleftheria Tseliou, Olga Smoliak, Andrea LaMarre and Christopher Quinn-Nilas present discursive psychology as a critical and applied approach to communication in everyday life. To exemplify their argument, these authors offer a selective review of the application of discursive psychology to a range of topics. Chapter 21 completes the communication domain with a focus on public deliberation. Until recently, the practice of public deliberation has not received much attention in applied social psychology. Kieran O'Doherty and Karla Stroud argue that central to work in this area is the assertion that people affected by decisions should have a voice in collective decision-making processes that influence their lives. These authors also propose that social psychologists are well placed to contribute to efforts to enhance deliberative processes by which members of the public come together in attempts to arrive at collective conclusions on key social issues.

Domain eight offers an exploration of scholarship in the area of **education**. Applied social psychologists conduct research and develop programmes in a range of educational settings to address various concerns from communities, educators and students. In Chapter 22 Louise Alexitch outlines the contributions of applied social psychologists to several areas of education to illustrate the value of a social cognition perspective in this domain. The primary focus in this chapter is on students, their perceptions and beliefs about their own abilities and learning environments. In this vein, Alexitch reviews four primary areas of scholarship relating to academic self-concepts, teacher expectations, social comparisons and student motivation, which are central to student success. In the second and final chapter (Chapter 23) in this domain, Anne Galletta offers a critical (liberation) and community-orientated approach to consider the importance of participative action projects in education. These projects involve educators, youth and social psychologists engaging in critical inquiry and action together.

Human beings live somewhere and engage with others in a range of physical and social environments. Domain nine cogitates scholarship that addresses the **environment and place**; topics that have seen rapid growth in attention in recent years. Chapter 24 tackles the twin issues of how social psychologists can help reduce environmentally harmful behaviour patterns and promote pro-environmental behaviour in order to reduce harmful emissions. In this chapter, Heather Truelove, Wesley Schultz and Ashley Gillis review theory and research on behaviour change and make useful recommendations for actions to address environmental concerns. In the following chapter (Chapter 25), Alexander Bridger, Sophia Emmanouil and Rebecca Lawthom provide a critical perspective on the social psychology of place. These authors argue for a psychogeographical turn in applied social psychology as a way of embracing the importance of material and social contexts in understanding the everyday conduct of social lives. This approach is exemplified through an example from the authors' own research into urban gentrification. Chapter 26 adopts a community approach to environmental issues and outlines strategies for social changes necessary to address environmental issues. Here, Bianca Dreyer and Manuel Riemer propose that more research in this area is important but not sufficient for supporting such changes. These authors argue that social psychologists need to do more to cooperate with social movements and community groups. They provide practical exemplars of this type of action-research that is contributing to positive social change.

For over 100 years, scholar practitioners in applied social psychology have worked to address crime and 'anti-social' behaviour. Domain ten encompasses two chapters that provide excellent introductions to work in the domain of **criminal justice, law and crime**. In Chapter 27, Fabiana Alceste, Aria Amrom, Johanna Hellgren and Saul Kassin examine social psychological research with a direct bearing on the criminal justice system. The authors focus, in particular, on social psychological factors related to different forms of evidence, processes whereby guilt and innocence are adjudicated (correctly or incorrectly) and laypeople's perceptions of justice. Chapter 28 completes the contributions to the Handbook with an illustration of a critical and community orientated perspective on the injustices of criminal victimisation and the need to explore such issues within historically specific socio-political contexts. Mandy Morgan, Leigh Coombes, Stephanie Denne and Melissa Rangiwananga exemplify their approach through the case of domestic violence.

In conclusion, we are excited to present a collection of chapters, which showcases many of the cutting-edge dimensions of contemporary Applied Social Psychology as an evolving sub-disciplinary area focused on understanding and responding to social issues. Of course, we make no claims to exhaustiveness. By necessity, we have omitted important work that should be recognised as applied social psychology. Nor do we claim that our specific structure of this Handbook is the only, or even best, way of categorising work in the sub-discipline. However, we do believe that we have succeeded in collecting, in one place, an impressive array of practitioner-scholars that together provide a complex and nuanced foundation for the work of applied social psychologists into the future.

REFERENCES

Adelman, C. (1993). Kurt Lewin and the origins of Action Research. *Educational Action Research, 1*(1), 7–24.

Billig, M. (2014). Kurt Lewin's leadership studies and his legacy to social psychology: Is there nothing as practical as a good theory? *Journal for the Theory of Social Behaviour, 45*(4), 440–457.

Campbell, D. (1981). The Kurt Lewin Memorial Award Presentation. *Journal of Social Issues, 37*(1), 205–206.

Cartwright, D. (1979). Contemporary social psychology in historical perspective. *Social Psychology Quarterly, 42*, 82–93.

Fryer, D (1986). The social psychology of the invisible: An interview with Marie Jahoda. *New Ideas in Psychology, 4*(1), 107–118.

Gergen, K. (1973). Social psychology as history. *Journal of Personality and Social Psychology, 26*, 309–320.

Gruman, J., Schneider, F., & Coutts, L. (2017). *Applied Social Psychology: Understanding and Addressing Social and Practical Problems* (3rd edn.). Thousand Oaks, CA: SAGE.

Guthrie, R. (2004). *Even the Rat was White: A Historical View of Psychology* (2nd Ed.). Boston: Pearson.

Herman, E. (1995). *The Romance of American Psychology: Political Culture in the Age of Experts.* Los Angeles: University of California.

Hill, D. (2006). Theory in Applied Social Psychology: Past mistakes and future hopes. *Theory & Psychology, 16*(5), 613–640.

Hodgetts, D., Drew, N., Stoltie, O., Sonn, C, Nikora, N., & Curtis, C. (2010). *Social Psychology and Everyday Life*. Basingstoke: Palgrave/MacMillian.

Hodgetts, D., & Stolte, O. (2017). *Urban Poverty and Health Inequalities: A Relational Approach.* London: Routledge.

Jahoda, M. (1992). Reflections on Marienthal and after. *Journal of Occupational and Organizational Psychology, 65*, 355–358.

Jahoda, M., Lazarsfeld, P., & Zeisel, H. (1933/1971). *Mariethal: A Sociography of an Unemployed Community*. London: Tavistock.

Lewin, K. (1946). Action research and minority problems. *Journal of Social Issues, 2(4)*, 34–46.
Lewin, K. (1951). In D. Cartwright (Ed.), *Field Theory in Social Science: Selected papers*. New York: Harper & Row.
Lubek, I., & Apfelbaum, E. (2000). A critical gaze and wistful glance at hand-book histories of social psychology: Did the successive accounts of Gordon Allport and successors historiographically succeed? *Journal of the History of the Behavioral Sciences, 36*, 405–428.
Marrow, A. (1969). *The Practical Theorist: The Life and Work of Kurt Lewin*. New York: Basic Books.
McDougall, W. (1908). *An Introduction to Social Psychology*. London: Methuen.
Murphy, J. (1998). Using social psychology. In R. Sapsford, A. Still, D. Miell, R. Stevens, & M. Wetherall (Eds.). *Theory and Social Psychology* (pp. 161–190). Thousand Oaks, CA: Sage
Nelson, G. B., & Prilleltensky, I. (2010). *Community Psychology: In Pursuit of Liberation and Well-being* (2nd edn.). New York: Palgrave Macmillan.
Pe-Pau, R., & Perfecto-Ramos, P. (2012). Philippines. In D. Baker (Ed.). *The Oxford Handbook of the History of Psychology* (pp. 395–411). Oxford: Oxford University Press.
Ross, E. (1908). *Social psychology: An Outline and a Sourcebook*. New York: Macmillan.
Rutherford, A., Unger, R., & Cherry, F. (2011). Reclaiming SPSSI's sociological past: Marie Jahoda and the Immersion Tradition in social psychology. *Journal of Social Issues, 67(1)*, 42–58.
Sawyer, T. (2000). Francis Cecil Sumner: His views and influence on African American higher education. *History of Psychology, 3*(2), 122–141.
Staeuble, I. (2004). De-centering western perspectives: Psychology and the disciplinary order in the first and third world. In A. C. Brock., J. Louk, & W. Van Horn (Eds.). *Rediscovering the History of Psychology: Essays Inspired by the Work of Kurt Danger* (pp. 183–205). New York: Kluwer.
Stagner, R. (1986). Reminiscences about the founding of SPPSI. *Journal of Social Issues, 42*(1), 35–42.
Stam, H. (2006). Introduction: Reclaiming the *social* in social psychology. *Theory & Psychology, 16*, 587–595.
Stephens, R. (1998). Dimensions of distinguishing between theories in social psychology. In R. Sapsford, A. Still, D. Miell, R. Stevens, & M. Wetherell (Eds.). *Theory and Social Psychology* (pp. 45–64). Thousand Oaks, CA: Sage.
Sumner, F. (1924). Core and context in the drowsy state. *American Journal of Psychology, 35*(2), 307–308.
Sumner, F. (1928). Environic factors which prohibit creative scholarship among Negros. *School and Society, 22*, 294–296.
Tuffin, K. (2005). *Understanding Critical Social Psychology*. London/Thousand Oaks/New Delhi: Sage.
Watkins, M., & Shulman, H. (2008). *Toward Psychologies of Liberation*. London: Palgrave MacMillan.

PART I

Culture and Indigeneity

1

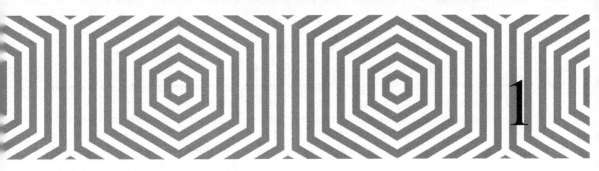

Acculturation and its Application: A Conceptual Review and Analysis

Saba Safdar and Fons J. R. van de Vijver

ACCULTURATION: A CONCEPTUAL REVIEW AND ANALYSIS

In this chapter, a review of acculturation literature is provided by examining a selection of research that is conducted in the Americas, Europe, Oceania, Asia, and Africa. Firstly, we provide a brief historical overview of how acculturation has been conceptualized and operationalized based on an anthropological definition and discuss some of the criticisms that have been raised within this framework. Our argument is that the transition in the literature from unidimensional, to bidimensional, and to emerging multidimensional models reflects the changing reality of immigration and the way immigrants negotiate their allegiances with relevant cultures surrounding them in the acculturation context.

Secondly, we review several contemporary acculturation models and frameworks that have been used to examine key factors in understanding the process of adjustment of newcomers in their settling society. Additionally, we discuss the emerging models of acculturation. In describing these acculturation models, we describe how antecedents, mediating, and outcome factors are involved in feedback loops, whereby output variables will have an impact on acculturation orientations.

Thirdly, we review the literature on acculturation of refugees, focusing on characteristics that set refugees apart from other acculturating groups. The multiple sources of stress for this group are examined. Additionally, the importance of contextual and personal factors in adjustment of refugees is discussed.

Fourthly, we discuss the application of this line of work in different sociocultural contexts. We will examine and compare adjustment of newcomers in different societies within the framework of governmental policies and host society attitudes. We also examine the impact of the larger demographic conditions on sociocultural adjustment of newcomers. We describe studies that compare a single ethnic group in multiple societies (such as studies of Turkish and Iranian immigrants in different Western countries).

Definition of Acculturation

Studies of psychological acculturation can be taken to have started when Graves (1967) coined the term psychological acculturation. The earliest use of acculturation terminology goes back to the nineteenth century, when social scientists applied the term to the changes in indigenous groups as a result of colonization. Within this context, acculturation was used to describe cultural shifts from 'uncivilized' and 'savage' culture to civilized European culture (e.g., McGee, 1898). Acculturation within this framework was viewed as a one-dimensional development from culture A to culture B (see Safdar et al., 2013, for a review). The one-dimensional model, however, was criticized as it is possible to identify with both the heritage culture and the culture of the settlement society (Berry, 1980; van Oudenhoven et al., 2006).

Anthropologists, Redfield et al., (1936: 149) defined acculturation as 'those phenomena which result when groups of individuals having different cultures come into continuous first-hand contact, with subsequent changes in the original patterns of either or both groups'. This definition is widely used by social scientists and cited extensively in the acculturation literature. However, the definition has been criticized as viewing the construct at a group level and providing no insight to its psychological mechanism at the individual level and what aspects of 'original patterns' change (Chirkov, 2009). In response to these criticisms, and in line with the acculturation literature examining individual change in terms of the behavioral (sociocultural adaption) and the cognitive-affective (psychological adaptation) domains (Searle and Ward, 1990), Safdar and colleagues (2013) proposed a working definition of acculturation which is mainly the same definition that Redfield et al. (1936: 215) proposed, with minor modifications. It states that acculturation process are, 'those phenomena which result when groups of individuals with different cultures come into contact, with subsequent changes in the original patterns of either or both groups, or in behavioural or psychological change in individuals from either or both groups'. The authors not only specified patterns of change, they also removed the inclusion of 'continuous' and 'first-hand' from the original definition as these are not necessary types of contact in order for change to occur. This is particularly true in the modern world, where technology has increased and altered types of contact with 'others'.

Acculturation Strategies

Berry's acculturation strategies

More than four decades ago, Berry (1974; 1980) considered intercultural strategies. In his original work, Berry (1974) considered three dimensions in response to intercultural contact. The first dimension was preference for maintaining ones' heritage culture. The second dimension was preference for having contact with the larger society. The third dimension was the role of societal policies in facilitating or constraining the first two preferences. How groups and individuals respond to these dimensions defines *acculturation strategies*. At the individual level, when there is no preference to maintain heritage culture but value is seen in having contact with members of other ethno-cultural groups, *assimilation* is defined. When individuals prefer to maintain heritage culture but do not value having contact with members of other ethno-cultural groups, *separation* is defined. When there is an interest to maintain heritage culture and also have contact with other groups, *integration* is the outcome. Lastly, when individuals have no interest either in maintaining the original culture or in having contact with other groups, *marginalization* is the outcome. These acculturation strategies are from the point of view of individuals and members of non-dominant groups and referred to as AIMS (Assimilation, Integration, Marginalization, Separation), highlighting the acculturation goals of individuals (Berry and Safdar, 2007).

Although individuals strive toward their acculturation goals, they do not have the freedom to choose their AIMS. Many dominant groups enforce particular forms of acculturation, which limit the choices that individuals and non-dominant groups can make. In the 1980 formulation, Berry included the role of the dominant society in impacting the strategies adopted by non-dominant peoples. That is, the mutual or reciprocal character of these strategies was proposed. At the group level, the dominant group sets up *acculturation expectations* toward non-dominant ethnocultural groups (Berry, 1974; 1980). These expectations are in the forms of policies, regulations, and ideologies (Berry, 1974; 1980). When the dominant group expects non-dominant groups to assimilate, *melting pot* is the outcome, and when separation is expected, *segregation* is the outcome. Similarly, when diversity is accepted, *multiculturalism* is the outcome, and when marginalization is forced, *exclusion* is the outcome (Berry, 1980; Berry and Safdar, 2007).

The Interactive Acculturation Model (IAM)

Bourhis et al. (1997) compare acculturation strategies between members of the non-dominant group and the receiving society. The IAM proposes five acculturation strategies and expectations. At the individual level, these are *assimilation*, *separation*, *integration*, *marginalization*, and *individualism*. The first four correspond to Berry's (2003) acculturation strategies. *Individualism* refers to a tendency to be defined as an individual rather than a member of a cultural group. At the group level, acculturation expectations are *assimilation*, *segregation*, *integration*, *exclusion*, and *individualism*. Similarly, the first four correspond to Berry's (2003) acculturation expectations. *Individualism* refers to when members of the dominant group hold the belief that people should be defined as individual rather than members of an ethno-cultural group. There is limited empirical support for the usefulness of inclusion of *individualism* as an important distinction within acculturation strategies and expectation (Safdar et al., 2013).

According to the IAM model, if members of both groups share the same acculturation preference, *concordance* occurs, but when members of the two groups do not share the same acculturation preference, *discordance* emerges. The *concordance* and *discordance* acculturation preferences lead to three acculturation outcomes: *consensual, problematic*, and *conflictual.*

Concordance Model of Acculturation (CMA)

Piontkowski et al. (2000) proposed the CMA, which also refers to consensual, problematic, and conflictual acculturation outcomes, and it is based on both Berry's (1997) fourfold acculturation strategies and Bourhis and colleagues' (1997) IAM framework. According to the CMA, there are four levels of concordance and discordance between immigrants and receiving society. When the attitudes between the two groups match, there is a *consensual level.* When the attitudes of the two groups do not match in terms of heritage cultural maintenance, there is a *culture-problematic level* relational outcome. When the attitudes between the two groups do not match in terms of participating in the larger society, there is a *contact-problematic level* relational outcome. Lastly, when immigrants and members of the larger society have mismatched attitudes toward both maintenance of heritage culture and participating in the larger society, *the conflictual level* is the outcome. It has been reported that, when there is discordance between the immigrant group and the receiving society in terms of maintaining heritage culture and having contact with the larger society, members of both groups are more likely to report intergroup anxiety and perceive high levels of realistic (e.g., perception of economic loss and job loss) and symbolic threats (e.g., perception of difference in values and beliefs; Rohmann et al., 2006).

Models of Acculturation

Berry's acculturation framework

Berry (2003) proposed a bidirectional acculturation framework that incorporates variables at both group and individual levels. Variables at the group level capture contextual factors such as cultural values, degrees of diversity in the society, and sociopolitical characteristics of the groups. Variables at the individual level capture factors such as individual acculturation strategies, cultural identity, language proficiency, and family type (Berry, 2003). Variables at the cultural level include features of the two original cultural groups prior to their contact. Cultural variables focus on the nature of contact relationships between groups (e.g., temporary, permanent, colonization, etc.) and the resulting dynamic cultural changes in both groups and in the ethnocultural groups that emerge during the process of acculturation (Berry, 2003; Berry and Safdar, 2007). These cultural changes can be minor or substantial and range from being easily accomplished to being a source of major cultural disruption.

At the individual level, the psychological changes that individuals in all groups undergo, and their eventual adaptation to their new situations, should be considered (Berry, 2003). These changes can be a set of rather easily accomplished behavioral shifts (e.g., in ways of speaking, dressing, and eating) or they can be more problematic, producing acculturative stress (Berry, 1970; Berry et al. 1987), evidence of which is manifest as uncertainty, anxiety, and depression.

It has been argued that groups and individuals behave differently in multicultural settings, and depending on heritage cultural background, sociocultural characteristics of the society of settlement, and individual characteristics, the process of acculturation is different for individuals and cultural groups (Berry and Safdar, 2007). Adaptations can be primarily internal or *psychological* (e.g., sense of well-being or self-esteem) or *sociocultural* (e.g., intercultural contact, Berry, 2003; Ward, 1996).

Relative Acculturation Extended Model (RAEM)

The RAEM was developed by Navas et al. (2005). The RAEM makes a distinction between the ideal acculturation strategies preferred by immigrant groups and members of the receiving society and the actual strategies adopted by both groups. Additionally, the model distinguishes between seven domains, or spheres of acculturation options, to which immigrants and members of the receiving society adapt: economic, work, social, political, family, religious, and ways of thinking. Navas and colleagues (2005) made a distinction between peripheral and central domains. For example, in a study of African immigrants in Spain, it was found that immigrants and members of the receiving society coincide in peripheral domains (work, social, and economic) but they differ in central domains (family, religious, and ways of thinking; Navas et al., 2007). The advantage of division of acculturation domains into peripheral and central domains is the ability to predict intergroup conflict by focusing on some domains rather than others (Navas et al., 2007).

The Multidimensional Individual Difference Acculturation (MIDA) model

The MIDA model was proposed by Safdar and colleagues (Safdar et al., 2003; Safdar et al., 2009, see Figure 1.1) and rests on a number of theoretical approaches, including positive psychological functioning (Ryff and Singer, 1996), hassles and psychological distress (DeLongis et al., 1982), acculturation strategies (Berry, 1980), and identity (Phinney, 2003). Within the MIDA model, core variables at individual level that are relevant to the adaptation of newcomers in a variety of contexts have been incorporated. Specifically, adaptation is conceptualized in terms of psychophysical and sociocultural adaptation. This is consistent with the distinction that Ward and Kennedy (1994) made and referred to psychological adaptation as 'feeling well' and sociocultural adaptation as 'doing well'. In the MIDA model, level of engagement with heritage culture (*Ingroup Contact*) and members of the receiving society (*Outgroup Contact*) are conceptualized as sociocultural adaptation (i.e., doing well). Similarly, a low level of *Psychophysical Distress* is conceptualized as psychophysical adaptation (i.e., feeling well). It is proposed that newcomers' adaptation to a receiving society is predicted by individual level factors including social support, identity, family connection, language and cultural competence, and perception of hassles or discrimination (Safdar et al., 2003; 2009).

Psychosocial Resources consist of personal resilience, outgroup social support, and language and cultural competence. These variables reflect resources from the receiving society and those that are internal to the individual. *Connectedness* (also called *Co-national Connectedness*) consists of ingroup social support, family connection, and ethnic identity. These variables reflect individuals' ties to, and identification with, the heritage culture. *Hassles* include frequent irritants that individuals encounter and may include acculturation-specific hassles such as ethnic discrimination. It has been found that immigrants with high *Psychosocial Resources* tend to do better (high level of *Outgroup Contact*) and feel better (low level of *Psychophysical Distress,* Safdar et al., 2003, 2009, 2012). Similarly, it has been reported that immigrants with high *Connectedness* tend to do better (high level of *Ingroup Contact*; Safdar et al., 2003, 2009, 2012). *Hassles* tend to be associated with lower adaptation, specifically *Psychophysical Distress* (Safdar et al., 2009; 2012).

Safdar and colleagues (2003; 2012) incorporated the role of acculturation strategies as mediating variables in the MIDA model

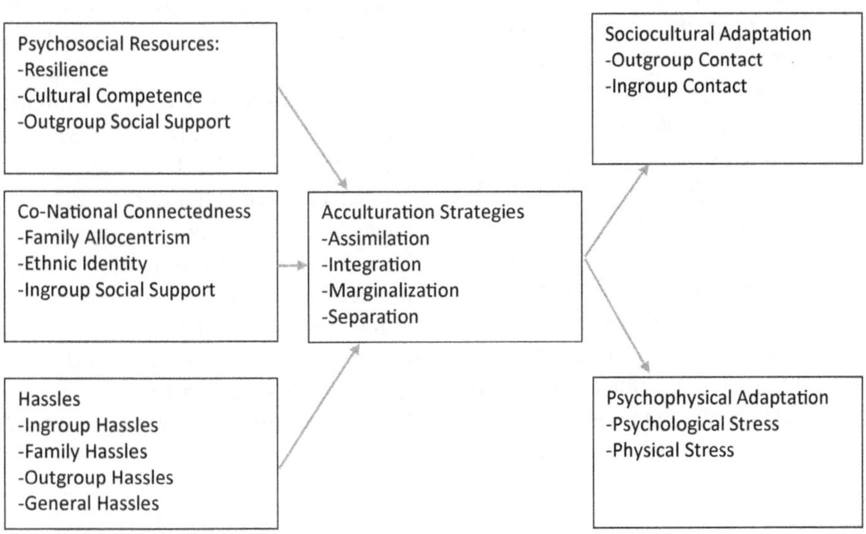

Figure 1.1 The Multidimensional Individual Difference Acculturation (MIDA) model (based on Safdar, Lay, & Struthers, 2003; Safdar, Struthers, & van Oudenhoven, 2009)

predicting adaptation. It was found that, among immigrants in Canada (i.e., Iranian, Indian, and Russian), *Separation* was associated with adaptation, specifically a high level of *Ingroup Contact.* Similarly, among the same group, *Assimilation* was associated with a high level of *Outgroup Contact.* Safdar and colleagues (2009) tested the MIDA model with samples of Iranian immigrants and refugees in the United States, the UK, and the Netherlands. They employed the two orthogonal dimensions of Berry's (1980) framework – a preference for maintaining heritage culture and a preference for engaging with the larger society – instead of the acculturation strategies as mediating variables. Similar to acculturation strategies, the researchers found that a preference for maintaining heritage culture was associated with adaptation, specifically a high level of *Ingroup Contact.* A preference for engaging with the larger society was associated with adaptation, specifically a high level of *Outgroup Contact* (Safdar et al., 2009).

Arends-Tóth and van de Vijver's acculturation model

The model depicted in Figure 1.2 is based on Arends-Tóth and van de Vijver's (2006; see also Celenk and van de Vijver, 2011; van de Vijver et al., 2016) acculturation model. It postulates that the acculturation process is an interaction of antecedent, mediating, and outcome factors. Antecedent factors refer to the context of acculturation and personal characteristics; examples of antecedent conditions are immigrant policies (Bloemraad et al., 2008; Bourhis et al., 1997; Helbling, 2013; Huddleston et al., 2011) and characteristics of the immigrant group (e.g., ethnic and linguistic vitality; Galchenko and van de Vijver, 2007; Giles et al., 1985; Harwood et al., 1994). Individual characteristics of the migrant, such as his or her personality, are also relevant. For example, there is evidence that exchange students with more extroversion, empathy, openness, and better communication skills fare better (Matsumoto and Hwang, 2013; van Oudenhoven and van der Zee, 2002). Mediating factors are acculturation strategies (or orientations as these are labeled in this model). These are meant to provide a link between contextual conditions and outcomes. Berry's (1997) model of acculturation strategies can be used here, but it is also possible to focus on the underlying dimensions (maintaining the ethnic culture and adopting the mainstream culture), starting from models that use three or even more dimensions (as discussed below in more detail). In all these models, acculturation orientations specify how migrants prefer to deal with the cultures surrounding them and how contextual conditions and their personal preferences shape these orientations. Outcome factors refer to 'being well' and 'doing well'. The former refers to mental health, using positive indicators, such as experienced health, resilience, or self-esteem, whereas the latter refers to competencies and networks in the ethnic and mainstream culture. School grades, job performance, and skills in the dominant language are examples of frequently studied skills related to the mainstream culture, whereas social support and ethnic language skills are examples of outcomes in the ethnic domain.

It can be concluded that the MIDA model and the model by Arends-Tóth and van de Vijver (2006) have important similarities to each other and to Berry's (2003) acculturation framework. In these models, psychological distress and ingroup and outgroup contacts are measures of adaptation and included as outcome variables. Similarly, the predictor variables in both models consist of individual characteristics, their perception of social context, and characteristics of the receiving society. Furthermore, these models include acculturation strategies as mediating variables. Arends-Tóth and van de Vijver's (2006), Berry's (2003), and Safdar and colleagues' (2003) models were developed independently. Their concordance supports the validity of the models. Overall, these models are based on a bidimensional approach

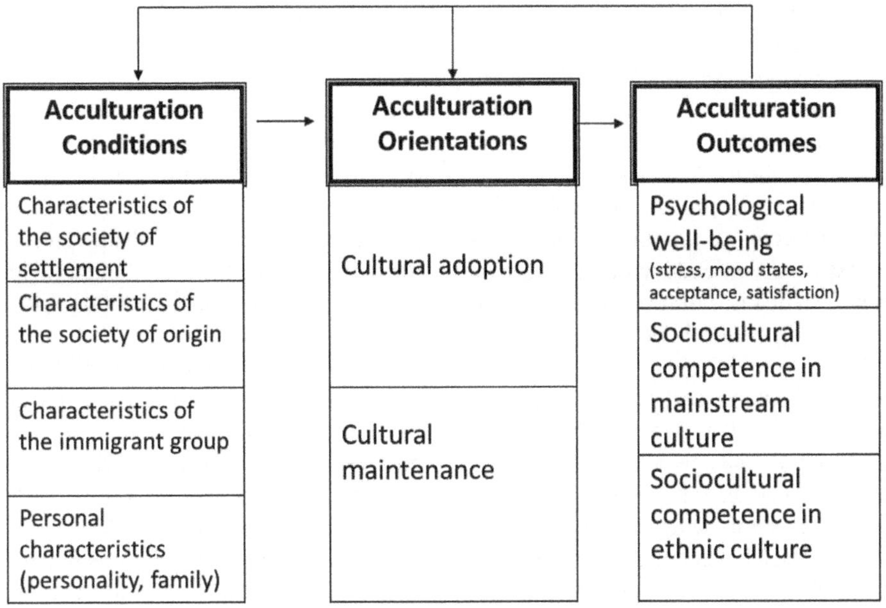

Figure 1.2 Conceptual framework of acculturation (adapted from Arends-Tóth & Van de Vijver, 2006)

to acculturation. They incorporate an a priori typology of acculturation. They also incorporate a range of factors that are central to examining acculturation of newcomers.

Emerging models

Migration patterns have been changing and will continue to change. For example, the group of expatriate employees is still growing (Finaccord, 2014). Student mobility has quadrupled in the last 25 years (to five million in 2014) (ICEF, 2015). The United Nations High Commissioner for Refugees (UNHCR) estimates that 65.3 million people, an unprecedented number, were displaced in 2016. Finally, popular destination countries, such as Canada, Australia, and New Zealand, report increases in permanent immigrants. These figures point to two important developments: firstly, to the best of our knowledge, the absolute number of migrants has never been larger before in human history; secondly, the nature of migration is changing. Notably, industrialized countries harbor large groups of both permanent and temporary migrants. These changes have a huge impact on cities in these industrialized countries, which have become truly multicultural. For urban dwellers, intercultural encounters have become more common in everyday life.

Acculturation patterns can be expected to be influenced by the type of acculturating group (Berry, 2006): acculturation will be different for the short-staying expat, than for the expat who will leave the country for another new country after a few years, than for the permanent migrants. So, acculturation is influenced by migration motive, length of stay, and the changing spatio-historical context in which it takes place. These changes should have implications for our conceptualizations of acculturation. The original unidimensional model of acculturation (Gordon, 1964), in which all immigrants gradually adjust to the dominant group in society, was mainly based on the acculturation patterns of European immigrants to the United States. Berry's (1997; see also Sam and Berry, 2016) bidimensional model was based on the observation that some immigrant groups are able to maintain their ethnic language and culture in the diaspora but are also well adjusted to the dominant society. We may need to adjust our models again to the changing pattern of acculturation in the world around us.

We describe two types of new acculturation models that set out to accommodate shortcomings of extant models and incorporate the new diversity. The first is tridimensional acculturation (Ferguson et al., 2012). These authors studied Jamaicans in the United States and found that these immigrants had three relevant cultures to which they related: their ethnic Jamaican culture, the new US culture, as well as the African-American culture. Jamaicans were found to identify with African Americans as a disadvantaged ethnic group but also as a resource for entertainment and hair care. The authors also studied adolescent Jamaicans in Jamaica and observed a phenomenon which they labeled 'remote acculturation', which refers to a process akin to Americanization. This group consumes US goods (clothing, food) and is interested in US culture (music, movies, television series). They adopt many elements of American culture, even though very few of them have ever visited the United States; hence the term remote acculturation.

The second type of model deals with the psychological consequences of globalization, which have been studied using related labels of multiculturalism (Chen et al., 2016), polyculturalism (Morris et al., 2015), and superdiversity (Vertovec, 1999; 2007). These concepts can be seen as generalizations of the concept of biculturalism (LaFromboise et al., 1993). The concept has become popular as it addresses a pivotal issue in acculturation: How do migrants negotiate their ethnic and mainstream background? For example, do they alternate between the cultures or do they combine (integrate) the two cultures?

A caveat is needed here. Multiculturalism as used here is very different from the concept with the same name that refers to the acceptance and support for the plural composition of society (Arends-Tóth and van de Vijver, 2003; Berry et al., 1997). Multiculturalism and polyculturalism in this chapter refer to the consequences of the many cross-cultural encounters in everyday life and the impact we all feel of the globalized culture. Modern (social) media play an important role in the dissemination of the culture. The group of people influenced by globalization is not restricted to immigrants, although it is in the nature of their migration that they will come across other cultures and globalization frequently. The domain of applicability of multiculturalism is not restricted to supranational entities. A good example can be found in post-apartheid South Africa. Since the abolishment of Apartheid in 1994 in South Africa, the concept of the Rainbow Nation has been promoted by various institutions in the country to instill a sense of inclusive identity that transcends ethnic boundaries as, historically, ethnic boundaries have always been rather impermeable. Multiculturalism is used here to promote inclusive identity and pride in the country's diversity (the rainbow as metaphor of the beauty of diversity). An important characteristic of the new acculturation framework is that the idea of contact between two cultures should be abandoned. Rather, it is assumed that 'individuals' relationships to cultures are not categorical but rather are partial and plural' (Morris et al., 2015: 631). The notion of tridimensional acculturation is here expanded to include any number of dimensions, dealing with any number of cultures. The same idea is used in superdiversity, which is a concept that was originally used to describe the neighborhoods in cities where many cultures live together, thereby forming a new, hybrid culture, based on, yet going beyond, the constituent cultures.

It could be argued that multiculturalism, polyculturalism, and superdiversity are not examples of acculturation. However, even if these concepts considerably differ from conventional unidimensional and bidimensional models of acculturation, we would argue that these concepts all comply with the basic definition of acculturation as referring to what happens when cultures come into prolonged, intense contact. Traditional models will need to be extended to relax two assumptions: (1) acculturation is about the contact of *two* cultures; (2) acculturation is about *physical* (or *first-hand*) encounters of people. In the new conceptualization, acculturation refers to the consequences of contacts between two or more cultures that are in actual or virtual contact, which could lead to changes in any of the cultures and/or the emergence of a new culture. The latter aspect (the emergence of a new culture) is also important in the new conceptualization. Globalization has led to a new culture, superdiversity can also lead to a cultural amalgam that is very specific for a city or neighborhood (van de Vijver et al., 2015).

Interesting as the concepts of tridimensional and remote acculturation, multiculturalism, polyculturalism, and superdiversity may be, they are still in their infancy and do not (yet) constitute a replacement of the extant acculturation frameworks. We still have little insight into the psychological processes of globalization, such as how to address domain specificity in these multiple identifications (as illustrated in the Jamaican example, target cultures are often identified within specific domains) and how individuals maintain a sense of coherence in the face of so many identifications. It may be instructive to use models of social and collective identities in acculturation research, as these fields have addressed several of the issues mentioned (Vignoles et al., 2011). The literature on identity also offers an interesting example for acculturation theory in its flexibility to define targets of identification. Acculturation is often strongly associated with ethnicity where the domains affected by acculturation may well go beyond ethnicity. For example, religious identity is an important aspect of many Muslim immigrants in Western countries whereas religion is not important for other groups (e.g., Statham et al., 2005). The same is true for language. An interesting example of the dissociation of identities among migrants can be found in Turkish and Moroccan immigrants in the Netherlands. Moroccan- and Turkish-Dutch tend to have a strong Muslim identity but the importance of their ethnic language (and linguistic identity) differs remarkably. After a few generations, Turkish-Dutch still tend to be able to speak Turkish, but Moroccan-Dutch tend to become Dutch monolinguals (Extra and Yagmur, 2010). This domain specificity is common in acculturation. Identities can be defined in different domains, such as ethnic identity, linguistic identity, and religious identity in the previous example. The acculturation literature and current assessments of acculturation are typically predicated on trait-like conceptualizations of acculturation in which preferences for maintenance or adoption are taken to hold across life domains. This approach will presumably have a limited applicability in studying modern types of acculturation (such as those dealing with globalization) that involve multiple dimensions and that are often very domain specific.

It can be concluded that, in our view, a new conceptual framework of acculturation is needed. The main reason is that the contexts in which acculturation takes place have changed, thereby limiting the applicability of conventional frameworks. Our argument is not so much that unidimensional and bidimensional models do no longer apply to acculturation but that new forms of acculturation require us to develop more flexible models. The need to develop new models may also be used as an opportunity to go beyond the often monodisciplinary focus of acculturation studies in psychology. Acculturation is studied in multiple disciplines which often work independently. Yet, a study of the domain specificity of acculturation processes may require multiple disciplines, such as anthropology to study the social context, economics to study consumption patterns and labor market participation, sociolinguistics to address language changes, and sociology to study housing patterns, to mention some examples.

ACCULTURATION OF REFUGEES AND OTHER IMMIGRANTS

There is an increasing interest in the acculturation of refugees, notably in Europe, which has witnessed the influx from places with humanitarian crises such as Syria. There is a number of characteristics of the group of refugees that sets them apart from other acculturating groups. An important characteristic is that they are forcibly displaced, usually without the option to return to their place of origin in the near future, and that they have experienced traumatic conditions, such as war, various types of violence, disease, famine, and death of family and friends. It is not surprising that much refugee literature deals with mental health and sociocultural adjustment to the new context.

Three types of factors have been shown to have a bearing on these outcomes. The first is related to the conditions prior to, and leading to, fleeing the country of origin: trauma, conditions in the host country, and personal resources. The most important variable that has been found to be consistently related to outcomes is trauma (e.g., Donà and Young, 2016; Fazel et al., 2012). The larger the frequency or severity of the traumas experienced, the more likely it is that Post-Traumatic Stress Disorder (PTSD) will have developed and that refugees will experience problems in their new cultural context (Knipscheer and Kleber, 2006).

Secondly, conditions in the receiving country are important moderators of acculturation outcomes for refugees (Steel et al., 2011). A first relevant condition is the legal status of the refugee (Da Lomba, 2010). Asylum procedures can take a long time and are accompanied by feelings of uncertainty and anxiety about the outcome. Individuals with a formal refugee status, which comes with the right to stay in the country, tend to experience less distress than persons still in the asylum procedure. The decision at the end of the procedure could be that the legal status is denied. Refugees with such a status can decide to stay in the country and become undocumented migrants, joining the ranks of migrants who entered the country using the services of human traffickers and who never applied for a legal status or were denied such a status. The considerable uncertainties of an undocumented status lead to serious stress in this group (Sullivan and Rehm, 2005). A second, well-documented source of stress is discrimination in the host country (Te Lindert et al., 2008). It has been found that immigrants and refugees tend to report discrimination (Berry et al., 2006a). The third source is the dispersion policy in a country. In many countries there is an explicit policy to disperse refugees from a single country so as to maximize the likelihood that refugees will adjust to the new culture and will lose ties with their ethnic culture; an example are Iranians in the Netherlands (Te Lindert et al., 2008). Such groups of dispersed refugees typically show high levels of sociocultural adjustment, although this is not always accompanied by high levels of subjective well-being. A fourth source of distress can be the drop in socioeconomic status and income after resettlement, even in the second generation (Connor, 2010). The new country may not recognize the certificates and professional experience of the refugees, which could imply that these refugees are not allowed to work in jobs they occupied in their country of origin. A fifth source of the stress is instability of the settlement, notably for children (Fazel et al., 2012). Many refugees do not directly travel from their country of origin to an address in the country of destination, but move from one place to another, in some cases from one country to another, before they reach a stable settlement. These long periods of being uprooted can be stressful for refugees. A final source of distress can be the absence of a social support network, which is typically the case in the first period in the new country (Fazel et al., 2012; Jasinskaja-Lahti et al., 2006).

Finally, personal factors are relevant in the adjustment process of refugees. There are indications that children with behavioral issues in the country of origin have more problems in adjusting to the new context (Fazel et al., 2012). Mental health issues prior to becoming a refugee tend to make it more difficult to deal with the distress in the country of settlement. The second factor refers to the personal or family situation at the time the expatriation process started in the situation in the country of settlement (Donà and Young, 2016). Family members can be a tremendous resource for each other in the expatriation process, although family relations can be a source of stress in refugee families when the second generation adjusts to the new cultural context much more quickly than the parents (Ho, 2010). Finally, the personal skills and characteristics that were described before as important moderators of the acculturation process, such as commendation skills, extraversion, and empathy, are also important for refugees.

The literature on refugees is replete with examples of mental health issues, negative emotionality, and distress. For some refugees, PTSD continues to make life hard, even after having stayed in the new country a long period of time. However, this emphasis on negative aspects of problems could easily distract the attention from the long-term outcomes in this group. Many refugees are able to successfully develop a new life in the acculturation context. The forced migration often creates an awareness that returning to the country of origin is not an option, which can create a strong motivation to learn the language and culture of the new country. Families that have a stronger assimilation preference tend to show more generation gaps and fewer conflicts.

Other groups with specific sociodemographic characteristics are temporary and voluntary acculturating groups, including tourists, international students, professional expats, and economic migrants. Examining acculturation of all these groups is beyond the focus of this chapter (see Safdar and Berno, 2016, for a review of acculturation of sojourners). However, we examine a distinction between economic migrants and other acculturating groups. Boski (2013: 1069) argued 'the driving force for economic immigrants is to escape poverty, to overcome unemployment, to improve their personal living condition, and to help their families at large'. He suggested that, instead of an acculturation paradigm, a *homo faber* model of immigrants is required that focuses on the centrality of work and particular motivation and stress that characterize this group (Boski, 2013). In particular, Boski (2013) found that Polish immigrants in Ireland worked harder, and were more conscientious, than Polish living in Poland and Irish nationals living in Ireland. He argued that this indicates that working hard is a consequence of the life condition of economic immigrants (i.e., a situational factor) rather than the result of acculturation (i.e., acquiring the values of the new culture or maintaining the values of the heritage culture). He also found that economic Polish migrants reported more distance from their peers. Boski (2013) argued that this is not a reflection of adaptation of separation strategy, rather it is due to the fact that economic migrants have little time and money to socialize with the majority.

IMPORTANCE OF SOCIOCULTURAL CONTEXT IN ACCULTURATION

Most studies in the early period of acculturation research addressed a single ethnic group in a single country at a single point in time. This design is still very common in acculturation research. Most of the work employing and testing unidimensional and bidimensional models is based on this design. However, over the years, it has become clear that this design has limitations. Studies employing these designs can provide valuable information about acculturation orientations and outcomes, but other features of acculturation may be more difficult to examine. For example, generational differences can be used as a proxy for developmental processes in acculturation, but longitudinal designs, following migrants over longer periods of time, provide more detailed information about acculturative changes. Also, comparing acculturation processes of different migrant groups in a single country (e.g., comparing refugees from multiple countries in Canada) or of a single migration group in multiple countries (e.g., comparing the acculturation of Syrian refugees in multiple European countries) are an important extension of the original paradigm (Sam and Berry, 2016). Such comparative acculturation studies allow for a more fine-grained analysis of how cultural context influences acculturation processes.

There is another argument why such designs will probably become more important. Conceptual models of acculturation tend to emphasize the role of context in acculturation; yet, its actual impact is infrequently studied. It is therefore quite natural that context is taken more seriously in our study designs. This can be done in multiple ways, such as asking migrants more subjective evaluations of their acculturation environment (e.g., asking for an evaluation of the acculturation climate), evaluating more objective aspects of the acculturation environment (e.g., examining the ethnic composition of the neighborhood), or choosing specific acculturation contexts that systematically vary in a presumably relevant acculturation aspect, such as country differences in multiculturalism policies. Below, we present examples of such comparative studies.

Yagmur (2016; see also Yagmur and van de Vijver, 2012) was interested in the acculturation of Turks in four different countries: Australia, France, Germany, and the Netherlands. These countries were chosen as they show large differences in multiculturalism policies. So, the interest was in identifying acculturation correlates of differences in multiculturalism policies. Of the four countries, Australia has the strongest support for a pluralist ideology, in which the state provides support for language classes and cultural activities to promote mother tongue maintenance alongside second language proficiency. With these policies, strong first language maintenance and successful socio-cultural integration would be expected for different generations of Turkish immigrants. France's policy is oriented on supporting nationhood, based on language assimilation. Social cohesion and national unity are taken to be best protected when everyone speaks the common language. Immigrants are encouraged to use French in the private sphere. In the Netherlands, the policy has long been oriented on integration (i.e., a combination of ethnic maintenance and adoption of Dutch culture), although more recently, the emphasis has shifted to assimilation. Germany has a strong tradition of homogenizing heterogeneity, with an emphasis on adoption of the main language and culture. Based on these findings, one would expect most language maintenance and the strongest ethnic orientation in Australia, followed by the Netherlands, and the strongest mainstream orientation and mastery of the dominant language in France and Germany.

Turkish identity was strongest in France and weakest in Australia and the Netherlands, whereas the mainstream (national) identity was strongest in Australia, followed by the Netherlands and France, and weakest in Germany. The preference to use the Turkish language was strongest in Germany and weakest in France. As could be expected, education was related negatively to Turkish identity, positively to mainstream identity, and negatively to preference to use Turkish. These findings suggest that multicultural policies have a bearing on core acculturation and language variables. Firstly, the French pressure on using the mainstream language has an effect, notably on more highly educated immigrants. It is interesting that Turks in Germany have the strongest preference to use Turkish. This latter finding is also reflected in the identity scores: contrary to what might be expected, Turkish immigrants feel the strongest ties with the mainstream culture and the weakest ties with their ethnic group in Australia, which is the country that uses least pressure to assimilate immigrants. The findings suggest that immigrants are most likely to adopt the mainstream identity and give up their ethnic identity when they are put under *least* pressure to do so.

In a similar study, acculturation of Iranian groups was examined in the United States, the UK, and the Netherlands (Safdar et al., 2009), which was then compared with acculturation of Iranians in Canada. The four countries differ in terms of acculturation policy and diversity index, which lead to different acculturation experiences for immigrants. Specifically, Canada is the only country with

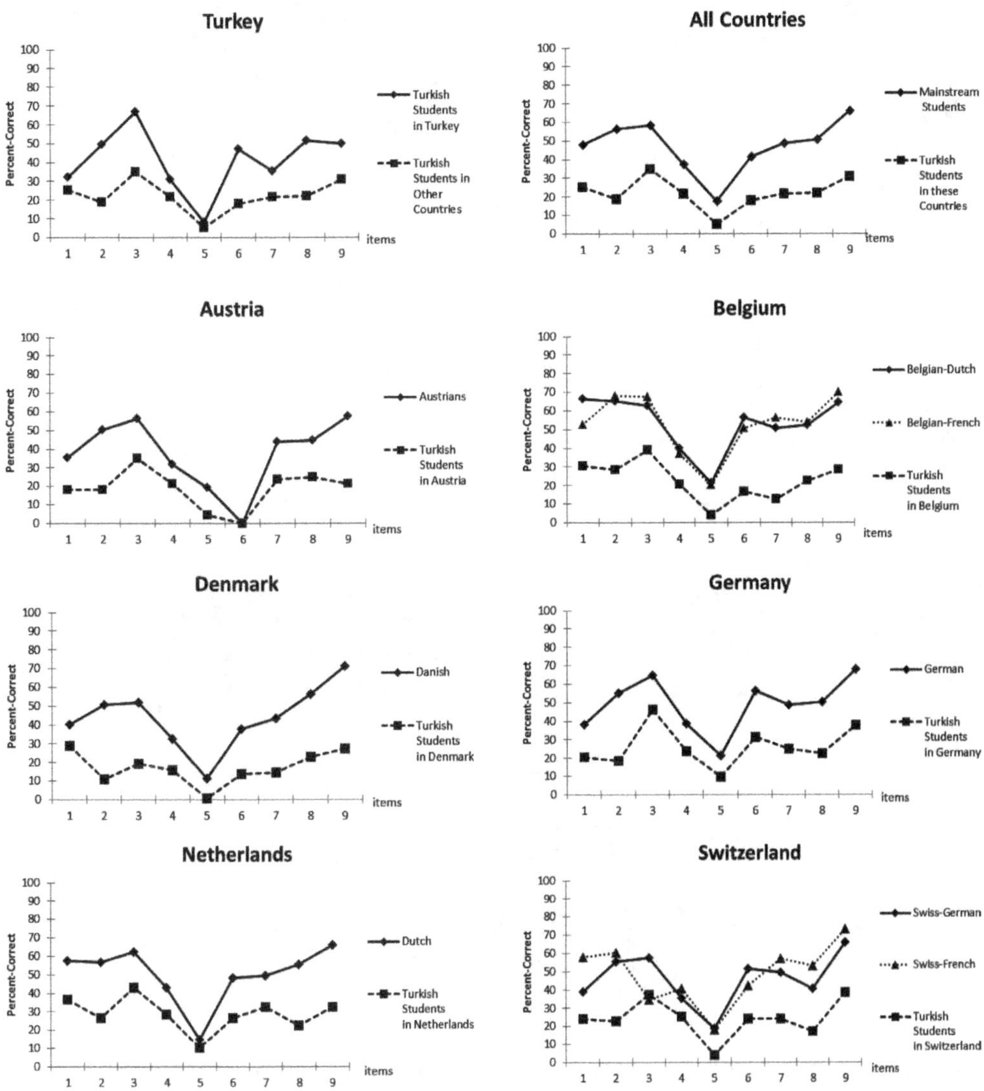

Figure 1.3 Percent-correct-values for PISA 2009 Released Reading Items (based on Arikan, Van de Vijver, & Yagmur, 2017)

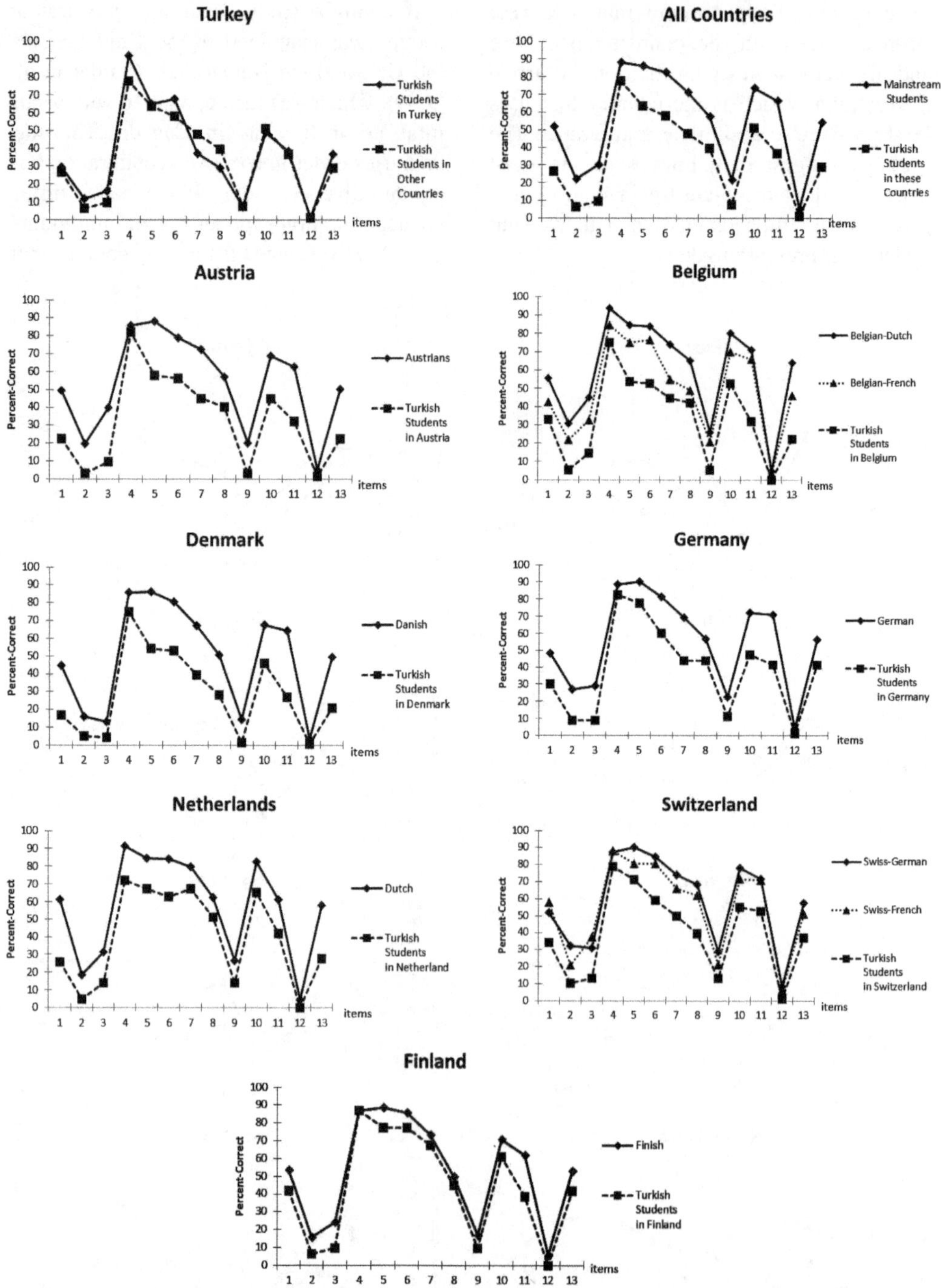

Figure 1.4 Percent-correct-values for PISA 2012 Released Mathematics Items (based on Arikan, Van de Vijver, & Yagmur, 2017)

an official multiculturalism policy, and both Canada and the United States rank higher than the UK and the Netherlands on the diversity index devised by Berry et al., (2006b). The researchers reported that Iranians living in Europe (i.e., the UK and the Netherlands) report poorer adaptation (i.e., higher psychophysical distress) than Iranians living in North America (i.e., Canada and the United States; Chuong and Safdar, 2008; Safdar and Lewis, 2007). Furthermore, Iranians living in North America reported higher levels of positive psychosocial functioning (e.g., resilience, social support, and cultural competence) than Iranians living in the UK (Chuong and Safdar, 2008). Although both these studies addressed individuals only coming from one ethnic culture and generalizations to other countries cannot be directly made, the results illustrate the importance of studying the context of acculturation.

Arikan et al., (2017) were interested in the educational performance of Turkish immigrants in different European countries. They analyzed reading and mathematics performance of mainstream and Turkish immigrants in Austria, Belgium, Denmark, Finland, Germany, the Netherlands, and Switzerland; data from native Turks were used as reference group. Data were derived from the 2009 and 2012 PISA (Programme for International Student Assessment) project, which assesses educational achievement among large probability samples of 15 year olds. Results are presented in Figures 1.3 (Reading) and 1.4 (Mathematics). As can be seen in both figures, immigrant students tended to show lower scores than mainstream students; the difference was larger for the reading test. Correcting for differences in individual background characteristics, such as socioeconomic status (typically lower for immigrant students than for mainstream students), reduced the group performance differences by about one third; yet, the differences remained highly significant. MIPEX scores of countries (Huddleston et al., 2011) were examined in the study. The Migrant Integration Policy Index (MIPEX) is is a measure of national integration policies, combining 167 policy indicators of migrants' opportunities to participate in society. MIPEX scores were used to predict of immigrant performance at country level (countries with higher scores give more legal rights to immigrants). These scores were significantly related to reading scores: immigrants living in countries with higher MIPEX scores showed higher reading scores; the association for mathematics was not significant. The difference could be a consequence of the more profound knowledge of the local language and culture that is required for reading than for math. Countries with higher MIPEX scores are more pluralistic and inclusive. It could well be that students in these countries identify more with the local culture (similar to what we found in the example of Turks in Australia, France, Germany, and the Netherlands; Yagmur, 2016); therefore, they could have a better knowledge of the local language and culture.

APPLICATIONS

Acculturation models are relevant for applied psychology. An important domain of application is test adaptations. There is extensive literature on how to adapt tests to make these suitable for a multicultural population (e.g., Hambleton et al., 2005; Suzuki and Ponterotto, 2008; van de Vijver, 2016). This literature addresses the question of how to identify and reduce cultural bias in assessment. Adaptations can involve simplification of language, removal of ethnocentrism, removal of implicit references to the dominant culture or references to cultural practices that are not widely shared. The procedures to adapt tests combine cultural and psychometric considerations. It should be noted that this literature has a procedural emphasis and does not describe cultural issues in depth; rather, it describes how cultural issues, when identified, can be incorporated in instruments

(Hambleton et al., 2005). Much of the literature deals with international comparisons, but generalizations to multicultural populations are obvious.

Another domain of application that has received ample attention is health-related treatment and intervention. Central in this work is the link between health behavior and acculturation; examples are work on smoking cessation in African Americans by Webb Hooper et al. (2012) and on implications of acculturation for lifestyle interventions among Latinos by Moreno and Johnston (2015). This literature shows that many health behaviors are influenced by acculturation and that migrants often slowly adopt the behaviors of their new cultural context with subsequent changes in health behavior. These findings point to the need for acculturation-informed interventions among immigrants.

There has been considerable debate about the question of the effectiveness of cultural adaptations of therapy and interventions. The topic has been studied so frequently that the first meta-analyses could be conducted (Castro et al., 2010; Griner and Smith, 2006). Castro et al. give an overview of procedures to implement cultural knowledge in therapies and interventions. Like the literature on test adaptations, the recommendations are procedural rather than cultural to make these widely applicable. The meta-analytic evidence strongly suggests that culturally adapted interventions are more effective. Therapists who speak the ethnic language are more effective than therapists working in the dominant language, and adaptations are more effective when dealing with migrants with low levels of adjustment to the dominant culture. The effects were mostly of medium size, suggesting that the 'one size fits all' approach in dealing with immigrants in therapy does not have a strong evidence base. Culture-informed therapy will, on average, create more change than a standard application of a therapy that has proven effective in the dominant group.

Furthermore, by understanding the factors that influence adjustment of newcomers, service providers, policy makers, and support programs are better equipped to facilitate settlement of migrants and refugees. Results of years of empirical evidence demonstrate that, when newcomers experience discrimination and stereotypes, they are likely to feel threatened and to reject the larger society (Berry, 2013; Gui et al., 2016). However, when newcomers experience inclusion and acceptance, they are more likely to adjust and engage with the larger society (Berry et al., 2006a; Gui et al., 2016). Similarly, when settling societies endorse assimilation or segregation policies, immigrants and refugees tend to have poorer well-being, higher levels of stress, and lower levels of adjustment (Berry, 1997; 2013). Conversely, promoting integration as a national policy is associated with better adjustment of newcomers and engagement with the larger society (Berry, 1997; 2013; Safdar et al., 2003; 2009; 2012). These are direct applications of acculturation research based on well-established psychological principles.

CONCLUSION

Overall, in our review, we demonstrated that acculturation is a process that migrants go through rather than only an outcome. Within the acculturation literature, a wide range of factors have been identified as central in examining the acculturation process. These factors include discrimination (Sam and Berry, 2016), linguistic vitality (Galchenko and van de Vijver, 2007), positive psychological functioning (Safdar et al., 2003), national and ethnic identity (Phinney, 2003), acculturation strategies of migrants (Berry, 1997), and acculturation expectations of the host culture (Bourhis et al., 1997). A successful acculturation process is measured in terms of 'doing well' (e.g., school adjustment, engagement with larger society) and 'being well' (e.g., self-esteem, low psychophysical stress, Gui et al., 2016). We reviewed several contemporary acculturation models that focus on specific individual and social characteristics of the migrating groups. We also demonstrated that acculturation is a bidirectional process. This means that successful acculturation not only depends on what immigrant groups do but also on characteristics of the host culture. We described studies of acculturation of one ethnic group in several social contexts to highlight the importance of sociocultural characteristics of host cultures in adjustment of migrants. Acculturation has moved from a rather peripheral phenomenon to an essential part of psychology. The large streams of voluntary and involuntary migration ensure that acculturation will continue to be a pivotal concept in the coming period.

REFERENCES

Arends-Tóth, J., & van de Vijver, F. J. R. (2003). Multiculturalism and acculturation: Views of Dutch and Turkish-Dutch. *European Journal of Social Psychology*, *33*, 249–266.

Arends-Tóth, J. V., & van de Vijver, F. J. R. (2006). Issues in conceptualization and assessment of acculturation. In M. H. Bornstein & L. R. Cote (Eds.) *Acculturation and parent–child relationships: Measurement and development* (pp. 33–62). Mahwah, NJ: Lawrence Erlbaum.

Arikan, S., van de Vijver, F. J. R., & Yagmur, K. (2017). PISA mathematics and reading performance differences of mainstream European and Turkish immigrant students. *Educational Assessment, Evaluation and Accountability*, *29*, 229–246.

Berry, J. W. (1970). Marginality, stress and ethnic identification in an acculturated aboriginal community. *Journal of Cross-Cultural Psychology*, *1*, 239–252.

Berry, J. W. (1974). Psychological aspects of cultural pluralism. *Culture Learning*, *2*, 17–22.

Berry, J. W. (1980). Acculturation as varieties of adaptation. In A. M. Padilla (Ed.), *Acculturation: Theory, models and some new findings* (pp. 9–25). Boulder, CO: Westview Press.

Berry, J. W. (1997). Immigration, acculturation, and adaptation. *Applied Psychology: An International Review*, *46*, 5–68.

Berry, J. W. (2003). Conceptual approaches to acculturation. In K. M. Chun, P. B. Organista, & G. Marin (Eds.), *Acculturation: Advances in theory, measurement, and applied research* (pp. 17–37). Washington, DC: American Psychological Association.

Berry, J. W. (2006). Mutual attitudes among immigrants and ethnocultural groups in Canada. *International Journal of Intercultural Relations*, *30*(6), 719–734.

Berry, J. W. (2013). Research on multiculturalism in Canada. *International Journal of Intercultural Relations*, *37*, 663–675.

Berry, J. W., Kim, U., Minde, T., & Mok, D. (1987). Comparative studies of acculturative stress. *International Migration Review*, *21*, 362–384.

Berry, J., & Safdar, S. (2007). Psychology of diversity: Managing of diversity in plural societies. In A. Chybicka & M. Kazmierczak (Eds.), *The psychology of diversity: Cultural and gender issues* (pp. 19–36). Cracow, Poland: Impuls.

Berry, J. W., Kalin, R., & Taylor, D. M. (1997). *Multicultural policy and ethnic attitudes in Canada.* Ottawa, ON: Minister of State for Multiculturalism, Printing and Supply Services in Canada.

Berry, J. W., Phinney, J. S., Sam, D. L., & Vedder, P. (2006a). Immigrant youth: Acculturation, identity, and adaptation. *Applied Psychology: An International Review*, *55*, 303–332.

Berry, J. W., Westin, C., Virta, E., Vedder, P., Rooney, R., & Sang, D. (2006b). Design of the study: Selecting societies of settlement and immigrant groups. In J. W. Berry, J. S. Phinney, D. L. Sam, & P. Vedder (Eds.), *Immigrant youth in cultural transition. Acculturation, identity, and adaptation across national contexts* (pp. 15–46). Mahwah, NJ: Lawrence Erlbaum Associates.

Bloemraad, I., Korteweg, A., & Yurdakul, G. (2008). Citizenship and immigration: Multiculturalism, assimilation, and challenges to the nation-state. *Annual Review of Sociology*, *34*, 153–179.

Boski, P. (2013). A psychology of economic migration. *Journal of Cross-Cultural Psychology*, *44*, 1067–1093.

Bourhis, R. Y., Moïse, L. C., Perreault, S., & Senéchal, S. (1997). Towards an interactive acculturation model: A social psychological approach. *International Journal of Psychology*, *32*, 369–386.

Castro, F. G., Barrera Jr, M., & Holleran Steiker, L. K. (2010). Issues and challenges in the design of culturally adapted evidence-based interventions. *Annual Review of Clinical Psychology*, *6*, 213–239.

Celenk, O., & van de Vijver, F. J. R. (2011). Assessment of acculturation: Issues and overview of measures. *Online Readings in Psychology and Culture, Unit 1*. Retrieved from http://scholarworks.gvsu.edu/orpc/vol8/iss1/10.

Chen, S. X., Lam, B. C., Hui, B. P., Ng, J. C., Mak, W. W., Guan, Y., Buchtel, E. E., Tang, W. C. S., & Lau, V. C. (2016). Conceptualizing psychological processes in response to globalization: Components, antecedents, and consequences of global orientations. *Journal of Personality and Social Psychology*, *110*, 302–331.

Chirkov, V. (2009). Critical psychology of acculturation: What do we study and how do we study it, when we investigate acculturation? *International Journal of Intercultural Relations*, *33*, 94–105.

Chuong, K., & Safdar, S. (2008). *Daily hassles in relation to psychological adjustment and distress among Iranian immigrants.* In D. Dupuis, & S. Rasmi (Co-Chair), Investigating acculturation from the perspectives of the receiving society and immigrant groups. Symposium conducted at the 69th Annual Convention of the Canadian Psychological Association. Halifax, Nova Scotia, Canada (June 12–14).

Connor, P. (2010). Explaining the refugee gap: Economic outcomes of refugees versus other immigrants. *Journal of Refugee Studies*, *23*, 377–397.

Da Lomba, S. (2010). Legal status and refugee integration: A UK perspective. *Journal of Refugee Studies*, *23*, 415–436.

DeLongis, A., Coyne, J. C., Dakof, G., Folkman, S., & Lazarus, R. S. (1982). Relationships of daily hassles, uplifts and major life events to health status. *Health Psychology*, *1*, 119–136.

Donà, G., & Young, M. (2016). Refugees and forced migrants. In D. L. Sam & J. W. Berry (Eds.), *The Cambridge handbook of acculturation psychology* (pp. 153–172). Cambridge, UK: Cambridge University Press.

Extra, G., & Yagmur, K. (2010). Language proficiency and socio-cultural orientation of Turkish and Moroccan youngsters in the Netherlands. *Language and Education*, *24*, 117–132.

Fazel, M., Reed, R. V., Panter-Brick, C., & Stein, A. (2012). Mental health of displaced and refugee children resettled in high-income countries: Risk and protective factors. *The Lancet*, *379*, 266–282.

Ferguson, G. M., Bornstein, M. H., & Pottinger, A. M. (2012). Tridimensional acculturation and adaptation among Jamaican adolescent-mother dyads in the United States. *Child Development*, *83*, 1486–1493.

Finaccord (2014). *Global expatriates: Size, segmentation and forecast for the worldwide market*. London, UK: Author.

Galchenko, I., & van de Vijver, F. J. R. (2007). The role of perceived cultural distance in the acculturation of exchange students in Russia. *International Journal of Intercultural Relations*, *31*, 181–197.

Giles, H., Rosenthal, D., & Young, L. (1985). Perceived ethnolinguistic vitality: The Anglo- and Greek-Australian setting. *Journal of Multilingual & Multicultural Development*, *6*(3–4), 253–269.

Gordon, M. M. (1964). *Assimilation in American life*. New York, NY: Oxford University Press.

Graves, T. D. (1967). Psychological acculturation in a tri-ethnic community. *Southwestern Journal of Anthropology*, *23*, 337–350.

Griner D., & Smith, T. B. (2006). Culturally adapted mental health interventions: A meta-analytic review. *Psychotherapy: Theory, Research, Practice, Training*, *43*, 531–548.

Gui, Y., Safdar, S., & Berry, J. (2016). Mutual intercultural relations among university students in Canada. *Frontiers: The Interdisciplinary Journal of Study Abroad,* XXVII, 17–32.

Hambleton, R. K., Merenda, P. F., & Spielberger, C. D. (Eds.). (2005). *Adapting educational tests and psychological tests for cross-cultural assessment*. Mawhaw, NJ: Erlbaum.

Harwood, J., Giles, H., & Bourhis, R. Y. (1994). The genesis of vitality theory: Historical patterns and discoursal dimensions. *International Journal of the Sociology of Language*, *108*, 167–206.

Helbling, M. (2013). Validating integration and citizenship policy indices. *Comparative European Politics*, *11*, 555–576.

Ho, J. (2010). Acculturation gaps in Vietnamese immigrant families: Impact on family relationships. *International Journal of Intercultural Relations*, *34*, 22–33.

Huddleston, T., Niessen, J., Chaoimh, E. N., & White, E. (2011). *Migrant Integration Policy Index III*. Retrieved from http://issuu.com/mipex/docs/migrant_integration_policy_index_mipexiii_2011?e=2578332/3681189#search.

ICEF. (2015). *The state of international student mobility in 2015*. Retrieved from http://monitor.icef.com/2015/11/the-state-of-international-student-mobility-in-2015/.

Jasinskaja-Lahti, I., Liebkind, K., Jaakkola, M., & Reuter, A. (2006). Perceived discrimination, social support networks, and psychological well-being among three immigrant groups. *Journal of Cross-Cultural Psychology, 37*, 293–311.

Knipscheer, J. W., & Kleber, R. J. (2006). The relative contribution of posttraumatic and acculturative stress to subjective mental health among Bosnian refugees. *Journal of Clinical Psychology, 62*, 339–354.

LaFromboise, T., Coleman, H. L. K., & Gerton, J. (1993). Psychological impact of biculturalism: Evidence and theory. *Psychological Bulletin, 114*, 395–412.

Matsumoto, D., & Hwang, H. C. (2013). Assessing cross-cultural competence: A review of available tests. *Journal of Cross-Cultural Psychology, 44*, 849–873.

McGee, W. J. (1898). Piratical acculturation. *American Anthropologist, 11*, 243–249.

Moreno, J. P., & Johnston, C. A. (2015). Considering the impact of acculturation on lifestyle interventions for Latinos. *American Journal of Lifestyle Medicine, 9*, 40–42.

Morris, M. W., Chiu, C. Y., & Liu, Z. (2015). Polycultural psychology. *Annual Review of Psychology, 66*, 631–659.

Navas, M., García, M. C., Sánchez, J., Rojas, A. J., Pumares, P., & Fernández, J. S. (2005). Relative acculturation extended model (RAEM): New contributions with regard to the study of acculturation. *International Journal of Intercultural Relations, 29*, 21–37.

Navas, M., Rojas, A. J., García, M., & Pumares, P. (2007). Acculturation strategies and attitudes according to the Relative Acculturation Extended Model (RAEM): The perspective of natives versus immigrants. *International Journal of Intercultural Relations, 31*, 67–86.

Phinney, J. S. (2003). Ethnic identity and acculturation. In K. M. Chun, P. B. Organista, & G. Marin (Eds.), *Acculturation: Advances in theory, measurement, and applied research* (pp. 63–81). Washington, DC: American Psychological Association.

Piontkowski, U., Florack, A., Hoelker, P., & Obdrzálek, P. (2000). Predicting acculturation attitudes of dominant and non-dominant groups. *International Journal of Intercultural Relations, 24*, 1–26.

Redfield, R., Linton, R., & Herskovits, M. J. (1936). Memorandum for the study of acculturation. *American Anthropologist, 38*, 149–152.

Rohmann, A., Florack, A., & Pointkowski, U. (2006). The role of discordant acculturation attitudes in perceived threat: An analysis of host and immigrant attitudes in Germany. *International Journal of Intercultural Relations, 30*, 683–702.

Ryff, C. D., & Singer, B. (1996). Psychological well-being: Meaning, measurement, and implications for psychotherapy research. *Psychotherapy and Psychosomatics, 65*, 14–23.

Safdar, S., & Berno, T. (2016). Sojourners: The experience of expatriates, students, and tourists. In D. L. Sam & J. W. Berry (Eds.), *The Cambridge handbook of acculturation psychology* (2nd edn.). Cambridge, United Kingdom: Cambridge University Press.

Safdar, S., & Lewis, J. R. (2007). Experience and impact of acculturation specific hassles among Iranians living in America, Britain, and the Netherlands. *Journal of Iranian Psychologists, 4(13)*, 1–18.

Safdar, S., Calvez, S., & Lewis, J. R. (2012). Multi-group analysis of the MIDA model: Acculturation of Indian and Russian immigrants in Canada. *International Journal of Intercultural Relation, 36*, 200–212.

Safdar, S., Choung, K., & Lewis, J. R. (2013). A review of the MIDA model and other contemporary acculturation models. In E. Tartakovsky (Ed.), *Immigration: policies, challenges and impact* (pp. 213–230). Hauppauge, NY: Nova Science Publisher.

Safdar, S., Lay, C., & Struthers, W. (2003). The process of acculturation and basic goals: Testing a multidimensional individual difference model with Iranian immigrants in Canada. *Applied Psychology: An International Review, 52*, 555–579.

Safdar, S., Struthers, W., & van Oudenhoven, J. P. (2009). Acculturation of Iranians in the

United States, the United Kingdom, and the Netherlands: A test of the multidimensional individual difference acculturation (MIDA) model. *Journal of Cross-Cultural Psychology, 40*, 468–491.

Sam, D. L., & Berry, J. W. (Eds.). (2016). *The Cambridge handbook of acculturation psychology.* Cambridge, UK: Cambridge University Press.

Searle, W., & Ward, C. (1990). The predictions of psychological and sociocultural adjustment during cross-cultural transitions. *International Journal of Intercultural Relations, 14*, 449–464.

Statham, P., Koopmans, R., Giugni, M., & Passy, F. (2005). Resilient or adaptable Islam? Multiculturalism, religion and migrants' claims-making for group demands in Britain, the Netherlands and France. *Ethnicities, 5*, 427–459.

Steel, Z., Momartin, S., Silove, D., Coello, M., Aroche, J., & Tay, K. W. (2011). Two year psychosocial and mental health outcomes for refugees subjected to restrictive or supportive immigration policies. *Social Science & Medicine, 72*, 1149–1156.

Sullivan, M. M., & Rehm, R. (2005). Mental health of undocumented Mexican immigrants: A review of the literature. *Advances in Nursing Science, 28*, 240–251.

Suzuki, L. A., & Ponterotto, J. G. (Eds.). (2008). *Handbook of multicultural assessment: Clinical, psychological, and educational applications* (3rd edn.). San Francisco, CA: Jossey-Bass.

Te Lindert, A., Korzilius, H., van de Vijver, F. J. R., Kroon, S., & Arends-Tóth, J. (2008). Perceived discrimination and acculturation among Iranian refugees in the Netherlands. *International Journal of Intercultural Relations, 32*, 578–588.

Van de Vijver, F. J. R. (2016). Test adaptations. In F. T. L. Leong, D. Bartram, F. M. Cheung, K. F. Geisinger, & D. Iliescu (Eds.), *The ITC international handbook of testing and assessment* (pp. 364–376). New York, NY: Oxford University Press.

Van de Vijver, F. J. R., Berry, J. W., & Celenk, O. (2016). Assessment of acculturation. In D. L. Sam & J. W. Berry (Eds.), *The Cambridge handbook of acculturation psychology* (pp. 293–314). Cambridge, United Kingdom: Cambridge University Press.

Van de Vijver, F. J. R., Blommaert, J. M. E., Gkoumasi, G., & Stogianni, M. (2015). On the need to broaden the concept of ethnic identity. *International Journal of Intercultural Relations, 46*, 36–46.

Van Oudenhoven, J. P., & van der Zee, K. I. (2002). Predicting multicultural effectiveness of international students: The Multicultural Personality Questionnaire. *International Journal of Intercultural Relations, 26*, 679–694.

Van Oudenhoven, J. P., Ward, C., & Masgoret, A. M. (2006). Patterns of relations between immigrants and host societies. *International Journal of Intercultural Relations, 30*, 635–657.

Vertovec, S. (1999). Conceiving and researching transnationalism. *Ethnic and Racial Studies, 22*, 447–462.

Vertovec, S. (2007). Super-diversity and its implications. *Ethnic and Racial Studies, 30*, 1024–1054.

Vignoles, V. L., Schwartz, S. J., & Luyckx, K. (2011). Introduction: Towards an integrative view of identity. In S. J. Schwartz, K. Luyckx, & V. L. Vignoles (Eds.), *Handbook of identity theory and research* (pp. 1–30). New York, NY: Springer.

Ward, C. (1996). Acculturation. In D. Landis, & R. Bhagat (Eds.), *Handbook of intercultural training* (2nd edn., pp. 124–147). Newbury Park, CA: Sage.

Ward, C., & Kennedy, A. (1994). Acculturation strategies, psychosocial adjustment, and sociocultural competence during cross-cultural transitions. *International Journal of Intercultural Relations, 18*, 329–343.

Webb Hooper, M., Baker, E. A., De Ybarra, D. R., McNutt, M., & Ahluwalia, J. S. (2012). Acculturation predicts 7-day smoking cessation among treatment-seeking African-Americans in a group intervention. *Annals of Behavioral Medicine, 43*, 74–83.

Yagmur, K. (2016). *Intergenerational language use and acculturation of Turkish speakers in four immigration contexts*. Frankfurt am Main, Germany: Peter Lang.

Yagmur, K., & van de Vijver, F. J. R. (2012). Acculturation and language orientations of Turkish immigrants in Australia, France, Germany, and the Netherlands. *Journal of Cross-Cultural Psychology, 43*, 1110–1130.

2

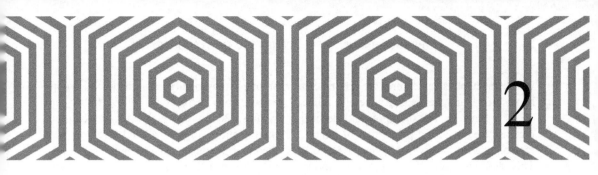

Heritage and (In)Equality: Social Psychology Applied to Race

Tracy A. McFarlane

OVERVIEW

A classic social psychological perspective on identity emphasizes the significance of social categories for individuals' secure identity formation, belonging, and affiliation (Hogg and Abrams, 1988; Tajfel and Turner, 1986). According to Stets and Burke (2000), societies present individuals with contrasting categories that vary based on power, status, and other socially defined values. Such group-based identity formation, together with role-based identification and the personal features of identity, provide the basis for achieving a full understanding of the self. Although critical for selfhood and psychological functioning, identity is not solely up to individual choice but is nested in the social meanings, norms, standards, and hierarchies of daily life.

With successive waves of international migration, globalization, and growing transnationalism, race has become even more ingrained as a feature of modern human experience across the globe. Enduring issues such as in-group/out-group distinctions, varying circumstances influencing identity salience, and even relatively modern social processes such as participation social movements are driven by the cognitive and motivational processes associated with who one is in society. Over time, human beings have learned to rely on patterns of categorizing each other, which include, but are not limited to, family, class, ethnicity, and race (Alleyne, 2005). As Markus (2008) points out, race and ethnicity have gained prominence in human consciousness, requiring psychologists to clearly define what race and ethnicity are and to explain why they matter. From an applied social psychology perspective, such conceptualizations are necessary for understanding and addressing racially infused matters of intergroup power, status, and exclusion.

Alleyne (2005) advances the view that race is a social construct based on features that may be transmitted genetically but vary in how they are perceived depending on time, place, and circumstances. Alleyne argues that visible racial physical features are salient, can be specified, and, hence, are generally relied on as a basis for classification and defines race as 'the socialized perception of phenotypical characteristics' (Alleyne, 2005: 2). This definition reflects a core assumption underpinning mainstream social science and, by extension, social psychological approaches to race. In critical psychological research, however, historical patterns of power relations are understood to direct race-related perceptions, behavior, and experiences. From a critical perspective, therefore, race reflects the hierarchical arrangement of social groups, rather than actual physical or behavioral group attributes (Durrheim et al., 2009). This view of race as a system of power acknowledges that the very use of the term, race, is racist. However, the use of race as a concept is necessary for identifying the past, present, and future effects of racism (Pascale, 2008).

Psychology has a history in which understandings of basic human psychological experience were based solely on middle-class persons who were predominantly Western, White (Markus 2008; Stevens, 2015), and male (Crawford and Unger, 2000). Therefore, the major theoretical foundations do not account for the experiences of human beings who do not share those characteristics, perspectives, or exposures. In fact, an assessment of how persons from Western, Educated, Industrialized, Rich, and Democratic (WEIRD) societies performed across studies of several psychological processes and outcomes (e.g., visual perception and spatial cognition) found that, in comparison with studies of humans outside such locales, WEIRD people's performance was actually unusual (Henrich et al., 2010). Critical approaches in psychology refute unexamined assumptions about characteristics presumably instilled by race, indigeneity, ethnicity, gender, sexual orientation, geographical location, and social class and bring the shaping power of social context into focus, while retaining respect for agency among traditionally marginalized groups and persons (Fox et al., 2009; Salter and Adams, 2013 Teo, 2009). These ongoing modifications in race-related psychological theories, practice, and research methodologies (Stevens, 2015) have contributed to less biased views of human nature in the discipline and, to some degree, society and influenced the implementation of racial equality policies and legislation.

On the heels of this transforming movement are claims of a post-race era. After all, the United States of America had a Black president. This contention is evident more in public discourse than in scholarly work but, while very few persons would completely deny that social inequalities exist, there are those willing to advance the argument that unfair treatment is no longer about race. Albeit premature, contested, and more explicit in some countries than in others, this controversy is illustrated in the following case, which unfolded in the UK media: the Equality and Human Rights Commission's (EHRC) analysis of race inequality in Great Britain found that Blacks were doing worst in several areas (2016). In the published review, the EHRC recommended full and immediate attention by the UK, Scottish, and Welsh governments to key areas of disparities: employment, education, crime, living standard, and healthcare. Journalist Michael White, commenting on the report, countered the EHRC's justification by highlighting improvements in British race relations and their effects. White concluded '… that class and culture are usually more important underlying determinants in many of these points of friction or distress' (2016). On the other hand, journalist Afuah Hirsch (2018) has reported her frustration at having to debate the current realities of race on a TV talk show, The Pledge:

> 'Life's moved on from race,' one of my fellow panelists told me on The Pledge. 'If it's well intentioned, it's not racism,' said another. All of this was, very ironically, good evidence of my point: that white fragility operates powerfully against progress; that there are those in our society,

including high-profile and influential people, who prefer defensiveness to a cold, hard analysis of the patterns of prejudice.

Evidently, race remains a critical social matter. The major social issues to which a social psychological approach to race has been applied, or should be applied, are evident in the high stakes areas of (im)migration, legal process, politics, economics, health, education, and environment. Cross-cutting themes of gender, age, social class (and/or socioeconomic status), and sexual orientation run through these social issues and demonstrate the intersectionality of master statuses involved in inequality and unfair treatment.

A critical, international approach to understanding culture, race, and indigeneity in applied social psychology reveals an imbalance in mainstream psychology discourse (Dafermos et al., 2013; Salter and Adams, 2013). Perspectives from the Caribbean, parts of South America, New Zealand, South Africa, and Australia are less known, while psychological studies of intergroup conflict and within-group struggles among racial and ethnic minorities living in diverse urban areas in the United States are most dominant in the literature. Between the margin and the center is a significant swathe of the human experience that remains underexplored and, at best, stereotyped. In this chapter, a wider global culture is explored to identify other conventions about race and illustrations of its role in the experience and practice of human distinctions.

A need exists for critical psychologists to make effective interventions into situations circumscribed by racial hierarchy and privilege. This chapter illustrates where, and how, social psychology has attended to interlinking concerns of inequality, oppression, and injustice across seemingly disparate milieus. Having detailed racial vulnerabilities due to stigma, prejudice, and discrimination and highlighted selected critical participatory approaches to ameliorating social inequality and the effects of intergroup conflict, the chapter concludes with the idea for a hopeful paradigm, *heritage identity*, whereby applied social psychologists may more fully engage the unique strengths and resistance resources of cultural, racial, and indigenous groups.

HOW DID WE GET HERE? SOCIAL PSYCHOLOGICAL PROCESSES OF RACIALIZATION

In a National Public Radio (NPR) interview in early August 2016, David Duke, former grand wizard of the Ku Klux Klan, defended the then US presidential candidate Donald Trump against claims that Trump was racist. Duke argued that, to be racist, one had to have hatred in one's heart for ethnic minorities. In the wake of the NPR interview, David Carr Fellow Greg Howard (2016) wrote a *New York Times Magazine* article in which he traced the public evolution of the word racist from the early twentieth century. This included references to assimilationist/segregationist policies to its post-civil rights era meaning, which has framed racism more in terms of the individual, human heart than with systemic practices or policies. According to Howard, a new definition for racism has evolved in public discourse, whereby anyone who makes any race-based assertion could, justifiably, be labeled racist. Consequently, he argued, it now appears useless to use the term race as a metric of difference in human experience.

Consensus on the definition of racism has not been achieved in the scientific literature. However, Clark et al. (1999: 805) provide a working definition: 'beliefs, attitudes, institutional arrangements, and acts that tend to denigrate individuals or groups because of phenotypic characteristics or ethnic group affiliation'. According to Clark and colleagues, racism may be intergroup (occurring between members of oppressed and non-oppressed groups) or intragroup (taking place between members of the same ethnic group). By pointing to White privilege, Wellman's (1993) explication extends the understanding of racism beyond regarding it to be evident only when the stigmatized is disadvantaged – the powerful are systematically advantaged by detriments to minorities. Racism, therefore, is systematic advantage and disadvantage due to race.

Social scientists are not always careful to define racism, even in studies designed to examine racism's effects (Yee et al., 1993). A review of empirical, quantitative studies, most of which were conducted in the United States among African Americans to investigate the relationship between racism and health, found that only 25% of the 138 studies (*n* = 34) included a definition of racism (Paradies, 2006). Among those studies that did, several defined racism as differential treatment by race. Still there was variation among the definitions in what constitutes racism. When the defining feature of racism was the effect of the experience, more definitions focused solely on the detrimental effects of racism than did those that also highlighted the privileges accrued through racism. When the characteristic features of racism lay in its antecedents, there was more attention to describing racism as being fueled either by an ideology of inferiority or superiority rather than being attributed to both. Further, Paradies (2006: 889) noted that 'only about half of these definitions recognized systemic racism (i.e. racism occurring through societal organizations, institutions, laws, policies, practices, etc.) as well as interpersonal racism (i.e. racist interactions between people)'.

Advocating for a critical consciousness of racism and its association with power, Tatum states, 'The dismantling of racism is in the best interests of everyone' (1997: 14). Not everyone would agree. For example, the narratives of White, mostly working-class males in the United States portray grief over their loss of privilege, which they perceived to be due to the gains of feminism and the invasion of racial and sexual minorities (Fine et al., 1997). On the other hand, negative emotions, such as anger or guilt, may be evoked by the realization that the benefits enjoyed by White people (e.g., access to desirable jobs, housing, or education) are due to ethnic minorities being denied a similar range of options (Tatum, 1997). Further, understanding racism to be systematic and not only personal prejudice challenges traditional notions of American meritocracy (Kwate and Meyer, 2010). Although racially based injustices are not enjoyed or suffered equally across (or within) racial groups, Tatum (1997) demonstrates that all persons are ultimately disadvantaged by racism: there are economic (e.g., racial tension in the workplace), social (e.g., falling away of interracial childhood friendships during adolescence), and psychological (e.g., fear of the other) costs of racism being paid by people of color *and* White people in America.

Psychological studies are producing results confirming the complex processes and outcomes involved in racism. For example, Kenrick et al. (2016) found that White participants' anxiety and perceptions of interracial bias influenced perceptual distortions (specifically, 'slowing bias' – similar to the expansion of time and the slowing of images that occur in the presence of a looming threat) in their assessment of Black confederates who were moving toward them. Similarly, Richeson and Shelton (2003) have demonstrated that being prejudiced may evoke physiological costs for prejudiced persons. Results of their experiment showed that levels of prejudice moderated the extent of cognitive impairment that followed when Whites engaged in cross-race interactions. Cognitive deficit, measured using a Stroop Test, was evident when highly prejudiced White participants interacted with Blacks. However, the effect was not found when high-prejudice White participants interacted with Whites or when low-prejudice White participants interacted with Blacks. These findings supported the authors' theory that when very prejudiced, high status persons have encounters requiring them to engage the target of their prejudice, this is stressful for them; the emotional and physiological effort of self-regulation evokes cognitive deficits. Research detailing the economic and psychic costs of racism is essential for advancing any arguments in favor of interrupting racial privilege and oppression.

CONTEXTS OF RACIAL DOMINANCE: TIME, PLACE, AND SOCIOHISTORICAL CONTEXT

Critical attention to race in psychology has been limited by the groups that have been the focus of such work. In the United States, where the majority of psychological studies are conducted, the focus has been primarily on people who are Black or White. Yet, throughout the world, societies affected by slavery and colonialism have witnessed the enactment of most racial atrocities (Houkamau et al., 2017; Sonn, 2010). Tuck and Wayne Yang (2012) highlight the stable and insidious nature of ideas of oppression by pointing to racialized views of, and acts toward, indigenous persons. For example, progressive people of European ancestry often claim Native American heritage or, in some other way, equate their knowledge of suffering with that of indigenous peoples. Further, immigrants and other groups who have been displaced by colonialism can become settlers who dominate, kill natives, and steal their land, while denying their culpability, maintaining their status, and ensuring their future advancement. Tuck and Wayne Yang point out that even ventures to create or enhance a critical consciousness of colonialism may serve as projects of distraction or means of assuaging guilt. They acknowledge the challenges involved in pursuing decolonization that does not seek to simply shift power from the oppressor to Native Peoples but endeavors to break centuries-old patterns of dominance.

Racism has been found to manifest in early childhood. According to Tatum (1997), three/four-year-olds who had never met a Native American, when asked to draw an Indian, produced menacing images with weapons and feathers. The children reported getting their ideas about Indians from a cartoon. Similarly, Tatum argued, the various stereotypes to which persons are exposed in early development become the foundation for pervasive adult prejudices and, more, are the inevitable product of being socialized in a racist society. Social systems, such as the education, health, and justice systems, are not apolitical or value free and, therefore, sustain disparities within racist societies. Within these systems are microcosms of society that reify and reproduce injustice.

Describing the education system as a mechanism whereby prejudice and injustices are reproduced, Tuck and Gorlewski (2016: 203) maintained,

> Neither knowledge nor the act of teaching is neutral or apolitical. What counts as knowledge, and how privileged knowledge is fostered and assessed, is largely promoted as natural, normal, and 'common sense.' In practice, however, the curriculum is contested, and all teaching is political; gaps represent deficits in socially constructed norms, not the students to whom the disparities are assigned. Curriculum, like policy, is socially constructed, and unless interrupted, schooling works to reinforce existing power relations.

For example, Olsen (1997) found that American (i.e., not immigrant) students described their school community using mostly racial and ethnic categories (e.g., Mexican, Black, White Smokers, and Mixed Race). While there was value in being friendly, fear and anger were frequent features in students' reports of their experience of the other. Consequently, '… the social life of the school was about groups isolating themselves by race' (Olsen, 1997: 64) and those lines were only crossed cautiously, primarily to facilitate the pursuit of shared interests among extracurricular activities.

Race-related practices within and across social settings are reflective of the values embedded in the broader cultural milieu.

Tuck and McKenzie (2015) argue for increases in critical place inquiry and striving for relational validity, whereby land, place, and relationships are recognized as being the very substance of the self. Accordingly, racial mixture across the world and throughout history provides a social case for recognizing the significance of location in human experiences of racial physical difference. Consider the persons labelled, 'mulatto', that is, of black and white heritage (colored, mestizo, creole, zambo, and quadroon are examples of other terms used to describe mixed-race identities; see Teo, 2004 for a more extensive list and a discussion of Hitler's influential assertions regarding what he referred to as racial crossing). Spencer (2011) claims that the mulatto label was always contested and posits that, unlike other designations that became problematic over time and were replaced (e.g., Negro), the term mulatto is simply being erased.

In the Caribbean, racial mixing has resulted in a continuum of skin color shades, with accompanying context-specific ascriptions of social value and power within that continuum (Alleyne, 2005). In the case of the Dominican Republic (DR), Rivera (2015) describes how the term mulatto emerged in that country against a historical backdrop of Spanish colonialism in a land of majority African descendants. According to Rivera, mulattos in the DR describe themselves as 'the whites of the land'. Arguing the relevance of Clarke and Clarke's (1947) study of doll selection for that nation's positioning in matters of race and color, Rivera advances two possible interpretations. He claims this instance of name searching may mean either that such persons are rejecting that which they were taught to despise – 'the white doll is good, and the doll is me' (Rivera, 2015: 111) or they are simply pretending to take on the label for the benefits that may be gained, knowing full well of their irrefutable blackness. A decontextualized analysis may construe evidence of self-denigration or denial. However, Rivera's recounting of the DR's history shows that the masses rejected Spanish domination and enslavement just as much as the elite appeared to turn their backs on their African ancestry, downplaying any affiliation with their Haitian neighbors. Citing Sidanius et al. (2001) finding that, in the DR, patriotism was unrelated to anti-black racism, Rivera concludes that self-definition in the DR is nuanced and the often-derided term 'mulatto' may offer a window to better understanding of racial dynamics in that country, but only if the historical context is engaged.

The importance of time, place, and sociohistorical context is also reflected in narratives collected in an investigation of self-definition among Jamaicans who claim mixed ancestry (Chin and McFarlane, 2013). Half of the respondents categorized themselves in one of the following two ways: they either confined themselves to one racial group from their mixed heritage or they chose not to identify with any racial label, claiming to not find race a meaningful category for their personal identity. The other half of the respondents reported choosing to identify equally with all the groups in their heritage. Contrary to the theory of biracial identity proposed by Rockquemore (1998), none of these bi/multiracial respondents reported varying their choice of racial category based on the situational context. Further, rather than using solely racial labels, most participants used a mix of racial and ethnic labels to describe themselves (e.g., Black Jamaican). For the Jamaican, living in a country where more than 90% of the population is of African ancestry, race is not as salient in the everyday experience to the extent that social class and skin color are. However, although the sub-group of Jamaicans who are of mixed ancestry are those we theorized to be most likely to have a language for expressing racial differentiation, our analysis of *how* they experienced difference was only partially aided by a model developed for use among a biracial Black/White American sample. These findings indicate the importance of culturally specific formulations of even cross-culturally shared experiences like being of mixed racial heritage. They also underscore the value of methodological approaches that go beyond identity labels (Ramkissoon et al., 2008) to better capture the legacies of slavery, colonialism, emancipation, and independence infused into Jamaicans' self-definition.

In our study of Jamaicans who self-identify as bi/multiracial, the inextricable relationship between ancestry and social class, and its consequences for personal and social well-being, emerged as an unanticipated significant finding (Chin and McFarlane, 2013). When asked what it was like to live as a person of mixed heritage in Jamaica, the predominant concern reported by these participants was being pre-judged by others to be of upper class or rich. Consequently, they reported being targeted for hand-outs or other favors. Since the bi-/multi-racial Jamaican is most likely to be a mix of African with either European, East Indian, Lebanese, Syrian, or Chinese, their skin color, hair texture, and even body size and shape are among those socioracial markers that have local denotations for classifying persons according to their ancestry (Alleyne, 2005; Markus, 2008). Further, in this setting, the Europeans, East Indians, Lebanese, Syrians, and Chinese have been disproportionately represented in the upper class. Therefore, the lighter complexion resulting from racial mixing sets such persons apart from the phenotypically African majority and signals an economic advantage that they may, or may not, actually possess. This perceived affluence based on skin color translates to an elevated social positioning that is like the experience of 'the coloureds' of South Africa (Sonn and Fisher, 2003), a mixed-ancestry group who enjoy advantages in employment, education, and living arrangements. Interestingly, persons of mixed heritage in Jamaica and the colored community in South Africa are 'in-betweens' socially *and* racially, but the value of their in-between status contrasts with that of the offspring of racially mixed pairings in Europe and the United States. Historically, in the latter contexts, racially mixed persons were assessed as being afflicted and lowering the social status of Whites (Teo, 2004; Tucker, 2004). As Durrheim et al. (2009: 198) observed, 'race and race categorizing are troubling in different ways in different contexts'.

SO WHAT? RACE-BASED EFFECTS OF STIGMA, PREJUDICE, AND DISCRIMINATION

Distorted information about minorities in the form of inaccuracies, unchallenged assumptions, and omissions reflect, reinforce, and reproduce ideas about the inadequacies that are supposedly characteristic of people of color (Tatum, 1997). Such messages shape a social ideology that leads to social distancing, underservice, hypervigilance, surveillance, marginalization, and exclusion. Pascale's (2008: 723) characterization of race as performative and 'both a social fabrication and a material reality' is demonstrated in routinely racist institutionalized practices within legal, economic, educational, and social structures (e.g., broken windows policing, low teacher expectations).

Cultural theorist Stuart Hall (1986: 25–6) defines ideology as '... the mental frameworks—the languages, the concepts, categories, imagery of thought, and the systems of representation—which different classes and social groups deploy in order to make sense of, define, figure out and render intelligible the way society works'. These social ideas constitute a 'material force' (Hall, 1986: 26) that influences and preserves hierarchical intergroup processes of social (in)equality, (in)justice, and (un)fair treatment. Such social ideas, therefore, drive the nature of social interactions of varying stakes, involving the seeking and delivery of services and business transactions.

Clark et al. (1999) reviewed research on intergroup racism in higher education, the restaurant industry, housing rental and sales, automotive sales, and hiring practices and identified a range of negative effects. Research evidence of the effects of perceived racism among diverse ethnic groups includes high incidence of reported stressful racial discrimination, cardiac-related diseases and conditions, lower levels of mastery, higher levels of psychological distress, anxiety, depression, interpersonal problems, and PTSD (Clark et al., 1999; Waelde et al., 2010). Further, Waelde and colleagues (2010) found race-related stress reported by Americans of European ancestry to be lower than reports from other ethnic groups. In the same study, reports of race-related stress by African Americans were higher than reports by Asian Americans and Hispanic Americans. In addition, more race-related event stressors were associated with more severe PTSD symptoms among ethnic minority participants, but exposure to race-related events was uncorrelated with PTSD symptom severity among White participants.

In the United States, racial and ethnic minorities experience health disparities at a higher rate than those who do not belong to these minority groups; these disparities are linked to the social, economic, and environmental disadvantages that come along with being oppressed under a racist system (Bahls, 2011). Epidemiological studies have reliably demonstrated that racial differences in physical and mental health are explained by variations in socioeconomic status social class, perceived discrimination, and stress (Williams et al., 1997). Further, in a refinement of the Theory of Fundamental Causes, which explains the connection between low socioeconomic status and poor health outcomes, Phelan and Link (2015) identified racism as being a path to health inequalities by way of unequal access to power, status, enriching environments, and services. The American Psychological Association, APA Working Group on Stress and Health Disparities (2017) details disproportionate exposure to stress among racial/ethnic minorities and low-income persons. This working group has explained the mechanisms whereby stress, a social determinant of health, creates vulnerabilities in mental and physical health for persons of color and low socioeconomic status.

Immigration: A Social Exemplar of the Relationship Between Race and Well-being

Attention to identity and adaptation among immigrants of color underscores the importance of critical social psychological approaches to race. Persons of African ancestry share a history of being targets of racial discrimination, yet there is diversity in their historical, cultural, national, ethnic, and religious heritage (Wright, 2004), which provides important linkages to understanding the range of psychological responses among that group. A critical approach to race in immigration involves going beyond using race as a category label, to taking seriously the related ethnic and racial identities of persons who relocate geographically. It also prioritizes incorporating into the analyses an account of how their affiliation with their countries of origin affects their adaptation (McFarlane, 2010).

There are complex relationships among perceived racism and other perceived forms of discrimination, group identification, well-being, and behavioral acculturation (Alamilla et al., 2017). This complexity is evident in the effect of discrimination on psychological distress, which can either be exacerbated or buffered by ethnic identity. The relationship between perceived discrimination and distress was examined among a US nationally representative sample of immigrant and US-born Asian respondents (Yip et al., 2008). In this sample, ethnic identity had both worsening and protective effects on well-being, with outcomes varying by age and whether respondents were born in the United States or were foreign-born.

Also important in studies of immigrant adaptation is attention to how immigrant racial and ethnic minority groups are perceived by majority groups in the host country. The social identities that are developed, supported, and contested when persons migrate, and the contextual factors and processes involved in cross-cultural identification, have been examined in studies of various groups migrating to varying geographical locations (e.g., Aveling and Gillespie, 2008; Deaux, 2006; Foner, 1987/2001; 2001; Phelps and Nadim, 2010). From these studies, we learn that the identities with which persons leave their country of origin are subject to the social representations they encounter when they move. This was evident among data I collected to investigate identity and stress among first-generation Jamaican immigrants to New York City (McFarlane, 1998). I asked a 33-year-old male who had been in the United States for 17 years to select a stressful experience for further discussion. Paul (a pseudonym) chose to recount his experiences of racism when he had just migrated as a high school student:

Paul: Coming here and going to high school, I had to face discrimination not only from, you know, from people of a different color, but also from people of my color, meaning Black Americans. You know, it was hard, it was hard trying to fit in, trying to be accepted. Not only from, I mean, Whites, but also from Blacks. I felt like an outcast, you know, it was real hard. And you would stand out, because you dressed different, you had an accent. The other time I experienced that was in the military, the military was bad, but let's take high school, and even outside of school, y'know, back in the 70's there weren't a lot of Jamaicans so it was just difficult trying to fit in, trying to be accepted.

Explaining how the children at school expressed their discrimination, he said:

Paul: Well, you'd get beat up, you'd get called names. Ahm, it was more from the Black kids than the White kids. I mean, when you left school and you'd go home, the White kids would go to their neighborhood and you and the Black kids would pretty much head in the same direction. You'd have to deal with that, you'd have to fight, you know, prove to them that you're not going to be pushed around. But they'd call you names and things like that. I don't think it really stopped until I left high school and went into the military. Then in the military now, it was different, you'd have to experience that from the White kids.

Tracy: And how long had you been living here before you went into the military?

Paul: Actually, three years, I did three years of high school, and went into the military when I was 17 and I stayed in the military for a period of four years. I mean that was hard adjustment, it's like going from one extreme to another. It's, it's tough, you know. Imagine going to school you have all these other factors that you have to deal with: you have to study, you have to pay attention in class. At the same time, you have to worry about fitting in, being liked by, you know, your counterparts. And when I look at myself today, in a sense, I find that I discriminate against Black Americans in how I feel –

Tracy: Really?

Paul: Yeah! I'm going to tell you, no matter how old you get, or no matter where you reach in life you'll never forget things that you went through. You always remember... no matter how much time passed, once you're scarred in a certain way,

> it's going to always remain with you for the rest of your life.

This personal account illustrates a process described by Sonn and Fisher (2003) as internalization, which involves returning the unfair treatment received, and is one of three possible responses to domineering intergroup contact (the other two are assimilation and accommodation). From their study of South African immigrants to Melbourne, Australia, Sonn and Fisher report evidence of participants reproducing the discrimination to which they were subjected and, in so doing, maintaining group difference. My study found that foreign-born Black persons not only experience racism from White persons but also from American-born Black persons and, as a result of internalization, they reciprocate these attitudes.

In academic discourse and in the media, disharmony among members of Black communities tends to get sensationalized and is the subject of what often amounts to little more than voyeurism on the part of some social scientists. However, a critical perspective is driven by the need for educators and researchers to develop and successfully implement programs to teach children to respect and value diversity in the classroom and in their communities. It is important to recognize the historical developments that lead to divergent experiences for different groups of persons of African ancestry. Diasporic nationalities are largely a function of the slave trade and, later, migration. Other participants in my study of first-generation Jamaican immigrants to New York City (McFarlane, 1998) reported having been told by White people that they were 'not like African Americans'. I interpret that as a 'divide and conquer' strategy used to pit Black people against each other, and which serves to further the interests of the dominant group by maintaining social disparities. Jamaicans, in this setting, are already socially in-between and, if they are without a strong ethnic identity, are vulnerable to social marginalization.

Race and/or ethnicity are robustly reported in psychological studies as being protective of psychological well-being for minority groups (e.g., Phinney, 1991); however, race (i.e., minority status) remains a threat to well-being in the twenty-first century (Kwate, 2014). Immigrants of color are subject to this vulnerability due to their race. Further, when salient racial, national, or ethnic identities serve as catalysts for people of color to discriminate against each other, the identities are no longer protective; they become counter-productive (intragroup racism has been identified as a mechanism of stress, see Clark et al., 1999) and block progress toward harmonious living, racial unity, and community advancement.

More work needs to be done to determine when, and where, minority racial social categories become vulnerability factors and the consequences this elicits in peoples' lives. Exemplifying the way forward, Veling et al., (2008) explored neighborhood density as an explanation for the high incidence of psychotic disorders reported in immigrant ethnic groups in Western Europe. Conducted in The Hague, results showed that the incidence of psychotic disorders among Moroccan, Surinamese, and Turkish immigrants, together and separately, was higher compared with the native Dutch. Further, after adjusting for neighborhood socioeconomic level, the incidence of psychiatric disorders among immigrants who lived in neighborhoods where the proportion of residents belonging to their group was low (i.e., low-density) was high compared to those who lived in high-density neighborhoods. Among the possible explanations the authors offer is the likelihood that ethnic enclaves provide the buffering effects of more social support availability and opportunities for positive ethnic group identification. They also proposed that living in their respective immigrant communities may reduce the likelihood of majority-group contact, hence reducing the probability of exposure to discrimination (a risk factor for schizophrenia and psychotic symptoms).

PROPOSING A 'STRENGTHS' PARADIGM FOR GOING FORWARD: HERITAGE IDENTITY

Identity conscious, participatory, and narrative methods are key to the incorporation of racially positioned knowledge in social psychology (Adams and Salter, 2011; Stevens, 2015). Psychologists have to grapple with developing methodologies and intervention strategies that work to eliminate those ways in which the discipline itself has normalized disparities by perpetuating a 'colorblind' ideology (Salter and Adams, 2013). We need research projects, programs, and interventions that are framed from the perspective of historically marginalized persons. Without these situated and dynamic approaches (Seedat et al., 2017), psychology will continue to reflect the broader economic and cultural power relationships and unequal opportunities by class and skin color that prevail across the globe.

Critical social psychological attention to race is benefitting from efforts, such as those of Stevens et al., (2017), to give voice to worldwide lived experiences of racism. Participatory projects conducted with American women of color, inmates (Cahill and Torre, 2007), street youth (Payne, 2013; 2014), and students in Northern Indigenous Canada (Tuck and Gorlewski, 2016), Uganda, and Vietnam (MacKenzie et al., 2015) provide examples of conceptual, methodological, reporting, and advocacy innovations involved in '… generating linkages with the psychology of oppression, colonial and post-colonial conditions, and liberation psychology' (Stevens, 2015: 183).

To better address situations of continued racial marginalization we, as a discipline, must become more accomplished in understanding the ongoing legacies of slavery and colonization that continue to shape peoples' lives in inequitable ways. In each setting, psychology research and programs are to be contextually grounded and informed by the identities and standpoint of those in whose interests they are proposed. Referring to Jamaica, Nettleford (2003) argues that the racial legacies of the plantation system are very much with us today. Race still matters. Therefore, race and ethnicity must be incorporated into social psychological analyses if we are to accurately document and address the lived realities of Caribbean existence today. History details the physical and psychological trauma of transplanted African slaves during colonization in the Caribbean. History also shows us that people of color have proven resilient in the face of discrimination. Despite the distressing features of this experience, a remarkable defiance and resilience mark the Caribbean path toward freedom and nationhood. Undoubtedly, the historical features, sociopolitical evolution, and current realities of Caribbean life underscore the importance of investigating subjectivities and structural underpinnings of race in this context.

In recognition of the importance of history for extending work on the social psychology of racism, I have been developing a Critical Participatory Action Research (CPAR) project to explore the relationship between heritage-related identity and psycho-social predictors of social problems. The study is part of a program of research intended to build a theory of identity in Jamaica and is hoped to contribute to understanding the meanings of culture, nationality, race, and ethnicity. The overarching research question is focused on articulating the sociocultural heritage that is the foundation of Jamaican identity and identifying those elements that explain the relationship of heritage identity to physical and psychological well-being. This new project builds on the work of sociohistorians Sherlock and Bennett (1998: 8), who chronicled events in Jamaica that reveal the complex interrelating effects of distress, outrage, and tenacity and posed the question, 'How does the Jamaican see himself or herself? Has he or she developed the self-pride, self-respect, the sense of self-esteem for which Marcus Garvey pleaded and which history justifies?'.

My *heritage identity* project constitutes a critical applied social psychology response that might be crafted to this historical context. The proposed project is designed to address the following key questions in Jamaica: What do 'race' and 'ethnicity' mean? And, how did these meanings come about? How is the identity of Jamaicans related to race, ethnicity, and nationality? What are the social costs and benefits of heritage identity? What are the possibilities (and cautions) for enhancing citizenship, nation building, and personal development through heritage identity? This new heritage identity initiative is attentive to the legacy of radical psychologies on which this perspective builds and the identities of which a focus on heritage must be mindful (Stevens, 2015).

This framework may have implications for wider diasporic studies of race. Across the undeniably distinct contexts of slavery, displacement, immigration, emancipation, and independence, the heritage identity project will stimulate questions such as, what were the potentially traumatizing social and political features beyond the Caribbean region and throughout the diaspora? Who are the heroes across post-colonial contexts? What resistance resources may be identified? What creative intervention techniques need to be reproduced, refined, and extended to foster resilience? Answers to such questions will be used to inform practical social change initiatives designed to address issues of racism, legacies of discrimination and efforts to promote positive personal and social identities across all levels: ranging from self-esteem and authenticity (micro level), interpersonal and within-group relations, power and status (meso level), and social movements (macrolevel) (Stets and Burke, 2000).

CONCLUSION

As a social construct, race remains an important concept for understanding the legacies of intergroup discrimination and injustice. Since the first generation of applied social psychology, issues of race, racism, intergroup power relations, and identities have remained of central concern. Explorations of racial differences in the early twentieth century contributed to a race science that was challenged by the first African American PhD in social psychology (Sumner, 1924; 1928) and his students (Guthrie, 1976). Still, understandings of race and it's effects remain deeply disturbing. More work needs to be done to develop effective responses to racism in social psychology and society at large. Also necessary is the development of psychologies that are less WEIRD and capable of understanding and responding to cultural differences in social practice and self-understandings. Work in this area is necessary to embrace the human potential that comes with our shared diversity. We also require a broader focus that extends well beyond racial attitudes, prejudice, and discrimination. In exploring issues of racism, we require an intersectional approach that reveals the interwoven nature of axes of inequality, oppression, and injustice that render particular groups of human beings the subjects of stigma, prejudice, and discrimination, whilst working systemically to impoverish lives. An important accompanying emphasis in this new generation of critical social psychology scholarship must be to broaden attention from focusing solely on group vulnerabilities to identifying cultural resistance resources that have facilitated the resilience of persons of color.

As is the case with any transformative effort, there is the need for attentiveness to potential risks. A key challenge in naming and addressing injustices is the risk of essentialism. Stevens (2015: 187) points out that Black Psychology scholars engaged in 'strategic essentialism' in order to achieve their critical objectives and acknowledged that this strategy comes with potential unintended consequences. As Teo (2004) and Howarth (2009) argue, by researching the issue of racism, social psychologists can inadvertently confirm the prejudicial view that racial minorities are a problem to be researched and managed. Efforts to research the antecedents and consequences of oppressive social categorization can result in substantiating the very categories we seek to eradicate. Rather than suggesting that social psychologists should therefore not work in this area due to the risks, I am proposing that we need to act with care and embrace the value of doing no harm. This requires us to begin to develop a new language for this work that allows us to move beyond the flawed language of ethnicity and race that has been discussed in this chapter (cf., Tatum, 1997). In my own work, I embraced the term heritage in an effort to overcome the crippling effects of the 'essence' and 'truth' with which some uses of the terms ethnicity and race are imbued. I have also embraced the assertion that we cannot change things without talking about them. Clarke and Braun's (2009) recommendation for critical gender scholarship is worth adopting in the critical race enterprise: highlighting the *processes* of social construction, norm setting, racial and ethnic stratification and inequality as the necessary path to dismantling their powerful effects.

Finally, critical social psychology applied to race in the twenty-first century is poised to be action oriented, reflecting meaningful engagement in the interest of radical social change. This chapter underscores the need to conduct race-related studies and interventions in a manner that starts with the local sociohistorical reality as foreground, rather than background. Influenced by the impressive cadre of classic work by DuBois, Fanon, Memmi, Freire, Cesaire, and other pioneering scholarship on coloniality, race and power, there is strong empirical support for the psychological effects of race and ethnicity and their role in shaping attitudes, beliefs, motivation, performance, and other psychological processes (Markus, 2008). Contemporary international scholarship using critical social psychological approaches to race spanning contexts marked by slavery, indigeneity, migration, colonization, displacement, marginalization, and exclusion are crucial for building coalitions for change. Identifying, engaging society with, and addressing race-based atrocities are vital strategies for preventing the occurrence of such events and for establishing shared understandings that are necessary for reversing legacy vulnerabilities. Our universal goal must be enhancing recognition of the agency of groups of color and ensuring their inclusion in society. This is essential for equitable social change.

ACKNOWLEDGEMENT

I am enormously indebted to Christopher C. Sonn of Victoria University, Melbourne, Australia for his invaluable comments on earlier versions of this chapter.

REFERENCES

Adams, G., & Salter, P. (2011). A critical race psychology is not yet born. *Connecticut Law Review, 43*(5), 1355–1377.

Alamilla, S. G., Kim, B. S. K., Walker, T., & Sisson, F. R. (2017). Acculturation, enculturation, perceived racism, and psychological symptoms among Asian American college students. *Journal of Multicultural Counseling and Development, 45*, 38–65. doi:10.1002/jmcd.12062

Alleyne, M. C. (2005). *The construction and representation of race and ethnicity in the Caribbean and the world.* Barbados: UWI Press.

American Psychological Association, APA Working Group on Stress and Health Disparities. (2017). *Stress and health disparities: Contexts, mechanisms, and interventions among racial/ethnic minority and low-socioeconomic status populations.* Retrieved from http://www.apa.org/pi/health-disparities/resources/stress-report.aspx

Aveling, E., & Gillespie, A. (2008). Negotiating multiplicity: Adaptive asymmetries within second-generation Turks' 'society of mind'. *Journal of Constructivist Psychology, 21*(3), 200–222. doi:10.1080/10720530802070635

Bahls, C. (2011). Health policy brief: Achieving equity in health. *Health Affairs*. Retrieved from http://healthaffairs.org/healthpolicybriefs/brief_pdfs/healthpolicybrief_53.pdf

Cahill, C., & Torre, M. E. (2007). Beyond the journal article: representations, audience, and the presentation of Participatory Action Research. In S. Kindon, R. Pain, & M. Kesby (Eds.), *Particpatory action research approaches and methods* (pp. 196–205). Abingdon: Routledge.

Chin, A., & McFarlane, T. (2013). *What are you? An exploration of biracial and multiracial identity experiences in Jamaica*. Poster presented at the National Multicultural Conference and Summit. Houston, TX.

Clark, R., Anderson, N. B., Clark, V. R., & Williams, D. R. (1999). Racism as a stressor for African Americans: A biopsychosocial model. *American Psychologist*, *54*, 805–816.

Clarke, V., & Braun, V. (2009). Gender. In D. Fox, I. Prilleltensky, & S. Austin (Eds.), *Critical psychology: An introduction* (2nd edn., pp. 232–249). Thousand Oaks, CA: Sage.

Crawford, M., & Unger, R. (2000). *Women and gender: A feminist psychology* (3rd edn.). Boston: McGraw Hill.

Dafermos, M., Markavos, A., Mentinis, M., Painter, D., & Triliva, S. (2013). The world is not enough: The dialectics of critical psychology. *Annual Review of Critical Psychology*, *10*, 1–34.

Deaux, K. (2006). *To be an immigrant*. New York: Russel Sage Foundation.

Durrheim, K., Hook, D., & Riggs, D. (2009). Race and racism. In D. Fox., I. Prilleltensky, & S. Austin (Eds), *Critical psychology: An introduction* (2nd edn., pp. 197–214). Thousand Oaks, CA: Sage.

Equality and Human Rights Commission (2016, August). Healing a divided Britain: the need for a comprehensive race equality strategy. Retrieved from https://www.equalityhumanrights.com

Fine, M., Weis, L., Addleston, J., & Marusza, J. (1997). White loss. In E. Seller & L. Weiss (Eds.), *Beyond black and white: New faces and voices in US schools* (pp. 283–301). NY: SUNY.

Foner, N. (Ed.). (1987/2001). *New immigrants in New York*. New York: Columbia University Press.

Foner, N. (Ed.). (2001). *Islands in the city: West Indian migration to New York*. Berkley: University of California Press.

Fox, D., Prilleltensky, I., & Austin, S. (2009). Critical psychology for social justice: Concerns and dilemmas. In D. Fox, I. Prilleltensky, & S. Austin (Eds.), *Critical psychology: An introduction* (2nd edn., pp. 3–19). Thousand Oaks, CA: Sage.

Guthrie, R. (1976). *Even the rat was white: A historical view of psychology*. New York: Harper and Row

Hall, S. (1986). The problem of ideology: Marxism without guarantees. *Journal of Communication Inquiry*, *10*, 28–44. doi: 10.1177/019685998601000203

Henrich, J., Heine, S. J. & Norenzayan, A. (2010). The weirdest people in the world? *Behavioral and Brain Sciences*, *33*(2–3), 61–83.

Hirsch, A. (2018, January 24). I've had enough of white people who try to deny my experience. *The Guardian*. Retrieved from https://www.theguardian.com

Hogg, M. A., & Abrams, D. (1988). *Social identifications: A social psychology of intergroup relations and group processes*. London & New York: Routledge.

Houkamau, C. A., Stronge, S., & Sibley, C. G. (2017). The prevalence and impact of racism toward indigenous Māori in New Zealand. *International Perspectives in Psychology: Research, Practice, Consultation*, *6*(2), 61–80. doi: 10.1037/ipp0000070

Howard, G. (2016, August 16). The easiest way to get rid of racism? Just redefine it. *The New York Times Magazine*. Retrieved from http://www.nytimes.com

Howarth, C. (2009) 'I hope we won't have to understand racism one day': Researching or reproducing 'race' in social psychological research? *British Journal of Social Psychology*, *48*(3), 407–426. doi: 10.1348/014466608X360727

Kenrick, A. C., Sinclair, S., Richeson, J., Verosky, S. C., & Lun, J. (2016). Moving while black: Intergroup attitudes influence judgments of speed. *Journal of Experimental Psychology: General*, *145*(2), 147–154. doi:10.1037/xge0000115

Kwate, N. O. A. (2014). 'Racism Still Exists': A public health intervention using racism 'countermarketing' outdoor advertising in a Black neighborhood. *Journal of Urban Health*, *91*(5), 851–872.

Kwate, N. O. A., & Meyer, I. H. (2010). The myth of meritocracy and African American health. *American Journal of Public Health*, *100*(10), 1831–1834.

MacKenzie, C. A., Christensen, J., & Turner, S. (2015). Advocating beyond the academy: Dilemmas of communicating relevant research results. *Qualitative Research*, *15*(1), 105–121. doi: 10.1177/1468794113509261

Markus, H. R. (2008). Pride, prejudice, and ambivalence: Toward a unified theory of race and ethnicity. *American Psychologist*, *63*(8), 651–670.

McFarlane, T. A. (1998, March). When racial identity supersedes ethnic identity: Jamaican immigrants reflect on encountering racism. In M. Fine (Chair), *The Politics of Identity*. Symposium conducted the annual meeting of the Ethnography in Education Research Forum, Philadelphia, PA.

McFarlane, T. A. (2010). Experiencing difference, seeking community: Racial, panethnic and national identities among female Caribbean-born US college students. *American Review of Political Economy: Special Issue on Caribbean Migration*, *8*(2), 87–114.

Nettleford, R. (2003). *Caribbean cultural identity: The case of Jamaica*. (2nd edn.). Princeton: Markus Wiener.

Olsen, L. (1997). *Made in America: Immigrant Students in our Public Schools*. New York: The New Press.

Paradies, Y. (2006). A systematic review of empirical research on self-reported racism and health. *International Journal of Epidemiology*, *35*, 888–901. doi: 10.1093/ije/dyl056

Pascale, C. M. (2008). Talking about race: Shifting the analytical paradigm. *Qualitative Inquiry*, *14*, 723–741. doi: 10.1177/1077800408314354

Payne, Y. A. (2013). Street PAR. Retrieved from http://www.thepeoplesreport.com/index.html

Payne, Y. A. (2014, August). 'Walk With Me': Organizing those from The Streets, A Community Development Effort. TEDx Wilmington. Retrieved from https://www.youtube.com/watch?v=PXNQ2C_d27A

Phelan, J. & Link, B. (2015). Is racism a fundamental cause of inequalities in health? *Annual Review of Sociology*, *41*, 311–330. doi. 10.1146/annurev-soc-073014-112305

Phelps, J. & Nadim, M. (2010). Ideology and agency in ethnic identity negotiation of immigrant youth. *Papers on Social Representations*, *19*, 13.1–13.27.

Phinney, J. S. (1991). Ethnic identity and self-esteem: A review and integration. Hispanic *Journal of Behavioral Sciences*, *13* (2), 193–208.

Ramkissoon, M., McFarlane, T. A. & Branche, C. (2008). Do race and ethnicity matter in Jamaica? Category labels versus personal self-descriptions of identity. *Journal of Caribbean Psychology*, *2*(2), 78–97.

Richeson, J. A., & Shelton, N. (2003). When prejudice does not pay: Effects of interracial contact on executive function. *Psychological Science*, *14*(3), 287–290. doi: 10.1111/1467-9280.03437

Rivera, P. R. (2015). The making of a mulatto community: Santo Domingo and the 'Colour Wave'. *Caribbean Quarterly*, *51*(4), 100–115.

Rockquemore, K. A. (1998). Between Black and White: Exploring the 'biracial' experience. *Race and Society*, *1*(2), 197–212.

Salter, P., & Adams, G. (2013). Toward a critical race psychology. *Social and Personality Compass*, *7*(11), 781–793. doi: 10.1111/spc3.12068

Seedat, M., Suffla, S., & Christie, D. J. (Eds.). (2017). *Emancipatory and participatory methodologies in peace, critical, and community psychology*. Cham, Switzerland: Springer. doi: 10.1007/978-3-319-63489-0

Sherlock, P., & Bennett, H. (1998). *The story of the Jamaican people*. Kingston: Ian Randle.

Sonn, C. (2010). Engaging with the Apartheid Archive Project: Voices from the South African diaspora in Australia, *South African Journal of Psychology*, *40*(4), 432–442. doi: 10.1177/008124631004000406

Sonn, C., & Fisher, A. (2003). Identity and oppression: Differential responses to an in-between status. *American Journal of Community Psychology*, *31*(1–2), 117–128. doi: 10.1023/A:1023030805485

Spencer, R. (2011). *Reproducing race: The paradox of generation mix*. Boulder, CO: Lynne Reinner.

Stets, J. E., & Burke, P. J. (2000). Identity theory and social identity theory. *Social Psychology Quarterly*, *63*(3), 224–237.

Stevens, G. (2015). Black psychology: Resistance, reclamation and redefinition. In I. Parker (Ed.). *Handbook of critical psychology* (pp. 182–190). NY: Routledge.

Stevens, G., Bell, D., Sonn, C., Canham, H., & Clennon, O. D. (2017). Transnational perspectives on black subjectivity. *South African Journal of Psychology*, *47*(4), 459 – 469. doi: 10.1177/0081246317737929

Sumner, F. (1924). Core and context in the drowsy states. *American Journal of Psychology*, *35*, 307–308.

Sumner, F. (1928). Environic factors which prohibit creative scholarship among Negros. *School and Society*, *22*, 294–296.

Tajfel, H., & Turner, J. C. (1986). The social identity theory of intergroup behavior. In S. Worschel, & W. Austin (Eds.), *Psychology of intergroup relations* (pp. 1–24). Chicago: Nelson-Hall.

Tatum, B. (1997). *'Why are all the black kids sitting together in the cafeteria?' And other conversations about race*. Basic Books: New York.

Teo, T. (2004). The historical problematization of 'mixed race' in psychological and human-scientific discourses. In A. Winston (Ed.). *Defining difference: Race and racism in the history of psychology* (pp. 79–108). Washington, DC: APA. doi:10.1037/10625-004

Teo, T. (2009). Philosophical concerns in critical psychology. In D. Fox, I. Prilleltensky, & S. Austin (Eds.), *Critical psychology: An introduction* (2nd edn., pp. 36–53). London: Sage.

Tuck, E., & Gorlewski, J. (2016). Racist ordering, settler colonialism, and edTPA: A participatory policy analysis. *Educational Policy*, *30*(1), 197–217.

Tuck, E., & McKenzie, M. (2015). Relational validity and the 'where' of inquiry: Place and land in qualitative research. *Qualitative Inquiry*, *21*(7), 633–638. doi: 10.1177/1077800414563809

Tuck, E., & Wayne Yang, K. (2012). Decolonization is not a metaphor. *Decolonization: Indigeneity, Education & Society*, *1*(1), 1–40.

Tucker, W. H. (2004). 'Inharmoniously adapted to each other': Science and racial crosses. In A. Winston (Ed.) *Defining difference: Race and racism in the history of psychology* (pp. 109–133). Washington, DC: APA. doi:10.1037/10625-004

Veling, W., Susser, E., Van Os, J., Mackenbach, J. P. Selten, J. P., & Hoek, H. W. (2008). Ethnic density of neighborhoods and incidence of psychotic disorders among immigrants. *American Journal of Psychiatry*, *165*, 66–73.

Waelde, L. C., Pennington, D., Mahan, C. Mahan, R., Kabour, M., & Marquett, R. (2010). Psychometric properties of the race-related events scale. *Psychological Trauma: Theory, Research, Practice, and Policy*, *2*(1), 4–11. doi: 10.1037/a0019018

Wellman, D. (1993). *Portraits of white racism*. (2nd edn.). Cambridge, England: Cambridge University Press. doi: 10.1017/CBO9780511625480

White, M. (2016, August 18). Race relations in 2016: much to deplore but plenty to applaud. *The Guardian*. Retrieved from https://www.theguardian.com

Williams, D., Yu, Y. Jackson, J., & Anderson, N. (1997). Racial differences in physical and mental health. *Journal of Health Psychology*, *2*(3), 335–351.

Wright, M. (2004). *Becoming Black: Creating Identity in the African diaspora*. Durham: Duke University Press.

Yee, A. H., Fairchild, H. H., Weizman, F., & Wyatt, G. E. (1993). Addressing psychology's problems with race. *American Psychologist*, *48*, 1132–1140. doi: 10.1037/0003-066X.48.11.1132

Yip, T., Gee, G. C., & Takeuchi, D. (2008). Racial discrimination and psychological distress: The impact of ethnic identity and age among immigrant and United States-born Asian adults. *Developmental Psychology*, *44*(3), 787–800. doi:10.1037/0012-1649.44.3.787

3

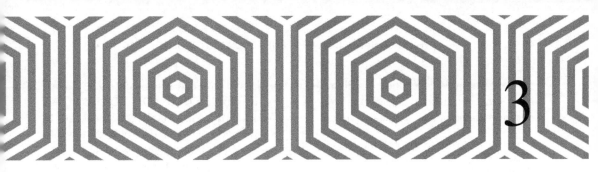

Decolonising Applied Social Psychology: Culture, Indigeneity and Coloniality

Christopher C. Sonn, Mohi R. Rua and Amy F. Quayle

There are various approaches in psychology that have sought to understand the role of culture in human functioning. Cross-cultural psychology has typically taken an approach described as 'etic', assuming that there are universal properties to culture that can be studied by comparing cultures on some observable dimensions. An emic approach is more evident in cultural psychology, which Shweder (1990: 1) described as 'the study of the way cultural traditions and social practices regulate, express, transform, and permute the human psyche, resulting less in psychic unity for humankind than ethnic divergences in mind, self, and emotion'. There has been longstanding interest in cultural matters and perspectives in various applied areas of psychology (e.g., Allwood and Berry, 2006; Gergen et al., 1996; Squire, 2000). Recent calls have advocated for critical engagement with 'culture' in applied psychology. For example, in community psychology, Kral et al. (2011) have called for a renewed and reimagined engagement with culture, and Harrell (2015) stated that human experience cannot be separated from culture. Yet, there remains a gap between recognising this and the ways in which research and practice are enacted.

While definitions of culture remain varied and contested, there is agreement about the importance of placing culture at the centre of our research and practice endeavours. In placing culture centrally, we have opted for an understanding of culture as situated, contested and socially constructed in the context of power relations. Misra and Gergen (1993: 226) wrote:

> ...culture is a historically situated, collective product constituted by the *values, beliefs, perceptions, symbols,* and other humanly created artifacts which are *transmitted* across generations through language and other mediums.... Culture is simultaneously a product of human action as well as a determinant of future action, a composite of meanings and associated traditions, which define, inform, and constitute the range of our understandings and investments.

Along with this conception of culture, we have been committed to engaging in a decolonising standpoint that seeks to disrupt:

> essentialist understandings of cultural matters that have served historically to marginalize others. This standpoint brings into clearer view ways in which power/privilege/oppression are reproduced and contested through racialized and ethnicized practices and discourses; that is, how social inequality is maintained and challenged through culture (Reyes Cruz and Sonn, 2015: 128).

The turn to decolonisation values a plurality of epistemologies, dialogical ethics, and importantly, is committed to affirming the experiences and knowledges of those who have been marginalised and oppressed (e.g., Adams et al., 2015). In this chapter, we begin by providing a brief overview of psychology, colonialism, and the calls for decolonisation. This is followed by an outline of some of the theoretical and methodological resources that we have utilised in our efforts to engage in decolonising praxis that centres culture and power to promote community wellbeing. We then discuss examples of research that deals with notions of indigeneity and culture. In the example from Aotearoa,[1] research with Māori[2] men is used to exemplify the ways in which Kaupapa Māori theory and method can be used to decolonise psychological research and practice in postcolonial contexts. The example from Australia brings liberation psychology to community arts and cultural development to contribute to decolonising research and practice.

PSYCHOLOGY, COLONIALISM AND DECOLONISATION

Psychology and Colonialism

Power is central to colonialism and has been a key concern for many groups in different countries around the world, where scholars and activists have advocated for the social transformation of oppressive societies and social and power arrangements (e.g., Coimbra et al., 2012; David, 2011; Dudgeon and Walker, 2015; Fine, 2006; 2012; Gone, 2011; Kessi and Boonzaier, 2016). Working towards the transformation of oppressive social systems and relations of power requires developing knowledge about colonialism and the various forms of oppression it has depended upon, including violence, exploitation and exclusion, cultural control and imperialism, which forced histories of dominated peoples into oblivion (Bulhan, 1985; Dutta et al., 2016; Fanon, 1967; Moane, 1999).

Often, forms of oppression were expressed in research and knowledge production practices, which came to construct and know inferior Others through Western worldviews and approaches (David, 2011; Enriquez, 1992; Teo, 2006). For example, in Aotearoa, historically, research has been 'done on the relatively powerless for the relatively powerful' (Gibbs, 2001: 674) and in accord with the worldview and values of the dominant Pākehā[3] group. Pākehā worldviews have been imposed on Māori, to the socio-cultural and historical disadvantage of Māori (Cooper, 2012; Stewart-Harawira, 2013). Consequently, many Māori have become suspicious of non-Māori researchers and their agendas (Gibbs, 2001; Smith, 1999). As Bishop (1998: 200) wrote:

> ...many misconstrued Māori cultural practices and meanings are now part of our everyday myths of New Zealand, believed by Māori and non-Māori alike, and traditional social and educational research has contributed to this situation. As a result, Māori people are deeply concerned about who researchers are answerable to. Who has control over the initiation, procedures, evaluations, construction, and distribution of newly defined knowledge?

In different areas of psychology, researchers continue to be critical of psychological research and practice that is ahistorical, acultural and decontextualised; what Seymour Sarason has referred to as Psychology Misdirected (Trickett, 2015). That is to say, a dominant version of psychology anchored in dispassionate objectivism and positivism and that subscribes to the view that there is a 'psychic unity of mankind' (Shweder, 1990) waiting to be discovered. Those critical of this approach advocate for an applied social psychology that contributes to building peaceful and inclusive societies that can foster the health and wellbeing of individuals and communities (Dudgeon and Walker, 2015; Sloan, 1996; Teo, 2006). Such approaches bring into question basic assumptions of 'psychic unity' and universalism and acultural, decontextualised psychology. In effect, these calls recognise that colonialism is not a phenomenon of the past but rather, as Maldonado-Torres (2007: 243) noted:

> … coloniality survives colonialism. It is maintained alive in books, in the criteria for academic performance, in cultural patterns, in common sense, in the self-image of peoples, in aspirations of self, and so many other aspects of our modern experience. In a way, as modern subjects we breathe coloniality all the time and every day.

An important task, then, for decolonisation is to engage with the process and practices of knowledge production in pursuit of liberation as well as with 'the psychosocial and sociocultural impacts of colonialism, racism, and the reproduction of privilege as part of the process of change to promote social justice and inclusion' (Sonn et al., 2013: 298).

Decolonising Methodologies and Liberation Approaches

There is a growing movement concerned with decolonising psychology and producing research and action that can contribute to liberation and empowerment (Adams et al., 2015; Dudgeon and Walker, 2015; Reyes Cruz and Sonn, 2015), and this orientation reflects a shift in applied social psychology. Central to decolonising applied social psychology is a change from a focus on individual blame deficit based approaches to viewing many social problems as the product of socio-economic structures of oppression within longer histories of slavery, colonialism and other systems of domination. Reyes Cruz and Sonn (2015) advocated for a decolonising standpoint from which to critically engage with notions of culture and diversity and dynamics of privilege and dispossession in communities. They noted that such a standpoint brings together theoretical and conceptual resources from various critical theory approaches such as Critical Race Theory (e.g., Ladson-Billings, 2003), feminist and postcolonial studies (Fine, 2006; Macleod and Bhatia, 2008), indigenous scholarship in Australia (Martin and Mirraboopa, 2003; Moreton-Robinson, 2016; Rigney, 2006) and, pivotally, liberation psychology (Martín-Baró, 1994; Montero, 2007; 2009; Seedat, 1997).

In the following sections, we provide selective examples of scholarship that has informed our work; namely, decolonising methodologies with links to indigenous scholarship in Aotearoa and liberation approaches with its roots in Latin America. Akin to the process of bricolage (Kincheloe, 2001), we bring these together because they have informed our own work and we have seen from our respective social locations that they share the goals of producing decolonial research and action.

Decolonising methodologies for Linda Smith is a process: '…which engages with imperialism and colonialism at multiple levels. For researchers, one of those levels is concerned with having a much more critical understanding of the underlying assumptions, motivations and values which inform research practices' (1999: 20). Smith (1999) has long advocated for the decolonising of Eurocentric theories and research methods in Aotearoa by prioritising indigenous worldviews, which continue to be marginalised as inferior and rejected as 'non-scientific' and superstitious nonsense (Cooper, 2012). In the Australian context, decolonising work is captured in the articulation of Aboriginal ways of knowing, doing and being (Martin and Mirraboopa 2003; Moreton-Robinson and Walter, 2009), as well as Rigney's (2006) work on indigenous and Indigenist frameworks. In Aotearoa, decolonising methodologies are reflected in the articulation of Kaupapa Māori theory and research practices as a form of colonial resistance, where Māori attempt to reclaim the indigenous research space (Cooper, 2012; Nikora, 2007; Smith, 1999; Smith, 2012; Stewart-Harawira, 2013).

Graham Smith (2012: 11) advocates Kaupapa Māori theory, as a 'space for thinking and researching differently, to center Māori interests and desires, and to speak back to the dominant existing theories in education'. Centering Māori aspirations is reflected in the applied nature of psychological research conducted by members of the Māori & Psychology Research Unit (MPRU) at the University of Waikato in Aotearoa, of which Mohi Rua is a principal investigator (Māori & Psychology Research Unit, 2016; Nikora, 2007). The MPRU has established itself as an internationally recognised indigenous research entity with a core goal of promoting excellence in research concerning the psychological needs, aspirations and priorities of Māori people. With an extensive number of reviewed articles, book chapters, books, conference presentations, keynote addresses, student theses and commissioned reports, the MPRU is recognised as a power house for Māori focused psychological research that centres Māori interest and desires. In defining Kaupapa Māori for research groups like the MPRU, Kaupapa Māori can be literally translated as 'Māori ideology – a philosophical doctrine, incorporating the knowledge, skills, attitudes and values of Māori society' (Moorfield, 2011: 65). Henry and Pene (2001: 235) described Kaupapa Māori as 'the Māori way or agenda…traditional Māori ways of doing, being and thinking, encapsulated in a Māori world view or cosmology'. Like the work of Linda Smith (1999) and the MPRU, Kaupapa Māori theory and research stem from the largely adverse influence of Eurocentric research that has dehumanised and dispossessed Māori people. A Kaupapa Māori approach legitimises Māori ways of being, values, core assumptions, ideas and knowledge as important aspects of research and theory (Jones et al., 2006; Smith, 1999; Smith, 2012).

A Kaupapa Māori approach to psychology in Aotearoa is particularly important, as mainstream psychology is heavily reliant on North American and British-based theories and quantitative methods that promote the individual over the collective (Hodgetts et al., 2010; Nairn et al., 2012; Waitoki and Levy, 2016). The use of a Kaupapa Māori approach has allowed indigenous psychologists of Aotearoa, like those associated with the MPRU, to position themselves more critically within the discipline, given that dominant Eurocentric knowledge has been regarded as being superior to indigenous worldviews and, as such, is rooted in European imperialism and colonialism (Jones et al., 2006; Nikora, 2007; Pihama et al., 2002; Waitoki and Levy, 2016). A Kaupapa Māori approach does not, however, discard all European knowledge, but instead views Eurocentric ways of knowing as possessing some insights whilst being generally relative to the cultural context of its development. The need for Kaupapa Māori approaches to psychology in Aotearoa is particularly evident today because of the failure of 'mainstream' psychological research to respond openly to indigenous knowledge and the survival or wellbeing of indigenous people (Nikora, 2007; Sefa Dei, 2013).

Another area of work that has been very influential in our efforts to decolonise psychology has its roots in Latin America. Montero (2007; 2009; Montero et al., 2016) has outlined the various fields of work developed to address the oppressive realities that characterise the lives of people in different countries in that region. These areas of scholarship include the critical pedagogy of Freire (1970, 1994) and his colleagues, the sociology and participatory methods advocated by Fals Borda (1979), Liberation Philosophy (Dussel, 1985/2003), and Dependency Theory and all inform what Montero et al. (2016)

refer to as a Liberation Paradigm. In Latin America, Martín-Baró (1994) proposed that psychology should develop a new praxis that recognised peoples' virtues, is based in the lived realities of the oppressed and that engages in the recovery of historical memory to de-ideologise taken for granted social realities in the process of reconstructing identities and communities. For Teo (2006: 180), developing liberation psychology means, 'that North American and European knowledge in psychology will be relativized from the perspective of the Latin American masses'.

Montero and Sonn (2009) have collected several examples of work illustrating how liberation psychology has spread and is being applied and developed in different countries. These applications included recovering cultural memory and accompanying displaced people in remaking their lives (Sacipa-Rodríguez et al., 2009) and social and historical analysis and critical deconstruction of mechanisms of oppression and their links to individual experiences (Moane, 1999; Sonn and Lewis, 2009). Importantly, these various examples of how liberation psychology is being utilised beyond Latin America advance psychology by looking at social issues 'with an ethical perspective expressed in the respect of the Other, and understanding that there is no liberation without the Other, whoever he/she is, because liberating oneself departs from the construction of the Other accepting his/her diversity' (Montero and Sonn, 2009: 6). Liberation approaches are concerned with producing knowledge through a relational epistemology, thereby challenging essentialist categorisation. The approach also advocates a praxis that does not separate theory from action but sees these as co-constituting. Within liberation approaches, the marginalised and excluded are valued as co-constructors of knowledge about their lives and the solutions required for addressing their challenges.

Kaupapa Māori and liberation psychology have shared commitments in disrupting coloniality and expanding our ecology of knowledge beyond privileged Western theories and methods (de Sousa Santos, 2007). This involves building knowledge from the standpoints of those who come from marginalised and excluded groups, valuing their diverse voices and forms of knowledge and mobilising those to foster strong individual and community identities. To support the marginalised and excluded voice, Watkins and Shulman (2008: 276) suggested that a decolonising praxis entails:

> ...claiming resources; testimonies, storytelling, and remembering to claim and speak about extremely painful events and histories; and research that celebrates survival and resilience and that revitalizes language, arts, and cultural practices. Communities beset by various forms of oppression, whose members have suffered from diminished senses of themselves by virtue of racism and classism, can use research to not only nurture community understanding, but to help preserve community and cultural practices.

While there are diverse approaches and methods, storytelling has consistently been advocated as both a way of knowing and doing within liberation and indigenous approaches to applied social psychology.

Ways of Knowing and Doing: Stories and Storytelling

Storytelling has been mobilised as a central methodology for decolonising and liberatory work. Some scholars argue that decolonising approaches reject research that is exclusively positivistic, reductionistic and objectivist as irrelevant and colonising (Evans et al., 2009). There is a focus on researching back, writing back and talking back (see hooks, 1990; Smith, 1999) – that is counter storytelling. Storytelling is vital to achieving these tasks. For Martin (2007: 46), writing from an Australian Aboriginal standpoint, 'Stories have power and give power':

> Stories are our law. Stories give identity as they connect us and fulfill our sense of belonging. Stories are grounding, defining, comforting and

embracing. Stories vary in their purpose and content and so Stories can be political and yet equally healing. They can be shared verbally, physically or visually. Their meanings and messages teach, admonish, tease, celebrate, entertain, provoke and challenge. (Martin, 2007: 45)

Stories are individual, social and ideological, and because they are produced in social contexts, they often reflect narratives that are socially and culturally available (Sonn et al., 2013). Stories are central to identity and community making processes. Individuals and communities do not always have equal access to resources, such as mass media for story and narrative production and circulation, and as a result, those in less powerful positions may be excluded or marginalised or their stories silenced, concealed or devalued, while dominant group stories may work to reinforce racism and existing power arrangements (Bell, 2010; Rappaport, 2000).

However, oppressed groups generate counter narratives. The emergence of such counter narratives reflects the ways in which those who are excluded and marginalised can still create stories, sometimes away from mainstream settings (including via social and alternative media) and these are important resources for individual and group identity construction (Sonn and Fisher, 1998). Counter narratives also provide insight into symbolic strategies of resistance and survival; in fact, stories can be deconstructed to make visible and challenge power dynamics, and thereby disrupt coloniality and epistemic violence (O'Nell, 1994).

The projects that we describe next have been produced in different contexts. The research example from Aotearoa reflects upon how homeless Māori men of central Auckland negotiate a positive sense of self, relationships and a place in our society, which is awash with negative characterisations of homeless people and Māori. In this example, Kaupapa Māori theory and practice is the enactment of decolonising work. The example from Australia is part of an effort to explore how arts and cultural practice can foster community and identity construction and to challenge coloniality (Sonn and Baker, 2016; Sonn and Quayle, 2012).

RECLAIMING CULTURE FROM A DECOLONISING STANDPOINT

Homeless Māori Men and Gardening in Aotearoa

As indigenous people of Aotearoa, Māori account for approximately 15% of the total population, and similar to the Aboriginal and Torre Strait Islander people of Australia, Māori suffer from some of the worst socio-economic indicators (Carson et al., 2007; Ministry of Health, 2010; 2015). The poor state of Māori health, in particular, is a personal, community, institutional and societal issue and has been directly attributed to the long-term impacts of colonisation and the social determinants of health (Durie, 2006; Walker, 1990; Wilkinson and Pickett, 2010). The impact of the socio-economic marginalisation of Māori is brought into stark relief when we consider issues such as homelessness. Māori experience homelessness in a disproportionate rate compared to non-Māori in Aotearoa due to the ongoing processes of colonisation, land dislocation and economic marginalisation (Groot et al., 2015; Hodgetts et al., 2016; King et al., 2015).

As well as documenting the plight of Māori homeless people, it is also important that applied social psychologists respond. Responses in Aotearoa occur in two primary forms. First, psychologists have been involved in designing and implementing services. Second, we have worked with social service agencies to document the impacts of their efforts to support homeless people. Here, we provide an example of the latter through a long and ongoing relationship between the MPRU (The University of Waikato) and the Auckland City Mission (ACM). As part of our ongoing collaborations, Māori staff from ACM invited members of the MPRU to document the functioning of a joint venture between the ACM and Ngāti Whātua ki ōrākei (local tribal group) designed to build community and social ties with homeless Māori men by encouraging them to grow food and replant native trees and shrubs on recently returned tribal land (Hodgetts et al., 2016; King et al., 2015). In understanding the importance of this gardening project, the concept of a community of practice provides insights, where shared endeavour and practices central to community participation enhance the men's sense of belonging and health (Wenger, 1998). The gardening group as a community provided an alternative to the oft-negative characterisation of homeless Māori men as lazy, undeserving, substance-abusing vagrants. The intent of our research was to extend our understanding of the nature of wellness-promoting practices for Māori men experiencing street homelessness in central Auckland. We were particularly interested in exploring the experiences of the men participating in the project and if they contributed to their sense of dignity, purpose, meaning and connectedness. However, to explore such issues, we had to meet the men formally and to ascertain if they were willing to host and work with us.

Our official engagement with these homeless Māori men (or 'streeties' as they liked to be known) in the gardening project began with a traditional Māori welcome, or *pōhiri*. Here, the 'streeties' led a Māori cultural process that drew upon their knowledge of Māori customs to appraise our intentions, to seek clarification on our personal histories and to connect through shared genealogical and tribal histories. In essence, the streeties were 'sussing us out', 'sizing us up', and checking out who we were and what we were about. The enactment of traditional Māori protocols is in contrast to popular accounts that often describe homeless Māori as culturally disconnected from the Māori world. In initiating a *pōhiri*, these men made it clear that, though they may be physically disconnected from the domiciled Māori world, they were by no means culturally disconnected. We were being invited into their world and under their terms as Māori men with significant cultural skills. The power dynamic and research agenda had been set by the streeties, and not us as researchers. To be led by the streeties reflects the importance of responding to the wishes of research participants in culturally appropriate ways.

Between October 2012 and April 2013, we spent every Tuesday and Thursday engaging through our participation in gardening with the men: five homeless Māori men aged between 50–70 years and two tribal representatives from Ngāti Whātua, who would garden with the men on these days. As researchers, there were four of us, all Māori men, ranging in ages between the mid-20s to the mid-60s. We immersed ourselves in the gardening project and engaged the streeties in subjective ways where we drew upon our 'feelings, emotions and lived experience, largely ignored by positivist approaches' (Tomaselli et al., 2008: 347). Drawing on indigenous methodologies and Kaupapa Māori theory, our approach to researching with the streeties was contrary to how our academic institutions teach research in psychology (Hodgetts et al., 2010; Smith, 1999; Smith, 2012; Waitoki and Levy, 2016). In fact, we sidelined psychology's detached approach, which is often concerned with the number of interviews and filling out forms, rather than the quality of relationships with interviewees (Hodgetts et al., 2016). We drew upon our Māori cultural competence to engage these senior Māori men, who happened to be homeless. This approach allowed us to respond to the cultural nuances of the streeties in how and when we could engage. As we worked together in the garden, we spent considerable time talking about all manner of topics and simply getting to know each other. This approach reflects the sociocultural importance of gardening in the Māori world as a place for communal engagement, kinship ties and traditional knowledge transmission (Moon, 2005).

Correspondingly, our first formal interview with the men did not occur until four months into gardening. During this four-month period, each of our research members would keep a journal of the day's events, casual conversations and activities. This journaling would happen away from the garden, often when we returned home, after which we would meet to compare notes. We also took photographs of our evolving relationships and the growing garden. We were even told that the oldest of the streeties, in his late 60s and someone who had spent 20 years on the streets, would not talk to us or be interviewed. This man became an active participant and key informant in the research process because we followed appropriate cultural practices in not pushing him to participate. We also interviewed tribal members who owned the land and helped facilitate the gardening project, and they were pivotal in making the streeties feel welcome. As one tribal member commented, 'we were trying to give them a place where they felt comfortable' (Rangatira, *tribal representative*).

Of significance in our research was the cultural guidance we received from a female tribal elder (Kahu) who worked in the garden alongside the streeties and our own research member, Tiniwai. Both Kahu and Tiniwai are kaumātua, or Māori cultural elders, knowledgeable in both Māori language and practices. They were of similar age to these elderly streeties, and the streeties trusted and respected Tiniwai and Kahu for their cultural positions. As kaumātua, the streeties saw them as pillars of Māori tradition who offer wisdom, humility and a living link to the past, as exemplified by the following *whakataukī* (proverbial saying) 'he kitenga kanohi, he hokinga whakaaro – to see a face is to stir the memory' (Dyall et al., 2013: 65). This whakataukī emphasises the important role kaumātua have in recounting lived connections with those ancestors long past and the traditions associated with their lived memories. The streeties recognised both Kahu and Tiniwai's authority as kaumātua, as we recognised the authority of these elderly Māori streeties as kaumātua and responded appropriately. The cultural sense of appreciation was mutual and reciprocal, as it needs to be in such settings.

As a research group, we also drew upon the Māori cultural practice of *manaakitanga* (nurturing relationships/caring) as an important principle for human relationships and caring for others (Mead, 2003). Manaakitanga is not just an abstract concept but a way of understanding one's own obligations to the welfare of others that often manifests in mundane everyday social practices. We cooked lunch together using the produce from the garden and culturally significant foods that embody manaakitanga and associated principles of generosity, hospitality and care for those present within the gardening group. In this regard, the cultural and material are interconnected (Breiger, 2000), rooted in a socio-historical context and a collective commitment towards ritualised and material practices of care. This is particularly important for men who live life on the margins of society and find it difficult to cook meals on the streets without being ushered on by security guards or the police. The mundane practice of cooking lunch undisturbed, using food that had been collectively grown, then sharing food with others, engendered social support, a sense of belonging, dignity, respect, compassion and connectedness. In this instance, the streeties are operationalising the concept of manaakitanga. As we shared food, we cared for each other and, in effect, we cared for ourselves materially, culturally and spiritually. Lunch time was that anchor point for each gardening day, where discussions over meals ranged from international politics of the Middle East, to sporting teams, tribal affiliations, tales of growing up and life on the streets.

Beyond lunch times, however, our engagements with the streeties ensured an exchange of gardening knowledge and practices, sharing traditional Māori names of vegetables, associated medicinal properties and the theorising of growing vegetables by the moon phases, in accordance with traditional Māori gardening practices. We also marvelled at one streetie's successful transplanting of watercress[4] from another part of Auckland to the garden. Tuku, as he came to be known, reminded us of the importance of watercress as a Māori food delicacy. Tuku's transplanting exploits reflected his ingenuity and determination to stay connected with an ancient food type. Tuku's watercress patch was his crowning glory, and he wanted to show it off. He invested vast amounts of time nurturing this crop. Everyone from the streeties, research team, folk from the marae and Auckland City Mission were impressed and ensured his watercress patch was tended to when Tuku was not at the garden.

Reading our experiences in engaging homeless Māori men, our approach to this research was essentially ethnographic in orientation as a way of understanding the streeties within their own lifeworlds or everyday settings (Griffin and Bengry-Howell, 2012; Hodgetts et al., 2016). Our use of a culturally-informed and immersive research strategy (Jahoda, 1992) highlighted the need for context-sensitive information about the streeties' life circumstances with relation to their narrative stories. We drew on participant-observation, visual and narrative methods to explore practices through which the streeties made sense of their lives in a society replete with public expectations and media images of homelessness (Groot et al., 2015; Hodgetts et al., 2016). In addition, and reflecting the shift away from ethnography as a technology of colonialism, our approach to this research was informed by Kaupapa Māori theory, where the Māori world view and epistemology provided a core framework for understanding, engaging with and analysing our participants' experiences and lifeworlds (Jones et al., 2006; Smith, 2012; Waitoki and Levy, 2016). With regard to Kaupapa Māori, these 'streeties' were still Māori cultural elders and were afforded cultural respect and deference regardless of their precarious situations. We took this cultural relationship seriously and their cultural competence in the Māori language and practices cemented this admiration. The streeties would sometimes converse with us in Māori during everyday conversations or formal interviews. As Māori researchers, we would reply in Māori, or at least as competently as possible, which for some of us, included fluency and, for some others, included understanding the conversation but replying in English. Our lifeworlds were not as distinct as one might believe and we found more in common with each other through our cultural sense of connectedness than differences. This was an important part of our research project, where the Māori cultural concept of *whanaungatanga*, or building and maintaining ongoing relationships, was of more importance than pushing the research agenda. If whanaungatanga was the goal for our research engagements, then the project motto became 'relationships first, research second'. Often, in psychology, the needs of the research precede the needs of the participants, so we were determined to reflect the work of Kaupapa Māori research principles in an attempt to question and decolonise Eurocentric research approaches.

Part of our engagement with the streeties included the Māori concept of *koha* or gifting without expectation in return. The exchange of koha is a typical function of the Māori world that affirms manaakitanga (caring for others), and promotes co-operation and reciprocation (Mead, 2003). Koha, for us, was also seen as a dialectical process where the gift of a research participant's time, knowledge and personal narrative is reciprocated with a gift from the researcher (Hodgetts et al., 2013). Koha reflects the value of gift exchange as an ethical principle of participative social psychological research and the anchoring of this research project within a Kaupapa Māori research approach. An example of koha occurred every Tuesday and Thursday, when we would buy both perishable and non-perishable food to share during lunch. Each time, we would buy more food than required for the day, and this was purposeful and guided by a tribal proverb, *Tūhoe moumou kai, moumou tāonga, moumou tangata ki te pō*. This ancient proverb encourages people to be plentiful in giving and caring for others where such giving will be reciprocated in your own time of need. The notion of buying more than required for 'lunch' also reflected our sense of manaakitanga (caring/hospitality) for the streeties beyond our engagement at the garden. We were obviously aware of their return to the streets and wanted them to take that extra food when the gardening day ended. Our intent was never made explicit or articulated as such, but the streeties knew what we were doing. They recognised this cultural practice. We knew, from a Māori cultural perspective, this practice was *tika*, or the Māori thing to do, and we let our culture guide us in this koha practice.

We also developed a photo book in recognition of our time with the streeties. The book recorded various events throughout our seven-month period, the growth of the garden and the various people involved in the garden. We gifted the book to each of the men. As a gardening group, we also planned fundraising ventures to pay for a fishing charter. The streeties loved fishing and would often fish off the rocks or the various wharves around the city. The precarious nature of the streeties lives meant ocean fishing on a charter boat was unattainable and the fundraising event was unsuccessful too, again reflecting the nature of their precarity (Standing, 2011). However, our research team spoke with the research funders about using funds to charter a fishing boat for the day and, to our surprise, the funder agreed. Together with members of Ngāti Whātua, the 'gardening group' got their wish: a chartered fishing trip on the Waitemata Harbour (Auckland). Both the photo book and the fishing trip were a koha, or a gift, to the streeties as a token of our appreciation. The fishing trip was also part of our research exit strategy with the tribal members of Ngāti Whātua, Auckland City Mission and the streeties.

The gardening project continued long after our time with the group had finished and, despite the experiences of homelessness for these Māori men, the gardening project provided respite from the harsh realities of living on the streets. The men used the Tuesdays and Thursdays as opportunities for social interaction, belonging, sense of worth and community through the mundane practice of gardening. This initiative was not about solving homelessness, but rather engaging these men in alternative realities and possibilities with the support of the domiciled community. As researchers, we recognised the nature of our roles was to record, engage and to be in conversation with our participants' stories. We were guided by our cultural knowledge in developing our relationships with these men and drew upon aspects of our psychology training to capture the everyday. We shared these insights with both the Auckland City Mission and Ngāti Whātua (tribal hosts), who reaffirmed their commitment to the project.

Counter Storytelling through Community Arts in Australia

In Australia, Indigenous people, who constitute approximately 3% of the total population, have a lower life expectancy, higher rates of suicide and self-harm and much higher rates of incarceration than other Australians (Australian Institute of Health and Welfare, 2014). Dominant cultural narratives of Aboriginal people in Australia construct them as 'the problem' in need of being 'fixed', while the ongoing history of dispossession and its legacy is often silenced or ignored (Walter, 2010).

In the town of Narrogin, in the Wheatbelt region of Western Australia (WA), the traditional custodians of the land, the Noongar people, have experienced community distress, as reflected in issues of suicide, racism and feuding (Davies, 2010). It is in this context, and in response to these challenges, that the Community Arts Network (CAN), a community arts and cultural development agency that has demonstrated a particular commitment to working with Noongar people, was invited to Narrogin to develop strategies for healing and community building.

The example we describe here is part of a broader programme of work exploring how community arts and cultural practice can contribute to Aboriginal self-determination and empowerment (Sonn and Quayle, 2012). The specific study reported draws from the work of Christopher Sonn and Amy Quayle, whose doctoral thesis focuses on CAN's Bush Babies project with Noongar people in Narrogin. It builds on previous work that showed that working at the indigenous/non-indigenous interface is a delicate and multilayered process, anchored in critical reflexivity. As noted by Walker et al. (2014: 207) reflexivity:

> …is about recognising and critically engaging our own subjectivities in the context of relating across cultural boundaries. It means examining our own social and cultural identities and the power and privilege we have because of these identities. It also requires that we engage with the political and ideological nature of practice and knowledge production and consider the implications of these for those we aspire to work with.

As several authors have written and we have argued based on our work over several years (see e.g., Sonn and Quayle, 2012), critically reflective practice is central in developing effective partnership in work with Aboriginal communities (Walker et al., 2014). Working in partnership requires time, building trust and developing personal relationships, similar to that described in the example above. The process involves working alongside cultural experts, listening and hearing and seeking advice. Often, this means not knowing, and being vulnerable because of this, but this is vital to the processes of jointly addressing the needs and aspirations of marginalised groups.

In CAN's practice, developing relationships, building trust and reciprocity have been central to working with Aboriginal communities, and the communities typically decide on projects and what they would like to do (Sonn et al., 2017). CAN's Rekindling Stories on Country strategy aimed to create opportunities for intergenerational dialogue and cultural transmission and the celebration of Noongar history, culture and language at a broader level. As part of this broader initiative, the Bush Babies project tells the stories of Noongar Elders from across WA who were born in the bush – stories about where they were born and what life was like for them growing up at this time. Many Aboriginal people were born in the bush because they were not allowed into hospitals; they lived on the fringes of towns near rubbish dumps, on 'Native' reserves and church controlled missions,[5] often separated from their families as part of the Stolen Generations (see Haebich, 2000). The Bush Babies project originated with a Noongar Elder who wanted to honour the Noongar Bush Babies and midwives who delivered them. The project has been delivered in many towns across the Wheatbelt since it began in 2010 and has made use of a variety of different arts practices, with the idea of renewing stories on country being the central thread (for more on Bush Babies see: http://www.canwa.com.au/project/bush-babies/; Quayle et al., 2016a). The Narrogin iteration of the project involved several components including: the collection of Bush Baby stories, and the creation of opportunities for intergenerational storytelling, and the Honouring our Elders portrait project and public exhibition(s).

Facilitated by Chronicle, a digital storytelling company, CAN organised a two-day storytelling workshop at the local high school involving four local Elders and approximately 12 Aboriginal and Torres Strait Islander media studies students. Elders shared stories of their lives growing up – often these were stories of being taken away from their families to a mission as a child or growing up on an Aboriginal reserve. They shared stories of suffering but also of resistance and survival. They emphasised to the young Aboriginal students to be proud to be Aboriginal. Students were then supported to create short digital stories using photographs and the recorded stories. CAN also recorded Bush Baby stories informally and, with the help of Chronicle, in a community setting. The aim was to create an archive of Bush Baby stories for current and future generations. Intergenerational storytelling was further encouraged through Storylines workshops with primary and high school students and their families. Students were able to explore the Storylines database, which is 'an online archive for the State Library's digitised heritage collections relating to Aboriginal history in Western Australia' (State Library of Western Australia, 2016).

The Honouring our Elders portrait project and exhibition emerged from the Narrogin community after the exhibition of photographs that had been taken as part of a previous Bush Babies project. A local non-indigenous artist saw a photo of Noongar Elder, Nana Purple, and asked if he could paint her portrait. This inspired the portrait project and exhibition, which sought to honour Noongar Elders through portraiture. Accompanying the portraits were short snippets of each Elder's story as well as the digital stories that had been produced by students. This project involved 10 non-indigenous and two Aboriginal artists who volunteered to paint the portraits of local Noongar Elders. The portraits were exhibited locally and also at the Western Australia (WA) Museum over a number of months. In 2016, this exhibition travelled around WA as part of Art on the Move.

Recovery of historical memory through storytelling, and documenting and exhibiting the stories of Elders are important strategies for decolonial work. Our subsequent analysis of the stories collected though the various stages of the project and conversational interviews has allowed us to witness the stories of Elders and also partner them in showing the ongoing dynamics of coloniality in the lives of Noongar people (Quayle et al., 2016b). The Elders' stories showed the circuits and consequences of dispossession (Fine and Ruglis, 2009) in the lives of Noongar people. The stories that they shared attested to the mechanisms of dispossession conveyed through their recollections of growing up on missions and reserves, the various forms of control that governed Noongar peoples' lives – the curfews, the permits, the segregation – and also highlighted the continued experience of structural, cultural and interpersonal violence. The stories were also testimonies of the intrapsychic and relational impacts of oppression (Quayle et al., 2016b), the effects of which are also experienced across generations. Importantly, though, the stories also conveyed the different psychological and embodied strategies people use, such as avoiding and ignoring racist behaviour, and the important role of Aboriginal cultural knowledge and practice in resistance and survival. These strategies of resistance and survival that were narrated are anchored in stories about traditions, places of cultural significance, and finding strength in culture, and country understood within Aboriginal frameworks. According to Bird-Rose (1996: 7):

> Country is a place that gives and receives life. Not just imagined or represented, it is lived in and lived with. Country in Aboriginal English is not only a common noun, but also a proper noun. People talk about country in the same way that they would talk about a person; they speak to country, sing to country, visit country, worry about country, feel sorry for country and long for country. People say that country knows, hears, smells, takes notice, takes care, is sorry or happy. Country is not a generalised or undifferentiated type of place such as one might indicate with terms like 'spending a day in the country' or 'going up to the country'. Rather, country is a living entity with a yesterday, today and tomorrow with a consciousness, and a will toward life. Because of this richness, country is home and peace: nourishment for body, mind and spirit [...].

Cultural connection to country is spiritual and, as Moreton-Robinson (2003) noted, relationship to country is central to belonging and identity. Meanings of country are passed on through story, song, art and dance. These are important counter stories in the Australian post-colonising context where Aboriginal people continue to be constructed as dysfunctional and often as passive victims in media and political discourse.

The stories collected and archived are resources for Aboriginal communities. They are part of processes of cultural reclamation, renewal and healing – they are the basis for community building practices. For non-indigenous people, Aboriginal stories are a challenge to the collective lies about the histories and culture of Aboriginal people as told by the powerful colonising group. Essentially, the stories, which are made public through arts and exhibitions, serve as an invitation to dialogue between the colonised and colonisers. As Quayle et al. (2016a) showed, the stories serve as a public pedagogy disrupting legitimising myths of 'inferiority', 'victimhood' and 'laziness'. In the words of one of the non-indigenous artists interviewed by Quayle: 'it's the project that has broken down barriers I think. It's a very non-threatening way to be in relationship, and most of the other ways you think of, it's one person telling another person how they should live…'. One Noongar Elder said: 'You know what, … [it's] done a lot for us, it's made us feel, back to where we should be as Aboriginal people but not only as Aboriginal people, as people, with respect for all people…'. These words are about being recognised and valued as people. As researchers in applied social psychology, we are learning and finding ways to work in solidarity with indigenous communities, creating new roles and methods for enacting liberation psychology.

SUMMARY AND CONCLUSION

In this chapter, we outlined how we are participating in applied social psychology research and action to contribute to the goals of decolonisation. In the projects that we have described, it is evident that forming connections with community based agencies and local communities is central to the goal of supporting efforts to challenge oppression at individual and group levels. Importantly, in the work of Māori, the very act of developing and articulating Kaupapa Māori is an exemplar of decolonising work. This is best described by what Pihama and colleagues (2002) refer to as a 'consciousness', where Māori notions of knowledge are valued and Pākehā hegemony is decentred. A Kaupapa Māori research approach does not necessarily prescribe the methodological tools for collecting empirical materials. It can, however, prescribe rules of engagement with Māori around what research is required, the implications of the research to both researcher and researched, the benefits of the research to the research group and the compensation of time and expense. Drawing on Kaupapa Māori to inform indigenous psychologies highlights the need to develop psychological knowledge that is understood and experienced by, and native to, the people it is designed for (Allwood and Berry, 2006; Kim et al., 2006; Waitoki and Levy, 2016).

The example of Kaupapa Māori, and the work by the MPRU as the foundation for an indigenous psychology, is part of a response to the decolonial project in psychology today (Hodgetts et al., 2010; Nikora, 2007; Waitoki and Levy, 2016). More specifically, this chapter contributes to work on indigenous psychologies that are anchored in a Māori understanding of being, which for Aotearoa, emphasises the retention of an identity as Māori and the centralising of Māori aspirations and priorities beyond those set by mainstream psychology. Drawing upon a Kaupapa Māori framework centres the importance of environment and culture in understanding indigenous people as interdependent and interconnected beings as opposed to Euro-American psychology that emphasises individualism, independence and self-sufficiency (Hodgetts et al., 2010; Nairn et al., 2012; Waitoki and Levy, 2016; Watkins and Shulman, 2008) – an important effort in redirecting applied social psychology.

While indigenous authors in Australia have developed similar approaches to Kaupapa Māori, the example from Australia takes a different path, drawing on the liberation paradigm to pursue decolonising work as non-indigenous researchers engaging with colonialism and racism. Central to CAN's Bush Baby project is the powerful epistemology and methodology of storytelling, which is pivotal to the process of deconstructing hegemonic cultural narratives. At the same time, this work involves sharing, elevating and strengthening narratives of resilience, resistance and survival. The recovery of historical memory (Martín-Baró, 1994) through storytelling using arts is central to cultural reclamation, identity affirmation and making place. This storytelling method is anchored in an epistemology that views knowledge as produced in, and through, social relations and relational ethics (Montero, 2007; 2009). Storytelling through community based arts and cultural practice creates spaces for participation and the representation of voices that have been routinely silenced. Engagement through indigenous arts and portraiture can trigger processes of problematisation and community self-expression of experiences of suffering aspirations, and healing. As noted by Watkins and Shulman (2008: 265),

> Liberation arts excel at the process of transformation. The right symbol or name in the right place can break silences, provide new insights, and reframe hierarchies in an instant. The conversations that follow can bring down barriers and transcend borders that seemed immovable.

As we expand our ways of knowing and doing, we are also called to engage with the politics of knowledge and representation, as key sites for decolonising praxis, which includes creating settings for dialogue and developing interventions into the cultural sphere through public art and installations.

In both the Australia and Aotearoa context, these forms of praxis are growing and part of the process of decolonising psychology (Dudgeon and Walker, 2015; Hodgetts et al., 2010; Waitoki and Levy 2016). Individual-level intervention and deficit models that frame human suffering as a result of personal shortcoming are contested in favour of explanations that understand such suffering as the result of historical, social, cultural and colonial dynamics (Trickett, 2015). As researchers and educators, we are engaging with alternative practices (documenting and archiving), forming disciplinary alliances and making public through arts modalities to tackle systems that inflict misery on peoples' lives (e.g., Adams et al., 2015; Coimbra et al., 2012; Dutta et al., 2016; Fine, 2006; Teo, 2015; Watkins and Shulman, 2008). These actions and processes are part of the generative process of building an ethical, relevant, just and culturally rooted applied social psychology.

Notes

1 The word 'Aotearoa' is the indigenous Māori word for New Zealand and it is increasingly used within the everyday vernacular of Māori and non-Māori. Referring to New Zealand as 'Aotearoa' is also a political statement, re-establishing the authority of Māori as the indigenous culture.
2 Indigenous people of Aotearoa/New Zealand.
3 Indigenous Māori term for British and European settlers to Aotearoa.
4 An aquatic plant which grows in running water.
5 Reserves and missions are places that Aboriginal people were forcibly relocated to, with missions typically run by churches and reserves run by government and sometimes churches (see Australian Institute of Aboriginal and Torres Strait Islander Studies, 2016).

REFERENCES

Adams, G., Dobles, I., Gómez, L. H., Kurtiş, T. & Molina, L. E. (2015). Decolonizing psychological science: Introduction to the special thematic section. *Journal of Social and Political Psychology*, *3*(1), 213–238.

Allwood, C., & Berry, J. (2006). Origins and development of indigenous psychologies: An international analysis. *International Journal of Psychology*, *41*, 243–268.

Australian Institute of Aboriginal and Torres Strait Islander Studies. (2016, August). *Mission and reserve records*. Retrieved from http://aiatsis.gov.au/research/finding-your-family/family-history-sources/mission-and-reserve-records

Australian Institute of Health and Welfare. (2014). *The health and welfare of Australia's Aboriginal and Torres Strait Islander peoples 2015*. Retrieved from https://www.aihw.gov.au/getmedia/584073f7-041e-4818-9419-39f5a060b1aa/18175.pdf.aspx?inline=true. Accessed 18 July, 2018.

Bell, L. A. (2010). *Storytelling for social justice: Connecting narrative and arts in antiracist teaching*. New York, NY: Taylor & Francis.

Bird-Rose, D. (1996). *Nourishing terrains: Australian Aboriginal views of landscape and wilderness*. Canberra, ACT: Australian Heritage Commission.

Bishop, R. (1998). Freeing ourselves from neocolonial domination in research: A Maori approach to creating knowledge. *International Journal of Qualitative Studies in Education*, *11*(2), 199–219.

Breiger, R. L. (2000). A tool kit for practice theory. *Poetics*, *27*(2–3), 91–115.

Bulhan, H. A. (1985). *Frantz Fanon and the psychology of oppression*. New York, NY: Plenum Press.

Carson, B., Dunbar, T., Chenhall, R. C., & Bailie, R. (Eds.). (2007). *Social determinants of Indigenous health*. Crows Nest, NSW: Allen & Unwin.

Coimbra, J. L., Duckett, P, Fryer, D., Makkawi, I., Menezes, I., Seedat, M., & Walker, C. (2012). Rethinking community psychology: Critical insights. *The Australian Community Psychologist*, *24*(2). 135–142.

Cooper, G. (2012). Kaupapa Maori research: Epistemic wilderness as freedom? *New Zealand Journal of Educational Studies*, *47*(2), 64–73.

David, E. J. R. (2011). *Filipino-American postcolonial psychology: Oppression, colonial mentality, and decolonization*. Bloomington, IN: Authorhouse.

Davies, K. (2010). A journalistic study of Narrogin's feuding families. *Research Journalism*, *1*(1), Retrieved from: http://ro.ecu.edu.au/cgi/viewcontent.cgi?article=1000&context=research_journalism

De Sousa Santos, B. (2007). *Beyond abyssal thinking: From global lines to ecologies of knowledge*. Retrieved from: http://www.eurozine.com/pdf/2007-06-29-santos-en.pdf. Accessed 18 July, 2018.

Dudgeon, P., & Walker, R. (2015). Decolonising Australian psychology: Discourses, strategies, and practice. *Journal of Social and Political Psychology*, *3*(1), 276–297.

Durie, M. (2006). *Whaiora: Maori health development* (2nd edn.). Melbourne, Vic: Oxford University Press.

Dussel, E. (2003). *Philosophy of Liberation*. Trans. A. Martinez & C. Morkovsky. Maryknoll, NY: Orbis Books. Original work published in 1985.

Dutta, U., Sonn, C. C., & Lykes, M. B. (2016). Situating and contesting structural violence in community-based research and action. *Community Psychology in Global Perspective*, *2*(2), 1–20.

Dyall, L., Skipper, T., Kepa, M., Hayman, K., & Kerse, N. (2013). Navigation: process of building relationships with kaumātua (Māori leaders). *The New Zealand Medical Journal*, *126*(1368), 65–74.

Enriquez, V. G. (1992). *From colonial to liberation psychology: The Phillipine experience*. Quezon City: University of the Phillipines Press.

Evans, M., Hole, R., Berg, L. D., Hutchinson, P., & Sookraj, D. (2009). Common insights, differing methodologies: Toward a fusion of Indigenous methodologies, participatory action research, and white studies in an urban Aboriginal research agenda. *Qualitative Inquiry*, *15*(5), 893–910.

Fals Borda, O. (1979). Investigating reality in order to transform it: The Columbian experience. *Dialectical Anthropology*, *4*(1), 33–55.

Fanon, F. (1967). *Black skins, white masks*. New York, NY: Grove Press.

Fine, M. (2006). Bearing witness: Methods for researching oppression and resistance – A textbook for critical research. *Social Justice Research*, *19*(1), 83–108.

Fine, M. (2012). Troubling calls for evidence: A critical race, class and gender analysis of whose evidence counts. *Feminism & Psychology*, *22*(1), 3–19.

Fine, M., & Ruglis, J. (2009). Circuits and consequences of dispossession: The racialized realignment of the public sphere for US youth. *Transforming Anthropology*, *17*(1), 20–33.

Freire, P. (1970). *Pedagogy of the oppressed.* New York, NY: Continuum.

Freire, P. (1994). *Education for critical consciousness.* New York, NY: Continuum.

Gergen, K. J., Gulerce, A., Lock, A., & Misra, G. (1996). Psychological science in cultural context. *American Psychologist*, *51*(5), 496–503.

Gibbs, M. (2001). Toward a strategy for undertaking cross-cultural collaborative research. *Society and Natural Resources*, *14*, 673–687.

Gone, J. (2011). The red road to wellness: Cultural reclamation in a native First Nations community treatment centre. *American Journal of Community Psychology*, *47*, 187–202. doi: 10.1007/s10464-010-9373-2

Griffin, C., & Bengry-Howell, A. (2012). Ethnography. In C. Willig & W. Stainton-Rogers (Eds.), *The SAGE handbook of Qualitative Research in Psychology* (pp. 15–31). London, England: Sage.

Groot, S., Hodgetts, D., Nikora, L. W., Rua, M., & Groot, D. (2015). Pani me te rawakore: Home-making and Maori homelessness without hope or a home. In M. Kepa, M. McPherson & L. Manu'atu (Eds.), *Home: Here to stay* (Vol. 3, pp. 55–68). Wellington: Huia Publishers.

Haebich, A. (2000). *Broken circles: Fragmenting Indigenous families, 1800–2000.* Fremantle, WA: Fremantle Arts Centre Press.

Harrell, S. (2015). Culture, wellness, and world "PEaCE": An introduction to the person environment and culture emergence theory. *Community Psychology in Global Perspective*, *1*(1), 16–49.

Henry, E., & Pene, H. (2001). Kaupapa Maori: Locating Indigenous ontology, epistemology and methodology in the academy. *Organization*, *8*(2), 234–242.

Hodgetts, D., Chamberlain, K., Tankel, Y., & Groot, S. (2013). Researching poverty to make a difference: The need for reciprocity and advocacy in community research. *The Australian Community Psychologist*, *25*(1), 46–59.

Hodgetts, D., Drew, N., Sonn, C., Stolte, O., Nikora, L. W., & Curtis, C. (Eds.). (2010). *Social psychology and everyday life.* Basingstoke, England: Palgrave Macmillan.

Hodgetts, D., Rua, M., King, P., & Te Whetu, T. (2016). The ordinary in the extra-ordinary: Everyday lives textured by homelessness. In E. Schraube & C. Højholt (Eds.), *Psychology and the conduct of everyday life* (pp. 124–144). London, England: Routledge.

hooks, b. (1990). *Yearning: Race, gender, and cultural politics.* Boston, MA: South End Press.

Jahoda, M. (1992). Reflections on Marienthal and after. *Journal of Occupational and Organizational Psychology*, *65*, 355–358.

Jones, R., Crengle, S., & McCreanor, T. (2006). How Tikanga guides and protects the research process: Insights from the Hauora Tane project. *Social Policy Journal of New Zealand*, (29), 60–77.

Kessi, S., & Boonzaier, F. (2016). Resistance and transformation in postcolonial contexts. In C. Howarth & E. Andreouli (Eds.), *The Social Psychology of everyday politics* (Ch. 9). London, UK: Routledge.

Kim, U., Yang, K. S., & Hwang, K. K. (2006). *Indigenous and cultural psychology: Understanding people in context.* New York, NY: Springer.

Kincheloe, J. (2001). Describing the bricolage: Conceptualising a new rigor in qualitative research. *Qualitative Inquiry*, *7*(6), 679–692.

King, P., Hodgetts, D., Rua, M., & Te Whetu, T. (2015). Older men gardening on the marae: Everyday practices of being Maori. *AlterNative: An International Journal of Indigenous Peoples*, *11*(1), 14–28.

Kral, M. J., Ramírez García, J. I., Aber, M. S., Masood, N., Dutta, U., & Todd, N. R. (2011). Culture and community psychology: Toward a renewed and reimagined vision. *American Journal of Community Psychology*, *47*(1), 46–57.

Ladson-Billings, G. (2003). It's your world, I'm just trying to explain it: Understanding our epistemological and methodological challenges. *Qualitative Inquiry*, *9*(1), 5–12.

Macleod, C., & Bhatia, S. (2008). Postcolonialism and psychology. In C. Willig & W. Stainton-Rogers (Eds.), *The Sage handbook of qualitative psychology* (pp. 576–589). Thousand Oaks, CA: Sage.

Maldonado-Torres, N. (2007). On the coloniality of being: Contributions to the development of a concept, *Cultural Studies*, *21*(2–3), 240–270.

Māori & Psychology Research Unit. (2016). *Maori & Psychology Research Unit*. Retrieved from http://www.waikato.ac.nz/fass/research/centres-units/mpru

Martin, K. (2007). Aboriginal people, Aboriginal lands and Indigenist research: A discussion of research pasts and neo-colonial research futures. Unpublished dissertation, James Cook University, Cairns, Queensland, Australia.

Martin, K. & Mirraboopa, B. (2003). Ways of knowing, being and doing: A theoretical framework and methods for Indigenous and Indigenist research. *Australian Studies*, *27*(76), 203–214.

Martín-Baró, I. (1994). Towards a liberation psychology. In A. Aron & S. Corne (Eds.), *Writings for a liberation psychology: Ignacio Martín-Baró* (pp. 17–32). Cambridge, MA: Harvard University Press.

Mead, H. (2003). *Tikanga Maori: Living by Maori Values*. Wellington, New Zealand: Huia.

Ministry of Health. (2010). *The Social Report 2010*. Wellington: Ministry of Health.

Ministry of Health. (2015). *Tatau Kahukura: Māori Health Chart Book 2015* (3rd edn.). Wellington, New Zealand: Ministry of Health.

Misra, G., & Gergen, K. J. (1993). On the place of culture in the psychological sciences. *International Journal of Psychology*, *28*, 225–243.

Moane, G. (1999). *Gender and colonialism: A psychological analysis of oppression and liberation*. London, UK: Palgrave/McMillan.

Montero, M. (2007). The political psychology of liberation: From politics to ethics and back. *Political Psychology*, *28*(5), 517–533.

Montero, M. (2009). Community action and research as citizenship construction. *American Journal of Community Psychology*, *43*(1), 149–161.

Montero, M. & Sonn, C. (2009). About liberation and psychology: An introduction. In M. Montero & C. C. Sonn (Eds.), *Psychology of liberation: Theory and applications* (pp. 1–10). New York, NY: Springer.

Montero, M., Sonn, C. C., & Burton, M. (2016). Community psychology and liberation psychology: A creative synergy for an ethical and transformative praxis. In M. A. Bond, I. Serrano-García, & C. B. Keys (Eds.), *APA handbook of community psychology: Vol. 1. Theoretical foundations, core concepts, and emerging challenges*, (pp. 149–167). Washington, DC: American Psychological Association.

Moon, P. (2005). *A Tohunga's natural world: Plants, gardening and food*. Auckland, New Zealand: David Ling Publishing.

Moorfield, J. (2011). *Te Aka: Maori-English, English-Maori dictionary*. Auckland, New Zealand: Pearson.

Moreton-Robinson, A. (2003). I still call Australia home: Indigenous belonging in a white society. In S. Ahmed, C. Castaneda, A. Fortier, & M. Sheller (Eds.), *Uprootings/regroundings: Questions of home and migration* (p. 2340). Oxford, England: Berg.

Moreton-Robinson, A., & Walter, M. (2009). Indigenous methodologies in social research. In M. Walter (Ed), *Social research methods: An Australian perspective* (2nd edn., Ch. 22). South Melbourne, Vic: Oxford University Press.

Moreton-Robinson, A. (Ed.) (2016). *Critical Indigenous studies: Engagements in First world locations*. Tucson: The University of Arizona Press.

Nairn, R., Pehi, P., Black, R., & Waitoki, M. (Eds.). (2012). *Ka Tu, Ka Oho: Visions of a bicultural partnership in psychology: Invited Keynotes: Revisiting the past to rest the future*. Wellington: The New Zealand Psychological Society.

Nikora, L. W. (2007). Maori and psychology: Indigenous psychology in New Zealand. In A. Weatherall, M. Wilson, D. Harper & J. McDowell (Eds.), *Psychology in Aotearoa/New Zealand* (pp. 80–85). North Shore, New Zealand: Pearson Education.

O'Nell, T. D. (1994). Telling about whites, talking about Indians: Oppression, resistance and contemporary Indian identity. *Cultural Anthropology*, *9*(1), 94–126.

Pihama, L., Cram, F., & Walker, S. (2002). Creating methodological space: A literature review of Kaupapa Maori research. *Canadian Journal of Native Education*, *26*(1), 30–43.

Quayle, A., Sonn, C., & Kasat, P. (2016a). Community arts as public pedagogy: Disruptions into public memory through Aboriginal counter-storytelling. *International Journal of Inclusive Education*, *20*(3), 261–277.

Quayle, A., Sonn, C.C., & van den Eynde, J. (2016b). Narrating the accumulation of dispossession: Stories of Aboriginal Elders. *Community Psychology in Global Perspective,* 2(*2*), 79–96.

Rappaport, J. (2000). Community narratives: Tales of terror and joy. *American Journal of Community Psychology*, *28*(1), 1–24.

Reyes Cruz, M., & Sonn, C. C. (2015). (De)colonizing culture in community psychology: Reflections from critical social science. In R. D. Goodman, & P. C. Gorski (Eds.), *Decolonizing 'multicultural' counseling through social justice* (pp. 127–145). New York, NY: Springer.

Rigney, L.-I. (2006). Indigenist research and Aboriginal Australia. In J. Kunnie & N.I. Goduka (Eds.), *Indigenous peoples' wisdom and power: Affirming our knowledge through narratives* (pp. 32–50). Aldershot, England: Ashgate.

Sacipa-Rodríguez, S., Tovar-Guerra, C., Galindo Villarreal, L. F., & Bohórquez, R. V. (2009). Psychological accompaniment: Construction of cultures of peace among a community affected by war. In M. Montero & C. C. Sonn (Eds.), *Psychology of liberation: Theory and applications* (pp. 221–235). New York, NY: Springer.

Seedat, M. (1997). The quest for liberatory psychology. *South African Journal of Psychology*, *27*(4), 261.

Sefa Dei, G. J. (2013). Critical perspectives on indigenous research. *Socialist Studies/Etudes socialistes*, *9*(1), 27–38.

Shweder, R. A. (1990). Cultural psychology – What is it? In J. W. Stigler, R. A. Shweder, & G. Herdt (Eds.), *Cultural psychology: Essays on comparative human development* (pp. 1–43). Cambridge, England: Cambridge University Press.

Sloan, T. (1996). *Damaged life: The crisis of the modern psyche*. New York, NY: Routledge.

Smith, G. (2012). Interview: Kaupapa Maori: The dangers of domestication. *New Zealand Journal of Educational Studies*, *47*(2), 10–20.

Smith, L. T. (1999). *Decolonizing methodologies: Research and Indigenous peoples*. Dunedin, New Zealand: University of Otago Press.

Sonn, C. & Baker, A. (2016). Creating inclusive knowledges: Exploring the transformative potential of arts and cultural practice. *International Journal of Inclusive Education*, *20*(3), 215–228.

Sonn, C. C., & Fisher, A. T. (1998). Sense of community: Community resilient responses to oppression and change. *Journal of Community Psychology*, *26*(5), 457–471.

Sonn, C. C., & Lewis, R. (2009). Immigration and identity: The ongoing struggles for liberation. In M. Montero & C. C. Sonn (Eds.), *Psychology of liberation: Theory and applications* (pp. 115–134). New York, NY: Springer.

Sonn, C., & Quayle, A. (2012). Community psychology, critical theory and community development in Indigenous empowerment. In D. Bretherton & N. Balvin (Eds.), *Peace psychology in Australia* (pp. 261–282). New York, NY: Springer.

Sonn, C. C., Kasat, P., & Quayle, A. F. (2017). Creative responses to social suffering: Using community arts. In M. Seedat, S. Suffla, & D. Christie (Eds). *Emancipatory and participatory methodologies in peace, critical, and community psychology* (pp. 91–105). New York, NY: Springer.

Sonn, C. C., Stevens, G., & Duncan, N. (2013). Decolonisation, critical methodologies and why stories matter. In G. Stevens, N. Duncan, & D. Hook (Eds.), *Race, memory and the Apartheid Archive: Towards a transformative psychosocial praxis* (pp. 295–314). New York, NY: Palgrave Macmillan.

Squire, C. (2000). Reconfiguring psychology and culture. In C. Squire (Ed.), *Culture in psychology* (pp. 1–16). London, UK: Routledge.

Standing, G. (2011). *The precariat: The new dangerous class*. London, England: Bloomsbury Academic.

State Library of Western Australia. (2016). *Storylines*. Retrieved from: http://slwa.wa.gov.au/for/indigenous_australians/storylines.

Stewart-Harawira, M. (2013). Challenging knowledge capitalism. Indigenous research in the 21st century. *Socialist Studies/Etudes Socialistes*, *9*(1), 39–51.

Teo, T. (2006). *The critique of psychology: From Kant to postcolonial theory*. New York, NY: Springer Science & Business Media.

Teo, T. (2015). Essay on an aesthetics of resistance. In J. Cresswell, A. Haye, A. Larrain, M. Morgan, & G. Sullivan (Eds.), *Dialogue and debate in the making of theoretical psychology* (pp. 303–310). Concord, ON: Captus Press.

Tomaselli, K. G., Dyll, L., & Francis, M. (2008). Self and other: Auto-reflexive and indigenous ethnography. In N. K. Denzin, Y. S. Lincoln, & L. T. Smith (Eds.), *Handbook of critical and indigenous methodologies* (pp. 347–372). Thousand Oaks: CA: Sage.

Trickett, E. J. (2015). Seymour Sarason remembered: 'Plus ça change…', 'Psychology misdirected', and 'Community psychology and the anarchist insight'. *American Journal of Community Psychology, 56*, 197–204.

Waitoki, M., & Levy, M. (Eds.). (2016). *Indigenous psychology in Aotearoa/New Zealand*. Wellington: The New Zealand Psychological Society.

Walker, R. (1990). *Ka Whawhai Tonu Matau: Struggle without end*. Auckland, New Zealand: Penguin Books.

Walker, R., Schultz, C., & Sonn, C. (2014). Cultural competence: Transforming policy, services, programs and practice. In P. Dudgeon, H. Milroy, & R. Walker (Eds.), *Working together: Aboriginal and Torres Strait Islander mental health and wellbeing principles and practice* (2nd edn., pp. 195–220). Retrieved from: http://aboriginal.telethonkids.org.au/media/699863/Working-Together-Book.pdf

Walter, M. (2010). Market forces and Indigenous resistance paradigms. *Social Movement Studies: Journal of Social, Cultural and Political Protest*, 9(2), 121–137.

Watkins, M., & Shulman, H. (2008). *Toward psychologies of liberation*. Basingstoke, England: Palgrave MacMillan.

Wenger, E. (1998). *Communities of practice: Learning, meaning and identity*. Cambridge, England: Cambridge University Press.

Wilkinson, R. G., & Pickett, K. (2010). *The spirit level: Why greater equality makes societies stronger*. New York, NY: Bloomsbury Press.

PART II

Gender and Sexuality

4

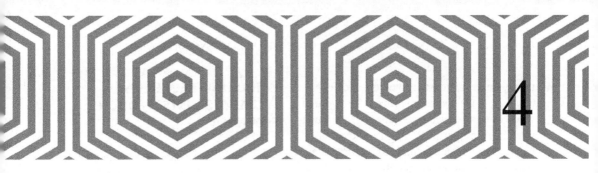

Interventions to Reduce Violence against Women: The Contribution of Applied Social Psychology

Paula C. Barata and Charlene Y. Senn

INTRODUCTION

We take the view that applied social psychology is not just about doing social psychology that is 'applicable' but rather involves specific efforts to ameliorate a social problem. It uses the theories, methods, and content knowledge of social psychology to move toward active solutions. One of the primary ways that social psychology has been used to address social problems within the area of gender is through the development and evaluation of specific interventions that draw on social psychological theories and methods, as well as gender research that has documented and sought to understand the problem.

We have chosen to focus our chapter on Violence Against Women (VAW) interventions. There are certainly examples of other worthy gender-based interventions that build on basic gender research and social psychological theory. For example, a number of eating disorder interventions build on research examining how social influences impact women's beliefs about their bodies (Becker et al., 2006; Cruwys et al., 2015). Many sexually transmitted infection risk-reduction interventions (e.g., to increase condom use) have also built on basic gender research and social psychological theories (e.g., Jemmott et al., 2014). Nevertheless, there are many examples of interventions within the VAW field and sufficient variety that allow us to demonstrate a number of different approaches. As VAW researchers, it is also the area with which we are most familiar.

We have included interventions that seek, as a primary goal, to change individual people's beliefs or behaviors in some way. For example, shelters for women who have experienced intimate partner violence (IPV) are a VAW intervention, but their primary goal is to provide options for women wanting to leave an abusive partner and not to change women's beliefs or behaviors in a specific direction. In our effort to highlight the role of social psychology, we have also avoided reviewing clinical interventions although many, based at least in part on social psychology, have been developed for women who have experienced abuse and men who have perpetrated abuse. Additionally, because one of our goals is to illustrate how social psychological theories have been incorporated into VAW interventions, we have also given priority to interventions and studies that have made those connections clear. Finally, the interventions selected for this chapter have used high quality designs. Not all of the interventions reviewed here used randomized clinical trials (RCTs), but most clearly sought to approximate this as a gold standard.

As noted above, one of our goals is to demonstrate how social psychological theories have been used in VAW interventions. Some interventions are driven by one particular theory, but in more complex interventions, multiple theories are often used for various purposes. We have structured the chapter to illustrate some of these variations. We begin with an intervention that has not benefited from a theoretical foundation, move to interventions that incorporate a particular theory, and then highlight complex interventions that use multiple theories. A second goal of this chapter is to illustrate the importance of strong feminist foundational knowledge in the development of VAW interventions. We make the argument that social theory[1] and strong empirical work alone are not enough to develop promising VAW interventions. The best interventions are grounded in a deep understanding of the role gender plays in VAW. Some of this content knowledge comes from social psychological literature, but it also borrows heavily from other disciplines. Our third goal is to highlight promising interventions in the VAW field, without being exhaustive. In highlighting particular interventions, we hope to illustrate some of the common struggles, limitations, and advantages as well as facilitate cross-pollination of ideas.

WITHOUT A THEORETICAL FOUNDATION INTERVENTIONS FLOUNDER

Some VAW interventions have been empirically evaluated but have loose theoretical foundations and imprecise mechanisms toward desired long-term outcomes. The interventions are rooted in a particular problem that is clearly articulated and defined (e.g., high rates of IPV), but how the interventions might ultimately lead to reduced VAW is less clear. Universal screening for IPV provides an illustrative example of how a lack of attention to theory led to conflicting conclusions about the merits of the intervention.

A number of healthcare settings have implemented universal screening for IPV. Universal screening is in operation when healthcare practitioners are required to ask all women about current or past experiences with IPV. There has been a great deal of empirical work on the outcomes of universal screening in a wide range of settings (e.g., emergency, antenatal, primary care, etc.), as evidenced by a number of reviews (Feder et al., 2009; O'Campo et al., 2011; O'Doherty et al., 2014). The stated rationale for universal screening is that IPV is very prevalent and associated with many negative physical and mental health outcomes (Campbell et al., 2009; Plichta, 2004), but the process through which universal screening might improve women's health is not well delineated. This has led to substantial debate in the literature (Cole, 2000; Taket et al., 2004) about the benefits versus potential adverse outcomes of screening as well as debate about the most appropriate outcome measures (e.g., increase in identification of victims of IPV, referrals to IPV services, better health, reduction in violence, etc.).

A Cochrane systematic review and meta-analysis identified 11 evaluation studies that compared a screening intervention to usual care (O'Doherty et al., 2014).

Their major finding was that identification of IPV increased with screening, but increased identification was not accompanied by increased referrals to IPV services. Only two studies measured subsequent IPV, only one study measured health outcomes, and neither of these outcomes improved with screening. The authors concluded that 'the current evidence does not support screening programs for intimate partner violence in healthcare settings' (O'Doherty et al., 2014: 4). Previous reviews have come to similar conclusions (Feder et al., 2009).

A concern with these reviews is that they have sought to understand whether screening 'works' with little attention to 'why' and 'how' screening might lead to better outcomes for victims of IPV (O'Campo et al., 2011). For example, the review by O'Doherty et al. (2014) excluded studies that included any structured follow-up with advocacy or counseling because they were interested in isolating the intervention to screening alone. Advocacy and counseling have long been seen as critical to effective support of women assaulted by their partners, but few women access formal services because of stigma and other social processes. Screening in emergency rooms and other general health services was proposed originally to decrease the need for victims to initiate help seeking and increase access to specialized referrals/resources. Early discussions revolved around whether generalist health practitioners could be trained to perform this relatively simple task that could increase access to appropriate care. To ignore the theoretical foundation for the practice in understanding its effectiveness is problematic because this review provides no direction regarding how to develop, improve, or evaluate a universal screening program.

In a different 'realist-informed' review of the empirical literature, O'Campo and colleagues (2011) used broader inclusion criteria to break down the theoretical underpinnings of screening interventions. After outlining the necessary components of a successful screening intervention through their review, they sought theoretical and empirical support for their conceptual framework. In the discussion of their paper, they used social cognitive theory (Bandura, 1986; 1988) to make sense of their findings. They argued that high provider self-efficacy for screening is a key process factor because the more successful programs did a number of different things that led to increased provider self-efficacy (i.e., institutional support, on-going training, effective screening protocols, and immediate referral access to support services). This conceptualization is extremely helpful (regardless of whether or not self-efficacy turns out to be the most important factor) because it provides some direction in evaluating the process through which universal screening may be most beneficial to women who have experienced IPV.

It is worth noting here that research on screening has been rigorous and has included a number of RCTs, and yet the conclusions reached are not very satisfying (i.e., we do not have enough evidence that screening works). This demonstrates that attention to careful methodological design by traditional standards cannot in, and of, itself provide the answer to whether an intervention is worthwhile. In part, this is because the intervention, although deceptively simple in this case (asking about IPV), is actually very complex (e.g., how and when is it asked?). It interacts in complex ways with other actions (e.g., what occurs in response to the question? Why were referrals not given?) and cannot be easily isolated to make it amenable to RCTs and meta-analyses. The inclusion of theory in the design of screening interventions would make these complexities visible and fundamentally change the approach to the evaluations.

THE BASICS: USING THEORETICAL PRINCIPLES TO SHIFT ATTITUDES

Some short VAW interventions are rooted very firmly in a single social psychological principle (a construct and its related theory), and some interventions are broader, but use a social psychological principle for a particular purpose (e.g., inducing cognitive dissonance to facilitate attitude change). In both cases, the psychological construct does not originate in VAW work and has been broadly applied to other social problems. The goal is usually a modest shift in attitude that could, with additional intervention, lead to a change in behavior or a reduction in violence.

Social norms approaches to VAW interventions fall into this category. These approaches are based on the premise that behavior is influenced by misperceptions about the behaviors and cognitions of others. As we will demonstrate in our example, a social norms approach to VAW can be brief and targeted. This can be beneficial when time for an intervention is limited. In combination with other approaches, and especially when the intervention begins with a deep understanding of VAW, the incorporation of a social norms approach can be useful.

Berkowitz (2003) wrote about the application of social norms theories to a number of health and social justice issues, including sexual assault prevention. He argued that most men hold misconceptions about other men's acceptance of sexual assault and that this inhibits them from speaking up when they hear sexist banter or see sexual harassment. He further argued that finding ways to correct these misconceptions would be useful to prevention efforts. An intervention targeting sexist attitudes has incorporated these ideas in an effort to reduce pluralistic ignorance, which is a cognitive error in which one incorrectly assumes that one's view (or behavior) is in the minority (i.e., is not the norm) when, in fact, it is common (Miller and McFarland, 1987). Kilmartin et al. (2008) designed a 20 minute small group intervention in which college men provided their personal views about sexism as well as their beliefs about other men's sexist views, learned about pluristic ignorance, and were provided with the groups' norms (i.e., descriptive norms) regarding sexist beliefs in graphic form. The graphs clearly showed that men's average sexist beliefs (the real group norm) were lower than their perceived sexist beliefs for the group. Compared to a control group of men that did not receive the intervention, men who received the intervention shifted their beliefs about other men's sexist views (i.e., pluralistic ignorance was reduced) at the three-week follow-up.

In the example above, correcting pluralistic ignorance *was* the intervention with no presumption that this change in beliefs leads immediately to behavior change, but one can see how correcting pluralistic ignorance could also be incorporated into a more complex intervention with multiple components in an effort to reduce VAW perpetration (rather than just sexist attitudes). For example, providing descriptive norms from their own community might also be expected to help engage participants. In an intervention for male perpetrators of IPV, a norms-based intervention was incorporated into a broader program that included motivational enhancement therapy followed by treatment (Mbilinyi et al., 2011). Here, the intervention included prevalence information about most men's IPV behaviors along with personalized information about their own IPV behaviors, making clear that their behavior was different from most men. The rationale for inclusion was that providing descriptive norms about IPV would highlight to participants that their behavior was problematic and would further motivate them to attend and actively engage in treatment and thus obtain more benefit from the treatment. The results were promising, with fewer incidents of self-reported IPV in the experimental group compared to the control group. Social norm techniques have also been incorporated into more complex intervention programs that use bystander theory, which we will discuss at length in another section (Berkowitz, 2003; Gidycz et al., 2011).

Another example is the incorporation of pledge sheets into a broader VAW intervention. Asking participants to make a written commitment to a particular cause by signing a pledge is thought to work through cognitive dissonance, which is the discomfort experienced when one holds two opposing attitudes or one's attitudes and behavior do not match (Festinger, 1957). Cognitive dissonance is theorized to motivate people to align their attitudes and their behavior because the experience of dissonance is uncomfortable; therefore, by making a personal (in writing) and/or public behavioral commitment, alignment between participants' cognitive commitment and overall attitude to doing their part to reduce sexual assault is strengthened (Banyard, 2014). Additionally, it is expected that they would be more likely to engage in appropriate behaviors in the future since not doing so would be uncomfortable. Oxfam's 'We Can' Campaign, which aims to reduce the social acceptance of VAW, includes the opportunity for individuals to sign a public pledge to take action against VAW, but this is a small component of a comprehensive intervention that includes workshops, street theater, and promotional booklets (Heise, 2011). Similarly, bystander approaches to sexual assault prevention sometimes include the signing of pledges that indicate their commitment to intervening in cases of sexual assault (Banyard et al., 2007).

In this section, we have reviewed ways in which a single social psychological principle has been used alone or has been incorporated into a broader VAW intervention. We would suggest that, in the above examples, the social psychological principles were incorporated appropriately. However, there can be dangers in applying social psychological theories to VAW work for the purposes of behavior change. For example, a sexual assault prevention intervention that included a cognitive dissonance component did have some concerning results. The intervention, designed for college men, included a 50 minute educational video and a cognitive dissonance exercise in which men in the experimental group wrote a list of arguments to convince a hypothetical character not to rape women (Stephens and George, 2009). Overall, compared to the control group, the experimental group demonstrated some positive effects, such as a decrease in rape-myth acceptance and an increase in victim empathy at the five week follow-up; however, these results were largely driven by low-risk men. High-risk men in the intervention group actually had higher rates of sexually aggressive behavior (82%) compared to high-risk men in the control group (47%) at five-week follow-up (Stephens and George, 2009). The authors did not speculate on the impact of the cognitive dissonance exercise or how it may have interacted with the educational video to produce this backlash effect; however, it is possible that half-heartedly writing arguments against rape could have trivialized the more powerful messages in the video or automatically induced counter arguments.

Norms-based interventions can also backfire because identifying descriptive norms (what people actually do/believe) can strengthen supportive attitudes toward sexual assault if the norms are themselves problematic. This backfire effect has been shown with norms-based interventions designed to curb college drinking (Russell et al., 2005). Using an intervention such as the one described by Kilmartin et al. (2008), which focuses on descriptive norms, would be unlikely to work with a group of men that hold strongly supportive attitudes about sexual assault. Rigorous evaluations are always needed to ensure outcomes of interventions are as intended.

GOING BEYOND THE BASICS: USING SOCIAL PSYCHOLOGICAL THEORIES TO CHANGE ATTITUDES AND BEHAVIOR

We agree with Banyard (2014: 348) that there is a 'need to combine prevention tools'. Successful interventions that have sought to change actual behavior have been more complex and do combine various psychological principles with a deep understanding of the gendered nature of VAW. The following sections introduce some of the most promising approaches.

Engaging Bystanders in Sexual Assault Prevention in Educational Settings

An approach that has gained substantial momentum is bystander intervention, especially regarding sexual assault and relationship violence on university campuses. Advocates of this approach draw heavily on an array of social psychological literature, including persuasion, social norms, helping behavior, and barriers to bystander intervention (Banyard et al., 2004). Especially foundational to this approach is Latané and Darley's (1969) and others' empirical work on the circumstances that enable or inhibit a person from intervening during an emergency in order to prevent a negative outcome (aka bystander theory). The foundational work on bystander behavior has demonstrated that, in order to intervene, a bystander must: notice and recognize a situation as an emergency, even when others are not reacting (overcome pluralistic ignorance); assume responsibility for helping (overcome diffusion of responsibility); know how to intervene and feel that their actions could make a difference (self-efficacy); and, ultimately decide to help despite possible costs to the bystander (cost–benefits analysis and evaluation apprehension). Applying this work to sexual assault prevention, bystander approaches tackle each of these issues by bringing awareness to the problem, encouraging people to take responsibility, and giving people concrete strategies and practice with intervening that emphasize the bystander's own safety. Bystander interventions are based on the premise that everyone has a role to play in preventing sexual assault because we are all potential witnesses to high-risk situations that provide an opportunity to interrupt a sexual assault (e.g., an intoxicated woman being led away from the party) and to mundane situations that reinforce acceptance of sexual assault (e.g., sexist jokes).

Two bystander intervention programs have been particularly well developed, evaluated, and taken up: *Bringing in the Bystander®* (Banyard et al., 2007; Moynihan et al., 2015) and *Green Dot* (Coker et al., 2011; 2017). However, there are a number of other bystander-based programs, including *InterACT*, *SCREAM* peer education, *Mentors in Violence Prevention*, *Step Up!*, the *Men's Project*, *Coaching Boys into Men*, the *Men's Program/Workshop*, and many variations across programs (for reviews of bystander programs see Coker and Clear, 2015 and Katz and Moore, 2013). Some incorporate motivational speeches (e.g., *Green Dot*) or theater (e.g., *InterACT*), but most include voluntary small group interactive workshops. The educational sessions can run from 90 minutes to seven hours over one or more sessions, and best practices suggest workshops should occur in small same-sex groups that are run by peer facilitators (men or a mixed-gender pair) (Katz and Moore, 2013). Despite differences in content or format, all programs attempt to increase the probability that a bystander will intervene in situations where the risk of sexual assault is elevated in order to change norms about sexual assault, interrupt an imminent sexual assault, and/or provide support to a sexual assault victim.

A number of programs have been evaluated using an experimental design with common outcome variables including, rape attitudes, bystander intent, efficacy, and behavior. As such, a meta-analysis was conducted for university bystander programs that included in-person training and a control group ($n = 12$). Katz and Moore (2013) found moderate effect sizes for bystander efficacy and intent to help and small effect sizes for rape-supportive attitudes, bystander helping behavior, and rape proclivity and no change in perpetration behavior. They suggested that bystander effects (e.g., bystander efficacy) may be more amenable to change with these interventions than outcomes more specifically associated with sexual assault (e.g., rape attitudes). It is also important to note that the long-term impact of bystander programs is not well known. Most of the programs included in the meta-analysis assessed outcomes shortly after training, with only three assessing behavioral outcomes a few months later. More recently, a few studies have examined longer-term follow-up. An evaluation of *Bringing in the Bystander®* (the longer 4.5 hour version) demonstrated some positive behavioral program effects at one-year follow-up. Students who participated in the program were more likely to have intervened with friends (but not strangers) compared to a control group; however, both groups demonstrated a decline in helping behaviors over time (Moynihan et al., 2015).

The goals of bystander programs, however, are ultimately to reduce rates of perpetration and victimization in the community through widespread bystander intervention by individuals. This is a more difficult outcome to measure; nevertheless, a few studies are emerging that examine behaviors at the community level. *Green Dot* has been evaluated at the population level over time in both a university sample and in a high-school sample. The university study compared an intervention campus with two comparison campuses and recruited a random sample of first year students into the study (Coker et al., 2016). Compared to the control campuses, students (men and women) attending the intervention school reported lower victimization rates of sexual harassment, stalking, incapacitated sex (too drunk or high to consent), and psychological dating violence; however, there were no differences in physically forced sex, coerced sex, or physical dating violence. There were also some changes for perpetration rates in sexual harassment and psychological dating violence, but the effects were present only for women's perpetration in two out of three of these domains. This is curious because women's violence against men was not what prompted any of these interventions given the much lower base rates. Additionally, there were no differences in the perpetration of unwanted sex or physical dating violence (Coker et al., 2016). The response rate in this study was not ideal (39%) and the campuses were not randomly assigned, but this study provided some evidence that a bystander intervention program can impact some types of victimization and perpetration at the population level.

A stronger long-term quasi-experimental evaluation of *Green Dot* was recently completed in high schools where implementation can reach the full community (Coker et al., 2017). This study examined perpetration and victimization behaviors such as forced sexual activity, incapacitated sexual activity, and physical dating violence across four years of *Green Dot* implementation. Compared to students in the control schools (usual care), students in the intervention schools demonstrated a decrease in sexual violence perpetration and victimization by year three of the four-year intervention. The effects, however, were more consistent for girls than for boys and reductions in perpetration were achieved only for girls (Coker et al., 2017). That is, there was a reduction in self-reported victimization rates in the interventions schools for both boys and girls, but a reduction in self-reported perpetration was only observed for girls by year three (Coker et al., 2017). Additionally, there is a significant *increase* in sexual perpetration for boys (but not girls) in year one (Coker et al., 2017, Appendix).

The results of the *Green Dot* evaluations are promising but difficult to interpret from a VAW perspective. Violence is reduced, but it is not clear that the program has adequately targeted gendered violence against women/girls. *Green Dot* attempts to have an impact on various types of power-based personal violence, and it may be that messages about VAW per se end up diluted.

Overall, bystander approaches have received a lot of attention and are quite promising. Approaching the problem from a community perspective that includes everyone (and especially men) in the solution has an intrinsic appeal, and as such, this approach has been adopted by a number of universities to address sexual assault against women and sometimes a broader array of interpersonal violence. This has also led to adaptations and add-ons that attempt to reach a broader audience or strengthen the effect of the program. For the most part, these changes have also borrowed heavily from social psychological theory.

Boosting the Impact of Sexual Assault Bystander Interventions by Applying More Theory

A number of other social psychology theories aimed at changing attitudes and behavior have been incorporated in different bystander intervention programs to reach a broader audience, boost program effects, or increase understanding of how programs work differentially for different audiences. An approach with the ability to reach many students is on-going social marketing through posters or announcements. The *Know Your Power®* Bystander Social Marketing Campaign (http://cola.unh.edu/prevention-innovations-research-center/know-your-power%C2%AE-bystander-social-marketing-campaign) targets sexual and relationship violence as well as stalking behaviors on college campuses with a number of images that bring attention to these problems and suggest ways to intervene. The campaign was carefully developed with pilot testing and community input through surveys and focus groups to model active bystander behaviors (Potter, 2012). A quasi-experimental evaluation that surveyed the campus community before and after a six-week campaign demonstrated a number of positive effects for students who saw the posters. These students increased their understanding of how to intervene, their willingness to intervene, and their actual involvement in intervention efforts (Potter, 2012).

Banyard et al. (2010) wrote a conceptual paper examining the merits of combining Prochaska and DiClemente's (1986) Transtheoretical Model of Change (TTM) with a bystander approach to sexual assault. Briefly, the TTM proposes five stages (i.e., precontemplation, contemplation, preparation, action, and maintenance) that people go through in efforts to make long-term behavioral changes. It has been widely used in efforts to change health behaviors (e.g., to quit smoking) and proponents of the model argue that measuring change between stages can more accurately assess program benefits for subgroups. Potter's (2012) *Know Your Power®* campaign incorporated a modified version of Prochaska and DiClemente's TTM to design the evaluation of the intervention. This allowed her to examine whether the campaign changed people's attitudes, regardless of where they were in their current attitudes toward the issue. This may be particularly important for social marketing campaigns that may resonate with people who are in a more advanced stage of readiness but create backlash for participants who have done very little thinking about the issue (e.g., in the precontemplation stage). In the one-year follow-up evaluation of *Bringing in the Bystander®*, Moynihan et al. (2015) found that 'readiness' to engage in bystander behavior, demonstrated by awareness of the problem of sexual assault at baseline, resulted in larger gains in actual bystander behavior. They went on to suggest that bystander programs should be tailored to participants' stage of change (not an easy task given the necessity of pre-screening).

As noted earlier, bystander approaches have also been combined with a social norms approach (Gidycz et al., 2011) to help facilitate more rapid, meaningful, and lasting changes for men. This combination has proved to be quite promising. Adaptation of an earlier program for men (Berkowitz, 1994) with a social norms component (Berkowitz, 2003) and a bystander approach resulted in a reduction in sexual aggression in men at a four-month follow-up and fewer associations with sexually aggressive peers (Gidycz et al., 2011). In this program, the 'norms correction component' (Gidycz et al., 2011: 724) occurred through small group discussion with the purpose of challenging 'traditional conceptions of masculinity that are associated with rape proclivity' (Gidycz et al., 2011: 724). That is, highlighting misperceptions in other men's attitudes allowed for an open discussion about sexist norms before the other components of the program (e.g., how to intervene appropriately as a bystander) were introduced (Gidycz et al., 2011). This program provides an excellent example of how multiple social psychological theories can be combined with a deep understanding of gender and VAW to produce behavior change.

Traditional social psychological principles, theories, and knowledge are likely to continue to be incorporated into bystander programs as they evolve. Recent calls have been made to better understand readiness and opportunities to help (Moynihan et al., 2015). Additionally, attention has been called to how social theories have already, in part, been incorporated into VAW prevention on university campuses and how further theoretical integration is needed as we move forward to build both more complex and yet also more focused and targeted prevention models (Banyard, 2014). In summary, bystander approaches to sexual violence in educational contexts have become increasingly complex and have incorporated a number of different social psychological theories. This is also true of other programs that seek to change community norms about VAW.

Engaging Communities in IPV Prevention

A review of programs in low- and middle-income countries identified a growing body of work that is addressing IPV by changing social gender norms and behavior (Heise, 2011: Ch. 2). Heise (2011) anchors her review in a much larger body of attitudinal research demonstrating the relationship between IPV and acceptance of male dominance and wife beating. She identified four broad categories of programs that are attempting to influence attitudes and shift norms: awareness campaigns, peer training and community workshops, gender transformative programming, and social norms marketing and 'edutainment' efforts (i.e., educational entertainment) (Heise, 2011).

The 'We Can' campaign, which was deployed in six South Asian countries to change attitudes and behaviors that support gender discrimination and violence, provides an illustrative example (Williams and Aldred, 2011). It is based on social cognitive theory (Bandura, 1986) and an adapted version of the Transtheoretical Model of Change (TTM) described earlier (Prochaska and DiClemente, 1986). However, the use of these theories in the 'We Can' campaign is intentionally loose in that there is acknowledgement that, 'Essentially, all models are wrong, but some are useful' (Williams and Aldred, 2011: 51). In other words, the theories are used to guide but are not followed dogmatically. The campaign itself works through alliance partner organizations and implements various activities, such as street theater, campaign booklets, and workshops (http://policy-practice.oxfam.org.uk/our-work/gender-justice/ending-violence-against-women/we-can). A key strategy is to recruit 'change makers' who work to change their own attitudes first and then, as we noted earlier, sign pledges to take action against VAW and are supported in a number of ways to bring the campaign message to others. A program evaluation used a mixed method approach and is described as 'realist', 'utilisation-focused', and 'participatory' (Raab, 2011: 47). It included in-depth interviews with allies and change makers (Williams and Aldred, 2011) as well as focus groups and surveys (Raab, 2011). The evaluation found that the campaign mobilized a large number of allies (over 3,000) and change makers (3.9 million) and provided some evidence that attitudinal and behavioral change was occurring for both change makers and the wider community (Raab, 2011). Unlike the majority of the bystander intervention evaluations reviewed in the previous section, the evaluation of 'We Can' is clearly not traditional, but traditional social psychological theory informed the development of the campaign.

FEMINIST INTERVENTIONS: CHALLENGING GENDER NORMS IN HETEROSEXUAL RELATIONSHIPS

Feminist theory, perhaps for obvious reasons, has had an impact on many VAW interventions, including those reviewed above; however, the extent to which interventions have incorporated a feminist understanding of gender and VAW vary. The interventions reviewed here foreground feminist theory in that the intervention itself is designed to challenge typical gender relations tied to VAW, but social theories and traditional research methodology were also used in the development and evaluation of these programs. The first group of interventions reviewed challenge gender norms in established intimate relationships by increasing women's economic power. The remaining interventions challenge gender norms through educational training and practice.

Economic Empowerment to Reduce IPV

A number of interventions have targeted women's economic empowerment as a means with which to prevent VAW. These interventions, largely employed in low- and medium-income countries, have used a number of strategies, such as providing women with financial literacy, vocational training, property ownership, cash transfers, and microfinance programs (Heise, 2011: Ch. 5). Building on both feminist and economic theories, these programs endeavor to increase women's relative economic power within the household in efforts to decrease IPV. Feminist theory suggests that women's economic empowerment should lead to decreases in VAW because it increases women's options and decreases their dependence on men. However, there is also evidence that short-term shifts in economic advantage within a household can increase VAW because these shifts challenge established gender norms that privilege men's power in the home (Heath, 2014; Macmillan and Gartner, 1999). Predictably, then, the results of economic empowerment interventions have been mixed. Some programs have shown a decrease in IPV and others an increase or no impact (Heise, 2011: Ch. 5). A critical factor in the success of economic empowerment may be the incorporation of programing that addresses women's empowerment issues more directly (e.g., discussion of gender roles and power relations) and breaks down social isolation (e.g., opportunities for women's group discussion). A successful economic empowerment program in Ecuador (Hidrobo et al., 2016) found that a critical component for their success was the inclusion of mandatory nutritional workshops that required women to leave the house and interact with other women in the program (Buller et al., 2016). Similarly, a microfinance program in South Africa found that, although women's economic situation improved in both experimental groups compared to the control group, a decrease in IPV was only significant in the group that also attended a program called 'Sisters for Life' that included discussions of gender roles and power relations (Kim et al., 2009).

Grabe (2010) has more explicitly examined the impact of a land ownership intervention program on Nicaraguan women's gender ideology and relationship power. Using a quasi-experimental design and a path analysis to examine mechanisms through which positive outcomes are obtained, she argued that landownership led to more progressive attitudes towards women, which had an impact on relationship power and partner control, which in turn, led to decreases in IPV. As is the case with many of these studies in the global south, this study took advantage of a preexisting non-governmental organization (NGO) program. In this case, the NGO provided landownership to women during a post-hurricane rebuilding strategy and also provided human rights and 'gender reflections' education. Additionally, women entitled to receive land through the program also had access to a women's organization that assisted them in obtaining titling to the land. Grabe (2010) measured participation in workshops, seminars, etc. aimed at women's empowerment and found a significant relationship between this kind of participation and landownership. Although landownership remained a better predictor of changes in gender-role ideology (attitudes toward women) than participation in empowerment programs, it may be that, for most women, *some* gender education is also needed for the benefits of economic empowerment to be fully realized. A second study on land ownership with women in both Nicaragua and Tanzania found that the proposed relationship between landownership, partner power, and IPV was similar in both countries (Grabe et al., 2015), both replicating and extending Grabe's earlier work. A thematic analysis of women's experiences with landownership in these two countries supported the notion that imbalanced gender relations were interrupted through women's landownership and that this had a direct impact on men's ability to perpetrate IPV (Grabe et al., 2015).

Empowering Women to Fight Back against Sexual Assault

Sexual assault resistance education programs are interventions designed to give women knowledge and skills to defend their sexual rights. Although there is a long tradition of feminist self-defense (e.g., WenDo; www.wendo.ca) and there are many self-defense workshops for women and girls available, they vary regarding the extent to which their content challenges gender norms, builds on VAW research and practice, and utilizes social theories. Most have not been evaluated in a rigorous manner. An exception is a program developed by the NGO *No Means No Worldwide* (https://www.nomeansnoworldwide.org/), which is premised on the belief that gender-related power imbalances are at the root of sexual VAW. The 12-hour program works to empower girls through self-esteem, self-efficacy, and verbal and physical self-defense. Descriptions of the program note that it is grounded in the health belief model and social learning theory and that the program content is delivered through role-playing, facilitated discussion, and extensive skills practice (Sarnquist et al., 2014). It is run with girls/young women (ages 14–21) in a high-school setting and facilitated by highly trained local women in their 20s. Two quasi-experimental studies (randomized by school) in Nairobi, Kenya, demonstrated significant and substantial decreases in forced and coerced sexual penetration victimization compared to a control group that received standard sexual education that included information about rape (Sarnquist et al., 2014; Sinclair et al., 2013). In addition to decreases in sexual assault, the program was also shown to reduce pregnancy related school dropout (Sarnquist et al., 2017). The authors attributed this to both a direct reduction of sexual assault but also to broader changes in empowerment that allowed girls and young women to exercise control over their own bodies and make decisions to delay marriage. RCTs in Malawi and Kenya are currently underway, but not yet available.

A number of feminist sexual assault resistance or 'risk-reduction' programs have been developed for North American university women, and a review of these programs found that five had been evaluated in controlled studies at the time of the review (Gidycz and Dardis, 2014). Most of the studies had a small number of participants, and the results were mixed with regards to a decrease in sexual assault. However, the only program with a one-year follow-up showed a reduction in sexual assault for women who voluntarily enrolled in a 30-hour empowerment self-defense course compared to a group of women enrolled in other courses (Hollander, 2014). Although Hollander's (2014) participants were not randomized to program, propensity matching was used to enhance the rigor of the comparison between groups. The program content has some overlap with the only resistance education program that has shown in an RCT to reduce rape in a sustained way.

After the Gidycz and Dardis (2014) review, another study demonstrated the effectiveness of a sexual assault resistance program using a RCT. The *Enhanced Assess, Acknowledge, Act* (EAAA) program reduced completed rape (from 9.8% in control to 5.2% in the program) and attempted rape (from 9.3% to 3.4%) at one-year follow-up (Senn et al., 2015), and significantly lower rates were maintained at 24 months (Senn et al., 2017). This program was developed by the second author of this chapter, so given our familiarity with it, we elaborate here on how its development was influenced by both a feminist understanding of VAW and by social theories.

The EAAA program is a 12-hour sexual assault resistance education program designed for first year university women (Senn et al., 2013, http://sarecentre.org/). The program itself was developed based on feminist scholarship about women's experiences of rape and how they interpret (cognitively) the behavior of, and respond (behaviorally) to, coercive male acquaintances who strategically use gendered socialization and normative heterosexual scripts to their advantage in addition to other coercive tactics. The program builds heavily on Nurius and Norris' (1996) cognitive ecological model of women's responses to sexual coercion, which as the name implies, considers both the cognitive appraisals that women make and the factors that play into those appraisals at different ecological levels. What is less apparent from the name is that their model is also strongly feminist in that it considers how gendered socialization and gendered peer interactions contribute to conflicting cognitive appraisals that make assessment of danger and forceful resistance difficult for women when sexual assault is perpetrated by men they know (e.g., women's socialization to maintain positive interpersonal relationships, etc.). The program also brings to life Rozee and Koss' (2001) conceptual research synthesis of the necessary components for a sexual assault resistance program, which they coined AAA. Their work is also feminist and builds on Nurius and Norris' (1996) cognitive ecological model. The first two As are cognitive and focus on critical stages of appraisal as women need to *Assess* a situation as risky and *Acknowledge* the danger before they can *Act*. In other words, the program teaches women to realistically assess risk when it is present (e.g., in men's behavior) and overcome feminine socialization when it puts them at a disadvantage in order to acknowledge that risk. This puts them in a better position to trust their perceptions and emotional responses quickly and to use forceful verbal and physical self-defense strategies known to lead to improved outcomes (Ullman, 2010; Tark and Kleck, 2014). The EAAA program also includes a feminist sexuality unit providing women with a rare opportunity to think about, and prioritize, their own sexual desires and values. Having a strong grounding in positive sexuality is also theorized to make acknowledgement of coercion and resistance to unwanted sex quicker and, therefore, more effective.

The psychological variables that were theoretically predicted to impact the rates of completed rape (perceptions of personal risk of rape by an acquaintance, rape myths, knowledge of effective resistance strategies, and self-defense self-efficacy) were changed in predicted directions (Senn et al., 2017). These outcome variables stem from the cognitive appraisal factors identified by Nurius and Norris (1996). Of particular importance given the high risk of re-victimization, the program also significantly reduced rape for women with a history of victimization (Senn et al., 2015). This is of particular note because earlier programs that had shown some promise had not been effective for women with a previous history of sexual assault (Hanson and Gidycz, 1993). It is likely that the EAAA program is effective for women with a history of sexual assault because the program carefully contradicts victim blaming and places 100% of the responsibility on perpetrators of sexual violence (Senn et al., 2008). Subgroup analysis with women who experienced rape demonstrated that self-blame was reduced for women who did the EAAA program compared to women in the control group (Senn et al., 2016). This is a testament to the program's strong feminist roots. Much attention was given to the sometimes subtle ways that survivors feel blamed when learning about sexual assault or when participating in mainstream self-defense training. Perceptions of blame can come from the content itself as well as from passing comments from other participants. The EAAA program script continually and explicitly challenges these myths, and facilitators were trained to identify victim blaming and deal with it quickly and effectively.

It is important to note here that the interventions in the previous sections that have focused on women through their economic empowerment or by empowering them to acknowledge and defend their sexual rights are the only interventions that have demonstrated a reduction in women's victimization. Other approaches have shown some success in changing attitudes and increasing prosocial behaviors. *Green Dot* has shown some reductions in some types of perpetration (mostly for girls). But only approaches focused on empowering women have shown a clear reduction in women's experiences of men's physical or sexual violence. Men are the only ones who can stop their initiation of perpetration behavior and they are entirely responsible for their actions, so these findings can be puzzling to understand. Empowering women economically likely creates a relationship and social context within which changes in men's behavior may be more quickly achieved. Empowering women to successfully resist men's violence has immediate results and an impact that does not require changes in men's behavior to be effective. We do not yet know whether the lessons men learn in these interactions with empowered women have lasting effects on them that generalize, but given social learning theory's lessons, we would expect that they would. Nevertheless, the burden of reducing VAW must always be the responsibility of men, and fortunately, there are some programs for men that deal critically with gender issues and have shown some effectiveness.

Teaching Men Not to be Violent

VAW programs for men that have built on feminist work have challenged gender norms and male privilege. All of the programs profiled here include bystander intervention elements because these are the only approaches that have shown some promise with older adolescent and adult men. However, they go beyond a bystander intervention approach by emphasizing feminist content that seeks to challenge normative gender relations and change boys and men's attitudes about women and about masculinity. The most widely adopted is the *Mentors in Violence (MVP) Program* developed by Jackson Katz (www.mvpstrat.com/about/). The historical roots of the program make clear that it was designed to challenge gender ideologies that privilege men and contribute to VAW (Katz et al., 2011). It was designed for men, especially men involved in hyper-masculine cultures (e.g., fraternities, sports teams, military, etc.), and the bystander approach was largely used because it 'offered a creative solution to one of the central challenges in gender violence-prevention education: how to engage men without approaching them as potential rapists and batterers' (Katz et al., 2011: 686). Although the program was initially designed for men, it was quickly adapted for women bystanders; however, it has not moved to a gender neutral approach to violence (Katz et al., 2011), so it seems appropriate to cover it here. The MVP has not been evaluated with an RCT, but a quasi-experimental evaluation comparing two high schools found some promising differences in attitudes toward gendered aggression and willingness to take action when witnessing gendered aggression (Katz et al., 2011). Ironically, given the roots of the program, a gender analysis of program effectiveness was not conducted. Rigorous testing and evidence of the program's effects on perpetrator or bystander behavior have not yet been accomplished.

A companion program to the *No Means No Worldwide* program profiled above with Kenyan girls has been developed for boys titled, *Your Moment of Truth* (YMOT). YMOT is a 12-hour after-school program provided in high schools (ages 15–22). It was developed over a two-year period to target the needs and experiences of Nairobi boys/young men, and its content is intended to promote gender equality, help develop positive masculinity, and teach boys/young men to safely intervene when they witness gender-based violence (Keller et al., 2017). YMOT was evaluated in a non-randomized design where high schools that received the program were compared to schools that received only the usual two-hour life skills class that included some sexual education (Keller et al., 2017). The results of a nine-month follow-up showed positive changes in attitudes toward women and rape myths compared to the comparison group. Although intervention participants noticed more gender-based violence, it is worth noting that both groups reported witnessing high levels of verbal harassment (52% versus 49%), physical threats (30% versus 25%) and physical or sexual assault (30% versus 27%). Critically, intervention participants were much more likely to successfully intervene (defined as stopping the violence) when witnessing these behaviors (Keller et al., 2017).

Programs for boys and young men provide an important and critical complement to the self-defense programs for girls and young women. Both sets of programs deal critically with gender issues and challenge normative heterosexual behavior that promotes VAW. This kind of programming is time consuming (often 12 hours or more), but if offered to enough people, could lead to normative changes about gender relations and VAW, which would be unlikely if only girls/women heard these messages. Only the programs for men, however, incorporated bystander approaches. As noted by Katz et al. (2011), this is needed to get buy-in, but it is concerning that, despite using bystander language and content to attract men to this kind of programming, authors have noted difficultly in recruiting male participants (Cissner, 2009; Stewart, 2014). This suggests that the men who most need to change their sexually violent behavior might be unlikely to participate. Whether or not longer programs that deal more in-depth with gender socialization can have an impact on men's own VAW behavior (for program participants) is not known, because the most promising programs have not reported rates of violence in program participants, despite this being a critically important outcome.

COMMON STRUGGLES AND TENSIONS

In reviewing VAW interventions for this chapter, we noted a number of struggles for these program developers and researchers that reoccurred or resonated with our own experiences with the EAAA program. There were also attempts to deal with these struggles or minimize perceived limitations. We have tried to highlight some of these throughout the chapter, but provide a fuller discussion and integration in this section.

Rethinking Ideas about Gold Standards in Intervention Assessment

At first glance, it would seem that VAW interventions are perfectly amenable to RCT evaluations by simply randomizing some people to the intervention and others to a control group. The reality is that (1) most VAW interventions are not a single component that can be easily manipulated, (2) what counts as a successful intervention outcome is not always easy to determine and may be both individual and community-wide, and (3) real people cannot always be randomized for practical or ethical reasons. We discuss each of these realities briefly below.

VAW interventions are multifaceted and trying to pinpoint and isolate the critical component(s) might be impossible or even counterproductive. As noted in an early section of this chapter, narrow conceptualizations of mandatory screening for IPV were problematic. Similarly, if economic empowerment interventions are operationalized in a very narrow way that only includes the economic incentive, they may be deemed unsuccessful, but the economic incentive may be critical in its interaction with other elements (i.e., educational empowerment) for reducing VAW. In other words, we could isolate each variable and determine that none of them work despite the fact that particular combinations might be very effective. Many of the educational interventions, including our own, are lengthy and require manualization and extensive training. The goal is to consistently deliver the intervention while knowing it will never be delivered exactly the same way twice because group dynamics and facilitator style will constantly change. However, sometimes delivering the intervention in exactly the same way is not a goal. Some interventions may require adaptation to different populations, but this variation in the implementation of the independent variable would be unacceptable or problematic for an RCT.

Similarly, the critical dependent variable is also not always easy to pinpoint or to measure appropriately. Ideally, we are interested in a reduction in VAW, but most interventions do not measure this. This has been identified as a legitimate problem (e.g., Schewe, 2007) because reductions in VAW often do not accompany other changes and can, in some cases, be increased (e.g., first year of the *Green Dot* program, which was noted earlier). However, in some circumstances, it may be inappropriate to measure VAW in the short term. For example, this may be inappropriate if the reduction in violence is not expected to occur immediately or if we initially expect an increase (i.e., in reported cases due to increased visibility or a reduction in victim blaming) or if a system wide influence is necessary for the change to be manifested. In these cases, identifying appropriate intermediate outcomes and measuring the primary outcome after an appropriate delay would make more sense. Relatedly, measuring changes in VAW at the population level is particularly challenging, but for some interventions, such as bystander approaches, the population level is where violence *should* be measured. This requires a long-term commitment to sustained intervention and measurement. It also requires an acceptance that the intervention itself might change and that other programs and activities are likely to come and go in that community during that time, which could interact with any program effects. It would be beneficial to track changes, but keeping everything static for the sake of the experimental design would be naïve and inadvisable. This also touches on the 'problem' of contamination. A rigorous experimental design tries to isolate exposure to the intervention to those in the experimental group only, but many of the interventions reviewed here are attempting to change norms in the wider community, so having an impact on others (including those in the control group) is actually a goal of the intervention. Trying to prevent this contamination could even be unethical. For example, in our RCT, women who participated in the EAAA program may have talked to other women about what they were learning (in fact, we encouraged it) and some of those other women might have been in our control group. We would not want to prevent those discussions and ultimately decided we would measure and assess the impact of 'contamination' to maintain our feminist goals and ensure that we could obtain funding and publish in mainstream journals (Senn et al., 2013; Senn et al., 2015).

Many of the interventions reviewed in this chapter were quasi experimental because they took advantage of naturally occurring variation in programming availability (e.g., Grabe, 2010; Hollander, 2014) or because the intervention was deliberately provided where it was most needed for ethical reasons (e.g., Sarnquist et al., 2014). The authors often describe this as a limitation because it does not meet the RCT gold standard; however, these evaluations still provide valuable evidence and researchers should be encouraged to do this important work. RCTs provide valuable evidence, but rigid acceptance of the experiment as a gold standard could itself be a limitation. For example, are we restricting the questions we ask to fit the design? Are we less likely to evaluate some interventions? Are we less likely to develop some interventions? And are we giving as much attention to process as outcome?[2]

Related to concerns about methodology, meta-analyses are often used to provide direction about whether an approach works. They can be extremely useful in summarizing a body of work and their results often carry a lot of weight, but even similar interventions may not be amenable to a traditional meta-analysis, and the conclusions about a group of interventions might even be counterproductive. There are many examples of interventions that teach women self-defense, but the programs vary so substantially in content (e.g., many focus on stranger sexual assault) and length that making conclusions about the group might tell you very little about whether a particular program should be implemented in a particular community. Additionally, meta-analyses have exclusion criteria that may be quite restrictive and may exclude some study designs or only include studies that measure common variables. These may, or may not, be the most important and revealing studies. When it comes to summarizing the literature on a particular VAW intervention, a realist informed review like the one by O'Campo and colleagues (2011) may provide the most useful information to those seeking to develop or implement a particular intervention in their community.

Problems When Targeting VAW Interventions at the Individual Level

We intentionally focused in this chapter on social interventions targeted at the individual level that sought to shift cognitions and behaviors. When it comes to VAW interventions, this level of focus creates some tension because we are aware that we are using an individual approach to deal with a social problem and that there are many limitations to doing so (Senn, 2011). For those of us who have focused on sexual assault resistance interventions for women, the tension includes wanting to give women the skills and knowledge that they need to overcome the barriers to fighting back against sexually coercive men they know, while also placing the responsibility for sexual assault on coercive men and on a society that, to a greater or lesser degree, supports a continuum of sexual violence. One of us has written at length about this tension (Senn, 2011). The economic empowerment programs address the social inequality through individual women and avoid the criticism of increasing women's responsibility for VAW because the intervention is not so obviously focused on what women do to resist VAW. However, these interventions also focus on women when the goal is to change men's behavior. For program developers who target men, there is little concern about victim blaming but there is a related tension. These programs must appeal to men in order to get them to participate and yet still hold coercive men responsible for their actions. It is difficult to recruit and retain men in VAW interventions even when they are enticed through bystander language (for a recent discussion of the broader issue of engagement of men see Casey et al., 2013). Additionally, interventions focused on men still need to be especially concerned with possible negative outcomes. Interventions can backfire and induce negative attitudes toward women in subsets of men (Bingham and Scherer, 2001; Stephens and George, 2009), usually the ones who most need to change their behavior, and this possibility needs to be carefully monitored.

Bystander approaches avoid targeting 'potential victims' or 'potential perpetrators' by teaching both men and women to intervene in various ways, but there is also a tension inherent in this approach. Targeting everyone as a bystander can risk becoming gender neutral, which is a criticism that has been levelled against the *Green Dot* program (Katz et al., 2011). We also know that there are gender differences in helping behavior (Eagly and Crowley, 1986), and intervening as a man is different from intervening as a woman. Without a critical understanding of that difference, bystander behavior risks reinforcing gender norms that can contribute to, rather than challenge, VAW. Benevolent sexism, which includes positive attitudes toward women in traditional roles (e.g., (certain) women should be protected) has been distinguished from hostile sexism, which includes overtly negative attitudes toward women (Glick and Fiske, 1996), but both reinforce gender norms and help to maintain patriarchy and VAW. Bystander approaches risk reinforcing benevolent sexism if the message men hear is that they need to police (bad) men and protect (good) women, and the message women hear is that they need to be protected. Recall that *Green Dot* demonstrated some behavioral changes at the population level in high schools for both perpetration and victimization, but only girls (not boys) in the intervention schools had lower sexual violence perpetration (Coker et al., 2017). Boys not only did not show this benefit, they showed a small, but significantly larger, rate of sexual perpetration in year one of the intervention. Unfortunately, the gender of the person who experienced the violence was not reported. Examining the impact of bystander approaches by gender is critical to understanding whether the program reduces violence against women and girls and, if it does not, to revising our interventions.

Is Applied Social Psychology Ignoring a Critical Step in VAW Interventions – Issues of Scale?

Interventions are usually developed on a small scale by community educators/activists, researchers, or teams that include both. If an intervention demonstrates promise, efforts to scale up the intervention and offer it more widely begin. Traditional applied social psychology has not taken a lead here, but understanding how best to move a promising intervention toward implementation is a critical step in ameliorating social justice problems. Moving from a successful evaluation to wider implementation is difficult (see, for example, the review by Durlak and DuPre, 2008). A number of issues need to be addressed, such as promoting the program, ensuring fidelity to the original intervention, providing materials and/or training to run the program, and monitoring and/or providing direction for adaptations. Throughout the chapter, we have provided a number of websites that showcase a particular intervention, but even creating and maintaining a website to provide visibility for an intervention requires resources. The needed resources, both time and money, to do this work can be prohibitive.

When the results of the EAAA program were published (Senn et al., 2015), our team received substantial media attention and this resulted in many inquiries about the program and an enthusiasm to take it up immediately. However, the program was not yet ready for broad implementation because the details of the transition from RCT to general practice (e.g., how to train large numbers of facilitators, produce the materials, ensure fidelity etc.) had not been worked out. To enable wider implementation of the EAAA program, the second author created a not-for-profit organization called the SARE Centre (http://sarecentre.org/), which provides training (we use a train-the-trainer model to transfer program expertise to university staff) and program material distribution. We are also conducting a four-year implementation research trial to monitor the implementation and establish the effectiveness of the program in real-world conditions. To do this, our previous evaluation team has expanded to include an expert in knowledge translation with experience in broad scale implementation (Gail McVey), but even with this addition, the learning curve on implementation has been steep. Moreover, requests for permission and assistance with adaptations for different audiences (e.g., graduate students, gay men, women in male-dominated industries) or contexts (e.g., assaulted women's shelters), currently exceed our capacity to assist. Applied Social Psychology theory and research can, and should, contribute to our understanding of how to bring effective VAW interventions to scale.

MOVING FORWARD AND CROSS-POLLINATION

Many VAW interventions have been interdisciplinary in that scholars and activists from different fields have worked together to create and evaluate these interventions. Some interventions also demonstrate the integration of different applied social traditions. For example, bystander interventions build on traditional social psychological theory, but proponents of this approach have argued effectively that these interventions also utilize a community psychology approach to sexual assault prevention because they invite everyone to take responsibility for sexual assault (Banyard et al., 2004). The We Can campaign (Williams and Aldred, 2011) also demonstrates this integration. The campaign uses social theory to guide program development but remains focused on community input in order to drive community change. Integration of feminist theory and research and traditional social psychology is seen in approaches that directly challenge gender norms and patriarchy such as economic empowerment programs (Heise, 2011), the EAAA program (Senn et al., 2015), and the Mentors in Violence Program (Katz et al., 2011). Although not always explicitly evident in the delivery of the program (to appeal to potential participants), almost all of the interventions in this field have built on feminist work that has challenged heterosexual norms that privilege male power and men's sexuality.

Different methodological traditions are also evident in this field but quantitative approaches have dominated in both the program development and evaluation of VAW interventions. There are few published examples of qualitative research for developing intervention content and process. Potter's (2012) social marketing campaign incorporated focus groups in the development of the campaign design and materials, although how the data were analyzed and incorporated was not clear from the published paper. It is possible that, similar to our own work on EAAA, others are also using some qualitative methods in the initial stages of program development, but this process is not being documented in the published literature. It may be that this preliminary work is perceived as insufficiently rigorous for publication or that, in the rush to design and implement the main study, the earlier work is left unwritten, but perhaps this trend is changing. A recent focus group study was published (Salazar et al., 2017) that describes the formative research that was undertaken to develop content for a web-based bystander intervention for male college students (Salazar et al., 2014).

Moving from development to evaluation, the incorporation of qualitative methods in the evaluation of VAW interventions stands to improve the rigor, interpretability, and application of interventions substantially. Hollander (2004; 2014), a sociologist, has used mixed methods across her evaluations of an empowerment self-defense course for university women. The most rigorous of these studies (2014) used qualitative interviews, open-ended survey items, and field notes to help provide context for, and interpretation of, the quantitative results. The use of qualitative methods led to the identification of important potential outcomes (e.g., embodiment) for future research that have not been included in other studies conducted in the field (Hollander, personal communication, 2016). Grabe et al. (2015) incorporated both quantitative and qualitative components of their evaluation of a women's landownership intervention. This triangulation of methods provided not only more convincing evidence of the impact of landownership, but better direction for moving forward and adapting the intervention to other locations. Given the benefits of using qualitative work for VAW interventions, we have to wonder why they are not incorporated (and published) more often. This situation is likely influenced by the positivist traditions underlying psychology specifically and evaluation research more generally. This affects the training of graduate students, who are then more comfortable and competent in designing surveys and experiments for their applied work. However, there is reason to be optimistic that things are changing. Both of our departments include applied social streams that provide training in both quantitative and qualitative methods.

The disciplinary, theoretical, and methodological integration that has occurred to date shows a willingness within the VAW field to combine approaches, and this has resulted in a number of promising interventions. Continuing in this direction will be critical if we are to make progress, and this Handbook provides an opportunity to continue this integration. For example, in Roen and Groot's chapter (in this Handbook), they demonstrate the utility of using an intersectional approach when working with trans* and gender diverse youth. Kimberle Crenshaw, who is widely credited with introducing the term intersectionality and developing the theory explicitly (1989), is a legal scholar. While her work quickly permeated into some disciplines (e.g., Women's and Gender Studies and Sociology), it is not, to our knowledge, taught in the core curriculum of most psychology graduate programs (even those with critical bents). It is unfortunate that an intersectional approach has not had more influence on VAW interventions, particularly in North America. This is somewhat surprising given that Crenshaw showed explicitly how an intersectional frame changed the understanding of violence against women of color (Crenshaw, 1991). VAW interventions vary considerably in how inclusive they are. We know from our own work that developing inclusive interventions is a considerable challenge (e.g., EAAA is inclusive of all students who identify as women across sexual identities). Developing interventions that go beyond inclusion to become truly intersectional will likely require new approaches and substantial transformation. This will be particularly important as programs are adapted to different contexts, but is also needed across the board. Application of intersectional theory enhances understanding and interpretation of the experiences of all women, not just those marginalized by ethnicity or class.

This chapter has demonstrated that social psychology has made substantial contributions to many VAW interventions, but has been most effective when used in combination with community psychology and interdisciplinary feminist approaches. We should continue to expand our cross-disciplinary teams to include members with diverse methodological and theoretical expertise. As we move forward, we need to do more to integrate current critical literature on gender and violence and ensure that qualitative designs play more than a supportive role in the development and evaluation of VAW interventions.

Notes

1 Throughout the chapter we use the term 'social theory' to mean social psychological theory.
2 Readers may be interested in an elaborated feminist critique by Michelle Fine (2012), who goes much further in questioning the demands for particular types of evidence on social justice grounds.

REFERENCES

Bandura, A. (1986). *Social foundations of thought and action: A social cognitive theory*. Englewood Cliffs, NJ: Prentice-Hall.

Bandura, A. (1988). Social cognitive theory and social referencing. In S. Feinman (Ed.), *Social referencing and social construction of reality*. New York, NY: Plenum.

Banyard, V. L. (2014). Improving college campus-based prevention of violence against women. *Trauma, Violence, & Abuse, 15*(4), 339–351. Retrieved from https://doi.org/10.1177/1524838014521027

Banyard, V. L., Eckstein, R. P., & Moynihan, M. M. (2010). Sexual violence prevention: The role of stages of change. *Journal of Interpersonal Violence, 25*(1), 111–135. Retrieved from https://doi.org/10.1177/0886260508329123

Banyard, V. L., Moynihan, M. M., & Plante, E. G. (2007). Sexual violence prevention through bystander education: An experimental evaluation. *Journal of Community Psychology, 35*(4), 463–481. Retrieved from https://doi.org/10.1002/jcop.20159

Banyard, V. L., Plante, E. G., & Moynihan, M. M. (2004). Bystander education: Bringing a broader community perspective to sexual violence prevention. *Journal of Community Psychology, 32*(1), 61–79. Retrieved from https://doi.org/10.1002/jcop.10078

Becker, C. B., Smith, L. M., & Ciao, A. C. (2006). Peer-facilitated eating disorder prevention: A randomized effectiveness trial of cognitive dissonance and media advocacy. *Journal of Counseling Psychology, 53*(4), 550–555. Retrieved from https://doi.org/10.1037/0022-0167.53.4.550

Berkowitz, A. D. (1994). A model acquaintance rape prevention program for men. In A. D. Berkowitz (Ed.), *Men and rape: Theory, research and prevention programs in higher education* (pp. 35–42). San Francisco, CA: Jossey-Bass.

Berkowitz, A. D. (2003). Applications of social norms theory to other health and social justice issues. In H. W. Perkins (Ed.), *The social norms approach to preventing school and college age substance abuse: A handbook for educators, counselors, and clinicians* (pp. 259–279). San Francisco, CA: Jossey-Bass.

Bingham, S. G., & Scherer, L. L. (2001). The unexpected effects of a sexual harassment educational program. *Journal of Applied Behavioral Science, 37*(2), 125–153. Retrieved from https://doi.org/10.1177/0021886301372001

Buller, A. M., Hidrobo, M., Peterman, A., & Heise, L. (2016). The way to a man's heart is through his stomach? A mixed methods study on causal mechanisms through which cash and in-kind food transfers decreased intimate partner violence. *BMC Public Health, 16*(1), 1–13. Retrieved from https://doi.org/10.1186/s12889-016-3129-3

Campbell, J. C., Baty, M. L., Laughon, K., & Woods, A. (2009). Health effects of partner violence: Aiming toward prevention. In D. J. Whitaker & J. R. Lutzker (Eds.), *Preventing partner violence: Research and evidence-based intervention strategies* (pp. 113–138). Washington, DC: American Psychological Association.

Casey, E. A., Carlson, J., Fraguela-Rios, C., Kimball, E., Neugut, T. B., Tolman, R. M., & Edleson, J. L. (2013). Context, challenges, and tensions in global efforts to engage men in the prevention of violence against women: An ecological analysis. *Men and Masculinities*, *16*(2), 228–251. Retrieved from https://doi.org/10.1177/1097184X12472336

Cissner, A. B. (2009). *Evaluating the Mentors in Violence Prevention program: Preventing gender violence on a college campus*. New York, NY: Center for Court Innovation.

Coker, A. L., Bush, H. M., Cook-Craig, P. G., DeGue, S. A., Clear, E. R., Brancato, C. J., Fisher, B. S., & Recktenwald, E. A. (2017). RCT testing bystander effectiveness to reduce violence. *American Journal of Preventive Medicine*, *52*(5), 566–578. Retrieved from https://doi.org/10.1016/j.amepre.2017.01.020

Coker, A. L., Bush, H. M., Fisher, B. S., Swan, S. C., Williams, C. M., Clear, E. R., & Degue, S. (2016). Multi-college bystander intervention evaluation for violence prevention. *American Journal of Preventive Medicine*, *50*(3), 295–302. Retrieved from https://doi.org/10.1016/j.amepre.2015.08.034

Coker, A. L., & Clear, E. R. (2015). New approaches to violence prevention through bystander intervention. In H. Johnson, B. S. Fisher, & V. Jaquier (Eds.), *Critical issues on violence against women: International perspectives and promising strategies* (pp. 221–232). New York, NY: Routledge.

Coker, A. L., Cook-Craig, P. G., Williams, C. M., Fisher, B. S., Clear, E. R., Garcia, L. S., & Hegge, L. M. (2011). Evaluation of Green Dot: An active bystander intervention to reduce sexual violence on college campuses. *Violence Against Women*, *17*(6), 777–796. Retrieved from https://doi.org/10.1177/1077801211410264

Cole, T. B. (2000). Is domestic violence screening helpful? *Journal of the American Medical Association*, *284*(5), 551–553. Retrieved from https://doi.org/10.1001/jama.284.5.551

Crenshaw, K. (1989). Demarginalizing the intersection of race and sex: A Black feminist critique of antidiscrimination doctrine, feminist theory and antiracist politics. *University of Chicago Legal Forum*, *1989*(1), 139–167. Retrieved from https://chicagounbound.uchicago.edu/cgi/viewcontent.cgi?article=1052&context=uclf

Crenshaw, K. (1991). Mapping the margins: Intersectionality, identity politics, and violence against women of color. *Stanford Law Review*, *43*(6), 1241–1299. Retrieved from https://doi.org/10.2307/1229039

Cruwys, T., Haslam, S. A., Fox, N. E., & McMahon, H. (2015). 'That's not what we do': Evidence that normative change is a mechanism of action in group interventions. *Behaviour Research and Therapy*, *65*, 11–17. Retrieved from https://doi.org/10.1016/j.brat.2014.12.003

Durlak, J. A., & DuPre, E. P. (2008). Implementation matters: A review of research on the influence of implementation on program outcomes and the factors affecting implementation. *American Journal of Community Psychology*, *41*(3–4), 327–350. Retrieved from https://doi.org/10.1007/s10464-008-9165-0

Eagly, A. H., & Crowley, M. (1986). Gender and helping behavior: A meta-analytic review of the social psychological literature. *Psychological Bulletin*, *100*(3), 283–308. Retrieved from https://doi.org/10.1037/0033-2909.100.3.283

Feder, G., Ramsay, J., Dunne, D., Rose, M., Arsene, C., Norman, R., Kuntze, S., Spencer, A., Bacchus, L., Hague, G., Warburton, A., & Taket, A. (2009). How far does screening women for domestic (partner) violence in different health-care settings meet criteria for a screening programme? Systematic reviews of nine UK National Screening Committee criteria. *Health Technology Assessment*, *13*(16), 1–140. Retrieved from https://doi.org/10.3310/hta13160

Festinger, L. (1957). *A theory of cognitive dissonance*. Stanford, CA: Stanford University Press.

Fine, M. (2012). Troubling calls for evidence: A critical race, class and gender analysis of whose evidence counts. *Feminism & Psychology, 22*(1), 3–19. Retrieved from https://doi.org/10.1177/0959353511435475

Gidycz, C. A., & Dardis, C. M. (2014). Feminist self-defense and resistance training for college students. *Trauma, Violence, & Abuse, 15*(4), 322–333. Retrieved from https://doi.org/10.1177/1524838014521026

Gidycz, C. A., Orchowski, L. M., & Berkowitz, A. D. (2011). Preventing sexual aggression among college men: An evaluation of a social norms and bystander intervention program. *Violence Against Women, 17*(6), 720–742. Retrieved from https://doi.org/10.1177/1077801211409727

Glick, P., & Fiske, S. T. (1996). The Ambivalent Sexism Inventory: Differentiating hostile and benevolent sexism. *Journal of Personality and Social Psychology, 70*(3), 491–512. Retrieved from https://doi.org/10.1037/0022-3514.70.3.491

Grabe, S. (2010). Promoting gender equality: The role of ideology, power, and control in the link between land ownership and violence in Nicaragua. *Analyses of Social Issues and Public Policy, 10*(1), 146–170. Retrieved from https://doi.org/10.1111/j.1530-2415.2010.01221.x

Grabe, S., Grose, R. G., & Dutt, A. (2015). Women's land ownership and relationship power. *Psychology of Women Quarterly, 39*(1), 7–19. Retrieved from https://doi.org/10.1177/0361684314533485

Hanson, K., & Gidycz, C. A. (1993). Evaluation of a sexual assault prevention program. *Journal of Consulting and Clinical Psychology, 61*(6), 1046–1052. Retrieved from http://dx.doi.org/10.1037/0022-006X.61.6.1046

Heath, R. (2014). Women's access to labor market opportunities, control of household resources, and domestic violence: Evidence from Bangladesh. *World Development, 57*, 32–46. Retrieved from https://doi.org/10.1016/j.worlddev.2013.10.028

Heise, L. L. (2011). *What works to prevent partner violence? An evidence overview*. London, UK: Department for International Development.

Hidrobo, M., Peterman, A., & Heise, L. (2016). The effect of cash, vouchers, and food transfers on intimate partner violence: Evidence from a randomized experiment in Northern Ecuador. *American Economic Journal: Applied Economics, 8*(3), 284–303. Retrieved from https://doi.org/10.1257/app.20150048

Hollander, J. A. (2004). 'I can take care of myself': The impact of self-defense training on women's lives. *Violence Against Women, 10*(3), 205–235. Retrieved from https://doi.org/10.1177/1077801203256202

Hollander, J. A. (2014). Does self-defense training prevent sexual violence against women? *Violence Against Women, 20*(3), 252–269. Retrieved from https://doi.org/10.1177/1077801214526046

Jemmott, J. B., Jemmott, L. S., O'Leary, A., Ngwane, Z., Icard, L. D., Heeren, G. A., Mtose, X., & Carty, C. (2014). Cluster-randomized controlled trial of an HIV/sexually transmitted infection risk-reduction intervention for South African men. *American Journal of Public Health, 104*(3), 467–473. Retrieved from https://doi.org/10.2105/AJPH.2013.301578

Katz, J., & Moore, J. (2013). Bystander education training for campus sexual assault prevention: An initial meta-analysis. *Violence and Victims, 28*(6), 1054–1067. Retrieved from https://doi.org/10.1891/0886-6708.VV-D-12-00113

Katz, J., Heisterkamp, H. A., & Fleming, W. M. (2011). The social justice roots of the Mentors in Violence Prevention model and its application in a high school setting. *Violence against Women, 17*(6), 684–702. Retrieved from https://doi.org/10.1177/1077801211409725

Keller, J., Mboya, B. O., Sinclair, J., Githua, O. W., Mulinge, M., Bergholz, L., Paiva, L., Golden, N. H., & Kapphahn, C. (2017). A 6-week school curriculum improves boys' attitudes and behaviors related to gender-based violence in Kenya. *Journal of Interpersonal Violence, 32*(324), 535–557. Retrieved from https://doi.org/10.1177/0886260515586367

Kilmartin, C., Smith, T., Green, A., Heinzen, H., Kuchler, M., & Kolar, D. (2008). A real time social norms intervention to reduce male sexism. *Sex Roles, 59*(3–4), 264–273. Retrieved from https://doi.org/10.1007/s11199-008-9446-y

Kim, J., Ferrari, G., Abramsky, T., Watts, C., Hargreaves, J., Morison, L., Phetla, G., Porter, J., & Pronyk, P. (2009). Assessing the incremental effects of combining economic and health interventions: The IMAGE study in South Africa. *Bulletin of the World Health Organization*, *87*, 824–832. Retrieved from https://doi.org/10.2471/BLT.08.056580

Latané, B., & Darley, J. (1969). Bystander 'apathy.' *American Scientist*, *57*(2), 244–268. Retrieved from http://www.jstor.org/stable/27828530

Macmillan, R., & Gartner, R. (1999). When she brings home the bacon: Labor-force participation and the risk of spousal violence against women. *Journal of Marriage and Family*, *61*(4), 947–958. Retrieved from http://www.jstor.org/stable/354015

Mbilinyi, L. F., Neighbors, C., Walker, D. D., Roffman, R. A., Zegree, J., Edleson, J., & O'Rourke, A. (2011). A telephone intervention for substance-using adult male perpetrators of intimate partner violence. *Research on Social Work Practice*, *21*(1), 43–56. Retrieved from https://doi.org/10.1177/1049731509359008

Miller, D. T., & McFarland, C. (1987). Pluralistic ignorance: When similarity is interpreted as dissimilarity. *Journal of Personality and Social Psychology*, *53*(2), 298–305. Retrieved from https://doi.org/10.1037/0022-3514.53.2.298

Moynihan, M. M., Banyard, V. L., Cares, A. C., Potter, S. J., Williams, L. M., & Stapleton, J. G. (2015). Encouraging responses in sexual and relationship violence prevention: What program effects remain 1 year later? *Journal of Interpersonal Violence*, *30*(1), 110–132. Retrieved from https://doi.org/10.1177/0886260514532719

Nurius, P., & Norris, J. (1996). A cognitive ecological model of women's response to male sexual coercion in dating. *Journal of Psychology & Human Sexuality*, *8*(1), 117–139. Retrieved from https://www.ncbi.nlm.nih.gov/pmc/articles/PMC4343209/

O'Campo, P., Kirst, M., Tsamis, C., Chambers, C., & Ahmad, F. (2011). Implementing successful intimate partner violence screening programs in health care settings: Evidence generated from a realist-informed systematic review. *Social Science and Medicine*, *72*(6), 855–866. Retrieved from https://doi.org/10.1016/j.socscimed.2010.12.019

O'Doherty, L. J., Taft, A., Hegarty, K., Ramsay, J., Davidson, L. L., & Feder, G. (2014). Screening women for intimate partner violence in healthcare settings: Abridged Cochrane systematic review and meta-analysis. *British Medical Journal*, *348*(g2913), 1–11. Retrieved from https://doi.org/10.1136/bmj.g2913

Plichta, S. B. (2004). Intimate partner violence and physical health consequences: Policy and practice implications. *Journal of Interpersonal Violence*, *19*(11), 1296–1323. Retrieved from https://doi.org/10.1177/0886260504269685

Potter, S. J. (2012). Using a multimedia social marketing campaign to increase active bystanders on the college campus. *Journal of American College Health*, *60*(4), 282–295. Retrieved from https://doi.org/10.1080/07448481.2011.599350

Prochaska, J. O., & DiClemente, C. C. (1986). Toward a comprehensive model of change. In W. R. Miller & N. Heather (Eds.), *Treating addictive behaviors* (pp. 3–27). New York, NY: Plenum Press.

Raab, M. (2011). *The 'We Can' campaign in South Asia, 2004–2011: External evaluation report*. Retrieved from the Oxfam Great Britain (OXFAM-GB) website: https://policy-practice.oxfam.org.uk/publications/the-we-can-campaign-in-south-asia-2004-2011-external-evaluation-report-146189

Rozee, P. D., & Koss, M. P. (2001). Rape: A century of resistance. *Psychology of Women Quarterly*, *25*(4), 295–311. Retrieved from https://doi.org/10.1111/1471-6402.00030

Russell, C. A., Clapp, J. D., & DeJong, W. (2005). Done 4: Analysis of a failed social norms marketing campaign. *Health Communication*, *17*(1), 57–65. Retrieved from https://doi.org/10.1207/s15327027hc1701_4

Salazar, L. F., Vivolo-Kantor, A., Hardin, J., & Berkowitz, A. (2014). A web-based sexual violence bystander intervention for male college students: Randomized controlled trial. *Journal of Medical Internet Research*, *16*(9). Retrieved from https://doi.org/10.2196/jmir.3426

Salazar, L. F., Vivolo-Kantor, A., & McGroarty-Koon, K. (2017). Formative research with college men to inform content and messages for a web-based sexual violence prevention program. *Health Communication*, *32*(9), 1133–1141. Retrieved from https://doi.org/10.1080/10410236.2016.1214219

Sarnquist, C., Omondi, B., Sinclair, J., Gitau, C., Paiva, L., Mulinge, M., Cornfield, D. N., &

Maldonado, Y. (2014). Rape prevention through empowerment of adolescent girls. *Pediatrics*, *133*(5), e1226–e1232. Retrieved from https://doi.org/10.1542/peds.2013-3414

Sarnquist, C., Sinclair, J., Omondi Mboya, B., Langat, N., Paiva, L., Halpern-Felsher, B., Golden, N. H., Maldonado, Y. A., & Baiocchi, M. T. (2017). Evidence that classroom-based behavioral interventions reduce pregnancy-related school dropout among Nairobi adolescents. *Health Education & Behavior*, *44*(2), 297–303. Retrieved from https://doi.org/10.1177/1090198116657777

Schewe, P. A. (2007). Interventions to prevent sexual violence. In L. Doll, S. Bonzo, J. Mercy, & D. Sleet (Eds.), *Handbook of injury and violence prevention* (pp. 223–240). New York, NY: Springer.

Senn, C. Y. (2011). An imperfect feminist journey: Reflections on the process to develop an effective sexual assault resistance programme for university women. *Feminism & Psychology*, *21*(1), 121–137. Retrieved from https://doi.org/10.1177/0959353510386094

Senn, C., Eliasziw, M., Barata, P. C., Thurston, W. E., Newby-Clark, I. R., Radtke, L., & Hobden, K. L. (2013). Sexual assault resistance education for university women: Study protocol for a randomized controlled trial (SARE trial). *BMC Women's Health*, *13*(25), 1–13. Retrieved from https://bmcwomenshealth.biomedcentral.com/articles/10.1186/1472-6874-13-25

Senn, C. Y., Eliasziw, M., Barata, P. C., Thurston, W. E., Newby-Clark, I. R., Radtke, H. L., & Hobden, K. L. (2015). Efficacy of a sexual assault resistance program for university women. *The New England Journal of Medicine*, *372*(24), 2326–2335. Retrieved from https://doi.org/10.1056/NEJMsa1411131

Senn, C. Y., Eliasziw, M., Hobden, K. L., Newby-Clark, I. R., Barata, P. C., Radtke, H. L., & Thurston, W. E. (2017). Secondary and 2-year outcomes of a sexual assault resistance program for university women. *Psychology of Women Quarterly*, *41*(2), 147–162. Retrieved from https://doi.org/10.1177/0361684317690119

Senn, C. Y., Hobden, K. L., & Eliasziw, M. (2016). *Effective rape resistance training: Can it reduce self-blame for rape survivors?* Paper presented at the American Psychological Association Convention, Denver, CO.

Senn, C. Y., Saunders, K., & Gee, S. (2008). Walking the tightrope: Providing sexual assault resistance education for university women without victim blame. In S. Arcand, D. Damant, S. Gravel, & E. Harper (Eds.), *Violence faites aux femmes* (pp. 353–372). Quebec City, QC: Les Presses de Universite du Quebec.

Sinclair, J., Sinclair, L., Otieno, E., Mulinge, M., Kapphahn, C., & Golden, N. H. (2013). A self-defense program reduces the incidence of sexual assault in Kenyan adolescent girls. *Journal of Adolescent Health*, *53*(3), 374–380. Retrieved from https://doi.org/10.1016/j.jadohealth.2013.04.008

Stephens, K. A., & George, W. H. (2009). Rape prevention with college men: Evaluating risk status. *Journal of Interpersonal Violence*, *24*(6), 996–1013. Retrieved from https://doi.org/10.1177/0886260508319366

Stewart, A. L. (2014). The Men's Project: A sexual assault prevention program targeting college men. *Psychology of Men & Masculinity*, *15*(4), 481–485. Retrieved from https://doi.org/10.1037/a0033947

Taket, A., Wathen, C. N., & MacMillan, H. (2004). Should health professionals screen all women for domestic violence? *PLOS Medicine*, *1*(1), 7–11. Retrieved from https://doi.org/10.1371/journal.pmed.0010004.g001

Tark, J., & Kleck, G. (2014). Resisting rape: The effects of victim self-protection on rape completion and injury. *Violence Against Women*, *20*(3), 270–292. Retrieved from https://doi.org/10.1177/1077801214526050

Ullman, S. E. (2010). *Talking about sexual assault: Society's response to survivors.* Washington, DC: American Psychological Association.

Williams, S., & Aldred, A. (2011). *Change making: How we adopt new attitudes, beliefs and practices; Insights from the We Can Campaign*. Retrieved from the Oxfam Great Britain (OXFAM-GB) website: http://policy-practice.oxfam.org.uk/our-work/gender-justice/ending-violence-against-women/we-can

5

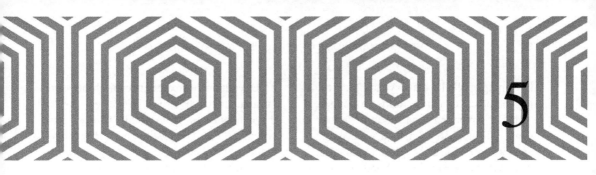

Trans* and Gender Diverse Youth: Applied and Critical Social Psychology Working in the Margins

Katrina Roen and Shiloh Groot

INTRODUCTION: INTERDISCIPLINARY AND PSYCHOLOGICAL PERSPECTIVES ON TRANS* AND GENDER DIVERSE YOUTH

In the past two decades, there has been a fundamental reduction in the age at which people begin identifying themselves as trans* or gender diverse (TGD) and a rapid rise in the number of children and young people presenting to psychologists with gender identity issues (at their own instigation or prompted by concerned adults, such as parents). This increase in clinical presentation, and decrease in age of presentation, has coincided with the introduction of puberty suppression as a way of relieving psychological distress among some young people who feel intensely at odds with their sexed body and the gendered expectations that go with that (Cohen-Kettenis et al., 2008). Two other shifts have gone hand-in-hand with these clinical developments: popular media representations of gender-crossing children (such as television documentaries) have drawn widespread attention to the possibilities of gender-crossing and puberty suppression, and the development of social media has enabled many TGD youth to record and publicise aspects of their gendered and bodily explorations, concerns, and transitions. Non-clinical research is now reporting that relatively high numbers of young people are identifying as transgender or questioning their gender (Clark et al., 2014).

Given that TGD youth have been the focus of increased research, clinical, and media attention in recent years, this chapter asks: What implications does this have for applied and social psychology? What intersections of (minoritised) identities and experiences need to be understood in order to work well with TGD youth? How can applied social psychologists draw from the interdisciplinary literature focusing on TGD youth in order to develop well-informed psychosocial approaches? We examine recent literature relating to TGD youth with a view to informing applied social psychological thinking and practice in this rapidly-evolving field.

This chapter relies on the term 'trans* or gender diverse' to refer to a wide range of gender expression and exploration that is now documented among children and young people. Some researchers refer to this spectrum of gendered possibilities with terms such as: gender independent, gender non-conforming, gender variant, gender creative (Pyne, 2014). However, it is important to note some might dis-identify with all of these terms, instead using conceptual terms drawn from indigenous languages to inform their identities (Driskill et al., 2011). An awareness of indigenous variation is essential as indigenous language terms are sometimes misappropriated and used interchangeably with terms such as transgender, but are best understood within their cultural context. This chapter seeks to address the broad gender terrain that lies outside of the Eurocentric,[1] prescribed, and normative binaries of girl/boy and woman/man. It also traverses ages and stages of life that can be quite distinct, i.e., childhood and youth, including early adulthood.

The developments that are seen, in clinical settings and in media representations, have implications for psycho-social understandings of trans* identities and gender diversity. These developments also have implications for applied social psychologists, who may come into contact with TGD children and youth and would ideally be equipped to work in a well-informed way with issues around gender-questioning, gender diversity, and gender transition.

The present chapter examines recent literature relating to TGD youth with a view to informing applied social psychology thinking and practice in this rapidly evolving field. We pay particular attention to intersectional issues, and the multiple layers of minoritisation that TGD youth can experience, by considering the realities of: TGD youth who are also minoritised in relation to culture and indigeneity, TGD youth who experience economic disadvantage and homelessness, and TGD youth who experience disability and/or mental health issues. We also consider the resilience of TGD youth who are now articulating and exploring new approaches to identity and embodiment, TGD youth who seek each other out in online and face-to-face settings to produce a sense of community, to build support networks, and to effect political change. We encourage applied psychologists to become well-informed about the shifts taking place as TGD youth develop a voice, challenge what health services offer, and articulate innovative ideas about gender and embodiment. We consider the implications of these shifts for applied and social psychology, and we point to specific issues to which psychologists might usefully be sensitive and take action. The kind of action we propose involves fostering allies for TGD youth and raising awareness of how cis-genderism[2] operates to exclude TGD youth.

Although TGD youth are disproportionately represented in homeless populations, TGD young people are often reluctant to seek assistance from social services and emergency shelters where they may encounter institutionalised violence, homophobia, and transphobia. Intersections of indigeneity, race and ethnicity, disability, and class further exacerbate the occurrence of institutionalised violence. A narrow focus on homelessness as the absence of physical shelter, and as evidence of social pathology in urban settings, effectively detaches TGD experiences of homelessness from the broader socio-political context of colonial societies. We suggest that, for applied social psychology to meaningfully address TGD youth homelessness, a decolonising approach can usefully be taken. We explain how this can reorient social policy interventions away from the management of 'deficiencies' or 'deviance' towards culturally relevant, community- and family-based programming that supports home-making.

Much research focusing on LGBT (lesbian, gay, bisexual, and trans*) youth tells us very little about TGD youth.[3] In this chapter, we aim to draw out psychologically-relevant findings from studies that do focus principally on TGD youth. We also draw cautiously on studies of LGBT youth, with the understanding that the perspectives and experiences of TGD youth are often under-represented in such studies.

MINORITISATION: AN INTERSECTIONAL APPROACH

What intersections of (minoritised) identities and experiences can usefully be understood for working well with TGD youth? How can applied social psychologists draw from the interdisciplinary literature focusing on TGD youth in order to develop well-informed psycho-social approaches? We suggest that intersectional and interdisciplinary approaches offer vital tools and understandings to applied social psychologists engaging with gender diversity.

Intersectional approaches allow for a focus that goes beyond single-factor ways of thinking about identity and, instead, takes into account the complex intersections of many aspects of a person's identity. As Nash puts it, intersectionality is 'the notion that subjectivity is constituted by mutually reinforcing vectors of race, gender, class, and sexuality' (Nash, 2008: 2). This means, for instance, paying attention to the fact that a particular TGD young person's life is not only affected by how they are gendered, but also by their age, culture, ability, religion, sexuality, and so on. Intersectional approaches emerged in the late 1980s and early 1990s in the context of critical race studies and, particularly, US legal theorising around the interrelated effects of racialisation and gendering (Nash, 2008). The term was coined by Kimberley Crenshaw (Crenshaw, 1989) and intersectional approaches have been taken up extensively within feminist research (Carastathis, 2014). The intersectional approach we take in this chapter, it is hoped, will draw attention to the complexity and diversity of TGD young people's lives and ensure that the focus is very specifically not centred on white, middle class, and otherwise privileged TGD youth.

Interdisciplinary research is a necessary resource for anyone working with TGD youth insofar as research-based knowledge on this topic spans education, sociology, psychology, gender studies, and social work and more. Focusing only on psychological literature relating to TGD youth would give a far more clinically oriented frame of reference than is useful for applied social psychologists. The current chapter uses literature across disciplines, drawing out points that are relevant from a social psychological perspective.

In reviewing literature relating to TGD youth and of relevance to applied social psychology, we pay particular attention to minoritisation. The lives of TGD youth represented in the literature (and this is even more so for those who are poorly represented) are often characterised by being multiply minoritised. Who it is possible to be and what it is possible to do are structured by the effects of minoritisation. The emotional well-being of TGD youth, the challenges faced, the search for a community of supportive and similar others, and the search for health and social care professionals who are well-informed about TGD youth issues are all conditioned by the sense of isolation, the experience of being misunderstood and misjudged, and the risk of being subject to exclusion and violence. That is, day-to-day experience for TGD youth is conditioned by the imposed effects of minoritisation.

Working well with TGD youth means working against the effects of minoritisation. This can be done by developing a framework of understanding that focuses attention on gendering as a process, rather than focusing on a discrete group of people (TGD youth). Understanding gendering as a process involves considering that all people are gendered, that gendering is a mulitfaceted phenomenon that is not well represented by straightforward binary categories (feminine/masculine), and that all people come to be positioned in diverse ways in relation to gender. In this sense, all people are part of the diverse spectrum of possibilities that are part of gendering. Viewed like this, TGD youth do not need to be constructed as a small or unusual minority group, standing out from an overwhelming majority of cis-gendered people (that is, people who are gendered in a way that is consistent with their sex at birth). Taking such a norm-critical perspective can help to reposition TGD youth as valid subjects and to expose the constructed nature of normative, binary gender. Nevertheless, hegemonic understandings of gender (as binary and tied to bodily sex) do produce minoritisation which has severe effects, including negative psychological consequences, for TGD young people.

DECOLONISING SEX AND GENDER

It is worth asking whether intersectionality permeates deep enough in challenging the Eurocentric bias of current psychological theory, teaching, and practice. Colonialism enforces an ideology of cis-genderism, which denigrates and pathologises gender identities that do not align with a person's assigned sex at birth or challenge Eurocentric gender norms (Shelton, 2015). This has significant implications for an applied social psychology which requires an examination of issues of power and privilege in modes of practice and the construction of knowledge (Sonn, 2006). Dissatisfaction with the unquestioned, derivative, and explicative nature of social psychological research that is deeply rooted in individualistic strands of Eurocentric psychology has led many indigenous researchers to look outside the discipline in order to begin solving the devastating problems within their own communities (Groot et al., 2012). Jean-Guy A. Goulet (1996: 683) echoed such frustrations when arguing that scholars of gender diversity have failed 'to consider indigenous constructions of personhood and gender'. Decolonisation provides a pathway for recovery, the re-establishment and legitimacy of cultural frameworks, and the assertion of rights – it is deeply rooted in indigenous ways of knowing, being, and doing (Hodgetts, 2010).

While indigenous TGD youth are predominantly acknowledged within the context of the LGB population, this is further complicated by the fact that colonialism, gender, sex, and sexuality are irrevocably intertwined and cannot usefully be extracted from one another. Understanding the nuances of pre-colonial gender diversity is severely hindered by colonising practices that were commonplace, such as massacres of indigenous peoples, accompanied by rape and sexual mutilation of both indigenous bodies and sacred symbols depicting histories of gender and sexual fluidity (Smith, 2011; Te Awekotuku., 2005). It is through these very mechanisms that Europeans were able to colonise indigenous peoples in the first place. Similarly, Andrea Smith (2011) asserts that the maintenance of such patriarchal gender systems prevent decolonisation and the assertion of indigenous sovereignty.

Indigenous, aboriginal, and/or native, along with others, are dynamic and contested terms imposed on indigenous peoples (and, in some instances, misappropriated by other occupying groups to displace First peoples). We have relied upon the term indigenous to create links across oceans and between peoples but recognise the need to be sensitive to context. For example, it is important not to assert a monolithic link of indigenous gender variance within, and across, indigenous nations, colonial borders, and global networks (Driskill et al., 2011). First Nation Two-spirit is not comparable to categories of an indigenous Pacific (e.g., fa'afafine, takataapui etc), there is no single story. Further, indigenous linguistic terms conceptualising historical gender fluidity do not necessarily describe a minoritised group in indigenous societies that existed in oppositional difference to a gender majority (Driskill et al., 2011). For example,

Pasifika communities have long included mahu, vakasalewa, palopa, fa'afafine, akava'ine, fakaleiti (leiti), fakafifine (referred to using the acronym: MVPFAFF) (HRC, 2008). In recognition of such histories, and the ever-evolving communities they are drawn from, LGBT support networks in New Zealand align themselves with Pacific health organisations to provide the appropriate resources and support for Pasifika peoples.

With the imposition of Eurocentric democratic principles, indigenous TGD young people find themselves confronted with new oppressions in the name of 'custom and tradition' (Driskill et al., 2011). One such example is refugee youth who have made claims based on gender identity and, as such, have lived in defiance of social erasure, stigma, and violence in their countries of origin (Jordan, 2009). A decolonising approach when combined with intersectionality problematises assumptions that 'culture' is somehow implicated in the oppression of young TGD asylum seekers and refugees. Prioritising an essentialised view of culture at the expense of other relations or structures (such as class) may limit the opportunity for TGD refugees to use cultural frameworks as a means of challenging oppression (cf. Lugones, 2007).

When young people seeking asylum engage the refugee system, their applications are evaluated against expected trajectories of refugee flight and Eurocentric narratives of trans* identities, transition, or gender identity disorder (Jordan, 2009). Having already fled persecution, TGD refugee claimants' potential for safety and belonging is constrained when they do not conform to such conventions. Upon arrival in the destination country (not of their choosing and for which they are likely to be poorly prepared), young TGD refugees negotiate belonging and exclusion within and across multiple communities. This includes diasporic migrant and conational, LGBTGD, faith, and mainstream. The fortitude required to defy oppression, engage with a refugee system ill-equipped for (LGB)TGD applicants, the quotidian work of settling, and efforts to claim safety and belonging test the limits of what is possible (Jordan, 2009). For applied social psychology to be effective, it should be grounded in an awareness of imperialism, colonialism, capitalism, and other structures that impede the lives and well-being of TGD young peoples.

The history of relationships between a sovereign state and indigenous peoples is complex and has oftentimes been paternalistic and damaging. The ongoing colonisation of indigenous peoples perpetuates inequities which privilege white, cis-gender bodies and intellects while degrading indigenous gender variance (Abustan, 2015). The embodiment of such ideologies is experienced when indigenous peoples view themselves as bodies, without intellect, and incapable of self-governance (Finley, 2011). Indigenous peoples should be *self-critiquing* of indigenous constructions of 'tradition' and similar cultural nationalisms that are dependent on the exclusion of trans* and gender diverse people.

For example, Denetdale (2006) tells of how TGD Navajo youth left the Navajo Nation to move back to urban areas and to find a community of support as a consequence of cis/heteronormative Navajos. This represents a profound loss to the Navajo Nation. In the imperial construction of many such nation-states, it was these very kinship ties that were targeted by colonial regimes to eliminate gender and sexual diversity. Against cultural conservative efforts to discard diverse genders and sexualities as a colonial quality, Brooks (2008) reminds (LGB)TGD Abenaki that decolonisation compels the people to reject colonial outsider/insider binaries and asks instead how tradition invokes familial ties and invites relationships across difference.

Indigenous social psychologists are displacing non-indigenous conversations about indigenous people by building theories from the everyday knowledges drawn from their communities of origin (Groot et al., 2012). However, an uncritical politics of futurity and tradition can contribute to the reification of colonialism within Indigenous struggles for sovereignty. Cherokee queer/Two-spirit writer, scholar, and performer, Qwo-Li Driskill (2004) in their potent song titled 'We were stolen from our bodies' posits decolonising gender as one of the central facets of healing the legacy of historical trauma.

Too often, psychology (critical, feminist, and social included) has marginalised and ignored indigenous histories, socio-economic and political conditions, and worldviews (Groot et al., 2012). Further, non-indigenous scholars often apply Western concepts in ways that misappropriate indigenous diversely gendered phenomena. Until intersectionality as an approach employs decolonial theory, the risk of the continued privileging of Western assumptions is high. This is particularly so when intersectionality becomes a means of reifying identity politics rather than a tool that destabilises categories (Lugones, 2007). Non-indigenous applied social psychologists seeking to be allies must look beyond a glib examination of their own privileges and benefits from living in a settler colonial state, to actively listening to indigenous peoples. Drawing on, and supporting, indigenous research to decolonise psychology is critical but solidarity cannot occur in isolation. Immediately, globalisation, transnational activism, and a multitude of colonial histories and legacies become apparent. This should not only inform our (indigenous, non-indigenous, TGD, and cis-gender) work but must also be able to account for the geographic, linguistic, and political locations in an evolving global discipline (Groot et al., 2012).

HOME(LESS)NESS AND EXCLUSION

Until recently, homelessness among TGD youth has been studied almost exclusively in the context of homelessness in the broader LGBT population (Shelton, 2015; Yu, 2010). Although LGB and TGD people experiencing homelessness may have common needs, TGD young people are confronted with a range of unique challenges. For example, TGD youth are presented with significant barriers when attempting to change legal documents (e.g., official name and sex designation) and access social services related to gender transition (Shelton, 2015). While diverse sexualities have made some significant gains in social acceptance, gender diverse identities and expressions are not as widely recognised, protected, or affirmed by society and/or public policy (Lennon and Mistler, 2014; Shelton, 2015).

Homelessness is a serious societal concern involving material hardship and social marginalisation, which results in significantly poorer health outcomes and early death (Hodgetts et al., 2014). Research into homelessness is moving beyond individualistic risk factors associated with street life to explore protective factors that enable people to survive on the streets (Kidd and Davidson, 2007; Prince, 2008) and to discuss issues of identity (Groot et al., 2011). For example, Kidd and Davidson (2007) draw on the accounts of 208 homeless youth in New York and Toronto to document their accounts of survival and resilience linked to relational notions of the self, daily practices, and material and social circumstances. In the process, these authors point to the huge range of lives and survival strategies among young people experiencing homelessness. However, although most scholars readily agree that TGD people are over-represented in the homeless youth population, they remain severely under-represented in research and academic literature (Crossley, 2015).

Pathways into homelessness are complex, with many TGD people being rendered homeless at a young age due to ongoing abuse, mistreatment, and rejection by family members and the wider community (HRC, 2008). TGD people face prejudice and discrimination in housing, employment, healthcare, and education and can end up living on the streets or without permanent housing (HRC, 2008; Shelton, 2015; Yu, 2010). Research attests to street homeless people experiencing a profound sense of being worn down through constant exposure to wet and cold conditions, the unrelenting threat of violence and associated lack of sleep aggravated by the stress of vigilance, and bodily decline, including the loss of teeth (Groot et al., 2015). Those TGD young people who seek assistance from social services and emergency shelters are likely to encounter institutionalised oppression and violence, homophobia, and transphobia similar to that which excluded them from the realisation of home in the first place (Crossley, 2015; Shelton, 2015; Yu, 2010). Further, most shelters are segregated by assigned sex at birth, regardless of the individual's gender identity, and homeless TGD youth may even be ostracised by some agencies that serve their LGB peers (Choi et al., 2015).

Intersectionality provides a useful framework for capturing the overlapping minoritised identities that shape the lives of TGD young people experiencing homelessness and the ways in which differences between people intersect in institutional arrangements, social practices, and cultural discourses. Homelessness is not a neutral category but one that is intimately interwoven with other experiences of marginality. By way of illustration, the criminalisation of homelessness adds further complexity to the issue for TGD young people experiencing homelessness. The use of legislation to criminalise homelessness (e.g. through anti-begging laws) has often been deployed to both control how public space is used (Groot and Hodgetts, 2015) and to remove or exclude minoritised groups (including not only people who are homeless, but youth, racialised/visible minorities, and more generally, the poor) (cf. Groot and Hodgetts, 2012; Mitchell and Heynen, 2009).

Faced with discrimination at school and work, high rates of homelessness, and limited access to a community of support, some TGD youth engage in sex work to earn income or trade for housing and food. Because trans people, particularly trans girls and women of colour (including undocumented migrants), may be disproportionately represented among individuals engaged in street sex work, they are frequent targets of laws criminalising prostitution (Fletcher, 2013). Such policies inevitably reduce the access of TGD young people experiencing homelessness to much needed resources (Hunt, 2013).

Relative to the burgeoning body of literature documenting the lives of homeless adults, literature on indigenous, migrant, and refugee TGD young people experiencing homelessness is minimal at best (Groot et al., 2011). Further, of these few studies, many tend to have a Eurocentric and individualistic orientation and primarily focus on the barriers to care, perception of services, risk factors, and healthcare needs of this population (Crossley, 2015). This is despite empirical evidence that young people and those from ethnically, economically, and socially marginalised backgrounds are overrepresented in the homeless population (Hodgetts et al., 2014). Missing from the literature is a critical examination of the relational, structural, and cultural aspects of homelessness for TGD young people (Crossley, 2015; Groot et al., 2011).

A narrow focus on homelessness as the absence of physical shelter and as evidence of social pathology in urban settings effectively detaches TGD experiences of homelessness from the broader socio-political context of colonial societies. For example, homelessness is endemic to experiences of colonialism, not only at the personal, but also at the tribal and national level where many indigenous peoples have experienced over 150 years of being rendered out of place in their ancestral homelands (Groot and Peters, 2016). In such colonial contexts, many indigenous peoples live in impoverished and overcrowded conditions and, as such, are over-represented in the homeless population (as above). Institutionalised racism within the child-welfare, juvenile-justice, and criminal-justice systems further embeds experiences of homelessness for TGD young people of colour.

There is a significant lack of research on housing and accommodation issues for TGD youth from a refugee background (McMillan, 2009). Housing is not well covered in the literature, either as a standalone issue or in conjunction with a wider resettlement focus. This is surprising given that one of the main focuses of any country's response to refugees is resettlement, a notion bound up in ideas of home and housing. With the exception of LGBT asylum seekers applying for refugee status to another country (Jordan, 2009), there appears to be little research on TGD refugee youth experiences of home or being homeless. This inevitably leads to a lack of resources for working with migrant families in general and, as such, a lack of knowledge about families' cultural beliefs (already a problematic homogenous designation) regarding TGD people and sexuality and gender identity (Choi et al., 2015).

When defining homelessness, it is important to consider what the loss of a 'home' entails. More often than not, TGD young people experiencing homelessness have not developed a conventional attachment to a domiciled space due to distressing childhoods characterised by abuse, poverty, and family dysfunction (cf. Groot et al., 2012; Groot et al., 2015). TGD homeless young people have often been denied a 'conventional' home in both a physical and relational sense. Yet, there is more to these young peoples' lives than displacement and loss. For instance, beyond the stereotype of the middle-class youth falling prey to drug addiction and ending up on the street, many young people on the streets have come from youth detention facilities and foster homes (Reed-Victor and Stronge, 2002). Resilience for such young people is more about learning specific strategies for street life and establishing a community of support with other homeless people. The creation of judgement-free spaces, where meaningful and trusting relationships can be cultivated, is central to the delivery of health services for TGD young people experiencing homelessness (Trussell and Mair, 2010). The True Colors Residence, New York state's first permanent supportive housing facility for TGD youth with a history of homelessness, provides an exemplary model (Choi et al., 2015).

An awareness of existing policies is essential for applied social psychologists to be effective advocates in their work with TGD young people who are experiencing homelessness. Applied social psychologists are uniquely positioned to expand knowledge and awareness about the subject of social exclusion, deprivation, cultural displacement, poverty, and housing instability among TGD young people. Knowledge gained can assist policy makers and service providers conceptualise strategies, programmes, and public policies which recognise and accommodate the experiences and challenges specific to TGD young people experiencing homelessness. Further, a strength based-approach which critically examines the nature of resilience amongst homeless TGD young people has the potential to shift broader discourses regarding homelessness.

SELF-HARM, EMBODIED DISTRESS, AND DISABILITY

While research literature specifically focusing on TGD youth and homelessness is fairly sparse, research concerned with TGD youth and emotional and embodied distress more broadly is going through a period of rapid growth. Existing studies often use psycho-social indicators to assess the extent and effects of minoritisation faced by TGD children and youth. Various studies, for example, point to self-harming, suicidality, school drop-out, and substance abuse as indicators. Studies repeatedly show large disparities between TGD youth and other youth in relation to psycho-social measures.

While earlier studies on youth self-harm and suicidality have tended to work across age groups, or across a diverse LGBT spectrum, recent years have seen a rapid rise in the number of studies focusing specifically on TGD youth. Grossman and D'Augelli (2007) reported that, of 55 transgender youth studied, a quarter reported having attempted suicide and nearly half had thought seriously about killing themselves. The US National Transgender Discrimination Survey found that 41% of the 6,456 respondents indicated they have attempted suicide (Haas et al., 2014). In the Youth Chances UK survey, 25% of 956 young transgender respondents reported that they were currently self-harming, and a further 47% reported having self-harmed previously (Metro, 2016). Another UK-based survey of 120 reported that 48% of trans youth had attempted suicide at least once (Nodin et al., 2015).

Some researchers have focused on experiences of self-harm as well as harm-protective factors among TGD youth. One such study, carried out with 91 TGD students in Australia, suggests that, for TGD youth who have the opportunity to engage in online discussion, activism, or community events, this can help to counter the effects of discriminatory abuse. About a third of the sample reported that such involvement made them feel more resilient, eased their sense of depression, and reduced their thoughts of self-harm and suicide. Significantly, '24% of the survey participants reported that participating in activism stopped them engaging in an act of self-harm or suicide attempt' (Jones et al., 2016: 166).

Within the growing body of research concerned with TGD youth and self-harm, much attention is given to quantitative survey data showing the extent to which self-harm and suicidality can be issues for TGD youth. One of the studies that goes further conceptualises self-harm as embodied distress (McDermott and Roen, 2016) and explores the idea of distress being mapped onto trans* bodies via self-harm (Roen, 2016). In this work, emphasis is given to the notion of a queer and feminist bioethics which refuses to invalidate or pathologise the distress of TGD youth (Roen, 2016). Instead, what is opened up is discursive space for the gender diverse futures that might be envisaged by TGD youth. For this purpose, Ehrensaft's taxonomy of gender diversity possibilities is set out (Ehrensaft, 2011a, 2011b), and the importance of living with uncertainty (Möller et al., 2009) and not foreclosing identity (Wren, 2000) is underscored. The point is to open up for an envisaging of diverse futures that are not preconditioned by a sense of the inevitability of distress or the binary framing of medical sex reassignment (Roen, 2016). What can be taken from this work is that applied psychologists can be proactive in opening up discursive space – as well as making interventions at the structural and material level – contributing to the envisaging of diverse futures that neither involve pathologisation nor make binary gender outcomes a primary goal.

There is very little research literature addressing the intersection between TGD youth and disability. A systematic review of literature spanning education, health, and social sciences identified 24 anglophone works focusing on disability and LGBT youth published between 1995 and 2010 (Duke, 2011). Of these, there were only two studies focusing primarily on gender identity issues, and these were both clinical case studies concerning gender non-conforming children or young people with autism. What can be concluded from this metasynthesis, then, is that (i) there is a lack of research knowledge at the intersection of disability and TGD youth, (ii) most studies concerning LGBT youth and disability focus more directly on sexuality and have less to say about TGD youth, and (iii) when researchers do focus on TGD youth and disability, they are most likely to be taking a clinical approach. From this metasynthesis, it is also possible to observe that some researchers focusing on TGD youth regard gender non-conforming as a possible 'symptom' of autism. Clearly, there is much room for improvement here in terms of building research knowledge that positions TGD youth with disabilities as valid subjects and prioritising the perspectives and experiences of TGD youth with disabilities.

WELL-BEING AND COMMUNITY

Increasingly, researchers have turned to address questions of resilience among TGD youth, rather than only pointing to evidence of disadvantage and distress. Recent studies identify some helpful initiatives within schools (Jones et al., 2016), some address the potential for TGD youth to be supported effectively by allies (Harper and Singh, 2014), some highlight the value of parental support (Pyne, 2016; Riley et al., 2013), and some examine trans* young people's self-reported resilience strategies (Singh et al., 2014). One of the arenas where TGD youth are very proactively creating community and promoting well-being is online, and this is increasingly documented in research both within psychology and across the social sciences (McDermott and Roen, 2016; Raun, 2012). Other initiatives specifically seek to foster relational resilience among indigenous TGD youth, e.g., in New Zealand, Le Va's work in developing meaningful suicide prevention for young Pasifika peoples whose gender identity does not conform to colonial expectations (http://www.leva.co.nz/suicide-prevention/Rainbow). Non-government organisations, such as Le Va, work closely alongside people, families, communities, and services to provide the resources, tools, information, and support Pasifika TGD young people need for their physical, mental, social, and cultural well-being.

A growing body of literature addresses the experiences of parenting a gender non-conforming child, and much of this literature identifies opportunities for resilience. Some researchers point to the usefulness of parent support groups, where parents can meet others in a similar situation (Menvielle and Hill, 2010; Menvielle and Tuerk, 2002), some researchers examine how parents support their children, for example, by using discursive practices to frame their child's gender non-conformity positively (Rahilly, 2013).

Riley and collaborators, who have researched the needs of gender variant children and their parents, emphasise the importance of networks of support, including other families with gender diverse children, and a wider community (including religious groups, clubs, and schools) that offers support and acceptance (Riley et al., 2011; Riley et al., 2013). Professionals across various sectors and specialisms, including applied social psychology, might usefully work together to promote such networks of understanding and support.

A growing number of studies have pointed towards the value of the internet for promoting resilience among TGD youth. Robinson and colleagues, for example, found that transgender youth were particularly likely to have drawn from the internet where they were able to access both sophisticated understandings about gender, sex, and sexuality (Robinson et al., 2014). Developing such understandings can provide a base for collective thinking that works against the isolating and individualising perspectives that may leave some TGD youth feeling alone and hopeless.

Jones and colleagues have studied TGD youth in Australia, with a particular focus on the role of networks and activism in promoting resilience. This research suggests that, while compared with cis-gendered same-sex attracted youth, TGD youth may be more likely to have suffered discriminatory physical abuse and to have engaged in self-harm, they were also more likely to have talked with people in their networks about their identity and to have sought help or to have engaged in activism (Jones and Hillier, 2013). Significantly, in a following paper, it is reported that 91% of TGD youth research participants (n = 189) reported taking part in activism (Jones et al., 2016). Here, activism is defined very broadly, including 'liking' an activist Facebook page, signing a petition, attending a march or rally, creating an activist blog, writing to a member of parliament, uploading a video to the internet, speaking at, or helping to organise, a march or rally. Most described positive effects of this activist participation, such as: feeling better about their gender identity, having fun, and feeling part of a larger community (Jones et al, 2016). Such research substantially underscores the importance of the work that is being done by TGD youth to find similar others, to build community, to speak out against transphobia and cis-genderism, to support one another in the face of adversity. It also points to the importance of the internet as a forum where this work can take place and where TGD young people explicitly engage with one another around themes of identity, harm reduction, and supporting one another in the face of adversity: all themes that are taken up by other researchers too (e.g., Henriksen, 2014; McDermott and Roen, 2016; Raun, 2012).

In terms of making practical suggestions for enhancing TGD youth resilience and contributing to the work that applied social psychologists might do, one particularly useful approach is to focus on the process of developing allies for TGD youth (Harper and Singh, 2014). This approach builds on Lev's transgender emergence model, although Lev's model was not intended specifically for youth (Lev, 2004). According to this model, transgender emergence is understood to include various stages such as: developing awareness of gender identity issues, seeking information and reaching out, beginning to tell others about one's gender identity and exploring questions of labelling and identification, exploring questions about transition and possibly body modification, then acceptance and posttransition issues. Understanding this process could help to identify points where allies can contribute sensitively.

In considering how families might become allies for TGD youth, Harper and Singh usefully explain that families often fear for their children and, in the case of a TGD young person, may be worrying about issues of safety, schooling, and future success (Harper and Singh, 2014). When these fears are at the fore, families can be ill-equipped to support and advocate for TGD children and young people. The emphasis, then, is on supporting families to come to a place of acceptance from which they can then support children and young people. In working with families to become supporters and advocates, it may be useful to draw from a notion of an action continuum, such as that proposed by Adams et al. (2007). This continuum relates to the stages a person might go through in the process of becoming an advocate. The starting point, at worst, might be that the person actively contributes to, or denies, the social injustices faced by TGD youth. Movement along the continuum might see that same person beginning to recognise social injustice and eventually being willing to take some action, possibly by educating themselves about the issues, educating others and raising awareness, offering support and encouragement, and eventually initiating change and preventing social injustices faced by TGD youth (Harper and Singh, 2014). Being aware of this continuum, and the potential for movement towards being more supportive and possibly engaging in advocacy, might help in recognising opportunities for change based in psychological understandings.

Drawing from Harper and Singh's thinking about ally development, we suggest that, in order for psychologists to be able to contribute to this kind of change, what is required is self-reflection: being able to facilitate supportive contexts for TGD youth, or produce opportunities for allies and advocates to emerge, requires one to have reflected on one's own relationship to gender identity questions. This initial process of self-reflection and learning could usefully involve a sensitisation to language use, a developing awareness of institutionalised structures and taken-for-granted features of one's local context that are likely to exclude TGD youth. This means, for example, noticing where toilets and changing rooms only cater to binary-gendered people, and learning to use pronouns that go beyond the binary (e.g., ze/hir/hirs and they/them/theirs) (Harper and Singh, 2014).

Harper and Singh write about the role of psychoeducation in helping family members and other (potential) allies to develop their capacity to support and advocate for TGD youth. It can be useful to draw attention to the point that gender fluidity in childhood, and beyond, is not uncommon and has existed throughout history and across cultures. Drawing attention to identity terms and pronoun preferences can also be part of this process of psychoeducation.

IMPLICATIONS FOR APPLIED AND CRITICAL PSYCHOLOGY

Throughout this chapter, we have raised a number of important questions for applied social psychologists to consider, which we now hope to provide some summarising answers to in this section. We have encouraged applied psychologists to become well-informed about the shifts taking place as TGD youth develop a voice, challenge what health services offer, lobby for trans-inclusive educational spaces, and articulate innovative ideas about gender and embodiment. We considered the implications of these shifts for applied and social psychology and pointed to specific issues to which psychologists might usefully be sensitive. In order to develop a knowledge-base that is useful for applied social psychologists, we emphasised the importance of drawing from critical psychology, from norm-critical understandings, and from interdisciplinary research.

In drawing together ideas from interdisciplinary research, we have selected research that has the potential to inform psycho-social perspectives and can contribute to interventions that promote well-being. We have written about the experiences, challenges, and resilience of TGD youth with a view to showing how applied social psychologists might usefully contribute in this complex and rapidly changing field of work. We have taken a social justice approach that draws understandings from critical psychology, and we point to the usefulness of queer understandings to applied psychological work concerning TGD youth.

By taking an interdisciplinary approach, it is possible to draw insights from a diverse range of school-based research, health and social care research, gender and sexuality studies, and other social science approaches, such as sociological research. All of these fields do address the psycho-social contexts and well-being of TGD youth in some way. The question we are addressing in this final section is: How can interdisciplinary research inform applied social psychological approaches to TGD youth?

Working with TGD youth issues has many parallels with working with minoritised groups in general. Social justice approaches offer particular insight into ways of working with minoritised groups, stigma, and social inequalities, and for this reason, may be especially useful in the development of applied social psychological work on TGD youth issues. Sexuality and gender studies also offer insights about sexuality and gender minoritisation that stand to make a useful contribution. Concepts such as heteronormativity, cis-genderism, and transphobia have been drawn from sexuality and gender studies and worked through the present chapter.

In addition to the interdisciplinary contributions to this chapter, we draw from critical psychologies (in which we include indigenous, feminist, and queer psychological work). We do this with the view that applied social psychology might best be able to meet TGD youth appropriately if critical understandings about identity, gender, embodiment, and reflexivity are brought into play. Critical psychologies offer ways of thinking about minoritisation that open up for the decentring of the norm, enabling a more respectful approach to non-conformity. Critical psychologies provide a poststructuralist critique of identity which opens up for the possibility of gender fluidity and for non-traditional gendering, without turning to pathologising labels or assumptions. Critical psychologies also open up for reflexive approaches that decentre scientific knowledge, prompt psychologists to question ourselves and our assumptions, and privilege the realities of minoritised others. This makes it possible to work respectfully, as a psychologist, with people who have often been rendered invalid subjects when viewed through the lens of psychology (Prilleltensky and Nelson, 2002).

Research with professionals who work with transgender people and their families suggests that the needs of gender variant children include:

> to be loved; to be listened to; to be respected and accepted; to be offered general, school and professional support; to be free to express their true gender; to have gender-variant friends; to be safe and have the same opportunities as other children; and to have access to a delayed puberty where indicated. (Riley et al., 2013: 648)

Importantly for applied social psychologists, the kind of information felt to be supportive and helpful to families with a gender non-conforming child is information about gender diversity, about the idea that gender does not conform to a clear binary, and that there are sources of information for gender diverse children and young people (Riley et al., 2013). This frees parents up from the sense of having to be the primary source of knowledge about something they may feel they do not know much about.

In practical terms, there are numerous strategies and interventions that could be useful for applied social psychologists seeking to work well in relation to TGD children and young people. These might include the following points, which we conceptualise in relation to, first, developing awareness, and then taking action:

- Being aware of spaces where TGD young people engage with one another (e.g., online, at some schools, and some youth groups). Facilitating the development and maintenance of these spaces when possible, and ensuring that these spaces are genuinely accessible to a diverse range of TGD youth, not only a privileged few.
- Exploring issues within TGD communities and concerning various aspects of TGD lives, and not assuming that TGD people are homogenous and all hold similar views.
- Noticing who could be a strategic ally in the production of TGD youth-friendly spaces, e.g., some parents, some school staff, some decision-makers, and some health professionals. Facilitating an active shift towards ally development.
- Becoming sensitive to the workings and signs of transphobic and cis-genderist understandings, e.g., the building of spaces designed only for binary genders such as toilets and changing rooms; the development of written forms that force people to tick binary sex/gender boxes; ways of addressing people that assume binary gender that can be read from bodily cues in a straightforward way.
- Working with intersectionality and decolonisation in ways that do not treat this as an academic exercise. Learning, reflecting on, and understanding the patterns and effects of oppression, taking action with others (clients, colleagues etc), and most importantly – listening instead of speaking over.
- Intervening appropriately when you see the workings of transphobic and cis-genderist thinking in action. This means creatively developing intervention strategies that raise awareness, challenging current practices and assumptions, and providing alternatives.
- Helping friends, colleagues, and others to become sensitive to the unintended exclusionary effects of these day-to-day events and structures. Developing an awareness of the differential ways that these effects impact on TGD youth according to their socio-economic circumstances, living situation, colonisation, racialisation, education, and ability.
- Developing one's ability to notice contexts and situations where (some or all) TGD young people are likely to feel silenced, marginalised, excluded, and stigmatised, e.g., some families, schools, cultural contexts, religious groups, and sports groups. Working with leaders and others who are

strategically positioned to shift the exclusionary culture of that space.

- Transforming top-down and adultist programmes. Using participatory coalition work and public-awareness campaigns to help raise awareness of TGD at the community level.
- Familiarising oneself with research-based and TGD-youth-based understandings about the lived realities of TGD young people. Talking in a sensitive and informed way about the issues faced by TGD youth, and raising awareness of TGD youth perspectives, i.e., perspectives that challenge gender-normative assumptions and, therefore, counter the minoritisation of TGD youth.
- Becoming adept at identifying and bringing together people who are sensitive to these issues. Bringing together people who can think well about what kinds of changes are needed to promote well-being for a diverse range of TGD youth across a variety of contexts, e.g., in a local community, in an institutional context, in social and familial contexts.
- Mobilising services that address the serious family, social, emotional, educational, and economic conditions that impair TGD young peoples' safety, development, and future well-being.

Notes

1 The term 'Eurocentric' is used here to refer to viewpoints that emanate from dominant European, Anglo-American, Anglophone, or so-called 'Western' contexts.

2 Cis-genderism is the assumption that everyone fits unproblematically within a binary gender system and does not go through any gender transition in the course of their lives. Cis-genderist assumptions render TGD identities invisible and invalidate TGD experience.

3 Greytak and colleagues acknowledge this issue in their analysis of the extent to which school-based GLBT support initiatives actually do work to support transgender youth (Greytak et al., 2013).

REFERENCES

Abustan, P. (2015). Recovering and reclaiming queer and trans indigenous and Mestiza Pilipinx identities. *Journal of Mestizo and Indigenous Voices*, *1*(1), 1–10.

Adams, M., Bell, L., & Griffin, P. (Eds.). (2007). *Teaching for diversity and social justice* (2nd edn.). New York, NY: Routledge.

Brooks, L. (2008). Digging at the roots: Locating an ethical, native criticism. In C. S. Womack, D. H. Justice, & C. B. Teuton (Eds.), *Reasoning together: The native critics collective* (pp. 234–264). Norman: University of Oklahoma Press.

Carastathis, A. (2014). The concept of intersectionality in feminist theory. *Philosophy Compass*, *9*(5), 304–314.

Choi, S. K., Wilson, B. D. M., Shelton, J., & Gates, G. (2015). *The needs and experiences of lesbian, gay, bisexual, transgender, and questioning youth experiencing homelessness*. Los Angeles: The Williams Institute with the True Colors Fund.

Clark, T. C., Lucassen, M. F. G., Bullen, P., Denny, S. J., Fleming, T. M., Robinson, E. M., & Rossen, F. V. (2014). The health and well-being of transgender high school students: Results from the New Zealand Adolescent Health Survey (Youth'12). *Journal of Adolescent Health*, *55*(1), 93–99.

Cohen-Kettenis, P. T., Delemarre-van De Waal, H. A., & Gooren, L. J. G. (2008). The treatment of adolescent transsexuals: Changing insights. *Journal of Sexual Medicine.*, *5*(8), 1892–1897.

Crenshaw, K. W. (1989). Demarginalizing the intersection of race and sex: A black feminist critique of antidiscrimination doctrine, feminist theory and antiracist politics. *University of Chicago Legal Forum*, 139–167.

Crossley, S. (2015). Come out come out wherever you are: A content analysis of homeless transgender youth in social service literature. *PSU McNair Scholars Online Journal*, *9*(1), 4.

Denetdale, J. (2006). Chairmen, presidents, and princesses: The Navajo Nation, gender, and the politics of tradition. *Wicazo Sa Review*, *21*(1), 9–28.

Driskill, Q.-L. (2004). Stolen from our bodies: First nations two-spirits/queers and the journey to a sovereign erotic. *Studies in American Indian Literatures*, *16*(2), 50–64.

Driskill, Q.-L., Finley, C., Gilley, B. J., & Morgensen, S. L. (2011). *Queer indigenous studies: Critical interventions in theory, politics, and literature*. Tucson: University of Arizona Press.

Duke, T. S. (2011). Lesbian, gay, bisexual, and transgender youth with disabilities: A meta-synthesis. *Journal of LGBT Youth*, *8*(1), 1–52.

Ehrensaft, D. (2011a). Boys will be girls, girls will be boys: Children affect parents as parents affect children in gender nonconformity. *Psychoanalytic Psychology*, *28*(4), 528–548.

Ehrensaft, D. (2011b). *Gender born, gender made: Raising healthy gender-nonconforming children*. New York: The Experiment.

Finley, C. (2011). Decolonizing the queer native body (and recovering the native bull-dyke): Bringing 'sexy back' and out of native studies' closet. In Q.-L. Driskill, C. Finley, B. J. Gilley, & S. L. Morgensen (Eds.), *Queer indigenous studies: Critical interventions in theory, politics and literature* (pp. 31–42). Tucson: University of Arizona Press.

Fletcher, T. (2013). Trans sex workers: Negotiating sex, gender, and non-normative desire. In E. van der Meulen, E. M. Durisin, & V. Love (Eds.), *Selling sex: Experience, advocacy, and research on sex work in Canada* (pp. 65–73). Vancouver, Canada: UBC Press.

Goulet, J.-G. A. (1996). The 'Berdache'/two-spirit: A comparison of anthropological and native constructions of gendered identities among the Northern Athapaskans. *The Journal of the Royal Anthropological Institute*, *2*(4), 683–701.

Greytak, E. A., Kosciw, J. G., & Boesen, M. J. (2013). Putting the 'T' in 'resource': The benefits of LGBT-related school resources for transgender youth. *Journal of LGBT Youth*, *10*(1–2), 45–63.

Groot., S., & Hodgetts, D. (2012). Homemaking on the streets and beyond. *Community, Work & Family*, *15*(3), 255–271.

Groot., S., & Hodgetts, D. (2015). The infamy of begging: A case-based approach to street homelessness and radical commerce. *Qualitative Research in Psychology*, *12*(4), 349–366.

Groot, S., & Peters, E. (2016). Indigenous homelessness: New Zealand context. In J. Christensen & E. Peters (Eds.), *Indigenous homelessness: Perspectives from Canada, Australia and New Zealand*. Winnipeg, Canada: University of Manitoba.

Groot., S., Hodgetts, D., Nikora., L. W., & Leggat-Cook., C. (2011). A Māori homeless woman. *Ethnography*, *12*(3), 375–397.

Groot, S., Hodgetts, D., Nikora, L. W., Rua, M., & Groot, D. (2015). Pani me te rawakore: Home-making and Maori homelessness. In K. M., M. McPherson, & L. Manuatu (Eds.), *Home: Here to Stay*. Auckland: AlterNative.

Groot, S., Rua, M., Masters-Awatere, B., Dudgeon, P., & Garvey, D. (2012). Ignored no longer: Emerging indigenous researchers on indigenous psychologies. *Australian Community Psychologist*, *24*(1), 5–10.

Grossman, A. H., & D'Augelli, A. R. (2007). Transgender youth and life-threatening behaviors. *Suicide and Life-threatening Behavior*, *37*(5), 527–537.

Haas, A., Rodgers, P., & Herman, J. (2014). *Suicide attempts among transgender and gender non-conforming adults: Finding of the National Transgender Discrimination Survey*. Retrieved from https://williamsinstitute.law.ucla.edu/wp-content/uploads/AFSP-Williams-Suicide-Report-Final.pdf.

Harper, A., & Singh, A. (2014). Supporting ally development with families of trans and gender nonconforming (TGNC) youth. *Journal of LGBT Issues in Counseling*, *8*(4), 376–388.

Henriksen, C. (2014). *Hva kan blogger lære psykologer om kjønnsidentitetstematikk? [What can bloggers teach psychologists about gender diversity?]*. (Unpublished thesis, Clinical Psychology Degree Programme), University of Oslo, Norway.

Hodgetts, D. (2010). *Social psychology and everyday life*. Basingstoke; New York: Palgrave Macmillan.

Hodgetts, D., Stolte, O., & Groot, S. (2014). Homelessness, Overview. *Encyclopedia of Critical Psychology* (pp. 883–888). New York: Springer.

Health Research Council (HRC) (2008). *To be who I am: Report of the inquiry into discrimination experienced by transgender people = Kia noho au ki tōku anō ao: he pūrongo mō te uiuitanga mō aukatitanga e pāngia ana e ngā tāngata whakawhitiira*. Retrieved from https://www.hrc.co.nz/files/5714/2378/7661/15-Jan-2008_14-56-48_HRC_Transgender_FINAL.pdf. Auckland, New Zealand.

Hunt, S. (2013). Decolonizing sex work: Developing an intersectional indigenous approach. In E. van der Meulen, E. M. Durisin, & V. Love (Eds.), *Selling sex: Experience, advocacy, and research on sex work in Canada* (pp. 82–100). Vancouver, Canada: UBC Press.

Jones, T., & Hillier, L. (2013). Comparing trans-spectrum and same-sex-attracted youth in Australia: Increased risks, increased activisms. *Journal of LGBT Youth*, *10*(4), 287–307.

Jones, T., Smith, E., Ward, R., Dixon, J., Hillier, L., & Mitchell, A. (2016). School experiences of transgender and gender diverse students in Australia. *Sex Education*, *16*(2), 156–171.

Jordan, S. R. (2009). Un/convention(al) refugees: contextualizing the accounts of refugees facing homophobic or transphobic persecution. *Refuge*, *26*(2), 165.

Kidd, S. A., & Davidson, L. (2007). 'You have to adapt because you have no other choice': The stories of strength and resilience of 208 homeless youth in New York City and Toronto. *Journal of Community Psychology*, *35*(2), 219–238.

Lennon, E., & Mistler, B. J. (2014). Cisgenderism. *TSQ: Transgender Studies Quarterly*, *1*(1–2), 63–64.

Lev, A. I. (2004). *Transgender emergence: Therapeutic guidelines for working with gender variant people and their families*. New York: Haworth.

Lugones, M. (2007). Heterosexualism and the colonial/modern gender system. *Hypatia*, *22*(1), 186–209.

McDermott, E., & Roen, K. (2016). *Queer youth, suicide and self-harm: Troubled subjects, troubling norms*: Basingstoke, UK: Palgrave Macmillan.

McMillan, N. (2009). *Long-term settlement of refugees: An annotated bibliography of New Zealand and international literature*. Wellington, New Zealand: Department of Labour.

Menvielle, E., & Hill, D. B. (2010). An affirmative intervention for families with gender-variant children: A process evaluation. *Journal of Gay and Lesbian Mental Health*, *15*(1), 94–123.

Menvielle, E., & Tuerk, C. (2002). A support group for parents of gender non-conforming boys. *Journal of the American Academy of Child and Adolescent Psychiatry*, *41*, 1010–1013.

Metro. (2016). *Youth Chances: Integrated Report*. Retrieved from London, UK: https://www.metrocentreonline.org/sites/default/files/2017-04/National%20Youth%20Chances%20Intergrated%20Report%202016.pdf.

Mitchell, D., & Heynen, N. (2009). The geography of survival and the right to the city: speculations on surveillance, legal innovation, and the criminalization of intervention. *Urban Geography*, *30*(6), 611–632.

Möller, B., Schreier, H., Li, A., & Romer, G. (2009). Gender identity disorder in children and adolescents. *Current Problems in Pediatric and Adolescent Health Care*, *39*(5), 117–143.

Nash, J. C. (2008). Re-thinking intersectionality. *Feminist Review*, *89*(1), 1–15.

Nodin, N., Peel, E., Tyler, A., & Rivers, I. (2015). *The RaRE research report: Risk and resilience explored*. London: PACE.

Prilleltensky, I., & Nelson, G. (2002). *Doing psychology critically: Making a difference in diverse settings*. London: Palgrave Macmillan.

Prince, L. (2008). Resilience in African American women formerly involved in street prostitution. *The ABNF Journal*, *19*(1), 31–36.

Pyne, J. (2014). Gender independent kids: A paradigm shift in approaches to gender non-conforming children. *Canadian Journal of Human Sexuality*, *23*(1), 1–8.

Pyne, J. (2016). "Parenting is not a job … it's a relationship": Recognition and relational knowledge among parents of Gender non-conforming children. *Journal of Progressive Human Services*, *27*(1), 21–48.

Rahilly, E. (2013). The parental transition: A study of parents of gender non-conforming children. In F. Green & M. Friedman (Eds.), *Chasing rainbows: Exploring gender fluid parenting practices* (pp. 170–182). Toronto: New Demeter Press.

Raun, T. (2012). *Out online: Trans self-representation and community building on YouTube*. (PhD thesis). Roskilde University, Denmark. Retrieved from http://rudar.ruc.dk//bitstream/1800/10666/1/Tobias_final_with_front_page_pfd.pdf

Reed-Victor, E., & Stronge, J. (2002). Homeless students and resilience: Staff perspectives on individual and environmental factors. *Journal of Children and Poverty*, *8*(2), 159–173.

Riley, E. A., Sitharthan, G., Clemson, L., & Diamond, M. (2011). The needs of gender-variant children and their parents according to health professionals. *International Journal of Transgenderism*, *13*(2), 54–63.

Riley, E. A., Sitharthan, G., Clemson, L., & Diamond, M. (2013). Recognising the needs of gender-variant children and their parents. *Sex Education*, *13*(6), 644–659.

Robinson, K. H., Bansel, P., Denson, N., Ovenden, G., & Davies, C. (2014). *Growing up queer: Issues facing young Australians who are gender variant and sexuality diverse*. Melbourne: Young and Well Cooperative Research Centre.

Roen, K. (2016). The body as a site of gender-related distress: Ethical considerations for gender variant youth in clinical settings. *Journal of Homosexuality: Mapping Queer Bioethics*, *63*(3), 306–322.

Shelton, J. (2015). Transgender youth homelessness: Understanding programmatic barriers through the lens of cisgenderism. *Children and Youth Services Review*, *59*, 10–18.

Singh, A. A., Meng, S. E., & Hansen, A. W. (2014). 'I am my own gender': resilience strategies of trans youth. *Journal of Counseling and Development*, *92*(2), 208.

Smith, A. (2011). Queer theory and Native studies: The heteronormativity of settler colonialism. In Q.-L. Driskill, C. Finley, B. J. Gilley, & S. L. Morgensen (Eds.), *Queer indigenous studies: Critical interventions in theory, politics, and literature* (pp. 43–65). Tucson: University of Arizona Press.

Sonn, C. C. (2006). Multiple belongings? Reflection on the challenges of reconstructing Apartheid-imposed identities in Australia after immigration. In G. Stevens, V. Franchi, & T. Swart (Eds.), *A race against time: Psychology and challenges to deracialisation in South Africa* (pp. 335–348). Pretoria, South Africa: University of South Africa.

Te Awekotuku., N. (2005). Reka Anō: Same sex lust and loving in the Ancient Māori world. In A. J. Laurie & L. Evans (Eds.), *Outlines: Lesbian and gay histories of Aotearoa* (pp. 6–9). Wellington: Lesbian & Gay Archives of New Zealand.

Trussell, D. E., & Mair, H. (2010). Seeking judgment free spaces: poverty, leisure, and social inclusion. *Journal of Leisure Research*, *42*(4), 513.

Wren, B. (2000). Early physical intervention for young people with atypical gender identity development. *Clinical Child Psychology and Psychiatry*, *5*(2), 220–231.

Yu, V. (2010). Shelter and transitional housing for transgender youth. *Journal of Gay & Lesbian Mental Health*, *14*(4), 340–345.

6

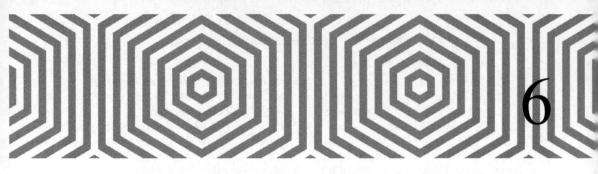

The Social Psychology of Gender and Sexuality: Theory, Application, Transformation

Katherine Johnson and Antar Martínez-Guzmán

SETTING THE SCENE: THE PLACE OF GENDER AND SEXUALITY IN SOCIAL PSYCHOLOGY

Gender and sexuality are often periphery topics within social psychology. This is particularly so in programmes that lean on experimental approaches to understand the complexity of social behaviour without questioning why that knowledge is often founded on the notion of a psychological subject who is white and male. Yet, attention to gender and sexuality issues has enriched social psychology beyond the immediate topic in hand by highlighting the dominance of androcentric and heterosexist knowledge within the discipline more broadly. The influence of sexuality and gender research has also been under-estimated as a driving force in recent theoretical transformations. These have reimagined social psychology as *critical social psychology*, *psychosocial studies,* or *community psychology*, particularly in the UK. Even here, gender and sexuality topics remain on the margins, but feminist and queer scholarship have shaped the ethos of these novel forms of social psychology with their shared use of transdisciplinary critical theory, qualitative and participatory methods to focus on issues of power, experience and social change. Within this scholarship, mainstream psychology has often been an object of critique for its role in positioning women as intellectually and morally inferior to men (e.g. Ussher, 1991) and for medicalization and pathologizing lesbian, gay, bisexual and gender non-conforming people (e.g. Foucault, 1979/1990; Sedgwick, 1991). A detailed engagement with the complexity of the rich theoretical landscape that supports critical social psychology, psychosocial studies and community psychology is beyond the remit of this chapter (see Johnson, 2015 for an extended account applied to sexuality). Instead, we summarize three key theoretical shifts that have influenced the establishment of these novel forms of social psychology over the last 50 years and illustrate them through an applied focus on gender and sexuality research.

The first half of the chapter is organized thematically (i) 'the turn to language, identity and the problem of knowledge', (ii) 'affect, embodiment & subjectivity' and (iii) 'community, social justice, participation'. Each section explores the place of gender and sexuality research in relation to theoretical development and application, offers key empirical examples and, where appropriate, summarizes the methodological innovations aligned with each theme. In the second half of the chapter, we present detailed reflections on two of our current research projects with (i) trans youth in Brighton, UK, and (ii) activist women in Colima, Mexico. We do this by illustrating how the three themes have become increasingly entwined in the production of novel forms of applied social psychological research with marginalized groups to effect social change. This approach is practiced internationally and is variously organized under titles such as community/participatory psychology or psychosocial interventions in order to distinguish it from the experimental approach that dominates much of social psychology and the more theoretical strands of critical social psychology.

In the concluding section, we argue that gender and sexuality should not be seen as minority topics within applied social psychology. Engagements with gender and sexuality related topics have had a profound role in reshaping social psychology. Current interests in the intersection of gender and sexuality with other forms of marginalization, such as racialization and post/de-colonialism, illustrate the potential for further development of applied social psychology understandings of knowledge systems and concepts from beyond the global north in order to challenge the 'whiteness' of social psychological curricula and help reconfigure power relations that constrain gender and sexuality in both the global north and south.

KEY HISTORICAL DEVELOPMENTS

The Turn to Language, Identity and the Problem of Knowledge

The emergence of critical social psychology is commonly associated with the 'linguistic turn' that developed during the early twentieth century and had a significant impact across the social sciences and humanities, particularly in European contexts. The 'turn to language' was implicated in the so-called 'crisis in social psychology' that was widely debated in the UK (Parker, 1989). This unsettled the epistemological foundations of a discipline that had aligned itself with positivism and experimental methods in order to predict social behaviour but was questioned for its limited effect in creating a more just world. The 'turn' can be better defined as a vast and heterogeneous movement that shared a common ground of acknowledging the centrality of language for understanding both social reality and the nature of the knowledge produced about it. In terms of rethinking concepts of gender and sexuality, it offered a stark contrast to the well-established traditions that understood gender as a natural and universal fact, or (homo)sexuality as a perverse, but potentially biologically rooted, anomaly. Instead, it proposed an epistemological shift away from positivistic tenets that thought of language as a transparent means of representation, to one that recognized the active and constructive role of language and social meaning in defining gender relations and sexual practices. This turn has been at the heart of subsequent approaches described in the UK as critical social psychology or psychosocial studies and, to a lesser extent, community psychology, which often takes language at face value.

Theoretical discussions and empirical research about sexuality and gender issues have been a crucial, and often overlooked, drive for articulating and invigorating this broad social constructionist perspective in human and social sciences. Feminist discussions about gender, for instance, have put into the spotlight the social and cultural nature of identities, roles and lived experiences for men and women (de Beauvoir, 1953). Similarly, authors like Michel Foucault (1979/1990) in France and Mary McIntosh (1968) in the UK produced early key texts that significantly contributed to the introduction of a discursive and constructionist standpoint. In the same line, the US-based feminist philosopher Judith Butler's (1990) conception of gender performativity had a major impact on social and feminist psychological perspectives, emphasizing the centrality of discourse for the production of identities, bodies and the politics that regulate and disrupt them. In contrast to mainstream psychological approaches, gender and sexuality were no longer understood as individual traits or personal attributes, but rather as social categories and discursive constructs located in specific historical scenarios or emerging in social interaction. This turn, therefore, significantly challenged experimental social psychological accounts of gender and sexuality that rooted gender identity or sexual orientation in biological factors (i.e. hormones, genes, brain anatomy) and/or normative determinants of psychological development. Within the broad field of social constructionist perspectives, we sketch out two general theoretical and methodological trends through which gender and sexuality issues are approached, 'micro-social interaction' and 'poststructuralism'. Although there is substantial variability in actual research practices, these two lines heuristically encompass a wide-ranging landscape in applied critical social psychological research.

Micro-social interactionism

This approach focuses on the comprehension and analysis of micro-social practices of interaction in everyday life. It is influenced by social theories and methodological innovations such as ethnomethodology, symbolic interactionism and conversation analysis. It pays attention to everyday interactions and the ordinary practices and activities through which men and women, homosexual or heterosexual subjects, live their lives and find their place in any given social context ruled by specific cultural norms. Here, social psychology overlaps with key sociological reference points, particularly those of Garfinkel's (1967) ethnomethodology that seeks to understand social action and patterns of social behaviour and Kessler and McKenna's (1978) subsequent study of transgenderism within this ethnomethodological framework. Within these approaches, gender expression and sexual practices are understood as emerging from communicative processes and interpersonal interaction in relation to the broader cultural norms that regulate them. Within critical social psychology, a new sub-field of Discursive Psychology emerged in the 1980s that was influenced by, and aligned with, this shift towards the analysis of micro-social interactionism and generated two widely accepted qualitative methods: discourse analysis (e.g. Potter and Wetherell, 1987) and conversation analysis (e.g. Atkinson and Heritage, 1984).

This focus on analyzing micro-social practices asks us to reconsider gender identities and the power relations between them as complex productions developed as a result of processes of social interaction, including elaboration of positions in discourse, labelling and dynamic self-identification (Speer and Stokoe, 2011). Rejecting that gender and sexuality can be reduced to essential biological or psychological cores, they look for the ways in which social meaning of sexuality and gender is achieved by specific patterns of communication and social exchanges. From this perspective, to understand gender and sexual identities and to account for sexual practices and relations, it is necessary to attend to the micro-processes of human interaction through which meaning is negotiated and co-created in ordinary scenarios.

An example of the application of this approach can be found in, '*Negotiating hegemonic masculinity: Imaginary positions and psycho-discursive practices*' (Wetherell and Edley, 1999). Here, the authors argue that the traditional ways of conceptualizing masculinity are insufficient as they offer a 'vague and imprecise account of the social psychological reproduction of male identities' (Wetherell and Edley, 1999: 335). They claim that concepts such as 'hegemonic masculinity' (Connell, 1987) are 'not sufficient for understanding the nitty gritty of negotiating masculine identities and men's identity strategies' (Wetherell and Edley, 1999: 336). In contrast, against the grain of mainstream psychological assumptions about innate masculine traits, they outline a critical social psychology of masculinity that understands 'how men position themselves as gendered beings'. This approach focuses on analyzing discursive strategies used by men to negotiate membership of gender categories and to explore how masculinity models work in practice and shows variation across specific social contexts. The emphasis is placed on how the concept of masculinity is negotiated in everyday interactions and how 'men take on the social identity of 'being a man' as they talk' (Wetherell and Edley, 1999: 336). They conclude that 'identification is a matter of *procedures in action* through which men live/talk/do masculinity' (Wetherell and Edley, 1999: 353). In this sense, the work is aligned with a strongly empirical tradition where issues of self-description and identification are accomplished in talk, and where the aim is to identify the complex and multiple discursive strategies mobilized in specific contexts in order to accomplish a variety of identity positions.

Another important account in this line is Susan Speer's (2005) *Gender Talk: Feminism, Discourse and Conversation Analysis*. Speer pays close attention to 'sex differences' in language use (i.e. how men and women talk differently) but also to the ways in which discourse produces specific gender identities and power dynamics between them. She argues that the gendered nature of social relations can be traced through specific language strategies used by speakers, and the gender and sexuality assumptions that are embedded within them. In order to do so, she endorses an agenda of 'a fine-grained, data-driven form of analysis' which draws on insights from the sociological perspective of conversation analysis and discursive psychology. She suggests this offers a means for 'advancing an understanding of how gender, sexuality and prejudice are constituted in talk, and grounds our feminist politics'. This is considered to be an approach that works at 'ground level' or from 'the bottom up' as it looks to interaction and 'participants' orientations' to show how discourse is gendered, rethinking, for example, 'cognitive-psychological' understandings of gender prejudices and heterosexism. This methodological orientation is considered helpful for reorganizing the relationship 'between the 'macro-social' structural realm of gender norms' and 'the cognitive-psychological realm of thoughts, feelings, identity, and prejudicial attitudes and beliefs' (Speer, 2005: 12). For Speer, the 'external' social structural context (the macro realm) and the 'internal' psychological context (the cognitive realm) 'are constituted, oriented to, and reproduced in the 'micro-interactional', discursive realm' (Speer, 2005: 12). Thus, *Gender Talk* is an important example of the application of conversation analysis and discursive psychology to feminist examinations of the power asymmetries between men and women and the constitution of gender identities categories, masculinity and femininity.

Poststructuralism

The second constructionist perspective in critical social psychology is associated with a historical and genealogical approach, influenced by a range of poststructuralist thought (e.g. Foucault 1969; 1979/1990) and related forms of critical theory, such as feminist performative theory (Butler 1990; 1993), psychoanalysis (Lacan, 1988) and philosophy (e.g. Derrida 1976). This perspective also states that sexual and gender identities are not uniform or standard phenomena, and that their meanings and social roles have varied throughout history. An important focus has been on the historical analysis of the shifting meanings of gendered bodies and sexualities, as a result of mechanisms of reality production that not only oppress and regulate but also, and especially, incite forms of resistance. The work of Michel Foucault (e.g. 1979) is a particular influence here in terms of a constructionist perspective that looks into the interplay between gender/sexuality and scientific truth, as well as other authoritative discourses. This reading proposes an understanding of homosexuality and other non-normative gender and sexual categories as manufactured, or brought into being, by psychological-legal apparatus that both shape and regulate them in specific medical and political regimes. Following Butler (1990; 1993), it also seeks to illustrate the systematic process of naturalization of gender identities and roles through citation practices and highlights the power differential involved in this naturalization. In this sense, this perspective seeks to explain the origin, the social meaning and continually changing forms of sexual and gendered subjects, as well as the power relations that arise among them.

It should be noted that not all feminists (e.g. Jackson and Scott, 2010) have been convinced by a Foucauldian inspired social constructionist approach because of its limited engagement with gender oppression and perceived lack of sensitivity to issues of agency. Yet, it is not always possible to disentangle the theoretical roots of either a social interactionist or Foucauldian inspired poststructuralist approach. For example, Celia Kitzinger is a well-known proponent of social interactionist and discursive approaches to sexuality (e.g. Frith & Kitzinger, 2001) but her ground breaking text within social psychology, *The Social Construction of Lesbianism* (Kitzinger, 1987) can also be interpreted as a Foucauldian-inspired poststructuralist analysis of lesbian sexuality. Here, Kitzinger argues that a new liberal humanist discourse about lesbianism emerged after homosexuality was removed from the *Diagnostic and Statistical Manual of Mental Disorders* (DSM). Despite its liberationist potential, she argues that the shift from pathologization towards a 'gay-affirmative' perspective in psychology also acted to oppress lesbians by developing a depoliticized, individualistic framework that celebrated lesbianism as a 'sexual preference', rather than as a political stance against the 'patriarchal oppression of women' (Kitzinger, 1987: vii). While Kitzinger's argument overlooks the role of desire between women, it offers a rare example of research focused on lesbianism and illustrates how discourses that emerge from psychology become embedded within people's personal narratives as a way of self-explanation.

Another example of the poststructuralist approach can be found in Jane Ussher's (2006) *Managing the Monstrous Feminine*, which sets out an analysis of 'discursive practices' involved in the construction and regulation of the female body. Specifically, she examines how scientific (i.e. medicine, psychology), legal and popular culture (i.e. mythology, literature and film) discourses combine to produce representations of femininity and the reproductive body that position women as dangerous, weak and sick. Discussing cases of discursive constructions around the 'fecund body' and its markers (e.g. menstruation, pregnancy and menopause), Ussher argues that these discourses produce an 'idealised femininity as embodied pathology' and, more widely, function to monitor differences and asymmetries between men and women. Representations analyzed by the author 'reflect and construct the regimes of truth within which women become "woman"' (Ussher, 2006: 20). Following a constructionist perspective that emphasizes discursive practices, Ussher argues there is no 'natural' female body that prefigures discourse, but rather femininity is enacted within a regulated discursive framework that naturalizes the reproductive female body. In this process, science has played an important role in developing the pathologizing disciplinary practices which position the reproductive body as an object of surveillance and regulation 'central to the performance of normative femininity' (Ussher, 2006: 20).

With a clear Foucauldian influence, Ussher argues that medical and psychological experts and institutions become key elements in positioning woman as objects of treatment and intervention aimed at controlling and reducing the threatening femininity. Ussher's work also pays attention to 'women's narratives of resistance', exemplifying how this constructionist perspective frequently takes into account marginalized groups and subjects' discourses, and explores how these problematize meta-narratives and hegemonic discourses on gender and sexuality. Through interviews in different English-speaking countries, she aims to understand 'the complex and sometimes seemingly contradictory ways in which contemporary Western women simultaneously accept and resist the discourses and practices associated with the fecund body' (Ussher, 2006: 14). The author suggests surveillance strategies and pathologizing discourses can be challenged, disturbed or undermined by women's particular lives and narratives, through developing a 'different language' to account for experience. At both the individual and collective level, women can, and have, engaged in processes of resistance, negotiation and transformation of forms of knowledge that position 'the fecund body as site of danger, disease, or debilitation'. They do this by creating new frameworks where women are 'active questioning subjects, rather than passive objects or simple projections of man's unconscious fears and fantasies' (Ussher, 2006: 154).

These heterogeneous lines of work share some common features as part of a wider shift towards the analysis of discourses, social meaning and representation practices in the study of gender and sexuality. Whether emphasizing more micro-linguistic practices of interaction or wider cultural/ideological discourses and practices, they argue for an anti-essentialist conception of the gendered subject and their sexual experiences, as well as for the contingency of sexual categories and gender identities, and the material and political effects they have on the social world. As a consequence, in contrast to experimental social psychological approaches, critical social psychology demonstrates that gender and sexuality can be understood through models of complex variation; draws attention to the place of gender norms in regulating conduct and desires; and assists in developing applied interventions to challenging stigma and pathologization of non-normative gender and sexualities in everyday language.

Embodiment, Subjectivity, Affect

Even as the 'turn to language' was emerging, another shift in emphasis began taking place in critical social psychology. In response to the increasingly familiar worry that more theoretical strands of critical social psychology were failing to sufficiently engage with the *materiality* of the body and people's lived experiences, some psychologists began to reach for new theories, methods and concepts to explore social psychological phenomena. In fits and starts, over subsequent years, another wave of research emerged that drew attention to 'the body' beyond its relationship to discourse and representation. Concepts such as 'embodied subjectivity', 'embodiment' and, most recently, 'affect' were used to rethink the psychological subject in relation to lived experiences, feelings and the embodied process of being and becoming. Alan Radley (1991: 4) was one of the first to ask what social psychology has contributed to understandings of the body, lamenting that 'the topic appears to be entirely peripheral to the discipline's main aims' while suggesting that this can perhaps be explained at a superficial level by the opposition between 'the social' and 'the biological'.

In a review of the history of social psychology, he argued that engagements with the body prior to 1990 could only be found at the margins of the discipline in topics such as gender differences or psychoanalysis – both of which have since had significant influence in the subsequent theoretical turns to embodiment and affect. He argued that 'the body has [only] made an appearance at the fringe of social psychology, within studies of individuals who are, in some important way, marginalized in the social world' (Radley, 1991: 16). This is an important, and often overlooked, point. The work on the disciplinary margins in topics related to gender and sexuality inequality and oppression, produced by feminist and queer scholars, has had a major influence in reshaping key theoretical trajectories in psychology, but the importance of feminist and queer thought is often erased from generalist social psychological accounts of theoretical development (e.g. Brown and Stenner, 2009). In this section, we outline two subsequent theoretical shifts in critical social psychology, the turn to embodiment and the turn to affect, drawing specific attention to their influence in examples of applied social psychological research in topics related to gender and sexuality.

Embodiment

The seminal text *Changing the Subject* (Henriques et al., 1984) drew attention to the discursive and cultural conditions of subjectivity, or how we experience ourselves. Two subsequent social psychological texts, both published in 1998, stand out as setting the scene for what became known as the 'turn to embodiment', extending attention to how this experience was lived. The first, *Reconstructing the Psychological Subject: Bodies, Practices, Technologies* (Bayer and Shotter, 1998) noted that within critical social psychology analyses of discursive practices entailed an overemphasis on 'linguistic, conversational and literary devices' (Bayer and Shotter, 1998: 4) which, rather than offering something new, often ended up reinstating many of the binaries it aimed to undo. This criticism was seen as crucial to avoid a potential dead end in social psychological research. It ushered in a series of debates about subjectivity, matter and the body, topics that were widely represented in the second seminal text The Body and Psychology (Stam, 1998). Here, rather than the body being conceived as an object of social constructionism, as epitomized in phrases such as 'written on the body', scholars sought new theories, concepts and methods to explore experience in ways that might avoid dualistic separations between mind/body and nature/culture. At the heart of this shift to the question of embodiment was an epistemological dilemma about the relationship between biology and social, nature and culture. Feminists have long been suspicious about any recourse to an ontological grounding of gender differences in biology, evolution and neuroscience, the approach that dominates much experimental social psychology. Instead, feminist perspectives favoured understanding biology and bodily meanings in relation to cultural inscriptions, rather than distinct from, and/or as a precursor to, culture meaning (e.g. Fausto-Sterling, 1992). The turn to embodiment within critical social psychology sought new ways of understanding the dynamic interaction between nature and culture, discourse and materiality.

As part of this process, a range of sources were drawn on, including feminism, actor-network theory, feminist science studies and phenomenology. Bayer and Shotter (1998: 13) set out a thesis to 'reenchant social constructionism' and 'do psychology differently' by extending the use of the term *practice* to include bodily and embodied elements that promote 'situated knowledges for social change'. The emphasis on 'practices of the body' is central to research produced in feminist psychology on gender-related topics. For example, the poststructuralist work already discussed by Jane Ussher (2006: 169) used a range of theoretical and methodological approaches to extend her analysis and highlight the relationship between discursive and material practices that regulate the female reproductive body. By analyzing cultural representations alongside interviews and memory work, she weaved a material-discursive narrative about how women resist normative accounts of the female body as abject and promote alternative visions of the reproductive life cycle as 'an opportunity to connect with feelings, with embodiment' and to reflect 'on the meanings associated with being a woman at different stages in life'. Nevertheless, in this analysis, materiality does not figure in an ontologically distinct manner and, as in much poststructuralist analyses (e.g. Butler, 1993), the body and materiality appear to collapse into discourse.

Affect

In the last decade, the use of terms such as embodiment have begun to be entwined with another new emphasis described as the so-called 'turn to affect'. In a detailed summary of a complex field that spreads across the humanities and social science, Margaret Wetherell (2012: 11) suggests that the topic based interest in affect 'leads to a focus on embodiment, to attempts to understand how people are moved, and what attracts them, to an emphasis on repetitions, pains and pleasures, feelings and memories'. She defines affect as 'embodied meaning making' and states her preference for the term *affective practices,* noting that the affective turn (particularly outside of social psychology) offers a paradigm shift 'away from discourse and disembodied talk and texts, towards more vitalist, 'posthuman' and process-based perspectives'. It could be interpreted from this that the turn to affect is not a turn to something new, but an extension of the dilemmas already identified in the turn to embodiment. Within critical social psychology, affect has introduced a greater focus onto the realm of feelings, bodily states and experiences (e.g. Cromby, 2015), as well as topics related to emotions (Greco and Stenner, 2008), that brings with it a greater attention to ontology – what it means to *be*.

For some (e.g. Johnson, 2015), drawing on Eve Sedgwick's work in queer studies has entailed moving away from an emphasis on epistemological critiques or 'paranoid readings' that are associated with deconstructive linguistic techniques of critical social psychology in order to accentuate experiences, feelings and community (for the purpose of social change). This shift is also emphasized within 'new materialist' feminist (e.g. Coole and Frost, 2010). Here, topics about the psychological realm, such as depression (e.g. Cvetkovich, 2012), have been analyzed in terms of their affective dynamics and political potential. A key figure in this contemporary field who is of particular interest to social and applied psychology is Elizabeth Wilson. Her work has long sat at the intersections of feminist theory and psychology, and she has authored articles and books on the relationship between cognitive science and embodiment (Wilson, 1998) and feminism and the neurological body (Wilson, 2004). In her recent publication, *Gut Feminism* (2015), she takes issue with some feminist's lack of engagement with biology, asking how feminists might make better use of biology and pharmaceutical data. Her approach is to ask 'How do biological data arrest, transform, or tax the theoretical foundations of feminist theory?' (Wilson, 2015: 3) rather than what can biology do for feminism? Wilson offers a radical departure from poststructuralist endeavours to address bodily practices that end up favouring talk and culture by taking 'biomedical data seriously but not literally, moving them outside the zones of interpretative comfort they usually occupy'. Her argument is not for a 'return to biology' at the expense of culture, rather for taking biology seriously when exploring the entanglements of body and brain that generate depressive states to understand 'the remarkable intra-actions of melancholic and pharmaceutical events in the human body' (2015: 13).

Wilson's approach is part of a movement within the humanities and social sciences to develop transdisciplinary engagements beyond dualist conceptions of mind/body, nature/culture, epistemology/ontology which have also reconfigured some approaches within social psychology. Here, the descriptor 'psychosocial' has grown in popularity, particularly among some critical social psychologists, associated with the 'turn to language' as a way of drawing attention to active attempts to suture together notions of psychic life and materiality, interior–exterior divisions (e.g. Frosh, 2010). It is this approach that is applied in Johnson's (2015) monograph, *Sexuality: A Psychosocial Manifesto*. In an overview of twentieth and twenty-first century theorizing of sexuality, Johnson weaves a narrative that seeks to stitch together conceptual impasses in the field of sexuality: between psychology and historicism, biology and social constructionism, identity and subjectivity. Yet the psychosocial is not just a theoretical approach to apply to the phenomena we seek to understand. It is also a call to 'reimagine the psychological through theoretical enrichment with other disciplinary interpretations and critiques' (Johnson, 2015: 177) and greater emphasis on the role of participatory research methods for the transformation of marginal lives. In this way, we see again how those engaged with research on gender and sexuality are contributing to the broader reshaping of applied social psychology by developing novel approaches to challenge inequalities and foster social justice.

Social Transformations: Participation, Community, Social Justice

This third shift within social psychological theory and practice can also be traced to recent developments which place greater emphasis on themes related to social justice and community participation. This movement, often referred to as community psychology, has been of particular importance in the Latin American context, where societies have suffered from extreme inequality and political oppression with significant consequences for the lives of individuals and groups (Montero, 2003). Influenced by ideas coming from pedagogy for liberation (Freire, 2000), liberation psychology (Martín-Baró, 1998), participatory action-research (Fals-Borda, 1984) and an emerging community psychology (e.g. Serrano-García et al, 1987), this movement sought to create a politically engaged and militant psychology, directed towards the needs of oppressed groups and marginalized realities of their particular context. At the same time, this movement sought to challenge the dominant approach of experimental social psychology, that originated mostly in English-speaking and developed countries, which emphasized the individual and understood the subject as primarily a passive entity of social action.

The relation between these 'liberation' and community approaches with the field of gender and sexuality has not been straightforward. As has been noted, feminist perspectives and critical studies in gender and sexuality share important epistemological and methodological concerns and orientations. For instance, both are interested in examining the implicit (social and political) assumptions of dominant paradigms in social psychology and pay special attention to the way cultural values and ideological assumptions shape knowledge production and disciplinary practices. They also share an interest in analyzing power relations and acknowledging social and historical context as a key element for understanding phenomena. Moreover, both have questioned the subject/object dichotomy in theory, methodology and application and have argued for an action-oriented and emancipatory position towards knowledge. Community psychology perspectives have found traction in global studies that focus on gender equality because of its attempt to address power differentials through action-orientated research approaches that work on social justice issues identified at a local level.

Within applied social psychology programmes, there is some evidence of feminists working on topics related to gender violence and community-based responses (e.g. Bostock et al., 2009). Nevertheless, to a good extent, community psychology and sexuality/gender studies have maintained rather distant positions. As Mulvey (1988) argues, despite their compatibility, community psychology and feminist psychology have not been significantly combined or integrated. Cosgrove and McHugh (2000) have suggested that liberation and community psychology often operate with an essentialist and non-problematized notion of gender that tends to homogenize and universalize some gender models. Therefore, while gender is usually understood as an 'independent variable' in community approaches, 'primary methods for understanding [gender] experience have been methods that support rather than challenge dichotomous, context-free conclusions' (Cosgrove and McHugh, 2000: 825). For this reason, critical social psychologists have been largely suspicious of community psychology perspectives which are seen to lack a deep theoretical engagement with issues of power.

In a systematic review of the content of North American community psychology journals, Wasco and Bond (2010) argue that gender is rarely a focal topic for community psychology and is instead included as a grouping value. Inclusion of a gendered analysis is often only within the realm of focusing on 'women's issues', particularly mental health and motherhood, and there is very little consideration of men and masculinities within community psychology approaches. They conclude that:

> Despite community psychology's value of social justice and our use of oppression theories to recognize systemic forces and structures that privilege agent identities (e.g., heterosexuals, men) over target identities (e.g., gay men/lesbians, women), our review did not find as much empirical work as we had anticipated related to gendered oppression. (Wasco and Bond, 2010: 26)

One explanation for this could be that the authors only included North American journals within their analysis, and if they had extended to European and Australasian publications there might have been a wider representation of the type of work found. However, even in publications such as the *Journal of Applied Social & Community Psychology*, a core focus on either gender or sexuality is rare, despite its greater overlap with critical social psychology approaches to issues of truth, power and social justice. There are, of course, some noted exceptions, including two special editions on feminism and community psychology published by the *American Journal of Community Psychology* (Bond et al, 2000a; 2000b), which included analyses of the relationship between feminism and community psychology (e.g. Angelique and Culley, 2000; Bond and Mulvey, 2000) and subsequent attempts to draw attention to women's concern through a feminist and community psychology lens (e.g. Angelique et al., 2001; Angelique & Culley, 2003; Gridley and Turner, 2010). It is also possible to identify a line of applied work interested in the connection between gender studies and feminist perspectives within action-oriented and 'activist' research in the field of psychology. For instance, Montenegro et al. (2011) have discussed the relation between globalization, exploitation and gender inequalities and its impact and confrontation in the Latin American context. Showing the bridges that have characterized the relationship between the feminist scholarship and activism, authors call attention to the importance of geopolitical contexts, as well as diverse axes of discrimination, to move forward a transnational feminism that productively articulates with psychology.

We are only aware of a very limited number of researchers working on LGBT issues within community psychology perspectives. Despite the potential for community psychology and action-based research being identified over 20 years ago for their radical potential for sexual minorities (Garnets,

1994), it has yet to be fully delivered. Based in the United States, Harper and Schneider (2003) have been at the forefront, identifying the impact of oppression on LGBT communities and the need for health and wellbeing to be addressed through a social change agenda. In the UK, Johnson (2007; 2011) has delivered a number of community psychology projects in collaboration with LGBT groups in the field of mental health, stigma and suicidal distress. These have taken a participatory-action research approach and produced outcomes that have changed policy and practice in the local area, leading to improved service provision and support options. Following on from this, we have developed a new partnership reflecting on the role of community psychology and action-based methods when working with groups who are as interested in changing how they are represented, as well as the oppression they face (Johnson and Martínez-Guzmán, 2013). Here, in contrast to the North American community psychology focus, we filter our action orientation method through a critical social psychology lens, drawing attention to issues of representation and affect in the process of creating lasting social transformation for marginalized groups.

CRITICAL APPLICATIONS: TWO EMPIRICAL EXAMPLES

In this section, we reflect on two applied social psychological projects we are currently working on, situating our reflections in relation to the development of critical social, psychosocial and community psychology perspectives on gender and sexuality. In the first example, Johnson outlines her research project *Trans Youth: what matters?* which is working with a trans youth group in the UK via a creative-arts based methodology to explore topics that participants define as important to them. In the second example, Martínez-Guzmán introduces a social change project that involves activist women in Mexico. This project draws on narrative interviews, photovoice and reflexive groups to consider the relationship between gender and social action. In our accounts, we provide a brief overview of the two studies and outline the methodological procedures before attempting to unpack the social psychological influences at play in the conception, interpretation and impact of our applied research. The purpose of our reflections is to illustrate how the three novel strands that have emerged in applied social psychology have begun to entwine in contemporary scholarship in the European and Latin American context. Our argument is not that one strand is preferable to another but rather the turn to language, embodiment and social action represent an enhancement of the strategies that critical social psychologists and psychosocial researchers use to inform and improve the life conditions of the people they work with. These brief introductions to our research also demonstrate the reach of these contemporary applied social psychological perspectives, from debates on identity construction, anti-normativity and community-belonging to feminist activism and gender equality in postcolonial contexts.

Trans Youth: What Matters?

Context and rationale

Critical social psychological research that seeks to understand transgender experience has a long, complex and contested history. Within this, we cannot fail to acknowledge the role of psychology in debates about whether gender diversity should be seen as a form of pathology as well as explanatory accounts for cross-gender identification as an unusual developmental pathway (see Johnson, 2017). Feminists have also shaped a range of understandings, from radical feminist critiques of trans women and children that rely on essentialist notions of gender (e.g. Brunskell-Evans and Moore, 2017; Jeffreys, 2014) to poststructuralist-informed critiques of the clinical management of gender and sexuality norms and limiting the proliferation and diversification of gender subjectivities (e.g. Butler, 2004; Roen, 2011).

In the context of childhood and adolescence, these debates become even more heightened. Concerns have been raised about the ethics of medical intervention when young people are still developing physically, emotionally and socially, and these are contrasted against the risk of not intervening when someone is exhibiting distress (Johnson, 2017). In the UK, there is a fractious public debate about the increasing numbers of young people, particularly natal females, identifying as trans, including trans non-binary, and whether schools, health professions and parents are equipped to properly support them. Within the limited literature there is a variety of accounts from clinical, parent and 'transcritical' perspectives (e.g. Brill and Kenney, 2016; Brunskell-Evans and Moore, 2017; Wren, 2014) but a notable gap in research from the perspective of trans young people. This research was developed in an attempt to address that gap.

Methodological approach

This study draws on a range of approaches familiar to applied social psychologists. It was conceived via a collaborative relationship with a local youth group that specialized in supporting trans youth. We decided to use participatory creative methods as they are recognized as accessible for children and young people (Reavey and Johnson, 2017) and offer flexibility for participants by encompassing a range of techniques from painting, drawing, plasticine or clay modelling, collage and LEGO™. In contrast to more traditional qualitative approaches, these methods are considered participatory because they shift the focus of agency so that the participants determine the topics to be discussed, rather than responding to a set of preconceived interview questions.

The research began with two familiarization visits to the youth group. The group meets every fortnight and attendance varies from session to session but generally includes some people who have attended for two or more years as well as first time attendees in most meetings. In the first familiarization meeting, I introduced myself to the young people and the focus on wanting to understand what matters were of importance to them. We had a brief discussion about issues such as pathologization, mental health and access to services as possible topics. We also discussed the proposed approach to doing the research. They were familiar with using arts-based projects as part of their regular activities and had made a number of zines. They opted to use creative-arts and Lego™, rather than photovoice, as techniques to facilitate group discussions. I returned later for a second familiarization meeting once ethical approval had been granted by the university. On this occasion, the attendees were divided into two groups and discussed in more detail the issues that were important to them in terms of why they attended the group and their gender experiences in the day-to-day; these were then collated into five broad topics: belonging to the youth group; changing the gender world; gender dysphoria; trans identities; access to health services.

Twenty-one trans young people participated in the group discussions. The first theme attracted the most attendees, with 11 people opting to respond (in two groups); subsequent topics have attracted four to five participants. The activity involved spending 20 minutes making a visual representation of their thoughts and feelings about the topic. Each participant then offered an interpretation of the object they had created, before others offered their own observations, asking questions and sharing experiences. The group interview was recorded and transcribed. The analytic approach draws on a range of techniques familiar to social psychologists. Each topic has been read with attention to themes as well as to the way language is used to construct reality, identity positions and subjective experiences. The relationship between visual images and textual explanations offers the opportunity to reflect on some of the feelings associated with the topic through the affective realm – by asking the reader/viewer to sense how the young person might feel and embody their frustrations. Thus, a range of linguistic and visceral techniques are drawn on to interpret the data.

Key findings and observations

Within the individual transcripts for each topic, there are a number of shared and recurring themes. These include experiences of social isolation, difficulties finding emotional support and/or access to medical treatment, as well as accounts of dual-diagnoses, parental acceptance and rejection, explorations of identities, identifications and disidentifications with gender norms. As the key aim here is to locate this research project within broader trends in applied social psychology, I focus on a brief example:

1 Living in a binary gender system

All the participants expressed, at various points, frustrations with a binary gender system, even when they had a binary trans identity. For example, one participant, who identified as a binary trans man, used the activity in the week themed 'trans identities' to represent this (Figure 6.1).

Figure 6.1 'So this is a box with a big cross on it and then there's me on top and I'm refusing to go into the box because there's a big cross in the way. So I'm not being confined into a little box and a little label about my gender identity because even though I'm quite a binary trans person, like I'd say I'm a very binary trans person, I still don't want to just kind of submit to the cis kind of pressures that are put on trans people to appear as cisgendered as possible. So like C. painted my toenails and for me that's like a huge thing of resistance because I don't feel comfortable enough to do it outside but for me it like feels really good to know that they're done like that because I don't want to conform just because every cis person thinks that I should. So that's what mine represents.'

Within this account, gender is seen as a box that regulates who people are. Yet, agency for this regulation is attributed to cisgendered people, rather than to the restrictive nature of gender norms. This raises questions about how all gender is understood as normative, including trans identities, and that there is a perception of pressure to conform to those norms. The act of painting his toenails offers a form of resistance, but it is important to his male subjectivity that this remains hidden so it does not unsettle any 'outside' readings of his maleness. The image adds an additional dimension to the potential readings of this extract – pointing to visceral feelings of precariousness, firstly of teetering over a 'box' that may well entrap him in the expected norms of masculinity, alongside feelings of precarity that emerge from a lack of comfortableness in expressing a non-traditional notion of maleness (wearing nail polish on his toes) in the world.

Unpacking social psychological influences

This research is informed by, and draws on, all three traditions outlined in the previous section. In the first instance, the initial interpretation draws attention to gender as a powerful discourse that regulates the way young people present themselves, constraining more fluid gender expressions. Nevertheless, wearing nail polish on his toes offers the opportunity for resistance and subversion. This reading is clearly aligned with the poststructuralist approach in critical social psychology that analyzes language with a focus on power and subjectivity. The interpretation can be extended though by speculating on how *feelings* of uncomfortableness are embodied by pointing to the un-noted, but widely recognized, implications that public gender transgressions can result in material violence and even death. It could also point to a tension between medical and social transition, where a social identity transition unsupported by medical interventions heightens a sense of precarity because their body is not always read within the expected norms of masculinity as the physical transformations that take place during puberty are not yet available. However, once medical transition is in full swing and the young person's appearance is transformed via testosterone, they will increasingly be read as male and possibly cisgendered. This may conversely increase the likelihood that they will chose to show off their painted toenails in public, unsettling normative interpretations of the relationship between gender expression and bodies.

Here, the visual element of the research is particularly important as it can assist us in generating new understandings of some of the affective conditions of gender precarious positions and subjective feelings associated with gender dis/embodiment. The use of participatory creative-arts based methods in community psychology carries additional value in that they can act as a social intervention in themselves. Generating and sharing reflections on experiences in a group situation are not simply research data but also an opportunity to foster collective understanding, promote group cohesion and reduce the sense of isolation – a key issue described by these trans young people. Here, it should be noted that, in many respects, the research project was modelling the approach used by the youth group and that this activity of building relationships and confidence in how they perceived themselves and their gender identities is a vital element in their service provision. Finally, providing visual representations alongside textual explanations can improve the reach of research output by raising awareness of issues faced beyond a traditional academic audience. There is also the opportunity to challenge dominant representations of trans lives and re-story or re-frame experience and unsettle the gender norms that shape these.

Activist Women in a Mexican Province: Redefining Social Action

Context and rationale

The topic of social action and, in particular, activism and social movements is of interest for applied social psychology since these practices play an important role in contemporary social dynamics and the possibility of social change. In a Mexican context of increasing violence and insecurity (associated in part with drug trafficking and organized crime) alongside growing precariousness and corruption in the governmental institutions responsible for justice administration, social action and activism become urgent and indispensable tools for social life and community development.

The widespread conditions of violence, discrimination and oppression have been recently exacerbated in certain regions of the country and have particularly affected women, impacting on their capacity for social mobilization and political action. At both the individual and collective level, social conditions for women's self-determination and agency have shifted towards precariousness and uncertainty. In fact, the province of Colima, where the study discussed here is conducted, has recently declared a social and institutional emergency call regarding the increasing levels of violence against women and femicides.

Although community psychology and political psychology in Mexico and Latin America have paid attention to aspects related to social action and social change (Almeida and Sánchez, 2009; Burton and Kagan, 2005; Montero, 2007; 2010), less attention has been paid to the way gender saturates such practices and, in particular, how women undertake and engage in forms of activism and social transformation in contexts where they are systematically threatened with exclusion from public and political spaces. Against this background, this research project explores the trajectories of activist women as well as the ways in which they conceive and articulate social action and political participation in such conditions. More broadly, the study seeks to contribute to the understanding of the role of gender in the definition of social action and the way it impacts on processes of social transformation.

Methodological approach

Participants in this project are activist women working on different topics and fields that in some way share a general interest in combating conditions of injustice, enhancing community wellbeing and promoting more egalitarian social and environmental relations. Among the diverse fields of action, we find concern for human rights issues, including the defence of territory and natural resources, the promotion of LGBT rights, environmental rights, animal advocacy and protection, sexual and reproductive rights, and food sovereignty among others. The women involved are equally diverse, originating from rural and urban contexts, different socioeconomic status and age groups (from 18 to 65 years old). Similarly, they are involved with, or belong to, groups or organizations with different backgrounds and organizational structures (from informal collectives to established non-governmental organizations), including independent activists.

The study draws from two methodological strategies considered complementary to the research objectives. First, a narrative approach is used to explore identity and subjectivity. Narrative interviews allow participants to develop a discourse where different elements (characters, scenarios, events, meanings) are intertwined and arranged in the meaningful unity of a particular story or account. Exploration of the narratives constructed by the participants constitutes, from this perspective, a useful way to access the subjective experience and, simultaneously, the contextual and sociocultural conditions that frame it. It allows us to identify the canonical social forces that define what stories can be told and how, while acknowledging the active and agentive process through which participants plot together heterogeneous elements into a singular and personal account. Using feminist perspectives on narrative research, the process is understood as a narrative co-production (Balasch and Montenegro, 2003), where researcher and participant share and negotiate meanings in the cooperative building of a story. The narratives are conceived as methodological devices that can contribute to dislocate, transform or 'diffract' the institutional or canonical accounts that precede and pre-define the comprehension of a phenomenon. In this case, the narrative interviews were conducted with each participant to explore their activist trajectory, the factors that play a significant role in their political engagement and their perspective regarding the significance of gender in the development of these activities.

This approach was complemented by a second strategy. Photovoice is defined as a participatory research method that allows people to identify, represent and improve their community through a specific photographic technique (Wang and Burris, 1997). It was originally proposed as a methodological instrument particularly oriented towards groups and populations considered vulnerable or marginal. In fact, the first research experiences that gave rise to this method were focused on women living in poverty in rural areas, seeking to generate forms of expression and representation of their community problems to inform public policies. Photovoice enables reflexive exploration of the social environment in order to document processes of everyday life and to generate forms of visual representation of problems affecting the community. From this perspective, it is argued that the use of photographs can integrate relevant aspects for the analysis of a problem that often escape mere verbal means of interrogation. At the same time, through photographic creation, participants can express their ideas, conceptions, thoughts, relationships and forms of interaction, thus favouring the active involvement of the subjects in knowledge production from a personal and located standpoint. One of the highlights of this methodology is precisely the emotional and affective potential that photography can mobilize in the representations and understandings of social phenomena.

Participants were invited to take photographs related to their daily reality and their activist work in general. It was requested that they include aspects such as the scenarios and topics of interest, as well as the resources and tools of work, significant social actors or objects, obstacles and difficulties in the development of their activism and general appreciations of their political work. To this end, photographic cameras were offered, as well as a short training course on basic aspects of photographic composition for those who were interested. Some participants used their own devices for photographic production. Each participant selected a number of photographs that they considered especially significant to their experience or that expressed better their perspective on the subject and added a brief footer to each one, describing the meaning attributed to these images. The selected images are being shown through different platforms, including photographic exhibitions in different public and institutional spaces, as well as virtual sites.

Finally, reflexive groups have been developed where the research team and a number of participants (five to seven) get together with the aim of sharing and discussing experiences and perspectives from the different positions and viewpoints involved. Using the photographs as a means to stimulate or elicit conversation, participants elaborate on their practices and understandings, identify similarities and differences in their trajectories as well as common challenges. In accordance with an action-research perspective, these reflexive groups have become spaces for exchange, support and mutual learning, capable of generating forms of recognition, sorority and solidarity bonds.

Key findings and observations

Findings derived from the different methodological devices point to a number of aspects that allow better understanding of the social and political involvement of these women and, more broadly, to reconsider the role of gender in social action. Among some of the most salient issues are the conditions of vulnerability and insecurity that women face when undertaking activist work; some of them have received repeated threats and even had to change their residence because they perceive that their life was in danger. Gender power relations have also been significant to the experience of activism within the same groups and organizations. While women emphasize the importance of constructing collaboration networks and negotiating with a range of social actors, they also share the observation that their 'voice is less heard' than that of their male counterparts.

Despite these shared conditions hampering the activist practice of women, the way in which gender intersects with other social forces and axis of difference is also relevant.

For instance, women in rural contexts frequently conceive institutional and economic violence as the main obstacles (and motivators) for political action, while activists in urban areas place the struggle largely into the symbolic and representational arena, where narratives and places of enunciation are in dispute. Likewise, the trans activists construct narratives where physical violence and arbitrary arrests are relevant events defining the implications of their social action. Thus, the study illustrates the importance of exploring the intersections between gender and other social forces that condition and define women's social action in a context particularly marked by symbolic and material violence.

On the other hand, the methodological approach enables us to make visible the situated and contextual nature of social action, rooted in the participants' lives. One of these lines relates to the way in which women's conception of activism is permeated and frequently driven by their everyday life and domestic spaces. In contrast to an understanding of social action in terms of what one participant called the 'war model', where activism takes place in the public and institutional arena, away from the issues of personal life and through an 'us-against-them' narrative, women's conception of activism blurs the relationship between the public and the private and places the political as central to everyday personal spaces. Similarly, in contrast with the politics 'of confrontation' that prevail in the discourses present in the context of the study, participants put forward an ethics of care and solidarity, generating ties and associations that communicate seemingly unrelated spaces, social actors and political resources. For example, a participant working in the topic of animal protection and wellbeing captured the following image, shown in Figure 6.2.

Figure 6.2 'Doing the laundry is the first thing I can remember that was taught to me as a woman. The washing machine for me is a machine that helps women liberation.'

In this image, the participant has portrayed her freshly washed clothes, drying in the sun in her backyard. In the description, she refers to the washing machine as a technological device that contributes to a 'liberation' experience as it allows escaping, to some extent, one of the tasks imposed on her by the established and expected gender roles in her community. In this way, the participant places domestic tasks and intimate spaces at the centre for the comprehension of a gendered social order and the possibility for agency and emancipation.

In her narrative account, the participant relates the origins of her interest in animal advocacy issues:

> Since I was a little girl, there have always been animals in my house. My grandmother had birds, dogs and even a horse. And I remember, I always like to tell this story… I felt a lot of empathy with the dog and the horse, because we were being hit with the same whip! (laughs) So I thought 'it really hurts, so the dog and the horse must be in pain too'… Because they would beat us all three, and… well, other kids as well; animals and kids. So I felt very close to the dog, and we played a lot and I used to take care of him.

In her narrative, the participant articulates early experiences and family relationships with particular forms of violence but, at the same time, with ties of care and empathy. This narrative accounts for power relations rooted in everyday settings and makes visible a form of violence that is normalized in this particular context. Likewise, it politicizes events, experiences and affective dispositions usually considered of the private realm, blurring the contours traditionally established between the personal and the political, particularly regarding social action. Finally, the participant suggests that particular stories are chosen and told in strategic ways, perhaps aiming to be persuasive with specific audiences or constructing a particular stand or position in a political discussion.

Unpacking applied social psychological influences

In this study, some of the theoretical tools of the social psychological approaches previously discussed come into contact. On the one hand, the narrative approach takes language as an active and constructive practice where events, meanings and social actors are entangled to produce particular discursive actions, identity positions and political stances. Through the narrative account, it is possible to trace both of the discursive traditions mentioned as part of the linguistic turn in critical social psychology. Narratives can be understood as interactional and micro-social practices where rhetorical strategies are used to generate particular effects on an audience (i.e. positioning non-human animals as oppressed beings deserving empathy and sharing with children these forms of oppression). At the same time, narratives elaborated by participants are conditioned by, and reflect, historical moments and geopolitical contexts where they are displayed (i.e. cultural values, normalized power relations and conceptions about social actors are evidenced). Moreover, informed by a poststructuralist perspective, narratives can be understood as situated discourses that problematize or challenge hegemonic or dominant narratives about what counts as social action and the role that gender plays in its configuration.

On the other hand, it is possible to find in this study an approach to knowledge and research as action-oriented, a distinctive feature of both community psychology and feminist perspectives. This reading allows for an understanding of participants as active agents, who are involved in researching their own realities via, for example, photo production and the characterization of their environments. An action-research sensibility is also integrated, as can be observed in the reflexive groups that enable spaces of learning, interchange and building social and emotional bonds that might result in transformative experiences for participants themselves. Likewise, photographic exhibitions constitute a strategy not only for knowledge dissemination but also for denouncing particular social problems and advancing political demands.

Finally, narratives and images produced by activist women can operate as symbolic dispositives that intervene in a symbolic and political dispute over how social problems are to be defined and how social transformation is to be conceived, making visible the heterogeneous positions of women in a particular set of power relations and the relevance of gender for understanding social change.

CONCLUSIONS AND FUTURE DIRECTIONS

In this chapter, we have set out three dominant tropes in contemporary applied social psychological research that is orientated towards critical, psychosocial and community psychology perspectives. We have attempted to demonstrate how research on topics related to gender and sexuality is not just informed by these epistemological and methodological threads, but has been central to their emergence and evolution. In the presentation of examples from our own research, we have attempted to demonstrate the interrelationship of these theoretical strands as we attempt to understand gender and sexuality within specific geopolitical contexts (UK and Mexico) by attending to shared concern for representations, materiality and the drive to social action to improve lived experiences and challenge inequalities. However, our interpretations are already embedded within our own ideological frameworks that emerge from receiving training in critical social psychology in the UK and Spain. It is important to remain vigilant to the fact that critical histories of sexualities research (in particular) tend to be dominated by AngloAmerican perspectives that favour a scholarly canon with its roots in Freud and Foucault (see Johnson, 2015), which reinforces the idea that the psychological subject is white and male. Feminist psychology has long offered an alternative to this within social psychology (e.g. Wilkinson, 1996), and the international journal *Feminism & Psychology* continues to increase the visibility of topics related to women, gender more broadly (e.g. masculinities, transgender, non-binary) and sexualities, as well as set the agenda for feminist psychological research that extends beyond the UK and United States.

Nevertheless, concepts such as intersectionality that draw specific attention to the relationship between race and gender (Crenshaw, 1989) are under explored in all iterations of social psychology compared to other social sciences. Critical social and community psychological perspectives have begun to counter this by drawing attention to the importance of indigenous theories and knowledge, as well as the influence of southern theorists such as Franz Fanon (1952/2017) and Gloria Anzaldúa (1987) who have developed their own powerful and nuanced understandings of the psychosocial conditions of living on the margins, embodying the borders of gender, sexuality and race, often in postcolonial conditions. It is here that applied social psychologists need to make further developments in order to theorize gendered and sexual experiences and identities with attention to race and colonialism. Increasingly, academics and activists are forming international and global alliances that ask questions about whose knowledge and experience counts. Within these, we need to be able to acknowledge shared experiences of gender and sexuality inequalities but not presuppose that global social change movements (such as Western notions of feminism or LGBT rights) should be based on concepts developed in the global north, often in contexts where practices of racialization, and the colonial histories associated with them, remain unexamined. Such strategies risk developing neo-colonial interventions and erasing local forms of knowledge (Connell, 2007). In contrast, sensitive explorations and collaborations that cross geographical borders offer the opportunity to develop new understandings of gender and sexuality that can inform and challenge the 'whiteness' of the social psychology curriculum and assist in the reconfiguration of the power relations that constrain gender and sexuality in both the global north and south.

REFERENCES

Almeida, E., & Sánchez, M. E. (2009). Desarrollo comunitario y desarrollo humano: aportes de una sinergía ONG-Universidad. *Sinéctica*, (32), 11–13.

Angelique, H., & Culley, M. (2000). Searching for feminism: An analysis of community psychology literature relevant to women's concerns. *American Journal of Community Psychology*, *28*, 793–813.

Angelique, H., & Culley, M. (2003). Feminism found: An examination of gender consciousness in community psychology. *Journal of Community Psychology*, *31*, 189–209.

Angelique, H., Campbell, R., & Culley, M. (2001). The anemic state of women's health in community psychology. *Community Psychologist*, *34*, 22–24.

Anzaldúa, G. (1987) *La Frontera/Borderlands: The new mestiza*. San Francisco: Aunt Lute Books.

Atkinson, J. M., & Heritage, J. (Eds.). (1984). *Structures of social action: Studies in conversation analysis*. Cambridge: Cambridge University Press

Balasch, M., & Montenegro, M. (2003). Una propuesta metodológica desde la epistemología de los conocimientos situados: Las producciones narrativas. *Encuentros en Psicología Social*, *1*(3), 44–48.

Bayer, B. M., & Shotter, J. (Eds.). (1998). *Reconstructing the psychological subject: Bodies, practices, and technologies*. London: Sage.

Bond, M. A., & Mulvey, A. (2000). A history of women and feminist perspectives in community psychology. *American Journal of Community Psychology*, *28*, 599–630.

Bond, M. A., Hill, J., Mulvey, A., & Terenzio, M. (Eds.). (2000a). Special issue part I: Feminism and community psychology I [Special issue]. *American Journal of Community Psychology*, *28*(5), 585–755.

Bond, M. A., Hill, J., Mulvey, A., & Terenzio, M. (Eds.). (2000b). Special issue part II: Feminism and community psychology II [Special issue]. *American Journal of Community Psychology*, *28*(6), 759–911.

Bostock, J., Plumpton, M., & Pratt, R. (2009). Domestic violence against women: Understanding social processes and women's experiences. *Journal of Community & Applied Social Psychology*, *19*(2): 95–110.

Brill, S., & Kenney, K. (2016). *The transgender teen: A handbook for parents and professionals supporting transgender and non-binary teens*. New Jersey, USA: Cleis Press.

Brown, S. D., & Stenner, P. (2009). *Psychology without foundations: History, philosophy and psychosocial theory*. London: Sage.

Brunskell-Evans, H., & Moore, M. (2017). *Transgender children and young people: Born in your own body*. Cambridge: Cambridge Scholars Publishing.

Burton, M., & Kagan, C. (2005). Liberation social psychology: learning from Latin America. *Journal of Community & Applied Social Psychology*, *15*(1), 63–78.

Butler, J. (1990) *Gender trouble and the subversion of identity*. New York and London: Routledge.

Butler, J. (1993) *Bodies that matter*. New York and London: Routledge.

Butler, J. (2004). *Undoing gender*. London: Routledge.

Connell, R. (1987). *Gender and power: Society, the person and sexual politics*. Stanford, CA: Stanford University Press.

Connell, R. W. (2007) *Southern Theory: The global production of knowledge*. Cambridge: Polity Press.

Coole, D., & Frost, S. (2010). *New materialisms: Ontology, agency, and politics*. Durham & London: Duke University Press.

Cosgrove, L., & McHugh, M. (2000). Speaking for ourselves: Feminist methods and community psychology. *American Journal of Community Psychology*, *28*, 815–838.

Crenshaw, K. (1989). Demarginalizing the intersection of race and sex: a Black feminist critique of antidiscrimination doctrine, feminist theory and antiracist politics. *University of Chicago Legal Forum*, *140*, 139–167.

Cromby, J. (2015). *Feeling bodies: Embodying psychology*. London: Palgrave.

Cvetkovich, A. (2012). *Depression: A public feeling*. Durham, NC: Duke University.

De Beauvoir, S. (1953). *The second sex* [1949]. Trans. H. M. Parshley. London: Jonathan Cape.

Derrida, J. (1976). *Of grammatology* [1967]. Trans. Gayatri Chakravorty Spivak (pp. 247–272). Baltimore: Johns Hopkins University Press.

Fals Borda, O. (1984. *Resistencia en el San Jorge*. Bogotá: Carlos Valencia.

Fanon, F. (1952/2017). *Black skin, white mask – New edition*. London: Pluto Press.

Fausto-Sterling, A. (1992). *Myths of gender: Biological theories about women and men.* New York: Basic Books.

Foucault, M. (1969). *The archaeology of knowledge*. London: Tavistock Press.

Foucault, M. (1979/1990). *The history of sexuality, Volume 1: An introduction*. Harmondsworth: Penguin Books.

Freire, P. (2000). *Pedagogy of the oppressed.* New York: Continuum.

Frith, H., & Kitzinger, C. (2001). Reformulating sexual script theory: developing a discursive psychology of sexual negotiation. *Theory and Psychology*, *11*(2): 209–232.

Frosh, S. (2010). *Psychoanalysis outside the clinic: Interventions in psychosocial studies*. London: Palgrave.

Garfinkel, H. (1967). *Studies in ethnomethodology.* Englewood Cliffs, NJ.

Garnets, L. D., & D'Augelli, A. R. (1994). Empowering lesbian and gay communities: A call for collaboration with community psychology. *American Journal of Community Psychology*, *22*, 447–470.

Greco, M., & Stenner, P. (2008). *Emotions. A social science reader.* London: Routledge.

Gridley, H., & Turner, C. (2010). Gender, power and community psychology. In G. Nelson, & I. Prilleltensky (Eds.), *Community psychology: In pursuit of liberation and well being* (2nd edn., Ch. 18, pp. 389–406). Basingstoke, UK: Palgrave MacMillan.

Harper, G. W., & Schneider, M. (2003). Oppression and discrimination among lesbian, gay, bisexual, and transgendered people and communities: A challenge for community psychology. *American Journal of Community Psychology*, *31*, 243–252.

Henriques, J., Hollway, W., Urwin, C., Venn, C., & Walkerdine V. (Eds.) (1984/1998). *Changing the subject: Psychology, social regulation and subjectivity*. London and New York: Methuen.

Jackson, S., & Scott, S. (2010). Rehabilitating interactionism for a feminist sociology of sexuality. *Sociology*, *44*(5), 811–826.

Jeffreys, S. (2014). *Gender hurts: A feminist analysis of the politics of transgenderism.* Abingdon, Oxfordshire: Routledge, Taylor & Francis Group

Johnson, K. (2007). Researching suicidal distress with LGBT communities in the UK: Methodological and ethical reflections on a community-university knowledge exchange project. *The Australian Community Psychologist*, *19*(1): 112–123.

Johnson, K. (2011). Visualising mental health with an LGBT community group. In P. Reavey (Ed.), *Visual methods in psychology: Using and interpreting images in qualitative research*. London: Routledge.

Johnson, K. (2015). *Sexuality: A psychosocial manifesto.* Cambridge: Polity Press.

Johnson, K. (2017). Beyond boy and girl: gender diversity in childhood. In L. O'Dell, C. Brownlow, & H. Bertilsdotter Rosqvist (Eds.) *Different childhoods: Non-normative development and transgressive trajectories*. London: Routledge.

Johnson, K., & Martínez-Guzmán, A. (2013). Rethinking concepts in participatory action-research and their potential for social transformation: post-structuralist informed methodological reflections from LGBT and trans-collective projects. *Journal of Applied Social & Community Psychology*, *23*(5), 405–419.

Kessler, S. J., & McKenna, W. (1978). *Gender: An ethnomethodological approach*. Chicago: University of Chicago Press.

Kitzinger, C. (1987). *The social construction of lesbianism*. London: Sage.

Lacan, J. (1988). *The seminar of Jacques Lacan Book II: The ego in Freud's theory and in the technique of psychoanalysis 1954–55.* Trans. S. Tomaselli, Ed. J.-A. Miller. New York: Norton.

Martín-Baró, I. (1998). *Writings for a liberation psychology*. New York: Harvard University Press.

McIntosh, M. (1968/1981). The homosexual role. In K. Plummer (Ed.) *The making of the modern homosexual*. London: Hutchinson.

Montero, M. (2003). *Teoría y práctica de la psicología comunitaria: la tensión entre comunidad y sociedad.* Barcelona: Paidós.

Montero, M. (2007). The political psychology of liberation: From politics to ethics and back. *Political Psychology, 28*(5), 517–533.

Montero, M. (2010). Fortalecimiento de la ciudadanía y transformación social: Área de encuentro entre la Psicología Política y la Psicología Comunitaria. *Psykhe (Santiago), 19*(2), 51–63.

Montenegro, M., Capdevila, R., & Figueroa Sierra, H. (2011). Editorial introduction: Towards a transnational feminism: Dialogues on feminisms and psychologies in a Latin American context. *Feminism & Psychology, 22*(2), 220–227.

Mulvey, A. (1988). Community psychology and feminism: Tensions and commonalities. *Journal of Community Psychology, 16*, 70–83.

Parker, I. (1989). *The crisis in modern social psychology, and how to end it*. London and New York: Routledge.

Potter, J., & Wetherell, M. (1987). *Discourse and social psychology: Beyond attitudes and behaviour*. London: Sage.

Radley, A. (1991). *The body and social psychology*. New York: Springer Science & Business Media.

Reavey, P. & Johnson, K. (2017). Visual approaches: using and interpreting images in qualitative psychology. In C. Willig & W. Stainton-Rogers (Eds.) *The SAGE handbook of qualitative research in psychology* (2nd edn.). London: Sage.

Riger, S. (2016). On becoming a feminist psychologist, *Psychology of Women Quarterly, 40*(4): 479–487.

Roen, K. (2011). The discursive and clinical production of trans youth: Gender variant youth who seek puberty suppression. *Psychology & Sexuality, 2*(1), 58–68.

Sedgwick, E. K. (1991). How to bring your kids up gay: The war on effeminate boys. *Social Text, 29*, 18–27.

Serrano-García, I., López, M. M., & Rivera-Medina, E. (1987). Toward a social-community psychology. *Journal of Community Psychology, 15*, 431–446.

Speer, S. A. (2005). *Gender talk: Feminism, discourse and conversation analysis*. London & New York: Routledge.

Speer, S., & Stokoe, E. (Eds.) (2011). *Conversation and gender*. Cambridge: Cambridge University Press.

Stam, H. J. (Ed.). (1998). *The body and psychology*. London: Sage.

Ussher, J. M. (1991). *Women's madness: Misogyny or mental illness*. London: Harvester Wheatsheaf.

Ussher, J. M. (2006). *Managing the monstrous feminine: Regulating the reproductive body*. London & New York: Routledge.

Wang, C., & Burris, M. A. (1997). Photovoice: Concept, methodology, and use for participatory needs assessment. *Health Education & Behavior, 24*(3), 369–387.

Wasco, S. M., & Bond, M. A. (2010). The treatment of gender in community psychology research. In J. C. Chrisler & D. R. McCreary (Eds.), *Handbook of gender research in psychology, Vol. 2. Gender research in social and applied psychology* (pp. 613–641). New York, US: Springer Science + Business Media. http://dx.doi.org/10.1007/978-1-4419-1467-5_26

Wetherell, M. (2012). *Affect and emotion: A new social science understanding*. London: Sage.

Wetherell, M., & Edley, N. (1999). Negotiating hegemonic masculinity: Imaginary positions and psycho-discursive practices. *Feminism & Psychology, 9*(3), 335–356.

Wilkinson, W. (1984).

Wilkinson, S. (1996). *Feminist social psychologies: International perspectives*. Milton Keynes: Open University Press.

Wilson, E. (1998). Loving the computer. In H. Stam (Ed.) *The body and psychology* (pp. 71–93). London: Sage.

Wilson, E. A. (2004). *Psychosomatic: Feminism and the neurological body*. Durham & London: Duke University Press.

Wilson, E. A. (2015). *Gut feminism*. Durham & London: Duke University Press.

Wren, B. (2014). Thinking postmodern and practising in the enlightenment: Managing uncertainty in the treatment of children and adolescents. *Feminism & Psychology, 24*(2), 271–291.

PART III

Politics

7

Towards an Applied Social Psychology of Democratic Citizenship

Colin Scott and Allison Harell

INTRODUCTION

Civic participation is a core requirement of a healthy, functioning democracy (Pander, 2003; Schlozman et al., 2012). In pluralist societies, the equality of participation across minority groups is an important indicator of the quality of democracy (Eggert and Giugni, 2010). Yet, in many advanced democracies, electoral participation, a cornerstone of democratic vitality, is in decline (Blais, 2000), while the participation of new immigrant citizens raises concern among some host society members as to 'whose side' they are on (Hindriks et al., 2015; Verkuyten, 2018; Verkuyten et al., 2016).

Psychologists from a range of sub-fields have applied their training to inform public policy (Maton, 2017), and social psychologists, in particular, have a history of taking action to affect social change (e.g., Lewin, 1946). Social psychological interventions rooted in theories of intergroup contact (Allport, 1954) and common ingroup identification (Gaertner and Dovidio, 2000) have proven quite effective at improving intergroup attitudes in laboratory experiments and cross-sectional studies (Dovidio et al., 2016; Pettigrew and Tropp, 2006). Field experiments are a promising method for applied research on prejudice and discrimination reduction in the real world (Bertrand and Duflo, 2017) and political scientists are increasingly leveraging insights from social psychology to test the causal effects of voter mobilization initiatives. However, causal inferences of the efficacy of social psychological interventions outside of the laboratory are the exception (Paluck and Green, 2009a). As a result, policy makers and public servants lack the practical advice needed to incorporate social psychological insights into their planning and decision-making (Brown et al., 2012; Er-rafiy et al., 2010; Paluck and Green, 2009a; Pettigrew, 2011; Wills, 2010).

In this chapter, we draw on literatures from psychology and political science to illustrate the greater potential for applied social psychologists to guide civic organizers and policy practitioners concerned with encouraging more equitable participation. Social psychological research is increasingly moving beyond the individual level by engaging with institutional and societal forces (e.g., Guimond et al., 2013; Himmelweit and Gaskell, 1990; Howarth et al., 2013). Combining insights from the political and psychological sciences, the study of political psychology has grown into an interdisciplinary field aimed at advancing our understanding of the interactions between individuals and their political environments (Huddy et al., 2013). There are many avenues and opportunities to advance applications of social psychology to politics. Here, we focus on strategies for facilitating electoral engagement, racial biases and their influence on political preferences, and the role of diversity policy in affecting intergroup relations and immigrant integration. While the emphasis on voter mobilization, racial biases, and immigrant integration policy by no means capture the breadth of the psychological study of politics, they represent key areas where social psychology can inform practitioners working to address contemporary challenges to democratic citizenship.

MOBILIZING ELECTORAL ENGAGEMENT

Declining voter turnout is a challenge to many democracies (Blais, 2000; Schlozman et al., 2012). Low levels of voter turnout among youth are linked to generational differences in political attitudes, such as interest in politics and a sense of civic duty (Barnes and Virgint, 2010; Blais et al., 2004; Blais and Loewen, 2011). Participation gaps between younger and older adults are not necessarily a sign of apathy but may be due, in part, to greater skepticism with the way democracy works (Gidengil and Bastedo, 2014). Institutional factors also shape the ways in which citizens participate in elections. The electoral system, political campaigns, and degree of party competition shape voters' considerations (Blais, 2006; Blais and Dobrzynska, 1998; Blais et al., 2004; Duverger, 1955; Lijphart, 1994). In federal political systems with multiple levels of government (i.e., provincial and federal), voters face greater cognitive demands to correctly place responsibility for policy outcomes at the appropriate level of government (Cutler, 2004). In many jurisdictions, voter identification legislation is becoming increasingly strict and commonplace, with recent evidence linking these laws to lower voter turnout among certain ethnic and political groups (Braconnier et al., 2017; Hajnal et al., 2017). Political scientists are leveraging psychological research to develop and test interventions designed to better mobilize and inform citizens. In this regard, there is much opportunity for applied social psychologists to partner with scholars from allied fields, in addition to policy practitioners and community organizers working to improve voters' engagement with elections.

Field Experiments to Mobilize Voter Turnout

Participation gaps are widespread in even the most advanced industrial democracies (Schlozman et al., 2012). To address this challenge, political scientists are increasingly drawing on psychological theory to inform interventions designed to motivate voters' interest and participation in elections (for reviews, see Gerber and Green, 2017; Green and Gerber, 2015; Green et al., 2013). Commonly referred to as 'Get-Out-The-Vote' initiatives, a number of strategies have been developed and tested using large-scale field experiments to assess what strategies work for mobilizing voter turnout.[1] Participants are randomly sampled (usually at the household level) and assigned to experimental conditions or a control group at random. Numerous types of treatments have been tested, but in general, Get-Out-The-Vote initiatives vary relevant source characteristics (e.g., canvassers' gender, ethnicity or party affiliation); the medium of contact (e.g., in person, over the phone, or through the mail); or the persuasive content of message delivered to the recipient. A large empirical literature on the effects of voter mobilization interventions demonstrate that interventions that employ direct face-to-face contact with participants have a larger effect on voter turnout than interventions delivered over the phone or through the mail (Gerber and Green, 2000; Green and Gerber, 2015; Green et al., 2003).

In designing voter mobilization initiatives, psychological research on social pressure and behavioural compliance (Cialdini and Trost, 1985) has played an important role in the development of the persuasive messages that are central to the experimental treatment. Messages designed to mobilize voters typically have three components (Green and Gerber, 2010: 331–332): first, treatment messages make the recipient aware of existing social norms (e.g., that voting is a normative civic duty); second, they remind the recipient of their compliance with a desired outcome (e.g., whether the recipient voted or not in a previous election); and, finally, they leverage social pressure by making the recipient aware that their participation is public record (e.g., that, in certain jurisdictions, records of whether someone voted or not are available). Simply reminding citizens whether or not they voted is public record and observable to others has been shown to increase voter turnout (Davenport, 2010; Green et al., 2013; Green and Gerber, 2010; Panagopoulos, 2013; 2014), particularly if the respondent abstained in the previous election (Gerber et al., Green & Larimer, 2008; 2010; Rogers et al., 2017).

Voter mobilization initiatives are most effective when they are conducted under conditions of face-to-face contact and tend to have larger effects among those who report less interest in politics (Gerber and Green, 2017). In some cases, increases in voter turnout have been driven largely by greater turnout among first-time and occasional voters in some contexts (Nyman, 2017), an encouraging finding as low levels of voter turnout among young adults are a major concern for electoral participation (Blais, 2000; Blais et al., 2004). Even in electoral systems that follow some form of proportional representation and where voter turnout tends to be higher (Blais and Carty, 1990), door-to-door canvassing experiments are still shown to modestly increase (by 3.6 percentage-points) the probability of voting (Nyman, 2017). Furthermore, evidence suggests that the positive effects of voter mobilization initiatives can extend to other people, having indirect mobilizing effects on others not receiving the treatment (Nickerson, 2008). This 'contagion' effect suggests that door-to-door voter mobilization interventions might be even more powerful and cost-effective as the treatment effect may have an indirect effect on other voters in the household as a result of their contact with the individual receiving the treatment.

In their guiding text for researchers, Alan Gerber and Donald Green (2012: xvii) remark that, '[a]lthough field experiments are sometimes dismissed as prohibitively expensive, difficult, or ethically encumbered, experience shows that a wide variety of field experimental studies may be conducted with limited resources and minimal risk to human subjects.' Despite their limited use by social psychologists (Paluck and Green, 2009a), field experiments are well suited to examining social psychological processes in naturalistic settings and offer practitioners insights on strategies to influence attitude and behavioural change in the real world. Field experiments have a number of advantages over other research designs commonly used in social psychology and have the potential to overcome many of the limitations that hinder social psychologists' ability to inform policy practitioners (Pettigrew,

2011). First, while laboratory experiments have been very important at advancing our knowledge of how psychological processes function in political decision-making (e.g., Iyengar, 1994; Iyengar et al., 1984; Lau and Redlawsk, 2001; 2006), they suffer from low levels of external validity and are reliant on non-probabilistic sampling. Field experiments have the potential to overcome these limitations by testing psychologically informed interventions in a natural setting, such as with eligible voters during an election campaign (but see Desposoto, 2016 for a discussion of ethical challenges). Field experiments also lend to behavioural measurement; in certain jurisdictions, researchers interested in mobilizing electoral participation are able to draw on administrative records of whether an individual has voted or not. While these data are not available in all jurisdictions, wherever possible behavioural outcomes should be used to overcome limitations of self-report measures of electoral participation, which are prone to social desirability. Readers interested in a comprehensive review of field experiment methodology, including their design, analysis, and interpretation, as well as a discussion of common challenges and proposed solutions in contexts relevant to political participation, are referred to Gerber and Green (2012).

A caveat to the finding that encouraging participation leads to modest improvements in voter turnout is that not all individuals respond the same way to voter mobilization interventions employing persuasive appeals. Although the effects of social pressure messages have been shown to persist even after several months (Davenport et al., 2010), some evidence suggests there is potential for a 'backlash' among individuals that respond negatively to social pressure. Mann (2010) demonstrates that gentler social pressure treatments can still be effective at mobilizing voter turnout, cautioning researchers to avoid potentially threatening messages, which may inadvertently suppress turnout among some recipients.

Careful attention should be paid to the detection of heterogeneous treatment effects when designing and analyzing field experiments to mobilize voter turnout (Enos et al., 2014; Gerber and Green, 2012, chapter 9). Heterogeneous treatment effects occur when the effect of the experimental manipulation is conditioned by participant characteristics. For example, Alan Gerber and colleagues (2013) demonstrate how treatment effects from some Get-Out-The-Vote initiatives are conditioned by personality traits, with individuals higher in openness to experience being particularly susceptible to persuasive messaging imbedded in voter mobilization treatments. Attention to treatment effects are important in voter mobilization experiments in order to ensure that treatment effects do not inadvertently suppress turnout for certain individuals, particularly those who are already least likely to vote. Otherwise, although voter mobilization interventions may increase overall voter turnout on average, they may actually augment disparities in political participation by decreasing the propensity to vote among certain groups of people (Enos et al., 2014). Researchers designing interventions that incorporate social pressure manipulations should pay particular attention to heterogeneous treatment effects.

Cognitive Biases and Political Decision-Making

Political campaigns are elaborate attempts at persuasion with voters bombarded by competing messages and information on the ideological, social, and policy positions of candidates and parties. Dual process theories of attitude change and persuasion distinguish between two routes to information processing: a central, systematic route guided by effortful consideration of the information at hand; and, a peripheral, heuristic route relying on environmental cues when cognitive resources such as interest and knowledge are limited (Chaiken, 1980; Petty and Cacioppo,

1986). Bernard Berelson and colleagues (1954: 308) have remarked that a

> democratic citizen is expected to be well informed about political affairs. He [sic] is supposed to know what the issues are, what their history is, what the relevant facts are, what alternatives are proposed, what the party stands for, what the likely consequences are. By such standards the voter falls short.

Given that the psychological burden of seeking out and processing all relevant and available political information is cognitively demanding (e.g., Downs, 1957), it is no surprise that the use of cognitive shortcuts are pervasive in the searching and processing of political information (Brady and Sniderman, 1985; Conover and Feldman, 1989; Lau and Redlawsk, 2006).

To compensate for this lack of information, voters rely heavily on cues taken from their political environments (Brady and Sniderman, 1985; Conover and Feldman, 1989; Popkin, 1991; Sniderman et al., 1991). One of the most pernicious and well-documented sources of bias in the processing of political information is motivated reasoning leading to partisan favouritism (Campbell et al., 1960; Jerit and Barabas, 2012; Lodge and Hamil, 1986; Taber and Lodge, 2006). Although heuristic use is an adaptive way of making decisions when information processing is constrained by time and other resources (Gigerenzer, 2000; Simon 1957), cognitive shortcuts do not always allow voters to act as though they were fully informed (Bartels, 1996) and, in some cases, motivate voters to avoid or reject information that discredits a prior belief or opinion (e.g., Nyhan and Reifler, 2010; Redlawsk, 2002; Taber and Lodge, 2006). Citizens tend to learn 'politically congenial facts and for resisting uncongenial ones' (Jerit and Barabas, 2012: 682) and use social cues on the Internet to avoid negative information about their political preferences (Pierce et al., 2017). Research drawing on system justification theory (Jost et al., 2004) shows how, paradoxically, many individuals from disadvantaged groups are ideologically motivated to justify the existing social order, even when the status quo undermines group interests (Hoffarth and Jost, 2017).

In an effort to better inform voters, a number of online tools have been developed to facilitate voters' engagement and knowledge about candidates' policy positions during campaigns. With estimates of usage exceeding one-quarter of the electorate in some Western European democracies (Marschall, 2014), the proliferation of online voting advice applications (VAAs) are increasingly popular tools designed to help voters make informed decisions about where candidates and political parties stand on important ideological, policy, and social issues (e.g., Enyedi, 2016; Fossen and Anderson, 2014; Garzia, 2010; Mahéo, 2016; 2017), guiding voters through the increasingly complex information environment of political campaigns by helping users reduce the costs of identifying the party that best reflects their views about key campaign issues (Dinas et al., 2014; Dumont and Kies, 2015; Fossen and Anderson, 2014). Past research has shown that VAAs can mobilize voters and stimulate electoral participation. For example, research conducted during the 2006 Dutch parliamentary election estimates VAAs account for a 4.4% increase in turnout after controlling for confounding variables (Gemenis and Rosema, 2014) and that the greatest potential for change is among younger users who are less knowledgeable about politics (Fivsaz and Nadig, 2010; Mahéo, 2016). Other researchers have found similar results in Canada, supporting the evidence that VAAs can have a slight effect on stimulating political interest and mobilizing behaviours, but these effects are conditioned by political interest (Mahéo, 2016; 2017).

The estimation of treatment effects from VAAs is challenging due to self-selection into the treatment, as the primary users of the applications are also those who are most likely to vote and be interested in politics.

VAA use is driven largely by educated, politically interested men (Hooghe and Teepe, 2007), the same groups of users that, on average, are more likely to form party preferences as a result of VAA use (Mahéo, 2016). As Mahéo (2016: 406) notes, 'while this is good news, as we obtain further evidence of VAAs' educational utility, it leads us to conclude that VAAs may be missing their target.' Younger and less educated citizens typically report less interest in politics, less engagement in elections, and less knowledge about political issues (Barnes and Virgint, 2010; Blais and Loewen, 2011; Blais et al., 2004; Delli Carpini and Keeter, 1996). A major challenge for future applied research using VAAs is overcoming issues of sampling, non-compliance, and to further investigate the possibility of hetereogenous treatment effects among VAA users with different partisan attachments, biases, and levels of political information and interest. As Valérie-Anne Mahéo (2016: 406) suggests, 'one possibility for voter education campaigns and organizations would be to consider combining VAA use with follow-up discussion or with another information activity' to help less politically sophisticated users process information and make the most of it.

Richard Lau and David Redlawsk (2006: 15) consider voters' ability to select the candidate or party that is most congruent with their own ideological values and beliefs as 'correct voting', noting how '[t]he simple act of voting is not so simple if people fail to make good choices.' While VAAs have been evaluated with respect to their impact on voter turnout, political interest, and the formation of political preferences, less is known about their effect on information processing. Applied psychologists interested in political cognition and information processing can play an important role in designing and evaluating VAA tools by examining how the information presented by VAAs may be mitigated by partisan biases or whether their use affects information searching behaviour. There is some evidence to suggest that VAAs may deter users from voting when results reveal discordances between users' preferences and the estimated political positions of political parties and candidates (Dinas et al., 2014). Future evaluations of VAAs should test for whether these tools run the risk of inadvertently suppressing turnout among users who are not closely matched to any particular candidate or party. Understanding how VAA use affects political cognition is an important avenue for improving the development of tools to help voters make political choices. Although VAAs have been used in campaigns in one form or another for some time, it is only recently that researchers are investigating the extent to which these online tools can increase electoral engagement and help users make more informed political choices.

Individuals who can mobilize greater cognitive resources have been shown to rely less on partisan cues (Dalton, 1984). The extent to which VAAs are able to help users overcome cognitive hurdles like seeking out and processing large amounts of political information, or avoiding and discounting information that runs against partisan beliefs, are important avenues for future research. Political cognition researchers have developed methodological tools such as dynamic process tracing that allows researchers to investigate voters' information searching behaviour and its effects on decision in campaign environments (e.g., Lau and Redlawsk, 2001; 2006; Pierce et al., 2017). Finally, attempts to correct false or unsubstantiated political beliefs are prone to being ignored or even increase misperceptions, an effect which varies by political ideology (Nyhan and Reifler, 2010). Tools designed to help users become more active and critical consumers of political information must also guard against 'backlash' effects, which might inadvertently heighten partisan biases or make recipients *even more* likely to stay home on Election Day. Incorporating VAAs into political cognition research in both laboratory and field settings can offer insights into how information interventions are working (or not) to facilitate political decision-making. Ultimately, whether the presentation of candidates' positions along policy and ideological dimensions helps voters make more informed choices is a matter for future research.

RACIAL BIASES, POLITICAL ATTITUDES, AND INTERGROUP RELATIONS

In culturally diverse societies, the equality of participation across minority groups is an important indicator of the quality of democracy (Eggert and Giugni, 2010). However, persistent racial biases present a significant challenge to the integration and participation of immigrant minorities. State policies towards citizenship and integration reflect ideological norms about how newcomers are expected to participate in the larger society (Bourhis et al., 1997; Guimond et al., 2013). A growing body of research in social and political psychology has focused on how institutional or ideological support for diversity and the integration of immigrants can attenuate or enhance racial biases among host society members, influencing intergroup attitudes by shaping the ideological climate into which newcomers must adapt and integrate (Bourhis et al., 1997; Guimond et al., 2013; Kauff et al., 2013; Levin et al., 2012; Richeson and Nussbaum, 2004; Scott and Safdar, 2017).

Changing individuals' perceptions of 'standard' or 'desirable' behaviour is one way to usher in social change (Tankard and Paluck, 2016). As perceptions of perceived norms change so too do intergroup attitudes. Drawing on the case of the US Supreme Court's ruling in favour of same-sex marriage, for example, Tankard and Paluck (2017) demonstrate how institutional support for a hierarchy-attenuating policy (i.e., marriage equality) can influence individual perceptions of how socially normative support for group equality is. According to social dominance theory, 'ideologies that promote or maintain group inequality are the tools that legitimize discrimination' (Pratto et al., 1994: 741). Normative messages about the hierarchical nature of intergroup relations have been shown to motivate exclusionary attitudes and behaviours among dominant majority group members (Ho et al., 2012; Jost and Thompson, 2000; Levin et al., 2012; Pratto et al., 1994; 2000; Sibley and Duckitt, 2008). A social psychological lens applied to integration policy offers policy practitioners an analytical framework through which to assess the effects of diversity and integration policies on intergroup relations and the equality of participation across minority groups.

Maintaining harmonious intercultural relations in multinational contexts, where perceptions of cultural insecurity and political tensions between competing host communities could run high, is a significant challenge for policy makers. In such scenarios, cultural anxieties about intergroup relations risk becoming institutionalized in policy initiatives. We begin this section by examining ways in which racial biases perpetuate inequality by shaping majorities' policy preferences and how social psychological theories of intergroup contact and common identification offer strategies to improve intergroup attitudes. In the following section, we close this chapter by discussing how competing integration policy frameworks for managing diversity can be designed with these strategies in mind to undermine such biases and promote inclusion. We advocate for greater partnership between social psychologists and policy makers in the design and evaluation of integration policy to better provide policy practitioners with the tools needed to examine the effects of integration policy on intergroup relations.

Racial Biases and Political Preferences

Within political science, the study of racial attitudes falls into two camps (for an overview, see Bobo and Fox, 2003; for a critique of both approaches, see Sniderman and Carmines, 1997). Social psychological approaches tend to view prejudice as negative evaluations about an individual's moral or social characteristics based on group membership. While explicit prejudice falls easily within this camp, there is a rich literature on more implicit forms of racial prejudice which suggest that prejudices persist in forms of subtle racism or racial resentment (Kinder and Sears, 1981; Meertens and Pettigrew, 1997; Pettigrew and Meertens, 1995). Social structural approaches, in contrast, view hostile attitudes towards race-targeted policies as a reflection of real conflict between groups over social and economic resources (Blumer, 1958; Esses et al., 1998; Sears et al., 2000). If social identities are a mask through which we understand the political world, it is easy to see how other policies could become associated with specific groups, thereby activating prejudicial thinking.

Racial biases exert a strong effect on support for policy initiatives that aim to attenuate inequality (Bobo and Kleugal, 1993; Dixon et al., 2007; Feldman and Huddy, 2005). Those who hold more prejudicial attitudes consistently oppose anti-discrimination policy measures such as preferential hiring (Bobo and Kluegel, 1993; Breugelmans and van de Vijver, 2004); are less generous with welfare spending and social assistance in general (Harell et al., 2016); and oppose affirmative action policies (Bobo and Kleugal, 1993; Feldman and Huddy, 2005) or other policy initiatives that strive for racial integration (Dixon and Durrheim, 2004; Dixon et al., 2007; Jackman and Crane, 1986). Welfare policies in the United States context have been heavily imbued with racial content in the minds of many citizens (Gilens, 1999; Katz, 1989; Mendelberg, 2001; Winter, 2008), and there is increasing evidence that such racialized frames extend to welfare state policies more generally across Anglo-Saxon democracies such as Canada and the UK (Harell et al., 2016). Such findings have serious implications for the shared social safety net that states have put in place since the mid-twentieth century. For example, citizens (and particularly white citizens) tend to view benefits that target needy citizens as disproportionately benefiting racial minorities (Gilens, 1999); and, when given explicit cues about benefits going to a racial outgroup, citizens' support for such benefits tends to decrease (Gilens, 1999; Harell et al., 2016; Iyengar, 1991). Immigration flows from developing countries bring a more racially and religiously diverse immigrant population into receiving countries, making conflicts over reasonable accommodation and access to state resources more likely to incite racial biases and discrimination. Similar to welfare support, an important body of research looks at how intergroup evaluations influence support for crime policies. Past research has suggested that racial prejudice predicts support for crime-related spending (Barkan and Cohn, 2005) as well as the death penalty (Bobo and Johnson, 2004) and that juries are more likely to convict black defendants in non-capital cases (Williams and Burek, 2008).

Racial biases exert powerful effects on the lived experiences of immigrant minorities by shaping their perceptions of threat and discrimination and influencing their attachment to, and participation in, the larger society. Social psychology research points to the importance of attachment to the host society and feelings of relative deprivation in motivating immigrants' political participation (see Simon and Klandermans, 2001). For example, feelings of relative deprivation are associated with decreased confidence in political institutions (Corning, 2000; Klandermans et al., 2001; Pettigrew et al., 2008) and a decreased attachment to the host society in favour of a psychological shift in identification away from the majority group and towards the immigrant minority group (Branscombe, et al., 1999). In some cases, persistent perceptions of threat and discrimination may lead newcomers to develop an oppositional identity against the host society (Verkuyten and Yildiz, 2007). As social identity theory would suggest, minority group members' perceptions of threat and insecurity have been linked to an increase in identification and emotional attachment to the minority group (Jetten et al., 2001). Longitudinal research illustrates how immigrants who experience psychological distress report more negative integration outcomes eight years later, including more negative attitudes towards the host society and poorer psychological wellbeing (Jasinskaja-Lahti et al., 2009). Interventions to undermine racial biases and foster more welcoming attitudes towards immigrants and their participation in the larger society are an important avenue for applied social psychological research.

Contact and Shared Identification as Strategies to Reduce Racial Biases

Social psychological research on the cognitive and motivational processes affected by intergroup contact and social categorization have much potential to inform our knowledge of the political world by offering policy makers insight into the ways in which our social identities colour our interactions and evaluations of others (Allport 1954; Dovidio et al., 2003; Pettigrew and Tropp, 2006; Pettigrew et al., 2011; Tajfel and Turner, 1986). Research on immigration and intercultural relations have examined how different interventions that promote intergroup contact and common identification can be effective at reducing racial biases, prejudice, and discrimination (e.g., Dovidio and Gaertner, 2000; Dovidio et al., 2016; Gaertner and Dovidio 2012; Pettigrew and Tropp, 2006; Sam and Berry, 2010). Social psychological processes that underlie stereotypes and discrimination are central in explaining the persistence of biases in the implementation and delivery of social services. At a time when anxieties over immigration are especially salient, identifying these processes, and assessing the ways in which policy initiatives enhance or attenuate group hierarchy and inequality, is pertinent to the effective management of diversity in plural societies.

Gordon Allport (1954) proposed that intergroup contact, under conditions of low intergroup competition and inequality, shared goals, and institutional supports are effective ways to reduce prejudice and improve intergroup relations. A large body of empirical research on the contact hypothesis generally supports this argument ($\bar{r} = -.21$, Pettigrew et al., 2011; see also Hewstone and Swart, 2011; Pettigrew and Tropp, 2006), even for individuals that strongly endorse hierarchical intergroup relations and are especially predisposed to prejudice and discrimination (Kteily et al., 2017). In some contexts, however, exposure to increased diversity has been negatively associated with social trust, membership in associations, and political engagement (Putnam, 2007), with some evidence to suggest that simply being in the presence of diverse others can lead to more negative intergroup attitudes (Blumer, 1958; Enos., 2014; Giles and Buckner, 1993). The so-called 'threat hypothesis' suggests that as an area becomes increasingly diverse, outgroup hostility tends to increase with research supporting the conclusion that diversifying areas are associated with greater outgroup animosity (Branton and Jones, 2005; Oliver and Mendelberg, 2000). In short, despite a large body of research highlighting the benefits of contact, without attention to the conditions that generate intergroup anxieties stemming from intergroup competition of material and symbolic resources, the positive effects of intergroup contact are likely to be mitigated or even reversed.

Experimental manipulations of direct intergroup contact are especially challenging (Pettigrew and Tropp, 2006; but see Enos, 2014). As such, there is a lack of causal evidence in naturalistic settings to provide empirical guidance for policy makers looking to improve attitudes and overcome intergroup conflict (Paluck and Green, 2009a: 352; see also Paluck, Green and Green, in press). However, the positive effects of intergroup contact do not only arise from first-hand experience with diversity; indirect forms of contact have also been shown to improve intergroup attitudes by reducing intergroup anxiety with the help of interventions predicated on imagined contact and mental imagery (Birtel and Crisp, 2015; Crisp and Turner, 2009; Crisp et al., 2011; Turner and Crisp, 2010; West et al., 2017). Interventions that leverage indirect contact reduce prejudice towards cultural minorities by targeting individuals' distorted cognitions about cultural outgroups (see Birtel and Crisp, 2015), reducing the intergroup anxiety that contributes to negative attitudes and avoidance of contact (Crisp and Turner, 2009). In post-conflict settings, imagined contact interventions embedded in media initiatives have been shown to have mixed effects on intergroup attitudes. Bilali and Vollhardt (2015) report the findings from a field experiment drawing on a media intervention designed to promote reconciliation and perspective taking in post-conflict Rwanda, with similar programmes taking place around Africa's Great Lakes region (see also Bilali and Vollhardt, 2013; Paluck, 2009; Paluck and Green, 2009b). Coordinated with the support of the Dutch non-governmental organization Le Beneveloncija (www.labenevolencija.org), media initiatives in the form of a radio drama that leverages the narratives and discussions of fictional characters from diverse cultural groups have been used to promote educational messages emphasizing intergroup commonalities and the promotion of a shared vision of the future, while also celebrating diversity. These field experiments involving indirect contact initiatives demonstrate that media intervention can lead to positive impacts on certain social attitudes, including social distance and victim conscientiousness, but may also reduce tolerance and cooperative behaviour toward certain community members in others (cf. Paluck, 2010).

Common group identification has been shown to increas the integration efforts of host society members by promoting norms of resource sharing between majority group members and immigrant minorities and weakening racial biases of dominant group members. A shared identification between members from different groups has been tied to reduced social distance and more positive attitudes towards others following ethnic conflict (Cehajic et al., 2008). According to the Common Ingroup Identity Model (Dovidio and Gaertner, 2000; Gaertner and Dovidio, 2012), if both ingroup and outgroup members share a common superordinate group membership, cognitive motivations that drive ingroup favouritism should generalize to the 'embedded outgroup', resulting in a reduction in intergroup anxiety that motivates dominant group members to avoid intergroup contact. Shared identification has been shown to have positive effects for dominant and non-dominant group members alike. For immigrants integrating into new societies, the development of dual identification with both heritage and host societies has been shown to motivate the political participation of migrants in Western European democracies (Simon and Grabow, 2010; Simon and Ruhs, 2008) and lead to better adaptation outcomes during cross-cultural transition (Nguyen & Benet-Martínez, 2007; Sam and Berry, 2010). From the perspective of majority group members, experimental primes of a common ingroup had more welcoming attitudes towards the integration and participation of cultural minorities and demonstrated greater willingness to support the integration of newcomers by volunteering in an organization and donating money to a charity (Kunst et al., 2015).

ACCULTURATION AND THE POLITICAL PSYCHOLOGY OF INTEGRATION POLICY

Public policies can play a powerful role in defining and promoting a shared sense of national belonging that reflects the identity of host society members and public opinion towards how newcomers should integrate. Yet, policy makers' assumptions about how newcomers will adapt and integrate do not always align with the lived experiences of immigrants and sojourners (e.g., Scott et al., 2015). As a result, the development of integration policies risks being one-sided, neglecting the reciprocal nature of acculturation and cross-cultural adaption (Berry, 1997; Bourhis et al., 1997). While integration policy is situated within broader economic, political, and sociocultural contexts, intergroup relations are central to the management of integration and diversity.

Integration policy frameworks have a powerful influence on normative beliefs and perceptions of how newcomers ought to participate in society by encouraging or undermining the conditions for positive intergroup contact and shared identification between dominant majorities and immigrant minorities. Different ideological orientations towards immigrant integration are institutionalized in public policy frameworks that shape the conditions under which newcomers are able to participate in the larger society (Bourhis et al., 1997; Guimond et al., 2013). Integration policies and normative discourses around integration may enhancing or attenuating the effects of individual predispositions on expressions of prejudice among majority group members, depending on the degree to which integration frames endorse group-based social hierarchy (Guimond et al., 2013; Kauff et al., 2013; Levin et al., 2012; Pelletier-Dumas et al., 2017; Scott and Safdar, 2017; Verkuyten, 2005). Social psychologists are increasingly engaging with the effects of diversity policy on intergroup relations (Berry, 1984; Bourhis et al., 1997; Guimond et al., 2013; Levin et al., 2012; Pelletier-Dumas et al., 2017). Greater partnership between social psychologists and policy makers offers practitioners and organizations seeking to better manage immigrant integration and intercultural relations a framework through which to assess how such policies can lead to different relational outcomes between host society members and immigrant minorities.

Acculturation and Immigrant Integration Policy

Integration policy is predicated on acculturation ideologies that define the strategies used to manage intercultural relations. Acculturation refers to a reciprocal processes of psychological and sociocultural adaptation that takes place when immigrant minorities and host communities enter into prolonged intercultural contact (Berry, 1997; 2005). Although much psychological research on acculturation has emphasized the strategies and experiences of non-dominant immigrant groups, as a process of bidirectional change, acculturation frameworks are also apply to investigate how national host communities respond to cultural diversity (Bourhis et al., 1997; 2010). At a general level, the strategies individuals use to manage the acculturation experience vary along two dimensions: (1) the extent to which maintenance of newcomers' heritage cultural characteristics and identities are considered to be important and valued, both by immigrant minorities as well as dominant majorities; and, (2) the degree to which contact and participation in the host community is desired and encouraged (Berry, 1997). These two acculturation strategies are generally independent (Arends-Tóth and van de Vijver, 2007) and have a strong influence on intercultural relations (Berry, 2005). Social psychological research suggests that immigrants who are able and willing to maintain their heritage cultural identity while adopting the values and practices of the host society are able to integrate with the most positive adaptation outcomes (Berry, 1997; Nguyen and Benet-Martínez, 2007; Sam and Berry, 2010; Zagefka and Brown, 2002); perceive lower levels of discrimination (Berry et al., 2006);

and report decreased levels of acculturative stress, negative self-esteem, and anti-social behaviours (Berry et al., 2006; Jasinskaja-Lahti et al., 2009; Pascoe and Smart Richman, 2009). Integration policies that permit the adoption and maintenance of multiple cultural identities are desirable because they permit immigrants to share a common identification with members of the host community while still maintaining the psychosocial resources from their heritage cultural identity (Berry, 2005; Dovidio et al., 2016; Zagefka and Brown, 2002).

Integration ideologies are institutionalized through public policy frameworks (Guimond et al., 2013) and influence individual attitudes and behaviours by creating a social climate conducive to a given ideological perspective (Bourhis et al., 1997). By regulating the conditions under which newcomers can participate in the host society, integration policies help define the national ingroup, shaping the way we think about group membership. Cross-national analyses point to significant variation in the degree to which Western immigrant-receiving societies adopt pro-diversity integration policy frameworks to manage intercultural relations (e.g., MIPEX, 2016). Immigrant minorities share 'a vulnerability to the tolerance or rejection of dominant host communities whose demographic strength, prestige, and institutional power within the national state can result in much acculturative pressure' (Bourhis et al., 2010: 782). In multinational societies, competing nation-building projects present an added challenge to the integration of newcomers (Banting and Soroka, 2012). In such contexts, the politics of immigrant integration are not simply a case of 'old' citizens against 'new' ones; rather, important divisions 'within the ranks of the "old" shape the country's response to the "new" (Banting and Soroka, 2012: 157–158).

A major challenge for immigrant integration policy is to determine how to accommodate diversity, 'while respecting the rights of everyone, in particular the rights of immigrants and members of minorities, who, in this relationship, are usually the most vulnerable citizens' (Bouchard, 2015: 3). Faced with significant levels of international migration, policy makers are tasked with successfully integrating newcomers and managing the cultural anxieties of host society members who may feel threatened by increased cultural diversity (Pratto and Lemieux, 2001). In 1971, Canada outlined a federal policy of multiculturalism as a framework to manage intercultural relations (Berry, 1984; 2006; 2013; Kymlicka, 1998). Multiculturalism places strong emphasis on the maintenance of heritage cultural identities while encouraging the full, equitable participation of all ethnocultural groups in the life of the larger society (Berry, 2006). As a pluralist integration framework, multiculturalism goes beyond the presence of cultural diversity by promoting the full participation of newcomers in the host society in an equitable manner. To accomplish this goal of mutual acceptance among all ethnic and cultural groups, Canadian multiculturalism policy is driven by three components (Berry, 1984; 2006): a cultural component that financially and socially encourages the maintenance and development of all cultural identities; a social component that prioritizes intergroup contact and participation; and a communication component which emphasizes the learning of national languages (i.e., English or French) to facilitate integration and mutual adaptation of acculturation.

In contrast to assimilationist policies where newcomers' participation is predicated on rejecting their heritage cultural identities in exchange for the values and practices of the host society, multiculturalism is a hierarchy-attenuating strategy for managing cultural diversity (Levin et al., 2012). Generally, multicultural messages have been shown to improve intergroup attitudes (Guimond et al., 2013, Guimond et al., 2014; Richeson & Nussbaum, 2004; Verkuyten, 2005) by attenuating the relationship between social dominance orientation and measures of prejudice (Levin et al., 2012; Scott and Safdar, 2017). However, when interactions are conflictual (Vorauer and Sasaki, 2011), or when individuals feel culturally threatened and insecure (Berry et al., 1977), multiculturalism receives less support and may even trigger more negative intergroup outcomes in certain settings (but see Scott and Safdar, 2017).

Multiculturalism is challenged in societies where cultural insecurity and perceptions of threat are high, leading some policy makers to embrace alternative integration strategies that favour colour-blind individualism or an alternative interculturalism framework that promotes diversity while placing greater emphasis on the cultural values of the dominant majority group (Bouchard, 2015; 2016). Both approaches de-emphasize the egalitarian principle of multicultural integration frames, and an important avenue for future applied social psychology research on integration policy is to investigate the extent to which alternative and emerging integration frameworks influence intercultural relations. Immigration policies 'must accommodate the goals and needs of members of majority and minority groups – preferably simultaneously', and as such, an understanding of groups' goals and motivations is 'critical for designing appropriate policies to improve intergroup relations' (Dovidio et al., 2016: 35). While pluralist integration policies expect newcomers to adopt the public values of the host society while celebrating diversity through financial and social supports to maintain heritage cultural practices in accordance with existing legal norms, civic policies adopt a colour-blind approach, ignoring cultural differences with little to no official promotion of minority cultures. Colour-blind integration frameworks risk making dominant group members less aware of the unique challenges faced by minority group members (Kunst et al., 2015). As such, policy makers should assess the extent to which integration strategies succeed in promoting a shared identity and attachment to, as well as a sense of belonging in, the host society.

CONCLUSIONS

There are many avenues to continue building an applied social psychology of democratic citizenship. By informing the development of civic engagement interventions and offering policy practitioners the tools needed to manage diversity and integration, social psychological research is playing an increasingly active role by looking beyond the individual level to investigate the interactive effects of social and political forces on citizens' attitudes and behaviours in their political environments. New opportunities are emerging for applied social psychologists to engage with civic organizers and policy practitioners to work together in addressing challenges to democratic citizenship. In this chapter, we have examined research at the intersection of social psychology and politics in an effort to showcase how social psychological research is being put into practice to overcome some challenges facing advanced democracies. Designing effective strategies to 'get out the vote' and help citizens make more informed political decisions have been shown to lead to modest improvements in electoral engagement. At the same time, policy frameworks that manage the integration of immigrant minorities have been linked to persistent racial biases that undermine equal participation in culturally plural societies. Concerns regarding voters' engagement with elections, persistent racial biases, and the equality of participation from cultural minorities are just some of the significant challenges that advanced industrialized democracies are facing. Emerging challenges to democratic citizenship are multifaceted, and as such, greater collaboration between applied researchers from social psychology and allied disciplines, in partnership with civic organizers and policy makers, is needed.

Note

1 For a detailed overview of the design, analyses, and interpretation of field experiments, including discussion of core concepts, and methodological and statistical, see Gerber and Green (2012) and John (2017). For a discussion of ethical challenges in conducting field experiments in political science and public policy, see Desposoto (2016).

REFERENCES

Allport, G. W. (1954). *The nature of prejudice*. Boston: Addison Wesley.

Arends-Tóth, J. & van de Vijver, F. (2007). Acculturation attitudes: A comparison of measurement methods. *Journal of Applied Social Psychology, 37*, 1462–1488.

Banting, K., & Soroka, S. (2012). Minority nationalism and immigrant integration in Canada. *Nations and Nationalism, 18*(1), 156–176.

Barkan, S. E., & Cohn, S. F. (2005). Why whites favor spending more money to fight crime: The role of racial prejudice. *Social Problems, 52*(2), 300–314.

Barnes, A., & Virgint, E. (2010). Youth voter turnout in Canada: 1. Trends and issues. *In Brief* series, 2010-19-E. Ottawa, ON: Library of Parliament.

Bartels, L. M. (1996). Uninformed votes: Information effects in Presidential elections. *American Journal of Political Science, 40*(1), 194–230.

Berelson, B., Lazarsfeld, P. F., & McPhee, W. N. (1954). *Voting: A study of opinion formation in a presidential campaign*. Chicago: University of Chicago Press.

Berry, J. W. (1984). Multicultural policy in Canada: A social psychological analysis. *Canadian Behavioural Science, 16*(4), 353–370.

Berry, J. W. (1997). Immigration, acculturation and adaptation. *Applied Psychology: An International Review, 46*, 5–68.

Berry, J. W. (2005). Acculturation: Living successfully in two cultures. *International Journal of Intercultural Relations, 29*, 697–712.

Berry, J. W. (2006). Mutual attitudes among immigrants and ethnocultural groups in Canada. *International Journal of Intercultural Relations, 30*, 719–734.

Berry, J. W. (2013). Research on multiculturalism in Canada. *International Journal of Intercultural Relations, 37*(6), 663–675.

Berry, J. W., Kalin, R., & Taylor, D. M. (1977). *Multiculturalism and ethnic attitudes in Canada*. Ottawa: Supply and Services Canada.

Berry, J. W., Phinney, J. S., Sam, D. L., & Vedder, P. (2006). Immigrant youth: Acculturation, identity, and adaptation. *Applied Psychology, 55*(3), 303–332.

Bertrand, M. & Duflo, E. (2017). Field experiments on discrimination. In A. V. Banarjee, & E. Duflo (Eds.), *Handbook of economic field experiments* (Vol. 1). Amsterdam: Elsevier.

Bilali, R., & Vollhardt, J. R. (2013). Priming effects of a reconciliation radio drama on historical perspective-taking in the aftermath of mass violence in Rwanda. *Journal of Experimental Social Psychology, 49*(1), 144–151.

Bilali, R., & Vollhardt, J. R. (2015). Do mass media interventions effectively promote peace in contexts of ongoing violence? Evidence from Eastern Democratic Republic of Congo. *Peace and Conflict: Journal of Peace Psychology, 21*(4), 604.

Birtel, M. D. & Crisp, R. J (2015). Psychotherapy and social change: Utilizing principles of cognitive-behavioural therapy to help develop new prejudice-reducing interventions. *Frontiers in Psychology, 6*, Article 1771.

Blais, A. (2000). To vote or not to vote? The merits and limits of rational-choice theory. Pittsburgh, PA: University of Pittsburgh Press.

Blais, A. (2006). What affects voter turnout? *Annual Review of Political Science, 9*, 111–125.

Blais, A., & Carty, R. K. (1990). Does proportional representation foster voter turnout? *European Journal of Political Research, 18*, 167–181.

Blais, A., & Dobrzynska, A. (1998). Turnout in electoral democracies. *European Journal of Political Research, 33*(2), 239–261.

Blais, A., & Loewen, P. (2011). *Youth electoral engagement in Canada*. Ottawa, Canada: Elections Canada.

Blais, A., Gidengil, E., & Nevitte, N., (2004). Where does turnout decline come from? *European Journal of Political Research, 43*, 221–236.

Blumer, H. (1958). Race prejudice as a sense of group position. *Pacific Sociological Review, 1*(1), 3–7.

Bobo, L. & Kluegel, J. (1993). Opposition to race-targeting: Self-interest, stratification ideology, or racial attitudes. *American Sociological Review*, *58*(4), 443–464.

Bobo, L. D., & Fox, C. (2003). Race, racism, and discrimination: Bridging problems, methods, and theory in social psychological research. *Social Psychology Quarterly*, *66*(4), 319–332.

Bobo, L. D., & Johnson, D. (2004). A taste for punishment: Black and white Americans' views on the death penalty and the war on drugs. *Du Bois Review: Social Science Research on Race*, *1*(1), 151–180.

Bouchard, G. (2015). *Interculturalism: A view from Quebec*. Toronto: University of Toronto Press.

Bouchard, G. (2016). Quebec interculturalism and Canadian multiculturalism. In N. Meer, T. Modood, & R. Zapata-Barrero (Eds.), *Multiculturalism and interculturalism: Debating the dividing lines*. Edinburgh, Scotland: Edinburgh University Press.

Bourhis, R., Moise, C., Perreault, S., & Senécal, S. (1997). Towards an interactive acculturation model: A social psychological approach. *International Journal of Psychology*, 32, 369–386.

Bourhis, R. Y., Montaruli, E., El-Geledi, S., Harvey, S. P., & Barrette, G. (2010). Acculturation in multiple host community settings. *Journal of Social Issues*, *66*(4), 780–802.

Braconnier, C., Dormagen, J., & Pons, V. (2017). Voter registration costs and disenfranchisement: Experimental evidence from France. *American Political Science Review*, *111*(3): 584–604.

Brady, H. E., & Sniderman, P. M. (1985). Attitude attribution: A group basis for political reasoning. *American Political Science Review*, *79*(4), 1061–1078.

Branscombe, N. R., Schmitt, M. T., & Harvey, R. D. (1999). Perceiving pervasive discrimination among African-Americans: Implications for group identification and well-being. *Journal of Personality and Social Psychology*, 77, 135–49.

Branton, R. and Jones, B. (2005) Reexamining racial attitudes: The conditional relationship between diversity and socioeconomic environment, *American Journal of Political Science*, *49*(2), 359–372.

Breugelmans, S. M. & Van De Vijver, F. (2004). Antecedents and components of majority attitudes toward multiculturalism in the Netherlands. *Applied Psychology: An International Review* *53*(3), 400–422.

Brown, R., de Visser, R., Dittmar, H., Drury, J., Farsides, T., Jessop, D., & Sparks, P. (2012). Social psychology and policy making: Past neglect, future promise. *Public Policy Research*, *18*(4), 227–234.

Campbell, A., Converse, P., Miller, W. & Stokes, D. P. (1960). *The American Voter*. New York: John Wiley & Sons.

Cehajic, S., Brown, R., & Castano, E. (2008). Forgive and forget? Antecedents and consequences of intergroup forgiveness in Bosnia and Herzegovina. *Political Psychology*, *29*(3), 351–367.

Chaiken, S. (1980). Heuristic versus systematic information processing and the use of source versus message cues in persuasion. *Journal of Personality and Social Psychology*, *39*(5), 752–766.

Cialdini, R. B., & Trost, M. R. (1985). Social influence, social norms, conformity, and compliance. In D. T. Gilbert, S. T. Fiske, & G. Lindzey (Eds.), *The handbook of social psychology* (Vol. 2). New York: Oxford University.

Conover, P. J., & Feldman, S. (1989). Candidate perception in an ambiguous world: Campaigns, cues, and inference processes. *American Journal of Political Science*, *33*(4), 912–940.

Corning, A. F. (2000). Assessing perceived social inequity: A relative deprivation framework. *Journal of Personality and Social Psychology*, *78*, 463–477.

Crisp, R. J., & Turner, R. N. (2009). Can imagined interactions produce positive perceptions?: Reducing prejudice through simulated social contact. *American Psychologist*, *64*(4), 231–240.

Crisp, R. J., Birtel, M. D., and Meleady, R. (2011). Mental simulations of social thought and action: trivial tasks or tools for transforming social policy? *Current Directions in Psychology*, *20*, 261–264.

Cutler, F. (2004). Government responsibility and electoral accountability in federations. *Publius: The Journal of Federalism*, *34*(2), 19–38.

Dalton, R. J. (1984). Cognitive mobilization and partisan dealignment in advanced industrial democracies. *The Journal of Politics*, *46*(1), 264–284.

Davenport, T. C. (2010). Public accountability and political participation: Effects of a face-to-face feedback intervention on voter turnout of public housing residents. *Political Behavior*, *32*(3), 337–368.

Davenport, T. C., Gerber, A. S., Green, D. P., Larimer, C. W., Mann, C. B., & Panagopoulos, C. (2010). The enduring effects of social pressure: Tracking campaign experiments over a series of elections. *Political Behavior*, *32*(3), 423–430.

Delli Carpini, M. X. & Keeter, S. (1996). *What Americans know about politics and why it matters*. Yale University Press: New Haven, USA.

Desposato, S. (2016). *Ethics and experiments: Problems and solutions for social scientists and policy professionals*. New York, NY: Routledge.

Dinas, E., Trechsel, A. H., & Vassil, K. (2014). A look into the mirror: Preferences, representation and electoral participation. *Electoral Studies*, *36*, 290–297.

Dixon, J., & Durrheim, K. (2004). Dislocating identity: Desegregation and the transformation of place. *Journal of Environmental Psychology*, *24*(4), 455–473.

Dixon, J., Durrheim, K., & Tredoux, C. (2007). Intergroup contact and attitudes toward the principle and practice of racial equality. *Psychological Science*, *18*(10), 867–872.

Dovidio, J. F., & Gaertner, S. L. (2000). Aversive racism and selection decisions: 1989 and 1999. *Psychological Science*, *11*(4), 315–319.

Dovidio, J., Gaertner, S. L., & Kawakami, K. (2003). Intergroup contact theory: The past, present, and the future. *Groups Processes and Intergroup Relations*, *6*(1), 5–21.

Dovidio, J. F., Gaertner, S. L., Ufkes, E. G., Saguy, T., & Pearson, A. R. (2016). Included but invisible? Subtle bias, common identity, and the darker side of 'we.' *Social Issues and Policy Review*, *10*(1), 6–46.

Downs, A. (1957). *An economic theory of democracy*. New York: Harper.

Dumont, P. & Kies, R. (2015). Les systèmes d'aide au vote: Défis et potentialités. *Revue Internationale de Politique Comparée*, *22*(2), 297–318.

Duverger, M. (1955). Partis politiques et classes sociales. In *Partis politiques et classes sociales en France*. Paris: Presses de Sciences Po (PFNSP).

Eggert, N., & Giugni, M. (2010). Does associational involvement spur political integration? Political interest and participation of three immigrant groups in Zurich. *Swiss Political Science Review*, *16*(2), 175–210.

Enos, R. D. (2014). Causal effect of intergroup contact on exclusionary attitudes. *PNAS*, 111(10): 3699–3704.

Enos, R. D., Fowler, A., & Vavreck, L. (2014). Increasing inequality: The effect of GOTV mobilization on the composition of the electorate. *The Journal of Politics*, *76*(1), 273–288.

Enyedi, Z. (2016). The influence of voting advice applications on preferences, loyalties and turnout: An experimental study. *Political Studies*, *64*(4), 1000–1015.

Er-rafiy, A., Brauer, M., & Musca, S. C. (2010). Effective reduction of prejudice and discrimination: Methodological considerations and three field experiments. *Revue Internationale de Psychologie Sociale*, *23*(2), 57–95.

Esses, V., Jackson, L. M., & Armstrong, T. L. (1998). Intergroup competition and attitudes toward immigrants and immigration: An instrumental model of group conflict. *Journal of Social Issues*, *54*(4), 699–724.

Feldman, S. & Huddy, L., (2005). Racial resentment and white opposition to race-conscious programs: Principles or prejudice? *American Journal of Political Science*, *49*(1), 168–183.

Fivaz, J., & Nadig, G. (2010). Impact of Voting Advice Applications (VAAs) on voter turnout and their potential use for civic education. *Policy & Internet*, *2*(4), 167–200.

Fossen, T., & Anderson, J. (2014). What's the point of voting aid applications? Competing perspectives on democracy and citizenship. *Electoral Studies*, *36*, 244–251.

Gaertner, S. L., & Diviodio, J. F. (2000). *Reducing Intergroup Bias: The Common Ingroup Identity Model*. New York, N.Y: Routledge.

Gaertner, S. L., & Dovidio, J. F. (2012). Reducing intergroup bias: The Common Ingroup Identity Model. In P. A. M. Van Lange, A. W. Kruglanski, & E. T. Higgins (Eds). *Handbook of theories of social psychology* (Vol. 2, pp. 439–457). Thousand Oaks, CA: Sage.

Garzia, D. (2010). The effects of VAAs on users' voting behaviour: An overview. In L. Cedroni, &

D. Garzia (Eds.) *Voting advice applications in Europe: The state of the art*. ScriptaWeb: Napoli

Gemenis, K., & Rosema, M. (2014). Voting advice applications and electoral turnout. *Electoral Studies*, *36*, 281–289.

Gerber, A. S., & Green, D. P. (2000). The effects of canvassing, telephone calls, and direct mail on voter turnout: A field experiment. *The American Political Science Review*, *94*(3), 653–663.

Gerber, A. S. & Green, D. P. (2012). *Field experiments: Design, analysis and interpretation*. New York, NY: W. W. Norton & Company.

Gerber, A. S., & Green, D. P. (2017). Field experiments on voter mobilization: An overview of a burgeoning literature. In A. V. Banarjee, & E. Duflo (Eds.) *Handbook of economic field experiments* (Vol. 1). Amsterdam: Elsevier.

Gerber, A. S., Green, D. P., & Larimer, C. W. (2008). Social pressure and voter turnout: Evidence from a large-scale field experiment. *American Political Science Review*, *102*(1), 33–48.

Gerber, A. S., Green, D. P., & Larimer, C. W. (2010). An experiment testing the relative effectiveness of encouraging voter participation by inducing feelings of pride or shame. *Political Behavior*, *32*(3), 409–422.

Gerber, A., Huber, G. A., Doherty, D., Dowling, C. M., & Panagopoulos, C. (2013). Big Five personality traits and responses to persuasive appeals: Results from voter turnout experiments. *Political Behavior*, *35*, 687–728.

Gidengil, E., & Bastedo, H. (2014). *Canadian democracy from the ground up: Perceptions and performance*. Toronto, Ontario: University of Toronto Press.

Gigerenzer, G. (2000). *Adaptive thinking: Rationality in the real world*. New York: Oxford University Press.

Gilens, M. (1999). *Why Americans hate welfare: Race, media and the politics of antipoverty policy*. Chicago, IL: University of Chicago Press.

Giles, M. W., & Buckner, M. A. (1993). David Duke and Black threat: An old hypothesis revisited. *The Journal of Politics,* 55(3), 702–713.

Green, D. P., & Gerber, A. S. (2010). Introduction to social pressure and voting: New experimental evidence. *Political Behavior*, *32*, 331–336.

Green, D. P. & Gerber, A. S. (2015). *Get out the vote: How to increase voter turnout*. Washington, DC: Brookings Institution Press.

Green, D. P., Gerber, A. S., & Nickerson, D. W. (2003). Getting out the vote in local elections: Results from six door-to-door canvassing experiments. *The Journal of Politics*, *65*(4), 1083–1096.

Green, D. P., McGrath, M. C., & Aronow, P. M. (2013). Field experiments and the study of voter turnout. *Journal of Elections, Public Opinion and Parties*, *23*(1), 27–48.

Guimond, S., Crisp, R. J., de Oliveira, P., Kamiejski, R., Kteily, N.,.... Tougas, F., Sidanius, J., Zick, A. (2013). Diversity policy, social dominance, and intergroup relations: Predicting prejudice in changing social and political contexts. *Journal of Personality and Social Psychology*, *104*(6), 941–958.

Guimond, S., de la Sablonnière, R., & Nugier, A. (2014) Living in a multicultural world: Intergroup ideologies and the societal context of intergroup relations, *European Review of Social Psychology*, (*25*)1, 142–188

Hajnal, Z., Lajevardi, N., & Nielson, L. (2017). Voter identification laws and the suppression of minority votes. *The Journal of Politics*, *79*(2), 363–379.

Harell, A., Soroka, S., & Iyengar, S. (2016). Race, prejudice and attitudes toward redistribution: A comparative experimental approach. *European Journal of Political Research*, *55*(4), 723–744.

Hewstone, M., & Swart, H. (2011). Fifty-odd years of inter-group contact: From hypothesis to integrated theory. *British Journal of Social Psychology*, *50*(3), 374–386.

Himmelweit, H. T., & Gaskell, G. (1990). *Societal psychology*. Newbury Park, CA: Sage.

Hindriks, P., Verkuyten, M., & Coenders, M. (2015). The evaluation of immigrants' political acculturation strategies. *International Journal of Intercultural Relations*, 47, 131–142.

Ho, A. K., Sidanius, J., Pratto, F., Levin, S., Thomsen, L., Kteily, N., & Sheehy-Skeffington, J. (2012). Social dominance orientation: Revisiting the structure and function of a variable predicting social and political attitudes. *Personality and Social Psychology Bulletin*, 38, 583–606.

Hoffarth, M. R., & Jost, J. T. (2017). When ideology contradicts self-interest: Conservative opposition to same-sex marriage among sexual minorities – A commentary on Pinsof and Haselton. *Psychological Science*, *28*(10), 1521–1524.

Hooghe, M., & W. Teepe. (2007). Party profiles on the web: An analysis of the log files of nonpartisan interactive political internet sites in the 2003 and 2004 election campaigns in Belgium. *New Media and Society*, *9*(6), 965–985.

Howarth, C., Campbell, C., Cornish, F., Franks, B., Garcia-Lorenzo, L., ... Mannell, J., Reader, T., & Tennant, C. (2013). Insights from Societal Psychology: The contextual politics of change. *Journal of Social and Political Psychology*, *1*(1), 364–384.

Huddy, L., Sears, D. O., & Feldman, S. (2013). Introduction: Theoretical foundations of political psychology. In L. Huddy, D. O. Sears, & J. S. Levy (Eds.) *The Oxford handbook of political psychology*. Oxford University Press: Oxford, UK.

Iyengar, S. (1991). *Is anyone responsible? How television frames political issues*. Chicago: University of Chicago Press.

Iyengar, S. (1994). *Is anyone responsible?: How television frames political issues*. Chicago: University of Chicago Press.

Iyengar, S., Kinder, D. R., Peters, M. D., & Krosnick, J. A. (1984). The evening news and presidential evaluations. *Journal of Personality and Social Psychology*, *46*(4), 778–787.

Jackman, M. R., & Crane, M. (1986). Some of my best friends are black...: Interracial friendship and whites' racial attitudes. *Public Opinion Quarterly*, *50*(4), 459–486.

Jasinskaja-Lahti, I., Liebkind, K., & Solheim, E. (2009). To identify or not to identify? National disidentification as an alternative reaction to perceived ethnic discrimination. *Applied Psychology*, *58*(1), 105–128.

Jerit, J., & Barabas, J. (2012). Partisan perceptual bias and the information environment. *Journal of Politics*, *74*(3), 672–684.

Jetten, J., Spears, R., & Manstead, A. S. (2001). Similarity as a source of differentiation: The role of group identification. *European Journal of Social Psychology*, *31*(6), 621–640.

John, P. (2017). *Field experiments in political science and public policy: Practical lessons in design and delivery*. New York, NY: Routledge.

Jost, J., Banaji, M. R., & Nosek, B. A. (2004). A decade of system justification theory: Accumulated evidence of conscious and unconscious bolstering of the status quo. *Political Psychology*, *25*(6), 881–919.

Jost, J. T., & Thompson, E. P. (2000). Group-based dominance and opposition to equality as independent predictors of self-esteem, ethnocentrism, and social policy attitudes among African Americans and European Americans. *Journal of Experimental Social Psychology*, *36*(3), 209–232.

Katz, M. (1989). *The undeserving poor: From the war on poverty to the war on welfare*. New York: Pantheon Books.

Kauff, M., Asbrock, F., Thörner, S., & Wagner, U. (2013). Side effects of multiculturalism: the interaction effect of a multicultural ideology and authoritarianism on prejudice and diversity beliefs. *Personality & Social Psychology Bulletin*, *39*(3), 305–320.

Kinder, D., & Sears, D. (1981). Prejudice and politics: Symbolic racism versus racial threats to the good life. *Journal of Personality and Social Psychology*, *40*(3), 414–431.

Klandermans, B., Roefs, M., & Olivier, J. (2001). Grievance formation in a country in transition: South Africa, 1994–1998. *Social Psychology Quarterly*, *64*, 41–54.

Kteily, N. S., Hodson, G., Dhont, K., & Ho, A. K. (2017). Predisposed to prejudice but responsive to intergroup contact? Testing the unique benefits of intergroup contact across different types of individual differences. *Group Processes & Intergroup Relations*.

Kunst, J. R., Thomsen, L., Sam, D. L., & Berry, J. W. (2015). 'We are in this together': Common group identity predicts majority members' active acculturation efforts to integrate immigrants. *Personality and Social Psychology Bulletin*, *41*(10), 1438–1453.

Kymlicka, W. (1998). *Finding our way: Rethinking ethnocultural relations in Canada*. Toronto: Oxford University Press.

Lau, R. R., & Redlawsk, D. P. (2001). Advantages and disadvantages of cognitive heuristics in political decision-making. *American Journal of Political Science*, *45*(4), 951–971.

Lau, R. R., & Redlawsk, D. P. (2006). *How voters decide: Information processing during an election campaign*. New York: Cambridge University Press.

Levin, S., Matthews, M., Guimond, S., Sidanius, J., Pratto, F., Kteily, N., Pitpitan, E. V., & Dover, T. (2012). Assimilation, multiculturalism, colorblindness: Mediated and moderated relationships between social dominance orientation and prejudice. *Journal of Experimental Social Psychology*, *48*(1), 207–212.

Lewin, K. (1946). Action research and minority problems. *Journal of Social Issues*, *2*(4), 34–46.

Lijphart, A. (1994). Democracies: Forms, performance, and constitutional engineering. *European Journal of Political Research*, *25*(1), 1–17.

Lodge, M., & Hamill, R. (1986). A partisan schema for political information processing. *American Political Science Review*, *80*(2), 505–520.

Mahéo, V.-A. (2016). The impact of voting advice applications on electoral preferences: A field experiment in the 2014 Quebec election. *Policy & Internet*, *8*(4), 391–411.

Mahéo, V. A. (2017). Information campaigns and (under) privileged citizens: An experiment on the differential effects of a voting advice application. *Political Communication*, *12*, 1–19.

Mann, C. B. (2010). Is there a backlash to social pressure? A large-scale field experiment on voter mobilization. *Political Behavior*, *32*(3), 387–407.

Marschall, S. (2014). Profiling users. In D. Garzia, & S. Marschall (Eds.), *Matching voters with parties and candidates*. Colchester: ECPR Press.

Maton, K. I. (2017). *Influencing social policy: Applied psychology serving the public interest*. New York, USA: Oxford University Press.

Meertens, R. W., & Pettigrew, T. F. (1997). Is subtle prejudice really prejudice? *The Public Opinion Quarterly*, *61*(1), 54–71.

Mendelberg, T. (2001). *The race card: Campaign strategy, implicit messages, and the norm of equality*. Princeton, NJ: Princeton University Press.

MIPEX. (2016). Migrant Integration Policy Index. Retrieved from http://www.mipex.eu/.

Nguyen, A. M. D., & Benet-Martínez, V. (2007). Biculturalism unpacked: Components, measurement, individual differences, and outcomes. *Social and Personality Psychology Compass*, *1*(1): 101–114.

Nickerson, D. W. (2008). Is voting contagious? Evidence from two field experiments. *American Political Science Review*, *102*(1), 49–57.

Nyhan, B., & Reifler, J. (2010). When corrections fail: The persistence of political misperceptions. *Political Behavior*, *32*, 303–330.

Nyman, P. (2017). Door-to-door canvassing in the European elections: Evidence from a Swedish field experiment. *Electoral Studies*, *45*, 110–118.

Oliver, J. E., & Mendelberg, T. (2000). Reconsidering the environmental determinants of white racial attitudes. *American Journal of Political Science*, *44*(3), 574–589.

Paluck, E. L. (2009). What's in a norm? Sources and processes of norm change. *Journal of Personality and Social Psychology*, *96*(3), 594–600.

Paluck, E. L. (2010). Is it better not to talk? Group polarization, extended contact, and perspective taking in Eastern Democratic Republic of Congo. *Personality and Social Psychology Bulletin*, 36(9), 1170–1185.

Paluck, E. L., & Green, D. P. (2009a). Prejudice reduction: What works? A review and assessment of research and practice. *Annual Review of Psychology*, *60*, 339–367.

Paluck, E. L., & Green, D. P. (2009b). Deference, dissent, and dispute resolution: An experimental intervention using mass media to change norms and behavior in Rwanda. *The American Political Science Review*, *103*, 622–644.

Paluck, E. L., Green, S. A., & Green, D. P. (in press). The contact hypothesis re-evaluated. *Behavioral Public Policy*, 1–30. doi:10.1017/bpp.2018.25

Panagopoulos, C. (2013). I've got my eyes on you: Implicit social-pressure cues and prosocial behavior. *Political Psychology*, *35*(1), 23–33.

Panagopoulos, C. (2014). Watchful eyes: Implicit observability cues and voting. *Evolution and Human Behavior*, *35*(4), 279–284.

Pander, R. (2003). Can mandated political representation increase policy influence for disadvantaged minorities? Theory and evidence from India. *American Economic Review*, *93*(4), 1132–1151.

Pascoe, E. A., & Smart Richman, L. (2009). Perceived discrimination and health: A meta-analytic review. *Psychological Bulletin*, *135*(4), 531–554.

Pelletier-Dumas, M., de la Sablonnière, R., & Guimond, S. (2017). The role of assimilation and multiculturalism for the relation between social dominance orientation and prejudice: The case of Anglophones and Francophones in Québec. *Journal of Cross-Cultural Psychology*, *48*(6), 874–891.

Pettigrew, T. F. (2011). Toward sustainable psychological interventions for change. *Peace and Conflict: Journal of Peace Psychology*, *17*(2), 179–192.

Pettigrew, T. F. & Meertens, R. W. (1995). Subtle and blatant prejudice in Western Europe. *European Journal of Social Psychology*, *25*(1), 57–75.

Pettigrew, T. F. & Tropp, L. R. (2006). A meta-analytic test of intergroup contact theory. *Journal of Personality and Social Psychology*, *90*(5), 751–783.

Pettigrew, T. F., Christ, O., Wagner, U., Meertens, R. W., Van Dick, R., & Zick, A. (2008). Relative deprivation and intergroup prejudice. *Journal of Social Issues*, *64*, 385–401.

Pettigrew, T. F., Tropp, L. R., Wagner, U., & Christ, O. (2011). Recent advances in intergroup contact theory. *International Journal of Intercultural Relations*, *35*, 271–280.

Petty, R. E. & Cacioppo, J. T. (1986). *Communication and persuasion: Central and peripheral routes to attitude change*. New York: Springer-Verlag.

Pierce, D. R., Redlawsk, D. P., & Cohen, W. W. (2017). Social influences on online political information search and evaluation. *Political Behavior*, *39*(3), 651–673.

Popkin, S. L. (1991). *The reasoning voter: Communication and persuasion in presidential campaigns*. Chicago, IL: University of Chicago Press.

Pratto, F., & Lemieux, A. F. (2001). The psychological ambiguity of immigration and its implications for promoting immigration policy. *Journal of Social Issues*, *57*(3), 413–430.

Pratto, F., Liu, J. H., Levin, S., Sidanius, J., Shih, M., Bachrach, H., & Hegarty, P. (2000). Social dominance orientation and the legitimization of inequality across cultures. *Journal of Cross-Cultural Psychology*, *31*(3), 369–409.

Pratto, F., Sidanius, J., Stallworth, L. M., & Malle, B. F. (1994). Social dominance orientation: A personality variable predicting social and political attitudes. *Journal of Personality and Social Psychology*, *67*, 741–763.

Putnam, R. D. (2007). E pluribus unum: Diversity and community in the twenty-first century. The 2006 Johan Skytte Prize Lecture. *Scandinavian Political Studies*, *30*(2), 137–174.

Redlawsk, D. P. (2002). Hot cognition or cool consideration? Testing the effects of motivated reasoning on political decision-making. *Journal of Politics*, *64*(4), 1021–1044.

Richeson, J. A., & Nussbaum, R. (2004). The impact of multiculturalism versus colorblindness on racial bias. *Journal of Experimental Social Psychology*, *40*(3), 417–423.

Rogers, T., Green, D. P., Ternovski, J., & Ferrerosa Young, C. (2017). Social pressure and voting: A field experiment conducted in a high-salience election. *Electoral Studies*, *46*, 87–100.

Sam, D. L., & Berry, J. W. (2010). Acculturation: When individuals and groups of different cultural backgrounds meet. *Perspectives on Psychological Science*, *5*(4), 472–481.

Schlozman, K. L., Verba, S., & Brady, H. E. (2012). *The unheavenly chorus: Unequal political voice and the broken promise of American democracy*. Princeton, NJ: Princeton University Press.

Scott, C. & Safdar, S. (2017). Threat and prejudice against Syrian refugees in Canada: Assessing the moderating effects of multiculturalism, interculturalism, and assimilation. *International Journal of Intercultural Relations*, *60*, 28–39.

Scott, C., Safdar, S., Desai Trilokekar, R., & El Masri, A. (2015). International students as 'ideal immigrants' in Canada: A disconnect between policy makers' assumptions and the lived experiences of international students. *Comparative and International Education*, *43*(3), Article 5.

Sears, D. O., Sidanius, J., & Bobo, L. (Eds.). (2000). *Racialized politics: The debate about racism in America*. Chicago, IL: University of Chicago Press.

Sibley, C., & Duckitt, J. (2008). Personality and prejudice: A meta-analysis and theoretical review. *Personality and Social Psychology Review*, *12*(3), 248–279.

Simon, H. (1957). *Administrative behavior: A study of decision-making processes in administrative organization*. New York, USA: The Free Press.

Simon, B. & Grabow, O. (2010). The politicization of migrants: Further evidence that politicized collective identity is a dual identity. *Political Psychology*, *31*(5): 717–738.

Simon, B., & Klandermans, B. (2001). Politicized collective identity: A social psychological analysis. *American Psychologist*, *56*(4), 319.

Simon, B., & Ruhs, D. (2008). Identity and politicization among Turkish migrants in Germany: The role of dual identification. *Journal of Personality and Social Psychology*, *95*(6), 1354–1366.

Sniderman, P. M., & Carmines, E. G. (1997). *Reaching beyond race*. Cambridge, MA: Harvard University Press.

Sniderman, P. M., Brody, R. A., & Tetlock, P. E. (1991). *Reasoning and choice: Explorations in political psychology*, Cambridge, MA: Cambridge University Press.

Taber, C., & Lodge, M. (2006). Motivated skepticism in the evaluation of political beliefs. *American Journal of Political Science*, *50*(3), 755–769.

Tajfel, H., & Turner, J., C. (1986). The social identity theory of intergroup behavior. In W. G Austin, & S. Worchel (Eds.), *Psychology of intergroup relations* (2nd edn.). Chicago: Nelson-Hall.

Tankard, M. E., & Paluck, E. L. (2016). Norm perception as a vehicle for social change. *Social Issues and Policy Review*, *10*(1), 181–211.

Tankard, M. E., & Paluck, E. L. (2017). The effect of a Supreme Court decision regarding gay marriage on social norms and personal attitudes. *Psychological Science*, *28*(9), 1334–1344.

Turner, R. N. & Crisp, R. J. (2010). Imagining intergroup contact reduces implicit prejudice. *British Journal of Social Psychology*, 49, 129–142.

Verkuyten, M. (2005). Ethnic group identification and group evaluation among minority and majority groups: Testing the multiculturalism hypothesis. *Journal of Personality and Social Psychology*, *88*(1), 121–138.

Verkuyten, M. (2018). The struggle over political power: Evaluating immigrants' political party representation. *Social Psychology and Personality Science*, *9(4): 419–425*.

Verkuyten, M., Hindriks, P., & Coenders, M. (2016). Majority members' feelings about political representation of Muslim immigrants. *Social Psychology*, *47*, 257–269.

Vorauer, J. D., & Sasaki, S. J. (2011). In the worst rather than the best of times: Effects of salient intergroup ideology in threatening intergroup interactions. *Journal of Personality and Social Psychology*, *101*(2), 307–320.

Verkuyten, M., & Yildiz, A. A. (2007). National (dis)identification and ethnic and religious identity: A study among Turkish-Dutch Muslims. *Personality and Social Psychology Bulletin*, 33(10), 1448–1462.

West, K., Hotchin, V., & Wood, C. (2017). Imagined contact can be more effective for participants with stronger initial prejudices. *Journal of Applied Social Psychology*, *47*(5), 282–292.

Williams, M. R., & Burek, M. W. (2008). Justice, juries, and convictions: The relevance of race in jury verdicts. *Journal of Crime and Justice*, *31*(1), 149–169.

Wills, M. (2010). Psychological research and immigration policy. *Journal of Social Issues*, *66*(4), 825–836.

Winter, N. (2008). *Dangerous frames: How ideas about race and gender shape public opinion*. Chicago, IL: University of Chicago Press.

Zagefka, H., & Brown, R. (2002). The relationship between acculturation strategies, relative fit and intergroup relations: Immigrant-majority relations in Germany. *European Journal of Social Psychology*, *32*(2), 171–188.

8

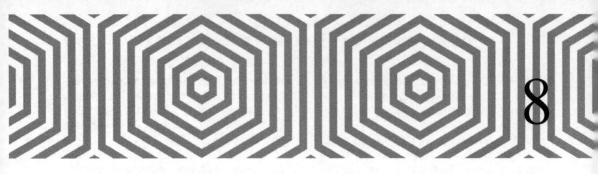

Critical Social Psychology of Politics

Eleni Andreouli and Lia Figgou

INTRODUCTION

In this chapter, we develop a critical social psychological perspective for the study of politics with a focus on the particular topic of citizenship in the context of immigration. The chapter is divided in two main parts. We start by making a distinction between politics as an object of study for social psychology and politics as part of academic social psychological work (i.e. the politics of social psychology as a discipline). We argue that critical social psychology is concerned with both types of politics, that is, both with exploring the political aspects of social psychological issues and with interrogating the political roots and consequences of social psychological knowledge. We also argue that the establishment of social psychology as a discipline is closely linked to an interest in deeply political topics. Social psychologists have often explicitly connected their topics of investigation with political realities, or even with specific political projects. However, the image of a politically interested social psychology has been in tension with the vision of objective science which motivated many of the discipline's founding scholars. The connection of social psychological knowledge with politics has been a contentious topic throughout the history of the discipline, and it became particularly important in discussions of the so-called 'crisis of social psychology'. Politics, therefore, constitutes a key interest for critical social psychology. The chapter suggests that an important contribution of critical social psychology to the study of politics is exploring what lay social actors construct as political and ideological in an era in which the end of politics is proclaimed, and understanding the ways in which such 'everyday politics' connect with broader socio-political contexts. These ideas are exemplified in the second part of the chapter through a discussion of critical social psychological work on citizenship, which serves as an example within the larger field of social psychology and politics. We draw together work from critical social and political psychology to examine the ways in which broader ideological themes become implicated into lay political discourses. The chapter discusses empirical studies from the emerging critical social psychology of citizenship to show that citizenship and immigration are treated as issues that can be dealt with through technocratic practices, which are constructed as consensual and above politics. However, as we show, contemporary discourses about the 'ideal citizen' are not value-free, but they are underpinned by ideologies such as neoliberalism. The chapter concludes by considering the implications of a critical social psychology of politics for social change.

THE POLITICS OF SOCIAL PSYCHOLOGY

It is definitely a truism to suggest that social psychology is related to politics. According to Nesbitt-Larking and Kinnvall (2012), by adopting a 'social problem' orientation, social psychological theory and research have historically paid close attention to topics distinctively and deeply political, such as mass psychology and collective action, intergroup relations and racism, fascism and authoritarianism. Nevertheless, the relation between psychology and politics is not always transparent and it 'stands in need of explanation' (Tileagă, 2013: 4). Any account of this relationship is constituted, but also limited, by epistemological positions and priorities. Therefore, while, from one perspective, politics may be seen as a topic of social psychological inquiry, from another perspective, it may also be considered as part of academic social psychological work.

Accounts of the relation between politics and social psychology usually unfold through a consideration of the history of the discipline, through attention to changes in the constitutive schemes that psychologists have used, in order to produce the object of their discipline (Danziger, 1994; Fine, 2006). These changes, according to Danziger (1994: 5), concern 'the ends' rather than 'the means' of research practice. To start with a widely cited early example from the history of social psychology, Le Bon's (1896) work on the 'pathology' of the crowd, is seen to constitute a response to the need for new means of social control and order generated by the industrialisation of European and North American cities (Reicher, 2001). As Moscovici (1985) put it, Le Bon's crowd psychology provided a diagnosis of the danger of collective movements and offered a cure at the same time, by constituting a guidebook on political leadership style that proved to be useful and effective for leaders such as Hitler, Mussolini, and Stalin.

Historical accounts also attribute the expansion of the 'social attitudes' research paradigm – which affected the establishment of social psychology as a discipline – to political changes that took place in the United States in the first decades of the previous century. Danziger (1997) suggests that early attempts to measure attitudes were accompanied by explicit claims on the political utility of the task. Samelson (1978), on the other hand, considers the interest in exploring 'race attitudes' to constitute a significant reversal. According to his account, while until the 1920s a great deal of psychological research was preoccupied with the identification of mental differences between human 'races', by 1940, this concern was supplanted by an interest in measuring intergroup attitudes. Samelson maintains that this reversal did not constitute the result of an internal failure of 'race psychology', but external, contextual factors had a major contribution. Immigration policy changes in the United States (such as the Immigration Restriction Law of 1924) diminished the need for psychological research to provide justifications for the exclusion of certain nationalities due to their presumed inferiority. Moreover, the influx of ethnic minority professionals in the field of psychology and the leftward shift of psychologists during the period of the Great Depression can be considered to have exerted some influence in the same direction. Finally, during the Second World War, the need to unite America against Nazi Germany was another reason to leave behind research on supposed inherent race differences.

Historical accounts maintain that the anti-fascist spirit exerted persistent influence on social psychological research from the late 1930s onwards. The seminal work of Kurt Lewin and his colleagues (Lewin et al., 1939) explored the implications of different styles of leadership – democratic, autocratic, and laissez-faire – on group structure and member behaviour and concluded that democratic leadership was not only more effective but it was also appreciated by group members. Adorno and his colleagues (1950), on the other hand, considering that fascism met enthusiastic support because it managed to appeal to people's subjective-emotional needs, attempted to reconcile the notion of political ideology with personality dynamics and individual attitudes. According to Nicholson (1997), the 1950s and 1960s were filled with studies that focused on conformity (Asch, 1956), obedience to authority (Milgram, 1963), and the avoidance of dissonance (Festinger, 1964). The political significance of these studies, conducted while the horror of the Holocaust was fresh in memory, has been largely highlighted. Their (unintended) consequences, related to the fact that they prioritised compliance and conformity as a research question, have also been indicated. As other commentators have argued, by fashioning a discipline organised primarily around variables of consensus and dissonance reduction, social psychologists have repressed or under-theorised contradiction (Billig, 1987), coercion and hegemony, dissent and revolution (Fine, 2004).

While the way in which anti-fascism has influenced the political economy of social psychological knowledge production has been highlighted, other influences, such as Marxism, have been relatively neglected. Anti-communist purges of universities are deemed to have influenced this inattention. According to Harris (1996: 73), for example, one may sense a Marxist influence behind the Asch experiments and, in particular, behind the finding that two persons can resist conformity to an erroneous social norm, while a single person will bend to the opinion of the majority. Nevertheless, 'the political cleansing of existing histories prevents us from knowing how Solomon Asch's experience of solidarity with a small political minority – Communist faculty at Brooklyn College – contributed to his discovery of this important principle in social and experimental psychology.'

The way in which anti-communism in the United States influenced the political and institutional development of American psychology from 1935 to 1955 is also reflected in Nicholson's (1997) account of the transformation of the professional model proclaimed by the Society for the Psychological Study of Social Issues (SPSSI) and by Goodwin Watson as one of its founders. According to this account, while in 1936, SPSSI's statement of purpose called upon psychologists to abandon political disinterestedness and to employ a politically motivated conception of scientific research, less than ten years later, in 1945 (when SPSSI launched its *Journal of Social Issues*), this politically motivated statement gave way to the liberal vision of (politically disinterested) scientific progress. According to Nicholson, this change can certainly be attributed to the political persecution of communists and, in this case, of Watson in particular. Nevertheless, there are other factors that should be taken into account. Early psychologists had invested much effort, time, and resources for the discipline to be accredited with the necessary reputation of accuracy and scientific objectivity. The vision of a politically motivated psychology has not been compatible with the epistemology of an objective science.

The way in which existing epistemological choices and conceptual tools reflected the politics of psychology as a discipline and restricted the range of potential research questions (and answers) has been pointed out by Danziger (1997) in his account of the use of attitude scales in *The Authoritarian Personality* (Adorno et al., 1950). The concept of attitudes and its measurement technology, according to this account, were incompatible with the original research question of Adorno and his colleagues' project. Attitude scales could be used to identify individual differences but they were unable to capture social consciousness as a coherent integrated whole that reflected a certain socio-political culture. By using the concept and research technology of attitudes, the authors of *The Authoritarian Personality* ended up with an account that focused on styles of thinking (e.g. cognitive rigidity) instead of historically specific beliefs. This has had, according to Billig (1982), important consequences on the way in which some of this project's conclusions were reinterpreted and used by researchers with a totally different political agenda to the one of the authors of *The Authoritarian Personality*. When the war against fascism gave way to the Cold War, authors like Eysenck (1954) and Rokeach (1960) sharpened the distinction between content of beliefs and style of thinking, in order to suggest that cognitive rigidity characterised communists as well as fascists.

The study of individual cognitive processes became – among others – a focus of critique in the so-called 'crisis' of social psychology. The following two sub-sections discuss this 'crisis' and explore the implications for the study of the political, respectively.

The Politics of the Crisis and Beyond

The 'crisis' of social psychology refers to historical debates that developed around the late 1960s and early 1970s, at a period in which scholars on both sides of the Atlantic openly questioned some core assumptions of the discipline regarding scientific knowledge and truth, the metaphors of human mind that dominated social psychological texts, and the capacity of the experimental method to capture the situated, context-specific nature of meaning and to appreciate the richness of human experience. It is beyond the scope of the present chapter to elaborate on these critiques in detail or to cast light on the multifaceted issues that have been raised (but see Armistead, 1974; Elms, 1975; Faye, 2012; Parker, 1989). We will briefly consider, however, the political context of these critiques as well as their implications for a social psychology of politics.

According to Spears (1997), the crisis was characterised by a rather clear left-liberal political agenda. The post-war generation of the late 1960s explicitly criticised the world order and protested inside and outside universities against those state institutions that paid service to this order. The practices and institutions of psychology were very often identified with this old-world order (Rose, 1985). In the same vein, Faye (2012) maintained that the 'crisis' in social psychology reflected a larger crisis in American society. The same issues that were debated during the crisis, according to Faye, had been contentious throughout the history of the discipline. They had never caused, however, the forceful debates of the 1970s. Outside pressures and a 'language of crisis' that was prevalent at the time contributed to social psychologists' increasing consideration of their discipline's detachment from societal concerns.[1]

The idea that the discipline should take into account the political and historical context of research and knowledge production (Israel and Tajfel, 1972) was central in the crisis debates. According to Gergen (1973), history constitutes a better model than physical science for social psychology. Psychological knowledge is not only produced within a certain political and cultural milieu, and reflects its values, but it also exerts influence on social values and cultural practices. An example is Moscovici's (1961/2008) study of how psychoanalysis became incorporated into everyday common sense in France. Moscovici (1972) further considered the way in which research questions are related to certain social and political contexts and suggested that a distinct European tradition in social psychology should be based on the social theoretical production of Europe and on European political history.

These debates brought to the fore another issue that is important for our current consideration of the relation between social psychology and politics: the issue of the relation between scientific and everyday knowledge. The critique of positivism and its epistemological foundations opened the way to reconsider this relation and to compare lay and social scientific concepts and categories. Authors like Harré (1974) questioned the status of scientific interpretative resources and tools and supported the need to trust the experience and interpretation of research participants and to avoid privileging expert knowledge over common sense.

The crisis and its repercussions are commonly considered to have influenced the development of what is identified as critical social psychology. While, in some contexts, critical social psychology tends to be treated as identical to the 'turn to discourse' that took off in the late 1980s and early 1990s, it constitutes a broader movement that brought together feminist, social constructionist, poststructuralist, and qualitative research perspectives (Augoustinos, 2013). What is seen to have united these perspectives is the objective of a politically progressive psychology, a psychology concerned with politics, oppression, and social change (Parker, 2013). In fact, critical social psychology is usually defined by its perspective on the relation between psychological knowledge and politics, or rather by its preoccupation and concern with the politics of the discipline. To quote from Hepburn (2003: 1):

> So critical social psychology is critical of society or at least some basic elements of its institutions, organization or practices. But critical social psychology (sometimes shortened to CPS) is critical in another basic sense: It is critical of psychology itself. It asks questions about its assumptions, its practices and its broader influences.

Nevertheless, it would be misleading to overemphasise the convergence between critical social psychologists. Critical social psychology can hardly be seen as a homogenous field and it would be more easily defined by those (ontological and epistemological) premises that it opposes rather than by those that are shared between its various strands. European critical social psychological traditions have significant differences with those traditions developed in the United States and they both differ from the psychology of liberation that flourished in Latin America (e.g. Martín-Baró, 1994; Montero, 2007). In particular, it would be misleading to suggest that an approach to the relation between politics and social psychology constitutes common ground amongst critical social psychologists and promotes a 'collective' identity (Condor, 1997). The possibility for social change and the lack of compatibility of certain epistemological positions (e.g. relativism) with radical politics constitute points of disunity and heated debate (Parker, 1999).

Bearing in mind the diversity of approaches between – as well as within – critical camps, and also considering that our own perspective is situated in a particular geographical and scholarly context, we will proceed to sketch what we see as an important project of critical social psychology in the era of neoliberalism when the end of ideology has been proclaimed.

Critical Social Psychology and the Political in the Era of the 'End of Ideology'

In a highly influential paper, Weltman and Billig (2001) argued that political psychology would benefit by importing the concepts and analytic lens of discursive and rhetorical psychology. Such a project, according to the authors, would enable the study of the details of political rhetoric and it would highlight the dilemmas and contradictions of a political ideology that attempts to refute its ideological and political character by being disguised as common sense. In particular, analysis of interviews with local officials in the Midlands of England indicated, according to Weltman and Billig, two main contradictions. First, while most politicians claimed the need for social change, at the same time they did their best to prove their personal stability. Second, despite the fact that they were apparently affiliated with certain political parties and inevitably mobilised their affiliation in their arguments, they argued against the parochialism of the left–right division and for the need to support consensual, less ideologically divisive politics.

Weltman and Billig's work seems – more than a decade later – to be particularly topical. Decisions in institutions of crisis-ridden Europe are commonly constructed as indisputable technocratic issues to which there are no alternatives, and coalitions between parties with deep ideological differences are represented as the ideal type of governing (Figgou, 2016). On the other hand, populist arguments based around xenophobia, immigration restriction, and violation of citizenship rights usually mobilise concerns about the failure of the political 'establishment'. Hence, a representation of politics as dirty and corrupted is juxtaposed to the blamelessness and the purity of lay social actors who are represented as against (conventional) politics (Clarke, 2010).

Research on the politics of the everyday has been, however, immensely limited (but see Howarth and Andreouli, 2017). As Condor (2016) has maintained, political and social psychologists tend to restrict their focus of attention to their conceptions of politics and the political, neglecting what these concepts mean to lay social actors. Condor claims that this stance is predicated on the assumption that politics constitutes a distinct domain that requires competences, deep knowledge, and refined attitudes that are not available to lay people. On the contrary, based on empirical findings, Condor asserts that, when people do not have available domain-specific knowledge, they justify their attitudes towards political events by employing generic political idioms and ideological values.

To study common sense conceptions of politics does not mean to take lay representations at face value or to ignore the macrorealities of social life. Politics constitutes a product of social practices and social interaction but also the broader context of values and practices within which specific interactions take place. Hence, a social psychological study of politics involves a focus on the 'thinking society' (Moscovici, 1984) and its institutions as well as an approach to language, communication, and interaction as the arena in which political ideologies are intersubjectively produced and reproduced. As Tileagă (2013) notes, a critical social and political psychological approach is interested not simply in how the world becomes intelligible to political psychologists but, more importantly, in how the world becomes intelligible to lay social actors in concrete social contexts.

TOWARDS A CRITICAL SOCIAL PSYCHOLOGY OF CITIZENSHIP

Drawing on the ideas presented above, in this section, we elaborate further a critical social psychological perspective on politics. We focus specifically on a topic that has recently attracted the attention of social psychologists, namely, citizenship. We do not suggest here that citizenship is the only, or the main, topic in the field of a critical social psychology of politics. In recent years, however, citizenship has become a key concept in the study of politics in social psychology, particularly in the European context. This reflects, to an extent, the fact that citizenship appears to be an important concept of contemporary political vocabularies. In what follows, we first introduce the concept of citizenship and highlight its importance in contemporary politics and then present a critical social psychology approach to the study of citizenship, with an emphasis on immigration contexts.

'The Era of Citizenship'

It can be argued that we live in an 'era of citizenship', in a time, that is, when citizenship has become a crucial concept for understanding and engaging with contemporary politics, particularly in European and other Western contexts. This is evident in 'formal' state-based politics in Western countries, whereby citizenship is increasingly used as a tool for enhancing social cohesion and dealing with presumed security threats, namely, terrorism. In the UK, for example, since the early 2000s, there have been efforts to link British citizenship with national belonging, so that, more than a legal status, citizenship becomes a meaningful bond uniting British nationals. This, presumably, is a solution for problems of integration caused by immigration. Citizenship is also employed in more transgressive politics, with calls, for example, for more cosmopolitan forms of citizenship as a means for creating inclusive and equal societies. In this context, as Condor (2011) has observed, citizenship has become a matter of critical reflexive concern.

Academic research has responded to such societal challenges with an 'explosion' of studies on citizenship in the past couple of decades (Kymlicka and Norman, 1994, in Condor, 2011). Scholarly work on citizenship is increasingly diversified and multidisciplinary, engaging the entirety of the social sciences. In addition to the traditional focus on social, political, and civil rights (Marshall, 1964), there is now work in diverse areas such as sexual citizenship, ecological citizenship, post-national and multicultural citizenship, among many others. This proliferation and expansion of work on citizenship reflects the diversification of contemporary political life and rights claims, particularly the complexities of identity-based politics in the Western world. While, traditionally, the citizen has been understood as the adult male (Marshall, 1950: 24), more recently there has been a focus on exploring 'the diverse communities to which we belong, the complex interplay of identity and identification in modern society, and the differentiated ways in which people now participate in social life' (Hall and Held, 1989: 176).

In addition to the proliferation of citizenship rights claims, Isin (2009) notes that the scales, sites, and acts of citizenship are also expanding. For example, the range of actions that is understood as constituting political behaviour is changing. Blogging, for instance, has become a new way for expressing political views and seeking to assert political influence. In terms of sites, social media, for example, have become important sites of political action and they are frequently used for political campaigning. Crucially, for the social psychological approach adopted in this chapter, citizenship is increasingly located in the field of everyday life: it is not only politicians who 'do' politics but lay citizens themselves. Contemporary identity-based politics, mentioned above, is an example of how the distinction between what is personal or private and what is political or public is blurred. There are myriad examples of how the political has 'spread over' to the everyday and vice versa – e.g. campaigns against 'everyday sexism'. It seems that politics is nowadays played out in diverse spheres and with diverse political actors, each with their own position, agenda, and interests. Together, these points suggest that 'who is a citizen' and 'what citizenship is' are not straightforward issues, but they are reconfigured in line with changing political claims and struggles. This calls for a reconsideration of the multiple spheres in which contemporary politics play out, particularly the ways in which 'formal' institutional politics relate to 'lay' politics of everyday life.

Principles of a Critical Social Psychology of Citizenship

While, as it was argued above, social psychology has paid attention to various political topics, the concept of citizenship has been remarkably absent from the discipline (Condor, 2011). Where citizenship has been salient in scholarly work, this is often in a rather de-politicised manner, such as in organisational studies (see review by Stevenson et al., 2015). To offer an account of the politics of citizenship from a critical social psychological perspective, we will draw on work from the emerging critical social psychology of citizenship, which has recently begun to take shape (Stevenson et al., 2015).

We will develop two main arguments: (1) a critical social psychology of citizenship should focus on the different, multifaceted, and contested conceptions of citizenship; (2) a critical social psychology of citizenship should take into account the different ways in which politics of the everyday are related to 'big' institutional politics.

Haste (2004: 414) argues that a key issue for social psychologists is to explore the dynamics of the citizenship construct by asking 'how do we construct individuals as citizens, and how do we construct the concept of citizenship itself'. Citizenship, in other words, is not only something that people 'have' but also something that people 'do'. This is eloquently shown by Barnes et al. (2004) in a heavily cited critical social psychological study of citizenship. Taking a discursive approach, Barnes et al. (2004) studied letters of complaint in relation to the settlement of 'new age travellers' in a local community in England and illustrated the ways in which the identity of the citizen could be mobilised in order to construct arguments against new travellers. Positioning themselves as 'concerned citizens', local residents could claim an entitlement over how the local space could be managed. At the same time, new travellers were positioned as violating the norms of good citizenship. Their presence in public space was seen as illegitimate and unwarranted on the basis of normative representations about public behaviour which reify power imbalances between those who are controlled (e.g. squatters, travellers) and those who have the capacity to discipline others deemed to act in disorderly ways (Di Masso, 2012). It follows that a group's social position can allow it more or less voice to define what is considered 'appropriate' or 'normal' citizenship.

A key question here is who counts as a political actor in analyses of citizenship? In traditional analyses of citizenship and politics, political actors are considered to be the official political institutions (e.g. states or interstate organisations) and other political agents who may operate outside government or state structures (e.g. activists, civil society organisations, pressure groups) but are nonetheless understood as being politically active. Contrary to this view of the political actor as a specialised political expert, ordinary citizens are assumed to be observers or recipients of political processes, but they are not seen as being actors themselves.

In fact, there is an interesting paradox when considering the role of citizens in politics. On the one hand, 'ordinary' citizens are 'enrolled' as participants in contemporary strategies of neoliberal governance (Clarke, 2010). For example, in the 2010 UK government's 'Big Society' political agenda, citizens were called to engage in politics, particularly in matters of local governance. This is supposedly an empowering approach that takes power away from politicians and gives it to the people. It can be construed as a means of governing through ordinary people. On the other hand, however, the valorisation of citizens as valuable political actors is premised precisely on the fact that ordinary citizens are depoliticised (Clarke, 2010;

Neveu, 2015). In an era of great disaffection from institutionalised forms of politics, ordinary people are considered simultaneously below politics, because they are concerned with everyday matters, and above politics, because they have not been contaminated by a corrupt political system (Clarke, 2010). In this context, common sense often becomes a tool of political rhetoric (Condor et al., 2013; Hall and O'Shea, 2015). Politicians claim that they speak on behalf of the people and that their policies represent common sense. As such, common sense becomes a 'contested arena' (Hall and O'Shea, 2015: 55).

Against this background, critical social psychology has the potential to examine common sense in its own right and, thus, to explore the politics of everyday life from the perspectives of citizens themselves. As Neveu (2015: 150) argues, '[a]pproaching citizenship processes 'from the ordinary' is a fruitful perspective from which the political dimensions of usually unseen or unheard practices and sites can be grasped'. A social psychological approach can uncover and interrogate the politics of the ordinary and the everyday, thus adding nuance to a black-and-white state-centric understanding of politics.

Contrary to assertions of post-ideological politics (Weltman and Billig, 2001), a critical social psychological approach exposes the nuances and complexities of everyday ideologies, which often go unnoticed. In that respect, Billig and colleagues' (1988) analysis of everyday 'lived' ideologies is particularly useful. For Billig et al. (1988), ideology is not a formal system of political principles but a network of 'common-sensical' ideas, which provide the symbolic material for everyday political reasoning. Hall and O'Shea (2015) have, for example, examined some of the ways in which neoliberalism has 'infiltrated' common sense, so that the logic of the market, with its principles of self-interest and individualism, becomes a background given in contemporary political thinking. However, everyday ideologies are not closed, but they can contain the seeds for argumentation and debate. Indeed, in their brief, but insightful, analysis of online comments in *The Sun* newspaper regarding controversial welfare reforms in 2013 in the UK, Hall and O'Shea, (2015) found that while benefits claimants are commonly demonised under a neoliberal logic that diminishes social responsibility, there were also counter-voices against neoliberal politics and competitive individualism. Billig and colleagues (1988) suggest that everyday ideologies are structured around dilemmas. For instance, the dominant ideological theme of individualism in contemporary free-market neoliberal societies may be countered by the theme of social responsibility. Pursuing one's self-interest and contributing to society are both valued ideals. While neoliberal values have become hegemonic, the value of justice based on social solidarity may also be part of common sense and can be drawn upon to argue against an individualistic view of justice. Such dilemmas, therefore, provide the raw material for argumentative thinking and social debate (Billig, 1987). This rhetorical approach draws attention to what Haste (2004: 415) has called 'ideology in process'. In adopting this perspective, critical social psychologists explore the strategic dimension and the functions of everyday political discourse, both in the micro context of a given interaction and the macro sociopolitical context.

For instance, in his study of young people's conceptions of employment rights and responsibilities, Gibson (2011) showed that lay thinking is structured around a fundamental ideological tension between the right to welfare and the responsibility to contribute to society. To resolve this dilemma, participants employed the trope of effortfulness, arguing that 'making an effort' should be a precondition for receiving unemployment benefits. However, this dominant focus on individual effort was disrupted in the context of talk about immigration. In that context, participants put forward a more societal explanation of unemployment as the result of immigration. Gibson's research highlights some of the ways in which broader norms and ideologies (e.g. the ideology of individualism) find their way into lay political thinking and are actively negotiated in specific interactions and argumentative contexts. This study further shows that 'individualistic' and 'solidaristic' ideologies coexist and can both be drawn upon in different ways. Furthermore, both these ideological themes can be used to exclude others, either because they are considered 'lazy' or because they are not 'one of us', therefore, ultimately reinforcing the ideology of liberal individualism, on the one hand, and nationalism (cf. Billig, 1995), on the other.

The dominant juxtaposition of politics with supposedly non-political common sense entails another interesting and fairly neglected question – the extent to which lay constructions of the political share the assumptions identified in formal political discourse. In a recent study (Figgou, 2016), lay people accounted for the electoral success of the neo-Nazi party of Golden Dawn in Greece in terms of a distinction between the political system and Golden Dawn, portraying Golden Dawn as being against politicians and above politics. Widely shared in these accounts was also a categorical distinction between ideology and non-ideology driven voters. The former were considered to constitute a small minority, while the latter, the vast majority of voters, were portrayed as everyday people who were driven by despair and indignation. Of course, more research is needed in order to understand not only the public understandings of politics and the political but also the ways in which these are employed in certain social and rhetorical contexts towards certain rhetorical ends.

These studies, and others in the field, show the micro-performances of citizenship in everyday life. But they also show that these everyday manifestations of politics do not occur in a vacuum; they are contingent on the social and political context in which they take place. Issues of power are very important in this regard. A critical analysis is not only concerned with the ways in which citizenship is constructed but also with which definitions of citizenship acquire more legitimacy than others. Put differently, critical social psychology is interested in exploring how different political actors may have differential 'epistemological power' to construct normative accounts of citizenship, while other voices may be marginalised.

In some cases, individuals or groups do not have the societal position and resources to become political agents and participate as citizens. The notion of denizenship illustrates this point. Turner (2016) argues that today denizenship can be used to describe not only foreign residents with limited rights in a country but also people with full citizenship rights formally who are nonetheless excluded in various ways. Turner (2016) notes that, following the financial crisis of 2008, austerity measures (such as increased taxation and limited public spending for health and welfare) have diminished citizens' social rights across many Western countries. At the same time, neoliberal employment practices and the decline of trade unions have left many in precarious work conditions. This means that people who are citizens 'on paper' do not have access to opportunities and rights that would allow them to participate in the civil sphere. These considerations highlight the relevance of social class for work on citizenship and for social and political psychology in general (Hodgetts and Griffin, 2015).

This discussion of the links between the micro and the macro levels of analysis draws our attention to the need to be careful not to overemphasise everyday politics at the expense of state politics. Indeed, this is precisely the discourse of right-wing populism that has recently been spreading in Europe and that valorises the ordinary citizen while devaluing the formal political structures (Figgou, 2016). In our view, the state and other formalised political institutions remain powerful political actors and ought to be acknowledged in social psychological work. As we have argued in previous work

(Andreouli et al., 2016b), these powerful actors can be said to construct hegemonic and normative representations about the meanings and boundaries of citizenship. For instance, considering citizenship in immigration contexts, state laws and policies have crucial authority in defining who is entitled to citizenship and under what criteria – as the next section will show, drawing on research examples from European contexts.

Citizenship and Immigration

Studying processes of exclusion has been central in the critical social psychology of citizenship as it has begun to take shape in recent years (Stevenson et al., 2015). In that regard, much social psychological work on citizenship has focused on contexts of immigration. In what follows, we discuss work from the social psychology of citizenship and immigration, paying particular attention to three 'common-sensical' assumptions that inform political reasoning about citizenship and immigration, which have been studied in relevant research: the 'essentialised' citizen, the 'deserving' citizen, and the 'rational' citizen. These are not mutually exclusive categories; rather, they correspond to intersecting representations and norms of 'good citizenship'.

The 'essentialised' citizen

Much of the social psychology of citizenship has paid particular attention to national citizenship, drawing links between the concept of identity (so central as it is in the discipline) and the concept of citizenship. Some researchers have studied how different conceptions of nationhood and national identity are reflected in different representations of citizenship. The distinction between ethnic and civic representations of the nation has been very important in this field. The former refers to an understanding of the nation as an ethnic community, with a shared ancestry and culture, while the latter prioritises common territory and political values. In their study on essentialism and citizenship in the Greek context, Kadianaki and Andreouli (2017) found that Greek citizenship was largely essentialised in public debates about a new citizenship law in Greece. In that study, Greek citizenship was represented in terms of an ethnic essence that is inherited from generation to generation, but it cannot be otherwise obtained. These findings offer support to previous research showing that ethnic representations of nationhood can be associated with strong anti-immigration views (Pehrson et al., 2009).

Non-essentialist narratives were also identified in Kadianaki and Andreouli's (2017) study. These were based on ideas of civic participation and cultural integration, whereby becoming Greek was seen as a choice rather than an inevitable biological fact. Still, however, culture could be used in essentialist ways; cultural assimilation and 'shedding' one's heritage culture were often discussed as criteria for granting Greek citizenship to migrants. These findings resonate with the broader politics of cultural integration as they are played out in Western liberal democracies. Citizenship tests, ceremonies, and the like have now become a precondition for citizenship acquisition in most countries of the West in recent years, pointing to a 'thickening' of citizenship alongside a more general 'disillusionment' with multiculturalism, which is now routinely seen as a threat to social cohesion. While this representation of citizenship in terms of cultural assimilation appears exclusionary, it can also be used to argue for opening up citizenship to migrants. In Kadianaki and Andreouli's (2017) study, it was found that some migrants used arguments of cultural assimilation in order to claim their right to become Greeks – often compared to other migrants, who were described as not integrated. Therefore, essentialism is an ideologically laden representational tool that can be used strategically to support both arguments for inclusion and exclusion (Figgou, 2013).

Nevertheless, as we have previously suggested (Andreouli et al., 2016b), it can be argued that the emphasis on cultural assimilation, on the part of both ethnic majorities and minorities, masks an underlying ethnic essentialism, since arguments around cultural assimilation are often rhetorically used to 'compensate' for the lack of migrants' ethnic ties with the 'host' society. Therefore, we can further argue that ethnic nationalism constitutes a banal ideological framework (cf. Billig, 1995) which incorporates within it not only the ethnic/non-ethnic dichotomy but also the dichotomy between culturally integrated or compatible/culturally not integrated or non-compatible.

It is not only the national citizenship category that can be essentialised. Figgou (2015), in her research in Greece, has shown, for instance, that the category of the 'illegal immigrant' can be essentialised as a personality trait that indicates migrants' moral character. Therefore, essentialisation appears to be a key ideological tool for excluding migrants – particularly those who are seen 'undeserving'. This latter theme is further explored below.

The 'deserving' citizen

Research within the social psychology of citizenship has drawn attention to the distinction between 'deserving' and 'undeserving' citizens, which seems to frame many contemporary discourses around citizenship in relation to immigration issues. For instance, Andreouli and Dashtipour (2014) and Andreouli and Howarth (2013) have shown that representations of British citizenship are structured around a fundamental tension between deserving and undeserving migrants. The former are those who contribute to the economy and integrate into British culture, while the latter are those who are seen as lacking the potential to integrate and who are also seen as abusing Britain's welfare system. This dualism between the 'good' and the 'bad' immigrant can be used to present Britain as a welcoming and tolerant society that helps those in 'genuine' need (the so-called 'genuine asylum seekers') but excludes those migrants who are seen as opportunists seeking to exploit Britain's resources for their personal benefit. This way, anti-immigration views against 'bad' migrants are presented as reasonable and legitimate, while maintaining an image of Britain as a tolerant country.

Moreover, Andreouli and Howarth (2013) have shown that this dualistic representation of migrants also permeates public policy discourses around citizenship and naturalisation in the UK. An analysis of public policy documents on naturalisation showed that at the heart of the UK's 'earned citizenship' policies lies a distinction between migrants who are seen as an economic resource and migrants who are seen as abusers of British resources and hospitality. Public policy on naturalisation operates as a bordering mechanism which distinguishes between 'elite' (predominantly wealthy, skilled, mainly Western) migrants and 'non-elite' migrants (predominantly poor, unskilled migrants from the Global South). While this anti-immigration discourse is seemingly based on civic responsibilities (e.g. financial contribution of migrants) more so than on ethnic criteria, Andreouli and Howarth (2013) have shown that civic and ethnic criteria overlap so that 'non-elite' migrants from the Global South who are seen as lacking both the financial and the ethno-cultural capital to integrate in the society.

Given recent trends in the West to introduce citizenship tests and ceremonies as a means for assessing migrants' potential to integrate, several social psychologists have explored the meanings of citizenship as manifested in these new spaces and rituals of performing citizenship. Certainly, such new political initiatives respond to an increasing anxiety about a presumed lack of social cohesion in contemporary Western nation-states – which is commonly attributed to immigration. In this context, Gray and Griffin (2014) analysed one of the editions of the *Life in the*

UK handbook that is used for the citizenship test in the UK and which assesses would-be citizens on their knowledge of the country. Gray and Griffin observed that the test aims to counter the presumed negative cultural impact of immigration in Britain by teaching British culture to migrants. Through this practice, British citizenship emerges as a matter of technical expertise, not as a matter of political participation.

Overall, it could be argued that there is a general trend in Western nation-states of representing citizenship as a privilege that has to be earned through criteria of economic contribution, cultural integration, and emotional commitment (Andreouli and Howarth, 2013). As we showed above, the criterion of effortfullness (see Gibson, 2011) is key in contemporary discourses of citizenship as it is used to navigate the ideological tension between rights (to welfare, humanitarian protection, freedom of movement etc.) and duties in liberal conceptions of citizenship.

The 'rational citizen'

Many social psychological studies on citizenship and immigration, particularly those falling within the broader field of critical discursive psychology, have focused on processes of identity management in relation to everyday talk about immigration. Much of this work has been devoted to studying the ways in which people present themselves as reasonable and seek to rhetorically 'dodge the identity of prejudice' (Wetherell and Potter, 1992). This often takes the form of the 'I'm not racist, but…' disclaimer, which is employed in immigration-related discussions to disclaim a racist identity while putting forward anti-immigration arguments that can potentially be heard as prejudiced (Augoustinos and Every, 2010; Goodman, 2010). For instance, Hanson-Easey and Augoustinos (2010), in the Australian context, and Capdevila and Callaghan (2008), in the UK context, have shown that political discourse against asylum seekers is based on seemingly pragmatic and de-racialised arguments, which present the exclusion of asylum seekers as a reasonable response to dealing with immigration-related problems. As Billig and colleagues (1988) have observed, the modern liberal ideal of reason dictates a 'norm against prejudice'. This means that citizens are expected to be rational and non-prejudiced. In this ideological context, negative views towards outgroups should be justified on the basis of reasonable arguments rather than 'irrational' prejudice.

Further findings, documented in recent critical social psychological studies on immigration and race talk (Augoustinos and Every, 2010; Goodman and Burke, 2010), suggest that social actors are not only concerned about complying with the norm against prejudice, they are also cautious about attributing opposition to immigration to some form of racism. Apart from the widely studied taboo against racism, a taboo against making accusations of racism is also prevalent. By complying with this latter norm, citizens demonstrate their solidarity to other citizens who are seen as more vulnerable to the implications of immigration. Moreover, similar concerns around accusing others of fascism and ideological extremity have been found in research in the context of discussing the electoral success of extreme right parties (Figgou, 2016). More broadly, an 'end of racism' narrative (Andreouli et al., 2016a), i.e. denying the very existence of racism in contemporary societies and arguing that it is a 'thing of the past', draws on a more fundamental discourse about the end of politics which characterises neoliberal ideology. Neoliberalism promotes the economisation of political activity so that it is construed as a matter of 'cold' calculation of risks and benefits, rather than a matter of ideological preferences and/or prejudices. In this way, the 'ideal' citizen under neoliberalism is a technocratic, rational, and pragmatic calculator (cf. Brown, 2016). Somewhat paradoxically, then, the citizen emerges as a non-political and non-ideological subject.

CONCLUSIONS: A SOCIAL PSYCHOLOGY FOR SOCIAL CHANGE

In this chapter, we have outlined a critical approach to the study of politics in social psychology. We started by reflecting on the relationship between (social) psychology and politics and then we outlined a perspective on the critical social psychology of politics, particularly regarding the study of citizenship. Certainly, our chapter is limited in that we neglected other aspects of politics that are important in contemporary societies. In particular, while we discussed the boundaries between citizenship/non-citizenship, our focus was on how citizenship is enacted, less so on how it may be denied. For instance, issues around deportation (see, for example, an interesting collection of works by De Genova and Peutz, 2010) also clearly have important socio-psychological ramifications (e.g. in terms of identity and displacement). At the same time, our scope has been limited to European and Western contexts (for a discussion of Latin American Liberation Psychology, see for example, Montero, 2007). Nevertheless, our examination of citizenship has given us some insights about the value of a critical social psychology of politics. In this final section, we review some key arguments of the chapter and examine their implications for social change.

One can think of two ways that a critical social psychological approach relates to social change. The first has to do with studying social change and the second has to do with contributing to social change. Regarding the study of processes of social change, as we have suggested in this chapter, a critical approach takes into consideration both the level of institutions (for example, state polices on citizenship and immigration) and the level of everyday life (the ways in which citizenship is enacted and negotiated in concrete everyday settings). This dual focus on the macro and micro scale allows us to study both stability, i.e. the ways that dominant ideologies (for example, about the norms defining 'good citizenship') remain dominant and 'commonsensical', *and* change, i.e. the ways in which processes of claims making within a 'battle of ideas' (Moscovici and Markova, 2000: 275) can contest dominant meanings.

This perspective allows us to interrogate the very notion of social change. Change is often a rhetorical trope employed by politicians to justify their decisions and agendas. We can see that when politicians predicate their arguments on the need for social and political change against previous governments and/or against 'the establishment' more generally. The concept of social change is also commonly interlinked with the concepts of the active citizen and active participation. In the approach outlined above, we have emphatically maintained that it is the processes of 'doing' citizenship that we are interested in, because this focus on action and practice challenges the reification of the citizenship category (cf. Reicher and Hopkins, 2001). However, from a critical perspective, the meanings of action, participation, and active citizenship should not be taken at face value, but they should be interrogated. Norms of 'active citizenship' promote particular types of political action and participation as appropriate and acceptable. Voting, for example, is considered to be fundamental as a citizenship right and obligation and as a cost-effective way of political participation (while abstaining from voting in the elections is considered as a-political and even as problematic). Norms of 'active citizenship', whereby individual citizens are expected to take individual responsibility for the matters that concern them (which can be described as governance through the responsibilisation of citizens (Rose, 1989/1999)), are reflected on what we earlier called the 'rational citizen', the self-interested and self-contained subject who acts in their own best interests. Hegemonic norms of 'good citizenship', built on the basis of a narrow conception of individual participation, can be critiqued on the grounds that they limit citizens' capacity to form more collective movements.

With regards to contributing to social change, we have argued that the key merit of a critical approach is that it studies the ways in which ideologies become embedded in everyday common sense. This reinforces their power because the ideological underpinnings of 'thinking as usual' (Schütz, 1944) are not easily reflected upon, but they are routinely taken as a given. As such, a critical approach has the potential to uncover the ideological foundations of 'common-sensical' assumptions, such as the assumption that citizenship is only deserved by those with sufficient economic, social, and cultural capital (e.g. migrants who are seen as adequately assimilated) under a neoliberal model of politics, thus limiting the political voice of lower socio-economic classes and non-nationals. This emphasis on studying the politics of common sense is particularly important nowadays with the rise of right-wing populists who claim to speak on behalf of 'ordinary' people (see Wodak, 2015). In this context, it is imperative that we take a critical look at common sense and its ideological dimensions. This critical approach to politics can denaturalise dominant ideologies and open up a space for imagining alternative politics and developing new political narratives. This approach expands the notion of the political to include transgressive political action; for example, going beyond dominant notions of the 'active citizen' to study 'activist citizens' (Isin, 2009), citizens who engage with politics in non-normative ways (for example, by staging protests, occupations, and so on – or even by acting as whistle-blowers against objectionable state practices) with the aim to disrupt the status quo. In our view, critical social psychology can be aligned with progressive social movements that serve social justice.

Note

1 Faye also cites House (1977), according to whom the 'crisis' also reflects the lack of interchange between psychological and sociological variants of social psychology and the inability to formulate theories that incorporate different (psychological and societal or sociological) levels.

REFERENCES

Adorno, T. W., Frenkel-Brunswik, E., Levinson, D. J., & Sanford, R. N. (1950). *The authoritarian personality*. New York: Harper and Row.

Andreouli, E., & Dashtipour, P. (2014). British citizenship and the 'other': An analysis of the earned citizenship discourse. *Journal of Community & Applied Social Psychology, 24*(2), 100–110.

Andreouli, E., & Howarth. C. (2013). National identity, citizenship and immigration: Putting identity in context. *Journal for the Theory of Social Behaviour, 43*(3), 361–382.

Andreouli, E., Greenland, K., & Howarth, C. (2016a). 'I don't think racism is that bad any more': Exploring the 'end of racism' discourse among students in English schools. *European Journal of Social Psychology, 46*(2), 171–184.

Andreouli, E., Kadianaki, E., & Xenitidou, M. (2016b). Citizenship and social psychology: An analysis of constructions of Greek citizenship. In C. Howarth, & E. Andreouli (Eds.), *The social psychology of everyday politics* (pp. 87–101). London: Routledge.

Augoustinos, M. (2013). Discourse analysis in psychology: What's in a name? *Qualitative Research in Psychology, 10*(3), 244–248.

Augoustinos, M., & Every, D. (2010). Accusations and denials of racism: Managing moral accountability in public discourse. *Discourse & Society, 21*(3), 251–256.

Armistead, N. E. (1974). *Reconstructing social psychology*. Oxford: Penguin.

Asch, S. E. (1956). Studies of independence and conformity: A minority of one against a unanimous majority. *Psychological Monographs: General and Applied, 70*, 1–70.

Barnes, R., Auburn, T., & Lea, S. (2004). Citizenship in practice. *British Journal of Social Psychology, 43*, 187–206.

Billig, M. (1982). *Ideology and social psychology*. Oxford: Blackwell.

Billig, M. (1987). *Arguing and thinking: A rhetorical approach to social psychology*. Cambridge: Cambridge University Press.

Billig, M. (1995). *Banal nationalism*. London: Sage.

Billig, M., Condor, S., Edwards, D., Gane, M., Middleton, D., & Radley, A. (1988). *Ideological dilemmas: A social psychology of everyday thinking*. London: Sage.

Brown, W. (2016). Sacrificial citizenship: Neoliberalism, human capital, and austerity politics. *Constellations*, *23*(1), 3–14.

Capdevila, R., & Callaghan, J. E M. (2008). 'It's not racist. It's common sense'. A critical analysis of political discourse around asylum and immigration in the UK. *Journal of Community and Applied Social Psychology*, *18*, 1–16.

Clarke, J. (2010). Enrolling ordinary people: governmental strategies and the avoidance of politics?, *Citizenship Studies*, *14*(6), 637–650.

Condor, S. (1997). And so say all of us? Some thoughts on 'experiential democratization' as an aim for critical social psychologists. In T. Ibáñez, & L. Íñiguez (Eds.), *Critical Social Psychology* (pp. 111–146). London: Sage.

Condor, S. (2011). Towards a social psychology of citizenship? Introduction to the Special Issue. *Journal of Community & Applied Social Psychology*, *21*, 193–201.

Condor, S. (2016). Public opinion and the problem of information. In C. Howarth, & E. Andreouli (Eds.), *The social psychology of everyday politics* (pp. 189–205). London: Routledge.

Condor, S., Tileaga, C., & Billig, M. (2013). Political rhetoric. In L. Huddy, D. O. Sears, & J. S. Levy (Eds.), *The Oxford handbook of political psychology* (2nd edn., pp. 262–297). Oxford: Oxford University Press.

Danziger, K. (1994). *Constructing the subject: Historical origins of psychological research*. Cambridge: Cambridge University Press.

Danziger, K. (1997). *Naming the mind: How psychology found its language*. London: Sage.

De Genova, N., & Peutz, N. (2010). *The Deportation regime: Sovereignty, space, and the freedom of movement*. Durham, NC: Duke University Press.

Di Masso, A. (2012). Grounding citizenship: Toward a political psychology of public space. *Political Psychology*, *33*(1), 123–143.

Elms, A. C. (1975). The crisis of confidence in social psychology. *American Psychologist*, *30*(10), 967.

Eysenck, H. J. (1954). *The psychology of politics*. London: Routledge and Kegan Paul.

Faye, C. (2012). American social psychology: Examining the contours of the 1970s crisis. *Studies in History and Philosophy of Science Part C: Studies in History and Philosophy of Biological and Biomedical Sciences*, *43*(2), 514–521.

Festinger, L. (1964). *Conflict, decision, and dissonance* (Vol. 3). Stanford, California: Stanford University Press.

Figgou, L. (2013). Essentialism, historical construction, and social influence: Representations of Pomakness in majority talk in Western Thrace (Greece). *British Journal of Social Psychology*, *52*, 686–702.

Figgou, L. (2015). Constructions of 'illegal' immigration and entitlement to citizenship: Debating an immigration law in Greece. *Journal of Community & Applied Social Psychology*, *26*(2), 150–163.

Figgou, L. (2016). Everyday politics and the extreme right: Lay explanations of the electoral performance of the neo-Nazi political party 'Golden Dawn' in Greece. In C. Howarth, & E. Andreouli (Eds.), *The social psychology of everyday politics* (pp. 206–221). London: Routledge.

Fine, M. (2004). Witnessing whiteness/Gathering intelligence. In M. Fine, L. Weis, L. Powell Pruitt, & A. Burns (eds.), *Off white: Readings on power, privilege and resistance* (pp. 245–256). New York: Routledge.

Fine, M. (2006). Bearing witness: Methods for researching oppression and resistance – A textbook for critical research. *Social Justice Research*, *19*(1), 83–108.

Gergen, K. J. (1973). Social psychology as history. *Journal of personality and social psychology*, *26*(2), 309.

Gibson, S. (2011). Dilemmas of citizenship: Young people's conceptions of un/employment rights and responsibilities. *British Journal of Social Psychology*, 50(3), 450–468.

Goodman, S. (2010). 'It's not racist to impose limits on immigration': Constructing the boundaries of racism in the asylum and immigration debate. *Critical Approaches to Discourse Analysis across Disciplines*, *4*(1), 1–17.

Goodman, S., & Burke, S. (2010). 'Oh you don't want asylum seekers, oh you're just racist'. A discursive analysis of discussions about whether it's racist to oppose asylum seeking. *Discourse and Society*, *21*(3), 325–340.

Gray, D., & Griffin, C. (2014). A journey to citizenship: Constructions of citizenship and identity in the British citizenship test. *British Journal of Social Psychology*, *53*, 299–314.

Hall, S., & Held, D. (1989). Citizens and citizenship. In S. Hall & M. Jacques (Eds.), *New times: The changing face of politics in the 1990s* (pp. 173–188). London: Lawrence & Wishart.

Hall, S., & O'Shea, A. (2015). Common-sense neoliberalism. In S. Hall, D. Massey, & M. Rustin (Eds.), *After neoliberalism? The Kilburn manifesto* (pp. 52–68). London: Lawrence and Wishart.

Hanson-Easey, S., & Augoustinos, M. (2010). Out of Africa: Accounting for refugee policy and the language of causal attribution. *Discourse & Society*, *21*(3) 295–323.

Harré, R. (1974). Blueprint for a new science. In N. E. Armistead (Ed.), *Reconstructing social psychology* (pp. 3–25). Oxford: Penguin.

Harris, B. (1996). Psychology and Marxist politics in the United States. In I. Parker, & R. Spears (eds) *Psychology and society: Radical theory and practice* (pp. 64–78). London: Pluto Press.

Haste, H. (2004). Constructing the citizen. *Political Psychology*, *25*(3), 413–439.

Hepburn, A. (2003). *An introduction to critical social psychology*. London: Sage.

Hodgetts, D., & Griffin, C. (2015). The place of class: Considerations for psychology. *Theory & Psychology*, *25*(2), 147–166.

House, J. S. (1977). The three faces of social psychology. *Sociometry*, *40*(2), 161–177.

Howarth, C. & Andreouli, E. (Eds.). (2017). *The social psychology of everyday politics*. London: Routledge.

Isin, E. F. (2009). Citizenship in flux: The figure of the activist citizen. *Subjectivity*, *29*, 367–388.

Israel, J., & Tajfel, H. (1972). *The context of social psychology: A critical assessment*. London: Academic Press.

Kadianaki, I., & Andreouli, E. (2017). Essentialism in social representations of citizenship: an analysis of Greeks' and migrants' discourse. *Political Psychology*, 38(5), 833–848.

Le Bon, G. (1896). *The crowd: A study of the popular mind*. London: Ernest Benn.

Lewin, K., Lippitt, R., & White, R. K. (1939). Patterns of aggressive behavior in experimentally created 'social climates'. *The Journal of Social Psychology*, *10*(2), 269–299.

Marshall, T. H. (1950). *Citizenship and social class and other essays*. Cambridge: Cambridge University Press.

Marshall, T. H. (1964). *Class, citizenship and social development*. New York: Doubleday.

Martín-Baró, I. (1994). Toward a liberation psychology. In A. Aron, & S. Corne (Eds. & Trans.), *Writings for a liberation psychology* (pp. 17–32). Cambridge, MA: Harvard University Press.

Milgram, S. (1963). Behavioral study of obedience. *The Journal of Abnormal and Social Psychology*, *67*(4), 371–378.

Montero, M. (2007). The political psychology of liberation: From politics to ethics and back. *Political Psychology*, *28*(5), 517–533.

Moscovici, S. (1961/2008). *Psychoanalysis: Its image and its public*. Cambridge: Polity Press.

Moscovici, S. (1972). Theory and society in social psychology. In J. Isreal, & H. Tajfel (Eds.), *The context of social psychology: A critical assessment*. London: Academic Press.

Moscovici, S. (1984). The phenomenon of social representations. In R. Farr, & S. Moscovici (Eds.), *Social representations*. Cambridge: Cambridge University Press.

Moscovici, S. (1985). *The age of the crowd: A historical treatise on mass psychology*. Cambridge: Cambridge University Press.

Moscovici. S. and Markova, I (2000). Ideas and their development: a dialogue between Serge Moscovici and Ivana Markova. In G Duveen (Ed), *Social representations: explorатuions in social psychology*. Oxford: Polity Press, pp. 224–286.

Nesbitt-Larking, P., & Kinnvall, C. (2012). The discursive frames of political psychology. *Political Psychology*, *33*(1), 45–59.

Neveu, C. (2015). Of ordinariness and citizenship processes. *Citizenship Studies*, *19*(2), 141–154.

Nicholson, I. (1997). The politics of scientific social reform, 1936–1960: Goodwin Watson and the Society for the Psychological Study of Social Issues. *Journal of the History of the Behavioral Sciences*, *33*(1), 39–60.

Parker, I. (1989). *The crisis in modern social psychology – and how to end it*. London: Routledge

Parker, I. (1999). Critical psychology: critical links. *Annual Review of Critical Psychology, 1*(1), 3–18.

Parker, I. (2013). Discourse analysis: Dimensions of critique in psychology. *Qualitative Research in Psychology, 10*(3), 223–239.

Pehrson, S., Vignoles, V. L., & Brown, R. (2009). National identity and anti-immigrant prejudice: Individual and contextual effects of national definitions. *Social Psychology Quarterly, 72*(1), 24–38.

Reicher, S. (2001). The psychology of crowd dynamics. In M. A. Hogg & R. S. Tindale (Eds.), *Blackwell handbook of social psychology: Group processes* (pp. 182–208). Oxford: Blackwell.

Reicher, S., & Hopkins, N. (2001). Psychology and the end of history: A critique and a proposal for the psychology of social categorization. *Political Psychology, 22*(2), 383–407.

Rokeach, M. (1960). *Open and closed mind*. New York: Basic Books.

Rose, N. (1985). *Psychology, politics and society in England 1869–1939*. London: Routledge and Kegan Paul.

Rose, N. (1989/1999). *Governing the soul: The shaping of the private self* (2nd edn.). London: Free Association Books.

Samelson, F. (1978). From 'race psychology' to 'studies in prejudice': Some observations on the thematic reversal in social psychology. *Journal of the History of the Behavioral Sciences, 14*(3), 265–278.

Schütz, A. (1944). The stranger: An essay in social psychology. *American Journal of Sociology, 49*(6), 499–507.

Spears, R. (1997). Introduction. In T. Ibáñez, & L. Íñiguez (Eds.), *Critical social psychology* (pp. 1–26). London: Sage.

Stevenson, C., Dixon, J., Hopkins, N., & Luyt, R. (2015). The social psychology of citizenship, participation and social exclusion: Introduction to the special thematic section. *Journal of Social & Political Psychology, 3*, 1–19

Tileagă, C. (2013). *Political psychology: Critical perspectives*. Cambridge: Cambridge University Press.

Turner, B. S. (2016). We are all denizens now: on the erosion of citizenship. *Citizenship Studies, 20*(6–7), 679–692.

Weltman, D., & Billig, M. (2001). The political psychology of contemporary anti-politics: A discursive approach to the end-of-ideology era. *Political Psychology, 2*, 367–381.

Wetherell, M., & Potter, J. (1992). *Mapping the language of racism: Discourse and the legitimation of exploitation*. London: Harvester Wheatsheaf.

Wodak, R. (2015). *The politics of fear: What right-wing populist discourses mean*. London: Sage.

9

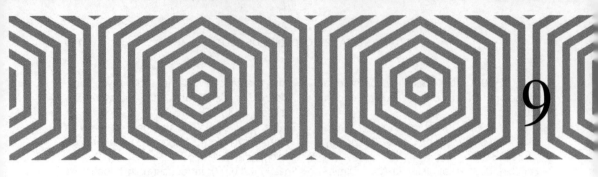

Macropsychology: Challenging and Changing Social Structures and Systems to Promote Social Inclusion

Malcolm MacLachlan, Joanne McVeigh, Tessy Huss and Hasheem Mannan

INTRODUCTION

Applied social psychology seeks to develop a psychological understanding of practical social problems and to use this to intervene and ameliorate such problems (Schneider et al., 2017). We see our description of macropsychology as a particular style of applying social psychology and one that likely differs from many others in this volume. While much of our work *thinks through* an applied social psychology ethos (for instance, its theories and methods), it does not necessarily *think of* that ethos in its execution. In *doing* macropsychology, the praxis may often be infused with cognate theories and methods, including from outside psychology; not selected to enhance applied social psychology per se, but rather to make an intervention more likely to succeed in its own right. Many of the social problems that may be addressed at the macropsychology level are necessarily constituted of factors related to, but distinct from, an applied social psychology analysis. Within such an amalgam of theoretically inspired and systematically executed interventions at the macro level, applied social psychology has much to offer.

In 2006, the National Institutes of Health in the United States noted that 'although behavioral and social sciences have contributed greatly to the understanding, prevention, and treatment of many of today's pressing health problems, there is growing recognition that with improved methodologies, behavioral and social sciences *could do more* to address *the complexity* of these problems'. The research agency continued by describing what 'more' might mean: 'Complexity results from the interaction of *multiple factors* … further compounded as the relationships between these components *change over time* … occurring within a context of *nested hierarchies*, from *micro to macro* levels … relationships among which *change over time* and *across development*' (italics added; National Institutes of Health, 2006).

It is our contention in this chapter that psychology could contribute in a much greater capacity to understanding or implementing the complexity of social change, particularly at the macro level.

A macro perspective in psychology, which has been termed macropsychology, has been slow to develop. Psychology has focused on 'understanding down' by dismantling complex behaviour into subcomponents that are proximate, individualistic, subcutaneous or reductive, which is often constructed as conferring 'insight'. Yet, as Smail (n.d.) argues, 'one cannot hope to understand the phenomena of psychological distress, nor begin to think what can be done about them, without an analysis of how power is distributed and exercised within society'. If psychology is to contribute to truly managing the complexity of life, then more 'understanding up' is needed. This requires addressing how psychology can both influence and be influenced by social institutions, systems and policies, and allowing it to develop 'outsight'.

While much has been achieved by 'understanding down' psychology, at least some practitioners also recognise, and are frustrated at, the discipline's failure to address the social settings and conditions in which people live, and in which their problems therefore arise. These are social settings and conditions that an applied social psychology can contribute to addressing. Jordan (2014: 364) asserts that 'counselling and psychotherapy cannot fully alleviate the symptoms unless … [they] can treat the cause (the political and historical constellations that shape the era) and *yet that cause is the exact subject psychology is not allowed to address*' (italics added). In this chapter, we allow psychology to address some of the political and historical constellations that influence behaviour.

Two decades ago, Marsella (1998: 1282) argued that psychology is 'now embedded in an entangled web of global economic, political, social, and environmental events and forces', and he critiqued the discipline for its failure to address globalisation. He noted that psychology was contained in a focus on individuals, services provided in clinics and offices, and that it was largely dominated by the interests of psychology as a profession, rather than service to the community. Of particular relevance to us here is Marsella's plea that psychology pay more attention to the 1948 Universal Declaration of Human Rights (United Nations, 2015) and to developing psychology's potential social activist role. The increasing rate of globalisation makes the continued neglect of these areas even more problematic (Marsella, 2012). Much of psychology implicitly explores what is optimal, good or 'right' for human beings. Yet psychology continues to eschew advocating for social structures or policies that promote what is right for humans – human rights.

The application of macropsychology to guide the implementation of policy is evident. For example, the Social and Behavioral Sciences Team (SBST) at the US White House Office of Science and Technology Policy was established as a federal interagency research and advisory group on using social and behavioural science to improve government programmes (Winerman, 2015). Areas in which the SBST works to apply behavioural science include improving access of children from low-income families to free or reduced price school meals and empowering inmates released from prison to successfully reintegrate into their communities (National Science and Technology Council, 2016). These are critically important initiatives. Yet, even here, psychology is used more to implement policy than it is to determine policy.

The American Psychological Association has also played an active role in using psychological evidence to promote inclusive public policy. Anderson (2015) suggests that immigration is one of numerous national and global issues that psychological research and best practice can provide policy-makers with valuable evidence. We assert that psychology should not only be providing policy-makers with evidence, but psychologists should be involved in making policy; in ensuring it is developed in inclusive ways and implemented fairly.

Importantly, the historical involvement of psychologists in policy processes also contains several negative exemplars. In her account of psychology's rise to public power, Herman (1995: 10) questions: 'What exactly have psychological experts done? Have they spoken the truth or manufactured deception? Have they expanded the realm of freedom or perfected the means of control?' Herman continues by asserting: '[Psychology] has served to complicate, and often obscure, the exercise of power in recent U.S. history, but it has also legitimised innovative ideas and actions whose aim has been to personalise, and expand, the scope of liberty' (Herman, 1995: 15).

MACROPSYCHOLOGY

Macropsychology may be defined as 'the application of psychology to factors that influence the settings and conditions of our lives' (MacLachlan, 2014: 851). Macropsychology is a perspective, not a subdiscipline, and its scope is therefore very broad and cross-sectoral. Let us briefly consider just some of the elements of this breadth.

Bronfenbrenner (1979) distinguished between micro-, meso- and macro-systems. For example, the reproduction of macro level systems in micro level interactions is explored through work on the 'conduct of everyday life' from the Northern European critical psychology tradition (Højholt and Schraube, 2016; Holzkamp, 2016). In the realm of rehabilitation, at the micro level, adaptation to the loss of a limb can, for instance, present significant psychological challenges in terms of coping efforts, mood or activity (Desmond and MacLachlan, 2002). At the meso level, disability can, however, promote positive identity, well-being and powerful advocacy among disabled people's organisations (DPOs); or it can subject individuals or groups to stigma, discrimination and prejudice (MacLachlan et al., 2014; Mji et al., 2011). At the macro level, as we will see, social policies, social institutions and social structures can facilitate or hinder inclusion. All of these levels have strong behavioural components. The potential of psychology – unique among the social sciences – is then to link these different levels together in a system that traverses these levels, *a meta* (interlinked) system recognising the interplay of individual, group and population behaviour. In essence then, macropsychology asks: 'How can psychology operate more effectively as a population science?'

Central to macropsychology is the assertion that psychological characteristics and social settings co-construct one another. An intriguing example of this comes from a recent study on individual problem solving and the social structure of communities arising from different systems of agricultural production. Talhelm et al. (2014) argued that living in an area that has a history of growing rice makes people more interdependent than those who live in an area with a history of growing wheat – due to the greater level of collective activity and cooperation necessary in more labour intensive and less mechanised rice production. They compared 1,162 Han Chinese participants across six sites on a series of problem-solving tests designed to assess analytic (matching to categories) and holistic (matching to relationships) thinking. The researchers also assessed participants' degree of individualism or collectivism (through their drawing of, and representation of, themselves relative to others in a sociogram) and, separately, their in-group loyalty (by preferred allocations of rewards to their own group). They found that people in rice-growing areas were more interdependent and holistic in their problem solving than were those from wheat-growing areas (having controlled for a number of potentially confounding variables) (Talhelm et al., 2014). This, then, is one way in which the broader context in which people live – the sort of work historically carried out in an area – may influence how they think and act. Another interesting example of social context influencing psychological characteristics is the finding that, where the prevailing sex-ratio has more men than women, people expect men to spend more money on a St. Valentine's Day gift, a dinner entrée and an engagement ring (Griskevicius et al., 2012). Again, as with the Talhelm et al. (2014) study, this study illustrates how a social context may strongly influence psychological characteristics. One way to think about these relationships is through their macro (societal level psychology), meso (group level psychology) and micro (individual level psychology) interaction.

However, the macro → meso → micro relationship is not just a one-directional relationship but can work both ways. Therefore, micro, or individual level, psychology may also strongly impact on macro, or societal level, psychology. For instance, using large population samples, Obschonka et al. (2016) found that, in the US and UK, regional variations in personality were associated with economic resilience during the economic crash.

The researchers used the Big Five personality factors (extraversion, openness, conscientiousness, emotional stability and agreeableness), in addition to computing an entrepreneurial personality profile. They demonstrated that (controlling for a range of confounding factors) more emotionally stable regions and regions with a more prevalent entrepreneurial personality profile experienced a significantly lower economic slowdown. A possible micro–meso–macro relationship (individual personality–activity of business organisations–regional economic indicators) can thus be inferred from these data. These linkages – constituting a meta-systems approach – are the essence of how a macro perspective in psychology can complement, rather than compete with, individual and group perspectives, which are much more familiar and much better developed within psychology.

We are, however, much more familiar with sociological or economic analysis operating at the macro or societal level. For instance, it is well established that the socioeconomic circumstances in which people live influence their psychological well-being. This is demonstrated by the classic studies of Brown and Harris (1978) on depression in London or the more recent work on social inequity by Wilkinson and Pickett (2010), some of the effects of which have been traced down to the micro (individual) level of cardiovascular reactivity (Steptoe and Kivimäki, 2012). Similarly, some of the core propositions of societal psychology (Himmelweit, 1990; Hodgetts et al., 2010) also strongly resonate with a macro perspective; for instance, awareness of sociocultural context, the interdependence of the individual and the collective, the importance of social systems and hierarchies, the broader environment and the inherent interdisciplinary nature of the topics of interest.

There is also much excellent work and debate concerning how large-scale empirical psychology (surveys, Big Data, meta-analyses and randomised controlled trials) can be put into policy and practice, stimulating the development of implementation science. In the research field, it is often assumed that 'putting into real-world practice' is somehow easier than doing the original, often abstracted, research. However, what can be put into policy and practice is ultimately constrained by the social structures, systems and power relationships that prevail. It is for that reason that we now focus on some attempts to address these issues. These attempts are, as one might expect, engaging with situations comprised of multiple factors; they are complex, messy and changing. It is also often the case that, in seeing change, we must see contribution rather than attribution as the more likely claim for success; something that may not satisfy a stronger commitment to logical positivism.

SOCIAL INCLUSION

According to Dukes (1999: 1), 'social and political institutions set the context for individual and group behaviour and are meant to provide the resources individuals need to survive. How people act and live is shaped in large part by the social structures in which they find themselves'. We seek to illustrate the macro perspective, the social structures, by focusing on the particular area of social inclusion, albeit across several sectors. Much of this chapter draws on our own research and practice concerned with promoting social inclusion for persons with disabilities, although in a manner that seeks to recognise the intersectionality of situations that marginalise or disempower people. This work has addressed policy, institutional and systems issues. As a backdrop to this, we have been guided by several social psychological theories concerning equity, identity and empowerment, but most especially the theory of social dominance (Sidanius and Pratto, 1999). In each of the examples below, we have sought to counter social dominance through the adoption of methods that take context and/or process into account.

We describe three projects. First, a realist synthesis is outlined of policy and governance literature with a particular focus on context. Second, we describe the development of policy analysis instruments with a focus on policy change. Third, we discuss a project involving working with the Theory of Change approach to produce systems, institutional and structural change.

Project 1: Realist Synthesis of Policy Literature

Harris et al. (2015) argue that the adoption of realist methods to examine complex public health issues is rapidly increasing. Policymakers need to understand why, and how, a programme might work in one context but not in another and how to adapt interventions to local contexts (Westhorp, 2014). Realist synthesis is an approach to reviewing research evidence on complex social interventions, which enables explanatory analyses of how, why and for whom interventions work, or do not work (Pawson et al., 2004). As an emerging approach to evidence review, realist synthesis is particularly useful for exploring the effects of complex interventions because it is based on the premise that an understanding is needed of how interventions work in different contexts and why (Rycroft-Malone et al., 2010). Realist approaches assume that nothing works everywhere for everyone and that context significantly shapes programme outcomes (Westhorp, 2014). This clearly challenges the idea of identifying universal laws within psychology because it sees behaviour as being dependent on particularities that vary. Research that obscures or controls for context – as much psychological research does – restricts our knowledge of how, when and for whom an intervention can be effective (Wong et al., 2013).

A realist synthesis may follow similar steps to a traditional systematic review, with some exceptions – such as inclusion of multiple types of information, an iterative process and a focus on explaining why an intervention works, or does not work, rather than simply its outcome or an averaging of its outcomes (Rycroft-Malone et al., 2010). To explore the relationship between context and outcome, realism uses the concept of 'mechanism' (Wong et al., 2013), represented in Pawson and Tilley's (1997) formula as 'mechanism + context = outcome'. Realism upholds that mechanisms are important as they generate outcomes and that context is important as it alters the processes by which an intervention generates outcomes (Wong et al., 2013).

Context–mechanism–outcome pattern configurations (CMOs) are therefore propositions that indicate what it is about a programme that works, for whom, and in what circumstances (Pawson and Tilley, 1997). In realist inquiry, the cause–effect relationship (for example, as represented by X causes Y) is rigorously explored by attempting to determine how a causal outcome (O) between two events (X and Y) is actually brought about (the mechanism (M)) through the context (C) in which the relationship occurs (McVeigh et al., 2016). Instead of comparing changes for a group of people who have participated in a programme with people who have not, as is conducted in a randomised controlled or quasi-experimental design, a realist evaluation compares CMOs within programmes (Greenhalgh et al., 2015). For example, it might explore if a programme works more or less effectively, and through which different mechanisms, across different localities, and how and why (Greenhalgh et al., 2015).

We undertook a realist synthesis to provide recommendations to the World Health Organization (WHO) on policy-related leadership and governance of health-related rehabilitation services in less resourced settings (McVeigh et al., 2016). For this study, a two-stage approach was used: a systematic search and realist synthesis of the relevant literature, followed by a Delphi survey of the views of expert stakeholders on the results generated by the realist synthesis. These two approaches were used to combine the authority and contextual focus of a systematic search and realist synthesis of the literature, with further expert stakeholder feedback provided by the Delphi survey to triangulate, refine and achieve consensus on results. However, here our experts also constituted service users, service providers and policy-makers, and all had an equal voice in the anonymous group consensus process offered by a Delphi study (Hasson et al., 2000).

Table 9.1 provides a sample CMO from a study we included in our review and the associated Delphi statements. The study reported the scaling up of a depression treatment programme in primary care in Chile (Araya et al., 2012). Combining many studies from which we identified a range of CMOs, several broad principles emerged from the findings: participation of persons with disabilities in policy processes; collection of disaggregated disability statistics and development of health information systems; explicit promotion in policies of access to services for all subgroups of persons with disabilities and service-users; strong intersectoral coordination; and 'institutionalising' of rehabilitation programmes by aligning them with pre-existing ministerial models of healthcare (McVeigh et al., 2016).

It is important to point out that many of the authors of the studies we reviewed actually paid little attention to context–mechanism interactions; these being extracted by us across different studies. Such information is often embedded in reports and research papers, but not necessarily explicitly discussed by the authors. The comparative approach, however, helps to identify contextual variations between studies. By using a realist synthesis to provide recommendations on policy-related leadership and governance of health-related rehabilitation services in less resourced settings, evidence on this research area was accumulated that would likely not have been generated with other empirical approaches. Realist methods, however, lend themselves to such complexity, offering a rich 'messy' perspective – one that psychology is uniquely positioned to understand, even if it has often been opposed to such complexity (MacLachlan, 2014).

Project 2: Development of Policy Analysis Instruments

Complex and multidimensional phenomena such as social exclusion must be addressed through equally complex responses (Mathieson et al., 2008; Percy-Smith, 2000; World Bank, 2013). Such interventions, individually or collectively, must change the behaviour and attitudes of socially dominant groups and empower vulnerable groups in the process by improving the terms of their engagement with society at large (Fraser, 1998; Silver, 2015; World Bank, 2013).

Table 9.1 Illustration of a realist analysis of a published study and our use of it to develop Delphi statements

Contexts	*Mechanisms*	*Outcome*	*CMO (context–mechanism–outcome configuration)*	*Delphi survey statements*
1. (i) A national disease-burden study was conducted. (ii) Two large psychiatric morbidity surveys were conducted. (iii) Other studies showed that depression was also very common among primary care patients. (iv) A trial was conducted of the cost-effectiveness of an improved treatment for depression through primary care in Chile. (v) A randomised controlled trial of a programme to improve the management of depressed women in the primary care setting showed positive results. (vi) The ministry of health hired an academic institution to undertake a small-scale evaluation of the effectiveness of the programme.	1. (i) The psychiatric morbidity surveys were used to advocate for more resources for the depression treatment programme. (ii) The studies were based on local data. (iii) The Mental Health Unit at the Ministry of Health leveraged available evidence effectively. (iv) A workable action plan was presented to policy-makers. (v) There was ongoing communication between the research team and those designing the programme.	1. The Ministry of Health decided that depression would become the country's third highest health priority for 2002.	When scientific evidence on a disease burden is collected (**intervention**) and used to advocate for more resources, based on local data, and effectively leveraged and presented to policy-makers with a workable action plan (**mechanisms**), a specific health issue can be established as a national health priority (**outcome**) – even in a context of socioeconomic challenges, such as in a low- or middle-income country (**context**).	1. Governments should provide adequate levels of funding for the collection of disability statistics using both quantitative and qualitative research methods, including disaggregated information, to enable a situational analysis of disability. 2. Information collected on disability should be disseminated proactively, succinctly, quickly, and in a language and format that decision-makers and persons with disabilities can easily and quickly understand.

Conceptually, such policy interventions span multiple levels; policies encouraging behavioural and attitudinal changes can take place at the interpersonal, the small group or organisational and structural level (Cook et al., 2014; Fisher and Purcal, 2017).

Interventions at the structural level are initiated by governments and usually take the form of national policies, legislation and laws (Cook et al., 2014; Fisher and Purcal, 2017). Fisher and Purcal (2017) suggest that the effectiveness of interventions at the structural level is contingent on reinforcement of related or complementary interventions at lower levels. Oftentimes, national policies or strategies will include programmes targeting the micro and meso levels as part of an overarching, longer-term strategy to end discrimination and to realise certain socio-economic and political rights for specific vulnerable groups. We contend that interventions at the structural level need to be socially inclusive, both in their content and their development and implementation.

We have reported elsewhere the development of EquiFrame, a tool that assesses the extent to which the actual *content* of existing policies – 'policy on the books' – promotes social inclusion and human rights (see Amin et al., 2011; MacLachlan et al., 2012; Mannan et al., 2011). EquiFrame identifies the degree of commitment of a policy to 21 core concepts of human rights and inclusion of 12 vulnerable groups. The framework has now been used to analyse over 80 such policies in Europe, Africa and Asia. EquiFrame has been, or is currently being, used to develop new, or revise existing, policies in South Africa (disability and rehabilitation policies), Malawi (National Health Policy and National Health Research Policy), Sudan (to guide the development of all future health policies), Malaysia (Science and Technology Funding Policy), and in Cambodia and Timor-Leste. In the Lao People's Democratic Republic, it has been used with Handicap International to support the process of developing a Policy/Strategy/Action Plan on disability. EquiFrame has also been used for training and capacity building for policy development, revision and analysis of existing policies for staff from the United Nations Educational, Scientific and Cultural Organization (UNESCO), International Labour Organization (ILO), WHO, United Nations Development Programme (UNDP) and United Nations Children's Fund (UNICEF) as part of the United Nations Partnership to Promote the Rights of Persons with Disabilities (UNPRPD) (see MacLachlan et al., 2016).

In addition to the content of policy documents, our work has also focused on the process of their development and implementation. We are interested in the experiences of inclusion in these processes for those groups most marginalised and vulnerable in society (Huss and MacLachlan, 2016). We have therefore developed a complementary tool to EquiFrame, called EquIPP (Equity and Inclusion in Policy Processes), to support the development and implementation of inclusive policies (Huss and MacLachlan, 2016; MacLachlan et al., 2016). Similar to EquiFrame, EquIPP provides a Likert-scale score of inclusion across a number of relevant domains, producing scoring and mapping that identifies instances of the policy process where considerations of equity and inclusion are strong or weak. EquIPP is the product of collaborative work with UNESCO's Management of Social Transformations (MOST) programme and the UNPRPD (see UNDP, 2016). EquIPP proposes 17 Key Actions to support the development of an inclusive and equitable policy process (see Table 9.2). It was trialed in Malaysia, Cambodia and Timor-Leste as a precursor to the establishment of UNESCO's Inclusive Policy Lab.

EquiFrame and EquIPP are therefore complementary tools to support the content and process of inclusive policies. For example, using both EquiFrame and EquIPP, we conducted an analysis of social inclusion and equity in Malawi's National HIV and AIDS Policy review process (Chinyama et al., 2017). This research was conducted over two phases. First, we used EquiFrame to assess the *content* of the policy with regards to its coverage of 21 core concepts of human rights and inclusion of 12 vulnerable groups. Second, we assessed the engagement of vulnerable groups in the policy *process* using EquIPP. For the latter, ten interviews were conducted with a purposive sample of representatives of civil society organisations, public sector and development partners who participated in the policy revision process. Further data were collected using documentation of the policy process. Our findings highlighted that the policy had a relatively high coverage of core concepts of human rights and vulnerable groups, although with some

Table 9.2 Key actions and definitions of domains within EquIPP (Equity and Inclusion in Policy Processes)

Key Action	*Definition*
Key Action 1: Set up inclusive and participatory mechanisms	This Key Action involves detailing a public engagement strategy for the purpose of policy development/revision.
Key Action 2: Ensure the highest level of participation	This Key Action involves maximising the quality of participation and ensuring that all relevant stakeholders participate directly or are adequately represented in policy deliberations.
Key Action 3: Strengthen cross-sectoral cooperation	This Key Action involves strengthening communication and the flow of information across government departments and the integration of plans and policies.
Key Action 4: Strengthen inter- governmental cooperation	This Key Action involves the harmonisation of national and local level initiatives through the creation of an overarching policy framework.
Key Action 5: Plan according to need	This Key Action involves the adoption of participatory planning techniques to tailor policy provisions to local complexity of needs.
Key Action 6: Specify actions by which social needs will be addressed	This Key Action involves the identification of explicit projects, programmes and interventions to address social needs and level the playing field and promote social inclusion.
Key Action 7: Build equity considerations into budgets	This Key Action involves the prioritisation and funding of programmes, projects and interventions specifically designed to benefit vulnerable groups in government budgets.
Key Action 8: Minimise gaps between real and planned budgets	This Key Action involves creating a favourable and participatory oversight environment to monitor anticipated and actual expenditure.
Key Action 9: Devise a responsive and flexible implementation plan	This Key Action involves developing a detailed and overarching implementation plan in a participatory manner, and which should involve key stakeholders, including relevant government sectors, local governments, service users and service providers.
Key Action 10: Adopt the most inclusive selection methodology	This Key Action involves taking necessary steps to ensure that beneficiaries are identified in the most inclusive manner to yield a maximum of policy coverage.
Key Action 11: Select the most appropriate implementation partners	This Key Action involves mobilising the non governmental, civil society and private sector for the operationalisation of social inclusion policies.
Key Action 12: Encourage cooperation between agencies and service providers	This Key Action involves strengthening the links between implementers on the ground to deliver a more tailored and holistic response to social inclusion.
Key Action 13: Collect qualitative and quantitative data	This Key Action involves setting up mixed and multi-methods monitoring and evaluation frameworks in a participatory manner.
Key Action 14: Integrate, aggregate, disaggregate and share data	This Key Action involves integrating, aggregating, disaggregating and sharing data to monitor and evaluate policies across multiple domains and over time.
Key Action 15: Select appropriate indicator dimensions	This Key Action involves the participatory design of an indicator framework to measure appropriate social outcomes.
Key Action 16: Share information with policy beneficiaries	This Key Action involves taking steps to ensure equitable access to all information relating to policy benefits.
Key Action 17: Share information with the policy community	This Key Action involves taking steps to ensure equitable access to all information relating to the policy more broadly.

omissions, such as the failure to mention the aged population, ethnic minorities, those living away from services and displaced populations. We also found that reasonable steps were taken to engage and promote the participation of vulnerable groups regarding the planning, development, implementation, monitoring and evaluation processes of the policy, although similarly with some notable exceptions. For example, evidence collected from the majority of interview participants and documentation of the policy process indicated that the final revised policy lacked proper dissemination to the actual beneficiaries. Accordingly, although our analyses of the Malawi HIV and AIDS Policy indicated commitment to core concepts of human rights, inclusion of vulnerable groups and inclusive processes, we also highlighted areas where social inclusion and equity could be strengthened (Chinyama et al., 2017).

We briefly report the application of EquIPP to the National Disability Policy process of Timor-Leste and the associated National Action Plan. According to the 2016 Timor-Leste Demographic and Health Survey, 15% of the population aged five or older reported some level of difficulty in at least one domain of functioning (General Directorate of Statistics, Ministry of Health and ICF, 2018). In this small island State, persons with disabilities experience stigma and discrimination in many life domains (OHCHR, 2011). Based on principles of action research, together with our UN partners, the project in Timor-Leste sought to engage a variety of local stakeholders from various ministries and civil society (the National Working Group) as co-investigators in the process of policy assessment with the aim of fostering a structured group learning experience. Some of the major barriers identified included a low level of priority accorded to disability inclusion within the country's development agenda. Focal points had been appointed within individual ministries, yet were unable to prioritise disability-related activities within their ministries. In a mid-term review of the National Action Plan, conducted by Handicap International Indonesia and Timor-Leste Programme (2016), the authors also noted that many of the focal points had not received formal training on disability.

Progress on disability inclusion was further impeded by very few disability-related activities in Ministries' annual business plans, which in turn, limited the budgetary and human resources allocated to the implementation of the National Action Plan. Consequently, persons with disabilities have benefitted little from the national policy to date. Nonetheless, the national policy and the associated action plan were both developed with significant input from persons with disabilities and their representative organisations and, as such, reflect their needs and interests. Thus, in the case of Timor-Leste, persons with disabilities were included as part of the process of policy development but have not benefited from inclusive implementation of polices; rather, other interests have prevailed. By tracking this process through EquIPP, we can point to the elements of implementation that have been unsatisfactory and determine if this is due to lack of resources, commitment or other overriding interests by more dominant groups.

Assessing the inclusiveness of policy processes allows us to identify barriers and facilitators of social change. It provides an opportunity to flag significant obstacles and to address or rectify them when policies are eventually revised. Most importantly, however, policy assessments, through the use of methodologies such as EquiFrame and EquIPP, can tell us much about the priority accorded to issues of inclusion of vulnerable groups and about prevailing negative attitudes and behaviours in society.

Project 3: Using the Theory of Change Approach

'Decent Work' is the clarion call for the ILO. Decent Work Country Programmes are developed in each country in which the ILO works, with the participation of national governments, employers' and workers' organisations – thus fulfilling the ILO's remit of bringing this tripartite of stakeholders together. The Decent Work Agenda has four primary objectives – promotion of rights at work, employment, social protection and social dialogue – which provide the basis for the 19 outcomes that Decent Work seeks to achieve. Here, we describe one of the projects that aimed to contribute to achieving these goals. PROPEL was funded by Irish Aid and focused on Promoting Rights and Opportunities for People with Disabilities in Employment through Legislation (PROPEL). It fitted into the ILO's broader programme priority outcomes by targeting two of their 19 outcomes – skills development ('Skills development increases the employability of workers, the competitiveness of enterprises and the inclusiveness of growth'; ILO Outcome 2) and the elimination of discrimination ('Discrimination in employment and occupation is eliminated'; ILO Outcome 17) – by contributing to the promotion of employment opportunities (ILO, 2013). The PROPEL Programme operated over four years (2012–2016) and spanned six countries (three in Africa, comprising Botswana, Ethiopia and Zambia; and three in Asia, comprising Indonesia, Vietnam and China). Specific initiatives to achieve the above outcomes differed in each country.

Our role was to provide knowledge management support to the overall programme. This was achieved through a combination of activities. We conducted intensive training workshops with the Country Leads of each programme, coming together yearly at ILO headquarters in Geneva. In these workshops, we provided information on research that we believed was relevant to the purpose of the project. We also worked with participants to establish how such knowledge could most usefully inform what they were trying to achieve in their own country. Our own inputs included presentations and discussions on prejudice, diversity and inclusion; barriers and facilitators of access to services; establishing indicators; assessing the inclusiveness of policy; understanding disability and inclusion related statistics; and developing a Theory of Change for each country. We also used Quality Circles/Action Learning Sets, which were conducted virtually, to begin with at monthly intervals and then less frequently as the project developed. Furthermore, we offered personal coaching to help Country Leads think through some of the challenges and blockages they faced in trying to change social policies and social structures in very complex and differing social, cultural and economic environments.

Here, we describe the global Theory of Change (the theory of how the programme might work across all of the countries) and then provide a few examples of specific outcomes in different countries. The Theory of Change approach (see Connell and Kubisch, 1998) identifies long-term goals and then maps out the precursors and the interactions between these – including necessary preconditions – to make these goals achievable. It allows for complex interacting factors, rather than simpler linear causality, and it can incorporate multiple stakeholders, facilitators and barriers. Adopting a rights-based approach, the project sought to facilitate more inclusive work for persons with disabilities through addressing both supply and demand side characteristics. From the supply side, it sought to create better access of persons with disabilities to skills development. From the demand side, it sought to encourage the private sector to be more open to employing persons with disabilities.

The Theory of Change that guided us, as the people responsible for the knowledge management for the project, is presented in Figure 9.1. This has four distinct components, but each of these components also has one common element – Disability Equality Training. This training was provided by an independent consultant (Maureen Gilbert) who worked in each of the countries on the project, where she provided training that

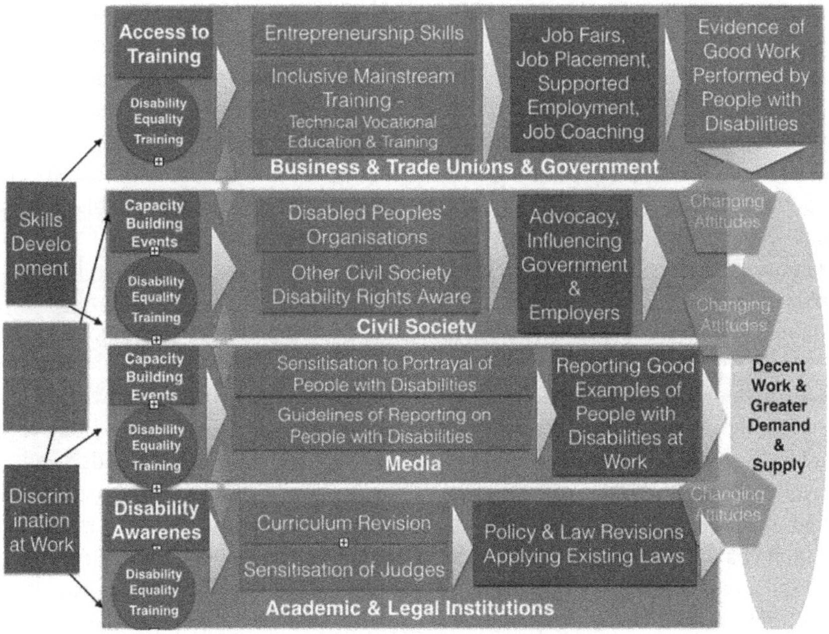

Figure 9.1 The Theory of Change developed for knowledge management of the International Labour Organization's PROPEL programme

enhanced sensitivity to disability and to the idea of persons with disabilities as equal people. The training was conducted primarily by using experiential exercises that encouraged not only an intellectual identification with persons with disabilities, their human rights and need for social inclusion and participation, but also an emotional one. Importantly, this emotional identification was aimed at promoting a rights-based, social model view. Therefore, a charity, individualised, medical model view was not utilised, which often diminishes the value of some views and elevates the dominance of other (of professional) views.

In addition to this Disability Equality Training, the programme had four areas that mutually complemented each other, aiming to produce changes that we believed were required to ensure decent work for persons with disabilities. Promoting skills through disability-inclusive vocational training was the first component. We – the overall programme team working across, and located in, each of the six countries – worked with government bodies in charge of vocational training and through them with Technical Vocational Education and Training (TVET) Centres. These centres aim to promote knowledge and skills acquisition for work, interfacing the needs of employers and the skills potential of clients. For instance, PROPEL provided advice and support in adjusting the physical environment, the teaching methods and materials, the curriculum and the attitudinal environment within the centres in order to make them more accessible. This was a particular focus in China, Ethiopia and Zambia.

A second component of PROPEL was supporting employment of persons with disabilities in the private sector by seeking to change the attitudes of employers and workers, advocating for a human rights-based approach and building a business case for disability inclusion. As part of this component, PROPEL facilitated mediation and placement services and supported employment services targeting persons with intellectual disabilities.

These supports were often provided by DPOs or other civil society organisations. We also promoted national business and disability networks, which built on the expertise of the ILO Global Business and Disability Network and encouraged businesses to be more welcoming to the inclusion of persons with disabilities. This component was most evident in China, Ethiopia, Indonesia, Vietnam and Zambia.

A component that very clearly relates to applied social psychology is the third component of challenging stereotypes through working with the media, who – sometimes unwittingly – promote negative stereotypes of persons with disabilities, reinforcing stigma and negative attitudes that constitute an important barrier to employment. We worked with media outlets, often in cooperation with DPOs, in developing guidelines for more balanced, rights-based and fairer reporting on disability issues. More than this, we encouraged positive reporting of persons with disabilities, highlighting impressive examples of persons with disabilities making excellent contributions at work. Such impression management can change attitudes, facilitate disability-friendly workplaces and more positive societal views in general. Media initiatives were undertaken in China, Ethiopia, Indonesia, Vietnam and Zambia.

The fourth component of PROPEL focused on revising policies and legislation. Addressing discrimination often necessitates revision of existing policies and laws, at times the development of new legislation, and sometimes better application of existing laws intended to prevent discrimination regarding access to, or at, work. Here, we supported DPOs to develop advocacy skills so that they could more effectively highlight to policy-makers the need to address employment opportunities for persons with disabilities. In some cases, this meant meeting with, and giving direct advice to, policy-makers. However, we also took a longer-term approach in some cases, working with law faculties of universities to support curriculum development (new modules) to present disability and access to employment as fundamental human rights issues. Law students were encouraged to conduct research projects on issues concerning disability, and we offered significant prizes for the best projects. We supported addressing legal and policy aspects in Botswana, China, Ethiopia, Indonesia, Vietnam and Zambia.

Some of the outcomes associated with the project included a strengthened enabling policy environment in Ethiopia to promote access of young men and women with disabilities to quality vocational training; future lawyers and judges' knowledge and capacity to promote disability rights issues in Vietnam; and enhanced capacity of Constituents on disability management in employment for persons with disabilities due to use of practical guidelines developed in Bahasa, Indonesia (ILO and Irish Aid, 2015).

The Theory of Change developed for PROPEL was clearly ambitious, and how it was applied differed in each of the programme countries. It embraces the complexity of social contexts and acknowledges the need to work around power-relationships, including those that are implicit and expressed through prejudice and stigma at the individual level. Such an approach is clearly not linear. Rather, the success of an intervention is claimed through lines of plausible causality, in a system where there are multiple actors and multiple outcomes; where contribution is a more realistic claim than singular attribution. Is an applied social psychology comfortable with this level of ambiguity? If not, then we may be removing ourselves from the very contexts where psychology can have greatest, but less attributable, impact.

CONCLUSION

The focus of psychology has conventionally been on micro and meso issues, at the individual and group level. Conrad (2007) argues that processes of medicalisation have led to the 'individualisation of social problems' and therefore disregard social forces that affect well-being. Similarly, Jordan (2014) suggests that many psychological researchers regard the concept of 'self' as bounded, transhistorical and decontextualised. According to Cushman (1990: 609), 'while psychologists have been treating the empty self, they have, of necessity, also been constructing it, profiting from it, and not challenging the social arrangements that created it'. In contrast, a macropsychology explores how to establish social systems that are most likely to promote a sense of value, inclusion and participation (MacLachlan, 2014) and address broader contextual factors and international practices and policy (Carr and MacLachlan, 2014). Scaling up to a macropsychology – one that addresses the wider scope of promoting the well-being of individuals, groups, nations and global society – can guide policy and support well-being on a national and global scale (MacLachlan, 2014).

The earliest use of the term 'macropsychology' that we could find dates back to Katona in 1979, who – in an economic context – wrote:

> Psychology is overwhelmingly micro because it is only the individual who reacts, learns, thinks, and has emotions. Social psychology also analyses mostly how individual behavior is influenced by belonging to groups, although group norms and social forces are occasionally discussed. Does macropsychology therefore belong in sociology, or is it something hazy and unnecessary? (Katona, 1979: 120–1)

Unfortunately, this provocative question did not stimulate much reaction. We believe that a macro perspective is more necessary now – in an increasingly globalised world – than it has ever been in psychology. We also admit that it has been, and is likely to continue to be, 'hazy'. In our view, macropsychology is more about a perspective, an ethos and methodologies than it is about definitive outcomes; although they would, of course, be very nice too. However, in an interdisciplinary world, with a focus on multicausal problems and with multiple pathways to solutions, applied social psychology has much to contribute to developing a macro perspective, promoting psychology as a population science and addressing major social challenges and opportunities in the twenty-first century.

REFERENCES

Amin, M., MacLachlan, M., Mannan, H., El Tayeb, S., El Khatim, A., Swartz, L., Munthali, A., Van Rooy, G., McVeigh, J., Eide, A., & Schneider, M. (2011). EquiFrame: A framework for analysis of the inclusion of human rights and vulnerable groups in health policies. *Health and Human Rights*, *13*(2), 1–20.

Anderson, N. B. (2015). Psychology's contributions to understanding immigration. *Monitor on Psychology*, *46*(1). Retrieved from http://www.apa.org/monitor/2015/01/ceo.aspx

Araya, R., Alvarado, R., Sepúlveda, R., & Rojas, G. (2012). Lessons from scaling up a depression treatment program in primary care in Chile. *Revista Panamericana de Salud Pública*, *32*(3), 234–240.

Bronfenbrenner, U. (1979). *The ecology of human development: Experiments by nature and design*. Cambridge, MA: Harvard University Press.

Brown, G. W., & Harris, T. (1978). *Social origins of depression: A study of psychiatric disorder in women*. New York, NY: Free Press.

Carr, S. C., & MacLachlan, M. (2014). Humanitarian work psychology. *The Psychologist*, *27*(3), 160–163. Retrieved from https://thepsychologist.bps.org.uk/volume-27/edition-3/humanitarian-work-psychology

Chinyama, M. J., MacLachlan, M., McVeigh, J., Huss, T., & Gawamadzi, S. (2017). An analysis of the extent of social inclusion and equity consideration in Malawi's national HIV and AIDS policy review process. *International Journal of Health Policy and Management*, *6*, 1–11.

Connell, J. P., & Kubisch, A. C. (1998). Applying a theory of change approach to the evaluation of comprehensive community initiatives: Progress, prospects, and problems. *New Approaches to Evaluating Community Initiatives*, *2*, 1–16.

Conrad, P. (2007). *The medicalization of society: On the transformation of human conditions into treatable disorders.* Baltimore, MD: Johns Hopkins University Press.

Cook, J. E., Purdie-Vaughns, V., Meyer, I. H., & Busch, J. T. A. (2014). Intervening within and across levels: A multilevel approach to stigma and public health. *Social Science & Medicine*, *103*, 101–109.

Cushman, P. (1990). Why the self is empty: Toward a historically situated psychology. *American Psychologist*, *45*(5), 599–611.

Desmond, D., & MacLachlan, M. (2002). Psychosocial issues in the field of prosthetics and orthotics. *Journal of Prosthetics and Orthotics*, *14*(1), 19–22.

Dukes, E. F. (1999). Structural forces in conflict and conflict resolution in democratic society. In H-W. Jeong (Ed.), *Conflict resolution: Dynamics, process and structure* (pp. 155–172). Brookfield, VT: Ashgate.

Fisher, K. R., & Purcal, C. (2017). Policies to change attitudes to people with disabilities. *Scandinavian Journal of Disability Research*, *19*(2), 161–174.

Fraser, N. (1998). *Social justice in the age of identity politics: Redistribution, recognition, participation*. Berlin, Germany: Wissenschaftszentrum Berlin für Sozialforschung.

General Directorate of Statistics (GDS), Ministry of Health, & ICF. (2018). *Timor-Leste Demographic and Health Survey 2016.* Dili, Timor-Leste and Rockville, MD: GDS and ICF. Retrieved from https://www.dhsprogram.com/pubs/pdf/FR329/FR329.pdf

Greenhalgh, T., Wong, G., Jagosh, J., Greenhalgh, J., Manzano, A., Westhorp, G., & Pawson, R. (2015). Protocol – the RAMESES II study: Developing guidance and reporting standards for realist evaluation. *BMJ Open*, *5*, e008567.

Griskevicius, V., Tybur, J. M., Ackerman, J. M., Delton, A. W., Robertson, T. E., & White, A. E. (2012). The financial consequences of too many men: Sex ratio effects on saving, borrowing, and spending. *Journal of Personality and Social Psychology*, *102*(1), 69–80.

Handicap International Indonesia & Timor-Leste Programme. (2016). *Planning forwards: Report of the mid-term review of the National Action Plan for People with Disabilities (2014–2018).* Report prepared by the Mid-Term Review Team.

Harris, P., Friel, S., & Wilson, A. (2015). 'Including health in systems responsible for urban planning': A realist policy analysis research programme. *BMJ Open*, *5*(7), 1–7.

Hasson, F., Keeney, S., & McKenna, H. (2000). Research guidelines for the Delphi survey technique. *Journal of Advanced Nursing*, *32*(4), 1008–1015.

Herman, E. (1995). *The romance of American psychology: Political culture in the age of experts.* Berkeley, CA: University of California Press.

Himmelweit, H. (1990). *Societal psychology (SAGE Focus Editions).* Thousand Oaks, CA: Sage.

Hodgetts, D., Drew, N., Sonn, C., Stolte, O., Nikora, L. W., & Curtis, C. (2010). *Social psychology and everyday life*. Basingstoke, England: Palgrave Macmillan.

Højholt, C., & Schraube, E. (2016). Introduction: Toward a psychology of everyday living. In E. Schraube & C. Højholt (Eds.), *Psychology and the conduct of everyday life* (pp. 1–14). Hove, England: Routledge.

Holzkamp, K. (2016). Conduct of everyday life as a basic concept of critical psychology. In E. Schraube & C. Højholt (Eds.), *Psychology and the conduct of everyday life* (pp. 65–98). Hove, England: Routledge.

Huss, T., & MacLachlan, M. (2016). *Equity and inclusion in policy processes (EquIPP): A framework to support equity & inclusion in the process of policy development, implementation and evaluation*. Dublin, Ireland: Global Health Press. Retrieved from https://global-health.tcd.ie/assets/doc/The%20EquIPP%20manual%2013th%20April%202016.pdf

ILO (International Labour Organization). (2013). *The Director-General's Programme and Budget Proposals for 2014–15 (317th Session, Geneva, 6-28th March 2013).* Geneva, Switzerland: ILO. Retrieved from http://www.ilo.int/wcmsp5/groups/public/—ed_norm/—relconf/documents/meetingdocument/wcms_203480.pdf

ILO (International Labour Organization), & Irish Aid. (2015). *Irish AID–ILO Partnership Programme 2012–15: Progress Report 2014.* Retrieved from http://www.ilo.org/wcmsp5/groups/public/—dgreports/—exrel/documents/genericdocument/wcms_369809.pdf

Jordan, M. (2014). Moving beyond counselling and psychotherapy as it currently is – Taking therapy outside. *European Journal of Psychotherapy & Counselling, 16*(4), 361–375.

Katona, G. (1979). Toward a macropsychology. *American Psychologist, 34*(2), 118–126.

MacLachlan, M. (2014). Macropsychology, policy, and global health. *American Psychologist, 69*(8), 851–863.

MacLachlan, M., Amin, M., Mannan, H., El Tayeb, S., Bedri, N., Swartz, L., Munthali, A., Van Rooy, G., & McVeigh, J. (2012). Inclusion and human rights in health policies: Comparative and benchmarking analysis of 51 policies from Malawi, Sudan, South Africa and Namibia. *PLoS ONE, 7*(5), e35864.

MacLachlan, M., Mannan, H., Huss, T., Munthali, A., & Amin, M. (2016). Policies and processes for social inclusion: Using EquiFrame and EquIPP for policy dialogue. Comment on 'Are sexual and reproductive health policies designed for all? Vulnerable groups in policy documents of four European countries and their involvement in policy development'. *International Journal of Health Policy and Management, 5*(3), 193–196.

MacLachlan, M., Mji, G., Chataika, T., Wazakili, M., Dube, A. K., Mulumba, M., Massah, B., Wakene, D., Kallon, F., & Maughan, M. (2014). Facilitating disability inclusion in poverty reduction processes: Group consensus perspectives from disability stakeholders in Uganda, Malawi, Ethiopia, and Sierra Leone. *Disability and the Global South, 1*(1), 107–127.

Mannan, H., Amin, M., MacLachlan, M., & the EquitAble Consortium. (2011). *The EquiFrame manual: A tool for evaluating and promoting the inclusion of vulnerable groups and core concepts of human rights in health policy documents.* Dublin, Ireland: The Global Health Press. Retrieved from https://global-health.tcd.ie/assets/doc/EquiFrame%20Manual_May19_2011.pdf

Marsella, A. J. (1998). Toward a 'global-community psychology': Meeting the needs of a changing world. *American Psychologist, 53*(12), 1282–1291.

Marsella, A. J. (2012). Psychology and globalization: Understanding a complex relationship. *Journal of Social Issues, 68*(3), 454–472.

Mathieson, J., Popay, J., Enoch, E., Escorel, S., Hernandez, M., Johnston, H., & Rispel, L. (2008). *Social exclusion: Meaning, measurement and experience and links to health inequalities. A review of literature (WHO Social Exclusion Knowledge Network Background Paper 1).* Geneva, Switzerland: WHO. Retrieved from http://www.who.int/social_determinants/publications/socialexclusion/en/

McVeigh, J., MacLachlan, M., Gilmore, B., McClean, C., Eide, A. H., Mannan, H., Geiser, P., Duttine, A., Mji, G., McAuliffe, E., Sprunt, B., Amin, M., & Normand, C. (2016). Promoting good policy for leadership and governance of health related rehabilitation: A realist synthesis. *Globalization and Health, 12*(49), 1–18.

Mji, G., Gcaza, S., Swartz, L., MacLachlan, M., & Hutton, B. (2011). An African way of networking around disability. *Disability & Society, 26*(3), 365–368.

National Institutes of Health. (2006). *Facilitating interdisciplinary research via methodological and technological innovation in the behavioral and social sciences (R21).* Bethesda, MD: National Institutes of Health. Retrieved from http://grants.nih.gov/grants/guide/rfa-files/RFA-RM-07-004.htm

National Science and Technology Council (Executive Office of the President of the United States). (2016). *Social and Behavioral Sciences Team 2016 annual report.* Retrieved from https://www.whitehouse.gov/sites/whitehouse.gov/files/images/2016%20Social%20and%20Behavioral%20Sciences%20Team%20Annual%20Report.pdf

Obschonka, M., Stuetzer, M., Audretsch, D. B., Rentfrow, P. J., Potter, J., & Gosling, S. D. (2016). Macropsychological factors predict regional economic resilience during a major economic crisis. *Social Psychological and Personality Science, 7*(2), 95–104.

OHCHR (Office of the High Commissioner for Human Rights). (2011). *Report on the rights of persons with disabilities in Timor-Leste.* Retrieved from http://www.ohchr.org/Documents/Countries/TP/UNHR_Report2011_en.pdf

Pawson, R., Greenhalgh, T., Harvey, G., & Walshe, K. (2004). *Realist synthesis: An introduction* (ESRC Research Methods Programme, University of Manchester, RMP Methods Paper 2). Retrieved from https://www.researchgate.net/publication/228855827_Realist_Synthesis_An_Introduction

Pawson, R., & Tilley, N. (1997). *Realistic evaluation*. London, England: Sage.

Percy-Smith, J. (Ed.). (2000). *Policy responses to social exclusion: Towards inclusion?* Maidenhead, England: Open University Press.

Rycroft-Malone, J., McCormack, B., DeCorby, K., & Hutchinson, A. (2010). Realist synthesis. In K. Gerrish & A. Lacey (Eds.), *The research process in nursing* (6th edn., pp. 303–320). Oxford, England: Wiley-Blackwell.

Schneider, F. W., Gruman, J. A., & Coutts, L. M. (2017). Defining the field of applied social psychology. In J. A. Gruman, F. W. Schneider, & L. M. Coutts (Eds.), *Applied social psychology: Understanding and addressing social and practical problems* (3rd edn., pp. 3–26). Thousand Oaks, CA: Sage.

Sidanius, J., & Pratto, F. (1999). *Social dominance: An intergroup theory of social hierarchy and oppression*. Cambridge, England: Cambridge University Press.

Silver, H. (2015). *The contexts of social inclusion (DESA working paper no. 144).* New York, NY: United Nations Department of Economic and Social Affairs. Retrieved from http://www.un.org/esa/desa/papers/2015/wp144_2015.pdf

Smail, D. (n.d.). *Social power and psychological distress: A social materialist approach to clinical psychology.* Retrieved from http://davidsmail.info/introfra.htm

Steptoe, A., & Kivimäki, M. (2012). Stress and cardiovascular disease. *Nature Reviews Cardiology*, *9*(6), 360–370.

Talhelm, T., Zhang, X., Oishi, S., Shimin, C., Duan, D., Lan, X., & Kitayama, S. (2014). Large-scale psychological differences within China explained by rice versus wheat agriculture. *Science*, *344*(6184), 603–608.

UNDP (United Nations Development Programme). (2016). *Connections: Building partnerships for disability rights. An overview of results from the first UNPRPD funding round.* New York, NY: UNDP. Retrieved from mptf.undp.org/document/download/16578

United Nations. (2015). *Universal Declaration of Human Rights.* New York, NY: United Nations. Retrieved from http://www.un.org/en/udhrbook/pdf/udhr_booklet_en_web.pdf

Westhorp, G. (2014). *Realist impact evaluation: An introduction*. London, England: Overseas Development Institute. Retrieved from https://www.odi.org/sites/odi.org.uk/files/odi-assets/publications-opinion-files/9138.pdf

Wilkinson, R., & Pickett, K. (2010). *The spirit level: Why equality is better for everyone.* London, England: Penguin Group.

Winerman, L. (2015). *The White House says more federal programs should tap behavioral science.* Washington, DC: American Psychological Association. Retrieved from http://www.apa.org/monitor/2015/11/upfront-white-house.aspx

Wong, G., Westhorp, G., Pawson, R., & Greenhalgh, T. (2013). *Realist synthesis: RAMESES training materials.* Retrieved from http://www.ramesesproject.org/media/Realist_reviews_training_materials.pdf

World Bank. (2013). *Inclusion matters: The foundation for shared prosperity. New Frontiers of Social Policy (advance edition).* Washington, DC: World Bank. Retrieved from http://siteresources.worldbank.org/EXTSOCIALDEVELOPMENT/Resources/244362-1265299949041/6766328-1329943729735/8460924-1381272444276/InclusionMatters_AdvanceEdition.pdf

PART IV

Health and Mental Health

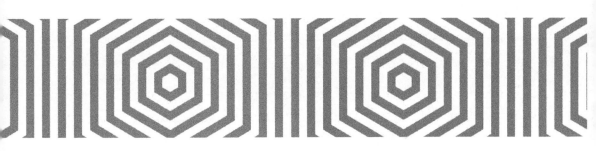

10

Social Cognitive Approaches to Health Issues

Benjamin Giguère, R. Thomas Beggs and Fuschia M. Sirois

Social cognition and health psychology are, in many ways, an odd couple. Social cognition is concerned with general processes and causal explanations. As such, it has tended to be exploratory, looking for the increasingly novel and counter-intuitive processes involved in perceiving, attending to, remembering, thinking about, and making sense of people, objects, events, and ourselves. By contrast, health psychology has tended to focus on specific phenomena tied to practical issues of physical, mental, and social well-being, which tend to be of concern to scholars, practitioners, and lay people. In terms of the contrast, Taylor (1982) noted that the fascinating qualities of social cognitive research may not be appreciated by a large audience, compared to the broad appeal of the specific issues of concern to health psychology.

There is a group of scholars and practitioners that work at the crossroads of these two domains, using social cognitive theories to benefit the physical, mental, and social health of individuals and communities. Although they may not explicitly identify as such, they are, at least in part, applying social psychology to health. This chapter aims to review applied research focusing on social cognitive approaches to health issues, with an emphasis on interventions aimed at cognitive and behavioural change. Although this mission statement may appear narrowly focused, the body of relevant literature is impressive.

Our chapter, which is not an exhaustive review, is divided into four key sections. In the first section, we provide a brief overview of the context in which social cognition merges with health psychology. In the second section, we review social cognitive theories commonly used in health research. In the third section, we focus on the use of social cognitive theories in interventions to encourage health-related changes. In the fourth section, we discuss challenges associated with research and interventions drawing on social cognition to foster health change.

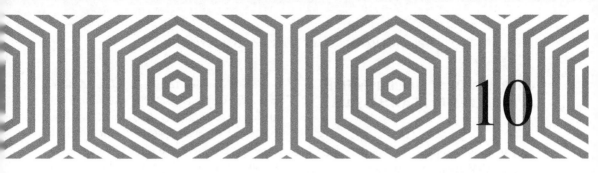

OVERVIEW OF SOCIAL COGNITIVE APPROACHES TO HEALTH ISSUES

Broadly speaking, social cognition is concerned with the processes involved when people think about, and make sense of, the world around them. Specifically, these cognitive processes involve attending to (and/or selecting) information about, interpreting information about, making decisions about (judging), and storing and retrieving information about people and ourselves, as well as objects, states, and events (see Moskowitz, 2005). For the most part, these processes have been assumed to vary on a continuum. At one end are processes that primarily aim to systematically consider information, typically at the expense of mental energy. At the other end are processes that primarily focus on conserving mental energy, at the expense of the systematic consideration of information. Among these energy-saving strategies, relying on socially learned expectations (e.g., schemas, categories, behavioural scripts, expected outcomes) and cognitive 'shortcuts' (e.g., availability heuristics, confirmation bias), are some of the most commonly researched and reported. At the route of social cognitive approaches is the assumption that these processes are key to understanding the influence of macro and meso level factors on individuals at the micro level.

Health behaviour research crosses multiple disciplines. When applied to health issues, social cognitive approaches are typically concerned with social cognition as it pertains to the understanding of practical issues related to physical, mental, and social health and wellbeing. As such, social cognitive approaches tend to examine health-related phenomena at an individual level, focusing on intra-personal factors and their interaction with perceptions of the social environment. The emphasis on micro level factors, namely social cognitive processes, is a distinctive feature of these approaches when applied to health.

This distinctive feature is reflected in the common methods used by research in this area. Indeed, typically, knowledge has been generated by using studies with relatively small sample sizes that often rely on correlational or experimental designs. In such studies, the unit of analysis is generally a person or a person's response at one or multiple time points. The emphasis on processes is also reflected in the common applications of the knowledge generated to address health-related issues. For example, the approaches can offer insight into the specific element of an intervention to influence individual decision-making and behaviour (e.g., Rothman and Salovey, 1997).

This approach can be contrasted with others used in the context of health research, such as public health, which tend to examine health-related phenomena using multi-level approaches, combining macro, meso, and micro factors. They also tend to rely on much larger samples, in which the unit of analysis is sometimes a person but will also often include other factors such as institutions, jurisdictions, and organizations. The contrast is also reflected in the application of knowledge. The distinctive contribution of social cognitive approaches is often less amenable to tackling health-related societal problems at multiple levels when compared to other disciplines that study health-related societal problems.

The distinctive features are well-illustrated in the prevalent social cognitive theories applied to understand health, but perhaps even more so in the attention given to the emphasis on the use of theory to explain the social cognitive processes assumed to underlie health-related behaviours. Trying to explain 'why people act that way' allows for unique novel contributions in this area of research. A good example of such a contribution comes from the work of Shelley Taylor. One of her seminal articles reports on a study conducted with cancer patients (Taylor, 1982) and revealed how the application of social cognitive theories can provide insight in health issues. Specifically, it provided insight into how different attributions of the causes of breast cancer can provide a helpful sense of psychological control. As she illustrates by her focus on the theoretical implications of her work, the role of theory is highly valued from a social cognitive perspective.

Researchers who have embarked in work at the junction between social cognition and health are often faced with a careful balancing act between the universalist assumptions of social cognitive theories and the specifics of the health issues they are examining. As applied scholars and practitioners know, rarely will one theory be sufficient to understand the complexity of a specific behaviour. At the same time, most of applied social psychology is guided by Lewin's often quoted take on theory: 'there is nothing as practical as a good theory' (1943: 118). Because of the emphasis on theory from a social cognitive perspective, we opted to structure this chapter in some ways by theoretical approach.

SOCIAL COGNITIVE THEORIES COMMONLY APPLIED IN HEALTH CONTEXTS

Multiple reviews of the literature have examined the cognitive and behavioural theories that are commonly used in the context of health research (e.g., Armitage and Conner, 2000; Noar, 2005), including one focusing on interventions (Davis et al., 2015). For the most part, these reviews converge to suggest that the most frequently used theories in the context of health research are the Health Belief Model (HBM; Becker, 1974), Theories of Reasoned Action (TRA; Fishbein and Ajzen, 1975) and Planned Behaviour (TPB; Ajzen, 1991), Social Cognitive Theory (SCT; Bandura, 1986), and the Transtheoretical Model of Change (TTM; Prochaska and DiClemente, 1984). Of these, all but the TTM have clear roots in social cognitive principles – as its name implies, the TTM was not meant to be rooted in any one single theoretical perspective.

While the assumptions and propositions of these theories vary greatly, they do share some similarities. For the most part, social cognitive theories applied to health phenomena tend to assume that health-related actions are the result of rational decision-making processes that involve the deliberate and systematic processing of information. The commonality of this assumption reflects their common roots in expectancy-value theories, such as proposed by Lewin and his colleagues (e.g., Lewin et al., 1944). These theories suggest that the likelihood a behaviour will occur depends on the sum total of the product of the expectancy and value of the outcome(s) of the behaviour (see Feather, 1982).

These theories also hold that social cognitions are the primary causal agent of health-related actions. Although they use distinct terminology for these cognitions, most of these theories suggest that attitudinal beliefs of individuals, social norms, a sense of efficacy and control, and intentions to engage in actions play an important role in the health-related behaviours that people engage in. Overall, they also hold that these cognitions are accessible to awareness and that they tend to operate through conscious processes. Guided by these notions, these theories typically suggest that individuals enact actions that appear rational to them at the moment they are performed. However, decades of research and campaigns focusing on cognitions such as fear-appeals, risk perceptions, and attitudes suggest that the link between our cognitions and our actions is not as direct or seemingly rational as one would assume.

In order to address this lack of concordance, other social cognitive theories have been elaborated. These approaches draw on both social cognition research and early work on fear appeals that showed counter-intuitive patterns of behaviour when people are made to fear certain health outcomes. For instance, Gollwitzer's Implementation Intentions (IIs, see Gollwitzer, 1999) offers one such alternative to a purely rational approach by focusing on action control strategies that aim to ensure that 'good intentions' get translated into actual behaviour. Social norm approaches generally offer another alternative. For example, norms-based research has shown that people often act in ways similar to others, even when faced with information suggesting that they should not, and that they also typically underestimate the influence of norms on their actions (see Cialdini, 2005; Miller and Prentice, 2016). Finally, cognitive dissonance is often discussed in the literature as a counterpoint to the argument that people are rational actors.

In this section, we review applied social cognitive work tied to the HBM, SCT, TPB, IIs, Social Norm approaches, and cognitive dissonance. However, we do not discuss the TTM. The importance of this approach for understanding the process of health behaviour change is well established. However, our focus in the current chapter is on social cognitive theories and the TTM offers limited explanations of the social cognitive processes assumed to underlie each of the steps (cf., Armitage and Conner, 2000). Protection Motivation Theory, which is also a common theory, is discussed later in the section reviewing social cognitive models developed specifically to explain health attitude and behaviour change.

Health Belief Model

A focus on health attitudes was first introduced by the HBM (Janz and Becker, 1984). The HBM was developed by US Public Health Service social psychologists in the 1950s to help understand why people do, or do not, take action to prevent, detect, or control illness. The overall premises of the model are that people have a desire to avoid illness, and to get well when ill, and that they have concordant beliefs that certain actions will either prevent illness or improve an existing condition (Janz and Becker, 1984). As such, the HBM assumes that people are rational beings who will favour being healthy and avoid illness, and will act accordingly.

The model relies on a series of four central sets of cognitions related to illness (Janz and Becker, 1984). *Perceived susceptibility* refers to a person's perception of the risk of acquiring a health-related condition. *Perceived severity* refers to perceptions of how serious a condition would be if it were acquired, or of how serious it is if the person already has it. *Perceived benefits* are the extent to which a person believes that a health-promoting behaviour will be effective in preventing or controlling a health condition. Finally, *perceived barriers* refer to obstacles or costs associated with following through with a health-promoting behaviour. Thus, according to the HBM, people are more likely to engage in health behaviours if they believe they are susceptible to a health condition, if they believe the condition could have serious consequences for their health, and if they believe a course of action with health benefits and few obstacles is available to them.

Outside of these four major dimensions of the HBM are minor factors that have generally received less attention by researchers. *Cues to action* refer to stimuli that trigger the health-related decision-making process; these cues could be internal (e.g., physical symptoms) or external (e.g., mass media communication). *Modifying variables* are generally socioeconomic factors that can affect perceptions of the four main dimensions. Lastly, self-efficacy was added to the HBM in 1988 in response to the recognition of its important role in motivating health-related actions (Rosenstock et al., 1988). In the HBM, self-efficacy typically refers to someone's confidence in their ability to perform a health behaviour successfully.

The HBM has been used for a wide variety of behaviours (see Abraham and Sheeran, 2005). For instance, smoking, prescription drug taking, cancer screening, condom use, continuous positive airway pressure therapy (CPAP), and exercise have all been investigated using the HBM (see Carpenter, 2010, and Janz and Becker, 1984, for reviews).

Overall meta-analyses have reported small effect sizes for the four main individual factors of the HBM. For example, Harrison et al. (1992) observed that, while most of the factors were significantly associated with behavioural outcomes retrospectively and prospectively, the effect sizes were relatively small; susceptibility had an estimated correlation of $r = .15$, severity $r = .08$, benefits $r = .13$, and costs $r = .21$. Perceived benefits and costs performed better in retrospective studies than in prospective studies, raising the issue that perhaps these factors are less useful in predicting behaviour than they are in explaining it post hoc (Harrison et al., 1992).

The findings of Harrison and colleagues were replicated by Carpenter (2010), who reports that severity and susceptibility had small weighted correlations, with estimated correlations of .15 and .05, respectively. Benefits and barriers were more strongly correlated with behaviour, with estimated weighted correlations of .27 and .30, respectively. A meta-analysis by Sheeran et al. (2014) focused on experimental work that examined the effect of perceived severity yielded results that aligned with previous findings, suggesting that perceived severity had a small effect size on intentions ($d = .32$) and behaviour ($d = .34$).

It is worth noting that the effect of each of the factors was considered in isolation from each other. It is possible that there are interactions between these sets of cognitions, and that the effect of the model would be larger than that which would be expected based on the effect size of each of the factors. For example, it could be that people need to first perceive they are susceptible to a condition with severe outcomes to motivate them to look for accessible health-promoting behaviours. Unfortunately, there is no standard method of combing the factors, and therefore, not enough research has been done on combined models to warrant their inclusion in a meta-analysis. It is also possible that the factors are sharing variance, meaning that a combined model would explain less variance than the sum of each of the factors' variance. It is also worth noting that, since the HBM includes four sets of cognitions, examining their interactions may present unique challenges; analyses could require a four-way interaction.

Finally, the support for the causal role of the HBM factors is mixed. Most research assessing the HBM involves correlational designs, often cross-sectional in nature, and there are inherent challenges to these designs when examining causality. We did not find any large body of research that has examined the HBM systematically by manipulating all its proposed sets of cognitions. Future work examining the HBM using randomized control studies, particularly if blind or possibly double blind, to examine the effect of the factors on health behaviours would provide valuable information about the value of this model in applied settings.

The reputation of the HBM is also affected by its link to adverse effects and to misuse by industry to support practices that encourage unhealthy behaviours. For example, Balbach et al. (2006) review how tobacco industry executives used the focus on individual rational choice of the HBM to shift the blame from their companies onto the consumers. This argument was possible because HBM-based research gives little attention to sociostructural forces. Specifically, research derived from the HBM approach failed to systematically recognize the role of industry in framing information about smoking and health.

In sum, the HBM is one of the original models used in order to understand health decisions. The components of the model have been widely studied to help explain a range of health behaviours. Current findings suggest that individual components of the model are linked to health-related intentions and behaviours, typically with small effect sizes (cf., Cohen, 1992). The studies have relied primarily on correlational designs and examined the components of the model individually. Therefore, experimental research designs would help understand what causal role the factors of the HBM have in people's health decisions. The examination of the interaction of the factors of the HBM may also help further understand the model.

Social Cognitive Theory

SCT (Bandura, 1986) addresses both socio-structural and personal determinants of behaviour. The theory has been used to explain multiple domains of human thoughts and behaviour, including health. The theory assumes that people are agentic thinkers and, as with other social cognitive approaches, that their thoughts serve determinative functions. It argues that people engage in a dynamic construction of thoughts about future courses of action in response to changing situational demands. People assess the functional value and efficacy of these courses of actions based on their expected outcomes and make the necessary changes. These processes are set in an interactive triadic reciprocal causation framework: behavioural patterns, environmental events, and internal cognitive, affective, and biological states are assumed to operate as interacting determinants of human behaviour.

Other factors in the model include *collective efficacy*, which is typically defined in terms of perceptions that a group can bring about a desired outcome, and *environmental determinants* of behaviour. The latter includes *incentive motivation* (punishments and rewards) and *facilitation* (resources and environmental supports). Collectively, these factors are seen as influencing goals and behaviour (Bandura, 2004).

Health researchers have typically focused on two factors of SCT that influence the likelihood that a person will take a health-related course of action: expected outcomes and self-efficacy. As defined by Bandura (1977: 193), an outcome expectancy is 'a person's estimate that a given behaviour will lead to certain outcomes'. Thus, a person must first expect that the benefits of performing a course of action outweigh the costs of doing so (i.e., physical, social, and self-evaluative outcome expectations). Bandura (1977) argued that the outcomes expected from a course of action are largely dependent on people's perception of how successful they will be in performing specific actions in specific contexts. Thus, Bandura originally argued that self-efficacy had a causal impact on expected outcomes but that expected outcomes did not have a causal effect on self-efficacy. This original notion has been questioned by researchers, and it is currently often assumed that the causal relationship between expected outcomes and self-efficacy is bidirectional (see Williams, 2010).

SCT, in particular expected outcomes and self-efficacy, has been applied to many health behaviours, such as prescription drug adherence, physical exercise, risky sexual behaviours, medical screening, and addictive behaviours (see Bandura, 1998; Luszczynska and Schwarzer, 2005). In one study, for example, patients who had been hospitalized for an acute myocardial infarction were assigned to an SCT-based treatment programme (DeBusk et al., 1994). The treatment programme supplemented usual care with activities aimed at increasing patients' sense of self-efficacy, such as monitoring. Those in the SCT group were more likely to quit smoking, had lower LDL cholesterol, and improved functional capacity compared to the control group.

A meta-analysis of 54 studies that examined the influence of self-efficacy on smoking cessation reported small effect sizes when self-efficacy was assessed prior to quitting (Cohen's $d = -0.17$; Gwaltney et al., 2009). The same study reported that, when self-efficacy was assessed after a quitting attempt, the effect was larger (Cohen's $d = -0.37$). Sheeran and colleagues (2016) conducted a meta-analysis examining the impact of experimentally manipulated self-efficacy on a range of health outcomes. Their results revealed medium effect size self-efficacy on health-related behavioural intentions (Cohen's $d = 0.51$) and a smaller effect for health-related behaviour (Cohen's $d = 0.47$).

Other studies have tended to focus exclusively on the expected outcomes components of SCT. For example, Hull and Bond (1986) conducted a meta-analysis examining the influence of alcohol outcome expectancies on consumption and reported a large effect ($Z = 5.10$). In a more recent meta-analysis, Reich et al. (2010) examined the effect of implicit and explicit alcohol outcome expectancies. They observed a small to medium effect between implicit measures of expectancies and alcohol consumption ($r = .35$), and, in line with Bond and Hull, they observed a large effect between explicit expectancies and alcohol consumption ($r = .41$).

SCT does share many points with other social cognitive theories commonly used in the context of health. For instance, it holds, as a central tenet, that cognitions are a primary causal determinant of behaviour. Also, most social cognitive models now include the notion of self-efficacy, or a version of it. For example, as we discuss further in the TPB section, the concept of perceived behavioural control in that theory is akin to the concept of self-efficacy. There are some notable differences, however. One important difference between the HBM and SCT is SCT's treatment of self-efficacy. Whereas self-efficacy is a somewhat tangential concept in the HBM, it is central to SCT. In SCT, self-efficacy is assumed to have a direct effect on health behaviours and indirect effects through its influence on outcome expectations, sociostructural factors, and goals (Bandura, 2004).

Another major difference from the HBM, and other theories including the TPB, is SCT's fundamental assumption that the relationship between a person, their behaviour, and their environment is reciprocal – the person is altered by the environment but also can alter it and elicit particular responses from it (Bandura, 1986; 2004). As part of this reciprocal relationship, SCT recognizes that groups of people can alter the environment in order to alter behaviour. For example, groups of people working for public health agencies use the media to encourage people to reduce smoking or increase healthy eating.

There may also be more useful aspects of SCT, in terms of applications to health, than those researchers have tended to focus on – namely self-efficacy and expect outcomes (see Bandura, 1998; 2004). In particular, the theory asks researchers and practitioners to consider perceived and actual sociostructural factors that may set barriers to healthy practices, as well as the interactions between these personal and sociostructural factors. In this, SCT aims to cut across levels (micro, meso, and macro) to understand how social cognitive processes shape human behaviour dynamically.

In sum, SCT holds that people form beliefs about behaviours and their likely outcomes in response to their changing social environment. The theory has some similarities with the other theories reviewed, but its focus on self-efficacy is an important distinguishing factor. Self-efficacy has generally been shown to have a medium effect size on intentions and a smaller effect size on behaviour (e.g., Gwaltney et al., 2009). The research on SCT has been somewhat focused on the micro, individual level; future research may benefit from investigating the theory across the meso and macro levels as well.

Theory of Planned Behaviour

The TRA (Fishbein and Ajzen, 1975) and TPB (Ajzen, 1991) departed from previous theories by proposing that intentions are the most proximal determinant of behaviour. The models propose that the intention to perform a behaviour is shaped by two conceptually independent components: an attitudinal component and a normative component, which are assumed to have additive effects on behavioural intentions. The attitudinal component reflects the favourableness of the evaluation of the behaviour. On the basis of an expectancy-value approach to attitudes, Fishbein and Ajzen (1975) proposed that people's expectations about the consequences of behaviour were weighted by the importance or value placed on these consequences, and this combination shaped attitudes. The normative component of the model, termed *subjective norm*, refers to people's perception of the extent to which others who are important to them expect them to engage, or not engage, in a behaviour.

Ajzen (1991) revised the TRA and introduced the TPB. The TPB proposes that, to account for nonvolitional behaviours accurately, it is necessary to consider the extent to which individuals perceive the behaviours to be under their personal control. This third determinant of intentions is called *perceived behavioural control.*

In a meta-analysis of studies drawing on the TPB, Armitage and Conner (2001) observed that the factors posited by the theory accounted for 39% of variance in behavioural intentions and 27% of variance in behaviour. In line with past reviews (e.g., Ajzen, 1991; Sheppard et al., 1988), they also observed that the subjective norm construct is generally the weakest predictor of intentions.

McEachan et al. (2011) conducted a more specific meta-analysis focusing exclusively on prospective studies targeting health-related behaviours. Their results illustrated that the predictive validity of TPB varied by type of health behaviour. Physical activity and diet behaviours were better predicted (23.9% and 21.2% variance explained, respectively) than risky behaviours, detection behaviours, safer sex, and abstinence from drugs, which were more poorly predicted (between 13.8% and 15.3% variance explained). Intentions accounted for the most variance in behaviour across behaviour types. Attitudes were the strongest predictor of intentions for all types of behaviour, with the exceptions of risk behaviours, for which they were equal to perceived behavioural control, and detection behaviours, for which perceived behavioural control was the strongest predictor. As with previous meta-analyses, McEachan et al. (2011) observed that subjective norms were generally the weakest predictor.

The lack of predictive value of subjective norms has been attributed, at least in part, to a combination of issues of conceptualization and measurement. Subjective norms are conceptualized in terms of social pressure applied globally on a person's motivation. However, the relevance of different groups to a behaviour may vary as a function of context. For example, norms about alcohol consumption for a university student on a campus are more likely to be shaped by their peers and friends on campus, while norms about alcohol consumption for that same student are more likely to be shaped by their parents when they meet their future inlaws. Moreover, adults are rarely under direct and explicit social pressure to enact certain actions. Indeed, subjective norms have been observed to have lower predictive value for adults compared to adolescents (see McEachan et al., 2011).

Given that the TPB is more recent than its predecessors, it has benefited from the insights provided by the research examining these earlier models. As such, it does share similarities with some of them. Among these, there are similarities between the notions of perceived behaviour control and the concept of self-efficacy from the SCT. In addition, the TPB adopted an expectancy-value approach to attitude, which is similar to the approach that underlies the core sets of cognitions in the HBM.

Overall, the TPB appears to offer some improvement in terms of predictive value over theories that preceded it, particularly when compared to the HBM. For example, Bish et al. (2000) compared the ability of the HBM and the TPB to predict intentions to complete cervical smear tests and observed that the HBM accounted for 4% of the variance in intentions while the TPB accounted for 51% of the variance. These results align with those of other work comparing the HBM and TPB (e.g., Conner and Norman, 1994; Quine et al., 1998; Weinstein, 1993).

Perhaps because of its popularity, the TPB has often been the focus of critics. The size of the effects garnered by the theory has been criticized (see Sniehotta et al., 2014). Another frequent criticism is aimed at a central tenet of the TPB: that attitude, subjective norms, perceived behavioural control, and intentions are sufficient to account for behaviour. These critics argue, directly or indirectly, that the model is too reductionist and that it needs to be supplemented by other variables (e.g., Kam et al., 2008).

The TPB has also been criticized for focusing on the proximal determinants of behaviour, leaving out explanations as to what factors influence these proximal determinants (cf., Conner and Armitage, 1998). As already discussed, another frequent criticism focuses on the conceptualization and operationalization of the main components of the TPB, particularly subjective norms.

In sum, the TPB is an important and often-used theory in understanding health behaviours. The theory focuses on the factors that influence intentions to act. Meta-analyses have indicated that the factors of the TPB generally have medium to large effects on intentions and small to medium effects on behaviour. While these studies have generally found a smaller effect for subjective norms in the TPB model, the way that norms were originally conceptualized in the model does present some problems. A novel approach to norms, as well as a greater consideration of how meso and macro factors may shape the cognitions proposed under the TPB, may provide important and valuable theoretical and applied insights.

Implementation Intentions

Peter Gollwitzer and his colleagues took particular interest in the gap between intentions and behaviour. They realized that the time between when a goal is set and when a goal is acted upon is often long, which leads to people failing to act (see Gollwitzer, 1999). To explain the intention–behaviour gap, they introduced the idea that intentions often require an implementation plan. Specifically, Gollwitzer differentiated IIs from broader goal intentions. A goal intention is simply something that someone wants to achieve, such as wanting to lose 10 pounds. They proposed that setting such goal intentions is merely a first step to enacting a course of action, and that planning how to achieve the goal, getting started, and completing goal striving are equally important steps. As a result, they introduced the concept of an II, which is the act of committing to how, when, and where the goal will be achieved (see Gollwitzer, 1999).

From an II perspective, good intentions are more likely to be acted upon if a person has IIs – an 'if/then' plan – in place. For example, an II could take the following form: *if* I get home from work by 5 pm on a given day, *then* I will go to the gym. Importantly, the desired behaviour – going to the gym – is now part of a specific plan. If a person had such a plan in place and they got home from work at 4:45 pm, they would not have to consider all possible options to occupy their evening, such as trying a new recipe or just flopping in front of a screen. Rather, with an implementation plan, the desired, pre-selected response often becomes efficient, immediate, and automatic (Brandstatter et al., 2001).

Through the II process, many of the issues that impede goal completion are resolved (see Gollwitzer, 1999). For instance, procrastination is reduced because the decision to act has already been made. Distractions are also reduced, as other possible goal pursuits are no longer in competition with the previously decided-upon action. The need for willpower is reduced, as the environmental cues one selected (the 'ifs' in the intention) direct the behaviour (the 'then').

As with its predecessors, this approach was not elaborated specifically for health behaviours, although it is commonly used in that context (see Gollwitzer and Sheeran, 2006). The efficacy of IIs is supported by a sizeable body of research, which uses various types of designs and behaviours (see Sheeran et al., 2005 for a review specific to health). In their meta-analysis, Gollwitzer and Sheeran (2006) report that the overall impact of forming IIs on goal achievement in the context of health behaviours was Cohen's d of 0.59, with a 95% CI of 0.52 to 0.67, which can be characterized in the range of medium size. Interestingly, IIs appeared to have stronger effects for individuals facing mental health issues (e.g., schizophrenic patients, frontal lobe patients, and heroin addicts), with large effect sizes observed in these populations.

Two recent meta-analyses have also looked at the effects of IIs on diet (Adriaanse et al., 2011) and exercise (Bélanger-Gravel et al., 2013). For diet, IIs were found to be effective at increasing the intake of healthy foods ($d = 0.59$) but were less effective in decreasing the intake of unhealthy foods ($d = 0.29$; Adriaanse et al., 2011). The authors observed that the methodological quality of the studies meta-analysed moderated the effect size estimates. Specifically, studies that used better control groups resulted in smaller effect size estimates, while studies that used better outcome measures reported larger effect size estimates. For exercise behaviours, Bélanger-Gravel et al. (2013) report a standard mean difference of 0.31, 95% CI [0.13, 0.35], for IIs at post intervention, which they qualify as a small to medium effect.

As with the theories reviewed previously, implementation intention has obvious connections to past work, particularly to the TPB. This link has been examined by some researchers. For instance, Sheeran and Orbell (2000) randomly assigned women to a cervical cancer screening implementation condition or to a control. They observed that, although TPB variables (i.e., attitudes, subjective norms, perceived behavioural control and intentions) provided good predictors of screening attendance, IIs provided a better one. This pattern of result had been observed in other studies (e.g., breast self-examination, Orbell et al., 1997), supporting the incremental value of the II approach.

Since it does draw on elements of some of its theoretical predecessors, the theory shares some of their critiques, such as reductionism. In particular, the II approach assumes that people are willing and able to engage in a particular behaviour or behaviour change. It offers little in terms of explaining what makes someone willing and able to engage in a behaviour or behaviour change. Critiques aside, II is arguably among the simplest, most effective forms of applied social psychological interventions technique relying on cognitive approaches to influence the prevalence of health-related behaviour among large groups of people over time (e.g., Adriaanse et al., 2011; Bélanger-Gravel et al., 2013; Gollwitzer and Sheeran, 2006).

In sum, II was developed to address the gap between intentions and behaviour. The work suggests that the likelihood of goal attainment increases by committing to how, where, and when that goal will be pursued. A central aspect of the theory is that people who create if/then plans for desired behaviours reduce barriers to goal attainment. Research has suggested that IIs are generally effective for health behaviours, with effect sizes typically in the medium range. IIs require relatively low cost and resources intervention techniques. As such, they offer currently one of the most cost-effective avenues for interventions to increase the likelihood of the occurrence of health-related behaviours across large groups of individuals.

Social Norm Theories

Although often underestimated by lay people and scholars alike, social norms have been increasingly recognized as a powerful source of influence on behaviour (see Cialdini, 2005). From a social cognitive perspective, norms are typically conceptualized as perceived norms, which are stored in memory and retrieved when prompted by situational cues. These norms are assumed to capture our perceptions of how people typically think, feel, or act in a given situation. From this information, we infer what is typically perceived as normal and acceptable in a given context, which forms basis for comparative judgements to guide and evaluate our own thoughts, feelings, and actions.

The direct presence of others is not a requirement of most theoretical approaches for normative influence to occur; in part because norms can become internalized. This notion is supported by numerous studies in which the influence of norms was observed regardless of the absence of observers (e.g., Aarts and Dijksterhuis, 2003; Deutsch and Gerard, 1955; Giguère et al., 2016; Postmes et al., 2001). Normative influence can also occur without the need for conscious awareness (e.g., Aarts and Dijksterhuis, 2003; Nolan et al., 2008). As such, for most approaches, the influence of social norms does not necessitate that individuals hold rational explicit cognitions for them to act in a certain way.

One challenge when reviewing the role of norms from a social cognitive perspective in the context of health is the range of conceptualizations and operationalizations of the notion of norms in the scholarly literature. A few more well-known, distinct conceptualizations of norms can be found. The TPB defines norms as *subjective norms*, which are assumed to represent what important others expect someone to think, feel, or do, and these norms are expected to operate mainly through external pressures. The Focus Theory of Normative Conduct distinguishes between *descriptive norms*, which describe what is typical or normal, and *injunctive norms*, which capture 'what constitutes morally approved and disapproved conduct' (Cialdini et al., 1990: 1015). The Social Identity Approach to normative influence focuses on the notion of *group norms*, which are defined as the accepted or implied rules of how behaviourally-relevant ingroup members should, and do, behave (see Smith and Louis, 2009; Turner, 1991); these group norms can be either descriptive or injunctive in nature.

The importance of normative influence on behaviour has been questioned, primarily due to the mixed support in research on subjective norms (cf., Armitage and Conner, 2001). As we previously discussed, subjective norms have faced conceptualization and operationalization issues. Social Identity Approaches to norms have aimed to address some of these issues (see Smith and Louis, 2009). The approach extends the notion of norms beyond external prescriptions that are dependent on the extent to which one believes a behaviour is expected and observable by important others. It proposes that, when specific group memberships form a salient basis for self-definition, individuals construct context-specific ingroup norms based on what they perceive as the prototypical ingroup beliefs, attitudes, feelings, and behaviours. From this perspective, the influence of norms occurs through a cognitive process which brings a group membership to become the salient basis for self-definition – a process called self-categorization, which is independent of social pressure (see Turner, 1991).

Multiple studies have supported the value of this approach in the context of health behaviours. In two studies, Terry and Hogg (1996) observed that group norms were positively associated with intentions to use sunscreen and that this relationship was moderated by the degree to which someone identified with the behaviourally-relevant reference group. The influence of group norms has been supported with a host of health-related behaviours, including smoking (e.g., Schofield et al., 2003), alcohol consumption (e.g., Giguère et al., 2014; Neighbors et al., 2008), substance use (e.g., Verkooijen et al., 2007), healthy eating (e.g., Louis et al., 2007; Stok et al., 2012), flu vaccination (e.g., Falomir-Pichastor et al., 2009), and physical activity (e.g., Chatzisarantis et al., 2009).

The potential value of social norms in understanding health behaviours is further supported by research examining alternatives to the subjective norms conceptualization. Rivis and Sheeran (2003) report a meta-analysis that examined descriptive norms as an additional predictor to the factors proposed by the TPB in the context of health behaviours. Their results suggest that descriptive norms account for variance incrementally above subjective norms in predicting intentions and behaviour ($\Delta R^2 = .05$).

Manning (2009) conducted a meta-analysis to examine the role of descriptive and injunctive norms on behaviour, with an emphasis on health behaviours. His results revealed that descriptive norms had a greater influence on behaviour compared to injunctive norms ($r = .34$ and .28, respectively), particularly when behaviours were not socially approved, were more socially motived, and more pleasant. Overall, it appears that, in most cases, descriptive norms seem to have a greater effect in predicting behaviour compared to other conceptualizations of norms. The literature also suggests that descriptive norms tend to have greater influence on unhealthy behaviours than healthy ones (see Rivis and Sheeran, 2003).

Central to most theories about the influence of norms is their cognitive salience. Indeed, the Focus Theory of Normative Conduct (Cialdini et al., 1990) argues that the salience of norms is the primary determinant of the influence of norms. Situational factors influencing the salience of norms are thus important factors in understanding normative influence. As such, the use of experimental designs in which the salience of normative information is manipulated is well suited to understanding normative influence.

Providing insight in this approach, Sheeran and colleagues (2016) conducted a meta-analysis examining experimental research focusing, in part, on norms. They report that experimentally-induced changes in norms were associated with a small to medium effect of change in intentions ($d = .49$) and behaviour ($d = .36$). Importantly, their findings suggested that a change in norms was sufficient to change behaviour, even without changes in attitudes and self-efficacy. Interestingly, their findings also suggest that the influence of norms on behaviour was, in part, independent of their influence on intentions. This finding aligns with the idea that the influence of norms can occur directly, bypassing individuals' conscious intentions.

Some important questions about social norms with important implications for health behaviours remain understudied, particularly from a social cognitive perspective. Among these, how people identify the norm in a given situation is central to understanding the impact of norms on health behaviours. The work of Prentice and Miller (1993) is among the few that have focused on this question. Their investigation on campus alcohol consumption norms revealed that students made a systematic error in their identification of norms by overestimating the degree to which alcohol consumption was normal. They suggest that this misperception may be due to a biased display of public support for the normative behaviour and a biased encoding of the public behaviour of others. Their work, along with others (e.g., Kashima et al., 2013), suggests that people tend to apply the normative information they observe from a few salient exemplars to all members of a social category, such as defined by a group or a community. The implications of this cognitive process in the case of health behaviours are important. It is likely that, in the case of health-behaviour norms, unhealthy exemplars are more salient, and thus lead to a biased perception of norms in an unhealthy direction. Beyond identifying norms, other aspects that would benefit from further investigations with particular relevance to health include how norms change over time, how multiple norms interact to influence behaviour, and how to best use norms-based interventions to affect beliefs and behaviours.

Social norms and the social comparison process linked to them underlie much theorizing in social cognitive models. The notion of norms is part of the SCT and the TPB. There are interesting parallels between a norm-based approach and II. Norms provide information about which action is desirable, along with how, when, and where the action will be achieved. Similarly, the II approach focuses on if/then plans to pre-commit to how, when, and where a goal-related action will be performed. A norm-based approach may offer one avenue to provide insight in the source of naturally occurring IIs. The possible interactions between norms and other types of cognitions also remain an understudied area with much potential. For example, Walker et al. (2011) suggest that perceiving social norms encouraging marijuana use can be associated with a lower sense of self-efficacy in avoiding using marijuana.

In sum, the multiple social cognitive theories about social norms and their influence seem to converge on a few important issues. First, social norms have a meaningful influence on behaviour, including health behaviours. Second, the influence of norms on behaviour can occur through their impact on intentions or directly on behaviour. Third, multiple different conceptualizations of norms can be found in the field. Of these conceptualizations, descriptive norms appear to have the strongest and most consistent influence on health-related behaviours across studies.

Cognitive Dissonance

The overarching idea of cognitive dissonance is that psychological inconsistency makes people experience an uncomfortable state of arousal (Festinger and Carlsmith, 1959). People tend to maintain logical consistency both between their cognitions and between their cognitions and their behaviours. Failure to maintain such consistency leads most people to experience a state of unpleasant arousal, which can only be resolved by removing the inconsistency. Thus, this approach focuses on instances when people believe that they are acting freely but think or behave in ways they did not intend, or which they would not perceive as rational.

To highlight the nature of cognitive dissonance and dissonance reduction, Festinger (1957) described someone who is a cigarette smoker. This person is engaged in a behaviour that they know is harmful to their health, which results in dissonance. Festinger proposed the person would engage in ongoing attempts to rid themselves of this dissonance. For instance, they could change their behaviours by quitting smoking. Alternatively, they could change their beliefs about the effects of smoking, by choosing to reject, downplay, or question the science showing that smoking is bad for their health. They could also change their other beliefs by deciding that it is better to 'live fast and die young' than it is to live a longer, less exciting life. If any of these strategies are successful, the person will have eliminated the uncomfortable dissonance that arose from the knowledge that smoking was harmful to their health.

Drawing on the idea of cognitive dissonance and on analogies with disease inoculation, William McGuire and his colleagues (e.g., Papageorgis and McGuire, 1961) surmised that people tend to defend their beliefs, including health beliefs, by avoiding exposure to inconsistent information. In doing so, they may leave themselves in a position where they are unmotivated and inexperienced in developing supporting arguments for their beliefs and in refuting counter-arguments. McGuire and his colleagues thus proposed that a process of inoculation could prepare people to address the content of specific arguments that they might encounter. The effectiveness of this method has been demonstrated through interventions with adolescents to inoculate them against smoking (e.g., Evans et al., 1978). They were exposed to a review of pro-smoking arguments that they may encounter and given time to come up with counter-arguments. The presence of these practiced counter-arguments effectively increased adolescents ability to resist peer pressure, which led to reduced smoking rates (Evans et al., 1978). Banas and Rains (2010) conducted a general meta-analysis of inoculation theory. The mean effect size of inoculation was $d = 0.43$ when compared to participants who were not inoculated, and the 95% CI ranged from 0.39 to 0.48.

Dissonance-based field studies and interventions have been used to address condom use (e.g., Stone et al., 1994) and eating disorders (e.g., Stice et al., 2007) among other behaviours (see Freijy and Kothe, 2013, for a review). A meta-analysis of eating disorder interventions showed that the presence of dissonance-related content was associated with significantly reduced body dissatisfaction ($z = 2.10$), thin ideal internalization ($z = 2.22$), dieting ($z = 2.78$), negative affect ($z = 2.39$), and eating pathology ($z = 3.11$) but not changes in body mass ($z = -0.57$; Stice et al., 2007), effect sizes which are classifiable in the small to medium range (cf., Cohen, 1992).

In sum, cognitive dissonance provides a theoretical perspective to understand why and how people continue problematic health behaviours. In general, meta-analysis shows that inoculation has a small to medium effect size. Future research should consider conflicting thoughts and beliefs around health behaviours, as their presence may help explain the general disconnect between intentions and behaviour.

SOCIAL COGNITION AND HEALTH BEHAVIOUR CHANGE

As illustrated by the social cognitive theories that are commonly applied to health, this domain of research has been primarily focused on the factors predicting health-related behaviours. This 'predictive research' typically uses self-report measures of social cognitions to predict intentions and/or behaviour; often using cross-sectional or longitudinal survey designs. Many would argue, however, that the key goal of social cognitive research is not to merely explain and predict health behaviour but to foster behaviour change through interventions that induce changes in social cognitions (cf., Conner and Norman, 2005; Rutter and Quine, 2002).

The social cognitive research into behaviour change is generally based on one of three different strategies, which are not mutually exclusive. First, some research uses experimental designs to examine hypotheses, which typically have arisen from 'predictive research', about behaviour change. Second, some research examines social cognitive models that focus solely on behaviour change. Finally, some research targets intervention programmes, which typically combine multiple behaviour change techniques and which are often social cognitive in nature. These strategies all focus on examining the effect of changes in social cognitions on behaviour change. We describe each in further detail in the following three sections.

Experimental Examination of Predictive Models

The focus on the causal influence of social cognitions on behaviour underlies the use of experimental methods; the intent being to establish a strong argument for causality. Experimental approaches do bring complementary evidence to the primarily correlational methods used in 'predictive research'. The assumption behind much of the 'predictive research' is that experimental manipulations of, and interventions to change, social cognitions observed to predict health-related behaviours will lead to changes in behaviour similar in magnitude and direction to the effect sizes observed in predictive research. Evidence that certain social cognitive processes co-occur with a certain behaviour, however, does not necessarily mean that induced changes in these social cognitive processes will result in comparable changes in behaviour. For example, it may be that both the social cognitive process and the health-related behaviour are caused by a third variable. Although this issue can be partly addressed in longitudinal prospective studies that aim to predict future occurrences of behaviour using social cognitions, such designs do not fully address this issue, particularly as it pertains to behaviour change. Therefore, experimental research that examines whether changes in social cognitions lead to the expected changes in behaviour can offer a unique contribution to the domain.

In addition, from a behaviour change perspective, the manipulations used in these experiments are often amenable to be adapted to intervention techniques or directly inform their design. For example, work that revealed that university student drinking norm misperception was associated with student problematic drinking led to research manipulating norm perceptions in order to correct misperceptions, which ultimately lead to intervention programmes focusing on correction of norms misperceptions (see Perkins, 2002, for a more complete discussion of evolution of alcohol misuse norm-based interventions).

There is a steadily increasing body of knowledge examining some of the key predictions derived from social cognitive models. For aspects of some theories, the body of available knowledge has now been the subject of meta-analyses. For example, Webb and Sheeran (2006) conducted a meta-analysis of 47 studies that used experimental methods to examine the relationship between intentions and behaviour, focusing primarily on health-related behaviour. They reported that a medium to large change in intentions ($d = 0.66$) led to a small to medium change in behaviour ($d = 0.36$). Their results support the notion that induced intention changes did impact behaviour; albeit less than what would have been expected based on predictive research.

In another meta-analysis of 204 studies, Sheeran and colleagues (2016) examined the effect of experimental changes in self-efficacy, norms, and attitudes on intended or actual health-related behaviour. They reported that these factors have medium-sized effects on intentions ($d = 0.51$, 0.49, and 0.48, respectively). They also reported that changes in norms and attitudes had a small effect on behaviour ($d = 0.36$ and 0.38, respectively), while self-efficacy had a medium effect ($d = 0.47$). Finally, they also note that, overall, the effect sizes were larger for manipulations that aimed at increasing a target behaviour instead of decreasing it. Importantly for comparisons with past meta-analyses focusing on correlational studies, they reported that effect sizes from correlational studies were generally larger than those from experimental studies.

The different results between predictive correlational and experimental research suggest that the presumption that the observations from correlational work will be essentially the same as those from experimental work is likely unfounded. Overall, it appears that effect sizes may be smaller with induced social cognitive changes. This highlights the need for care when applying the results of primarily correlational work in the context of health behaviour change, such as when attempting to estimate the possible effects of social cognitive interventions to induce change.

Social Cognitive Models of Behaviour Change

From its inception, social psychology has been concerned with addressing social issues. Therefore, it is not surprising that some social cognitive models specifically focus on health change and prevention. The most common application of social psychology to health has involved attempts to change health-related attitudes. Early work by Irving Janis, Howard Leventhal, and other scholars often explored the use of fear appeals to motivate people to change such life-threatening habits as cigarette smoking (see Leventhal, 1970). For example, Janis and Feshbach (1953) examined the impact of fear appeals of various strengths on conformity to dental hygiene recommendations. The rationale for the study was that if you can alert people to health threats and raise their concern, you can motivate them to change their behaviour. Counter-intuitively, their work demonstrated that minimal fear appeals produced greater conformity than stronger fear appeals.

Protection Motivation Theory (Rogers, 1975) and its later revisions (e.g., Maddux and Rogers, 1983; Rogers, 1983) are social cognitive theories that focus on explaining the impact of such fear-appeals on attitudes and behaviour. Its impetus was to understand how induced changes in social cognition can lead to changes in behaviour – as opposed to generally explain how social cognitions influence behaviour. The theory is typically understood to propose that two categories of social cognitive processes are the primary determinant of protection motivation: threat appraisal (e.g., fear; perceived vulnerability to a health threat) and coping appraisal (e.g., perceived response efficacy; self-efficacy). Threat appraisal is proposed to increase maladaptive coping (e.g., denial; fatalism) and to motivate protective behaviours (e.g., getting screened for cancer). Coping appraisal is proposed to decrease maladaptive coping and to increase protection motivation. Protection motivation is typically operationalized in terms of behavioural intentions. Results of meta-analyses suggest that threat appraisals have effects generally characterized as small to medium on intentions ($.10 < r$'s $< .20$) while coping appraisals have effects generally characterized as medium ($-.34 < r's < .33$; Milne et al., 2000). Their results, along with others, suggest that coping appraisals generally have larger effects than threat (see also Floyd et al., 2000). With regards to subsequent behaviour, the results of Milne et al. suggest effects best characterized as very small for threat appraisals ($-.04 < r's < .12$) and small to medium for coping appraisals ($-.25 < r's < .22$).

The usefulness of fear appeals in terms of promoting health changes remains controversial. Efforts to instil fear or feelings of threat can sometimes backfire, making people less, rather than more, receptive to health-related communications (see Gerrard et al., 1996). There are, however, some notable successful applications of fear-arousing approaches to motivating healthy behaviour change. For example, Fong et al. (2009) offer a compelling review of numerous studies from multiple countries that show decreased smoking rates after the introduction of graphic pictorial anti-smoking images on cigarette packs.

A meta-analysis by Witte and Allen (2000) helped further clarify the use of fear-appeals in health promotion campaigns by revealing that they tend to produce greatest behaviour change when they are used in combination with high-efficacy messages. That is, fear appeals work best when the message also promotes the individual's sense of self-efficacy to change the behaviour and their sense that the behaviour change can help them to avoid the fear-provoking outcome.

Other models of social cognitive behaviour change have also been proposed. Among these, there has been a recent emergence of research and intervention programmes to promote changes through the use of social norms (see Miller and Prentice, 2016). In the context of health, the most frequent use of this approach has been to curtail problematic alcohol consumption, primarily in college students. Three main forms of norm-based interventions have been used: personalized normative feedback interventions, group-based approaches, and social norm marketing approaches.

First, in personalized normative feedback interventions, individuals are provided with feedback about their own behaviour and the behaviour of a relevant reference group. This approach typically highlights discrepancies between the person's actions and those of the group in a way that encourages a desired outcome (see Lewis and Neighbors, 2007, for an example). Second, group-based approaches have used small group discussions led by facilitators to provide opportunities for participants to compare their perspectives and to motivate them to engage in behaviour change. This approach can be quite effective due to the fact that participants often believe that others have endorsed a new behaviour (see Schroeder and Prentice, 1998, for an example). Third, Social Norm Marketing Approaches (SNMAs) involve the use of mass media communication to disseminate a factual message about the incidence of some desirable behaviour to a target audience (see DeJong et al., 2006, for examples).

This distinction between individualized (e.g., interaction with expert, computer generated feedback), small group with possibility of communication among members, and mass social marketing approaches as modes of delivery is one that can be applied to most behaviour change techniques derived from social cognitive research. Of these, social marketing approaches offer unique opportunities to address health issues by reaching a large target audience in a cost-effective way (see Lee and Kotler, 2011).

In terms of the types of behavioural change techniques used, providing information (e.g., behaviour outcomes; risk awareness) is among the most common one in intervention research drawing on social cognitive approaches. This technique does align well with the central defining feature of social cognitive approaches, which is that cognition is a primary determinant of behaviour. Other techniques commonly observed in the literature include skill focused techniques (e.g., skill building) and goal-setting. Abraham and Michie (2008) conducted a systematic review and coding of published interventions and manuals and proposed a taxonomy of 26 techniques of health behaviour change – the majority of which are social cognitive in nature. Michie et al. (2011) offered a revised taxonomy of 40 techniques. These taxonomies offer unique opportunities for the field to identify which combination of techniques maximizes effectiveness and minimizes risk. We strongly recommend that applied research considers them in their work.

Intervention Programmes

Intervention programmes can be broadly defined as a collection of activities typically drawing on a combination of intervention techniques to reach predefined objectives. In the context of health, programmes typically include activities aimed at health promotion or the prevention of unhealthy behaviours to impact the overall health of a group of individuals. Typically, researchers are involved in what could be best described as pilot interventions, trial interventions, or programme efficacy studies (cf., Bégin et al., 2009). These are typically time-limited activities and are smaller scale compared to actual programmes, which are typically managed by public and/or non-profit organizations.

Applied social psychologists tend to use one of three approaches to examine intervention programmes. In the first, they focus on the development of a specific intervention programme that then they implement (*researcher-driven programmes*). For example, the Brief Alcohol Screening and Intervention for College Study (BASICS) is based primarily on SCT and Social Norm Theory and uses these theoretical bases to address problematic alcohol consumption on campuses (Dimeff et al., 1999). Fachini et al. (2012) report a meta-analysis of randomized control studies of this standardized, manualized intervention. Their results showed a reduction in alcohol consumption (−1.50 drinks per week, 95% CI: −3.24 to −0.29) and alcohol-related problems (mean difference: −0.87, 95% CI: −1.58 to −0.20) at 12 months follow up after the BASICS programme.

The second approach involves examining intervention programmes being implemented by stakeholders (i.e., individuals who have a vested interest in the possible programme) (*stakeholder-driven programmes*). Typically, this type of work is done when stakeholders want to pilot test intervention programmes to identify possible issues with implementation and/or to evaluate effectiveness before implementation on a wider scale (e.g., expanding the target audience, running the programme on a permanent basis). Finally, in some cases, applied social psychologists will engage in collaborations with stakeholders to design, implement, and evaluate either a complete intervention programme or some of its components (*collaborative programmes*).

Although many interventions are evaluated in part, or over a brief period of time, there are some cases in which applied social psychologists have been able to focus their work on ongoing full-scale intervention programmes. Among these, the work of Geoffrey Fong as part of the International Tobacco Control Policy Evaluation Project is one of the most noteworthy. The collaborative project focuses on how intervention techniques derived from tobacco control policies implemented by different governments influence social cognitions and the resulting behaviour change. The work also includes indicators of the public health and economic impacts (see Fong et al., 2006). This collaborative project is remarkable for many reasons. Of particular importance to the present topic is the focus on the causal chain that impacts intervention programmes: starting with policy, which promotes intervention techniques, which impact social cognitions, which then impact behaviours (see Fong et al., 2006). This project suggests that policy-level changes can indeed impact social cognitions and behaviour. It provides an excellent example for applied social psychologists to follow.

CHALLENGES AND FUTURE DIRECTIONS

The main focus of social cognitive theories when applied in a health context can be defined as to seek out the most parsimonious set of processes that will account for the most meaningful amount of statistical variance in the physical, psychological, and/or social health of large groups of people. The typical ultimate goal is to use the knowledge generated through this theory-informed research to design interventions aimed at changing behaviour to improve the overall physical, psychological, and/or social health of large groups of individuals.

A few of the relevant social cognitive processes are featured in several theories and have therefore received more focus in the applied research literature. Among these processes, the notions of behavioural intentions and self-efficacy are two that clearly stem from social cognitive applied research in the area of health (cf., Conner and Norman, 2005).

The notion of behavioural intentions as a proximal determinant of health behaviour is common to the TPB and the II approaches, as well as more recent applications of the HBM and SCT. As we have reviewed herein, the evidence seems clear: Setting intentions to engage in a course of health-related actions increases the likelihood that these actions will be carried out. The effect sizes that have been observed tend to be typically characterized as small to medium, according to prevailing rules of thumb (cf., Cohen, 1992). Interestingly, the impact of intention setting on behaviour is enhanced when combined with an implementation plan. As such, among social cognitive approaches, II offers one of the most resource effective modes of intervention to induce behaviour change, when appropriate to utilize given the context.

The concept of self-efficacy is central to SCT, it is part of recent work on the HBM, it is also part of the TPB, in terms of the notion of perceived behavioural control, and it is part of the rationale for IIs. As we have reviewed herein, the evidence also seems clear: An increased sense of self-efficacy is associated with increases in the likelihood that people will engage in healthy behaviours. As with intentions, the effect sizes tend to be typically characterized as small to medium according to prevailing rules of thumb (cf., Cohen, 1992).

Social cognitive approaches have shown promise in contributing to health-related behaviour change among groups of individuals. Indeed, this area of research and practice has tremendous potential to significantly impact societies. Projects like the International Tobacco Collaboration, which document the impact of policies on social cognitions, behaviour, and health (see Fong et al., 2006) offer astonishing examples of this potential.

There are, however, multiple challenges ahead. Although some clear patterns are emerging out of the research into social cognitive models applied to health, there remains much work to be done in consolidating the knowledge about current models. The research on behaviour change and intervention programmes remains limited, and research that allows the inference of causality is particularly lacking. Such work is fundamental to bridging our understanding of the social cognitive determinants of health with interventions that address health issues. Finally, the research thus far has generally focused on social cognitive models that assume individuals act as rational beings who are primarily focused on being 'healthy' as defined by current prevailing consensus in medicine. Theoretical alternatives to these assumptions should be proposed and investigated.

Consolidating Knowledge of Current Models

The focus of current approaches is to build cumulative knowledge to understand some of the causes of health-related behaviours. This approach lends itself to the use of meta-analytical techniques, which aligns with current statistical recommendations (see Cumming, 2014; Ioannidis, 2005). Indeed, there are multiple important meta-analyses that help synthesize the knowledge derived from social cognitive research (e.g., Armitage and Conner, 2001; Sheeran et al., 2014; Sheeran, et al., 2016; Webb and Sheeran, 2006). These meta-analyses tend to rely on the 'small', 'medium', and 'large' effect size categories that Cohen hesitatingly introduced in 1988. Although they facilitate interpretation of results, as evidenced by our use of these categories in this chapter, such a 't-shirt size' approach to interpreting effect sizes has disadvantages, such as implying that factors with smaller effect sizes are trivial in understanding health behaviour (cf., Marks, 1996).

As this domain of research moves forward, a more nuanced interpretation of effect sizes may be beneficial, as sometimes even small effect sizes can be meaningful (see Cohen, 1988; Thompson, 2006). It should be recognized at the outset that, given that health behaviours are the result of biological, psychological, and social factors, as well as their interactions, the notion that any one approach could account for the majority variance in a health behaviour is likely not a realistic expectation. Thus, while constantly searching for more predictive value, we should be modest in our expectations of how much variance a factor or theory can account for.

It may also be useful to distinguish the type of outcome being examined. Three broad types of outcomes can often be observed in this area: *social cognitive outcomes*, *behavioural outcomes*, and *impacts on health. Cognitive outcomes* are typically the cognitions assumed to underlie the motivation for a behaviour, such as attitudes and intentions. *Behavioural outcomes* are typically the individual-level proximal actions that affect health. The *impact on health* is typically defined in terms of morbidity and/or mortality, and is assumed to be affected by the re-occurrence of health behaviours over time. Given that the ultimate goal is to impact the overall health of groups of individuals, understanding health impact should be viewed as of greater value than understanding behaviour, and understanding behaviour should be viewed as of greater value than understanding cognition.

Thus, a small percentage of variance explained in health impact may be more meaningful than a small percentage of variance explained in cognition.

Another issue in terms of consolidating our understanding of current prevailing models is that the research examining these models has tended to focus on some aspects of theories, and not others. Indeed, few of the studies examining social cognitive models rigorously apply the theories they draw from (see Painter et al., 2008). The trend in the literature seems to be to study the components that lend themselves to self-report measures and generally to omit those that require more involved research designs. For example, in SCT, expected outcomes and self-efficacy have received much more empirical research attention compared to reciprocal determinism and collective efficacy. As such, researchers may make greater contributions to the field by a careful and complete examination of the current prevailing models than by suggesting new models. To fully examine the current models in terms of their ability to predict health-related behaviours, researchers may need to learn different methodological approaches, use multi-method approaches, and engage in interdisciplinary collaborations.

From Predicting to Intervention

One of the most important challenges in this area of work, if not the most important challenge, will be to increase the focus on interventions. Although there seems to be wide interest in applying social cognitive models of health to behaviour change interventions, there is still limited research that informs these models. For example, of the 18,000 records examined by Sheeran and colleagues (2016), only 204 tested the effects of changes of attitude, norms, and/or efficacy on intentions or behaviour. A focus on interventions will further consolidate the knowledge derived from current prevailing social cognitive models and contribute to the fulfillment of the goal of addressing health issues that affect large groups of individuals.

There are many important challenges to conducting intervention research. These studies are typically quite demanding. The design, conduct, and reporting of intervention studies often require more time, effort, and resources than other types of research, particularly if they involve a collaboration between researchers and non-academic stakeholders. Some challenges are particularly notable for social cognitive intervention studies conducted in the context of health.

One such specific challenge, which is rarely discussed, involves the possible risks to participants of intervention studies and the increased demands these risks place on researchers. The prevailing logic behind pursuing intervention programmes often seems to be that doing anything is better than doing nothing. The assumption is that trying out an intervention comes at no additional risk. Unfortunately, this is not always the case. There have been documented adverse effects of intervention programmes, which are often referred to as 'boomerang effects'. For example, Wechsler et al. (2003) observed that some social norm marketing intervention campaigns aimed at reducing alcohol consumption among college students ended up increasing alcohol consumption. In another example, Mann et al. (1997) used group discussion to reduce the prevalence of eating disorders among female students. Unfortunately, the programme led participants to perceive that eating disorders were more common than they did prior to the intervention.

The consideration of possible adverse effects is crucial to intervention research, particularly when the interventions focus on health outcomes. Researchers must design intervention studies that minimize, monitor, and contain potential adverse effects. A notable example of such a containment strategy comes from the sustainability literature. Schultz et al. (2007) conducted a field study examining a norm-based intervention to reduce energy consumption. Anticipating that a normative message might have a boomerang effect on people who were already low energy consumers, the researchers included an additional norm-based feedback to prevent such a result (see Truelove, Schultz and Gillis, Chapter 24).

Another specific challenge arises from the assessment of intervening variables. Examining expected intervening variables is crucial to the contribution of social cognitive intervention research. For example, if researchers test an intervention designed to change perceived norms about drinking on a college campus in order to decrease alcohol consumption, they cannot only measure changes in alcohol consumption. They must also determine if the intervention influenced perceived norms if they want to establish a causal chain (see Spencer et al., 2005). Collection of this information often requires the participation of the stakeholders or their staff, who may not be aware of the importance of this information or have resources and time to gather it, and thus may not systematically collect it.

Finally, the potential contributions of intervention research to our knowledge depend largely on the willingness and capacity of researchers to share the details and results of their interventions with transparency; the dissemination of findings is crucial, whether results support the effectiveness of the attempted intervention or not. To this end, adhering to open science principles (Nosek et al., 2015), using standard measures of behaviour change whenever possible (e.g., Semaan et al., 2002), and adhering to the suggestions of Davidson et al. (2003) may prove invaluable. Specifically, Davidson et al. (2003) recommend that researchers report (a) the content or elements of the intervention, (b) the characteristics of those delivering the intervention, (c) the characteristics of the participants, (d) the setting, (e) the mode of delivery, (f) the intensity, (g) the duration, and (h) adherence to delivery protocols. Adhering to these suggestions is an important challenge for researchers, since many scholarly outlets are not suitable to follow the above suggestions. This failure of scholarly outlets often leads researchers and practitioners, who may not have access to these scholarly outlets, to publish their work in the 'grey literature' (i.e., material and research produced and distributed outside the traditional commercial/academic channels).

In considering knowledge mobilization, researchers should be mindful that stakeholders may want to limit sharing details and data. As such, researchers should ensure to negotiate a knowledge mobilization plan with their stakeholder partners at the outset of their collaboration. As part of this process, researchers should strive for openness and transparency to maximize the potential benefits of the intervention study to our knowledge base. Researchers and practitioners could also contribute to the field by using open access platforms (e.g., the Open Science Framework) to share their grey literature publications.

The extra demands of intervention research have important repercussions for researchers, such as a lower scholarly publication rate. Researchers must rise up to these challenges. Intervention research is central to our ability to clearly demonstrate the value of our scholarship to society. Without such research, advocating for our fields will become challenging, if not impossible (see Cialdini, 2009). Beyond the egoistical costs to our own fields, the failure to engage in the increasing demand for social cognitive interventions for health-related behaviours may leave stakeholders without any expert support. This lack of expertise may create a situation where waves of poorly planned interventions are conducted, resulting in either indications of poor intervention effectiveness or in a failure to assess any effectiveness at all. These failed interventions will have real costs to real people. Moreover, they may create a body of findings suggesting social cognitive approaches to health are of little value.

For researchers to successfully rise up to the challenges of intervention research, they will need the support of their peers and their fields. Undoubtedly, a shift to increased intervention work will require many researchers, stakeholders, institutions, journal editors, journal publishers, grant reviewers, and multiple others to change their default way of thinking when it comes to research. Central to this shift will be a move from an overemphasis on discovery to a recognition of the fundamental role of integration and application in the development of knowledge (see Boyer, 1990).

This shift will also require a change in training for some applied social psychology graduate programmes in order to prepare their graduates to engage in intervention research. For example, graduate students should all be required to complete programme evaluation courses and to gain experience working with non-academic stakeholders through practicums or work placements. Through such steps, applied social psychology can increase its ability to affect positive change in the world.

Future Directions

Theory is central to the discipline of applied social psychology and to the development of effective interventions (e.g., Michie and Prestwich, 2010). Theories are essential to identifying the causes of behaviours and thus to understand behavioural change. For the most part, the social cognitive theories that have been applied in a health context assume that people are both rational thinkers, who systematically consider information, and motivated to be healthy, as defined by current prevailing medical models (cf., Conner and Norman, 2005).

This assumption is somewhat surprising. The field of social psychology is composed of research that documents numerous instances where normal individuals act in ways that otherwise they would not have, and which often appear irrational or abnormal (see Krueger and Funder, 2004). Social psychology typically explains people's otherwise seemingly irrational or abnormal actions using some type of biased social cognitive processes. This perspective on social cognition, and how it is used to understand human behaviour, seems at odds with the notion of social cognition as it is often applied in the context of health.

There are some notable exceptions in the literature that illustrate the potential value of drawing more broadly on social psychological research into social cognition. For example, the work of Stone and colleagues (1994) suggests that inducing hypocrisy in adolescents by making them aware of the difference between their stated condom use beliefs and their actual behaviour could increase their subsequent condom purchases. Given that failures to act in an intended way or in the best interest of one's health seem to be at the root of many of the health issues, researchers may find some insights by examining social cognition more broadly.

A central assumption to many social cognitive theories is that macro and meso level factors will impact individuals at the micro level. For example, this multi-level assumption is well illustrated by the notion of reciprocal determinism that is found in Bandura's Social Cognitive Theory. Unfortunately, the multi-level hypotheses of these theories have not been the subject of much research in the context of health. This is surprising, given that the role of the social environment in health behaviour and health promotion interventions is well-established (see Stokols, 1992; Taylor and Sirois, 2014). Examinations of the interaction between sociostructural factors and individual-level social cognitions may help address some of the theoretical questions related to prevailing social cognitive health models. For example, it may help to explain the factors that influence the naturally occurring formation of attitudes and intentions. A multi-level approach may also help to understand the role of sociodemographic factors that affect health, such as socioeconomic status, gender, and race-ethnicity. This approach may also broaden the scope of social cognitive research, which typically focuses on self and other perceptions, by focusing on perceptions of systems, such as the health care system. However, investigating these avenues will most likely require the use of different research methodologies than are commonly used, including the use of qualitative research and interdisciplinary collaborations. It may also require that researchers and practitioners draw on social psychology theories that are not traditionally used in the context of health.

Social Identity Approaches, a term used to encompass Social Identity Theory (Tajfel and Turner, 1979) and Self-Categorization Theory (Turner et al., 1987), may be particularly well-suited to connect social cognitions and social structures in the context of health. In fact, Social Identity Theory emerged, in part, as a response to a concern that social psychology was becoming overly focused on micro level phenomena (see Taylor and Brown, 1979). This theory aims to bridge the gap between micro and macro levels, postulating that people act not only as individuals but also as group members with shared perceptions, goals, and identity. The theory has been used in the context of health-related behaviours (see Haslam et al., 2009) and offers many interesting avenues. For example, it is well suited to examining the impact of large-scale social changes on health, as well as to understanding the origins of social movements in response to reforms that would decrease access to health care.

The concept of self-identity is also a central notion of much of social psychological research. Although also not a theory per se, there is an extensive body of social cognitive research focusing on the self and identity, which is typically defined in terms of knowledge about who we are and our ability to be an active agent affecting our environment. There have been some critiques which hold that the concept of the self is of little value in the context of predicting behaviour (e.g., Conner and Armitage, 1998), but the notion of the self has been placed at the centre of social cognitive approaches to health behaviour (see Conner and Norman, 2005). In particular, the concept of self-regulation has been proposed as integral to understanding the role of social cognition on health behaviours (e.g., Sirois, 2004; see Conner and Norman, 2005).

Increasingly, self and identity regulation are being recognized as having important implications for health behaviours, insomuch as the processes involved can shape the motivational significance of the beliefs that underlie people's decisions to manage their health (Shepperd et al., 2011). Future work that focuses on the role of self/identity-regulation strategies in health would expand our understanding of when factors such as social norms may help or hinder health behaviour change. For example, individuals may engage in unhealthy behaviours, such as drinking and smoking, because they are linked to a desired identity (Shepperd et al., 2011), in which case the norms associated with this identity will be more salient than those that suggest such behaviours are undesirable.

One of the key challenges for social cognitive approaches applied to health is the limited generalizability of the findings due to the nature of the participants used in most studies. For the most part, social cognitive models applied to health have been studied using WEIRD participants: those who are in Western, Educated, Industrialized, Rich and Democratic contexts (Henrich et al., 2010). It is now clear that these participants are unique in many ways, including social cognitive processes, and as such, do not provide a strong basis for generalizations (see Henrich et al., 2010). Unfortunately, most researchers examining social cognitive models of health behaviour implicitly, or explicitly, assume that their findings with WEIRD participants are universal. As with intervention research, engaging in research with non-WEIRD populations has greater costs for the researcher and limited institutionalized advantages (see Henrich et al., 2010). That said, at the very least, researchers and practitioners should recognize any limitations in their work related to a restricted cultural context. As with intervention research, investment in conducting cultural, cross-cultural, and international research is central to the ability of this domain to address health issues on a large scale.

CONCLUSION

Overall, social cognitive approaches applied to health issues affecting groups of individuals are of tremendous value because of the prevailing desire to understand causes of behaviour and its changes. For example, this work allows us to understand which particular elements impact the effectiveness of an intervention, which in turn, allows us to answer a very common question asked by stakeholders: 'What do I need to include in my intervention for it to work?' The value of this approach has been demonstrated through successful intervention programmes, such as the Tobacco Control Policy Evaluation Project (Fong et al., 2006).

The approach is not without critiques. For example, the focus on parsimonious causes that helps inform effective intervention programmes often comes at the costs of reductionism. Although the approach has shown its value, there remain multiple challenges. For instance, there is a pressing need for more research focusing on behaviour change and intervention programmes. There are also many other possible avenues for social cognitive approaches to contribute to health issues. The connection between macro, meso and micro levels of explanation that underlies many social cognition approaches seems under-represented in empirical social cognitive health research.

In the end, it is worth the effort required to rise up to these challenges, in order to better understand and address the collective causes of health issues shared among large groups of people.

REFERENCES

Aarts, H., & Dijksterhuis, A. (2003). The silence of the library: Environment, situational norm, and social behaviour. *Journal of Personality and Social Psychology*, *84*, 18–28.

Abraham, C., & Michie, S. (2008). A taxonomy of behavior change techniques used in interventions. *Health Psychology*, *27*, 379–387.

Abraham, C., & Sheeran, P. (2005). The Health Belief Model. In M. Conner and P. Norman (Eds.) *Predicting health behaviour: Research and practice with social cognition models* (pp. 28–80). Berkshire: Open University Press.

Adriaanse, M. A., Vinkers, C. D. W., De Ridder, D. T. D., Hox, J. J., & De Wit, J. B. F. (2011). Do implementation intentions help to eat a healthy diet? A systematic review and meta-analysis of the empirical evidence. *Appetite*, *56*, 183–193.

Ajzen, I. (1991). The theory of planned behaviour. *Organizational Behaviour and Human Decision Processes*, *50*, 179–211.

Armitage, C. J., & Conner, M. (2000). Social cognition models and health behaviour: A structured review. *Psychology and Health*, *15*, 173–189.

Armitage, C. J., & Conner, M. (2001). Efficacy of the Theory of Planned Behaviour: a meta-analytic review. *British Journal of Social Psychology*, *40*, 471–499.

Balbach, E. D., Smith, E. A., & Malone, R. E. (2006). How the health belief model helps the tobacco industry: individuals, choice, and 'information'. *Tobacco Control*, *15*(Suppl. 4), 37–43.

Banas, J. A., & Rains, S. A. (2010). A meta-analysis of research on inoculation theory. *Communication Monographs*, *77*, 281–311.

Bandura, A. (1977). Self-efficacy: Toward a unifying theory of behavioural change. *Psychological Review*, *84*, 191–215.

Bandura, A. (1986). *Social foundations of thought and action: A social sognitive theory.* Englewood Cliffs, NJ: Prentice Hall.

Bandura, A. (1998). Health promotion from the perspective of social cognitive theory. *Psychology and Health*, *13*, 623–649.

Bandura, A. (2004). Health promotion by social cognitive means. *Health Education & Behaviour*, *31*, 143–164.

Becker, M.H. (1974) The health belief model and sick role behavior. *Health Education Monographs, 2*, 409–419.

Bégin, M., Eggerston, L., & Macdonald, N. (2009). A country of perpetual pilot projects. *Canadian Medical Association Journal, 180*, 1185.

Bélanger-Gravel, A., Godin, G., & Amireault, S. (2013). A meta-analytic review of the effect of implementation intentions on physical activity. *Health Psychology, 7*, 23–54.

Bish, A., Sutton, S., & Golombok, S. (2000). Predicting uptake of a routine cervical smear test: A comparison of the health belief model and the theory of planned behaviour. *Psychology and Health, 15*, 35–50.

Boyer, E. (1990). *Scholarship reconsidered: Priorities of the professoriate*. Princeton, NJ: Carnegie Foundation for the Advancement of Teaching.

Brandstatter, V., Lengfelder, A., & Gollwitzer, P. M. (2001). Implementation intentions and efficient action initiation. *Journal of Personality and Social Psychology, 81*, 946–960.

Carpenter, C. J. (2010). A meta-analysis of the effectiveness of Health Belief Model variables in predicting behaviour. *Health Communication, 25*, 661–669.

Chatzisarantis, N. L. D., Hagger, M. S., Wang, C. K. J., & Thøgersen-Ntoumani, C. (2009). The effects of social identity and perceived autonomy support on health behaviour within the Theory of Planned Behaviour. *Current Psychology, 28*, 55–68.

Cialdini, R. B. (2005). Basic social influence is underestimated. *Psychological Inquiry, 16*, 158–161.

Cialdini, R. B. (2009). We have to break up. *Perspectives on Psychological Science, 4*, 5–6.

Cialdini, R. B., Reno, R. R., & Kallgren, C. A. (1990). A focus theory of normative conduct: Recycling the concept of norms to reduce littering in public places. *Journal of Personality and Social Psychology, 58*, 1015–1026.

Cohen, J. (1988). *Statistical power analysis for the behavioral sciences.* Routledge

Cohen, J. (1992). A power primer. *Psychological Bulletin, 112*, 155–159.

Conner, M., & Armitage, C. J. (1998). Extending the theory of planned behaviour: A review and avenues for further research. *Journal of Applied Social Psychology, 28*, 1429–1464.

Conner, M., & Norman, P. (1994). Comparing the health belief model and the theory of planned behaviour in health screening. In D. R. Rutter and L. Quine (Eds.) *Social psychology and health: European perspectives* (pp. 1–24). Aldershot: Avebury.

Conner, M., & Norman, P. (2005). *Predicting health behaviour* (2nd edn.). McGraw-Hill, UK: Open University Press.

Cumming, G. (2014). The new statistics: Why and how. *Psychological Science, 25*, 7–29.

Davidson, K. W., Goldstein, M., Kaplan, R. M., Kaufmann, P. G., Knat- terund, G. L., Orleans, C. T., Spring, B., Trudeau, K. J., & Whitlock, E. P. (2003). Evidence-based behavioural medicine: What is it and how do we achieve it? *Annals of Behavioural Medicine, 26*, 161–171.

Davis, R., Campbell, R., Hildon, Z., Hobbs, L., & Michie, S. (2015). Theories of behaviour and behaviour change across the social and behavioural sciences: A scoping review. *Health Psychology Review, 9*, 323–344.

DeBusk, R. F., Miller, N. H., Superko, H. R., Dennis, C. A., Thomas, R. J., Lew, H. T., Berger, W. E. III, Heller, R. S., Rompf, J., Gee, D., Kraemer, H. C., Bandura, A., Ghandour, G., Clark, M., Shah, R. V., Fisher, L., & Taylor, C. B. (1994). A case-management system for coronary risk factor modification after acute myocardial infarction. *Annals of Internal Medicine, 120*, 721–729.

DeJong W., Kessel Schneider, S., Comberg Towvim, L., Murphy, M. J., Doerr, E. E., Simonsen, N. R., Mason, K. E., & Scribner, R. A. (2006). A multisite randomized trial of social norms marketing campaigns to reduce college student drinking. *Journal of Studies on Alcohol, 67*, 868–879.

Deutsch, M., & Gerard, H. (1955). A study of normative and informational social influences upon individual judgment. *Journal of Abnormal and Social Psychology, 51*, 629–636.

Dimeff, L. A., Baer, J. S., Kivlahan, D. R., & Marlatt, G. A. (1999). *Brief alcohol screening and intervention for college students: A harm reduction approach*. New York: Guilford Press.

Evans, R. I., Rozelle, R. M., Mittelmark, M. B., Hansen, W. B., Bane, A. L., & Havis, J.

(1978). Deterring the onset of smoking in children: Knowledge of immediate physiological effects and coping with peer pressure, media pressure, and parent modeling. *Journal of Applied Social Psychology*, *8*, 126–135.

Fachini, A., Aliane, P. P., Martinez, E. Z., & Furtado, E. F. (2012). Efficacy of brief alcohol screening intervention for college students (BASICS): A meta-analysis of randomized controlled trials. *Substance Abuse Treatment, Prevention, and Policy*, *7*, 40.

Falomir-Pichastor, J. M., Toscani, L., & Despointes, S. H. (2009). Determinants of flu vaccination among nurses: The effects of group identification and professional responsibility. *Applied Psychology*, *58*, 42–58.

Feather, N. T. (Ed.) (1982). *Expectations and actions: Expectancy-value models in psychology*. Hillsdale, NJ: Erlbaum.

Festinger, L. (1950). Informal social communication. *Psychological Review*, *57*, 271–282.

Festinger, L. (1957). *A theory of cognitive dissonance*. Evanston, IL: Row, Peterson.

Festinger, L., & Carlsmith, J. M. (1959). Cognitive consequences of forced compliance. *The Journal of Abnormal and Social Psychology*, *58*, 203–210.

Fishbein, M., & Ajzen, I. (1975). *Belief, attitude, intention, and behaviour*. New York: Wiley.

Floyd, D. L., Prentice-Dunn, S., & Rogers, R. W. (2000). A meta-analysis of research on Protection Motivation Theory. *Journal of Applied Social Psychology*, *30*, 407–429.

Fong, G. T., Cummings, K. M., Borland, R., Hastings, G., Hyland, A., Giovino, G. A., Hammond, D., & Thompson, M. E. (2006). The conceptual framework of the International Tobacco Control (ITC) Policy Evaluation Project. *Tobacco Control*, *15*(Suppl. III), iii3–iii11.

Fong, G. T., Hammond, D., & Hitchman, S. C. (2009). The impact of pictures on the effectiveness of tobacco warnings. *Bulletin of the World Health Organization*, *87*, 640–643.

Freijy, T., & Kothe, E. J. (2013). Dissonance-based interventions for health behaviour change: A systematic review. *British Journal of Health Psychology*, *18*, 310–337.

Gerrard, M., Gibbons, F. X., Benthin, A. C., & Hessling, R. M. (1996). A longitudinal study of the reciprocal nature of risk behaviours and cognitions in adolescents: What you do shapes what you think and vice versa. *Health Psychology*, *15*, 344–354.

Giguère, B., Lalonde, R. N., & Taylor, D. M. (2014). Drinking too much and feeling bad about it? How identification moderates experiences of guilt and shame following the transgression of group norms. *Personality and Social Psychology Bulletin*, *40*, 617–632.

Giguère, B., Sirois, F. M., & Vaswani, M. (2016). Delaying things and feeling bad about it? A norm based approach to understanding procrastination. In T. A. Pychyl & F. M. Sirois (Eds.), *Perspectives on procrastination, health, and well-being*. Toronto, Canada: Elsevier.

Gollwitzer, P. M. (1999). Implementation intentions: Strong effects of simple plans. *The American Psychologist*, *54*, 493–503.

Gollwitzer, P. M., & Sheeran, P. (2006). Implementation Intentions and goal achievement: A meta-analysis of effects and processes. *Advances in Experimental Social Psychology*, *38*, 69–119.

Gwaltney, C. J., Metrik, J., Kahler, C. W., & Shiffman, S. (2009). Self-efficacy and smoking cessation: A meta-analysis. *Psychology of Addictive Behaviours*, *23*, 56–66.

Harrison, J. A., Mullen, P. D., & Green, L. W. (1992). A meta-analysis of studies of the health belief model with adults. *Health Education Research*, *7*, 107–116.

Haslam, S. A., Jetten, J., Postmes, T., & Haslam, C. (2009). Social identity, health and well-being: An emerging agenda for applied psychology. *Applied Psychology*, *58*(1), 1–23.

Henrich, J., Heine, S. J., & Norenzayan, A. (2010). The weirdest people in the world? *Behavioural and Brain Sciences*, *33*(2–3), 61–83.

Hull, J. G., & Bond, C. F. (1986). Social and behavioural consequences of alcohol consumption and expectancy: A meta-analysis. *Psychological Bulletin*, *99*(3), 347–360.

Ioannidis, J. P. A. (2005). Why most published research findings are false. *PLOS Medicine*, *2*(8), e124–e126.

Janis, I. L., & Feshbach, S. (1953). Effects of fear-arousing communications. *Journal of*

Abnormal and Social Psychology, *48*(1), 78–92.

Janz, N. K., & Becker, M. H. (1984). The Health Belief Model: A decade later. *Health Education Quarterly*, *11*(1), 1–47.

Kam, J. A., Matsunaga, M., Hecht, M. L., & Ndiaye, K. (2008). Extending the Theory of Planned Behaviour to predict alcohol, tobacco, and marijuana use among youth of Mexican heritage. *Prevention Science*, *10*, 41–53.

Kashima, Y., Wilson, S., Lusher, D., Pearson, L. J., & Pearson, C. (2013). The acquisition of perceived descriptive norms as social category learning in social networks. *Social Networks*, 1–9.

Krueger, J. I., & Funder, D. C. (2004). Towards a balanced social psychology: Causes, consequences, and cures for the problem-seeking approach to social behaviour and cognition. *Behavioural and Brain Sciences*, *27*, 313–327.

Lee, N., & Kotler, P. (2011). *Social marketing: Influencing behaviours for good*. Los Angeles, CA: SAGE Publications.

Leventhal, H. (1970). Findings and theory in the study of fear communications. *Advances in experimental social psychology*, *5*, 119–186.

Lewin, K. (1943). Psychology and the process of group living. *The Journal of Social Psychology*, *17*, 113–131.

Lewin, K., Dembo, T., Festinger, L., & Sears, P. S. (1944). Level of aspiration. In J. M. Hunt (Ed.), *Personality and the behaviour disorders* (pp. 333–378). New York: Roland.

Lewis, M. A., & Neighbors, C. (2007). Optimizing personalized normative feedback: The use of gender-specific referents. *Journal of Studies on Alcohol and Drugs*, *68*, 228–237.

Louis, W. R., Davies, S., Smith, J. R., & Terry, D. J. (2007). Pizza and pop and the student identity: The role of referent group norms in healthy and unhealthy eating. *Journal of Social Psychology*, *147*, 57–74.

Luszczynska, A., & Schwarzer, R. (2005). Social Cognitive Theory. In M. Conner & P. Norman (Eds.), *Predicting health behaviour* (2nd edn., pp. 127–169). McGraw-Hill, UK: Open University Press.

Maddux, J. E., & Rogers, R. W. (1983). Protection motivation and self-efficacy: A revised theory of fear appeals and attitude change, *Journal of Experimental Social Psychology*, *19*, 469–479.

Mann, T., Nolen-Hoeksema, S., Huang, K., Burgard, D., Wright, A., & Hanson, K. (1997). Are two interventions worse than none? Joint primary and secondary prevention of eating disorders in college females. *Health Psychology*, *16*, 215–225.

Manning, M. (2009). The effects of subjective norms on behaviour in the theory of planned behaviour: A meta-analysis. *British Journal of Social Psychology*, *48*, 649–705.

Marks, D. F. (1996). Health psychology in context. *Journal of Health Psychology*, *1*, 7–21.

McEachan, R. R. C., Conner, M., Taylor, N. J., & Lawton, R. J. (2011). Prospective prediction of health-related behaviours with the Theory of Planned Behaviour: A meta-analysis. *Health Psychology Review*, *5*, 97–144.

Michie, S., & Prestwich, A. (2010). Are interventions theory-based? Development of a theory-coding scheme. *Health Psychology*, *29*, 1–8.

Michie, S., Ashford, S., Sniehotta, F. F., Dombrowski, S. U., Bishop, A., & French, D. P. (2011). A refined taxonomy of behaviour change techniques to help people change their physical activity and healthy eating behaviours: The CALO-RE taxonomy. *Psychology and Health*, *26*, 1479–1498.

Miller, D. T., & Prentice, D. A. (2016). Changing norms to change behaviour. *Annual Review of Psychology*, *67*, 339–361.

Milne, S. Sheeran, P., & Orbell, S. (2000). Prediction and intervention in health-related behavior: A meta-analytic review of Protection Motivation Theory. *Journal of Applied Social Psychology*, *30*, 106–143.

Moskowitz, G. (2005). *Social cognition*. New York, NY: Guilford Press.

Neighbors, C., O'Connor, R. M., Lewis, M. A., Chawla, N., Lee, C. M., & Fossos, N. (2008). The relative impact of injunctive norms on college student drinking: The role of reference group. *Psychology of Addictive Behaviours*, *22*, 576–581.

Noar, S. M. (2005). Health Behaviour Theory and cumulative knowledge regarding health behaviours: are we moving in the right direction? *Health Education Research*, *20*, 275–290.

Nolan, J. M., Schultz, P. W., Cialdini, R. B., Goldstein, N. J., & Griskevicius, V. (2008). Normative social influence is underdetected. *Personality and Social Psychology Bulletin*, *34*, 913–923.

Nosek, B. A., Alter, G., Banks, C., Borsboom, D., Bowman, S. D., Breckler, S. J., & Yarkoni, T. (2015). Promoting an open research culture. *Science*, *348*, 1422–1425.

Orbell, S., Hodgkins, S., & Sheeran, P. (1997). Implementation intentions and the theory of planned behaviour. *Personality and Social Psychology Bulletin*, *23*, 945–954.

Orbell, S., & Sheeran, P. (1998). 'Inclined abstainers': A problem for predicting health-related behaviour. *British Journal of Social Psychology*, *3*, 151–165.

Painter, J. E., Borba, C. P. C., Hynes, M., Mays, D., & Glanz, K. (2008). The use of theory in health behaviour research from 2000 to 2005: A systematic review. *Annals of Behavioural Medicine*, *35*, 358–362.

Papageorgis, D., & McGuire, W. J. (1961). The generality of immunity to persuasion produced by pre-exposure to weakened counterarguments. *Journal of Abnormal and Social Psychology*, *62*, 475–481.

Perkins, H. W., Haines, M., & Rice, R. (2005). Misperceiving the college drinking norm and related problems: A nationwide study of exposure to prevention information, perceived norms and student alcohol misuse. *Journal of Studies on Alcohol*, *66*, 470.

Postmes, T., Spears, R., Sakhel, K., & De Groot, D. (2001). Social influence in computer-mediated communication: The effects of anonymity on group behaviour. *Personality and Social Psychology Bulletin*, *27*, 1242–1254.

Prentice, D. A., & Miller, D. T. (1993). Pluralistic ignorance and alcohol use on campus: Some consequences of misperceiving the social norm. *Journal of Personality and Social Psychology*, *64*, 243–256.

Prochaska, J. O., & DiClemente, C. C. (1984). *The transtheoretical approach: Crossing traditional boundaries of therapy.* Homewood, IL: Dow Jones Irwin.

Quine, L., Rutter, D. R., & Arnold, L. (1998). Predicting and understanding safety helmet use among schoolboy cyclists: A comparison of the theory of planned behaviour and the health belief model. *Psychology & Health*, *13*, 251–269.

Reich, R. R., Below, M. C., & Goldman, M. S. (2010). Explicit and implicit measures of expectancy and related alcohol cognitions: A meta-analytic comparison. *Psychology of Addictive Behaviours*, *24*, 13–25.

Rivis, A., & Sheeran, P. (2003). Descriptive norms as an additional predictor in the theory of planned behaviour: A meta-analysis. *Current Psychology*, *22*, 218–233.

Rogers, R. W. (1975). A protection motivation theory of fear appeals and attitude change. *The Journal of Psychology*, *91*, 93–114.

Rogers, R. W. (1983). Cognitive and physiological processes in fear appeals and attitude change: a revised theory of protection motivation. In J. T. Cacioppo and R. E. Petty (Eds.) *Social psychophysiology: A source book* (pp. 153–176). New York, Guilford Press.

Rosenstock, I. M., Strecher, V. J., & Becker, M. H. (1988). Social learning theory and the health belief model. *Health Education Quarterly*, *15*, 175–183.

Rothman, A. J., & Salovey, P (1997). Shaping perceptions to motivate healthy behavior: The role of message framing. *Psychoogical Bulletin*, *121*, 3–19.

Rutter, D., & Quine, L. (Eds.) (2002). *Changing health behaviour: Intervention and research with social cognition models*. Buckingham: Open University Press.

Schofield, P. E., Pattison, P. E., Hill, D. J., & Borland, R. (2003). Youth culture and smoking: Integrating social group processes and individual cognitive processes in a model of health-related behaviours. *Journal of Health Psychology*, *8*, 291–306.

Schroeder, C., & Prentice, D. (1998). Exposing pluralistic ignorance to reduce alcohol use among college students. *Journal of Applied Social Psychology*, *28*, 2150–2180.

Schultz, P. W., Nolan, J. M., Cialdini, R. B., Goldstein, N. J., & Griskevicius, V. (2007). The constructive, destructive, and reconstructive power of social norms. *Psychological Science*, *18*, 429–434.

Semaan, S., Des Jarlais, D. C., Sogolow, E., Johnson, W. D., Hedges, L. V., Ramirez, G., Flores, S. A., Norman, L., Sweat, M. D., & Needle, R. (2002). A meta-analysis of the effect of HIV prevention interventions on the sex behaviours of drug users in the United States. *Journal of Acquired Immune Deficiency Syndrome*, *30*(Suppl. 1), S73–S93.

Sheeran, P. (2002). Intention–behaviour relations: A conceptual and empirical review. *European Review of Social Psychology*, *12*, 1–30.

Sheeran, P., & Orbell, S. (2000). Using implementation intentions to increase attendance for cervical cancer screening. *Health Psychology*, *19*, 283–289.

Sheeran, P., Harris, P. R., & Epton, T. (2014). Does heightening risk appraisals change people's intentions and behaviour? A meta-analysis of experimental studies. *Psychological Bulletin*, *140*, 511–543.

Sheeran, P., Maki, A., Montanaro, E., Avishai-Yitshak, A., Bryan, A., Klein, W. M. P., Miles, E., & Rothman, A. J. (2016). The impact of changing attitudes, norms, and self-efficacy on health-related intentions and behaviour: A meta-analysis. *Health Psychology*, *35*, 1178–1188.

Sheeran, P., Milne, S., Webb, T. L., & Gollwitzer, P. M. (2005). Implementation intentions. In M. Conner and P. Norman (Eds.), *Predicting health behavior: Research and practice with social cognition models* (2nd ed.). Milton Keynes, UK: Open University Press.

Shepperd, B. H., Hartwick, J., & Warshaw, P. R. (1988). The theory of reasoned action: A meta-analysis of past research with recommendations for modications and future research. *Journal of Consumer Research*, *15*, 325–343.

Shepperd, J. A., Rothman, A. J., & Klein, W. M. P. (2011). Using self- and identity-regulation to promote health: Promises and challenges. *Self and Identity*, *10*, 407–416.

Sirois, F. M. (2004). Procrastination and intentions to perform health behaviours: The role of self-efficacy and the consideration of future consequences. *Personality and Individual Differences*, *37*, 115–128.

Smith, J. R., & Louis, W. R. (2009). Group norms and the attitude–behaviour relationship. *Social & Personality Psychology Compass*, *3*, 19–35.

Sniehotta, F. F., Presseau, J., & Araújo-Soares, V. (2014). Time to retire the theory of planned behaviour. *Health Psychology Review*, *8*, 1–7.

Spencer, S. J., Zanna, M. P., & Fong, G. T. (2005). Establishing a causal chain: Why experiments are often more effective than mediational analyses in examining psychological processes. *Journal of Personality and Social Psychology*, *89*, 845–851.

Stice, E., Shaw, H., & Marti, C. N. (2007). A meta-analytic review of eating disorder prevention programs: Encouraging findings. *Annual Reviews in Clinical Psychology*, *3*, 207–231.

Stok, F. M., De Ridder, D. T. D., de Vet, E., & de Wit, J. B. F. (2012). Minority talks: The influence of descriptive social norms on fruit intake. *Psychology and Health*, *27*, 956–970.

Stokols, D. (1992). Establishing and maintaining healthy environments: Toward a social ecology of health promotion. *American Psychologist*, *47*, 6–22.

Stone, J., Aronson, E., Crain, A. L., Winslow, M. P., & Fried, C. B. (1994). Inducing hypocrisy as a means of encouraging young adults to use condoms. *Personality and Social Psychology Bulletin*, *20*, 116–128.

Tajfel, H., & Turner, J. C. (1979). An integrative theory of intergroup conflict. In W. G. Austin & S. Worchel (Eds.), *The social psychology of intergroup relations* (pp. 33–48). Monterey, CA: Brooks-Cole.

Taylor, D. M., & Brown, R. J. (1979). Towards a more social social psychology. *British Journal of Social and Clinical Psychology*, *18*, 173–179.

Taylor, S. E. (1982). Social cognition and health. *Personality and Social Psychology Bulletin*, *8*, 549–562.

Taylor S. E., & Sirois F. M. (2014). *Health psychology*. New York: McGraw-Hill.

Terry, D. J., & Hogg, M. A. (1996). Group norms and the attitude-behaviour relationship: A role for group identification. *Personality and Social Psychology Bulletin*, *22*, 776.

Thompson B. (2006). *Foundations of behavioural statistics: An insight-based approach*. New York: Guilford.

Turner J. C. (1991). *Social influence*. Milton Keynes, UK: Open University Press.

Turner, J. C., Hogg, M. A., Oakes, P. J., Reicher, S. D., & Wetherell, M. S. (1987).

Rediscovering the social group: A self-categorization theory. Oxford: Blackwell.

Verkooijen, K. T., De Vries, N. K., & Nielsen, G. A. (2007). Youth crowds and substance use: The impact of perceived group norm and multiple group identification. *Psychology of Addictive Behaviours*, *21*, 55–61.

Walker, D. D., Neighbors, C., Rodriguez, L. M., Stephens, R. S., & Roffman, R. A. (2011). Social norms and self-efficacy among heavy using adolescent marijuana smokers. *Psychology of Addictive Behaviours*, *25*, 727–732.

Webb, T. L., & Sheeran, P. (2006). Does changing behavioural intentions engender behaviour change? A meta-analysis of the experimental evidence. *Psychological Bulletin*, *132*, 249–268.

Wechsler, H., Nelson, T. E., Lee, J. E., Seibring, M., Lewis, C., & Keeling, R. P. (2003). Perception and reality: A national evaluation of social norms marketing interventions to reduce college students' heavy alcohol use. *Journal of Studies on Alcohol and Drugs*, *64*, 484–494.

Weinstein, W. D. (1993) Testing four competing theories of health-protective behaviour. *Health Psychology*, *12*, 324–333.

Williams, D. M. (2010). Outcome expectancy and self-efficacy: Theoretical implications of an unresolved contradiction. *Personality and Social Psychology Review*, *14*, 417–425.

Witte, K., & Allen, M. (2000). A meta-analysis of fear appeals: implications for effective public health campaigns. *Health Education & Behaviour*, *27*, 591–615.

11

Critical Health Psychology: Applications for Social Action

Tracy Morison, Antonia Lyons and Kerry Chamberlain

An important area within applied social psychology is the health and wellbeing of individuals, communities, and societies and how this is related to broader social, cultural, and global contexts. Drawing on the insights and methods of social psychology, critical health psychology works to interrogate these relationships to improve health and wellbeing outcomes. In this way, it extends beyond the more conventional approaches to physical health and wellbeing found in traditional health psychology (Horrocks and Johnson, 2012). Critical health psychologists are interested in advancing new psychological understandings of health and illness. Like applied social psychologists, they are also committed to finding ways to contribute to the transformation of an unhealthy world (Murray and Poland, 2006). These two features delineate the 'critical' in critical health psychology. Taking such an approach to health psychology, therefore, means opening one's eyes to new ways of seeing health-related issues (Lyons and Chamberlain, 2017).

Critical health psychology has recently developed into a popular, vibrant, and diverse area of scholarship in its own right (Horrocks and Johnson, 2012). Of course, like most academic fields, critical health psychologists do not all see eye to eye on particular issues (Stam, 2006). Nevertheless, there are a number of common aims and interests that could be said to define this area of scholarship, as outlined by the *International Society for Critical Health Psychology*, namely: (1) a dissatisfaction with the positivist assumptions of much conventional psychology and its lack of engagement with broader social and political issues; (2) an interest in various critical theories and approaches to knowledge, such as social constructionism, post-modernism, feminism, and Marxism; (3) the use of various qualitative and participatory methods of research, such as discourse analysis, narrative inquiry, action research, and ethnography; (4) an awareness of the social, political, and cultural dimensions of health and illness, such as poverty, racism, and sexism; and (5) an active commitment to reducing human suffering and improving the conditions of life, especially for socially marginalised members of society (https://ischp.info/). From these broad principles, it is clear that a prominent concern for critical health psychology is the application of knowledge for the benefit of society. Though they might not always agree as to how to go about achieving these overarching objectives, critical health psychologists are generally united in their commitment to deepening social analysis for social justice purposes (Lyons and Chamberlain, 2017; Murray and Poland, 2006).

The commitment to social justice has become increasingly prominent in critical health psychology; the field has 'become increasingly ambitious and visionary' (Hepworth, 2006: 334). Today, in the face of widespread neoliberal consumer-capitalism, addressing the social inequality and injustice that underpin global health issues has become a priority of growing urgency (Brown and Baker, 2012). Consequently, a growing number of critical health psychologists consider that they ought to be part of a moral project of individual and social transformation, rather than accepting (and even reinforcing) the status quo (Murray, 2012a). This project of transformation has required 'radically different approaches … new agendas, theories and methods' (Hepworth, 2006: 332), as we discuss in this chapter.

This chapter is divided into four parts. In the first part, we provide a brief historical discussion of the emergence and growth of critical health psychology, where we highlight its early influences, points of departure, and, particularly, its continued concern with addressing social injustice. In the second section, we focus on the 'call to action', which has necessitated greater attention to how knowledge is generated and applied in critical health psychology, including attempts to re/connect method, theory, and practice and to bridge the academic and non-academic worlds. In the third part, we turn to promising methodological developments in contemporary critical health psychology, showcasing the opportunities for justice-oriented work afforded by innovative methodologies. Finally, in the fourth part, we consider two areas for future work that critical health psychology researchers need to take into account as they respond to the discipline's call to action.

THE CRITICAL TURN IN HEALTH PSYCHOLOGY

Psychology's engagement with physical health and wellbeing emerged from an awareness of the limitations of approaching health issues exclusively from a narrow biomedical perspective. Psychologists turned their attention to issues of medical care as they noted how the broader environment played a part in people's physical health and wellbeing. These factors included the role of escalating healthcare costs, the HIV pandemic, the role that behaviour plays in health, and the growing view of health as an individual responsibility. In order to realise the ideal of 'health for all' (Mahler, 1981) proposed by the World Health Organization, early health psychologists argued that health and illness need to be understood more holistically and studied in terms of the ways that the psychological and social worlds work together with the biological or physical (Igarashi, 2015). This view informed Engel's (1977) foundational 'bio-psycho-social' framework, which remains an important lens in traditional health psychology.

Increasingly, however, scholars raised concerns that these efforts to recognise the contextual factors of health and illness did not go far enough. They argued that achieving health for all required health psychology to expand its focus further. Until then, following the neo-behaviourist view of dominant US-based psychology, much work in health psychology focused on the individual and an assumption that changing individual behaviours that 'cause' poor health could allow people to enjoy healthy lives (and significantly reduce State medical expenditure) (Igarashi, 2015). For example, Matarazzo (1982: 12) urged scholars to 'aggressively investigate and deal effectively with the role of the individual's behaviour and lifestyle in health and dysfunction'.

This kind of individualised focus frequently centred on 'social cognition' – how individuals make sense of social phenomena (Horrocks and Johnson, 2014; Lyons and Chamberlain, 2017) – and worked to reduce questions of health 'to instrumental, technical problems of management and control' (Igarashi, 2015: 175). This is best evidenced in the use of health behaviour models, still in use today. The Health Belief Model (Rosenstock, 1974) and the Theory of Planned Behaviour (Ajzen, 1985) are two well-known examples. These models map out causal relationships between attitudes, beliefs, and cognitions and particular health-related behaviours. Health issues are therefore explained chiefly at the individual level. As a result, proposed solutions or interventions frequently take the form of rationalistic education-type interventions that try to change individual behaviours (Murray and Chamberlain, 2014). However, critics argue that these explanations and solutions to a large extent ignore how 'health behaviours' are shaped by the wider context; by social relationships, institutions, media, political economies, and so on. This leaves a great deal unexplained and fails to capture the complex, multifaceted, sometimes contradictory nature of people's behaviour (Mielewyczyk and Willig, 2007; Murray, 2000; Murray and Poland, 2006).

Taking issue with this view, critics maintained that such constrained individualistic approaches do not meaningfully consider the enmeshment of health and illness in wider social, cultural, political, and historical contexts (Horrocks and Johnson, 2014). They argued that health psychology must also tackle the material, structural, and justice concerns that underpin global health problems (for example, malnutrition, HIV/AIDS) as well as address the experiential, deeply personal, and bodily nature of health/illness (Stam, 2006). Extending this argument, critical scholars, like Murray (2012a; 2012b), have questioned whether a health psychology that tries to be scientific can, in fact, deal with the root causes of poor health, which are unavoidably shaped by the broader socio-cultural context.

While adopting narrower positivist methods has helped professionalise health psychology, it has also placed limits on what it is able to achieve. Increasingly, scholars pointed out that this positivistic bent had rendered the field politically ineffective (Murray, 2012a; 2012b). Positivist theories and methods not only obscure the functioning of social contexts and structures, but their emphasis on individualism and scientific neutrality also discourages meaningful political engagement and action that can transform the conditions that foster poor health (Murray, 2012a; Murray and Poland, 2006).

Consequently, traditional (or 'mainstream') health psychology has also been implicated in *perpetuating* the inequality that underpins poor health. Critical scholars have shown how its individualistic ontology of selfhood dovetails neatly with the neoliberalism of capitalist societies (for example, Brown and Baker, 2012). Neoliberalism – and its strong emphasis on personal choice and responsibility – is a significant driver of rising inequality. This ideology discourages (direct) state responsibility for citizens' welfare, as seen in calls across the developed world for 'lean healthcare' and the privatisation of services in a range of contexts. By helping to maintain a neoliberal ideology, traditional health psychology is seen as contributing to its ends: health outcomes are situated within the logic of personal choice, with self-management and responsibility promoted as the keys to health and wellbeing (Brown and Baker, 2012; Horrocks and Johnson, 2014).

As a result, critical health psychologists have argued for different ways of working that extend the focus of health psychology research and practice.

Critical health psychology has thus developed as a way of extending the aims and reach of more conventional approaches, particularly those that have not meaningfully included the social dimensions of health (Chamberlain and Murray, 2009; Horrocks and Johnson, 2014). This turn occurred within the context of a more general dissatisfaction, particularly among social psychologists, with psychology's continued lack of social relevance. This turn was therefore part of the broader project of critical psychology, which aimed to evaluate psychological theories and practices in order to show how they are implicated in perpetuating social injustice (Parker, 2007; Prilleltensky, 1997).

The emerging field of critical health psychology was profoundly influenced by developments in social psychology and the turn to qualitative methodologies, particularly those emphasising the importance of language and power (for example, Edwards and Potter, 1992; Gergen, 1985; Potter, 1996; Potter and Wetherell 1987). The critical turn in health psychology was spurred also by health-oriented research in sociology, anthropology, and other social science disciplines that took a broader view of health and illness. This included work on 'healthism' (Herzlich, 1973), victim blaming (Ryan, 1971), and social representations and lay understandings of illness (d'Houtaud and Field, 1984). Critical epistemologies and social theories (for example, social constructionism, Marxism, and feminism) enabled health psychologists to emphasise the importance of, *inter alia*, socio-cultural, political, and economic dynamics in keeping people healthy, shaping health outcomes, determining healthcare access, and framing illness experiences (Lyons and Chamberlain, 2017).

Over the years, critical health psychologists have pioneered new ways of doing health research and championed the use of qualitative methodologies (Chamberlain and Murray, 2017). This has led to a surge of interest in qualitative methodologies in health psychology more broadly. As the editors of a recent special issue of *Health Psychology* note, 'increasingly, health (and other) psychologists are turning to qualitative methods to complement or contest the more established approaches' (Gough and Deatrick, 2015: 289). The growth of qualitative research in health psychology, they contend, is also related to 'increasing policy and practitioner emphasis on patient/client experiences and practices pertaining to prevention, illness, and service use' (Gough and Deatrick, 2015: 290).

Critical health psychology research has played a crucial role in highlighting interconnections between social disadvantage and health. Qualitative methods have been useful in this regard; they highlight the importance of context and meaning in people's health practices and show how 'power, economics and macrosocial processes influence and/or structure health, health care, health psychology, and society at large' (Marks, 2002: 15). Research in a range of contexts has focused on people from marginalised groups, including sexual minorities (for example, Morison and Lynch, 2016; Peel and Thomson, 2009), those from the impoverished contexts (for example, Hodgetts et al., 2011), racial and ethnic minorities (for example, Brondolo et al., 2009), and people with disabilities (for example, Finlay et al., 2015; Rohleder and Swartz, 2009). Feminist health psychologists have also pointed to the interconnection of various forms of marginalisation – rooted in racial, geographical, economic, class-based, and other differences – highlighting how these shape the dis/advantage that particular people/groups experience (for example, Macleod, 2012; Macleod et al., 2018).

In recent years, questions have been raised about the extent to which qualitative language-based research, especially discourse analysis, can actually contribute to social action. The concern is that a persistent focus on language potentially diverts attention from broader real-life issues (Johnson, 2012; Murray, 2012b). A growing tension has developed within critical health psychology between critique and social action. On one hand is the pressing need to address suffering and inequality and to improve health outcomes. On the other hand, there is the conviction that researchers must continue to provide nuanced accounts of the political and moral dimensions of health issues – questions best answered by means of qualitative methodologies grounded in critical theories (Cornish and Gillespie, 2009). Murray (2014) maintains that, while improving people's lives has *always* been a core value of critical health psychology, the objective of contributing to personal and social transformation has, to some extent, been underplayed in favour of work focused on critique. In the following section, we turn to the application and practical use of knowledge: we provide a brief background to the call to action in critical health psychology and then discuss how contemporary researchers have responded to this call and attempted to reconcile the critique–praxis tension.

RESPONDING TO THE CALL TO ACTION

A central and pressing question in critical health psychology has been how, and to what extent, social action is its goal (see Hepworth, 2006). Concerns about the relevance and purpose of psychological knowledge are hardly new among critically-minded scholars. As far back as the 1980s critical social psychologists were calling for greater consideration of the applied and practical use of their research. Potter and Wetherell (1987: 174), for instance, argued that 'over and above amassing of research findings and the furtherance of careers…the image of a benign body of practitioners waiting to read the journals of pure scientists and put research findings into practice is heart-warming, but unrealistic'. Such sentiments seem particularly pertinent to health psychology, when the objects of study are frequently, and literally, matters of life and death.

More than a decade ago, Lee (2006: 358) asked critical health psychologists: 'Will we continue to be all talk and no action, will we continue to produce powerful rhetoric for a small audience of true believers or will we act to make a difference?' This question remains relevant. In light of creeping neoliberalism, rising fascism, and widening inequity witnessed around the world, the need for engagement and action within social and health psychology is now considered more urgent than ever and the call for researchers to come down from the ivory tower has intensified (Fine, 2016). Within critical health psychology, the need for less 'talk' and more 'action', as per Lee's (2006) plea, has pushed researchers to think more carefully about the ways that knowledge is produced and applied in critical health psychology, and how to reconnect method, theory, and practice.

In responding to the call to action, contemporary qualitative research in health psychology is presented with a challenge, namely to 'reforge [the] connection between research and practice and to consider ways of increasing the impact of qualitative research' (Murray, 2014: 585). Lyons and Chamberlain (2017: 542) assert that the insights gained from qualitative research on people's health and illness experiences 'can be used to support, assist, and provide more effective and targeted care for specific people, groups and communities, and lead to the revision of health policies and health care practices'. To achieve this, researchers have had to carefully consider how critique, and a focus on language, can respond to the material conditions of people's lives. Some researchers have adopted a pragmatic approach, viewing the knowledge they generate as a tool for social action with the potential to promote positive change (Cornish and Gillespie, 2009; Murray, 2014). In a somewhat similar vein, Murray (2012a) has proposed a critical approach to social action: the imbrication of a critical lens within applied research, both at the interpersonal level (for example, exploring illness experiences and social location) and the group level (for example, working with communities to challenge oppressive social relations). This involves taking into account the socio-historical context, connections between personal and socio-structural levels, and the structural bases of health/illness.

Discursive researchers have also addressed the issue of the social relevance of language-based research. Some have attended to the ways that findings from discursive studies can usefully inform public health practice. For instance, Horrocks and Johnson (2014) investigated child immunisation practices among working-class mothers in the UK to show how dominant discourses of motherhood govern women's decisions to vaccinate, despite recent controversy surrounding vaccination. Their analysis illuminates webs of power in operation: dominant gendered ideologies shape and provoke mothers' compliance, despite potentially worrying information about vaccination safety. Such an analysis, they argue, makes visible the broader social 'landscape' of health information and health promotion and offers opportunities to transform and reconstruct dominant ideologies. This may involve using qualitative and participatory research in working with people, as well as lobbying for change, and creating receptive social environments for less oppressive approaches to health promotion.

Similarly, discursive studies can generate useful data for health campaigns and messaging (Gibson et al., 2014). For example, Bowleg and colleagues (2015) show how gendered discourses shaped accounts of safer sex practices and condom use for Black heterosexual men in the United States. Research by Gibson et al. (2014; 2015) shows how information on Australian breast cancer websites was presented in morally-loaded and culturally-specific ways, constraining the choices of those targeted by the sites (white, heterosexual, middle-class women) and potentially excluding others from information and support services. Findings from such studies can inform health campaigns and messaging to provide inclusive, culturally-competent information (Gibson et al., 2014). Such insights also have value for informing large-scale research and for adding nuance to public health campaigns (Horrocks and Johnson, 2014). The challenge is how to make this knowledge accessible and available beyond the academy, essentially producing useful knowledge for wider audiences.

Research aimed at achieving social justice and changing oppressive circumstances demands knowledge of different kinds. Although the creation of academic knowledge, in the form of books and articles, is valuable and should not be abandoned, it is important to go beyond these traditional forms of academic dissemination to produce what might be called 'practical knowledge', aimed at achieving change and improving lives. This is the position of the scholar-activist (Murray, 2012b; Routledge and Derickson, 2015), where scholarship and activism are intertwined, mutually fostering and stimulating one another (Suzuki and Mayorga, 2014). The concern here is with how the influence of research findings can be maximised beyond academia, both during and after the research (Murray, 2014).

Translating research knowledge for these ends requires time and commitment from researchers and may also demand collaborations to access necessary skills. There are many ways in which this may be accomplished (Mayan and Daum, 2016). Chamberlain and Hodgetts (2017) describe a range of disseminations that arose from the Family100 project, a longitudinal community-oriented project conducted with 100 families living in poverty in Auckland, New Zealand. Working in partnership with a community agency, the research shared knowledge through: case-based workshops to develop skills for the staff of the agency which fostered the research; case studies developed from the research data and presented to High Court judges to increase their understandings of the everyday lives of people living in poverty; publications to disseminate the research findings to community audiences (Auckland City Mission, 2014; Garden, 2014); and presentations and workshops delivered to a range of relevant agencies, including Treasury, the Families Commission, and the local City Council. These knowledge-sharing activities necessitated the translation of academic research into content that was informative and helpful for each particular audience.

Another example of dissemination, focused on delivering research findings about the social determinants of health to lay community audiences, is provided by the American Public Health Association. They developed a range of materials to disseminate the effects of inequalities in education, housing, and income using infographics and online stories using *Storify* (American Public Health Association, 2016). Such work is premised on an ethics of reciprocity, based on equality and exchange (Maiter et al., 2008), where researchers are committed to delivering outputs beyond the academy that will benefit the community in return for the collaboration of community members in research processes. Such attempts to bridge the academic/non-academic divide are also evident in community-oriented critical health psychology research, which involves deeper and multi-layered engagements with research participants. These approaches are participatory in nature, in the sense that they engage with, rather than research on, participants (Mayan and Daum, 2016).

Proponents of such participatory approaches argue that social critique is more effective when it engages with, and is grounded in, the material realities of participants' lives (Fine, 2016; Hodgetts et al., 2014). Acknowledging this 'rich basket of critical knowledge percolating in the margins' (Fine, 2016: 362) – what Fine terms 'radical marginality' (Fine, 2016: 350) – is essential to ethical and effective social justice research. In this vein, Fine (2016: 358) argues for participatory research based upon four principles that can be useful in community-oriented critical health psychology: (1) take seriously that expertise is widely distributed but that wisdom about injustice is experiential, 'cultivated in the bodies and communities of those most intimately wounded'; (2) link research on oppression to research on privilege; (3) understand how the 'contact zones of divergent standpoints' produce powerful research on history, social structures, and people's lives; and (4) consider how the validity and impact of research is increased when designed alongside social justice movements and distributed in 'outputs' based upon meaningful engagement with social justice movement actions and community life (for example, community performances, social media, legal cases, academic writing). It is clear that issues of power and privilege are therefore at the forefront of arguments for using participatory and emancipatory methods (Murray and Chamberlain, 2014). Working with communities is envisaged not simply as producing better research but as part of an ethical position that values local knowledges and maintains a keen awareness of the intricacies of speaking about/for/with the 'Other'.

Community approaches can make a fundamental difference for participants' lives. For example, in community-led research on HIV in rural South Africa, Campbell et al. (2007) sought to facilitate a 'health-enabling social environment' – social contexts that support effective HIV/AIDS management. The researchers adopted a collaborative approach in order to contribute to contextual changes that could enable more effective community-led HIV/AIDS management. While potentially powerful, this kind of work also has its challenges. For example, in this case, difficulties were related to 'working at the community level in highly conservative patriarchal communities to tackle problems which may be shaped by economic and political processes over which local people have little control' (Campbell et al., 2007: 347).

Another example of community-oriented health psychology work is provided by the Family100 project, which demonstrated how 'adversity associated with urban poverty gets under the skin and into the minds of those affected through processes of "embodied deprivation"' (Hodgetts et al., 2014: 98). The researchers aimed to 'look locally and work systemically' (Hodgetts et al., 2014: 98) by engaging in a range of activities and forms of advocacy within and beyond the community, as described above (see also, Chamberlain and Hodgetts, 2017). This project makes a strong case for moving beyond one-off, localised interventions and working to address structural issues – in this instance poverty – in community health psychology research.

Participatory approaches can also be combined with other qualitative methods, like discursive approaches, to enhance the impact of research findings (Johnson, 2012). The combined use of qualitative methods (also known as pluralism) potentially expands the depth and scope of the data generated (Chamberlain et al., 2011) and can facilitate the reach to wider audiences. We turn now to discuss some promising new developments in contemporary critical health psychology that hold potential for research focused on social change.

PROMISING DEVELOPMENTS FOR SOCIAL CHANGE

In recent years the social sciences have produced a number of innovative ways of generating data and working with participants (Chamberlain et al., 2011). Many of these facilitate participatory and emancipatory work. Within critical health psychology, the kinds of analytical questions that are now being asked have promoted methodological innovation (Lyons and Chamberlain, 2017). We focus here on two particular developments that have potential to enhance research that can produce change by expanding research impacts and facilitating participant involvement in research design and implementation (Murray, 2014). These are the use of new technologies and arts-based approaches, which we discuss in turn with examples of work for each.

New technologies, and especially social media technologies, have facilitated innovative ways of carrying out qualitative research in health psychology (Morison et al., 2015). As technologies expand, researchers are increasingly utilising them to collect and generate data through novel means. Social networking and digital technologies have provided fruitful avenues for health-based research (Lupton, 2017), providing original data and enhanced possibilities for working with participants, and producing practical knowledge.

One such avenue, though not uncomplicated, is the possibility of creating virtual spaces that are more egalitarian than offline locations. This is evident in the 2015 online participatory project with deaf Australians by Ferndale et al., which involved the creation of a deaf-friendly virtual space for research. The researchers were able to use internet-based technologies to promote collaboration and ensure that the study was informed by the expertise and needs of Australians living with deafness. They were also able to use tools to enhance participation and communication (for example, interpreters, captioning), as well as to try to compensate for the interactional dynamics that create power differentials between hearing and deaf people.

Digital technologies and social media are increasingly embedded in people's worlds and have consequences for health and well-being. One recent research project has explored this in relation to the drinking practices and drinking cultures of young adults in Aotearoa New Zealand, drawing on multiple approaches and multiple methods. The use of a range of methods, including digital technologies, provided nuanced insights about young people's drinking cultures that could not have been generated using traditional offline methods (or, indeed, a single approach to data generation). These approaches showed the vast amount of alcohol marketing that is taking place 'under the radar' on social media and the lack of regulation in this field (Goodwin et al., 2014; Lyons et al., 2015). In addition, online technologies have proved useful in providing different avenues for disseminating research findings, making these available to participants, and reaching broader non-academic audiences. Online dissemination of the research findings aimed to change the ways that young people engage with alcohol marketing (and Facebook privacy settings) and inform policy makers about the influences of alcohol marketing through social media. There is great potential in harnessing new technologies for both researching particular health-based topics and disseminating knowledge more broadly.

Another promising development within health research is the use of creative arts, such as creative writing, performance, and visual arts, as a means to obtain and develop different forms of knowledge and bring such knowledge to the attention of wider audiences, with potential for effecting transformation and social justice agendas. Interest in arts-based health research methods has grown rapidly in recent years (de Jager et al., 2016; Leavy, 2015; Rolling, 2013).

Body mapping is one such method that is particularly useful for exploring health-based issues and for projects with a participatory or social justice orientation (de Jager et al., 2016). This visual, story-based method is used with groups and involves 'creating body maps using drawing, painting or other art-based techniques to visually represent aspects of people's lives, their bodies' (Gastaldo et al., 2012: 5). The technique was originally developed as a group art therapy tool for South African women living with HIV/AIDS and evolved into an advocacy tool, with the body maps used for community mobilisation and advocacy around HIV treatment (Morgan and Bambanani Women's Group, 2003). Boyce (n.d.) provides an overview of this project and examples of body maps. Subsequently, body mapping has been developed as a research tool (Gastaldo et al., 2012) and applied to other health issues, such as sexual abuse trauma (Zoldbrod, 2015).

Other arts-based methodologies include art for activism, photo-voice and performative approaches (for example, Murray and Crummet, 2010; Rossiter et al., 2008; see also Boydell et al. (2012) for a review). Such methods were employed by Murray and colleagues in a participatory action research project concerned with ageing in a disadvantaged urban setting. In this project, artwork was used as a means for understanding older persons' experiences, enhancing their confidence and wellbeing, and as an advocacy tool. Arts-based methods can help with 'reducing stigma, increasing awareness and giving voice to perspectives that would otherwise remain un-seen/heard' (de Jager et al., 2016: para. 29). These methods have the potential to empower participants, their communities, and even society at large. These examples show how, when 'employed in the research process, the arts enable an examination of the everyday in imaginative ways that draw attention to the cruelties and contradictions inherent in neoliberal society' (Foster, 2016: 1). Of course, arts-based methods are not devoid of power differentials, embedded, for example, in cultural perceptions and meanings of the arts, different technological competencies, and access to technologies (Morison et al., 2015). Nevertheless, creative methods do lend themselves to more egalitarian ways of doing research and create opportunities for scholar-activism. Many arts-based approaches (such as body mapping, discussed above) have an explicit social justice agenda and also offer a number of other benefits, including therapeutic effects, promoting collaborative and reflective research processes, encouraging embodied awareness, as well as their use as a knowledge translation strategy (de Jager et al., 2016; Leavy, 2015). Such approaches are therefore useful in participatory and emancipatory research projects for generating data, engaging broader audiences, critical consciousness raising, and advocacy purposes (Foster, 2016; Murray, 2014).

CRITICAL ISSUES FOR RESPONDING TO CALLS TO ACTION

Our final consideration turns to critical questions that are relevant to contemporary critical health psychology and which require further attention from researchers, particularly with regard to the applied and practical use of research findings. We single out two issues here, although many others could be raised. The first is the question of the materiality of health and illness. This question has surprisingly received relatively limited attention, given that the topics of health psychology research frequently concern material effects and flesh-and-blood matters. The second issue is somewhat more practical in nature, but no less weighty, namely: the politics of knowledge production. This issue centres on questions such as, by whom, and for whom, is health psychology knowledge produced? We discuss each issue in turn.

There has been a recent concern across the social sciences to address issues of materiality (for example, Fox, 2016). However, this has not been very visible within psychology, even though it has considerable relevance for health psychology, especially in relation to specific questions about bodies and embodiment, technologies of treatment, and spaces of care. Concerns have grown within critical health psychology, and other critical qualitative arenas of work, that the material world has been ignored in favour of advancing critique and undertaking research with a dominant focus on talk and text.[1] Questions have been raised about what long-standing qualitative approaches, which privilege meaning and language, may 'leave out' of their analyses. These questions have initiated a number of theoretical and methodological developments (Chadwick, 2017) around the 'turn to bodies' (Cromby, 2015) and the 'sensory/affective turn' (Wetherell, 2012; 2013).

Scholars working in these areas have argued that more comprehensive theorising is needed. For example, Lyons et al. (2014) argue that we need to generate deeper theoretical understandings of gendered embodiment in order to get to grips with the intricacies of particular health practices. Others have alerted us to the need for 'embodied qualitative methodologies' (Chadwick, 2017: 54). These two endeavours are not mutually exclusive, of course. Chadwick (2017) argues that successfully developing such methodologies is dependent on a suitable theory of embodied being.

In critical health psychology, the issue of materiality is a growing area of interest requiring further theoretical and methodological innovation (Lyons et al., 2014). There continues to be a range of responses to the debate about materiality and some methodological innovations. Attempts have been made to orient qualitative research to the material dimensions of health and illness. For example, in a study of cardiovascular functioning during couples' conversations, Lyons and Cromby (2010) theorised and explored how the performative and social constructionist nature of language has physiological correlates. Cromby's (2005) notion of 'embodied subjectivity' has been used by researchers to understand and theorise Scottish women's drinking as a gendered *and* embodied practice and show how physical space and bodily enjoyment, felt emotions, and physical pleasures are crucial to drinking practices (Lyons et al., 2014). In a similar vein, Chadwick (2017: 58) attempts to 'find new theoretical and methodological ways of approaching, tracing and representing the bodies already in our qualitative data and analyses'. In her research on South African women's birthing narratives, she employs notions of multi-vocality and poetic analytic devices to disrupt conventional transcription processes in order to 'listen for the body', described as a process of reading between the lines for 'the fleshy ways in which words, sounds, phrases and stories were told' (Chadwick, 2017: 64) by participants (see also Brown et al., 2011; Cromby, 2015). Taking materiality in another direction, Caronia and Mortari (2015) document how spaces and artefacts of an intensive care unit shape the practices that occur within it and frame the moral order of the medical care that is enacted there.

Such work provides inspiration for further work in this area. Future studies could, for instance, draw insights from research invoking materiality (Hout et al., 2015: Maller, 2015) or from materialist adaptations of performativity within feminism in order to investigate how embodied subjects 'do' health or illness in various ways (Nentwich and Morison, 2017). Similarly, novel qualitative methodologies may also provide fertile grounds for those seeking to foreground materiality. Methods like body mapping, for instance, potentially incorporate multi-sensory, embodied, and contextualised ways of meaning making (Thomas and Mulvey, 2008). Alongside the proliferation of new technologies, we are witnessing a turn to visual data generation (for example, photographs, art, filming) and multi-modal analyses that potentially offer ways of attending to the material world (Gough and Lyons, 2016).

The second issue we want to consider in this section is the politics of knowledge production, particularly the politics of location and decolonising and indigenising critical health psychology. Critical health psychologists continue to scrutinise their own positionalities – as researchers, practitioners, and academics – and the power relationships associated with the socially privileged positions they occupy. Attention has been paid to power dynamics between researchers and the individuals or communities they work with (for example, Ben-Ari and Enosh, 2013). Less consideration has been given to the politics *within* health psychology. Such concerns are not simply related to individual opportunities (for health psychologists), but also to how the production and application of knowledge are shaped by socio-historical and geopolitical factors.

As postcolonial feminist scholars have cautioned, geographical and social location can work in the interest of privilege and power, favouring particular readings while undermining or silencing others (Giroux, 2009). Health psychology's Euro-American heritage means that relations of knowledge production are structured in terms of centre and periphery (Yen, 2016). For example, Yen (2016: 87) illustrates how South African (health) psychologists' work is evaluated within 'conditions of knowledge production, which favour single-author high impact journal publications and narrow disciplinary specialisation, and the interests of the Anglophone heartland of psychology, rather than engagement, transgressive inquiry, and the promotion of a truly postcolonial scholarship'. Such scholarship generally does not reflect the concerns of the global South, as determined by those who live there. Instead, health psychology continues to be dominated by the vicissitudes of Northern research agendas and funding priorities. In practical terms, this has translated into disproportionate attention and funding dedicated to health issues that are of concern in the developed global North, such as such as stress, coronary heart disease, cancer, and obesity.

In contrast, Teo (2015) argues that various forms of internationalisation (that is, the global imposition of Western psychology) can be tempered by cooperation with indigenous approaches. It is heartening, therefore, to witness a revived interest in decolonising higher education and indigenising knowledge production. This interest has, in part, been stirred by a number of protests and grass root social movements criticising continued racial and economic inequity and discrimination in higher education across the globe (Fine, 2016). These include the Chilean student protests (Long, 2011), 'Black on campus' and 'Black Lives Matter' student-led protests in US universities, the Million Student March against student debt, also in the United States (Hartocollis and Bidgood, 2015; Harvin, 2016; Thomas, n.d.), the 'Rhodes Must Fall' protests originating in South Africa and taken up in the UK (Elgot, 2016), and ongoing 'Fees Must Fall' demonstrations in South Africa, supported by students in New York and London (Davids and Waghid, 2016). Essentially, decolonising/indigenising involves transforming what counts as legitimate knowledge, challenging, transforming, and/or replacing Northern theories and methodologies with home grown, locally-relevant approaches. Calls for transforming spaces of knowledge production, and knowledge itself, are particularly urgent in former colonies such as India, South Africa, New Zealand, and Australia (Dudgeon and Walker, 2015; Sherwood, 2013; Zavala, 2013).

There have been some moves within critical social psychology toward challenging the hegemony of Western perspectives and understandings within the discipline. We now note, for instance, that some undergraduate social psychology textbooks include indigenous psychologies that grapple with issues of knowledge integration (for example, Hodgetts et al., 2010). Further, indigenised social psychology textbooks offer counter perspectives on social psychology topics (for example, Macapagal et al., 2013; Ratele, 2006). Critical health psychologists, in contrast, have not yet adequately begun to engage with questions of decolonisation and indigenising of knowledge and practice within the discipline.

For critical health psychologists, calls for transformation would mean working toward 'producing new knowledges and discourses which challenge typical psychological conceptions; providing a range of Indigenous-led strategies, solutions, tools, and methods to support critical reflexivity; and acknowledging power relations and white privilege' (Dudgeon and Walker, 2015: 292). Some progress has been made, such as the use of participatory research to improve aboriginal people's access to health services in Australia (Durey et al., 2016). However, there is still much to be done in this regard within critical health psychology.

CONCLUSION

Applied social psychologists and critical health psychologists are united by the desire to make a real difference in people's lives. Spurred by the ideals of social transformation and justice in the arena of health and wellbeing, critical health psychology extends its view beyond more individualistic approaches, foregrounding broader contexts in issues surrounding health and illness. The sub-discipline continues to challenge itself to produce socially relevant and useful knowledge and, in this regard, offers useful insights around health and wellbeing, as well as methodological and theoretical innovations, for applied scholarship in social psychology.

The ideal of social transformation, we have argued, has always been fundamental for critical health psychologists, but as the field has developed, and as social inequity has widened globally, it has become a more pressing objective (Murray, 2014). The challenge for critical health psychology has been to maintain its critical edge, rooted in a strong history of critical thinking and nuanced critique, while at the same time responding to the practical concerns and material realities that shape people's lives (Cornish and Gillespie, 2009). We have considered some of the ways that the discipline has risen to this challenge, in attempts to reconnect theory, method, and practice, and in working to bridge the academic and the non-academic worlds.

It is clear that critical health psychology has continued to develop, to respond to changing social contexts, to be open to new ways of working, and to seek new forms of knowledge. In this chapter, we have highlighted two particular areas for future growth: questions of materiality and embodiment and responding to the politics of knowledge, especially in regard to the task of decolonisation and indigenisation. More work is certainly needed, in these areas and beyond, if we are to achieve the original ambition that was the genesis of health psychology: improved health for all. Some advances made in these areas within applied social psychology offer inspiration for critical health psychology.

In thinking about the future of critical health psychology, now a recognised and established field, we offer a final thought. We began by asserting that critical health psychology is essentially about 'new ways of seeing'. In closing, we suggest that, to retain this quality, and to continue to 'see differently' – with the fundamental aim of making a difference in people's lives – critical health psychology must embrace Fine's (2016) 'radical marginality'. We suggest this not only in the sense that she means – of working with those at the margins of society (although this is imperative) – but also in a disciplinary sense. Critical psychology has in some ways been the rebel, the young upstart who defies the conventional and the traditional. As it reaches maturity, it must maintain this powerful resistant stance, particularly in the face of widening global inequalities.

Note

1 This is particularly relevant to discursive work influenced by the Loughborough School (i.e., Edwards and Potter, 1992), which takes a more micro-analytic perspective than (often more pragmatic) critical psychology work in other contexts.

REFERENCES

Ajzen, I. (1985). From intentions to actions: A theory of planned behavior. In J. Kuhl and J. Beckmann (Eds.), *Action control: From cognition to behavior* (pp. 11–39). Berlin: Springer-Verlag.

American Public Health Association. (2016). *Infographics: Social determinants of health.* Retrieved from http://thenationshealth.aphapublications.org/content/infographics-social-determinants-health

Auckland City Mission. (2014) *Demonstrating the complexities of being poor: An empathy tool.* Auckland: Auckland City Mission. Retrieved from http://www.aucklandcitymission.org.nz/latest-news/resources/

Ben-Ari, A., and Enosh, G. (2013). Power relations and reciprocity: Dialectics of knowledge construction. *Qualitative Health Research, 23*(3): 422–429.

Bowleg, L., Heckert, A. L., Brown, T. L., and Massie, J. S. (2015). Responsible men, blameworthy women: Black heterosexual men's discursive constructions of safer sex and masculinity. *Health Psychology, 34*(4): 314–327.

Boyce, A. (n. d.). *Body maps: A presentation based on the work of the Bambanani Women's Group, Khayelitsha, Cape Town, South Africa*. [PowerPoint slides]. New York, USA: Institute for African Development Cornell University. Retrieved from https://www.powershow.com/view/2ba3e-NWM1M/Body_Maps_a_presentation_based_on_the_work_of_the_Bambanani_Womens_Group_Khayelitsha_Cape_Town_So_powerpoint_ppt_presentation?skipadult=1

Boydell, K. M., Gladstone, B. M., Volpe, T., Allemang, B., and Stasiulis, E. (2012, January). The production and dissemination of knowledge: A scoping review of arts-based health research. In *Forum Qualitative Sozialforschung/Forum: Qualitative Social Research* (Vol. 13, No. 1).

Brondolo, E., Gallo, L. C., and Myers, H. F. (2009). Race, racism and health: disparities, mechanisms, and interventions. *Journal of behavioral medicine, 32*(1), 1.

Brown, B. J., and Baker, S. (2012). *Responsible citizens: Individuals, health, and policy under neoliberalism*. London and New York: Anthem Press.

Brown, S. D., Cromby, J., Harper, D. J., Johnson, K., and Reavey, P. (2011). Researching 'experience': Embodiment, methodology, process. *Theory and Psychology, 21*(4): 493–415.

Campbell, C., Nair, Y., and Maimane, S. (2007). Building contexts that support effective community responses to HIV/AIDS: A South African case study. *American Journal of Community Psychology*, *39*(3–4): 347–363.

Caronia, L., and Mortari, L. (2015). The agency of things: How spaces and artefacts organize the moral order of an intensive care unit. *Social Semiotics*, *25*(4): 401–422.

Chadwick, R. (2017). Embodied methodologies: challenges, reflections and strategies. *Qualitative Research*, *17*(1), 54–74.

Chamberlain, K., and Hodgetts, D. (2017). Collecting qualitative data with hard-to-reach groups. In U. Flick (Ed.), *The SAGE handbook of qualitative data collection (pp. 668–685).* London: Sage.

Chamberlain, K., and Murray, M. (2009). Critical Health Psychology. In D. Fox, I. Prilleltensky, and S. Austins (Eds.), *Critical psychology: An introduction* (2nd edn., pp. 144–158). London: Sage.

Chamberlain, K., and Murray, M. (2017). Qualitative research in health psychology. In C. Willig, and W. Stainton Rogers (Eds.), *The SAGE handbook of qualitative research in psychology* (2nd edn., pp. 431–449). London: Sage.

Chamberlain, K., Cain, T., Sheridan, J., and Dupuis, A. (2011). Pluralisms in qualitative research: From multiple methods to integrated methods. *Qualitative Research in Psychology*, *8*(2): 151–169.

Cornish, F., and Gillespie, A. (2009). A pragmatist approach to the problem of knowledge in health psychology. *Journal of Health Psychology*, *14*(6): 800–809.

Cromby, J. (2005). Theorising embodied subjectivity. *International Journal of Critical Psychology*, *15*, 133–150.

Cromby, J. (2015). *Feeling bodies: Embodying psychology*. Basingstoke, UK: Palgrave Macmillan.

De Jager, A., Tewson, A., Ludlow, B., and Boydell, K. (2016). Embodied ways of storying the self: A systematic review of body-mapping. *Forum Qualitative Sozialforschung/Forum: Qualitative Social Research*, *17*(2): Art. 22.

D'Houtaud, A., and Field, M. (1984). The image of health: Variations in perception by social class in a French population. *Sociology of Health and Illness*, *6*(1): 30–60.

Davids, N., and Waghid, Y. (2016). #FeesMustFall: History of South African student protests reflects inequality's grip. *Mail and Guardian.* Retrieved from http://mg.co.za/article/2016-10-10-feesmustfall-history-of-south-african-student-protests-reflects-inequalitys-grip

Dudgeon, P., and Walker, R. (2015). Decolonising Australian psychology: Discourses, strategies, and practice. *Journal of Social and Political Psychology*, *3*(1): 276–297.

Durey, A., McEvoy, S., Swift-Otero, V., Taylor, K., Katzenellenbogen, J., and Bessarab, D. (2016). Improving healthcare for Aboriginal Australians through effective engagement between community and health services. *BMC Health Services,* 16: 224–237.

Edwards, D., and Potter, J. (1992). *Discursive psychology*. London: Sage.

Elgot, J. (2016). 'Take it down!': Rhodes Must Fall campaign marches through Oxford. *The Guardian*. Retrieved from https://www.theguardian.com/education/2016/mar/09/take-it-down-rhodes-must-fall-campaign-marches-through-oxford

Engel, G. L. (1977). The need for a new medical model: A challenge for biomedicine. *Science*, *196*: 129–136.

Ferndale, D., Watson, B., and Munro, L. (2015). Creating deaf-friendly spaces for research: Innovating online qualitative enquiries. *Qualitative Research in Psychology*, *12*(3): 246–257.

Fine, M. (2016). Just methods in revolting times. *Qualitative Research in Psychology*, *13*(4): 347–365.

Finlay, W. L., Rohleder, P., Taylor, N., and Culfear, H. (2015). 'Understanding' as a practical issue in sexual health education for people with intellectual disabilities: A study using two qualitative methods. *Health Psychology*, *34*(4): 328–338.

Foster, V. (2016). *Collaborative arts-based research for social justice*. London: Routledge.

Fox, N. J. (2016). Health sociology from post-structuralism to the new materialisms. *Health*, *20*(1), 62–74.

Garden, E. (2014). *Speaking for ourselves.* Auckland: Auckland City Mission. Available at http://www.aucklandcitymission.org.nz/latest-news/resources/

Gastaldo, D., Magalhães, L., Carrasco, C., and Davy, C. (2012). *Body-map storytelling as research: Methodological considerations for telling the stories of undocumented workers through body mapping.* Available at www.migrationhealth.ca/undocumented-workers-ontario/body-mapping

Gergen, K. J. (1985). The social constructionist movement in modern psychology. *American Psychologist*, *40*(3): 266–275.

Gibson, A. F., Lee, C., and Crabb, S. (2014). 'If you grow them, know them': Discursive constructions of the pink ribbon culture of breast cancer in the Australian context. *Feminism and Psychology*, *24*(4): 521–541.

Gibson, A. F., Lee, C., and Crabb, S. (2015). Reading between the lines: Applying multimodal critical discourse analysis to online constructions of breast cancer. *Qualitative Research in Psychology*, *12*(3): 272–286.

Giroux, H. A. (2009). Paulo Freire and the politics of postcolonialism. In A. Kempf (Ed.), *Breaching the colonial contract* (pp. 79–89). Netherlands: Springer.

Goodwin, I., Lyons, A. C., Griffin, C., and McCreanor, T. (2014). Ending up online: Interrogating mediated youth drinking cultures. In B. Roberts and A. Bennett (Eds.), *Mediated youth cultures* (pp. 59–74). Basingstoke, UK: Palgrave Macmillan.

Gough, B., and Deatrick, J. A. (2015). Qualitative health psychology research: Diversity, power, and impact. *Health Psychology*, *34*(4): 289–292.

Gough, B., and Lyons, A. C. (2016). The future of qualitative research in psychology: Accentuating the positive. *Integrative Psychological and Behavioral Science*, *50*(2): 234–243.

Hartocollis, A., and Bidgood, J. (2015). Racial discrimination protests ignite at colleges across the US. *New York Times.* Retrieved from http://www.nytimes.com/2015/11/12/us/racial-discrimination-protests-ignite-at-colleges-across-the-us.html?smid=fb-nytimesandsmtyp=cur

Harvin, M. (2016). Racism, civil rights and the struggle for equality still issues in higher education today. *Education News.* Retrieved from https://www.goodcall.com/news/racism-civil-rights-and-the-struggle-for-equality-still-issues-in-higher-education-today-04039

Hepworth, J. (2006). The emergence of critical health psychology: Can it contribute to promoting public health? *Journal of Health Psychology*, *11*(3): 331–341.

Herzlich, C. (1973). *Health and illness: A social psychological analysis* (Trans. D. Graham). London: Academic Press.

Hodgetts, D., Chamberlain, K., Tankel, Y., and Groot, S. (2014). Looking within and beyond the community: Lessons learned by researching, theorising and acting to address urban poverty and health. *Journal of Health Psychology*, *19*(1): 97–102.

Hodgetts, D., Drew, N., Stolte, O., Sonn, C, Nikora, N., and Curtis, C. (2010). *Social psychology and everyday life*. Basingstoke: Palgrave MacMillan.

Hodgetts, D., Stolte, O., Radley, A., Leggatt-Cook, C., Groot, S., and Chamberlain, K. (2011). 'Near and far' social distancing in domiciled characterisations of homeless people. *Urban Studies*, *48*(8), 1739–11753

Horrocks, C., and Johnson, S. (2012). *Advances in health psychology: Critical approaches.* Basingstoke, UK: Palgrave Macmillan.

Horrocks, C., and Johnson, S. (2014). A socially situated approach to inform ways to improve health and wellbeing. *Sociology of Health and Illness*, *36*(2): 175–186.

Hout, A., Pols, J., and Willems, D. (2015). Shining trinkets and unkempt gardens: On the materiality of care. *Sociology of Health and Illness*, *37*(8): 1206–1217.

Igarashi, Y. (2015). Health psychology: Towards critical psychologies for well-being and social justice. In I. Parker (Ed.), *Handbook of critical psychology* (pp. 173–81). London: Sage.

Johnson, S. (2012). Working with the tensions between critique and action in critical health psychology. In C. Horrocks and S. Johnson (Eds.), *Advances in health psychology: Critical approaches* (pp. 17–28). Basingstoke, UK: Palgrave Macmillan.

Leavy, P. (2015). *Method meets art: Arts-based research practice* (2nd edn.). New York: Guilford Press.

Lee, C. (2006). Critical health psychology: Who benefits? *Journal of Health Psychology*, *11*(3): 355–359.

Long, G. (2011, August 11). Chile student protests point to deep discontent. *BBC News.* Retrieved from http://www.bbc.com/news/world-latin-america-14487555.

Lupton, D. (2017). *Digital health: Critical perspectives*. London: Routledge.

Lyons, A. C., and Chamberlain, K. (2017). Critical health psychology. In B. Gough (Ed.), *Handbook of critical social psychology* (pp. 533–556). Basingstoke, UK: Palgrave MacMillan.

Lyons, A. C., and Cromby, J. (2010). Social psychology and the empirical body: Rethinking the relationship. *Social and Personality Psychology Compass*, *4*(1): 1–13.

Lyons, A. C., Emslie, C., and Hunt, K. (2014). Staying 'in the zone' but not passing the 'point of no return': Embodiment, gender and drinking in mid-life. *Sociology of Health and Illness*, *36*(2): 264–277.

Lyons, A. C., Goodwin, I., McCreanor, T., and Griffin, C. (2015). Social networking and young adults' drinking practices: Innovative qualitative methods for health behaviour research. *Health Psychology*, *34*(4): 293–302.

Macapagal, M. E., Ofreneo, M. A., Montiel, C. J., and Nolasco. J. (2013). *Social psychology in a Philippine context.* Quezon City, Philippines: Ateneo de Manila University Press.

Macleod, C. (2012). Feminist health psychology and abortion: Towards a politics of transversal relations of commonality. In C. Horrocks and S. Johnson (Eds.), *Advances in health psychology* (pp. 153–168). Basingstoke, UK: Palgrave Macmillan.

Macleod, C., Chiweshe, M., and Mavuso, J. (2018). A critical review of sanctioned knowledge production concerning abortion in Africa: Implications for feminist health psychology. *Journal of Health Psychology*, *23*(8), 1096–1109.

Mahler, H. (1981). The meaning of Health For All by the year 2000. *World Health Forum*, *2*(1): 2–21.

Maiter, S., Simich, L., Jacobson, N., and Wise, J. (2008). Reciprocity: An ethic for community-based participatory action research. *Action Research*, *6*(3): 305–325.

Maller, C. J. (2015). Understanding health through social practices: Performance and materiality in everyday life. *Sociology of Health and Illness*, *37*(1): 52–66.

Marks, D. F. (2002). Freedom, responsibility and power: Contrasting approaches to health psychology. *Journal of Health Psychology*, *7*, 5–19.

Matarazzo, J. D. (1982). Behavioral health's challenge to academic, scientific, and professional psychology. *American Psychologist*, *37*(1), 1–14.

Mayan, M., and Daum, C. (2016). Beyond dissemination: Generating and applying qualitative evidence through community-based participatory research. In K. Olson, R. Young, and I. Schultz (Eds.), *Handbook of qualitative health research for evidence-based practice* (pp. 441–452). New York: Springer.

Mielewczyk, F., and Willig, C. (2007). Old clothes and an older look: The case for a radical makeover in health behaviour research. *Theory and Psychology*, *16*(6): 811–837.

Morgan, J., and Bambanani Women's Group. (2003). *Long life: Positive HIV stories*. Cape Town: Double Storey Books.

Morison, T., and Lynch, I. (2016). 'We can't help you here': The discursive erasure of sexual minorities in South African public sexual and reproductive health services. *Psychology of Sexualities Review*, *7*(2): 7–25.

Morison, T., Gibson, A. F., Wigginton, B., and Crabb, S. (2015). Online research methods in psychology: Methodological opportunities for critical qualitative research. *Qualitative Research in Psychology*, *12*(3): 223–232.

Murray, M. (2000). Reconstructing health psychology: An introduction. *Journal of Health Psychology*, *5*(3): 267–271.

Murray, M. (2012a). Social and health psychology in action. In D. Sheffield and M. Forshaw (Eds.), *Health psychology in action* (pp. 128–149). London: Wiley-Blackwell.

Murray, M. (2012b). Critical health psychology and the scholar-activist tradition. In C. Horrocks, and S. Johnson (Eds.), *Advances in health psychology: Critical approaches* (pp. 29–43). London: Palgrave.

Murray, M. (2014). Implementation: Putting analyses into practice. In U. Flick (Ed.), *The SAGE handbook of qualitative data analysis* (pp. 585–599). London: Sage.

Murray, M., and Chamberlain, K. (2014). Health psychology. In T. Teo (Ed.), *Encyclopaedia of critical psychology* (pp. 844–850). New York: Springer.

Murray, M., and Crummett, A. (2010). 'I don't think they knew we could do these sorts of things': Social representations of community and participation in community arts by older people. *Journal of Health Psychology*, *15*(5), 777–785.

Murray, M., and Poland, B. (2006). Health psychology and social action. *Journal of Health Psychology*, *11*(3): 379–384.

Nentwich, J. C., and Morison, T. (2017). Performing the self. In C. Travis and J. W. White (Eds.), *APA Handbook of the psychology of women* (pp. 209–228). Washington: American Psychological Association.

Parker, I. (2007). Critical psychology: What it is and what it is not. *Social and Personality Psychology Compass*, *1*(1): 1–15.

Peel, E., and Thomson, M. (2009). Lesbian, gay, bisexual, trans and queer health psychology: Historical development and future possibilities. *Feminism and Psychology*, *19*(4): 427–436.

Potter, J. (1996). *Representing reality: Discourse, rhetoric and social construction*. London: Sage.

Potter, J., and Wetherell, M. (1987). *Discourse and social psychology: Beyond attitudes and behaviour*. London: Sage.

Prilleltensky, I. (1997). Values, assumptions, and practices: Assessing the moral implications of psychological discourse and action. *American Psychologist*, *52*(5): 517–535.

Ratele, K. (Ed.) (2006) *Inter-group relations: South African perspectives*. Pretoria, South Africa: Juta and Company Ltd.

Rohleder, P., and Swartz, L. (2009). Providing sex education to persons with learning disabilities in the era of HIV/AIDS: Tensions between discourses of human rights and restriction. *Journal of Health Psychology*, *14*(4): 601–610.

Rolling, J. H. (2013). *Arts-based research*. New York: Peter Lang.

Rosenstock, I. M. (1974). The health belief model and preventive health behavior. *Health Education Monographs*, *2*(4): 354–386.

Rossiter, K., Kontos, P., Colantonio, A., Gilbert, J., Gray, J., and Keightley, M. (2008). Staging data: Theatre as a tool for analysis and knowledge transfer in health research. *Social Science & Medicine*, *66*(1): 130–146.

Routledge, P., and Derickson, K. (2015). Situated solidarities and the practice of scholar-activism. *Environment and Planning D: Society and Space*, *33*(3): 391–407.

Ryan, W. (1971). *Blaming the victim*. New York: Pantheon.

Sherwood, J. (2013). Colonisation – it's bad for your health: The context of Aboriginal health. *Contemporary Nurse*, *46*(1): 28–40.

Stam, H. J. (2006). Physician, heal thyself: The fate of the professional-cum-critic. *Journal of Health Psychology*, *11*(3): 385–389.

Suzuki, D., and Mayorga, E. (2014). Scholar-activism: A twice told tale. *Multicultural Perspectives*, *16*(1): 16–20.

Thomas, D. (n.d.). UC Riverside invokes #Mizzou during a march for free tuition. *Los Angeles Times*. Retrieved from http://www.latimes.com/local/education/la-me-edu-million-student-march-uc-riverside-mizzou-20151112-htmlstory.html

Thomas, E., and Mulvey, A. (2008). Using the arts in teaching and learning: Building student capacity for community-based work in health psychology. *Journal of Health Psychology*, *13*(2): 239–250.

Teo, T. (2015). Critical psychology: A geography of intellectual engagement and resistance. *American Psychologist*, *70*(3): 243–254.

Wetherell, M. (2012). *Affect and emotion: A new social science understanding*. London: Sage.

Wetherell, M. (2013). Affect and discourse – what's the problem? From affect as excess to affective/discursive practice. *Subjectivity*, *6*(4): 349–368.

Yen, J. (2016). Psychology and health after apartheid: Or, why there is no health psychology in South Africa. *History of Psychology*, *19*(2): 77–92.

Zavala, M. (2013). What do we mean by decolonizing research strategies? Lessons from decolonizing, Indigenous research projects in New Zealand and Latin America. *Decolonization: Indigeneity, Education and Society*, *2*(1): 55–71.

Zoldbrod, A. P. (2015). Sexual issues in treating trauma survivors. *Current Sexual Health Reports*, *7*(1): 3–11.

12

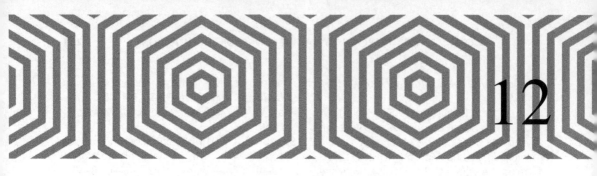

Community Based Mental Health in Cultural Contexts: From Deinstitutionalisation to Engaged and Authentic Community Based Care

Neil Drew and Michael Adams

Notwithstanding the divisiveness of the 'crisis' in social psychology and the enduring dominance of the experimental positivist approaches, applied social psychologists have a long tradition of making a difference at the coalface of community concerns (Hodgetts et al., 2010). Applied social psychologists bring a strong ethic of what is known variously as praxis or reflective practice, which grounds practice in strong evidence-based research (including the many interpretations of what constitutes evidence). Social psychological theories and methods offer a unique and diverse canon from which practitioners from many allied disciplines may draw succour in their everyday efforts to seek solutions to social and community concerns.

In this chapter, we will demonstrate that applying overly Eurocentric understandings of human beings and mental health concerns to Indigenous communities has proven problematic and necessitates disciplinary reflection and adaptation to ensure we respond to, and meet, the actual needs of local people. Similarly, the nexus between the dominant discourses of mental health (and ill-health) and Indigenous understandings and cultural constructions of health has been fraught and problematic, usually to the detriment of Indigenous peoples (Dudgeon et al., 2014). For example, Aboriginal and Torres Strait Islander people in Australia take their own lives at 1.6 times the national rate for non-Indigenous people (Australian Indigenous HealthInfoNet, 2016). In the far north of Western Australia, the rate is estimated at almost ten times the national rate (McHugh et al., 2016). A study by the Kimberley Mental Health and Drug Service audited suicides in the Kimberley region from 2005–2014 and found that the Indigenous suicides rate was 74 per 100,000, which they believe is almost certainly an underestimation (McHugh et al., 2016). On the available evidence, conventional interventions and programmes to address the issue have proven hopelessly inadequate (Silburn et al., 2014).

This is not to say that there are no theories or concepts that can guide collaborative efforts to address community mental health concerns in Indigenous settings. The applied social psychological theories we invoke in this chapter include critical scholarship on whiteness and identity, as well as notions of social justice, cultural safety, responsiveness, and competence. We will demonstrate how, when these interpretive lenses are brought into authentic conversation with one another in a safe and collaborative intercultural space, there is an opportunity for a deeper appreciation of the mutual benefit of knowledge exchange in cultural contexts. This approach offers the best chance for meaningful, strength-based work that addresses pressing community mental health concerns.

Many contemporary applied social psychologists realise the need to pragmatically embrace both interdisciplinarity in their everyday work and inter sub-disciplinarity (Hodgetts et al., 2010). In the history of social psychology, the so-called crisis is a well-worn path and, while the debates have raged for decades, often to the detriment of the development of the discipline, there was much good that emerged to transform and reenergise social psychology. These days, some authors have advocated a rapprochement of sorts (Hodgetts et al., 2010), a far more ecumenical approach to social psychology that suggests that there are lessons to be learned across ontological and epistemological borders. Social psychology has grown into a mature and exceedingly productive area of enquiry and action that seeks to understand the mutuality between people and their social world (cf. Cartwright, 1979; Jost and Kruglanski, 2002). It is important to seek an appreciation of the insights from our own and aligned social sciences in addressing complex societal issues such as mental health in Indigenous community settings.

This chapter reflects and draws on the lived experiences of Neil Drew, a non-Indigenous applied social psychologist, and Uncle Mick Adams, an Australian Aboriginal Elder, social work scholar and leading academic researcher. We will examine the contribution that applied social psychology has made to the interdisciplinary enterprise of community mental health in in Australian Indigenous settings. In doing so, we will describe the emergence of the natural helper in community based mental health as the apotheosis of community mental health care. The community mental health workforce is generally under resourced, overburdened and, on that account, at risk of burnout and high turnover. Natural helpers, also referred to as lay health workers and lay educators (Simoni et al., 2011), have been found to be a cost effective, productive and empowering resource in a diverse range of settings throughout the world, but particularly in developing countries (Auger and Verbiest, 2007; van Ginnekin et al., 2013). The natural helper movement recognises the inherent strength and resilience of indigenous communities and their capacity to manage their own mental health as authentic health practitioners not merely the subjects of mental health interventions (Auger and Verbiest, 2007; Patel et al., 2011; Pincock, 2007). Lay health workers are a crucial, but vastly underutilised and often taken-for-granted, resource.

This chapter also foregrounds the importance of social psychologists working with approaches to care that resonate culturally with Indigenous communities. The lay helper approach to community mental health has particular resonance for Aboriginal and Torres Strait Islander peoples in Australia (Drew, 2014; Owen, 2006). As such, we will draw on our academic work and applied research with Aboriginal and Torres Strait Islander people to illustrate ways of working with natural helpers to foster genuine grass roots engagement with the people who possess the cultural knowledge required to make culturally safe and appropriate choices and action. In doing so, we also demonstrate ways of working with Aboriginal and Torres Strait Islander people and communities that have led to the honour of being embraced as natural helpers ourselves.

TAKING A CASE-BASED APPROACH TO COMMUNITY MENTAL HEALTH

We offer a case-based exploration of the experiences of the two authors. In doing so, we demonstrate the utility of case-based approaches for elucidating the nuances and complexities of working in a cultural setting on community mental health concerns. We have adopted a case orientation as this reflects the importance of applied social psychologists immersing themselves in what Gergen (1988: 10) called the 'hurly-burly' of everyday life. We also use the case-based orientation to foreground the importance of meaningful relationships between scholars and local residents in trying to address social issues, such as community mental health. The quality of these relationships fosters a climate of authentic knowledge co-design and co-production that is crucial to socially transformative practice. Case-based research offers promise of reinvesting applied social psychology with the truly social.

Our two case studies are brought into conversation with one another to examine the way that a non-Indigenous researcher and an Indigenous researcher engage in case-based research, negotiating the complexities of *everyday* practice. Of particular interest to applied social psychologists should be the realisation that the case-based approach applies not only to the co-production of knowledge in relation to the phenomenon of interest but also to the co-production (co-construction) of the scholar/practitioner. These two cases present a tapestry of intricately woven elements that are not prescriptive but rather are illustrative of the *kinds* of issues that confront applied social psychologists working in community mental health settings. Both represent an orientation towards principled practice, which we discuss in detail below, that finds form in the unfolding relationships that characterise community life. Underlying both cases is an understanding that the way we approach our work allows us to discover who we are, where we are from, and where we may go with the local community. It is important to note that, while we have similar lived experiences, we have not worked together or studied the same discipline, therefore the chapter is unique as it includes different understandings, perspectives and worldviews.

The first case focuses on Neil Drew, a fourth generation non-Indigenous Australian with cultural roots in the MacLeod clan from the Isle of Skye on my father's side and the Mossops and Frys on my mother's side. I grew up in Papua New Guinea during the transition of those countries to independence from Australia in the 1960s and 1970s. Returning to Australia as a teenager in the mid 1970s, I became acutely aware of the general antipathy many non-Indigenous Australians displayed towards the first peoples of Australia. I entered into university as a provisional applicant where I completed an undergraduate degree in social psychology. It was during this time that I undertook a volunteer role in an Aboriginal and Torres Strait Islander health service. In the intervening 30 years, I have had the great privilege to be mentored and supported through a range of activities with Aboriginal and Torres Strait Islander communities throughout Australia. It is these experiences that culminated in the development of the tripartite framework for trust building and engagement that is described in this chapter.

The second case focuses on Uncle Mick Adams, a descendent of the Yadhiagana/Wuthathi people of Cape York Peninsula in Queensland on his father's side and the Gurindji people of Central Western Northern Territory on his mother's side. I grew up in a place called Parap Camp in a suburb in Darwin in Australia's Northern Territory. The Parap Camp was intended to be a temporary housing solution for a maximum of eight years. As a young boy, I did not see the value in schooling and have referred to myself as a 'high school dropout by way of choice' (Adams, 2016). Later in life, I enrolled in the Aboriginal Task Force at the South

Australian Institute of Technology and subsequently gained two undergraduate degrees, a Master's degree and a PhD. I have spent most of my working life living and learning in Aboriginal and Torres Strait Islander communities throughout Australia.

THE CONTEXT FOR COMMUNITY MENTAL HEALTH CARE: THE EMERGENCE OF THE NATURAL HELPER

The institutional confinement of people for reasons such as mental illness has been practiced for centuries within Europe and its colonies. 'Madhouses' and asylums were utilised not so much for rehabilitation but rather to remove the afflicted people from the public gaze. In ancient Greece and Rome, asylums were places where people could seek refuge and sanctuary (Yohanna, 2013). Still others saw 'modern' institutionalisation as a mechanism for social control (Mac Suibhne, 2011). The movement towards the deinstitutionalisation of patients with a mental illness can be traced to the 1960s and the seminal publication of the work of Canadian sociologist Erving Goffman. His 1961 undercover work *Asylums: Essays on the social situation of mental patients and other inmates* shone a very bright light on the institutional practices and experiences of inmates (Mac Suibhne, 2011). The impetus for deinstitutionalisation was firmly planted in the zeitgeist of civil rights in the 1960s and 1970s; the idea that institutionalising people with mental illnesses was inhumane. There was also hope that emerging medications could cure and, of course, save money by reducing the need for institutionalisation (Accordina et al., 2001; Yohanna, 2013).

Many benefits were anticipated from the processes of deintitutionalisation and some were realised. With appropriate levels of support, people with mental health issues experienced the positive benefits of improved access to services, positive adaptation to community and improved family contact (Drake, 2014). Nevertheless concerns about the processes of deinstitutionalisation emerged very soon after the project commenced. The process of deinsititutionalisation began in haste with inadequate thought and based on a number of unfounded assumptions, such as that people would have a place to live, that they would have family support systems in place and that community services were adequately resourced to support them (Accordina et al., 2001). Community attitudes towards community housing for people with serious mental health concerns were often negative, resulting in the closure of, or failure to establish, housing (Wilmoth et al., 1987).

Three key elements of deinstitutionalisation have been identified; a shift away from dependence on mental hospitals, an increase in the number of transinstitutional beds in hospitals and the development of community based mental health services (Sealy and Whitehead, 2004: 250). They noted, however, that while the release of patients from mental hospitals was quick, the development of transinstitutional arrangements and the resourcing of community mental health services was slow (Sealy and Whitehead, 2004). As early as the 1980s, it was stridently noted that the 'massive, unplanned discharges without adequate follow up has led to large numbers of uncoordinated nursing home placements, where people live in unhealthy, dangerous conditions' (Brown, 1980: 315). So, people with mental health concerns are disproportionately represented in suboptimal housing conditions, including homelessness and boarding houses (Drake, 2014). According to Drake (2014), the processes of transinstitutionalisation simply shifted people from traditional institutions to community based accommodation that nevertheless had many of the negative attributes of the institutions from which they had transitioned, such as 'congregate care, regimentation and material deprivation' (Drake, 2014: 243).

Getting people out of institutional care required large scale investment in community based services. This cycling of resources was, on the whole, not forthcoming. In a report to the World Health Organzation, Thornicroft and Tansella (2003) noted that the evidence shows quite conclusively that community based care cost about the same as hospital-based care and that the quality of service is closely related, not surprisingly, to expenditure. Thornicroft and Tansella (2003) offer nine principles for balanced community based mental health services, autonomy, continuity, effectiveness, accessibility, comprehensiveness, equity, accountability, coordination and efficiency.

Mobilisation of the natural helper network is a 'natural', and much needed, extension of community based mental health services. This is particularly true in rural, regional and remote areas where retention of the mental health workforce is an ongoing concern (Cosgrave et al., 2015). Authentic support and training for this defacto health workforce has delivered myriad dividends and adds further balance to the model of balanced care. International evidence attests to the importance of the natural helper, also known variously as lay health workers or lay health educators (van Ginnekin et al., 2013). These are people who are 'naturally' turned to for help in times of crisis. They have always been there, and will always be there, yet are unrecognised, under resourced and overburdened. They are often the ordinary, unremarked members of the community who provide a vital essential service for their communities. Definitions of natural helpers (lay educators, lay health workers) vary widely, with some paid but most unpaid (Auger and Verbiest, 2007)

The natural helper concept resonates in many cultural contexts because it mobilises community members who have the trust and confidence of their community and know the language and customs of the people (Auger and Verbiest, 2007). These are trusted members of community who can bridge the gap between community members and the mental health services they require. This is particularly relevant in the Aboriginal and Torres Strait Islander communities where levels of trust and confidence in services provided by representatives of the dominant culture are low. The reason for low levels of trust and confidence are shared with many Indigenous groups around the world that have been subjected to colonialist oppression since the period of settlement. There is also wide recognition among indigenous scholars that colonisation has had profound effects on the wellbeing of colonised peoples (Sherwood, 2014).

In the following section, we provide a snapshot of the health of Australian Aboriginal and Torres Strait Islander people as further evidence of the need for culturally appropriate methods for engagement and collaboration to address the health concerns that are, by any yardstick, a national disgrace.

THE CONTEXT FOR COMMUNITY BASED MENTAL HEALTH CARE: ABORIGINAL AND TORRES STRAIT ISLANDER HEALTH

The health outcomes for the Aboriginal and Torres Strait Islander peoples of Australia are, like many indigenous people from around the world, significantly worse than the health of settler peoples (Australian Indigenous HealthInfoNet, 2016). The health of Aboriginal and Torres Strait Islander peoples is affected by a range of factors, including the conditions in which many indigenous peoples live and the social determinants of health such as education and employment. As a direct consequence of colonisation, indigenous peoples have suffered the loss of language, land and access to natural resources (Adams, 2014). Indigenous peoples also face racism, discrimination and marginalisation within settler society. Collectively, these have become known as the cultural determinates of health. Paradies (2016) provided a scathing summary of colonial practices that have impacted on indigenous peoples including, 'war, displacement, forced labour, removal of children, relocation, ecological destruction, massacres, genocide, slavery, (un) intentional spread of deadly diseases, banning of indigenous languages, regulation of marriage, assimilation and eradication of social cultural and spiritual practices'. Experiences of the enduring impact of colonisation have culminated in transgenerational trauma or historical trauma (Kirmeyer et al., 2014). The 4Cs of historical trauma include *colonial injury* as a result of the behaviour of colonial powers; *collective impacts* to represent the impact not just for individuals but also across the entire community; *cumulative effects* that, in essence, 'build up' over time and; *cross generational* impacts that resonate across generations (Kirmeyer et al., 2014; Paradies, 2016).

While the self-evident truth of health inequalities is inescapable, discursive portrayals in the public domain exacerbate negative expectations. For example, media portrayals of the health of Aboriginal and Torres Strait Islander peoples are overwhelmingly negative, with a recent study indicating that over 70% of stories were negative compared with 15% positive (Stoneham, 2014). These representations predominantly ignore the historical and colonial causes of mental distress in indigenous communities, focusing instead on individual behaviour patterns and, in doing so, legitimising intrusive policies and practices that do not serve Aboriginal and Torres Strait Islander people. The deeply racist and deficit-focused narrative has a long tradition in psychology. For example, Sigmund Freud made a psychological comparison between Australian Aboriginal people and his neurotic patients. His comments exemplify the attitudes of the colonists. In his book *Totem and Taboo* (1950) he observed that there was merit in drawing comparisons between the psychology of 'primitive people' and the psychology of neurotics. He wrote '… I shall select as the basis of this comparison the tribes that have been described by anthropologists as the most backward and miserable of savages, the Aborigines of Australia, the youngest continent' (Freud, 1950: 2). He goes on to write:

> …they do not build houses or permanent shelters; they do not cultivate the soil; they keep no domesticated animals except the dog; they are not even acquainted with the art of making pottery… chiefs and kings are unknown among them; communal affairs are decided by a council of elders. It is highly doubtful whether any religion, in the shape of a worship of higher beings, can be attributed to them. (Freud, 1950: 2)

These deficit narratives that are reproduced through public discourse today work to decontextualise and homogenise the experiences of Aboriginal and Torres Strait Islander people in ways that would not be tolerated if applied to members of the settler society.

It is now widely acknowledged that there is a need to shift from 'deficit' thinking to more strengths-based approaches. Many authoritative institutions and organisations have made public commitments to promote strengths-based approaches in the public discourse on Aboriginal and Torres Strait Islander issues. The shift to a strengths-based narrative serves to recognise and honor the resilience and persistence of Aboriginal and Torres Strait Islander people's culture and to recalibrate the narrative away from stereotypical, homogenising and racist views; it actively works to shift from a discourse of despair to a discourse of resilience, persistence and hope. At the same time, it offers hope of productive work in the intercultural space shared by Aboriginal and Torres Strait peoples and their non-Indigenous counterparts (Nakata, 2013). This dialogue has the capacity to forge pathways forward that are unobscured by the weight of negative expectations and self-fulfilling prophesy (Houston, 2016).

As noted above, in relation to Aboriginal and Torres Strait Islander health, there is increased recognition of the importance of a number of culturally determined 'health protecting factors', including connection to land, culture, spirituality and ancestry; kinship and; self-determination, community governance and cultural continuity (Dudgeon et al., 2014). Strengths-based approaches embrace and endorse strategies, programmes and policies that embody these health protective factors as part of a decolonising agenda (Dudgeon et al., 2014).

In Australia, the peak body representing psychologists has recognised that they have been complicit in both the production and the perpetuation of deficit narratives. In September 2016, the Australian Psychological Society issued a formal apology to Aboriginal and Torres Strait Islander people. This peak body representing psychologists felt that the apology was a necessary and long overdue statement that will be an important part of healing relations between mainstream psychology and Aboriginal and Torres Strait Islander peoples. The entire apology may be read on the Australian Psychological Society webpage (https://www.psychology.org.au/).

Such apologies from professional groups are important, but also must be followed by concerted effort to address the alarming trends in Aboriginal and Torres Straight Island mental health. In 2012–13, 69% of Aboriginal and Torres Strait Islander adults experienced at least one significant stressor in the previous 12 months and were 2.7 times as likely as non-Indigenous people to feel high, or very high, levels of psychological distress. One particularly alarming figure indicates that, in 2012–13, the hospitalisation rate for assault was 34 times higher for Indigenous women than for other women. In 2013, the death rate for International Classification of Diseases (ICD) 'Intentional self-harm' (suicide) for Aboriginal and Torres Strait Islander people was 2.2 times the rate reported for non-Indigenous people. Between 2001 and 2010, the age adjusted suicide rate was 21.4 per 100,000 for Aboriginal and Torres Strait Islander people and 10.3 per 100,000 for non-Indigenous people. Alarmingly, the suicide rate for the far north of Western Australia, where Drew's case study was undertaken, is many times higher at 74 per 100,000 (McHugh et al., 2016).

Addressing the health disparities that are reflected in these statistical trends is the key focus for our work, as outlined below. We focus first on what a non-indigenous psychologist can do and then what is being done by an Indigenous scholar and Elder.

POSITIONING MYSELF (NEIL) AS A NON-INDIGENOUS PRACTITIONER IN ABORIGINAL AND TORRES STRAIT ISLANDER COMMUNITIES

Oombulgurri, the former Forrest River Mission and the site for this case study that commenced in 2005, was a remote Aboriginal community that was located on the traditional meeting grounds of the Dadaway and comprised mainly of members of the Stolen Generations. It was an hour and a half by boat, 15 minutes by light aircraft and 18 hours by four wheel drive from the far northern town of Wyndham. Oombulgurri is also near the site of the Forrest River massacres that occurred in 1926. By some estimates, over 50 Aboriginal women and children were killed and their bodies burned in retaliation for the death of a pastoralist killed by an Aboriginal man defending his wife. The bones of those killed were recovered, blessed in the Forrest River Mission Church and interred on the escarpment overlooking the community. A cairn and a large steel cross mark the spot. Two officers were charged for the massacre, but they were dismissed for lack of evidence.

The population of Oombulgurri varied from as many as 300 to as few as 25 depending on the time of year and other family, social and cultural circumstances and obligations.

In late 2008, Oombulgurri was declared a 'dry' (alcohol-free) community, an outcome of the coroner's report into over 20 deaths of young people by suicide across the Kimberley, with several of the suicides of young people taking place in Oombulgurri. Before that time, alcohol was freely available in the community and there were regular alcohol-fuelled violent incidents and allegations of child sexual abuse. In 2011, Oombulgurri was closed as unviable and the residents relocated to Wyndham. One elderly woman was 'relocated' to the tidal swamp outside Wyndham due to severe housing shortages that were not planned for. She lived in a tent and fresh water and food were delivered to her each day. She said to Drew, 'Neil, I was stolen once before and taken to the Forest River mission… now I feel as though I have been stolen again'.

Community leaders wanted to develop their capability to support their people in need but felt that they lacked the knowledge and skills. They also needed to help themselves. As one leader said, thumping his clenched fist against his chest, 'How can I help my community when my own heart is full of pain? We need to develop confidence. We need someone to walk alongside us as we develop confidence using the skills we develop in workshops. One-off workshops are great but there is no follow up'. The core purpose of our work was not to create more services. The core purpose of the programme was to mobilise and support this natural helper network.

Over the next several years, the programme developed as a process of 'living and learning together'. We were not asked to 'do' anything other than to engage in long-term relationship development and trust building; then 'whatever happens will be better than it would otherwise be'. I lived for two months of each year in the community, working on projects determined and guided by the community.

As a non-Indigenous person, it was crucially important that I 'position' myself in relation to the work I was undertaking with the natural helper network in Oombulgurri. To do this, I was primarily guided by the Aboriginal leaders in the community. The key challenge was to integrate my background and training in applied social psychology with the wisdom and knowledge of the Aboriginal and Torres Strait Islander people I was working with. As I listened and learned, it became apparent that there were a number of theories and approaches to applied social psychology that spoke directly to the experiences, aspirations and expectations of the community regarding how I (we) should engage and work. The many conversations, activities, experiences over the several years that the programme has been in existence fostered and encouraged 'living and learning together' that led to the co-construction and co-design of the tripartite framework for trust building. The framework guides my engagement with, and understandings of, the experiences of Aboriginal and Torres Strait Islander people. The key to appreciating the tripartite framework is the realisation that it is indeed a co-construction, not a retro fit or imposition of Western knowledges, to co-opt Aboriginal and Torres Strait islander ways of knowing. The articulation of the framework in presentations, publications and training has always been done with the explicit approval, support and encouragement of those who jointly 'own' the intellectual property of the framework. As part of the Wundargoodie Youth and Community Wellbeing Programme, the tripartite framework for principled practice achieved its clearest articulation. Also, and importantly, the tripartite framework provides some clear and achievable mechanisms for enacting decolonising practice (Dudgeon and Walker, 2015).

Social and cultural psychology has made a material and positive contribution to understanding Aboriginal and Torres Strait Islander health, particularly through the lens of whiteness. This, coupled with an understanding of Aboriginal and Torres Strait Islander Terms of Reference, provides a dual lens through which practice at the coalface of mental health concerns may be interrogated as part of a commitment to reflective and decolonising practice (Adams et al., 2014; Drew 2014; 2015; Morgan and Drew, 2010). As non-Indigenous practitioners, we must not only acknowledge but also accept that our 'whiteness' is inextricably bound to the enduring impacts of colonisation, racism and discrimination that characterises many Aboriginal and Torres Strait Islander people's experience of the health system with which they interact (or, more likely, do not interact) (Ali and Sonn, 2009; Green et al., 2007). This enables us to position ourselves in ways that not only empower the community members we work with but also to engage in an ongoing project of depowering ourselves as part of our commitment to decolonising practice (Drew, 2015). Adopting Aboriginal and Torres Strait Islander Terms of Reference requires that we accept the sovereignty of Aboriginal and Torres Strait Islander people as the regional stewards of Australia and that we embrace, respect and acknowledge the centrality of culture, country and knowledges to their lived experience in all areas of individual and community life (Oxenham, 2000).

The model of principled practice is an explicit acknowledgement of the power differentials that exist between Aboriginal and Torres Strait Islander peoples and non-Indigenous researchers that predominantly represent the colonialist discourses and practices that have dominated approaches to community mental health. There are three 'legs' to the framework that guide my practice in Aboriginal and Torres Strait Islander communities. They are: moral exclusion, moral complexity and procedural fairness. A commitment to principled practice means we must (re)position ourselves as on ongoing process of identity and meaning making as we come to understand ourselves in relation to our work and engagement in cultural contexts.

The first leg of the tripartite framework is moral exclusion. Many people and groups feel that they are not afforded fair treatment by those with whom they interact. In many instances, they feel that not only are they not afforded fair treatment, they believe that the other party does not want to afford them fair treatment. To be positioned this way in relation to others is to be morally excluded, or outside the scope of justice (Opotow, 1990; 2008).

That moral exclusion exists is contrary to many people's belief that a concern for justice is ubiquitous. Yet, there are myriad instances where clearly this is not supported. Moral philosophers have argued that the boundaries for the scope of justice are not clear cut. Some argue that all sentient beings should be included within the scope of justice while others argue for a much broader and expansive moral envelope to include other life forms. The social psychological literature on the whole assumes moral inclusion (Opotow, 1990)

Excluding people from the scope of justice involves a process known as de-legitimisation (Bandura, 1990). As we saw above in relation to Aboriginal and Torres Strait Islander health, the media, in particular, is implicated in framing stories that serve to de-legitimise the experiences of Aboriginal and Torres Strait Islander peoples in ways that position them outside the scope of justice in mainstream society and enable politicians to prosecute policy positions that would otherwise be extremely difficult to justify (Stoneham, 2014).

Such processes of symbolic power and exclusion have material implications in terms of how social issues are faced by communities, including Oombulgurri, that require reasoned responses by applied social psychologists to promote morally inclusive, socially transformative counter narratives that deal with the moral complexities at play (Hodgetts et al., 2010).

The second leg is moral complexity. Moral complexity provides the counterpoint to moral enormity (Fellman, 2009). For many people, the treatment of Aboriginal and Torres Strait Islander people since colonisation is a morally enormous event in which the colonists are implicated in systematic practices that many consider genocidal. Morally enormous events promote moral clarity through the creation of binary opposites of 'good' and 'bad', moral and immoral (Fellman, 2009). Moral complexity, on the other hand, suggests that it is more complex. Good and bad reside within and amongst us in ways that are too nuanced and 'complex' to allow the creation of binaries. While we may expect Aboriginal and Torres Strait Islander people to prefer moral enormity, given the history of genocidal practices since invasion and continued symbolic violence perpetrated by governmental, media and public discourses, for many, moral complexity speaks more directly to their lived experiences. As applied social psychologists, we must grapple with moral complexities and associated issues of equity and justice. Complex (or so-called wicked) problems require complex solutions (Drew, 2014). To prefer moral enormity relieves us of our obligation to engage fully in complex spaces and provides tacit support for the conclusion that morally complex people and situations are effectively beyond redemption. Our pursuit of the unambiguous stance of moral enormity and a failure to grapple with moral complexity can be stultifying and disabling in very real and everyday ways.

The final element of the tripartite framework is procedural fairness. The social psychology of justice for much of its history in the discipline was concerned primarily with distributive fairness; the fairness of resource distributions (Lind and Tyler, 1992; Lind and Tyler, 1988). It wasn't until the mid 1970s that there was a burgeoning interest in procedural fairness; the fairness of the ways in which distributions are made. There are some key concepts that have informed applied social psychological practice in cultural contexts. The first is the crucial distinction between decision control and process control, most clearly articulated in the seminal work of Thibaut and Walker (1975). When there is a measure of control over the decision making it is referred to as decision control. Process control, on the other hand, refers to control over the processes by which decision are made (Thibaut and Walker, 1975). This elegant observation has shaped much of the subsequent research on procedural fairness. While it is ubiquitously evident, issues of procedural fairness and justice mean different things to different people in different circumstances (Törnblom, 1992). This underscores the importance of context in applied social psychology.

A number of rules or criteria for procedural fairness have been identified, from the instrumental – such as knowledge of the procedures – to more values based propositions – such as respect and dignity (Lind and Tyler, 1988; Tyler & Lind, 1992). Most people can, and do, identify not only when the criteria for procedural fairness have been violated but also which of the rules has been broken (Hodgetts et al., 2010). In practical terms for an applied social psychologist, procedural justice effects are essentially quite simple. If we perceive that we have been treated in a procedurally fair way then we are more likely to be happy with, and accept, the outcomes and be satisfied with the treatment we have received. Experiences of perceived procedural unfairness lead to anger, resentment and resistance.

Another central insight is that people learn about their standing or status in the group based on their perceptions of procedural justice. So, not only do people make judgements about how procedures lead to outcomes, they also, at a deeper level, come to understand where they sit in the so-called 'pecking order' impacting sense of identity and sense of belonging (Tyler and Lind, 1992). More recent work has extended this to an elaboration of the individual and organisational elements of procedural fairness (Blader and Tyler, 2003). This is particularly important for applied social psychologists working in this space. The model argues that people make judgements about the quality of decisions and the quality of the treatment they receive at both the organisation level and at the level of the individual representing the organisation.

Finally, and perhaps most importantly with respect to work at the cultural interface, is that perceptions of procedural fairness have a direct impact on levels of trust and confidence (Lind and Tyler, 1988). Violations of procedural fairness diminish trust and confidence, while perceptions that procedures are fair enhance trust and confidence. Aboriginal people have been denied (or perceive themselves to have been denied) procedural fairness for most of the period of colonisation. Policies, practices and processes have systematically denied them voice. For every criteria for procedural fairness, there are instances of the failure of governments, organisations and individuals to afford procedural fairness. It is little wonder that Aboriginal and Torres Strait Islander people feel disenfranchised, alienated and mistrustful of non-Indigenous regimes (see, for example, Altman and Hinkson, 2007). It is little wonder too that identity – or, more precisely, lack of identity – is implicated in suicide and self-harm (Silburn et al., 2014).

The tripartite framework is an example of knowledge brokerage and co-production. While it is couched for academic purposes in stylised academic language here, the framework emerged after several years of 'living and learning together' with Aboriginal people. While most community members with whom we have worked do not speak about their experiences in this way, their experiences of being morally excluded, in morally complex contexts while being subject to procedurally unfair practices are undeniable. Importantly, the framework provides an interpretive lens through which pathways for action and social transformation may be examined in ways responsive to historical and contemporary intergroup relations between our Indigenous and settler communities.

In summary, the first case highlights ways in which an applied social psychologist was able to bring his disciplinary training into an authentic conversation with the Aboriginal people of Oombulgurri to co-construct a way of working and engaging with the natural helper networks to prevent Aboriginal youth suicide. The development of the tripartite framework as a shared framework for understanding exemplifies the ways in which principled engagement in the intercultural space can yield important positive outcomes for the community and the social psychologist. The second case examines the lived experience of a senior Aboriginal scholar, living and working in a wide range of communities.

ENGAGING AUSTRALIAN ABORIGINAL AND TORRES STRAIT ISLANDER PEOPLE: AN INSIDER'S PERSPECTIVE

I (Uncle Mick), in my work throughout Australia, draw on my lived experience as an Aboriginal and Torres Start Islander man to render my commitment to socially transformative practice self-evident. I consider myself a natural helper in Australian Aboriginal and Torres Strait Islander communities. My approach to working with community is deeply rooted in an understanding of the issues and concerns of the everyday lives of Aboriginal and Torres Strait Islander people that I myself have lived. In this section, I discuss my research as the cased-based exemplar for understanding the importance of cultural ways of working (Adams, 2015a). In undertaking my PhD and conducting other research studies, I use my cultural understandings to get men talking about the very sensitive topics of sexual and reproductive issues, mental health and suicide in ways that many other academic researchers have failed to achieve.

I work to engage other Indigenous Australian's from a cultural insider's perspective. Of particular relevance here is the concept of an appreciation of the Australian Aboriginal history (Adams, 2014; Tatz, 2001) as well as an interpretation of the Aboriginal Life Set. This orientation enables us to look out beyond the landing of James Cook and look at how Aboriginal people structured themselves as hunters and gathers (Adams, 2015b).

Archaeological evidence demonstrates that Aboriginal people have been present in Australia for at least 50,000 years. Australian Aboriginal and Torres Strait Islander people had a complex society with high levels of self-determination over all life aspects, including ceremony, spiritual practices, medicine, birthing, child rearing, relationships, management of land and systems and law. People had a healthy diet of protein and plants that contained adequate mineral and vitamins and ate very little fat, sugar and salt (Flood, 2006; Fredericks et al., 2012). As the sovereign people, Aboriginal and Torres Strait Islander people were able to determine, monitor and evaluate individual, family and community health and wellbeing. Most of the treatment provided to Aboriginal and Torres Strait Islander people was provided by traditional spiritual healers, self-care and through traditional remedies (Couzos and Murray, 2008; Fredericks et al., 2012).

Aboriginal peoples embrace all phenomena and life as part of a vast and complex system-reticulum of relationships which can be traced directly back to the ancestral Totemic Spirit Beings of The Dreaming. The Dreaming establishes the structures of society, rules for social behaviour and the ceremonies performed to ensure continuity of life and land. The Dreaming governs the laws of community, cultural lore and how people are required to behave in their communities (Adams, 2015b).

Traditionally, the Aboriginal family was a collaboration of clans composed of mothers, fathers, uncles, aunties, brothers, sisters, cousins and so on. This size of family was the norm but is recognised in today's terms as an 'extended family'. Life prior to colonisation was straightforward and love was abundant. The ways were easy but intelligent, slower but knowledgeable and simple. It was a way of life that survived for hundreds of thousands of years, undisturbed and untouched (Adams, 2002; Adams and Danks, 2005; Adams and McCoy, 2011; Fejo-King, 2013; Walker, 1993). The roles of family members were set according to individual positions in the tribe, and families would live together in a communal environment with responsibilities being shared throughout the family. These included child rearing, cooking, hunting and the teaching of knowledge by tribal elders. Failure to carry out his or her responsibilities meant that the rest of the family suffered. The men were the hunters, usually tracking down larger animals like kangaroo or emu, while women supplied the family with berries, nuts and roots (Adams and McCoy, 2011; Fejo-King, 2013, Sam, 1992).

It is very important to understand the purpose of the kinship system, which basically enabled Aboriginal people to work out exactly where they stood in relation to each other within the tribal system. The kinship system provided a mental map of social relationship and behaviour, particularly how you would greet, address and act towards other members within the tribe. The kinship system controlled potential conflict situations, ensured that obligations were fulfilled and maintained security within the group structure (Adams, 2002; 2014; Adams and McCoy, 2011; Fejo-King, 2013).

As a researcher, I incorporate both etic (outsider) and emic (insider) roles throughout the consultation and research process. This is because the configuration of Aboriginal and Torres Strait Islander communication patterns and methodologies is entwined through Aboriginal and Torres Strait Islander terms of reference that incorporate an Indigenous worldview. The Aboriginal and Torres Strait Islander terms of reference are applied to capture the voices, emotions and actions and real understanding of the respondents' view of their world and the experiences that have shaped their world. This methodology enables the stakeholders to openly discuss their concerns and to develop knowledge that has the potential to assist them to proactively control their lives (Adams, 2001; Fejo-King, 2013).

The Aboriginal and Torres Strait Islander's ways of conducting relationships and working create and promote richer understandings of Aboriginal and Torres Strait Islander cultures and concerns. It is also important to engage in ways that respond to Aboriginal clan histories, cultural diversities and expectations, past and present, and how current social and political issues impact on the lives of Indigenous Australians (Adams, 2015a).

Accordingly, applied social psychologists theories and practices are based on the principles of non-Indigenous principles and ideas. Correspondingly, applied social psychologists do not understand, recognise or reference Aboriginal and Torres Strait Islander ways of knowing, being and doing within their scope of practice (Adams 2015a). To understand the health and wellbeing of Aboriginal and Torres Strait Islander peoples requires us to accept and understand the historical, cultural, physiological, psychosocial, economic, environmental and political context (Adams, 2015a). For example, the Australian Association of Social Workers observed that if social workers in Australia are to uphold the profession's core values of respect for Aboriginal and Torres Strait Islander peoples and people from other cultures' social justice and professional integrity, it is essential that culturally responsive practice becomes integrated into their continuing professional development throughout their careers (Australian Association of Social Workers, 2016). This means that the Eurocentric worldview that still dominates applied social psychologists needs to be brought into conversation with and revised to better respond to the needs of Aboriginal and Torres Straight Island peoples and how we understand causality and control, express and communicate emotional distress, think about and feel about others, as well as our very different life circumstances.

I have observed that universal dimensions of behaviour and empirically derived classifications are imposed by Eurocentric psychologists on other cultures without any real understanding that these categories may not be applicable to this group. For example, the label of abnormality is often erroneously applied to a range of behaviours that the settler society may find objectionable but these same behaviours are often quite acceptable within Aboriginal and Torres Strait Islander contexts as part of our 'normal' lifestyles. That is to say, when an Aboriginal and Torres Strait Islander person says that non-human beings were related to them and that they have to talk and respect these entities as they would other members of their own family, that would be accepted in Aboriginal and Torres Strait Islander society but would be seen as abnormal or a bit looney in the settler society.

As another example, an old man was talking to a medical practitioner, telling him how he went bush every week to talk to his father. The practitioner showed semi interest in the old man, just to make conversation, without taking any real notice of what the old man was trying to tell him. Later, the old man eventually came around to tell the practitioner that his father had been dead for ten years and that a tree now took the place of his father. The practitioner immediately sat up straight; got the pen and paper out; started to take full interest in what the old man was saying; and started to make in-depth conversation with the old man. Moreover, the practitioner was showing more interest, not so much in the story but in the old man's abnormality.

The examples above speak to how the composition of Aboriginal and Torres Strait Islander communication patterns and wellness are entwined within Aboriginal terms of reference that incorporate Indigenous worldviews. Correspondingly, many non-Aboriginal academics describe Aboriginal experiences and relationships from 'outside' perspectives and, in doing so, often jump to invalid conclusions. They often draw inaccurate conclusions about issues they cannot always fully understand. This is partly because the Indigenous knowledge frameworks are often much broader and more robust than the more atomised or de-compartmentalised psychological frameworks.

When I set out to undertake my PhD ground breaking research study on male sexual and reproductive health, I was very aware that it was difficult enough to get non-Indigenous men to talk about such a sensitive issue and repeatedly advised that it would be impossible to engage Aboriginal and Torres Strait Islander males in such conversations. Dominating my conversations with other academics were assumptions about men based on non-Indigenous men that lead to the underestimation of the capability and knowledge of Aboriginal and Torres Strait Islander men and what we are willing to talk about. Although 'officially' the student in the university context, I was the expert in the communicating context and knew that other indigenous men would talk to me about these issues. In order to ensure my Supervisor understood the Aboriginal and Torres Strait Islander ways of working and engaging, I took him on a field trip with me to a remote island community to talk about and promote the interest of my research study. When we arrived, he could not believe, or truly understand why, when people saw me they would come up and talk openly about family relationships and connections without prompting; who was living; who had passed on; how we played football [sports] together and so on; other than the purpose of our visit to the community. He was more interested and expected us to have a meeting as soon as we got there. The valuable lesson here for my supervisor and other non-Aboriginal researchers is that, when conducting research in such settings, one is not doing research *on* the community using ethical frameworks and methods developed in other cultural settings. One needs to conduct research *with* the community, drawing on expected relational practices, ways of being and interacting.

The impact of non-Aboriginal and Torres Strait Islander worldviews with the associated structures of control and power on the providers of social, educational and health has, at times served to diminish the position of Aboriginal and Torres Strait Islander researchers. What I provide here is an example of the balance of academic requirements with the Aboriginal and Torres Strait Islander ways of working. This was an appropriate learning experience for my supervisor and he was more alerted to, and willing to accept, my methodology for the research by the time of our second field visit.

This is not to say that applied social psychology theories and practices do not offer critical assessment tools or insights into the development, and effective delivery, of mental health services. It is to argue that such technologies and insights work best when subsumed within Indigenous frameworks and cultural practices and enacted through an ethics of share responsibility and control. We require partners in action who are willing to work with us rather than impose interventions on us. The profession will benefit from continued efforts to explore the intricate interactions of context, discourse and theory along the lines offered by Neil in the previous section. As Connolly and Harms (2015) propose, paying attention to culture and diversity is critically important when thinking about the application of theory in practice. Imported theories can offer insights and be used positively to increase understanding when trying to help people work out difficulties in their lives. Connolly and Harms (2015) also argue that theories can be used to impose professional ideas in ways that are prejudicial to the interests of clients or lack synchronicity with their concerns and worldviews. A more participative and culturally open approach on the part of non-indigenous psychologists is crucial for the profession to enact the spirit of the formal apology offered by the Australian Psychological Society and to address the disadvantages and inequities and epistemic violence that Aboriginal and Torres Strait Islander people often face at the front-end of mental health service delivery.

AN EFFECTIVE APPROACH TO ADDRESSING ABORIGINAL COMMUNITY MENTAL HEALTH

As can be seen from the case studies presented by the authors, each has made a commitment to principled practice, one from a non-Indigenous perspective with a commitment to principled practice and the other from the perspective of an Aboriginal man immersed in the indigenous Australian Life Set (Adams, 2015b). While the trajectory towards engaged transformative practice has been quite different for each, there are some common features that are elaborated below in the spirit of partnership and shared learning.

While Uncle Mick is a natural helper with deep cultural knowledge that he brings as part of his lived experience as an Aboriginal Elder, Drew was afforded the opportunity to develop as a natural helper guided by the community. Both speak of the importance of honouring Aboriginal and Torres Strait Islander ways of knowing and being. The tripartite framework provides the scaffolding upon which Drew was able to (re)construct his professional identity and practices in the Aboriginal and Torres Strait Islander life world(s) described by Uncle Mick. The social psychological theories that evolved as part of the tripartite framework provide an interpretive lens through which his everyday practice could be viewed and held accountable in ways that are culturally appropriate and responsive.

Respect for Indigenous knowledges and worldviews is fundamental. This foundational commitment is evident in the tripartite framework and infuses the work of Uncle Mick. The tripartite framework makes no sense without a clear commitment to Aboriginal and Torres Strait Islander Terms of Reference and Uncle Mick is unequivocal in his belief that a deep understanding of Aboriginal and Torres Strait Islander knowledges and worldviews is a nonnegotiable expectation for authentically engaged practice. From this fundamental position some other observations may be drawn about the work of applied social psychologists in this context.

First, **interdisciplinarity**. The theories and methods utilised in everyday practice are, by necessity, drawn from an eclectic mix of areas. Of particular relevance and importance has been indigenous knowledge and practice, indigenous, community and liberation psychologies (and liberation theologies), all of which can be draw upon by applied social psychologists in order to guide ethical practice and respond more effectively to the mental needs of Aboriginal and Torres Straight Island Communities (see also Sonn, Rua and Quayle, Chapter 3, this collection). Again, this call for interdisciplinarity echoes from the past (e.g. Tajfel, 1978) and requires us to realise that disciplinary boundaries, along with those between psychologists, social workers and community members, are porous and artificial in applied contexts.

Second is **epistemological and ontological pluralism**. Applied social psychologists working in the intercultural space need to take seriously the cultural context and the importance of both negotiating a shared understanding and accommodating with respect the intrinsic value of Indigenous knowledge in their own right. In Throgmorton's (2000) terms, we need to understand the distinctiveness and the overlaps in our interpretive communities as we seek 'experience near'. Aboriginal and Torres Strait Islander knowledge systems are older and wiser by a significant order of magnitude than those of settler society and, while colonialist practices have sought to eradicate them, they persist in resilient and increasingly revitalised cultures.

Third is **knowledge brokerage**. A key to effective, engaged practice is to ensure that research findings and other key elements of quality evidenced-based practice are dialectically-orientated translational research. Translational research is known by a variety of terms: knowledge transfer, knowledge exchange, utilisation science, knowledge mobilisation, impact, value; all of which mean essentially the same thing, notwithstanding the interdisciplinary debates that have flourished in the published literature (Hall, 2011; Leadbetter et al., 2011). We refer to the *activity* as translational research and the *process* as *knowledge exchange*. This is particularly important in the area of Aboriginal and Torres Strait Islander health because it emphasises the bidirectional nature of the activity. We must acknowledge the importance of Indigenous ways of knowing and being and work to avoid reproducing power relations that lead to moral exclusion of Aboriginal and Torres Strait Islander people. Knowledge exchange needs to be an authentic exchange characterised by co-design, co-production and co-construction of knowledge-based material to inform practice and policy in Aboriginal and Torres Strait Islander health (Barnes et al., 2011). In this way, knowledge exchange becomes a decolonising and socially transformative practice (Hall, 2011; Smylie, 2011; Smith, 1999) that can be informed by the five principles of Begoray and Banister (2011). These are; contextuality (creating a space of relatedness and connection in Indigenous context), collaboration (researchers, mentors and the elders meet regularly and work collaboratively to develop ideas in conjunction with cultural awareness and appropriateness), reciprocity (it encourages knowledge sharing from researchers, mentors and consultants to Indigenous communities, as well as creating awareness of Indigenous health problems to a wider community), relationality (it emphasises the importance of establishing and sustaining a meaningful relationship between researchers and Indigenous communities, and it requires researchers to be culturally sensitive), reflexivity (it is the reflection about the Indigenous health programme).

Fourth is **social justice**. The pursuit of social justice is a foundational aspiration for applied social psychologists. They eschew the archaic notions of universal truth and objectivity and are, as Gergen so eloquently described, free to 'join in the hurly burly of cultural life – to become an active participant in the construction of culture' (Gergen, 1988: 10). Of particular importance has been the vast literature on the social psychology of justice. Though still largely rooted in the experimental traditions, the social psychology of justice provides an important lens through which we can understand the dynamics of justice (or, more precisely, injustice) in our everyday lives. While a relative obsession with distributive fairness dominated the field for many years, insights from the body of work on procedural fairness and the scope of justice has found particular resonance in applied social psychological practice with Indigenous peoples. A deep understanding of the social psychology of justice provides clear signposts for action to redress injustice in ways that foster authentic social transformation.

Fifth is **reflective and principled practice**. Reflective practice embodies commitments to praxis and a continual engagement between knowledge production and knowledge exchange. This is also known as the tension between *evidence-based practice* and *practice-based evidence*. Principled practice not only acknowledges values-based practice, it attempts to clearly articulate a set of principles and values that underpin both reflection and action. The tripartite framework for trust building is one example of how a non-Indigenous applied social psychologist (re)positioned himself through a process of reflective commitment to principled practice (see also Drew, 2014).

CONCLUDING COMMENTS

The importance of engagement with local knowledge systems cannot be overstated in terms of applied social psychology practice. The work of first author Drew has been simply stated by the community leaders he works with as 'living and learning together'. That is an elegant summary of the principles and practices outlined in this chapter. 'Living and learning together' is about knowledge co-production and shared understandings in the intercultural space. For Drew, knowledge co-production is undertaken guided by principled practice.

For the second author, Uncle Mick, the co-production is a function of the shared identity as Aboriginal and Torres Strait Islander people while remaining respectful of the rich diversity of Aboriginal and Torres Strait Islander cultures throughout Australia. For Uncle Mick, his capacity to live and learn together stems from his deep commitment to cultural ways of working as an Aboriginal man. His engagement with a very wide range of Aboriginal and Torres Strait Islander communities mirrors his experiences outlined in the case-based practice of researching Aboriginal men and their health. The outcomes from his research, while 'traditional' in some respects, could only be achieved by living and learning together.

The applied social psychology described in this chapter is about matching our activities to the natural ebb and flow of everyday life in community. Our work is not about prevention, intervention or postvention; it is about authentic engagement in the everyday activities of both the community natural helpers and the community members. This harks back to the early work of applied social psychologists such as Marie Jahoda.

The key to engaged practice is the development of strong trusting relationships. It is a given that psychologists and others working in Aboriginal and Torres Strait Islander communities take responsibility for ensuring that they have received cultural competence training (Walker et al., 2014). There is a necessary precursor to undertaking this training. While cultural competence training is a reflective activity, it is important to position yourself in the intercultural space (Nakata, 2013). As part of the Wundargoodie Aboriginal Youth and Community Wellbeing Programme, the tripartite framework for principled practice was developed to provide the reflective lens through which engaged practitioners could view themselves and their work. The tripartite framework is firmly grounded in social psychological theories and is relationship building, trust building and identity making. Uncle Mick has emphasised the importance of engaging with the Aborigine Life Set (Adams, 2015b).

Earlier in this chapter, we described the emergence of natural helpers as the 'natural' progression in community based mental health care. It should be apparent that the applied social psychologist, as engaged practitioner, will become part of an extended natural helper network. This can only be achieved if there is an authentic commitment to the principles and practices outlined in the two case studies.

The authentically engaged applied social psychologist eschews the expert role but does not relinquish the expertise that he or she possesses and may bring to the co-construction, co-design and co-production of community led initiatives for positive social transformation such as natural helping.

In closing, applied social psychologists have much to offer the world in which they live and work. It is important that they 'be in the world' and immerse themselves in the everyday, as was evident in the work of the foundational generation of our sub-discipline. The case-based approach to everyday practice adopted in this chapter offers one mode of immersion research that synchronises with the expectations of Aboriginal and Torres Strait Islander people regarding ways of working. These ways of working are at the very heart of socially transformative practice in all life realms, particularly health and mental health. The journey from institutionalisation to deinstitutionalisation to community mental health service and, finally, to the recognition of natural helpers has been arduous, challenging and frustrating no doubt for generations of applied social psychologists. By embracing principled practice as a process of engagement, we were never sure where we would end up, but we were always confident that it would be a better place than it would otherwise be.

REFERENCES

Accordina, M., Porter, D., & Morse, T. (2001). Deinstitutionalization of persons with severe mental illness: Context and consequences. *Journal of Rehabilitation*, *75*: 16–21.

Adams, M. (2001). *How Aboriginal and Torres Strait Islander men care for their health: An ethnographic study*. (Master of Arts thesis). Centre for Aboriginal Studies, Curtin University of Technology, Perth.

Adams, M. (2002). Establishing a national framework for improving the health and well-being of Aboriginal and Torres Strait Islander males. *Aboriginal and Islander Health Worker Journal 26*(1), 11–12.

Adams, M. (2014). *Men's business: A study into Aboriginal and Torres Strait Islander men's sexual and reproductive health*. Canberra, ACT: Magpie Goose Publishing.

Adams, M. (2015a). Utilising appropriate methodology and social work practices: Consulting with Aboriginal and Torres Strait Islander males. In C. Fejo-King, & J. Poona (Eds.), *Emerging from the margins, first Australians' perspectives of social work* (pp. 81–116). Canberra, ACT: Magpie Goose Publishing.

Adams, M. (2015b). Aboriginal Life Set, mental health and suicide. In C. Fejo-King, & J. Poona (Eds.), *Reconciliation and Australian social work past and current experiences informing future practice*. Canberra, ACT: Magpie Goose Publishing.

Adams, M. (2016) *My journey through the academic mist*. Canberra, ACT: Magpie Goose Publishing.

Adams, M., & Danks, B (2005) *What do you do when your mate is telling you that he is thinking about committing suicide: A study with Aboriginal and Torres Strait Islander males talking about the effects of suicide.* Canberra, ACT: The Office of Aboriginal and Torres Strait Islander Health.

Adams, M., & McCoy, B. (2011). Lives of Indigenous Australian men. In R. Thackrah, & K. Scott (Eds.), *Indigenous Australian health and cultures. An introduction for health professionals* (pp. 127–151). Frenchs Forest, NSW: Pearson Australia.

Adams, Y., Drew, N., & Walker, R. (2014). Principles of practice in mental health assessment with Aboriginal Australians. *Working together: Aboriginal and Torres Strait Islander mental health and wellbeing principles and practices* (2nd edn., pp. 243–260). Canberra, ACT: Commonwealth of Australia.

Ali, L., & Sonn, C. (2009). Multiculturalism and whiteness: Through the experiences of second generation Cypriot Turkish. *Australian Journal of Community Psychology*, *21*, 24–38.

Altman, J., & Hinkson, M. (Eds). (2007). *Coercive reconciliation: Stabilise, normalise, exit Aboriginal Australia*. Melbourne: Arena Publications.

Auger, S., & Verbiest, S. (2007). Lay health educators' roles in improving patient education. *NC Medical Journal*, *68*, 334.

Australian Association of Social Workers. (2016). *Preparing for culturally responsive and inclusive social work practice in Australia: Working with Aboriginal and Torres Strait Islander peoples – January 2015*. Updated April 2016. Available at: https://www.aasw.asn.au/document/item/7006

Australian Indigenous HealthInfoNet. (2016). Overview of Aboriginal and Torres Strait Islander health status, 2015. Perth, WA: Australian Indigenous HealthInfoNet.

Bandura, A. (1990). Selective activation and disengagement of moral control. *Journal of Social Issues*, *46*, 27–46.

Barnes, H., Henwood, W., Kerr, S., Mcmanus, V., & McCreanor (2011) Knowledge translation and Indigenous research. In E. Banister, B. Leadbeater, & E. A. Marshall (Eds). *Knowledge translation in context: Indigenous, policy, and community settings* (pp. 161–180). Toronto: University of Toronto Press

Begoray, D., & Banister, E. (2011). Knowledge translation and adolescent girls' sexual health education in Indigenous communities. In E. Banister, B. Leadbeater, & E. A. Marshall (Eds). *Knowledge translation in context: Indigenous, policy, and community settings* (pp. 143–160). Toronto: University of Toronto Press

Blader, S., & Tyler, T. (2003). A four component model of procedural justice: Defining the meaning of a 'fair' process. *Personality and Sopcial Psychology Bulletin*, *29*, 747–758.

Brown, P. (1980). Social implications of deinstitutionalization. *Journal of Community Psychology*, *8*: 314–322.

Cartwright, D. (1979). Contemporary social psychology in historical perspective. *Social Psychology Quarterly*, *1*: 82–93.

Connolly, M., & Harms, L. (2015). *Social work: From theory to practice*, (2nd edn.). Cambridge: Cambridge University Press.

Cosgrave, C., Hussain, R., & Maple, M. (2015). Retention challenge facing Australia's rural community mental health services: Service manager's perspectives. *The Australian Journal of Rural health*, *23*: 272–276.

Couzos, S. & Murray, R. 2003. *Aboriginal Primary Health Care, An Evidence-based Approach*. Oxford: Oxford University Press.

Drake, G. (2014). The transinstitutionalisation of people living in licensed boarding houses in Sydney. *Australian Social Work*, *67*: 240–255.

Drew N. (2014). Living and learning together: Principled practice for engagement and social transformation in the East Kimberley region of Western Australia. In R. Reinhart, K. Barbour, & C. Pope (Eds.), *Ethnographic worldviews: Transformations and social justice* (pp. 77–91). Dordrecht, Netherlands: Springer.

Drew, N. (2015). Social and emotional wellbeing, natural helpers, critical health literacy and translational research: connecting the dots for positive health outcomes. *Australasian Psychiatry*, *23*(6), 620–622.

Dudgeon, P., & Walker, R. (2015). Decolonising Australian psychology: Discourses, strategies, and practice. *Journal of Social and Political Psychology*, *3*(1), 276–297.

Dudgeon, P., Wright, M., Paradies, Y., Garvey, D., & Walker, I. (2014). Aboriginal social, cultural and historical contexts. In P. Dudgeon, H. Milroy, & R. Walker (Eds.), *Working together: Aboriginal and Torres Strait Islander mental health and wellbeing principles and practice* (2nd edn., pp. 3–24). Canberra, ACT: Department of The Prime Minister and Cabinet.

Fejo-King, C. (2013). *Let's talk kinship: Innovating Australian social work education, theory, research and practice through Aboriginal knowledge*. Canberra, ACT: Christine Fejo-King Consulting.

Fellman, M. (2009). *Moral complexity and the Holocaust*. Lanham, Maryland: University Press of America.

Flood, J. (2006). *The Original Australians: Story of the Aboriginal People*. Allen and Unwin, Sydney.

Fredericks, B., Lee, V., Adams, M., & Mahoney, R. (2012). *Aboriginal and Torres Strait Islander Health*. In M. L. Fleming, & E. Parker (Eds.), *Introduction to public health* (2nd edn., pp. 350–372). Chatswood, NSW: Churchill Livingstone Elsevier.

Freud, S. (1950). *Totem and Taboo: Some points of agreement between the mental lives of savages and neurotics*. London: Routledge & Kegan Paul.

Gergen, K. (1988). *Towards a postmodern psychology*. Invited address. International Congress of Psychology, Sydney, Australia.

Green, M., Sonn, C., & Matsebula, J. (2007). Reviewing whiteness: Theory, research and possibilities. *South African Journal of Psychology*, *37*, 389–419.

Hall, B. (2011). Foreword. In E. Banister, B. Leadbeater, & E. A. Marshall (Eds). *Knowledge translation in context: Indigenous, policy, and community settings* (pp. vii–x). Toronto: University of Toronto Press.

Hodgetts, D., Drew, N., Sonn, C., Nikora, L., & Curtis, C. (2010). *Social Psychology and Everyday Life*. London: Palgrave Macmillan.

Houston, S. (2016). We need transformative change in Aboriginal health. *Medical Journal of Australia*, *205*(1), 17–18.

Jost, J., & Kruglanski, A. (2002). The estrangement of social constructionism and experimental social psychology: History of the rift and prospects for reconciliation. *Personality and Social Psychology Review*, *6*: 168–187.

Kirmeyer, L., Gone, J., & Moses, J. (2014). Rethinking historical trauma. *Transcultural Psychiatry*, *51*(3), 299–319.

Leadbeater, B., Banister, E., & Marshall, E. (2011). How what we know becomes more widely known is context dependent and culturally sensitive. In E. Banister, B. Leadbeater, & E. A. Marshall (Eds). *Knowledge translation in context: Indigenous, policy, and community settings* (pp. 3–11). Toronto: University of Toronto Press.

Lind, A., & Tyler, T. (1988). *The social psychology of procedural justice*. New York: Plenum.

Mac Suibhne, S. (2011). Erving Goffman's *Asylums* 50 years on. *British Journal of Psychiatry*, *198*: 1–2.

McHugh, C., Campbell, A., Chapman, M., & Balaratnasingam, S. (2016). Increasing Indigenous self-harm and suicide in the Kimberley: An audit of the 2005–2014 data. *Medical Journal of Australia*, *205*: 33

Morgan, M., & Drew, N. (2010). Principled engagement: Gelganyem youth and community wellbeing program. In N. Purdie, P. Dudgeon, & R. Walker (Eds.), *Working together: Aboriginal and Torres Strait Islander mental health and wellbeing principles and practices* (pp. 253–265). Canberra, ACT: Commonwealth of Australia.

Nakata, M. (2013). The rights and blights of the politics in Indigenous higher education. *Anthropological Forum: A Journal of Social Anthropology and Comparative Sociology*, 1–15.

Opotow, S. (1990). Moral exclusion and injustice: An introduction. *Journal of Social Issues*, *46*, 1–20.

Opotow, S. (2008). 'Not so much as a place to lay our head…': Moral exclusion and inclusion in the American Civil War reconstruction. *Social Justice Research*, *21*, 26–49.

Owen, J. (2006). *Development of a culturally sensitive program delivering cardiovascular health education to Indigenous Australians, in south west towns of Western Australia with lay educators as community role models* (Unpublished Doctoral Thesis). University of Western Australia, Perth.

Oxenham, D. (2000). Aboriginal terms of reference. In P. Dudgeon, D. Garvey, & H. Pickett (Eds.) *Working with Indigenous Australians: A handbook for psychologists* (pp. 109–125), Perth, WA: Gunada Press.

Paradies, Y. (2016). Colonisation, racism and indigenous health. *Journal of Population Research*, *33*(1), 83–96.

Patel, V., Weiss, H., Chowdhary, N., Naik, S., Pednekar, S., Chatterjey, S., Bhat, B., Araya, R., King, M., Simon, G., Verdeli, H., & Kirkwood, B. (2011). Lay health worker led intervention for depressive and anxiety disorders in India: Impact on clinical and disability outcomes over 12 months. *The British Journal of Psychiatry*, *199*, 459–466.

Pincock, S. (2007). Vikram Patel: Promoting mental health in developing countries. *The Lancet*, *370*: 821.

Sam, M. (1992). *Through black eyes: A handbook of family violence in Aboriginal and Torres Strait Islander communities*. Victoria: SNAICC.

Sealy, P., & Whitehead, P. (2004). Forty years of deinstitutionalisation of psychiatric service in Canada: An empirical assessment. *Canadian Journal of Psychiatry*, *49*, 249–257.

Sherwood, J. (2014). Colonisation – It's bad for your health: The context of Aboriginal health. *Contemporary Nurse*, *46*(1), 28–40.

Silburn, S., Robinson, G., Leckning, B., Henry, D., Cox, A., & Kickett, D. (2014). Preventing suicide among Aboriginal Australians. In P. Dudgeon, H. Milroy, & R. Walker (Eds.), *Working together: Aboriginal and Torres Strait Islander mental health and wellbeing principles and practice* (2nd edn., pp. 147–164). Canberra, ACT: Department of The Prime Minister and Cabinet.

Simoni, J., Franks, J., Lehavot, K., & Yard, S. (2011). Peer interventions to promote health: Conceptual considerations. *American Journal of Orthopsychiatry*, *91*, 351–359.

Smith, L. (1999). *Decolonizing methodologies: Research and indigenous peoples*. London: Zed Books.

Smylie, J. (2011). Knowledge translation and indigenous communities: A decolonising perspective. In E. Banister, B. Leadbeater, & E. A. Marshall (Eds). *Knowledge translation in context: Indigenous, policy, and community settings* (pp. 181–200). Toronto: University of Toronto Press.

Stoneham, M. (2014). The portrayal of Indigenous health in selected Australian media. *The International Indigenous Policy Journal*, *5*. Retrieved from http://ir.lib.uwo.ca/iipj/vol5/iss1/5

Tajfel, H., & Fraser, C. (Eds.). (1978). *Introducing social psychology: An analysis of individual reaction and response*. New York, NY: Penguin Press.

Tatz, C (2001) *Aboriginal suicide is different: Aportrait of life and self-destruction*. Canberra, ACT: Aboriginal Studies Press.

Thibaut, J., & Walker, L. (1975). *Procedural justice: A psychological analysis*. New York: Wiley.

Thornicroft, G., & Tansella, M. (2003). *What are the arguments for community-based mental health care?* Copenhagen: WHO Regional Office for Europe.

Throgmorton, J. A. (2000). On the virtues of skilful meandering. *Journal of the American Planning Association*, *66*(4), 367–383.

Törnblom, K. (1992). The social psychology of distributive justice. In K. Scherer (Ed). *Justice Interdisciplinary Perspectives* (pp. 177–236). Cambridge: Cambridge University Press

Tyler, T., & Lind. (1992) A relational model of authority in groups. Advances in Experimental Social Psychology, 25, 115–191.

Van Ginnekin, N., Tharyan, P., Rao, G., Meera, S., Pian, J., Chandrashekar, S., & Patel, V. (2013). Non-specialist health worker interventions for the care of mental, neurological and substance abuse disorders in low and middle income countries. *Cochrane Database of Systematic Reviews*, (11), doi: 10.1002/14651858.CD009149.pub2.

Walker, Y. (1993). *Aboriginal family issues*. Family Matters, 35, 51-53.

Walker, R., Schultz, C., & Sonn, C. (2014). Cultural competence – transforming policy, services, programs and practice. In P. Dudgeon, H. Milroy, & R. Walker (Eds.), *Working together: Aboriginal and Torres Strait Islander mental health and wellbeing principles and practice* (pp. 195–220). Canberra, ACT: Commonwealth of Australia.

Wilmoth, G., Silver, S., & Severy, L. (1987). Receptivity and planned change: Community attitudes and deinstitutionalization. *Journal of Applied Psychology*, *72*, 138–145.

Yohanna, D. (2013). Deinstitutionalisation of people with mental illness: Causes and consequences. *Virtual Mentor*, *15*, 886–891.

PART V

Work

13

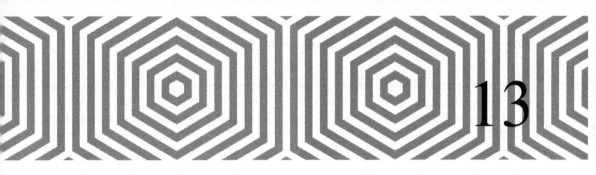

Social Cognition in the Workplace: The Future of Research on the Meaning of Work

Paul J. Maher, Deirdre O'Shea and Eric R. Igou

The desire to perceive life as meaningful is a core human motivation (Frankl, 1946: Fromm, 1947; Greenberg et al., 1990). High ratings of meaning in life are associated with better health (Steger et al., 2009a), decreased mortality (Krause, 2009), and slower age-related cognitive decline (Boyle et al., 2010), while low ratings are associated with depression, anxiety, and substance abuse (Harlow et al., 1986. For many people, jobs and occupations are enduring sources of such meaning (Emmons, 2003). Indeed, meaning of work scholarship has emerged as a rich field of research that has undergone rapid expansion over the last ten years or so. Research from organisational psychologists reveals that the ability to derive meaning from one's work is a key predictor of employee performance (Grant, 2008), occupational adjustment (Littman-Ovadia and Steger, 2010), and work satisfaction (Wrzesniewski et al., 1997). Moreover, experiencing work as meaningful leads people to experience life as more meaningful (Duffy and Sedlacek, 2007), particularly among those searching for meaning (Steger and Dik, 2009).

The psychosocial benefits of employment have long been recognised in social psychological literature (Fryer and Payne, 1984; Jahoda, 1982; Warr, 1987). Jahoda (1982) argued that the psychological benefits of employment stem from its latent functions, such as structure, collective purpose, and a sense of identity. These characteristics are also key components of one's sense of meaningfulness (Martela and Steger, 2016). Warr (1987) developed the vitamin model to address the fact that not all jobs are equal in the extent to which they benefit our well-being. He suggests that job characteristics can influence our well-being in a similar way to how vitamins impact our physical health. From this perspective, certain characteristics share a curvilinear relationship with mental health and can both hinder and benefit well-being (Warr, 2007). Likewise, Fryer (1986) suggests that bad jobs can negatively impact well-being and asserts that the negative impact of unemployment on well-being is dependent on the degree to which it obstructs one's ability to pursue valued goals (Fryer and Payne, 1984). In these models, and many others, benefits can be seen to stem from the ability of work to help us derive a sense of meaning from life (Wrzesniewski et al., 1997). People who feel their work is a calling also feel their lives are more meaningful (Duffy and Sedlacek, 2007). However, work may also challenge our ability to experience a sense of meaningfulness.

People face many challenges in deriving meaning from work and there is evidence to suggest that such challenges are becoming more commonplace. For example, boredom – an affective state characterised by lack of meaning, challenge, and attention (Van Tilburg and Igou, 2012; 2017b) – has increasingly been cited as the primary reason for people leaving their jobs (Mikulas, 2002). It has been found to be the second most common suppressed emotion at work (Mann, 2007). Likewise, precarious employment practices and the casualisation of labour have been on the rise for decades (Kalleberg, 2011). Such practices lead to workplace uncertainty and disrupt an individual's ability to gain a sense of meaningful identity from their occupational life. Over the past decade, social psychologists have become increasingly interested in how people maintain and defend their sense of meaning under such. However, evidence suggests that search for meaning in life is associated with lower well-being, in particular among older adults (Steger et al., 2009b), and experiences that threaten meaning can lead to increased stereotyping (Schimel et al., 1999) and political polarisation (Van Tilburg and Igou, 2016). Not all attempts to regulate meaning have negative consequences (Harmon-Jones et al., 1997; Van Tilburg and Igou, 2017a; Van Tilburg et al., 2013). For example, people can buffer themselves from the negative outcomes of meaning-regulation by reaffirming meaning elsewhere in non-threatened domains (e.g., in one's personal values or religiosity). This process is referred to as fluid compensation (Heine et al., 2006). In this chapter, we will discuss how individuals and organisations can capitalise on this process to help derive, and maintain, meaning in work.

Overall, we aim to bridge research on the meaning of work and the notion of meaning-regulation in social psychology to highlight the potential of a deeper focus on meaning-regulation in work contexts. We examine areas of synergy between these two perspectives and investigate how meaning-regulation may manifest in occupational settings and how it can be influenced. We will highlight the kind of meaning threats that are likely to be encountered through work and explore empirical evidence for psychological strategies that are directed at either maintaining or re-establishing a sense of meaningfulness, without negative consequences. We will also demonstrate how the meaning-regulation processes can address current limitations in our understanding of how people can best derive meaning from work.

SENSE OF MEANING

The roots of searching and finding meaning in life lie within human nature, that is, the ability to reflect on life and its meaning. For example, ancient Greek philosophers such as Plato, Aristotle, and Epicurus addressed the definition of meaning in life and its causes. In early theology, the questions of meaningfulness and purpose of life have been addressed by scholars such as Thomas of Aquinas and Meister Eckhart. Since the Renaissance, a long list of philosophers have discussed meaning in life and the human condition to strive for such experiences (e.g., Pascal, Kant, Hegel, Schopenhauer, Kierkegaard, Sartre). Psychology has also addressed the striving for meaning in life and conditions necessary for the experience of meaningfulness, for example, in the writings of Frankl (1946),

Fromm (1947), Maslow (1964), and Becker (1973). Although, meaning making processes and the centrality of sense of meaning in life have been addressed in academic psychology (e.g., Baumeister, 1991), it is in particular the research on mortality salience conceptualised by terror management theory (e.g., Greenberg et al., 1997) that has led to a bulk of research on existential psychological processes, including meaning making, and their importance for human social judgements, behaviour (e.g., Heine et al., 2006) and well-being (e.g., Wong, 2012).

Meaning is a difficult concept to define and within the field of industrial/organisational (I/O) psychology there are various conceptualisations, as we will discuss below. However, within social psychology, a consensus is beginning to emerge. At the most general level, meaning can be defined as 'relation' (Heine et al., 2006), as it is based on connections between people and the self (identities, thoughts, emotions, behaviours, memories, etc.) and with places and environments (Heine et al., 2006). Crucially, meaning in life is largely affected by people's experience of purpose, clear values, self-efficacy, and self-worth (Baumeister, 1991). Heine et al. (2006) point out that, given its centrality in life, a sense of meaning is a resource that people are motivated to defend. It is evidentially distinct from positive affect (Heintzelman and King, 2014a) and is comprised of both motivational and cognitive components.

The literature distinguishes two general forms of meaning. *Epistemic meaning* (e.g., Van Tilburg and Igou, 2013) concerns the extent to which experiences are characterised by reliable connections; the extent to which life 'makes sense' (Baumeister and Vohs, 2002). This is an essential element of how our cultural worldviews provide meaning (Dechesne and Kruglanski, 2004) and, in a more discrete sense, characterises the 'feeling of meaning'; a feeling related to whether or not stimuli are experienced as possessing an underlying coherence (Heintzelman and King, 2014b). *Teleological meaning* relates to the general need people have for wanting to feel significance (e.g., *my life matters*) and purpose (e.g., *my life has direction*) in their lives. Much of this aspect of meaning concerns the functionality of our behaviour. People judge behaviour as meaningful if it is viewed as *instrumental* in the pursuit of a *highly valued* goal (Van Tilburg and Igou, 2013). While epistemic and teleological meaning are partially distinct, psychometric research suggests they likely fall under the domain of a single higher-order factor (Krause and Hayward, 2014), reflecting our overall sense of meaning in life.

Importantly, a sense of meaningfulness is a psychological *experience* (e.g., Heintzelman and King, 2014b; Van Tilburg and Igou, 2013) that people monitor and frequently rate as high (Heintzelman and King, 2014a). However, certain experiences, which are referred to as meaning threats, can challenge this sense of meaning and elicit self-regulatory responses as part of a process referred to as meaning-regulation (Van Tilburg and Igou, 2011; Van Tilburg et al., 2013). Dating back to the theory of cognitive dissonance (Festinger, 1957), there has been a plethora of research demonstrating how forms of self-regulation result in defensive reactions to certain cognitive discrepancies/inconsistencies. In most cases, theorists have focused on specific areas of threat like self-discrepancy, uncertainty-management, and mortality salience (see Jonas et al., 2014). Theories of meaning-regulation, on the other hand, such as the meaning maintenance model (MMM; Heine et al., 2006), view each of these resources as relating to an overall sense of meaning in life and offer a more inclusive account of the threat/defensive literature.

REGULATING MEANING

Self-regulatory processes are at the heart of all goal-directed behaviour (Bandura, 1991) and undoubtedly play an important role in our working lives. According to the MMM, certain experiences threaten our sense of meaning and lead to compensatory responses. Research demonstrates that information that violates expectations, fosters uncertainty, or challenges one's ability to find purpose in life can serve as meaning threats (Proulx and Heine, 2006; Van Tilburg and Igou, 2012). For example, as we explained, boredom is an experience that challenges our sense of purpose (Van Tilburg and Igou, 2012), and experiences of boredom lead to lower ratings of meaning in life and attempts to regulate meaning. Similar responses are observed when people encounter music that violates expectations (Maher et al., 2013) or are repeatedly exposed to incongruent word-pairs (Randles et al., 2011). Thus, in the workplace, breaches in fairness, justice, psychological contracts and trust may all pose threats to meaning and prompt meaning-regulation. Finally, uncertainty (e.g., job insecurity, precarious working) is also associated with low levels of meaningfulness (Hogg, 2007) and results in motivations to restore a sense of order, clarity, and meaning (Heine et al., 2006). In the face of meaning threats such as these, people regulate meaning in many ways, some of which may have negative effects on work life and well-being (e.g., increased stereotyping, unhealthy eating). These meaning-regulation strategies can be grouped into two broad categories (Jonas et al., 2014), which we discuss below.

Proximal Versus Distal Defenses

The term *proximal defence* has been used to describe the *initial* responses to meaning threats, which are aimed at suppressing, or distracting and distancing oneself from the source of threat. These responses can have the most negative consequences. Various forms of proximal defences serve as strategies of meaning-regulation. They are associated with activation of the *behavioural inhibition system* (BIS; McNaughton and Corr, 2004), which increases attentional vigilance and avoidant behaviours. For example, in response to mortality salience (which renders life meaningless; Heine et al., 2006), people may escape or avoid self-awareness (Craig, 2009; Silvia, 2001). Bored individuals also engage in avoidant behaviours like unhealthy eating (Moynihan et al., 2015). Aside from the consequences for one's physical health, research has also demonstrated that poor diet can impair work performance (Boles et al., 2004) and that work stress, in turn, predicts poorer dietary habits (Kouvonen et al., 2005). This is one example of how proximal, work-related, meaning-regulation responses can lead to damaging cycles of behaviour.

In addition to these avoidant responses, proximal defences also involve an increase in vigilant attention that can exacerbate certain forms of bias. For example, in response to meaning threats, people exaggerate both positive and negative evaluations of stimuli (Holbrook and Sousa, 2013), show increased need for structure (Proulx et al., 2010), increased closed-mindedness (Kruglanski, 2004), and rely more heavily on stereotypes (Schimel et al., 1999). These processes serve as strategies for regulating meaning as they can facilitate an increased sense of order and clarity in the world. Perpetual activation of these proximal processes through the BIS can negatively impact well-being (Routledge et al., 2010) and disrupt the pursuit of everyday goals (Pyszczynski et al., 1999). Importantly, however, not every response to a meaning threat takes the form of proximal defence.

The discussion above demonstrates how proximal defences are initial responses that aim to deal directly with the sources of meaning threat. In contrast, distal defences most commonly occur after some delay. According to Jonas et al. (2014), when responding to meaning threats most people will down-regulate BIS activation (associated with proximal defence) by engaging in some form of approach orientated behaviour, for example by increasing their commitment to alternative values or groups and restoring a general sense of meaning. On an individual level, this may involve joining (or creating) clubs which align with ones identity/values or simply displaying images of value in one's workspace. On a broader level, institutions may aim to emphasise the positive benefits of their work for certain people or for society as a whole. Such a strategy may be beneficial when individuals are caught in challenging and meaningless jobs. Using meaning-regulation research, we will discuss the psychological mechanisms involved in the process.

Fluid Compensation

Meaning-regulation includes strategies that allow for flexibility for increasing and *re-establishing* a sense of meaning when facing a meaning threat. For example, when one receives negative feedback, self-esteem is likely to decline. Given that a positive self-view is a core human need, such a situation would qualify as a meaning-threat. Research demonstrates that people can regulate their sense of meaningfulness by reaffirming meaning elsewhere, in a domain that bears no relation to the threat (Heine et al., 2006), such as belongingness to others, which is also a core human need. This process has been termed *fluid compensation* (Proulx and Heine, 2006). Another example touches on death as a meaning threat and cultural worldviews as a source of meaning.

One of the most reliable findings in social psychology shows us that, in response to the meaninglessness induced by thinking about one's own inevitable death (mortality salience), people engage in worldview defence. By providing us with a sense of significance, purpose, and coherence, our cultural worldviews are a key source of meaning in life (Dechesne and Kruglanski, 2004). People bolster their adherence to cultural worldviews by, for example, engaging in ingroup favouritism and outgroup derogation (Greenberg et al., 2004). But mortality salience is not the only meaning threat that can trigger these responses. It is also displayed, for example, after people read absurd stories (Proulx et al., 2010), hear strange music (Maher et al., 2013), evaluate art perceived as meaningless (Landau and Greenberg, 2006; Proulx et al., 2010), or are bored (Van Tilburg and Igou, 2011).

Crucially, worldview adherence need not take the form of derogation or favouritism. People can affirm meaning by engaging in more socially beneficial behaviour. For example, bored people restore their sense of meaning in life by engaging in pro-social behaviour (Van Tilburg and Igou, 2017a). Van Tilburg and Igou (2017a) demonstrated that bored participants were motivated to give blood and donate to charity in an attempt to re-establish a sense of meaningfulness. Indeed, Grant (2007) has demonstrated that helping others in the workplace makes work more meaningful and engaging. Should the environment not provide such opportunities, people may alternatively engage in nostalgic reflection (Van Tilburg et al., 2013), which also promotes a sense of meaning, especially because nostalgic memories are centred on thoughts about positive relationships with others (Wildschut et al., 2010). Moreover, meaningful affirmations *buffer* against antisocial responses. For example, positive personality feedback (Harmon-Jones et al., 1997), affirmation of personal values (Schmeichel and Martens, 2005), and the affirmation of intrinsic religiosity (Jonas and Fischer, 2006) prevent a tendency to engage in derogation and favouritism after mortality salience.

Overall, social psychological research provides a strong framework for understanding how people experience a sense of meaning in life and how they are motivated to defend it. Given that family, religion, and work are typical sources from which people glean meaning (Emmons, 1997), work plays an important role in the meaning-regulation process.

MEANINGFUL WORK

Given the research we have discussed concerning a sense of meaningfulness and how it can be experienced/challenged, we suggest that a certain social or institutional context is necessary to experience meaningful work. Jobs that lack a basic level of stability, structure, or challenge will likely disrupt one's ability to derive meaning from work and life (Piotrowski et al., 2015). Without job security, work cannot provide the sense of coherence necessary for the experience of epistemic meaning. Similarly, it is difficult to maintain the teleological components of purpose and significance in work that is characterised as uncertain and unpredictable (Burgard et al., 2009). Ironically, Ross (2008) notes that, in the 1970s, efforts to make work more meaningful in the United States triggered a general decline of job security, as institutions focused on 'quality of work' while risk, uncertainty, and non-standard work arrangements proliferated. Such uncertain and unpredictable (i.e., precarious) working conditions reduce job satisfaction and can increase mental health problems (Benach and Muntaner, 2007). Today, political and economic factors have contributed to the growth of precarious employment practices (Kalleberg and Hewison, 2013; McCann, 2014) but such a macro-level discussion is beyond the scope of this chapter. Rather, we emphasise the need for stability and structure in our working lives and focus on how workers can derive meaning from work that provides this basic level of security necessary for meaningfulness to thrive. Much research from the field of I/O psychology has previously contributed to this topic.

The meaning of work has received attention in recent times as adding to both work performance and occupational health of employees, and additionally holds promise as an area that is particularly open to interventions. Much has been written on the meaning of work (see Rosso et al., 2010), including a number of theoretical reviews (e.g., Šverko and Vidović, 1995; Wrzesniewski et al., 2003). Combining the theoretical advances in the field of social psychology with applied research on the meaning of work provides fruitful avenues for future research and applications as it gives greater insight into the contextual features and self-regulatory mechanisms that are at work.

In particular, we suggest three ways in which a social psychological approach to meaning in life can help inform research on the meaning of work:

1 *Identifying meaning.* Using research from the field of social cognition to inform our conceptualisation of meaning divides the experience into two distinct, but related, features (epistemic and teleological). This can tell us something more about *how* people derive meaning from work.
2 *Identifying meaning threats.* The social cognitive perspective of meaning can help us predict when our jobs and work experiences can serve as a *threat* to our sense of meaning and disrupt our well-being and productivity.
3 *Identifying meaning-regulation processes.* Considering how people are motivated to defend and regulate their sense of meaning can help individuals more effectively experience meaning through their work and address any meaning threats that work may provide.

Work and employment have important roles to play in feelings of significance and purpose. Work that is characterised by high levels of positive influence and impact on others leads to a feeling of significance or that one is having a positive impact (Hackman and Oldham, 1976; Morgeson and Humphrey, 2006). The goal-directed nature of working, particularly when it is perceived to contribute to one's desired career path, creates a sense of direction and purpose that contributes to the overall sense of a meaningful life (Yeager and Bundick, 2009).

A broad range of applied psychological research highlights the importance of deriving meaning from one's work, demonstrating its relationship with job satisfaction (Wrzesniewski et al., 1997), performance levels (Grant, 2008), and engagement

(Kahn and Fellows, 2013). Furthermore, those who experience meaning in their work are three times more likely to remain in their organisations (Geldenhuys et al., 2014). The meaning of work literature has been reviewed many times before (e.g., Šverko and Vidović, 1995; Wrzesniewski et al., 2003), so here we discuss an integrative model put forward by Rosso et al. (2010) and provide a brief overview of the two key areas (job design and fit). In each case, we will extend this work by adopting a social cognitive perspective and highlight processes of epistemic and teleological meaning making.

HOW MEANING IS DERIVED FROM WORK

The work of Amy Wrzesniewski has been influential in advancing research on the meaning of work for individuals (e.g., Wrzesniewski, 1999, 2003). Indeed, there is a large range and variation of different theoretical perspectives present within the meaning of work research, but Rosso et al. (2010) provided a theoretical framework that aimed to capture and integrate the most common themes among them. They outline a distinction between the different ways people derive meaning by categorising different areas of research based on four sources of meaning; *agency*, *communion*, *self*, and *other*. They suggest that these four themes form two orthogonally related bi-polar pathways labelled as agency-communion and self-other. Work is purported to be most meaningful at the intersection of these dimensions. The self-other dimension reflects the fact that experienced meaningfulness can be viewed as internal to the self or external and involving others. The second dimension distinguishes agency (drive to separate, expand, and create) from communion (a drive to attach, connect, and unite). More importantly, the intersections of these dimensions reflect the areas where meaningful work resides: individuation (self-agency), contribution (other-agency), self-connection (self-communion), and unification (other-communion). Broadly speaking, these four intersections can be divided into two components relating to either teleological meaning (individuation and contribution) or epistemic meaning (self-connection, unification).

Dividing Rosso and colleagues' (2010) model into these two components offers a parsimonious view of how meaning is derived from work and also provides a more transparent distinction between different pathways. On the one hand, we can experience meaningfulness when we feel that we are significant and are pursuing a valued purpose (Heintzelman and King, 2014b; Pratt and Ashfort, 2003). On the other hand, meaning is experienced when we feel we understand our environments well and can relate features of the external world to ourselves and to each other (Heine et al., 2006). Individuation and contribution are clearly examples of the former, while self-connection and unification reflect more closely the latter. We will apply this dual perspective to two of the most well researched areas in the meaning of work literature: job design and work–role fit.

Job Design

Job design research focuses on key job characteristics that help foster the internal motivations that drive people to perform well at work. The job characteristics model was outlined by Hackman and Oldham (1976), who identified five work characteristics that make jobs more satisfying. These are *task variety* (the degree to which the job involves a variety of activities requiring different skills and talents), *task identity* (the degree to which an individual can complete a whole piece of work, from start to finish), *task significance* (the extent to which the work impacts on the lives of others), *autonomy* (the level of freedom or independence involved in carrying out the work), and *job feedback* (the extent to which the job provides an individual with clear feedback on their performance). Recently, Morgeson and Humphrey (2006) expanded upon this research with their 'work design' model, but it is this original job design framework that has more to say about experienced meaningfulness. According to Hackman and Oldham (1976), it is the first three work characteristics (*variety*, *identity*, and *significance*) that contribute to experienced meaningfulness and, through this pathway, increase job performance. From a social cognitive perspective, this last assumption is derived from a definition of meaningfulness that is predominantly focused on teleological components (e.g., my work matters, my work has direction). Hackman and Oldham (1976) define meaningfulness as the degree to which the individual experiences the job as one which is generally meaningful, valuable, and worthwhile.

The work characteristics model reflects features of both teleological and epistemic components of meaning. The teleological perspective focusing on *significance* and *purpose* is evident in the three characteristics assumed to contribute to experienced meaningfulness: variety, identity, and significance. In the case of task significance, perceiving that one's job benefits others will, in most cases, give one's work a highly valued purpose. Additionally, both variety and identity likely contribute to a sense of personal significance for the individual. Work may give one a sense of personal significance by making them feel like they matter and are a part of something bigger. Task variety promotes significance by making one feel their unique blend of talents is especially useful, while task identity helps us feel like we are contributing to something purposeful, increasing our sense of significance and providing a broader purpose to the work. These components resonate with Baumeister and Vohs' (2002) description of self-efficacy as one of the core requirements for meaning. It refers to a person's belief that they have the ability to contribute towards a positive outcome and make a difference (Baumeister and Vohs, 2002).

Alongside these features, an epistemic approach to meaning suggests that both task autonomy and job feedback should also aid experienced meaningfulness. Specifically, an epistemic perspective of meaning refers to how much we can understand and make sense of our environments and emphasises the importance of certainty, coherence, and connection (Heine et al., 2006). Receiving feedback is likely to contribute to greater understanding and a higher sense of coherence and certainty about one's job and work roles. Similarly, a level of autonomy is likely to promote certainty by giving individuals a greater sense of control over their working lives (Wrzesniewski and Dutton, 2001). For example, Antonovsky (1987) suggests that the meaningfulness subcomponent of a sense of coherence is dependent upon participation in decision making in working life. Research demonstrates that this component of coherence was resistant to change after an intervention delivered to unemployed people (Vastamäki et al., 2009). Only re-employment and, therefore, more active involvement in decision making brought about a significant change in meaningfulness among this group.

Taking this dual perspective on meaningfulness therefore suggests that all five job characteristics can contribute to meaningful work experiences through either epistemic or teleological pathways. Without this epistemic/teleological distinction, it is unclear why all five job characteristics would relate to meaning. Indeed, Hackman and Oldham (1976) originally hypothesised that only the teleological components – task variety, identity and feedback – would contribute towards experienced meaningfulness. Empirical research, however, supports the dual epistemic/teleological perspective. A large number of empirical studies have sought to test different aspects of Hackman and Oldham's job characteristics model and, to date, two meta-analyses focusing on this model have been conducted (Fried and Ferris, 1987; Humphrey et al., 2007). Broadly speaking, these analyses have provided support for the core assumptions of Hackman and Oldham's (1976) model, with some important caveats surrounding the role of experienced meaningfulness. Fried and Ferris (1987) found that experienced meaningfulness showed unexpectedly high correlations with job feedback and autonomy and was not strongly associated with task identity. Similarly, Humphrey et al. (2007) found that all five job characteristics were associated with experienced meaningfulness and they also tested causal pathways between these variables and job satisfaction. As expected, they found that experienced meaning partially mediated the link between task significance (i.e., impact on the lives of others) and job performance. However, they also found that the link between job feedback and job performance was fully mediated by experienced meaning.

Overall, adopting a broader conceptualisation of meaning that takes into account the role of epistemic and teleological facets helps explain how all five characteristics of the job design model contribute to experiencing meaning at work. Essentially, this is one example of how the social cognitive perspective broadens our view of what can constitute meaningful work or work experiences. Another avenue for deriving meaning from work comes in the form of work–role fit.

Meaning and Fit

Many meaning of work scholars suggest that perceiving some form of fit (e.g., person–job, work–role fit) between oneself and one's work contributes to a more meaningful work experience (Brief and Nord, 1990; Kristof, 1996; Shamir, 1991). Work–role fit can be defined as the degree to which one perceives compatibility between their self-concept and their working role. The fit-meaning association is also evident in research that focuses on identity and how work can provide meaning by helping one confirm or establish a valued identity (Swann et al., 2009). Empirical research supports the association between fit and meaning at work. For example, May (2003) conducted studies in a manufacturing environment and found that a sense of meaningfulness was significantly higher when individuals perceive a fit between themselves and their working role. In a separate study, this association was also found among workers at an insurance company (May et al., 2004). Furthermore, May et al. (2004) demonstrated that the relationship between work–role fit and engagement was fully mediated by experienced meaningfulness.

Brief and Nord (1990) suggest that this work–role fit fosters meaningfulness because when there is a match between work roles and one's self-concept it gives individuals an opportunity for them to express their values/beliefs. For example, individuals will feel their work is meaningful if it is consistent with aspects of their self-concept, like their attitudes (Bunderson and Thompson, 2009), values (Besharov, 2008), and identity (Elsbach, 2003). Similarly, Shamir (1991) suggests that people seek jobs that will allow them to remain true to their authentic self and cites evidence for how work tasks that are not inherently enjoyable can be experienced as both intrinsically motivating and meaningful if they are connected to components of an individual's self-concept. Taken together, these approaches highlight the teleological components of the fit-meaning association. In other words, fit is experienced as meaningful if it contributes towards the fulfilment of a broader purpose, like expressing one's values/beliefs or making one feel significant. Another view of the meaning-fit association takes a more epistemic perspective, highlighting how feelings of work engagement or immersion can contribute to an experience's meaningfulness.

A more epistemic perspective of the fit-meaning relationship sees high work–role fit as providing the ideal conditions for one to become immersed in one's work and generate a sense of flow or coherence. This sense of flow/coherence may subsequently give rise to greater feelings of meaningfulness. For example, Csikszentmihalyi (1975) defines flow as a state in which there is little distinction between the self and the environment. When in a state of flow, individuals require no external rewards or sources of motivation as they are fully absorbed in their activities. Flow is a peak experience of total absorption (Csikszentmihalyi, 1975), but in applying the concept to occupational settings, Kahn (1990) suggests that people vary in the degree to which they immerse themselves in their working tasks. Flow gives rise to a sense of coherence (Antonovsky, 1987) which may be experienced as meaningfulness. For example, lab studies by Heintzelman et al. (2013) demonstrate that engaging in tasks which are inherently coherent leads to greater ratings of meaning in life. If people come to associate work with feelings of coherence, they are more likely to rate it as meaningful.

Overall, viewing the meaning of work literature through the lens of social cognition and self-regulatory processes gives us a unique perspective on the different ways people experience meaning in the workplace. Taking this perspective highlights that, to date, there has been a predominant focus on teleological meaning, even though – as we have seen – there is much evidence for the influence of epistemic facets too.

This social cognitive perspective can help us uncover novel sources of meaning in the workplace. Heintzelman and King (2014b) suggest that, taking an epistemic point of view, one can see how routine and habits can contribute to experienced meaningfulness. For example, unemployed participants can attenuate the negative outcomes associated with their situation if they maintain routines and a rigid time structure (Van Hoye and Lootens, 2013). Moreover, finding more 'mundane' sources of meaning at work may be vital in helping us regulate our sense of meaning when it is under threat. From an epistemic perspective, meaning threats can take the form of expectancy violations (e.g., psychological contract breaches), cognitive inconsistencies (e.g., perceptions of injustice) and experienced uncertainty (e.g., job insecurity). In a world of work increasingly characterised by precarious employment (Kalleberg, 2011), such experiences are likely to be commonplace and this highlights the challenge of maintaining meaning in our everyday working environments., Thus, in the next section, we consider sources of meaning *threat* in the workplace.

THREATS TO ONE'S SENSE OF MEANING AT WORK

Given that our work roles are linked with our ability to derive meaning in our day-to-day lives, it is likely that certain work-related experiences may serve as particularly potent forms of meaninglessness or meaning threats. Indeed, Hogg (2007) suggested that the contemporary world of work is a strong and enduring source of uncertainty. As we discussed previously, people are inspired to respond to such experiences by defending their sense of meaning and will do so automatically and without awareness. When meaning-regulation takes the form of initial responses aimed at distancing/distracting ourselves from the threat (proximal defence), the effects can be counter-productive. By exacerbating cognitive bias (e.g., increased stereotyping) and increasing avoidance behaviours (e.g., unhealthy eating), proximal meaning-regulation responses resulting from work-related threats are likely to disrupt well-being and performance (Pyszczynski et al., 1999; Routledge et al., 2010).

There are many prevalent situations within the work domain which present clear threats to one's perceived meaning. For example, as we highlighted in the beginning, *precarious forms of employment*, which lead to job insecurity, have become increasingly more prevalent over the last half a century (see Kalleberg, 2011). Job insecurity is defined as a situation within which an employee lacks the assurance that their job will continue to exist in the future, and this naturally presents a high level of uncertainty at work. Research suggests that 45% of US workers experience job insecurity and, in certain cases, the experience is more damaging to health than unemployment (Burgard et al., 2009). Even on an organisational level, job insecurity can also be problematic as it can be a factor in organisational mergers and acquisitions (Hogg, 2001; Terry et al., 2001). As highlighted above, when individuals experience high levels of uncertainty, it can be appraised as a meaning threat and lead to forms of meaning-regulation (Heine et al., 2006). In the case of a merger, employees may deal with the uncertainty this fosters by identifying more strongly with the pre-merger organisation and therefore disrupt commitment to, and acceptance of, the new organisational structure (Hogg, 2001).

Another example for sources of meaning threats at work pertains to the *design of work* and, more specifically, to poorly designed jobs. Past research has demonstrated that poorly designed jobs are characterised by role ambiguity, role conflict, and lack of a clear purpose about the tasks one is asked to perform (Kahn et al., 1964; Vanishree, 2014). Activities that lack a clear purpose serve as a threat to our sense of meaning from a teleological perspective. Indeed, meta-analyses have consistently found that role ambiguity is negatively associated with work satisfaction, commitment, involvement, and performance (Fisher and Gitelson, 1983; Tubre and Collins, 2000). Furthermore, inadequate knowledge of the organisation's objectives and goals has been shown to increase levels of stress among employees (Idris, 2011). In certain circumstances, poorly designed jobs can also lead to boredom (Gemmill and Oakley, 1992).

I/O psychology research has highlighted *workplace boredom* as a major issue in modern day occupational settings (Cummings et al., 2016; Fisher, 1993; Loukidou et al., 2009). Cummings et al. (2016) cite statistics from an online workplace rating site with a sample of over 2,000 college graduates. Here, 61% of those surveyed stated that jobs were boring due to lack of challenge. Among this sample, administrative and manufacturing jobs were rated the most boring (Cummings et al., 2016). Boredom, appraised as low in purpose and attention and lacking challenge, leads to a reduced sense of meaning in life (Van Tilburg and Igou, 2012; 2017b). It is associated with absenteeism and poor retention rates (Fisher, 1993) as well as health problems (Britton and Shipley, 2010) and substance abuse (LePera, 2011). Research demonstrates that boredom triggers a search for meaning (Van Tilburg and Igou, 2012, 2017b) and, when this leads to distraction, it can have serious negative consequences in high risk settings. Dangerous incidents of boredom induced low attention and distraction have been reported among anaesthesiologists (Weinger, 1999), train drivers (Dunn and Williamson, 2011) and even airplane pilots (see Cummings et al., 2016).

Each of these scenarios provides an example of how meaning threats at work can have negative consequences. As such, it is important for employees and organisations to develop effective strategies of meaning-regulation which buffer against the negative effects of meaning threats. In the next section, we will review how the meaning-regulation literature can inform the development of such strategies and consider research from the organisational literature regarding attempts to address one form of meaning-regulation.

MEANING-REGULATION AT WORK

Broadly speaking, the meaning of work literature has not yet comprehensively addressed the issue of meaninglessness, meaning threat, or meaning-regulation at work.

However, one approach put forward by Wrzesniewski and Dutton (2001) builds upon the job design model to suggest ways in which individuals may enhance the meaningfulness they derive from work by introducing changes to their working life. This process has been termed *job crafting* (see also Berg et al., 2013), and here, we will review this approach and consider how it can be considered a form of meaning-regulation; i.e., a strategy for reaffirming or defending our sense of meaning. We then suggest additional strategies with a stronger basis in meaning maintenance models as novel areas for future applied research.

Job Crafting

While the job design approach highlights how work can be made more meaningful from the 'top-down' perspective, the job crafting approach aims to emphasise how employees themselves can make alterations to better cultivate the experience of meaning through work (Berg et al., 2013). Wrzesniewski and Dutton (2001) define *job crafting* as 'the physical and cognitive changes individuals make in the task or relational boundaries of their work'. Crafters are encouraged to reshape the boundaries of their job through a combination of three different techniques. This first form of crafting involves changing *task* boundaries. This is achieved by altering the number and type of tasks done at work or by altering the amount of time and energy devoted to different tasks. The second form of crafting involves changing the *relational* boundaries of work. This is achieved by adjusting the types of interactions people have with others at work. One can change how, when, or with whom they interact most on the job. Finally, the third form of crafting involves changing the *cognitive* boundaries of their job. This is achieved by changing the way one perceives their job and the relationships within it. So one could reframe their view of a certain task by considering how it is a small part of a much wider process that may, for example, encourage positive societal change. Overall, crafters can use any combination of these three techniques to help experience more meaning for their work.

Job crafting interventions may offer promise for tackling threats to meaning in the work domain. For example, crafting has been shown to impact adaptive performance during organisational change (Van Mersbergen, 2012), which can be considered a threat to one's meaning. Van Mersbergen (2012) found that a job crafting intervention increased perceptions of job resources and decreased perceptions of job demands, which in turn, has a positive effect on work engagement and positive emotions. The results also demonstrated that the intervention had an impact on adaptive performance. Although this research did not examine it, one potential explanation for the relationship between job crafting and adaptive performance may be via the reduction of meaning threats. As we outlined above, organisational change and its inherent uncertainty can be considered a meaning threat, and crafting one's job may give individuals a sense of control and autonomy, thus modifying their threat appraisal. This perspective has not been investigated to our knowledge, but presents an important avenue for future research. Past literature has called for a greater focus on understanding the underlying mechanisms of the intervention (Lyubomirsky and Layous, 2013; Michel et al., 2015; Nielsen and Randall, 2012), and to date, job crafting interventions have not focused on the reduction of meaning threats as a mechanism.

Despite Wrzesniewski and Dutton (2001) providing support for the fact that job crafting is a meaning making strategy, little of the now considerable body of research on job crafting has subsequently examined whether meaning is a mechanism through which job crafting has its effects on well-being, work engagement, and performance (Petrou et al., 2012; van den Heuvel et al., 2015). However,

Tims et al. (2016) conducted a three wave weekly study to understand the impact of job crafting on person–job fit and meaningfulness. Their results demonstrated that those who crafted their jobs by increasing their job resources (e.g., support, autonomy), challenging job demands (such as participating in new projects), and decreasing their hindering job demands (e.g., reducing their emotional job demands) reported higher person–job fit during the next week. A higher demands-ability fit in turn related to more meaningfulness in the final week of the study. This research demonstrates that job redesign interventions, which move the focus away from the characteristics of the job to the fit between the job demands and employees abilities to meet these demands, have potential to influence the sources of meaning at work for individuals.

However, while empirical evidence provides support for job crafting as a meaning making strategy (Berg et al., 2013), there are some key limitations that constrain its effectiveness. It is clear that not all jobs will be conducive to job crafting. In particular, the first two forms of job crafting (task and relational) require a degree of autonomy that not every employee is fortunate enough to experience. Indeed, Lyons (2008) found that the likelihood of engaging in job crafting is dependent upon an employee's perceived level of control. Across different sectors and job levels, many positions require jobs to be performed in a uniform or strictly procedural way. For example, there is likely to be little employee autonomy on a manufacturing line. Similarly, an accountant position can involve highly regimented routines that include little scope for crafting. These issues are a particularly strong limitation if we are to consider job crafting as a tool for meaning-regulation. This is because a job lacking autonomy is also likely to be one where experiencing meaningfulness may be challenging. Furthermore, it is likely that those working in highly regimented positions will experience high levels of boredom on the job. As such, the only job crafting solution available to individuals in such situations would be some form of cognitive reframing; that is, changing how they perceive their job. However, the efficacy of this technique may, at times, be limited to certain job types. There is evidence to suggest that, in some instances, this form of crafting may have negative consequences, leading people to see their work as more meaningless. For example, individuals who aim to reframe their work by linking it to an 'unanswered calling' (see Wrzesniewski et al., 1997) can experience regret and frustration at the fact that their current job clearly cannot be linked to a broader more valuable purpose (Berg et al., 2010). In this case, the strategy is likely to backfire and increase experiences of meaninglessness or meaning threat.

Nevertheless, job crafting can be an effective way to establish and reaffirm a sense of meaningfulness at work. However, given the limitations we highlight above, many employees across different disciplines are unlikely, or unable, to use job crafting as a strategy for meaning-regulation. So what can employees do when restrained by a lack of autonomy or opportunities to reframe their positions? This is when a 'distal' form of meaning-regulation, specifically fluid compensation, can prove fruitful.

Fluid Compensation

As we explained previously, *Fluid Compensation at Work* refers to the process whereby meaning is regulated by reaffirming meaning elsewhere, even if this alternative meaning source bears no relation to the threat (Heine et al., 2006). Research in I/O psychology already provides examples of such meaning-regulation strategies taking place in occupational settings. For instance, Elsbach (2003) outlines how workers who use non-territorial workspaces (e.g., 'hot-desks') perceive a threat to their workplace identity. Employees in this situation will engage in identity affirmation by, for example, displaying family pictures or symbols of educational achievement on portable artefacts. Such fluid compensation is not disruptive and, as such, can be contrasted with the other common response to this situation; simply refusing to move desks (Elsbach, 2003). In another example of work-related fluid compensation, Ashforth and Kreiner (1999) explain how employees with socially stigmatised jobs establish strong occupational and work group cultures. In other words, employees in these situations establish shared and deeply held systems of values and norms. Many may expect the opposite to be the case, assuming that these workers would be more likely to distance themselves from one another and from their stigmatised roles. However, from a meaning-regulation perspective, the workers' identity affirming strategy may help reaffirm a sense of meaningfulness in their work (Beyer, 1981).

Organisations and individuals can capitalise upon the interchangeable nature of fluid compensation strategies. In other words, reaffirming values and meaningful affiliations helps us maintain a sense of meaningfulness and buffers us from the effects of meaning threats, *regardless of the source of the threat.* If a job is lacking in autonomy and a cognitive reframing strategy is not effective, individuals can compensate by, for example, fostering feelings of nostalgia (Van Tilburg et al., 2013). Alternatively, organisations can provide more opportunities for employees to engage in meaning affirmation. Grant (2007) outlines how organisations can design certain jobs in a way that emphasis the prosocial impact of their work by, for example, increasing contact with beneficiaries. Grant (2007) discusses this as a way to motivate employees. As we have seen, opportunities to engage in pro-social behaviour can act as a form of meaning-regulation (Van Tilburg and Igou, 2017) but, equally, so can many alternative ways to affirm social identity, even if it is as simple as displaying a symbol (Elsbach, 2003).

PRACTICAL APPLICATIONS AND INTERVENTIONS TO ENHANCE MEANING

This chapter shows the potential for meaning of work research to be enhanced by considering social psychological approaches to meaning and meaning-regulation. We have demonstrated the potential of job crafting interventions for harnessing meaning in work environments. In this final section, we consider additional ways in which meaning and meaning-regulation can be practically applied through the design and implementation of interventions to enhance meaning and the effective regulation of meaning in work environments. As we outlined, deriving meaning from work can come from both teleological (significance and purpose) and epistemic (sense-making and understanding) sources. From a teleological perspective, work will feel more meaningful if it has greater purpose or social significance.

Enhancing Meaning at Work

A study conducted by Clauss et al. (2018) evaluated the effectiveness of a positive work reflection designed to promote meaning on psychological resources and exhaustion. This study examined a daily intervention asking caregivers to reflect on a positive and meaningful event that happened during their working day for two working weeks. The results demonstrated that, compared to a control group, emotional exhaustion and fatigue decreased for those in the intervention group. Furthermore, the study found that the psychological resources of hope and optimism increased in the intervention group for those with a high need for recovery. This research demonstrated that interventions designed to promote reflection on epistemic meaning can have a positive impact on psychological well-being and psychological resources.

Prosocial aspects of job design present a further avenue for enhancing sources of meaning at work. As we have highlighted, Grant (2007) proposed a model of relational job design which focuses on the job impact on beneficiaries and contact with beneficiaries, which could indirectly impact on an individual's social worth, self-determination, and competence. Michaelson et al. (2014) suggest that meaningfulness can be cultivated through a social identity approach, and building on these two perspectives, Arieli et al. (2014) implemented a benevolence intervention which aimed to develop values of benevolence which reflect the motivation to help and care for others. Findings demonstrated that their 30 minute intervention did indeed increase benevolence values and, in turn, increased participant's willingness to volunteer to help others. Although this intervention did not assess whether meaningfulness increased, the next logical step for future research is to examine whether such interventions that tap sources of meaning do indeed enhance meaning in the workplace.

Decreasing Meaning Threats

Another way to intervene to enhance the meaning of work is to decrease meaning threats, and this can also be done by enhancing the 'teleological' aspects of meaning. As we stated, boredom represents a prominent threat to meaning in the workplace that can have severe negative consequences. Despite this, there is little research in I/O psychology aimed at addressing this problem. However, evidence from the educational domain suggests certain interventions can reduce boredom and increase engagement. Like work, education is an achievement context and so applying techniques from this area to occupational settings should prove fruitful. Specifically, techniques that aim to increase intrinsic motivation, or interest, at work will help eliminate boredom and its consequences. For example, Hulleman et al. (2010) tested an intervention based in a utility-value approach, aimed at helping students find value and meaning in their work. The intervention was a ten minute writing task which asked participants to explain how the work they were doing was relevant to their lives. Compared to controls, students who took part in the intervention showed an increase in situational interest beyond the intervention, both in a lab study and in a longitudinal field study. The increase in utility value also transferred to higher performance. Such an intervention fosters meaningfulness from a teleological perspective. In other words, it increases one's ability to find significance and purpose in their work.

Meaning threats, such as boredom at work, may also be tackled from an epistemic perspective by increased feelings of absorption or flow. Eastwood et al. (2012) refer to 'task-related imagination' as a strategy for increasing intrinsic motivation by turning a task into a game or 'mental cinema'. When the content of one's imagination is related to the task at hand, this will increase task absorption and, by extension, meaning (Csikszentmihalyi, 1975). Recently, a related intervention, known as *gamification*, has been tested as a way to increase intrinsic motivation. Gamification involves adding game-like elements (e.g., leader boards, challenges, scoring, badges) to non-game settings (e.g., work). Like other interventions to improve intrinsic motivation, this technique has been particularly successful in education (Barata et al., 2013). It has also been proposed as a way to reduce boredom in drivers (Schroeter et al., 2014). There is already some evidence supporting the efficacy of this technique in work settings (e.g., Flatla et al., 2011), though more research is needed. Overall, reviews demonstrate that gamification has been a successful way to increase motivation and engagement across many different contexts (Hamari et al., 2014), including in the work domain.

Interpersonal Sense-Making

Sense-making has been theorised to be an important component of meaning maintenance

(Proulx and Inzlicht, 2012). Job crafting interventions that focus specifically on the relational aspect of crafting and on interpersonal sense-making hold the potential to reduce meaning threats. Employees actively shape their own meaning through their sense-making of cues received from co-workers and the tendency to pursue particular types of cues (Wrzesniewski et al., 2003). An individual's self-perspective is co-founded through social interactions; hence, a cue received from a co-worker that is interpreted as significant will have an impact on the meaning one constructs of their job, role, and self (Wrzesniewski et al., 2003). The interpersonal sense-making model of workplace meaning considers how employees make sense of a person's motives for acting in a particular way. Considering whether an act was intentional or not on the part of another person has the ability to increase, or decrease, the impact of affirmative/dissaffirmative cues on the meaning of work (Wrzesniewski et al., 2003). This idea is supported by attribution theory (Fiske and Taylor, 1991; Kelley, 1971) and considers how an individual uses information to arrive at a causal explanation for the occurrence of particular events.

An intervention that influences sense-making cues that individuals exhibit, as well as the way in which they interpret the cues of others, should influence the meaning of work for individuals. Relational job crafting may provide employees with the opportunity to actively craft their interpersonal relationships into higher quality connections, therefore enhancing their work experience, and consequently, work meaning as well as increasing job commitment and positive attitudes (Chiaburu and Harrison, 2008; Salancik and Pfeffer, 1978). Relational job crafting can be easily developed as a workplace intervention. A relational job crafting intervention which utilises the model of interpersonal sense-making to encourage employees to notice the affirmative social cues received from co-workers within their work and reappraise the dissaffirmative relational cues has the potential to positively impact the meaning of work.

An interpersonal sense-making intervention may also work by decreasing the extent to which individuals perceive meaning threats and fostering a greater sense of meaning through both epistemic and teleological pathways. From a teleological perspective, interpersonal sense-making can foster feelings of belongingness and give one the impression that they are part of something bigger than themselves. From an epistemic perspective, sense-making enhances our ability to feel connected and experience work in a more coherent fashion. It also highlights how future research on job crafting can be refocused to investigate how interventions specifically influence meaning. Past research on civility interventions would support this line of reasoning. Civility interventions in the workplace have shown that increasing civil behaviours among co-workers fosters trust and positive attitudes and decreases distress (Laschinger et al., 2012; Leiter et al., 2011; Leiter et al., 2012). Future research would benefit from investigating whether such interventions have their effects via the reduction of meaning threats.

CONCLUSION

Overall, the research reviewed here demonstrates how important our sense of meaning is to our everyday working lives. Experiencing meaningfulness at work is associated with a host of positive outcomes and there are many different ways individuals and organisations can help cultivate this experience. Furthermore, if this sense of meaning is threatened or disrupted, people will be motivated to repair, reaffirm, and create new meaning. This can disrupt one's ability to function optimally at work and lead to undesirable outcomes such as cognitive bias, absenteeism, disengagement, and outgroup derogation. However, as meaning-regulation research demonstrates, psychological responses triggered by meaning threat can be used relatively interchangeably to address this threat. Reaffirming values and meaningful affiliations or engaging in nostalgic reflection can help us maintain a sense of personal meaningfulness and buffer us from the effects of meaning threats, regardless of the source of that threat. We adopted a social cognitive perspective and examined meaning at work by distinguishing teleological and epistemic forms of meaning and meaning-regulation processes. By integrating this with research from I/O psychology, we gave examples for practical interventions aimed at increasing our sense of meaning at work and reducing the impact of meaning threats.

Applying the concept of meaning-regulation to organisational research can help scholars gain a greater understanding of work behaviour and performance. It should also inspire future research aimed at investigating the many different ways people regulate meaning in the workplace. Ultimately, this knowledge will help organisations and individuals reach their full potential at work and in everyday working life.

REFERENCES

Antonovsky, A. (1987). Health promoting factors at work: The sense of coherence. In R. Kalimo, M. A. El-Batawi, & C. L. Cooper (Eds.), *Psychosocial factors at work and their relation to health* (pp. 153–167). Geneva, CH: World Health Organization.

Arieli, S., Grant, A. M., & Sagiv, L. (2014). Convincing yourself to care about others: An intervention for enhancing benevolence values. *Journal of Personality*, *82*, 15–24. 2004

Ashforth, B. E., & Kreiner, G. E. (1999). 'How can you do it?': Dirty work and the challenge of constructing a positive identity. *Academy of Management Review*, *24*, 413–434.

Bandura, A. (1991). Social cognitive theory of self-regulation. *Organizational Behavior and Human Decision Processes*, *50*, 248–287.

Barata, G., Gama, S., Jorge, J., & Gonçalves, D. (2013, September). Engaging engineering students with gamification. Paper presented at the *5th International Conference on Games and Virtual Worlds for Serious Applications (VG-Games).* Washington, DC: IEEE Computer Society Press.

Baumeister, R. F. (1991). *Work, work, work, work. Meanings of Life* (pp. 116–144). New York, NY: The Guilford Press.

Baumeister, R. F., & Vohs, K. D. (2002). The pursuit of meaningfulness in life. In C. R. Snyder & S. J. Lopez (Eds.), *The handbook of positive psychology* (pp. 608–618). New York, NY: Oxford University Press.

Becker, E. (1973). *The denial of death*. New York, NY: Simon & Schuster.

Benach, J., & Muntaner, C. (2007). Precarious employment and health: developing a research agenda. *Journal of Epidemiology and Community Health*, *61*(4), 276–277.

Berg, J. M., Dutton, J. E., & Wrzesniewski, A. (2013). Job crafting and meaningful work. In B. J. Dik, Z. S. Byrne, & M. F. Steger (Eds.), *Purpose and meaning in the workplace* (pp. 81–104). Washington, DC: American Psychological Association.

Berg, J. M., Grant, A. M., & Johnson, V. (2010). When callings are calling: Crafting work and leisure in pursuit of unanswered occupational callings. *Organization Science*, 21, 973–994.

Besharov, M. L. (2008). Mission goes corporate: Understanding employee behavior in a mission-driven business. (Unpublished doctoral dissertation). Harvard Business School, Boston, MA.

Beyer, J. M. (1981). Ideologies, values, and decision making in organizations. In P. C. Nystrom and W. H. Starbuck (Eds.), *Handbook of organizational design Vol. 2* (pp. 166–202). New York: Oxford University Press.

Boles, M., Pelletier, B., & Lynch, W. (2004). The relationship between health risks and work productivity. *Journal of Occupational and Environmental Medicine*, *46*(7), 737–745.

Boyle, P. A., Buchman, A. S., Barnes, L. L., & Bennett, D. A. (2010). Effect of a purpose in life on risk of incident Alzheimer disease and mild cognitive impairment in community-dwelling older persons. *Archives of General Psychiatry*, *67*, 304–310.

Brief, A. P., & Nord, W. R. (1990). *Meanings of occupational work*. Lexington: Lexington Books.

Britton, A., & Shipley, M. J. (2010). Bored to death? *International Journal of Epidemiology*, *39*, 370–371.

Bunderson, J. S., & Thompson, J. A. (2009). The call of the wild: Zookeepers, callings, and the double-edged sword of deeply meaningful work. *Administrative Science Quarterly*, *54*, 32–57.

Burgard, S. A., Brand, J. E., & House, J. S. (2009). Perceived job insecurity and worker health in the United States. *Social Science & Medicine*, *69*(5), 777–785.

Chiaburu, D. S., & Harrison, D. A. (2008). Do peers make the place? Conceptual synthesis and meta-analysis of coworker effects on perceptions, attitudes, OCBs, and performance. *Journal of Applied Psychology*, *93*(5), 1082-1103.

Clauss, E., Hoppe, A., O'Shea, D., Gonzalez-Morales, M. G., Steidle, A., & Michel, A. (2018). Promoting personal resources and reducing exhaustion through positive work reflection among caregivers. *Journal of Occupational Health Psychology*, *23*(1), 127–140.

Craig, A. D. (2009). How do you feel—Now? The anterior insula and human awareness. *Nature Reviews Neuroscience*, *10*, 59–70.

Csikszentmihalyi, M. (1975). Play and intrinsic rewards. *Journal of Humanistic Psychology*, *15*, 41–63.

Cummings, M. L., Gao, F., & Thornburg, K. M. (2016). Boredom in the workplace: A new look at an old problem. *Human Factors: The Journal of the Human Factors and Ergonomics Society*, *58*, 279–300.

Dechesne, M., & Kruglanski, A. (2004). Experimental existentialism and the concept of closure. In J. Greenberg, S. L. Koole, & T. Pyszczynski (Eds.), *Handbook of experimental existential psychology* (pp. 247–262). New York, NY: Guilford Press.

Duffy, R. D., & Sedlacek, W. E. (2007). The presence of and search for a calling: Connections to career development. *Journal of Vocational Behavior*, *70*, 590–560.

Dunn, N., & Williamson, A. (2011, July). *Monotony in the rail industry: The role of task demand in mitigating monotony related effects on performance*. Paper presented at the Ergonomics Australia–HFESA 2011 Conference, Sydney, Australia.

Eastwood, J. D., Frischen, A., Fenske, M. J., & Smilek, D. (2012). The unengaged mind: Defining boredom in terms of attention. *Perspectives on Psychological Science*, *7*, 482–495.

Elsbach, K. D. (2003). Relating physical environment to self-categorizations: Identity threat and affirmation in a non-territorial office space. *Administrative Science Quarterly*, *48*(4), 622.

Emmons, R. A. (1997). Motives and life goals. In R. Hogan, J. Johnson, & S. Briggs (Eds.), *Handbook of personality psychology*, San Diego, CA: Academic Press.

Emmons, R. (2003) Acts of Gratitude in Organizations. In K.S. Cameron, J.E. Dutton, & R.E. Quinn (Eds.), *Positive organizational scholarship* (pp. 81–93). San Francisco: Berrett-Koehler.

Festinger, L. (1957). *A theory of cognitive dissonance*. Stanford, CA: Stanford University Press.

Fisher, C. D. (1993). Boredom at work: A neglected concept. *Human Relations*, *46*, 395–417.

Fisher, C. D., & Gitelson, R. (1983). A meta-analysis of the correlates of role conflict and ambiguity. *Journal of Applied Psychology*, *68*, 320.

Fiske, S. T., & Taylor, S. E. (1991). *Social cognition* (2nd edn.). New York: McGraw-Hill.

Flatla, D. R., Gutwin, C., Nacke, L. E., Bateman, S., & Mandryk, R. L. (2011). Calibration games: making calibration tasks enjoyable by adding motivating game elements. In *Proceedings of the 24th Annual ACM Symposium on User Interface Software and Technology* (pp. 403–412). Santa Barbara, CA: ACM.

Frankl, V. E. (1946). *Man's search for meaning.* Boston: Beacon Press.

Fried, Y., & Ferris, G. R. (1987). The validity of the job characteristics model: A review and meta-analysis. *Personnel Psychology*, *40*(2), 287–322.

Fromm, E. (1947). *Man for himself*. New York, NY: Holt, Rinehardt, & Winston.

Fryer, D. (1986). Employment deprivation and personal agency during unemployment: A critical discussion of Jahoda's explanation of the psychological effects of unemployment. *Social Behaviour*, *1*(1), 3–23.

Fryer, D., & Payne, R. (1984). Proactive behaviour in unemployment: Findings and implications. *Leisure Studies*, *3*(3), 273–295.

Geldenhuys, M., Łaba, K., & Venter, C. M. (2014). Meaningful work, work engagement and organisational commitment. *South African Journal of Industrial Psychology*, *40*(1), doi:10.4102/sajip.v40i1.1098

Gemmill, G., & Oakley, J. (1992). The meaning of boredom in organizational life. *Group & Organization Management*, *17*(4), 358–369.

Grant, A. M. (2007). Relational job design and the motivation to make a prosocial difference. *Academy of Management Review*, *32*, 393–417.

Grant, A. M. (2008). The significance of task significance: Job performance effects, relational mechanisms, and boundary conditions. *Journal of Applied Psychology*, *93*, 108–124.

Greenberg, J., Koole, S. L., & Pyszczynski, T. (2004). *Handbook of experimental existential psychology*. New York: Guilford Press.

Greenberg, J., Pyszczynski, T., Solomon, S., Rosenblatt, A., Veeder, M., Kirkland, S., & Lyon, D. (1990). Evidence for terror management theory II: The effects of mortality salience on reactions to those who threaten or bolster the cultural worldview. *Journal of Personality and Social Psychology*, *58*(2), 308.

Greenberg, J., Solomon, S., & Pyszczynski, T. (1997). Terror management theory of self-esteem and cultural worldviews: Empirical assessment and conceptual refinements. In M. P. Zanna (Ed.), *Advances in experimental social psychology* (Vol. 29, pp. 61–139), Orlando, FL: Academic Press.

Hackman, J. R., & Oldham, G. R. (1976). Motivation through design of work – Test of a theory. *Organizational Behavior and Human Performance*, *16*(2), 250–279.

Hamari, J., Koivisto, J., & Sarsa, H. (2014). Does gamification work? – A literature review of empirical studies on gamification. In *2014 47th Hawaii International Conference on System Sciences* (pp. 3025–3034). Washington, DC: IEEE Computer Society Press.

Harlow, L. L., Newcomb, M. D., & Bentler, P. M. (1986). Depression, self-derogation, substance use, and suicide ideation: Lack of purpose in life as a mediational factor. *Journal of Clinical Psychology*, *42*, 5–21.

Harmon-Jones, E., Simon, L., Greenberg, J., Pyszczynski, T., Solomon, S., & McGregor, H. (1997). Terror management theory and self-esteem: Evidence that increased self-esteem reduces mortality salience effects. *Journal of Personality and Social Psychology*, *72*, 24–36.

Heine, S. J., Proulx, T., & Vohs, K. D. (2006). The meaning maintenance model: On the coherence of social motivations. *Personality and Social Psychology Review*, *10*(2), 88–110.

Heintzelman, S. J., & King, L. A. (2014a). Life is pretty meaningful. *American Psychologist*, *69*(6), 561.

Heintzelman, S. J., & King, L. A. (2014b). (The feeling of) meaning-as-information. *Personality and Social Psychology Review*, *18*(2), 153–167.

Heintzelman, S. J., Trent, J., & King, L. A. (2013). Encounters with objective coherence and the experience of meaning in life. *Psychological Science*, *24*(6), 991–998.

Hogg, M. A. (2001). Social categorization, depersonalization, and group behavior. In M. A. Hogg & R. S. Tindale (Eds.), *Blackwell handbook of social psychology: Group processes* (pp. 56–85). Oxford, England: Blackwell.

Hogg, M. A. (2007). Uncertainty–identity theory. In M. P. Zanna (Ed.), *Advances in experimental social psychology* (Vol. 39, pp. 69–126). San Diego, CA: Academic Press.

Holbrook, C., & Sousa, P. (2013). Supernatural beliefs, unconscious threat, and judgment bias in Tibetan Buddhists. *Journal of Cognition and Culture*, *13*, 33–56.

Hulleman, C. S., Godes, O., Hendricks, B. L., & Harackiewicz, J. M. (2010). Enhancing interest and performance with a utility value intervention. *Journal of Educational Psychology*, *102*, 880.

Humphrey, S. E., Nahrgang, J. D., & Morgeson, F. P. (2007). Integrating motivational, social, and contextual work design features: a meta-analytic summary and theoretical extension of the work design literature. *Journal of Applied Psychology*, *92*, 1332.

Idris, M.K. (2011). Over time effects of role stress on psychological strain among Malaysian public university academics. *International Journal of Business and Social Science*, *2*(9), 154–161.

Jahoda, M. (1982). *Employment and unemployment: A social-psychological analysis*. London: Cambridge University Press.

Jonas, E., & Fischer, P. (2006). Terror management and religion: Evidence that intrinsic religiousness mitigates worldview defense following mortality salience. *Journal of Personality and Social Psychology, 91*, 553–567.

Jonas, E., McGregor, I., Klackl, J., Agroskin, D., Fritsche, I., Holbrook, C., & Quirin, M. (2014). Threat and defense: From anxiety to approach. *Advances in Experimental Social Psychology, 49*, 219–286.

Kahn, W. A. (1990). Psychological conditions of personal engagement and disengagement at work. *Academy of Management Journal, 33*, 692–724.

Kahn, W. A., & Fellows, S. (2013). Employee engagement and meaningful work. In B. J. Dik, Z. S. Byrne, & M. F. Steger (Eds.) *Purpose and meaning in the workplace* (pp. 105–126). Washington, DC: American Psychological Association.

Kahn, R. L., Wolfe, D. M., Quinn, R. P., Snoek, J. D., & Rosenthal, R. A. (1964). *Organizational stress: Studies in role conflict and ambiguity*. Oxford: John Wiley.

Kalleberg, A. L. (2011). *Good jobs, bad jobs: The rise of polarized and precarious employment systems in the United States, 1970s–2000s*. New York: Russell Sage Foundation.

Kalleberg, A. L., & Hewison, K. (2013). Precarious work and the challenge for Asia. *American Behavioral Scientist, 57*(3), 271–288.

Kelley, H. H. (1971). *Attribution in social interaction*. New York: General Learning Press.

Kouvonen, A., Kivimäki, M., Cox, S. J., Cox, T., & Vahtera, J. (2005). Relationship between work stress and body mass index among 45,810 female and male employees. *Psychosomatic Medicine, 67*(4), 577–583.

Krause, N. (2009). Meaning in life and mortality. *The Journals of Gerontology Series B: Psychological Sciences and Social Sciences, 64*, 517–527.

Krause, N., & Hayward, R. D. (2014). Assessing stability and change in a second-order confirmatory factor model of meaning in life. *Journal of Happiness Studies, 15*, 237–253.

Kristof, A. L. (1996). Person-organization fit: An integrative review of its conceptualizations, measurement, and implications. *Personnel Psychology, 49*(1), 1–49.

Kruglanski, A. W. (2004). *The psychology of closed-mindedness*. New York, NY: Psychology Press.

Landau, M. J., & Greenberg, J. (2006). Play it safe or go for the gold? A terror management perspective on self-enhancement and protection motives in risky decision making. *Personality and Social Psychology Bulletin, 32*, 1633–1645.

Laschinger, H. K. S., Leiter, M. P., Day, A., Gilin-Oore, D., & Mackinnon, S. P. (2012). Building empowering work environments that foster civility and organizational trust: Testing an intervention. *Nursing Research, 61*, 316–325.

Leiter, M. P., Day, A., Oore, D. G., & Laschinger, H. K. S. (2012). Getting better and staying better: Assessing civility, incivility, distress, and job attitudes one year after a civility intervention. *Journal of Occupational Health Psychology, 17*, 425–434.

Leiter, M. P., Laschinger, H. K. S., Day, A., & Oore, D. G. (2011). The impact of civility interventions on employee social behavior, distress, and attitudes. *Journal of Applied Psychology, 96*, 1258–1274.

LePera, N. (2011). The relationships between boredom proneness, mindfulness, anxiety, depression, and substance use. *New School Psychology Bulletin, 8*, 15–25.

Littman-Ovadia, H., & Steger, M. (2010). Character strengths and well-being among volunteers and employees: Toward an integrative model. *The Journal of Positive Psychology, 5*, 419–430.

Loukidou, L., Loan-Clarke, J., & Daniels, K. (2009). Boredom in the workplace: More than monotonous tasks. *International Journal of Management Reviews, 11*, 381–405.

Lyons, P. (2008). The crafting of jobs and individual differences. *Journal of Business and Psychology, 23*, 25–36.

Lyubomirsky, S., & Layous, K. (2013). How do simple positive activities increase well-being? *Current Directions in Psychological Science, 22*, 57–62.

Maher, P. J., Van Tilburg, W. A. P., & Van Den Tol, A. J. M. (2013). Meaning in music: Deviations from expectations in music prompt outgroup derogation. *European Journal of Social Psychology, 43*, 449–454.

Mann, S. (2007). The boredom boom. *The Psychologist, 20*, 90–93.

Martela, F., & Steger, M. F. (2016). The meaning of meaning in life: Coherence, purpose and significance as the three facets of meaning. *Journal of Positive Psychology*, *11*(5), 1–15.

Maslow, A. H. (1964). *Religions, values, and peak experiences*. Columbus, OH: Ohio State University Press.

May, D. R. (2003). Fostering the human spirit at work: Toward an understanding of the influences on employees' experienced meaningfulness at work. Unpublished manuscript.

May, D. R., Gilson, R. L., & Harter, L. M. (2004). The psychological conditions of meaningfulness, safety and availability and the engagement of the human spirit at work. *Journal of Occupational and Organizational Psychology*, *77*, 11–37.

McCann, D. (2014). Equality through precarious work regulation: lessons from the domestic work debates in defence of the Standard Employment Relationship. *International Journal of Law in Context*, *10*, 507–521.

McNaughton, N., & Corr, P. J. (2004). A two-dimensional neuropsychology of defense: Fear/anxiety and defensive distance. *Neuroscience & Biobehavioral Reviews*, *28*, 285–305.

Michaelson, C., Pratt, M. G., Grant, A. M., & Dunn, C. P. (2014). Meaningful work: Connecting business ethics and organization studies. *Journal of Business Ethics*, *121*, 77–90.

Michel, A., O'Shea, D., & Hoppe, A. (2015). Designing and evaluating resource-oriented interventions to enhance employee well-being and health. *Journal of Occupational and Organizational Psychology*, *88*, 459–463.

Mikulas, W. L. (2002). *The integrative helper: Convergence of Eastern and Western traditions*. Pacific Grove, CA: Brooks/Cole.

Morgeson, F. P., & Humphrey, S. E. (2006). The Work Design Questionnaire (WDQ): Developing and validating a comprehensive measure for assessing job design and the nature of work. *Journal of Applied Psychology*, *91*(6), 1321–1339.

Moynihan, A. B., Van Tilburg, W. A. P., Igou. E. R., Wisman, A., Donnelly, A. E., & Mulcaire, J. (2015). Eaten up by boredom: Consuming food to escape awareness of the bored self. *Frontiers in Psychology*, *6*: 369.

Nielsen, K., & Randall, R. (2012). Opening the black box: Presenting a model for evaluating organizational-level interventions. *European Journal of Work and Organizational Psychology*, *22*, 601–617.

Petrou, P., Demerouti, E., Peeters, M. C. W., Schaufeli, W. B., & Hetland, J. (2012). Crafting a job on a daily basis: Contextual correlates and the link to work engagement. *Journal of Organizational Behavior*, *33*, 1120–1141.

Piotrowski, M., Kalleberg, A., & Rindfuss, R. R. (2015). Contingent work rising: Implications for the timing of marriage in Japan. *Journal of Marriage and Family*, *77*(5), 1039–1056.

Pratt, M. G., & Ashforth, B. E. (2003). Fostering meaningfulness in working and at work. In K. S. Cameron, J. E. Dutton, & R. E. Quinn (Eds.), *Positive organizational scholarship: Foundations of a new discipline* (pp. 309–327). San Francisco, CA: Berrett-Koehler.

Proulx, T., & Heine, S. J. (2006). Death and black diamonds: Meaning, mortality, and the meaning maintenance model. *Psychological Inquiry*, *17*, 309–318.

Proulx, T., & Inzlicht, M. (2012). The five 'A's of meaning maintenance: Finding meaning in the theories of sense-making. *Psychological Inquiry*, *23*, 317–335.

Proulx, T., Heine, S. J., & Vohs, K. D. (2010). When is the unfamiliar the uncanny? Meaning affirmation after exposure to absurdist literature, humor, and art. *Personality and Social Psychology Bulletin*, *36*, 817–829.

Pyszczynski, T., Greenberg, J., & Solomon, S. (1999). A dual-process model of defense against conscious and unconscious death-related thoughts: An extension of terror management theory. *Psychological Review*, *106*, 835–845.

Randles, D., Proulx, T., & Heine, S. J. (2011). Turn-frogs and careful sweaters: Non-conscious perception of incongruous word pairings provokes fluid compensation. *Journal of Experimental Social Psychology*, *47*(1), 246–249.

Ross, A. (2008). The new geography of work: Power to the precarious? *Theory, Culture & Society*, *25*(7–8), 31–49.

Rosso, B. D., Dekas, K. H., & Wrzesniewski, A. (2010). On the meaning of work: A theoretical integration and review. *Research in Organizational Behavior*, *30*, 91–127.

Routledge, C., Ostafin, B., Juhl, J., Sedikides, C., Cathey, C., & Liao, J. Q. (2010). Adjusting to death: The effects of mortality salience and self-esteem on psychological well-being, growth motivation, and maladaptive behavior. *Journal of Personality and Social Psychology*, *99*(6), 897–916.

Salancik, G., & Pfeffer, J. (1978). A social information processing approach to job attitudes and Task Design. *Administrative Science Quarterly*, *23*(2), 224–253.

Schimel, J., Simon, L., Greenberg, J., Pyszczynski, T., Solomon, S., Waxmonsky, J., & Arndt, J. (1999). Stereotypes and terror management: Evidence that mortality salience enhances stereotypic thinking and preferences. *Journal of Personality and Social Psychology*, *77*(5), 905–926.

Schmeichel, B. J., & Martens, A. (2005). Self-affirmation and mortality salience: Affirming values reduces worldview defense and death thought accessibility. *Personality and Social Psychology Bulletin*, *31*, 658–667.

Schroeter, R., Oxtoby, J., & Johnson, D. (2014, September). AR and gamification concepts to reduce driver boredom and risk taking behaviours. In *Proceedings of the 6th International Conference on Automotive User Interfaces and Interactive Vehicular Applications* (pp. 1–8). Santa Barbara, CA: ACM.

Shamir, B. (1991). Meaning, self and motivation in organizations. *Organization Studies*, *12*, 405–424.

Silvia, P. J. (2001). Nothing or the opposite: intersecting terror management and objective self-awareness. *European Journal of Personality*, *15*, 73–82.

Steger, M. F., & Dik, B. J. (2009). If one is looking for meaning in life, does it help to find meaning in work? *Applied Psychology: Health and Well-Being*, *1*(3), 303–320.

Steger, M. F., Mann, J. R., Michels, P., & Cooper, T. C. (2009a). Meaning in life, anxiety, depression, and general health among smoking cessation patients. *Journal of Psychosomatic Research*, *67*, 353–358.

Steger, M. F., Oishi, S., & Kashdan, T. B. (2009b). Meaning in life across the life span: Levels and correlates of meaning in life from emerging adulthood to older adulthood. *The Journal of Positive Psychology*, *4*(1), 43–52.

Šverko, B., & Vidović, V. V. (1995). Studies of the meaning of work: Approaches, models and some of the findings. In D. E. Super & B. Šverko (Eds.), *Life roles, values and careers: International findings of the work importance study*. San Francisco, CA: Jossey-Bass.

Swann, W. B., Jr., Johnson, R. E., & Bosson, J. (2009). Identity negotiation at work. In B. Staw, & A. Brief (Eds.), *Research in organizational behavior.* (Vol. 29, pp. 81–109). Amsterdam: Elsevier.

Terry, D. J., Carey, C. J., & Callan, V. J. (2001). Employee adjustment to an organizational merger: An intergroup perspective. *Personality and Social Psychology Bulletin*, *27*, 267–280.

Tims, M., Derks, D., & Bakker, A. B. (2016). Job crafting and its relationships with person-job fit and meaningfulness: A three-wave study. *Journal of Vocational Behavior*, *92*, 44–53.

Tubre, T. C., & Collins, J. M. (2000). Jackson and Schuler (1985) revisited: A meta-analysis of the relationships between role ambiguity, role conflict, and job performance. *Journal of Management*, *26*, 155–169.

Van den Heuvel, M., Demerouti, E., & Peeters, M. C. W. (2015). The job crafting intervention: Effects on resources and well-being at work. *Journal of Occupational and Organizational Psychology*, *88*, 511–532.

Van Hoye, G., & Lootens, H. (2013). Coping with unemployment: personality, role demands, and time structure. *Journal of Vocational Behavior*, *82*, 85–95.

Van Mersbergen, J. (2012). *The test and evaluation of a job crafting intervention in healthcare.* (Master of Science in Innovation Management), TUE, Eindhoven.

Van Tilburg, W. A. P., & Igou, E. R. (2011). On boredom and social identity: A pragmatic meaning-regulation approach. *Personality and Social Psychology Bulletin*, *37*, 1679–1691.

Van Tilburg, W. A. P., & Igou, E. R. (2012). On boredom: Lack of challenge and meaning as distinct boredom experiences. *Motivation & Emotion*, *36*, 181–194.

Van Tilburg, W. A. P., & Igou, E. R. (2013). On the meaningfulness of behavior: An expectancy × value approach. *Motivation and Emotion*, *37*, 373–388.

Van Tilburg, W. A. P., & Igou, E. R. (2016). Going to political extremes in response to boredom. *European Journal of Social Psychology*, *46*(6), 687–699.

Van Tilburg, W. A. P., & Igou, E. R. (2017a). Can boredom help? Increased prosocial intentions in response to boredom. *Self and Identity*, 16(1), 82–96.

Van Tilburg, W. A. P., & Igou, E. R. (2017b). Boredom begs to differ: Differentiation from other negative emotions. *Emotion.* 17(2), 309–322.

Van Tilburg, W. A. P., Igou, E. R., & Sedikides, C. (2013). In search of meaningfulness: Nostalgia as an antidote to boredom. *Emotion*, *13*, 450–461.

Vanishree, P. (2014). Impact on role ambiguity, role conflict and role overload on job stress in Small and Medium scale industries. *Research Journal of Management Science*, *3*, 10–13.

Vastamäki, J., Moser, K., & Paul, K. I. (2009). How stable is sense of coherence? Changes following an intervention for unemployed individuals. *Scandinavian Journal of Psychology*, *50*, 161–171.

Warr, P. B. (1987). *Work, unemployment and mental health*. Oxford: Oxford University Press.

Warr, P. (2007). *Work, happiness, and unhappiness*. Mahwah, NJ: Lawrence Erlbaum.

Weinger, M. (1999). Vigilance, boredom, and sleepiness. *Journal of Clinical Monitoring and Computing*, *15*, 549–552.

Wildschut, T., Sedikides, C., Routledge, C., Arndt, J., & Cordaro, F. (2010). Nostalgia as a repository of social connectedness: The role of attachment-related avoidance. *Journal of Personality and Social Psychology*, *98*, 573.

Wong, P. T. P. (Ed.) (2012). *The human quest for meaning: Theories, research, and applications* (2nd edn.). New York, NY: Routledge.

Wrzesniewski, A. (1999). *Jobs, careers, and callings: Work orientation and job transitions.* Doctoral dissertation, University of Michigan.

Wrzesniewski, A. (2003). Finding positive meaning in work. In K. S. Cameron, J. E. Dutton, & R. E. Quinn (Eds.), *Positive organizational scholarship*. San Francisco, CA: Berrett-Koehler Publishers, Inc.

Wrzesniewski, A., & Dutton, J. E. (2001). Crafting a job: Revisioning employees as active crafters of their work. *Academy of Management Review*, *26*(2), 179–201.

Wrzesniewski, A., Dutton, J. E., & Debebe, G. (2003). Interpersonal sensemaking and the meaning of work. *Research in Organizational Behavior*, *25*, 93–135.

Wrzesniewski, A., McCauley, C., Rozin, P., & Schwartz, B. (1997). Jobs, careers, and callings: People's relations to their work. *Journal of Research in Personality*, *31*, 21–33.

Yeager, D. S., & Bundick, M. J. (2009). The role of purposeful work goals in promoting meaning in life and in schoolwork during adolescence. *Journal of Adolescent Research*, *24*, 423–452.

14

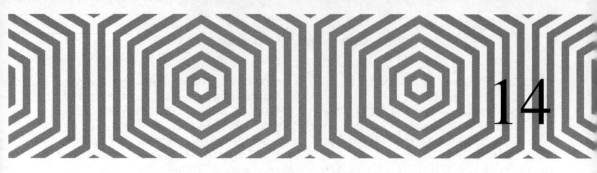

Applied Social Psychologies, the Neoliberal Labour-Market Subject and Critique

David Fryer

OPENING ORIENTING COMMENTS

Contributing authors to this book were invited by the Editors to include a hands-on, autobiographical element in setting out their approach and to locate the contemporary, nationally bounded, culturally specific, theoretically particular nature of their approach within wider historical, international, culturally and theoretically diverse alternative approaches. I start this chapter by inscribing that genre of writing.

After graduating with an undergraduate degree in psychology, a Master's degree in philosophy and, in 1978, a transdisciplinary PhD which was meant as, simultaneously, a contribution to the sociology of knowledge, to the history of psychology, to the philosophy of explanation and to transdisciplinary scholarship in epistemics, I was effectively unemployable in the British academic world of the time. I signed on, became officially unemployed, claimed unemployment benefit and engaged in job search rituals. Eventually, in February 1981, I was offered and accepted a job as a Post-Doctoral Researcher in the Social and Applied Psychology Unit at Sheffield University. I was paid to engage in research into applied social psychological aspects of unemployment and also to teach research methods to occupational psychology Master's students. This post-doctoral period led to a series of academic jobs in public universities and private sector Higher Education providers as lecturer, senior lecturer, reader and, eventually, professor. However, my career as an applied social psychologist began as a member of the unemployed.

Over three and a half decades later, my career as an applied social psychologist is ending as, what some would discursively position, a member of the precariat. Since being made redundant from a position as Head of Research at a private sector Higher Education provider, my working life has become a cocktail of quasi-employment-related activities. I am (at some times) paid to work part-time as a sessional academic teacher in the burgeoning Higher Education private-sector which has flourished under neoliberal governments. This is profoundly insecure work: contracts for paid work are not issued until days before a teaching term begins and such contracts are cancelled immediately the staff–student ratio is deemed insufficiently profitable by the employer. As a member of the private sector academic precariat, I am (at some times) paid: to teach in courses problematically accredited by others; to illuminate a syllabus problematically designed by others; to explain material problematically written by others; and to mark against criteria problematically set and deployed by others – all of the above strictly in line with market considerations. I (at some times) do occasional brief, part-time, paid, sessional, academic teaching in the increasingly neoliberalised public university sector, where I also (at some times) do unpaid academic work supervising PhDs as an 'honorary' appointee. I discursively position myself: at some times as part-time employed; at other times as under-employed; at other times as unemployed; and at still other times as post-employed. I could be positioned (at all times) as a member of the precariat. Writing of the precariat, Standing (2014) wrote: 'essentially, their labour is insecure and unstable, so that it is associated with casualisation, informalisation, agency labour, part-time labour, phoney self-employment and the new mass phenomenon of crowd-labour'. In addition, I often work unpaid on what I sometimes position as my 'own' academic scholarship and research projects but, at other less self-deluding times, I acknowledge that my 'own' academic projects are also constituted by the neoliberalised academic 'industry'. For example, I spend much of 'my' time and energy, as now, writing (unpaid) copy for vastly profitable publishing companies dominated by commercial considerations (see Fryer and Duckett, 2014). Rather than part-time-employed, un-employed, under-employed, precariously-employed, or any of the other terms used above, I prefer to position myself as de-ployed, to signify the reversal of employment and the active maneuvering involved in the reproduction of the human means of production in the neoliberal labour market.

I thus began my academic life as an applied social psychologist as one of the millions of people who made up 'the unemployed' and I am ending it as one of the billions of people de-ployed under neoliberalism to serve the interests of capital and those who profit from it.

I am not, and have not been, alone throughout this period. The numbers of people estimated to be currently unemployed are vast. The International Labour Organization (ILO, 2017) asserts that 'over 201 million' are unemployed globally in 2017 with 'an additional 2.7 million unemployed people globally' becoming unemployed in 2018. As a member of the de-ployed I am, according to the ILO, in 2017 one of 1.4 billion people worldwide who are in 'vulnerable forms of employment … typically subject to high levels of precariousness'. According to the ILO, '42 per cent of total employment in 2017', globally, is precarious, with 'almost one in two workers in emerging countries … in vulnerable forms of employment, rising to almost four in five workers in developing countries'. Moreover, 'the number of workers in vulnerable forms of employment is projected to grow globally by 11 million per year'.

How is one to make sense of employment, unemployment and de-ployment? I have spent much of the last 35 years of my 'working' life considering this question.

Apart from 'my' personal experience of unemployment and precarity, as a post-doctoral researcher, I was intensively, if informally, mentored for more than 20 years by Marie Jahoda, the doyenne of psychological research in relation to unemployment (Fryer, 1986a; 1986b; 1986c; 1987; 1992; 1997; 1999; 2001a; 2001b; Fryer and Jahoda, 1998a; 1998b; 2000; Fryer, 1999). I learned more than I can say working at the Social and Applied

Psychology Unit at the University of Sheffield under the direction of Peter Warr (Fryer and Warr, 1984) and with Roy Payne (Fryer and Payne, 1984a; 1984b; 1984c; 1986). I held Visiting Researcher positions at Flinders University, where I learned still more about unemployment-related research from Norm Feather (Fryer and Feather, 1994) and at the University of Adelaide, where I learned even more about unemployment-related research from Tony Winefield (Fryer and Winefield, 1998; Winefield and Fryer, 1996). More recently, I have been learning from work in a very different tradition from the modernist tradition exemplified above: I have enjoyed a huge learning curve regarding the seismic implications for the applied social of employment, un-employment and de-ployment of researchers drawing upon the oeuvres of Michel Foucault (Fryer and Stambe, 2014a; 2014b; 2014c; 2015; Marley and Fryer, 2014; Stambe and Fryer, 2012).

The most important of this learning has been learning what, and how NOT, to think i.e. to engage critically: 'those who are separated from what they can do, can, however, still resist; they can still not do' (Agamben, 2011: 45).

For a long period of time, I had discursively positioned my 'knowledge' about psychological aspects of various forms of participation in, and exclusion from, the capitalist labour market, achieved (apparently) through so many years of painstaking research, as 'extensive'. For a long period of time, I had also discursively positioned my 'knowledge' as 'authentic': after all, it had been acquired through diverse means, including through 'lived experience', but gradually I came to position that 'knowledge' as enslaving rather than liberating, in the sense of Horkheimer (1982), and I came to regard my 'lived experience' as more informative about the apparatus of interconnected societal elements within which I am constituted and reconstituted than about the authenticity of my phenomenological experience. I came to position my understanding of 'the applied social psychology' of em-ployment, un-employment and de-ployment and of myself as central to the ways I am governed. Indeed, I came to see my previous version of 'critique' as, actually, performance of compliant thinking within the dominant neoliberal box rather than emancipatory thinking about that problematic neoliberal box from outside it.

In this chapter, I offer an account of key psychological research into unemployment from the 1930s to the present day. This may appear at first sight merely of 'academic' historical interest, inserted to set the context for contemporary scholarship, but that is not how it is intended. The 1930s were an inscription of problematic discourses which are dominant to this day. The discourses which are positioned in this chapter as less problematic are still today subjugated discourses. As a piece of critical scholarship, this chapter interrogates dominant systems of applied social psychological knowledge statements which were given the status of scientific truth through the work of Jahoda, Warr, myself in my early career and others and tries to uncover how these are related to the constitution of oppressive power relations. Two core propositions, in particular, underpin this chapter in a pincer movement of resistance to dominant ways of making sense of employment, unemployment and de-ployment.

One core proposition of this chapter is that applied social psychologies of work have been, and still are, central in the twentieth and twenty-first century to the constitution of versions of unemployment and of the unemployed subject required for contemporary versions of neoliberal capitalism to reproduce the necessary human means of production. This was evident first in selective psy-complexified 'knowledging' and 'truthing', psy-complex discourses, practices etc. through which claims are given the status of knowledge or truth in relation to the qualitative research 'literature' on 'consequences of unemployment'. This became reinforced through decontextualising quantitative focus on aspects of alleged 'consequences' of unemployment for 'psychological well-being'. It was still further reinforced by processes of theoretical truthing in relation to the alleged psychological deprivation central to unemployment.

The second core proposition of this chapter is that the prime task of critique in relation to: 'the heterogeneous knowledges, forms of authority and practical techniques that constitute psychological expertise', produce 'positive knowledges, plausible truth claims, and apparently dispassionate expertise' and 'have had a key role in constructing "governable subjects"' i.e. the psy-complex (Rose, 1999: vii–viii) is not to reform or radicalise them but to undermine, neutralise and replace them. From a critical standpoint, applied social psychology is just one more version of the psy complex. This is, of course, a Foucauldian position.

Before proceeding further, we will unpack how 'critique' is used in this chapter.

WHAT IS IT TO ENGAGE IN CRITIQUE?

According to Horkheimer, critical psychology is, fundamentally, concerned with liberation of 'human beings from the circumstances that enslave them' (Horkheimer 1982: 244). Most applied social psychologists would agree that liberation from enslavement is a 'good thing' but be unlikely to agree on what enslaves human beings, what liberation from enslavement involves and whether or not it is the role of applied social psychologists to liberate people from enslavement.

MARXIST AND FREUDIAN CRITIQUE

Horkheimer was Director of the Institute for Social Research ('the Frankfurt School'), whose work was heavily informed by Marxism, psychoanalysis and anti-positivism. Consistently with this, Kagan et al. (2011) wrote that,

> what is meant by the term 'critical' is an approach that tries to understand a social reality through introduction of another more penetrating frame of reference, one that has to do with a general theory of human society (or at least late capitalist society) understood in terms of contradictions between different social interests and economic processes of exploitation, capital accumulation, and so on

and describe themselves as 'comfortable with' 'the Frankfurt School of Marxist intellectuals concerned with questions of culture and its relation to society (e.g. Adorno, Horkheimer, Marcuse, Fromm, Habermas)' (Kagan et al., 2011: 12). Marxism is a powerful contemporary influence on the work of critical scholars (e.g. Parker, 1997; 2007; Seedat et al., 2001) and, crucially here, Marie Jahoda.

Psychoanalysis is clearly also 'an approach that tries to understand a social reality through introduction of another more penetrating frame of reference' (Kagan et al., 2011: 12). Psychoanalysis is a powerful contemporary force within critique and the work of critical psychologists (e.g. Hollway and Jefferson, 2000; Parker, 2009; 2015; 2018) and, crucially here, Marie Jahoda (1977).

There are other approaches to understanding social realities through introduction of other, more penetrating, frames of reference (emancipatory disability studies, feminisms, liberation theory, postcolonial theory, queer theory, etc.) but they have not, as yet, been influential in the applied social psychology of (un)employment in ways comparable to Marxism and psychoanalysis.

The work of Marie Jahoda, most influential of all research into 'consequences' of labour market (non) participation, is underpinned by both Marxism and psychoanalysis but is also methodologically 'Kantian'.

KANTIAN CRITIQUE

Kant wrote: 'Enlightenment is man's release from his self-incurred tutelage. Tutelage is man's inability to make use of his understanding without direction from another … Sapere aude! 'Have courage to use your own reason!' – that is the motto of enlightenment.' (Kant, 1784 in Lotringer, S. (1997: 29). Consistently with this, while they do not mention Kant specifically, Halpern and Butler (2011:30) write of critical thinking: 'researchers generally agree that it involves an attempt to achieve a desired outcome by thinking rationally in a goal-oriented fashion and reasoning in an open-ended manner'. Halpern and Butler (2011: 30) refer explicitly to: 'critical thinking, or thinking like a psychological scientist'. By 'thinking like a psychological scientist', they mean thinking like a metropolitan (Connell, 2007), post-positivist scientist, where 'thinking critically' is thinking within the dominant post-positivist frame of reference. Thinking like a metropolitan psychological scientist is precisely the antithesis of what critical thinking is within Marxist, Freudian or Foucauldian frames of reference. As we will see, the research of mainstream applied social psychologists into (un)employment research is characterised by commitment to this *anti-critical* 'critical' frame of reference.

FOUCAULDIAN CRITIQUE

As both Kant and Foucault noted in relation to 'sapere aude', Frederick II countered: 'Let them reason all they want to as long as they obey' (Foucault, 1978/1990/1997 in Lotringer, 1997: 49). For Foucault to engage in critique was to do anything but obey. Foucault (1997: 46) wrote:

> I would … propose, as a very first definition of critique, this general characterisation: the art of not being governed quite so much' … 'how not to be governed like that, by that, in the name of those principles, with such an objective in mind and by means of such procedures, not like that, not for that, not by them … critique finds its anchoring point in the problem of certainty in its confrontation with authority

(Foucault, 1978/1990/1997 in Lotringer, 1997: 44). Within this frame of reference, enslavement is positioned as having multiple loci of accomplishment, including compliance achieved through subjection/re-subjectivation, oppressive power-knowledge systems which take both productive and restrictive forms, and the broader project of governmentality and liberation is positioned as achieved by critical resistance (see: Fryer and Fox, 2015; Marley and Fryer 2014; Nic Giolla Easpaig et al. 2014; Rose, 1999).

THE JAHODA LEGACY

The intellectual legacy of Marie Jahoda to the contemporary applied social psychology of (un)employment is, for better or worse, almost impossible to overstate.

Jahoda was centrally responsible for two extended field studies in the 1930s. The first was a brilliant community study carried out in the early 1930s in Marienthal in Austria and published in 1933 in Leipzig in Germany as *Die Arbeitslosen von Marienthal: Ein soziographischer Versuch uber die Wirkungen langdauernder Arbeitslosigkeit mit einem Anhang zur Geschichte der Soziographie* (Osterreichischen Wirtschaftspsychologischen Forschungsstelle, 1933). This translates literally as *The Unemployed of Marienthal: a sociographic essay on the effects of long term unemployment with an appendix on the history of sociography*, but it was published in English as *Marienthal: The Sociography of an Unemployed Community* (Jahoda et al., (1971) and republished in a new edition with a new foreword in 2002). The influence of this field study is incalculable. The second was an equally brilliant organisational case study in Cymavon, Wales. The influence of this second study is near negligible because, although completed in 1938, it was withheld from publication by Jahoda until 1987, i.e. for nearly half a century, for personal rather than scientific reasons. It was published as: *Unemployed Men at Work* (Jahoda, 1938/1987).

The members of the Marienthal research team were overwhelmingly active members of the *Austro-Marxist* Social Democratic Party, albeit a 'Marxism that had omitted ... crude dogmatisms ... and implanted into Marxism a sturdy shot of empiricism adopted from Ernst Mach's philosophy of science and his followers in the Vienna Circle of Logical Positivism' (Fleck, 2002: xxiii).

Jahoda was also heavily involved in *psychoanalysis* shortly before being heavily involved in the Marienthal study as a researcher and author of the main text. The research began in autumn 1931, and in 1930 and 1931 Marie Jahoda underwent psychoanalysis with her analyst, Heinz Hartmann: one of only two psychoanalysts to receive their training analysis from Sigmund Freud.

The Marienthal research, according to Jahoda (1983), 'pushed towards sociology by its Austro-Marxist roots, was forced by its tie with psychology to deal systematically with complex subjective experiences'. The underpinning of the research in Marienthal by Austro-Marxism and psychoanalysis is important as both Marxism and psychoanalysis are penetrating frames of reference which transform how social reality is understood.

Writing several years after the Marienthal study, Lazarsfeld claimed that 'unemployment tends to make people more emotionally unstable than they were previous to unemployment', that 'there is a general lowering of morale with unemployment' (Eisenberg and Lazarsfeld, 1938). However, although the work in Marienthal is often discursively positioned as revealing deleterious mental health consequences of unemployment for the mental health of *unemployed individuals*, actually Jahoda stated unambiguously in 1933 that: '*The object of this investigation was the unemployed community, not the unemployed individual*' and, moreover, that '*the whole field of psychopathology was omitted*' (Jahoda et al., 2002: 2).

Moreover, the Marienthal text is far more nuanced than many later and secondary sources imply. In Marienthal, the consequences of unemployment on the community and the families which made it up are positioned as multifaceted, with negative, positive and ambivalent states co-existing at the same time. For example, although 70% of the families in Marienthal with which the researchers worked were positioned as 'resigned' and although the criteria for resignation indeed included: 'no plans, no relation to the future, no hopes, extreme restriction of all needs beyond the bare necessities', the criteria for resignation also included: 'maintenance of the household, care of the children, and an overall feeling of well-being'. Moreover, a further 23% were positioned as 'unbroken', the criteria for which included 'maintenance of the household, care of the children, subjective well-being, activity, hope and plans for the future, sustained vitality' etc. Thus, 93% of the families were deemed to be characterised by well-being with children and household well looked after (Fryer, 1987: 84–6).

Lazarsfeld also claimed that, with lengthening unemployment, people move through stages from shock via optimism, then pessimism, to fatalist resignation (Eisenberg and Lazarsfeld, 1938) and, as Jahoda summarised: 'our basic insights into the effects of unemployment eventually emerged: a diminution of expectation and activity, a disrupted sense of time, and a steady decline into apathy through a variety of stages and attitudes' (Jahoda et al., 2002: 2). However, although it might be supposed that such stages are manifestations of an intra-psychic psychological dynamic independent of the social world, the stages of 'attitude' described by Jahoda et al. (1971) were carefully discursively positioned as anchored to stages of deepening poverty. Thus, Jahoda et al. (2002: 81–2) divided members of the unemployed community about which they produced and legitimated knowledge claims into four categories 'according to their basic attitude' and they also reported the 'average income per consumer unit in each of these four attitude categories'. These were: those with an 'unbroken' attitude (averaging 34 Schillings income per month); those with a 'resigned' attitude (averaging 30 Schillings income per month); those with an attitude of being 'in despair' (averaging 25 Schillings income per month); and those with an 'apathetic' attitude (averaging 19 Schillings income per month). The authors commented that this information: 'is not only significant for the connection it establishes between a family's attitudes and its economic situation: it also allows us to foresee at approximately what point the deterioration in income will push a family into the next lower category' (Jahoda et al., 2002: 81), explicitly: 'economic deterioration carries with it an almost calculable change in the prevailing mood' (Jahoda et al., 2002: 82). They even spelled out the difference five Schillings made 'between being unbroken, resigned, in despair, or apathetic' (Jahoda et al., 2002: 82): the 'difference of approximately five Schillings a month means the difference between … having the children's shoes repaired or keeping the children at home, between occasionally having a cigarette or having to pick up butts on the street.' (Jahoda et al., 2002: 82).

In the Welsh study, *Unemployed Men at Work*, Jahoda (1938/1987: 2) (the fieldwork was carried out in 1935) referred to 'the disastrous economic and human consequences of unemployment' and referred to a grey literature document (now untraceable) produced by The Order of Friends in 1930 which claimed the consequences of unemployment on the family were as follows:

> under such circumstances the father … grows slack and spiritless … his wife and home suffer accordingly and the children are brought up in an atmosphere of unhappiness and unrest made worse by malnutrition. The rot that follows – economic, social, political, and moral – is deep rooted and is accompanied by an apathy more deadly than the spread of an extremist political doctrine. (Cited in Fryer and Ullah, 1987: 2)

However, Jahoda (1938/1987) also emphasised the less severe impact of unemployment in the Eastern Valley than that in Marienthal saying 'unemployment, though extremely unpleasant, was less psychologically destructive in South Wales than in Austria or within the Subsistence Production Society than outside it' (Fryer, 1987: 85). The Subsistence Production Society's 400 volunteers worked for the unemployment allowance and were paid no extra but the purchasing power of unemployment allowance increased by a third. Jahoda elaborated that 'nothing worse than resignation was found in the Eastern Valley, in Marienthal despair and compete apathy were discovered' (Fryer, 1987: 84) and commented that this 'may have been mainly because of the size and permanence of the unemployment allowance in Wales' (Fryer, 1987: 85). The emphasis of Jahoda and of Lazarsfeld in the 1930s was thus overwhelmingly on the material effects of poverty and economic insecurity rather than the psychological effects of unemployment.

Jahoda's Austrian and Welsh field studies were important and influential but they were not the only relevant studies carried out in the 1930s. Frew (1935) claimed that records over a six-year period showed the health of children in chronically unemployed families showed deterioration with respect to both dental health and moderate cases of rickets (both associated with nutritional deficit). Yet Frew (1935) also claimed that the health of children in these same unemployed families showed improvements in other respects: reduction in *severe* cases of rickets, *improvements* in height, weight and in how well children were clothed and with 'greater interest … shown by the parents in the care of the children'. Israeli (1935) claimed unemployed people were confused and worried about the future but also claimed they were calm 'towards the past'. Bakke (1933) claimed unemployment led for some to: mental exhaustion; reduced self-confidence; bewilderment; disheartenment; hopelessness; demoralisation; despondency, and Pilgrim Trust (1938) claimed that 'when a man is out of work, anxiety is part of a vicious circle, and the more he worries, the more he unfits himself for work'. Yet Bakke (1933) also reported in relation to jobless men that 'very few of them were worrying. There was a feeling of security in the face of their experience and prospect'. Bakke (1940), based on research between 1930 and 1939 in the United States, claimed that unemployment was associated with reduced sense of control, reduced family cohesion, reduced social integration. However, importantly, he also claimed: 'unemployment does not destroy family harmony … it merely acts as an irritant on whatever tendencies are already present' and he emphasised the resilience of families in the face of unemployment: 'almost as soon as the family is attacked by the disease of unemployment, the restorative process is set in motion aimed at the renewal of the ability of the family to fulfill its economic and social role'. Carnegie UK Trust (1943) claimed that 'the central problem' faced by young unemployed men was 'maintaining self-respect' rather than anything worse. Three points deserve emphasis.

Firstly, the studies reviewed above carried out by both Jahoda and other researchers in the 1930s did not actually emphasise particularly negative psychological impacts *of unemployment* per se on adults. As far as the psychological impact of unemployment on children is concerned, some claimed this was deleterious but in mostly minor ways, others claimed that unemployment had no negative impact at all on children's health, nutritional standards or family functioning, and some even claimed that, in the face of unemployment, families demonstrated resilience and parenting improved. The psychological impact *of unemployment* per se on mental health, while mentioned, was not emphasised in the investigations associated with Jahoda and others in the 1930s. This is extraordinary because subsequently the work of Jahoda was widely taken to emphasise the psychological consequences of *unemployment per se*.

Secondly, the destructive role of economic insecurity, poverty and 'want' associated with unemployment, rather than unemployment itself, was emphasised by other researchers, as well as by Jahoda and Lazarsfeld, in the causation of psychological and health problems. Eisenberg and Lazarsfeld (1938) claimed: 'just having a job itself is not as important as having a feeling of economic security'. Bakke (1933) attributed the security of the British jobless men to 'unemployment insurance' which 'has reduced starvation, ill health, poverty and the like' and claimed that, when unemployment insurance was in place, unemployment had no impact at all on children's health, nutritional standards, religious, legal or political radicalisation. Bakke (1940) later made a series of claims, based on a variety of knowledge-claim-legitimation-practices between 1930 and 1939, that the impact of unemployment – or rather unemployed poverty – was worse in the United States, where crucially, there was no unemployment insurance, than in the UK. Pilgrim Trust (1938) claimed that, for both employed and unemployed people, 'the economic level at which families were living … was such as to cause anxiety, and in some case physical deterioration'. This is extraordinary because subsequently the work in the 1930s was widely taken to emphasise the deleterious psychological rather than economic consequences of unemployment.

Thirdly, the psychological difficulties later attributed primarily to unemployment per se were positioned by Jahoda in the 1930s as primarily consequences of previous *em*ployment, not as consequences of *un*employment. For example, writing of the Subsistence Production Society (SPS), Jahoda (1938/1987: 2) wrote an objective 'less explicitly expressed but certainly present in the SPS, was to overcome the 'disastrous consequence' *of employment*, under the conditions that had prevailed in the Eastern Valley'. It is particularly striking that what researchers have come to regard as the classic psychological consequences of *un*employment are positioned instead, in the Eastern Valley investigation, as consequences of *em*ployment. Jahoda (1938/1987) referred to: irregularity as 'the normal way of living' (Fryer, 1987: 88) as 'work in the mines communicated a jazzlike rhythm to life in a miner's family and home'; as 'the social life of the local community' was fragmented by competing religions in the community; as the capacity for collective action was almost exhausted by trades unionism; as a 'most depressing atmosphere' was produced by lack of open space and overcrowded housing; as 'fatalism' was created by 'daily contact with danger and death' in the mines; by 'continuous physical and mental tension' and 'constant anxiety for the future' being created during slumps.

This is especially extraordinary because, while the psychological difficulties attributed to *un*employment per se were positioned by Jahoda in the 1930s as primarily consequences of previous features of *em*ployment, the later Jahoda positioned the consequences of *un*employment per se as the consequences of *deprivation of* employment. Jahoda is widely known for an account of what causes the alleged negative psychological consequences of unemployment which is not only independent of, and inconsistent with, the conclusions of the prior fieldwork in many respects but actually incorporates opposite assumptions. Jahoda claimed that, although the 'manifest', i.e. intended function of employment, is to earn a living, employment also has 'latent', i.e. unintended, functions (an imposed time structure, engagement in regular social contact, participation in a collective purpose, receipt of a social identity and required regular activity), the deprivation of which – by unemployment – is responsible for the 'psychological consequences' of 'unemployment' (Jahoda, 1982).

This, still hugely influential, explanatory account of what it is about unemployment that is psychologically problematic was developed by Marie Jahoda many years after the fieldwork in Austria and Wales and owed more to Marxist and Freudian frames of reference than to empirical work. Jahoda (1982) wrote: 'Marx and Freud ... make visible the invisible: Freud by explaining man to himself, Marx by explaining society to men' (Jahoda, 1982: 69). In relation to Freud, Jahoda writes:

> current psychological responses to unemployment can with somewhat greater confidence than in the past be attributed to the absence of a job not just to restricted finances ... it is as yet not possible to infer systematically from current empirical research what these responses are. On the other hand, an analysis of employment as an institution makes it possible to specify some broad categories of experience, enforced on the overwhelming majority of those who participate in it ... to the extent that these categories of experience have become a psychological requirement in modern life, the unemployed will suffer from their absence ... support for the psychological deprivation of the unemployed – comes from Freud's psychological thought. His aphorism that work is man's strongest tie to reality (Freud, 1930) and its reversal – unemployment loosens man's grip on reality – must be understood within his general conception of human needs. (Jahoda, 1982: 59–60)

Jahoda's explanatory account is deeply problematic in a number of ways (Fryer, 1986a). However, here I will confine myself to ideological grounds: Jahoda's explanatory account discursively positions the unemployed subject as passively dependent upon employment as constructed under capitalism to maximise employer profits for psychological health. Ironically, given her Marxist position, Jahoda's applied social psychological texts discursively positioned the twentieth century capitalist labour market as providing social structures which, whether they liked it or not, were essential for workers' psychological health. This did not escape the attention of the Establishment's London newspaper, *The Times*. Extraordinarily, on 27th September 1993, *The Times* carried a report by the then Science Editor about 'Professor Marie Jahoda's theory' and a linked 'Leading article' which concluded 'the very constraints of working life are what make it satisfying ... being compelled to take part by some force outside of personal whim ... seems to be the key factor in making paid work a more valuable source of psychological well-being'.

Fryer (1986a; 1986d) proposed an alternative, meta-explanatory approach, not in terms of the psychologically benevolent structures of employment (of which the unemployed person was deprived or in deficit) but in terms of the restriction of agency by unemployment, which was socially constructed to ensure that the unemployed were insecure, relatively poverty-stricken and powerless (Fryer, 1986a; 2006; Fryer and Fagan, 1994; 2003). This was followed up by scholarship-warranted writing emphasising the agency-inhibiting, destructive problems intrinsic to being unemployed as opposed to being not-employed; that is, exploring the role of unemployed poverty (Fryer, 1990; McGhee and Fryer, 1989), lack of control over the future and drawing attention to the glaring differences between the experiences of those made unemployed and of those laid off for an equivalent period of time but with a return to the previous employment already collectively negotiated (Fryer and McKenna, 1987; 1988; McKenna and Fryer, 1984). Other writing drew attention to the positive experiences of some unemployed people in some ways despite deprivation of employment (Cassell et al., 1988; Darwin et al., 1987; Fryer and Payne, 1984a). However, problematically, like Jahoda, Fryer's explanatory account reinscribed the traditional modernist 'agency/structure' binary in the form of separate realms of individualised, subjective agency and contextual social structure. It also reinscribed the profoundly problematic notion of a foundational, ontologically-persistent, 'unitary, rational subject' (Henriques et al., 1998). See also: Fryer, 2012; 2014; 2017).

Jahoda followed Alfred Marshall in positioning work as 'an exertion or mind or body undergone partly or wholly with a view to some good other than the pleasure derived directly from work' (Jahoda, 1982: 9). For Jahoda, employment on the other hand 'refers to work under contractual arrangements involving material rewards' (Jahoda, 1982: 8). For Jahoda, 'unemployment should be contrasted with employment, not with work' (Jahoda, 1982: 11) and was the absence of paid, contractually obligated and regulated work. Jahoda noted that volunteering, housework, do-it-yourself, hobbies, parenting, children's homework, work in the 'black' economy were 'economically relevant forms of work' (Jahoda, 1982: 9) but were not employment as defined. Jahoda insisted 'for the purposes of a social-psychological approach to the world of work it is necessary to distinguish clearly between three forms of work: that captured in Marshall's broad definition, employment as regulated by contractual arrangements, and other economic activities not so regulated' (Jahoda, 1982: 9). Although Jahoda claimed that only employment could serve all the 'latent functions' necessary for well-being and mental health, other forms of work, e.g. parenting, volunteering etc., could serve some of them.

Such an approach looks naïve and dated, to say the least, to a contemporary scholar. Naïve because parenting, when understood as reproduction of the human means of production, housework, when understood as maintaining the working health and fitness of the employee, etc. are very definitely economically relevant to the functioning of neoliberal capitalism. Dated because we live in the era of the zero hours contract (a contract of employment where no work is guaranteed) and the gig economy in which workers are positioned as independent contractors with no protection against unfair dismissal; no right to redundancy payments, no right to receive the national minimum wage, nor paid holiday nor pay when ill.

In summary, there is a dramatic contrast between early Jahoda – who emphasised the deleterious health consequences of poverty and economic insecurity rather than the deleterious psychological consequences of unemployment and the role of psychologically noxious features of prior employment in the experience of unemployment – and the later Jahoda – who emphasised the deleterious psychological consequences of unemployment and the causal role in that of the deprivation of psychologically benevolent features of former employment rather than of income.

Note that I am NOT here endorsing either the claim that unemployment causes psychological problems or the claim that poverty causes psychological problems. I am observing that a body of knowledge claims have been deployed first to support one thesis then to support another. It is important to realise that, although the majority of research in the 1930s emphasised the negative consequences of *poverty, insecurity and poor-quality* employment, this same research has been widely taken to emphasise the negative *psychological* consequences of *unemployment.* The problem was repositioned as primarily a psychological one. Later, the solutions were repositioned as psychological too.

THE WARR LEGACY

The Marienthal researchers' research methods were mostly qualitative but most researchers whose conclusions were summarised above deployed what are now traditional mainstream quantitative knowledge-claim warranting-strategies. Frew (1935) warranted his claims by reference to systematic analysis of medical records of hundreds of children over a seven-year period. Israeli (1935) warranted his claims by reference to quantitative analysis of three short quantitative psychology questionnaires completed by hundreds of unemployed people from the north west of England and Scotland. Pilgrim Trust (1938) warranted their claims by reference to a large (1,086) random sample of men and women from the live files of the Unemployment Assistance Board in six towns selected to represent degrees of prosperity (from prosperous to 'specially distressed' areas) being interviewed by a team of interviewers generating data on a huge array of factors including: family composition, income, outgoings, previous occupation, employment record, appearance, health, domestic standards, home atmosphere, employability, attitudes and social relations. Carnegie UK Trust (1943) warranted their claims by reference to interviews in a longitudinal design, interviewing a sample of young unemployed men five times over three years between 1936 and 1939. Note that I am not here contrasting qualitative and quantitative methods and endorsing one as opposed to the other. Both are ways of truthing claims which are of more interest within the frames of reference of the sociology of knowledge, the philosophy of science and the politics of ideas than they are within epistemological or ontological frames of reference.

These quantitative knowledge-claim warranting studies are the methodological precursors of the later work of Warr, Feather, Winefield and others and all are examples of a particular form of scientific rationality: thinking like a metropolitan scientist within the dominant post-positivist frame of reference.

If unemployment had been comprehensively psychologised in the 1930s and further psychologised by Jahoda's changing emphasis, that psychologisation intensified during the 1970s and 1980s through research dominated by attempts to answer the question of whether 'unemployment' caused 'poor mental health' (so-called 'social causation') or whether 'poor mental health' predisposed a person to 'unemployment' (so-called 'individual drift'). The 'gold standard' of this sort of research is the large scale quantitative survey, ideally longitudinal, with standardised measures of aspects of mental health and psychological well-being (deemed reliable and valid) sophisticatedly analysed. Quantitative longitudinal studies with standardised measures deemed reliable and valid tracked large, carefully matched, samples of people in and out of employment-related transitions. Some followed groups of adults from employment into unemployment, some followed groups of adults from unemployment into employment but some of the best – within their own frame of reference – were conducted with young people. Many such studies have been done, but three longitudinal research programmes have been particularly influential. The first was the 1980s research programme based at the Social and Applied Psychology Unit in Sheffield, England (see Warr, 1987 for an overview). The second program was based at The Flinders University of South Australia (see Feather, 1990; O'Brien, 1986; for overviews). The third was based at the University of Adelaide (see Winefield et al., 1993; 2017). In brief, such studies provided powerful evidence within a mainstream modernist frame of reference that unemployment causes, rather than merely results from, poor psychological health. Statistically sophisticated meta-reviews pooled data from a variety of studies (e.g., McKee-Ryan et al., 2005; Paul and Moser, 2009). There was widespread agreement that 'unemployment' is not only associated with, but 'causes', individual misery and mental health problems, including anxiety, depression, negative self-esteem, dissatisfaction with life, social dislocation, community dysfunction and population morbidity (see also: Classen and Dunn, 2012; Jefferies et al., 2011; Keily and Butterworth, 2013; Kim et al., 2012). While caveats, criticisms and controversies have been raised in relation to this huge body of research, they are mostly relatively minor and overwhelmingly raised within the frame of reference of such research, rather than of it. It is now difficult to contest, within the dominant modernist research frame of reference, the claim that 'employment' has a positive impact and unemployment a negative impact upon the 'psychological well-being' of 'unemployed people.' While still trying to explicate a causal relationship, research in the 1990s and 2000s also focused on the different 'effects of unemployment' between individuals and identifying 'moderators' which can be used to fine tune intervention technologies, e.g., Paul and Moser (2009). The accumulated research about the 'psychological costs' of 'unemployment' is vast. Even in 2011, Maynard and Feldman (2011), for example, were able to report that their systematic search of relevant databases had revealed 31,839 peer-reviewed works with 'unemployment' in the abstracts published in the previous 50 years.

Warr and other positivist unemployment researchers typically paid lip service to Jahoda's definitions of work, employment and unemployment but actually proceeded in practice to position unemployment however it was positioned politically in terms of eligibility for State funded unemployment benefit/job seekers' allowance, or whatever it was called in differing contexts. In the 1980s, in the UK, frequent changes in eligibility to financial support almost always reduced the number of people positioned as unemployed. Thus, Warr (1987) gave accounts of work employment and unemployment similar to Jahoda's (e.g. 'employment … typically takes the form of a contractual relationship between an individual and an employer' (Warr, 1987: 56)) except that he stipulated that he excluded illegal contractual work from employment and added a category of the 'non-employed … adults below the age of retirement who have no job and are not seeking one' (Warr, 1987: 57).

However, the samples of 'unemployed' people actually recruited into research studies were taken from those eligible to sign on for unemployment benefit. Over time, the way the number of 'unemployed' people was officially determined came to reflect the ILO social survey operationalisation:

> The unemployed comprise all persons above a specified age who during the reference period were: without work, that is, were not in paid employment or self-employment during the reference period; currently available for work, that is, were available for paid employment or self-employment during the reference period; and seeking work, that is, had taken specific steps in a specified recent period to seek paid employment or self-employment. (https://stats.oecd.org/

glossary/detail.asp?ID=2791) (International Labour Organization, 1982)

The above, dominant, approaches position both 'unemployment' and 'mental health' as 'real' and independent and then claim a causal relationship between them which is truthed by means of 'psy science', thus legitimating psy as a science capable of demonstrating real causal relationships between real 'things'.

THE FOUCAULT LEGACY

Within a Foucauldian critical frame of reference, the research of psychological and other social scientists widely discursively positioned as uncovering the relationship between independent phenomena, 'unemployment' and 'mental health', actually contributes to the *constitution* of unemployment, the *constitution* of 'mental ill-health' and the *constitution* of a causal relationship between them. 'Unemployment' and 'mental health' are positioned as 'real' only insofar as they are discursively constituted as real within problematic dominant discourses and apparatuses. Because 'unemployment' and 'mental health' are discursively constituted does not mean they are 'imaginary' in a conventional sense and does not mean they have no material effects. The oppression of people (including the auto-oppression achieved through subjective reconstitution) is not illusory nor imagined but is contingent on the persistence of the apparatus of interconnected constructed and maintained social elements which produce and maintain them.

Likewise, the 'labour market' and 'mental health' are 'real' only in the sense that they are constituted, legitimated and deployed to material effect through interconnected politico-economic policies, 'active labour market' technologies, welfare bureaucracies, discursive systems etc. as well, of course, as the knowledge-work of social and psy-complex scientists of unemployment and of mental health.

A key task in understanding and contesting 'unemployment' and the psychological states allegedly caused by it is, to cite Foucault, 'to reveal the interconnections between a whole set of practices coordinated with a particular regime of truth which make what does not exist' (unemployment, depression, anxiety etc. and the relationship between them) … 'nonetheless become something, something however that continues not to exist' (Foucault, 2010: 19).

The alleged relationship between 'unemployment' and 'mental health' is, from this standpoint, revealed as not to do with 'natural' and inevitable psychological consequences of depriving a person of employment-related, psychologically necessary, structures nor of frustrating the agency of the individual person but a set of interconnected manifestations of social violence necessary to constitute a neoliberal capitalist labour market and its subjects which functions optimally in the interests of neoliberal elites. What is important to focus upon here is not those who constituted as in the category, unemployed or employed, but rather on how constitution is accomplished, in whose interests constitution is accomplished and how constitution can be resisted.

Within a Foucauldian frame of reference, in relation to (un)employment and the individual subject, knowledge systems 'about' 'unemployment' and 'the unemployed subject' directly imply, and are implied by, power relations which produce neoliberal subjects in ways which both enable and simultaneously constrain what they are, and can be, in relation to the labour market. The neoliberal labour market subject, including the unemployed subject, does not, within this frame of reference, exist prior to power-knowledge but rather is constituted by being 'power-knowledged' via authorities such as unemployment researchers and social scientists whose work warrants: theories of unemployment; 'measurement of' unemployed people's 'well-being' and 'mental health'; the accumulation of statistics about the scale of 'unemployment'; 'documentation' of unemployed people's 'lived experience' and, crucially, by unemployed people coming to know themselves, i.e. power-knowledge themselves through the discourses available to them, including those discourses whose constitution is accomplished at least partly through the work of applied social psychological unemployment researchers.

Dominant power-knowledged discursive systems of statements constituting the neoliberal labour market subject position workers as both 'human capital' and entrepreneurs of themselves. Whereas classic neoliberalism is widely regarded as a political rationality based in deregulation and absolute non-intervention, as Foucault recognised, contemporary 'neo liberal governmental intervention is no less dense, frequent, active, and continuous than in any other system. It has to intervene on society as such, in its fabric and depth' (Foucault, 2010: 145).

This intervention includes the re-subjectification of the neoliberal labour market subject as 'unemployed', 'employed' etc., socially and historically produced identities, which are infoldings of the social exteriority. A network of interconnected, socially constituted, social elements, including discourses of unemployment and mental health; a network whose primary function is to control inflation, reduce wage costs, discipline those in work, etc. also simultaneously reconstitutes neoliberal subjects. This network also constitutes immiseration of the members of that category and (re)constitutes the subjectivity of 'the unemployed' in such ways as to (re)produce the compliant human means of production required by the employers, shareholders and government within the contemporary version of the precarious neoliberal capitalist labour market. For more detail see: Fryer, 2017; Fryer and Stambe, 2014a; 2014b; 2015; Rose, 1999; Stambe and Fryer, 2012.

CLOSING DIS-ORIENTING COMMENTS

As noted at the outset of this chapter, contributing authors to this book were encouraged to include an autobiographical element, to locate the contemporary, nationally bounded, culturally specific, theoretically particular nature of their approach within wider historical, international, culturally and theoretically diverse alternative approaches.

Although within some frames of reference – or, as I would prefer to put it, discourses – it is uncontroversial to use terms like 'autobiographical' and related terms such as 'lived experience', to contrast the 'subjective' with the 'objective', to assume incremental historical change from the past to the present, to contrast nations and so on, within the critical frame of reference within which this chapter is written, such manoeuvres are resisted. The use of a term like 'autobiography' in dominant discourse brings with it a commitment to the rational, unitary, ontologically-persisting, individual person who can give a coherent account of events over time having witnessed them. This use is rejected in favour of a subject in a constant process of reconstitution.

Within the critical frame of reference within which this chapter is written, the 'knowledge' of the neoliberal unemployed subject is not positioned as to be taken seriously because based on 'authentic' 'lived experience' compared, for example, with the expertise of the neoliberal unemployment researcher subject, nor is the 'knowledge' of the latter positioned as to be taken seriously because based on 'objective' 'scientific' 'research'. Rather, both are positioned as discursively constituted claims which can be legitimated and delegitimated within differing 'truthing' and 'knowledging' 'regimes'.

The terms 'truthing' and 'knowledging' are used to refer to the processes through which claims are given the status of 'truth' and interrelated 'truthed' claims, and practices associated with them, are given the status of knowledge within different regimes of truth. Notions of 'actual' 'truth' and 'falsity' are not coherent within the critical frame of reference within which this chapter is written. The truthing regimes and practices of both unemployed people and unemployment researchers are subjected to the same critical processing as the truthing regimes and practices of alchemists and phrenologists.

Within the critical frame of reference within which this chapter is written, assumptions of gradual incremental gains in 'knowledge' are rejected in favour of diverse discontinuous 'knowledges' which are truthed simultaneously or successively through diverse and discontinuous regimes of truth. This frame of reference troubles assumptions of progress from the past to the present and of nation-specific knowledge.

In this chapter, I focused on a critical approach which draws heavily on the work of Foucault and those who have developed his work. Critique is never static or completed, so while I endorse a Foucauldian approach here and for now, I acknowledge, indeed emphasise, that Foucauldian approaches to critique are interim positions which must themselves be subjected to critique.

The version of Foucauldian critique inscribed within this chapter rejects the notion of a foundational, ontologically-continuous, 'unitary, rational subject' (Henriques et al., 1998). Rather, the subject is positioned as constituted and reconstituted, within 'dispositifs' ('thoroughly heterogeneous ensembles consisting of discourses, institutions, architectural forms, regulatory decisions, laws, administrative measures, scientific statements, philosophical, moral and philanthropic propositions… the apparatus itself is the system of relations that can be established between these elements' (Foucault, 1980: 194)), from moment to moment 'amid economic and political reforms, violence, and social suffering' (Biehl et al., 2007). The positioning of the subject as (re)constituted applies, of course, not only the unemployed person (the neoliberal-(un)employed-subject), the expected focus of this chapter, but also the researcher-subject, the author-subject, the reader-subject, the reviewer-subject, the publisher-subject and, of course, the Editor-subject!

ACKNOWLEDGEMENTS

I acknowledge that this chapter draws in places upon other papers I have published over many years.

I acknowledge the contributions of Rose Stambe to my thinking during the several years we have worked together and thank anonymous referees and the Editors for valuable feedback on previous versions of this chapter.

REFERENCES

Agamben, G. (2011). On what we can not do. In *Nudities* (ch. 5, pp. 43–45). Stanford: Stanford University Press.

Bakke, E. W. (1933). *The unemployed man*. London: Nisbet.

Bakke, E. W. (1940). *Citizens without work*. New Haven: Yale University Press.

Biehl, J., Good, B., & Kleinman, A. (Eds.) (2007). *Subjectivity: Ethnographic investigations*. Berkeley: University of California Press.

Carnegie UK Trust. (1943). *Disinherited youth: A survey 1936–39*. London: T. A. Constable Ltd.

Cassell, C., Fitter, M., Fryer, D., & Smith, L. (1988). The development of computer applications by unemployed people in community settings. *Journal of Occupational Psychology*, *61*, 89–102.

Classen, T. J., & Dunn, R. A. (2012). The effect of job loss and unemployment duration on suicide risk in the United States: a new look using mass layoffs and unemployment insurance claims. *Health Economics*, *21*, 338–350.

Connell, R. (2007). *Southern theory*. Crows Nest, NSW: Allen and Unwin.

Darwin, J., Fitter, M., Fryer, D., & Smith, L. (1987). Developing information technology in the community with unwaged groups. In P. Bjerknes, P. Ehn, & M. Kyng (Eds.), *Computers and democracy*. Aldershot: Avebury/Gower.

Eisenberg, P., & Lazarsfeld, P. F. (1938). The psychological effects of unemployment. *Psychological Bulletin*, *35*, 358–390.

Feather, N. T. (1990). *The psychological impact of unemployment*. New York: Springer Verlag.

Fleck, C. (2002). Introduction to the transaction edition. In M. Jahoda, P. F. Lazarsfeld, & H. Zeisel (Eds.), *Marienthal: The sociography of an unemployed community with a new introduction by Christian Fleck* (pp. vii–xxx). New Brunswick: Transaction Publishers.

Foucault, M. (1978/1990/1997). What is critique? Text of a lecture given in May 1978 to the French Society of Philosophy, later published in French in 1990 in the *Bulletin de la Societe francaise de philosophie* and published in English translation in 1997. See: Lotringer (1997: 41–81).

Foucault, M. (1980). The confession of the flesh. In C. Gordon (Ed.), *Power/Knowledge selected interviews and other writings* (pp. 194–228). New York: Pantheon Books.

Foucault, M. (2010). *The birth of biopolitics*. London: Palgrave MacMillan (Originally given as Lecture 1 at the College de France 1978–9 as The Birth of Biopolitics).

Freud, S. (1930). *Civilisation and its discontents*. London: Hogarth.

Frew, H. W. O. (1935). The effect of continual unemployment on health of school children in a depressed area. *Glasgow Medical Journal*, *123*, 8–13.

Fryer, D. (1986a). Employment deprivation and personal agency during unemployment: a critical discussion of Jahoda's explanation of the psychological effects of unemployment. *Social Behaviour*, *1*(3), 3–23.

Fryer, D. (1986b). The social psychology of the invisible: an interview with Marie Jahoda. *New Ideas in Psychology*, *4*(1), 107–118.

Fryer, D. (1986c). Employment deprivation and personal agency during unemployment. *Social Behaviour*, *1*(3), 3–23.

Fryer, D. (1986d). On defending the unattacked: a comment on Jahoda's defence. *Social Behaviour*, *1*, 31–32.

Fryer, D. (1987). Monmouthshire and Marienthal: sociographies of two unemployed communities. In D. Fryer, & P. Ullah, *Unemployed people: Social and psychological perspectives* (pp. 74–93). Milton Keynes: Open University Press.

Fryer, D. (1990). The mental health costs of unemployment: towards a social psychological concept of poverty. *British Journal of Clinical and Social Psychiatry*, *7*(4), 164–176.

Fryer, D. (1992). Das Unsichtbare sichtbar machen – David Fryer im Gesprach mit der Sozialpsychologin Marie Jahoda. In A. Wacker (Ed.), *Die Marienthal-Studie – 60 Jahre spater, Marie Jahoda funf und achtzigsten Geburtstag* (pp. 19–35). Universities of Hannover and Oldenburg: Agis texte Band 2.

Fryer, D. (1997). *Interview with Professor Marie Jahoda*. Commissioned by the American Psychological Association (Division 27) for archival video records. American Psychological Association (Division 27) Archives. Issued in 2000 as a two-volume compact disc in the *Exemplars of Community Psychology* series.

Fryer, D. (2001a). Marie Jahoda 1907–2001: Eine Wurdigung. In J. Zempel, J. Bacher, & K. Moser (Eds.), *Erwerbslosigkeit – Ursachen, Auswirkungen und Interventionen* (pp. 437–440). Opladen: Leske + Budrich.

Fryer, D. (2001b). Marie Jahoda (1907–2001). In C. Fraser, B. Burchell, D. Hay, & G. Duveen (Eds.), *Introducing social psychology* (pp. 320–321). Cambridge: Polity Press.

Fryer, D. (2006). Insecurity, the restructuring of unemployment and mental health. In T. Kieselbach, A. H. Winefield, C. Boyd, & S. Anderson (Eds.), *Unemployment and health: International and interdisciplinary perspectives*. Bowen Hills, Qld: Australian Academic Press.

Fryer, D. (2012). Critical differences: the development of a community critical psychological perspective on the psychological costs of unemployment. In T. Kieselbach, & S. Mannila (Eds.), *Unemployment, precarious work and health. Research and policy issues*, (pp. 473–489). Wiesbaden: VS - Verlag für Sozialwissenschaften.

Fryer, D. (2014). Unemployment: 2031–2036. In T. Teo (Ed.), *Encyclopaedia of critical psychology*. New York: Springer.

Fryer, D. (2017). Counter-inscription: writing as an engaged method of resistance and liberation. In M. Seedat, & S. Suffla, S (Eds.), *Community, liberation and public engagement: Beyond formulaic method*. New York, Springer.

Fryer D., & Duckett P. (2014). Publishing. In T. Teo (Ed.), *Encyclopaedia of critical psychology* (pp. 1605–1610). Springer, New York,

Fryer, D., & Fagan, R. (1994). The role of social psychological aspects of income in the mental health costs of unemployment. *The Community Psychologist*, *27*(2), 16–17.

Fryer, D., & Fagan, R. (2003). Towards a community psychological perspective on unemployment and mental health research. *American Journal of Community Psychology*, *32*(1/2), 89–96.

Fryer, D., & Feather, N. (1994). Intervention research techniques. In C. Cassell, & G. Symon (Eds.), *Qualitative methods in organizational and occupational psychology* (pp. 230–247). London: Sage.

Fryer, D., & Fox, R. (2015). Community psychology: Subjectivity, power and collectivity. In I. Parker (Ed.), *Handbook of critical psychology*. London: Routledge.

Fryer, D., & Jahoda, M. (1998a). Marie Jahoda and David Fryer in conversation. *Journal of Community and Applied Social Psychology*, *8*(2), 89–100.

Fryer, D., & Jahoda, M. (1998b). *Professor Marie Jahoda in interview: The origins of a social psychologist*. Video interview. Commissioned by the British Psychological Society for the *BPS Archives*.

Fryer, D., & Jahoda, M. (2000). *Video interview with Professor Marie Jahoda*. Commissioned by the American Psychological Association (Division 27) for archival records. Published in a two-volume compact disc in the *Exemplars of Community Psychology* series.

Fryer, D., & McKenna, S. (1987). The laying off of hands: Unemployment and the experience of time. In S. Fineman (Ed.), *Unemployment: Personal and social consequences* (pp. 47–73). London: Tavistock.

Fryer, D., & McKenna, S. (1988). Redundant skills: temporary unemployment and mental health. In M. Patrickson (Ed.), *Readings in organizational behaviour* (pp. 44–70). New South Wales: Harper and Row.

Fryer, D., & Payne, R. L. (1984a). Pro-activity in unemployment: findings and implications. *Leisure Studies*, *3*, 273–295.

Fryer, D., & Payne, R. L. (1984b). Book borrowing and unemployment. *Library Review*, 32, 196–206.

Fryer, D., & Payne, R. L. (1984c). Working definitions. *Quality of Working Life*, *1*(5), 13–15.

Fryer, D., & Payne, R. L. (1986). Being unemployed: a review of the literature on the psychological experience of unemployment. In C. L. Cooper, & I. Robertson (Eds.), *International review of industrial and organizational psychology* (pp. 235–278). Chichester: Wiley.

Fryer, D., & Stambe, R. (2014a). Neo-liberal austerity and unemployment: Critical psychological issues. *The Journal of Critical Psychology, Counselling and Psychotherapy*, *14*(4), 256–266.

Fryer, D., & Stambe, R. (2014b). Work and the crafting of individual identities from a critical standpoint. *Australian Community Psychologist*, *26*(1), 8–17.

Fryer, D., & Stambe, R. (2014c). Neo-liberal austerity and unemployment: critical psychological issues. *The Psychologist*, *27*(4), 244–249.

Fryer, D., & Stambe, R. (2015). Unemployment and mental health. In J. Wright (Ed.), *International encyclopedia of social and behavioral sciences* (2nd edn., Vol. 24, pp. 733–737). Oxford: Elsevier.

Fryer, D., & Ullah, P. (Eds.) (1987). *Unemployed people: Social and psychological perspectives*. Milton Keynes: Open University Press.

Fryer, D., & Warr, P. B. (1984). Unemployment and cognitive difficulties. *British Journal of Clinical Psychology*, *23*, 67–68.

Fryer, D., & Winefield, A. H. (1998). Employment stress and unemployment distress as two varieties of labour market induced psychological strain: an explanatory framework. *Australian Journal of Social Research*, *5*(1), 3–18.

Fryer, D. (1999). Marie Jahoda: a social psychologist for and in the real world. In Isaksson, K., Hogstedt, K., Eriksson, C., & Theorell, T. (Eds.), *Health effects of the new labour market* (pp. 5–10). New York: Kluwer Academic/Plenum Publishers.

Halpern, D. F., & Butler, H. A. (2011). Critical thinking and the education of psychologically literate citizens. In J. Cranney, & D. S. Dunn (Eds.), *The psychologically literate citizen: Foundations and global perspectives* (pp. 27–40). New York: Oxford University Press.

Henriques, J., Hollway, W., Urwin, C., Venn, C., & Walkerdine, V. (1998). *Changing the subject: Psychology, social regulation and subjectivity*. London: Routledge.

Hollway, W., & Jefferson, T. (2000). *Doing qualitative research differently free association, narrative and the interview method*. London: Sage.

Horkheimer, M. (1982). *Critical theory*. New York: Seabury Press.

International Labour Organization. (1982). *Resolutions concerning economically active population, employment, unemployment and underemployment*. Adopted by the 13th International Conference of Labour Statisticians. Retrieved from http://www.ilo.org/global/statistics-and-databases/standards-and-guidelines/resolutions-adopted-by-international-conferences-of-labour-statisticians/WCMS_087481/lang–en/index.htm

International Labour Organization. (2017). *World employment and social outlook: Trends 2017*. Retrieved from http://www.ilo.org/global/research/global-reports/weso/2017/WCMS_541211/lang–en/index.htm

Israeli, N. (1935). Distress in the outlook of Lancashire and Scottish unemployed. *Journal of Applied Psychology*, *19*, 67–69.

Jahoda, M. (1938/1987). Unemployed men at work. In D. Fryer, & P. Ullah (Eds.), *Unemployed people: Social and psychological perspectives* (pp. 1–73). Milton Keynes: Open University Press.

Jahoda, M. (1977). *Freud and the dilemmas of psychology*. London: The Hogarth Press

Jahoda, M. (1982). *Employment and unemployment: A social-psychological analysis*. Cambridge: Cambridge University Press.

Jahoda, M. (1983). The emergence of social psychology in Vienna: An exercise in long-term memory. *British Journal of Social Psychology*, *22*, 343–349.

Jahoda, M., Lazarsfeld, P. F., & Zeisel, H. (1971). *Marienthal: The sociography of an unemployed community*. Chicago: Aldine.

Jahoda, M., Lazarsfeld, P. F., & Zeisel, H. (2002). *Marienthal: The sociography of an unemployed community with a new introduction by Christian Fleck*. New Brunswick: Transaction Publishers.

Jefferies, B. J., Nazareth, I., Marston, L., Moreno-Kustner, B., Sellón, J. Á., Svab, I., & King, M. (2011). Associations between unemployment and major depressive disorder: evidence from an international, prospective study (the predict cohort). *Social Science & Medicine*, *73*, 1627–1634.

Kagan, C., Burton, M., Duckett, P., Lawthom, R., & Siddiquee, A. (2011). *Critical community psychology*. Chichester: BPS Blackwell.

Kant, I. (1784/1997). In S. Lotringer (Ed.), *The politics of truth: Michel Foucault* (1997: pp. 29–37). Cambridge, MA: Semiotext(e).

Keily, K. M., & Butterworth, P. (2013). Social disadvantage and individual vulnerability: a longitudinal investigation of welfare receipt and mental health in Australia. *Australian & New Zealand Journal of Psychiatry*, *47*(7), 654–666.

Kim, I. H., Muntaner, C., Vahid, S. F., Vives, A., Vanroelen, C., & Benach, J. (2012). Welfare states, flexible employment and health: a critical review. *Health Policy*, *104*, 99–127.

Lotringer, S. (Ed.). (1997) *The politics of truth: Michel Foucault*. Cambridge, MA: MIT Press.

McGhee, J., & Fryer, D. (1989). Unemployment, income and the family: an action research perspective. *Social Behaviour*, *4*, 237–252.

McKee-Ryan, F., Song, Z., Wanberg, C. R., & Kinicki, A. J. (2005). Psychological and physical well-being during unemployment: a meta-analytic study. *Journal of Applied Psychology*, *901*, 53–70.

McKenna, S., & Fryer, D. (1984). Perceived health during lay-off and early unemployment. *Occupational Health*, *36*(5), 201–206.

Marley, C., & Fryer, D. (2014). Social change through critical knowledge work: the case of ADHD. *The Journal of Critical Psychology, Counselling and Psychotherapy*, *14*, 11–19.

Maynard, D. C., & Feldman, D. C. (Eds.) (2011). *Underemployment: psychological, economic, and social challenges*. Springer: New York.

Nic Giolla Easpaig, B., Linn, S., Humphrey, R., & Fryer, D. (2014). A queer-theoretical approach to community health psychology. *Journal of Health Psychology*, *19*(1), 117–125.

O'Brien, G. E. (1986). *Psychology of work and unemployment*. Chichester: Wiley.

Osterreichischen Wirtschaftspsychologischen Forschungsstelle. (1933). *Die Arbeitslosen von Marienthal: Ein soziographischer Versuch uber die Wirkungen langdauernder Arbeitslosigkeit*. Leipzig: Hirzel.

Parker, I. (1997). Psychology, subjectivity and resistance. *Forum Kritische Psychologie*, *38*, 136–145.

Parker, I. (2007). *Revolution in psychology: Alienation to emancipation*. London: Pluto Press.

Parker, I. (2009). *Psychoanalytic mythologies*. London: Anthem Press.

Parker, I. (2015). *Psychology after psychoanalysis: Psychosocial studies and beyond*. Abingdon/New York: Routledge

Parker, I. (2018). *Psy-Complex in question: Critical review in psychology, psychoanalysis and social theory*. Winchester and Washington: Zero Books.

Paul, K. I., & Moser, K. (2009). Unemployment impairs mental health: meta-analyses. *Journal of Vocational Behaviour*, *74*, 264–282.

Pilgrim Trust (1938). *Men without work*. Cambridge: Cambridge University Press.

Rose, N. (1999). *Governing the soul: The shaping of the private self*. London: Free Association Press.

Seedat, M., Duncan, N., & Lazarus, S. (2001). *Community psychology: Theory, method and practice. South African and other perspectives*. Cape Town: Oxford University Press.

Stambe, R., & Fryer, D. (2012). Answering back to governmentality. In C. Chapman, K. Kellehear, M. Everett, A. Lane, M. Cassaniti, S. Robertson, J. Peters, L. Prowse, M. Hilton, & T. Trauer (Eds.), *Recovering citizenship, contemporary TheMHS in mental health services*. Brookvale: Acorn Press.

Standing, G. (2014). The precariat and class struggle. Published as: O precariado e a luta de classes, *Revista Crítica de Ciências Sociais*, *103*(May), 9–24. http://www.guystanding.com/files/documents/Precariat_and_Class_Struggle_final_English.pdf

Warr, P. (1987). *Work, unemployment and mental health*. Oxford: Clarendon Press.

Winefield, A. H., & Fryer, D. (1996). Some emerging threats to the validity of research on unemployment and mental health. *The Australian Journal of Social Research*, *12*(1), 115–134.

Winefield, A. H., Delfabbro, P. H., Winefield, H. R., Duong, D., & Malvaso, C. (2017). The psychological effects of unemployment and unsatisfactory employment on young adults: findings from a 10-year longitudinal study. *The Journal of Genetic Psychology*, *178*(4), 246–251.

Winefield, A. H., Tiggemann, M., Winefield, H. R., & Goldney, R. D. (1993). *Growing up with unemployment: A longitudinal study of its psychological impact*. London: Routledge.

15

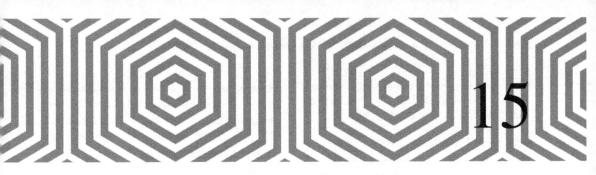

Standing Up for Sustainable Livelihoods: From Poverty to Prosperity

Stuart C. Carr

Ask yourself: What are the biggest issues in the world today? If you said 'poverty', you are in high company. Two rounds of global consultations over two decades by the United Nations (2016; Annan, 2000) have named poverty the primary challenge facing our global community. Primary how? 'Poverty' is not just about money (Carr and Sloan, 2003). Having enough money certainly frees people up and enables them to develop their talents and aspirations (Sen, 1999). What poverty actually 'is' are poverties of opportunity – structural barriers to good health, education, occupation, equity, clean environment (Annan, 2000; United Nations, 2016). Multi-faceted, poverty is thereby a core, structural, applied issue in global *community* psychology (Marsella, 1998).

Asked how to *combat* poverties of opportunity in everyday life, people will often spontaneously think of, and mention, a particular mid-level structure – 'jobs' (Galinha et al., 2016; Narayan et al., 2000; Narayan and Petesch, 2002). Not just poor-quality, poorly paid, precarious work, i.e., 'working poverty' (World Bank, 2012). People want opportunity for work that is 'decent' (Blustein, 2016; Galinha et al., 2016; ILO, 2013). To qualify as 'decent', work must meet people's aspirations, shorter-term (e.g., a job, a living wage) and longer-term (e.g., decent career prospects), for a dignified life for themselves and families, at work and in their communities (ILO, 2014). A decent job can be life-changing (Tuason, 2010). Poverty reduction is therefore an applied issue in both global community and *work* psychology (Carr, 2013).

Pari Passu, community and work psychology point towards *sustainable livelihood.* To be sustainable,

> A livelihood comprises the capabilities, assets (stores, resources, claims and access) and activities required for a means of living: A livelihood is sustainable which can cope with and recover from stress and shocks, maintain or enhance its capabilities and assets, and provide sustainable livelihood opportunities for the next generation; and which contributes net benefits to other livelihoods

[i.e., community] at the local and global levels and in the short and long term. (Chambers and Conway, 1991: 6, parenthesis added)

Sustainable livelihood is a *multiplier*.

Originating as a response to extreme material poverty in rural and remote communities (Chambers and Conway, 1991), the term 'sustainable livelihood' has since been applied to different types of community and challenge, including urban communities where the world's majority now reside (United Nations, 2014) and to the capacity to recover from natural or manmade disasters (respectively, Krantz, 2001; Blaikie et al., 2004). Wider still, the qualifier 'sustainable' directly connects the 'sustainable' in sustainable livelihood with the most integrated structure for human development over the next 15 years – the United Nations (2016) 'Sustainable Development Goals', or 'SDGs'.

The SDGs are a reminder that if poverty is structural and multifaceted then its reduction must be too. In Figure 15.1, eradicating poverty in all its forms everywhere, including low, mid and higher income countries, is paramount (SDG 1). Interrelated, SDGs 2 to 17 support this primary objective. Foundational are access to decent health and educational services (SDGs 2, 3 and 4). SDG 5 spans gender equity during school and into work. SDGs 8–12 extend the ethos of equity into decent work (SDG 8), economic inclusion (SDG 9), reducing income inequality (SDG 10), building inclusive communities (SDG 11) and more sustainable consumption (SDG 12). These will help sustain (versus destroy) the environment (SDG 13–15) and enable more peaceful societies (SDG 16). Underlining SDGs 1–16 is a process goal – SDG 17 Partnership (Figure 15.1). Partnership, of course, requires people to work and commune together, across a variety of sectors and disciplines – including psychologists!

Sustainable livelihood is thus central, and pivotal, in *every one of the SDGs*.

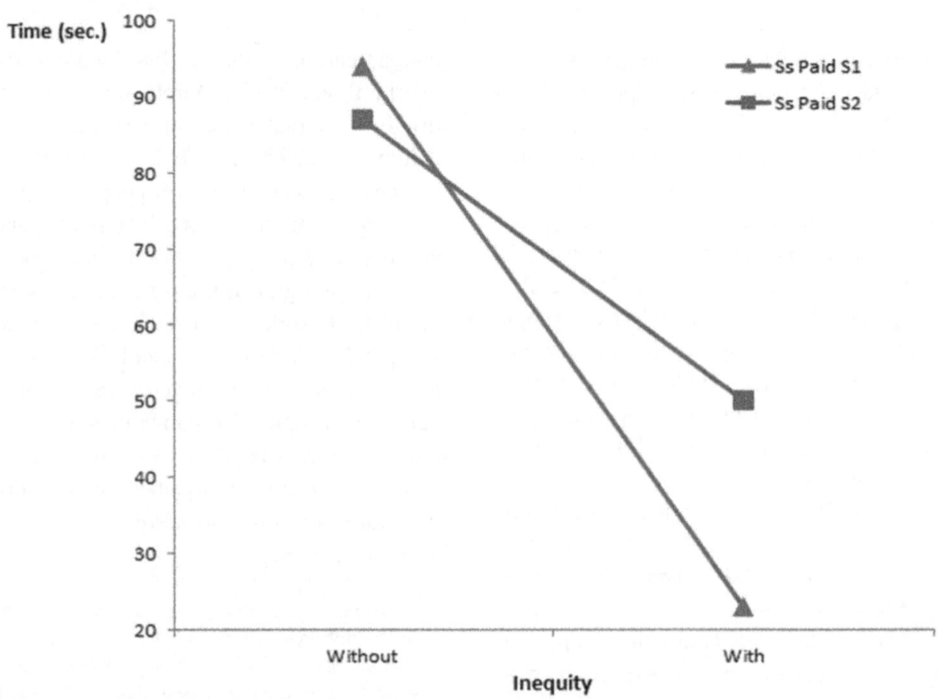

Figure 15.1 Double demotivation from dual salaries in the laboratory

Source: Carr et al. (1995), adapted by H. Jones.

From a lofty macro level, 'jobs' are defined somewhat abstractedly (by the World Bank, 2012: 5) as 'activities that generate income, monetary or in kind, without violating human rights'. Even using this limited definition (ILO, 2016), there are at least 200 million people in the world who remain 'unemployed [despite] actively looking for work' (ILO, 2016: 5, parenthesis added). Job creation is very important for economic inclusion (SDG 8; Fryer, Chapter 14, this volume). On that side of the jobs fence, from a global population of seven billion, three billion people *do* have 'jobs' (ILO, 2016). Shockingly, however, half of those jobs are classified (by the World Bank and the ILO) as employment that is 'vulnerable' – meaning unsafe, irregular, insecure, informal, poorly paid, often in subsistence agriculture and industrial sweatshops, e.g., in the garment industry, and in domestic work (ILO, 2015).

Expanding the definition of work from jobs to 'livelihood' allows for, and duly recognizes, the existence of unpaid work (such as domestic labour), children helping out in a family enterprise, illegal and indentured work such as sexual slavery, bonded labour (Singh and Tripathi, 2010) and any other form of work that violates human rights (World Bank, 2012). Through this more inclusive lens, inestimable numbers of livelihoods around the world are not sustainable but instead 'precarious' (Standing, 2014). Their role in poverty perpetuation cannot be underestimated, or overlooked, by any social psychology that genuinely claims to be 'applied', or as representing the 99% (SDG 10).

The ethos of the SDGs, like their predecessors the Millennium Development Goals (Annan, 2000), is Humanitarian. They are concerned primarily with promoting and enabling human welfare and wellbeing. Extemporizing this applied, pro-social ethos is 'Humanitarian work psychology' (Berry et al., 2011). Humanitarian work psychology is a relatively recent development (Lefkowitz, 2016). It challenges extant occupational stereotypes (Carr et al., 2014) that work psychology is merely a servant of power (Baritz, 1960; Bergman and Jean, 2016; Brief, 2000). It asks how organizations may best serve and empower workers – financially, occupationally, socially; furthermore, it specifically allows for 'shared prosperity' between one group and the other (SDG 10).

Insofar as a sustainable livelihood can empower people's choices in life (Sen, 1999), it may not only (1) inform but also (2) be informed by, Humanitarian work psychology (Carr, 2007). The Humanitarian focus itself has at least two main foci, which together form an *ethical* framework (Lefkowitz, 2016) for the rest of this chapter: (1) Humanitarian work, in particular applications of social psychology to community and Non-Government Organization (NGO) work to reduce poverty (Carr et al., 1998; MacLachlan et al., 2012); and (2) making work in *general* more accountable to Humanitarian standards (Carr and MacLachlan, 2014; Carr et al., 2012; United Nations, 2016).

HUMANITARIAN WORK | PSYCHOLOGY

Humanitarian work takes many forms, ranging from famine and other disaster relief (Vandaveer and Rizzuto, 2014) to maternal/child health (Vallières and McAuliffe, 2016) to empowerment camps for girls (Berry et al., 2014); from building wells and sanitation systems (Godbout, 2014) to training entrepreneurs (Bischoff et al., 2014); from combating homelessness (Kandola, 2014) to advocating for the rights of refugees and asylum seekers (Viale, 2014). Such diverse and multiple forms of Humanitarian service are reflected all across the SDGs (Figure 15.1). They are undertaken in a range of different sectors, from grass-roots 'self-help' and non-government to government welfare organizations, government-to-government 'bilateral' aid agencies (Carr, 2013), workers' cooperatives (Grace and

Associates, 2014), and in multi-lateral agencies like the UN itself to multi-national Corporate Social Responsibility, or 'CSR' (Osicki, 2016).

No single chapter can possibly span all of these forms of work, or diverse types of organization, and related livelihoods. Nevertheless, practice-based experiences may help to identify some wide-ranging barriers to sustainable Humanitarian service – first of all, since Humanitarian work is a human service, from service-*facing*, *community* perspectives; and secondly, to sustainable livelihood amongst the Humanitarian *workforce* – who might, or might not, be from the community that the work is meant to serve.

Community Perspectives

From a service-facing viewpoint, and rather surprisingly perhaps, the form that Humanitarian assistance takes is quite often simply not needed, or wanted. One example often springs to my mind, when living and working as a teacher in Malaŵi: a brand new Mercedes fire engine was donated by a European bilateral aid agency, to the local town services. Sadly, the truck was too wide for the narrow streets and lanes, meaning that it was very soon damaged. It needed hydrants to work – yet there were few, if any, in the municipality. There was a drought, and the water reservoir was empty. There was inflation, so that spare parts, which rely on foreign exchange rates to purchase, were unaffordable. And so on. Within just weeks, the truck was parked up in the yard, where it fell into disrepair and disuse, not only useless but a drain on resources for the community it was meant to serve. Size mattered, but as is often the case, e.g., from water and sanitation to health care services, less might have been more, in particular more *sustainable* (MacLachlan, 1996). As in many other memories, from outdated books to ultra-modern (read costly to maintain) computers, the service here was misaligned: first, with community need; and, second, with what service workers' communities can sustain.

Welfare services a different kind of example. Food banks, for instance, are supposed to serve the nutritional needs of people who are displaced or homeless. They are found all over the world, from Bogotá in Colombia (which has one of the largest volumes of internally displaced in the world) to Auckland in New Zealand (which is now one of the most unequal economies in the OECD). Across these very diverse settings, people – in one case anecdotally and in the other reportedly (Family 100 Research Project, 2014) – prefer to go hungry than face demeaning treatment from desk staff. Queuing up for welfare and being barked at, or talked down to, through an iron grille is demeaning (personal experience). So is being filmed with your own child whilst an aid worker pleads for sponsorship (subtext: Incapable parent). In each example, the service interfaces poorly with what people actually need and want (Godbout, 2014). From their perspective, their treatment – and with it the service itself – is unsustainable.

Taken together, what these examples suggest is that Humanitarian work can cut across the grain of everyday human factors – not simply material needs and wants but, just as importantly, *social* factors. They include, for instance, basic needs to be treated with dignity and respect by any human and service employee. A similar point applies to the services themselves. In the powerful and poignant words of one widely respected Indigenous community leader: 'We want health, housing and education, but not at the expense of losing our own soul, our own identity, a say in our lives: We refuse to sacrifice the essence of what makes us Aboriginal people' (Dodson, 1998: 8).

In this case, what Humanitarian 'assistance' *symbolizes* is deeply problematic – by conflicting with valued freedoms (Sen, 1999). Sometimes that conflict is material as well as symbolic. In terms of earning a daily living, becoming a 'recipient' of Humanitarian services may ironically *compete* directly with earning a sustainable livelihood. Aid has opportunity costs. Being 'aided' can include anything from not being able to tend one's community garden, or small-holding because one is working elsewhere to assemble donated aid equipment, dig a donated well, or unload donated foodstuffs, unwanted second-hand clothes or books (Carr et al., 1995). Personal occupational time is finite. Digging our own garden is preferable to (read more sustainable than) working as an aid 'recipient'. Mantras and monikers like 'helping people to help themselves' or 'to fish' become trite and patronising. Neither partnership nor reciprocity (Lough, 2016), they actually *impose* on, and may subtract from, sustainable livelihood.

Humanitarian work, then, easily becomes a challenge to a range of human factors, such as autonomy, identity and equity (MacLachlan et al., 2012). At the core of these human factors is a paradox: By its very nature, Humanitarian service work *mirrors* the very indignities it is meant to dissolve. It is not the changes it wants to see in the world. Furthermore, Humanitarian services should ideally, if they are sincere, be in the business of making themselves redundant. From an organizational perspective, this inconvenient truth is contradictory too. After all, organizations do not normally exist to not exist! And if empowerment is motivating, we cannot expect them to readily disempower themselves (!).

How can such apparent contradictions be resolved? The SDGs (Figure 15.1) indicate that Humanitarian goals can, and should, serve specific, overarching goals. A practical problem with the SDGs, though, is that they are quite macro – they do not readily translate into everyday actions (Easterly, 2006). This critique of macro-level goals implies a role for behavioural principles to be applied effectively to poverty eradication (MacLachlan and McAuliffe, 2003). Indeed, through a series of 'high-level' summits held in Rome (2002), Paris (2005), Accra (2008) and Busan (2011), the United Nations have identified and iterated a set of behavioural principles for implementing the SDGs sustainably (OECD, 2016a). They have not so far though – to the best of my knowledge – translated applications (OECD, 2016a). The rest of this section thus parses these so-called Paris principles into everyday practice (Gloss and Foster-Thompson, 2013).

Ownership is a familiar principle in social and community psychology but also in UN-speak. In the latter, communities will set their own strategies for poverty reduction. An example from Humanitarian work would be the Office of Aboriginal Development in Australia, which initially set out to aid Indigenous communities in remote Far North Australia to develop enterprises (Ivory, 2003). It soon became apparent (Ivory, 2003) that the only 'help' that might be needed, given the region's ancient trading routes and enterprising values, was advice about how to navigate government 'red tape'. In other words, government was more of a barrier than an enabler to Indigenous enterprise. Once recognized, the service was adapted to community aspirations for sustainable livelihoods (by charting how to navigate the red tape). Thereafter, community-based enterprises, from Indigenous tourism to Indigenous cosmetics, thrived (Ivory, 2005).

Local Ownership is a foundation for what the UN terms *Alignment* (OECD, 2016a). According to this principle, donor countries should align behind community objectives and use local systems to achieve them. Looking back at our anecdotal examples above, clearly they were not aligned with community values, or systems, municipal or social. An example of the inverse can be found in job selection, and performance management, for Humanitarian workers in church-based Humanitarian services across sub-Saharan Africa and Southern Asia (Manson and Carr, 2011). Expatriate Humanitarian mission-workers whose values aligned not just with international 'HQ' but, more importantly, with what *local communities valued* were more job satisfied, engaged in their work and satisfied with life – each indicative of job motivation and performance (Manson and Carr, 2011). Analogously perhaps, in an innovative application of attribution theory, judges who were trained to role-play the circumstances of homelessness and street-life became more sensitized to rehabilitation options (Hodgetts et al., 2013).

In each of these examples, success was arguably achieved by *operationalizing* a macro principle – of alignment – at an everyday middle level – in the workplace.

Alignment is a precursor in turn to *harmonization*. This means that Humanitarian agencies, and workers in them, coordinate, simplify procedures and share information to avoid duplication (OECD, 2016a). In human service sectors such as welfare systems and international aid, people in need can find themselves spending more time being referred from one agency to the next, or overrun by a plethora of aid agencies who themselves can drain and pollute resources (Godbout, 2014). In UN-speak, services have become 'fragmented'. Adopting a more harmonized approach would consist of services that wrap around client to cover all needs, rather than struggling to connect with a service that actually meets their needs. Wraparound services like these can be found in youth services, for example, whereby youth workers, and the agencies they represent, work in a more coordinated roundtable arrangement with the client, rather than in separate, oftentimes fragmented, bureaucracies (Bergquist and Gammon, 2015).

Principles of ownership, alignment and harmonization of Humanitarian services are *inputs* to poverty eradication rather than actual outcomes from them. The principle of *Results* requires that Humanitarian service stays focused on real and measurable impact on development (OECD, 2016a). For example, Humanitarian organizations in Cambodia have focused on partnering with private sector organizations to enable women beer sellers aspiring to escape precarious pay and sexually unsafe conditions to safer, more decent hospitality jobs in hotels (Lee et al., 2010). A key part of the programme of services developed by the NGO ('Sirchesi') has been a tracking system for ensuring that the women actually do go on to develop safe and decent careers, with commensurate rises in quality of life and living for themselves and their families.

Under *Mutual Accountability*, Humanitarian donors and partners are accountable for development results (OECD, 2016a). An example of how this principle applies to social psychology is found in the study of environmental disasters, including persistent drought related to climate change (Hayati et al., 2010). Hayati et al. (2010) found, whilst drought hurts health and education, Humanitarian assistance packages had been favouring the least needy farmers, who possessed the stronger paperwork skills to apply for soft loans. Like Ivory (2003), and others in enterprise development (Berry et al., 2014; Bischoff et al., 2014; Klinger et al., 2013), their work highlights how, and where, Humanitarian systems can direct more resources; in this case, towards training that empowers the poorer farmers with numeracy skills.

Skills development in any workforce is termed, in poverty reduction, *Capacity Development,* meaning explicitly the ability of local, relatively indigenous workers to self-manage their own future (OECD, 2016a). Capacity development is also often code for practices that enable sustainable livelihoods locally *within* the Humanitarian sector. Surprisingly perhaps, barriers to working effectively in this sector, according to workers themselves, are often not in the work itself, however challenging and daunting the tasks may be. Instead, the devil is in the detail. It is everyday organizational hassles that can be the straw to break the proverbial camel's back (Vergara and Gardner, 2011).

As we now consider, they include workforce relations, work conditions and the dynamics in-between.

Workforce Perspectives

The fundamental paradox in Humanitarian work, replicating and reflecting the structural inequities it aims to remove, is not restricted to relations with communities. A stunning and widespread example concerns the remuneration that Humanitarian forces themselves are paid. As we saw above, whilst money is not central in itself, it does enable other freedoms, and it can symbolize how much a person's reference group is valued, respected and treated fairly.

Against that yardstick for social justice, NGO employees are often treated very differently based solely on their community of origin – which, by most standards, is unfair. Host national employees, often highly skilled and experienced, tend to be paid a far lower rate than their equally skilled international counterparts. In one Pacific Island community, where the gap approached double figures, the double standard is called 'economic apartheid' (Marai et al., 2010; Marai, 2014). Locally aligned research on dual salaries, conducted across six low-income countries, found amongst local workers that they are despised as excessive, unfair, demotivating, conducive of brain drain. Ironically, they *strip* capacity from local communities, workforces and sustainable livelihoods (UNDP, 2014). They undermine relationships (McWha & MacLachlan, 2011); prevent partnerships (SDG 17).

This research has also engaged in partnership (SSG 17) with local communities to co-articulate options for more sustainable livelihoods, and thereby capacity development. Identified by local workforce representatives themselves, some options in practice included more ownership of the job description, alignment with community aspirations during job selection (above), harmonization of pay systems across expatriate and host national groups, and accountability via remuneration based on actual performance rather than ethnicity. Practicable measures like these, we believe, would help combat brain drain and enable capacity.

Belief on its own is not enough to change workplace practices, however. Despite the mounting evidence against their sustainability, dual salaries remain stubbornly in place. They are going nowhere in a hurry. Evidence-based belief is not enough either. Perhaps the SDGs will give an accountability boost to the case for wages reform, towards single rather than double standards. At an everyday organizational level, e.g., amongst NGOs, Humanitarian work psychologists have argued that this too is wishful thinking (Saner and Yiu, 2012). Instead, specific *skills* are required, and need to be cultivated in a new cadre of workers, to take the SDGs and evidence from research into practice: A set of 'new diplomacies' and new diplomats (Saner and Yiu, 2016).

In the case of dual salaries and Humanitarian workforce development, new diplomacies have included working in partnership (Figure 15.1, SDG 17) with the international NGO sector. Some major NGOs had become concerned by the injustice of the dual salary system as reported in work surveys of their employees. Focused on the SDGs (Figure 15.1), members of a network of international NGOs, the Core Humanitarian Standard (CHS) Alliance, are trialling various alternative policy options, e.g., paying Humanitarian workers on a single salary ladder in each country where they operate (http://www.chsalliance.org/news/blog/fair-pay).

Links with salary survey experts and researchers will enable this project to discern which policy options work best in which types of context, e.g., disaster relief work versus human rights advocacy, to foster capacity and sustainability. More importantly, we are working in partnership with NGO umbrella organizations like the CHS Alliance, which actively promotes good practices in Humanitarian workforce development. To that extent, any practice-based, evidence-informed protocol that emerges will already be owned, aligned, harmonized, results-driven and mutually accountable to the NGO sector and its donors.

Box 15.1 Critical incidents from dual salaries in low-waged Solomon Islands

LOCAL PERSPECTIVE

'Australians are coming in with a higher and higher and better lifestyle, making a lot of money… what they might get in one week is what Solomon Islanders might live on in a year…that's just sure to engender some bitterness eventually' (Church Leader)

EXPATRIATE PERSPECTIVE

'I was introduced to your work recently during a visit to the Solomon Islands, when an employee was talking about her experiences in this location, in particular her guilt regarding the gulf that exists between herself and the local islanders' (Aid Counsellor)

Source: Marai et al. (2010); Carr et al. (2013: 501).

New-ish diplomacies like these have a potential to be applied across other sectors, e.g., towards capacity building in education (SDG 4). In international high schools, for instance, dual salaries have been linked with double dips in motivation and wellbeing (Marai, 2002/3). There may be analogous applications to be made across organizations within the Tertiary Education sector (Marai, 2014), for instance universities across the Commonwealth. My own introduction to dual salaries came through an experience working as a lecturer in Malaŵi, working alongside several internationally recruited academic staff; all employed on *local* salary packages. All subsequently became senior professors in leading universities across the Pacific, Europe and the United States. Given our global community's commitment to the SDGs, we have since advocated to the Association of Commonwealth Universities (ACU) that now is the time to be partnering with research to better align and harmonize efforts to render pay and benefits for all academic staff in low income countries fair (Project ADDUP, 2016).

The deeper issue reflected in dual salary structures is inequality. The mini-narratives in Box 15.1 remind us that the motivational and performance fallout from dual salaries will spill over from organizations into the communities they are pre-supposed to serve. Dual structures are not confined to the non-profit, Humanitarian sector, or indeed just higher education. They are an institution – across a range of sectors and livelihoods, from private to public services and civil society work (Carr et al., 2010; Leung et al., 2014). Why are 'middle' classes even remotely important in poverty eradication? At a macro-economic level, because flourishing in the middle tends to trickle down to more human services and employment for lower income groups (ILO, 2013). At a more meso level, local professionals are often role models, sources and reflections of community, indigenous aspiration. At a workplace level, dual salaries are largely taboo. They are largely taboo because of power relations and the risk of losing one's job. Speaking truth to power, against the concrete ceiling of dual salaries, is more safely done through partnership – including research partnerships with Humanitarian | work psychology.

HUMANITARIAN | WORK PSYCHOLOGY

Experimental representations have been used to probe how dual salaries affect levels of intrinsic motivation. In real workplaces, intrinsic motivation is linked to organizational citizenship. In Figure 15.1, we see what happened to intrinsic motivation levels during an informative experimental representation of the motivational fallout from dual salaries. Individuals were each paid relatively trivial sums for working on a task that was intrinsically interesting, and then observed during a free choice period – a measure of intrinsic motivation. At random, participants were paid either $1 or $2 for participating, either 'With' or 'Without' knowledge about the Inequity. This enabled the study to tease out some of the effects of money per se from those of socio-economic inequality, i.e., absolute from relative income.

Without knowledge of the inequity there was no difference in motivation levels. In absolute terms, amount of money did not matter. With knowledge of inequity, however, motivation levels for the same amount caused a significant main effect – a drop not solely in the underpaid group but also, surprisingly perhaps, in the overpaid group.

In other words, there was a *double* demotivation.

Why and how did *both* groups become demotivated? Some clues emerged. Accounting for significant amounts of variance in the double demotivation effect in Figure 15.1 were at least two factors, one structural and absolute (pay condition per se), the other psychological and relative (individual differences in equity sensitivity). Of the two effects, the larger was the structural pay condition, not personality traits like equity sensitivity (McLoughlin and Carr, 1997). Structural inequality (SDG 10) was primary (for both pay groups).

How representative are the sums of money in Figure 15.1 to real life? One has to wonder about reactions outside the laboratory, where larger sums and real livelihoods are at stake. Would motivation from overpayment drop more, or less? In Box 15.1, we can understand that the internationally waged aid worker became sufficiently demoralized by pay inequality to seek counselling. After all, they may have become an aid worker precisely to help *reduce* inequality. Analogous results have been found as we saw in international high schools (Marai, 2002/3).

Across other real livelihoods, e.g., in the private sector, possible reasons for, and of, demotivation, respectively, were less evident (Carr et al., 2010). In field surveys of dual salaries, there was a threshold for acceptability (Carr et al., 2010). Workers from both sides tended to accept that a wage gap *ratio* of some kind was fair – to reflect added costs of relocation, mortgages, school fees, re-entry, etc. Between 2/3:1 was the modal reported acceptable ratio. The actual ratio frequently tended to exceed this fairness threshold, averaging 4:1 and ranging anywhere from 2:1 to 10:1. Consistent with the idea of a threshold, dual salaries were least problematic at the lower end of the threshold ratio spectrum. As the ratio climbed towards double figures, the higher-paid began to rate their own abilities higher than their local counterparts rate theirs, *even though they were statistically no different* (Marai et al., 2010).

Balance theories (of multiple denominations) predict that working harder to justify the extra money is unsustainable (especially with ratios in double figures which would rapidly lead to burnout!). More likely, ironically in the name of justice, people might start to inflate their own abilities psychologically to help rationalize the difference ('I/we must be worth the money'). Someone who *thinks* they are better than they really are is likely to work less hard than if there was less self-inflation. They may also receive less help from their local colleagues, e.g., during cross-cultural adjustment ('You're the expert, you do the work!'), contributing to early returns and lost capacity in the host country. To these extents, the expatriates too would become demotivated.

Crucially, systems theory predicts that, in the mid- to longer-term, double standards are unsustainable. Any subtle process of demotivation amongst the better off would insidiously undermine social relations, including insidious denigration of local peers over time (Carr, 2000; 2013). As time wears on, the relatively privileged become increasingly disparaging of the relatively deprived group, increasingly blaming them for their own hardship. Simultaneously, the relatively deprived group become increasingly disengaged from the relatively privileged counterparts, as the latter grow increasingly aloof. And so on. Each adjustment triggers an equal and opposite reaction. The more privileged, the more easily it is triggered, and the quicker it degenerates into outright conflict, and even hatred. Amongst food bank workers, expect the full-time, professional workers, not the volunteer students or part-timers, to be rudest – and loathed.

This is the dynamic nub, the value-add from systems theory, to double demotivation processes. The more one group distances, or disengages, from supporting and cooperating with the other, in what members feel is a legitimate form of equity restoration, the more the other's equity restoration – in this case self-inflation – is reinforced. Self-inflation sets off another round of disengagement, and so on. Across developmental time, therefore, the net result is an insidiously *escalating* double demotivation; in effect, a double vicious circle. Eventually, every double standard becomes unsustainable (Carr, 2013).

Why make so much, in this chapter, of dual salaries? They are an elephant-in-the-room against human development work and sustainable livelihoods (MacLachlan et al., 2012). They are also emblematic of workplace inequality in general, and incomes 'at' work in particular (ILO, 2013). They remind us that income inequality is often most proximal, and salient, at work, inside an organization and across its supply chains. Escalating double demotivation could apply in principle to any form of economic apartheid, in any inequitable workplace or inter-community inequality (SDG 10, Figure 15.1). Plus, the inequality need not be confined to any one sector (Box 15.2). As Box 15.2 indicates, escalation of disengagement can occur between government and non-government sectors.

Living Wages

As well as being relatively deprived, studies of dual salary systems have found that local workers 'inside' dual salary structures are often poor in the absolute too – they experience *non*-living wages (Carr et al., 2010). This is a common point across professional workers in health and education (SDGs 2–5), across many low- and middle-income countries (Carr et al., 2011), even though (as we have seen) a thriving middle-classes is often essential for relative and absolute poverty to be reduced across societies as a whole (ILO, 2013).

But how can precarious wages be combated?

The most direct way to tackle income inequality and enable more sustainable

Box 15.2 Kenya cracks down on foreign NGO workers, citing wage disparity

The [NGO] Board, a government institution that is responsible for regulating the NGO sector in Kenya, claims that there are thousands of expats working without appropriate permits and cites the large wage disparity between locals and foreigners as one of the main reasons behind the tougher stands… 'I realized that no matter what I did, I would raise about a certain rank and get paid a higher salary because I was a local hire,' Helen said in an interview…

…In 2013 the current government tried to amend the Public Benefits Organizations Act, which regulates the operations of NGOs and civil society in Kenya, in an attempt to restrict and monitor the external funding for these organizations… An estimated 240,000 people work in the NGO sector in Kenya, and it is undeniable that NGOs play a vital role in providing essential services where the government fails. But the sector is also marred by a variety of challenges, with wage disparity being one of the many…

Source: Abridged from de Fazio (2016), with parentheses added.

livelihoods, within or between organizations in a supply chain, is by wage distribution – in this case, lowering the wage ceiling and raising the wage floor.

At the top end of the wage spectrum, the ILO (2013) has shown this and challenged exorbitant Chief Executive Officer (CEO) wages. This ILO World of Work Report (2013) calls them out for being a global drain on resources from wage budgets; for reducing the prospects of job creation; for exacerbating wage inequalities with labour (SDG 10, Figure 15.1); and for significantly exacerbating, rather than reducing, world poverty (SDG 1). Double demotivation theory adds to these costs the risk of demotivation, through self-inflation, e.g., from CEO salaries that are 500 times those of the shopfloor.

Capping CEO wages is one policy tool that has been invoked in The Netherlands, and again in Kenya, as a pre-condition for government funding in the NGO sector. Sadly though, this macro-level tool has been less visible in other sectors, including the private sector in which 9/10 of the world's 'jobs' are held (UNDP, 2014).

At the other end of the wage spectrum are the 'working poor' (ILO, 2013). Working poverty has arguably become more of an issue than unemployment and equal in magnitude to the issue of poverty per se. In 2016, the world contains up to 702 million people who daily face extreme poverty, defined today as living on less than $1.90 a day (World Bank, 2016). Astoundingly, some 327 million, approaching *half* of these 702 million people who live in 'extreme' poverty (recently redefined from $1.25 to $1.90 per day) are actually also 'working' (ILO, 2016)! Moreover, almost a billion more of the three billion total in jobs earn just $1.90–$5.00, not every hour but per *day* (ILO, 2016). Clearly, working poverty through precarious livelihood is a major global issue.

Legal safety nets are simply not working (Cunniah, 2012). Many of the world's 1.5 billion 'vulnerable' workers (70% of whom are in sub-Saharan African countries) work in the informal sector (ILO, 2016). There, by definition, they are not even protected by insufficient legal minima – Minimum Wages. Job formalization is clearly an issue for poverty eradication (SDG 1). Yet even amongst those that do have formal jobs – from pickers in the tea industry in Malaŵi (Oxfam, 2014) to blue collar occupations across the United States (Smith, 2015) – their own country's legal Minimum Wage is increasingly *in*sufficient to make ends meet (ILO, 2016). Today, a further major challenge has opened up, with the availability of global labour markets enabling outsourcing and a global race-to-the-bottom on wages (Collins and Mayer, 2010).

Collectively, what these statistics tell us is that unemployment per se is not the major issue in eradicating poverty (for SDG 1). A wider and deeper issue today is actually access to *decent work* (Figure 15.1, SDG 8). This starts with, and is predicated on, earning a living income (UNDP, 2014). Paradoxically, it has become *working* poverty, through non-living wages, that is now arguably 'the' most fundamental, Humanitarian challenge for Humanitarian I work psychology today (Bergman and Jean, 2016).

Surprisingly enough, perhaps, work psychology knows very little indeed about the very low tail end of the income distribution at work, compared to its middle and upper-waged counterparts (Judge et al., 2010; see also Card et al., 2012; Mumford and Smith, 2012). Where living wages *are* calculated, they tend to be set by fiat – econometrically, through the average price of a shopping basket for instance, which is then used, circularly, to calculate the wage that would be needed to buy it. Nowhere in the process are people's own everyday experiences, and qualities of life and work life, calibrated alongside the money.

This exclusive focus on econometrics creates a space for Humanitarian work psychology to make a contribution. Specifically, we can begin to develop more inclusive ways of monetizing the financial returns of work, less

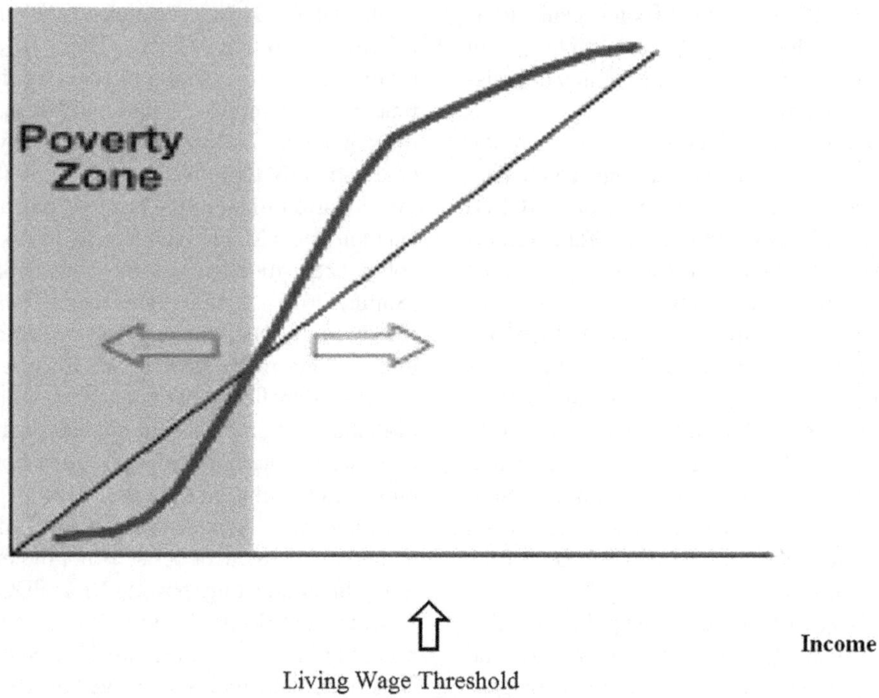

Figure 15.2 Potential relationships between income and thriving

Source: Carr et al. (2016a).

for the employer and more *for the employee* (Carr et al., 2016a). 'How' we do this matters a great deal – it is a new diplomacy. A difficult balancing act; on the one hand, it must serve labour whilst, on the other hand, it must ultimately be persuasive to management, especially perhaps in the vast private sector.

Figure 15.2 theorizes the Humanitarian I work psychology of a living wage. First, it draws from the concept of a poverty trap and poverty trap theory (solid S-Shaped line). This argues that people on low incomes are often trapped below, or on, the waterline (≈), e.g., by loan sharks, or unexpected bills, or added costs of finding a job, such as travel to work. Only above a certain Living Wage Threshold do they earn enough to start thriving, e.g., saving, sending kids to school, enjoying some quality of life, and work–life balance. This point is crucial – literally pivotal in fact – because it means that *only if wages reach that living threshold* will there ever be any pivot from working poverty towards thriving.

A potential problem for the continuous blue line is that there is a competing theory, which has different wage policy implications (the dotted blue line). According to diminishing marginal returns, which is based on just noticeable difference theory in psychology, any increment in wages, however small, will enable thriving – and especially so at lower levels. In other words, a dollar means much more to someone with zero dollars than the same dollar does to anyone with 100. This idea fits with, and supports, monetarist policies to grow jobs (SDG 8 – Job creation in Figure 15.1) by keeping wages low ('Grow now, share later'), as opposed to more humanistic mantras that decent wages should come first and economic growth second ('Share now, grow later').

Diplomatically, we might say that neither of these economic policy camps has so far prevailed, although the former has arguably had more time to prove itself (Cunniah, 2012).

A preliminary study of the relationship between lowered wages and capabilities has recently been conducted in New Zealand (Carr et al., 2016b). Household income was compared with measures of life and workplace capability. The shape of the functions linking these capabilities back to household income, controlling for dependents and income streams, was reportedly more akin to the continuous than the discontinuous blue line in Figure 15.2. There was reported to be a 'pivot' range between NZ30K and NZ40K dollars household income gross per annum. As income traversed this pivotal range (Yao et al., 2016), qualities of life and work life changed from predominantly negative (e.g., job and life DIS-satisfaction) to positive (e.g., job and life Satisfaction). In the lower category, a majority of people inside the 30Ks bracket reported *not* having enough to make ends meet. At household incomes above NZ$40K, there was a significant shift, with a majority of people inside that bracket reporting they *were* making ends meet. Most importantly perhaps (Yao et al., 2016), people's subjective quality of life typically tended to be more positive in the 40Ks range than in the 30Ks bracket (Box 15.3).

Only a minority of New Zealand employers in this study were officially 'Living Wage employers'. A Living Wage employer in this sense guarantees all employees are paid at, or above, the Living Wage campaign figure at the time (NZ$18.80/hour). Interestingly enough, when household income bracket itself was controlled (along with dependants etc.), there was a further statistically significant increment in subjective work and life capabilities for the employee responding to the survey (Carr et al., 2016b). In other words, there may have been a symbolic fillip to and from the quality of work and work life when working in a living wage workplace.

This study was conducted in a single economy in a relatively high-income country and must be regarded with caution. Far more extensive studies, particularly in very low-income communities inside a range of countries (including New Zealand) are lacking. Project GLOW (Global Living Organizational Wage) seeks to narrow that gap. It will build capacity to systematically probe the relationships between the *lowest* ranges of income and qualities of life, and work life, over countries (across entire supply chains, including garment factories, agricultural workers and domestic workers); over time (five decades and generations); and over multiple indicators of human capabilities (quantitative and qualitative). It will include new diplomats to carry the research into organizational policy. GLOW's goal is thus to build new interdisciplinary and inter-sectoral capacity for sustainable livelihoods, through a global–local network of

Box 15.3 Living wage pivot ranges

30Ks INCOME PERSPECTIVE

'I am unable to meet my weekly commitments and have to juggle payments around.'

40Ks income perspective

'It covers the basics and a bit of extra, but I'm not able to buy a house or go away on holidays or anything like that.'

Source: Yao et al. (2016).

practice-based service, research and teaching hubs.

One of the mantras in Figure 15.2 – grow now share later or share now grow later – will turn out to be the more strongly supported by actual data, anchored in people's everyday quality of life, in the community and at work. That information will develop academic 'theory'. Yet what about changing actual wage policies, to benefit people and combat working poverty? 'Which' new diplomacies will work?

Knowing about and how to use labour codes, as supportive and essentially prosocial accountability structures, are a useful starting point (Jayasinghe, 2016). According to the OECD Guidelines for Multinational Enterprises (OECD, 2011; 2016b), for example, the nub of eradicating working poverty is to strike a balance between decent work for the employees and economic viability for the organization (Saner and Yiu, 2016). Such tasks may be 'tricky' – read diplomatic – without an evidence-based, *business* case for living wages; without sector wide cooperation (Nieuwenkamp, 2016: 3). Research is already starting to show that there can be efficiency gains that come from people feeling that they are being treated fairly at work, including being paid fairly (Card and Krueger, 1994; Coulson et al., 2015). GLOW is developing aligned, reliable and valid measures of income and capabilities associated with them. Hence, there could be a more 'Humanitarian' emphasis on links between wages and living, between decent work and *shared* prosperity (SDG 10, Figure 15.1).

The living wage may also become a new diplomacy tool in itself. It clearly links with ideas like Fair Trade, which aids some of the 12.6 million people working in 2.6 million agricultural and other cooperatives worldwide (Grace and Associates, 2014), and cash transfers (conditional or not, as in Universal Basic Income). It is also quite clearly already capturing the global imagination (if in doubt, google it/them). Trump and Brexit are scary augurs for the growing power of appeals to emotion and mistrust of social science expertocrats, including the research they produce and publish. But emotional appeals can cut both ways. The living wage is not just an intellectual abstraction, or a research concept, or a theory or a study in a journal. It stirs positive emotions; standing up against inequality and adverse impact and for sustainable livelihoods. In the 'UK', for instance, the living wage has a potential to help address SDG 5, since the majority of workers on lower pay are often women, especially older women and single mothers (Wright, 2016).

As Wright (2016) points out, for livelihoods to become more *sustainable*, particularly for smaller to medium enterprises, employers will need to be convinced of the efficiency gains as well as benefits to society. Drawing some connection between living wages and consumer loyalty might help in that regard. Highlighting links with CSR and, more broadly, OSR (for organizational social responsibility) is a case in point. Most of the research on CSR seems to be obsessed with highlighting the gains it brings to the employer (recruitment, reputation, profits, etc.), not the community. It has been more focused on 'C-sr' than 'c-S-r' (Carr, 2013). This foregrounding of benefits for corporations gives the lie to the research's own service to power, not social responsibility. Yet, the same research field tends to identify consumer scepticism about the sincerity of CSR as being a major barrier to its credibility with the public. Citizens/customers do not believe in the sincerity of a firm's 'C-sr' unless the 'C' in question pays its own workers a living wage (Erdogan et al., 2016).

In the public (and customer's) eye, 'c-S-r' may begin at home, with living wages. This particular bottom-line may provide diplomatic leverage for 'C-sr' by realigning living wages with shared interests. In the process, the greater good of shared prosperity might better be served.

Free Movement

Throughout history, freedom of movement has been an enabler of human thriving and forcible displacement, like colonization and neo-colonialism, the reverse (Carr, 2010). Reminding us of the latter injustice was the 2016 Rio Olympiad. For the first time ever, one of the 'countries' competing was country-less, forcibly displaced: 'Team Refugee Olympic Athletes' represented the refugees in the world today. Their team reminded the world that they are the size of a major country. According to the United Nations High Commissioner for Refugees (UNHCR), 65.3 million people are currently displaced by conflict and persecution, a figure four times greater than the previous decade and up by almost six million since the previous year alone (UNHCR, 2016). Closing borders is not a solution to this Humanitarian crisis (UNHCR, 2016). Nor is putting up *city* walls: Globally there are even more people – 40.8 million of them, in fact – who are forcibly displaced *in*side their own countries (UNHCR, 2016).

Adding to these global mobility statistics, in 2013, there were at least 244 million people in the world who live abroad worldwide, most of them of working age (United Nations, 2016). Many more of them – 740 million – have moved from country to cities within their country (IOM, 2015). An unknown number have literally mobilized to escape from poverty, including by making a decent living (Jackson et al., 2005). Seeking socio-economic freedoms, these human beings are often disparagingly referred to as 'economic migrants'. Ironically nonetheless, the very same 'diaspora nations' can, and do, make a huge economic contribution to their host as well as home nations (Carnegie Endowment for International Peace, 2009). They can do so, for example, by responding to recovering labour market demand and through remittances, respectively. In a purely business sense too, inclusion of diversity can be a significant stimulus and advantage for group innovation and creativity, over the mid- to longer-term (West, 2002).

Unfortunately, there are many structural barriers to such shared prosperity through free movement, for mobile populations of all kinds. Many of them are related to a goal of many so-called 'migrants': finding a decent job, a sustainable livelihood. Standing in the way are often mid-level barriers. They include precarious employment, lower-than-living wages, prejudice and discrimination (IOM, 2010; UNDP, 2009), even against the relatively skilled (for a review, Carr, 2013).

Overcoming such barriers to free movement, and the freedoms that it can bring, will require a range of flexible and socially responsible macro-level policy measures. The options range from flexible immigration and temporary visas to job creation and inclusive labour rights (Ghosh, 2011). In terms of new diplomacies, through its International Organization of Employers, the private sector has been working in alliance with the Global Forum for Migration and Development and The Hague Process on Refugees and Migration, to explore a range of policy options to facilitate a 'migration-development nexus' (Matthews, 2014).

Mid-level, much of the societal prejudice and discrimination that migrant populations experience manifests in the workplace (Al-Ariss and Őzbilgin, 2010). Logically, therefore, workplaces are also probably where much can be done to *combat* barriers to poverty reduction, in particular through humane workplace practices. These mid-level opportunities range from (1) creating humane workspaces and places in the first place to (2) enabling decent work practices in private sector firms (UNDP, 2014).

With respect to (1), social enterprises are one type of organization that can enable free movement towards sustainable livelihood. Social entrepreneurship can reduce the barriers facing migrant populations, including refugees (UNDP, 2014: 105). A social enterprise called Hathay Bunano is designed to prevent urban poverty and precarious livelihood in the garment industry by providing sustainable livelihood to women in rural Bangladesh (http://www.pebblechild.com). It employs and trains rural women to produce handcrafted items and pays a living wage through fair trade. The enterprise has been sufficiently profitable to ensure sustainability – it operates independently of public donors (UNHCR, 2012). Another example is the social enterprise called 'Technology for Tomorrow', which is based in Uganda. It employs refugees in the production of goods that address challenges in refugee settings – such as low-cost solutions for feminine hygiene (Humanitarian Innovation Project, 2013). These two cases exemplify and instantiate the role that social dynamics can play in women's empowerment (Schein, 2012) and in meeting SDG 5 (Figure 15.1).

With respect to (2), commercial enterprises have been urged to apply a range of relatively localized measures to help overcome prejudice and discrimination, increasing access to decent work and returns on 'investment' for migrants and firms alike (UNDP, 2014). Discrimination and prejudice can happen in at least two major phases of employment, termed 'access bias' and 'discrimination bias' (Carr, 2013; Levashina et al., 2014). The former means that people cannot get their foot in the proverbial employment door or, where they can, are hired for jobs well below their skills level (Maynard et al., 2010). The latter means that people are denied equal employment opportunities over time once they have secured employment, for example in career advancement (Lim and Ward, 2003; Mace et al., 2005; Mahroum, 2000).

Designed, in theory, to help prevent such barriers are Trade Blocs and politico-economic unions. Often constituted legally through treaties of one kind or another, some of the salient examples across the global economy include the EU (European Union), Mercasur (Latin America), EAC (East African Community), SADC (South African Development Community), ASEAN (Association of East Asian Nations) and CER (Australasia). Their macro-level logic includes, in theory, the enablement of free movement, e.g.., of labour. In practice, however, there are often prejudicial barriers against people from both outside and inside these so-called 'free trade, and movement of labour' zones (Carr, 2010).

A mid-level, organizational barrier to free movement can arise where least expected. For example, within SADC and the EAC, Humanitarian | work psychology can include bias against enabling decent jobs for 'immigrants' from neighbouring countries, who common sense might suggest will receive the warmest reception, in favour of sojourners from countries *out*side of the union. Similarity can sometimes resonate inversely with host communities and organizations (Carr et al., 2001). Social and societal psychology reasons for these barriers range from realistic conflict and relative deprivation to intergroup comparison and the socio-political dynamics of social identity.

Difference can be a source of fear and exclusion, too. Prejudice and discrimination are widely found against groups whose 'difference' is perceived as threats to internal security, religious beliefs and so on (Podsiadlowski and Ward, 2010). Similarity attraction and social dominance preservation are some of the major reasons why, at an organizational level, people specifically from economically poorer countries often find themselves at the back of the hiring queue – even though they may need the opportunity for sustainable livelihood most of all (Coates and Carr, 2005).

The reader will recognize these reasons for socio-economic, socio-cultural and socio-political exclusion – Applied Social psychologists know them well. Frequently, they are implicit, for example not recognizing 'foreign' qualifications or not hiring or promoting people because they do not have enough 'Kiwi experience'. We already know, then, that they need to be 'called out'. Ethically, research should speak truth to the power of these 'defensive routines' (Argyris, 1998), which are reflections of implicit prejudice and discrimination.

Ironically, psychology remains relatively silent during what is arguably one of the greatest-ever Humanitarian crises – the need for wealthier societies, and employers, to be more inclusive towards the globally, nationally and locally displaced. Access to a decent, sustainable livelihood can be a pivotal enabler of such inclusion. Research on its own though is not enough. Practice-based advocacy, for example by structuring job descriptions and job selection processes, as well as processes for fairly appraising, evaluating and rewarding job performance, can go some of the way towards redressing the imbalance. Bias and discrimination are harder to practice when there are agreed-upon goals, good answers, good performance and so on. Activism, for example by partnering with living wage movements along global supply chains (above), may be a next, logical step towards sustainable livelihoods.

Goal Setting

Using goals, and goal setting, to promote sustainable livelihoods at a workplace level is implied in the SDGs themselves (Figure 15.1). The emphasis here is on the process – setting goals – and on doing so locally. Not at a macro level but at everyday 'meso' levels, for example in a community garden, small-scale croft or allotment, or in employment in domestic work. In theory, goal setting, when conducted under conditions of ownership, alignment and accountability, can be empowering for individual and group livelihoods (Figure 15.3).

Figure 15.3 is a distillation of Figure 15.1 through the lens of systems theory dynamics. It focuses on the systems archetype, Escalation (Senge, 1992). It integrates the dynamics of high performance cycles with psychological sense of empowerment, with one process feeding the other, in dynamic unison (UNDP, 2014). Although empirical research does not yet directly support such a virtuous duet for empowerment and goals, capability theory (Sen, 1999) and liberation psychology (Freire, 1972; Sánchez et al., 2003) do infer that empowerment begets empowerment.

Specifically from Figure 15.3, to the extent that firms decide to reward performance in

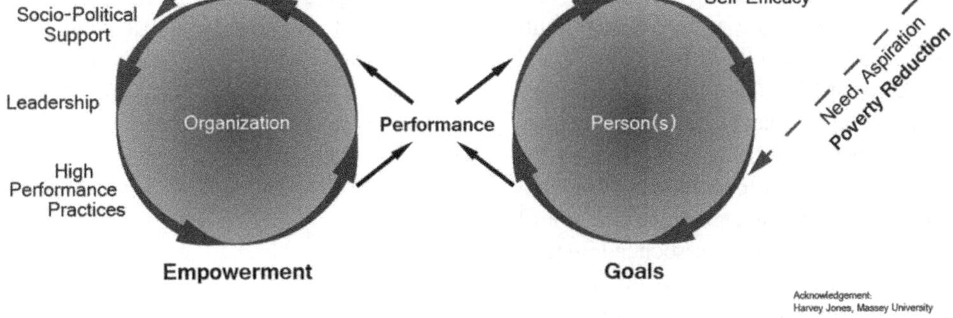

Figure 15.3 Goal setting and empowerment

Source: Extracted and adapted from UNDP (2014). Acknowledgement: Alexander Gloss.

with enhanced *work design characteristics*, support and leadership that includes rewards for high performance, it would be logical to expect that *empowerment* itself can become self-reinforcing. Figure 15.3 proposes that this can occur through a sense of self-efficacy, which can be either personal or social, that meets one's own individual or collective goals, at work and in life. Hence, Figure 15.3 predicts a positive double performance cycle in which skills, and sustainable livelihoods, are capacitated by Decent Work practices, on the one hand (ILO, 2013), and through inherent human agency on the other (Sen, 1999).

An application of such goal-setting ideas can be found in the groundbreaking anti-poverty work of Ruth Kanfer and colleagues (Meyer et al., 2016). Funded by the Bill and Melinda Gates Foundation, Meyer et al. (2016) focused on improving health service outcomes, specifically reducing child mortality rates and improving maternal health, in remote Bihar State in rural India. Bihar is one of India's most populated, poorest and gender disparate states. Project Ananya (Sanskrit for 'unlike the others') was staffed by Frontline Primary Healthcare Workers – some paid, others unpaid, some trained and others untrained – who were working largely independently from one another and with very few resources.

Aligning their approach with barriers identified by the frontline health care workers themselves, with relatively collectivist social norms and with difficult, but attainable, goals commensurate with preset public health outcomes, researchers and workers co-designed and implemented a team-based programme of goal setting. In keeping with this ethos, and on the insistence of the teams themselves, the performance was incentivized with team rewards, which in this case, consisted not of money but home goods associated locally with quality of life, such as cooking utensils.

This brief summary cannot possibly do justice to the achievements of the programme staff through this partnership with research and goal setting. Nonetheless, 'all accounts suggest that the …program is having a robust impact on the … health outcomes it was intended to improve. This conclusion is consistent with the changes…regarding the overall effectiveness and cohesion among teams' (Meyer et al., 2016: 109). Changes at the mid, termed 'meso'-organizational level, have addressed previously fragmented health services to the extremely poor. This has been achieved, according to Kanfer and colleagues, by being focused on improving team motivation and performance, which have made a real difference in Project Ananya.

In addition to outlining 'how' work psychology can be applied at the base of the (health opportunities) pyramid, Meyer et al. (2016) discussed a number of learning points from the process itself. They ranged from assessment challenges to questioning the meaning of work in different socio-cultural, socio-political and socio-economic settings. A key lesson though for applied social psychology is that IO interventions may easily be *mis*-applied to produce unsustainable efficiency gains from an already under-resourced cadre of professional workers (Kanfer and Meyer, 2015). As we saw, many frontline workers worked pro bono – and incentives were accordingly non-material (homeware items). This does *not* mean, however, that cost-effective team building should substitute for decent work conditions amongst those workers – including living wages, a decent 'wedge' (Kanfer and Meyer, 2015).

This brings us back full circle to the very beginning of our journey – that people are often seeking a way out of poverty and hardship via the dignities and freedoms enabled by having a decent, sustainable livelihood (Galinha et al., 2016).

CONCLUSIONS

Is this chapter 'diplomatic'? Perhaps some of the 'new' diplomacies will already be familiar to social and community psychologists.

Certainly, however, the context for their application is quite new. Across sectors, and interdisciplinary, it includes, for example, dealing with the SDGs, OECD Country Reporting Officers for keeping corporations accountable to the general public (OECD, 2016c) and, in general, an inter-organizational, supply chain, partnered nature of work life today. It may well include emotion and activism, or as it was once expressed in a heated forum, 'hearts and flowers AND nuts-and-bolts'. Either way, anti-poverty, pro-community work psychology is being centrally driven by human aspirations towards a decent, sustainable livelihood. This fundamental goal has meaning and gravitas, at both macro and meso levels. It can be socially facilitated, and instantiated, through meso-level structures in a diverse range of workplaces, across an array of sectors. Research on its own is never enough. We need research, practice and foundationally perhaps, teaching new diplomacies. Ultimately, standing up for sustainable livelihoods is about prospering through partnership.

ACKNOWLEDGEMENTS

Too many colleagues and teams have contributed to this chapter to name. I can only leave the References to do some of the talking.

REFERENCES

Al-Ariss, A., & Őzbilgin, M. (2010). Understanding self-initiated expatriates: Career experiences of Lebanese self-initiated expatriates in France. *Thunderbird International Business Review, 52*, 275–285.

Annan, K. (2000). *We, the peoples*. New York: United Nations.

Argyris, C. (1998). A conversation with Chris Argyris: The father of organizational learning. *Organizational Dynamics, 27*, 21–33.

Baritz, L. (1960). *The servants of power: A history of the use of social science in American industry*. Middletown, CT: Wesleyan University Press.

Bergman, M. E., & Jean, V. A. (2016). Where have all the workers gone? A critical analysis of the under-representativeness of our samples relative to the labor market in the industrial-organizational psychology literature. *Industrial and Organizational Psychology, 9*, 84–113.

Bergquist, R., & Gammon, R. (2015). *Introduction to wraparound*. Wellington: Werry Centre for Infant, Child and Adolescent Mental Health.

Berry, M., Kuriansky, J., & Butler, M. (2014). A multidisciplinary approach to solving global problems: The case of psychologists collaborating on a girls' empowerment program in Africa. In W. Reichman (Ed.), *Industrial and Organizational Psychology help the vulnerable: Serving the underserved* (pp. 73–91). Basingstoke, UK: Palgrave-Macmillan.

Berry, M., Reichman, W., MacLachlan, M., Klobas, J., Hui, H. C., & Carr, S. C. (2011). Humanitarian work psychology: The contributions of organizational psychology to poverty reduction. *Journal of Economic Psychology, 32*, 240–247.

Bischoff, K. M., Gielnik, M. M., & Frese, M. (2014). Entrepreneurship training in developing countries. In W. Reichman (Ed.), *Industrial and Organizational Psychology help the vulnerable: Serving the underserved* (pp. 112–119). Basingstoke, UK: Palgrave-Macmillan.

Blaikie, P., Cannon, T., Davis, I., & Wisner, B. (2004). *At risk: Natural hazards, people's vulnerability, and disasters*. New York: Routledge.

Blustein, D. L. (2016). Decent work: A psychological perspective. *Frontiers in Psychology, 7*, article 407.

Brief, A. P. (2000). Still servants of power. *Journal of Management Inquiry, 9*, 342–351.

Card, D., & Krueger, A. B. (1994). Minimum wages and employment: A study of the fast-food industry in New Jersey and Pennsylvania. *The American Economic Review, 84*, 772–793.

Card, D., Mas, A., Moretti, E., & Saez, E. (2012). Inequality at work: The effect of peer salaries on job satisfaction. *American Economic Review, 102*, 2981–3003.

Carnegie Endowment for International Peace. (2009). Migrants and the global financial crisis. *Policy Brief 83*, November, 1–7.

Carr, S. C. (2000). Privilege, privation, and proximity: 'Eternal triangle' for development? *Psychology and Developing Societies*, *12*, 167–176.

Carr, S. C. (2007). I/O psychology and poverty reduction. *The Industrial Psychologist*, *45*, 43–50.

Carr, S. C. (Ed.) (2010). *The psychology of global mobility*. New York: Springer.

Carr, S. C. (2013). *Anti-poverty psychology*. New York: Springer.

Carr, S. C., & MacLachlan, M. (2014). Humanitarian work psychology. *The Psychologist*, *27*(3), 160–163.

Carr, S. C., & Sloan, T. S. (Eds.) (2003). Poverty and psychology: From global perspective to local practice. New York: Springer.

Carr, S. C., Eltayeb, S., MacLachlan, M., Marai, L., McAuliffe, E., & McWha, I. (2013). Aiding international development: Some fresh perspectives from Industrial/Organizational Psychology. In J. Olsen-Buchanan, L. Koppes-Bruan, & L. F. Thompson (Eds.), *Using industrial-organizational psychology for the greater good* (pp. 490–528). New York: Routledge/SIOP New Frontiers Series.

Carr, S. C., Leggatt-Cook, C., Clarke, M., MacLachlan, M., Papola, T. S., Pais, J., Thomas, S., Normand, C., & McAuliffe, E. (2011). *What is the evidence of the impact of increasing salaries on improving the performance of public servants, including teachers, nurses and mid-level occupations, in low- and middle-income countries: Is it time to give pay a chance?* Systematic Review. London: UKAID.

Carr, S. C., MacLachlan, M., & Furnham, A. (Eds) (2012) *Humanitarian work psychology*. Basingstoke, UK: Palgrave-Macmillan.

Carr, S. C., MacLachlan, M., & McAuliffe, E. (1998). *Psychology of aid*. London: Routledge.

Carr, S. C., McAuliffe, E., & MacLachlan, M. (2014). Servants of Empowerment. In W. Reichman (Ed.), *Industrial and Organizational Psychology help the vulnerable: Serving the underserved* (pp. 143–163). Basingstoke, UK: Palgrave-Macmillan.

Carr, S. C., McWha-Hermann, I., Furnham, A., MacLachlan, M., Marai, L., Munthali, A., Pais, J., & Peniop, J. (2016). Dual salaries for development workers: Undermining fairness, sustainability, and performance. *The Association of Commonwealth University, Bulletin*, *188*, 18–19.

Carr, S. C., McWha, I., MacLachlan, M., & Furnham, A. (2010). International-Local remuneration differences across six countries: Do they undermine poverty reduction work? *International Journal of Psychology*, *45*(5), 321–340. Global Special Issue on Psychology and Poverty Reduction.

Carr, S. C., MacLachlan, M., Zimba, C., & Bowa, M. (1995). Community aid abroad: A Malawian perspective. *Journal of Social Psychology*, 135, 781–783.

Carr, S. C., Parker, J., Arrowsmith, J., & Watters, P. A. (2016a). The Living Wage: Theoretical integration and an applied research agenda. *International Labour Review*, *155*, 1–24.

Carr, S. C., Parker, J., Arrowsmith, J., Watters, P. A., & Jones, H. (2016b). Can a 'living wage' springboard human capability? An exploratory study from New Zealand. *Labour & Industry*, *26*, 34–39.

Carr, S. C., Rugimbana, O., Walkom, E., & Bolitho, F. H. (2001). Selecting expatriates in developing areas: 'Country-of-Origin' effects in Tanzania. *International Journal of Intercultural Relations*, *25*(4), 441–457.

Chambers, R. C., & Conway, G. R. (1991). Sustainable rural livelihoods: Practical concepts for the 21st century. *IDS (Institute of Development Studies), Discussion Paper 296.* Brighton, UK: University of Sussex.

Coates, K., & Carr, S. C. (2005). Skilled immigrants and selection bias. *International Journal of Intercultural Relations*, *29*, 577-99.

Collins, J. L., & Meyer, V. (2010). *Both hands tied: Welfare reforms and the race to the bottom in the low-wage labor market*. Chicago, IL: University of Chicago Press.

Coulson, A. B., Bonner, J., & the Living Wage Foundation. (2015). *Living Wage employers: Evidence of UK business cases*. Strathclyde, UK: University of Strathclyde Business School.

Cunniah, D. (2012). Foreword: Social justice and growth – the role of the minimum wage. *International Journal of Labor Research*, *4*, 5–6.

de Fazio, M. I. (2016). Kenya cracks down on foreign NGO workers citing wage disparities. *Humanosphere*, July 6.

Dodson, P. (1998). *Will the circle be broken? Cycles of survival for Indigenous Australians*. Darwin, Australia: North Australia Research Unit/Australian National University.

Easterly, W. (2006). *The white man's burden*. Harmondsworth, UK: Penguin.

Erdogan, B., Bauer, T., & Taylor, S. (2016, April). *The influence of management commitment to the ecological environment on employees*. NSF/SIOP Corporate Social Responsibility Summit, Anaheim, California, April 12–13.

Family 100 Research Project. (2014). Speaking for ourselves: The truth about what keeps people in poverty from those who live it. Auckland: Auckland City Mission.

Freire, P. (1972). *Pedagogy of the oppressed*. New York: Herder & Herder.

Galinha, I. C., Garcia-Martín, M. A., Gomes, C., & Oishi, S. (2016). Criteria for happiness among people living in extreme poverty in Maputo, Mozambique. *International Perspectives in Psychology: Research, Practice, Consultation, 5*, 67–90.

Ghosh, B. (2011). *The global economic crisis and migration: Where do we go from here?* Geneva: IOM.

Gloss, A. E., & Foster-Thompson, L. (2013). I-O psychology without borders: The emergence of Humanitarian work psychology. In J. Olson-Buchanan, L. Koppes, & L. F. Thompson (Eds.), *Using industrial-organizational psychology for the greater good: Helping those who help others* (pp. 353–393). New York: Routledge.

Godbout, J. (2014). Exploring Haiti from an organizational psychology perspective: Lessons learned along the way. In W. Reichman (Ed.), *Industrial and Organizational Psychology help the vulnerable: Serving the underserved* (pp. 131–142). Basingstoke, UK: Palgrave-Macmillan.

Grace, D., and Associates. (2014). *Measuring the size and scope of the cooperative economy*. Madison, WI: UN Secretariat, Department of Economic and Social Affairs/Division of Social Policy and Development.

Hayati, D., Yazdanpanah, M., & Karbalee, F. (2010). Coping with drought. *Psychology and Developing Societies, 22*, 361–383. Global Special Issue on Psychology and Poverty Reduction.

Hodgetts, D., Chamberlain, K., Tankel, Y., & Groot, S. (2013). Researching poverty to make a difference: The need for reciprocity and advocacy in community research. *The Australian Community Psychologist, 25*, 35–48. Global Special Issue on Psychology and Poverty Reduction.

Humanitarian Innovation Project. (2013). *Technology and Innovation in Kampala*—June 2013 (Mission Report 4). Retrieved from https://www.refugee-economies.org/assets/downloads/HIP-Mission-Report-4-FINAL.pdf

ILO (International Labour Organization). (2013). *World of Work Report, 2013: Repairing the economic and social fabric*. Geneva: ILO.

ILO (International Labour Organization). (2014). *World of Work Report, 2014: Developing with jobs*. Geneva: ILO.

ILO (International Labour Organization). (2015). *Cooperatives and the world of work No. 2 – Cooperating out of isolation: Domestic workers' cooperatives*. Geneva: ILO.

ILO (International Labour Organization). (2016). *World Employment Social Outlook: Trends 2016*. Geneva: ILO.

IOM (International Organization for Migration). (2010). *Migration and the economic crisis in the European Union: Implications for policy*. Brussels: IOM.

IOM (International Organization for Migration). (2015). *World Migration Report: Migrants and Cities: New Partnerships to manage mobility*. Geneva: IOM.

Ivory. B. (2003). Poverty and enterprise. In S. C. Carr, & T. S. Sloan (Eds.), *Poverty and psychology: From global perspective to local practice* (pp. 251–266). New York: Springer.

Jackson, D. J., Carr, S. C., Edwards, M. E., Thorn, K., Allfree, N., Hooks, J. J., & Inkson, K. (2005). Exploring the dynamics of New Zealand's talent flow. *New Zealand Journal of Psychology, 34*(2), 110–116.

Jayasinghe, M. (2016). The operational and signaling benefits of voluntary labor code adoption: Re-conceptualizing the scope of human resource management in emerging economies. *Academy of Management Journal, 59*, 658–677.

Judge, T. A., Piccolo, R. F., Podsakoff, N. P., Shaw, J. C., & Rich, B. L. (2010). The relationship between pay and job satisfaction:

A meta-analysis. *Journal of Vocational Behaviour*, *77*, 157–167.
Kandola, B. (2014). Increasing resilience among people who are homeless. In W. Reichman (Ed.), *Industrial and Organizational Psychology help the vulnerable: Serving the underserved* (pp. 186–203). Basingstoke, UK: Palgrave-Macmillan.
Kanfer, R., & Meyer, R. D. (2015). Improving motivation and performance among front-line healthcare workers in rural India. In I. McWha, D. C. Maynard, & M.O. Berry (Eds.), *Humanitarian work psychology and the global development agenda* (pp. 110-122). New York: Routledge.
Klinger, B., Khwaja, A. I., & del Carpio, C. (2013). *Enterprising psychometrics and poverty reduction: Innovations in poverty reduction*. New York: Springer.
Krantz, L. (2001). *The sustainable livelihood approach to poverty reduction*. Stockholm: Swedish International Development Cooperation Agency.
Lee, H., Pollock, G., Lubek, I., Niemi, S., O'Brien, K., Green, M., Bashir, S., Braun, E., Kros, S., Huot, V., Ma, V., Griffiths, N., Dickson, B., Pring, N., Sohkurt Huon-Ribeil, K., Lim, N., Turner, J., Winkler, C., Wong, M. L., Van Merode, T., Dy, B. C., Prem, S., & Idema, R. (2010). Creating new career pathways to reduce poverty, illiteracy and health risks, while transforming and empowering Cambodian women's lives. *Journal of Health Psychology*, *15*, 982–992. Global Special Issue on Psychology and Poverty Reduction.
Lefkowitz, J. (2016). The maturation of a profession: A work psychology for the new Millennium. In I. McWha-Hermann, D. C. Maynard, & M. O'Neill Berry (Eds.), *Humanitarian work psychology and the global development agenda: Case studies and interventions* (pp. 200–204). New York: Routledge. Global Special Issue on Psychology and Poverty Reduction.
Leung, K., Lin, X., & Lin, L. (2014). Compensation disparity between locals and expatriates in China: A multilevel analysis of the influence of norms. *Management International Review*, *54*, 107–120.
Levashina, J., Hartwell, C. J., Morgeson, F. P., & Campion, M. A. (2014). The structured employment interview: Narrative and quantitative review of the research literature. *Personnel Psychology*, *67*, 241–293.
Lim, A., & Ward, C. (2003). The effects of nationality, length of residence, and occupational demand on the perceptions of 'foreign talent' in Singapore. In K. S. Yang, K. K. Hwang, P. B. Pedersen, & I. Daibo (Eds.), *Progress in Asian Social Psychology* (Vol. 3, pp. 427–459). Westport, CT: Praeger.
Lough, B. J. (2016). *Reciprocity in international volunteer cooperation*. Oslo: Fredskorpset.
Mace, K. A., Atkins, S. G., Fletcher, B., & Carr, S. C. (2005). Immigrant job hunting, labour market experiences, and feelings about occupational life in New Zealand: An exploratory study. *New Zealand Journal of Psychology*, *34*(2), 97-109.
MacLachlan, M. (1996). From sustainable change to incremental improvement: The psychology of community rehabilitation. In S. C. Carr, & J. F. Schumaker (Eds.), *Psychology and the developing world* (pp. 26–37). Westport, CT: Praeger.
MacLachlan, M., Carr, S. C., & McAuliffe, E. (2012). *The aid triangle: Recognizing the human dynamics of dominance, justice and identity*. New York: Zed Books.
MacLachlan, M., & McAuliffe, E. (2003). Poverty and process skills. In S. C. Carr, & T. S. Sloan (Eds.), *Poverty and psychology: From global perspective to local practice* (pp. 267–84). New York: Springer.
Mahroum, S. (2000). High-skilled globetrotters: Mapping the international migration of human capital. *R & D Management*, *30*, 23–32.
Manson, J., & Carr, S. C. (2011). Improving job fit for mission workers by including expatriate and local job exerts in job specification. *Journal of Managerial Psychology*, *26*(6), 465–484. Global Special Issue on Psychology and Poverty Reduction.
Marai, L. (2002/3). Double demotivation and negative social affect among teachers in Indonesia. *South Pacific Journal of Psychology*, *14*, 1–7.
Marai, L. (2014). Dual salary and workers' well-being in Papua New Guinea. In W. Reichman (Ed.), *Industrial and Organizational Psychology help the vulnerable: Serving the underserved* (pp. 120–130). Basingstoke, UK: Palgrave-Macmillan.

Marai, L., Kewibu, V., Kinkin, E., Peniop, J. P., Salini, C., & Kofana, G. (2010). Remuneration disparities in Oceania: Papua New Guinea and Solomon Islands. *International Journal of Psychology*, *45*, 350–359. Global Special Issue on Psychology and Poverty Reduction.

Marsella, A. J. (1998). Toward a Global Community Psychology: Meeting the needs of a changing world. *American Psychologist*, *53*, 1282–1291.

Matthews, J. (2014). *GFMD 2013–2014 Engagement with the Private Sector. Global Forum on Migration and Development*. International Organization of Employers, and The Hague Process on Refugees and Migration, 12 March, ILO, Geneva.

Maynard, D., Ferdman, B., & Holmes, T. (2010). Mobility and inclusion. In S. C. Carr (Ed.), *The psychology of global mobility* (pp. 211–234). New York: Springer.

McLoughlin, D., & Carr, S. C. (1997). Equity sensitivity and double de-motivation. *Journal of Social Psychology*, *137*, 668–670.

McWha, I., & MacLachlan, M. (2011). Measuring relationships between workers in poverty-focused organizations. *Journal of Managerial Psychology*, *26*, 485–499. Global Special Issue on Psychology and Poverty Reduction.

Meyer, R., Kanfer, R., & Burrus, C. (2016). Improving motivation and performance among frontline healthcare workers in rural India. In I. McWha-Hermann, D. C. Maynard, & M. O'Neill Berry (Eds.), *Humanitarian work psychology and the global development agenda* (pp. 100–112). New York: Routledge.

Mumford, K., & Smith, P. N. (2012). *Peer salaries and employee satisfaction*. Bonn: Institute for the Study of Labour.

Narayan, D., & Petesch, P. (2002). *Voices of the Poor: From many lands* (especially Ch. 16). New York: Oxford University Press.

Narayan, D., Chambers, R., Shah, M. K., & Petesch, P. (2000). *Voices of the Poor: Crying out for change* (especially Ch. 3). New York: Oxford University Press.

Nieuwenkamp, R. (2016). Scaling up living wages in global supply chains. *OECD Insights*, May, 1–4.

OECD (Organisation for Economic Co-operation and Development). (2011). *OECD guidelines for multinational enterprises*. Paris: OECD.

OECD (Organisation for Economic Co-operation and Development). (2016a). *The high-level fora on aid effectiveness: A history*. Paris: OECD.

OECD (Organisation for Economic Co-operation and Development) (2016b). Global Forum on Responsible Business Conduct: The New edition of Guidelines for Multinational Enterprises, Paris, OECD, June 6–9.

OECD (Organisation for Economic Co-operation and Development). (2016c). *Implementing the OECD guidelines for multinational enterprises: The national contact points from 2000 to 2015*. Paris: OECD.

Osicki, M. (2016). Leadership development via Humanitarian work: IBM's efforts in Nigeria. In I. McWha-Hermann, D. C. Maynard, & M. O'Neill Berry (Eds.), *Humanitarian work psychology and the global development agenda: Case studies and interventions* (pp. 56–68). New York: Palgrave.

Oxfam. (2014). *Steps towards a living wage in global supply chains*. Oxfam Issue Briefing, December, 1–16.

Podsiadlowski, A., & Ward, C. W. (2010). Global mobility and bias in the workplace. In S. C. Carr (Ed.), *The psychology of global mobility* (pp. 279–300). New York: Springer.

Project ADDUP. (2016). Building responsible universities: Are dual salaries undermining fairness, sustainability and performance? *Bulletin of the Association of Commonwealth Universities*, in press.

Sánchez, E., Cronick, K., & Wiesenfeld, E. (2003). Poverty and community. In S. C. Carr, & T. S. Sloan (Eds.), *Poverty and psychology: From global perspective to local practice* (pp. 123–146). NewYork: Springer.

Saner, R., & Yiu, L. (2012). The new diplomacies and Humanitarian work psychology. In S. C. Carr, M. MacLachlan, & A. Furnham (Eds.), *Humanitarian work psychology* (pp. 129–165). Basingstoke, UK: Palgrave-Macmillan.

Saner, R., & Yiu, L. (2016). Looking on the bright side. *Global Focus*, *10*, 53–57.

Schein, V. (2012). Women, work and poverty: Reflections on research for social change. In S. C. Carr, M. MacLachlan, & A. Furnham (Eds.), *Humanitarian work psychology* (pp. 249–265). Basingstoke, UK: Palgrave-Macmillan.

Sen, A. (1999). *Development as freedom*. Oxford, UK: Oxford University Press.

Senge, P. (1992). *The fifth discipline*. Sydney: Random House.

Singh, S., & Tripathi, R. C. (2010). Why do the bonded fear freedom? *Psychology and Developing Societies*, *22*, 249–297. Global Special Issue on Psychology and Poverty Reduction.

Smith, L. (2015). Reforming the minimum wage: Toward a psychological perspective. *American Psychologist*, *70*, 557–65.

Standing, G. (2014). *A precariat charter: From denizens to citizens*. New York: Bloomsbury.

Tuason, M. T. (2010). The poor in the Philippines. *Psychology and Developing Societies*, *22*, 299–330. Global Special Issue on Psychology and Poverty Reduction.

UNDP (United Nations Development Programme). (2009). *Human Development Report 2009: Overcoming barriers: Human mobility and development*. New York: United Nations.

UNDP (United Nations Development Programme). (2014). *Barriers and opportunities at the base of the pyramid: The role of the private sector in inclusive development.* Istanbul International Centre for Private Sector in Development (IICPSD): UNDP.

UNHCR (United Nations High Commissioner for Refugees). (2012). *Livelihood programs: UNHCR Operational Guidelines*. Geneva: UNHCR.

UNHCR (United Nations High Commissioner for Refugees). (2016). *Global forced displacement hits record high*. Geneva: UNHCR.

United Nations. (2014). *Revision of world urbanization prospects*. New York: United Nations.

United Nations. (2016). *Transforming our world: the 2030 Agenda for sustainable development.* Retrieved from https://sustainabledevelopment.un.org/post2015/transformingourworld

Vallières, F., & McAuliffe, E. (2016). Reaching MDGs 4 and 5: the application of organisational psychology to maternal and child health programme sustainability in Sierra Leone. In I. McWha-Hermann, D. C. Maynard, & M. O'Neill Berry (Eds.), *Humanitarian work psychology and the global development agenda: Case studies and interventions* (pp. 15–27). New York: Routledge.

Vergara, J., & Gardner, D. H. (2011). Stressors and psychological wellbeing in local Humanitarian workers in Colombia. *Journal of Managerial Psychology*, *26*, 500–507. Global Special Issue on Psychology and Poverty Reduction.

Viale, T. (2014). Challenges of the ultimate messengers. In W. Reichman (Ed.), *Industrial and Organizational Psychology help the vulnerable: Serving the underserved* (pp. 12–32). Basingstoke, UK: Palgrave-Macmillan.

Vandaveer, V. V., & Rizzuto, T. E. (2014). In the wake of disaster: Facilitating business recovery. In W. Reichman (Ed.), *Industrial and Organizational Psychology help the vulnerable: Serving the underserved* (pp. 204–226). Basingstoke, UK: Palgrave-Macmillan.

West, M. A. (2002). Sparkling fountains or stagnant ponds: An integrative model of creativity and innovation implementation in work groups. *Applied Psychology*, *51*, 355–387.

World Bank. (2012). *Work Development Report: 2013: Jobs*. Washington, DC: World Bank.

World Bank. (2016). *Global Monitoring Report*. New York: World Bank.

Wright, A. (2016). Comments on the introduction of the National Living Wage. *HR Review*, March, 1–2. http://www.hrreview.co.uk/analysis/analysis-reward/comments-introduction-national-living-wage/61809, accessed August 1, 2018.

Yao, C., Parker, J., Arrowsmith, J., Carr, S. C., & Jones, H. (2016, June/July). *Is there a 'tipping range' for a living wage? Qualitative evidence on the link between pay and perceived work-life quality*. British Universities Industrial Relations Association Conference, Leeds, June 29–July 1.

PART VI

Ageing

16

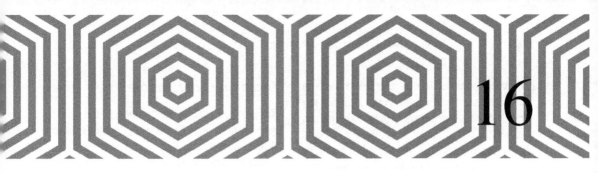

Ageing in Context: Ageism in Action

Donatienne Desmette, Hélène Henry and Stefan Agrigoroaei

Populations are ageing worldwide at a rate unprecedented in human history. As Park et al. (2015: 2) emphasized, '*population aging is set to dominate the social context for the twenty-first century with major social, political, cultural and economic implications*'. In many societies, older people are perceived as being a threat to the society's future well-being because of their overconsumption of resources, through pensions and use of health systems (Cronshauw, 2012). Such sociostructural changes in intergenerational relations have the potential to increase discrimination toward older people (North and Fiske, 2012). In fact, there is evidence that age discrimination has increased rather than decreased in recent years in the European Union (EU) (Gutman and Dunleavy, 2015). Demographic changes pose significant challenges for society and researchers. Challenges for people and institutions are to ensure respect for, and quality of life of, older people in those societies where individuals can expect to live longer lives. Issues for researchers are to understand the roots of age discrimination to highlight efficient interventions in order to acknowledge negative views of ageing and to prevent their potential deleterious effects.

A first aim of this chapter is to provide a general overview of social psychological theories that are relevant to understanding attitudes toward older adults. These attitudes are examined through the lens of ageism, which refers to a process of systematic stereotyping and discrimination of people because they are old or perceived as old (Butler, 1987; Bytheway, 2005). As a major framework of studies on social perceptions of age, ageism is a key concept for researchers and practitioners interested in ageing (Nelson, 2005). The first section of the chapter defines ageism and presents theoretical frameworks that contribute to explaining why ageism still exists.

The second section examines causes and consequences of ageism and under what conditions these consequences are more prominent. These issues are addressed in two domains: health and work. Indeed, the surge in the ageing population worldwide has resulted in some newer and more profound challenges in terms of older adults' employment as well as the healthcare of older people (Levy and MacDonald, 2016; North and Fiske, 2012). First, we examine research on how ageism interferes with healthy ageing. We show the deleterious effects of institutionalized age-based attitudes and behaviors on the quality of healthcare services received by older adults. Second, we demonstrate that ageism also exists in the workplace. For example, research has extensively found that workers may become subjected to prejudiced opinions of others as soon as they are perceived as 'old'. In the two domains (i.e., health and work), particular attention is devoted to the role of context in ageism. We conclude this section by examining several methodological issues that contribute to explaining some current limitations in research on ageism.

Finally, the third section examines which intervention programs can reduce ageism and/or its effects. Health and employment contexts pose substantial and timely public policy implications (Levy and MacDonald, 2016). However, age discrimination is a complex issue that cannot just be proscribed with law (Taylor, 2001) and monitoring multi-level intervention programs may be required. In the last section of the chapter, we present paths for psychosocial-based interventions at the individual, organizational, and societal levels.

THE ROOTS OF AGEISM

What is ageism? Does it affect younger and older people similarly? In which way is it different from sexism and racism? Which theories contribute to explain age-related discrimination? This section offers some answers to these questions.

Focus on Older People

Research has consistently shown that stereotype content about various age groups differs (Finkelstein et al., 2015; Hummert, 1990). For example, with the same list of traits, Hummert (1990) found different clusters of perceptions when applied to older people (e.g., perfect grandparent, severely impaired) or to young people (e.g., mature young professional, member of underclass). Although studies on young individuals are still relatively scarce (Finkelstein et al., 2015; Greenberg et al., 2002), young adults as well as older adults have been shown to be discriminated against because of their age, in the workplace and the society at large (Finkelstein et al., 2013; Gartska et al., 2005; Snape and Redman, 2003). However, the consequences of age discrimination are more pervasive for older than for younger adults (Nelson, 2005). For example, older workers are more willing than younger workers to quit their job when they perceive that they experience discrimination because of their age (von Hippel et al., 2013), even when perceptions of discrimination are similar between the older and the younger workers (Snape and Redman, 2003). Moreover, while everyday discrimination demonstrated a strong relationship with job satisfaction for both younger (20–34-year-old) and older (55–71-year-old) workers, general psychological well-being was impacted in the older workers but not in the younger workers (Taylor et al., 2013). Therefore, despite the fact that age discrimination not only affects older but also younger individuals, researchers have most often focused predominantly on ageism against older individuals as the 'most troubling and consequential form of ageism' (Greenberg et al., 2002: 27).

The Irrational and Covert Age Differentiation

Researchers have suggested some unique aspects of ageism compared to other forms of discrimination (Greenberg et al., 2002; Nelson, 2016). In particular, ageism is considered irrational because everyone may expect to become older and therefore a member of the prejudiced age group (Gartska et al., 2005; Packer and Chasteen, 2006). Moreover, people are often unaware of ageism because of institutionalization of age segregation (Hagestad and Uhlenberg, 2005). Indeed, age segregation exists in many social institutions because, in contrast to sex or race, chronological age is included as an eligibility criterion for participation, such as access to pension funds or to work accommodations (Baruch et al., 2014; Hagestad and Uhlenberg, 2005). This institutionalization of age segregation (Hagestad and Uhlenberg, 2005) contributes to making ageism more difficult to detect than racism and sexism and to legitimating age discrimination as a fair treatment (Nelson, 2016; Palmore, 1999).

Despite the use of common age categories of 'older adults' and 'older workers', ageing is a multidimensional, multidirectional process characterized by well-documented individual differences (Baltes et al., 1999). In other words, people from the same age group often differ in terms of their *functional age* (Sterns and Miklos, 1995). Mental and physical health, cognitive abilities, motivation, and performance depend on individual factors, such as personal trajectories and contextual influences (Hess, 2005; Kanfer and Ackerman, 2004). In particular, there are *social contexts* that can lead to people feeling or being perceived as older than they actually are. Indeed, age is a social construct and specific expectations are associated with certain age categories (Giles and Reid, 2005; Sterns and Miklos, 1995). There are positive and negative stereotypes (e.g., Hummert, 1990) but, in general, negative expectations are more widespread than the positive ones regarding the aged (Bal et al., 2011; Cuddy et al., 2005; Kite et al., 2005; McCarthy and Heraty, 2017) and they increase with the target's age (Hummert, 1990).

Theoretical Insights

Studies that investigate ageism in social psychology often refer to theories such as the stereotype content model (Fiske et al., 2002) that predicts age prejudice through an ambivalent stereotype (e.g., Cuddy et al., 2005), social identity theory that explains age prejudice through self-enhancement (e.g., Chasteen, 2005), and more recently the intergenerational perspective that analyses ageism as the product of the dynamic between generations in a society (e.g., North and Fiske, 2012).

Ambivalent stereotype: The compassionate ageism

Beyond the description of traits related to age groups, the tripartite view of ageism (Finkelstein and Farrell, 2007) distinguishes between stereotypes, affects, and behaviors. This approach investigates how age-related stereotypes (i.e., generalized beliefs about the qualities and characteristics of a particular age group, Finkelstein et al., 2015) are related to the way people feel (i.e., affect component) and consequently act (i.e., the behavioral component) with the outgroup members (Finkelstein, 2015). The stereotype content model (Fiske et al., 2002) proposes that stereotypes of older people may be characterized along two independent axes: warmth and competence. Cuddy and colleagues (Cuddy and Fiske, 2002; Cuddy et al., 2005) found that, as a group, older adults are rated high in warmth and low in competence (i.e., elderly people are viewed as possessing far fewer competence traits than warmth traits). This pattern of stereotype determines a compassionate ageism toward older people, with pity as the main emotion endorsed toward this group. These authors noticed that older individuals may also elicit some more positive emotions (e.g., admiration) because they are viewed as a cooperative (i.e., warm) group. However, because perceptions of low-status and frailty are often dominant, feelings of pity toward older adults are more pervasive.

Noticeably, negative stereotypes toward older people have been shown to transcend cultural boundaries (Cuddy et al., 2005). Although prevailing beliefs on age suggest that Eastern cultures hold older adults in higher esteem than Western cultures do due to stronger collectivist norms and filial piety (e.g., Cheng and Chan, 2006), whether cultural traditions translate into actual differences in attitudes is less clear (North and Fiske, 2015). In fact, studies have shown that benevolent ageism seems to be prevalent in Western as well as in Eastern societies. Analyzing perceptions of older adults in 26 cultures, Löckenhoff et al. (2009) found that there was a widespread cross-cultural consensus about the basic patterns of ageing (e.g., perceived age-related declines in physical attractiveness and increases in wisdom and received respect). A recent meta-analysis revealed that attitudes toward ageing and the aged were even more negative in the East than in the West (North and Fiske, 2015). In fact, analyses of moderators showed that ageism was strongest in regions and countries with recent rises in population ageing. In other words, beyond cross-cultural aspects, the structure of populations should be taken into account because it may have a detrimental effect on intergenerational relations (Löckenhoff et al., 2009; North and Fiske, 2015).

Finally, older individuals may themselves contribute to age-inequalities through self-fulfilling prophecies, such as stereotype threat (Steele and Aronson, 1995), whereby negative meta-stereotypes (a person's beliefs regarding the stereotype that members of another group hold about one's own group; Finkelstein et al., 2015) are explicitly made salient (Abrams et al., 2006) or implicitly activated (Hess et al., 2003; Levy, 1996). This point will be examined more closely in the section devoted to ageism in the health domain.

Self-enhancement in response to a threat to social identity

People define themselves and others in terms of age categories such as 'younger' (e.g., 18–30 years old, Gartska et al., 2005), 'middle-aged' (e.g., 35–55 years), and 'older' (75 years and over) adults. Age group identification is at the heart of a growing research interest, in particular in the work domain (Levy and MacDonald, 2016). Most research that addresses age categorization has employed social identity theory (Tajfel and Turner, 1986). Social identity theory postulates that individuals seek self-enhancement in maintaining that their own group is superior to others. However, age is different from gender and race: the boundaries between age groups are permeable. In the normal course of life, younger individuals will become members of an older age group and older people can remember having been younger (Chasteen, 2005; Gartska et al., 2005). Similar to studies using terror management theory (Martens et al., 2005; Solomon et al., 1991), which show that anxiety related to ageing and thoughts about one's own mortality increase prejudice toward older adults, social identity theory suggests that older adults may elicit negative attitudes because they represent a future social membership that is threatening for younger people. According to this perspective, negative attitudes toward older people can be seen as a strategy of younger people to maintain a positive social identity of their own age group by distancing themselves from the lower status of older people (Desmette et al., 2015; Packer and Chasteen, 2006). However, experimentally increasing participants' status was shown not to reduce negative bias (e.g., perceived dissimilarity between age groups, social distance) toward older people (Chasteen, 2005). In other words, beyond the intergroup dimension, ageing per se seems to be a specific phenomenon in eliciting age-related prejudice. Several studies have also examined how older adults' own age-related social identity contributes to shape their behavior (Abrams et al., 2006; Chasteen, 2005; Desmette and Gaillard, 2008; Gartska et al., 2005). These studies will be discussed in more detail in the section focused on ageism in the work domain.

The intergenerational perspective

Western modern societies have made old age an 'isolated island' and this segregation contributes to fostering ageism (Hagestad and Uhlenberg, 2005). Based on contact theory (Allport, 1954; Pettigrew, 1998), studies show ageism reduction when younger individuals are in contact with older people (Pettigrew and Tropp, 2006). The positive effects of intergenerational contact may be explained by the reduction of anxiety that young people feel when they interact with older people (Harwood et al., 2005). Similarly, intergenerational contact was shown to buffer deleterious effects of stereotype threat on older people's cognitive performance through reduction of their anxiety toward younger people (Abrams et al., 2006).

The recent succession, identity, and consumption model (North and Fiske, 2012; 2013) develops a challenging conceptualization of the intergenerational approach to ageism. This model proposes that ageism depends on sociostructural characteristics of relations between generations. Ageism happens when younger people perceive that older people violate prescriptive age stereotypes in three domains: they fail to pass down enviable resources (succession), they overconsume shared resources (consumption), and/or they fail to act their age (identity). In other words, this model postulates the conditions by which tensions between younger and older age groups can occur and when they can be resolved in society at large (North and Fiske, 2012; 2013) and in the workplace (North and Fiske, 2015). This approach is especially promising in a changing environment where more generations will co-exist and where competition for resources between age groups is likely to grow.

AGEISM: WHAT IS THE PICTURE?

Despite the fact that studies have also investigated ageism in domains such as communication and media, the vast majority of studies has focused on healthcare and employment (e.g., Lagacé, 2015; Nelson, 2002). Indeed, on the one hand, these fields have repeatedly shown empirical evidence of ageism. On the other hand, changes in demography may reinforce the psychosocial conditions of ageism in domains where older adults are likely to be seen as threatening for collective resources. This chapter will present relevant findings – while not exhaustive – on ageism in the health and work domains.

In the domain of health, empirical evidence is generally obtained with retired individuals (mainly 65+ years old). In the work domain, the focus is on working adults generally labeled as 'older workers'. In fact, there remains no established chronological age at which to define an 'older worker': researchers variously refer to the age from 40 or 45 years old, which often corresponds to employment policies, to 65 years old, which largely coincides with statutory pension provision (McCarthy et al., 2014). However, studies frequently use age 50 as the threshold.

Ageism and Health

Individual differences in health and health trajectories are traditionally described in terms of chronological age. However, a robust message that emerges from multiple studies is that age-related differences in health, broadly defined, are better understood by taking into account the subjective constructions or subjective experiences of age and ageing. For instance, other indicators, such as subjective age (e.g., how old one feels), are more reliably associated with health and mortality rates. Also, perceived age (i.e., how old a person looks to others), generally used by clinicians as a global indicator of physical health, represents a valid biomarker of ageing that predicts survival among older adults (Christensen et al., 2009). Ageing occurs within sociocultural contexts, and in this section, we argue that, because apparent age is a social cue people use to adjust their behaviors and attitudes, how old a person is perceived by others can interfere with his/her general level of health. Besides age-differentiated behaviors that imply appropriate responses oriented toward older adults (Hagestad and Uhlenberg, 2005), and the sporadic situations of discrimination in favor of older adults (Palmore, 1999), there is consistent evidence that ageism is pervasive at the institutional level in healthcare settings. Therefore, our first goal is to illustrate the ageist attitudes and practices observed among healthcare professionals, by providing a non-exhaustive list of studies and theoretical explanations. At the individual level, health in older adults can also be conceptualized as a result of their own perceptions and beliefs (meta-stereotypes). Thus, the second goal of this section is to present empirical evidence and theoretical models focused on the health consequences of stereotype threat, internalized age stereotypes (stereotype embodiment), and perceived age discrimination.

Ageism in healthcare

Ageism in medical settings is well documented. General negative attitudes toward older patients are prevalent among health professionals (Grant, 1996) and there is evidence that they can be transmitted from faculty to students (Fajemilehin, 2004; Happell and Brooker, 2001; McLafferty and Morrison, 2004). In line with the tripartite model, these negative attitudes affect the quality of care received by older patients. The main quantifiable, behavioral indicators of the intentional or subconscious discrimination against older patients examined in the literature are: the likelihood of under- or overdiagnosing, the quality of the treatment, and the likelihood of preventive care and inclusion in clinical trials. First, with respect to the diagnosis process, on average, older patients are asked fewer open-ended questions and physicians request fewer details about their conditions. Moreover, in the presence of the same symptoms and background information, case histories of older individuals are more likely to be described as pathological and to be associated with a poorer prognosis (Gatz and Pearson, 1988). Second, older patients are also more likely to receive inappropriate medical treatment. An illustrative, national study was carried out in the UK by Peake et al. (2003) with a focus on lung cancer patients from three age groups: under 65 years, 65–74 years, and 75 years and older. Despite the evidence that older patients respond to chemotherapy and surgery as well as younger adults with the same functional status, 'older patients are less likely to receive active treatment of any sort' (Peake et al., 2003: 174). Importantly, while ageism among health professionals remains one of the main explanations, it is also possible that older adults tend to decline treatment when offered (Peake et al., 2003). Third, compared to younger counterparts, older patients are less likely to be involved in preventive care practices. For example, according to Arber et al. (2004), when working with older individuals (i.e., a 75-year-old) compared to younger individuals (i.e., a 55-year-old), general practitioners are less likely to ask and give advice about their smoking and alcohol consumption habits. Using hypothetical descriptions of patients with angina, Harries et al. (2007) have shown that those over 65 years were less likely, for example, to be given a cholesterol test, exercise tolerance testing, angiography, or to be referred to a cardiologist. In addition, older adults are significantly underrepresented in clinical research trials.

Other examples of observable manifestations of ageism were identified by analyzing the patterns of interaction between physicians and older patients. Healthcare professionals do not only tend to reinforce dependent behaviors in older adults but they also display paternalistic behaviors, impatience, while speaking loudly, more slowly, with exaggerated pronunciation and simple sentence structure (i.e., overaccommodation and baby talk; Nelson, 2005).

While misconceptions, ignorance, and value judgments can be the main ingredients of such ageist behaviors, healthcare professionals can also base their decisions on empirically verified information. For instance, while deciding the appropriateness of a medical procedure for a younger or older patient, they can simply use the information available in mortality tables and compare the possible outcomes. Along the same lines, Tsuchiya et al. (2003) made the distinction between three categories of ageism in the healthcare system. The first type of ageism is health maximization ageism (younger adults would be given priority because they would have a larger number of quality-adjusted life years). The other two types are productivity ageism (giving priority to younger adults because they are perceived as being socially and economically more productive; e.g., 'the 35-year old could give a lot to society if given an extra five years'), and fair innings ageism (one's individual expected remaining healthy life years are compared with an average and those who fall below average are preferred). Fair innings ageism is equivalent to upweighting health gains in those who have accumulated less lifetime health (e.g., 'the five-year-old has lived less life and deserves a chance').

Generally, patterns of discriminatory behaviors and negative attitudes have their origins in a set of biased assumptions (negative stereotypes) shared by healthcare professionals. For example, advanced age is systematically and ineluctably associated with disease, functional limitations, cognitive decline, and comprehension problems. Adults of all ages perceive older people as having a lower potential to live longer and healthy lives (Tsuchiya et al., 2003). Moreover, older adults are perceived as being less likely to benefit from certain treatments. This is in line with some studies showing that experience with older adults and the amount and the quality of knowledge are critical determinants of attitudes toward ageing. Generally, the more (accurate) knowledge and experience healthcare providers have, the more positive their attitudes (e.g., Stewart et al., 2005).

The influence of context

Several experimental studies have examined the role of context and shown that the simple exposure of older participants to negative age stereotypes can have physical health consequences. For instance, Levy et al. (2008) documented increased cardiovascular response to stress (e.g., increased blood pressure) among older adults subliminally exposed to negative age stereotypes. This paradigm involving implicit priming was also used to examine whether the activation of negative age stereotypes translates into poorer cognitive performance. Indeed, Hess et al. (2004) have shown that older adults achieved lower recall memory scores when negative stereotypes were implicitly primed, compared to situations that activated positive stereotypes. These results show that, while performing cognitive tests, older adults are vulnerable to age-based stereotype threat (see Lamont et al., 2015, for a meta-analysis). Stereotype threat, as defined by Steele and Aronson (1995: 797) refers to 'being at risk of confirming, as self-characteristic, a negative stereotype about one's group'. The majority of the stereotype threat experimental studies involve an explicit activation of stereotypes. The two main categories of cues used in experimental studies are the presentation of negative expectations about ageing (e.g., 'past research has shown memory decline with age') and the activation of negative age stereotypes by framing the task as stereotype-relevant (e.g., 'this task measures your memory abilities'). As expected, the pattern of results usually obtained (e.g., Desrichard and Köpetz, 2005; Hess et al., 2003; 2004; Rahhal et al., 2001) is characterized by lower cognitive scores among older adults.

Recently, Sindi et al. (2013) experimentally created contexts of cognitive evaluation that were considered unfavorable for older adults (and consequently favorable for younger adults). Specifically, they manipulated the location of testing, the age of the experimenter, time of testing, the type of task, and importantly, in line with the stereotype threat literature, the task instructions. A setting was considered unfavorable for older adults when the testing location was not known by older adults, the session was scheduled in the afternoon, the testing was conducted by a younger research assistant, the stimuli were more familiar for younger adults, and the instructions emphasized the memory component of the task. The results have shown that older adults tested in an unfavorable environment displayed increased levels of cortisol and a steeper forgetting rate in memory performance. To summarize, contextual features can account for the poorer cognitive and physical outcomes observed, on average, among older adults and can be targeted by intervention programs.

Older patients as victims and perpetrators: The role of meta-stereotypes

In the general framework of age-stereotypes, attitudes, and discriminatory behaviors, the efforts to understand individual differences in health among older adults also include the analysis of their own perceptions and beliefs. Ageist beliefs can be internalized by older adults and become their own personal beliefs about ageing. Negative stereotypical beliefs applied to the self are embodied, often unconsciously, in one's behavior and health (Allen, 2016; Levy, 2009). Multiple studies have shown that internalized negative assumptions about ageing translate into poorer outcomes, such as health problems (e.g., worse hearing, higher functional limitations), lower sense of control over health, and even higher risk of mortality (e.g., Levy, 2003; Levy et al., 2002; 2006; Wurm et al., 2007). In contrast, older adults with more positive views of ageing have better physical health and higher survival rates, over and above the role of traditional predictors such as sex and socioeconomic status (Levy et al., 2002).

The role of individual variables

At the individual level, the health consequences of ageism can also be examined through the lens of perceived age discrimination. Even though not all discriminatory behaviors are perceived as such by older adults, perceived unequal, unfair treatment based on age is highly prevalent (Ayalon, 2014). The general, robust message that emerges from the literature is that day-to-day perceived age discrimination could represent a source of chronic stress, with evident negative consequences on mental and physical health and well-being (e.g., Luo et al., 2012; Yuan, 2007). Along the same lines, perceived age discrimination can also impact health behaviors, personal beliefs (e.g., sense of control), and social interactions (e.g., Yuan, 2007). For example, higher levels of perceived age discrimination translate into a lower likelihood of visiting health professionals and into a reduced level of social engagement (Rippon et al., 2014). Interestingly, Stephan et al. (2015) showed that perceived age discrimination also contributes to older subjective age. Those exposed to everyday age-related discriminatory experiences tend to feel older than their actual age.

Several studies have shown that some individuals are more susceptible than others to report age discrimination. A recent study (Voss et al., 2016) showed an interesting positive association between perceived discrimination and one's own views on ageing. In other words, those who report higher levels of discrimination are those with more negative views on ageing. In other studies (e.g., Rippon et al., 2014), perceived age discrimination was more common in male, more educated, less wealthy, and retired participants, although the results are not always consistent. For instance, Yuan (2007) found that employed persons tend to report more age discrimination. Nevertheless, a robust association is observed in the literature between age and perceived age discrimination, with older adults reporting higher levels of discrimination. Using data from a national longitudinal survey of women in the United States (Gee et al., 2007), an analysis of self-reported age discrimination across the adult life course revealed a curvilinear association, with higher levels in the 20s, a drop in the

30s, followed by a gradual rise and a peak in the 50s. Taken together, these results can help identify the most vulnerable categories of adults, in terms of perceived age discrimination, that should be targeted by prevention and intervention programs.

Ageism and Work

Fostered by (past) employment policies (e.g., mandatory retirement or early retirement plans) that reinforce age frontiers and stereotypes, ageism remains one of the least acknowledged prejudices in the workplace (Bayl-Smith and Griffin, 2014; McCarthy and Heraty, 2017). However, demographic changes involve facing new challenges to prevent ageism and manage intergenerational relationships in a workforce with ever increasing age diversity (North and Fiske, 2015). This section gives an overview of research on ageism applied to the workplace and presents some theoretical implications. We first present an overview of ageism in the workplace and then investigate the role of the context. Finally, we introduce recent research on the impact of ageism on older workers.

Ageism in the workplace

Research has shown that older workers are hired less often than younger workers, more often dismissed from jobs, and denied promotions, training or other career development opportunities (see the reviews of Finkelstein and Farrell, 2007; Posthuma and Campion, 2009; Truxillo et al., 2017). In general, managers prefer younger workers to older workers, even when both are equally qualified. For example, a field study using fictitious job applications with similar qualifications showed that older applicants (46 years old) received significantly fewer invitations for interviews than younger ones (31 years old; Ahmed et al., 2012). In three laboratory studies, Abrams et al. (2016) demonstrated that younger targets (around 20 years old) were preferentially recommended for hiring over older ones (about 60 years old), even when the rational argument of the 'return on investment' (i.e., which would be lower for the older candidate) was made irrelevant by making the time perspective similar (e.g., both candidates applied for a short-term position). Unfair differential treatment has also been observed in situations of performance assessment. In a laboratory study, Rupp et al. (2006) asked participants to make recommendations for a younger and an older worker after professional failure in a high level position. They found that the failure in performance led to more punitive recommendations for the older target (e.g., demotion) than for the younger one (training), due to internal attributions for the older workers (i.e., expectations of future failure for the older employee because of age-related incompetence).

The influence of context

Contextual variables that may moderate the extent of ageism are micro-level aspects of the research situation that make age more or less salient, such as the research design and the amount and type of information as well as more meso-level aspects of the situation like organizational age and sociostructural relations between generations.

First, research designs that activate direct comparison between younger and older targets have been shown to increase the likelihood of ageism. Typically, researchers manipulate age salience by asking participants to have absolute decisions in between-subject designs (e.g., by asking participants if they would hire an older worker) versus comparative decisions in within-subject design (e.g., by asking participants whether to hire an older or a younger candidate among two). Within-subject designs result, in general, in larger differences between younger and older workers than between-subject research designs (Bal et al., 2011; Kite et al., 2005). Other studies make the age more or less salient in varying the age diversity in the applicant pool (i.e., Cleveland and Hollmann,

1990). Despite the relatively limited evidence, the more the older workers represent a smaller portion in an age diverse context (i.e., the more they are in solo status, Kanter, 1977), the more likely the age stereotype will be activated (e.g., Kunze et al., 2013). Congruently with social identity (Tajfel and Turner, 1986) and self-categorization (Turner, 1999) theories, when age is made salient in the social context (i.e., in within-subject designs or when older people are few in a younger group), young evaluators (e.g., managers) may self-categorize as a member of the young workers group and they will then tend to focus on age and to ignore other social and individual characteristics.

Second, the amount and type of information have been shown to moderate the likelihood of ageism. In general, when more information about individuals or the job is introduced, the perceivers may individuate the particular older person they are evaluating (Finkelstein and Farrell, 2007; Gordon and Arvey, 2004). Individuation processes would encourage evaluators to focus on the abilities of individuals rather than their membership in the older workers' group (Perry and Finkelstein, 1999). The typical method in these studies is to compare attitudes (e.g., a hiring decision) about an older worker versus a younger worker under conditions where there is individuating information provided (e.g., the personal or work history) and where there is not. The type of information has also been shown to moderate age bias such that when participants are informed about aspects related to an individual's job performance (e.g., skills, abilities) rather than to some category (e.g., job title), less age bias is found (Gordon and Arvey, 2004).

Finally, managers hold stereotypes on organizational age (e.g., industry age norms, retirement age norms) that strongly contribute to defining a worker as an older worker (Lawrence, 1988; McCarthy et al., 2014). According to social role theory (Eagly, 1987), viewing people in particular social roles contributes to shaping beliefs about groups: because people observe the role-driven behavior, they come to associate the characteristics of these roles with the individuals who occupy them. Because an important social role is employment, which is occupied predominantly by younger people while older adults are (early) retirees, people draw the conclusion that younger adults are more likely to have agentic traits (e.g., self-confidence, energy) than older adults (Kite et al., 2005; Levy and MacDonald, 2016). Congruently, many jobs have a perceived 'correct age': they should be held by employees of a certain age group (Cleveland and Shore, 1992; Lawrence, 1988; McCarthy et al., 2014). In hiring decisions, for example, managers engage in a matching process, whereby applicant- and job-related cues are matched to determine the extent to which the applicant is suitable for the job in question. When the job-related cues provide a mismatch between the job age norms and the applicant age, age bias is more likely to appear. Mismatch effect has been shown to be stronger for older workers (Perry and Finkelstein, 1999). As an example, Diekman and Hirnisey (2007) presented to young participants a younger candidate versus an older candidate who applied either to a younger-typed context (i.e., a growing company) or to an older-typed context (i.e., a traditional company). They found that the older applicant was less often proposed for hiring than the younger candidate in the younger-typed (i.e., mismatching) context while no difference emerged in the older-typed (i.e., matching) context. On the positive side, older workers may be more positively evaluated than younger workers when they hold envied managerial positions because of the fit between the stereotype of experience related to age and the high status function (Chattopadhyay and Marsh, 1999).

Sociostructural aspects of relations between generations

Analyzing ageism toward older workers according to the succession, consumption, and identity model (North and Fiske, 2012; 2013),

North and Fiske (2016) underline the role of sociostructural aspects of relations between age groups. In experimental studies, they showed that perceptions of resource scarcity for their own group increased the likelihood that young participants (i.e., students and younger workers) were prejudiced toward an older worker who was presented as violating prescriptive stereotypes such as being reluctant to retire. Conversely, Henry et al. (2015) showed that, when all age groups are provided with human resource (HR) practices that fulfill their lifespan needs (i.e., developmental needs for younger and generativity needs for older workers), intergenerational contact was improved and, consequently, age bias was reduced.

As a whole, these findings demonstrate that ageism results from the interplay between age stereotypes and the context characteristics that are likely to make them more, or less, threatening for those who are viewed as 'older workers'. Moreover, older workers themselves may contribute to ageism and its consequences.

Older workers: Victims and perpetrators

In many Western countries, older workers retire earlier than the official pension age of the country or the minimum age to access the full-pension benefits (e.g., Desmette and Vendramin, 2014). Employers' stereotypes that people over a certain age are no longer qualified (or motivated) to work (e.g., McCann and Giles, 2002) may contribute to explain why older workers want to withdraw from work. However, (early) retirement may also be conceived as a strategy to cope with a social identity (Tajfel and Turner, 1986) perceived as devalued, through individual mobility or psychological disengagement from the threatening domain. In this section, we examine older workers' reactions to ageism and how they may inadvertently contribute to perpetuate age stereotypes.

Several studies confirmed that retirement decisions/intentions are more common in older workers who perceive that they are discriminated against because of their age (Snape and Redman, 2003; von Hippel et al., 2013) or when the context makes salient the negative stereotypes rather than positive stereotypes of their age group (Gaillard and Desmette, 2010). In a set of studies, Lagacé and colleagues (Lagacé et al., 2008; Laplante et al., 2010) showed that early retirement was the final step of a de-identification process from the work domain when they perceived HR discriminatory practices and denigrating language. Other studies highlighted that the more the older workers identify themselves as an older worker, the more they were willing to retire early (Desmette and Gaillard, 2008; Zaniboni et al., 2010) and to compete with younger workers (Desmette and Gaillard, 2008). In fact, age-related social identity might be more important than perceived discrimination in predicting work-related attitudes in older workers (Levy and MacDonald, 2016).

Social identity also may be a positive component of psychosocial age and have favorable consequences for older workers' attitudes in the workplace. For example, feeling good about being an older worker (i.e., affective identification) appears to have positive effects: the higher the affective identification with the older workers' group, the lower the psychological disengagement from work (Desmette and Gaillard, 2008). Furthermore, Bayl-Smith and Griffin (2014) showed that self-categorization as a late-career worker (i.e., cognitive identification) was consecutive to age discrimination in the organization, with negative consequences on participants' job engagement (i.e., feeling good in the job). However, this relationship was nonsignificant for individuals who had a high affective identification as a 'late-career worker'. In other words, affective identification with the group of older workers buffered the negative effects of discrimination.

To sum up, studies show that older workers often are victims of ageism but, paradoxically, they can also contribute to perpetuate age stereotypes such as the stereotype 'willing to retire older worker' when they disengage from the ageist work domain.

Methodological Issues

Despite the increasing number of studies on ageism, our understanding of this concept remains somewhat limited, partially because of methodological issues (Nelson, 2016). The first issue relates to tools used to measure ageism. Two main methodological approaches are prominent in the literature. The first is to use questionnaires to directly assess general ageist attitudes. In this respect, one of the most used direct scales is the Fraboni Scale of Ageism, which appears to be the first to measure ageism using the tripartite model (Rupp et al., 2005). The second method involves using fictional vignettes of targets presented as either young or old. Indirect and implicit measures (e.g., Implicit Association Test) are used to go beyond the overt expression of prejudice and to elicit a nuanced and potentially more accurate picture of its extent (Levy and Macdonald, 2016; Taylor et al., 2013). However, implicit ageism in real life is difficult to estimate and it is usually inferred based on observations of behaviors and practices.

The second methodological issue concerns the operationalization of age perceptions using negative terms. Indeed, most of the researchers use the definition proposed by Butler (1987). As a consequence, they tend to focus more on the negative dimensions of attitudes toward older people. Studies based on the stereotype content model and its extension, the bias map model (Cuddy et al., 2007), have shown that more positive perceptions, emotions, and behaviors toward older adults can also be included as measures (Iweins et al., 2012; 2013). In this perspective, future assessments should allow more positive perceptions (Levy and MacDonald, 2016).

Finally, study designs and analytic strategies in research on ageing and ageism should consider the lifespan perspective in order to better analyze how perception of ageing can change across the life course. In this respect, measuring age as a continuous variable and longitudinal design should help to better understand ageing and the social construction of age as a fluid process (Levy and MacDonald, 2016).

HOW TO REDUCE AGEISM? OVERVIEW OF INTERVENTION PROGRAMS

The previous sections of this chapter have highlighted the detrimental consequences of ageism among older individuals in the healthcare sector as well as in the workplace. Despite this evidence, up to now, research has focused more on understanding antecedents and consequences of ageism, rather than suggesting actual interventions to reduce it (Truxillo et al., 2015b). In this last section, we aim to give some guidance for intervention programs. Specifically, we present empirical evidence for interventions that can be implemented to prevent ageism or to reduce its negative effects for individuals, organizations, and society.

Individual Level

Interventions aimed at individuals can be implemented to reduce negative effects of ageism on older individuals. On the one hand, older people need to be educated about ageism and stereotypes, to recognize them and to resist the negative influence of stereotype threat (Chrisler et al., 2016). On the other hand, managers and healthcare providers should also be aware that negative age stereotypes may bias their behaviors toward older individuals.

Older individuals

In order to reduce negative effects of stereotype threat, interventions which reframe older individuals' cognitions may be implemented (Finkelstein et al., 2015; North and Fiske, 2015). As an example, task instructions could avoid making salient the memory component of a certain test for older people. Kang and Chasteen (2009) asked older women to recall a prose passage. Results showed that older women who were told that the study aims to investigate reading comprehension and impression formation skills (i.e., no-threat condition), rather than the memory ability (i.e., threat condition), performed the recall task better. Other findings lead us to conclude that older people would benefit more from preventive, rather than challenging, goals. Barber and Mather (2013) found that, under stereotype threat, older adults' working memory performance was impaired when the reward of recalling was gain-based (i.e., when they gain money for each word correctly recalled). In contrast, their performance was improved when the reward was loss-based (i.e., when they lost money for each word forgotten). Consequently, employers and healthcare providers might value 'prevention-focused' mentalities among older individuals in order to help them to be less sensitive to effects of negative meta-stereotypes (North and Fiske, 2015).

Another way to reduce negative effects of meta-stereotypes consists of affirming positive aspects of personal or social identity (Derks et al., 2011; Finkelstein et al., 2015). In their study, Kang and Chasteen (2009) found that older women's age-group identification was associated with poorer performance in a recall task, suggesting that strongly age-identified older adults are more sensitive to stereotypical declines in memory performance. On this basis, employers and healthcare providers should make salient positive older adults' achievements to increase age positive social identity (in particular the affective components of social identity, e.g., Bayl-Smith and Griffin, 2014; Desmette and Gaillard, 2008) and reduce their vulnerability to stereotype threat.

Managers and healthcare providers

Regarding interventions designed to reduce ageism, changing mindsets of managers and healthcare providers may be promising. In particular, healthcare professionals as well as managers may be unaware of their negative bias toward older individuals and older workers. Unconscious bias refers to opinions about different social groups that operate outside of individuals' conscious awareness (Grewal et al., 2013). Unconscious bias training may contribute to reduce ageism. Such training makes individuals aware of both their biases and the consequences on decision-making when they are not recognized (Murphy and Cross, 2017).

In this respect, healthcare professionals should be better educated about gerontology and positive aspects of ageing (Chrisler et al., 2016), especially because age bias is poorly recognized among the healthcare professions (Blunt-Bugental and Hehman, 2007). In the healthcare context, some educational training to recognize, reduce, and manage bias in general has been developed (Teal et al., 2012). However, some caution is needed when implementing unconscious bias training. For instance, several studies (e.g., Knapp and Stubblefield, 2000; Williams et al., 2007) found that improving knowledge through training in gerontology did not impact the attitudes toward older adults. The focus on age-decline per se might, in fact, reinforce stereotypes of dependency and frailty (North and Fiske, 2015). Nevertheless, a recent study (Boswell, 2012) focusing on four simultaneous preductors of trainee ageism (i.e., knowledge of ageing, ageing anxiety, quantity of contact with older adults, and compassion) found significant associations, with the exception of contact with older adults. However, the study only measured the frequency of contact. It was suggested that the quality of contact, rather than its frequency, is more predictive of intergenerational attitudes.

In addition, employers and managers should be trained to identify common age stereotypes and informed that their own judgment of older workers may be biased. For instance, trainers could reduce stereotypes among managers (and other people working with older individuals) by sharing scientific results showing that the characteristics typically associated with older individuals are equally distributed across age groups (Kmicinska et al., 2016). These training sessions should also inform participants about the negative effect of ageism on treatment recommendations (Madan et al., 2001), on organizational performance (Kunze et al., 2011), and on evaluations (Kmicinska et al., 2016). In line with this, Ries et al. (2013) designed a promising training program for supervisors. This training consists of two modules: the first aims at recognizing diversity as a resource, while in the second module supervisors are instructed to discuss strategies to manage age diversity and draw practical implications. An evaluation showed that the training had a positive impact four months later as it decreased salience of age differences, increased appreciation of age diversity, and reduced age stereotypes in supervisors. Once again, we recommend to practitioners to be cautious when implementing such diversity training, because other studies found that diversity training may activate, rather than reduce, bias (e.g., Duguid and Thomas-Hunt, 2015; Kalev et al., 2006).

Organizational Level

The literature suggests some interventions that could be implemented in organizations and in healthcare institutions. In particular, improving intergenerational contact among age groups and creating an age diversity climate may contribute to reduce ageism.

Improving intergenerational contact

Several studies show that improving intergenerational contact among age groups may help to reduce ageism and its consequences. For instance, Bernard et al. (2003) assessed the effect of an intervention in which medical students were assigned a senior mentor (a community-dwelling older person). These students had to interview the mentor once per semester. Results showed that those students held more positive attitudes toward ageing compared to the students in the control group. Meta-analytic findings confirmed that intergenerational contact reduces age bias (Pettigrew and Tropp, 2006). Accordingly, Truxillo et al. (2015a) suggest that interventions that increase the positive exposure to others of different ages should be implemented in organizations, either through focused interventions or structured discussion to reduce explicit and implicit stereotypes. In the same way, Finkelstein et al. (2015) suggest implementing social interventions such as team-building to solidify bonds among team members of different ages, to increase honesty in communication, and to create a sense of identity within the team.

In particular, it seems important to foster dual identity (i.e., when subgroup and superordinate group identities exist simultaneously, Gaertner et al., 1996). For instance, Iweins et al. (2013) found that high-quality contact between workers of different ages was related to positive perceptions of older workers through dual identity combining age and organization components. Therefore, managers should emphasize superordinate and organization-focused goals and identities and foster group members to work toward a superordinate goal (North and Fiske, 2015).

Beyond reducing ageism, intergenerational contact also benefits older people themselves. Abrams et al. (2006) found that stereotype threat resulted in worse performance at a cognitive abilities test only among retired adults who had experienced less positive intergenerational contact previously.

Henry et al. (2015) found that, in an organizational context which provided generativity opportunities (i.e., job features that pertain to passing knowledge and sharing with younger generations), intergenerational contact reduced older workers' prejudice toward younger workers.

Creating an organizational age diversity climate

As a support to positive intergenerational contact, organizations and health institutions should promote policies that value and implement age diversity (Chrisler et al., 2016; Iweins et al., 2013; Kydd and Fleming, 2015; Truxillo et al., 2015a). Studies that examine effects of the age diversity climate (i.e., employees' perceptions that their organization supports an age-diverse workforce and takes active steps to integrate employees of all age groups, Boehm et al., 2014), in general, reveal that a positive age-related diversity climate reduces ageism (Iweins et al., 2013; Wegge et al., 2012). However, age practices that are viewed as favoring older workers because of their age may have reverse effects. Younger workers who were experimentally presented with an organization that hired an older worker in an age-diversity program compared to a control condition displayed more negative stereotypes as well as more negative feelings (contempt) and negative behaviors (e.g., harassment; Iweins et al., 2012). Therefore, age-friendly contexts, rather than contexts favorable for a specific age group, should be overtly implemented (e.g., age-neutral recruiting policies, age-neutral career and promotion systems, or equal access to training irrespective of age, Boehm et al., 2014). In the healthcare sector, older patients should be included in clinical trials, except if there is a non-age related reason to exclude them (Bowling, 1999; Chrisler et al., 2016). Moreover, health promotion campaigns should include older people since health can be improved at any age (Chrisler et al., 2016; Levy, 2009).

Societal Level

By creating policies to proscribe age discrimination and to enhance age diversity in the workforce, society may also contribute to reduce ageism.

Anti-discrimination laws

In the 1970s and the 1980s, older people were actively encouraged to retire early (Walker, 1985). Afterwards, the ageing of the workforce has led many countries to introduce measures to increase the employment rate of workers older than 50 years (e.g., recommendations by the EU and the Organisation for Economic and Co-operative Development, OECD), and age discrimination employment laws have been implemented across the globe (e.g., the Age Discrimination Employment Act of 1967 in the United States, ADEA; The Employment Equality Acts of 2004 in the EU). These anti-discrimination employment laws vary from one country to another depending on the protected 'target' (i.e., only older workers or older and younger workers alike), the criteria of classification (i.e., there is a separate age law or the law also protects other groups, such as groups based on race, religion, or ethnicity), and the degree of enforcement and regulatory control. They define the entities covered (e.g., private entities and government agencies), the practices covered (e.g., recruitment, hiring, training, benefits) as well as the administrative procedures that should be carried out by the victims of discrimination (Gutman, 2012; Gutman and Dunleavy, 2015).

Increasing age diversity in the workforce

Despite these anti-discrimination laws, age discrimination has grown exponentially in recent years in the UK and in the EU in general (Gutman and Dunleavy, 2015). As highlighted by Taylor (2001), age discrimination is a complex issue, difficult to proscribe with law, and important questions remain (e.g., should legislation apply to people of any age?). Moreover, proscribing discrimination brings only a partial solution. Governments should review employment legislation in order to make sure, on the one hand, that older workers will receive the same job opportunities as workers of other ages (Taylor, 2001). In Belgium, like in other countries, public policies have been implemented to increase age diversity in the workforce. For instance, employers may receive incentives from the government, such as taxes reduction, to hire a worker aged over 50 (Desmette and Vendramin, 2014). However, such practices should be implemented carefully because they may be seen as preferential treatment by other groups and reinforce ageist attitudes in the workplace (Iweins et al., 2012). On the other hand, employers should be encouraged to make flexible arrangements regarding retirement as one cause of institutional ageism is related to mandatory retirement at fixed ages (Walker and Taylor, 1993). Related to that, retirement ages should be based on job-related criteria rather than on age solely (Gutman and Dunleavy, 2015). There is also some evidence that bridge employment (i.e., transitional jobs between full-time employment and complete retirement, Schultz, 2003) may help retirees to maintain their psychological well-being (Wang, 2007). Moreover, Ng et al. (2016) found that negative retirement stereotypes (e.g., negative thoughts about mental health during retirement) were negatively associated with survival. These results highlight the importance for social policies to promote the adoption of positive mindsets regarding older adults' physical and mental health and the encouragement to work at older ages – at least when working conditions are favorable.

CONCLUSION

The general framework of this chapter was social cognition and ageing, with a focus on ageism, a phenomenon extensively examined in the literature on social perception. In the first section, we addressed the theoretical explanations of ageism. The second section referred to what we know about the manifestations of ageism in two of the most investigated settings, the health and work domains. The answers to these two questions suggest, on the one hand, that age is a social construct and that older people are perceived as members of a disadvantaged group. Theories based on stereotypes, such as the stereotype content model (Fiske et al., 2002) and, as well, social identity theory (Tajfel and Turner, 1986), have been shown to be useful for understanding attitudes toward older individuals (Chasteen, 2005; Iweins et al., 2013). Moreover, these theories can also inform about the reactions of older individuals' to age stereotypes and discrimination (e.g., Abrams et al., 2006; Lagacé et al., 2008).

On the other hand, compared to other forms of discrimination, ageism presents some particularities. Indeed, older adults represent a particularly permeable category. Everybody expects to become a member of the older group. Packer and Chasteen (2006) have shown that seeing yourself as older reinforces the negative attitudes toward older people as a whole. Regarding stereotypes, competence (Cuddy et al., 2005) would benefit from distinguishing between the more fluid sub-dimension of adaptability (Warr and Pennington, 1993), which is negatively related to ageing, and the more crystallized sub-dimension of efficiency, which increases with age due to experience. In other words, discrimination of people because of old age should be considered as conceptually different from discrimination in general. Moreover we consider that, even though younger adults are also targets of prejudice and deserve attention, the notion of ageism should be restricted to older individuals. As presented by Butler (1987), ageism is, in essence, oriented toward the aged and the ageing process itself. In addition, there is evidence that the negative consequences of age discrimination are more deleterious for older people than for younger individuals.

With respect to our second goal, we have shown that compassionate ageism leads to reducing older individuals' rights and opportunities in two of the most investigated settings, the health and work domains. For instance, there is evidence for lower quality of treatment of older patients (Harries et al., 2007) and lower employment opportunities for older workers (Posthuma and Campion, 2009). In addition, we also presented older individuals not only as victims of ageism but as active agents that interiorize and apply the ageist beliefs to themselves. One's negative views on ageing translate into poorer physical and cognitive health outcomes. Negative age meta-stereotypes and age discrimination are experienced by older individuals as sources of stress (Luo et al., 2012) and they negatively impact their performance and well-being (Abrams et al., 2006; Luo et al., 2012; Taylor et al., 2013).

We have also emphasized that some contextual characteristics may contribute to making the individuals 'older', both in the eyes of the younger adults and in their own eyes. For example, age differences are larger in contexts that activate negative age stereotypes. In addition to social psychology theories, the lifespan approach can represent a useful framework to better understand perceived age and its consequences. In particular, one of the postulates of socioemotional selectivity theory (Carstensen et al., 1999) is that, as people age, they tend to perceive their future time to live as limited. Studies found that perception of future time in one's working life (i.e., Occupational Future Time Perspective, OFTP) may be influenced by the social context, such that negative age meta-stereotypes are negatively associated with OFTP (Bal et al., 2015) while an organizational climate for successful ageing is positively associated with OFTP (Zacher and Yang, 2016). These studies confirm that the combination of social psychology and lifespan theories into an integrative theoretical framework is a promising route for progress in the understanding of ageing.

In the last section of this chapter, we examined what professional and lay people can do to reduce and prevent ageism. Three main messages emerge from the multiple examples of interventions that we have provided. First, we have to be cautious when we apply theoretical models outside of the lab. The majority of the recommendations are empirically based. However, only a few of them have been tested in a real-world environment (Truxillo et al., 2015b). Second, interventions may be implemented at individual, organizational, and societal levels. We consider that society and organizations should be the primary focus. Researchers and policy-makers should join forces to plan and implement more age-heterogeneous environments in order to reduce institutionalized ageism (Hagestad and Uhlenberg, 2005). They should also collaborate to evaluate the long-term effects of their programs on ageist beliefs and behaviors. Third, prominent inter-individual differences among older adults should be recognized (Hess, 2005; Sterns and Miklos, 1995). Therefore, as mentioned by Finkelstein (2015), policies should avoid adopting 'one-size-fits-all' measures and consider individual situations when they aim to answer age-related questions. However, HR managers and policy makers should remember that such 'preferential treatment' based on age is likely to provoke the unintended effect of ageism (Iweins et al., 2012). Nevertheless, difficulties cannot be reasons to avoid taking steps to prevent or reduce ageism when it happens.

REFERENCES

Abrams, D., Eller, A., & Bryant, J. (2006). An age apart: The effects of intergenerational contact and stereotype threat on performance and intergroup bias. *Psychology and Aging, 21*, 691–702.

Abrams, D., Swift, H. J., & Drury, L. (2016). Old and unemployable? How age-based stereotypes affect willingness to hire job candidates. *Journal of Social Issues*, *72*, 105–121.

Ahmed, A. M., Andersson, L., & Hammarstedt, M. (2012). Does age matter for employability? A field experiment on ageism in the Swedish labour market. *Applied Economics Letters*, *19*, 403–406.

Allen, J. O. (2016). Ageism as a risk factor for chronic disease. *The Gerontologist*, *56*, 610–614.

Allport, G. (1954). *The nature of prejudice*. Cambridge, MA: Addison-Wesley Publishers.

Arber, S., McKinlay, J., Adams, A., Marceau, L., Link, C., & O'Donnell, A. (2004). Influence of patient characteristics on doctors' questioning and lifestyle advice for coronary heart disease: A UK/US video experiment. *British Journal of General Practice*, *54*, 673–678.

Ayalon, L. (2014). Perceived age, gender, and racial/ethnic discrimination in Europe: Results from the European Social Survey. *Educational Gerontology*, *40*, 499–517.

Bal, A. C., Reiss, A. E., Rudolph, C. W., & Baltes, B. B. (2011). Examining positive and negative perceptions of older workers: A meta-analysis. *The Journals of Gerontology, Series B: Psychological Sciences and Social Sciences*, *66*, 687–698.

Bal, P. M., de Lange, A. H., Van der Heijden, B. I. J. M., Zacher, H., Oderkerk, F. A., & Otten, S. (2015). Young at heart, old at work? Relations between age, (meta-)stereotypes, self-categorization, and retirement attitudes. *Journal of Vocational Behavior*, *91*, 35–45.

Baltes, P. B., Staudinger, U. M., & Lindenberger, U. (1999). Lifespan psychology: Theory and application to intellectual functioning. *Annual Review of Psychology*, *50*, 471–507.

Barber, S. J., & Mather, M. (2013). Stereotype threat can both enhance and impair older adults' memory. *Psychological Science*, *24*, 2522–2529.

Baruch, Y., Sayce, S., & Gregoriou, A. (2014). Retirement in a global labour market: A call for abolishing the fixed retirement age. *Personnel Review*, *43*, 464–482.

Bayl-Smith, P. H., & Griffin, B. (2014). Age discrimination in the workplace: Identifying as a late-career worker and its relationship with engagement and intended retirement age. *Journal of Applied Social Psychology*, *44*, 588–599.

Bernard, M. A., Mcauley, W. J., Belzer, J. A., & Neal, K. S. (2003). An evaluation of a low-intensity intervention to introduce medical students to healthy older people. *Journal of the American Geriatrics Society*, *51*, 419–423.

Blunt-Bugental, D. B., & Hehman, J. A. (2007). Ageism: A review of research and policy implications. *Social Issues and Policy Review*, *1*, 173–216.

Boehm, S., Kunze, F., & Bruch, H. (2014). Spotlight on age-diversity climate: The impact of age-inclusive HR practices on firm-level outcomes. *Personnel Psychology*, *67*, 667–707.

Boswell, S. S. (2012). Predicting trainee ageism using knowledge, anxiety, compassion, and contact with older adults. *Educational Gerontology*, *38*, 733–741.

Bowling, A. (1999). Ageism in cardiology. *British Medical Journal*, *319*, 1353–1355.

Butler, R. (1987). *Ageism. The encyclopedia of ageing*. New York: Springer.

Bytheway, B. (2005). Ageism and age categorization. *Journal of Social Issues*, *61*, 361–374.

Carstensen, L. L., Isaacowitz, D. M., & Charles, S. T. (1999). Taking time seriously: A theory of socioemotional selectivity. *American Psychologist*, *54*, 165–181.

Chasteen, A. (2005). Seeing eye-to-eye: Do intergroup biases operate similarly for younger and older adults? *International Journal of Aging and Human Development*, *61*, 123–139.

Chattopadhyay, A., & Marsh, R. (1999). Changes in living arrangement and familial support for the elderly in Taiwan. *Journal of Comparative Family Studies*, *30*, 523–537.

Cheng, S. T., & Chan, A. C. M. (2006). Filial piety and psychological well-being in well older Chinese. *The Journals of Gerontology: Series B, Psychological Sciences and Social Sciences*, *61*, 262–269.

Chrisler, J. C., Barney, A., & Palatino, B. (2016). Ageism can be hazardous to women's health: Ageism, sexism, and stereotypes of older women in the healthcare system. *Journal of Social Issues*, *72*, 86–104.

Christensen, K., Thinggaard, M., McGue, M., Rexbye, H., Hjelmborg, J. V. B., Aviv, A.,

Vaupel, J. W. (2009). Perceived age as clinically useful biomarker of ageing: Cohort study. *British Medical Journal*, *339*, 1–8.
Cleveland, J. N., & Hollmann, G. (1990). The effects of the age-type of tasks and incumbent age composition on job perceptions. *Journal of Vocational Behavior*, *36*, 181–194.
Cleveland, J. N., & Shore, L. M. (1992). Self- and supervisory perspectives on age and work attitudes and performance. *Journal of Applied Psychology*, *77*, 469–484.
Cronshauw, S. (2012). Aging workforce demographics in Canada: Occupational trends, work rates, and retirement projections. In J. W. Hedge, & W. C Borman (Eds.), *The Oxford handbook of work and aging* (pp. 98–114). New York: Oxford University Press.
Cuddy, A. J. C., & Fiske, S. T. (2002). Doddering but dear: Process, content, and function in stereotyping of older persons. In T. D. Nelson (Ed.), *Ageism: Stereotyping and prejudice against older persons* (pp. 3–26). Cambridge: A Bradford Book.
Cuddy, A. J. C., Fiske, S. T., & Glick, P. (2007). The BIAS map: Behaviors from intergroup affect and stereotypes. *Journal of Personality and Social Psychology*, *92*, 631–648.
Cuddy, A. J. C., Norton, M. I., & Fiske, S. T. (2005). This old stereotype: The pervasiveness and persistence of the elderly stereotype. *Journal of Social Issues*, *61*, 267–285.
Derks, B., Scheepers, D., Van Laar, C., & Ellemers, N. (2011). The threat vs. challenge of car parking for women: How self- and group affirmation affect cardiovascular responses. *Journal of Experimental Social Psychology*, *47*, 178–183.
Desmette, D., & Gaillard, M. (2008). When a 'worker' becomes an 'older worker': The effects of age-related social identity on attitudes towards retirement and work. *Career Development International*, *13*, 168–185.
Desmette, D., & Vendramin, P. (2014). Bridge employment in Belgium: Between an early retirement culture and a concern for work sustainability. In C. M. Alcover, G. Topa, E. Parry, F. Fraccaroli, & M. Depolo (Eds.), *Bridge employment: A research handbook* (pp. 70–89). Lancaster University, UK: Routledge.
Desmette, D., Iweins, C., & Yzerbyt, V. (2015). Agîsme et gestion des âges: Quelles implications pour les travailleurs âgés en Belgique? In M. Lagacé (Ed.), *Représentations et discours sur le vieillissement: La face cachée de l'âgisme* (pp. 147–172). Québec: Presses de l'Université Laval.
Desrichard, O., & Köpetz, C. (2005). A threat in the elder: The impact of task-instructions, self-efficacy and performance expectations on memory performance in the elderly. *European Journal of Social Psychology*, *36*, 537–552.
Diekman, A. B., & Hirnisey, L. (2007). The effect of context on the silver ceiling: A role congruity perspective on prejudiced responses. *Personality and Social Psychological Bulletin*, *33*, 1353–1366.
Duguid, M. M., & Thomas-Hunt, M. C. (2015). Condoning Stereotyping? How Awareness of Stereotyping Prevalence Impacts Expression of Stereotypes. *Journal of Applied Psychology*, *100*, 343–359.
Eagly, A. H. (1987). *Sex differences in social behaviour: A social-role interpretation*. Hillsdale, NJ: Lawrence Erlbaum Associates, Inc.
Fajemilehin, B. R. (2004). Attitudes of students in health professions toward caring for older people: Needed curricula revisions in Nigeria. *Educational Gerontology*, *30*, 383–390.
Finkelstein, L. M. (2015). Older workers, stereotypes, and discrimination in the context of the employment relationship. In M. Bal, D. Kooij, & D. Rousseau (Eds.), *Aging workers and the employment relationship* (pp. 13–32). London: Springer.
Finkelstein, L. M., & Farrell, S. K. (2007). An expanded view of age bias in the workplace. In K. Shultz, & G. Adams (Eds.), *Aging and work in the 21st century* (pp. 73–108). Hillsdale, NJ: Lawrence Erlbaum.
Finkelstein, L. M., King, E. B., & Voyles, E. C. (2015). Age metastereotyping and cross-age workplace interactions: A meta-view of age stereotypes at work. *Work, Aging and Retirement*, *1*, 26–40.
Finkelstein, L. M., Ryan, K. M., & King, E. B. (2013). What do the young (old) people think of me? Content and accuracy of age-based metastereotypes. *European Journal of Work and Organizational Psychology*, *22*, 633–657.
Fiske, S. T., Cuddy, A. J. C., Xu, J., & Glick, P. (2002). A model of (often mixed) stereotype

content: Competence and warmth respectively follow from perceived status and competition. *Journal of Personality and Social Psychology*, *82*, 878–902.

Gaertner, S. L., Dovidio, J. F., & Bachman, B. A. (1996). Revisiting the contact hypothesis: The induction of a common ingroup identity. *International Journal of Intercultural Relations*, *20*, 271–290. Special Issue: International Congress on Prejudice, Discrimination and Conflict, Jerusalem, Israel.

Gaillard, M., & Desmette, D. (2010). (In)validating stereotypes about older workers influences their intentions to retire early and to learn and develop. *Basic and Applied Social Psychology*, *32*, 86–95.

Gartska, T. A., Hummert, M. L., & Branscombe, N. R. (2005). Perceiving age discrimination in response to intergenerational inequity. *Journal of Social Issues*, *61*, 321–342.

Gatz, M., & Pearson, C. G. (1988). Ageism revised and the provision of psychological services. *American Psychologist*, *43*, 184–188.

Gee, G. C., Pavalko, E. K., & Long, J. S. (2007). Age, cohort and perceived age discrimination: Using the life course to assess self-reported age discrimination. *Social Forces*, *86*, 265–290.

Giles, H., & Reid, S. A. (2005). Ageism across the lifespan: Towards a self-categorization model of ageing. *Journal of Social Issues*, *61*, 389–404.

Gordon, R. A., & Arvey, R. D. (2004). Age bias in laboratory and field settings: A meta-analytic investigation. *Journal of Applied Social Psychology*, *34*, 468–492.

Grant, L. D. (1996). Effects of ageism on individual and health care providers' responses to healthy aging. *Health and Social Work*, *21*, 9–15.

Greenberg, J., Schimel, J., & Mertens, A. (2002). Ageism: Denying the face of the future. In T. D. Nelson (Ed.), *Ageism: Stereotyping and prejudice against older persons* (pp. 27–48). London: A Bradford Book.

Grewal, D., Ku, M. C., Girod, S. C., & Valantine, H. (2013). How to recognize and address unconscious bias. In L. W. Roberts (Ed.), *The academic medicine handbook: A guide to achievement and fulfillment for academic faculty* (pp. 405–412). New York: Springer.

Gutman, A. (2012). Age-based laws and regulations. In J. W. Hedge, & W. C. Borman (Eds.), *The Oxford handbook of work and aging* (pp. 606–628). New York: Oxford University Press.

Gutman, A., & Dunleavy, E. (2015). A comparison of EEO law on workforce aging across English-speaking countries. In L. Finkelstein, D. Truxillo, F. Fraccaroli, & R. Kanfer (Eds.), *Facing the challenges of a multi-age workforce: A use-inspired approach* (pp. 283–310). New York: Routledge.

Hagestad, G. O., & Uhlenberg, P. (2005). The social separation of old and young: A root of ageism. *Journal of Social Issues*, *61*, 343–360.

Happell, B., & Brooker, J. (2001). Who will look after my grandmother? Attitudes of student nurses toward the care of older adults. *Journal of Gerontological Nursing*, *27*, 12–17.

Harries, C., Forrest, D., Harvey, N., McClelland, A., & Bowling, A. (2007). Which doctors are influenced by a patient's age? A multi-method study of angina treatment in general practice, cardiology and gerontology. *Quality & Safety in Health Care*, *16*, 23–27.

Harwood, J., Hewstone, M., Paolini, S., & Voci, A. (2005). Grandparent-grandchild contact and attitudes toward older adults: Moderator and mediator effects. *Personality and Social Psychology Bulletin*, *31*, 393–406.

Henry, H., Zacher, H., & Desmette, D. (2015). Reducing age bias and turnover intentions by enhancing intergenerational contact quality in the workplace: The role of opportunities for generativity and development. *Work, Aging and Retirement*, *1*, 243–253.

Hess, T. M. (2005). Memory and aging in context. *Psychological Bulletin*, *131*, 383–406.

Hess, T. M., Auman, C., Colcombe, S. J., & Rahhal, T. A. (2003). The impact of stereotype threat on age differences in memory performance. *The Journals of Gerontology, Series B: Psychological Sciences and Social Sciences*, *58*, 3–11.

Hess, T. M., Hinson, J. T., & Statham, J. A. (2004). Explicit and implicit stereotype activation effects on memory: Do age and awareness moderate the impact of priming? *Psychology and Aging*, *19*, 495–505.

Hummert, M. L. (1990). Multiple stereotypes of elderly and young adults: A comparison of structure and evaluations. *Psychology and Aging*, *5*, 182–193.

Iweins, C., Desmette, D., & Yzerbyt, V. (2012). Ageism at work: What happens to older workers who benefit from preferential treatment? *Psychologica Belgica*, *52*, 327–349.

Iweins, C., Desmette, D., Yzerbyt, V., & Stinglhamber, F. (2013). Ageism at work: The impact of intergenerational contact and organizational multi-age perspective. *European Journal of Work and Organizational Psychology*, *22*, 331–346.

Kalev, A., Kelly, E., & Dobbin, F. (2006). Best practices or best guesses? Assessing the efficacy of corporate affirmative action and diversity policies. *American Sociological Review*, *71*, 589–617.

Kanfer, R., & Ackerman, P. L. (2004). Aging, adult development, and work motivation. *Academy of Management Review*, *29*, 440–458.

Kang, S. K., & Chasteen, A. L. (2009). The moderating role of age-group identification and perceived threat on stereotype threat among older adults. *The International Journal of Aging and Human Development*, *69*, 201–220.

Kanter, R. (1977). *Men and women of the corporation*. New York: Basic Books.

Kite, M. E., Stockdale, G. D., Whitley, B. E., Jr., & Johnson, B. T. (2005). Attitudes toward older and younger adults: An updated meta-analysis. *Journal of Social Issues*, *61*, 241–266.

Kmicinska, M., Zaniboni, S., Truxillo, D. M., Fraccaroli, F., & Wang, M. (2016). Effects of rater conscientiousness on evaluations of task and contextual performance of older and younger co-workers. *European Journal of Work and Organizational Psychology*, 25, 707–721.

Knapp, J. L., & Stubblefield, P. (2000). Changing students' perceptions of aging: The impact of an intergenerational service learning course. *Educational Gerontology*, *26*, 611–621.

Kunze, F., Boehm, S. A., & Bruch, H. (2011). Age diversity, age discrimination climate and performance consequences – a cross organizational study. *Journal of Organizational Behavior*, *32*, 264–290.

Kunze, F., Boehm, S., & Bruch, H. (2013). Age, resistance to change, and job performance. *Journal of Managerial Psychology*, *28*, 741–760.

Kydd, A., & Fleming, A. (2015). Ageism and age discrimination in health care: Fact or fiction? A narrative review of the literature. *Maturitas*, *81*, 432–438.

Lagacé, M. (2015). *Représentations et discours sur le vieillissement: La face cachée de l'âgisme*. Québec: Presses de l'Université Laval.

Lagacé, M., Tougas, F., Laplante, J. D., & Neveu, J.-F. (2008). La santé en péril: Les répercussions de la communication âgiste sur le désengagement psychologique et l'estime de soi des infirmiers de 45 ans et plus. *Revue Canadienne du Vieillissement*, *27*, 285–299.

Lamont, R. A., Swift, H. J., & Abrams, D. (2015). A review and meta-analysis of age-based stereotype threat: Negative stereotypes, not facts, do the damage. *Psychology and Aging*, *30*, 180–193.

Laplante, J., Tougas, F., Lagacé, M., & Bellehumeur, C. (2010). Facilitators and moderators of psychological disengagement among older workers: The contribution of group status, meaning of work status and collective self-esteem. *The Journal of Diversity in Organizations, Communities & Nations*, *10*, 195–208.

Lawrence, B. S. (1988). New wrinkles in the theory of age: Demography, norms, and performance ratings. *Academy of Management Journal*, *31*, 309–337.

Levy, B. (1996). Improving memory in old age through implicit self-stereotyping. *Journal of Personality and Social Psychology*, *71*, 1092–1107.

Levy, B. R. (2003). Mind matters: Cognitive and physical effects of aging self-stereotypes. *The Journals of Gerontology, Series B: Psychological Sciences and Social Sciences*, *58*, 203–211.

Levy, B. R. (2009). Stereotype embodiment: A psychological approach to aging. *Current Directions in Psychological Science*, *18*, 332–336.

Levy, B. R., Ryall, A. L., Pilver, C. E., Sheridan, P. L., Wei, J. Y., & Hausdorff, J. M. (2008). Influence of African American elders' age stereotypes on their cardiovascular response to stress. *Anxiety, Stress, and Coping*, *21*, 85–93.

Levy, B. R., Slade, M. D., & Gill, T. M. (2006). Hearing decline predicted by elders' stereotypes. *Journals of Gerontology: Psychological Sciences*, *61*, 82–87.

Levy, B. R., Slade, M. D., Kunkel, S. R., & Kasl, S. V. (2002). Longevity increased by positive self-perceptions of aging. *Journal of Personality and Social Psychology*, *83*, 261–270.

Levy, S. R., & MacDonald, J. L. (2016). Progress on understanding ageism. *Journal of Social Issues*, *72*, 5–25.

Löckenhoff, C. E., De Fruyt, F., Terracciano, A., McCrae, R. R., De Bolle, M., Costa, P. T. Jr., Aguilar-Vafaie, M. E., Ahn, C.-K., Ahn H. N., Alcalay, L., Allik, J., Avdeyeva, T. V., Barbaranelli, C., Benet-Martinez, V., Blatny, M., Bratko, D., Cain, T. R., Crawford, J. T., Lima, M. P., Fickova, E., Gheorghiu, M., Halberstadt, J., Hrebıckova, M., Jussim, L., Klinkosz, W., Knezevic, G., Leibovich de Figueroa, N., Martin, T. A., Marusic, I., Anwar Mastor, K., Miramontez, D. R., Nakazato, K., Nansubuga, F., Pramila, V. S., Realo, A., Rolland, J.-P., Rossier, J., Schmidt, V., Sekowski, A., Shakespeare-Finch, J., Shimonaka, Y., Simonetti, F, Siuta, J., Smith, P. B., Szmigielska, B., Wang, L., Yamaguchi, M., & Yik, M. (2009). Perceptions of aging across 26 cultures and their culture-level associates. *Psychology and Aging*, *24*, 941–954.

Luo, Y., Xu, J., Granberg, E., & Wentworth, W. M. (2012). A longitudinal study of social status, perceived discrimination, and physical and emotional health among older adults. *Research on Aging*, *34*, 275–301.

Madan, A. K., Aliabadi-Wahle, S., & Beech, D. J. (2001). Ageism in medical students' treatment recommendations: The example of breast-conserving procedures. *Academic Medicine*, *76*, 282–284.

Martens, A., Goldenberg, J. L., & Greenberg, D. J. (2005). A terror management perspective on ageism. *Journal of Social Issues*, *61*, 223–239.

McCann, R., & Giles, H. (2002). Ageism in the workplace: A communication perspective. In T. D. Nelson (Ed.), *Ageism: Stereotyping and prejudice against older persons* (pp. 163–199). Cambridge, MA: MIT Press

McCarthy, J., & Heraty, N. (2017). Ageist Attitudes. In E. Parry, & J. McCarthy (Eds.), *The Palgrave handbook of age diversity and work* (pp. 399–422). London: Macmillan.

McCarthy, J., Heraty, N., Cross, C., & Cleveland, J. (2014). Who is considered an 'older worker'? Extending our conceptualisation of 'older' form an organisational decision maker perspective. *Human Resource Management Journal*, *24*, 374–393.

McLafferty, I., & Morrison, F. (2004). Attitudes towards hospitalized older adults. *Journal of Advanced Nursing*, *47*, 446–453.

Murphy, C., & Cross, C. (2017). Gender, age, and labour market experiences. In E. Parry & J. McCarthy (Eds.), *The Palgrave handbook of age diversity and work* (pp. 561–582). London: Macmillan.

Nelson, T. D. (2002). *Ageism: Stereotyping and prejudice against older persons*. Cambridge, UK: Bradford Books.

Nelson, T. D. (2005). Ageism: Prejudice against our feared future self. *Journal of Social Issues*, *61*, 207–221.

Nelson, T. D. (2016). Promoting healthy aging by confronting ageism. *American Psychologist*, *71*, 276–282.

Ng, R., Allore, H. G., Monin, J. K., & Levy, B. R. (2016). Retirement as meaningful: Positive retirement stereotypes associated with longevity. *Journal of Social Issues*, *72*, 69–85.

North, M. S., & Fiske, S. T. (2012). An inconvenienced youth? Ageism and its potential intergenerational roots. *Psychological Bulletin*, *138*, 982–997.

North, M. S., & Fiske, S. T. (2013). Act your (old) age: Prescriptive, ageist biases over succession, consumption, and identity. *Personality and Social Psychology Bulletin*, *39*, 720–734.

North, M. S., & Fiske, S. T. (2015). Intergenerational resource tensions in the workplace and beyond: Individual, interpersonal, institutional, international. *Research in Organizational Behavior*, *35*, 159–179.

North, M. S., & Fiske, S. T. (2016). Resource scarcity and prescriptive attitudes generate subtle, intergenerational older-worker exclusion. *Journal of Social Issues*, *72*, 122–145.

Packer, D. J., & Chasteen, A. L. (2006). Looking to the future: How possible aged selves influence prejudice toward older adults. *Social Cognition*, *24*, 218–247.

Palmore, E. B. (1999). *Ageism: Negative and positive*. New York: Springer Publishing Company.

Park, H. -J., Li, W. W., Cummings, S. M., & Ponnuswami, I. (2015). Introduction: Mental health in an ageing world. In W. W. Li, S. M., Cummings, I. Ponnuswami, & H.-J. Park (Eds.), *Aging and mental health: Global perspectives* (pp. 1–10). New York: Nova Sciences Publishing.

Peake, M. D., Thompson, S., Lowe, D., & Pearson, M. G. (2003). Ageism in the management of lung cancer. *Age and Aging, 32*, 171–177.

Perry, E. L., & Finkelstein, L. M. (1999). Toward a broader view of age discrimination in employment related decisions: A joint consideration of organizational factors and cognitive processes. *Human Resource Management Review, 9*, 21–49.

Pettigrew, T. F. (1998). Intergroup contact theory. *Annual Review of Psychology, 49*, 65–85.

Pettigrew, T. F., & Tropp, L. R. (2006). A meta-analytic test of intergroup contact theory. *Journal of Personality and Social Psychology, 90*, 751–783.

Posthuma, R. A., & Campion, M. A. (2009). Age stereotypes in the workplace: Common stereotypes, moderators, and future research directions. *Journal of Management, 35*, 158–188.

Rahhal, T. A., Hasher, L., & Colcombe, S. J. (2001). Instructional manipulations and age differences in memory: Now you see them, now you don't. *Psychology and Aging, 16*, 697–706.

Ries, B. C., Diestel, S., Shemla, M., Liebermann, S. C., Jungmann, F., Wegge, J., & Schmidt, H.-H. (2013). Age diversity and team effectiveness. In C. M. Schlick, E. Frieling, & J. Wegge (Eds.), *Age-differentiated work systems* (pp. 89–118). Berlin: Springer.

Rippon, I., Kneale, D., de Oliveira, C., Demakakos, P., & Steptoe, A. (2014). Perceived age discrimination in older adults. *Age and Ageing, 43*, 379–386.

Rupp, D. E., Vodanovich, S. J., & Credé, M. (2005). The multidimensional nature of ageism: Construct validity and group differences. *Journal of Social Psychology, 145*, 335–362.

Rupp, D. E., Vodanovich, S. J., & Credé, M. (2006). Age bias in the workplace: The impact of ageism and causal attributions. *Journal of Applied Social Psychology, 36*, 1337–1364.

Schultz, K. S. (2003). Bridge employment: Work after retirement. In G. A. Adams and T. A. Beehr (Eds.), *Retirement: Reasons, processes, and results*. New York: Springer.

Sindi, S., Fiocco, A. J., Juster, R.-P., Pruessner, J., & Lupien, S. J. (2013). When we test, do we stress? Impact of the testing environment on cortisol secretion and memory performance in older adults. *Psychoneuroendocrinology, 38*, 1388–1396.

Snape, E., & Redman, T. (2003). Too old or too young? The impact of perceived age discrimination. *Human Resource Management Journal, 13*, 78–89.

Solomon, S., Greenberg, J., & Pyszczynski, T. (1991). Terror management theory of self-esteem. In C. R. Snyder, D. R. Forsyth, C. R. Snyder, & D. R. Forsyth (Eds.), *Handbook of social and clinical psychology: The health perspective* (pp. 21–40). Elmsford, NY: Pergamon Press.

Steele, C. M., & Aronson, J. (1995). Stereotype threat and the intellectual test performance of African Americans. *Journal of Personality and Social Psychology, 69*, 789–811.

Stephan, Y., Sutin, A. R., & Terracciano, A. (2015). How old do you feel? The role of age discrimination and biological aging in subjective age. *PLOS ONE, 10*, e0119293.

Sterns, H. L., & Miklos, S. M. (1995). The aging worker in a changing environment: Organizational and individual issues. *Journal of Vocational Behavior, 47*, 248–268.

Stewart, J., Giles, L., Paterson, J., & Butler, S. (2005). Knowledge and attitudes towards older people: New Zealand students entering health professional degrees. *Physical & Occupational Therapy in Geriatrics, 23*, 25–36.

Tajfel, H., & Turner, J. C. (1986). The social identity theory of intergroup behavior. In S. Worchel, & W. Austin (Eds.), *Psychology of intergroup relations* (2nd edn., pp. 7–24). Chicago: Nelson-Hall.

Taylor, P. (2001). Older workers and the cult of youth: Ageism in public policy. In I. Glover, & M. Branine (Eds.), *Ageism in work and employment* (pp. 271–284). Aldershot, Hampshire, UK: Ashgate.

Taylor, P., McLoughlin, C., Meyer, D., & Brook, E. (2013). Everyday discrimination in the workplace, job satisfaction and psychological wellbeing: age differences and moderating variables. *Ageing and Society*, *33*, 1105–1138.

Teal, C. R., Gill, A. C., Green, A. R., & Crandall, S. (2012). Helping medical learners recognise and manage unconscious bias toward certain patient groups. *Medical Education*, *46*, 80–88.

Truxillo, D. M., Cadiz, D. M., & Hammer, L. B. (2015a). Supporting the aging workforce: A review and recommendations for workplace intervention research. *Annual Review of Organizational Psychology and Organizational Behavior*, *2*, 351–381.

Truxillo, D. M., Finkelstein, L. M., Pytlovany, A. C., & Jenkins, J. S. (2015b). Age discrimination at work: A review of the research and recommendations for the future. In A. J. Colella, & E. B. King (Eds.), *The Oxford handbook of workplace discrimination*. New York: Oxford University Press.

Truxillo, D. M., Fraccaroli, F., Yaldiz, L. M., & Zaniboni, S. (2017). Age discrimination at work. In E. Parry, & J. McCarthy (Eds.), *The Palgrave handbook of age diversity and Work* (pp. 447–472). London: Macmillan.

Tsuchiya, A., Dolan, P., & Shaw, R. (2003). Measuring people's preferences regarding ageism in health: Some methodological issues and some fresh evidence. *Social Science & Medicine*, *57*, 687–696.

Turner, J. C. (1999). Some current issues in research on social identity and self-categorization theories. In N. Ellemers, R. Spears, & B. Doosje (Eds.), *Social identity* (pp. 6–34). Bodmin, Cornwall (GB): MPG Books Ltd.

von Hippel, C., Kalokerinos, E. K., & Henry, J. D. (2013). Stereotype threat among older employees: Relationship with job attitudes and turnover intentions. *Psychology and Aging*, *28*, 17–27.

Voss, P., Wolff, J. K., & Rothermund, K. (2016). Relations between views on ageing and perceived age discrimination: A domain-specific perspective. *European Journal of Ageing*, *14*, 5–15.

Walker, A. (1985). Early retirement: Release or refuge from the labour market. *The Quarterly Journal of Social Affairs*, *1*, 211–229.

Walker, A., & Taylor, P. (1993). Ageism versus productive aging: The challenge of age discrimination in the labour market. In S. Bass, F. Caro, & Y. Chen (Eds.), *Achieving a productive ageing society*. London: Auburn House.

Wang, M. (2007). Profiling retirees in the retirement transition and adjustment process: examining the longitudinal change patterns of retirees' psychological well-being. *The Journal of Applied Psychology*, *92*, 455–474.

Warr, P., & Pennington, J. (1993). Views about age discrimination and older workers. In *Age and employment: Policies and practices* (pp. 75–106). London: Institute of Personnel Management.

Wegge, J., Jungmann, F., Liebermann, S., Shemla, M., Ries, B. C., Diestel, S., & Schmidt, K.-H. (2012). What makes age diverse teams effective? Results from a six-year research program. *Work: A Journal of Prevention, Assessment & Rehabilitation*, *41*, 5145–5151. Special Issue: 18th World Congress on Ergonomics – Designing a sustainable future.

Williams, B., Anderson, M. C., & Day, R. (2007). Undergraduate nursing students' knowledge of and attitudes toward aging: Comparison of context-based learning and a traditional program. *Journal of Nursing Education*, *46*, 115–120.

Wurm, S., Tesch-Römer, C., & Tomasik, M. J. (2007). Longitudinal findings on aging-related cognitions, control beliefs, and health in later life. *The Journals of Gerontology Series B: Psychological Sciences and Social Sciences*, *62*, 156–164.

Yuan, A. S. V. (2007). Perceived age discrimination and mental health. *Social Forces*, *86*, 291–311.

Zacher, H., & Yang, J. (2016). Organizational climate for successful aging. *Frontiers in Psychology*, *7*, 1007.

Zaniboni, S., Sarchielli, G., & Fraccaroli, F. (2010). How are psychosocial factors related to retirement intentions? *International Journal of Manpower*, *31*, 271–285.

17

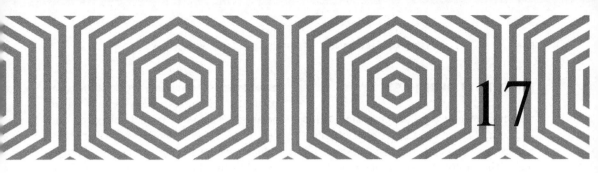

Social Policy and Social Identities for Older People

Mary Breheny and Christine Stephens

OVERVIEW

Population ageing, changing gender and family role expectations, and increased responsibility for individual experience have changed what it means to be an older person today. These social changes make a new set of identities available for older people based around imperatives to live a long and healthy life, contribute to family and community, and resist decline and dependency. These identities are provided by dominant discourses of older age, which are developed in research and policy, and become part of everyday discourse through media and popular culture representations of the rights and responsibilities of older age. From a social constructionist perspective, people negotiate their identity through everyday talk by using shared linguistic and social resources. Although new identities of 'successful' ageing appear to be a positive shift for older people from earlier representations of ageing as decline and withdrawal, such positive identities are not equally available to all older people. The capability to identify as ageing successfully depends largely on physical, material, and social resources. Older people rich in such resources can locate themselves firmly within a valued ageing identity and reap all the benefits of the shift to viewing ageing as a time of opportunity. Older people in poor health, and with limited material and social resources, are excluded from such positive versions of later life, although they are not excluded from the expectations of healthy living, independence, and contribution required of the virtuous citizen. To address the damaging effects of such social identities, we need to move beyond successful ageing limited to expectations for health promotion and productivity to view healthy ageing as reflecting the availability of supportive social environments across the life course that enable people to live well in later life.

IDENTITY IN OLDER AGE

Societies categorise people according to life stage or age and assign tasks, rights, responsibilities, and appropriate behaviours accordingly. Thus, different age groups gain social identities as well as power in relation to one another (Calasanti, 2007). Schneider and Ingram (1993) have described how groups who are affected by public policy come to be characterised by stereotypes such as 'deserving', 'honest', or 'selfish', which structure their public identities. Hudson and Gonyea (2012) drew on this conceptualisation to describe how the representation of older people has shifted from 'dependants', a characterisation which was dominant well into the twentieth century, to 'contenders'. This has correspondingly shifted attitudes to older people from compassionate ageism and collective responsibility for the aged to an ideological swing towards individual responsibility and intergenerational conflict (Binstock, 2010). This shift has repositioned older people as no longer deserving by virtue of their age alone and increasingly in competition with other age groups for scarce resources.

From a social constructionist perspective, people negotiate a positive identity for themselves in everyday talk by using such shared linguistic and social resources. Everyday language reproduces societal and individual relationships of power within specific social contexts (Powell and Biggs, 2004). Paying attention to the ways in which particular constructions arise, strengthen, and dominate our understandings of social relations, while alternative understandings are neglected, or fall out of favour, reveals these powerful relationships. Wearing (1995) used discursive analysis to describe the dominant discourse of ageing in the 1990s as one which constructed older people as inferior on biological grounds. Wearing argued that this construction worked to isolate and disempower older people. The subject position of one in biological decline was taken up by older people themselves to 'incorporate and perpetuate powerlessness' (Wearing, 1995: 265). Using particular discourses makes certain subject positions, such as 'dependent elder' or 'successful ager', available for a speaker. These subject positions are constituted by the rights and obligations to say certain kinds of things in certain situations (Harre and Gillett, 1994). Consequently, an older person's talk about independence and health does not represent a detached account of their life but a particular version of events produced in a specific context to present themselves as a certain type of person. Language is not neutral; it conveys morally laden messages that categorise how older people should be and act, and therefore, enable or constrain what can be said and done (Katz, 2000). Accordingly, different ways of talking about older age provide different subject positions which have implications for identity in later life. In the following sections, we will unpack the ways in which recent discourses of ageing have been shaped by social changes and the ways in which social policy has contributed to shifting discourses of ageing which alter the social identities available to older people.

SHIFTING IDENTITIES FOR OLDER PEOPLE

Expectations for later life are not fixed but are always changing in response to prevailing social and economic conditions. Just like younger people, older people negotiate their identities in the context of the present situational, cultural, and historical moment (Biggs, 2001). The main drivers of change over the life course of the current cohort of older people are population ageing, changing expectations for the role of a person in society, and an increased focus on individual responsibility for living circumstances.

The world's populations are ageing. Population ageing means that there is both a rise in the average age of the population as well as a growing proportion of older people within populations. According to the World Health Organization (WHO, 2012), between 2000 and 2050, the proportion of the world's population aged over 60 years will double from 11% to 22%. As people live longer, particularly in developed countries, the nature of being old is also changing. Since the 1940s, older people in many countries have generally had greater life expectancy, rising standards of living, better health, and are more likely to have a longer retirement following working life (MacKean and Abbot-Chapman, 2012). These demographic changes influence the social identities available to older people.

Although, arguably, increased longevity and improved health into older age is a positive change for society, population ageing has not been greeted with enthusiasm. Population ageing and increased numbers of older people has been interpreted as a frightening demographic change with catastrophic implications for health and social care services. Robertson (1999) has labelled this characterisation of changing population structure as 'apocalyptic demography', in which an increasing older population is represented as destabilising the wellbeing of society as a whole. Martin et al. (2009) are among those who have noted this new form of ageism, which is seen in media accounts using alarmist metaphors of a 'time bomb' or 'tidal wave' to describe older people about to engulf the population. This produces a tension between population ageing as a sign of increased population health with additional time spent in good health versus increased longevity as a fearful change with older people living longer with poor health. These two alternative accounts of this demographic shift recur in policy and media accounts of population ageing.

This change in population structure has occurred alongside a shift in Western countries towards differentiation of the individual life course. Expectations of appropriate life course trajectories are now less circumscribed by family and gender roles and more closely aligned with the pursuit of individually directed goals (Blaikie, 1999). What it means to be a person of any age is increasingly based on living 'my life' as an individual project (Beck and Beck-Gernsheim, 2002). As a result, identity formation has become more intimately shaped by individual choices, understood as the 'do-it-yourself' biography (Beck and Beck-Gernsheim 2002). People are expected to take responsibility for their financial, social, and physical wellbeing and manage their own lives according to individual life goals. Such expectations profoundly influence social identities. Beck and Beck-Gernsheim (2002) argue that such changes have created a generational divide, with older people's social identities linked to family and gender roles. However, older people also describe life as an individual project in pursuit of self-directed goals (Henricksen and Stephens, 2010), often interpreting this as a shift due to ageing rather than as a broader cross-generational shift in identity formation (Breheny and Stephens, 2017). From an individualisation perspective, older age reflects the culmination of a lifetime of individual choices, and older people are viewed as responsible for managing their own life trajectories.

Individualisation of biography dovetails with the dominant neoliberal economic ideology of the twenty-first century. Neoliberalism refers to the restructuring that has occurred since the 1970s that celebrates unhindered markets as the most effective means of achieving economic growth and public welfare (Bell and Green, 2016). The implications of these market fundamentalist ideals are far more than economic. They have had a profound impact on how we understand the role of the individual in society (Somers and Block, 2005). Neoliberal ideology valorises independence, rationality, hard work, and individual responsibility for outcomes (Coburn, 2000). Within a neoliberal worldview, people are positioned as responsible for minimising risk and maintaining health and activity (Petersen, 1996). Social policy reflects and reinforces this version of right conduct to suggest that self-care, responsible lifestyles, and constant activity are the route to individual and societal wellbeing (Katz and Marshall, 2003; Pond et al., 2010). Neoliberalism implies that making good choices and having positive outcomes are equally possible for all older people (Holstein and Minkler, 2003). From this perspective, inequalities in circumstances no longer reflect social and structural inequities, but are re-cast as the inevitable outcome of freedom of choice (Ayo, 2012). Because people are responsible for their choices, the solution to inequalities becomes encouraging people to choose right conduct. This correspondingly shifts responsibility for outcomes in later life from the collective or state to the individual (Biggs et al., 2017).

Over the lifetimes of the current cohort of older people, there have been huge changes in the role that people are understood to play in managing their own health (Ayo, 2012). The current approach is often referred to as 'healthism' (Crawford, 1980), in which people are encouraged to take responsibility for their own health and consequently held accountable for any failures in health. To be viewed as healthy, people are expected to engage in a range of practices including physical activity, management of diet, consumption of products and health services, and to display commitment to increasing their knowledge of health and wellbeing (Ayo, 2012). Healthism is particularly detrimental for older people because, as they age, they are more likely to experience loss of physical abilities (Stephens, 2017).

These social changes influence the social identities available to older people to negotiate their place in the world (Biggs, 2005). Together, population ageing, individualisation, and healthism have altered later life from a time of withdrawal and dependency to a time for pursuing health. These changes make available a new set of identities for older people based around imperatives to live a long and healthy life, actively manage their contribution and participation, and resist decline and dependency.

SUCCESSFUL AGEING POLICIES

Since the 1970s, a political economy approach to gerontology (e.g., Estes 1979; Minkler and Estes, 1999; Townsend, 1981; Walker, 1981) has drawn the attention of researchers to the influence of ideologies and economic, political, and social processes on the identities of older people. In the later twentieth and early twenty-first centuries, social policy responses to population ageing have shifted from a focus on care toward the promotion of independence, participation, and wellbeing for older people. Today, social policy in the United States, Europe, and Australasia is framed in terms of promoting health and independence among older people to reduce the burden on health and welfare systems and maximise their contribution to society (Stenner et al., 2011). Such policies are largely based on WHO (World Health Organization, 2002) recommendations to promote active ageing. An important influence on research, intervention, and public policy within this framework has been Rowe and Kahn's (1997) successful ageing model of intervention to promote maintenance of high mental and physical functioning, ongoing social engagement, and avoidance of disease and disability. These powerful notions of active and successful ageing have driven much research and intervention in terms of the most effective and efficient ways to promote wellbeing (Dupuis and Alzheimer, 2008). Such policy encourages older people to responsibly plan and manage their own lives as they age.

These policy accounts of what older age can, and should, be focus on four intersecting aspects: physical health, independence, social participation, and contribution. Health in older age is seen as central to the social identity of older people. Health is also linked to independence, as older people in good health are viewed as able to avoid reliance on others. Independence is often used as a marker of successful ageing, and identifying the factors that enhance independence among older people is often claimed in policy documents to be of vital importance.

The importance of social connection in the lives of older people is also a key focus of ageing policy. Research has consistently demonstrated the benefits of social integration for the aged (Holt-Lunstad et al., 2010), and social exclusion has been linked to poor health among older people (Cacioppo et al., 2015). Accordingly, social integration is recommended in policy both for its health benefits and because it is advantageous for the wider community. In particular, policy suggestions for social integration link the beneficial effects of social participation to the value of older people as contributors to the community through paid or voluntary work situations (Biggs, 2001). Within social policy, activities such as work, volunteering, or mentoring are suggested as pathways to social inclusion. Martinson and Halpern (2011) note the recent focus of active ageing policy discourse on volunteering and civic engagement as the route to a valued identity in later life.

FROM POLICY TO IDENTITY VIA THE MEDIA

These accounts of what older age can and should be provide the foundation for valued social identities. Representations of ageing are developed in social science theory, research and policy, and are reflected and reproduced through media and popular culture representations of what it means to be an older person (Laliberte Rudman, 2006; Wearing, 1995). These are not inevitable ways of viewing older age; they are a version of later life developed in response to wider social forces and imperatives (Biggs, 2001; Powell, 2001).

Government social policies are one very strong influence on the ways in which people are seen as a certain sort of person in society. Townsend's (1986) influential work pointed theorists and researchers to the key role of governmental social policy in constructing versions of old age. Biggs (2001) has described how policy is typically an attempt to address a perceived social problem which, in turn, implicitly or explicitly characterises people in terms of valorised or tainted identities. In this way, policies about ageing contribute to discourses of ageing which shape what it means to be an older person today across a variety of domains, including social relationships, social contribution, and healthy ageing.

The media are a prominent route by which social policy is made available for consumption and debate. The media powerfully construct ageing identities by describing the attributes of successful, independent, healthy, or contributing elders. Rozanova (2010) found that discourses of successful ageing in the print media reproduced recognisable neoliberal policy imperatives of older people as individually responsible for ageing successfully. Similarly, popular media headlines encourage older people to defy old age or refuse to age, suggesting that ageing is a choice that people make. Pronouncements such as: 'It's no accident that I've reached age 88 in great health' (Vernon, 2015) promote healthy ageing as reflecting the application of careful self-management. The social policy notion of successful ageing has been taken up by the media and used to present successful older people as defying age-related decline and achieving in areas traditionally associated with younger people. These include feats of physical strength, such as weightlifting, or extreme activities, such as skydiving. Because these activities are typically associated with youth, undertaking them in older age is used as evidence of ongoing youth with headlines such as: 'What Dilys Price the 82-year-old skydiver can teach you about eternal youth' (Johnston, 2016). Such defiance of ageing (which is shown by its very newsworthiness to be anomalous) becomes a representation of what it means to age well and successfully. The concern is not the representation of these feats as possible but as normative. Gawande (2014) has critiqued these expectations by saying:

> We're always trotting out some story of a ninety-seven-year-old who runs marathons, as if such cases were not miracles of biological luck but reasonable expectations for all. Then, when our bodies fail to live up to this fantasy, we feel as if we somehow have something to apologize for. (Gawande, 2014: 28)

Harris et al. (2016) analysed a media video promoting maintenance of health in older age. Using a split screen comparison of a healthy older person alongside an unhealthy older person, they demonstrated that this video framed health as a simple choice. A lack of health in later life was viewed 'not as a normal part of life, but as an affliction brought about by a failure of will' (Harris et al., 2016: 383). Such media representations frame ageing successfully as resisting ageing itself so that older people are encouraged to identify with youth and vigour.

Successful ageing also includes financial preparation. Older people are exhorted to have bank accounts as 'healthy as they are' (Johnson, 2015) so that health and wealth are intertwined in the media representation of identity in later life. The media also represent older age as a time of leisure through promotion of international travel and luxury consumption (Ylänne-McEwen, 2000). Nussbaum and Coupland (2004: 238) refer to this representation as the 'golden years of a leisure-filled existence'. This leisure lifestyle is part of the story of what older age is able to offer the well-prepared. In the same way as health is presented as a virtuous choice, financial security is an important aspect of a successful ageing identity linked to rational economic decision making. Those who are unable to enjoy golden years of leisure and luxury are represented as having failed to prepare for later life.

The careful management of health and finances as one ages is framed as desirable not only for older people themselves but as beneficial for society as a whole in the context of population ageing (Harris et al., 2016). One online newspaper exhorted older people to: 'exercise more if they want to live longer and ensure they are not a burden on the already stretched public health system' (Torrie, 2013). Similarly, older people who make contributions to the economy through consumption or continued paid employment are constructed as valuable members of society (Wilinska and Cedersund, 2010), while those in poverty are represented as ill-prepared for later life and burdensome (Hurley et al., 2017). Older people who understand this responsibility to age well for the benefit of society describe self-care as a societal responsibility rather than selfish pursuit (Laliberte Rudman, 2015). In this context, individual achievement of health and wealth is valorised as a contribution to the general economy and wellbeing of all.

Although government policy accounts focus on later life as a positive opportunity and the media portray physically active and financially secure seniors enjoying life, this conflicts with alternative equally widespread discourses of later life as a time of dependency and vulnerability (Fealy et al., 2012). Ageing as decline and loss previously dominated policy and public representations of ageing. Although 'successful' ageing was conceived, in part, to counter such representations (Martinson and Halpern, 2011), both remain as alternative discourses and together shape media representation of later life (Rozanova, 2010). Older people can engage in health-promoting and age-defying activities to position themselves as ageing successfully or they can resist this version of ageing and be positioned by default as declining into dependency. Media representations alternate between these discursive possibilities, depicting both active and independent older people as flourishing and later life as a time of physical decline into dependency (Hodgetts et al., 2003). Successful ageing discourse suggests that older people are able to choose between these alternatives. Successful ageing is personified by 'the self-regulating old-but-youthful person who remains productive and maintains good health through the life course, thereby avoiding becoming a burden to others' (Harris et al., 2016: 378). Older people construct their identity based upon such accounts to negotiate a positive identity as the capable and useful older adult presented in policy discourse and reproduced in media accounts of successful ageing.

HOW DO SUCCESSFUL AGEING IDENTITIES FUNCTION?

A focus on the positive aspects of later life has promoted opportunities for older people to remain involved in their communities, to extend paid employment and contribute to voluntary organisations, and has increased expectations for a productive and healthy life beyond traditional retirement age. Although these identities appear to be a positive shift for older people from earlier expectations of ageing as decline and withdrawal, such positive identities are not equally available to all older people. The capability to identify as ageing successfully depends largely on maintaining mental and physical health and access to material and social resources. Older people rich in such resources can locate themselves firmly within a positive and valued ageing identity and, consequently, reap all the benefits of the shift to viewing ageing as a time of opportunity. Social science enquiry has contributed to critiques of the ways in which these discourses position older people in the twenty-first century in ways that can be oppressive and deny lifelong inequalities and the experiences of embodied ageing.

Ageing in a Material World

Attention to successful ageing implies that making good choices and having positive outcomes are equally possible for all older people (Holstein and Minkler, 2003). An emphasis on individual responsibility for health and independence neglects the social and physical conditions that may limit universal access to a healthy and engaged older age (Waitzkin et al., 1994). The ideal of successful ageing takes little account of lifelong inequalities and different opportunities for different groups of people to age successfully (Holstein and Minkler, 2003). Several authors (e.g., Estes et al., 2003; Minkler and Estes, 1999; Portacolone, 2011; Walker, 1981) have pointed to the broader influence of economic, political, and social processes on the health of older people. Age intersects with other inequalities, such as socioeconomic status (Victor, 2010), gender (Calasanti, 2007), and minority group status (Minkler, 1996), to shape health trajectories throughout life, and these inequalities are exacerbated in old age. In particular, successful ageing is most difficult for those older people who have experienced a lifetime of poor health and low wage insecure employment and, consequently, reach later life least physically and financially able to maintain their own wellbeing. Successful ageing policies ignore these inequalities and promote an ageing identity that is only attainable by a privileged few (Estes et al., 2003; Holstein and Minkler, 2003; Minkler and Estes, 1999; Portacolone, 2011). Such a narrow focus reinforces the social exclusion of marginalised older people who are unable to live up to the ideal of the active, healthy, and socially engaged older person (Ranzijn, 2010).

Poor, ill, and disconnected older people, as well as healthy, wealthy, and engaged older people, live in the same society which is shaped by social policy and media exhortations to age well. Thus, older people with low levels of living standards and poor health may be excluded from active participation, but they are not excluded from aspirations to age well. Breheny and Stephens (2010) found that older people with higher living standards acknowledged privilege but also took personal credit for being a virtuous older person looking forward to a secure future as a reward.

For example, one participant and interviewer worked together to develop a description of the future located firmly within discourses of successful ageing.

Interviewer: I would like, you know, to put your mind to the future, do you have any concerns as you grow older, or when you and your husband grow older?

Susan: No, I feel like I've lived a fairly privileged and satisfying life really. In that we have this home which is us, we've built it ourselves. We have a boat, up the road in a marina, we walk on we walk off, we sail, we kayak, I paint, I write, I have a private practice and do work I really enjoy, my husband and I are great friends, grandchildren and our children give us a lot of joy and my husband has brought me peace by giving my son security.

Interviewer: That's really optimistic when you are looking to the future that you've got all those (...). What about your own retirement and is your husband working?

Susan: My husband's been retired since he turned 50, although he has never worked so hard in his life, he has built me this house and developed the garden.

Interviewer: So do you have concerns about your own and your husband's health or financial security and stuff for the future. Are they issues for you?

Susan: No.

Interviewer: That's good. You have years to look forward to of more of the same, would that sound right?

Susan: Yes, more of the same and probably a lot more pleasant.

What was not foregrounded in this sort of talk was the financial security and structural advantage that supported their virtuous successful ageing. Participants who reported financial struggles and considerable health limitations also took responsibility for their circumstances and also talked about being positive. These lower income older people positioned themselves as good citizens through references to hard work, making good choices, and taking responsibility for their present situations. In an example of this sort of talk, a 65-year-old participant who lived in severe hardship described at various times a life of labour which has mis-shaped her spine, domestic abuse causing disability, and serious chronic illness. She finally said:

...I've got a heart murmur and I've got a chronic pulmonary disease in my lungs. That's my latest one. [Interviewer: Oh gosh.] But I'm fine.

Interviewer: But you're still very cheerful, that's nice. [Anna: Yeah.] That's really good and you've got a positive attitude.

Anna: There's people a lot worse off than me. When I look at my friend who is in the wheelchair through Agent Orange in Vietnam, there is nothing wrong with me. I just need to look at him and I realise how damn lucky I am.

Interviewer: Well you've got a lovely attitude and I think that's nice.

Anna: Thank you, well you've got to get by don't you.

This extract makes clear the interviewer's role in encouraging a positive attitude. Together, interviewee and interviewer position Anna as a virtuous older person despite poor health and economic circumstances. It could be argued that recourse to a positive attitude is indeed the virtuous solution to dealing with debilitating health problems in later life. However, Anna's focus on a positive attitude and 'getting by' supports social structures that reinforce disadvantage rather than challenging the underlying structures that promote inequalities. This story of being thankful in the context of considerable material disadvantage works to promote stoic attempts to cope with adversity rather than addressing the conditions that contribute to this situation. The analysis (see Breheny and Stephens, 2010) illustrated that although older people may be excluded from enjoying the material conditions on which a successful later life is built, they are not excluded from the impact of these dominant constructions of later life on their identity as older citizens.

The Imperative of Physical Health

Good health is central to a virtuous identity (Crawford, 2006), and within successful ageing discourse, good health is seen as the *product* of certain practices, rather than as a way of being generally well. Research with older people in New Zealand, Australia, and Canada has shown that many focus on diet, exercise, and mental stimulation as activities undertaken intentionally to promote health and defy an ageing body (Laliberte Rudman, 2015; Pond et al., 2010). They often described ageing in terms of what 'they 'should' be doing for fitness or health, such as walking or swimming, even though those things were not a part of their lives' (Burden, 1999: 32).

There are two main concerns about the effect of this focus on health. First, this talk includes a moral dimension in which people position themselves and others as virtuous or irresponsible depending on their body's condition and how well they engage in health-related practices. In other words, health promotion discourse leads to individual responsibility and blaming, and people feel ashamed of their ill health. These 'healthism' effects are already well recognised through the work of people like Crawford (2006) or Lupton (1995). Because the body itself has become a demonstration of virtuous ageing, older people who display good health and physical functioning can take pride in the condition of their body. For example, after describing his physical health and flexibility, a 77-year-old participant in a recent study summed up his good health by saying: 'I boast about it a lot and I'm entitled to'. The interviewer agreed: 'I know' (from Breheny and Stephens, 2017). This entitlement to pride in the condition of one's body in older age means that those whose bodies display age-related decline are ashamed. The effect is to blame the individual for failure to age successfully, while ignoring the complexities of life that impact on health (Waitzkin et al., 1994). Those experiencing embodied decline accept responsibility for their poor health. Older people in poor health or with mobility limitations may avoid going out in public to avoid displaying poor health or age-related decline (Breheny and Stephens, 2017).

The second effect of a focus on healthism is denial of ageing and death. While the focus of successful ageing discourse is on the maintenance of health and avoidance of decline, it is particularly difficult for older people to be subjected to these expectations of maintaining fitness because they are so much more likely to suffer disability or general loss of physical abilities due to ageing. There is no space within health promotion discourse for the effects of ageing itself on bodies and no recognition of the inevitability of death. The contradiction of these ideals and the actual reality of physical decline were beginning to be noticed by some study participants (Pond et al., 2010). One man who promoted his health through annual check-ups, healthy eating, growing fresh produce, and keeping fit had, nevertheless, recently noticed changes which caused him to express his sense of dissonance between health promotion advice and his own experience:

> I know that I'm not as strong as I used to be, even, although I consider I live an active life, you know, I'm out there planting trees and digging and chopping and sawing and I'm a bit concerned about whether I need to do more to look after my general fitness. I would have thought I shouldn't have to … I've often wondered whether I should start some kind of fitness regime along those lines but it's rather annoying when you've been out working all day and you come in physically tired and you still feel that you might need more exercise. It just doesn't quite add up somehow.

This man was disappointed that, despite being very active, his strength was declining. He was worried because health promotion advice would be to *increase* his physical activity. There is little mention of rest and relaxation in health promotion. Other participants expressed surprise when adherence to ideal health protective behaviour failed, and they felt betrayed by health promotion discourse. These were people who had followed all health promotion advice and *still* fell ill. They felt bewildered by the mismatch between their virtuous behaviour and poor health.

Furthermore, death is absent in successful ageing discourse. Harris et al. (2016) noted that, even in a video exhorting older people to live well in their last ten years, there is no mention of what exists at the end for those committed to making health last. Constructions of successful ageing deny the inevitably of death and construct a version of ageing in which people may never grow old (Powell and Biggs, 2004). Gawande (2014) argues that a failure to confront death underlies our inability to deal sensibly with ageing. Ironically, the absence of death from the story of successful ageing may make it more difficult for older people to age well. As people age, awareness of the proximity to death focuses attention on what they themselves value (Breheny and Stephens, 2017; Carstensen, 2006). The neglect of any recognition of physical decline and death in current ageing discourse promotes a radical new, and potentially disappointing, version of the meaning of being old.

A focus on maintaining physical health stigmatises the actual physical signs of ageing, undervalues the real experiences of growing old, and denies the complexity of gains and losses in older age. The dangers of such a pervasive influence on daily practice for older people may be found in suggestions that relentless activity and virtuous diets might allow us to live forever. This creates difficulties for those who are experiencing changes in energy and strength levels. Instead of resting a little as people age, they must engage in increasing levels of self-surveillance and discipline.

Maintaining Independence

Social policy and media accounts of ageing promote independence and self-reliance as the hallmark of successful ageing (Ranzijn, 2010; Rozanova, 2010). Many older people position themselves in terms of a self-reliant virtuous actor (Holstein and Minkler, 2003; Laliberte Rudman, 2006), and this may mean it is difficult for some older people to even imagine becoming dependent as they age (Smith et al., 2007). Positioning themselves as independent has implications for what older people can do, and particularly for their ability to ask for help and support (Ranzijn, 2010; Robertson, 1999). Older people may be strongly self-reliant, but the focus on avoidance of dependency may have negative consequences when older people face challenges for which they would benefit from support and care.

For some older people attempting to maintain an independent identity, accepting help can be worse than not meeting some everyday needs. For example, older people who were ill or disabled revealed these stances by saying:

> I won't let anyone help me. She [my friend] knew that I was in bed and she would come in and make me a cup of coffee and she'd say 'do you want to go and have a shower', 'I can do it thank you'; and when I get that tone people know leave her alone, let her fall over but leave her alone. (from Breheny and Stephens, 2012)

> Natasha said 'I'll come up once a fortnight and do your housework for you' but I can't have her coming up every fortnight without paying her and we're only on the pension because we smoke here I can't afford it. (from Breheny et al., 2014)

Maintaining an independent identity enables freedom to determine the arrangements of care and a sense of individual control over decision making, but these accounts demonstrate the weight of such freedom: refusing needed assistance from friends or family while taking responsibility for poverty. These extracts further demonstrate that an independent identity may be managed in ways that are potentially detrimental to physical capability. Physical capability is most difficult to achieve for older people who have experienced a lifetime of poor health and low wage insecure employment and, consequently, reach later life least physically and financially able to maintain their independence. Denied other claims to successful ageing, such older people may yet manage an independent identity through refusal to accept help. In this way, dependence and independence are not bodily states but social identities (Fine and Glendinning, 2005).

The promotion of independence also has implications for relationships of care. In the context of exhortations to remain independent, older people may resist care and support, as they fear becoming a burden on others as they age (Kemp and Denton, 2003; Portacolone, 2011). Many will become unavoidably less able to manage on their own and may be at risk of avoiding help seeking or legitimate social support. For example, one participant responded to a question about moving closer to his sister by saying:

> No. I mean the only reason you'd do that is if you were really ill and then you'd be a burden. The opposite if anything. (from Breheny and Stephens, 2012)

This sort of response can be understood in terms of the absence of any valued identity as the recipient of care in older age. Seeking and accepting help can be viewed as maintaining connectedness between people (Fine and Glendinning 2005), which acknowledges their fundamental interdependence (Robertson, 1999). Rather than focusing on dependence as linked with decline and disengagement, interdependence may be constructed as part of reciprocity and connectedness throughout life.

PARTICIPATION IN SOCIETY

One of the main expectations of an actively participating member of society is that they should help others (Martinez et al., 2011), and for older people, this is often understood in terms of 'volunteering'. Martinson and Halpern (2011) have noted the recent focus of active ageing policy discourse on volunteering and civic engagement. Although social policy may now emphasise volunteering, it is not a new idea, and older people are often keen to participate or see themselves as important providers in the community (e.g., Heenan, 2010). Many older people want to contribute to their communities in various ways, such as providing financial and practical support to family and friends, through charitable donations, and by formal volunteering (Stephens et al., 2015a). They described these roles as a community service and as a pleasure, often in terms of what they themselves gained from the experience. Volunteering fosters a sense of belonging, increased self-worth and enjoyment (Townsend et al., 2014), and offers opportunities for generativity (Narushima, 2005). Volunteering has also been shown to have many positive health effects for volunteers (Anderson et al., 2014). Although people have various motives for volunteering (Narushima, 2005), it appears that the altruistic aspect of volunteering is particularly beneficial (Anderson et al., 2014). A key way in which the social function and the benefits of helping others have been theorised is in terms of reciprocity.

Reciprocity is often understood simply as a social exchange of benefits, with each party expecting some return; however, Gouldner (1960) also pointed to reciprocity as a moral norm. Thompson (2013) has drawn upon this socially based theorising to understand reciprocity in terms of socially constructed identities. Moral values such as social obligation and returning benefits to society, being able to give something back, are often reported as motives for volunteering (see Stephens et al., 2015b). Those who are not able to contribute may feel a burden on others, which is an uncomfortable moral position given the moral norm of reciprocity. Thus, social contribution provides a positive identity for those in later life through a sense of fulfilling reciprocal obligations of return for both past and future benefits.

Walker (2008) has critiqued the ways that an active ageing approach to social policy now focuses on the ideals of productive contribution. Once volunteering becomes part of these wider discourses of productivity and is related, through norms of reciprocity, to the worth of all older people in society, then we must raise concerns about those who cannot contribute in this way. Although volunteering has been shown to be especially beneficial to those with lower incomes (Dulin et al., 2012; Morrow-Howell et al., 2009), not all people are able to volunteer, and this is particularly true for people of low socioeconomic status. Research also shows that disadvantaged people do not have the same opportunities to volunteer as wealthier people do (Tang et al., 2010; Warburton et al., 2004). The reasons for lack of participation by members of lower socioeconomic groups may be found in a common set of barriers: poor health, disability, lack of transportation, and finances (e.g., Stephens et al., 2015b; Warburton, et al., 2004). Furthermore, structural and material exclusion from participation has been shown to lead to wider social exclusion. While noting the importance of reciprocity to the maintenance of social integration and social ties, Offer (2012) has described the way in which inability to reciprocate among low income families leads to lack of social integration and withdrawal from community involvement. Thus, the lack of ability to contribute in various ways leads to further withdrawal from community activities, and having few resources to contribute means that older people are often excluded from social exchanges (Komter, 1996). Older people must work harder to maintain an identity as a contributing citizen, and those with fewer resources are even less able to meet the ideal of the contributing active older person (Martinson and Halpern, 2011). The moral norm of reciprocity is highlighted by current active ageing policies, which include a focus on contribution and volunteering, but this becomes a psychological burden when people are unable to reciprocate:

> I feel I'm useless. I can't do anything for anybody now. I couldn't even go and help a neighbour out you know because I just can't see. (...) I'm no use now. (Grace, age 88, from Mansvelt, 2017)

Even for those older people able, and willing, to contribute in this way, declining health often means that identities such as 'able contributor' cannot be sustained as they age. If a society highlights moral obligations to participate and, in particular, to volunteer time to others without support for that engagement, it further oppresses those who are already unable to live up to the ideals of successful ageing.

THE PROBLEMS OF SUCCESSFUL AGEING

Paying attention to the construction of ageing identities within successful ageing discourse alerts us to three overarching problems. These are the homogenising and oppressive nature of ideologies of successful ageing, the moral positioning of older people within ageing discourses, and the suppression of other possible ageing identities.

First, successful ageing discourse constructs older people as a homogenous group. In talking about 'older people' as a population group to be studied, we tend to forget that 'age' is only about number of years lived, and people of older age are as diverse as everybody else in all other ways. Health and wellbeing levels differ, and these are related to differences in social class, race, ethnicity, gender, education level, and material wealth or deprivation. In the twenty-first century, as people live longer and life choices are broader, this diversity continues to increase. Furthermore, most research on the experience of ageing has focused on white, middle-class older people in developed countries (Dupuis and Alzheimer, 2008). Older people from many minority groups, those living in poverty, and those living in less developed areas of the world are not accounted for.

Second, people construct their identity on the basis of understandings of older age as an individual project of healthy activities and contribution to community (Ekerdt and Koss, 2016). These dominant discourses of ageing shape understandings of appropriate activities for a virtuous older person in today's society (Laliberte Rudman, 2006). These discourses become part of a moral imperative to spend time in later life on 'keeping fit' as well as 'giving back' (see Dorfman, 2013). These moralising discourses about how one should spend one's time become a psychological burden when people are unable to stay well, participate, or contribute. In a neoliberal milieu, those who age successfully appear to do so on their own merits, while those who fail to age well must struggle to be recognised as good citizens.

A third problem is that a dominant discourse of successful ageing (with allied discourses of productive, healthy, and active ageing) suppresses other discourses of ageing. There are alternative discourses which provide differently valued identities. For example, discourses of 'time' acknowledge that time is limited and thus support pursuing pleasure in later life (Breheny and Stephens, 2017). Other discourses position later life as a time of contemplation, spirituality, or rest (Martinson, 2006). The dominance of current constructions of ageing drives alternative discourses, such as care, respect for elders, or preparation for death, as appropriate aspects of ageing, into the background. Many older people are working hard to attain the ideals of fitness and active contribution despite changing needs, while those who fail to conform to the successful ageing ideal may be reproached and disdained by those (young or old) who can display healthy and flexible bodies.

ALTERNATIVE FRAMEWORKS FOR UNDERSTANDING AGEING

Current policy versions of successful ageing are not ultimately concerned with what older people value but what makes older people *of value*. To achieve a well-supported and well-resourced older age, ageing policy needs to 'go beyond promoting the self-reliance of older people surviving alone in their own homes and aim to promote community responsibility for socially and emotionally rewarding lives in old age' (Plath, 2002: 46). This will involve a shift from identifying all older people in terms of the physical changes that older people may experience (Grenier, 2005; Wiles, 2011). Reductions in physical capability need not be associated with an identity as dependent and burdensome. Examining older people's talk about later life experiences and their own valued activities suggests that a broader conceptualisation of wellbeing is required to address the problems created by 'successful ageing' policies. This conceptualisation needs to include the voices of older people who struggle to meet expectations for 'successful' ageing and pay more attention to the role of enabling environments that will support improvements in wellbeing for all.

Sen's (1987) capability approach provides a framework for this broader conceptualisation of ageing well that can inform both research and social change. The capability approach focuses on a person's 'capability' or the extent to which they are able to function in ways that they value. This conceptualisation is able to include the reality of embodied ageing and the social location of older people's lives. 'Capability' describes the level of peoples' freedom to pursue the lives that they themselves have reason to value and focuses on the aspects of their environment that prevent valued functioning in these ways (Sen, 1992; 1993). Paying attention to capability is particularly important for understanding the wellbeing of older people who have different levels of physical capacity as they age (Stephens and Breheny, 2018). Rather than drawing upon normative definitions that reproduce dominant discourses in which physical health, independence, and productivity are produced by individuals, the capability approach focuses on the needs of older people themselves.

In practice, this means that, rather than inquiring about levels of particular predefined attributes of success, people assess their freedom to achieve their own valued functionings. For example, Venkatapuram (2011) argues that health may be seen as the capability to achieve a cluster of connected capabilities, like the capability to be warm, or to be secure, to attend social gatherings, or enjoy customary pleasures. Stephens et al. (2015a) demonstrated the use of a capability approach to identify a cluster of such connected capabilities valued by older people. Similarly, Grewal et al. (2006), analysed data from interviews with older people in the UK to identify five important attributes of quality of life. They identified the capability to achieve valued functionings of attachment, role, enjoyment, security, and control as markers of quality of life. Anand and van Hees (2006) also assessed wellbeing using a capability perspective to shift the perspective from individual achievement. Rather than inquiring about levels of actual social participation, or quality of the environment, participants assessed their levels of choice in these areas.

Focusing on a person's capability, or the extent to which they are able to function in ways that they value, shifts the ways in which we generally talk about ageing and wellbeing from a focus on all older people remaining young and fit to recognising the values of older people in their actual circumstances (Stephens, 2017). From a capabilities perspective, physical health is not a commodity that people are responsible for maintaining, but a valued functioning that depends upon supportive resources provided in communities (Sen, 1992; 1993). The social and physical environment is viewed as integral to the experience of ageing.

Using this approach, we can be critical of policy that encourages physical and relational independence and naturalises self-reliance. Drawing on Sen's recognition of supportive environments and communities, ageing policy could equally address demographic ageing by increasing support for community members to care for one another (Horrell et al., 2015; Portacolone, 2011). The presence of a range of sources of support enables older people to view themselves as navigating supportive communities rather than experiencing dependence (Hammarström and Torres, 2010). Viewing care in terms of interdependence and autonomy provides broader support for older people and their carers and may assist in providing appropriate material and community support for members of an ageing population, many of whom will face some degree of decline and need. Supportive communities should also include positive identities for older people who experience limitations and frailties, not just for older people capable of reproducing normative expectations for active and successful ageing.

Sen's capability approach provides the basis for distancing our construction of the wellbeing of older people from the oppressive ideals of individual responsibility and from the denial of physical ageing. The capability approach is a socially based and ethically oriented way to understand the wellbeing of older people which has the potential to address the critiques summarised above. It frames people's wellbeing in terms of their capability to function in the ways that they value. In doing so, this framework focuses on social rather than individual responsibility for health, on wellbeing rather than healthism, and allows for freedom rather than oppression (Stephens and Breheny, 2018). The capability approach shifts our understandings of the basis of wellbeing among older people to their social and environmental context by considering people's freedom to make valued choices. Differences in the capacity to choose the life that is valued reflect structurally produced access to lifelong advantage or disadvantage. Because the dominant discourses which underpin research and social policy have powerful effects, the adoption of this approach can influence the way in which ageing is constructed by all, including older people themselves.

Shifting from a focus on personal responsibility to age successfully, with its moral implications, to recognition of the impact of the social and material context on wellbeing, will enable all older people to age well within supportive environments that account for differences in capability. From a capabilities perspective, policy and intervention would focus on promoting a valued social identity for all elders, regardless of their physical health, level of reliance on others, or capacity to contribute. Sen's capability approach is a theoretical approach to social justice as well as a field of praxis and a framework for social change. It suggests the development of understanding what people actually value, followed by support from the whole of society to enable older people to maintain a valued identity and participate in ways that are valued in their society.

REFERENCES

Anand, P., & Van Hees, M. (2006). Capabilities and achievements: An empirical study. *The Journal of Socio-Economics, 35*(2), 268–284.

Anderson, N. D., Damianakis, T., Kröger, E., Wagner, L. M., Dawson, D. R., Binns, M., Bernstein, S., Caspi, E., & Cook, S. L. (2014). The benefits associated with volunteering among seniors: A critical review and recommendations for future research. *Psychological Bulletin, 140*(6), 1505–1533.

Ayo, N. (2012). Understanding health promotion in a neoliberal climate and the making of health conscious citizens. *Critical Public Health, 22*(1), 99–105.

Beck, U., & Beck-Gernsheim, E. (2002). *Individualization: Institutionalized individualism and its social and political consequences*. London: Sage.

Bell, K., & Green, J. (2016). On the perils of invoking neoliberalism in public health critique, *Critical Public Health, 26*(3), 239–243.

Biggs, S. (2001). Toward critical narrativity: Stories of aging in contemporary social policy. *Journal of Aging Studies, 15*, 303–316.

Biggs, S. (2005). Beyond appearances: perspectives on identity in later life and some implications for method. *Journals of Gerontology: Psychological Sciences and Social Sciences, 60B*(3), S118–S128.

Biggs, S., McGann, M., Bowman, D., & Kimberley, H. (2017). Work, health and the commodification of life's time: Reframing work–life balance and the promise of a long life. *Ageing and Society, 37*(7), 1458–1483.

Binstock, R. H. (2010). From compassionate ageism to intergenerational conflict? *The Gerontologist, 50*(5), 574–585.

Blaikie, A. (1999). *Ageing and popular culture*. Cambridge: Cambridge University Press.

Breheny, M., & Stephens, C. (2010). Ageing in a material world. *New Zealand Journal of Psychology, 39*, 41–48.

Breheny, M., & Stephens, C. (2012). Negotiating a moral identity in the context of later life care. *Journal of Aging Studies, 26*, 438–447.

Breheny, M., & Stephens, C. (2017). Spending time: The discursive construction of leisure in later life. *Annals of Leisure Research, 20*(1), 39–54.

Breheny, M., Stephens, C., & Mansvelt, J. (2014). 'That's life isn't it': Investigating inequalities in older age. In M. Roche, J. Mansvelt, R. Prince, & A. Gallagher (Eds), *Engaging Geographies: Landscapes, Life Courses, and Mobilities (pp. 101–116)*. Newcastle upon Tyne: Cambridge Scholars Publishing.

Burden, J. (1999). Leisure as process and change: What do older people say? *Annals of Leisure Research, 2*(1), 28–43.

Cacioppo, J. T., Cacioppo, S., Capitanio, J. P., & Cole, S. W. (2015). The neuroendocrinology of social isolation. *Annual Review of Psychology, 66*(1). 733–767.

Calasanti, T. (2007). Bodacious berry, potency wood and the aging monster: Gender and age relations in anti-aging ads. *Social Forces, 86*(1), 335–355.

Carstensen, L. L. (2006). The influence of a sense of time on human development. *Science, 312*(5782), 1913–1915.

Coburn, D. (2000). Income inequality, social cohesion and the health status of populations: The role of neo-liberalism. *Social Science & Medicine, 51*, 135–146.

Crawford, R. (1980). Healthism and the medicalization of everyday life. *International Journal of Health Services. 10*(3), 365–388.

Crawford, R. (2006). Health as a meaningful social practice. *Health, 10*(4), 401–420.

Dorfman, L. T. (2013). Leisure activities in retirement. In M. Wang (Ed.), *The Oxford handbook of retirement* (pp. 339–353). New York: Oxford University Press.

Dulin, P. L., Gavala, J., Stephens, C., Kostick, M., & McDonald, J. (2012). Volunteering predicts happiness among older Maori and non-Maori in the New Zealand health, work, and retirement longitudinal study. *Aging & Mental Health, 16*(5), 617–624.

Dupuis, S. L., & Alzheimer, M. (2008). Leisure and ageing well. *World Leisure Journal, 50*(2), 91–107.

Ekerdt, D. J, & Koss, C. (2016). The task of time in retirement. *Ageing and Society, 36*, 1295–1311.

Estes, C. L. (1979). *The aging enterprise*. Michigan: Jossey-Bass Publishers.

Estes, C. L., Biggs, S., & Phillipson, C. (2003). *Social theory, social policy and ageing: A critical introduction*. Maidenhead: Open University Press.

Fealy, G., McNamara, M., Treacy, M. P., & Lyons, I. (2012). Constructing ageing and age identities: A case study of newspaper discourses. *Ageing & Society, 32*(1), 85–102.

Fine, M., & Glendinning, C. (2005). Dependence, independence or inter-dependence? Revisiting the concepts of 'care' and 'dependency'. *Ageing & Society, 25*, 601–621.

Gawande, A. (2014). *Being mortal: Illness, medicine and what matters in the end*. Profile Books. Kindle Edition.

Gouldner, A. W. (1960). The norm of reciprocity: A preliminary statement. *American Sociological Review, 25*(2), 161–178.

Grenier, A. M. (2005). The contextual and social locations of older women's experiences of disability and decline. *Journal of Aging Studies, 19*(2), 131–146.

Grewal, I., Lewis, J., Flynn, T., Brown, J. Bond, J., & Coast, J. (2006). Developing attributes for a generic quality of life measure for older people: Preferences or capabilities? *Social Science & Medicine, 62*, 1891–1901.

Hammarström, G., & Torres, S. (2010). Being, feeling and acting: A qualitative study of Swedish home-help care recipients' understandings of dependence and independence. *Journal of Aging Studies, 24*(2), 75–87.

Harré, R., & Gillett, G. (1994). *The discursive mind*. London: Sage.

Harris, R., Wathen, C. N., Macgregor, J. C. D., Dennhardt, S., Naimi, A., & Ellis, K. S. (2016). Blaming the flowers for wilting: Idealized aging in a health charity video. *Qualitative Health Research, 26*(3), 377–386.

Heenan, D. (2010). Social capital and older people in farming communities. *Journal of Aging Studies, 24*(1), 40–46.

Henricksen, A., & Stephens, C. (2010). An exploration of the happiness-enhancing activities engaged in by older adults. *Ageing International, 35*, 311–326.

Hodgetts, D., Chamberlain, K., & Bassett, G. (2003). Between television and the audience: Negotiating representations of aging. *Health, 7*, 417–438.

Holstein, M. B., & Minkler, M. (2003). Self, society and the 'new gerontology'. *The Gerontologist, 43*, 787–796.

Holt-Lunstad, J., Smith, T., & Layton, J. B. (2010) Social relationships and mortality risk: a meta-analytic review, *PLoS Medicine, 7*(7), e1000316.

Horrell, B., Stephens, C., & Breheny, M. (2015). Capability to care: Supporting the health of informal caregivers of older people. *Health Psychology, 34*(4), 339–348.

Hudson, R. B., & Gonyea, J. G. (2012). Baby Boomers and the shifting political construction of old age. *Gerontologist, 52*(2), 272–282.

Hurley, K., Breheny, M., & Tuffin, K. (2017). Intergenerational inequity arguments and the implications for state-funded financial support of older people. *Ageing & Society, 37*(3), 561–580.

Johnson, G. (2015). *Super seniors face danger of outliving their savings*. Retrieved from http://www.theglobeandmail.com/globe-investor/retirement/retire-planning/

super-seniors-in-danger-of-outliving-their-savings/article27302767/

Johnston, J. (2016). *'I can't imagine life without it!' What Dilys Price the 82-year-old skydiver can teach you about eternal youth*. Retrieved from http://www.dailymail.co.uk/femail/article-3617026/I-t-imagine-life-without-Dilys-Price-82-year-old-skydiver-teach-eternal-youth.html

Katz, S. (2000). Busy bodies: Activity, aging and the management of everyday life. *Journal of Aging Studies*, *14*, 135–152.

Katz, S., & Marshall, B. (2003). New sex for old: Lifestyle, consumerism, and the ethics of aging well. *Journal of Aging Studies*, *17*(1), 3–16.

Kemp, C. L., & Denton, M. (2003). The allocation of responsibility for later life: Canadian reflections on the roles of individual, government, employers and families. *Ageing & Society*, *23*, 737–760.

Komter, A. E. (1996). Reciprocity as a principle of exclusion: Gift giving in the Netherlands. *Sociology*, *30*, 299–316.

Laliberte Rudman, D. L. (2006). Shaping the active, autonomous and responsible modern retiree: An analysis of discursive technologies and their links with neo-liberal political rationality. *Ageing & Society*, *26*(2), 181–201.

Laliberte Rudman, D. (2015). Embodying positive aging and neoliberal rationality: Talking about the aging body within narratives of retirement. *Journal of Aging Studies*, *34*, 10–20.

Lupton, D. (1995). *The imperative of health: Public health and the regulated body*. London: Sage.

MacKean, R., & Abbot-Chapman, J. (2012). Older people's perceived health and wellbeing: The contribution of peer-run community organisation. *Health Sociology Review*, *21*(1), 47–57.

Mansvelt, J. (2017). Reciprocity in uncertain times: Negotiating giving and receiving across time and place among older New Zealanders. In A. Ince, & S. M. Hall (Eds), *Sharing economies in times of crisis: Practices, politics and possibilities*. (pp. 50-65). Abingdon: Routledge

Martin, R., Williams, C., & O'Neill, D. (2009). Retrospective analysis of attitudes to ageing in the Economist: Apocalyptic demography for opinion formers? *BMJ*, *339*, b4914.

Martinez, I. L., Crooks, D., Kim, K. S., & Tanner, E. (2011). Invisible civic engagement among older adults: Valuing the contributions of informal volunteering. *Journal of Cross Cultural Gerontology*, *26*, 23–37.

Martinson, M. (2006). Opportunities or obligations? Civic engagement and older adults. *Generations*, *4*, 59–65.

Martinson, M., & Halpern, J. (2011). Ethical implications of the promotion of elder volunteerism: A critical perspective. *Journal of Aging Studies*, *25*, 427–435.

Minkler, M. (1996). Critical perspectives on ageing: New challenges for gerontology. *Ageing & Society*, *16*, 467–487.

Minkler, M., & Estes, C. L. (1999). Critical gerontology: Perspectives from political and moral economy. Amityville, NY: Baywood.

Morrow-Howell, N., Hong, S. I., & Tang, F. (2009). Who benefits from volunteering? Variations in perceived benefit. *Gerontologist*, *49*(1), 91–102.

Narushima, M. (2005). 'Payback time': community volunteering among older adults as a transformative mechanism. *Ageing and Society*, *25*(4), 567–584.

Nussbaum, J. F., & Coupland, J. (Eds) (2004). *Handbook of communication and aging research* (2nd edn.). Mahwah, NJ: Lawrence Erlbaum Associates.

Offer, S. (2012). The burden of reciprocity: Processes of exclusion and withdrawal from personal networks among low-income families. *Current Sociology*, *60*, 788–805.

Petersen, A. R. (1996). Risk and the regulated self: The discourse of health promotion as politics of uncertainty. *Journal of Sociology*, *32*, 44–57.

Plath, D. (2002). Independence in old age: shifting meanings in Australian social policy. *Just Policy: A Journal of Australian Social Policy*, *26*, 40–47.

Pond, R., Stephens, C., & Alpass, F. (2010). Virtuously watching one's health: Older adults' regulation of self in the pursuit of health. *Journal of Health Psychology*, *15*(5), 734–743.

Portacolone, E. (2011). The myth of independence for older Americans living alone in the Bay Area of San Francisco: A critical reflection. *Ageing & Society*, *31*, 803–828.

Powell, J. L. (2001). Theorizing gerontology: The case of old age, professional power, and social policy in the United Kingdom. *Journal of Aging and Identity*, *6*, 117–135.

Powell, J. L., & Biggs, S. (2004). Ageing, technologies of self and bio-medicine: A Foucauldian excursion. *International Journal of Sociology and Social Policy*, *24*(6), 17–29.

Ranzijn, R. (2010). Active ageing – Another way to oppress marginalized and disadvantaged elders? Aboriginal elders as a case study. *Journal of Health Psychology*, *15*, 716–723.

Robertson, A. (1999). Beyond apocalyptic demography: Toward a moral economy of interdependence. In M. Minkler, & C. L. Estes (Eds.), *Critical gerontology: Perspectives from political and moral economy* (pp. 75–90). New York: Baywood.

Rowe, J. W., & Kahn, R. L. (1997). Successful aging. *The Gerontologist*, *37*, 433–440.

Rozanova, J. (2010). Discourse of successful aging in The Globe and Mail: Insights from critical gerontology. *Journal of Aging Studies*, *24*, 213–222.

Schneider, A., & Ingram, H. (1993). The social construction of target populations. *American Political Science Review*, *87*, 334–347.

Sen, A. (1987). *The standard of living (the Tanner lectures)*. G. Hawthorne (Ed.). Cambridge: Cambridge University Press.

Sen, A. (1992). *Inequality re-examined*. New York, NY: Russell Sage Foundation.

Sen, A. (1993). Capability and well-being. In M. C. N. A. Sen (Ed.), *The quality of life* (pp. 30–53). Oxford: Clarendon Press.

Smith, J. A., Braunack-Mayer, A., Wittert, G., & Warin, M. (2007). 'I've been independent for so damn long!': Independence, masculinity and aging in a help seeking context. *Journal of Aging Studies*, *21*, 325–335.

Somers, M. R., & Block, F. (2005). From poverty to perversity: Ideas, markets, and institutions over 200 years of welfare debate. *American Sociological Review*, *70*(2), 260–287.

Stenner, P., McFarquhar, T, & Bowling, A. (2011). Older people and 'active ageing': Subjective aspects of ageing actively. *Journal of Health Psychology*, *16*(3), 467–477.

Stephens, C. (2017). From success to capability for healthy ageing: Shifting the lens to include all older people. *Critical Public Health*, *27*(4), 490–498.

Stephens, C., & Breheny, M. (2018). *Healthy ageing: A capability approach to inclusive policy and practice.* London: Routledge.

Stephens, C., Breheny, M., & Mansvelt, J. (2015a). Healthy ageing from the perspective of older people: A capability approach to resilience. *Psychology and Health*, *30*(6), 715–731.

Stephens, C., Breheny, M., & Mansvelt, J. (2015b). Volunteering as reciprocity: Beneficial and harmful effects of social policies to encourage contribution in older age. *Journal of Aging Studies*, *33*, 22–27.

Tang, F., Morrow-Howell, N., & Choi, E. (2010). Why do older adult volunteers stop volunteering? *Ageing & Society*, *30*(5), 859–878.

Thompson, S. (2013). Reciprocity and old age. In *Reciprocity and dependency in old age* (pp. 35–65). New York: Springer.

Torrie, B. (2013). *Exercise more and live longer, elderly urged.* Retrieved from http://www.stuff.co.nz/national/health/8243478/Exercise-more-and-live-longer-elderly-urged.

Townsend, P. (1981). The structured dependency of the elderly: A creation of social policy in the twentieth century. *Ageing & Society*, *1*(1), 5–28.

Townsend, P. (1986). Ageism and social policy. In C. Phillipson, & A. Walker (Eds.), *Ageing and social policy* (pp. 15–44). London: Gower.

Townsend, M., Gibbs, L., Macfarlane, S., Block, K., Staiger, P., Gold, L., Johnson, B., & Long, C. (2014). Volunteering in a school kitchen garden program: Cooking up confidence, capabilities, and connections. *Voluntas*, *25*(1), 225–247.

Venkatapuram, S. (2011). *Health justice: An argument from the capabilities approach.* Cambridge: Polity.

Vernon, S. (2015). *7 pillars of successful ageing.* CBS News. Retrieved from http://www.cbsnews.com/news/7-pillars-to-successful-aging/

Victor, C. R. (2010). *Ageing, health and care.* Bristol: The Policy Press.

Waitzkin, H., Britt, T., & Williams, C. (1994). Narratives of aging and social problems in medical encounters with older persons. *Journal of Health and Social Behavior*, *35*, 322–348.

Walker, A. (1981). Towards a political economy of old age. *Ageing and Society*, *1*, 73–94.
Walker, A. (2008). Commentary: The emergence and application of active aging in Europe. *Journal of Aging & Social Policy*, *21*, 75–93.
Warburton, J., Oppenheimer, M., & Zappala, G. (2004). Marginalizing Australia's volunteers: The need for socially inclusive practices in the non-profit sector. *Australian Journal on Volunteering*, *9*(1), 33–40.
Wearing, B. (1995). Leisure and resistance in an ageing society. *Leisure Studies*, *14*(4), 263–279.
Wiles, J. (2011). Reflections on being a recipient of care: Vexing the concept of vulnerability. *Social & Cultural Geography*, *12*(6), 573–588.
Wilinska, M., & Cedersund, E. (2010). 'Classic ageism' or 'brutal economy'? Old age and older people in the Polish media. *Journal of Aging Studies*, *24*(4), 335–343.
World Health Organization. (2002). *Active Ageing: a policy framework*. Retrieved from http://whqlibdoc.who.int/hq/2002/who_nmh_nph_02.8.pdf
World Health Organization. (2012). *Aging and life course: Interesting facts about ageing*. Retrieved from http://www.who.int/ageing/about/facts/en/
Ylänne-McEwen, V. (2000). Golden times for golden agers: Selling holidays as lifestyle for the over 50s. *Journal of Communication*, *50*(3), 83–99.

18

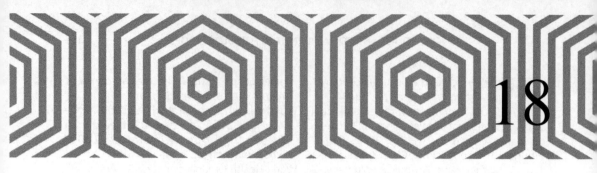

Successful Ageing and Community

Wendy Wen Li and Alma Au

INTRODUCTION: WORLD POPULATION AGEING

The United Nations' report *World Ageing Population 2015* points out that the number of older people (namely, those aged 60 years or over) has increased considerably in recent years in most countries and regions. Moreover, this growth is projected to accelerate in the coming decades. Between 2015 and 2030, the number of older people in the world is projected to grow by 56%, from 901 million to 1.4 billion. It is projected that by 2050 the global population of older people will double in size from 2015, reaching nearly 2.1 billion. Globally, the number of the 'oldest-old' people (namely, those aged 80 years or over; United Nations, 2015a) has risen faster than the number of older people overall. In 2015, there were 125 million people aged 80 years or over. It is projected that in 2050 the number of oldest-old persons will reach 434 million, which would be triple the 2015 number.

The trend of population ageing is clearly demonstrated in developed countries, such as the United States, Australia and New Zealand. In the United States, there were 43.1 million people aged over 65 years in 2013. As a result, older people constituted 13.7% of the US population, which is roughly one in every seven Americans (Administration on Aging, 2014). Due to the ageing of the 'baby boomers' (who were born approximately between the years 1946 and 1964; Li and Jackson, 2016), the older population is projected to rapidly increase in coming years. By 2040, the number of older people is expected to reach 79.7 million, which is a rise of 21% (Cummings and Trecartin, 2016). Australia's population is projected to increase from 21.5 million in 2011 to between 36.8 and 48.3 million by 2061 (Australian Bureau of Statistics, 2013a). By 2061, the age structure of the population is expected to significantly change (Li and Jackson, 2016). In 2011, three million people were aged 65 years and over, a number that is projected to grow to between nine million and 11.1 million in 2061 (Australian Bureau of Statistics, 2013a). In 2013, the number of people aged over 75 years represented 6.4% of the national population. By 2060, that group is expected to constitute 14.4% of the population (Productivity Commission, 2013). Similarly in New Zealand, older adults also constitute a significant proportion of the population (Park and Adamson, 2016). In 2013, there were 607,032 people aged 65 or over, accounting for 14.3% of all New Zealanders (Statistics New Zealand, 2014). The number of older people is projected to more than double between 2015 and 2050, constituting more than one-quarter of the New Zealand national population (Park and Adamson, 2016). By 2050, the number of the oldest-old group is expected to more than quadruple from 73,317 in 2013 to over a quarter of a million by 2050 (Statistics New Zealand, 2006).

Putting the developed world aside, countries such as China, India and Uganda have also experienced significant population ageing. China has one of the most ageing societies and also has the largest elderly population in the world (Li et al., 2016). The 2010 Census indicated that the total population of China was nearly 1.4 billion. In 2010, the number of people aged 60 and over was 178 million, constituting 13.3% of the national population. There were 119 million people aged 65 years and older, accounting for 8.9% of the population. In addition, 16.6% of the population were under 15 years old, which is a decrease of 23% from 2000. Meanwhile, the number of people in the age group of 60 and over increased by 2.9% over the same period (National Bureau of Statistics of China, 2011). India is the world's second most populated country after China, with an estimated population of 1.21 billion in 2011. The overall population in India is estimated to grow 55% by 2050, and the population aged 60 years and above is projected to increase by 26% (Ponnuswami and Udhayakumar, 2016). Uganda has a differing population age structure compared to the aforementioned countries: only 5% of Uganda's 24.2 million people were aged 60 years and above and 50% were under 15 years old in 2002. However, the ageing population has increased by nearly 1% from 4.1% in 1991, which suggests that the elderly population in Uganda is growing quickly. It is projected that the number of people aged 60 years and above in Uganda will double to three million in less than ten years (Kyaddondo, 2016).

Population ageing around the world has stimulated intense debates regarding whether ageing is a risk or an opportunity. From a negative viewpoint, some believe that population ageing is the 'greying of humanity'; a threat to world budgets that may bring a worldwide economic crisis (Socolovsky, 2002). However, many argue that ageing should be celebrated and viewed from a positive perspective. This positive perspective maintains that older people have skills, knowledge and experience and can make valuable contributions to society. One of the most influential concepts that promotes the positive perspective of ageing is successful ageing (DiPietro et al., 2012; Eyler et al., 2011; Provencher et al., 2014; Rowe and Kahn, 1997 Vance, 2012; Verny et al., 2015). The concept of successful ageing challenges the stigmatic view associated with old age, a view that regards older adults as a burden on society. It acknowledges that older people can function at a high level both cognitively and socially, and make a great contribution to society.

A REVIEW OF THE CONCEPTS OF BIOLOGICAL AND COGNITIVE SUCCESSFUL AGEING

From the 1950s to the early 1980s, research in ageing had a longstanding emphasis on biological losses in older persons, and normality was the key concept in gerontology studies (Rowe and Kahn, 1987). These studies considered that normal ageing referred to minimal physiological loss, the absence of disease and disability or other age-related changes to physical functions. The concept of normal ageing implies that older people with decline in the capacity to metabolise a glucose load, lower bone density and impaired cognitive function (which are the results of the biological change when people age) cannot age successfully (Vaillant and Mukamal, 2001). At this time, people who did not fit in the definition of normal ageing were labelled by gerontologists as abnormal (Tornstam, 1992) or maladjusted (Lynott & Lynott, 1996).

This strong emphasis on high functioning and capacity in older people is manifested in Rowe and Kahn's (1987) successful ageing model. In their seminal study 'Human aging: Usual and successful aging', published in *Science*, Rowe and Kahn (1987) proposed that research on successful ageing should focus on people who have above average physiological and psychosocial characteristics in their later life. Rowe and Kahn categorised these people as 'successful agers' as opposed to 'usual agers' (Lupien and Wan, 2004). Rowe and Kahn's definition of successful ageing includes three main components – 'low probability of disease and disease-related disability, high cognitive and physical functional capacity, and active engagement with life" (Rowe and Kahn, 1997: 433). Figure 18.1 illustrates Rowe and Kahn's model of successful ageing.

In Rowe and Kahn's model, low probability of disease is associated with minimal changes and even absence of disease and of risk factors for disease. High functional level refers to physical and cognitive capacities for activities. Active engagement with life includes interpersonal relations and productive activity (Rowe and Kahn, 1997). This model has been popular in ageing studies. Many of the later models of successful ageing have been developed based on Rowe and Kahn's model (DiPietro et al., 2012).

One of the newer approaches is the *successful cognitive ageing model*. Successful cognitive ageing focuses on successful brain ageing instead of the traditional focus on neuropathological cognitive defects (Verny et al., 2015). Successful brain ageing is concerned with enhancing brain capacity to prevent the loss of information processing capacity and *cognitive* reserve (Daffner, 2010). While acknowledging that cognitive performance declines in most areas when people age, the theory of successful cognitive ageing argues that there are compensatory mechanisms in human beings' cognitive systems to compensate age-related dysfunction in a homeostatic manner (Eyler et al., 2011; Verny et al., 2015). There are a number of factors that have been considered to support cognitive reserve and functioning. These factors include a variety of lifestyle factors, such as mental stimulation, cognitive leisure activities, social stimulation, active lifestyle, cognitive remediation and physical activities (Vance, 2012).

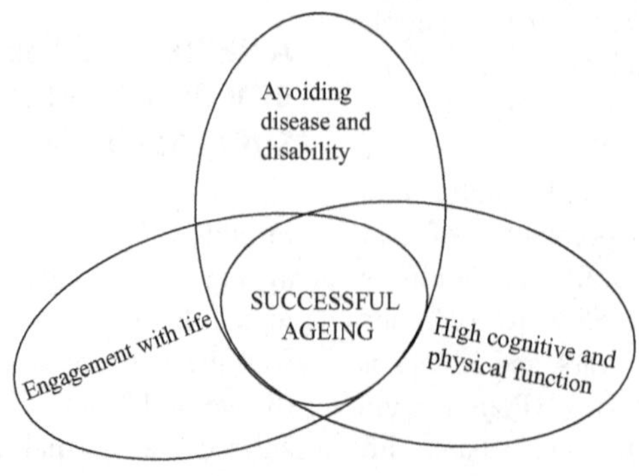

Figure 18.1 Rowe and Kahn's model of successful ageing

Source: Reproduced according to the figure in Rowe and Kahn (1997: 434)

Rowe and Kahn's model and the later successful cognitive ageing model provide biologically and cognitively grounded consideration for understanding successful ageing. However, despite the advantages of these models, they fail to recognise that a disease-free older age is unrealistic for most people (Bowling and Dieppe, 2005). As a result, the models appear to suggest that older people with physical illness and cognitive impairment may not be able to age successfully. Using a dualist perspective of illness–healthiness relations, the models consider successful ageing as an objective and physical construct, which is separate from 'subjective successful ageing' where people believe they age successfully although they have some physical illness or cognitive impairment. The models also suggest that successful ageing depends on an individualistic set of practices determined by factors that relate to active lifestyles (Crowther et al., 2002). As pointed out by Katz (2013), active lifestyle is closely linked to status hierarchies and social contexts, and an active lifestyle also requires adequate resources. Rowe and Kahn's biological model and the successful cognitive ageing model place emphasis on individual responsibilities for successful ageing, which may result in downplaying the influence of social constraints and inequalities in successful ageing.

To adequately address social constraints and inequalities in successful ageing, an incorporation of research in the area of ageing from a community perspective is required. The community approach to successful ageing recognises the important role that community plays in successful ageing. The approach also acknowledges older people's skills and capacities that support them to age successfully in their community (Provencher et al., 2014).

SUCCESSFUL AGEING IN THE COMMUNITY

Traditionally, the concept of community refers to the geographical area where people live in a bounded geographical area in a small rural town, a neighbourhood or even a city (Bradshaw, 2008). The term 'community without propinquity', coined by Webber (1964), challenges the traditional concept of proximal community and proposes that community can exist among people who share common interests and interaction but who do not share a common locality. This concept provides the theoretical foundation of Anderson's concept of imagined community. An imagined community refers to communities as 'being distinguished, not by their falsity/genuineness, but by the style in which they are imagined' (Anderson, 1987: 7). In Anderson's view, people of an imagined community who internalise an image of that community are interconnected members who have shared interests. Anderson proposes that the imagination of the community and the sense of connectedness are as essential as the physical environment of a community. Bringing these definitions together, Provencher et al. (2014) define community as a physically bounded or virtual place, a set of shared interests and a sense of belonging.

The notion of ageing in place (AIP), which closely links to the concept of community, was adopted in policy initiatives in the agreement among the countries in the Organisation for Economic Co-operation and Development (OECD) in 1994. The policy initiatives aim to support older persons to remain living at home and also to improve older people's well-being, independence and social participation. If remaining at home is not possible, the alternative should be that older people live in a supportive environment close to their communities (Organisation for Economic Co-operation and Development, 1994). For example, AIP has been a central theme of Australian ageing policy since then, particularly in community care (Commonwealth of Australia, 2009). It is widely accepted that the majority of older Australians should live in their community for as long as possible, rather than moving to residential aged care. In 2011, 94% of Australians aged 65 years and over lived in their own homes (Australian Bureau of Statistics, 2013b). New Zealand also adopts AIP in aged care policy and advocates that older adults make their own choices about where to live, and the policy also provides support to their successful ageing in the community rather than moving into residential care (Li et al., 2014).

Later, AIP was adopted as a philosophy of aged care following the introduction of policy initiatives (Li, 2013). Here, the philosophical concept of AIP is fundamentally concerned with experiences of community life (Li et al., 2014). It promotes community as a place where older people feel safe, secure, protected and empowered, and where older people can establish and maintain a sense of belonging through their everyday activities. AIP is thus aligned with the principles of community psychology: empowerment; freedom of choice; and consultation. These are three sets of linked values in ageing from a community perspective, allowing older people to make decisions about their living arrangements in later life.

AIP emphasises the role of community in empowering older people to age successfully. Within this context, empowerment refers to the expansion of resources and enhancement of capabilities of older people to participate in, negotiate with and influence the processes of policy and decision making. Therefore, older people have greater control over their own lives and can make decisions on where to live (Naranyan, 2007; Rappaport, 1981; 1987). According to Rappaport (1987), the concept of empowerment consists of not only individual determination over one's own life but also democratic participation in the life of the community at a community and social level. From the perspective of empowerment, AIP can be seen as an intentional ongoing process in the local community where older people live, which involves mutual respect, critical reflection, caring and group participation (Nelson and Prilleltensky, 2005). Through this process, older people can gain greater access to, and control over, the resources that support them ageing in the community.

Freedom of choice is a value that is strongly associated with AIP. The well-being of older people is partly dependent on the freedom of choice they can enjoy in their daily life. In relation to AIP, freedom of choice includes two aspects: process and opportunity. The opportunity aspect suggests that freedom is not only a choice between alternatives but also about the opportunities of where to live that are provided to older people. In other words, freedom of choice gives older people the ability to live as they would like, to choose living arrangements that they prefer (Sen, 1990) and to receive support to do so. The process aspect advocates that older people are part of the decision making process regarding where to live in their later life. This means that older people are seen as active agents rather than passive service recipients. Hence, from the perspective of freedom of choice, AIP policy not only needs to aim to improve the opportunities that older people have, but also strive to strengthen and improve the processes involved (Lebmann, 2011).

Consultation with citizens (particularly older people) has become integral to the development, implementation and evaluation of AIP policies in many countries. Such consultation is regarded as a process through which people influence and share control over initiatives, decisions and resources that affect the citizens' abilities to age in place (Cuthill, 2001). The consultation process is an active involvement of the community, which provides the community with ownership of AIP initiatives, thereby enhancing the prospects of a sustainable outcome. Consultation also generates improved social justice outcomes (Crase et al., 2005). Hence, the consultation process may advance the legitimacy of policy decisions in relation to AIP, enhance the quality of the decision and, in so doing, produce greater efficacy of AIP policy (Holland, 2002).

It is clear that AIP could not be implemented without support from communities.

As defined by Wilkinson (1991), a community is a place in which people experience society directly. It is at a community level that policies are translated into practice. It is also at the community level that older persons connect themselves to society through participation. A community is thus a dynamic social and geographical entity, which provides a platform for older people to respond to the issues that affect their successful and healthy ageing.

The connection to place is therefore an essential concept in older people's ageing in the community. Here, the notion of place is understood beyond the common-sense level that refers to a place mainly as a physical space. More importantly, it also refers to social, relational and cultural contexts within which older people connect with the physical places they experience (Hodgetts et al., 2010). Therefore, place is a social construct that marks older people's experience (Hodgetts et al., 2010; Li et al., 2010a; 2014). Places provide contexts for older people to reflect on their life journeys and to be involved in community activities. As people age, important places often are those that mark older people's particular experiences (Manzo, 2005). Those experiences are part of people's development in the life course, in that they are events that help move people's life journey forward. Because 'awareness of the past is an important element in the love of a place' (Tuan, 1974: 99), these subjective experiences with places are constructed by the development of place bonding (Vorkinn and Riese, 2001).

Place is also a process through which older people reflect their identities. Place is not a fixed geography. It is continuously shaped and reshaped, negotiated and renegotiated within different contexts and at different times. In that sense, place is not mute (Li et al., 2010a). It tells something about the person who creates and uses it. For example, a house in which older people move is a physical space. When they make efforts to transform the house into their home, they reshape the physical space and turn it into a place that reflects their history, identities, desires and culture (Li et al., 2010a). In doing so, older people use home to say things about themselves (Williams, 2002). Many older people regard the communities surrounding them as their homes and symbols of their identities. In that regard, home and community can be seen as an outward magnification of an inner reality, reflecting both the older person's identity and their relationships to society (Li and Tse, 2015).

AIP accordingly can be conceptualised as emplaced ageing by bringing the concepts of home and community together. At an individual level, emplaced ageing highlights that older people develop and maintain attachments to place through their lifetime experience, such as making decisions of where to live, owning a house and turning a house into a home. Their identities become bound up with their experience of place and their identification of community. At the community level, emplaced ageing provides a theoretical conception to understand a new phenomenon in which communities can become new sites of aged care that provide services to support older people to successfully age in the community. As a result, the aged care system for those who age in the community may no longer be hospital-based or illness related. Rather, older people may move from hospitals to communities, such as in the Hong Kong case of successful ageing and volunteering in the community (outlined in the later sections of this chapter).

MIGRANTS' SUCCESSFUL AGEING IN THE COMMUNITY

Running parallel with the trend of population ageing is human movement across international borders as a result of globalisation. The United Nations' *International Migration Report 2015* suggested that the population of international migrants worldwide has continued to increase rapidly over the past 15 years, with a total of 244 million international migrants in 2015 (United Nations, 2015b). That is a rise from 222 million in 2010 and 173 million in 2000. Of the 244 million international migrants, 104 million (43%) were born in Asia. Among these Asian migrants, India and China were the countries that had the largest diasporas in the world in 2015. India had 16 million, followed by China with ten million.

It is impractical that this chapter covers all migrant groups who are successfully ageing in their host countries. The chapter will hone in on successful ageing of Chinese migrants in Australia and New Zealand, because the Chinese migrant population is one of the largest migrant groups in the world. Many of the issues and experiences discussed below are also typical for older migrants from other ethnic groups. Therefore, the discussion of Chinese migrant ageing in Australia and New Zealand should provide insights into ageing in the community for Chinese migrants living in other countries and for older migrants from other ethnic groups.

The Chinese people have a long history of international migration. It is estimated that there were over 40.3 million Chinese residing in 148 countries and regions outside mainland China in 2011 (Poston and Wong, 2016). Among these Chinese migrants, there is a group of older Chinese adults who are either long-term settlers or recent immigrants to Western countries who wish to reunite with their adult children. For these older Chinese people, their experiences and practices of successful ageing in their communities are likely to be different from their local counterparts. One of the features of successful ageing in the community for older Chinese migrants is the cultivation of a sense of community.

A sense of community is concerned with the belonging to a community where members share similarities, establishing reciprocal relations and facilitating the satisfying of needs of the individual members of that community (Pretty et al., 2007; Sarason, 1974; Sonn, 2002). Earlier work on sense of community has focused on setting-specific local community (Li et al., 2014). This focus could be seen to imply that successful ageing happens in the local, native community. However, globalisation and the rapid development of media technologies open up multiple ways for people to develop their sense of community, both physically in local community and virtually in social media. Because of this development of technologies, research into sense of community is required to move beyond local settings to include international communities in which people are connected through the use of communication technologies. The following cases offer insights into how older Chinese migrants establish senses of community in Australia and New Zealand.

Tan and colleagues' study (Tan et al., 2010) aimed to explore the life experiences and views on successful ageing of older Chinese-Australians. In the study, Chinese-Australians were operationally defined as participants who identified themselves as Chinese, were from South-east Asian and North-east Asian countries and who had at least one Chinese parent. The sample consisted of ten Chinese-Australians who were born between 1927 and 1950 (age range 55 to 78 years) with the mean age being 60 years. More than half of the participants were not involved in paid work. In addition, half of the participants lived with their spouse or partner and the other half lived with other family members. Eight out of ten participants had completed tertiary education. Participants had good English language abilities and skills, rating both their oral and written English between 'good' and 'excellent'. This indicated that participants were comfortable with the English language and therefore are able to communicate with ease in Australia. The results of Tan's study revealed that the participation in local community and volunteering provided the participants with a sense of meaningful engagement and a sense of community. The older Chinese-Australians regarded active participation in community as central to their successful ageing in Australia.

The participants in the study reported that they felt volunteer work increased their well-being and life satisfaction (Tan et al., 2010). The findings indicate that volunteering promotes people to engage with the community in a meaningful way, which in turn, contributes to sustaining good mental and physical health in their later life.

Differing from Tan's study on older Chinese migrants (who were long-term settlers and had good English language skills), Li's study (2013) focused on the experiences of ageing in the community among older Chinese-New Zealanders who were new migrants and had limited English abilities and skills. The term 'older Chinese immigrant' in that study referred to people who were currently staying in New Zealand with permanent residency or New Zealand citizenship, and who had immigrated to New Zealand from mainland China under the family reunion programme, and were 60 years of age and over. A total of 32 participants (18 females and 14 males), ranging in age from 62 to 77 years, participated in the study. All participants had lived in New Zealand for less than 15 years. At the time of the first interview in 2008, ten participants lived with their adult children; 22 participants lived with their spouse only or lived alone, seven of these lived in state houses while 14 lived in private rentals and one lived in a retirement village. Thirty-one out of 32 participants considered that they had very limited English skills. None of them were involved in paid work. The participants' primary source of income was means-tested emergency grants, a form of social benefit in New Zealand, of no more than NZ$10,000 per annum.

Although the background of the participants in Li's study was rather different from those in Tan's study, the participants in both studies shared similarities in relation to their local community involvement. Similar to Tan et al.'s participants, Li's participants were actively involved in weekly activities co-ordinated by local Chinese organisations. Every week, the community activities provided the older Chinese migrants with a place. In this place, they could express, share and validate their emotions with their peers, which offered them a sense of community. Again, similar to Tan et al.'s participants, many of Li's participants were involved in volunteering, with the participants regarding volunteering as a crucial process that shaped the construction of their cultural self. Volunteering nurtured their construal of a sense of community and strengthened them to claim membership in the local community.

Looking beyond the local setting as in Tan et al.'s study, Li's study also explored how a sense of community was cultivated in the transnational community. According to Castles (2002), the transnational community refers to communities that are established beyond national borders, and the identities of the individuals in the community are not primarily based on attachment to a specific territory. For the older Chinese immigrants, emotional and cultural connections with their birth country played a central role in the construction of their virtual sense of community in the transnational community in which they were involved (Li et al., 2010a). For example, the participants utilised satellite television to watch Chinese news and entertainment programmes. These programmes produced by their home country not only provided them with news and entertainment but also the virtual sense of community that fulfilled their emotional bond with China. They also used Chinese social media, such as *WeChat*, to communicate with their families and friends in China. Online communication offered the older Chinese migrants opportunities to virtually participate in the community activities in China (Li et al., 2014).

Tan et al.'s and Li's studies illustrate that their participants were not passive recipients of care. They cared for others and actively made contributions to the community, through volunteering for example. Volunteering is engaging in an activity through which people intend to help others without receiving pay or other material compensation for their time and services (Okun and Schultz, 2003; Wilson, 2006). As discussed previously, volunteering provides older adults with a way to maintain meaningful social roles and to continue to actively participate in society, which is essential for older people to develop a sense of community where they are ageing. Research has shown that volunteering is significant for the psychological well-being of older people (Cheng and Heller, 2009; Morrow-Howell et al., 2009). This is also evident in the Hong Kong case presented below.

SUCCESSFUL AGEING AND VOLUNTEERING IN THE COMMUNITY

Similar to other developed countries and regions, Hong Kong's population projection also shows a marked transformation in age structure. According to the latest projected results, the Hong Kong Resident Population is expected to increase from 7.24 million in mid-2014 to a peak of 8.22 million in mid-2043, and then decline to 7.81 million by mid-2064. Population ageing is expected to continue. Excluding foreign domestic helpers, the proportion of elderly people aged 65 and over is projected to increase from 15% in 2014 to 23% in 2024 and 30% in 2034, and further rise to 36% in 2064. The labour force is projected to increase slightly from 3.60 million in 2014 to 3.65 million in 2018, and then decrease to 3.43 million in 2031. It is then expected to hover between 3.42 million and 3.43 million until 2038, before decreasing to 3.11 million in 2064 (Census and Statistics Department of the Government of the Hong Kong Special Administration Region, 2015).

As Hong Kong is experiencing population ageing at an unprecedented rate, the policy of AIP in the Hong Kong community needs to take population ageing into account. Hong Kong has developed strategies to address AIP. In the 1970s, the Hong Kong government launched the Urban Redevelopment Program, which consisted of public housing and territory-wide development strategies. According to Chui's report, from 1973 onwards, the government delivered the Ten-Year Housing Programme (TYHP) that adopted a two-pronged approach. On the one hand, the government's public housing estates were extended from the urban areas to the then rural and sparsely populated New Territories. On the other hand, the government redeveloped the land in the urban area occupied by old public housing estates by launching a Comprehensive Redevelopment Plan (CRP). In 1988, the Long-Term Housing Strategy was launched as the extension of the TYHP over two decades from 1988 to 2009. These housing programmes have offered priority and support to older people (Chui, 2008).

Meanwhile, productive ageing has been promoted in Hong Kong to support older people ageing successfully in the community. Many older people in Hong Kong are capable of continuing in employment for longer. These employed older people make continuing contributions to society through taxation and have active social engagement through their employment. The phenomenon of older people continuing to be involved in paid work in their later life is aligned with the concepts of productive ageing and successful ageing. Similar to successful ageing, productive ageing takes a positive approach to ageing and can be defined as any activities by an older individual that produce a good or service for society, whether paid or unpaid (Morrow-Howell et al., 2001.) Typical areas of interest of productive ageing include the aforementioned continued employment in older persons and volunteering.

As previously mentioned, volunteering is a form of social participation and community engagement which plays a vital role in productive and successful ageing. Social participation and community engagement are important dimensions of successful ageing in the community, can lead to a significant improvement in physical and mental health and quality of life of older adults and can also improve quality of community life for older people (Chong et al., 2013; Taylor et al., 2004). Volunteering provides older adults with opportunities to actively maintain meaningful social roles and to contribute to their community (Morrow-Howell et al., 2009). Volunteering is also important for the maintenance of both physical and psychological health for older persons because it offers opportunities for physical activities and developing social networks (Cheng and Heller, 2009). The following are examples of how older adult (aged between 55 to 65) and young adult (aged between 18 to 21) volunteers support the successful ageing of dependent older adults in Hong Kong communities.

The Institute of Active Ageing (IAA) of the Hong Kong Polytechnic University views Hong Kong's demographic change as an excellent opportunity to support the city's development into a society that is better equipped to meet the needs and potential of its ageing population. Adopting an evidence-based model and interdisciplinary model, various life-long educational opportunities are offered to empower older members of society to attain healthy and active ageing through facilitating their participation in volunteer work and employment. One innovative project involves training senior citizens as paraprofessionals to implement a telephone support programme for dementia caregivers. A randomised controlled trial was carried out to test whether telephone psychoeducation combined with an enhanced behavioural activation (BA) module had a better effect on the well-being of Alzheimer's caregivers than psychoeducation alone. Ninety-three caregivers, including 66 adult children and 30 spouse/peer caregivers participated in the study. Five senior citizens (aged between 55 to 65) were trained as paraprofessionals to deliver BA to enhance cost-effectiveness and sustainability. For the first four weeks, all participants received the same psychoeducation. For the psychoeducation with the BA group, 51 participants received eight biweekly phone sessions of planning and practice on pleasant event scheduling and improving communications. For the control group, 45 participants received eight biweekly sessions of general support without any practice. As compared to the control group, the group with enhanced BA reported significantly decreased levels of depressive symptoms and enhanced relationships with the care recipients (Au, 2015; Au et al., 2015a). The findings suggested that skill-based training can be successfully administered through trained senior citizen volunteers.

In another related project, 36 university students were invited to partner with older adult volunteers (aged between 55 to 65) in providing support through home visits to marginalised and frail elders over eight weekly sessions. In negotiation with the service organisation, student volunteers were required to design a creative task that would enhance the health and well-being of the service recipients in the community. The results suggested that students demonstrated significantly positive changes in their motivation to serve others and the search for meaning in life (Au et al., 2015b). This project is an example of an intergenerational approach to ageing. According to So and Shek (2011), an intergenerational approach to ageing can simultaneously address the social issues of age-segregation and also the negative perception of older people among younger people. Through intergenerational volunteering programmes, older adults can help young people to develop the awareness, skills and self-confidence necessary to navigate difficult life obstacles. As the young volunteers provide support to older adults, they can apply and synthesise what they have learnt to problems encountered in real-life situations. Meanwhile, intergenerational volunteering programmes can provide the older volunteers with an intergenerational learning opportunity. For example, older volunteers may benefit from having younger volunteers' teach them how to use different technologies (e.g., computers and social media) and, therefore, may appreciate the important role that technology may serve in their lives (Spiteri, 2016).

Volunteering can have a positive impact on the older volunteers themselves. Chong et al. (2013) examined the factors related to volunteerism and explored the relationship between volunteerism and successful ageing across three age groups. A total of 1,170 Hong Kong Chinese respondents aged between 15 and 79 years were recruited for the study via a random household survey. Compared with younger and midlife adults, older adults were motivated to volunteer by societal concern and esteem enhancement. Participation in voluntary work was associated with three positive ageing outcomes: good health; caring engagement with significant others; and productive engagement in the community. The findings suggested great potential in promoting volunteering in old age because older volunteers tended to contribute more hours than younger volunteers did. Taken together, findings of volunteering examples in Hong Kong contribute to the literature by offering a framework for developing sustainable and accessible community care.

CHAPTER SUMMARY

Building upon a critical review of the biological and cognitive concepts of successful ageing, this chapter has provided an overview of ageing from a social psychology standpoint. This has been achieved by defining the concept of successful ageing from a community perspective. Successful ageing employs concepts such as empowerment, freedom of choice and consultation to discuss the diversity and complexity of ageing in the community. Based on the discussion, the cases of migrant successful ageing in Australia and New Zealand and volunteering in Hong Kong offer possible applications of successful ageing in the community.

These cases of ageing in the community reflect the notion of 'care in the community' and 'care by the community' (Chui, 2008), which are two important dimensions that support the implementation of AIP (Li, 2011; 2013). 'Care in the community' refers to the provision of care within the locality of the older person. 'Care by the community' promotes the commitment that the members of the community care for and support older people to live in the community. The practices of both care in the community and care by the community are grounded in mutual acquaintance between the caregivers and the cared-for (Chui, 2008).

Nevertheless, there is considerable concern over the sustainability of community care. Culturally, it is anticipated that family self-reliance will continue to dominate the provision of community care under the Chinese cultural aged care philosophy, namely filial piety. Filial piety denotes the respect and care for older people. Adult children are traditionally expected to live with their ageing parents to provide financial, physical and emotional support (Li et al., 2010b; Li and Jackson, 2016). However, the Chinese cultural heritage of filial piety among Chinese communities in Western countries and in Hong Kong has weakened, and the co-residence of older people and their adult children has been significantly decreased (Chui, 2008). Older people cannot rely upon their adult children to live with them and look after them in their everyday life. Thus, the sustainability of community care is essential for successful ageing in the community. Community-based home care services for older people have been demonstrated to play a significant role in maintaining the sustainability of community care (Chui, 2008). To further sustain community-based home care, more training programmes and volunteering opportunities that engage independent young and older adults to help with the frail elderly are needed (Au et al., 2016). In doing so, AIP can be bolstered with the strong foundation of generation integration. Although these insights into successful ageing in the community are concluded from the Chinese cases shared in this chapter, they can also offer similar implications to successful ageing in other cultures.

As noted previously, Rowe and Kahn's model (1987) and the successful cognitive ageing model suggest an absolute dichotomy of health and illness. This dichotomy views the older person out of context, pulling meaning of ageing out of the community. In addition, the dichotomy appears to exclude the older person's personal or individual experience by overlooking how the social psychological phenomenon of successful ageing is contained in the process of negotiation and interaction with people and the environment (Li, 2013). Therefore, successful ageing should not be regarded as a privilege for people without physical illness. Rather, it can be conceptualised as productions of subjectivity that are embedded in the psychical, cultural and social world.

Furthermore, the Chinese cases discussed in this chapter demonstrate that social policies and community play an important role in supporting older people to participate and live in the community in the ways they choose. According to Li (2013), policymaking (including writing of AIP policies) is largely informed by the model of calculative rationality. This model refers to the process of simply calculating and choosing the best and most efficient means to attain a given policy goal. As a result of this model, older people's opinions in relation to where they will live in their later lives may be overlooked. It is therefore essential to promote broader participatory political engagement from a range of stakeholders, including older people, when producing AIP policies. As a result, the policy-making process will respond to the complex needs of successful ageing in the community and reflect the principles of community psychology: empowerment, freedom of choice and consultation.

REFERENCES

Administration on Aging. (2014). *The Older Population. Administration for Community Living. U.S. Department of Health and Human Services*. Retrieved from http://www.aoa.gov/Aging_Statistics/Profile/2013/3.aspx.

Anderson, B. (1987). Imagined communities: Reflections on the origin and spread of nationalism (4th edn.). London, UK: Verso.

Au, A. (2015). Volunteer assisted telephone support for dementia caregivers. *Clinical Gerontologist*, *38*(3), 190–202.

Au, A., Gallagher-Thompson, D., Wong, M. K., Leung, J., Chan, W. C., Chan, C. C., … Chan K. (2015a). Behavioral activation for dementia caregivers: Scheduling pleasant events and enhancing communications. *Clinical Interventions in Aging*, *10*, 611–619.

Au, A., Ng, E., Gardner, B., Lai, S., & Chan, K. (2015b). Proactive aging and intergenerational mentoring program to promote the well-being of older adults: Pilot studies. *Clinical Gerontologist*, *38*(3), 203–210.

Au, A., Yip, H. M., Chan, W.C., Xue, B., & Tsien, T. (2016). Ageing and mental health in Hong Kong: Challenges and Innovations. In W. W. Li, S. Cummings, I. Ponnuswami, & H. Park (Eds.), *Ageing and mental health: Global perspectives* (pp. 81–96). New York, NY: Nova Science Publishers.

Australian Bureau of Statistics. (2013a). *Gender indicators, Australia, Jan 2013 (cat no. 4125.0)*. Retrieved from http://www.abs.gov.au

Australian Bureau of Statistics. (2013b). *Where and how do Australia's older people live?* Retrieved from http://www.abs.gov.au/ausstats/abs@.nsf/Lookup/2071.0main+features602012-2013

Bowling, A., & Dieppe, P. (2005). What is successful ageing and who should define it? *British Medicine Journal*, *331*(7531), 1548–1551.

Bradshaw, T. (2008). The post-place community: Contributions to the debate about the definition of community. *Community Development*, *39*(1), 5–16.

Castles, S. (2002). Migration and community formation under conditions of globalization. *International Migration Review*, 36(4), 1143–1168.

Census and Statistics Department of the Government of the Hong Kong Special Administration Region. (2015). *Hong Kong Population Projections for 2015 to 2064.*

Hong Kong, China: Government of the Hong Kong Special Administration Region.

Cheng, S.-T., & Heller, K. (2009). Global aging: Challenges for community psychology. *American Journal of Community Psychology, 44*, 161–173.

Chong, A. M. L., Rochelle T. L., & Liu, S. (2013). Volunteerism and positive aging in Hong Kong: A cultural perspective. *International Journal of Aging and Human Development, 77*, 211–231.

Chui, E. (2008). Ageing in place in Hong Kong – Challenges and opportunities in a capitalist Chinese city, *Ageing International, 32*(3), 167–182. DOI: 10.1007/s12126-008-9015-2

Commonwealth of Australia. (2009). *Moving or staying put: Deciding where to live in later life*. Brisbane: Australia National Seniors Productive Ageing Centre.

Crase, L., Dollery, B., & Wallis, J. (2005). Community consultation in public policy: The case of the Murray-Darling Basin of Australia. *Australian Journal of Political Science, 40*, 221–237.

Crowther, M., Parker, M., Achenbaum, W. A., Larimore, L., & Koenig, H. (2002). Rowe and Kahn's model of successful aging revisited: Positive spirituality – The forgotten factor. *The Gerontologist, 42*(5), 613–620.

Cummings, S., & Trecartin, S. (2016). Mental health and ageing: The United States. In W. W. Li, S. Cummings, I. Ponnuswami, & H. Park (Eds.), *Ageing and mental health: Global perspectives* (pp. 51–66). New York, NY: Nova Science Publishers.

Cuthill, M. (2001). Developing local government policy and processes for community consultation and participation. *Urban Policy and Research, 19*(2), 183–202.

Daffner, K. R. (2010). Promoting successful cognitive aging: A comprehensive review. *Journal of Alzheimer's Disease, 19*(4), 1101–1122.

DiPietro, L., Singh, M. F., Fielding, R., & Nose, H. (2012). Successful aging. *Journal of Aging Research, 2012*, 1–2.

Eyler, L., Sherzai, A., Kaup, A., & Jeste, D. (2011). A review of functional brain imaging correlated of successful cognitive aging. *Biological Psychiatry, 70*, 115–122.

Hodgetts, D., Drew, N., Sonn, C. C., Stolte, O., Nikora, N., & Curtis, C. (2010). *Social psychology and everyday life*. London, UK: Palgrave.

Holland, I. (2002). Consultation, constraints and norms: The case of nuclear waste. *Australian Journal of Public Administration, 61*, 76–86.

Katz, S. (2013). Active and successful aging: lifestyle as a gerontological idea. *Recherches sociologiques et anthropologiques (Sociological and Anthropological Research), 44*(1), 33–49.

Kyaddondo, B. (2016). Old age mental health in Uganda. In W. W. Li, S. Cummings, I. Ponnuswami, & H. Park (Eds.), *Ageing and mental health: Global perspectives* (pp. 183–196). New York, NY: Nova Science Publishers.

Lebmann, O. (2011). Freedom of choice and poverty alleviation. *Review of Social Economy, 69*(4), 439–463.

Li, W. W. (2011). Filial Piety, parental piety and community piety: Changing cultural practices of elderly support among Chinese migrant families in New Zealand. *OMNES: The Journal of Multicultural Society, 2*(1), 1–30.

Li, W. W. (2013). *Shifting selves in migration: Home, ageing in place and well-being*. Beijing, China: Central Compilation & Translation Press.

Li, W. W., Hodgetts, D., & Ho, E. (2010a). Gardens, transition and identity reconstruction among older Chinese immigrants to New Zealand. *Journal of Health Psychology, 15*(5), 786–796.

Li, W. W., Hodgetts, D., Ho, E., & Stolte, O. (2010b). From early Confucian texts to ageing care in China and abroad today: The evolution of filial piety and its implications. *Journal of US-China Public Administration, 7*(7), 48–59.

Li, W. W., Hodgetts, D., & Sonn, C. (2014). Multiple senses of community among older Chinese migrants to New Zealand. *Journal of Community and Applied Social Psychology, 24*(1), 26–36.

Li, W. W., Huang, X., Li, H., & Chen, Y. (2016). Aged care and mental health in China. In W. W. Li, S. Cummings, I. Ponnuswami, & H. Park (Eds.), *Ageing and mental health: Global perspectives* (pp. 151–166). New York, NY: Nova Science Publishers.

Li, W. W., & Jackson, K. (2016). Ageing and mental health in Australia. In W. W. Li, S. Cummings, I. Ponnuswami, & H. Park (Eds.), *Ageing and mental health: Global perspectives* (pp. 13–32). New York, NY: Nova Science Publishers.

Li, W. W., & Tse, S. (2015). Problem gambling and help seeking among Chinese international students: narratives of place identity transformation. *Journal of Health Psychology, 20*(3), 300–312.

Lupien, S., & Wan, J. N. (2004). Successful ageing: From cell to self. *Philosophical Transactions of the Royal Society of London, 359*, 1413–1426.

Lynott, R., & Lynott, P. (1996). Tracing the course of theoretical development in the sociology of aging. *The Gerontologists, 36*, 749–760.

Manzo, L. C. (2005). For better or worse: Exploring multiple dimensions of place meaning. *Journal of Environmental Psychology, 25*, 67–86.

Morrow-Howell, N., Hinterlong, J., & Sherraden M. (2001). *Productive aging concepts and challenges.* Baltimore, MD: T56 The John Hopkins University Press.

Morrow-Howell, N., Hong, S.-I., & Tang, F. (2009). Who benefits from volunteering? Variations in perceived benefits. *The Gerontologist, 49*(1), 91–102.

Narayan, D. (2007). Empowerment. *Journal of Ambulatory Care and Management, 30*(2), 120–125.

National Bureau of Statistics of China. (2011). *Communiqué of the National Bureau of Statistics of People's Republic of China on Major Figures of the 2010 Population Census (No. 1).* Retrieved from http://web.archive.org/web/20131108022004/http://www.stats.gov.cn/english/newsandcomingevents/t20110428_402722244.htm

Nelson, G., & Prilleltensky, I. (2005). *Community psychology: In pursue of liberation and well-being*. New York, NY: Palgrave MacMillan.

Okun, M. A., & Schultz, A. (2003). Age and motives for volunteering: Testing hypotheses derived from socioemotional selectivity theory. *Psychology and Aging, 18*(2), 231–239.

Organisation for Economic Co-operation and Development. (1994). *New orientations for social policy*. Paris, France: Author.

Park, H., & Adamson, C. (2016). Ageing and mental health in diversity: A New Zealand experience. In W. W. Li, S. Cummings, I. Ponnuswami, & H. Park (Eds.), *Ageing and mental health: Global perspectives* (pp. 67–80). New York, NY: Nova Science Publishers.

Ponnuswami, I., & Udhayakumar, P. (2016). Gerontological mental health in India. In W. W. Li, S. Cummings, I. Ponnuswami, & H. Park (Eds.), *Ageing and mental health: Global perspectives* (pp. 167–180). New York, NY: Nova Science Publishers.

Poston, D., & Wong, J. H. (2016). The Chinese diaspora: The current distribution of the overseas Chinese population. *Chinese Journal of Sociology, 2*(3), 348–373.

Pretty, G., Bishop, B., Fisher, A., & Sonn, C. (2007). Psychological sense of community and its relevance to well-being and everyday life in Australia. *The Australian Community Psychologist, 19*(2), 6–25.

Productivity Commission. (2013). *An ageing Australia: Preparing for the future*. Retrieved from www.pc.gov.au

Provencher, C., Keating, N., Warburton, J., & Roos, V. (2014). Ageing and community: Introduction to the Special Issue. *Journal of Community & Applied Social Psychology, 24*, 1–11.

Rappaport, J. (1981). In praise of paradox: A social policy of empowerment over prevention. *American Journal of Community Psychology, 9*, 1–25.

Rappaport, J. (1987). Terms of empowerment/exemplars of prevention. *American Journal of Community Psychology, 15*, 121–148.

Rowe, J., & Kahn, R. (1987). Human aging: Usual and successful. *Science, 237*(4811), 143–149.

Rowe, J., & Kahn, R. (1997). Successful aging. *The Gerontologist, 37*(4), 433–440.

Sarason, S. B. (1974). *The psychological sense of community: Prospects for a community psychology*. San Francisco, CA: Jossey-Bass.

Sen, A. K. (1990). Welfare, freedom and social choice: A reply. *Louvain Economic Review, 56*, 451–485.

So, K. M., & Shek, D. T. (2011). Elder lifelong learning, intergenerational solidarity and positive youth development: The case of Hong Kong. *International Journal of Adolescent Medicine and Health, 23*(2), 85–92.

Socolovsky, J. (2002). *Greying of humanity a threat to world budgets*. Retrieved from http://www.smh.com.au/articles/2002/04/07/1017206292613.html

Sonn, C. C. (2002). Immigration adaptation: Understanding the process through sense of community. In A. T. Fisher, C. C. Sonn, & B. J. Bishop (Eds.), *Psychological sense of community: Research, applications, and implications* (pp. 205–222). New York, NY: Kluwer Academic/Plenum Publishers.

Spiteri, D. (2016). What do older people learn from young people? Intergenerational learning in 'day centre' community settings in Malta. *International Journal of Lifelong Education*, *35*(30), 235–253.

Statistics New Zealand. (2006). *Demographic aspects of New Zealand's ageing population*. Retrieved from http://www.stats.govt.nz/browse_for_stats/ people_and_communities/older_people/demographic-aspects-nz-ageing-population.aspx

Statistics New Zealand. (2014). *2013 Census ethnic group profiles*. Retrieved from http://www.stats.govt.nz/browse_for_stats/snapshots-of-nz

Tan, J., Ward, L, & Ziaian T. (2010). Experiences of Chinese immigrants and Anglo-Australians ageing in Australia: a cross-cultural perspective on successful ageing. *Journal of Health Psychology*, *15*(5), 697–706.

Taylor, A. H., Cable, N. T., Faulkner, G., Hillsdon, M., Narici, M., & Van Der Bij, A. K. (2004). Physical activity and older adults: A review of health benefits and the effectiveness of interventions. *Journal of Sports Sciences*, *22*(8), 703–725.

Tornstam, L. (1992). The quo vadis of gerontology: On the gerontological research paradigm. *The Gerontologist*, *32*, 318–326.

Tuan, Y.-F. (1974). *Topophilia: Study of environmental perception, attitudes and values*. Englewood Cliffs, NJ: Prentice Hall.

United Nations. (2015a). *World population ageing 2015*. New York, NY: Author.

United Nations. (2015b). *International migration report 2015*. New York, NY: Author.

Vaillant, G., & Mukamal, K. (2001). Successful aging. *The American Journal of Psychiatry*, *158*(6), 839–847.

Vance, D. (2012). Potential factors that may promote successful cognitive aging. *Nursing: Research and Reviews*, *2*, 27–32.

Verny, M., Moyse, E., & Krantic, S. (2015). Successful cognitive aging: Between functional decline and failure of compensatory mechanisms. *Biomedical Research International*, *2015*, 1–4.

Vorkinn, M., & Riese, H. (2001). Environmental concern in a local context: The significance of place attachment. *Environment and Behavior*, *33*, 249–263.

Webber, M. (1964). Urban place and the non-place realm. In M. Webber (Ed.), *Explorations into urban structure* (pp. 79–153). Philadelphia, PA: University of Pennsylvania Press.

Wilkinson, K. (1991). *The community in rural America*. New York, NY: Greenwood Press.

Williams, G. (2002). Changing geographies of care: employing the concept of therapeutic landscapes as a framework in examining home space. *Social Science & Medicine*, 55, 141–154.

Wilson, J. (2006). Volunteering. *Annual Review of Sociology*, *26*, 415–440.

PART VII

Communication

19

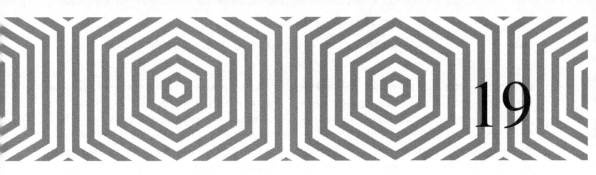

Social Cognition and Communication: From Attitudes and Persuasion to Cross-Cultural Psychology, Social Representations, Discourse, and the Technologies of Digital Influence

James H. Liu, Homero Gil de Zúñiga and Trevor Diehl

OVERVIEW

Communication and language, while central in human social life, have not been the preferred terms of engagement in the field of social psychology. Rather, persuasion directed at individuals and the subsequent processes of attitude formation have been the focus since the early twentieth century and continue to preoccupy researchers today. In the seminal work of Carl Hovland and colleagues at Yale, communication was conceptualized as messages shared among rational, information-processing individuals. The primary aim of communication, according to these scholars, was attitude change (see Hovland, Janis, & Kelley, 1953, or Petty and Cacioppo, 1986 for an overview). Psychological research on attitudes became important during the World Wars as part of the American government's propaganda efforts targeted at the home population. Though our understanding of how attitude change works is much more nuanced, its enduring prevalence in the field prompted one researcher to note that attitude change is 'the most distinctive and indispensable concept in contemporary American social psychology' (Albarracin and Vargas, 2009: 394).

The purpose of this chapter is to expand the focus of attention from experimental work on attitude formation and persuasion directed at individuals to a broader conception of communication and persuasion between people as members of social networks and collectives, endowed with pre-existing structures (both intra- and inter-individual) that function with agency in dealing with persuasion. We conceptualize attitudes not as properties of individuals but as representational profiles (Sibley and Liu, 2013) that link people to communities through shared meanings. According to this approach, meanings are communicated through social structures of friendship, kinship, and group identity. These are dynamic structures imbued with meaning that can be analyzed through cultural, representational, and discursive lenses. Given that we view persuasion as flowing through social networks and communities, we recognize the importance of action research (Lewin, 1946), where people (as individuals and in collectives) are engaged co-creators of social action, especially when it comes to institutions. The ability of individuals to link with others through emerging communication technologies, while under-researched, is a topic that we signal as important for the development of theories that consider communication as embedded in social structures.

The evolution from individual to representational and group paradigms took place over the last century. The individual-focused 'persuasion paradigm' left an indelible mark on communication theory and social psychology. Propaganda research, in part inspired by the growth of fascism in Europe and in part driven by commerce and public relations, became the template for media effects research after the wars. In its initial guise, as proposed by Lazarsfeld and Merton (1948), the so-called transmission, or hypodermic needle, effect in communication assumed a direct, one-way flow of messages from the center to the populace. For example, this assumption guided the works of the 'Father of Public Relations' Edward Bernays (1928/2005) whose application of communication theory mainly served the purposes of those with money and/or authority. Elites at the time saw mass media as a vehicle for social control and manipulation in democratic societies.

Assumptions about the nature of audiences began to shift after the war. In particular, as resources in post-war societies were channeled toward domestic life and consumerism, the nature of public life also shifted. In response, researchers updated their assumptions about audience effects to reflect the growing influence of group, membership, and community based social ties – such as churches, political parties, and community organizations. Communication effects were not quite direct, but instead filtered through opinion leaders in the group; what Katz and Lazarsfeld called the 'two-step flow' of communication (1966).

In this chapter, we review some classic research following the 'persuasion paradigm' but quickly introduce parallel and overlapping ideas that treat individuals as part of a social system, where communication acts result in forming shared understanding (or representations, see Moscovici, 1961/2008, or common ground, see Kashima, 2014). Shared meanings are further enabled through technologies that bind people, not only as part of linguistic and cultural communities but also as individuals with agendas who can be agents of change (Ford and Ford, 1995). We examine, in detail, three different research lenses for examining how people associate with one another: cultural, representational, and discursive. None of these approaches is without limitation, and we discuss these in light of their ability to describe and explain social and community based action.

After describing these three orientations in terms of social cognition, culturally elaborated meanings, and communication, we consider the role of communications technology in 'making people'. The idea of persuasion as a message between two information processors is opened up to a wider vision of people as agents living in networks of social life and shared meaning, who make use of the technologies that enable them to achieve aims that vary from time to time, and across different places and cultures (Ford, Ford, & D'Amelio, 2008; Liu and MacDonald, 2016).

We close with a consideration of the role of communications technology as one of the driving forces in globalization that, together with capitalism and mass migration, are shaping collective futures for the interconnected strands of humanity. In this milieu, we consider some avenues open to the twenty-first-century citizen interested in making a difference with communications-oriented social science and social science research.

THE 'PERSUASION PARADIGM' IN SOCIAL PSYCHOLOGY AND COMMUNICATION THEORY

The 'persuasion paradigm' is at the heart of mainstream social psychology as a discipline. The foundation of this approach is: a source transmits an information-rich message to another, who processes this information and responds by either changing (or not changing) their attitudes and behaviors (Albarracin and Vargas, 2009; Hovland et al., 1953). The analysis of 'who says what to whom with what effect' decomposes communication into four useful components: the source (who said it), the message (what was said), the recipient (to whom), and consequences (persistence of message retention and attitude, or behavioral change). The social psychological literature often does not clarify that sources of information are not always individuals, but rather can be institutions. Messages may be carefully designed by professionals to achieve an outcome desired by an institution (as in advertising). A message could be from an authority that flows through mass communications channels (as in a Twitter feed from a politician) with immense power. Typically in the literature the source is treated as though it were an individual, and as though communications were democratic or egalitarian; that is, without examining the power dynamics underpinning any persuasion attempt.

In the 1980s and 1990s, researchers seized on the zeitgeist of the times for integrating accumulated evidence from the persuasion paradigm to develop the Elaboration Likelihood Model (Petty and Cacioppo, 1986: ch. 9) and the Heuristic-Systematic Model of information processing (Chaiken and Trope, 1999). These models highlight the idea that there are two pathways towards persuasion: one a central or systematic route, where a person pays careful attention to message content, and the other a peripheral or heuristic route, where the person is less motivated to pay attention to details of the message and allows peripheral features (i.e., information processing shortcuts) to decide their reaction. They tended to privilege rational information processing (the central or systematic route) and bundle everything else (including emotions, most often operationalized as mood – Bechara and Damasio (2005) – and situational constraints) into the peripheral or heuristic route.

The emergence of these 'dual-processing models' (Chaiken and Trope, 1999) has been highly influential across the social and natural sciences. The different names and processes for similar hypotheses concerning cognitive-motivational systems (e.g., central/peripheral and systematic/heuristic) remain to be disentangled from related terms, such as automatic versus controlled or implicit/explicit, but it is clear that there will be continued research efforts in this direction.

One shortcoming of the dual-process approach is that, although a simple idea on the surface, the empirical implications of certain assumptions in these models are rather complex. For example, rational thought processes may be accessed heuristically, through memory, depending on the sophistication of the individual (Egidi, 2017). In addition, scholars argue that systemic processing is influenced by social factors, like group norms (Kahneman, 2003). Others have argued that heuristic processing is also biased, depending on the message source or other factors (Chaiken and Maheswaran, 1994). Thus, by the early 1990s, fewer scholars argued that communication effects were direct. Scholars became increasingly concerned with identifying the intervening factors between message reception and attitude change (or formation).

A Shift to the Social Sphere and the Deliberative Turn

Around the same period, social psychology and communications scholars began to look at political discussion following a persuasion attempt as a hitherto ignored area of inquiry. Sparked by seminal works of Jurgen Habermas and James Fishkin, rational debate in political decision-making became a sort of normative standard for scholars. These accounts of attitude change incorporated a direct critique of the claim that a democracy could be predicated on persuasion by mass media. Instead, a counterclaim was made that public decisions should be made in formalized settings, where participants are more or less equally informed, and consensus is made through debate (Fishkin, 1991; Habermas and McCarthy, 1985). The notion of a 'public sphere' between the state and civil society, Habermas argued, was a check on ruling elites and a mark of government by the people (Habermas, 1991: xi).

The deliberative turn is important for three reasons. First, it represents a shift away from simple persuasion models and attitude formation and draws attention to democratic participation. Second, attributes of discursive processes are formally introduced into the research tradition. Third, and perhaps most importantly, the notion of public spheres firmly opens the door to communication as a socially grounded act; one that is contextual depending on the historical and political factors of the culture. Before turning to these issues in depth, we show how discussion and participation have been incorporated into the now classic dual-process models. These updated models were later complemented by alternative theories, but these later accounts are still grounded in the social and discursive implications of the deliberative turn.

From Classic Persuasion to Discussion, Mediation, and Participation

Informed by the role of political discussion in creating a participatory public sphere, scholars updated the classic persuasion theory and formalized a version of the dual-process model. Two complementary theoretical accounts serve as foundational explanations for how dual-processing models might work in practice, beyond their original laboratory contexts. On the one hand, the *communication mediation model*, as introduced by McLeod and colleagues (1999), claims that, for people to be involved in civic and political life, the information they consume from mass media is often processed (or mediated) through interpersonal discussion. That is, people are often exposed to information from the news (from institutions), and this serves as 'fuel' for political discussions with others (Gamson, 1992). These efforts, in turn, will make them more likely to participate in the political sphere. In this vein, discussion serves as a sort of social/societal reasoning mechanism; the effect of information alone, whether it is processed heuristically or systematically, may not be sufficient to exert long-lasting persuasive effects (Cho et al., 2009; Gil de Zúñiga and Valenzuela, 2011; Shah et al., 2007).

On the other hand, the *cognitive mediation model* contends that there are also individual cognitive processes of how information affects individuals. When people consume information, they may reflect on that information at a later time and think about ways it relates to their lives. Reflection reorganizes their ideas, helps elaborate upon them, and this mechanism will lead them to engage in active behavior (Bandura, 2001; Eveland, 2004; Jung, Kim, & Gil de Zúñiga, 2011). This process not only takes place when an individual initially 'consumes' information, but also when they subsequently engage in discussion with others (or ruminate). In short, the cognitive elaboration of news or information provided in discussions also mediates the effect of information over individuals' behavior. The literature in social psychology derived from the elaboration likelihood model (see Petty, Brinol, & Priester, 2009) did not extend far enough beyond the laboratory and immediate persuasion effects to integrate these more extended effects. Both models (cognitive and communication mediation) are particularly useful in the modern information environment. This is because most messaging is filtered through mass media and interpersonal friend networks.

Heuristic and systematic ways of processing information, as well as the different social modes in which information is mediated in today's highly networked communication contexts, are key in explaining why, and how, people get persuaded and partake of civic and political activities (Evans, 2008). The 'deliberative turn' in communications theory was key in facilitating these developments. In social psychology, parallel thinking about the role of discussion and reflection in mediating communication effects took place in a similar vein. Social representations theory (Moscovici, 1961/2008), for example, complements these approaches but also more directly addresses the social sphere in which communications take place. In other words, individual changes in attitudes or cognition are mediated via interpersonal discussion. In turn, shared representations of attitude/belief objects are produced through conversations with others (Sibley and Liu, 2013; Sibley, Liu, & Kirkwood, 2006). The next section digs into the ramifications of alternate forms of communications mediation models.

THE CONTENT-BASED PARADIGMS OF CROSS-CULTURAL PSYCHOLOGY, SOCIAL REPRESENTATIONS THEORY, AND DISCURSIVE PSYCHOLOGY

Advances in communications theory have extended classic social psychological models of persuasion beyond the laboratory and into the naturalistic communicative contexts where persuasion actually takes place. Classic models have simultaneously been challenged and augmented by three alternative 'fringe movements' coming from three separate areas of social and cross-cultural psychology. These take different angles in identifying the communities of thought, feeling, and action that mediate responses to persuasion.

In contrast with the classic approach, which is focused on individual information processing, these alternative approaches focus attention on culture and content. Although Cross-Cultural Psychology (CCP), Social Representations Theory (SRT), and Discursive Psychology (DP) have separate strengths and weaknesses, they share the premise that important causal features of information processing are difficult (if not impossible) to ascertain using experimental methods. They share the critique that experimental methods ignore the common ground (Kashima, 2014): persuasion is contingent on *shared content and beliefs about 'reality' that inflect the course of information processing.*

They also illuminate different ways in which a person may bind to a community. CCP focuses on culture – often at an abstract level, for example, in differentiating between individualistic and collectivist cultures (Triandis, 1995). SRT and DP both focus on groups within a society or communities that share particular systems of meaning, but emphasize different aspects of the constitution of groups and the construction of meaning.

Cross-Cultural Psychology (CCP)

Following publication of Markus and Kitayama's (1991) classic paper, Cross-Cultural Psychology's criticisms are probably familiar to social psychologists today. Cross-Cultural Psychology points out the problems of relying on a limited database:

most experiments are done on Western undergraduates. Making conclusions from such a limited sample is tantamount to overgeneralizing from so-called WEIRD, or White, Educated, Industrialized, Rich, and Democratic, samples that dominate experimental research (Heinrich, Heine, & Norenzayan, 2010). One of the risks of such an approach is that these 'WEIRDos' may have an independent sense of self that is constructed out of the material conditions afforded by industrialization (leading to individualism and an independent self-construal). This produces information processing outcomes different from those common in more traditional/collectivistic societies. In these societies, an interdependent sense of self is normative (Inglehart and Baker, 2000; Markus and Kitayama, 1991).

While accumulated research (for a review, see Smith, Fischer, & Vignoles, 2013) has taken some of the edge off Markus and Kitayama's (1991) original formulation – which made virtually every mainstream theory of motivation, cognition, and emotion in social psychology contingent upon a person's self-construal (as independent or interdependent) – the fact remains that experimental procedures administered to East Asian (or other non-Western) populations often yield different results compared to the same procedures administered to Westerners. These differences are typically not mediated by self-construal (so the cause of the differences is less than certain). Our best guess is that normative influences, that is, the rewards and costs of social interaction, shape outcomes (Smith et al., 2013). So, for example, modesty is frequently observed as a communications style for East Asians that does not function in the same way as it does for North Americans (Tafarodi, Shaughnessy, Yamaguchi, & Murakoshi, 2011); but the reason people behave more modestly in Japan could be that they are concerned about negative perceptions of self-aggrandizement by others, rather than because they have lower self-esteem than Canadians.

Regardless of the proximal causal mechanism of cross-cultural differences, the cautionary tale is the same: be careful when you assume that some experimental condition is the 'cause' of differences obtained between a treatment and control group. The shared cultural background of these individuals may condition the results obtained, such that, when the same procedures are administered to an experimental and control group with a *different* cultural background, a different result may appear (e.g., no difference between the experimental and control group, and therefore a failure to replicate, see Markus and Kitayama, 1991; Smith et al., 2013). The basic lesson here is that for human thought, behavior, motivation, and emotion, *content inflects process*.

As an illustration of this principle, consider the case of cognitive dissonance theory (Festinger and Carlsmith, 1959), among the most popular and influential of social psychology theories of attitude change in the 1960s and 1970s and now part of the canon of received knowledge taught in undergraduate textbooks. Cognitive dissonance theory claims that inconsistency among attitudes, behavior, values, and beliefs is aversive to the individual; particularly when the inconsistency involves a valued aspect of the self (Stone and Cooper, 2001). The individual will be motivated to reduce dissonance, typically by changing their attitudes and preserving valued aspects of the self-concept. Heine and Lehman (1997) found no effect of cognitive dissonance among Japanese using the 'Free Choice Paradigm', where North Americans typically overvalue their choice after it is freely made, compared to a rejected, but previously valued, alternative (also known as post-decision dissonance or the choice justification effect). They argued,

> Making a difficult choice, and the accompanying concerns that choice was not optimal are simply not as psychologically threatening to the Japanese. We contend that, unlike those with an independent view of the self, the possibility that one has made a poor decision may not implicate core

aspects of identity for the interdependent self .... (Heine and Lehman, 1997: 397)

Kitayama, Snibbe, Markus, & Suzuki (2004: 528) refined this formulation by arguing that 'Asians may show dissonance effects when their behaviors are made public, as public scrutiny may produce worries about interpersonal rejection'. They reported that 'Japanese justified their choices by spreading alternatives only when self-*relevant social others were salient (italics added).* In contrast, European Americans justified their choices in all conditions' (Kitayama et al., 2004: 531; italics added). In other words, East Asians only showed cognitive dissonance when their decisions might affect relationships with relevant (significant) others, whereas for Euro-Americans, dissonance is produced by fears of incompetence, as indicated by making a wrong decision.

This is a perfect illustration of content inflecting process. The process of cognitive dissonance does appear in both East Asian and North American culture, but the triggers for producing this aversive state appear to depend on self-construal. For interdependent East Asians, dissonance appears only when decisions are made that impact interpersonal harmony with significant others, but for Euro-Americans, it is the individual's autonomous fear of making a bad decision (and hence displaying incompetence) that is the trigger. Hence, dissonance is a much more easily observed phenomenon in North America as compared to Japan. Americans and Canadians appear to over-value their independent abilities at making good decisions more than Japanese, who tend to be more aware of the situational and interpersonal constraints on the quality and impact of their decision-making.

In this line of experimental research, the process of communication is not overtly theorized – but presumably, in interdependent societies, the process of communication between significant others must be implicated in naturalistically occurring cognitive dissonance. Public behavior affects the reputation of the person in question through others in their social environment talking about them (e.g., criticizing them for their inappropriate decisions). Hence, the social environment for communication (Habermas, 1991; McLeod et al., 1999; Sherif, 1936) appears absolutely crucial for realizing the exact form and frequency of psychological phenomena, like cognitive dissonance obtained in laboratory contexts.

Beyond differences in individuals, what are the implications of culture for attitudes and persuasion among people in society? The evidence is tangential, as the work in cross-cultural psychology is mainly based on laboratory experiments on individuals or surveys of people in society. However, there is research holding that collectivistic cultures possess high-context norms for communication that require implicit knowledge and careful processing of environmental factors (or context, see Hall, 1959). Individualistic cultures are theorized to be more direct (or low-context) in their communications norms: this presumably allows newcomers to enter into society more easily. Norms are more influential on behavior in collectivistic societies, whereas attitudes are more influential in individualistic societies (Triandis, 1995). Furthermore, in the domain of leadership studies (Cheng, Chou, Wu, Huang, & Farh, 2004), in collectivistic cultures there is more deference to leaders and greater expectations for them providing top-down directions in organizations. Putting this together, and focusing on East Asian forms of collectivism, Liu (2015) claimed that relational obligations of an ethical and normative nature could slow down the dissolution of social structures by neo-liberal market forces. This happens by embedding the individual in binding relationships to meaningful collectives like family and the workplace. Ho, Peng, Lai & Chan (2001) therefore argued for methodological relationalism as a research strategy for East Asian societies, where the relationship, not the individual, is the basic unit of analysis.

Social Representations Theory (SRT)

Whereas a basic unit of analysis for CCP is typically culture, the idea that content inflects process permeates SRT as well. In contrast to CCP, SRT focuses on communication processes between, and within, groups in a given society and the dynamics of representation (or meaning) involved in this (Moscovici, 1988). The idea of social representations is that different collectives (typically within a country, but sometimes across cultures as well) hold different representations (or shared knowledge, beliefs, and feelings) of a social object that is structured in ways that make changing attitudes towards this object a function of properties of the social object. These properties include knowledge structures surrounding this object and what this object means for a collective.

According to Moscovici (1963: 251), 'social representation is defined as the elaborating of a social object by the community for the purpose of behaving and communicating'. Drawing from SRT, Sibley and Liu (2013: 161) advanced the concept of a 'representational profile as a set of discretely measureable attitudes that are bound together by a common interpretation within a group to make sense of and communicate within a social context about a social object'. This 'enable[s] the empirical mapping of dynamics between a representation, the people who hold it, and identity and action in group life' (Sibley and Liu, 2013: 161). They further elaborated a representational profile as a 'system [of meaning] that grasps together the ensemble of discrete attitudes in the context of communicating them intelligibly to people who may, or may not, agree with this point of view' (Sibley and Liu, 2013: 162).

What the concept of a representational profile does is locate a discrete attitude as part of a larger ensemble of meaning that is used in communications by members of different collectives who agree and disagree with one another. When an attitude is part of a social representation (e.g., profile), it is likely to be much harder to change on a long-term basis (see Liu, Sibley, & Huang, 2014). This is because any new information that comes through a persuasion attempt may be countered by naturalistically occurring information that comes through a person's social networks. Furthermore, a person might be emotionally invested in a particular point of view because of the meanings attached to particular words or discourses associated with this view (Wagner, Valencia, & Elejabarrieta, 1996).

For example, Sibley and Liu (2013) identified 12.9% of a national sample of New Zealanders as having a 'pro-bicultural representational profile' – that is, in favor of a range of social policies to improve things for Māori, the indigenous people of New Zealand (a disadvantaged minority and also signatories of the foundational document for the establishment of the contemporary state – the Treaty of Waitangi, see Orange, 2004). These people were more likely to vote for the Māori Party – a relatively newly formed political party focused on indigenous rights – and 45% of Māori were pro-bicultural, compared to only 5% of New Zealand Europeans. To attempt to turn attitudes toward bicultural policy issues more negative in this collective (as compared to the other profiles, like Bivalent, Moderate Differentiated, or Anti-Bicultural) would likely encounter social pushback – as the person would be more likely to talk to other Māori Party supporters and other Māori people for whom bicultural policy issues are likely to have salience and importance.

This pushback may also take place cognitively and motivationally, as Abric's (2003) formulation of a central nucleus of social representation predicts. The central nucleus is an emotionally engaged set of attitudes and beliefs meaningful for the person: it is conceptualized as more stable than peripheral elements of a social representation that come and go (Wagner et al., 1996). For the 'pro-bicultural' representational profile, knowledge of the Treaty of Waitangi (and violations of it, see

Liu and Robinson, 2016) and how important it is for New Zealand's claim to sovereignty provide the theory/meaning that knits the different attitudinal elements of support for bicultural policy together as part of a central nucleus of representation for biculturalism. Other attributes, like the physical appearance of Māori as brown-skinned, may be more peripheral.

Thus, attitudes towards 'Reserving places for Māori students to study medicine' (a sample item on the bicultural policy scale used by Sibley and Liu, 2013) would likely not be independent from a system of meaning about colonization and its aftermath. This attitude might be motivated by, and connected to, a broader system of meaning, compared to, say, attitudes towards which soap to use or what soap opera to watch. The differences between these are not likely to be confined to differences between central and peripheral route information processing; it is the difference between changing an isolated piece of information versus something that is part of a meaningful body of knowledge.

Discursive Psychology (DP)

CCP and SRT have not assailed the epistemological foundations of mainstream psychology to the extent of DP (Edwards and Potter, 1992). Inspired by the deliberative turn in social sciences, content is again at the front and center. However, DP views interpersonal communication through a commitment to social constructionism, wherein attitudes are positioned as ephemeral artefacts of social cognition as a research paradigm, and talk and text are positioned as more deserving of research attention. According to Potter and Weatherall (1987: 6), 'social texts do not merely *reflect* or *mirror* objects, events and categories pre-existing in the social and natural world. Rather, they actively *construct* a version of those things. They do not just describe things, they *do* things. And being active, they have social and political implications'.

The language of psychological science is problematized as a means of constructing accounts that appear to be 'scientific' but can be deconstructed as *versions* or *accounts* rather than objective descriptions of fact. This is a more extreme form of the challenges to scientific validity aimed at the mainstream by CCP. Instead of aiming to correct/extend the factual and theoretical basis of psychological science, DP attempts to replace experimental and quantitative survey methods with the study of social text and competing accounts (Edwards and Potter, 1992). These accounts are markers for communities of practice.

A powerful illustration of a discursive approach to psychology is Potter and Edwards (1990). They deconstruct consensus information, one of the three types of information that determine causal attribution according to Kelley's (1967) highly influential covariation model. Potter and Edwards (1990: 408) focus on how discourse on consensus is functionally oriented to accomplish certain social actions; that is, 'how people construct versions specifically in order to make certain conclusions inferable… discourse analysis takes the constructed nature of such accounts, and the way these constructions provide a basis for interferences of different kinds as a central focus of study'.

In Kelley's (1967) covariation model, consensus information (along with distinctiveness and consistency) is treated as one of three types of information used to make attributions for the cause of an event. In Potter and Edwards' (1990) deconstruction of a newspaper article about a political briefing, claims about consensus are used intentionally by actors to warrant (or support) their conflicting accounts about what happened at the meeting. In the information processing theory of Kelley (1967), consensus is treated as an objective input for the person who, like a naïve scientist, uses this information to compute the likely cause of an event. In Potter and Edwards (1990), consensus information is constructed as a claim that is used to warrant (justify) journalists' claims that a highly-ranked politician told them that he was thinking of means-testing pensioners' benefits. When this caused controversy, the politician claimed, 'the journalists had got together and their 'fevered imagination' had produced 'a farrago of invention' whose accounts bear no relation whatever to what I said' (Potter and Edwards, 1990: 411).

The journalists used consensus information to undermine the politician's account of the meeting, writing 'How on earth did the Chancellor, as a former journalist, manage to mislead so many journalists at once about his intentions?', 'is the Chancellor saying that every journalist who came to the briefing… misunderstood what he said', and 'The reporters, it seemed, had unanimously got it wrong. Could so many messengers really be so much in error? It seems doubtful…' (Potter and Edwards, 1990: 412). The politician counter-argued that the journalists colluded together to produce this consensus because the actual briefing was far less newsworthy.

It is the factuality of consensus information that is used to undermine an alternative account of an event, not the consensus information itself that is the subject of interest according to DP. Variability between versions, either produced by different people or by the same person at different occasions, is grist for the mill for a social constructionist approach to social psychology. As Potter and Edwards (1990: 421) argue, 'Consensus and independence, then, are not merely an analyst's categories for theorizing about what people say, but may be studied as categories that the speakers themselves flexibly deploy in the course of rhetorical work'. 'Facts' are to be interrogated as part of a rhetorical social process rather than established in an 'objective manner' as in scientific inquiry. Attribution is not theorized as abstract reasoning, as in the Kelley covariation model, but rather 'phenomena previously understood this way are more coherently seen as constitutive parts of activities such as blamings and rebuttals' (Potter and Edwards, 1990: 421).

Social constructions are clearly part of the 'common ground' (Kashima, 2014) that allow a people, and groups within a culture, to operate in a coherent manner – to maintain continuity amid change (Liu, Fisher Onar, & Woodward, 2014). In the main, however, scholars from developing parts of the world like Asia have eschewed DP's call for a radical epistemological departure from the Western scientific mainstream but heeded CCP's call for more culturally grounded work (Kashima, 2005). There are two reasons for this: the first is that people in developing countries tend to admire science and the idea of historical progress more than people living in developed countries, where these are pretty much taken for granted (Páez, Liu, Bobowik, Basabe, & Hanke, 2016). The second is that epistemologically, traditionally collectivist societies like those in Asia focus on holism as the basis for their philosophy, not the analytical/separationist approach favored by the social constructionists (who position themselves in opposition to positivist versions of science; for extended discussion, see Liu, 2011).

According to Kashima (2005: 35), 'If we take a view that intentionality is materially realized, meaning is part of a causal chain, and social scientific investigation is also part of complex causal processes, we can adopt a monist ontology, in which human nature is not distinct from, but continuous with, material nature'. Asian philosophy privileges holism above analytical forms of separation – this may have prevented systematic advance in science historically, but it also favors a more active, engaged, and holistic social science today; one focused on social change for public good rather than reifying scientific categories that aren't much use in daily life (Liu, 2014). In the final part of this chapter, we consider the roles technology, science, and social science may play in constructing global futures.

THE ROLE OF COMMUNICATION TECHNOLOGIES IN 'MAKING PEOPLE'

There is much that can be taken away from approaches to the problem of attitudes and persuasion that pay deeper attention to the ways in which content inflects process. This may be applied to analyzing how technology produces, reproduces, and communicates culture and its contents. Kashima asserts that Asian social psychology has no problem in accepting these basic premises:

> 1. Culture is socially and historically constructed, 2. People construe themselves using concepts and other symbolic structures that are available, 3. People develop a theory of mind (i.e., a theory of how the mind works) to understand others. 4. People have beliefs about the world, and they act on those beliefs. 5. People engage in meaningful action. 6. Culture is constitutive of the mind. (Kashima, 2005: 20)

This is a manifestly constructionist epistemic position that is simultaneously part of a holistic scientific enterprise that uses quantitative methods in the main, but is open to qualitative methods and studies social change (see Yang, 2000 for theory of how this can be encompassed).

Digital communication technologies are harbingers of change that are having a profound impact across the globe. A visible example is the explosion of social media across the world with billions of users. Today, the importance of communication technologies is key to shaping how people communicate with each other, the way they get their news, how they keep entertained, and even the way they shape their own personal identities (Gil de Zúñiga, Molyneux, & Zheng, 2014; Papacharissi, 2015). This is because they operate using network structures. Network structures might undermine some of the social organizing principles of modernity established in the last 200 years. Since the industrial revolution, modern society has been bound by a top-down, one-way flow of communication, often characterized by information scarcity and top-down broadcasting structures (Bimber, 2003). The reorganization of social life around networked structures tends to decentralize power structures; digital networks lead to a free flow of information in multiple directions, and lower the costs of communication. These can disrupt economic systems through the development of peer-to-peer sharing and the 'free culture' of the internet (Benkler, 2004).

Digital network structures increase the speed of interpersonal communication, encourage information sharing, and offer new models for economic activity. The internet, social media, and mobile smart phones influence people through changes in social relations – on the one hand, they extend reach but, on the other, they allow minority views to thrive and connect with other minority views. Hence, the idea of representational profiles (Sibley and Liu, 2013) – as communities or collectives of individuals who share knowledge structures constructed through communication and motivated by systems of meaning – appears to be even more valuable as a research tool. These representational profiles may transcend boundaries of distance and culture and produce new forms of shared understanding – for instance, about heroes and villains in world history (Hanke, Liu, Sibley, Paez, Gaines, Moloney, et al., 2015) – shared by individuals across, rather than just within, cultures. The utilization of digital technology simultaneously allows the construction of global consciousness by removing distance as a barrier, but it also feeds pockets of resistance against such a mainstream by allowing dissidents to more easily form coalitions (Liu and Macdonald, 2016).

The use of these technologies has an enormous influence on how people learn new information, participate in politics, and organize social protest movements (Aday, Farrell, Lynch, Sides, Kelly, & Zuckerman, 2010). They also enable citizens to act as journalists and political pundits, outside of the traditional news industry. Networks allow politicians to talk directly to constituencies and create a space for 'e-government' to engage local communities to solve local problems or to upset the status quo. Networks also disrupt economic activity when sharing replaces the need for markets and property rights; for example, with Wikipedia, travel information, or open source software. They allow forms of agency and loosely networked types of alliances that might not have been possible without such freedom of communications (see Ford, Ford, & D'Amelio, 2008; Liu, Ng, Gastardo-Conaco, & Wong, 2008), and this can contribute to pluralism, at least within democratic states.

Following literature on the digital divide, countries with internet access and skills are able to take advantage of increased productivity, enhanced leisure time, and new forms of media, shopping, and social interaction (Norris, 2001). One takeaway from this burgeoning literature is that media effects depend on how the technology is used. For example, people who use the internet tend to score lower on depression tests, but only when they use it to talk to friends and family (Bessiere et al., 2008). Similarly, those that use the internet and social media for news and information tend to participate in politics and have higher levels of political knowledge (Kenski and Stroud, 2006). On the other hand, those that use the internet and communication technologies for entertainment and escapism avoid politics entirely (Prior, 2005). In another example, cell phones have been heralded for improving the quality of life for peoples across sub-Saharan Africa (Aker and Mbiti, 2010) – but the same technologies have been blamed for social isolation in Japan, where more young people refuse to live lives independent of their parents or even leave the house (Stip et al., 2016). Networks mediate the general effect of digital technology on individuals, but the specific influences depend on how they are used. In short, and regardless of whether we highlight the positive or negative ways in which digital media and new technologies affect people, their role in shaping people's lives is unquestionable and conditioned by content – by the choices people make in using this technology.

Among CCP's basic units of analysis, the country may become increasingly difficult to analytically sustain in the Digital Age, where information sharing is exponentially increasing at the same time as plural networks of sociality and meaning are being constructed. Digital technology allows choice in social interaction partners, choice in social networks, and choice of unbridled amounts of information in whatever domain information is desired. This may undermine cross-cultural differences, bringing about hybridity and pockets of similarity and difference that both transcend and increase pluralism with national boundaries (Appiah, 2005; Hermans and Dimaggio, 2007). The internet does not, however, transcend language differences.

GLOBALIZATION AND SOCIAL ACTION

With the rise of social media and friend networks, communication theory has developed perspectives where the role of direct mass persuasion effects is considered to be outdated relative to network models based on social psychology. These theories suggest that mass communication works as a stimulus, and the effect depends on how an individual reacts to the message in their social milieu. Discussion frequency, network attributes, and cognitive reasoning all play roles in mediating communication effects – social cognition in communications theory should thus be entering into an era of fuller connectivity, taking the isolated individual out of the lab, and bringing theories of individual functioning into their place as part of 'thinking societies' (Moscovici, 1961/2008).

As communication technology develops at a blistering pace, researchers have struggled to adapt older paradigms to the new communication environment. At no time has the modality and technology of communication (e.g., face to face versus telephone versus television and the internet) been a focus of attention. We argue that this 'technology blindness' limits the practicality and applicability of social psychology, particularly across cultures where the access to, and acceptance of, technology varies considerably. An important direction for the future is to conceptualize how organized social action can flow through different social networks mediated by different types of communications technology. Very little is currently available, for example, to theorize about how people living in countries with poor traditional infrastructure but with access to the internet (e.g., through satellite technology) can develop economically through alternative models and alternative social networks (Acker and Mbiti, 2010).

One goal of the current chapter has been to bring the literature on discursive, cross-cultural, and representational turns in social psychology into dialogue with the role of modality and technology of communication in its effects on attitudes and persuasion. Contextual, cultural, and content based features of communications may be very important if the goal is to succeed in group level persuasion. Situating the individual within a cultural context that includes technology is eminently practical as a communications strategy for the field.

Furthermore, the flow of communication between interest groups as manifested by action research, originated by Lewin in the 1940s–1950s and subsequently extended by qualitative researchers into participant action research, is raised as an alternative approach to applying communications and psychology research. While successful actions are less common than calls for it, action research remains a 'gold standard template' for producing a reciprocally engaged social science, where people are acknowledged as change agents that turn the probability fields afforded by technology into history (like the amazing rise of East Asian societies to wealth and modernity in a short time, see Tu, 1996). Conceptualizing persons as change agents needs to take into account the discursive repertoires prevalent at a time and place in a culture's history, thus leveraging social constructionism to a more active place in producing public good than has heretofore been seen in critical psychology as a movement (see Fox, Prilleltensky, & Austin, 2009).

Action research has not found a home in wealthy countries where publish or perish rules the academy (Liu et al., 2008). But it may thrive in developing societies with access to digital technology (and hence advanced knowledge and literature) and political elites willing to invest in social science as a collective good (Liu and Macdonald, 2016). The emergence of an academic culture that privileges good practice and making contributions to public good rather than publication for its own sake might only emerge in pockets, but these may grow through the interconnectedness of the internet and its ability to allow people to form collectives of choice.

A final thought concerns the digital influence of technology on group thinking. Social media and the internet make it increasingly easy for groups to form into clusters, which might work as a welcoming place where different kinds of marginalized groups find a voice, versus isolating themselves from one another. However, on the other hand, the internet and information technologies have facilitated an informational process by which individuals may easily get exposure only to information they agree with. This is termed 'selective exposure', where the internet provides opportunities for individuals to get their information from partisan sources. Several scholars (i.e., Colleoni, Rozza, & Arvidsson, 2014; Iyengar, Hahn, Krosnick, & Walker, 2008; Stroud, 2010) have taken a cautious view of new technologies because of this: selective exposure to information, partisan sorting, and identity politics effectively create an 'echo chamber', where only attitude-consistent information is shared. This leads to less of a civil public sphere and effectively hamstrings the democratic order (Herbst, 2010; Theriault, 2008). On the other hand, several authors highlight the capacity of information technologies, with social media at the forefront, to expand people's political discussion networks and get exposed to different views and information.

In this environment, it remains an open question how often this takes place and, if so, how. In other words, what makes 'echo chambers' form or dissipate? This is a question of central importance to the twenty-first century, where the process of 'making people' is inescapably intertwined with globalization and globalizing technologies.

REFERENCES

Abric, J.-C. (2003). *Methode d'Étude des Représentations Sociales* (Methods of Studying Social Representations). Paris: Érés (In French).

Aday, S., Farrell, H., Lynch, M., Sides, J., Kelly, J., & Zuckerman, E. (2010). Blogs and bullets: New media in contentious politics. *Peaceworks, 65*, 1–31. Washington, DC: United States Institute of Peace. Retrieved from http://www.usip.org/publications/blogs-and-bullets-new-media-in-contentious-politics

Aker, J. C., & Mbiti, I. M. (2010). Mobile phones and economic development in Africa. *The Journal of Economic Perspectives, 24*(3), 207–232.

Albarracin, D., & Vargas, P. (2009). Attitudes and persuasion: From biology to social responses to persuasive intent. In S.T. Fiske, D.T. Gilbert, & G. Lindzey (Eds.), *Handbook of social psychology* (5th edn.), pp. 394–427). New York: Wiley.

Appiah, K.A. (2005). *The ethics of identity*. Princeton: Princeton University Press.

Bandura, A. (2001). Social cognitive theory of mass communication. *Media Psychology, 3*(3): 265–299.

Bechara, A., & Damasio, A. R. (2005). The somatic marker hypothesis: A neural theory of economic decision. *Games and Economic Behavior, 52*(2), 336–372.

Benkler, Y. (2004). Sharing nicely: On shareable goods and the emergence of sharing as a modality of economic production. *Yale Law Journal, 114*(2), 273–358.

Bernays, E. (2005) [1928]. *Propaganda*. Brooklyn, NY: Ig Publishing.

Bessiere, K., Kiesler, S., Kraut, R., & Boneva, B. S. (2008). Effects of Internet use and social resources on changes in depression. *Information, Community & Society, 11*(1), 47–70.

Bimber, B. (2003). *Information and American democracy: Technology in the evolution of political power*. Cambridge, UK: Cambridge University Press.

Chaiken, S., & Maheswaran, D. (1994). Heuristic processing can bias systematic processing: Effects of source credibility, argument ambiguity, and task importance on attitude judgment. *Journal of Personality and Social Psychology, 66*, 460–460.

Chaiken, S., & Trope, Y. (1999). *Dual-process theories in social psychology*. New York: Guilford Press.

Cheng, B. S., Chou, L. F., Wu, T. Y., Huang, M. P., & Farh, J. L. (2004). Paternalistic leadership and subordinates responses: Establishing a leadership model in Chinese organizations. *Asian Journal of Social Psychology, 7*(1), 89–117. DOI: 10.1111/j.1467-839X.2004.00137.x

Cho, J., Shah, D. V., McLeod, J. M., McLeod, D. M., Scholl, R. M., & Gotlieb, M. R. (2009). Campaigns, reflection, and deliberation: Advancing an O-S-R-O-R model of communication effects. *Communication Theory, 19*(1), 66–88.

Colleoni, E., Rozza, A., & Arvidsson, A. (2014). Echo chamber or public sphere? Predicting political orientation and measuring political homophily in Twitter using big data. *Journal of Communication, 64*(2), 317–332.

Edwards, D., & Potter, J. (1992). *Discursive psychology*. London: Sage.

Egidi, M. (2017). Schumpeter's picture of economic and political institutions in the light of a cognitive approach to human behavior. *Journal of Evolutionary Economics, 27*(1), 139–159.

Evans, J. S. B. T. (2008). Dual-processing accounts of reasoning, judgment, and social cognition. *Annual Review of Psychology, 59*, 255–278.

Eveland, Jr., W. P. (2004). The effect of political discussion in producing informed citizens: The roles of information, motivation, and elaboration. *Political Communication, 21*(2), 177–193.

Festinger, L., & Carlsmith, J. M. (1959). Cognitive consequences of forced compliance.

Journal of Abnormal and Social Psychology, *58*, 203–211.

Fishkin, J. S. (1991). *Democracy and deliberation: New directions for democratic reform*. New Haven: Yale University Press.

Ford, J. D., & Ford, L. W. (1995). The role of conversations in producing intentional change in organizations. *The Academy of Management Review*, *20*(3), 541–570.

Ford, J. D., Ford, L. W., & D'Amelio, A. (2008). Resistance to change: The rest of the story. *Academy of Management Review*, *33*(2), 362–377.

Fox, D., Prilleltensky, I., & Austin, S. (2009). *Critical psychology: An introduction* (2nd edn.). Los Angeles: Sage.

Gamson, W. A. (1992). *Talking politics*. Cambridge: Cambridge University Press.

Gil de Zúñiga, H., & Valenzuela, S. (2011) The mediating path to a stronger citizenship: Online and offline networks, weak ties, and civic engagement, *Communication Research*, *38*(3), 397–421.

Gil de Zúñiga, H., Molyneux, L., & Zheng, P. (2014). Social media, political expression, and political participation: Panel analysis of lagged and concurrent relationships. *Journal of Communication*, *64*(4), 612–634.

Habermas, J. (1991). *The structural transformation of the public sphere: An inquiry into a category of bourgeois society*. Boston: MIT Press.

Habermas, J., & McCarthy, T. (1985). *The theory of communicative action* (Vol. 2). Boston: Beacon Press.

Hall, E. T. (1959). *The Silent Language*. New York: Doubleday.

Hanke, K., Liu, J, H., Sibley, C., Paez, D., Gaines, Jr., S. P., Moloney, G., et al. (2015). 'Heroes' and 'Villains' of world history across cultures. *PLoS One*, *10*(2): e0115641.

Heine, S. J., & Lehman, D. R. (1997). Culture, dissonance, and self-affirmation. *Personality and Social Psychology Bulletin*, *23*(4), 389–400.

Henrich, J., Heine, S. J., & Norenzayan, A. (2010). The weirdest people in the world. *Behavioral and Brain Sciences*, *33*, 61–135.

Herbst, S. (2010). *Rude democracy: Civility and incivility in American politics*. Philadelphia: Temple University Press.

Hermans, H., & Dimaggio, G. (2007). Self, identity, and globalization in times of uncertainty: A dialogical analysis. *Review of General Psychology*, *11*(1), 31–61.

Ho, D. Y. F., Peng, S. Q., Lai, A. C., Chan, S. F. F. (2001). Indigenization and beyond: Methodological relationalism in the study of personality across cultural traditions. *Journal of Personality*, *69*(6), 925–953.

Hovland, C. I., Janis, I. L., & Kelley, H. H. (1953). *Communication and persuasion: Psychological studies of opinion change*. New Haven: Yale University Press.

Inglehart, R., & Baker, W. E. (2000). Modernization, cultural change, and the persistence of traditional values. *American Sociological Review*, *65*, 19–49.

Iyengar, S., Hahn, K. S., Krosnick, J. A., & Walker, J. (2008). Selective exposure to campaign communication: The role of anticipated agreement and issue public membership. *The Journal of Politics*, *70*(1), 186–200.

Jung, N., Kim, Y., & de Zúniga, H. G. (2011). The mediating role of knowledge and efficacy in the effects of communication on political participation. *Mass Communication and Society*, *14*(4), 407–430.

Kahneman, D. (2003). Maps of bounded rationality: a perspective on intuitive judgment and choice. *The American Economic Review*, *93*(5), 1449–1475.

Kashima, Y. (2005). Is culture a problem for social psychology? *Asian Journal of Social Psychology*, *8*, 19–38.

Kashima, Y. (2014). Meaning, grounding, and the construction of social reality. *Asian Journal of Social Psychology*, *17*(2), 81–95.

Katz, E., & Lazarsfeld, P. F. (1966). *Personal Influence: The part played by people in the flow of mass communications*. New Brunswick, NJ: Transaction Publishers.

Kelley, H. H. (1967). Attribution theory in social psychology. In D. Levine (Ed.), *Nebraska symposium on motivation*. Lincoln: University of Nebraska Press.

Kenski, K., & Stroud, N. J. (2006). Connections between Internet use and political efficacy, knowledge, and participation. *Journal of Broadcasting & Electronic Media*, *50*(2), 173–19

Kitayama. S., Snibbe, A.C., Markus, H.R., Suzuki, T. (2004). Is there any 'free' choice? Self and dissonance in two cultures, *Psychological*

Science, 15(*8*), 527-533 https://doi.org/10.1111/j.0956-7976.2004.00714.x2.

Lazarsfeld, P., & Merton, R. K. (1948). Mass communication, popular taste and organized social action. *Media Studies*, 18–30.

Lewin, K. (1946). Action research and minority problems. *Journal of Social Issues*, *2*(4), 34–46.

Liu, J. H. (2011). Asian epistemologies and contemporary social psychological research. In N. Denzin, & Y. Lincoln (Eds.), *Handbook of qualitative research* (4th edn., pp. 213–226). Thousand Oaks, CA: Sage.

Liu, J.H. (2014). What Confucian philosophy means for Chinese and Asian psychology today: Indigenous roots for a psychology of social change. *Journal of Pacific Rim Psychology, 8*(2), 35–42.

Liu, J.H. (2015). Globalizing indigenous psychology: An East Asian form of hierarchical relationalism with worldwide implications. *Journal for the Theory of Social Behavior, 45*(*1*), 82-94.

Liu, J. H., & Macdonald, M. (2016). Towards a psychology of global consciousness. *Journal for the Theory of Social Behavior*, *46*(3), 310–334.

Liu, J. H., Fisher Onar, N., & Woodward, M. (2014). Symbologies, technologies, and identities: Critical Junctures Theory and the multi-layered Nation-State. *International Journal of Intercultural Relations*, *43*, 2–12.

Liu, J. H., Ng, S. H., Gastardo-Conaco, C., & Wong, D. S. W. (2008). Action research: A missing component in the emergence of social and cross-cultural psychology as a fully interconnected global enterprise. *Social & Personality Psychology Compass*, *2*(3), 1162–1181.

Liu, J.H., & Robinson, A.R. (2016). One ring to rule them all: Master discourses of enlightenment- and racism- from colonial to contemporary New Zealand. *European Journal of Social Psychology*, *42*(*2*), 137-155.

Markus, H. R., & Kitayama, S. (1991). Culture and the self: Implications for cognition, emotion, and motivation. *Psychological Review*, *98*(2), 224–253.

McLeod, J. M., Scheufele, D. A., & Moy, P. (1999). Community, communication, and participation: The role of mass media and interpersonal discussion in local political participation. *Political Communication*, *16*(3), 315–336.

Moscovici, S. (1961/2008). *La psychanalyse, son image et son public (Psychoanalysis, its image and its public)*. Paris: Presses Universitaires de France. (English translation by Polity Press, Cambridge UK).

Moscovici, S. (1963). Attitudes and opinions. *Annual Review of Psychology*, *14*, 231–260.

Moscovici, S. (1988). Notes towards a description of social representations. *European Journal of Social Psychology,* 18(3), 211–250.

Norris, P. (2001). *Digital divide: Civic engagement, information poverty, and the Internet worldwide*. Cambridge, UK: Cambridge University Press.

Orange, C. (2004). *An illustrated history of the Treaty of Waitangi*. Wellington, New Zealand: Bridget Williams Books.

Páez, D., Liu, J. H., Bobowik, M., Basabe, N., & Hanke, K. (2016). Social representations of history, cultural values, and willingness to fight in a war: A collective-level analysis in 40 nations. *Asian Journal of Social Psychology*, *19*, 347–361.

Papacharissi, Z. (2015). *Affective publics: Sentiment, technology, and politics*. Oxford: Oxford University Press.

Petty, R. E., & Cacioppo, J. T. (1986). *Attitudes and persuasion: Classic and contemporary approaches.* Dubuque, IA: Wm. C. Brown Publishers.

Petty, R. E., Brinol, P., & Priester, J. R. (2009). Mass media attitude change: Implications of the Elaboration Likelihood Model of persuasion. In J. Bryant, & M. B. Oliver (Eds.), *Media effects: Advances in theory and research* (3rd edn., pp. 125–164). New York: Routledge.

Potter, J., & Edwards, D. (1990). Nigel Lawson's tent: Discourse analysis, attribution theory and the social psychology of fact. *European Journal of Social Psychology*, *20*, 405–424.

Potter, J., & Weatherall, M. (1987). *Discourse and psychology: Beyond attitudes and behavior.* London: Sage.

Prior, M. (2005). News vs. entertainment: How increasing media choice widens gaps in political knowledge and turnout. *American Journal of Political Science*, *49*(3), 577–592.

Shah, D. V., Cho, J., Nah, S., Gotlieb, M. R., Hwang, H., Lee, N. J., Scholl, M., & McLeod, D. (2007). Campaign ads, online messaging, and participation: Extending the

Communication Mediation Model. *Journal of Communication*, *57*, 676–703.

Sherif, M. (1936). *The psychology of social norms.* New York: Harper & Bros.

Sibley, C. G., & Liu, J. H. (2013). Relocating attitudes as components of representational profiles: Mapping the epidemiology of bicultural policy attitudes using Latent Class Analysis. *European Journal of Social Psychology*, *43*, 160–174.

Sibley, C. G., Liu, J. H., & Kirkwood, S. (2006). Toward a social representations theory of attitude change: The effect of message framing on general and specific attitudes toward equality and entitlement. *New Zealand Journal of Psychology*, *35*(1), 3–13.

Smith, P. B., Fischer, R., & Vignoles, V. (2013). Chapter 7. Self and identity processes. In P. B. Smith, R. Fischer, V. L. Vignoles, & M. H. Bond (Eds.), *Understanding social psychology across cultures: Engaging with others in a changing world* London: Sage.

Stip, E., Thibault, A., Beauchamp-Chatel, A., & Kisely, S. (2016). Internet addiction, Hikikomori syndrome, and the prodromal phase of psychosis. *Frontiers in Psychiatry*, *7*(6). https://doi.org/10.3389/fpsyt.2016.00006

Stone, J., & Cooper, J. (2001). A self-standards model of cognitive dissonance. *Journal of Experimental Social Psychology*, *37*(3), 228–243.

Stroud, N. J. (2010). Polarization and partisan selective exposure. *Journal of Communication*, *60*(3), 556–576.

Tafarodi, R. W., Shaughnessy, S. C., Yamaguchi, S., & Murakoshi, A. (2011). The reporting of self-esteem in Japan and Canada. *Journal of Cross-Cultural Psychology*, *42*(1), 155–164.

Theriault, S. M. (2008). *Party polarization in Congress*. Cambridge: Cambridge University Press.

Triandis, H. C. (1995). *Individualism and collectivism.* Boulder, CO: Westview Press.

Tu, W. M. (Ed.) (1996). *Confucian traditions in East Asian modernity*. Cambridge, MA: Harvard University Press.

Wagner, W., Valencia, J., & Elejabarrieta, F. (1996). Relevance, discourse and the 'hot' stable core social representations – A structural analysis of word associations. *European Journal of Social Psychology*, *35*(3), 331–351.

Yang, K. S. (2000). Monocultural and cross-cultural indigenous approaches: The royal road to the development of a balanced global psychology. *Asian Journal of Social Psychology*, *3*, 241–264.

20

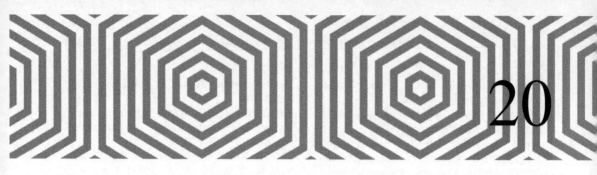

Discursive Psychology as Applied Science

Eleftheria Tseliou, Olga Smoliak, Andrea LaMarre and Christopher Quinn-Nilas

In this chapter, we propose that discursive psychology (DP) is an applied approach to the study of the social world. DP is a trend of discourse analysis (Potter & Hepburn, 2005) originally developed mostly by social psychology scholars in the United Kingdom. Applied social psychology, a distinct and rapidly growing branch of social psychology, highlights the importance of empirically investigating applied and practical matters, highly relevant for peoples' everyday practices. Applied social psychologists often aim to determine real-world implications of social psychological work, including interventions for everyday problems (Gruman, Schneider, & Coutts, 2017).

Similarly, applied research has been central to DP since its emergence (e.g., Edwards & Potter, 1992). The 'applied' nature of DP is evident in two ways: in its focus on applied topics, but also in the distinct approach discursive psychologists take to understanding and examining phenomena, namely an interest in 'studying the world as it happens' (Wiggins & Hepburn, 2007, p. 281). We begin the chapter with a brief overview of DP, including its origins, current developments, and basic tenets. While doing so, we highlight the applied approach that DP undertakes in theorizing psychological phenomena. We then offer a selective overview of DP research across a variety of topics, which demonstrates how DP is particularly concerned with the study of applied matters, while also highlighting what DP distinctly offers in the study of these topics. We conclude by exploring the implications of DP for applied social psychology.

ORIGINS, TENETS, AND STRANDS OF DISCURSIVE PSYCHOLOGY

It is not easy to define DP in a straightforward way given the several different accounts of its origins and the diversity in current DP trends (e.g., Potter, 2010; Tileagă & Stokoe,

2016). The term DP usually points to what Augoustinos and Tileagă (2012, p. 405) refer to as 'the Loughborough school of social psychology', meaning the intellectual heritage of psychologists like Michael Billig, Derek Edwards, David Middleton, Jonathan Potter, and Margaret Wetherell, who revisioned mainstream social psychology through a discursive – or linguistic – lens. Although the term 'discursive psychology' was introduced by Edwards and Potter (1992) in their seminal book *Discursive Psychology*, the origins of DP can be traced back to three earlier works (Billig, 1987; Edwards & Mercer, 1987; Potter & Wetherell, 1987).

DP developed through attempts to bring discourse analysis, rhetorical and critical perspectives into social psychology (Hepburn & Jackson, 2009; Hepburn & Potter, 2011). 'Discourse analysis' is an umbrella term pointing to a variety of approaches across disciplines usually clustered under the epistemological turn in social sciences, known as the 'discursive turn' (Bozatzis, 2014; Tseliou, 2013; 2018). This shift to an alternative paradigm in social sciences introduced the idea that the use and social history of language should be considered constitutive of any phenomenon, including scientific knowledge. This implied a social constructionist perspective on knowledge as socially, historically, and locally constructed (Burr, 2015). Both the initial proposal for introducing discourse analysis in social psychology (Potter & Wetherell, 1987) and its subsequent development in DP (Edwards & Potter, 1992) promoted this epistemological shift from uncovering 'true' or 'correct' versions of social reality to recognizing that multiple realities may coexist and seeing language as the primary means through which versions of reality are constructed and negotiated in social interaction. The main idea was that social psychology should turn to discourse or language use as the object of study instead of treating language as a means to get access to 'inner' cognitive processes.

In DP, the focus turns to how versions of reality are *constructed* (i.e., actively assembled through language and interactions) and negotiated and to the functions that such constructions serve in the context of their production (e.g., Edwards & Potter, 1992). By 'functions', we mean the ways in which people use language to achieve certain practical purposes (e.g., request, accuse, deny, invite). Language is thus treated as social action or a way to get things done in interaction (Austin, 1962). Furthermore, language use is treated as attending to variable functions depending on the particular occasion and on the rhetorical and the institutional context (Potter, 2011; 2012a; Wiggins & Potter, 2008). This interest in constructed and functional characteristics of language use, as well as in variability, is further attuned to how people mobilize classic *psychological* processes and psychosocial categories, such as memory, attribution, emotion, traits, or prejudice, in their talk-in-interaction (Edwards, 1997; 2012; Edwards & Potter, 1992; Potter, 1996). A 'classic' model which epitomizes DP key notions is the Discursive Action Model (DAM) (Edwards & Potter, 1993), originally introduced as a way to reconceptualize attributions and memory in discursive terms.

Wiggins (2017, p. 4) defined DP as 'a theoretical and analytical approach to discourse which treats talk and text as an object of study in itself, and psychological concepts as socially managed and consequential in interaction'. This focus on language use denotes a (micro-oriented or bottom-up) strand of DP, which has been inspired by Wittgenstein's and Austin's linguistic philosophy with a pragmatic approach to language and interest in language use as performative or as *doing things*. It also heavily draws on conversation analysis (a micro-level, turn-by-turn approach to understanding language as constitutive, see Sacks, Schegloff, & Jefferson, 1974), rooted in ethnomethodology, to the extent that it is difficult to differentiate many contemporary DP contributions from conversation analysis (Parker, 2012; Potter, 2010). Micro-oriented

DP focuses on the details and sequentiality of language use in naturally occurring sets of data, like transcribed videotaped therapy sessions, courtroom talk, and academic lectures and emphasizes participants' perspectives; that is, the way that people themselves make sense of their interactions.

DP is also rooted in a critical perspective committed to a radical, political stance which aimed at disciplinary change and the reconceptualization of social psychology (Billig, 2012; Parker, 2012). The latter was evident in early attempts (e.g., Billig et al., 1988; Potter & Wetherell, 1987) to approach language not only at the micro-level of its use in everyday interactions but also in relation to a macro-level of context. Here, language is approached as constitutive of everyday discursive practices in ways resonant with wider socio-political, historical, and ideological conditions. Potter and Wetherell (1987) deployed the notion of 'interpretive repertoires' to denote the semantic resonance of language use with social history. Put simply, interpretative repertoires suggest that we do not invent the content of discourse with each interaction. Instead, there are systematic and historically constituted ways to talk about an 'object', which become commonsensical, vary across cultures, and in some cases, become culturally established as privileged (Potter, 2011; Potter & Wetherell, 1987).

Billig et al. (1988) also advanced the notion of ideological dilemmas, which signified an attempt to approach language use as a terrain where ideology is downplayed and constructed on an everyday, practical basis. Ideological dilemmas, evident in how people may describe events in conflicting and contradictory ways, go beyond individual choices between options. Rather, the concern is with the 'moral and ideological complexities' of a dilemma (Billig et al., 1988, p. 12) or with how meaning-making is socially and culturally embedded. In describing experiences and events, people may *simultaneously* draw on different, even conflicting, ideologies or cultural systems of ideas and ideals (e.g., conservative and liberal, collectivist and individualist, patriarchal and egalitarian).

In addition to attending to the constructed and functional nature of language, critical DP scholars (e.g., Bozatzis, 2009; Goodman & Speer, 2007; Tileagă, 2009; Wetherell & Edley, 2014) explore how language *constructs* certain versions of reality. This 'both/and' position, introduced by Wetherell (1998), highlights the possibility of combining analyses of the micro-details of talk with post-structuralist readings of texts by retaining an analytic emphasis on notions like interpretative repertoires and ideological dilemmas (for examples, see Bozatzis, 2009; Goodman & Speer, 2007; Tileagă, 2009; Wetherell & Edley, 2014).

DP's commitment to the study of how the 'psychological' is intersubjectively and socially performed and, therefore, its advancement of an applied perspective is evident in its origins and influences. In the remainder of the introduction section, we will pursue this line of argumentation by highlighting some key tenets of DP.

DISCURSIVE PSYCHOLOGY AS AN APPLIED FRAMEWORK

We argue that DP introduces an applied perspective to the study of psychological phenomena (see also Wiggins & Hepburn, 2007). There are at least two ways in which this is accomplished. Firstly, the topics of study chosen by DP scholars are often of applied relevance to everyday life and examinations of social structures. As we will make evident in the next section, DP has been deployed for the study of a wide range of applied matters, such as processes of counseling or health encounters, police interrogations, or judicial decision-making. DP is also widely deployed for the study of institutional practices, as well as for the study of how policy is done in everyday practice (Wiggins & Hepburn, 2007).

Secondly, DP presumes that psychological phenomena are people's practical accomplishments constituted in everyday social interaction and offers a wide set of methodological tools for the study of these phenomena in discursive terms. By focusing on what people actually *do* in the course of their interactions (Hepburn & Potter, 2011), DP provides an understanding of what constitutes a psychological phenomenon in the actual interactional, discursive practice, where it is evoked (Edwards, 2012; Wiggins & Potter, 2008). For example, little is known about how a complaint, a threat, a prejudiced belief, or a therapist's formulation about clients' problems is performed in the actual, natural settings of peoples' everyday practices. What DP offers is an empirical exploration of these phenomena in the natural settings of their occurrence, using 'a direct focus on human action' (Hepburn & Potter, 2011, p. 2) to explicitly orient to practical approaches for understanding social life. DP produces detailed analyses of how people 'do psychology' in everyday life, including institutional settings. By exploring talk-in-interaction and texts as contextually-bound, DP offers a wide range of possibilities for depicting in detail what a range of key practices may actually look like or how problems may get constructed or addressed, for example, in education, counselling, health, politics, and other areas. In that sense, DP offers a naturalistic, applied approach to social psychology (Potter, 2012b). The critical strands of DP introduced above (e.g., Wetherell, 2007) are also directly aimed at introducing social change by highlighting processes of ideological reproduction and thus by problematizing certain patterns of discourse use. Critical DP helps unmask the constraining aspects of discourse use, which may privilege certain practices and understandings and marginalize others due to its historical and ideological constitution.

In the remainder of this chapter, we will present a selective review of DP studies, including a variety of topics *across* disciplines or sub-disciplines, which highlight the application of DP. We will show how DP has been, and is currently, deployed for the study of a wide range of applied topics. Our review of DP studies is selective and aimed at illustrating applications of DP rather than being systematic or exhaustive. Our aim was to explore the use of DP in topics usually identified as applied (see Gruman et al., 2017; Steg, Leiser, Buunk, & Rothengatter, 2017). Our illustrative examples concern studies where authors refer to the use of DP and not studies which undertake a discourse analytic or rhetorical approach without mentioning the use of DP.

APPLICATIONS OF DISCURSIVE PSYCHOLOGY: THE STUDY OF THE 'PSYCHOLOGICAL' AS SOCIAL PRACTICE

The overview of DP research that follows includes a variety of topics from a number of disciplines, including health psychology, education, environmental psychology, sport psychology, clinical psychology, political psychology, and more. These topics concern social justice issues like discrimination, embodied practices like health, nutrition, and exercise, environmental issues like nature and geographical space, professional encounters like health care, psychotherapy, and counseling, organizational themes like leadership and management, technology and computer-mediated communication, educational processes as well as legal issues and political discourse. Thus, DP studies have, as key focus, the study of both ordinary, everyday discourse but also of institutional and political discourse. Different sub-sections depict different facets of everyday life from the 'local' to the 'institutional'. Within each sub-section, we present indicative examples of DP studies that explicate how a range of psychological phenomena or notions like attitudes, prejudice, identity, beliefs, or attributions are discursively performed in action.

ADDRESSING SOCIAL JUSTICE ISSUES: IDENTITY CONSTRUCTION AND PREJUDICE IN TALK

Since its origins, DP presented key themes in social psychology (e.g., attitudes, attributions, prejudice, and identity) as discursive accomplishments in talk in interaction (Edwards & Potter, 1992; Potter & Wetherell, 1987). DP research has provided pertinent insight on how *gender* and *ethnic/national identities* are debated and constructed in talk and has enhanced understanding of social justice issues, such as the discursive accomplishment of *sexism* and *racism*. For example, DP research (e.g. Stokoe, 2015) has illustrated how speakers built their prejudiced claims to appear to be non-prejudiced or as mere descriptions of events and people.

Investigating the 'isms' (e.g., sexism, racism, classism, ableism) from a DP perspective allows researchers to explore how social categories like gender and category-based marginalization and privilege are built in interaction. By focusing on interaction, DP analysis allows for nuanced understandings of social identity as built and resisted in talk, and of less direct and subtler operations of prejudice. The DP literature demonstrates strategies that people use in their talk to guard against allegations of being racist, sexist, etc. and how these strategies serve to further entrench marginalization and oppression of members of certain social groups (Hanson-Easey, Augoustinos, & Moloney, 2014; Stokoe, 1998). It also foregrounds the need to move beyond pre-determined categorization of minority groups in particular and facilitates exploration of how people construct their belonging (or non-belonging) to different groups in a way that leads to new insight into membership categorization (Stokoe, 1998).

Analysis of gender and sexism with a DP lens extends understanding of how, when, and where sexism operates in contemporary society and highlights the limits and possibilities of talk for expanding or contracting gender categories. For example, Stokoe's (1998) analysis of gender in academic discourse highlights how making statements about the non-sexist nature of one's talk often actually *enabled* sexism to persist and limited listeners' possibilities for refuting sexism. Edley and Wetherell (1997) used a critical discursive approach to explore the construction of masculine identities through broader cultural understandings of the 'traditional' and 'changed' masculine ideal. The young men the authors interviewed had different access to social status and privilege in a school context based on how well they performed 'new' or more progressive masculinity (Edley & Wetherell, 1997).

With respect to *racism*, DP has been acknowledged for its ability to tune into racism shrouded in the 'norm against prejudice' (Billig, 1988, p. 95), allowing researchers to acknowledge racism as something that is *done*, rather than something that exists de facto (Bozatzis, 2009; Durrheim, Greener, & Whitehead, 2015). DP research has helped to unravel the ways in which prejudice intersects with the discursive construction of national identities (Condor, 2000) or citizenship (Figgou, 2016). For example, in her work on nationalism and race in England, Condor (2000) demonstrated how participants tread delicately around the subject of national identity, using linguistic strategies to distance themselves from statements that might be perceived as racist. Disclaimers are examples of such strategies, where racism is denied in statements like 'I am not against immigrants, but…' (van Dijk, 1992). An approach like DP is essential to understanding that disclaimers do not necessarily mean that racism does not exist.

Issues like racism and sexism bear policy implications but are also associated with the risk of violence. Sexual violence, for example, is also constructed in talk and around gendered ideologies; gendered power is either enforced or deconstructed in the way that perpetrators talk about such acts (e.g., Burt, 1980). This interplay between gender and violence was highlighted in the analysis by LeCouteur and Oxlad (2011) who focused on how men who had engaged in violent or abusive behavior talked about their behavior. They found that men described their partners as having violated gender norms in their relationships, positioning their partners as improperly occupying the category of 'woman'. Focusing on discourse in the study of violence allows us to move beyond attempts to understand what a perpetrator was *thinking*, and toward an analysis of how violent behaviors are presented as reasonable and justifiable and how others may endorse or challenge such claims.

DISCURSIVE EMBODIED PRACTICES: HEALTH, NUTRITION, AND EXERCISE

Discursive psychological research has also offered insight on the discursive construction of embodied practices concerning matters of applied relevance, like health, nutrition, and exercise and highlighted how *agency*, *accountability*, and *attributions* are interactionally negotiated and accomplished. Overall, by addressing embodied practices as discursive accomplishments, DP research has forwarded consideration of the social and cultural contexts of physical activity, *health*, and well-being (Seymour-Smith, 2015; Wiggins, 2017).

In the area of *health*, in particular, DP has shed light on how patients themselves put together descriptions of illness or health (e.g., being legitimately ill) and what actions such descriptions achieve in situated contexts of their use. As Seymour-Smith (2015, p. 378) remarked, 'studying the actual practices of people "doing" health and illness in situ is fascinating and enlightening and allows us to examine real-life health and illness issues as they unfold'. DP work has explored how people manage (attribute, endorse, resist, etc.) accountability for being healthy or ill, or for dealing with illness appropriately, in relation to topics such as coeliac disease (Veen, te Molder, Gremmen, & van Woerkum, 2010), chronic fatigue syndrome (Horton-Salway, 2001; Tucker, 2004), infertility (de Kok, 2009; de Kok & Widdicombe, 2010), suicide (Horne & Wiggins, 2009; Wiggins, McQuade, & Rasmussen, 2016), weight management (Cranwell & Seymour-Smith, 2012), diabetes (Peel, Parry, Douglas, & Lawton, 2005), and dementia (Lawless, Augoustinos, & LeCouteur, 2017), among other topics. de Kok and Widdicombe (2010), for example, examined illness narratives, specifically causes of infertility. The participants first denied, then specified, causes of infertility. Denials functioned to display a lack of entitlement to medical knowledge and as a defense against a potential inference that speakers may have personal experiences with the causes of infertility they describe (e.g., STD or abortion). The authors stressed the value of studying people's own illness beliefs in situations of their production to understand not only the content of illness beliefs but also speakers' interactional concerns in producing these beliefs.

DP research on *nutrition*, *weight*, and *eating disorders* has brought the interactional context in which people consume food (Wiggins, Potter, & Wildsmith, 2001) and the broader socio-political contexts of eating and embodiment to the fore. It has reformulated eating as something people do interactionally, investigating eating 'intentions', 'motivations', and 'causes' as participants' concerns (Wiggins et al., 2001, p. 14). By highlighting the interactional context in which people consume food (Wiggins et al., 2001), and the broader socio-political contexts of eating and embodiment, DP has shed light on the politics of discourse around food and on the societal constraints and constructions of eating, wellness, and body. DP has been applied to the topics of food disgust (Wiggins, 2013), food, physiology, and eating practices (Wiggins et al., 2001), evaluation and enjoyment of food (Sneijder & te Molder, 2006), gluten-free diets (Veen et al., 2010) and body size and weight (Hepburn & Wiggins, 2005). For example, Wiggins (2009) explored talk within the context of treatment for weight management in the United Kingdom. Her analysis revealed how clients framed themselves as responsible for their weight gain. As this analysis and others show, people draw on broader discourses of the link between food, body size, and morality, promoting the idea that fatness is a signifier for laziness (Rice, 2007) and that 'over' eating signifies a loss of control (Burns, 2004). This is problematic insofar as it limits agency by repeatedly positioning fat people pursuing weight loss as occupying a 'sick role' that requires constant self-action. In an analysis of the construction of people with eating disorders on the TV program *Dr. Phil*, LaMarre and Sutherland (2014) identified discursive strategies used to constitute people as 'eating disordered' and as accountable for their disorders. Taking a DP approach helps to tease out the way that morality is interactionally constructed in relation to size and eating practices (Wiggins, 2009) and creates the possibility of creating space for meaningful and helpful professional encounters (e.g., in psychological or nutritional counseling).

Relatedly, DP has been used to understand *sport* and *exercise*, beginning nearly two decades ago (e.g., McGannon & Mauws, 2000). Since its entrance into the field, DP has been applied to a range of topics, including athletes' accounts of their success and failure in competition (Locke, 2003; 2004), construction of a soccer fan identity (Miller & Benkwitz, 2016), athletes' accounts of taking prohibited substances (Lamont-Mills & Christensen, 2008), bodily self-surveillance and self-discipline in elite sport (Cosh, Crabb, Kettler, LeCouteur, & Tully, 2015), women's participation in physical activities (e.g., McGannon & Schinke, 2013) and constructions of elite athletes' identity (e.g., Cosh, Crabb, & Tully, 2015).

An example of a DP in sport psychology comes from Locke (2004), who examined how athletes talk about their failures and successes. Athletes in her study diluted personal agency to appear modest in accounting for good performance and removed personal agency (i.e., allocated blame to external forces) in discussing poor performance. Cosh et al. (2015) analyzed interactions between elite athletes and sport staff during routine practices of body composition testing and identified discursive practices used to constitute athletes as needing ongoing self-monitoring and improvement around eating. The authors argued that such constructions were limiting and potentially left athletes vulnerable to unhealthy eating and exercise regiments. Cosh, Crabb, and Tully (2015) analyzed news articles to explore retirement of elite athletes. Within these articles, athletes were constructed as both the cause and the cure for their transitioning difficulties and distress. Overall, by identifying the discursive practices and the cultural meanings which shape athletes' identities, behaviors, and experiences, DP research has expanded understanding of physical activity as practiced.

WIDENING THE LENS: THE DISCURSIVE CONSTRUCTION OF NATURE, GEOGRAPHICAL SPACE, TECHNOLOGY, AND COMPUTER-MEDIATED COMMUNICATION

DP has also been deployed to investigate how the 'psychological' is downplayed in a wider layer of context, namely that of *nature/environment*. The discursive study of the environment is marginalized within environmental and social psychology, which remains largely dominated by individualist perspectives on environmental phenomena and change (Batel, Castro, Devine-Wright, & Howarth, 2016). However, discursive psychologists have explored a range of topics related to environment (for an overview, see

Aiello & Bonaiuto, 2016). These include place identity and attachment (Di Masso, Dixon, & Durrheim, 2014; Hugh-Jones & Madill, 2009; McKinlay & McVittie, 2007), sense of place (Cantrill, 1998), scientists' discourse about environmental events (Callaghan & Augoustinos, 2013) and specific geographical features (Wallwork & Dixon, 2004). In doing so, DP researchers have highlighted how the environment and people's place in it are constantly interpreted and contested (Hajer & Versteeg, 2005). DP studies have approached the 'natural' and built features of the environment not as objectively given but as constructed and as resources for social action (Dixon & Durrheim, 2000). Thus, DP research has helped to illuminate how different meanings concerning the environment and place and ways to address environmental problems are formulated, promoted, and resisted.

Di Masso, Dixon, and Pol (2011), for example, explored place as a discursive construct, investigating the construction of access to and 'proper' uses and beneficiaries of places. They showed how different constructions of the same space in Barcelona were mobilized to justify different plans for the space's 'development' (e.g., making space available to private investors). In a related series of studies (Hugh-Jones & Madill, 2009; McKinlay & McVittie, 2007), DP scholars have investigated place-identity and people's attachment to places. For example, Hugh-Jones and Madill (2009) examined interview accounts of residents of a small English village. Among various conclusions, the authors noted that residents constructed themselves as willing and able to live in the area with extreme weather conditions, the constructions which allowed claiming the distinctiveness of place-identity and deserved belonging to the village.

Discursive psychological research has also expanded to a different kind of space, delineated by the increasing use of *technology*. DP research on *computer-mediated communication* has addressed a variety of topics, including racism (e.g., Durrheim et al., 2015; Simmons & LeCouteur, 2008), veganism (Sneijder & te Molder, 2009) and health conditions (e.g., Guise, Widdicombe, & McKinlay, 2007; Horne and Wiggins, 2009; Lawless, Augoustinos, & LeCouteur, 2017; Smithson et al., 2011). For example, Burke and Goodman (2012) analyzed internet discussions on the topic of asylum seeking. They were particularly interested in how Nazi-related language was used to both support and oppose asylum seeking and express and challenge racism tradespeople seeking asylum in the United Kingdom. The study offers concrete recommendations regarding helpful, and less helpful, rhetoric for challenging negative views toward asylum seekers and sheds light on discursive strategies used to constitute collective identities and distinctions and hierarchies in groups' identities (e.g., *us* versus *them*). Lawless et al. (2017) investigated how information about dementia risk prevention is presented on non-profit dementia organization websites. They found that risk management is individualized through the way dementia is constructed in talk, with self-responsibility being presented as an essential and morally-bound aspect of maintaining brain health. The study highlights that constructing the onus as being on the individual minimizes the importance of broader contextual factors impacting health (e.g., socio-economic status, education). This reproduces neoliberal health discourse and increases risks for stigmatization, victim blaming, and has implications for how these individuals are treated by government and health care practitioners (Lawless et al., 2017).

FROM 'LOCAL' TO INSTITUTIONAL AND POLITICAL DISCOURSE: ORGANIZATIONS, PROFESSIONAL ENCOUNTERS, EDUCATION, MASS-MEDIA, LAW, AND POLITICS

Discursive psychologists have been particularly keen to extend the study of how psychological notions are discursively accomplished in institutional discourse. This sub-section includes DP studies that have investigated discourse from organizations and professional encounters, such as medical settings and psychotherapy or counseling, educational processes, mass-media discourse, as well as judicial discourse and political discourse.

DP has been deployed for the study of *health encounters* or interaction between health professionals and people in need of medical care, including mental health care and *counseling/psychotherapy*. It has thus elucidated how health advice and treatment are delivered and received in various health care settings (e.g., medical, help-line, counseling), including why, and how, patients resist health advice and treatment adherence (e.g., Auburn, 2010; Hepburn & Potter, 2011; Locke & Horton-Salway, 2010). Furthermore, it has contributed to a growing understanding of the minutia of the psychotherapy/counseling process, approached as a joint accomplishment by therapist and clients, particularly in the case of systemic and constructionist therapies with respect to problem formulation and blame attributions (Diorinou & Tseliou, 2014; Patrika & Tseliou, 2016). Sutherland, LaMarre, Rice, Hardt, and LeCouteur (2017) have used DP to explore the 'new sexism' through an analysis of couple therapy sessions. Their analysis revealed a range of discursive strategies used by couples to endorse egalitarian ethos while simultaneously excusing and justifying male partners' limited domestic and childcare contributions. Such DP research has increased understanding of health care and patient resistance as joint, discursive accomplishments. It has thus promoted a reflexive awareness on behalf of practitioners of possible implications of their actions in their interaction with patients allowing them to reflexively modify and tailor health information and treatment to recipients (Seymour-Smith, 2015).

DP has also provided unique insights into *management*, *leadership*, and *organizational change*. Such insight concerns the micro-dynamics responsible for the day-to-day operation of organizations. Organizations are comprised of people, and DP provides insight into the 'rich surface' (Edwards, 2006) of interaction between people that is applicable to all types of organizational research. Studies have focused, for example, on prejudice in the workplace (Dick, 2013), ownership talk during consultations (Kykyri, Puutio, & Wahlstrom, 2010), diversity in employment (McVittie, McKinlay, & Widdicombe, 2008) and organizational change (Mueller & Whittle, 2011; Whittle, Suhomlinova, & Mueller, 2010).

Studies using DP have shown that certain discursive practices are deployed when attempting to translate new management ideas into practice across the organization. Whittle et al. (2010) examined the talk of private–public partnerships in the United Kingdom and concluded that organization members who want to instigate change (i.e., leaders, managers) used a variety of discursive practices to constitute change as beneficial to all recipients. One of these practices was coined 'funnel of interests', which involved the active negotiation and realignment of how recipients view change in order to emphasize its benefits and minimize its perceived disadvantages (Whittle et al., 2010). In this way, leaders or other instigators of organizational change 'funnel' the diverse interests and concerns of the change recipients to align everyone's interests. Similarly, Mueller and Whittle (2011) outlined discursive practices, such as 'footing' (i.e., positioning one's self in different ways in relation to what is being said, such as through using terms such as 'we' or 'us), used to claim the absence of one's personal authorship of the changes and highlight the manager's limited agentic role. These practices added credibility to the managers' attempts at organizational change and increased uptake of proposed changes by the target audience (Mueller & Whittle, 2011).

As concerns *education* and *learning*, since Edwards' seminal work on the study of *classroom discourse* (Edwards & Mercer, 1987), there has been limited use of DP in the area of education despite the popularity of discourse analysis (Tseliou, 2015). DP studies challenge existing intrapsychic cognitive and behavioral models of knowing and examine learning as constituted jointly and interactionally by people. In doing so, DP studies present with an opportunity to understand how education is *performed*, how people conversationally and interactionally orient to their knowledge and learning, including people's positionality and power in, and beyond, classroom settings. Examples of DP work on *learning* and *education* include math teaching (Barwell, 2013), academic identity (McLean, 2012), teachers' identity (Oreshkina & Lester, 2015), gender-based discourse in sexual education interventions among South African high schoolers (Jearey-Graham & Macleod, 2017), and undergraduate students use of internet-based assessments in education (Lester & Paulus, 2011; Paulus & Lester, 2013). For example, Lester and Paulus (2011) examined 152 blog posts written by students as part of a course about their experiences and beliefs regarding dietary supplements. In this context, students actively negotiated and resisted presenting themselves as 'knowledgeable' through frequent use of disclaimers such as 'I don't know', and through talk that limited their accountability for their claims. The authors conclude that students don't see computer-supported talk in education as private, which has been assumed in previous work. Instead, students treat these types of online discussions as a publicly observable display of one's academic knowledge and expertise.

DP has also been deployed for the analysis of *mass-media discourse* on themes which cut across the topics raised in previous sections. For example, DP research has highlighted how *sexism* and *racism* seem to pervade mass-media discourse. Hanson-Easey and Augoustinos (2011) used critical DP to unpack the subtle operation of racism in radio talk-back shows in Australia. This work reveals the intricacies of the operation of racism in contemporary culture and situates this talk within broader exclusionary social structures, including criticism of refugees (Hanson-Easey et al., 2014) and laying blame on individuals from minority groups for 'integration problems' (Hanson-Easey & Augoustinos, 2012). While the linguistic practices used to invoke prejudice are complex, they hint at essentialist logics, presenting minority groups as homogeneous. Problematically, when groups and members of those groups are presented in essentialist terms, group membership can be used as a justification for exclusion, for instance, in immigration policy (Hanson-Easey et al., 2014). Venäläinen (2016, p. 426) similarly found that Finnish tabloids used gendered discourse to present female victims of sexual violence as deviant in order to 'preserve the normality of men'. Overall, in examining radio talk, DP has sought to identify discursive practices used in discussions across a range of topics, like eating disorders (Brooks, 2009), ethnic minority identity (Merino & Tileaga, 2011) or the concept of 'defectiveness' within evangelical Christian discourse (Xanthopoulou, 2010).

DP has been used for the study of institutional discourse concerning the *law*, such as police interrogations (e.g., Edwards, 2006; 2008) or courtroom and judicial discourse (e.g., MacMartin & Wood, 2005; Wood & MacMartin, 2007) and has provided insight on a series of law-related themes, such as criminal intent (Edwards, 2008), which seem to intersect with psychological matters like ascribing blame or expressing remorse. Instead of treating legal decisions as outcomes of cognitive states and as existent prior to legal activities, DP has approached them as situated, discursively constituted practices. For example, Wood and MacMartin (e.g., MacMartin, 2002; MacMartin & Wood, 2005; Wood & MacMartin, 2007) investigated the discursive constitution of *judicial decisions* in cases of childhood sexual abuse. MacMartin (2002) showed how evidence of a child's post-abuse contact with the perpetuator can be used to discount a complaint of sexual abuse, highlighting the need for further education of judges (e.g., that children are often abused by people children know).

Similarly, DP has been used to gain understanding of how *police interrogations* work in actual practice (e.g., Edwards, 2006; 2008) given an interest on how police interrogations exert psychological pressures on suspects to confess (Nadler & Mueller, 2017). For example, Edwards (2006) argued that actions can be given a generalized quality and showed that suspects used the first-person dispositional *would* constructions (e.g., 'I wouldn't hurt an old lady', 'I wouldn't do that') to constitute themselves as particular kinds of people (i.e., incapable of immoral conduct of this kind). Such constructions were used to deny the offence and undermine a witness's accusatory testimony. Police officers used third-person *would* constructions (e.g., 'why (0.6) this lady: (0.3) would wanna (0.7) lie') to challenge suspects' refutation of accusatory testimony.

In the area of *politics*, DP has been applied to the study of institutional discourse across a variety of topics intersecting with psychological matters like prejudice or attributions, including political ideology (Edwards & Potter, 1992; Kurz, Augoustinos, & Crabb, 2010; Weltman & Billig, 2001), apologies for historical injustices (e.g., Augoustinos, Hastie, & Wright, 2011), and sexism and racism in politics (e.g., Burke & Goodman, 2012; Sorrentino & Augoustinos, 2016). Such DP research has highlighted the discursive and rhetorical dimension of political discourse, which has been largely overlooked within political psychology and political sciences (Finlayson, 2004). For example, Weltman and Billig (2001) interviewed British politicians to identify practices used to construct persuasive arguments in political debate. Politicians in this study denied being ideological (e.g., endorsing 'left' or 'right' politics) while simultaneously promoting specific ideological viewpoints. Similarly, Rapley (1998) studied Pauline Hanson's speech to Parliament in which she expresses her views on immigration. Rapley showed how Hanson constructed herself as an in-group member (ordinary Australian), someone who is credible to speak on behalf of Australians, and simultaneously mitigated potential accusations for coming across as racist by constructing prejudice against immigration as factual. Finally, DP has been utilized to analyze political discourse on matters like climate change (Kurz et al., 2010) thus contributing to the study of 'the discursive limits of the ways in which the issue of climate change is constructed in public debate' (Kurz et al., 2010, p. 601).

IMPLICATIONS OF DISCURSIVE PSYCHOLOGY: RECONSIDERING THE 'PSYCHOLOGICAL' AND THE 'INSTITUTIONAL' AS APPLIED

In our selective overview of DP studies, we have explored examples that illustrate the utility of DP for the study of a variety of topics of applied relevance, from the 'local' to the 'institutional'. By giving examples of DP studies, we have shown how DP proposes an applied perspective to the study of psychological phenomena in that it forwards an understanding of how these are actively constructed in interaction. In that sense, it highlights how people produce states, outcomes, problems, and interventions in specific interactions and settings.

More specifically, by situating the psychological in the social, and by allowing for the exploration of how ideology is performed by people (Billig et al., 1988), DP provides a particularly useful frame for exploring social issues within contemporary contexts. For example, in the case of forms of discrimination, like racism or sexism, DP provides a way to capture how discrimination is *enacted* through interaction, despite people's awareness of the unacceptability of social exclusion. Such reflexive awareness of subtle ways of prejudice and discrimination can have direct implications for change in everyday and institutional practices. Similarly, DP research contributes to an applied perspective concerning embodied, everyday practices, like nutrition, exercise, and health or 'hot topics' of the day, like environmental issues. DP-derived knowledge in such issues can have direct implications for practical interventions concerning everyday life. For example, by highlighting how constructions of places and human–place relations may carry significant social and ideological consequences (e.g., development of environmental policy, social exclusion, resistance to environmental change, use of space) (e.g., Di Masso et al., 2014), DP's study of environmental issues can transform related practices and policy decisions.

Further to its merit for an applied reconsideration of the 'local', DP-derived insight on professional, organizational, and institutional practices bears further applied value. DP's engagement with extending the 'psychological' to the 'institutional' widens the scope of practical relevance and applications from the 'local' to the wider setting of policy, interventions, and professional practice.

DP research can inform health care practice, including psychotherapy/counseling practice, in that it can provide increased understanding of how practitioners and clients jointly and discursively construct the process of treatment. Such reflexive awareness of sides of practice which usually remain obscured can significantly add to the transformation of psychotherapeutic and counseling practice (Patrika & Tseliou, 2016). Knowledge generated in DP studies can also help professionals co-construct or 'bring forth' culturally marginalized and less pathologizing identities for people seeking health care (Peel et al., 2005). Thus, DP knowledge can also be used in the training of health providers (Potter & Hepburn, 2005), psychotherapists, and counselors. Similarly, organizations can use the knowledge derived by DP research concerning the micro-dynamics of organizational operation to inform the application of change and to more effectively translate their organization level changes. As concerns education, DP can help to open up space for exploring education as interactionally performed and, in that sense, as more than a top-down force or unidirectional model. Such knowledge can help to reflexively appraise educational practices as well as policy and identify ways of pushing education in new directions wherein various forms of knowledge are honored.

Finally, DP research on legal issues and political discourse can also hold applied value. Applying a DP lens to investigate law and criminal justice can illuminate how justice is *done*, and this can identify areas of change in the legal system or clarify specific changes to be made. By advancing the rhetorical investigation of political discourse, DP can also contribute to the creation of social and political change, a welcome contribution toward addressing practical, real-life problems in politics (Winter, 2000).

CONCLUSION

In this chapter, we have presented DP as applied science. By providing an indicative selection of DP studies across a variety of topics of applied relevance, we have argued that DP is inherently applied. Overall, we have argued that DP can illuminate how everyday and institutional practices are performed in the context of peoples' discursive interactions across a variety of discourse types, including ordinary and institutional discourse. We have also argued that DP allows for a reconsideration of the psychological as social practice and, when endorsing a critical perspective, it further allows for scrutinizing how ideology is downplayed at local and institutional practices. We do not consider the project of introducing DP as applied science finalized. For example, there is still work in progress concerning the methodological applicability of DP to the study of the embodied aspects of discourse or to the study of emotions (Wetherell, 2012). Furthermore, along with others (Wiggins & Hepburn, 2007), we think that DP needs to address wider issues concerning what should be considered as applied research and whom it should concern. Both theory and findings can bear implications for practice and this can equally concern members of the different groups studied (e.g., counselors and clients) (Wiggins & Hepburn, 2007). Nevertheless, with this chapter, we have highlighted that it is worthwhile to explore the potential of DP for applied social psychology.

ACKNOWLEDGEMENTS

We would like to acknowledge Nikos Bozatzis and Georgios Abakoumkin for their helpful comments in earlier drafts of this chapter.

REFERENCES

Aiello, A., & Bonaiuto, M. (2016). Rhetorical approach and discursive psychology: The study of environmental discourse. In M. Bonnes, T. Lee, & M. Bonaiuto (Eds.), *Psychological theories for environmental issues* (pp. 235–270). New York, NY: Routledge.

Auburn, T. (2010). Cognitive distortions as social practices: An examination of cognitive distortions in sex offender treatment from a discursive psychology perspective. *Psychology Crime and Law*, *1–2*, 103–123. https://doi.org/10.1080/10683160802621990

Augoustinos, M., & Tileagă, C. (2012). Twenty five years of discursive psychology. *British Journal of Social Psychology*, *51*(3), 405–412. https://doi.org/10.1111/j.2044-8309.2012.02096.x

Augoustinos, M., Hastie, B., & Wright, M. (2011). Apologizing for historical injustice: Emotion, truth and identity in political discourse. *Discourse & Society*, *22*(5), 507–531. https://doi.org/10.1177/0957926511405573

Austin, J. L. (1962). *How to do things with words*. Oxford, UK: Clarendon Press.

Barwell, R. (2013). Discursive psychology as an alternative perspective on mathematics teacher knowledge. *ZDM*, *45*(4), 595–606. https://doi.org/10.1007/s11858-013-0508-4

Batel, S., Castro, P., Devine-Wright, P., & Howarth, C. (2016). Developing a critical agenda to understand pro-environmental actions: Contributions from Social Representations and Social Practices Theories. *Wiley Interdisciplinary Reviews: Climate Change*, *7*(5), 727–745. https://doi.org/10.1002/wcc.417

Billig, M. (1987). *Arguing and thinking: A rhetorical approach to social psychology*. Cambridge, UK: Cambridge University Press.

Billig, M. (1988). The notion of 'prejudice': Some rhetorical and ideological aspects. *Text: Interdisciplinary Journal for the Study of Discourse*, *8*(1–2), 91–110. https://doi.org/10.1515/text.1.1988.8.1-2.91

Billig, M. (2012). Undisciplined beginnings, academic success, and discursive psychology. *British Journal of Social Psychology*, *51*(3), 413–424. https://doi.org/10.1111/j.2044-8309.2011.02086.x

Billig, M., Condor, S., Edwards, D., Gane, M., Middleton, D., & Radley, A. (1988). *Ideological dilemmas: A social psychology of everyday thinking*. London, UK: Sage.

Bozatzis, N. (2009). Occidentalism and accountability: Constructing culture and cultural difference in majority Greek talk about the minority in Western Thrace. *Discourse & Society*, *20*(4), 431–453. https://doi.org/10.1177/0957926509104022

Bozatzis, N. (2014). The discursive turn in social psychology: Four nodal debates. In N. Bozatzis, & Th. Dragonas (Eds.), *The discursive turn in social psychology* (pp. 25–50). Chagrin Falls, Ohio: Taos Institute Worldshare Books.

Brooks, S. (2009). Radio food disorder: The conversational constitution of eating disorders in radio phone-ins. *Journal of Community and Applied Social Psychology*, *19*(5), 360–373. https://doi.org/10.1002/casp.1021

Burke, S., & Goodman, S. (2012). 'Bring back Hitler's gas chambers': Asylum seeking, Nazis and Facebook – a discursive analysis. *Discourse & Society*, *23*(1), 19–33. https://doi.org/10.1177/0957926511431036

Burns, M. (2004). Eating like an ox: Femininity and dualistic constructions of bulimia and anorexia. *Feminism and Psychology*, *14*, 269–295. https://doi.org/10.1177/0959353504042182

Burr, V. (2015). *Social constructionism* (3rd edn.). London, UK: Routledge.

Burt, M. R. (1980). Cultural myths and supports for rape. *Journal of Personality and Social Psychology*, *38*, 217–30. http://dx.doi.org/10.1037/0022-3514.38.2.217

Callaghan, P., & Augoustinos, M. (2013). Reified versus consensual knowledge as rhetorical resources for debating climate change. *Revue Internationale de Psychologie Sociale*, *26*(3), 11–38.

Cantrill, J. G. (1998). The environmental self and a sense of place: Communication foundations for regional ecosystems management. *Journal of Applied Communication Research*, *26*, 301–318. https://doi.org/10.1080/00909889809365509

Condor, S. (2000). Pride and prejudice: Identity management in English people's talk about 'this country.' *Discourse & Society*, *11*, 175–205. https://doi.org/10.1177/0957926500011002003

Cosh, S., Crabb, S., Kettler, L., LeCouteur, A., & Tully, P. J. (2015). The normalisation of body regulation and monitoring practices in elite sport: A discursive analysis of news delivery sequences during skinfold testing. *Qualitative Research in Sport, Exercise and Health*, *7*(3), 338–360. https://doi.org/10.1080/2159676X.2014.949833

Cosh, S., Crabb, S., & Tully, P. J. (2015). A champion out of the pool? A discursive exploration of two Australian Olympic swimmers' transition from elite sport to retirement. *Psychology of Sport and Exercise*, *19*, 33–41. https://doi.org/10.1016/j.psychsport.2015.02.006

Cranwell, J., & Seymour-Smith, S. (2012). Monitoring and normalising a lack of appetite and weight loss. A discursive analysis of an online support group for bariatric surgery. *Appetite*, *58*(3), 873–881. https://doi.org/10.1016/j.appet.2012.01.029

De Kok, B. C. (2009). 'Automatically you become a polygamist': 'Culture' and 'norms' as resources for normalisation and managing accountability in talk about infertility. *Health*, *13*, 197–217. https://doi.org/10.1177/1363459308099684

De Kok, B. C., & Widdicombe, S. (2010). Interpersonal issues in expressing lay knowledge: A discursive psychology approach. *Journal of Health Psychology*, *15*(8), 1190–1200. https://doi.org/10.1177/1359105310364437

Di Masso, A., Dixon, J., & Durrheim, K. (2014). Place attachment as discursive practice. In L. C. Manzo & P. Devine-Wright (Eds.), *Place attachment: Advances in theory, methods and applications* (pp. 75–86). New York, NY: Routledge.

Di Masso, A., Dixon, J., & Pol, E. (2011). On the contested nature of place: 'Figuera's Well,' 'The Hole of Shame' and the ideological struggle over public space in Barcelona. *Journal of Environmental Psychology*, *31*(3), 231–244. https://doi.org/10.1016/j.jenvp.2011.05.002

Dick, P. (2013). The politics of experience: A discursive psychology approach to understanding different accounts of sexism in the workplace. *Human Relations*, *66*(5), 645–669. https://doi.org/10.1177/0018726712469541

Diorinou, M., & Tseliou, E. (2014). Studying circular questioning 'in situ': Discourse analysis of a first systemic family therapy session. *Journal of Marital and Family Therapy*, *40*(1), 106–121. https://doi.org/10.1111/jmft.12005

Dixon, J., & Durrheim, K. (2000). Displacing place-identity: A discursive approach to locating self and other. *British Journal of Social Psychology*, *39*, 27–44. https://doi.org/10.1348/014466600164318

Durrheim, K., Greener, R., & Whitehead, K. A. (2015). Race trouble: Attending to race and racism in online interaction. *British Journal of Social Psychology*, *54*(1), 84–99. https://doi.org/10.1111/bjso.12070

Edley, N., & Wetherell, M. (1997). Jockeying for position: The construction of masculine identities. *Discourse and Society*, *8*(2), 203–217. https://doi.org/10.1177/0957926597008002004

Edwards, D. (1997). *Discourse and cognition*. London, UK: Sage.

Edwards, D. (2006). Facts, norms and dispositions: Practical uses of the modal verb would in police interrogations. *Discourse Studies*, *8*(4), 475–501. https://doi.org/10.1177/1461445606064830

Edwards, D. (2008). Intentionality and *means rea* in police interrogations: The production of actions as crimes. *Intercultural Pragmatics*, *5*(2), 77–199. https://doi.org/10.1515/IP.2008.010

Edwards, D. (2012). Discursive and scientific psychology. *British Journal of Social Psychology*, *51*(3), 425–435. https://doi.org/10.1111/j.2044-8309.2012.02103.x

Edwards, D., & Mercer, N. M. (1987). *Common knowledge: The development of understanding in the classroom*. London, UK: Routledge.

Edwards, D., & Potter, J. (1992). *Discursive psychology*. London, UK: Sage.

Edwards, D., & Potter, J. (1993). Language and causation: A discursive action model of description and attribution. *Psychological Review*, *100*(1), 23–41. http://dx.doi.org/10.1037/0033-295X.100.1.23

Figgou, L. (2016). Constructions of 'illegal' immigration and entitlement to citizenship: Debating an immigration law in Greece. *Journal of Community and Applied Social Psychology*, *26*, 150–163. https://doi.org/10.1002/casp.2242

Finlayson, A. (2004). Political science, political ideas and rhetoric. *Economy and Society*, *33*(4), 528–549. https://doi.org/10.1080/0308514042000285279

Goodman, S., & Speer, S. A. (2007). Category use in the construction of asylum seekers. *Critical Discourse Studies*, *4*(2), 165–185. https://doi.org/10.1080/17405900701464832

Gruman, J. A., Schneider, F. W., & Coutts, L. M. (2017) (Eds.), *Applied social psychology: Understanding and addressing social and practical problems* (3rd edn.). Thousand Oaks, CA: Sage.

Guise, J., Widdicombe, S., & McKinlay, A. (2007). 'What is it like to have ME?': The discursive construction of ME in computer-mediated communication and face-to-face interaction. *Health*, *11*(1), 87–108. https://doi.org/10.1177/1363459307070806

Hajer, M., & Versteeg, W. (2005). A decade of discourse analysis of environmental politics: achievements, challenges, perspectives. *Journal of Environmental Policy & Planning*, *7*(3), 175–184. https://doi.org/10.1080/15239080500339646

Hanson-Easey, S., & Augoustinos, M. (2011). Complaining about humanitarian refugees: The role of sympathy talk in the design of complaints on talk back radio. *Discourse and Communication*, *5*(3), 247–271. https://doi.org/10.1177/1750481311405588

Hanson-Easey S., & Augoustinos M. (2012). Narratives from the neighbourhood: The discursive construction of integration problems in talkback radio. *Journal of Sociolinguistics*, *16*(1), 28–55. https://doi.org/10.1111/j.1467-9841.2011.00519.x

Hanson-Easey, S., Augoustinos, M., & Moloney, G. (2014). 'They're all tribals': Essentialism, context and the discursive representation of Sudanese refugees. *Discourse & Society*, *25*(3), 362–382. http://doi.org/10.1177/0957926513519536

Hepburn, A., & Jackson, C. (2009). Rethinking subjectivity: A discursive psychological approach to cognition and emotion. In D. Fox, I. Prilleltensky, & S. Austin (Eds.), *An introduction to critical psychology* (2nd edn., pp. 188–219). London, UK: Sage.

Hepburn, A., & Potter, J. (2011). Threats: Power, family mealtimes, and social influence. *British Journal of Social Psychology*, *50*(1), 99–120. https://doi.org/10.1348/014466610X500791

Hepburn, A., & Wiggins, S. (Eds.) (2005). Developments in discursive psychology. *Discourse & Society*, *16*(5), 595–601. https://doi.org/10.1177/0957926505054937

Horne, J., & Wiggins, S. (2009). Doing being 'on the edge': managing the dilemma of being authentically suicidal in an online forum. *Sociology of Health & Illness*, *31*(2), 170–184. https://doi.org/10.1111/j.1467-9566.2008.01130.x

Horton-Salway, M. (2001). Narrative identities and the management of personal accountability in talk about ME: A discursive psychology approach to illness narrative. *Journal of Health Psychology*, *6*(2), 247–259. https://doi.org/10.1177/135910530100600210

Hugh-Jones, S., & Madill, A. (2009). The air's got to be far cleaner here: A discursive analysis of place-identity threat. *British Journal of Social Psychology*, *48*(4), 601–624. https://doi.org/10.1348/014466608X390256

Jearey-Graham, N., & Macleod, C. I. (2017). Gender, dialogue and discursive psychology: A pilot sexuality intervention with South African High-School learners. *Sex Education*, 1–16. https://doi.org/10.1080/14681811.2017.1320983

Kurz, T., Augoustinos, M., & Crabb, S. (2010). Contesting the 'national interest' and maintaining 'our lifestyle': A discursive analysis of political rhetoric around climate change. *British Journal of Social Psychology*, *49*(3), 601–625. https://doi.org/10.1348/014466609X481173

Kykyri, V. L., Puutio, R., & Wahlström, J. (2010). Inviting participation in organizational change through ownership talk. *The Journal of Applied Behavioral Science*, *46*(1), 92–118. https://doi.org/10.1177/0021886309357441

LaMarre, A., & Sutherland, O. (2014). Expert opinion? A micro-analysis of eating disorder talk on Dr. Phil. *The Qualitative Report*, *19*(43), 1–20. Retrieved from https://nsuworks.nova.edu/tqr/vol19/iss43/2

Lamont-Mills, A., & Christensen, S. (2008). 'I have never taken performance enhancing drugs and I never will': Drug discourse in the Shane Warne case. *Scandinavian Journal of Medicine & Science in Sports*, *18*(2), 250–258. https://doi.org/10.1111/j.1600-0838.2007.00639.x

Lawless, M., Augoustinos, M., & LeCouteur, A. (2017). 'Your brain matters': Issues of risk and responsibility in online dementia prevention information. *Qualitative Health Research*. Advance online publication. https://doi.org/10.1177/1049732317732962

LeCouteur, A., & Oxlad, M. (2011). Managing accountability for domestic violence: Identities, membership categories and morality in perpetrators' talk. *Feminism & Psychology*, *21*(1), 5–28. https://doi.org/10.1177/0959353510375406

Lester, J. N., & Paulus, T. M. (2011). Accountability and public displays of knowing in an undergraduate computer-mediated communication context. *Discourse Studies*, *13*(6), 671–686. https://doi.org/10.1177/1461445611421361

Locke, A. (2003). 'If I'm not nervous, I'm worried, does that make sense?': The use of emotion concepts by athletes in accounts of performance. *Forum Qualitative Sozialforschung/Forum: Qualitative Social Research*, *4*(1), Art. 10. http://dx.doi.org/10.17169/fqs-4.1.752

Locke, A. (2004). Accounting for success and failure: A discursive psychological approach to sport talk. *Quest*, *56*, 302–320. https://doi.org/10.1080/00336297.2004.10491828

Locke, A., & Horton-Salway, M. (2010). 'Golden age' versus 'bad old days': A discursive examination of advice giving in antenatal classes. *Journal of Health Psychology*, *15*(8), 1214–1224. https://doi.org/10.1177/1359105310364439

MacMartin, C. (2002). (Un)reasonable doubt? The invocation of children's consent in sexual abuse trial judgments. *Discourse & Society*, *13*, 9–40. https://doi.org/10.1177/0957926502013001002

MacMartin, C., & Wood, L. A. (2005). Sexual motives and sentencing: Judicial discourse in cases of child sexual abuse. *Journal of Language and Social Psychology*, *24*, 129–159. https://doi.org/10.1177/0261927X05275735

McGannon, K. R., & Mauws, M. K. (2000). Discursive psychology: An alternative approach for studying adherence to exercise and physical activity. *Quest*, *52*, 148–165. https://doi.org/10.1080/00336297.2000.10491707

McGannon, K. R., & Schinke, R. J. (2013). 'My first choice is to work out at work; then I don't feel bad about my kids?': A discursive psychological analysis of motherhood and physical activity participation. *Psychology of Sport and Exercise*, *14*(2), 179–188. https://doi.org/10.1016/j.psychsport.2012.10.001

McKinlay, A., & McVittie, C. (2007). Locals, incomers and intra-national migration: Place identities and a Scottish island. *British Journal of Social Psychology*, *46*, 171–190. https://doi.org/10.1348/014466606X96958

McLean, N. (2012). Researching academic identity: Using discursive psychology as an approach. *International Journal for Academic Development*, *17*(2), 97–108. https://doi.org/10.1080/1360144X.2011.599596

McVittie, C., McKinlay, A., & Widdicombe, S. (2008). Organizational knowledge and discourse of diversity in employment. *Journal of Organizational Change Management*, *21*(3), 348–366. https://doi.org/10.1108/09534810810874822

Merino, M. E., & Tileagă, C. (2011). The construction of ethnic minority identity: A discursive psychological approach to ethnic self-definition in action. *Discourse & Society*, *22*(1), 86–101. https://doi.org/10.1177/0957926510382834

Miller, P. K., & Benkwitz, A. (2016). Where the action is: Towards a discursive psychology of 'authentic' identity in soccer fandom. *Psychology of Sport and Exercise*, *23*, 40–50. https://doi.org/10.1016/j.psychsport.2015.11.002

Mueller, F., & Whittle, A. (2011). Translating management ideas: A discursive devices analysis. *Organization Studies*, *32*(2), 187–210. https://doi.org/10.1177/0170840610394308

Nadler, J., & Mueller, P. A. (2017). Social psychology and the law. In F. Parisi (Ed.), *The Oxford handbook of law and economics* (Vol. 1). Oxford, UK: Oxford University Press.

Oreshkina, M., & Lester, J. N. (2015). A discursive psychology approach to the study of pre-service teachers' written reflections about teacher effectiveness. *Teaching Education*, *26*(4), 422–438. https://doi.org/10.1080/10476210.2015.1034680

Parker, I. (2012). Discursive social psychology now. *British Journal of Social Psychology*, *51*(3), 471–477. https://doi.org/10.1111/j.2044-8309.2011.02046.x

Patrika, P., & Tseliou, E. (2016). Blame, responsibility and systemic neutrality: a discourse analysis methodology to the study of family therapy problem talk. *Journal of Family Therapy*, *38*(4), 467–490. https://doi.org/10.1111/1467-6427.12076

Paulus, T. M., & Lester, J. N. (2013). Making learning ordinary: Ways undergraduates display learning in a CMC task. *Text & Talk*, *33*(1), 53–70. https://doi.org/10.1515/text-2013-0003

Peel, E., Parry, O., Douglas, M., & Lawton, J. (2005). Taking the discursive biscuit? A discursive approach to managing diet in Type 2 Diabetes. *Journal of Health Psychology*, *10*, 779–791. https://doi.org/10.1177/1359105305057313

Potter, J. (1996). *Representing reality: Discourse, rhetoric and social construction.* London, UK: Sage.

Potter, J. (2010). Contemporary discursive psychology: Issues, prospects and Corcoran's awkward ontology. *British Journal of Social Psychology*, *49*, 691–701. https://doi.org/10.1348/014466610X486158

Potter, J. (2011). Discursive psychology and discourse analysis. In J. P. Gee, & M. Handford (Eds.), *Routledge handbook of discourse analysis* (pp. 104–119). London, UK: Routledge.

Potter, J. (2012a). Discourse analysis and discursive psychology. In H. Cooper (Ed.), *APA handbook of research methods in psychology: Vol. 2. Quantitative, qualitative, neuropsychological, and biological* (pp. 119–138). Washington, DC: American Psychological Association.

Potter, J. (2012b). Re-reading discourse and social psychology: Transforming social psychology. *British Journal of Social Psychology*, *51*(3), 436–455. https://doi.org/10.1111/j.2044-8309.2011.02085.x

Potter, J., & Hepburn, A. (2005). Discursive psychology as a qualitative approach for analysing interaction in medical settings. *Medical Education*, *39*, 338–344. https://doi.org/10.1111/j.1365-2929.2005.02099.x

Potter, J., & Wetherell, M. (1987). *Discourse and social psychology: Beyond attitudes and behaviour.* London, UK: Sage.

Rapley, M. (1998). 'Just an ordinary Australian': Self-categorization and the discursive construction of facticity in 'new racist' political rhetoric. *British Journal of Social Psychology*, *37*(3), 325–344. https://doi.org/10.1111/j.2044-8309.1998.tb01175.x

Rice, C. (2007). Becoming the fat girl: Emergence of an unfit identity. *Women's Studies International Forum*, *30*, 158–174. https://doi.org/10.1016/j.wsif.2007.01.001

Sacks, H., Schegloff, E. A., & Jefferson, G. (1974). A simplest systematics for the organization of turn-taking for conversation. *Language*, *50*, 696–735. http://dx.doi.org/10.2307/412243

Seymour-Smith, S. (2015). Applying discursive approaches to health psychology. *Health Psychology*, *34*(4), 371. http://dx.doi.org/10.1037/hea0000165

Simmons, K., & LeCouteur, A. (2008). Modern racism in the media: constructions of the possibility of change' in accounts of two Australian riots'. *Discourse & Society*, *19*(5), 667–687. https://doi.org/10.1177/0957926508092248

Smithson, J., Sharkey, S., Hewis, E., Jones, R. B., Emmens, T., Ford, T., & Owens, C. (2011). Membership and boundary maintenance on an online self-harm forum. *Qualitative Health Research*, *21*(11), 1567–1575. https://doi.org/10.1177/1049732311413784

Sneijder, P., & te Molder, H. F. (2006). Disputing taste: Food pleasure as an achievement in interaction. *Appetite*, *46*(1), 107–116. https://doi.org/10.1016/j.appet.2005.03.002

Sneijder, P., & te Molder, H. (2009). Normalizing ideological food choice and eating practices. Identity work in online discussions on veganism. *Appetite*, *52*(3), 621–630. https://doi.org/10.1016/j.appet.2009.02.012

Sorrentino J., & Augoustinos, M. (2016). 'I don't view myself as a woman politician, I view myself as a politician who's a woman': The discursive management of gender identity in political leadership. *British Journal of Social Psychology*, *55*(3), 385–406. https://doi.org/10.1111/bjso.12138

Steg, L., Leiser, K., Buunk, A. P., & Rothengatter, T. (2017) (Eds.). *Applied social psychology: Understanding and managing social problems* (2nd edn.). Cambridge, UK: Cambridge University Press.

Stokoe, E. H. (1998). Talking about gender: The conversational construction of gender categories in academic discourse. *Discourse & Society*, *9*(2), 217–240. https://doi.org/10.1177/0957926598009002005

Stokoe, E. (2015). Identifying and responding to possible-isms in institutional encounters: Alignment, impartiality, and the implications for communication training. *Journal of Language and Social Psychology*, *34*(4), 427–445. https://doi.org/10.1177/0261927X15586572

Sutherland, O., LaMarre, A., Rice, C., Hardt, L., & LeCouteur, A. (2017). New sexism in couple therapy: A discursive analysis. *Family Process*, *56*(3), 686–700. https://doi.org/10.1111/famp.12292

Tileagă, C. (2009). The social organization of representations of history: The textual accomplishment of coming to terms with the past. *British Journal of Social Psychology*, *48*(2), 337–355. https://doi.org/10.1348/014466608X349487

Tileagă, C., & Stokoe, E. (2016). Introduction: The evolution of discursive psychology: From classic to contemporary themes. In C. Tileagă & E. Stokoe (Eds.), *Discursive psychology: Classic and contemporary issues* (pp. 1–12). New York: Routledge.

Tseliou, E. (2013). A critical methodological review of discourse and conversation analysis studies of family therapy. *Family Process*, *52*(4), 653–672. https://doi.org/10.1111/famp.12043

Tseliou, E. (2015). Discourse analysis and educational research: Challenge and promise. In Th. Dragonas, K. Gergen, S. McNamee, & E. Tseliou (Eds.), *Education as Social Construction: Contributions in theory, research and practice* (pp. 263–282). Chagrin Falls, OH: Taos Institute Worldshare Books Publications. Retrieved from: https://www.taosinstitute.net/education-as-social-construction-contributions-to-theory-research-and-practice

Tseliou, E. (2018). Conversation analysis, discourse analysis and psychotherapy research: Overview and methodological potential. In O. Smoliak, & T. Strong (Eds.), *Therapy as discourse: Practice and research*. London, UK: Palgrave MacMillan.

Tucker, I. (2004). 'Stories' of chronic fatigue syndrome: An exploratory discursive psychological analysis. *Qualitative Research in Psychology*, *1*(2), 153–167. https://doi.org/10.1191/1478088704qp008oa

Van Dijk, T. A. (1992). Discourse and the denial of racism. *Discourse & Society*, *3*(1), 87–118. https://doi.org/10.1177/0957926592003001005

Veen, M., te Molder, H., Gremmen, B., & van Woerkum, C. (2010). Quitting is not an option: An analysis of online diet talk between celiac disease patients. *Health*, *14*(1), 23–40. https://doi.org/10.1177/1363459309347478

Venäläinen, S. (2016). 'She must be an odd kind of woman': Gendered categorizations in accounts of lethal intimate partner violence in Finnish tabloid news. *Feminism & Psychology*, *26*(4), 426–443. https://doi.org/10.1177/0959353516655370

Wallwork, J., & Dixon, J. A. (2004). Foxes, green fields and Britishness: On the rhetorical construction of place and national identity. *British Journal of Social Psychology*, *43*, 21–39. https://doi.org/10.1348/014466604322915962

Weltman, D., & Billig, M. (2001). The political psychology of contemporary anti-politics: A discursive approach to the end-of-ideology era. *Political Psychology*, *22*(2), 367–382. https://doi.org/10.1111/0162-895X.00245

Wetherell, M. (1998). Positioning and interpretative repertoires: Conversation analysis and post-structuralism in dialogue. *Discourse & Society*, *9*(3), 387–412. https://doi.org/10.1177/0957926598009003005

Wetherell, M. (2007). A step too far: Discursive psychology, linguistic ethnography and questions of identity. *Journal of Sociolinguistics*, *11*(5), 661–681. https://doi.org/10.1111/j.1467-9841.2007.00345.x

Wetherell, M. (2012). *Affect and emotion: A new social science understanding*. London, UK: Sage Publications.

Wetherell, M., & Edley, N. (2014). A discursive psychological framework for analyzing men and masculinities. *Psychology of Men and Masculinities*, *15*(4), 355–364. http://dx.doi.org/10.1037/a0037148

Whittle, A., Suhomlinova, O., & Mueller, F. (2010). Funnel of interests: The discursive translation of organizational change. *The Journal of Applied Behavioral Science*, *46*(1), 16–37. https://doi.org/10.1177/0021886309357538

Wiggins, S. (2009). Managing blame in NHS weight management treatment: Psychologizing weight and 'obesity'. *Journal of Community & Applied Social Psychology*, *19*(5), 374–387. https://doi.org/10.1002/casp.1017

Wiggins, S. (2013). The social life of 'eugh': Disgust as assessment in family mealtimes. *British Journal of Social Psychology*, *52*(3), 489–509. https://doi.org/10.1111/j.2044-8309.2012.02106.x

Wiggins, S. (2017). *Discursive psychology: Theory, method and applications*. London, UK: Sage.

Wiggins, S., & Hepburn, A. (2007). Discursive research: Applications and implications. In A. Hepburn, & S. Wiggins (Eds.), *Discursive research in practice: New approaches to psychology and interaction* (pp. 281–291). Cambridge, UK: Cambridge University Press.

Wiggins, S., & Potter, J. (2008). Discursive psychology. In C. Willig, & W. Stainton-Rogers (Eds.), *The Sage handbook of qualitative research in psychology* (pp. 73–90). London, UK: Sage.

Wiggins, S., McQuade, R., & Rasmussen, S. (2016). Stepping back from crisis points: The provision and acknowledgment of support in an online suicide discussion forum. *Qualitative Health Research*, *26*(9), 1240–1251. https://doi.org/10.1177/1049732316633130

Wiggins, S., Potter, J., & Wildsmith, A. V. (2001). Eating your words: Discursive psychology and the reconstruction of eating practices. *Journal of Health Psychology*, *6*, 5–15. https://doi.org/10.1177/135910530100600101

Winter, D. G. (2000). Power, sex, and violence: A psychological reconstruction of the 20th century and an intellectual agenda for political psychology. *Political Psychology*, *21*(2), 383–404. https://doi.org/10.1111/0162-895X.00194

Wood, L. A., & MacMartin, C. (2007). Constructing remorse: Judges' sentencing decisions in child sexual assault cases. *Journal of Language and Social Psychology*, *26*, 343–362. https://doi.org/10.1177/0261927X07306979

Xanthopoulou, P. (2010). The production of 'defectiveness' as a linguistic resource in broadcast evangelical discourse: A discursive psychology approach. *Discourse & Society*, *21*(6), 675–691. https://doi.org/10.1177/0957926510381221

21

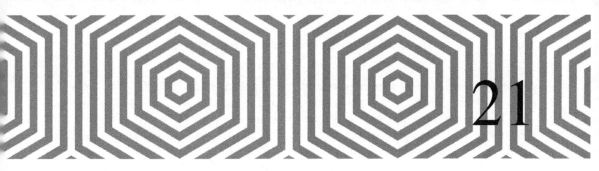

Public Deliberation and Social Psychology: Integrating Theories of Participation with Social Psychological Research and Practice

Kieran C. O'Doherty and Karla Stroud

INTRODUCTION

Even though the theory and practice of public deliberation have received significant attention across the social sciences, to date, social psychology's role in this movement has been marginal. The idea that those who are affected by a decision should also have a voice in making that decision has a long history. Indeed, democracy is based on that idea. However, even in democratic societies there are constraints on how much ordinary people can influence high level policy decisions. For many important and contentious issues, most of us do not have a direct voice in decisions that affect our lives in crucial ways.

Deliberative democracy is a political philosophy that posits that political decisions should arise from the engagement of lay citizens in democratic processes, and democracy should involve the respectful exchange of reasons to justify collective decisions (Gutmann and Thompson, 2004; Weinstein and Kahane, 2010). Its basic premise is that individuals from all walks of life should have the opportunity to participate in discussions about important social issues and that these discussions are taken into account in policy decisions.

Public deliberation is one particular instantiation of deliberative democratic principles. It is a particular kind of public conversation that aims to involve a diversity of individuals in collectively working toward solutions to a social problem. The term 'deliberation' holds very specific meaning in this regard. Chambers (2003: 309) provides the following definition:

> Generally speaking, we can say that deliberation is debate and discussion aimed at producing reasonable, well informed opinions in which participants are willing to revise preferences in light of discussion, new information, and claims made by fellow participants. Although consensus need not be the ultimate aim of deliberation, and participants are expected to pursue their interests, an overarching interest in the legitimacy of outcomes (understood as a justification to all affected) ideally characterizes deliberation.

A public deliberation is thus a particular event in which members of the public convene in an attempt to arrive at collective conclusions about a social issue, and they do so while following the norms of deliberation. That is, they become informed about the issues at hand, they engage with each other respectfully and revise their opinions based on new information and the perspectives of other participants, and they work together toward civic minded solutions.

Public deliberation has enjoyed a rich history as a form of democratic practice. Uses of deliberation can be traced back to the city states of Ancient Greece and the Roman Republic as early as the sixth century BCE, where collective decisions on issues of public relevance were made after extensive debate between advocates of diverse views (Richards and Gastil, 2016). In colonial New England during the seventeenth century, town hall meetings were institutionalized as methods for the expression of public opinion (Richards and Gastil, 2016). Early eighteenth century Europe saw physical spaces such as coffee shops and salons utilized for individuals to meet and engage in public debates (Finlayson, 2005).

Although public deliberation has a celebrated history, its popularity has ebbed and flowed with the political, cultural, and social atmosphere, as well as technological advancements of the times. Currently, deliberative democracy is experiencing a resurgence, both within academia and as a practical method of public engagement. Websites such as participedia.com are devoted to showcasing deliberative projects in the form of case studies and descriptions of methods used in public deliberations taking place across the globe. Scholarly publications such as *The Journal of Public Deliberation* have been created to publish articles based solely on the theoretical and empirical investigation of public deliberation. Formal organizations that are dedicated to the promotion, organization, and design of public deliberations, such as the Kettering Foundation and The Pew Charitable Trusts, have also been instituted.

Applied social psychologists are often concerned with seeking solutions to social issues. Many of us are also concerned with social justice and understanding social problems from the perspective of those who experience them. Perhaps more importantly, applied social psychologists also work toward change. One important level at which social change takes place is through influencing public policy. Public deliberation has the potential to achieve all of these goals. In light of this, our chapter has two goals. The first is to argue for the use of public deliberation as a form of social psychological practice. Social psychologists who are interested in participatory approaches and in influencing policy will find in public deliberation a practical mechanism that supports these purposes. The second goal is to identify particular areas of research where social psychological expertise has the potential to contribute to public deliberation theory and practice.

We begin with a brief overview of *deliberative democracy* theory and the normative ideals typically seen to underlie deliberative democratic practice. We then focus specifically on *public* deliberation as a form of deliberative democratic practice. In line with the first goal of this chapter, we argue that public deliberation can be understood as social psychological practice and provide guidelines for the design and implementation of deliberation processes. We focus, in particular, on recruitment and selection of participants, information provision to support meaningful deliberation, structuring the deliberative process, and evaluation of the quality of deliberation. We then turn to the second goal of the chapter, which is to identify several areas of research in which scholarship on public deliberation stands to benefit from the contributions of social psychologists. We highlight, in particular, potential contributions from experts on cognitive heuristics and biases, group dynamics and decision making, framing, discursive psychology, cultural psychology, critical psychology, and phenomenological psychology.

DELIBERATIVE DEMOCRACY

Public deliberation is a specific instantiation of broader deliberative democratic principles. We therefore provide a brief overview of the foundations of deliberative democracy as they relate to our discussion, before focusing more specifically on public deliberation. Although deliberative democracy is not usually seen as a replacement for representative democracy, it does shift the focus away from voting and instead focuses on the communicative processes that precede the development of collective decisions. Legitimacy of public decisions, therefore, lies not in the aggregation of independent individual votes, but rather in public articulation and explanation to justify public policies (Chambers, 2003: 308). Indeed, Dryzek and Niemeyer (2010) suggest that deliberative democracy is primarily a theory of legitimacy.

Advocates for deliberative democracy argue that the discussion of issues of public relevance should not involve only experts and politicians but also members of the public who reflect a wider diversity of perspectives (Gastil and Keith, 2005; Ryfe, 2005). Although experts bring important knowledge to any discussion, their perspectives often reflect narrow personal or professional interests (MacLean and Burgess, 2010). More importantly, the rationale for seeking public input in particular decisions relies, in part, on the democratic imperative to involve those affected by a particular policy in the development of that policy (Dryzek, 2001; Goodin, 2007). This observation is particularly pertinent in situations where policy decisions are made in the bureaucratic sphere with no direct involvement of wider publics or elected officials (MacKenzie and O'Doherty, 2011). There are obvious limitations to the number of issues for which public input can be sought. Even if public apathy for engaging in political processes could be dramatically reduced, we cannot all be involved in all public decisions that affect us. In this context, Warren (1996) suggests a distinction between political (contentious) versus settled issues. While settled issues can be dealt with more routinely, Warren argues that contentious issues require meaningful public input. Indeed, Warren and Pearse (2008) have argued that when democracies fail to incorporate citizen concerns into policy, this can result in declining voter turnout and broad discontent with governing bodies who come to be perceived as untrustworthy. In some cases, the failure to incorporate broader public concerns in policy may not be due to a lack of willingness on the part of decision makers but rather unclear or unstable citizen preferences such that governing bodies cannot adequately reflect their interests in policy decisions (Fung, 2008). In both instances, proponents of deliberative democracy have proposed that such *democratic deficits* (Fung, 2008; Warren and Pearse, 2008) require citizen engagement frameworks to contribute to the development and articulation of public preferences, ideally allowing government to be more responsive to citizen interests (Fung, 2008).

Gutmann and Thompson (1997) argue that, while disagreement is an inevitable component of democracies, it is possible for members of a society to deliberate about their disagreements in ways that contribute to the overall improvement of society. A commonly cited principle of deliberative democracy is, therefore, mutual respect among participants (Gutmann and Thompson, 2004; Mansbridge et al., 2012). The goal of deliberation is not necessarily to change people's opinions or values but rather to guide them to appreciate that there is worth in different perspectives. For example, Gutmann and Thompson (2004: 93) state,

> citizens who seriously disagree over policies such as the legalization of abortion, capital punishment and pornography can share other substantive standards: they can recognize that their own moral commitments might turn out to be wrong even though they now have good reason to believe them to be true; they can value public deliberation

> as a critical means of subjecting their moral commitments to critical scrutiny (and possibly changing them in the future); and they can give serious consideration to opposing points of view as a manifestation of their respect for morally reasonable people.

A related aspect of deliberative democratic ideals is the exchange of reasons and justifications for particular perspectives (Chambers, 2003). Gutmann and Thompson (2004) refer to this as mutual reason-giving and argue that participants in a discursive exchange should not only provide justifications for their particular perspectives; they should also seriously consider new information and moral arguments, as well as being open to re-assess information and arguments they may have previously encountered. For members of the public to express well-reasoned positions, they must be provided with relevant information and exposed to the perspectives and opinions of others. Indeed, deliberative systems are said to have an epistemic function, such that they 'produce preferences, opinions and decisions that are appropriately informed by facts and logic and are the outcome of substantive and meaningful consideration of relevant reasons' (Mansbridge et al., 2012: 11). Often the quality of deliberation rests upon the extent to which participants are provided with relevant and accurate information (Fishkin et al., 2000).

Deliberative democrats also advocate for political equality. In the context of deliberation, equality does not mean that each perspective is given equal weight but rather that each individual is permitted to express their preference free from social inequalities traditionally produced by wealth and power (Moore and O'Doherty, 2014). Accordingly, in line with reason giving, all individuals are required to provide accounts that support their positions. This principle has been criticized as being exclusionary by some, and we return to this point later in this chapter.

Ultimately, the goal of deliberative democracy is not simply to come to decisions but rather to come to mutual decisions that are justified by the reasons on which they are based (Gutmann and Thompson, 2004). Even when individuals disagree about particular issues, through sharing perspectives and articulating their reasoning respectfully, they may come to agreement on shared goals and values. Consequently, through participating in deliberative processes, individuals come to appreciate positions that extend beyond a limited self-interest (Gutmann and Thompson, 2004), and they are expected to collectively come to conclusions that are accepted more broadly in the public sphere (MacKenzie and O'Doherty, 2011). Gutmann and Thompson (1997) therefore suggest that deliberation improves collective decision making and enhances the legitimacy of associated policies by basing them on questions of common rather than exclusively individual interest, by encouraging mutual respect among individuals even in the face of strong moral disagreement, and by basing decisions on greater individual and collective understanding.

We have provided this background on deliberative democracy as a foundation to understand the principles underlying public deliberation. However, public deliberation, is typically conceived of as a much narrower and more specific practice. In particular, while deliberative democratic principles are often taken to suggest that all members of a society who are affected by a particular decision should have a voice in making that decision, public deliberations tend to involve only a subset of the society. An important concept in the instantiation of many forms of public deliberation in this context is that of a minipublic. A minipublic is a group of people that is constituted in such a way as to be small enough to enact principles of deliberation, and representative enough to be considered democratic (Goodin and Dryzek, 2006). Although minipublics are generally not representative in a political sense (i.e., members are not formally elected), nor in a statistical sense (though some larger deliberative designs may emphasize criteria for the deliberating group to be statistically representative of the population), they can be constructed to maximize the diversity of perspectives that exist in a given population (Longstaff and Burgess, 2010). Because minipublics only involve a relatively small number of people in deliberative democratic processes, they have important limitations to enacting macropolitical goals of deliberative democracy (Chambers, 2009). Nevertheless, they have an important role in the design of broader deliberative systems (Curato and Boker, 2016; Niemeyer, 2014). In addition, there are several ways in which minipublic deliberations can affect broader public and political spheres, such as directly influencing public policy, informing public debates, legitimating policy development processes, and building constituencies (Goodin and Dryzek, 2006; see also Mackenzie and O'Doherty, 2011).

As the foregoing discussion illustrates, the ideals of deliberative decision making require that high standards be satisfied. Moreover, much of the extensive literature on deliberative democracy is theoretical with no clear guidance as to how deliberative principles might be applied in practice. For example, when a new law or policy is considered that potentially affects the residents of an entire country, it is not clear who precisely should be involved in deliberative conversations. How should conversations be structured, and what kind of information should be provided to participants in the deliberation? Finding answers to these questions is critical for applied social psychologists who seek to incorporate public deliberation into their work. There is now also a substantial literature relating to methodology on public deliberation. In the next section, we draw on this literature systematically to provide detailed guidelines for the design and implementation of public deliberation processes.

IMPLEMENTING PUBLIC DELIBERATION

Public deliberation is a very particular instantiation of deliberative democratic ideals in the sense that it involves a discrete event or set of processes that are designed and implemented purposefully to achieve specific participatory aims. The purpose of this section is therefore to provide a detailed discussion of the design and implementation of public deliberation processes.

When theoretical ideals of deliberative democracy are applied to settings in which members of the public are invited to consider an issue and provide input for policy, we can speak of public deliberation. In such events, members of the public are recruited, provided with information about a particular topic, engage in debate, and ultimately come to a decision about policy recommendations grounded within a collective understanding of the issues (O'Doherty et al., 2012b). Public deliberation can be realized in many forms and existing approaches and methods are not governed by any one specific framework. Warren (2009) estimates that there are likely close to 100 different deliberative designs. Current models include National Issues Forums, deliberative polling, consensus conferences, planning cells, and citizen juries, to name but a few. Extensive descriptions and examples of these models go beyond the scope of this chapter and can be found in Gastil and Levine (2005). What all of these models have in common is that they aim to include ordinary citizens in debate surrounding issues of policy relevance (Dryzek and Niemeyer, 2010) and therefore place decision making in the public sphere, rather than behind closed doors (Barnes, 2008). Nevertheless, choices in the design of a deliberative forum can have both practical and conceptual implications (Button and Ryfe, 2005). The social and institutional contexts in which a public deliberation might be convened vary; therefore, the design of deliberative forums needs to be tailored, paying attention to factors such as representation and recruitment, framing, forum design, facilitation, and synthesis of results (O'Doherty et al., 2012a).

Representation and Recruitment

The notion of 'the public' is an abstraction. Therefore, recruiting a sample of participants for public deliberation constitutes a very particular 'public' whose input on an issue is sought. Therefore, there are important theoretical and practical considerations in precisely how individuals are selected to be part of a particular public deliberation process. Public deliberation events can involve small groups of 10–12 individuals and up to thousands, depending on the particular design that is implemented. Because deliberation relies on in-depth communication among participants, there are limits to the number of people that can participate in any one given deliberative event. Even for public deliberations that involve thousands of people, there are many more millions of people that may be affected by a given policy that are not involved in the deliberation. Decisions about who, precisely, is chosen to participate and what processes are used to recruit and select participants in a deliberation therefore warrant close consideration. In making these decisions, Fung (2006: 67) suggests asking the following questions: 'are they [participants] appropriately representative of the relevant population or the general public? Are important interests or perspectives excluded? Are participants responsive and accountable to those who do not participate?'.

When issues are contentions, there is often more than one interest group claiming to represent public interests. And often there is disagreement among, and within, different groups. It is therefore crucial for the legitimacy of a deliberative public forum that it is positioned beyond partisan interests (O'Doherty et al., 2012a). Participants need to be chosen to reflect this. Although self-selection can never be fully eliminated (participants always have the choice to agree or decline an invitation to participate), there are methods for minimizing its influence (Longstaff and Burgess, 2010). Of particular concern in this regard are (1) disproportionate participation in deliberative events of individuals with higher educational attainments and affluence and (2) disproportionate participation of individuals with vested interests relating to the issue under consideration. A high degree of self-selection may lead to a decrease in the range of perspectives represented in a deliberative forum and thus undermine its legitimacy (Ryfe, 2005). Organizers can thus either purposively invite participants, opting to select those who are less likely to participate (e.g., minorities, economically disadvantaged individuals), or randomly select participants in such a way that greater representativeness is achieved (Fung, 2006). Random selection, in particular, offers benefits over self-selection as more diverse perspectives will be expressed, and those who participate are more likely to represent those who do not (Dryzek and Niemeyer, 2010).

Another issue to consider is the possible inclusion of experts in the design of a deliberative event. Experts generally represent narrow professional or personal perspectives (MacLean and Burgess, 2010), and while some designs permit experts to deliberate directly with lay citizens, such a design risks discussions being dominated by expert positions, marginalizing the voices of lay citizens (O'Doherty et al., 2012a). An alternative way of including expert positions is to have experts serve as information sources and give presentations to deliberants but not otherwise participate in the deliberation (see below, 'Information Provision'). Such individuals might have expertise in legal or ethical implications of particular positions and can provide information to participants, while other speakers might represent particular groups (e.g., cultural, ethnic minorities, personal experience related to the topic). Such experts will, of course, vary depending on the topic of the public deliberation.

Finally, it should be noted that the objective of convening a deliberative forum may be to incorporate the views of particular stakeholder groups into policy decisions, as opposed to those of a broader public (e.g., Hodgetts et al., 2014). In such cases, selection of participants will, of course, be much more targeted.

Regardless of the method chosen for recruitment, it is important to consider that the participants in any given public deliberation cannot be representative of population views because the majority of the population has not been exposed to technical information and perspectives of others the same way that deliberation participants have been. Therefore, although consideration of how to constitute the group of participants who take part in a deliberation is critical, the validity of conclusions should not be judged simply by how representative the sample was, but rather by understanding the extent to which participants engaged in deliberation and took into account relevant information and diverse perspectives (O'Doherty et al., 2013).

Information Provision

While critics of deliberation have expressed concerns over the competence of ordinary citizens to engage in discussions about complex issues, research suggests that they make excellent deliberators, regardless of issue complexity (Dryzek and Niemeyer, 2010). Nevertheless, deliberants need up to date and accurate information to engage in meaningful deliberation. A key component of successful deliberation, therefore, is the provision of sufficient information to ensure that deliberants have a foundation upon which to base their positions (Gutmann and Thompson, 2004).

Information can be provided to participants in a range of modalities, such as written materials, videos, online materials, and presentations by expert speakers at the deliberation event. Using more than one modality also facilitates uptake owing to differences in learning styles among participants. Providing information for public engagement on a controversial topic is open to criticisms of undue framing favoring vested interests (Petersen, 2007). Therefore, information materials will generally need to be produced specifically for a public deliberation event, as pre-existing materials may be framed in ways that reflect particular institutional or partisan interests. Friedman (2007) suggests that information provided to deliberants is 'framed for deliberation'. Rather than attempting to provide information in a neutral or objective manner, framing for deliberation involves providing information from multiple perspectives. If expert or key stakeholder speakers are used to inform deliberants, for example, each speaker need not attempt to be neutral in their portrayal of issues; rather, all speakers collectively should be chosen to span a range of competing perspectives. For example, a deliberation about salmon genomics on the West Coast of Canada involved explicit consideration of the role of salmon aqua culture and wild fisheries (O'Doherty et al., 2010). The interests of these two industries are generally seen to be in conflict with each other in various ways. Information provision for this deliberation, therefore, sought to provide information from each of these (and other) perspectives to provide deliberants with a foundation for their discussions, as opposed to attempting to provide a singular account.

Deliberation Structure: Questions, Tasks, Facilitation, Analysis

In addition to considering the framing of information provided to participants, it is also important to consider how questions and tasks posed to deliberants are framed. Questions posed to participants can range on a spectrum from very open to very specific. Openly defined deliberations allow participants to discuss issues they deem to be important, essentially taking the discussion in any direction they like. Deliberations that are governed by specific questions keep the discussion confined to issues more narrowly, as deemed important by the organizers.

However, such a design also risks leaving little room to discuss unanticipated points of view (O'Doherty et al., 2012a). When questions are framed openly, participants may feel a greater sense of legitimacy associated with the outcomes of the deliberation, and such framing allows for the inclusion of unanticipated points of view. However, such framing can also pose difficulties for the integration of recommendations into existing policies (O'Doherty and Burgess, 2013; O'Doherty et al., 2012a). Given these tensions, it can be helpful to understand the conditions under which a particular method of framing is most appropriate. Specific framing may be most useful when policy frameworks are already in place, while open framing may be most useful when norms and policies have yet to be developed (O'Doherty and Burgess, 2013).

It can also be useful to combine open and specific formats of framing. For example, a public deliberation about ethical implications of human tissue biobanking (the BC Biobank Deliberation) was conducted in British Columbia, Canada, in 2007 (see Burgess et al., 2008). At the time, little was known about public views on the topic of biobanks. The deliberation was therefore structured in an open manner, with few or no constraints imposed by the organizers regarding the direction of conversations during the deliberation. This open structure was instantiated by giving participants the very broad task of designing a biobank for British Columbia. The BC Biobank Deliberation was followed by another public deliberation, the BC BioLibrary Deliberation in 2009 (O'Doherty et al., 2012b). In contrast to the earlier public deliberation, the BC BioLibrary Deliberation used a very narrow focus on specific questions that were posed to participants. This narrow framing was justified, in part, by using the results of the previous (open frame) deliberation as a foundation for which kinds of issues could be regarded as relatively settled and which ones were more contentions (Warren, 1996) and therefore required further examination. For example, the issue of whether biobanks had broad in principle public support was very much at the center of the first (BC Biobank) deliberation. Because one of the main outcomes of this deliberation was strong in principle support for biobanks, in principle support was presumed in the second (BC BioLibrary) deliberation, and discussion could focus on finer details about the ethical operation of biobanks (see O'Doherty and Hawkins, 2010, for a fuller discussion). It is also possible to design deliberations that include both open and specific question formats. For example, a deliberation in Canada about the use of microbial genomics for bioremediation of unexploded ordinance involved two phases of deliberation. In the first phase, deliberants worked toward setting an agenda of topics for further discussion. In the second phase, they worked toward collective positions on those topics (O'Doherty et al., 2013).

An important consideration related to framing and the posing of questions and tasks is the role facilitators play in conducting public deliberations. Facilitators have an important role not only in ensuring that participants adhere to norms of deliberation (respectful exchange, providing reasons for propositions, etc.) but also in ensuring that the results of a public deliberation are meaningful. While scholars suggest that facilitators should not represent a particular vested interest in the issue, they should have some familiarity with the topic such that they are able to recognize points of tension and different positions, and to ensure that the discussion remains on topic (O'Doherty et al., 2012a). It should be emphasized, however, that the role of facilitators in deliberation is a neglected topic of study that requires urgent scholarly attention.

Finally, consideration needs to be given to how the results of a public deliberation should be conceived and reported (O'Doherty, 2013). Some scholars argue that statically measuring opinions is inadequate and therefore qualitative analyses are necessary (O'Doherty, 2017;

Walmsley, 2011). Specifically, Walmsley explains that qualitative methods can aid in the investigation of particular theoretical claims, such as whether participants consider the positions of others, if they change their own arguments and perspectives, incorporating aspects of other's arguments, and in what ways consensus might be reached when there has been disagreement. As deliberation can involve many days of conversation, in both plenary and break-out groups, it is by no means obvious which particular statements should be recognized as 'final' and who should be the person or group to articulate and report on the official outcomes of the deliberation. It is tempting to think that all proceedings of the deliberation could simply be subjected to a thematic or content analysis, the results of which could be taken to constitute the outcomes of the deliberation. This, however, would be a mistake. Because participants in deliberation are expected to move from the expression of individual opinions to articulating civic solutions, and because they are expected to continuously consider new information and other perspectives in coming to conclusions, a mechanism is required that differentiates the expression of the final collective positions of the deliberating group from other statements made by participants. This has been referred to elsewhere as the deliberative output of the deliberation (O'Doherty and Burgess, 2009) or the deliberative public opinion of the group (O'Doherty, 2017). Ideally, the deliberative process is itself structured in such a way that facilitators guide participants to the expression of collective positions, which are then documented as the official conclusions of the group. Analysis of the deliberation to report on its outcomes would then focus primarily on documenting these collective positions. Of course, additional thematic analysis of all the conversations preceding the articulation of collective positions is useful at that point to provide greater understanding of the group's reasoning that led up to their conclusions (O'Doherty, 2013).

Evaluating the Quality of Deliberation

Deliberation is intended to bring change. However, whether the change that is ultimately effected through deliberative processes is in line with deliberative principles cannot be assumed. When misused, or in spite of the intentions of the organizers, failures of deliberative processes can 'produce more harm than good' (Dorr Goold et al., 2012: 11). For instance, when the outcomes of a deliberative process are determined more by the powerful voices of some participants than the exchange of reasons and perspectives, uptake in policy could magnify, rather than alleviate, social inequalities. Or, if the process is perceived to be tokenistic because of insufficient opportunity to discuss aspects of an issue deemed most relevant by the deliberants (as opposed to the organizers), the deliberative process may lead to disengagement and cynicism.

Empirical evaluation of deliberative processes is therefore critical, and such evaluation needs to be based on a sound theoretical foundation. A number of different frameworks have been suggested for evaluating quality of deliberation (e.g., Abelson et al., 2003; Black et al., 2009; Cobb and Gano, 2012; de Vries et al., 2010; 2011; Steenbergen et al., 2003). Across different approaches, Dorr Goold et al. have suggested several common criteria that can be used to assess the quality of deliberative events, which can be categorized as relating to structure, process, and outcomes of the deliberative event.

Under structure, Dorr Goold et al. (2012) point to the importance of ensuring:

- representativeness, such that people affected by the issues being discussed are appropriately selected to participate,
- the provision of adequate relevant and trustworthy information, and
- sufficient time to review information, reflect on it, discuss it with co-deliberants and, importantly, weigh trade-offs and work toward collective conclusions.

This latter point is often neglected in estimating the time it takes for everyone in a group of people to have a chance to speak and for disagreements and diverse perspectives to be worked out. Many structural elements can be assessed from analyzing the design of a deliberative event and from conducting post-deliberation surveys of participants.

With regard to process, Dorr Goold et al. suggest assessing the degree to which discussions in a given deliberation followed principles of deliberation. Questions to consider include:

- Were participants able to communicate freely, challenging one another, and accept or reject others' positions?
- Were attempts at persuasion based on reasons or appeals to values, as opposed to rhetorical skills or attempts to dominate?
- Was dialogue respectful?
- Were conclusions based on what is best for society as opposed to for particular individuals?

Process elements can be assessed using a combination of post-deliberation surveys and transcript analysis of event proceedings.

Finally, an assessment of outcomes focuses primarily on the impact that the deliberation has on both the individuals who participated in the event and on policy. Assessment of deliberation quality on the level of individual participants can focus on elements such as:

- Has participants' knowledge on the issues improved?
- Has there been a change in participants' views of other participants?
- Have participants become more active politically as a result of their participation in deliberation?
- Have their views of policy makers and experts working in the field changed?

Assessment on the level of policy impact is very challenging. Impacts on policy as a result of a public deliberation may take a long time to occur, at which point it will be difficult to attribute the policy change back to the deliberation. Nevertheless, awareness of the public deliberation among decision makers can be assessed, and decision makers can be interviewed about their intention to act on the outcomes of a deliberation. It should also be emphasized that a public deliberation can be of high quality even when it results in no direct policy change. For instance, existing policies gain in legitimacy if they are endorsed by a deliberative public forum. Policy makers can be more confident that their policies reflect informed public input, and the trust built between policy makers and publics through deliberation can lead to improved understanding and mutual support for future policy decisions (Dorr Goold et al., 2012).

PUBLIC DELIBERATION AS SOCIAL PSYCHOLOGICAL PRACTICE

As we have outlined above, public engagement processes have been used to inform policy on a wide range of issues, many of which are of interest to social psychologists. We therefore advocate that more applied social psychologists should take up public deliberation as a form of practice. We argue that theorizing, designing, and implementing deliberative public engagements aligns with applied social psychological goals. Not only can theorists and practitioners from other disciplines gain from the input of social psychologists; applied social psychologists stand to gain from making public deliberation their own and incorporating it as a key tool in their practice. In this section, we briefly examine three aspects of public deliberation as applied social psychological practice.

Public Deliberation as Intervention

In line with other chapters in this Handbook outlining social psychological interventions, public deliberation can be envisaged as a very particular kind of intervention that influences a range of social cognitive variables. For instance, public deliberation can act as an intervention to ameliorate deep cultural conflicts. When participants from diverse and conflicting cultural perspectives deliberate, it is possible for mutually acceptable solutions to be developed (Dembinksa and Montambeault, 2015; Luskin et al., 2014). In other words, both the transformative and improved decision making aspects of deliberation can be utilized to help tackle social issues that have long been of interest to social psychologists.

Luskin et al. (2014) discuss the findings from a deliberative poll conducted in Omagh in Northern Ireland. This district is characterized by a deep Catholic–Protestant divide in which schools are almost entirely comprised of either Catholic or Protestant pupils. Due to practical constraints (e.g., low enrollment), the government recommended greater collaboration and integration among schools. The Omagh Deliberative Poll was initiated to provide policy recommendations about the future of district schools. One-hundred and twenty-seven parents participated in the deliberative event. Participants completed a questionnaire that assessed their knowledge related to the relevant issues, their attitudes toward particular policies, and their beliefs about other community members. In addition to participants demonstrating greater learning and understanding of the issues, Luskin et al. (2014) found that, after deliberation, there was greater support for policies related to religious mixing and decreased support for policies that favored religious segregation. But perhaps the most important finding from this study was that, after deliberation, participants came to view members of the other religious community as more trustworthy and Catholics came to view Protestants as more open to reason.

Although much depends on the specific issues and communities concerned, as well as the particular instantiation of deliberative principles, cases such as these demonstrate at least the potential for deliberation to be used as a form of intervention to improve intergroup conflict.

Public Deliberation as Research Method

Public deliberation can also be conceptualized as a research method for gathering public input on an issue. As such, it can be compared to other social science research methodologies that are used to measure public opinion, such as surveys, polls, interviews, and focus groups. However, in contrast to these other methods, public deliberation offers distinctive advantages. In particular, traditional methods assume that members of the public have a familiarity with a topic of interest and that opinions about the topic are relatively enduring (O'Doherty et al., 2012b). When individuals are surveyed about particular issues about which they possess little information, it cannot be expected that responses reflect well-reasoned positions that would be valuable to policy makers. Public deliberation offers advantages over these methods because it promotes reflection (Gastil, 2008) and leads to the development of informed opinions.

Perhaps more radically, it has been argued that, specifically when it comes to measuring *public opinion*, there is no meaningful theoretical foundation underlying the use of surveys, polls, and focus groups (O'Doherty, 2017). The results of such instruments, rather than measuring public opinion, are better understood as producing and constructing a representation of public opinion. The use of public deliberation can therefore be understood as producing a different kind of outcome, a *deliberative public opinion*. Deliberative public opinion is a socially and historically situated construct with democratic legitimacy to the degree that it incorporates the diversity of views of the groups it purports to represent.

Beyond the deliberative outputs produced by a deliberative public engagement, deliberations produce large amounts of data.

These data can be analyzed along a number of dimensions, including:

- any substantive aspects of the topic of the deliberation (e.g., Hawkins and O'Doherty, 2010; Hodgetts et al., 2012; Nep and O'Doherty, 2013);
- the discursive processes underlying deliberation (e.g., Davies et al., 2006; O'Doherty and Davidson, 2010; Walmsley, 2010);
- the dominant discourses or societal representations of any particular phenomenon of interest (e.g., Walmsley, 2009).

In other words, public deliberation events constitute important data sources in their own right, with a particular structure distinctive from that of focus groups or other qualitative data sources (O'Doherty, 2012). Importantly, however, when used as a research method, public deliberation should not be understood as a way of measuring existing public opinion on an issue (O'Doherty, 2017). Because of the transformational nature of deliberation, participants gain new perspectives and develop deeper insights over the course of deliberation. Analysis of data from deliberative forums should recognize that these data are produced in a very particular setting and do not reflect participants' everyday lives in a straightforward way.

Public Deliberation as Political Mechanism

From an applied social psychological perspective, public deliberation can thus be understood both as an intervention and as a method for generating data. A third way to understand public deliberation is as a political mechanism. This understanding is arguably most in line with conceptions of public deliberation in political philosophy and political science, and it is also the understanding that has the most emancipatory value for applied social psychology.

Public deliberation is a practice that has the capacity to integrate diverse values, commitments, and life experiences of different individuals and groups and link these to collective decisions and practices. Public deliberation, therefore, is a mechanism that has the potential to:

1 produce intersubjective spaces for participants to explore, develop, and articulate individual and collective positions on social issues;
2 allow individual participants to situate their own values, experiences, and commitments relative to the collective space;
3 connect this plurality of cultural, social, and political aspects of individual and group psychology to policy frameworks, such that societal level structures may be designed and implemented in ways that foster well-being.

Public deliberation is therefore a practice very much in line with the goals and disciplinary interests of applied social psychology. However, in line with the opening remarks of this chapter, much depends on how we, as scholars, position ourselves, our research, and the participants with whom we interact. If we see ourselves as detached scientists, modeling the methods of the natural sciences in studying non-sentient objects, then conceiving of public deliberation as a form of social psychological intervention will be the extent of applying this approach in our practice. However, if we view people as *persons*, embedded within relational and societal frameworks and yet imbued with agency to act and interact with individual and collective purpose, then the adoption of deliberative approaches may allow for a much deeper applied social psychological practice.

SOCIAL PSYCHOLOGICAL CONTRIBUTIONS TO RESEARCH AND PRACTICE OF PUBLIC DELIBERATION

In general, psychology's contributions to public deliberation have been minimal. Investigations of the psychological factors influencing deliberation have tended to focus on intrapersonal characteristics such as personality factors and attachment styles (Kuhar, 2013). However, the potential of social psychology to contribute to the empirical literature on public deliberation has also been recognized (Delli Carpini et al., 2004; Mannarini, 2011; Mendelberg, 2002). Empirical research on public deliberation has tended to fall behind theoretical writings (Delli Carpini et al., 2004), which perhaps reveals the most pertinent niche for contributions from social psychology. Given that public deliberation is an inherently social activity, social psychology can help to understand the context dependent factors that may lead to the realization or failure of deliberative democratic ideals. Although deliberative democracy is a normative theory, such theory provides direction as to what questions to ask when testing claims empirically (Setälä and Herne, 2014).

In this final part of the chapter, we therefore examine areas of study in psychology, and in particular social psychology, that have direct relevance to the study of public deliberation. To date, social psychologists have tended not to focus their attention on public deliberation as an object of study. Nevertheless, particular areas of study and traditions of research have very evident relevance to the study of public deliberation. Our purpose here is to identify only a few such areas, calling for psychologists with this expertise to lend their skills to investigation of deliberative processes. Specifically, we discuss cognitive heuristics and biases, group dynamics and decision making, framing, discursive psychology, culture and social norms, power relations, and phenomenological analyses.

Cognitive Heuristics and Biases

Morrell (2014) suggests that the success of public deliberation can be threatened by the biases held by participants. He highlights three cognitive biases studied in social psychology that may adversely influence the outcomes of deliberation: attribution bias, in-group/out-group bias, and confirmation bias. Attribution bias refers to the systematic errors that individuals make when evaluating their own behavior and the behavior of others. For example, social psychological research suggests that individuals may make the fundamental attribution error such that they are more likely to attribute another's behavior to dispositional rather than situational factors. Morrell (2014) argues that, in deliberative situations where participants are required to come to agreement about the reasons underlying a decision, such an agreement would be difficult to achieve when attributional biases are at work. He uses the following example to illustrate his point:

> Imagine a situation where wealthy people think that their success arose from their own hard work and that the failure of the poorer people is simply because they are lazy. Poorer people, on the other hand, might attribute their failures to the system or their bad luck and the successes of the wealthy to their good luck or background. (Morrell, 2014: 162)

In such a situation, it would be difficult for such individuals to agree on a decision concerning social welfare programs. Another relevant social psychological finding is that of the in-group/out-group bias. This bias refers to the tendency for individuals to favor others they perceive to be like themselves (the in-group) over those they do not (the out-group). If mutual respect is a necessary condition for successful deliberation, then the operation of the in-group/out-group bias, according to Morrell (2014), would make it challenging for these conditions to be met.

Perhaps one of the most robust findings in the social psychological literature is that of the confirmation bias (Mercier and Landemore, 2012). The confirmation bias is the tendency to notice and interpret new information that confirms one's existing beliefs, while ignoring new information that may disconfirm them. The confirmation bias operates both among individuals and among groups of individuals reasoning together. If a necessary condition of deliberation is that participants listen closely and engage with each other's reasoning and arguments, then the confirmation bias can undermine such processes (Morrell, 2014).

Successful public deliberation projects demonstrate that participants do engage in meaningful deliberation that overcomes attribution bias, in-group/out-group bias, and confirmation bias to arrive at well-reasoned collective positions. This is evident in the collective recommendations produced by participants of the BC BioLibrary Deliberation (O'Doherty et al., 2012) and the RDX Deliberation (O'Doherty et al., 2013b). On a process level, Walmsley (2011) shows in a qualitative analysis how a group of deliberants came to develop consensus on a novel and emergent position relating to the compensation of donors to a biobank. Of interest, here, is how the analysis demonstrates the creative and civic-minded shifts in opinions that individual deliberants and the group as a whole engaged in to reach their conclusion, which clearly transcended typical understandings of attribution bias, in-group/out-group bias, and confirmation bias.

What is of interest, therefore, are the precise conditions under which biases hinder the success of deliberation and under which the successful application of deliberative norms assist individuals and groups overcome such biases. For example, Sunstein and Hastie (2008) note that some cognitive biases can be attenuated in certain conditions. The egocentric bias, for instance, which involves the tendency to believe that others think the same way that oneself does, can be corrected for when individuals are exposed to diverse viewpoints. Arguably, deliberation is therefore a powerful mechanism to assist overcoming recognized psychological biases and related phenomena such as motivated reasoning (see, for example, Kraft et al., 2015; Montpetit and Lachapelle, 2017) that contribute to divisiveness and problematic policy decisions. However, this is a hypothesis that needs to be further tested.

Group Dynamics and Decision Making

The length of time for which a deliberative minipublic is convened can vary from a single day to many years. However, even when established for only short periods of time, individuals brought together to participate in public deliberations constitute a group (Mannarini, 2011). It is therefore surprising that much of the analysis of deliberative forums is conducted at the level of the individual (e.g., measurement of individual participants' opinions pre- and post-deliberation). In contrast, Karpowitz and Mendelberg (2007) argue that the group, rather than the individual, is the more appropriate unit of analysis. What is certainly self-evident is that group dynamics affect both the quality and outcomes of deliberation.

Group decision making has been closely studied by social psychological researchers over the last 80 years. This has led some to criticize aspects of deliberation based on conclusions from social psychological studies. For example, Sunstein (2005) criticizes the practice of deliberation based on extensive social psychological research on small group discussion and identifies group polarization as a common threat to groups arriving at optimal conclusions. Group polarization is the tendency for groups to develop more extreme positions than those individuals held before they engaged with the group. Indeed, Sunstein (2002) warns that deliberation advantages those with extreme opinions because group preferences will tend to shift in their favor.

However, as Cobb (2012) points out, the research this criticism is based on pertains to group *discussion*, not *deliberation*. Group polarization tends to occur under particular conditions: when individuals already share a common position in relation to a particular issue. When individuals share common positions, each individual's confirmation bias will be augmented by the others in the group (Mercier and Landemore, 2012). But, for deliberation to occur, individuals must be exposed to, and engaged in, argumentation from different points of view (Cobb, 2012; Mercier and Landemore, 2012). Such a condition ensures that the confirmation bias of each individual is challenged by the information and opinions presented by other individuals because cognitive diversity is present. Indeed, when such a condition is met, depolarization tends to occur and beliefs and decisions are often more informed. Empirical evidence gives weight to these claims (Cobb, 2011). Social psychological studies of jury deliberation similarly demonstrate the benefits of careful and informed deliberation (see Chapter 27, in this Handbook).

In short, social psychological research programs have focused on decision making and group dynamics in small group discussions. This research has pointed out important failures in group decision making. The norms guiding deliberation and practice for instantiating public deliberation events contain elements that guard against such failures. However, systematic study of group dynamics in deliberative conversations still needs to be conducted, and the precise conditions that lead to success and failure in collective decision making in deliberation contexts need empirical elucidation.

Framing

The provision of relevant and balanced information for participants to consider is a core element of deliberation that is considered to be legitimate by both participants and evaluators. The issue of framing becomes relevant when making decisions about the provision of this information. Information can be provided in written form or be delivered verbally by individuals with varying positions on a particular topic of policy relevance, including those considered experts.

There is extensive psychological literature examining framing effects that can be applied to the study of public deliberation. The seminal work of Tversky and Kahneman (1981; 1987) found that the decisions people make are influenced by the way that information is presented. Therefore, any information that is presented is not neutral (Mannarini, 2011), and the framing of information will influence how individuals discuss a particular issue (Brewer and Gross, 2005). Recent research suggests that framing is influential within the context of deliberation and can have both negative and positive consequences.

In the context of public deliberation, two types of framing effects are important to consider: equivalency and issue framing effects (Druckman, 2004). Equivalency framing refers to the presentation of two different, but logically equivalent, statements (e.g., a 30% chance of rain today versus a 70% chance of no rain today). A framing effect occurs when the presentation of different frames leads to different responses by individuals (e.g., whether I bring an umbrella to work). In contrast, issue framing refers to the way in which descriptions emphasize particular considerations about an issue over others. Individuals exposed to such descriptions then form their opinion on the basis of these considerations (Druckman, 2004). Druckman and Nelson (2003) provide the example of a rally organized by a hate group. If a speaker frames the issue in terms of the right to free speech, listeners may be more likely to incorporate this into their opinion and support the rally on the basis of allowing people to speak freely. However, if a speaker were to frame the issue in terms of public safety, individuals hearing this speech are more likely to focus on public safety concerns and may be less likely to support the rally.

Framing clearly has important implications for the design and practice of public deliberation (see also 'Information Provision' above). Most obviously, if information presented to participants unduly frames issues in a particular way that biases the deliberation toward a particular outcome, this could undermine the legitimacy of the forum and its recommendations. However, appropriate framing may also facilitate successful deliberation (O'Doherty and Hawkins, 2010). Brewer and Gross (2005) found that common frames of reference allow people to have a shared understanding from which to approach and analyze a problem; this can be beneficial in the context of public deliberation. Additionally, while individuals may base their opinions on information they hear from elites (e.g., experts), conversation with other individuals may lessen the effects of elite framing. Therefore, when individuals are exposed to elite framing, but engage in conversations with individuals with different points of view, the effect of the elite framing is attenuated (Druckman and Nelson, 2003).

In sum, phenomena related to issue and equivalency framing are well studied in psychology. However, this knowledge has only been applied in very limited ways to the design and practice of public deliberation. Social psychologists have the potential to provide much value by focusing research on framing in the specific setting of public deliberation events.

Discursive Psychology

Although there has been an increase in empirical study of deliberation, there is still relatively little research on actual processes of public deliberation. With some notable exceptions (e.g., Davies et al., 2006; Steenbergen et al.,2003), empirical studies of deliberation often involve pre/post designs to measure the impact of deliberation on some variable of interest, and thus treat deliberation as a black box. What is required, therefore, is more extensive analysis of deliberative processes.

Discursive psychology (Edwards and Potter, 1992) is a branch of social psychology that is particularly suited to the study of communicative processes (see also Chapter 20, by Tseliou, Smoliak, LaMarre, and Quinn-Nilas, in this Handbook). Rather than viewing language as a vehicle for the expression of intrapsychic constructs (thoughts, feelings, attitudes, etc.), discursive psychology conceptualizes language as social action. Particular expressions are therefore not interpreted as a window on an individual's inner mental world, but rather as actions that serve particular purposes. Discursive psychology therefore presents a distinctive and valuable lens through which to analyze deliberative processes.

To date, only limited research along these lines has been conducted. Most notably, Davies et al. (2006) analyzed data collected from the National Issues for Health and Care Excellence (NICE) Citizens Council that took place in the United Kingdom between 2003 and 2004. This Citizens Council was composed of 30 individuals, reflective of the demographic characteristics of the general population. Through deliberation, the Citizens Council arrived at recommendations to inform the work of the NICE. Davies et al. demonstrated the relationship between discursive styles and their influence on the deliberation. For example, participants made use of adversarial discursive styles which mimicked interactions observed in political debates, as well as a discursive style that Davies et al. termed 'researcher speech style', which involved participants bringing information into the deliberation that they had learned elsewhere. Participants also used discursive styles that drew upon the exchange of personal stories. Storytelling appeared to be devalued as a discursive style within the context of this deliberation, and as a consequence, as the deliberation proceeded, participants came to draw upon more highly valued discursive styles and apologized when they did share personal anecdotes.

In another study, O'Doherty and Davidson (2010) drew on the discursive psychological notion of subject positions to gain a deeper understanding of deliberative communication processes. Davies and Harré (1990: 48) define positioning as 'the discursive process whereby selves are located in conversations as observably and subjectively coherent participants in jointly produced storylines'. O'Doherty and Davidson (2010) applied this framework to the analysis of a public deliberation about biobanking in British Columbia (Burgess et al., 2008). In particular, they investigated the ways in which participants in the deliberation drew on particular subject positions (e.g., those of 'patient' or 'Muslim' or 'white woman') to warrant particular arguments they were advancing. One of the conclusions of this study was that deliberation can indeed be an effective mechanism in creating an 'even playing field' for participants. The analysis showed that, on the whole, the status that individual participants held outside of the context of the deliberation was subordinate to the quality of the arguments and the reasoning presented. However, the ability of any given deliberation to achieve such a degree of equality may rely on particular structural elements, such as confining experts on the topic of the deliberation to the role of presenters and not including them as participants.

In short, discursive psychological analyses of deliberation are likely to provide valuable insights into processes of deliberation, but only little work in this regard has been conducted.

Power

Typical implementations of deliberation require that all participants are permitted to take part in the conversation and, when doing so, be allowed to introduce any claim they wish as well as question the claims of others without any internal or external pressure (Barnes, 2008). However, these conditions may not necessarily be met in practice. Indeed, instantiations of deliberative democracy have been criticized for reproducing structural inequalities (Walmsley, 2009).

Such criticism gains traction when we examine which types of discourse are privileged within deliberative exchanges. While rational arguments are often viewed as essential requirements of deliberation, some scholars have drawn attention to the exclusionary nature of such a restriction and argue that storytelling, emotion, and rhetoric be viewed as legitimate forms of communication within the context of deliberation (Young, 2000). Within the political science literature, theorists have debated the value of personal storytelling and reason-giving in the context of public deliberation (e.g., Gutmann and Thompson, 1996; Polletta and Lee, 2006; Young, 2000). Critics argue that traditionally marginalized groups, such as women, people with lower incomes, people with low educational attainment, and non-whites, may be at a disadvantage in presenting their views in deliberative settings because these groups are more likely to use, for example, storytelling over reasoned statements to advance their claims and preferences. As Hansen (2004: 119) has described 'deliberative democracy is not an equal process, as participants capable of arguing on rational, measurable and objective grounds are favoured through deliberative procedures'. Empirical examinations have investigated who tells stories, how stories are used, and how people respond to stories. Polletta and Lee (2006) examined the narrative claims made in an online deliberation designed to gather input into the design of Lower Manhattan after the September 11, 2001 terrorist attack. Although non-whites and those with low income and educational attainment were not less likely to use narrative claims, women were more likely to use narrative claims. However, an important caveat warrants mention. Regardless of group, those who saw themselves as advancing a minority viewpoint (e.g., experiences that they believed might not be shared by others) were more likely to make narrative claims compared to those who did not. Therefore, within this context, stories were seen as a legitimate means of communicating a claim. The authors also found that narrative claims were more likely than non-narrative claims to elicit a response from other participants. Indeed, when stories were told, they were more likely to elicit further narrative claims from other participants. When a narrative claim was made, participants would often respond with stories of their own that portrayed the connected nature of the stories, as well as advancing different points of view by telling corroborating stories with perhaps different implicit morals. Ultimately, the use of storytelling assisted the storytellers in identifying their own preferences, exposed values underlying positions, and also led to areas of agreement about particular issues. Such findings lend weight to Young's (2000) argument that forms of communication such as storytelling be supported in deliberative designs. The valuing of storytelling can create discursive space for individuals who may be disadvantaged by the emphasis placed on rational arguments.

Critical social psychologists, in particular, have important contributions to make to these debates. On the one hand, emancipatory claims for public deliberation should be subjected to careful scrutiny. On the other hand, deliberative ideals offer practical pathways for contributing to at least some of the social agendas of critical psychologists.

Phenomenological and Other Analyses of the Transformative Effects of Deliberation

An important claim for deliberation is that it is transformative for the participating individuals. Indeed, one of us (KO) has organized numerous public deliberations and invariably observed deliberants talking about how participating in the deliberation had changed their outlook on the issues they discussed and, more generally, how they related to others. Arguably, these are precisely the kind of phenomena that are of interest to psychologists.

One of the virtues of public deliberation is held to be that 'discussion produces better citizens: individuals who are more informed, active, responsible, open to arguments of others, cooperative, fair able to deal with problems, and ready to alter their opinions' (Pellizzoni, 2001: 66). In addition, proponents of deliberative democracy argue that participation in democratic institutions is likely to 'produce individuals with democratic dispositions. Such individuals would be more tolerant of difference, more sensitive to reciprocity, better able to engage in moral discourse and judgment, and more prone to examine their own preferences' (Warren, 1993: 209). And, of course, deliberation is held to be transformative in that participants gain greater knowledge of the relevant issues and perspectives, come to respect diverse perspectives, and eventually come to conclusions that are perceived as fair by all participants (Dembinksa and Montambeault, 2015).

Existing empirical research suggests that deliberation does indeed have transformative effects on the preferences of participants. For example, Niemeyer (2011) investigated the processes by which participant preferences changed during a citizen's jury convened in Australia to deliberate about what should be done with a controversial unsurfaced road. Participants were provided with five policy options and were asked to rank their preferences prior to, and immediately after, deliberation. Niemeyer showed that preferences changed from pre- to post-test and also investigated factors related to those changes. In particular, Niemeyer suggests that, prior to deliberation, participants' preferences were influenced largely by symbolic arguments strategically deployed by political forces. The deliberative process thus acted to open up participants' awareness to a wider range of concerns, which were taken into account in post-deliberation expressions of opinion. Similarly, a study on a consensus conference held on nanotechnologies in the United States suggests that, after deliberation, participants' ability to understand and engage with complex policy issues was increased (Cobb, 2011). Additionally, participants were more trusting of others after participation. Cobb argues that this is indicative of the capacity for deliberations to increase civic participation through building social capital. Finally, participants in this consensus conference became more knowledgeable about the issues and formed more informed preferences.

While these studies suggest that certain objective measures, such as knowledge, trust, and willingness to engage politically, may change as a result of participating in deliberation, they do not engage with the subjective experience of transformation that so many participants in public deliberations report anecdotally. Phenomenological and narrative analyses, and other qualitative approaches that focus on subjective experience, provide a novel opportunity for social psychological contributions to the empirical study of deliberation, and specifically the transformative effects and potential of deliberation.

CONCLUSION

In this chapter, we have argued that public deliberation should be taken up more broadly as a form of practice and a field of research for applied social psychologists. In making this argument, we have implied that, currently, there are not many social psychologists working in this field. However, many applied social psychologists advocate for participatory ideals in their research and are working with methodologies that support these ideals. In particular, community psychology, community based participatory research, and participatory action research, to name but a few, are all approaches that seek to involve people in knowledge generation and community decision making, rather than as objects of research to be studied. Many of these approaches are explored in other chapters of this Handbook, and some researchers have also connected broader participatory approaches to the notion of deliberation (e.g., Branney et al., 2017). However, public deliberation is quite distinct from other participatory approaches (Blacksher, 2013). In particular, in contrast to participatory research methodologies, public deliberation does not have its origins as a form of research, but rather as a political mechanism. Its original aims therefore have less to do with knowledge generation, and more with legitimacy of decisions made in the public sphere. However, as we have argued in this chapter, increased uptake of public deliberation by applied social psychologists is likely to lead to new theoretical and practical links being made and greater integration between epistemic and political programs.

Although the field of deliberative democracy is grounded in political philosophy and political science, the practice of public deliberation has benefitted from a wide range of disciplinary contributions. It would gain even further from the contributions of psychologists with expertise in a diverse set of methodologies and fields of research. More importantly, however, social psychologists could benefit from taking up public deliberation as their own form of practice. Public deliberation is a political mechanism that bridges the values and experiences of diverse publics with public policy. It is also a process that is transformational for the individuals who participate in it. Together, these characteristics make public deliberation an important tool for social psychological research and practice.

REFERENCES

Abelson, J., Forest, P. G., Eyles, J., Smith, P., Martin, E., & Gauvin, F.-P. (2003). Deliberations about deliberative methods: Issues in the design and evaluation of public participation processes. *Social Science & Medicine, 57*, 239–251.

Barnes, M. (2008). Passionate participation: Emotional experiences and expressions in deliberative forums. *Critical Social Policy, 28*(4), 461–481.

Black, L.W., Burkhalter, S., Gastil, J., & Stromer-Galley, J. (2009). Methods for analyzing and

measuring group deliberation. In L. Holbert (Ed.) *Sourcebook of political communication research: Methods, measures, and analytical techniques*, Routledge Communication Series. New York: Routledge, pp. 323–345.
Blacksher, E. (2013). Participatory and deliberative practices in health: Meanings, distinctions, and implications for health equity. *Journal of Public Deliberation*, *9*(1), Article 6.
Branney, P., Strickland, C., Darby, F., White, L., & Jain, S. (2017). Health psychology research using participative mixed qualitative methods and framework analysis: Exploring men's experiences of diagnosis and treatment for prostate cancer. In J. Brooks, & N. King (Eds.), *Applied qualitative research in psychology*. London: Palgrave, pp. 105–124.
Brewer, P. R., & Gross, K. (2005). Values, framing, and citizens' thoughts about policy issues: Effects on content and quality. *Political Psychology*, *26*(6), 929–948.
Burgess, M., O'Doherty, K., & Secko, D. (2008). Biobanking in British Columbia: Discussions of the future of personalized medicine through deliberative public engagement. *Personalized Medicine*, *5*(3), 285–296.
Button, M., & Ryfe, D. M. (2005). What can we learn from the practice of deliberative democracy? In J. Gastil, & P. Levine (Eds.), *The deliberative democracy handbook: Strategies for effective civic engagement in the 21st century*. San Francisco: Jossey-Bass Books, pp. 20–34.
Chambers, S. (2003). Deliberative democratic theory. *Annual Review of Political Science*, *6*, 307–326.
Chambers, S. (2009). Rhetoric and the public sphere: Has deliberative democracy abandoned mass democracy? *Political Theory*, *37*(3), 323–350.
Cobb, M. D. (2011). Creating informed public opinion: Citizen deliberation about nanotechnologies for human enhancements. *Journal of Nanopartical Research*, *13*(4), 1533–1548.
Cobb, M. D. (2012). Deliberative fears: Citizen deliberation about science in a national consensus conference. In K. C. O'Doherty, & E. Einsiedel (Eds.), *Public engagement and emerging technologies*. Vancouver, BC: UBC Press, pp. 115–132.
Cobb, M. D., & Gano, G. (2012). Evaluating structured deliberations about emerging technologies: Post-process participant evaluation. *International Journal of Emerging Technologies and Society*, *10*, 96–110.
Curato, N., & Boker, M. (2016). Linking minipublics to the deliberative system: a research agenda. *Policy Science*, *49*, 173–190.
Davies, B., & Harré, R. (1990). Positioning: The Discursive Production of Selves. *Journal for the Theory of Social Behaviour*, *20*(1), 43–63.
Davies, C., Wetherell, M., & Barnett, E. (2006). *Citizens at the centre: Deliberative participation in healthcare decisions*. Bristol: Policy Press.
Delli Carpini, M. X., Lomax Cook, F., & Jacobs, L. R. (2004). Public Deliberation, Discursive Participation, and Citizen Engagement: A Review of the Empirical Literature. *Annual Review of Political Science*, *7*, 315–344.
De Vries, R., Stanczyk, A., Wall, I. F., Uhlmann, R., Damschroder, L. J., & Kim, S. Y. (2010). Assessing the quality of democratic deliberation: a case study of public deliberation on the ethics of surrogate consent for research. *Social Science & Medicine*, *70*(12), 1896–1903.
De Vries, R., Stanczyk, A.E., Ryan, K.A., & Kim, S.Y.H (2011). A framework for assessing the quality of democratic deliberation: Enhancing deliberation as a tool for bioethics. *Journal of Empirical Research on Human Research Ethics*, 6(3), 19–30.
Dembinksa, M., & Montambeault, F. (2015). Deliberation for reconciliation in divided societies. *Journal of Public Deliberation*, *11*(1), Article 12.
Dorr Goold, S., Neblo, M. A., Kim, S. Y. H., de Vries, R., Rowe, G., & Muhlberger, P. (2012). What is good public deliberation? *Hastings Center Report*, *42*(2), 24–26.
Druckman, J. N. (2004). Political preference formation: Competition, deliberation, and the (ir)relevance of framing effects. *American Political Science Review*, *98*, 671–686.
Druckman, J. N., & Nelson, K. R. (2003). Framing and deliberation: How citizens' conversations limit elite influence. *American Journal of Political Science*, *47*(4), 729–745.
Dryzek, J. S. (2001). Legitimacy and economy in deliberative democracy. *Political Theory*, *29*(5), 651–669.
Dryzek, J., & Niemeyer, S. (2010). *Foundations and frontiers of deliberative governance*. New York: Oxford University Press.

Edwards, D., & Potter, J. 1992. *Discursive psychology*. London: Sage.
Finlayson, J. G. (2005). *Habermas: A very short introduction*. Oxford: Oxford University Press.
Fishkin, J. S., Luskin, R. C., & Jowell, R. (2000). Deliberative polling and public consultation. *Parliamentary Affairs*, *53*, 657–666.
Friedman, W. (2007). *Reframing 'framing'*. Public Agenda Occasional Paper Series, (1). Retrieved from https://www.publicagenda.org/files/Reframing%20Framing.pdf.
Fung, A. (2006). Varieties of participation in complex governance. *Public Administration Review*, 66–75.
Fung, A. (2008). Democratizing the policy process. In R. E. Goodin, M. Moran, & M. Rein (Eds.). *The Oxford handbook of public policy*. New York: Oxford University Press.
Gastil, J. (2008). *Political communication and deliberation*. Los Angeles: Sage.
Gastil, J., & Keith, W. M. (2005). A nation that (sometimes) likes to talk: A brief history of public deliberation in the United States. In J. Gastil, & P. Levine (Eds.), *The deliberative democracy handbook*. San Francisco, CA: John Wiley & Sons, Inc, pp. 3–19.
Gastil, J., & Levine, P. (Eds.) (2005). *The deliberative democracy handbook: Strategies for effective civic engagement in the twenty-first century*. San Francisco: Jossey-Bass.
Goodin, R. E. (2007). Enfranchising all affected interests, and its alternatives. *Philosophy and Public Affairs*, 35(1), 40–68
Goodin, R. E., & Dryzek, J. (2006). Deliberative impacts: The macro-political uptake of mini-publics. *Politics and Society*, *34*, 219–244.
Gutmann, A., & Thompson, D. (1996). *Democracy and disagreement*. Cambridge, MA: Harvard University Press.
Gutmann A., & Thompson, D. (1997). Deliberating about bioethics. *Hastings Center Report 27*(3): 38–41.
Gutmann, A., & Thompson, D. (2004). *Why deliberative democracy?* Princeton University Press.
Hansen, K. (2004). *Deliberative democracy and opinion formation*. University Press of Southern Denmark. Retrieved from http://www.kaspermhansen.eu/Work/Hansen2004.pdf
Hawkins, A. K., & O'Doherty, K. C. (2010). Biobank governance: a lesson in trust. *New Genetics and Society*, *29*(3), 311–327.
Hodgetts, K., Elshaug, A. G., & Hiller, J. E. (2012). What counts and how to count it: Physicians' constructions of evidence in a disinvestment context. *Social Science and Medicine*, *75*, 2191–2199.
Hodgetts, K., Hiller, J. E., Street, J. M. Carter, D., Braunack-Mayer, A. J., ... & the ASTUTE Health study group (2014). Disinvestment policy and the public funding of assisted reproductive technologies: Outcomes of deliberative engagements with three key stakeholder groups. *BMC Health Services Research*, *14*, 204–216.
Kahane, D., Weinstock, D., Leydet, D., & Williams, M. (2010). *Deliberative Democracy in Practice*. Vancouver: UBC Press.
Karpowitz, C. F., & Mendelberg, T. (2007). Groups and deliberation. *Swiss Political Science Review*, *13*(4), 645–662.
Kraft, P. W., Lodge, M., & Taber, C. S. (2015). Why people 'don't trust the evidence': Motivated reasoning and scientific beliefs. *The ANNALS of the American Academy of Political and Social Science*, *658*(1), 121–133.
Kuhar, M. (2013). Exploring psychological factors influencing deliberation. *Interdisciplinary Description of Complex Systems*, *11*(4), 415–426.
Longstaff, H., & Burgess, M. M. (2010). Recruiting for representation in public deliberation on the ethics of biobanks. *Public Understanding of Science*, *19*, 212–224.
Luskin, R. C., O'Flynn, I. Fishkin, J. S., & Russell, D. (2014). Deliberating across deep divides. *Political Studies*, *62*, 116–135.
MacKenzie, M. K., & O'Doherty, K. (2011). Deliberating future issues: Minipublics and salmon genomics. *Journal of Public Deliberation*, *7*(1): Article 5.
MacLean, S., & Burgess, M. M. (2010). In the public interest: Assessing expert and stakeholder influence in public deliberation about biobanks. *Public Understanding of Science*, *19*(4), 486–496.
Mannarini, T. (2011). Public involvement and competent communities: Towards a social psychology of public participation. *International Journal of Humanities and Social Science*, *1*(7), 66–72.
Mansbridge, J., Bohman, J., Chambers, S., Christiano, T., Fung, A., Parkinson, J.,

Thompason, D. F., & Warren, M. E. (2012). A systemic approach to deliberative democracy. In J. Parkinson, & J. Mansbridge (Eds.), *Deliberative systems*. Cambridge, UK: Cambridge University Press.
Mendelberg, T. (2002). The deliberative citizen: theory and evidence. In L. Delli Carpini, R. Huddy, & R. Shapiro (Eds.), *Research in micropolitics: Political decisionmaking, deliberation and participation* (pp. 151–193). Greenwich, CT: JAI Press.
Mercier, H., & Landemore, H. (2012). Reasoning is for arguing: Understanding the successes and failures of deliberation. *Political Psychology*, *33*(2), 243–258.
Montpetit, É., & Lachapelle, E. (2017). Policy learning, motivated scepticism, and the politics of shale gas development in British Columbia and Quebec. *Policy and Society*, 1–20.
Moore, A., & O'Doherty, K. (2014). Deliberative voting: Clarifying consent in a consensus process. *The Journal of Political Philosophy*, *22*(3), 302–319.
Morrell, M. (2014). Participant bias and success in deliberative mini-publics. In K. Gronlund, A. Bachtiger, & M. Setälä (Eds.), *Deliberative mini-publics: Involving citizens in the democratic process*. Colchester, UK: ECPR Press.
Nep, S., & O'Doherty, K. (2013). Understanding public calls for labeling of GM foods: Analysis of a public deliberation on GM salmon. *Society & Natural Resources*, *26*(5), 506–521.
Niemeyer, S. (2011). The emancipatory effect of deliberation: Empirical lessons from mini-publics. *Politics and Society*, *39*(1), 103–140.
Niemeyer, S. (2014). Scaling up deliberation to mass publics: harnessing mini-publics in a deliberative system. In K. Grönlund, A. Bächtiger, & M. Setälä (Eds.), *Deliberative mini-publics: Involving citizens in the democratic process* (pp. 177–202), Colchester: ECPR Press.
O'Doherty, K. C. (2012). Theorizing deliberative discourse. In K. C. O'Doherty, & E. F. Einsiedel (Eds.), *Publics and emerging technologies*. Vancouver: UBC Press, pp. 133–147.
O'Doherty, K. C. (2013). Synthesising the outputs of deliberation: Extracting meaningful results from a public forum. *Journal of Public Deliberation*, *9*(1), Article 8.
O'Doherty, K. C. (2017). Deliberative public opinion: Development of a social construct. *History of the Human Sciences*, *30*(4), 124–145.
O'Doherty, K., & Burgess, M. M. (2009). Engaging the public on biobanks: Outcomes of the BC Biobank Deliberation. *Public Health Genomics*, *12*(4), 203–215.
O'Doherty, K. C., & Burgess, M. M. (2013). Public deliberation to develop ethical norms and inform policy for biobanks: Lessons learnt and challenges remaining. *Research Ethics*, *9*(2), 55–77.
O'Doherty, K. C., & Davidson, H. J. (2010). Subject positioning and deliberative democracy: Understanding social processes underlying deliberation. *Journal for the Theory of Social Behaviour*, *40*(2), 224–245.
O'Doherty, K., & Hawkins, A. (2010). Structuring public engagement for effective input in policy development on human tissue biobanking. *Public Health Genomics*, *13*(4), 197–206.
O'Doherty, K. C., Burgess, M. M., & Secko, D. M. (2010). Sequencing the salmon genome: A deliberative public engagement. *Genomics, Society and Policy*, *6*(1), 16–33.
O'Doherty, K. C., Gauvin, F.-P., Grogan, C., & Friedman, W. (2012a). Implementing a public deliberative forum. *Hastings Center Report*, *42*(2), 20–23.
O'Doherty, K. C., Hawkins, A. K., & Burgess, M. M. (2012b). Involving citizens in the ethics of biobank research: Informing institutional policy through structured public deliberation. *Social Science and Medicine*, *75*, 1604–1611.
O'Doherty, K. C., MacKenzie, M. K., Badulescu, D., & Burgess, M. M. (2013). Explosives, genomics, and the environment: Conducting public deliberation on topics of complex science and social controversy. *Sage Open*, *3*, 1–17.
Pellizzoni, L. (2001). The myth of the best argument: Power, deliberation and reason. *British Journal of Sociology*, *52*(1), 59–86.
Petersen, A. (2007). Biobanks' 'engagements': Engendering trust or engineering consent? *Genomics, Society and Policy*, *3*(1), 31–43.

Polletta, F., & Lee, J. (2006). Is telling stories good for democracy? Rhetoric in public deliberation after 9/11. *American Sociological Review, 71*, 699–723.

Richards, R. C., & Gastil, J. (2016). Deliberation. In G. Mazzoleni (Ed.), *International encyclopedia of political communication*. Chichester, UK: John Wiley & Sons, pp. 1–13.

Ryfe, D. M. (2005). Does deliberative democracy work? *Annual Review of Political Science, 8*, 49–71.

Setälä, M., & Herne, K. (2014). Normative theory and experimental research in the study of deliberative mini-publics. In K. Gronlund, A. Bachtiger, & M. Setälä (Eds.), *Deliberative mini-publics: Involving citizens in the democratic process*. Colchester, UK: ECPR Press, pp. 57–75.

Steenbergen, M. R., Bächtiger, A., Spörndli, M., & Steiner, J. (2003). Measuring political deliberation: a discourse quality index. *Comparative European Politics, 1*(1), 21–48.

Sunstein, C. R. (2002). The law of group polarization. *The Journal of Political Philosophy, 10*(2), 175–195.

Sunstein, C. R. (2005). *Laws of fear: Beyond the precautionary principle*. Cambridge, UK: Cambridge University Press.

Sunstein, C. R., & Hastie, R. (2008). *Four failures of deliberating groups*. University of Chicago Law & Economics, Public Law & Legal Theory Working Papers No. 215. Retrieved from http://nrs.harvard.edu/urn-3:HUL.InstRepos:12809435

Tversky, A., & Kahneman, D. (1981). The framing of decisions and the psychology of choice. *Science*, 211, 453–458.

Tversky, A., & Kahneman, D. (1987). Rational choice and the framing of decisions. In R. M. Hogarth, & M. W. Reder (Eds.), *Rational choice*. Chicago: University of Chicago Press, pp. 67–94.

Walmsley, H. L. (2009). Mad scientists bend the frame of biobank governance in British Columbia. *Journal of Public Deliberation, 5*(1), Article 6.

Walmsley, H. L. (2010). Biobanking, public consultation, and the discursive logics of deliberation: Five lessons from British Columbia. *Public Understanding of Science, 19*(4), 452–468.

Walmsley, H. L. (2011). Stock options, tax credits or employment contracts please! The value of deliberative public disagreement about human tissue donation. *Social Science & Medicine 73*, 209–216.

Warren, M. E. (1993). Can participatory democracy produce better selves? Psychological dimensions of Habermas's Discursive Model of Democracy. *Political Psychology, 14*(2), 209–234.

Warren, M. E. (1996). Deliberative democracy and authority. *American Political Science Review, 90*, 46–60.

Warren, M. E. (2009). Governance driven democratization. *Critical Political Studies, 3*(1), 3–13.

Warren, M. E., & Pearse, H. (2008). Introduction: Democratic renewal and deliberative democracy. In M. E. Warren, & H. Pearse (Eds.), *Designing deliberative democracy: The British Columbia citizen's assembly*. New York: Cambridge University Press, pp. 1–19.

Weinstein, D., & Kahane, D. (2010). Introduction. In D. Kahane, D. Weinstock, D. Leydet, & M. Williams (Eds.), *Deliberative democracy in practice*. Vancouver, BC: UBC Press, pp. 1–18.

Young, I. (2000). *Inclusion and democracy*. New York: Oxford University Press.

PART VIII

Education

22

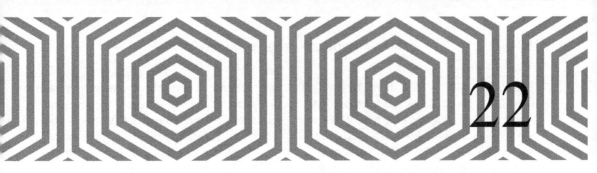

Applying Social Psychology to Education

Louise R. Alexitch

Social psychology has contributed significantly to the field of education, often by providing understanding about the challenges faced by schools, educators, students, and their parents. What factors help minority students to achieve? What reward structures will maximize students' love of learning? How can schools effectively integrate students from a variety of backgrounds? The approach taken by social psychologists has been to examine students' feelings, perceptions, and beliefs about school and their academic abilities, and to explore how these factors might intercept with the learning environment (Wilson & Buttrick, 2016). Attending school, after all, is very much an interpersonal process, and it is how the individual (in this case, the student) is both affected by, and in turn affects, the social environment (i.e., classroom structure, norms and expectations, reward contingencies) that is of particular interest to social psychologists. For example, a student's motivation to do well in a mathematics class will be shaped not only by her interest in math, but also by her parents' and teachers' expectations for her (and the importance that she places on these), societal norms regarding girls and mathematics, and perceptions about what is valued or considered successful in a classroom environment.

The current chapter looks at some important theories and research that may help to address some of the pressing issues mentioned above. While it is not a comprehensive review, the chapter will focus on four areas – motivation, academic self-concept, teacher expectations, and social comparison – that have made significant contributions to our understanding of how individuals succeed (and sometimes fail) within an academic context.

MOTIVATION, SELF-DETERMINATION, AND ACHIEVEMENT GOALS

Motivation in an academic context has generated a great deal of attention over the years from researchers, educators, students, and parents. Do students learn more effectively if they focus on academic performance? Are students better off in the long term if they are intrinsically motivated to learn? The following section will cover two theories of motivation that have dominated social psychology in the last 25 years: (1) Achievement Goal Theory and (2) Self-Determination Theory. Both theories outline how an individual's goals, perceived abilities, and performance can be significantly affected by the reward contingencies present in a classroom, as well as the structure of academic tasks. While Achievement Goal Theory conceptualizes motivation using discrete categories and orthogonal dimensions, Self-Determination Theory approaches motivation as occurring on a continuum from intrinsic to extrinsic. Both theories, however, advocate creating a social environment for students which emphasizes in-depth learning of subjects and deemphasizes performance indicators such as grades.

Achievement Goal Theory

Achievement Goal Theory (AGT) focuses on the nature of two goals: ***mastery goals*** (which emphasize the development of skills, competence, and understanding) and ***performance goals*** (which emphasize the demonstration of competence through grades, outperforming peers, and seeking approval of others) (Dweck, 1986; Elliot, 1999; Elliot & McGregor, 2001; Senko, Hulleman, & Harackiewicz, 2011). Mastery goals are associated with the idea that ability is changeable, that an individual can self-regulate learning, and is synonymous with a positive approach to learning. In contrast, performance goals are associated with the idea that ability is fixed and that the individual needs to demonstrate competence by outperforming others and being competitive rather than developing competence (Senko & Tropiano, 2016). Adopting mastery goals has been linked with a positive academic self-concept, greater sense of self-efficacy, more cooperative learning, greater persistence in academic tasks, and greater enjoyment of school and learning (Dweck, 1986; Harackiewicz, Barron, Tauer, & Elliot, 2002; Senko et al., 2011). Performance goals, on the other hand, have been linked with more negative outcomes, such as higher levels of anxiety and maladaptive academic behaviors such as self-handicapping (Dweck, 1986; Elliot, 1999; Elliot & McGregor, 2001).

Any parent, teacher, or educator looking at these findings would want to encourage students to take a mastery approach to school work rather than a performance approach. But when academic performance is examined in relation to mastery and performance goals, mastery goals do not necessarily produce better outcomes than performance goals. In fact, a number of studies (e.g., Harackiewicz et al., 2002; Senko et al., 2011) have found mastery goals to be only weakly related (or unrelated) to grades. To further complicate matters, performance goals do not always lead to negative outcomes and may predict higher academic performance than mastery goals (Midgley, Kaplan, & Middleton, 2001). In an effort to account for the inconsistent results obtained with performance goals, an additional dimension was incorporated into the mastery and performance goal dichotomy: ***approach-avoidance*** (Elliot, 1999; Elliot & Church, 1997). The resulting model now included four distinct achievement goals: mastery-approach, mastery-avoidance, performance-approach, and performance-avoidance. Each of these four achievement goal orientations has distinct antecedents and consequences. For example, students who adopt ***mastery-approach goals*** are driven by the need to achieve, self-determination, and wanting to master a task, resulting in greater understanding and more learning enjoyment. Those who adopt ***mastery-avoidance goals*** strive to avoid losing previously acquired skills and knowledge, resulting in higher levels of anxiety, disorganized study habits, and low self-determination. The latter is often displayed by perfectionists who are afraid of making mistakes or by aging adults who fear diminishing abilities and skills (Elliot, 1999; Elliot & McGregor, 2001). Although both types of mastery goals still reflect a genuine interest, mastery-avoidance goals have antecedents and consequences that are similar to those of performance-avoidance goals (Elliot, 1999; Elliot & Church, 1997).

Performance-approach and performance-avoidance goals have garnered the most research attention given their mixed effects on academic outcomes (Elliot, 1999; Elliot & McGregor, 2001; Senko et al., 2011). ***Performance-approach goals***, striving to outperform others and to appear talented, are associated with positive factors (e.g., better grades, need for achievement) and ***performance-avoidance goals***, striving to avoid doing worse than others or being seen as a failure, are associated with negative factors (e.g., poor academic performance, high test anxiety). Indeed, performance-approach goals are correlated with a positive academic self-concept, greater effort, and better performance than the three other goal orientations. But should we encourage students to adopt performance-approach goals rather than mastery-goals to improve their grades? Not necessarily. Unlike performance goals, mastery goals still lead to deeper processing of material, more love of learning, more use of adaptive strategies (e.g., seeking help, cooperative learning), and more persistence in the face of challenges (Senko et al., 2011; Senko & Tropiano, 2016). Harackiewicz et al. (2002) examined the interplay of incoming academic indicators (e.g., SAT scores), mastery and performance achievement goals, college grades, and interest in classes in predicting students' long-term success in college. Results showed that students' achievement goals in introductory courses were significant predictors of their future academic success. Specifically, students who adopted performance-approach goals generally attained higher grades in classes, and while mastery goals were not connected with grades, students who adopted mastery goals were more likely to enjoy lectures, showed continued interest in their course work, and were more likely to enroll in additional courses in their major.

The results of the Harackiewicz et al. (2002) study, and the recent work of others (e.g., Senko et al., 2011; Senko & Tropiano, 2016), suggest that, for students to have optimal motivation and academic achievement, they should adopt *both* mastery and performance goals, or rather, adopt goals that are most suitable to meet the demands of the educational situation. This has come to be known as the ***multiple goals perspective*** (Harackiewicz et al., 2002; Midgley et al., 2001; Senko et al., 2011). Students who have the ability and skills to shift between mastery and performance goals are at a greater advantage than those who stick to one orientation only. For example, a student can have a mastery-approach goal when learning material from a textbook but have a performance-approach goal when studying for a multiple-choice exam. Furthermore, a multiple goals orientation also implies that students can exercise more control over their learning, allowing for greater self-determination and self-regulation of learning (Harackiewicz et al., 2002; Senko et al., 2011). Although it is not yet clear whether encouraging students to take a multiple goals approach at the elementary or high school level is effective, there is mounting evidence that it is an adaptive approach at the post-secondary level (Harackiewicz et al., 2002).

Implications and Applications

Given that the social context can affect the type of goal orientations that students espouse, then messages conveyed in the learning environment, whether through classroom reward structures, peer or parental influences, or teachers' biases, would make some goals more salient to students over others (Maehr & Zusho, 2009; Urdan & Schoenfelder, 2006). Mastery goal orientation can be encouraged in students if they are assigned moderately challenging and meaningful academic work, if they are evaluated in a way that focuses on students' improvement, and if they are given choices about what tasks to work on (Maehr & Zusho, 2009; Urdan & Schoenfelder, 2006). In contrast, teachers might communicate to students that it is important to have grades that place you at the top of your class, thereby creating an atmosphere wherein outperforming one's peers (e.g., performance goals) is more important than learning and understanding course content (i.e., mastery goals) (Maehr & Zusho, 2009; Urdan & Schoenfelder, 2006). Teachers who use controlling behaviors, such as imposing strict deadlines for work, making numerous controlling statements about what students must know, or using a system of rewards and threats as a way to get students to work, will produce students who may adopt performance-avoidance goals. The result will be students who are overly concerned with avoiding negative evaluative reactions from teachers or peers rather than trying to do their best work (Midgley et al., 2001; Urdan & Schoenfelder, 2006).

Erturan-İlker (2014) investigated the differential effects of positive and negative feedback on students' achievement goals and the perceived motivational climate in a ninth-grade physical education class. Over the course of a six week period, students were required to learn volleyball skills through practices, drills, and exercises. Feedback was provided by the teacher to each student individually and focused on students' performance, ability, and effort, with half of the participants receiving positive feedback (e.g., 'You performed very well') and the other half of the participants receiving negative feedback (e.g., 'Your effort was poor'). Results showed that students in the positive feedback group showed a significant increase in their mastery- and performance-approach goals and a decrease in their performance-avoidance goals. Performance-avoidance goals, however, increased in the negative feedback group, with students in this group being more concerned about being worse (instead of better) than other students in learning volleyball skills. In addition, students in the positive feedback group perceived the classroom climate to be more mastery-oriented, whereas students in the negative feedback group perceived the classroom climate to be more oriented toward performance rather than learning.

Self-Determination Theory

Self-Determination Theory (SDT) distinguishes between behaviors that are performed of one's own volition and choice (***autonomous***) and behaviors which one feels pressured or directed to carry out (***controlled***) (Deci & Ryan, 1985; 2008). According to Deci and Ryan (2008), optimal conditions for individuals are those which meet the basic human needs of competence, relatedness, and autonomy, and these needs are more likely to be met by adopting intrinsic motivated goals. In SDT, five categories of motivation are placed along a continuum from the most autonomous (***intrinsic***) to the most controlled (***external regulation***). When individuals are intrinsically motivated in a particular context, they are engaging in activities that interest them, provide them with pleasure, and reflect the desire to learn, explore, and be challenged. At the other end of the continuum is external regulation, where individuals engage in activities to achieve some outcome that is externally dictated (e.g., seeking rewards, approval of others, avoiding negative outcomes) and where behavior is not considered to be self-determined. Between these two extremes are three additional types of motivation that vary in the degree to which the individual has internalized outside pressures or contingencies: (1) ***integrated regulation*** (external contingencies and cultural values have been incorporated into the self), (2) ***identified regulation*** (the activity is valuable only as it achieves some other internalized goal), and (3) ***introjected regulation*** (the activity is partially internalized and used to boost one's self-worth by seeking the approval of others) (Deci & Ryan, 1985; 2008).

In general, autonomous motivation (i.e., intrinsic, integrated, or identified) tends to yield better psychological health, positive well-being, and more effective performance on tasks than does controlled motivation (i.e., introjected, extrinsic) (Deci & Ryan, 2008). Indeed, pursuing goals with a focus on extrinsic elements is associated with poorer mental health, excessive social comparisons, greater anxiety and narcissism than pursuing goals with an intrinsic emphasis (Vansteenkiste, Simons, Lens, Sheldon, & Deci, 2004). When looking at the education field, it is generally considered that intrinsic, integrated, or identified regulation will have positive consequences for academic development, and external or introjected regulation will have negative consequences on academic development (Deci & Ryan, 2002; 2008; Guay, Ratelle, & Chanal, 2008). For example, as many Psychology students know, it is important to take a statistics course and get good grades in it, not because statistics is interesting (although some may come to love it) but because they recognize that it is vital to conducting research and in helping them achieve their career or academic goals. This is an example of identified regulation. In contrast, students may demonstrate introjected regulation in a school environment where there is a great deal of competition among students for grades. As we saw with AGT, the emphasis on performance has been found to lead to feelings of anxiety and pressure which can actually undermine intrinsic motivation to learn (Deci & Ryan, 2002).

In their review of SDT as applied to the education field, Guay et al. (2008) noted that students who are autonomously motivated toward academic work (i.e., intrinsic, integrated, or identified) have better in-depth learning, demonstrate a preference for challenging tasks, exhibit greater creativity, and show more satisfaction and enjoyment of school when compared to students who take a more extrinsic approach toward academic work. More autonomous motivation is associated with both short- and long-term academic achievement in general. Interestingly, while extrinsic motivation is still seen as undesirable, findings around introjected regulation and its consequences for students have been somewhat mixed (very similar to AGT and performance goals). For example, Vallerand, Fortier, and Guay (1997) noted that, while students who had dropped out of high school were more likely to have lower intrinsic motivation and lower identified regulation, students who persisted had higher levels of introjected regulation than those who had dropped out. Upon closer examination, however, while some positive behavioral outcomes may emerge from externally-regulated motivation (higher grades, more persistence in school), cognitive and affective outcomes are not positive when students are externally regulated (Deci & Ryan, 2002; 2008; Guay et al., 2008). For example, introjected regulation is associated with greater levels of school-related anxiety, possibly resulting from teacher and parental pressures to perform well, and may hinder the development of good interpersonal relations between students, their teachers, and their peers (recall the basic need of relatedness) (Deci & Ryan, 2008).

External regulation may also interfere with conceptual learning and in-depth processing of information (Guay et al., 2008; Vansteenkiste et al., 2004). In a field experiment with 200 Belgian college students studying to become teachers, Vansteenkiste et al. (2004) tested the SDT assumption that creating a classroom environment oriented toward intrinsic motivation yields better learning. Each teacher-in-training was in charge of a classroom in which they had to teach their students about recycling. In each classroom, students were divided into four groups, and teachers provided each group with a reading about recycling, as part of requiring students to learn about recycling. Students were given one of two goal conditions: (1) *intrinsic goal condition* (emphasis on helping the environment and the community) and (2) *extrinsic goal condition* (recycling helps save money by reusing materials). Half of the students in each goal condition received the reading worded in an *autonomy-supportive manner* (i.e., 'you can', 'if you choose') or in a *controlling manner* (i.e., 'you must', 'you have to'). Students were later measured on their motivation for reading the material, the level to which they had engaged in the topic (e.g., had done extra reading on reserve at library), and conceptual understanding of the material. Results showed that the intrinsic goal condition produced more positive learning outcomes, such as better in-depth processing of the material, test performance, and task persistence. Furthermore, findings showed that intrinsic goals were even more likely to be adopted when teachers framed them in an autonomy supportive manner. That is, the students were more likely to become fully engaged with the task and see its intrinsic value when they felt free to decide for themselves how to learn the material.

Implications and Applications

The Vansteenkiste et al. (2004) study and the work of others (e.g., Deci, 2009; Reeve, 2004) emphasize the importance of setting up classroom environments which can meet the basic needs of autonomy, competence, and relatedness as outlined by SDT. More specifically, Reeve (2004) argues that teachers need to provide an atmosphere for students which is ***autonomy supportive*** rather than controlling. Autonomy supportive teachers engage in more active listening, grant students time to engage in independent work, encourage students to ask questions, and are more empathic and responsive to students' needs (Deci & Ryan, 2002; Niemec & Ryan, 2009; Reeve, 2004). In terms of individual development, students who are exposed to an autonomy supportive school environment show higher levels of perceived competence, more self-determination, greater preference for challenge, and more creativity. Autonomy supportive classrooms also lead to more positive academic outcomes, such as better conceptual understanding of material and better overall comprehension (Deci & Ryan, 2002). Furthermore, Niemec and Ryan (2009) noted that an autonomy supportive environment helps a student meet his/her need for relatedness because it is easier for students to develop connections to peers, teachers, and others in a positive social climate. Because students want to maintain these good relationships, they may internalize the practices and values of those around them and, consequently, are likely to develop identified or integrated regulation with respect to school.

What about classroom environments that are controlling? In a controlling classroom, teachers tend to issue more directives to students, provide more criticism and negative feedback, impose more deadlines, and emphasize evaluation and grades (Deci & Ryan, 2002; Niemec & Ryan, 2009; Reeve, 2004). In this type of setting, the focus is on pleasing the teacher and meeting external demands rather than on personal development. Students may be better at memorization, may earn higher grades, and may do exactly what a teacher (as well as parents and the school system) expect, but they will also show less creativity, less flexibility in thinking, more surface learning of material, and poorer problem-solving (Deci & Ryan, 2002). So why use this teaching approach? Some researchers (e.g., Deci, 2009; Niemiec & Ryan, 2009; Reeve, 2004) have argued that the controlling environment used by teachers is often a function of external pressures put on teachers (such as the need to have high performing students) and is based on the perception from students, parents, and school systems that controlling teachers are somehow more 'competent'.

Deci (2009) advises that changing the school environment to one that emphasizes autonomy, competence, and need for belonging must be done at both the teacher and student levels. All parties involved in educating children need to be given the freedom to choose strategies for learning, so that all develop a sense of competence and effectiveness in their roles. This systemic approach is well represented by the ***First Things First (FTF)*** program in the United States. The FTF program is aimed at helping disadvantaged students to succeed and contains policies, curricula, and activities designed to satisfy the basic psychological needs for competence, autonomy, and relatedness in relation to schoolwork. There are three components to FTF: (1) small learning communities, (2) a family and student advocate system, and (3) autonomy-supportive instructional strategies. In the first component, students spend a majority of time with the same group of students and teachers across school years. The goal is to develop a sense of belonging among teachers, among students, as well as between teachers and their students. By getting to know their students over years, teachers are better able to help the student's autonomy development, and teachers are given power to make decisions regarding their students giving the teachers a sense of meaningfulness in their work. In the second component, teachers from the same learning community not only meet together to discuss a student's progress in school, but one teacher (advocate) also works as a liaison with families of students in their learning community. The goal here is to encourage families to be more involved in their child's education and to promote good relationships between teachers and parents. Finally, teachers also undergo extensive professional development that is tailored to address the needs of their learning community. Teachers plan and implement activities which are engaging and relevant to students' lives. Classroom activities not only meet the standards of the school district but are tailored for individual students so that students will have a greater likelihood of feeling competent. According to Deci (2009), when the FTF program is implemented correctly, it not only meets the needs of competence, autonomy, and relatedness but also improves educational outcomes for students.

ACADEMIC SELF-CONCEPT: PERCEIVING THE SELF IN AN ACADEMIC SETTING

A person's self-concept, developed through experiences and social interactions in one's environment, guides the way in which one behaves in a particular environment, and that behavior, in turn, further shapes one's identity (Marsh, 2016). Of interest in social psychology is how self-concept develops in a student as he/she is socialized within the educational setting and how self-concept can be significantly affected (either positively or negatively) by the cultural, racial, or gender expectations that others hold for a student. When we focus on the education setting, we refer to a specific dimension of the self-concept called ***academic self-concept.*** Academic self-concept is defined as a student's mental representation, perception, and self-evaluation of his/her academic abilities (Guay, Marsh, & Boivin, 2003; Marsh, 2016; Niepel, Brunner, & Preckel, 2014; Rodriguez, 2009; Seaton, Parker, Marsh, Craven, & Yeung, 2014). It includes how one perceives his/her abilities in either the general academic domain (e.g., 'I am a good student'; 'I am good at taking tests') or in specific academic areas (e.g., 'I am good at math but not good at history') (Marsh, 2016; Niepel et al., 2014; Pinxten, Wouters, Preckel, Niepel, De Fraine, & Verschureren, 2015). A positive academic self-concept has been associated with increased self-efficacy, better academic performance, greater commitment to school, and higher academic aspirations (Niepel et al., 2014; Pinxten et al., 2015; Salchegger, 2016).

One particular area of interest has been the nature of the relationship between academic self-concept and achievement (whether it is defined as grades, goals, or persistence in school). Recent studies (e.g., Guay et al., 2003; Marsh, Trautwein, Lüdtke, Köller, & Baumert, 2005; Seaton et al., 2014) have noted that the relation between academic self-concept and achievement is very likely to be a reciprocal one: that is, prior academic achievement affects academic self-concept, and prior academic self-concept affects subsequent academic achievement. Academic self-concept is believed to have motivational properties driving achievement (self-enhancement), and being successful or achieving one's goals may also result in a more positive academic self-concept (skill development) (Marsh et al., 2005). In a longitudinal study, Guay et al. (2003) examined the causal ordering of academic self-concept and achievement using Canadian elementary school children. At the end of each academic year, children provided information about their self-concepts across different subjects and teachers rated children's achievement in writing, reading, and mathematics. The results supported the reciprocal relationship between academic achievement and self-concept: as children grew older, their academic self-concept became more stable and more strongly correlated with academic achievement. Furthermore, they found that both self-enhancement (particularly in the younger children) and skill development operated across the age cohorts. Similarly, in tracking over 5,000 middle school students in Germany, Marsh et al. (2005) found evidence that prior academic self-concept predicts subsequent academic achievement beyond that explained by prior grades, standardized test scores, or interest in school.

The development of academic self-concept may also be tied to students' mastery and performance goals. For example, college students who have a positive academic self-concept are more likely to use elaborative cognitive learning strategies, see a college education as an important part of their identity, reflect on what they are learning, and are overall more likely to be intrinsically motivated to participate in higher education (Rodriguez, 2009). The relationship of mastery goals to academic self-concept, however, is mixed, with some researchers finding only a small (and inconsistent) relationship with self-concept, whereas performance approach goals seem to operate as a key link between academic self-concept and achievement (Niepel et al., 2014; Seaton et al., 2014). Specifically, performance-approach goals are related to positive changes in academic self-concept while performance-avoidance goals are related to negative changes in academic self-concept (Niepel et al., 2014). In a longitudinal study with high school students in Australia, Seaton et al. (2014) found performance approach goals were more strongly related to math achievement than were mastery goals. Having a positive self-concept, however, was associated with increases in both mastery and performance goal orientations, and having strong mastery and performance goals *initially* was associated with later development of a more positive self-concept.

What is it about performance goals that make them so critical to a student's self-concept? Recall that, in the previous section of the chapter, performance goals are often a reflection of how students see themselves (their abilities and performance) in relation to others in a specific context. Performance-approach goals involve striving to be better than others and wanting to be evaluated positively by teachers, whereas performance-avoidance goals involve fear of appearing worse than others (Senko et al., 2011). In both cases, performance goals necessitate making social comparisons with others in the classroom whereas mastery goals involve making more internal comparisons rather than social comparisons (Pinxten et al., 2015). This implies that the development of academic self-concept is significantly affected by the social environment (Niepel et al., 2014; Pinxten et al., 2015).

Development of Academic Self-Concept

Teacher and parental expectations, comparisons with one's classmates, and beliefs about one's abilities, all contribute to an individual's academic self-concept. The findings of Guay et al. (2003) and others (e.g., Marsh et al., 2005; Seaton et al., 2014) indicate that academic self-concept can change and that these changes are dependent upon the social environment. The academic self-concepts of young children start off very positive, and as they age, academic self-concept declines until it levels off in adolescence, and then it increases again in early adulthood (Guay et al., 2003; Marsh et al., 2005; Niepel et al., 2014). The decline in academic self-concept is not necessarily a bad thing. Young children have limited knowledge about their abilities and are only starting to learn about school, classmates, and teachers. These external entities provide the child with information about their relative academic strengths and weaknesses, leading to not only a decline in a very positive (and possibly unrealistic) academic self-concept but to a greater complexity (Guay et al., 2003; Marsh et al., 2005; Pinxten et al., 2015). Children come to learn which subjects they enjoy, how their performance compares to that of similar others, and which topics are more challenging for them. Pinxten et al. (2015) found that, even at a young age, children are able to differentiate their abilities across different domains and are able to engage in comparisons with their classmates.

Students will eventually internalize the expectations, values, and standards imposed by others, such that each student may evaluate his or her abilities, develop goals, and value specific academic domains that reflect those of their culture and society (Guay et al., 2003). Researchers from Western cultures such as North America, Europe, and Australia (e.g., Belfi, Goos, De Fraine, & Van Damme, 2012; Marsh et al., 2005) have noted, for example, that there are gender differences in academic self-concepts for specific areas of study and that these differences are consistent with gender stereotypes held in those cultures. For example, girls often have a more negative self-concept in mathematics and science when compared to boys, whereas boys have a more negative self-concept in language when compared to girls (Belfi et al., 2012). This is especially worrisome given that academic self-concept is significant predictor of academic achievement over the long term. If girls do not incorporate the idea of 'liking mathematics' or 'being good at science' into their academic self-concepts, it is unlikely that they will consider pursuing further education in these areas.

A similar pattern of results has been found when looking at racial differences in academic self-concepts and achievement. Cokley and his colleagues (Cokley & Moore, 2007; Cokley, McClain, Jones, & Johnson, 2011) have noted that a poorer academic self-concept may be one explanation for why African American students (especially males) show lower levels of achievement when compared to White American students. Just like most children, African American students start off enjoying school and are motivated to do well. Repeated negative experiences in school (e.g., teachers' low expectations, lack of culturally relevant materials, stereotypes about abilities of minorities), however, lead African American students to see themselves as incapable of academic success. As a result, many African American students may be even *disidentify* with school (Cokley & Moore, 2007), causing them to be less motivated to succeed, to devalue education, and to look for fulfillment elsewhere. At times, their academic self-concept may shift to domains that are deemed to be appropriate for their group (e.g., sports).

Disengagement from school is especially problematic for African American males than for their female counterparts. Cokley et al. (2011) examined academic disidentification, self-concept, and performance in a group of African American high school students. Findings showed that academic disidentification was present among male students but not female students. As students were followed over time, the correlation between academic self-concept and grades decreased in magnitude between younger and older students for males but not for females. Female students not only outperformed male students in terms of grades, but their academic self-concepts were more closely tied to academic achievement in a reciprocal manner: the better the girls performed in school, the more positive their academic self-concepts became, and the more academic success they experienced. In explaining these and similar findings, Cokley and his colleagues have observed that African American males experience an overall negative school environment (e.g., more likely to be punished, encounter negative views from teachers). African American females, in contrast, elicit more positive reactions from others so that, for them, school becomes more motivating than punitive.

Application: Improving Academic Self-Concept

The research on academic self-concept suggests that if we want to improve students' learning, motivation, and success, we need to focus on their perceptions of their academic abilities. That is, students need to identify with, and feel confident about, the likelihood of success in the school setting. This is especially important for students in minority groups or students who are under-represented in certain academic fields (e.g., girls in science).

Häussler and Hoffman (2002) wanted to increase girls' interest in science by adapting the middle school physics curriculum in Germany to be more 'girl-friendly' and thereby improving girls' academic self-concept as it relates to (in this case) physics. Data were collected at the beginning and end of the Grade 7 school year, and again at the beginning of the Grade 8 school year. While teaching concepts in physics typically involve the knowledge and manipulation of mechanical objects, Häussler and Hoffman (2002) felt that using more socially relevant examples might be more engaging for girls (e.g., teaching force and velocity by investigating how safety helmets work in protecting cyclists). In addition, teachers were trained to behave in ways that would promote a positive physics-related self-concept in girls. For example, if a girl signals that she is unable to do the task, the teacher is to avoid making any negative comments about the girl's ability but instead is to provide guidance on how to complete the task. Or, if a girl's performance is unsatisfactory, the teacher is to convey to the student that better performance is expected and to work out a plan to improve future achievement. Results showed that the altered curriculum did indeed have a significant positive effect on girls' interest and self-concept when compared to students who received traditional teaching in physics.

TEACHER EXPECTATIONS AND SELF-FULFILLING PROPHECY

Children's academic self-concept and perception of their abilities will be shaped by the people that they encounter in the school setting. One of the strongest influences on students is the teacher. The following section will focus on the nature of teachers' expectations and how these expectations may affect students for better or worse.

In the 1960s, Robert Rosenthal and Lenore Jacobson noticed that teachers had higher expectations for the achievement of good students in their classrooms and wondered whether these expectations could influence students' academic performance. In their classic experiment, *Pygmalion in the Classroom*

(1968), Rosenthal and Jacobson told teachers early in the school year that, based on the results of an IQ test, some of their students had above-average academic potential (a group labelled 'bloomers'). In actuality, these 'bloomers' had been randomly selected and were, on average, no smarter than the other students in class. The teachers were unaware that the information given to them about their students' IQ test scores was false, and the students were not told about the label given to them. By the end of the school year, the bloomers showed significant increases in their IQ scores when compared to students in the control condition. Remarkably, the teachers' expectations had come true. How did the improvement come about? Rosenthal and Jacobson suggested that because the teachers believed the bloomers to be above-average students, they began to treat these students differently. In-class observations revealed that teachers provided the bloomers with a more welcoming climate by giving them more attention, support, and encouragement. They gave these students more challenging material to learn, more constructive feedback on their schoolwork, and more opportunity to participate in class sessions.

Rosenthal and Jacobson's (1968) study generated decades of research, as well as controversy and criticism. ***Self-fulfilling prophecy***, as it came to be known, outlines how teachers' expectations (sometimes erroneous and biased) can change students' behavior and academic performance in a way that confirms the teachers' initial expectations (Dandy, Durkin, Barber, & Houghton, 2015; Jussim & Harber, 2005; Jussim, Robustelli, & Cain, 2009). The notion that teachers' perceptions may indeed bias their evaluations of students and predict students' achievement levels has a great deal of empirical support (Jussim & Harber, 2005; Madon, Jussim, & Eccles, 1997; McKown & Weinstein, 2002; Sorhagen, 2013; Weinstein, Gregory, & Strambler, 2004). In extensive reviews of the literature, however, some researchers (e.g., Jussim & Harber, 2005; McKown &Weinstein, 2002) have argued that teacher expectations may actually have only small effects on academic outcomes and that even the Rosenthal and Jacobson (1968) study itself produced only modest effects. Moreover, some research has shown that self-fulfilling prophecies in the classroom are not likely to accumulate over time and that the effect of negative teacher expectations may even dissipate over time (Jussim & Harber, 2005; Jussim et al., 2009).

So, which side is correct? Do teachers' perceptions of their students affect academic achievement? If the effects are only minimal and short term, do we need to worry about this? It seems difficult to believe that teachers have little influence on students' academic development given that individuals spend so much of their early life in a school setting. The next section will clarify some of these points by examining the nature of expectations, such as whether expectations have more of an impact in the early school years and whether expectations have differential consequences for specific groups of students.

How Teacher Expectations Work

Although some researchers have found that teacher expectations may have only small, fleeting effects on students' academic outcomes, nowhere is the potential impact of teacher expectations on student outcomes more evident than in elementary school (Jussim et al., 2009). Even students in first grade can detect differences in how teachers treat them versus other students in the class, and by fifth grade, these expectations become part of the student's self-concept (Weinstein et al., 2004). In these first school years, differences in children's abilities are made very salient to them: they are put into ability-based groupings, challenging materials are given to some students and not others, and students are made aware of their higher (or lower) performing classmates. These practices have the tendency to intensify the effects of self-fulfilling prophecies so that students begin to feel that they cannot move beyond their designated group, asking for help or expending extra effort may be a sign of poor ability, and learning is equivalent to getting good grades (Weinstein et al., 2004). Using students from across ten US school districts, Sorhagen (2013) found that academic achievements in high school were predicted by teacher expectations in the first grade. Specifically, students whose first-grade teachers had underestimated their abilities in math and reading-related areas performed significantly worse on standardized tests of math, reading comprehension, and verbal reasoning at age 15, regardless of how they scored on the standardized tests in first grade. The same pattern occurred for students whose teachers had over-estimated their abilities in first grade: these students performed better across a range of subjects when they reached high school. Moreover, Sorhagen (2013) found that not all students were affected equally. For example, the high school math achievement of children from poorer backgrounds was more affected by their first-grade teachers' expectations than children from more affluent backgrounds.

Teachers who hold expectations that strongly differentiate between high- and low-performing students create an atmosphere in which performance goals are stressed, making children feel that they are 'locked' into their group (Rubie-Davies, 2007; Weinstein et al., 2004). Teachers provide high achievers with more autonomy and support, while low-achieving children will be given more structured and repetitive work (Weinstein et al., 2004). On the other hand, teachers who do not hold such disparate expectations about high- and low-achieving students (or who have high expectations for *all* their students) create an overall more positive atmosphere for students where the focus is on mastery goals and on improving learning. Furthermore, as recommended through SDT, the latter foster more self-regulation and autonomy in their students (Rubie-Davies, 2007; Weinstein et al., 2004). In a study done with elementary school teachers in Auckland, New Zealand, Rubie-Davies (2007) found high-expectation teachers spent more time providing a framework for students' learning, provided students with more feedback, posed more complex questions to their students, and used more positive management techniques than did low-expectation teachers. When examining academic performance of students in their classes, the students' achievement levels mirrored their teachers' expectations.

Teacher Expectations of Student Subpopulations

Students from marginalized groups, such as African American, Hispanic, or Indigenous, seem to be especially vulnerable to teachers' views about them (Jussim & Harber, 2005; Jussim et al., 2009; McKown and Weinstein, 2002; Weinstein et al., 2004). Teachers also hold different expectations for girls and boys, leading to achievement gaps in particular areas such as mathematics and science (McKown & Weinstein, 2002; Robinson-Cimpian, Lubienski, Ganley & Copur-Gencturk, 2014). These expectations are often consistent with existing gender and ethnic stereotypes, further reinforcing the beliefs about academic ability differences in particular groups of students, and hence, becoming self-fulfilling prophecies for both the teachers and students themselves, who end up internalizing the stereotypes (Jussim et al., 2009; McKown & Weinstein, 2002).

In elementary school, girls have been found to be especially vulnerable to teachers' underestimations of their math abilities when compared to boys (McKown & Weinstein, 2002). Indeed, the gender bias in teachers' math expectations may have more of an impact over time and is not only limited to the early school years. As children become more socialized in the school setting, they begin to learn what is (and is not) expected of them, and this becomes incorporated into their academic self-concept. For example, McKown and Weinstein (2002) found that, in fifth grade (but not in first or third grade), teachers' expectations of math ability predicted year-end math achievement. Specifically, the underestimation for girls' math ability had an adverse effect on their math performance, but an overestimation of their math ability by teachers had little effect on their performance. This pattern of teacher expectations and resulting performance was not found for boys: teachers' underestimations of their math ability had little effect on their math performance. Robinson-Cimpian et al. (2014) also examined teacher expectations concerning mathematics proficiency in male and female students but argued that students' behaviors in class may be confounding how teachers rate a student's ability in a particular area. In their study, teachers perceived girls to be as equally proficient in math as similarly performing boys *only* when girls expended more effort, behaved better in class, and showed greater eagerness to learn. Essentially, this meant that teachers were consistently underrating girls' math ability by believing that girls' better performance in math was only achieved through extra effort.

Despite decades of findings that show Black and Hispanic children in the United States face discrimination and are more likely to be underserved by the educational system than are White children, teachers continue to underestimate the ability of Black and other minority students. Furthermore, while it may be argued that children in marginalized groups may be at a disadvantage due to poverty and disruptive home environments, a significant amount of the differences in the academic achievement of Black and White students may be attributed to stereotypic beliefs regarding the scholastic abilities of children in these groups (Rubie-Davies, Hattie, & Hamilton, 2006; Weinstein et al., 2004). For instance, teachers and parents (as well as the students themselves) believe that African American males are often thought to possess characteristics that are not conducive to academic achievement (e.g., propensity to violence, valuing athletics over academic subjects, lack of focus) (Jussim et al., 2009; Wood, Kaplan, & McLoyd, 2007). Wood et al. (2007) explored the expectations that African American youth had for themselves, as well as the expectations for academic success held by their parents and teachers. These expectations were examined in relation to the students' own perceptions of the school environment and their academic achievement. In general, male students reported lower expectations for their academic future, such as the likelihood that they would attend college, than did their female counterparts. Both teachers and parents also reported lower expectations for their male than female children's academic success, and these expectations correlated significantly with students' academic achievement at every grade level. Interestingly, when students rated the school environment to be positive, or when they perceived that teachers had positive expectations for their academic achievement, low parental expectations had less of an effect on students' academic performance. Wood et al. (2007) argued that a positive and encouraging school environment (such as supportive teachers) may offer some protective factors against the negative expectations held by the students and/or their parents.

Indigenous students, whether in Canada, the United States, Australia, or New Zealand, have also been subjected to negative effects of teacher expectations. Typically, Indigenous students are less successful in school than are their non-Indigenous counterparts, with overall lower school participation, poorer retention rates, experiences of racial prejudice and discrimination, and provision of poorer quality schooling. Rubie-Davies et al. (2006) examined teachers' expectations toward students from various ethnic groups attending elementary schools in New Zealand. Teachers' expectations at the beginning of the school year were higher than end-of-year actual achievement for all student groups except for Maori students. Even though Maori students had started off at the same level of achievement as the other groups in the classes, they made the least gains of all throughout the year. In contrast, Asian students showed the greatest gains in academic achievement through the year, with teachers holding the highest expectations for them. Teachers saw the Asian children as conscientious and industrious whereas the Maori children were believed to come from homes where education was not valued. Similar findings were also obtained by Dandy et al. (2015) using in-training teachers, experienced teachers, and students from Aboriginal, Asian, and European backgrounds in Australia. Both groups of teachers reported the highest expectations for Asian students and the lowest expectations for Aboriginal students. Asian students were rated as being more gifted academically, particularly in mathematics, and were viewed as working harder than either their European or Indigenous counterparts. Teachers rated Aboriginal students lower in ability and effort across all academic domains. Sadly, consistent with how teachers saw them, Aboriginal students themselves held negative expectations about their own and their group's future academic success.

Implications and Applications

Teachers are not always aware of the expectations they hold concerning certain groups of students, nor are they always cognizant of treating some groups of students differently from others (Gottfredson, Marciniak, Birdseye, & Gottfredson, 1995; Rosenthal & Jacobson, 1968). When interacting with students who they perceive to be low achieving, teachers may communicate their negative views through subtle behaviors, such as frequently interrupting students, making less eye contact, giving fewer smiles, or even assigning seats further away from the front of the classroom. Although teachers may not be aware that they are creating an unwelcoming learning and social environment for these students, the students themselves are very much aware.

The ***Teacher Expectations and Student Achievement (TESA)*** program (Gottfredson et al., 1995) is designed to make in-training teachers aware of the behaviors that they display when interacting with students from different achievement levels and to make teachers more sensitive to the way in which they respond to students. The program focuses on 15 classroom behaviors, divided into three categories: (1) response opportunities (e.g., amount of time waiting for students to answer, complexity of questions directed at students), (2) feedback to students (e.g., amount of praise given for success, feedback given on course work), and (3) personal regard (e.g., number of positive interactions, amount of eye contact with students). As part of the training, each teacher observes and gives feedback on the classroom behavior to at least three other teachers, and each teacher is also observed teaching and given feedback. In an evaluation of the program, Gottfredson et al. (1995) noted that students who had TESA-trained teachers performed better on achievement tests than did students whose teachers were not trained in the program. The researchers also found that the positive effects on students were greater at the earlier grades than in the later grades. Other evaluations of the TESA program (Cantor, Kester, & Miller, 2000) reveal that teachers find the training to be generally helpful, make use of many of the strategies outlined in the program, have more positive interactions with low-achieving students, and observe that their students develop more positive attitudes toward learning.

SOCIAL COMPARISON PROCESSES AND STUDENTS' ACHIEVEMENT

In the previous section, we saw the significant influence of teachers on students' academic development. Students, however, are not only affected by what their teachers think of them but also by their peers. Interactions between the teachers and students, as well as interactions among students, create a social environment that has a strong evaluative component. Students feel compelled to compare themselves to others in the classroom on social skills, physical appearance, performance in sports, as well as on academic performance (Dijkstra, Kuyper, van der Werf, Buunk, & van der Zee, 2008; Wehrens, Kuyper, Dijkstra, Buunk, & van Der Werf, 2010). While many academic indicators may seem, on the surface, to be objective, their interpretation by students, teachers, and parents is subjective. As we will see in this section, the types of comparisons that students make, and the context in which comparisons occur, can have substantial effects on students' academic self-concept, motivation to learn, and achievement.

The Basics of Social Comparisons

In any given situation, individuals may make upward, downward, or lateral social comparisons. The choice depends upon the motives for engaging in comparisons. Often, we prefer to compare ourselves to similar others for the purposes of self-evaluation (Blanton, Bunk, Gibbons, & Kuyper, 1999; Boissicat, Pansu, Bouffard, & Cottin. 2012; Buunk, Kuyper, & van der Zee, 2005; Dijkstra et al., 2008; Huguet, Dumas, Monteil, & Genestoux, 2001; Wehrens et al., 2010). This is referred to as a ***lateral comparison*** and is directed at others who share similar relevant characteristics such as gender, age, socioeconomic level, or key interests (Dijkstra et al., 2008; Wehrens et al., 2010). With ***upward comparisons***, the person's motivation is to improve, and thus, the comparison is made to another person who is performing better in a relevant area. Upward comparisons are thought to increase motivation to achieve, to foster a sense of self-efficacy, and to provide information to the individual on how to be more effective (Dijkstra et al., 2008; Huguet et al., 2001; Wehrens et al., 2010). ***Downward comparisons***, on the other hand, are driven by the need to self-enhance and are often used when individuals are under stress. These comparisons may help protect self-esteem and regulate anxiety levels but do not necessarily improve performance (Dijkstra et al., 2008; Huguet et al., 2001; Wehrens et al., 2010).

Beginning in preschool, children are capable of comparing themselves to their classmates and, as they age, come to rely on social comparison information to evaluate their abilities and develop their academic self-concept (Dijkstra et al., 2008). Early on, the primary motive for social comparisons is to acquire information about classroom norms and expectations for behavior (Dijkstra et al., 2008; Wehrens et al., 2010). As children get older, the reasons for making comparisons become more complex. Improving one's performance is key, and comparisons may involve strategies which help close the discrepancy between one's performance and that of others (Dijkstra et al., 2008; Huguet et al., 2001). By the time students reach high school, they will have been exposed to a much wider range of peers, and perceptions of their academic competencies in relation to others will based not just on one classroom but on numerous classrooms and, possibly, schools. Djikstra et al. (2008) noted that the social comparison motives of children under the age of seven are based on mastery-development goals of learning whereas older children are primarily motivated by evaluation of their performance in relation to others.

For the most part, students tend to engage in upward social comparisons, and these comparisons are associated with improvements in academic performance (Blanton et al., 1999; Buunk et al., 2005; Huguet et al., 2001; Marsh, Trautwein, Lüdke, & Köller, 2008). In a longitudinal study with high school students, Wehrens et al. (2010) found that the more favorable students' comparisons choices were, the higher their academic performance. The researchers concluded that students were performing better when comparing upward because it helped them to set challenging (but achievable) goals. Similar results were obtained by Huguet et al. (2001) in that students tended to choose same sex comparison targets who were slightly outperforming them in class. Again, the comparative evaluation choice helped students to see that it was possible to succeed at a task, thereby heightening motivation and feelings of self-efficacy (Huguet et al., 2001).

It seems almost counterintuitive that students would prefer to engage in comparisons with others who are doing better than they are so that they can also feel better about themselves. After all, we might expect some level of discouragement or resentment. Would not downward comparisons be more preferable? Gibbons, Lane, Gerrard, Reis-Bergan, Lautrup, Pexa, and Banton (2002) focused on how downward comparisons might operate in situations where (as in most classrooms) there is a range of performance levels among students. As with other studies, successful performers tended to use upward comparisons for continued self-improvement and rarely used downward comparisons. Students who were less successful, however, used downward comparisons to feel better. This especially occurred if students felt powerless to change their outcomes. For struggling students, therefore, downward social comparisons may help to regulate negative emotions and repair their self-image, even if it is only for the short term.

Recent research has revealed that the effects of social comparison on students' academic development will depend not only on whether the student engages in lateral, upward, or downward comparisons but also on the extent to which the student identifies with the target of the comparison (Boissicat et al., 2012; Wehrens et al., 2010). If a student identifies with the target (i.e., shares values, abilities, culture, etc.) or sees him/herself as part of the same group (referred to as ***identification or assimilation***), then the student will focus on the potential consequences of the situation for one's current or future situation when making a comparison (Boissicat et al., 2012; Buunk et al., 2005; Wehrens et al., 2010). In the case of identification, an upward comparison will be even more effective for the student because he/she will be able to visualize a successful outcome more easily (Buunk et al., 2005). Identification and a *downward comparison* may evoke anxiety and worry because (as with the upward comparison), the student might visualize him/herself in the same situation (Buunk et al., 2005; Wehrens et al., 2010). If, instead, students focus on the differences between themselves and the comparison target (referred to as ***differentiation or contrast***), then making comparisons will lead to very different consequences than those seen with identification. In the case of upward comparisons, a student might feel resentful of a more successful classmate and his/her academic self-concept may be negatively affected. In differentiation and downward comparisons, a student may feel contempt for the less successful peer or feel relief at doing better than the comparator, boosting his/her academic self-concept (Buunk et al., 2005; Djikstra et al., 2008).

Boissicat et al. (2012) examined the relationships between upward and downward comparisons, identification and differentiation conditions, and perceived school competence in French elementary school children. Results showed that downward identification and upward contrast were negatively related to perceived scholastic competence. That is, the more students identified with classmates who were performing poorly, and the more they saw themselves as different from successful classmates, the less academically able they felt. Upward identification and downward differentiation, however, were positively related to perceived school competence. Students who identified with classmates who were better performing, and who distanced themselves from poorly performing classmates, felt more academically competent.

Because students are often grouped with others who are similar in ability and are more likely to interact with peers who have a similar background, there is a greater likelihood that students will make more identification than differentiation comparisons (Buunk et al., 2005; Huguet et al., 2001; Wehrens et al., 2010). Also, students are motivated to feel positive better about themselves, and using upward identification is one way to accomplish this: students see themselves in their successful peers (Buunk et al., 2005). Therefore, upward identification serves as an important source of knowledge and motivation for the student, often leading to better academic performance (Dijkstra et al., 2008). But what happens to your academic self-concept or your beliefs about your academic competence if you have no choice but to identify with peers (either individually or as a group) who have lower levels of academic achievement? Altermatt and Pomerantz (2005) noted that low-achieving students who had a high-achieving best friend (upward identification comparison) improved their academic performance but their academic self-concepts suffered. On the other hand, low-achieving students who identified with (and compared themselves to) a similar low-achieving best friend did not improve their academic performance but their self-concept was positive. This may help explain why some studies have found that making upward social comparisons can have mixed effects on students' academic development: lower evaluations of one's competencies as a student but better academic performance – it all depends upon the degree of identification with the target (Blanton et al., 1999).

Gender and Social Comparisons

The choice of social comparisons, and the motives behind these comparisons, has been found to differ on the basis of gender (Buunk et al., 2005; Chazal, Guimond, & Darnon, 2012; Gibbons, Benbow, & Gerrard, 1994). For example, Buunk et al. (2005) noted that, when making downward comparisons, high school girls tended to show more sympathetic identification with the comparison target (i.e., feeling sorry for the other person) whereas boys showed more egocentric reactions and expressed anxiety that the target's performance might be indicative of their own future performance. Using first-year college students, Gibbons et al. (1994) found that both high- and low-performing college students lowered their preferred comparison choice (reducing the discrepancy between their own academic performance and that of their target) over a period of six months. Male students, however, reported higher performing initial comparison choices than did female college students, and low-performing males, in particular, decreased the number of comparisons that they made more than did low-performing female students. The researchers also noted that male students seemed to engage in social comparisons for self-protective motives to a greater extent than did female students.

Chazal et al. (2012) examined gender differences in academic self-concepts and social comparisons and how these differences might impact their academic choices in about 200 French high school students. As mentioned previously, in many Western cultures, boys develop self-concepts that reflect interest in mathematics and sciences, whereas girls' academic self-concepts reflect interest in language and arts disciplines. These self-concepts are often consistent with gender stereotypes and societal or cultural expectations. To examine how academic self-concepts might be affected when making social comparisons, one third of students were asked to compare themselves with boys in their class, another third of the students were asked to compare themselves with girls in their class, and the remaining students were not given any comparison instructions (control group). Results showed that evoking a comparison across gender lines was associated with accompanying adjustments in academic self-concepts, reported performance, and academic choices. For instance, culturally expected gender differences in academic self-concepts related to science and arts were obtained with the control group and the cross-gender comparison group. The gender differences, however, disappeared when students were asked to compare their self-concept with that of same sex peers: girls did not define themselves as less scientific than boys and boys did not define themselves as less arts-oriented than girls. Finally, when asked about their intention to enroll in higher education, girls were more likely to want to enroll in higher education than were boys when they compared themselves to their same sex peers, but boys were more likely to want to enroll in higher education than were girls when students had to make cross-gender comparisons.

Implications: The Downside of Ability Groupings

The research on gender and social comparisons suggests that the choice of comparison targets, whether in an identification or contrast situation, may affect a student's academic self-concept, motivation, and decisions. In classroom settings where students represent a range of academic abilities, each student may actively choose a comparison target who will boost one's self-esteem, motivate oneself to perform better or to distance oneself from failure. Students can identify with, or differentiate themselves strategically from, their peers through a combination of upward and downward social comparisons. But a common practice in many educational systems is that of ability grouping, which can result in a limited range of comparison choices (Marsh, 2016). Frequently, students who do poorly may be placed into classroom groups or special classes that will provide additional support to them or they may be held back a grade. Similarly, high-performing students might be accelerated beyond their grade level, put into classes with other high-ability students or may even start school at an earlier age (Marsh, 2016). We assume that, in the former situation (low-ability grouping), the effect on academic self-concept will be negative and that, in the latter situation (high-ability grouping), the effect on academic self-concept will be positive. Recent research, however, has not supported this assumption (Huguet et al., 2001; Marsh, 2016; Marsh et al., 2008).

In an extension of social comparison theory, Marsh and others (e.g., Marsh et al., 2008; Salchegger, 2016) proposed that a student's academic self-concept is significantly affected by the ability of other students in their school environment, in addition to perceptions of their own ability level; a phenomenon referred to as the ***Big Fish Little Pond Effect (BFLPE)***. The stronger the BFLPE is, the less realistic students' self-perceptions are of their abilities, such that high-ability students may see themselves as less competent than they actually are when they are placed in classroom groups or schools with other high-ability students (Salchegger, 2016). Interestingly, low achievers may see themselves as more competent when placed in low-ability groupings (Salchegger, 2016). Unlike classic social comparison theory, in BFPLE, students may use a generalized 'other' as the basis of comparison: that is, comparisons need not be limited to individual classmates but rather can be based on the average performance of an entire class or school (Marsh et al., 2008). In a large cross-cultural study, Marsh (2016) found a negative effect on academic self-concept for acceleration or skipping a grade and a positive effect on academic self-concept for retention (starting late, repeating grade).

These results are surprising given that many parents and educators would expect that placing a gifted child in an advanced class will ultimately lead to better academic outcomes. The critical factor, it seems, depends upon the relative weighting of the identification and differentiation effects when students make comparisons. Ability grouping for gifted students may have negative consequences for their academic self-concepts because they are no longer able to compare downward to enhance self-concept. Their choices for making downward comparisons and differentiation are now restricted (Dijkstra et al., 2008). Although there is a positive effect on students' academic self-concept in attending schools where the average ability is high due to identifying with a successful group, this is counterbalanced by the limited differentiation comparisons. Students may see themselves as less able than those around them and may feel that they do not belong to a successful group. The standards that students are expected to meet may improve their academic performance but the net effect of the BFLPE is negative on academic self-concept (Dijkstra et al., 2008; Marsh et al., 2008). At times, this may even lead high-ability students to pursue long-term academic and career goals that are below their potential (Salchegger, 2016).

These findings stress the need to create school systems and classroom environments that minimize the BFLPE. When comparing implicit, informal grouping of students (based on social and geographic factors) to explicit, formal grouping of students (i.e., school selectivity and ability tracking), the BFLPE has been found to be more pronounced in countries which practice explicit school tracking at earlier grades (Salchegger, 2016). Marsh (2016) and others (e.g., Altermatt & Pomerantz, 2005; Huguet et al., 2001; Salchegger, 2016) urge that heterogeneous ability classrooms or schools may be more positive for students' overall academic development than advancing students or placing them in highly selective schools.

CONCLUSION

Each child brings an identity, beliefs about his/her academic abilities, and assumptions about school before even stepping into a classroom for the first time. These individual factors interact with the school environment (i.e., teachers, peers, classrooms) to affect a student's self-concept, motivation to learn, and ultimately, academic success. This chapter highlighted how current educational practices (e.g., ability groupings) and new programs (e.g., First Things First) can have dramatic effects on students' academic outcomes, decisions, and goals. The application of social psychological theories, such as self-determination theory, in the design of educational programs has been especially effective in addressing gender and ethnic gaps in academic achievement.

REFERENCES

Altermatt, E. R., & Pomerantz, E. M. (2005). The implications of having high-achieving versus low-achieving friends: A longitudinal analysis. *Social Development*, *14*, 61–81. doi: 10.1111/j/1467-9507.2005.00291.x

Belfi, B., Goos, M., De Fraine, B., & Van Damme, J. (2012). The effect of class composition by gender and ability on secondary school students' well-being and academic self-concept: A literature review. *Educational Research Review*, *7*, 62–74. doi: 10.1016/j.edurev.2011.09.002

Blanton, H., Buunk, B. P., Gibbons, F. X., & Kuyper, H. (1999). When better-than-others compare upward: choice of comparison and comparative evaluation as independent predictors of academic performance. *Journal of Personality and Social Psychology*, *76*, 420–430. doi: 10.1037/0022-3514.76.3.420

Boissicat, N., Pansu, P., Bouffard, T., & Cottin, F. (2012). Relation between perceived scholastic competence and social comparison mechanisms among elementary school children. *Social Psychology of Education*, *15*, 603–614. doi: 10/1007/s11218-012-9189-z

Buunk, B. P., Kuyper, H., & van der Zee, Y. G. (2005). Affective response to social comparison in the classroom. *Basic and Applied Social Psychology*, *27*, 229–237. doi: 10.1207/s15324834basp2703_4

Cantor, J., Kester, D., & Miller, A. (2000, August). Amazing results! Teacher expectations and student achievement (TESA) follow-up survey of TESA-trained teachers in 45 states and District of Columbia. Paper presented at the Annual Meeting of the California Educational Research Association, Santa Barbara, CA. Retrieved from ERIC database (ED443801).

Chazal, S., Guimond, S., & Darnon, C. (2012). Personal self and collective self: When academic choices depend on the context of social comparison. *Social Psychology of Education, 15*, 449–463. doi: 10.1007/s11218-012-9199-x

Cokley, K., & Moore, P. (2007). Moderating and mediating effects of gender and psychological disengagement on the academic achievement of African American college students. *Journal of Black Psychology, 33*, 169–187. doi: 10.1177/0095798407299512

Cokley, K., McClain, S., Jones, M., & Johnson, S. (2011). A preliminary investigation of academic disidentification, racial identity, and academic achievement among African American adolescents. *The High School Journal, 95*, 54–68. doi: 10.1035/hsj.2012.0003

Dandy, J., Durkin, K., Barber, B. L., & Houghton, S. (2015). Academic expectations of Australian students from Aboriginal, Asian, and Anglo backgrounds: Perspectives of teachers, trainee-teachers, and students. *International Journal of Disability, Development, and Education, 62*, 60–82. doi: 10.1080/1034912X.2014.984591.

Deci, E. L. (2009). Large-scale school reform as viewed from the self-determination theory perspective. *Theory and Research in Education, 7*, 244–253. doi: 10.1117/1477878509104329

Deci, E. L., & Ryan, R. M. (1985). Intrinsic motivation and self-determination in human behavior. New York: Plenum.

Deci, E. L., & Ryan, R. M. (2002). The paradox of achievement: The harder you push, the worse it gets. In J. Aronson (Ed.), *Improving academic achievement: Impact of psychological factors on education* (pp. 61–87). Boston, MA: Academic Press.

Deci, E. L., & Ryan, R. M. (2008). Facilitating optimal motivation and psychological well-being across life's domains. *Canadian Psychology, 49*, 14–23. doi: 10.1037/0708-5591.49.1.14

Dijkstra, P., Kuyper, H., van der Werf, G., Buunk, A. P., & van der Zee, Y. G. (2008). Social comparison in the classroom: A review. *Review of Educational Research, 78*, 828–879. doi: 10.3102/0034654308321210

Dweck, C. S. (1986). Motivational processes affecting learning. *American Psychologist, 41*, 1040–1048. doi: 10.037/0003-066x.41.10.1040

Elliot, A. J. (1999). Approach and avoidance motivation and achievement goals. *Educational Psychologist, 34*, 149–169. doi: 10.1207/s15326985ep3403_3

Elliot, A. J., & Church, M. A. (1997). A hierarchical model of approach and avoidance achievement motivation. *Journal of Personality and Social Psychology, 72*, 218–232. doi: 10.1037/0022-3514.72.1.218

Elliot, A. J., & McGregor, H. A. (2001). A 2 × 2 achievement goal framework. *Journal of Personality and Social Psychology, 80*, 501–519. doi: 10.1037//0022-351

Erturan-İlker, G. (2014). Effects of feedback on achievement goals and perceived motivational climate in physical education. *Issues in Education Research, 24*, 152–161. Retrieved from http://www.iier.org.au/iier24/erturan-ilker.html

Gibbons, F. X., Benbow, C. P., & Gerrard, M. (1994). From top dog to bottom half: Social comparison strategies in response to poor performance. *Journal of Personality and Social Psychology, 67*, 638–652. doi: 10.1037/0022-3514.67.4.638

Gibbons, F. X., Lane, D. J., Gerrard, M., Reis-Bergen, M., Lautrup, C. L., Pexa, N. A., & Blanton, H. (2002). Comparison-level preferences after performance: Is downward comparison theory still useful? *Journal of Personality and Social Psychology, 83*, 865–880. doi: 10.1037/0022-3514.83.4.865

Gottfredson, D. C., Marciniak, E., Birdseye, A. T., & Gottfredson, G. D. (1995). Increasing teacher expectations for student achievement. *Journal of Educational Research, 88*, 155–163. doi: 10.1080/00220671.1995.9941294

Guay, F., Marsh, H. W., & Boivin, M. (2003). Academic self-concept and academic achievement: Developmental perspectives on their causal ordering. *Journal of*

Educational Psychology, *95*, 124–136. doi: 10.1037/0022-0663.95.I.124

Guay, F., Ratelle, C. F., & Chanal, J. (2008). Optimal learning in optimal contexts: The role of self-determination in education. *Canadian Psychology*, *49*, 233–240. doi: 10.1037/a0012758

Harackiewicz, J. M., Barron, K. E., Tauer, J. M., & Elliot, A. J. (2002). Predicting success in college: A longitudinal study of achievement goals and ability measures as predictors of interest and performance from freshman year through graduation. *Journal of Educational Psychology*, *94*, 562–575. doi: 10.1037// 0022-0663.94.3.562.

Häussler, P., & Hoffman, L. (2002). An intervention study to enhance girls' interest, self-concept, and achievement in physics classes. *Journal of Research in Science Teaching*, *39*, 870–888. doi: 10.1002/tea.10048.

Huguet, P., Dumas, F., Monteil, J. M., & Genestoux, N. (2001). Social comparison choices in the classroom: Further evidence for students' upward comparison tendency and its beneficial impact on performance. *European Journal of Social Psychology*, *31*, 557–578. doi: 10.1002/ejsp.81

Jussim, L., & Harber, K. D. (2005). Teacher expectations and self-fulfilling prophecies: Knowns and unknowns, resolved and unresolved controversies. *Personality and Social Psychology Review*, *9*, 131–155. doi: 10.1207/s15327957pspr0902_3

Jussim, L., Robustelli, S. L., & Cain, T. R. (2009). Teacher expectations and self-fulfilling prophecies. In K. R. Wentzel, & A. Wigfield (Eds.), *Handbook of motivation at school* (pp. 349–380). New York: Routledge.

Madon, S., Jussim, L., & Eccles, J. (1997). In search of the powerful self-fulfilling prophecy. *Journal of Personality and Social Psychology*, *72*, 791–809. doi: 10.1037/0022-3514.72.4.791

Maehr, M. L., & Zusho, A. (2009). Achievement goal theory: The past, present, and future. In K. R. Wentzel, & A. Wigfield (Eds.), *Handbook of motivation at school* (pp. 77–104). New York: Routledge/Taylor and Francis.

Marsh, H. W. (2016). Cross-cultural generalizability of year in school effects: Negative effects of acceleration and positive effects of retention on academic self-concept. *Journal of Educational Psychology*, *108*, 256–273. doi: 10.1037/edu000059

Marsh, H. W., Trautwein U., Lüdtke, O., & Köller, O. (2008). Social comparison and big-fish-little-pond effects on self-concept and other self-belief constructs: Role of generalized and specific others. *Journal of Educational Psychology*, *100*, 510–524. doi: 10.1037/ 0022-0063.100.3.510

Marsh, H. W., Trautwein U., Lüdtke, O., Köller, O., & Baumert, J. (2005). Academic self-concept, interest, grades, and standardized test scores: Reciprocal effects model of causal ordering. *Child Development*, *76*, 397–416. Retrieved from http://www.jstor.org/stable/3096511

McKown, C., & Weinstein, R. (2002). Modeling the role of child ethnicity and gender in children's differential response to teacher expectations. *Journal of Applied Social Psychology*, *32*, 159–184. doi: 10.1111/j.1559-1816.2002.tb01425.x

Midgley, C., Kaplan, A., & Middleton, M. (2001). Performance-approach goals: Good for what, for whom, under what circumstances, and at what cost? *Journal of Educational Psychology*, *93*, 77–86. doi: 10.1037/ 0022-00663.93.1.77

Niemiec, C. P., & Ryan, R. M. (2009). Autonomy, competence, and relatedness in the classroom: Applying self-determination theory to educational practice. *Theory and Research in Education*, *7*, 133–144. doi: 10.1117/1477 878509104318

Niepel, C., Brunner, M., & Preckel, F. (2014). Achievement goals, academic self-concept, and school grades in mathematics: Longitudinal reciprocal relations in above average ability secondary school students. *Contemporary Educational Psychology*, *39*, 301–313. doi: 10.1016/j.cedpsych.2014.07.002

Pinxten, M., Wouters, S., Preckel, F., Niepel, C., De Fraine, B., & Verschueren, K. (2015). The formation of academic self-concept in elementary education: A unifying model for external and internal comparisons. *Contemporary Educational Psychology*, *41*, 124–132. doi: 10.1016/j.cedpsych.2014.12.003

Reeve, J. (2004). Self-determination theory applied to educational settings. In E. L. Deci, & R. M. Ryan (Eds.), *Handbook of self-determination research* (pp. 183–203). Rochester, NY: University of Rochester Press.

Robinson-Cimpian, J. P., Lubienski, S. T., Ganley, C. M., & Copur-Gencturk, Y. (2014). Teachers' perceptions of students' mathematics proficiency may exacerbate early gender gaps in achievement. *Developmental Psychology*, *50*, 1262–1281. doi: 10.1037/a0035073

Rodriguez, C. M. (2009). The impact of academic self-concept, expectations and the choice of learning strategy on academic achievement: The case of business students. *Higher Education Research and Development*, *28*, 523–539. doi: 10.1080/07294360903146841

Rosenthal, R., & Jacobson, L. (1968). *Pygmalion in the classroom: Teacher expectations and student intellectual development*. New York: Holt.

Rubie-Davies, C. (2007). Classroom interactions: Exploring the practices of high- and low-expectation teachers. *British Journal of Educational Psychology*, *77*, 289–306. doi: 10.1348/000709906X101601

Rubie-Davies, C., Hattie, J., & Hamilton, R. (2006). Expecting the best for students: Teacher expectations and academic outcomes. *British Journal of Educational Psychology*, *76*, 429–444. doi: 10.1348/000709905X53589

Salchegger, S. (2016). Selective school systems and academic self-concept: How explicit and implicit school-level tracking relate to the Big-Fish-Little-Pond effect across cultures. *Journal of Educational Psychology*, *108*, 405–423. doi: 10.f037/edu000063

Seaton, M., Parker, P., Marsh, H. W., Craven, R. G., & Yeung, A. S. (2014). The reciprocal relations between self-concept, motivation and achievement: Juxtaposing academic self-concept and achievement goal orientations for mathematics success. *Educational Psychology*, *34*, 49–72. doi: 10.1080/01443410.2013.825232

Senko, C., Hulleman, C. S., & Harackiewicz, J. M. (2011). Achievement goal theory at the crossroads: Old controversies, current challenges, and new directions. *Educational Psychologist*, *46*, 26–47. doi: 10.1080/00461520.2011.538646

Senko, C., & Tropiano, K. L. (2016). Comparing three models of achievement goals: Goal orientations, goal standards, and goal complexes. *Journal of Educational Psychology*, *108*, 1178–1192. doi: 10.1037/edu0000114

Sorhagen, N. S. (2013). Early teacher expectations disproportionately affect poor children's high school performance. *Journal of Educational Psychology*, *105*, 465–477. doi: 10.1037/a0031754

Urdan, T., & Schoenfelder, E. (2006). Classroom effects on student motivation: Goal structures, social relationships, and competence beliefs. *Journal of School Psychology*, *44*, 331–349. doi: 10.1016/j.jsp.2006.04.003

Vallerand, R. J., Fortier, M. S., & Guay, F. (1997). Self-determination and persistence in a real-life setting: Toward a motivational model of high school dropout. *Journal of Personality and Social Psychology*, *72*, 1161–1176. doi: 10.1037/0022_3514.72.5.1161

Vansteenkiste, M., Simons, J., Lens, W., Sheldon, K. M., & Deci, E. L. (2004). Motivating learning, performance, and persistence: The synergistic effects of intrinsic goal contents and autonomy-supportive contexts. *Journal of Personality and Social Psychology*, *87*, 246–260. doi: 10.1037/0022-3514.87.2.246

Wehrens, M. J. P. W., Kuyper, H., Dijkstra, P., Buunk, A. P., & van der Werf, M. P. C. (2010). The long-term effect of social comparison on academic performance. *European Journal of Social Psychology*, *40*, 1158–1171. doi: 10.1002/ejsp.706

Weinstein, R. S., Gregory, A., & Strambler, M. J. (2004). Intractable self-fulfilling prophecies: Fifty years after Brown v. Board of Education. *American Psychologist*, *59*, 511–520. doi: 10.1037/0003-066X.59.6.511.

Wilson, T. D., & Buttrick, N. R. (2016). New directions in social psychological interventions to improve academic achievement. *Journal of Educational Psychology*, *108*, 392–396. doi: 10.1037/edu000111

Wood, D., Kaplan, R., & McLoyd, V. C. (2007). Gender differences in the educational expectations of urban, low-income African American youth: The role of parents and the school. *Journal of Youth and Adolescence*, *36*, 417–427. doi: 10.1007/s10964-007-9186-2

23

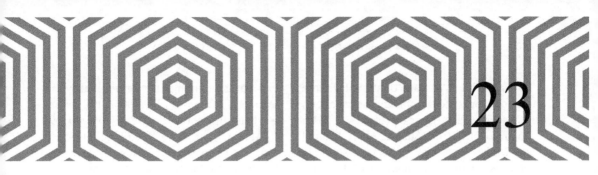

Critical Layering in Participatory Inquiry and Action: Praxis and Pedagogy in Seeking Educational Change

Anne Galletta

> [W]hat is deepest in the structural meaning of *the people* is its dynamic opening... (Martín-Baró, 1994: 184)

To provide a close-up view of applied social psychology in social and political contexts of education, this chapter explores complexity of thought and dialogue of understandings within several participatory action research (PAR) collectives. These collectives involve youth working with educators, members of the university, and broader community, representing layers of critical inquiry and action. In these intergenerational collectives, youth pursued questions about the constraints and opportunities available to them in an under-resourced Midwestern US urban school system. My intent is to underscore particular commitments in critical PAR through my tracing moments across these collectives that approached what social and liberation psychologist Ignacio Martín-Baró (1994) refers to as dynamic openings.

While the project particulars of this chapter focus on Cleveland, Ohio, the conditions of educational market reforms, high-stakes standardized testing, limited public participation in system governance, school privatization, and harsh disciplinary practices are part of the educational struggle for economically stressed communities of color in cities across the United States. Related to these conditions is the reach of a narrow philosophy of science embraced by many public agencies and much of US philanthropy, limiting what counts as knowledge in schools and invalidating methodologies viewed from a disciplinary center of privilege as outside 'science' (Stoudt et al., 2012).

In this chapter, I invite the reader to consider efforts to take to task psychological theory, method, and ethics in addressing social problems. In the local and global stratification of those stigmatized and accorded the low status or suspicion of the 'stranger' (Goffman, 1963), material and discursive conditions constrain and dehumanize. I employ the metaphor of *enclosure* used by social psychologists Henri Tajfel and John

Turner (1979) as a space of stasis for those accorded low status *or* potential space of creative social change (Fine and Halkovic, 2014; Stoudt et al., 2012; Subašic, 2012). Tajfel and Turner wrote that, in socially stratified societies, members of marginalized groups can secure higher social status through two options: (1) leave their existing group and join a group with higher social status through this social mobility or (2) undo the conditions of the status hierarchy through creative social change and alter the low status accorded to their group. The former is an individual strategy that does not alter existing relations of power. The latter is a collective strategy that disrupts these relations.

Social psychologist Erika Apfelbaum (1979) theorized power as expressed in a dependency relation, privileging one group and marginalizing the enclosed others through grouping processes, which are sustained and masked in degrouping – an illusion of social mobility, acts of tokenism, and opportunity accessed within conditionality. Apfelbaum's degrouping, like Tajfel and Turner's individual social mobility, is relatively conflict-free because it involves assimilation-like processes and does not pose questions about that which is normative within the social structure. However, there remains, nonetheless, the potential of regrouping, of questioning existing relations of power, reframing dominant narratives, and using conflict toward creative social change (Apfelbaum, 1979).

The work of Tajfel and Turner and Apfelbaum in the late 1970s offers conceptual space for recasting relationships and imagining Martín-Baró's dynamic opening. Locating stress points in the durability of privilege for those who cannot, or will not, 'turn white or disappear' (Fanon, 1952: 184) reveals the space of creative social change and regrouping. This space is theorized as both oppressively enclosed and potentially transformative. Brazilian critical educator Paulo Freire describes a site of liberatory struggle 'not as a closed world from which there is no exit, but as a limiting situation which they can transform' (Freire, 1970/2000: 49). Freire attributes this notion (Freire, 1970/2000: 99) to Álvaro Vieira Pinto, describing this space as *not* 'the impassable boundaries where possibilities end, but the real boundaries where all possibilities begin' (Vieria Pinto, 1960: 284).[1]

Drawing on Martín-Baró and Freire's understanding of limit situations and pursuing the social psychological metaphor of enclosure, this chapter offers illustrations of applied social psychological work through critical PAR. This work reflects core ethical and methodological commitments to analyze relations of power in the study of human experience and within the actual research endeavor. Within social psychology, this application of psychological theory, methods, and ethics through early efforts in PAR was evident in the work of Kurt Lewin (1948/1997). Lewin developed action research in the 1940s toward advancing science in the area of intergroup relations. For example, Lewin studied the dynamics of workshops in a project with the Connecticut State Advisory Board of the Interracial Commission. His interest was in increasing 'permanence' in improved intergroup relations and ongoing problem-solving concerning interracial and interethnic discrimination. The fullest expression of this effort was sustaining the relationship among teams subsequent to a single workshop gathering and providing the ongoing support of university academics. Lewin argued that these strategies 'should give a greater chance for permanency of the enthusiasm and group productivity and should multiply the power of the participants to bring about desired change' (Lewin, 1948/1997: 148). Conceptualizing a triangular relationship among action, research, and training, Lewin spoke in a compelling manner about action research:

> ...when I heard the delegates and teams of delegates from various towns present their plans for city workshops and a number of other projects to go into realization immediately, I could not help feeling that the close integration of action, training,

and research holds tremendous possibilities for the field of intergroup relations. (Lewin, 1948/1997: 149)

In Kurt Lewin's work, there is a bridging of theory and social realities and everyday practicies of communities, institutions, and/or groups. In her Preface to the 1948 publication of *Resolving Social Conflicts*, Gertrude Weiss Lewin recounted her husband's metaphor of the researcher's task as acting as a bridge across a gorge in order to connect the separated terrains of research and human experiences: 'The research worker can achieve this only if, as a result of a "constant intense tension," he [sic] can keep both theory and reality fully within his field of vision' (Lewin, 1948/1997: 10). The suspension of tension, as in the case of bridge construction, offers a metaphor for critical analysis and engagement characteristic of critical PAR. In Lewin's work, the press for transformation in human relations and in science is evident, sustaining tension between theory and lived realities, reconstructing the relational dimensions of knowledge production.

From Columbia, sociologist Orlando Fals-Borda wrote of PAR as research, adult education, and sociopolitical action: 'This experiential methodology implies the acquisition of serious and reliable knowledge upon which to construct power, or countervailing power, for the poor, oppressed and exploited groups and social classes—the grassroots—and for their authentic organizations and movements' (Fals-Borda and Rahman, 1991: 3). Collective inquiry takes place in the critical recovery of history, use of storytelling and popular culture, production of new knowledge, and sustained ownership of this knowledge by the people themselves (Fals-Borda and Rahman, 1991: 8–9). Countervailing power is established as information is collected through social validation, co-constructed by those *internally connected* to experiences of subordination and those *external to* this experience, whose involvement constitutes what Freire (1970/2000: 49) called a 'radical posture' of solidarity. This authentic commitment (Fals-Borda and Rahman, 1991: 4) represents *not* the detached gaze of an expert or the subject/object relationship between researcher and researched but, instead, a subject/subject set of relations through what Brazilian sociologist Maria Edy Ferreira writes as 'com[ing] to know *with* them the reality which challenges them' (Freire, 1970/2000: 110, footnote 23; my emphasis).

This solidarity is not facile nor is it innocuous. Social psychologist and critical PAR scholar María Elena Torre (2009: 110) theorizes PAR as a contact zone, 'a messy social space where very differently situated people could work together across their own varying relations to power and privilege'. In her work with collectives of youth and adults who bring to the projects very different histories, languages, identities, and ways of knowing, Torre extends the work of Pratt (1991), surfacing privilege not only within the phenomenon of study but also in the processes of inquiry and action through reciprocity, critical dialogue, and creative expression of things unsaid yet structurally and relationally present. In her work in New York and New Jersey with youth from under-resourced urban and wealthy suburban high schools researching educational inequities with adult allies, Torre notes, 'it was our work and responsibility to carve out a context not naively "vacated" by power issues, but strategically infused by and interrogating of them' (Torre, 2009: 117). In this sense, the Lewinian 'constant intense tension' sustains the dynamic opening as described by Martín-Baró. Deliberate attention to the social in terms of contextual layers of analysis, the political in terms of relations of power, and the ideological in terms of knowledge production is also evident in the work of critical psychologists (Collins, 2004; Hook, 2004). It demands a movement away from psychological imperialism toward more humanizing practices in knowledge production across disciplines and communities (Hook, 2004).

Within education, critical youth scholar Julio Cammerota and social psychologist and feminist Michelle Fine (2008) describe core principles of critical inquiry and action reflected in PAR processes in settings in which youth experience an intersection of oppressive conditions. Pedagogical sites include after-school programs, youth development organizations, community-based agencies, and sometimes schools. The research is conducted collectively, often intergenerationally. Knowledge production is deeply relational, with attention to relations of power that operate within, and outside of, the collective. Insider knowledge possessed by youth as it relates to the conditions of their lives and social and material realities they encounter are foregrounded in the research. Adult allies, such as community leaders, parents, academics, and graduate students may be a part of the collective, and the situated standpoints and resources they bring make visible other dimensions of the focus of inquiry.

As also noted by Cammarota and Fine (2008), critical PAR draws on key dimensions of critical race theory (CRT), which anchor PAR in the centrality of the social construction and material consequences of racism and the role of elites in structuring law to serve white interests (Bell, 1995). CRT conceptualizes racism as intersecting with other axes of oppression, such as gender identity, ethnicity, social class, immigration status, and sexuality (Crenshaw et al., 1995). Committed to social justice, CRT reveals prevailing discourses on educational opportunity as presuming neutrality and merit, as lacking a historical analysis, and possessing flawed claims of objectivity and 'color-blindness' (Ladson-Billings and Tate, 1995). It views experiential knowledge of marginalized groups as central to the study of social injustice and the transformation of oppressive structural conditions (Matsuda, 1995). Finally, CRT relies on a transdisciplinary perspective, drawing on history, sociology, critical policy studies, and other sources of theoretical frames for reversing the reproduction of racial inequities (Solórzano and Delgado-Bernal, 2001). These frames are central to the analyses conducted in critical PAR, and they provide entrée for collectives of youth and adults to creatively engage their local communities and distant agencies toward more humanizing practices in education, policing, health care, and immigration (Cammarota and Fine, 2008; Fox et al., 2010).

CRITICAL PAR COMMITMENTS TRACED IN FIVE PROJECT JUNCTURES

In this chapter, I pursue the theoretical possibilities outlined above and examine the processes of critical PAR. Within the chapter, I trace five junctures in several iterations of critical participatory inquiry and action: (1) the organic nature of PAR beginnings, responding to the realities of groups encountering historical moments; (2) the move toward critical engagement through layering of collective analyses; (3) situating individual lives in relationship with structural and historical conditions while keeping the analytical lens in motion; (4) recasting the relational space of enclosure in the classroom settings; and (5) attending to dynamic openings and closings of dialogic space in public forums. I 'interrupt' my narrative periodically to reflexively engage the reader in particular commitments in critical PAR. The organization of these reflexive writings is informed by the problem-posing process outlined by Freire (1970/2000).

In our project, which we named Lives in Transition (LiT), we formed a collective of adults and high school youth to inquire about, and act upon, problems youth encountered in their schools and neighborhoods, focusing on daily lived experiences as our data for 'reflection, discussion, and reconstruction' (Kemmis and McTaggart, 2005: 565). In the next section, I describe the first juncture that shaped subsequent inquiry and action in which the origins of the project took place.

Juncture One: Beginnings

In January of 2010, visual artist and critical educator vanessa jones and I collaborated with several teachers in a high school located in the Cleveland Hough neighborhood, historically the site in the 1960s of racial unrest and resistance to segregation in employment, education, and housing, still currently evident in the stress on neighborhood infrastructure and the daily lives of students and their families. We invited students from several classes to participate in a six-week project creating narratives from artistically rendered chronologies of their life experience. With the students, we traced the trajectory of individual experiences, noting transitional moments. We then filmed spoken word poetry or narratives by the students capturing a particular moment in time from their creative renderings.

A few days into the project, the school district announced the school would be closed at the end of the school year. The rationale for the closure was district 'transformation' in order to address three problems: a serious budget deficit, low test scores on state tests, and under-enrolled buildings in some of the district's most racially isolated and economically stressed neighborhoods. The six-week project timeframe ultimately extended well beyond June.

The remainder of the school year was tumultuous. We witnessed the response to the announcement, the opposition among some family members and youth and resignation among others, and the district's decision to move forward with the closure. The narratives of students' lives – the affection of a grandmother or joy of a sibling's birth, the loss of a loved one due to poor health or neighborhood violence, and the frequent changing of schools due to family moves – now included displacement to another high school. In one of its last days before the school closed, members of our then emerging PAR project photographed meaningful spaces within the building and documented final thoughts written by students in the school on long sheets of paper placed in different parts of the building. Returning with her camera, one young woman spoke of her response to what she had documented. She said to me, 'It feels like an eviction'.

This angle of vision, a view of displacement that held meaning for the youth researchers, provided the lens of study for the following year, as we worked with students transferred into school buildings a distance from their home and those within the buildings receiving the transferred students. Our research looked at the experience of school closure among youth. It led to a project with approximately ten students in two of the four receiving high schools. Data sources included autoethnographic texts, video footage from weekly sessions with the youth researchers, and mappings of students' transportation routes, poetry, photographs, newspaper clippings, district reports, state and federal documents, and archival materials. The youth researchers, educators, and university partners worked together to collectively study these data, contributing to a film, entitled *Lives in Transition: Eviction Notice*, which was produced by vanessa jones and Eric Schilling (2011). The film conveyed key concerns about school closure – need for transportation to receiving schools; impact of closure on achievement; the absence of youth and community participation in closure decision; and the uncertain future of the closed buildings. The film drew on history of the acceleration of school building in the 1960s to preserve segregation, connecting past with present in terms of a discourse of district improvement that obscured consequences for poor and working class youth of color. Youth from this collective traveled from Cleveland to New York City and later to Detroit to meet with other youth and adults who were also experiencing the closure of their schools.

While the events associated with this first early collective are documented elsewhere (Ayala and Galletta, 2012; jones et al., 2015), this project was then layered into the next iteration of critical inquiry and action, as several members of the first collective were involved in this later PAR project. Valerie Kinloch and Timothy San Pedro (2014) draw on the work of Bakhtin (1981) in conceptualizing the dialogic as 'the construction of a conversation between two or more people whereby the dialogic process of listening and speaking co-creates an area of trust between speakers–the space between' (Kinloch and San Pedro, 2014: 30). In this collaborative construction of meaning, 'dialogic spirals' suggest each project focus has dialogically engaged the next, layering its meaning making and acting as a catalyst for further inquiry and action.

Reflexive Interruption: What's the Nature of Relationship and Knowledge Construction in Critical PAR?

Here, I interrupt the description of the juncture to highlight a core commitment in critical participatory inquiry and action. This committment is that the research is *not on but with members of a community who share direct knowledge of the topic of interest*, and who often generate the focus of the research. This work is deeply relational in its investment to listen to each other and work horizontally in terms of power sharing. I note here one of six propositions established at the 1997 Action Research World Congress, reported by Doris Santos (2016: 26): 'PAR as pedagogy in action is, then, strongly based on the stories produced by participants' actions in the real socio-cultural world, which entails the construction of collective knowledge in more symmetrical relationships'.

The source of inquiry, then, is embodied and embedded within sociocultural and political contexts as lives are gendered, raced, classed, and shaped by relations of power. As Elizabeth R. Drame and Decoteau J. Irby (2016) write, the criticality of participatory research is found in its epistemic stance toward co-constructing knowledge. The authors note that knowledge is produced 'through the encounter between an indigenous (insider) knower who is tacitly familiar with a phenomenon and a person for whom a phenomenon is unfamiliar (outsider)' and the knowledge production is 'more complete than either of these ways of knowing alone' (Drame and Irby, 2016: 12). In theorizing Black Participatory Action Research (BPR), Drame and Irby note the ways in which participatory work can reproduce the power differentials and privilege it seeks to disrupt. Drame and Irby situate PAR as a space in which racial privilege is intricately embedded, and where 'academic researcher identities are inextricably linked to White supremacist institutions' (Drame and Irby, 2016: 7). As noted earlier by the work of Torre (2009) on the contact zone, the co-construction of inquiry and action requires an analysis of power relations within the collective.

Juncture Two: Toward Critical Engagement Through Layering of Collective Analyses

In the fall of 2012, we were aware that there was unfinished work from the earliest LiT collective. A mostly new group of high school youth came together to inquire into their educational experience. Some were from the same high schools from which students of the earlier collective had attended. In those buildings, I had come to know the educators, having spent considerable time in classrooms with students and teachers. However, to widen participation, I reached out to additional administrators in schools where teachers hoped their students might get involved. Below are field notes from my visits to schools to introduce myself and the project to educators:

> I sense some level of protection on the part of building level administrators for their students so as not to distract from the goal – passage of state tests and high school graduation. What reciprocity might I offer, and at what cost? At this time the most underresourced and academically strained schools are under such scrutiny by the school system and the state. And pressed by federal policy guidelines tied to funding in high-poverty schools. School closure remains a threat. School administrators get routinely moved from one building to another, or they are simply no longer here.
>
> My university credentials, white skin, and middle class background facilitate my initial access. Though I speak of the critical orientation of this work – perhaps not enough – the administrators appear most interested in the opportunities their students would have through the experience in a university setting. These resources speak more loudly to the educators, eager to connect their students with more research skills, creativity, technology, and social networks with faculty and students from the university.

Across the seven schools, 25 students participated in this next iteration of LiT. Some of the students were high achieving in their school, others had learning disabilities, and others struggled with academics in general. They reflected the district in terms of their socio-economic and racial background, as many of them were African American and from poor and working class neighborhoods.[2]

We gathered in November 2012 at the university, which became the space for our planning of a survey, analysis of the data, and developing creative products for reporting back. The youth discussed transitional moments in their lives and were interested in extending the work of the collective before them through the development of a survey. The survey would address school closure as well as transitional experiences in education, such as frequency in changing schools; transportation to and from school; relationships with other students and with teachers; classroom instruction; and youth voice. The seven high schools attended by the youth researchers were the sites of survey data collection and reporting back. The youth researchers spoke before the ninth grade students in their respective schools, inviting them to take the survey. We focused on the ninth grade because they had recently experienced a transition from a K-8 school into high school. Emphasizing the importance of voice reflected in survey data, the youth researchers promised the ninth grade students that they would be the first to get the results of the survey.

As a collective, we gathered in January of 2013 at the university to review the survey data. The team from Hamilton High School (pseudonym) focused on the theme of students not getting along with teachers and with their peers, which was evident in the survey data. Data from two questions in particular informed their discussion: 'How do students get along with each other in your school?' and 'How safe do you feel in school?'

The data were especially salient to the youth researchers from Hamilton because of an incident that had just happened involving a student-on-student fight that led to security and police involvement and the use of pepper spray on the students. The youth viewed this event as intertwined with the survey data results we were analyzing. This school was recently rebuilt and the new building generated a great deal of hope about what educational opportunities might be possible. During the meeting, the youth researchers replayed an excerpt from the evening news that covered the fight. The youth researchers noted the following in their early analysis coming out of the portrayal of violence in the newscast:[3]

Marcel: People say it's the school. I say it's the students.

Roy: It's basically gang-on-gang violence. We're put on the middle of [names several local neighborhoods] so basically everybody is beefing with each other, and we all are put in one place, so – they're gonna fight.

Marcel: We've got a big gym and a small gym and they shoved everybody in the small gym.
Brittany: It was for the [state tests].
Marcel: Because of [state tests], *but*, you know, you can't shove a bunch of kids in the small gym and expect nothing is gonna happen. So there was a couple of fights in the gym.
Marietta: Nobody broke it up.
Marcel: Nobody—by the time security got—only one security guard that finally got there
Anne: So what you're pointing to is a bigger problem than students being bad – you're talking about what we would say is a structural problem, right?
[youth researchers heads nodding, some 'right' responses]
Anne: A decision that was made [overcrowded gym during testing week] that created a situation that's not in the best interests of the students.
Brittany: And they did it again in day two [of testing].
...
Anne: This is deep...
Brittany & Marietta: Right.

The inclusion of the newscast by the youth was pivotal in opening up our analysis of the issue of safety. It reveals the tensions between viewing the data on school safety through the lens of human agency and/or structural considerations. In this exchange among the youth researchers, Marcel initiates his explanation of students as responsible for the violence in his school, echoed by Roy who describes the school at the center of gang activity. As action research scholars Kemmis and McTaggart (2005: 571) note, 'People not only are hemmed in by material institutional conditions, they frequently are trapped in institutional discourses that channel, deter, or muffle critique'. However, Marcel soon moves to a structural explanation, noting how overcrowded conditions in a small gym during a week of state testing and insufficient presence of security personnel contributed to the problem of one particular fight. In this juncture, we see the critical layering evident in the collective analyses.

In this shift, there is evidence of Martín-Baró's (1994) dynamic opening into contextual dimensions, as the youth note stresses from outside (conflict among neighborhood gangs) coalescing with those inside the school, such as overcrowding in a small space at a time of considerable anxiety over high-stakes state tests. Students cannot graduate from high school without passage of the state exams. The youth note that these conditions contributed to tensions in students being 'put in one place, so – they're gonna fight'.

Reflecting and extending the dialogic spiral as discussed by Kinloch and San Pedro (2014) and a process of inductive layering (Santos, 2016), the critical analyses of our collective moved us closer to taking action. Our first action-oriented step was to report back and problem pose with a wider group of individuals invested in the data. The youth returned to their respective schools and presented the results of the data to the ninth grade students to whom the youth had spoken the autumn before, now fulfilling their promise that students would be the first to learn the survey results. In the video they created, the Hamilton youth researchers featured the excerpt they found disturbing from the evening news. In this excerpt, the newscaster is standing outside Hamilton's newly built facility and noting the external aesthetics of the new high school. He contrasts the exterior of the school with what had occurred inside the facility, stating, 'It's absolutely a gorgeous building. However, what you're seeing repeatedly on the inside, it's ugly'.

In the creative product by the Hamilton team, the youth researchers juxtaposed the perspective of the televised evening news with the youth researchers' alternative newscast, which was more nuanced. In the video, Marietta plays the role of a journalist, and she interviews Roy on his views of attending Hamilton. Roy tells her, 'I like it. I like the fact that it's a new building and I get a good education there...I feel overall safe. Although we have our ups and downs, fights, and violence, I feel pretty much safe'. Similarly, Brittany appears unwilling to cast a sweeping generalization of the school and the students in it, responding, 'I feel very safe [pause]. Now look, I don't feel so safe when they be talking about shooting up our schools, and stuff. I don't feel safe'. Here the issue of the response to students' fighting on the part of security guards and police officers is noted, possibly intending to raise questions about the use of pepper spray on students as a means of restoring order. This creative product offered an opportunity for ninth grade students at Hamilton to critically engage on issues of safety, student conflict, the media portrayal of poor and working class students of color, high-stakes testing – forms of violence *within and outside* of the school doors. Through dialogic layering, the notion of 'violence' became deeply complicated and generative; it freed us from a one-dimensional view of the problem at the level of the individual. Freire (1970/2000) underscores the process through which one works out lived experience in relation to broader conditions:

> Reflection upon situationality is reflection about the very condition of existence: critical thinking by means of which people discover each other to be 'in a situation.' Only as this situation ceases to present itself as a dense, enveloping reality or a tormenting blind alley, and they can come to perceive it as an objective-problematic situation – only then can commitment exist. Humankind *emerge* from their *submersion* and acquire the ability to *intervene* in reality as it is unveiled. *Intervention* in reality – historical awareness itself – thus represents a step forward from *emergence*, and results from the *conscientizaçao* of the situation. *Conscientizaçao* is the deepening of the attitude of awareness characteristics of all emergence. (Freire, 1970/2000: 109)

While our analysis and reporting back reveal dimensions of 'reflection among situationality', the movement toward reframing a problem from entirely at the individual level of agency to a structural analysis reflects important points of critical engagement for our collective. However, the seductive pull of an individual level analysis often obscured attention to broader sociopolitical influences. Critical ethicist Monique Guishard (2009) cautions against the Freirian view of conscientizaçao, or critical consciousness, as linear, involving movement out of one stage into another. She notes that critical consciousness varies 'in form and expression across individuals and the contexts that facilitate its articulation' (Guishard, 2009: 103). Guishard outlines a theory that emphasizes 'emerging moments' of critical analysis taking place in multiple and interdependent contexts within and outside participatory collectives. Guided by this more 'dynamic polyphonic unit of analysis', Guishard notes, such a theory is responsive to 'ingenious strategies oppressed folks use while living with, challenging, surviving and thriving despite the intersecting oppressions of race, class, gender, and sexuality' (Guishard, 2009: 99).

Reflexive Interruption: How's Knowledge Constructed Among Individuals Positioned Very Differently Within Social Hierarchies?

Social psychologist Brett Stoudt, critical urban educational scholar Madeline Fox, and feminist and social psychologist Michelle Fine underscore the co-construction of knowledge within PAR (Stoudt et al., 2012). They employ black feminist Patricia Hill Collins' notion of situated standpoint in noting the angle of vision shared by members of a group similarly situated within hierarchical power relations. While arguing against notions of essentialism and noting heterogeneity within standpoint, the recognition of experiential bases of knowledge is central to their conceptualizing PAR. Situated standpoint provides what Sandra Harding refers to as 'strong objectivity', efforts to interrogate how prevailing ways of viewing social problems influence the focus of scientific study and how such focal areas are conceptualized. Harding (1992: 580) notes,

> Thus, democratizing the social order contributes to maximizing the objectivity of a society's sciences. In short, the most critical—'alien and possibly repugnant'— perspectives, because they conflict with the values and interests that have been conceptualized as neutral, are exactly what get dismissed a priori by objectivists. Thus the sciences are left complicitous with the projects of the most powerful groups in society. The neutrality requirement in not just ineffective at maximizing objectivity; it is an obstacle to it.

To illustrate the methodological utility of Collins' situated standpoint theory and realization of Harding's notion of strong objectivity, I draw on the work of colleagues at the Public Science Project, housed in the City University of New York Graduate Center, noting a critical PAR project, Polling for Justice (PFJ). The project focused on the experience among youth in New York City in terms of their experience of four sectors of public service: education, health care, housing, and criminal justice (Stoudt et al., 2012). PFJ consisted of 40 youth, joined by university faculty, graduate students, community organizers, and public health professionals. Stoudt et al. underscore their efforts to de-center objectivity as a criterion of validity and ethics in order to privilege all forms of knowledge:

> From the beginning, PFJ researchers contested the typical conflation of adult/White/well-educated perspective as objectivity. We did not, however, exclude such forms of expertise from the research, nor did we subordinate the knowledge of the academy to the knowledge of the youth. But we extended deliberately and critically the base from which knowledge and expertise would be cultivated: across disciplines, academy, community, and generations. *If, for instance, there were no youth on the research team, questions about relations with police would not have been asked and analyses would not have been made with the same depth and clarity.* With a diverse and multigenerational research team informed by lived experience, traditional bases of scientific knowledge, and critical theory/methods, we believe our 'expert validity' was enhanced as the academic monopoly on knowledge was challenged. (Stoudt et al., 2012: 182; my emphasis)

Analyzing quantitative and qualitative data collectively, with deliberate reflexive pauses to deepen their interpretation through performance of what they were seeing in the data, and pursuing additional data sources, PFJ found substantial differences in treatment of adolescents by the police across race, class, ethnicity, gender, and sexual orientation and vastly different levels of access to reproductive health care and care in physical and mental health, as well as education. To move from 'passive consumption' among a wider public concerning their findings and to stoke intergroup political solidarity toward addressing the flow of dispossession and advantage across public sectors, PFJ used embodied methodologies (Fox, 2011), such as performance, images, and audience engagement to foster 'mutual implication' (Stoudt et al., 2012: 187).

Juncture Three: Keeping the Analytic Lens in Motion

In the Lewinian tradition, LiT sought to 'multiply the power of the participants to bring about desired change' (Lewin, 1948/1997: 148) by returning the data to the ninth grade students, as promised. In this section, I trace our efforts to extend our analysis of the data and prepare for the action step of critically engaging a wider circle of youth in a second school through creative work. In preparation for reporting back to the ninth graders, the youth researchers from another school in the collective, Granite Hill High (pseudonym), planned a creative product that was both analytical and pedagogic; it would capture critical lines of analysis while also conveying the findings in an engaging manner for the ninth grade students.

In the earliest draft of their creative product, the youth focused on an issue that emerged from their study of the survey data, which revealed that, in their school, 83% of the ninth grade students reported students and teachers did not get along. From this discussion, the youth researchers filmed two scenarios – first what they initially called the 'wrong thing' followed by a scenario depicting the 'right thing'. In the first scene, conflict emerges between a student and teacher, with the teacher not responding to the student's questions about the steps involved in carrying out a math problem. The student persists in asking, the teacher appears to interpret the persistence as disrespect, and the interaction becomes confrontational, with the student walking out of the classroom as the teacher is shouting about reporting the student to the principal. In the second scene, the teacher explains how the math problem is carried out and asks the student if that makes sense to her. It is clear that the teacher is taking the time to determine if the student is understanding the steps in the math problem.

Several weeks later, we had our next session as a collective. During the meeting, we asked: how might we analyze these problems in relation to some of the other problems identified in the survey or raised in our discussions with the collective? Youth researcher La-Shaune Gullatt was momentarily distracted by two hand-sized rocks, which were bookends on the office shelf. The rocks were rough on the outside but sliced through on the inside, revealing various shades of color and geological design. The rocks became the subject of our discussion and a metaphor for critical analysis. Capturing this on video for the Granite Hill creative product, La-Shaune made the connection between analyzing what is happening in the first scenario (teacher and student conflict) in a one-dimensional manner versus looking at the conflict more closely with depth and layered detail. His comments are below:

> The first thing someone sees is that – or analyzes – is that they're just two people, they just don't like each other. What that could possibly mean is that – is just that. What they could do is that they should analyze it even more. They should see that there is something in the background that is causing it. Like these two rocks right here…

Coupled with music selected by another member of the Granite Hill group, the revised film segment powerfully introduced the possibility that there might be more to the teacher–student conflict in the scenario than meets the eye.

As a collective, we had explored the 'background' during several sessions. What everyday experiences in school were not accorded close study or questioning? In the Marxist tradition of 'relentless criticism of all existing conditions' (Marx, 1967: 212), critical PAR involves a practice of de-naturalizing institutional policies and practices. This involved, then, directing our observations 'toward previously inconspicuous phenomena' (Freire, 1970/2000: 82), 'in [their] deepest implications' (Freire, 1970/2000: 83) where the collective begins to 'single out elements from their "background awareness" and to reflect upon them' (Freire, 1970/2000: 83).

As we denaturalized normative practices in the schooling experience of youth, we explored implications of these practices, connecting these to the survey data. We drew lines of connection between data on 'getting along' and noted how school accountability policies intended for school improvement had resulted in school closure for two underperforming high schools, leading to increased changing of schools and considerable adjustments for students and teachers. Our discussion underscored how frequent changing of schools affected not only students but also teachers and might contribute to strained relations and compromised instruction. We talked about pressures on students and teachers to prepare students for standardized tests, with passage required for graduation. We also considered the history of racial and economic segregation in Cleveland and its suburbs. Our interpretation of the data on students 'getting along/not getting along' was informed by this shift in analytical focus across individual agency, structural conditions, and the

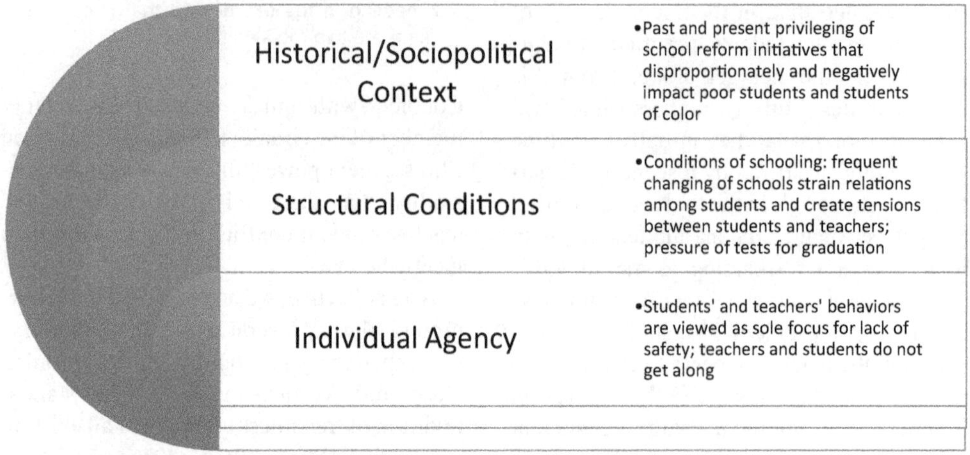

Historical/Sociopolitical Context
•Past and present privileging of school reform initiatives that disproportionately and negatively impact poor students and students of color
Structural Conditions
•Conditions of schooling: frequent changing of schools strain relations among students and create tensions between students and teachers; pressure of tests for graduation
Individual Agency
•Students' and teachers' behaviors are viewed as sole focus for lack of safety; teachers and students do not get along

Figure 23.1 Critical layering of analysis for ninth grade survey data

historical, as well as current, sociopolitical context. Figure 23.1 illustrates this critical layering.

In critical layering, then, the focus of one's analytic lens shifts from the study of individual lived experience to history, policy, and local economic conditions. In this manner, the analytic frame is in motion, holding in tension individual agency and broader economic, relational, and political conditions. This reflects the writing of feminists and critical theorists Lois Weis and Michelle Fine on what they refer to as oscillation (Weis and Fine, 2004), the analytic movement between theory and empirical data, and critical bifocality (Weis and Fine, 2012). Critical bifocality draws on the metaphor of visual space to offer a way of foregrounding the everyday experience and acts of agency while analytically *keeping present* that which may constitute the background – still integral to the whole, yet having the capacity to shift in focus. The use of foreground and background provides an analytic approach to exploring very different, but related, levels of analysis. Weis and Fine (2012: 176) define critical bifocality as the following:

> a dedicated theoretical and methodological commitment to a bifocal design documenting at once the linkages and capillaries of structural arrangements and the discursive and lived out practices by which privileged and marginalized youth and adults make sense of their circumstances.

In this manner, the ways of *seeing* a social problem can reframe it for the observer. In doing so, one might see the problem in a different way, thus altering how one talks about and addresses it. Lewin (1948/1997: 148–9) anticipated a radically changed unit of analysis in psychology, arguing, 'We will have to learn to handle these relatively large units of periods and social bodies without lowering the standards of validity and reliability to which we are accustomed in the psychological recording of the more microscopic units of action and periods of minutes or seconds of activity'. Reflecting Lewin's 'constant intense tension' bridging theory and lived realities, critical bifocality holds the possibility of disrupting a common or dominant view, creating room for institutions, laws, and policies to respond to the standpoint of those closest to the problem. Indigenous scholar Linda Tuhiwai Smith (1999) writes of the need for reframing of social problems to counteract the interventions employed to the detriment of Maori interests. Tuhiwai Smith situates Maori struggles within a historical frame, noting, for example, that social problems are 'not about psychological and individualized failure but about colonization or lack of collective self-determination' (Tuhiwai Smith, 1999: 152). In addition to reframing, Tuhiwai Smith includes 'retaining as much control over meanings as possible' (Tuhiwai Smith, 1999: 157–8) among her proposals for research in New Zealand and elsewhere that reflects indigenous commitments. Attention to reframing is evident in the next juncture.

Juncture Four: Dynamic Openings and Closings Toward Recasting the Relational Space of Enclosure – The Classroom Setting

Our reporting back occurred in classroom settings, typically the same classroom of the initial invitation to ninth grade students to participate in the survey. These settings were English classes, social studies classes, or student advisories that brought students together to meet informally and relationally with teachers. Sustaining the focus on Granite Hill, I show here our effort as a collective to create a dynamic opening for the ninth grade students in engaging them critically in the survey data results.

The first of five class periods of reporting back at Granite Hill was tough. It was the first class period of the day. The ninth grade students had not been prepared for our coming. As far as the ninth grade students were concerned, this was another social studies class. Unlike the brief amount of time we had asked for in introducing the survey several months earlier, this time we had asked for, and received, a full 30 minutes to discuss with the ninth grade students what had emerged in the survey data about their experience of school. Time off task from content in school was perceived by some administrators as costly in their efforts to ensure passing scores on the state tests, which influenced not only students' ability to graduate but also teachers' evaluation and, possibly, the school's future. Several administrators and teachers nonetheless viewed the class session as valuable engagement related to reporting back the survey findings.

In this first period of reporting back, there was interest among the ninth grade students in the creative product, the video the youth had prepared. Music, video, and graphics conveyed the survey data. In a segmented fashion, the video depicted a scene in which a teacher–student interaction becomes confrontational – the 'wrong-way' scenario – followed by a 'right-way' scenario. However, sandwiched in between was a scene with La-Shaune holding the rocks to convey critical analysis. He spoke to viewing problems beyond their surface level. How might the conflict between students and their teacher be understood with more depth? Employing the metaphor of the layered variation of colors and sediment evident when the rock's interior is made visible, La-Shaune suggested the need to make visible that which might be contributing to the teacher–student conflict. To speak to this, the video then rolls through some descriptive statistics from the survey to critically layer teacher–student conflict within structural conditions. As the data moved across the screen, they varied in their analytical lens between systemic conditions and acts of agency among students and teachers:

> Students change schools a lot...
> *Nearly 50% changed schools five to nine times before ninth grade*
>
> School closure...
> *35% students said elementary school closed*
>
> Getting to school may be difficult...
> *Cost and access are issues – bus shuttle has been helpful*
>
> Students said bullying is a problem...
> *Although 63% said students get along 'well' or 'very well'*
>
> 83% of students said...
> *Students and teachers do not get along very well*
>
> Students noted an emphasis on testing...
> *Students also reported that teachers helped and challenged them*
>
> More than half said teachers make them think deeply about ideas

While the enactments of school scenes, reflecting dimensions of the survey data, appeared to engage the ninth grade students, the metaphor of the rocks to symbolize critical layering and analysis fell flat. Suddenly, the reporting-back plan appeared to fizzle as the youth, Ms. J., a community member in the collective and retired teacher, and I grappled with how to support a dialogue. The period ended, and we spent the next class period, a free period without ninth grade students, brainstorming on how to report back in a way that was more accessible to the ninth grade students. Below is a transcript from our documentation through videotape of this moment of clarification among us as Ms. J. questioned for deeper understanding regarding the metaphor of the rocks. Here, she pressed for meaning in our effort to convey layers of lived experience – the small, or more immediate, problem – seen up close within broader sociopolitical and structural conditions – the big problems – often not visible:

Ms J.: I have a question, what do you mean when you're saying big problem and little problem? … I just want everybody to be on the same page, when you talk about big problems and little problems. I didn't hear it like big problem, little problem, but it's turned into big problem, little problem, cause when you first started talking about it, it was here's what you see on the outside and then here's the background

Isaac: …it can be interpreted in many different ways with the foreground is what you see, and then when you analyze and look to it, and then when it could be with the big problem and the little problem, it could be [for example] as far as the relocating schools—

Ms. J.: so the little problem, you're saying, is the changes [due to school closure]?

Isaac: the relationship between the teachers and the students

Ms. J.: so what's the big problem?

Isaac: what's causing—

Darren: how it got there—

Isaac: what's *causing* these small problems, like the altercations

Ms. J.: so the altercation is the big problem?

Isaac and Britanny together: no, the altercation is the *small* problem

La-Shaune: [quietly, in the background] but it can lead to big problems

Ms. J.: ok, the altercation is the little problem, ok

Isaac: because—and then we can just relate it back to the data because we did do videos based off the data that we received [indicating] more than half of our students said the students and the teachers don't have a great relationship

At this moment, the youth reflected on their efforts to reframe and foreground the broader social context in contrast to the tendency for the analytical lens to focus on individual behaviors. While they were unwilling to dismiss student–teacher conflict as either student resistance to learning or teacher disinterest in teaching, the youth were clear there were layers of consideration that cannot be subtracted from the analysis. The language of 'small' comes to signify that which is featured in the scenario. What is introduced in the data points scrolled across the screen constitutes the 'bigger' problems, what Freire (1970/2000: 82) referred to as 'previously inconspicuous phenomena "background"'. As noted above, Isaac identifies the lack of student–teacher relationships with the way in which students might not be known by teachers due to the relocation of students from closed buildings to receiving schools. In this manner, he anticipates the ways in which school closure and student relocation might create challenges for youth, socially and academically. Additionally, Isaac is very clear here that there is validity in this analytic reach, since it reflected the lived experience of the students,and the study of policies and practices we had engaged in during our sessions at the university.

In the case of Granite Hill, the students then reported back the remaining class periods, in between their lunch and their own class periods, with La-Shaune covering the last two class periods on his own. The level of engagement increased with La-Shaune suggesting to the students that they look carefully at the survey data that scrolled across the screen in the middle segment of the film. I added that the students think about how the data might connect with what was happening in the scenarios. With this scaffolding, some of the points in the video appeared to generate meaning. However, the exchange at Granite Hill was sometimes interrupted by students arguing with their teacher or each other. The classroom setting as it presented itself to us, physically and relationally, was a challenging space to do this dialogic work.

Juncture Five: Seeking to Engage a Wider Public

In the summer of 2014, our community member and former teacher Ms. J. secured a spot on the calendar of the Cleveland City Club for the youth to present. She argued for the opportunity, noting to the board of the City Club that the civic platform extended to local and national leaders had not been made accessible to youth. Given the organization's commitment to a robust exchange of ideas, the City Club board agreed to devote a session to youth involvement in research on education in their city. After some consideration of appropriate messages through the titling the event, the youth came up with *We the Students: More than Just a Number.*

Preparation for the event was another iteration of problem posing and critical dialogue. At this point, some of the youth had graduated from high school, or moved schools, and a core group of seven students met regularly to take on the task of presenting the survey results and capturing the process of PAR with a critical orientation.

In August of 2014, youth researchers La-Shaune Gullatt, Michael Sterritt, Jayme Thomas, and Taylor Watson, as well as critical urban educator Carly Evans and myself, presented the survey findings.[4] To further engage the audience, we asked youth in the audience to join us at the front of the room during segments of the presentation. Using embodiment methods (Fox, 2011), the youth from the audience 'spoke' the words and perspectives expressed in open-ended survey questions. These stories brought us closer to the lived experiences of students and their families dealing with school closure and access to transportation in a district shifting from neighborhood schools to a city-wide 'portfolio' of public and private school choices.

In the presentation, there was a skillful layering of lived experience in relation to historical and structural conditions. Youth researcher Taylor Watson said that 59% of the ninth grade students who took the survey said students and teachers don't get along very well. At the same time, Taylor said that there was evidence in the data of students reporting qualities in teaching the collective agreed were important, such as teachers encouraging critical thinking and challenging their students to work hard. She complicated the data further by noting that those who reported getting along with their teachers were more likely to also report their teacher focused only on the state exam. Taylor closed with a provocative question: 'Have students begun to equate good teaching with preparation for the state exam?' Later, in initially foregrounding structural conditions, Jayme Thomas acknowledged the serious consequences of school closure in contributing to academic struggle and school exit. She then spoke of the resilience she had gained partly as a result of what she learned about herself from her experience of school closure. Unwilling to narrate a single story of resilience *or* school exit, she spoke of the complexity of closure:

> For some students, school closure and just changing schools a lot has made them dropout and it's contributed to the dropout rate. And for me, I feel like this made me more resilient and a little more aware of the things that could happen and not become so affected by it, but nonetheless some students are not as resilient. (Galletta et al., 2014)

In Jayme and Taylor's critical layering, there is an epistemological shift and a move away from what Eve Tuck calls 'damage-centered' research (Tuck, 2009) that documents damage 'as a strategy for ensuring accountability and social change' but also 'reinforces and reinscribes a one-dimensional notion of these people as depleted, ruined, and hopeless' (Tuck, 2009: 409). And there is a move toward a 'desire-based' framework that 'complicates our understanding of human agency, complicity, and resistance' (Tuck, 2009: 420). To move toward such praxis, the history of disinvestment and disparity in access to educational opportunity is accompanied by that of resistance and strength, with clear lessons for youth in strategies for action, organizing, and working alongside adult allies toward engaging the public, impacting policy, and reversing inequalities. The LiT collective effectively presented the survey data and raised questions regarding the discourse of accountability and privatization of education in their city. In this way they drew on human agency, possessing a consciousness of history and current school reform efforts privileged as 'transformation' yet yielding alienating consequences.

For the presentation, our audience of 130 included a number of allies – educators, community members, and university students who had at one time been members, or supportive, of LiT. Also present were the district leadership and several high-level members of private foundations, which have heavily influenced the district policy. After we spoke, a member of the district leadership asked LiT members a question:

> I know we're not supposed to make a statement, but I'm incredibly proud of each of you. My question is [that] some of the issues you posed cannot be fixed through policy, so it's not something we can do as a district. So what can I do... to help make sure that the 5,000 educators of the Cleveland Metropolitan School District understand the issues that you're raising today?

In this statement, the expression of pride reflects the district leadership's recognition of the level of commitment among the youth researchers and the excellence of their presentation. At the same time, the pride expressed and the posing of this question obscured the goals of critical engagement and impeded our efforts in meaningful praxis in at least two ways: (1) it positions youth as in a particular relation with adults, delegitimizing their role in the research, which then may (2) erodes the validity of youth knowledge and analysis of their experience. Both of these processes recast relations and the epistemic underpinnings of this work. This is noted more generally in PAR by community psychologist and critical PAR scholar M. Brinton Lykes and educational policy analyst Walter M. Haney, who wrote, 'Within these continually changing relations, power is transformed and identity claims shift. However, these developing relationships are constrained by wider community dynamics which sometimes do not recognize the micro changes within our research relationships and processes' (Haney and Lykes, 2000: 288). Below are my thoughts, written as a retrospective field note:

> At once, the [leadership member's] expression of pride finds resonance with me. Yet there is a deflection of engagement. [Leadership member] does not respond to any of the core themes presented here. Why is there no substantive engagement with the data and perspectives the youth have offered?[5]

In the case of seeking to engage a wider public, we had approximated a dynamic opening in the embodiment of lived experience and the layering of this experience in relation to historical and structural conditions. However, we encountered unequal relations of power in the deflection of critical engagement on the part of the district leadership, reconfiguring the relational landscape and shuttering the transformative space.[6]

Reflexive Interruption: How Does the Struggle Outside the Collective Seep Within the Collective?

Critical PAR reflects a commitment to the collective as a site of inquiry and action where knowledge is co-constructed yet is not separate from the broader context of contestation and struggle within hierarchies of power. These two dimensions are sustained within one sentence here to convey the tension inherent in efforts to critically engage across difference and power and the need for reflexivity within institutions that are ill-prepared to counter the social reproduction of power differentials. Reflexivity is a process of searching for meaning as it relates to particular research experiences, events, and relationships, while exploring their ethical and methodological implications.

Drame and Irby (2016) describe three levels of critical reflexivity, extending work by Lai Fong Chiu (2006) and Ruth Nicholls (2009). Transparent *self*-reflexivity involves a self-questioning concerning assumptions and actions on the part of the individual researcher(s). *Interpersonal* reflexivity interrogates positionalities and the nature of relationships within, and beyond, the collective. *Collective* reflexivity 'holds the potential to reveal unanticipated outcomes of a research partnership, and when done as a group may reveal that participants experienced the project as "transformative, affirming, cathartic, or empowering" (Nicholls, 2009). It may also reveal the opposite' (Drame and Irby, 2016: 4–5).

In terms of collective reflexivity, as noted earlier, the original impetus for the critical PAR work outlined here was the response among students and their families toward school closure carried out as part of a district improvement plan. At the same time we began our work in the collective, there was an absence of attention to the deeply contextualized impact on children and youth directly experiencing these district policies and school practices (jones et al., 2015). In the years following, as we layered our work through several iterations of PAR, the district and state moved increasingly toward the privatization of education through legislation addressing educational funding and governance.

At the level of interpersonal reflexivity, while we worked toward solidarity, there were material and relational dimensions to our lives that distanced us. My position as a university faculty member had the potential for constraining critique and autonomy on the part of my graduate students and youth researchers who were collective members. My skin color, social class, and professional status, which I used as collateral for critical PAR in negotiating university resources and drawing on disciplinary privilege, also may have gotten in the way of my fully understanding the lived experiences of my students and the youth researchers.

At the level of self-reflexivity, the critical PAR work influenced deeply my scholarship and subjectivity. It required frequent interrogation of self in terms of what I might be missing, silencing, or amplifying. Psychology privileges detachment and neutrality on the part of the researcher and distance from her participants; however, these principles are deeply problematic within critical PAR, and critical psychology in general, and they can fail to make visible relations of power operating below the surface of individual lives, institutions, discourses, and social structures (Collins, 2004; Hook, 2004). Within my university, the leadership at several levels supported and invested in the policies of system transformation occurring in the school district. Our findings as a collective required analysis of this context of educational reform and conflicted with district assertions. This presented complex relationships entailing risk and privilege.

Risk and Privilege: Ethics and Critical PAR

The complexity of risk and privilege underscores not only tension as it relates to critical inquiry and action but also applied social psychology in general. This is evident in terms of institutional power as well as the long pursuit of science that fails to serve the communities presumed to be the benefactors of the inquiry (Drame and Irby, 2016; Guishard, 2009; Tuck, 2009). What counts as knowledge weighs heavily in the extent of its production, for which the academy has historically played a significant role. In this manner, social problems are framed according to angles of vision legitimized through the machinery of peer review, often reinforcing the world view of those enclosed within the privileged space of their discipline. These frames may prevail as accepted discourse. Epistemologically, applied work is challenging because it involves efforts to conduct social science and construct knowledge outside the positivist/post-positivist philosophy of science. This paradigm privileges relational distance between the researcher and participants and locates expertise within the academy in particular disciplines and discourses. Even as I write this chapter, I am conscious of the conditionality within relations of power underscored by Apfelbaum (1979) evident in the fragile Orlando Fals-Borda's subject–subject relationship (Fals-Borda, 2001) among those employing PAR methodologies. The very act of writing this chapter distances me from members of the collective, particularly the youth researchers, and reinscribes the subject–object relationship not reflective of critical PAR.

In terms of ethics, important understandings of vulnerability and protection, while based on a history of abuse and exploitation, remain hegemonic and static. Those working in applied social psychology are hard pressed to meaningfully communicate to institutional review boards their methodology and research design. The requirements within our respective disciplinary ethical principles and codes of conduct often reflect an orientation toward experimental study informed by a biomedical approach of conducting research (Guishard, Halkovic, Galletta, and Li, 2018). Such codes do not address questions that exist in PAR in terms of who owns the data, what is done with them, and who takes credit for the generation of themes and findings. For example, in my submission of a manuscript to a high-tiered disciplinary journal with a narrow view of science, my co-author and I were told by a reviewer that our inclusion of a young adult's authorship of a poem had breached confidentiality by including the name of this person. As is the case in this chapter, we had indicated in the manuscript that we would not use the creative work of another individual without seeking permission and providing credit.

I do not dismiss the need to think deeply about confidentiality and risk for participants – youth and adults. There are consequences we cannot anticipate. At the same time, it is important to consider when it may be appropriate to name the author of a poem or identify a member of a PAR collective at her or his request whose insights speak deeply to an individual or communal angle of vision, particularly if that standpoint is not visible within the literature or is silenced in some way. Locally and globally, there is room for further development in the area of ethical principles and professional codes of conduct as it relates to research in general and PAR in particular.[7]

CONCLUSION

There is considerable contestation over the direction of educational reform in the United States. Sustaining already profound shifts away from the collective good, federal and state policies focus on accountability through testing while students and teachers face instability, loss of public resources, and the increasing intrusion of privatized interests in their everyday school experience. For youth whose embodied or symbolic cultural markers position them on the periphery of social status, legal rights, and educational opportunities, the dominant pathway of individual social mobility does not offer freedom but estrangement. Within this context, critical PAR troubles the privileged arrangement of educational policies and practices. It expresses countervailing power and humanizes and democratizes the site of research.

This chapter employed Tajfel and Turner's social creativity as an analytic space to explore the disciplinary boundaries of social psychology through applied approaches in education. Critical praxis through collective inquiry and action among intergenerational collectives of adults and youth holds the possibility of Apfelbaum's notion of regrouping and Tajfel and Turner's idea of creative social change. There is the potential to imagine cognitive alternatives and to reframe existing discourse and symbolic representation within education, offering new frames that make visible potential practices of humanization in education. Tajfel and Turner (1979) pose social creativity as a route to changing unequal intergroup relations, recognizing the durability of social structures that maintain 'walls' or render the interests of marginalized groups as parenthetical (Apfelbaum, 1979). Bringing together youth, elders, university members, community leaders, and those from other professions, critical inquiry and action hold promise for fully realizing the meaning of Paulo Freire's limit situation, not as an enclosure but as a transformative space, reflecting Martín-Baró's dynamic openings. In doing so, PAR applies the social psychological in a critical manner, working ethically and methodologically toward the liberation of psychology.

Notes

1 According to Adrianne Aron and Shawn Corne, editors of Martín-Baró's collection of writings (Aron and Corne, 1991: 6–7), the concept of limit situation originated with Karl Jaspers and was further shaped by Ignacio Ellacuría. Ellacuria was the rector of the Universidad Centroamericana José Simeón Cañas (UCA). Along with Martín-Baró, Ellacuria was assassinated on November 16, 1989, by the Salvadoran government's elite counter-insurgency unit, trained at the US Army's School of Americas in El Salvador in the 1980s. Also murdered were four Jesuit priests, their housekeeper Julia Elba Ramos, and her teenage daughter Celina Maricet Ramos (United Nations, 1993: 45–54).

2 According to the Ohio Department of Education, students in the Cleveland school district in 2013–2014 reflected the following racial and/or ethnic background: 66% African American/Black; 15% Hispanic/Latino; 15% White/Non-Hispanic; 3% Multiracial; and 1% Asian or Pacific Islander. The district is designated by the state of Ohio as 100% economically disadvantaged. The district has shrunk in size over the last decade, as families have enrolled in charter schools, private religious schools, or engaged in homeschooling. The average daily attendance, as noted on the State Department of Education website, was 38,725 for the 2012–2013 school year. More recently, with the establishment of several schools receiving considerably more resources from private partnerships, the district has seen an increase in enrollment.

3 Discussion of Juncture Two draws from earlier writing (Giraldo-Garcia and Galletta, 2015), and we appreciate the permission to include this material here from the *Journal of Urban Learning, Teaching, & Research.* Pseudonyms are used for youth researchers depicted here who did not continue in the later years of the project.

4 Actual names of youth researchers are used for those who continued well into the project, publicly presented the work in several venues, and whose creative authorship is reflected in our scholarship. In keeping with ethics reflecting participatory methodologies, youth researchers were consulted about the inclusion of their names in this chapter. At the time of writing this chapter, these young adults remain in contact with me and have access to drafts of this manuscript.

5 After some time and persistence, several members of the LiT core group actually secured a private meeting with the district leadership, during which it engaged in the issues at a more productive level.

6 We were later able to further explore performance as a way to critically engage listeners and to elicit stories, repositioning those attending from audience to participant (Fox, 2011). This occurred through the support of the American Educational

Research Association (AERA) as part of its Education Research to Performance Youth Apprentice project, which featured youth engaged in research with faculty in education research. All ten teams participated in a preparatory workshop in December 2014 and reconvened in April 2015 in Chicago with other teams to feature our work at the AERA annual conference. This work was supported and nurtured by the 2014 AERA president Joyce E. King, social psychologist Michelle Fine, and AERA Director of Professional Development and Social Justice George L. Wimberly.

7 It appears that the British Psychological Society offers some nuanced consideration concerning participant voice and identity, which currently the American Psychological Association does not.

REFERENCES

Aron, A., & Corne, S. (Eds.) (1994). *Writings for a liberation psychology: Ignacio Martín-Baró*. Cambridge, MA: Harvard University Press.

Apfelbaum, E. (1979). Relations of domination and movements of liberation: An analysis of paper between groups. In W. G. Austin, & S. Worchel (Eds.), *The social psychology of intergroup relations*. Monterey, CA: Brooks-Cole.

Ayala, J., & Galletta, A. (2012). Documenting disappearing spaces: Erasure and remembrance in two high school closures. *Peace and Conflict: Journal of Peace Psychology, 18*(2), 149–155.

Bakhtin, M. M. (1981). Discourse in the novel. In M. Holquist (Ed.), *The dialogic imagination: Four essays* (pp. 259–422). Austin: University of Texas Press.

Bell, D. A., Jr. (1995). Brown v. Board of Education and the interest convergence dilemma. In K. Crenshaw, N. Gotanda, G. Peller, & K. Thomas (Eds.), *Critical race theory: The key writings that formed the movement* (pp. 20–29). New York, NY: New Press.

Cammarota, J., & Fine, M. (Eds.) (2008). *Revolutionizing education: Youth participatory action research in motion*. NY: Routledge.

Chiu, L. F. (2006). Critical reflection: More than nuts and bolts. *Action Research, 4*(2), 183–203.

Collins, A. (2004). Theoretical resources. In D. Hook, P. Kiguwa, N. Mkhize, I. Parker, E. Burman, & A. Collins (Eds.), *Critical psychology*. Cape Town, South Africa: Juta and Company.

Crenshaw, K., Gotanda, N., Peller, G., & Thomas, K. (1995). *Critical race theory: The key writings that formed the movement*. NY: The New Press.

Drame, E. R., & Irby, D. (2016). *Black participatory research: Power, identity, and the struggle for justice in education*. NY: Palgrave MacMillan.

Fals-Borda, O. (2001). Participatory (action) research in social theory: Origins and challenges. In P. Reason & H. Bradbury (Eds.), *Handbook of action research: Participative inquiry and practice* (pp. 27–37). Thousand Oaks, CA: Sage Publications.

Fals-Borda, O., & Rahman, M. A. (1991). *Action and knowledge: Breaking the monopoly with participatory action-research*. NY: The Apex Press.

Fanon, F. (1952). *Black skin, white masks*. London: Pluto Press.

Fine, M., & Halkovic, A. (2014). A delicate and deliberate journey toward justice. In P. T. Coleman, M. Deutsch, & E. C. Marcus (Eds.), *The handbook of conflict resolution: Theory and practice* (3rd edn.). San Francisco: Jossey-Bass.

Fox, M. (2011). Literate bodies: Multigenerational participatory action research and embodied methodologies as critical literacy. *Journal of Adolescent and Adult Literacy 55*(4), 343–345.

Fox, M., Mediratta, K., Ruglis, J., Stoudt, B., Shah, S., & Fine, M. (2010). Critical youth engagement: Participatory action research and organizing. In L. R. Sherrod, J. Torney-Purta, & C. A. Flanagan (Eds.), *Handbook of research on civic engagement in youth* (pp. 621–649). Hoboken, NJ: John C. Wiley & Sons, Inc.

Freire, P. (1970/2000). *Pedagogy of the oppressed*. New York, NY: Continuum International Publishing Group.

Galletta, A., Bisesi, A., Evans, C., Giraldo-Garcia, R., Gullatt, L., Sterritt, M., Thomas, J., & Watson, T. (2014). *We the students: More than just a number*. Presentation at City Club of Cleveland on August 7, 2014. https://www.cityclub.org/events/we-the-students-more-than-just-a-number

Giraldo-Garcia, R., & Galletta, A. (2015). What happened to our sense of justice? Tracing agency, inquiry, and action in a youth participatory action research (PAR) project. *Journal of Urban Learning, Teaching, & Research*, *11*, 91–98.

Goffman, E. (1963). *Stigma: Notes on the management of a spoiled identity*. New York: Simon & Schuster, Inc.

Guishard, M. (2009). The false paths, the endless labors, the turns now this way and now that: Participatory action research, and the politics of inquiry. *Urban Review*, *41*(1), 85–105.

Guishard, M., Halkovic, A., Galletta, A., & Li, P. (2018). Toward epistemological ethics: Centering communities and social justice in qualitative research. *Forum: Qualitative Social Research*, *19*(3). DOI: http://dx.doi.org/10.17169/fqs-19.3.3145

Haney, W., & Lykes, M. B. (2000). Practice, participatory research and creative research designs: The continuing evolution of ethical guidelines for research. In F. Sherman, & B. Torbert (Eds.), *Transforming social inquiry, transforming social action: New paradigms for crossing the theory/practice divide in universities and communities*. NY: Springer.

Harding, S. (1992). After the neutrality ideal: Science, politics, and "strong objectivity". *Social Research*, *59*(3), 567–587.

Hook, D. (2004). Critical psychology: The basic coordinates. In D. Hook (Ed.), *Critical psychology* (pp. 10–23). South Africa: UCT Press.

jones, v., & Schilling, E. (Producers) (2011). *Lives in Transition: Eviction Notice*. Video production. https://vimeo.com/27023571

jones, v., Stewart, C., Ayala, J., & Galletta, A. (2015). Expressions of agency: Contemplating youth voice and adult roles in participatory action research. In J. Conner, R. Ebby-Rosin, & A. Slattery (Eds.), *National society for the study of education yearbook: Student voice in American educational policy* (pp. 135–152). NY: Teachers College Press.

Kemmis, S., & McTaggart, R. (2005). Participatory action research: Communicative action and the public sphere. In N. K. Denzin, & Y. S. Lincoln (Eds.), *The SAGE handbook of qualitative research* (3rd edn., pp. 559–603). Thousand Oaks, CA: SAGE Publications.

Kinloch, V., & San Pedro, T. (2014). The space between listening and storying: Foundations for projects in humanization. In D. Paris, & M. T. Winn (Eds.), *Humanizing research: Decolonizing qualitative inquiry with youth and communities* (pp. 21–42). Thousand Oaks, CA: SAGE.

Ladson-Billings, G., & Tate, W. F., IV. (1995). Toward a critical race theory of education. *Teachers College Record*, *97*(1), 47–68.

Lewin, K. (1948/1997). *Resolving social conflicts: Selected papers on group dynamics*. Washington, DC: American Psychological Association.

Marx, K. (1967). In L. D. Easton, & K. H. Guddat (Eds.), *Writings of the young Marx on philosophy and society*. NY: Anchor Books.

Matsuda, M. (1995). Looking to the bottom: Critical legal studies and reparations. In K. Crenshaw, N. Gotanda, G. Peller, & K. Thomas (Eds.), *Critical race theory: The key writings that formed the movement* (pp. 63–79). New York, NY: New Press.

Nicholls, R. (2009). Research and indigenous participation: Critical reflexive methods. *International Journal of Social Research Methodology 12*(2), 117–126.

Pratt, M. L. (1991). Arts of the Contact Zone. *Profession*, *91*, 33–40.

Santos, D. (2016). Pedagogical practice and storytelling: Promoting educational change through participation. In B. Zufiaurre, & M. Perez de Villarreal (Eds.), *Positive psychology for positive pedagogical actions* (pp. 23–36). Hauppauge, NY: Nova Science Publishers, Inc.

Solórzano, D. G., & Delgado-Bernal, D. (2001). Examining transformation resistance through critical race theory and Lat/Crit theory framework: Chicano and Chicana students in an urban context. *Urban Education*, *36*(3), 308–342.

Stoudt, B. G., Fox, M., & Fine, M. (2012). Contesting privilege with critical participatory action research. *Journal of Social Issues*, *68*(1), 178–193.

Subašic, E. (2012). Where to from here for the psychology of social change? Future directions for theory and practice. *Political Psychology*, *33*(1), 61–74.

Tajfel, H., & Turner, J. C. (1979). An integrative theory of intergroup conflict. In W. G. Austin, & S. Worchel (Eds.), *The social psychology of intergroup relations*. Monterey, CA: Brooks-Cole.

Torre, M. E. (2009). Participatory action research and critical race theory: Fueling spaces for nos-otras to research. *Urban Review 41*(1), 106–120.

Tuck, E. (2009). Suspending damage: A letter to communities. *Harvard Educational Review, 79*(3), 409–427.

Tuhiwai Smith, L. (1999). *Decolonizing methodologies: Research and indigenous peoples*. NY: St. Martin's Press.

United Nations (1993). Report of the UN Truth Commission in El Salvador. http://www.derechos.org/nizkor/salvador/informes/truth.html

Vieira Pinto, Á. (1960). *Consciencia e realidade nacional* (Volume II). Rio de Janeiro: Ministerio da Educação e Cultura, Instituto Superior de Estudos Brasileiros.

Weis, L., & Fine, M. (2004). *Working method: Research and social justice*. NY: Routledge.

Weis, L., & Fine, M. (2012). Critical bifocality and circuits of privilege: Expanding critical ethnographic theory and design. *Harvard Educational Review, 82*(2), 173–201.

PART IX

Environment

24

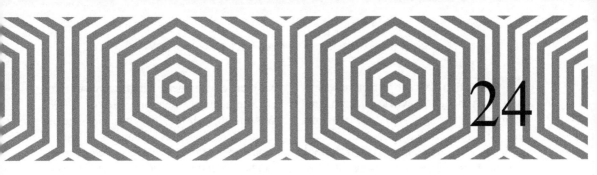

Using Social Psychology to Protect the Environment

Heather Barnes Truelove, P. Wesley Schultz and Ashley Jade Gillis

INTRODUCTION

Environmental problems are some of the most pressing issues of our time, and these problems are the direct result of human behavior. Overconsumption of natural resources, pollution of water, air, and land, and loss of biodiversity resulting from habitat destruction are just a few of the critical issues we face. As a case in point, the Earth's climate is warming at an unprecedented rate (IPCC, 2014), and the warming is the direct result of greenhouse gases emitted from human activity. World leaders have called upon scientific experts to assess the extent of the damage and to make recommendations about ways to mitigate this warming. Climate scientists have been called upon to measure and model the effects of increasing greenhouse gas concentrations in the atmosphere; biologists to study the damage to existing ecosystems from warming temperatures; and engineers to assess whether existing infrastructure can withstand rising sea level. All groups agree: projections are bad and will get worse with current levels of greenhouse gas emissions. Now what? How do we change things? How do we encourage people to reduce emissions? Considering the situation is already bad, how do people adapt when it gets worse? These questions can't be answered by the climate scientist or the biologist or the engineer. These questions must be answered by social and behavioral scientists and, particularly, psychologists who have an expertise in understanding human behavior (Clayton and Brook, 2005).

Increasingly, social psychologists are contributing to conversations regarding environmental problems such as climate change (Clayton et al., 2015a; 2015b; Schultz and Kaiser, 2012; Steg and Vlek, 2009). Social psychology, in particular, has been drawn upon to answer questions about people's relationships with the natural environment and to understand and promote pro-environmental behavior (PEB). Consider Kurt Lewin's (1936) formula describing behavior as a function of the interaction between person and environment. Although Lewin's 'environment' was mostly referring to the *social* environment, this formula has clear implications for the *natural* environment as well. Indeed, much of the psychology focusing on PEBs stems from social psychology. This chapter reviews the state of the research on social psychological approaches to promoting PEBs and points to fruitful areas for future research.

WHAT IS PEB?

What do the following behaviors have in common: purchasing an energy-efficient refrigerator, maintaining the correct tire pressure in your car, line drying laundry, and choosing a vegetarian meal instead of beef? Of course, they are all examples of PEBs. The efficient refrigerator uses less energy, the correct tire pressure requires less gasoline, the line drying saves energy from running the clothes dryer, and the beef substitution saves greenhouse gas emissions from livestock raising, transport, and refrigeration. Now that we've established what they have in common, think for a moment about how varied they are. They involve different domains: household, travel, food. They involve different financial resources, ranging from expensive to no cost. They involve different time commitments: one-time, monthly, daily. They have different impacts on the environment: major positive impact, little discernable impact. It should be no surprise that the sheer number of PEBs and the distinct differences between them make for a complicated field of study. To make the diverse array of PEBs manageable, researchers studying PEB have utilized varying strategies to group PEBs into categories.

Intent versus Impact

One important consideration when grouping PEBs into categories is the distinction between environmental impact versus pro-environmental intention (Stern, 2000; Whitmarsh, 2009). To measure PEBs, researchers generally compose a list of behaviors that could be considered environmentally friendly and then ask participants to report how often they engage in these behaviors. The more PEBs people do, and the more often they do them, the more they are presumed to behave pro-environmentally. However, PEBs vary greatly in terms of environmental impact. For example, suppose Simone turns off the faucet while brushing her teeth, waits for a full load of dishes before running the dishwasher, and unplugs her cell phone so it isn't charging overnight. Meanwhile, Rithvik recently installed attic insulation, but does none of the other things Simone does. Thus, on a four-item behavior list, Simone would appear more pro-environmental than Rithvik having done three-out-of-four PEBs versus one-out-of-four PEBs. But, who is really more pro-environmental? In terms of actual impact on the natural environment, it's clearly Rithvik because of the large energy savings that can result from using less energy to heat and cool the home following the insulation installation.

This example illustrates why researchers have found it useful to define PEBs in terms of *impact* rather than *intention* (Whitmarsh, 2009). *Impact-oriented* behaviors are those that actually affect the natural environment – altering the availability of natural resources regardless of the reason for adopting the behavior (Stern, 2000; Whitmarsh, 2009). In turn, *intent-oriented* behaviors are defined in terms of a person's motivation to positively alter the environment (Stern, 2000; Whitmarsh, 2009). From this distinction, researchers have noted that intent-oriented behavior does not necessarily coincide with a positive environmental impact (Gatersleben et al., 2002; Stern, 2000; Whitmarsh, 2009). In fact, some evidence suggests that members of the UK public who report engaging in intent-oriented behavior may actually conserve *less* than their non-intentional counterparts

(Whitmarsh, 2009). This divergence between intentions and impacts could result from misperceptions about the environmental consequences of different actions – a point to which we return later (Attari et al., 2010; Truelove and Parks, 2012; Whitmarsh, 2009). Overall, the impact–intent distinction has allowed researchers to focus on identifying high-impact behaviors and on people's beliefs and motives for behaving pro-environmentally (Gatersleben et al., 2002; Stern, 2000; Whitmarsh, 2009).

PEB Categorizations

General pro-environmental behavior

Out of the many ways to behave pro-environmentally, individuals can protest about environmental issues, vote for environmentally-friendly policies, purchase products with less packaging, and influence the actions of organizations or communities to which they belong. In fact, each one of these behaviors falls, respectively, into the four categories of general PEB proposed by Stern (2000): *activism*, *non-activist public-sphere behaviors*, *private-sphere behaviors*, and *other environmentally significant behaviors*. This categorization emerged empirically from a factor analysis of US residents' reported behavior and behavioral intentions, and each category has a distinct pattern of psychological and socio-demographic predictors (Stern, 2000). Stern (2000) further subdivided the category of private-sphere behaviors according to the type of decision involved: *purchase of major household goods or services*, *use and maintenance of environmentally important goods*, *waste disposal*, and *green consumerism* (Figure 24.1).

Similarly, Kaiser and colleagues' (2000) General Ecological Behavior (GEB) has been used to group PEB into six categories: *energy conservation*, *mobility and transportation*, *waste avoidance*, *consumerism*, *recycling*, and *vicarious, social behaviors toward conservation* (Kaiser and Wilson, 2000; Kaiser et al., 2003). Kaiser and Wilson (2004) compared the six-factor model of PEB to a unidimensional model of PEB using data from a sample of 895 Swiss residents. Results revealed that, although the six-factor model was a better statistical fit to the data, from a practical standpoint, the more complicated six-factor model did not predict the data appreciably better than the one-factor model. Considering PEBs are often highly correlated, thinking of PEB as one general class of behaviors can be useful (Kaiser and Wilson, 2004), though more recent work has continued to attempt to categorize PEBs into distinct clusters.

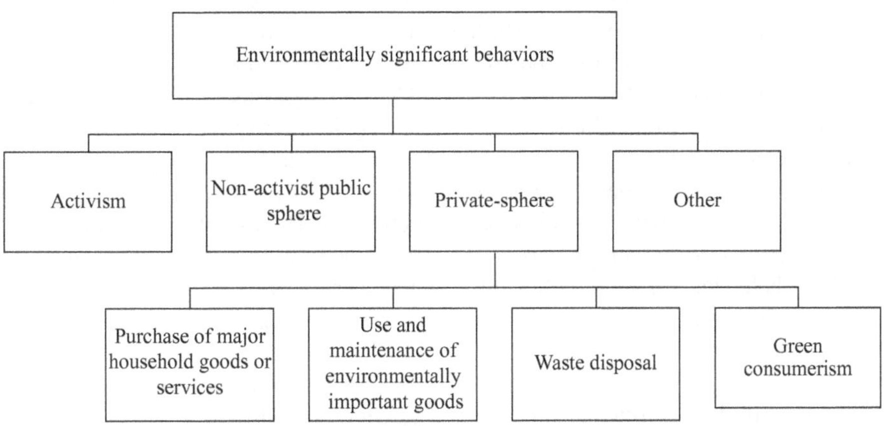

Figure 24.1 Depiction of Stern's (2000) classification of environmentally significant behavior

Household Energy Behaviors

Hear that buzzing sound? The marvels of technology are all around us and we need not look outside of our homes to see it – just think of how many products and devices are plugged into your walls. In the United States, for example, energy use in homes accounts for a whopping 38% of total national carbon emissions (Dietz et al., 2009). Research suggests that if residents adopted currently-available energy-efficient technologies and slightly altered how they used existing household technologies, the United States could reduce its household emissions by 20% and its total emissions by 7.4% (Dietz et al., 2009). This reflects two types of behaviors that researchers commonly refer to as *efficiency upgrades* and *curtailment behaviors*. Efficiency-improving actions, such as installing energy-efficient appliances and upgrading attic insulation, require a one-time financial investment. Curtailment behaviors like waiting until your dishwasher is full before running it and turning off computers before going to bed at night require no monetary expenditure but must be repeated frequently to achieve any significant savings. Researchers who have used this dichotomous behavior categorization have generally defined efficiency upgrades and curtailment behaviors in terms of how they perceive the consumer financial cost and frequency of the action. In terms of these two attributes, efficiency upgrades are high cost and low frequency and curtailment behaviors are low/no cost and high frequency (Karlin et al., 2014; Laitner et al., 2009).

However, determining whether specific PEBs qualify as curtailment or efficiency behaviors is not always clear-cut because not all household behaviors fit well within this dichotomy. Even though efficiency upgrades are marked by financial investment, sometimes behaviors that cost relatively little, or even nothing at all, like getting car tune-ups and maintaining the correct car tire pressure, are considered efficiency upgrades because they increase efficiency and are relatively infrequent (Gardner and Stern, 2008). Oftentimes, these infrequent low cost/no cost behaviors, which might be the easiest behaviors to promote, wind up getting neglected in behavior classification schemes (Karlin et al., 2014).

Dietz et al. (2009) provided a more refined view of household energy PEBs with their 'Behavioral Wedge'. In their categorization, Dietz et al. (2009) pack up the American house in five boxes that serve as further subdivisions of Stern's (2000) *purchase* and *use* of household goods categories: *weatherization* (e.g., improving attic insulation), *energy-efficient equipment* (e.g., buying an electric vehicle), *maintenance* (e.g., getting routine car tune-ups), *adjustments* (e.g. using cold rinse setting on washing machine), and *daily actions* (e.g., unplugging electronics not in use). This categorization scheme parcels out those infrequent low cost/no cost behaviors into maintenance behaviors (infrequent but habitual low cost actions) and adjustments (one-time no cost actions) rather than grouping them with other low cost actions (i.e., curtailment/daily) or other efficiency-improving actions (i.e., efficiency upgrades/energy-efficient equipment).

Laypersons' Perceptions of PEB

Dietz et al.'s (2009) categorization scheme for PEBs was driven mainly by the researchers' conceptualization as experts. Alternatively, Stern's (2000) was based on laypeople's perspectives as the categories emerged from factor analysis driven by data about how frequently people engage in the behaviors. The use of few attributes (such as frequency) to distinguish between PEBs is a major criticism of many of the existing layperson-driven categorization schemes (Karlin et al., 2014; Larson et al., 2015). More recent research has delved deeper into laypeople's perceptions of PEBs.

Research on laypersons' perceptions of PEBs has largely focused on the knowledge gap between experts and laypersons. Non-experts generally lack awareness about which behaviors mitigate climate change (Truelove and Parks, 2012) and which conserve the most energy (Attari et al., 2010) and water (Attari, 2014). When asked to identify the single-most effective action to reduce energy and water use, people most often report curtailment actions, with turning off the lights and taking shorter showers as the most commonly mentioned behaviors, rather than known higher impact efficiency actions (Attari et al., 2010; Attari, 2014). People also routinely misperceive the impact of their own behavior, underestimating their energy consumption by a factor of 2.8 (Attari et al., 2010) and water consumption by a factor of 2.0 (Attari, 2014). Additionally, people generally underestimate the impact of objectively high-impact behaviors and overestimate the impact of objectively low-impact behaviors (Attari et al., 2010; Attari, 2014; Truelove and Parks, 2012).

Not all research on laypersons' perceptions has been focused on inaccuracies, however. Researchers have also investigated perceptions of PEB costliness – an attribute that has otherwise been subject to researchers' perspectives (Tobler et al., 2012). As opposed to defining cost solely in monetary terms, Tobler et al. (2012) assessed perceived cost in terms of *time*, *inconvenience*, and *discomfort* in addition to *financial cost* among a Swiss sample. Transportation behaviors (e.g., avoiding car use for commuting to work and avoiding flights for holidays) were perceived as more costly than a category of PEBs that Tobler et al. (2012) define as 'low cost', which include PEBs like recycling paper, consuming seasonal food, and curtailment actions such as setting your thermostat lower in colder seasons and using warm water sparingly. Behaviors like electing politicians committed to climate protection, offsetting CO_2 emissions financially, and donating to climate protection projects were perceived as the most costly (Tobler et al., 2012). Subjective views about cost and misperceptions of environmental impacts, while of central importance, give us only a narrow view through the people's eye. Seeing the fuller picture requires investigating perceptions of additional PEB attributes and how these perceptions form.

Which Behaviors Should We Target?

Bridging together what is known about experts' categorizations and laypeople's perceptions, recommendations can be made about which PEBs should be targeted for interventions. We forward three non-mutually exclusive criteria that should be considered when selecting PEBs for interventions.

Environmental impacts of behavior

Perhaps the most obvious criterion for choosing behavior is its environmental impact – behaviors with higher impacts should generally be chosen over those with lower impacts. Given what we know about laypersons' (mis-)perceptions of environmental impact, expert knowledge should weigh heavily for behavior selection. Energy behavior researchers have composed lists of the most effective actions for reducing energy use (Gardner and Stern, 2008) and water use (Inskeep and Attari, 2014) in the home (Figure 24.2). These behaviors have the benefit of having quantifiable impacts – we can measure the kWh saved from installing an energy-efficient refrigerator and the gallons of water saved from installing a low-flow showerhead. Additionally, environmental scientists continue to enhance our understanding of the impacts of various actions through the use of life-cycle analysis, which better informs the prioritization of PEBs (Steg and Vlek, 2009).

Barriers to engaging in behavior

Effective interventions rely on identifying the barriers to behavior change and selecting PEBs with removable barriers. Researchers

Activity/Domain	*Efficiency action*	*Percent savings*	*Curtailment action*	*Percent savings*
Water-related actions				
Flushing	Replace standard toilets with WaterSense-labeled toilets	18.6%	Reduce daily toilet flushes by 25% (3.3 fewer flushes per household per day)	7.3%
Clothes washing	Replace clothes washer with an ENERGY STAR-labeled washer	16.7%	Only wash a full load of clothes (or adjust water level in washer to match load size)	7.9%
Showering	Replace standard showerheads with WaterSense-labeled showerheads	1.9%	Take shorter showers (5 min instead of 8.2 min)	8.2%
Faucet use	Install WaterSense labeled faucets (or equivalent flow-reducing aerator)	5.4%	Reduce the amount of time the faucet is left running by 2 min per day	4.4%
Dishwashing	Wash dirty dishes in an Energy Star-labeled dishwasher instead of hand-washing	2.1%	Do not pre-rinse dishes before putting in the dishwasher	0.4%
Energy-related actions				
Transportation	Buy a more fuel-efficient automobile (30.7 vs. 20 mpg EPA average-adjusted composite)	13.5%	Carpool to work with one other person	Up to 4.2%
Heating	Install/upgrade attic insulation and ventilation	Up to 5.0%	Turn down thermostat from 72 °F to 68 °F during the day and to 65 °F during the night	2.8%
Lighting	Replace 85% of all incandescent bulbs with equally bright CFL bulbs	4.0%	Do not leave one 60-watt bulb on all night	0.5%
Refrigeration/ Freezing	Install a more efficient refrigerator/ freezer (an Energy Star unit vs. a 19–21.4 ft^3 top-freezer unit bought from 1993–2000)	1.9%	Turn up the refrigerator thermostat from 33 °F to 38 °F and the freezer thermostat from –5 °F to 0 °F	0.5%
Clothes washing	Install a more efficient waster (an Energy Star washer vs. a 2001 or older non-Energy Star unit)	1.1%	Change washer temperature settings from hot wash, warm rinse to warm wash, cold rinse	1.2%

Figure 24.2 The abbreviated water and energy short lists for the American public

Note: Not all activities/domains are included. Only the actions with the highest savings for each activity/domain are included.
Source: Adapted and abbreviated from Gardner and Stern (2008) and Inskeep and Attari (2014).

have identified and organized barriers to PEB in several different ways. Lorenzoni et al. (2007) identified barriers perceived by the UK public at two levels: *individual* (e.g., lack of knowledge, distrust in information sources, belief that technology will save us) and *social* (e.g., lack of enabling initiatives, social norms, lack of action by governments and industry). Kollmuss and Agyeman (2002) also proposed a two-category scheme of *internal* (e.g., motivation, values, and knowledge) and *external* (e.g., factors related to institutions, economics, and society/culture) barriers. We can think of these barriers as *psychological* and *structural*, respectively, as Gifford (2011) has noted. Inherently, structural barriers are more difficult for interventions to address and this should factor into the behavior selection process. Gifford (2011) further distinguished psychological barriers, which exist within multiple levels, into seven categories: *limited cognition, ideologies, other people, sunk costs, discordance, perceived risks*, and *limited behavior*. Importantly, the many obstacles that prevent individuals from engaging in PEBs are interrelated, complex, and specific to certain people, behaviors, and contexts (Gifford et al., 2011; Lorenzoni et al., 2007).

With this in mind, we note that the most effective way of identifying the barriers of target behaviors, and determining whether interventions can remove these barriers, involves uncovering the specific barriers that the target audience perceives (McKenzie-Mohr, 2000; McKenzie-Mohr and Schultz, 2014).

Likelihood of successful behavior change

Determining the probability of successful behavior change involves assessing not just *whether* interventions can address the identified barriers but also *the extent* to which interventions can realistically address them (McKenzie-Mohr, 2011). Through a review of data on the most effective interventions to change PEBs, Dietz et al. (2009) calculated estimates of behaviors' *plasticity* – an indicator of how probable it is that people will adopt the behavior after an intervention. Their approach of determining behavior plasticity makes it possible to estimate the likelihood of success for different types of interventions (e.g., information campaigns, financial incentives, normative influence) and for specific behaviors (Dietz et al., 2009). Another simple indicator of the likelihood of success is whether the behavior is one-time or repetitive. Promoting habitual behavior is generally more difficult than one-time behaviors (McKenzie-Mohr, 2000), which has been confirmed by the low plasticity estimates of daily/curtailment behaviors (Dietz et al., 2009).

PEB SPILLOVER

In addition to evaluating an intervention's effectiveness at changing the targeted PEB, a flurry of recent research interest has centered on whether an intervention can also change non-targeted PEBs. Performance of one PEB is often assumed to positively spillover onto, or increase the likelihood of, additional PEBs (Department for Environment Food and Rural Affairs, 2008). Recycling is often viewed as this 'gateway' behavior, with policymakers hoping and assuming that if only the public would begin recycling then they would perform additional higher impact PEBs such as buying fuel-efficient cars and energy-efficient appliances. However, it's easy to imagine people you know who recycle committedly to justify driving an SUV (negative spillover). Clearly, both positive and negative spillover can occur. Recent research has investigated when, and why, they occur and what factors increase their likelihood (Nilsson et al., 2016).

Positive PEB spillover is mostly explained in the literature in terms of consistency and identity effects (for a synthesis of PEB spillover findings, see Truelove et al., 2014). Drawing on the social psychological theories of the Foot-in-the Door effect (Freedman and Fraser, 1966), Cognitive Dissonance theory (Festinger, 1957), and Self-Perception Theory (Bem, 1967), performance of an initial PEB is expected to activate salient identities (Cornelissen et al. 2008; Poortinga et al., 2013; Van der Werff et al., 2014) and elicit desires to be consistent in subsequent, related behavior (Van der Werff et al., 2014). When someone agrees to donate to an environmental organization, environmental identity is activated. If they are subsequently asked to volunteer for a beach clean-up, then the effects of their heightened identity and desires to be consistent make them more likely to join the clean-up effort compared to someone who had not previously donated (Figure 24.3).

Negative PEB spillover has mostly been explained in the literature in terms of licensing effects. According to moral licensing theory (Jordan et al., 2011; Zhong et al., 2009), people have a 'bank' of moral credits and they balance their credit across behaviors like a moral balance sheet (Dhar and Simonson, 1999; Merritt et al., 2010). Performance of a moral behavior results in a boost to the performer's moral self-worth, giving them some credits to burn. Thus, when asked to perform a subsequent moral behavior, the performer relies on their accrued moral credentials

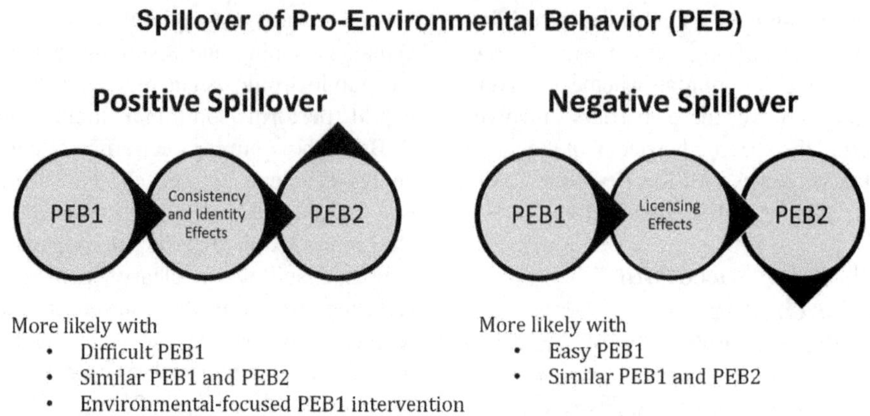

Figure 24.3 Positive and negative pro-environmental behavior (PEB) spillover conceptualization

and refuses the behavior, returning moral self-worth levels to a sort of stable baseline (Sachdeva et al., 2009). As seen with the Value–Belief–Norm (VBN) theory, PEB can be viewed as a type of moral behavior (Steg et al., 2005; Stern, 2000). Thus, applied to PEB, moral licensing suggests that when Isaac purchases an energy-efficient furnace, he may then be more likely to keep the heater running in the winter (Figure 24.7).

Increasing Positive Spillover and Decreasing Negative Spillover

Clearly, from an applied standpoint, increasing the potential for positive spillover while minimizing negative spillover is ideal. One thing researchers and policymakers should keep in mind is that behavioral difficulty matters. When the initial behavior is difficult, positive spillover is more likely to occur because the initial difficult behavior signals an environmental identity ('I must really be an environmentalist considering I've just performed such a difficult behavior'). With this activated identity, individuals are then more likely to display consistency effects, as described above (Gneezy et al., 2012). On the other hand, performance of an easy, initial behavior does not signal these identity effects and can result in negative spillover (Gneezy et al., 2012).

Additionally, spillover effects are amplified when the initial and subsequent behaviors are similar. Of course, individual perception is what matters most when determining whether behaviors are 'similar'. If someone views an initial behavior as environmentally friendly, then we expect performance of that behavior to activate consistency effects and positively spill over to other behaviors also perceived as environmentally friendly. Additionally, behaviors perceived to be in the same domain can lead to more positive or negative spillover, depending on the difficulty of the initial behavior. For example, doing an initial difficult weatherization behavior, such as buying an energy-efficient A/C unit, would be more likely to positively spill over to installing attic insulation than purchasing a fuel-efficient car. Additionally, the easy behavior of turning lights off when leaving a room would be more likely to negatively spillover to installation of energy efficient light bulbs than caulking around one's windows.

Finally, the framing of the intervention matters. Researchers have compared the effectiveness of intervention framing on eliciting positive PEB spillover, though few studies have been conducted in this area. One recent study in the United States found evidence of positive spillover from hotel towel reuse to turning lights off when leaving the hotel room after an intervention that elicited varying levels of commitment to reuse hotel towels upon guest check in (Baca-Motes et al., 2013). Looking at more long-term effects of spillover, among a sample of Danish students, both a monetary and a praise-focused intervention to increase green purchasing positively spilled over to a host of other PEBs six weeks later, though the effects were small (Lanzini and Thøgersen, 2014), and on an even longer time scale, among German samples, environmental (but not monetary) framing of an intervention to reduce electricity use positively spilled over to intention to perform a variety of additional PEBs (Steinhorst et al., 2015) and low carbon policy support (Steinhorst and Matthies, 2016).

MAJOR SOCIAL PSYCHOLOGICAL THEORIES APPLIED TO PEBS

It's clear that people perform numerous behaviors every day that affect the natural environment, and thus, there is considerable potential for encouraging PEBs. Interventions to promote these PEBs are most likely to be successful if they are grounded in theory (Schultz and Estrada-Hollenbeck, 2017). Several social psychological theories have been applied to PEBs, which has increased our understanding of the factors that relate to PEB performance and also pointed to areas potentially ripe for interventions. Although we touch on elements of each of these theories in our discussion below, we focus on the first four theories listed because they have been widely and recently used in the application of social psychology to PEB.

- Theory of Planned Behavior (Ajzen, 1991; Ajzen and Fishbein, 2005)
- Value–Belief–Norm theory (Stern et al., 1999)
- Protection Motivation Theory (Rogers, 1975; Rogers and Prentice-Dunn, 1997)
- Focus Theory of Normative Conduct (Cialdini et al., 1990)
- Social dilemmas (Kopelman et al., 2002)
- Cognitive dissonance (Dickerson et al., 1992; Festinger, 1957)
- Self-determination Theory (Deci and Ryan, 2011; Pelletier et al., 1998)
- Health Belief Model (Janz and Becker, 1984; Lindsay and Strathman, 1997; Nisbet and Gick, 2008)
- Norm Activation Model (Joireman et al., 2001; Schwartz, 1977)

Theory of Planned Behavior

Take a moment to think about the following questions. How many people do you know who are in favor of alternative energies (such as wind and solar power)? How many of these people actually use wind or solar power in their homes or purchase alternative energy sources from their utility companies? If you are like the authors, then your answer to the first question is probably 'a lot' and your answer to the second is 'not a lot'. The Theory of Planned Behavior (TPB) can help understand why pro-environmental attitudes don't always translate to PEB.

The Theory of Planned Behavior (TPB; Ajzen, 1991) and its predecessor the Theory of Reasoned Action (Fishbein and Ajzen, 1975) have been used in social psychology to predict a wide range of behaviors, including health behaviors, moral behaviors, goal-directed behaviors, and group performance, among others (Armitage and Conner, 2001). The major premises of the TPB are that behavior performance flows directly from intention to perform the behavior and intention is influenced by belief-driven attitudes, subjective norms, and perceived behavioral control (PBC), as defined below (Ajzen and Fishbein, 2005; Figure 24.4).

- **Attitudes**: positive or negative evaluations of performing the behavior
- **Subjective norms**: perceived pressures from important others to perform a behavior
- **Perceived behavioral control (PBC)**: beliefs about capability of performing the behavior

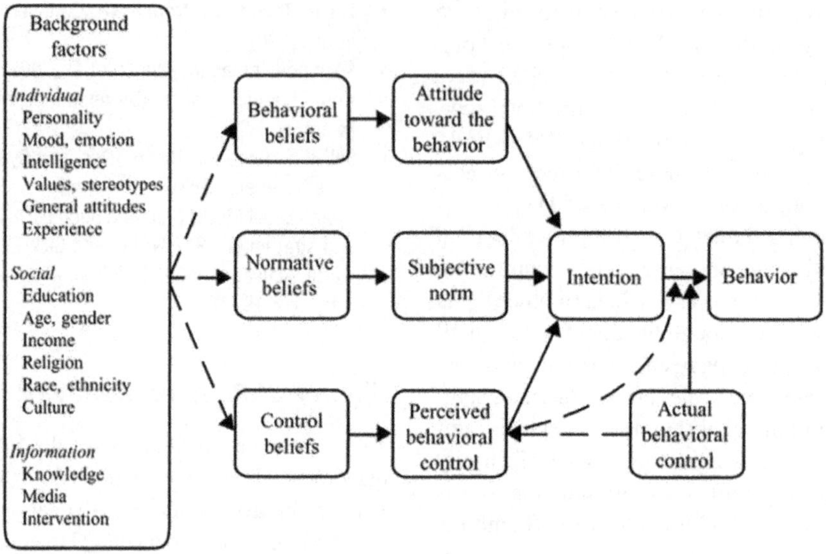

Figure 24.4 Depiction of the Theory of Planned Behavior

Source: Reproduced from Ajzen and Fishbein (2005).

The TPB easily lends itself to application to PEBs. For example, consider the case of Jimmy, who has a favorable attitude toward composting, feels social support from his neighbors and friends to compost (high subjective norm), and has the knowledge and skills needed to create a composting area in his backyard (high perceived behavioral control). We would expect Jimmy to be more likely to compost than Tony who, like Jimmy, has a favorable attitude toward composting but who knows few people who compost (low subjective norm) and doesn't have a backyard to his new apartment where he can compost (low perceived behavioral control).

Many studies have found support for the TPB in predicting PEB intention and performance. Specifically, the TPB has been successful at predicting Dutch and Canadian residents' intentions to use public and alternative transportation (de Groot and Steg, 2007a; Harland et al., 1999; Heath and Gifford, 2002), British residents' intentions to consume organic vegetables (Sparks and Shepherd, 1992), Canadian residents' intentions to compost and recycle (Taylor and Todd, 1995), US residents' intentions to stay at environmentally-friendly hotels (Han et al., 2010), and Dutch residents' intentions to use unbleached paper and energy saving light bulbs, and turn off the sink faucet while brushing teeth (Harland et al., 1999), as well as the actual use of public transportation among a Canadian sample (Heath and Gifford, 2002).

Further several studies have shown that interventions aimed at changing beliefs within the TPB (i.e., attitudes, subjective norm, and perceived behavioral control-related beliefs) can change behavior (Bamberg and Schmidt, 1998; Heath and Gifford, 2002; Litvine and Wüstenhagen, 2011). For example, Litvine and Wüstenhagen (2011) created a campaign that provided Swiss residents with information combatting common behavioral beliefs, normative beliefs, and control beliefs related to purchasing renewable energy. Messages emphasized the environmental benefits of purchasing green electricity (behavioral beliefs), that prominent citizens buy green electricity (normative beliefs), and the ease and convenience of the process (control beliefs). Those who received behavioral beliefs-focused information and those who received information simultaneously targeting all three TPB constructs were more likely to purchase renewable energy than controls who received no intervention.

Although the TPB has been relatively successful in its application to PEB, the TPB has been criticized for relying mostly on self-reported behavior instead of actual behavior and for the relatively weak strength of subjective norms to predict intention (Armitage and Conner, 2001). To the first point, there has been a simultaneous wide push within conservation psychology in general to focus on actual behavior instead of, or in addition to, self-reported behavior (e.g., working with utility companies to gather actual energy consumption instead of self-reported energy-related behavior performance) and many researchers are heeding this call (e.g., Baca-Motes et al., 2013; Litvine and Wüstenhagen, 2011; Schultz et al., 2007). In regard to the latter criticism, some have argued that subjective norms do not adequately capture the social pressures on people's behavior and that additional social and norm-related variables should be added to the TPB (Armitage and Conner, 2001). As a result, additional constructs have been added to the TPB to improve its ability to predict PEBs. Variables that have been studied as additions to TPB include:

- **Personal norms**: feelings of personal moral obligation to act (Harland et al., 1999; Kaiser, 2006; Litvine and Wüstenhagen, 2011; Nigbur et al., 2010)
- **Descriptive norms**: rates of adoption of a behavior in a given situation (Heath and Gifford, 2002; Nigbur et al., 2010),
- **Self-identity**: how one identifies oneself (Nigbur et al., 2010; Sparks and Shepherd, 1992)
- **Response efficacy**: belief that performance of behavior will have desired outcome (Lam, 2006; Litvine and Wüstenhagen, 2011).

Value–Belief–Norm Theory

Personal norms, the construct most commonly added to the TPB to predict PEB, are the central feature of the VBN theory of PEB (Stern, 2000). The VBN theory (Stern, 2000; Stern et al., 1999) grew out of Schwartz's (1977) moral norm-activation model of altruistic behavior, which argued that people acted altruistically because they were aware of harmful consequences to other people and because they felt personally responsible to take action. For example, if I saw someone get a flat tire after swerving to avoid hitting my kitten, I would likely feel a strong moral norm to help them.

Although the norm activation model was originally applied to helping other people, Stern extended Schwartz's model by suggesting that people act not just because of a recognition of consequences to other people but can also act out of a recognition of harm to the natural environment (Stern, 2000; Stern et al., 1999). Thus, the model could potentially explain people's PEB. For example, a person's decision to purchase a fuel-efficient automobile can be viewed as altruistic to the extent that the behavior comes out of a desire to lessen the effect of pollution on the self, others, and the biosphere.

Unlike the TPB, where intention is considered to be the main driver of behavior, in the VBN, personal norms are considered the main precursor of behavior. Pro-environmental norms are theorized to become activated when someone realizes that a valued object is threatened (awareness of consequences; AC) and that one's actions could alleviate the threat (ascription of responsibility, AR). As the VBN name implies, abstract values (i.e., egoistic, social-altruistic, and biospheric values) are thought to influence more specific beliefs, which in turn influence norms, and finally, behavior.

Values are abstract guiding principles (Schwartz and Bilsky, 1987; 1990). Three types of values are included in the VBN, as defined below (de Groot and Steg, 2007b; Stern, 2000).

- **Biospheric values**: value the natural environment for its inherent qualities
- **Egoistic values**: value the natural environment for the benefits it can bring to oneself
- **Social-altruistic values**: value the natural environment for the benefits it can bring to humans as a whole, society, family, or future generations

Beliefs are more specific than values. The VBN includes the following three beliefs:

- **New ecological paradigm**: a pro-environmental worldview (Dunlap and Van Liere, 1978; Dunlap et al., 2000)
- **Awareness of consequences (AC)**: recognition that environmental problems have negative consequences on valued objects, i.e., the biosphere (bio), self (ego), and society (social-altruistic) (Stern, 2000; Stern et al., 1999)
- **Ascription of responsibility (AR)**: feelings of responsibility to act to reduce environmental problems (Stern, 2000)

In the VBN, the main variables are thought to function as a mediation chain where each variable influences the next one in the causal chain, while not necessarily influencing behavior directly (Steg et al., 2005; Figure 24.5).

The VBN has been shown to predict a wide variety of PEBs, including support for energy policies among Dutch participants (Steg et al., 2005) and Americans' consumer behavior (Stern et al., 1999), environmental citizenship behaviors (Stern et al., 1999), willingness to sacrifice for environmental protection (Stern et al., 1999), and environmental activism (Stern et al., 1999). Although few researchers have tested the VBN in its entirety, several studies have tested models similar in spirit to the VBN, though using different measures of the constructs than those proposed by Stern. These VBN-esque models have been shown to predict political and activist behavior intention among Swedish residents (Gärling et al., 2003), support for pro-environmental tax policy among Korean students (Kim and Shin, 2015), intentions to purchase cloth diapers among Canadian mothers (Follows and Jobber, 2000), intentions to conserve energy among Italian homeowners (Fornara et al., 2016), and general PEB performance among Swedish individuals (Nordlund and Garvill, 2002). One of these studies substituted intention for norms, suggesting a hybrid between the VBN and TPB (Follows and Jobber, 2000).

VBN and TPB Hybrid

By now, you may be wondering which of these two theories is preferred when investigating PEBs. In a head-to-head comparison between the two theories in predicting German students' general PEB, the TPB was

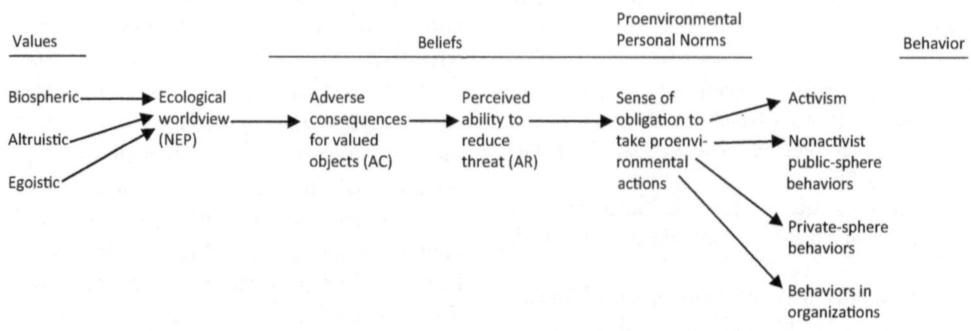

Figure 24.5 Depiction of the Value–Belief–Norm Theory

Source: Reproduced from Stern, 2000.

superior to the VBN in the amount of explained variance in behavior and also the modeling of the relationships between variables within the model (Kaiser et al., 2005). However, as is likely clear by now, several of the additions that have been proposed to the TPB exist within the VBN and vice versa. Thus, several studies have suggested a hybrid theory that incorporates key elements from each of the theories (Bamberg and Möser, 2007; Hunecke et al., 2001; Oom do Valle et al., 2005; Oreg and Katz-Gerro, 2006; Turaga et al., 2010).

Klöckner's (2013) meta-analysis of 56 different datasets predicting a variety of PEBs found that a hybrid VBN–TPB model with the addition of habit predicted PEB well. The TPB constructs of intention and PBC directly predicted behavior (along with habit); and attitude, personal norms and subjective norms directly predicted intention.

Protection Motivation Theory

Although much of the research predicting performance of PEBs has used the VBN, TPB, or some combination of the two, more recent research has applied the Protection Motivation Theory (PMT; Rippetoe and Rogers, 1987; Rogers, 1975; 1983) to PEBs. Historically, the PMT had been mostly applied to health risk communications and has been shown to be successful in doing so (Floyd et al., 2000).

The PMT argues that people evaluate potential threats through two successive appraisals. First, in the **risk appraisal**, they evaluate the risk of the threat by estimating the likelihood of the event and the severity of the threat should it occur. If the threat is deemed a risk, then, in the **coping appraisal**, they evaluate their ability to perform actions to reduce the threat (self-efficacy) as well as the behaviors' ability to actually reduce the threat (response efficacy). If they perceive they can cope with the threat, then they undertake protective behaviors. If they do not perceive that they can cope with the threat, then they may undertake maladaptive behaviors, such as fatalism, hopelessness, wishful thinking, and avoidance (Rippetoe and Rogers, 1987). The main variables of the PMT are defined below (Figure 24.6).

- **Risk perception**: beliefs about the likelihood and severity of an event
- **Self-efficacy**: belief that one is capable of performing an action
- **Response efficacy (outcome expectancy)**: belief that performance of an action will result in desired outcome

Applying PMT to PEBs is an easy transition. Many people are worried about environmental problems such as climate change; however,

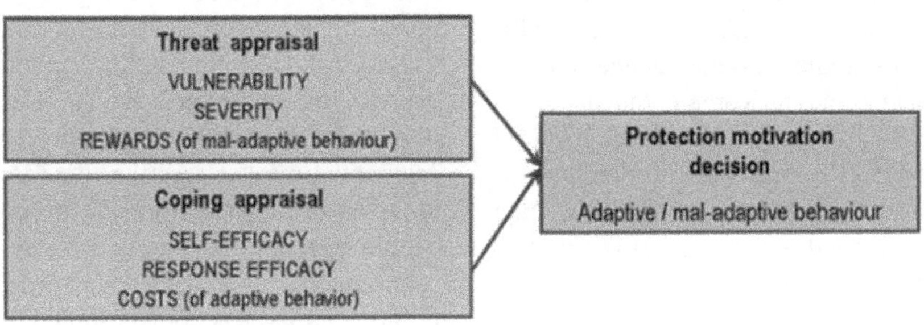

Figure 24.6 Protection Motivation Theory

Source: Reproduced from Bockarjova and Steg, 2014.

risk perceptions are not fully covered in the VBN or TPB. Additionally, neither VBN nor TPB adequately captures people's common feeling that their environmental efforts are just a drop in the bucket (Bonniface and Henley, 2008). These feelings certainly have a basis in truth. In actuality, the fact that I drive a fuel-efficient car will have no discernable impact on the environment. However, referring back to Dietz and Gardner's work (Dietz et al., 2009; Gardner and Stern, 2008), this behavior can have a huge impact if aggregated across millions of people. Nevertheless feelings of low response efficacy or outcome expectancy are not adequately captured in the VBN nor the TPB.

Recently, a handful of studies have used the PMT constructs to predict PEB (Bockarjova and Steg, 2014; Homburg and Stolberg, 2006; Zhao et al., 2016). For example, one study used the PMT variables to predict adoption of electric vehicles in the Netherlands (Bockarjova and Steg, 2014). Participants with stronger beliefs about the severity of problems caused by fossil fuel cars and their vulnerability to these problems, as well as weaker perceptions of the rewards of conventional vehicles, had greater intentions to buy electric vehicles. Additionally, those with high response efficacy and self-efficacy beliefs, as well as the perception of obtaining an electric vehicle as low cost, were more likely to intend to buy electric vehicles.

In the never-ending search for a comprehensive theory of PEB, some researchers have combined constructs from the TPB and PMT to predict climate change mitigating behaviors among Korean students (Kim et al., 2013), and a recent study used a hybrid of the PMT, TPB, and VBN to predict limiting meat consumption among Norwegian residents (Zur and Klöckner, 2014). Overall, constructs from PMT, VBN, and TPB have shown to be very important in predicting PEB, though simplifications and model tinkering and blending will likely continue long into the future.

Focus Theory of Normative Conduct

As noted above, the majority of the VBN, TPB, and PMT studies applied to PEB have been focused on predicting PEBs and PEB intentions, often with the assumption that changes to the main constructs of the theories would lead to changes in the behavior. However, several interventions have directly manipulated psychological concepts and elements from social psychological theories to change PEBs. Reviews of the literature have identified cognitive dissonance, commitment, goal-setting, modeling, feedback, and norms as major categories of social psychological interventions that have been implemented to change PEBs (Abrahamse et al., 2005; Osbaldiston and Schott, 2012). See Box 24.1 for descriptions of typical conservation psychology experiments that draw on commitment, goal-setting, and cognitive dissonance to change PEB.

We focus on normative messaging in detail in this section as it has been among the most effective interventions targeting PEBs (Abrahamse et al., 2005; Osbaldiston and Schott, 2012) and provides a nice illustration of how social psychological theories are tested over time in conservation psychology. As already mentioned above, *subjective norms*, a type of social norms, are expectations that important others want you to perform a certain behavior, and *personal norms* are feeling of moral obligation to perform an action. In addition to subjective norms, social norms include descriptive norms and injunctive norms. As a reminder, *descriptive norms* describe the common behavior of members of a group in a certain situation. In contrast, *injunctive norms* describe the commonly accepted or rejected behavior of people in a certain situation. In other words, descriptive norms describe what others do and injunctive norms describe what others should do.

The Focus Theory of Normative Conduct (Cialdini et al., 1990) argues that people will respond in line with normative information

Box 24.1 Example intervention studies in conservation psychology

Commitment. In commitment studies, researchers generally ask participants to make a commitment to change a PEB. Commitments can be written or verbal, public or private, specific or general. For example, Katzev and Johnson (1984) tested the effect of a specific commitment to reduce electricity use on electricity conservation among 90 American homeowners. Participants asked to commit to reducing their electricity consumption used less electricity during the intervention period of the study than controls and those who received a monetary incentive to reduce electricity. However, during the 18-day follow-up period and the longer two-and-a-half month follow-up period, there was no difference between groups (Katzev and Johnson, 1984).
Cognitive dissonance. Studies that draw on Cognitive Dissonance theory attempt to make salient that participants' previous behavior does not match their pro-environmental attitudes. For example, Dickerson et al. (1992) conducted a field experiment in a shower room of a US university's recreation facility. Participants were asked questions about their previous shower lengths (or not) and were asked to sign a public-commitment poster urging others to shorten their showers (or not). Participants were then unobtrusively timed in the public shower. Participants who were reminded of their previous wasteful behavior and who also made a public commitment urging others to take shorter showers were observed to take shorter showers than controls (Dickerson et al., 1992).
Goal-setting. When goal-setting is used, researchers ask participants to set a goal to reach a certain level of performance of a PEB, and feedback is usually given about participants' status in reaching that goal. Goals can be small or large and can set by the researcher or the participant. In one example lab study, McCalley and Midden (2002) had Dutch participants complete a series of computerized clothes-washing tasks. Participants with a goal to reduce the electricity use of their virtual washing machine and who received feedback about their progress toward the goal conserved more energy than controls. No differences were observed between whether the goal was participant- or researcher-set.

that is made salient to them (Cialdini et al., 1990). In a series of studies investigating the effect of norms on littering behavior in the United States, people returned to their cars from an event to find a handbill tucked under their windshield wiper blades (Cialdini et al., 1990). The researchers manipulated the environment to make different descriptive and injunctive norms salient. Participants were less likely to litter their handbill if there was no other litter around than if there was a lot of litter. However, the effect was even more pronounced when a confederate littered into the environment, drawing the participants' attention (i.e., focus) to the norm. Furthermore, when just one piece of litter was in an otherwise pristine environment, people were less likely to litter than if there was no litter or multiple pieces on the ground. Thus, the single piece of litter made the norm 'no one litters here' very salient, and people fell in line with the norm.

Normative messaging has also been applied to increase hotel guests' towel reuse. Although it is not most people's habits at home, in hotels many guests discard bath towels as dirty after one use. Reuse of towels can have considerable environmental impacts related to water, energy, and detergent use. Hotel companies have recognized the potential for environmental and financial savings in reducing one-time towel use of their guests and have created programs with reminders, prompts, and information leaflets displayed in hotel bathrooms to request that guests reuse their towels. Although a step in the right direction, research has shown that these programs could be more successful if they utilized social psychological norms. For example, several studies in the United States and Switzerland have provided feedback detailing social norms of guests' towel reuse to encourage others to reuse their towels as well (Goldstein et al., 2008; Schultz et al., 2008; Terrier and Marfaing, 2015). For example, Schultz et al. (2008) provided some guest rooms with descriptive and injunctive normative messages stating that fellow guests approved of towel reuse and that 75% of fellow guests reused their towels. Those in the normative condition used 25% fewer new towels compared to control rooms that were given the industry standard message.

More recently, normative feedback has been shown to reduce energy use in American homes (Schultz et al., 2007; 2015). In one study, people were provided with descriptive normative information about the average electricity use of others in their neighborhood. As in previous studies, one would expect that learning that others are performing a PEB would make people more inclined to also perform that PEB. But, Schultz and colleagues recognized that descriptive normative information can backfire for some people (Schultz et al., 2007).

Imagine this scenario. One day you and your neighbor Tom get your electricity bills from your utility company. Unbeknownst to you, Tom – who keeps his home icy in the summer and toasty in the winter *and* leaves the lights and TV on in the house all day while at work – used about 1500 kWh last month. You, however, keep your home tolerably warm in the summer and comfortably cool in the winter. You also diligently turn off your lights and TV when not in use. Not surprisingly, you used much less energy compared to Tom – just 680 kWh. When you're about to recycle the bill, you see another piece of paper in the envelope. It says that the average electricity use in your neighborhood is 1100 kWh. 'Wait…what?' The feedback that others are using more than you gives you a feeling of 'why should I be sacrificing all this if no one else is?' Alternatively, when your neighbor Tom gets the feedback that he uses much more than the average, he immediately feels feelings of guilt and concern. 'Wait…what? I should probably reduce my electricity use to be in line with everyone else.' Thus, the same message – descriptive normative feedback information – has had opposite effects. For Tom, someone acting less environmentally friendly than the norm, the descriptive feedback leads to more PEB, but for you, the feedback leads to less PEB. This sort of backfire is called the boomerang effect (Schultz et al., 2007).

All is not lost. Herein lies the power of injunctive norms. Remember that the Focus theory states that norms that are made salient will be followed. Now imagine that you get the same normative feedback on your bill, but you also have a smiley face emoticon next to your feedback reassuring you that you are doing the right thing (injunctive norm). Meanwhile, Tom gets a 'sad face' emoticon next to his feedback, reinforcing that his behavior is not the right thing. This kind of dual-normative approach, where injunctive and descriptive norms are used in tandem, has been shown to be successful in motivating electricity savings and counteracting the boomerang effect (Schultz et al., 2007). When residents were provided with descriptive normative information about the community's electricity use, those who were originally using more electricity than the norm decreased their electricity to be in line with the norm, while those originally using less electricity than the norm increased electricity use. However, when residents also received the corresponding injunctive smiley face or sad face on their bill, high users conserved even more and low users maintained their conservation (Schultz et al., 2007; Figure 24.7). These strategies have been effectively adopted by utility companies who have hired firms such as OPOWER to include injunctive and descriptive normative information in utility bills to reduce electricity usage (Allcott, 2011).

ADAPTATION TO CLIMATE CHANGE

Much of this chapter has focused on the application of social psychology to PEB performance with PEB defined as behavior that reduces humans' environmental impact. And this is where most other conservation psychology chapters in similar volumes end. However, despite attempts to curb our impact

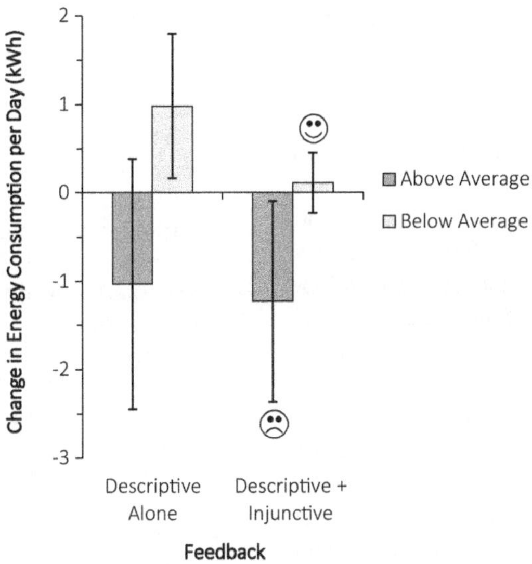

Figure 24.7 Results of Schultz et al.'s (2007) norm study. Difference between baseline daily energy consumption and daily energy consumption during the longer-term follow-up periods. Error bars show the 95% confidence interval of the pair-wise difference between usage during the follow-up period and during the baseline.

Source: Reproduced from Schultz et al.'s (2007) norm study.

now, human behavior over the last 150 years has created numerous, major environmental problems. Social psychology can greatly contribute to understanding not only how to reduce humans' impact on the environment but also how humans cope with adapting to these environmental problems. In recent years, there has been a recognition among those studying conservation psychology that much more research is needed to better understand adaptation to environmental problems, and specifically climate change adaptation (Reser and Swim, 2011).

Researchers have applied social psychological principles and theories to better understand climate change adaptation decisions made by a wide variety of groups including: peanut farmers in Australia (Marshall et al., 2012), residents of flood-prone homes in Germany (Grothmann and Reusswig, 2006), rice farmers in Sri Lanka (Truelove et al., 2015), homeowners in Britain (Bichard and Kazmierczak, 2011), farmers in Zimbabwe (Grothmann and Patt, 2005), and households in Kiribati (Kuruppu and Liverman, 2011). However, most of the work on the social psychology of climate change adaptation has been applied to the adaptation decisions of farmers in the developing world as their livelihoods make them especially vulnerable to climate impacts (Davidson, 2016). Interestingly, this work draws heavily on the PMT described above (Esham and Garforth, 2013; Grothmann and Patt, 2005; Keshavarz and Karami, 2016; Truelove et al., 2015). Specifically, applying the PMT to agricultural adaptation decisions, farmers who perceive a risk of a drought, and perceive it will be severe, are then expected to make a coping appraisal where they evaluate their capability of taking action and determine whether their action will make a positive difference in reducing the threat. Farmers who perceive a high risk and believe they can cope with the risk are then theorized to take protective action to mitigate the risk.

Recently, Truelove and colleagues proposed an addition to the PMT's coping and risk appraisals which they labeled the *social appraisal* (Truelove et al., 2015). The social appraisal includes an evaluation of perceived descriptive and injunctive norms in the community as well as community cohesion and identification. Considering farming is a very collective practice in much of the developing world, the addition of the social appraisal captures important variation between farmers and communities (Below et al., 2012; Esham and Garforth, 2013; Truelove et al., 2015). Although recent work on climate change adaptation has provided support for the PMT framing of adaptation decisions, additional research is clearly needed in this important area (Davidson, 2016) that continues to focus on farmers' agricultural adaptation but also further extends to other groups such as homeowners and residents in the developed world.

CONCLUSIONS

It is clear that changes to individual behavior, when aggregated across millions of people, can result in major improvements to our environment. Social psychologists' focus on classifying, predicting, and increasing PEBs has contributed a great deal to furthering our understanding of PEBs and the motivators and barriers to PEB. As environmental problems continue to grow, the opportunities for social psychologists to contribute to the conversations about environmental solutions will expand. The toolkit of social psychological theories and interventions makes social psychologists prime contributors to the discussion.

REFERENCES

Abrahamse, W., Steg, L., Vlek, C., & Rothengatter, T. (2005). A review of intervention studies aimed at household energy conservation. *Journal of Environmental Psychology, 25*(3), 273–291.

Ajzen, I. (1991). The theory of planned behavior. *Organizational Behavior and Human Decision Processes, 50*, 179–211.

Ajzen, I., & Fishbein, M. (2005). The influence of attitudes on behavior. In D. Albarracin, B. T. Johnson, & M. P. Zanna (Eds.), *The handbook of attitudes* (pp. 173–221). Mahwah, NY: Erlbaum.

Allcott, H. (2011). Social norms and energy conservation. *Journal of Public Economics, 95*(9–10), 1082–1095.

Armitage, C. J., & Conner, M. (2001). Efficacy of the Theory of Planned Behaviour: A meta-analytic review. *British Journal of Social Psychology, 40*, 471–499.

Attari, S. Z. (2014). Perceptions of water use. *Proceedings of the National Academy of Sciences, 111*(14), 5129–5134.

Attari, S. Z., DeKay, M. L., Davidson, C. I., Bruine, W., & Bruin, D. (2010). Public perceptions of energy consumption and savings. *Proceedings of the National Academy of Sciences, 107*(37), 16054–16059.

Baca-Motes, K., Brown, A., Gneezy, A., Keenan, E. A., & Nelson, L. D. (2013). Commitment and behavior change: Evidence from the field. *Journal of Consumer Research, 39*(5), 1070–1084.

Bamberg, S., & Möser, G. (2007). Twenty years after Hines, Hungerford, and Tomera: A new meta-analysis of psycho-social determinants of pro-environmental behaviour. *Journal of Environmental Psychology, 27*(1), 14–25.

Bamberg, S., & Schmidt, P. (1998). Changing travel-mode choice as rational choice: Results from a longitudinal intervention study. *Rationality and Society, 10*(2), 223–252.

Below, T. B., Mutabazi, K. D., Kirschke, D., Franke, C., Sieber, S., Siebert, R., & Tscherning, K. (2012). Can farmers' adaptation to climate change be explained by socio-economic household-level variables? *Global Environmental Change, 22*(1), 223–235.

Bem, D. J. (1967). Self-perception: An alternative interpretation of cognitive dissonance phenomena. *Psychological Review, 74*(3), 183–200.

Bichard, E., & Kazmierczak, A. (2011). Are homeowners willing to adapt to and mitigate the effects of climate change? *Climatic Change*, 633–654.

Bockarjova, M., & Steg, L. (2014). Can Protection Motivation Theory predict pro-environmental behavior? Explaining the adoption of electric vehicles in the Netherlands. *Global Environmental Change*, *28*(1), 276–288.

Bonniface, L., & Henley, N. (2008). 'A drop in the bucket': Collective efficacy perceptions and environmental behaviour. *Australian Journal of Social Issues*, *43*(3), 345–358.

Cialdini, R. B., Reno, R. R., & Kallgren, C. A. (1990). A focus theory of normative conduct: Recycling the concept of norms to reduce littering in public places. *Journal of Personality and Social Psychology*, *58*(6), 1015–1026.

Clayton, S., & Brook, A. (2005). Can psychology help save the world? A model for conservation psychology. *Analyses of Social Issues and Public Policy*, *5*(1), 87–102.

Clayton, S., Devine-Wright, P., Stern, P. C., Whitmarsh, L., Carrico, A., Steg, L., Swim, J., & Bonnes, M. (2015a). Psychological research and global climate change. *Nature Climate Change*, *5*(7), 640–646.

Clayton, S., Devine-Wright, P., Swim, J., Bonnes, M., Steg, L., Whitmarsh, L., & Carrico, A. (2015b). Expanding the role for psychology in addressing environmental challenges. *American Psychologist*, *71*(3), 199–215.

Cornelissen, G., Pandelaere, M., Warlop, L., & Dewitte, S. (2008). Positive cueing: Promoting sustainable consumer behavior by cueing common environmental behaviors as environmental. *International Journal of Research in Marketing*, *25*(1), 46–55.

Davidson, D. (2016). Gaps in agricultural climate adaptation research. *Nature Climate Change*, *6*(5), 433–435.

De Groot, J. I. M., & Steg, L. (2007a). General beliefs and the Theory of Planned Behavior: The role of environmental concerns in the TPB. *Journal of Applied Social Psychology*, *37*(8), 1817–1836.

De Groot, J. I. M., & Steg, L. (2007b). Value orientations to explain beliefs related to environmental significant behavior: How to measure egoistic, altruistic, and biospheric value orientations. *Environment and Behavior*, *40*(3), 330–354.

Deci, E. L., & Ryan, R. M. (2011). Self-determination theory. In P. A. M. Van Lange, A. W. Kruglanski, & E. T. Higgins (Eds.), *Handbook of theories of social psychology* (Vol. 1, pp. 416–433). Thousand Oaks, CA: Sage.

Department for Environment Food and Rural Affairs. (2008). *A framework for pro-environmental behaviours*. London: Department for Environment, Food and Rural Affairs.

Dhar, R., & Simonson, I. (1999). Making complementary choices in consumption episodes: Highlighting versus balancing. *Journal of Marketing Research*, *36*(1), 29–44.

Dickerson, C. A., Thibodeau, R., Aronson, E., & Miller, D. (1992). Using cognitive dissonance to encourage water conservation. *Journal of Applied Social Psychology*, *22*(11), 841–854.

Dietz, T., Gardner, G. T., Gilligan, J., Stern, P. C., & Vandenbergh, M. P. (2009). Household actions can provide a behavioral wedge to rapidly reduce US carbon emissions. *Proceedings of the National Academy of Sciences*, *106*(44), 18452–18456.

Dunlap, R. E., & Van Liere, K. D. (1978). The 'New Environmental Paradigm.' *Journal of Environmental Education*, *9*(4), 10–19.

Dunlap, R. E., Van Liere, K. D., Mertig, A. G., & Jones, R. E. (2000). Measuring endorsement of the New Ecological Paradigm: A revised NEP scale. *Journal of Social Issues*, *56*(3), 425–442.

Esham, M., & Garforth, C. (2013). Agricultural adaptation to climate change: Insights from a farming community in Sri Lanka. *Mitigation and Adaptation Strategies for Global Change*, *18*(5), 535–549.

Festinger, L. (1957). *A theory of cognitive dissonance*. Evanston, IL: Row.

Fishbein, M., & Ajzen, I. (1975). *Belief, attitude, intention, and behavior: An introduction to theory and research*. Reading, MA: Addison-Wesley.

Floyd, D. L., Prentice-Dunn, S., & Rogers, R. W. (2000). Meta-analysis of research on Protection Motivation Theory. *Journal of Applied Social Psychology*, *30*(2), 407–429.

Follows, S. B., & Jobber, D. (2000). Environmentally responsible purchase behaviour: A test of a consumer model. *European Journal of Marketing*, *34*(5/6), 723–746.

Fornara, F., Pattitoni, P., Mura, M., & Strazzera, E. (2016). Predicting intention to improve household energy efficiency: The role of value-belief-norm theory, normative and informational influence, and specific attitude. *Journal of Environmental Psychology, 45*, 1–10.

Freedman, J. L., & Fraser, S. C. (1966). Compliance without pressure: The foot-in-the-door technique. *Journal of Personality and Social Psychology*, *4*(2), 195–202.

Gardner, G. T., & Stern, P. C. (2008). The short list. The most effective actions U.S. households can take to curb climate change. *Environment: Science and Policy for Sustainable Development*, *50*(5), 12–25.

Gärling, T., Fujii, S., Gärling, A., & Jakobsson, C. (2003). Moderating effects of social value orientation on determinants of proenvironmental behavior intention. *Journal of Environmental Psychology*, *23*(1), 1–9.

Gatersleben, B., Steg, L., & Vlek, C. (2002). Measurement and determinants of environmentally significant consumer behavior. *Environment and Behavior*, *34*(3), 335–362.

Gifford, R. (2011). The dragons of inaction: Psychological barriers that limit climate change mitigation and adaptation. *The American Psychologist*, *66*(4), 290–302.

Gifford, R., Kormos, C., & McIntyre, A. (2011). Behavioral dimensions of climate change: Drivers, responses, barriers, and interventions. *Wiley Interdisciplinary Reviews: Climate Change*, *2*, 801–827.

Gneezy, A., Imas, A., Brown, A., Nelson, L. D., & Norton, M. I. (2012). Paying to be nice: Consistency and costly prosocial behavior. *Management Science*, *58*(1), 179–187.

Goldstein, N. J., Cialdini, R. B., & Griskevicius, V. (2008). A room with a viewpoint: Using social norms to motivate environmental conservation in hotels. *Journal of Consumer Research*, *35*(3), 472–482.

Grothmann, T., & Patt, A. (2005). Adaptive capacity and human cognition: The process of individual adaptation to climate change. *Global Environmental Change Part A*, *15*(3), 199–213.

Grothmann, T., & Reusswig, F. (2006). People at risk of flooding: Why some residents take precautionary action while others do not. *Natural Hazards*, *38*(1–2), 101–120.

Han, H., Hsu, L. T. (J.), & Sheu, C. (2010). Application of the Theory of Planned Behavior to green hotel choice: Testing the effect of environmental friendly activities. *Tourism Management*, *31*(3), 325–334.

Harland, P., Staats, H., & Wilke, H. A. M. (1999). Explaining proenvironmental intention and behavior by personal norms and the Theory of Planned Behavior. *Journal of Applied Social Psychology*, *29*(12), 2505–2528.

Heath, Y., & Gifford, R. (2002). Extending the Theory of Planned Behavior: Predicting the use of public transportation. *Journal of Applied Social Psychology*, *32*(10), 2154–2189.

Homburg, A., & Stolberg, A. (2006). Explaining pro-environmental behavior with a cognitive theory of stress. *Journal of Environmental Psychology*, *26*(1), 1–14.

Hunecke, M., Blobaum, A., Matthies, E., & Hoger, R. (2001). Responsibility and environment: Ecological norm orientation and external factors in the domain of travel mode choice behavior. *Environment and Behavior*, *33*(6), 830–852.

Inskeep, B. D., & Attari, S. Z. (2014). The water short list: The most effective actions U.S. households can take to curb water use. *Environment: Science and Policy for Sustainable Development*, *56*(4), 4–15.

IPCC. (2014). *Climate Change 2014: Synthesis Report. Contribution of Working Groups I, II and III to the Fifth Assessment Report of the Intergovernmental Panel on Climate Change Summary for Policymakers*. [Core Writing Team, R.K. Pachauri and L.A. Meyer (Eds.)]. Geneva, Switzerland: IPCC.

Janz, N. K., & Becker, M. H. (1984). The Health Belief Model: A decade later. *Health Education Quarterly*, *11*(1), 1–47.

Joireman, J. A., Lasane, T. P., Bennett, J., Richards, D., & Solaimani, S. (2001). Integrating social value orientation and the consideration of future consequences within the extended norm activation model of proenvironmental behaviour. *British Journal of Social Psychology*, *40*, 133–155.

Jordan, J., Mullen, E., & Murnighan, J. K. (2011). Striving for the moral self: The effects of recalling past moral actions on future moral behavior. *Personality and Social Psychology Bulletin*, *37*(5), 701–713.

Kaiser, F. G. (2006). A moral extension of the theory of planned behavior: Norms and anticipated feelings of regret in conservationism. *Personality and Individual Differences*, *41*(1), 71–81.

Kaiser, F. G., & Wilson, M. (2000). Assessing people's general ecological behavior: A cross-cultural measure. *Journal of Applied Social Psychology*, *30*, 952–978.

Kaiser, F. G., & Wilson, M. (2004). Goal-directed conservation behavior: The specific composition of a general performance. *Personality and Individual Differences*, *36*(7), 1531–1544.

Kaiser, F. G., Doka, G., Hofstetter, P., & Ranney, M. A. (2003). Ecological behavior and its environmental consequences: A life cycle assessment of a self-report measure. *Journal of Environmental Psychology*, *23*(1), 11–20.

Kaiser, F. G., Hubner, G., & Bogner, F. X. (2005). Contrasting the Theory of Planned Behavior with the Value-Belief-Norm model in explaining conservation behavior. *Journal of Applied Social Psychology*, *35*(10), 2150–2170.

Karlin, B., Davis, N., Sanguinetti, A., Gamble, K., Kirkby, D., & Stokols, D. (2014). Dimensions of conservation: Exploring differences among energy behaviors. *Environment and Behavior*, *46*(4), 423–452.

Katzev, R. D., & Johnson, T. R. (1984). Comparing the effects of monetary incentives and foot-in-the-door strategies in promoting residential electricity conservation. *Journal of Applied Social Psychology*, *14*(1), 12–27.

Keshavarz, M., & Karami, E. (2016). Farmers' pro-environmental behavior under drought: Application of protection motivation theory. *Journal of Arid Environments*, *127*, 128–136.

Kim, S., & Shin, W. (2015). Understanding American and Korean students' support for pro-environmental tax policy: The application of the Value–Belief–Norm Theory of environmentalism. *Environmental Communication*, *4032*, 1–21.

Kim, S., Jeong, S.-H., & Hwang, Y. (2013). Predictors of pro-environmental behaviors of American and Korean students: The application of the theory of reasoned action and protection motivation theory. *Science Communication*, *35*(2), 168–188.

Klöckner, C. A. (2013). A comprehensive model of the psychology of environmental behaviour – A meta-analysis. *Global Environmental Change*, *23*(5), 1028–1038.

Kollmuss, A., & Agyeman, J. (2002). Mind the Gap: Why do people act environmentally and what are the barriers to pro-environmental behavior? *Environmental Education Research*, *8*(3), 239–260.

Kopelman, S., Weber, J. M., & Messick, D. M. (2002). Factors influencing cooperation in commons dilemmas: A review of experimental psychological research. In E. Ostrom, T. Dietz, N. Dolsak, P. C. Stern, S. Stonich, & E. U. Weber (Eds.), *The drama of the commons* (pp. 113–156). Washington, DC: National Academies Press.

Kuruppu, N., & Liverman, D. (2011). Mental preparation for climate adaptation: The role of cognition and culture in enhancing adaptive capacity of water management in Kiribati. *Global Environmental Change*, *21*(2), 657–669.

Laitner, J. A. S., Ehrhardt-Martinez, K., & Mckinney, V. (2009). Examining the scale of the behaviour energy efficiency continuum. In *ECEEE 2009 Summer Study: Act! Innovate! Deliver! Reducing energy demand sustainably* (pp. 217–223). La Colle sur Loup, France: European Council for an Energy-Efficient Economy.

Lam, S.-P. (2006). Predicting intention to save water: Theory of Planned Behavior, response efficacy, vulnerability, and perceived efficiency of alternative solutions. *Journal of Applied Social Psychology*, *36*(11), 2803–2824.

Lanzini, P., & Thøgersen, J. (2014). Behavioural spillover in the environmental domain: An intervention study. *Journal of Environmental Psychology*, *40*, 381–390.

Larson, L. R., Stedman, R. C., Cooper, C. B., & Decker, D. J. (2015). Understanding the multi-dimensional structure of pro-environmental behavior. *Journal of Environmental Psychology*, *43*, 112–124.

Lewin, K. (1936). *Principles of topological psychology*. New York: McGraw Hill.

Lindsay, J. J., & Strathman, A. (1997). Predictors of recycling behavior: An application of a modified Health Belief Model. *Journal of Applied Social Psychology*, *27*(20), 1799–1823.

Litvine, D., & Wüstenhagen, R. (2011). Helping 'light green' consumers walk the talk: Results of a behavioural intervention survey in the Swiss electricity market. *Ecological Economics*, *70*(3), 462–474.

Lorenzoni, I., Nicholson-Cole, S., & Whitmarsh, L. (2007). Barriers perceived to engaging with climate change among the UK public and their policy implications. *Global Environmental Change*, *17*(3–4), 445–459.

Marshall, N. A., Park, S. E., Adger, W. N., Brown, K., & Howden, S. M. (2012). Transformational capacity and the influence of place and identity. *Environmental Research Letters*, *7*, 1–9.

McCalley, L. T., & Midden, C. J. H. (2002). Energy conservation through product-integrated feedback: The roles of goal-setting and social orientation. *Journal of Economic Psychology*, *23*(5), 589–603.

McKenzie-Mohr, D. (2000). Promoting sustainable behavior: An introduction to community-based social marketing. *Journal of Social Issues*, *56*(3), 543–554.

McKenzie-Mohr, D. (2011). *Fostering sustainable behavior: An introduction to community-based social marketing* (3rd edn.). Gabriola Island, BC: New Society.

McKenzie-Mohr, D., & Schultz, P. W. (2014). Choosing effective behavior change tools. *Social Marketing Quarterly*, *20*(1), 35–46.

Merritt, A. C., Effron, D. A., & Monin, B. (2010). Moral self-licensing: When being good frees us to be bad. *Social and Personality Psychology Compass*, *4/5*, 344–357.

Nigbur, D., Lyons, E., & Uzzell, D. (2010). Attitudes, norms, identity and environmental behaviour: Using an expanded theory of planned behaviour to predict participation in a kerbside recycling programme. *British Journal of Social Psychology*, *49*, 259–284.

Nilsson, A., Bergquist, M., & Schultz, W. P. (2016). Spillover effects in environmental behaviors, across time and context: A review and research agenda. *Environmental Education Research*, *4622*(November), 1–17.

Nisbet, E. K. L., & Gick, M. L. (2008). Can health psychology help the planet? Applying theory and models of health behaviour to environmental actions. *Canadian Psychology*, *49*(4), 296–303.

Nordlund, A. M., & Garvill, J. (2002). Value structures behind proenvironmental behavior. *Environment and Behavior*, *34*(6), 740–756.

Oom do Valle, P., Rebelo, E., Reis, E., & Menezes, J. (2005). Combining behavioral theories to predict recycling involvement. *Environment and Behavior*, *37*(3), 364–396.

Oreg, S., & Katz-Gerro, T. (2006). Predicting proenvironmental behavior cross-nationally: Values, the Theory of Planned Behavior, and Value-Belief-Norm Theory. *Environment and Behavior*, *38*(4), 462–483.

Osbaldiston, R., & Schott, J. P. (2012). Environmental sustainability and behavioral science: Meta-analysis of proenvironmental behavior experiments. *Environment and Behavior*, *44*(2), 257–299.

Pelletier, L. G., Tuson, K. M., Green-Demers, I., Noels, K., & Beaton, A. M. (1998). Why are you doing things for the environment? The Motivation Toward the Environment Scale (MTES). *Journal of Applied Social Psychology*, *28*(5), 437–468.

Poortinga, W., Whitmarsh, L., & Suffolk, C. (2013). The introduction of a single-use carrier bag charge in Wales: Attitude change and behavioural spillover effects. *Journal of Environmental Psychology*, *36*, 240–247.

Reser, J. P., & Swim, J. K. (2011). Adapting to and coping with the threat and impacts of climate change. *American Psychologist*, *66*(4), 277–289.

Rippetoe, P. A., & Rogers, R. W. (1987). Effects of components of protection-motivation theory on adaptive and maladaptive coping with a health threat. *Journal of Personality and Social Psychology*, *52*(3), 596–604.

Rogers, R. W. (1975). A Protection Motivation Theory of fear appeals and attitude change. *Journal of Psychology*, *91*, 93–114.

Rogers, R. W. (1983). Cognitive and physiological processes in fear appeals and attitudes change: A revised theory of protection motivation. In B. L. Cacioppo & L. L. Petty (Eds.), *Social psychophysiology: A sourcebook* (pp. 153–175). New York: Guilford.

Rogers, R. W., & Prentice-Dunn, S. (1997). Protection motivation theory. In D. S. Gochman (Ed.), *Handbook of health behavior research 1: Personal and social determinants.* (pp. 113 – 132). New York, NY: Plenum Press.

Sachdeva, S., Iliev, R., & Medin, D. L. (2009). Sinning saints and saintly sinners: The paradox of moral self-regulation. *Psychological Science*, *20*(4), 523–528.

Schultz, P. W., & Estrada-Hollenbeck, M. (2017). The USE of theory in applied social psychology. In L. Steg, K. Kaiser, A. P. Buunk, & J. A. Rothengatter (Eds.), *Applied social psychology: Understanding and managing social problems* (pp. 28–56). New York: Cambridge University Press.

Schultz, P. W., & Kaiser, F. G. (2012). Promoting pro-environmental behavior. In S. Clayton (Ed.), *The Oxford handbook of environmental and conservation psychology* (pp. 556–580). New York: Oxford University Press.

Schultz, P. W., Estrada, M., Schmitt, J., Sokoloski, R., & Silva-Send, N. (2015). Using in-home displays to provide smart meter feedback about household electricity consumption: A randomized control trial comparing kilowatts, cost, and social norms. *Energy*, *90*, 351–358.

Schultz, P. W., Khazian, A. M., & Zaleski, A. C. (2008). Using normative social influence to promote conservation among hotel guests. *Social Influence*, *3*(1), 4–23.

Schultz, P. W., Nolan, J. M., Cialdini, R. B., Goldstein, N. J., & Griskevicius, V. (2007). The constructive, destructive, and reconstructive power of social norms. *Psychological Science*, *18*(5), 429–434.

Schwartz, S. H. (1977). Normative influences on altruism. In L. Berkowitz (Ed.), *Advances in experimental social psychology* (Vol. 10, pp. 221–279). New York, NY: Academic Press.

Schwartz, S. H., & Bilsky, W. (1987). Toward a universal psychological structure of human values. *Journal of Personality and Social Psychology*, *53*(3), 550–562.

Schwartz, S. H., & Bilsky, W. (1990). Toward a theory of the universal content and structure of values: Extensions and cross-cultural replications. *Journal of Personality and Social Psychology*, *58*(5), 878–891.

Sparks, P., & Shepherd, R. (1992). Self-identity and the Theory of Planned Behavior: Assessing the role of identification with 'green consumerism.' *Social Psychology Quarterly*, *55*(4), 388–399.

Steg, L., & Vlek, C. (2009). Encouraging pro-environmental behaviour: An integrative review and research agenda. *Journal of Environmental Psychology*, *29*(3), 309–317.

Steg, L., Dreijerink, L., & Abrahamse, W. (2005). Factors influencing the acceptability of energy policies: A test of VBN theory. *Journal of Environmental Psychology*, *25*(4), 415–425.

Steinhorst, J., & Matthies, E. (2016). Monetary or environmental appeals for saving electricity? Potentials for spillover on low carbon policy acceptability. *Energy Policy*, *93*, 335–344.

Steinhorst, J., Klöckner, C. A., & Matthies, E. (2015). Saving electricity – For the money or the environment? Risks of limiting pro-environmental spillover when using monetary framing. *Journal of Environmental Psychology*, *43*, 125–135.

Stern, P. C. (2000). Toward a coherent theory of environmentally significant behavior. *Journal of Social Issues*, *56*(3), 407–424.

Stern, P. C., Dietz, T., Abel, T., Guagnano, G. A., & Kalof, L. (1999). A value belief norm theory of support for social movements: The case of environmental concern. *Human Ecology Review*, *6*(2), 81–97.

Taylor, S., & Todd, P. (1995). An integrated model of waste management behavior: A test of household recycling and composting intentions. *Environment and Behavior*, *27*(5), 603–630.

Terrier, L., & Marfaing, B. (2015). Using social norms and commitment to promote pro-environmental behavior among hotel guests. *Journal of Environmental Psychology*, *44*, 10–15.

Tobler, C., Visschers, V. H. M., & Siegrist, M. (2012). Addressing climate change: Determinants of consumers' willingness to act and to support policy measures. *Journal of Environmental Psychology*, *32*(3), 197–207.

Truelove, H. B., & Parks, C. D. (2012). Perceptions of behaviors that cause and mitigate global warming and intentions to perform these behaviors. *Journal of Environmental Psychology*, *32*(3), 246–259.

Truelove, H. B., Carrico, A. R., & Thabrew, L. (2015). A socio-psychological model for analyzing climate change adaptation: A case study of Sri Lankan paddy farmers. *Global Environmental Change*, *31*, 85–97.

Truelove, H. B., Carrico, A. R., Weber, E. U., Raimi, K. T., & Vandenbergh, M. P. (2014). Positive and negative spillover of pro-environmental behavior: An integrative review and theoretical framework. *Global Environmental Change*, *29*, 127–138.

Turaga, R. M. R., Howarth, R. B., & Borsuk, M. E. (2010). Pro-environmental behavior: Rational choice meets moral motivation. *Annals of the New York Academy of Sciences*, *1185*, 211–224.

Van der Werff, E., Steg, L., & Keizer, K. (2014). I am what I am, by looking past the present: The influence of biospheric values and past behavior on environmental self-identity. *Environment and Behavior*, *46*(5), 626–657.

Whitmarsh, L. (2009). Behavioural responses to climate change: Asymmetry of intentions and impacts. *Journal of Environmental Psychology*, *29*(1), 13–23.

Zhao, G., Cavusgil, E., & Zhao, Y. (2016). A protection motivation explanation of base-of-pyramid consumers' environmental sustainability. *Journal of Environmental Psychology*, *45*, 116–126.

Zhong, C.-B., Liljenquist, K., & Cain, D. (2009). Moral self-regulation: Licensing & compensation. In D. de Cremer (Ed.), *Psychological perspectives on ethical behavior and decision making* (pp. 75–89). Charlotte, NC: Information Age.

Zur, I., & Klöckner, C. A. (2014). Individual motivations for limiting meat consumption. *British Food Journal*, *116*(4), 629–642.

25

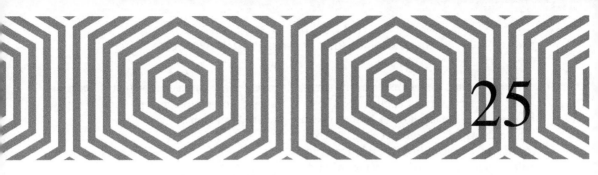

The Psychogeographical Turn in Applied Social Psychology

Alexander J. Bridger, Sophia Emmanouil and Rebecca Lawthom

Just as none of us is outside or beyond geography, none of us is completely free from the struggle over geography. That struggle is complex and interesting because it is not only about soldiers and cannons but also about ideas, about forms, about images and imaginings. (Said, 1993: 7)

INTRODUCTION

The question of how we come to make sense of our place in the world and where we locate ourselves in the world continues to be an important area of research, not only in applied social psychology but also in other academic disciplines such as human geography, philosophy and art. Social psychological research on place has enabled us to think about the relation of individuals to place and how human beings create identities in context. The premise of that research has been extremely important in aiming to reduce social conflict and for building positive relations between different communities. However, other writers have argued that the sense of who we are in the world has become 'emplaced' (Manzo, 2003) and that fixation of identities in specific places with subsequent causal effects needs re-examining. Whilst the focus of social psychological research more generally has been on studying attitudes in peoples' heads and analysing language, there has been scant focus on the practices of wandering through different places and what the impacts are of overarching social systems such as neoliberalism and consumer culture. Current social psychological research on place could therefore be usefully extended by considering the impacts of the wider political system of neoliberalism and consumerism upon peoples' everyday experiences of the world and by encouraging community reflections to build greater awareness of contemporary social conditions and to generate new avenues for social action. Taking such a stance requires a reconceptualisation of methods and theory and a psychogeographical turn in social psychological research is presented as one way in which to do further research.

In this chapter, we will explain why a psychogeographical turn in applied social psychology is needed and how such an approach can be drawn on to consider the commodification of everyday life. We will then provide a critical review of key studies of place from quantitative and qualitative applied social psychology. The strengths and limits of such work will then be assessed and the reasons why a turn to psychogeographical research is needed will be explored. After having discussed the main theoretical and historical arguments, we will then focus on explaining the psychogeographical approach in relation to the work of the situationists and their approach to analysing place and context. Reference will be made to the main research exemplar of a psychogeographical community group work project undertaken at the Hoot mental health drop-in centre in Huddersfield. Reference will also be made to the project activities, as well as documenting the experiences of participants and the impact to those involved and the host organisation. Themes explored through such work in relation to the project participants include the effects of neoliberal gentrification, the idea of consumer citizenship, inclusion and participation. The last section of this chapter will focus on the challenges and obstacles encountered through doing such work, and we will point to the multiplicity of ways in which to do psychogeographical work. In this chapter, reflexivity, ethics and professional conduct in relation to taking a caring approach to doing community work will also be discussed. Such a stance, we hope, further enhances the validity of this applied social psychological approach. Other challenges and issues that are encountered include discussion of dealing with multiple subject positions as an academic, doing community work and considering the question of what changes can be enabled as a result of doing such work. Having introduced what this chapter will be about, it is necessary to now move onto a critical review of current social psychological research on place, what psychogeography is and why it is necessary to take a psychogeographical turn in applied social psychology.

FROM A SOCIAL PSYCHOLOGY OF PLACE TO A PSYCHOGEOGRAPHICAL TURN IN APPLIED SOCIAL PSYCHOLOGY

It is important to begin with, outlining and reviewing the social psychological research on place, to present the case for a psychogeographical turn in applied social psychology. Readers will most likely be aware that the social psychological research on place is vast, ranging from studies on place identity, to intergroup conflict, the contact hypothesis and community based research. Social psychological and environmental psychological research have explored the relations of people to place. Altman's (1993) work on activity settings is important to start off with here. He argued that social relationships are always situated in what he referred to as activity settings. Within these settings, individuals draw on behaviours which are appropriate and normative to the context. For example, it would be an appropriate practice to queue in line to order a coffee in a coffee shop but it would be perceived as bizarre by other people to queue for a coffee and, when ready to place an order, to then go to the back of the queue and to engage with the whole process again. The example referred to here was an example of a social intervention by Jordan McKenzie (2008) at the Territories Reimagined: International Perspectives conference in Manchester. It is not clear what the purpose of the intervention was, though it does seem somewhat relevant to consider the notion of normative behaviours in social settings and what is appropriate and not appropriate behaviour. This work is thus important in terms of consideration of norms that govern social behaviour in specific settings.

However, such work needs to be extended in relation to considering questions of identity, place and belongingness, which will be discussed next.

Who we are, and how we come to define our sense of place in the world, is often bound up with where we live and what we do in our everyday lives. For this reason, social psychologists have applied social identity research in relation to belongingness, home and place. The relation of place in relation to identity moves us beyond the notion of identity tied simply to groups and to social processes. Any notion of identity therefore needs to be considered in relation to where identity is situated rather than with previous social identity work which presents its findings in an a-contextualised landscape. Indeed, two authors argued that:

> Like people, things and activities, places are an integral part of the social world of everyday life, as such, they become important mechanisms through which identity is defined and situated. (Cuba and Hummon, 1993: 112)

Individuals create many associations of place with home with specific memories (Cuba and Hummon, 1993), and through being in specific places, we formulate and create new identities (Twigger-Ross and Uzzell, 1996). Dixon and Durrheim (2004: 456) are quite critical of the mainstream experimental social psychological research on identity and place and argue that context should not be treated simply as an 'inert backdrop to social relations' or as having a 'negligible impact on the social psychological processes it frames'. Moreover, they also draw on arguments by Billig et al. (1988) in arguing that how people identify with places is essentially dilemmatic. Those arguments make sense and serve as an important way in which to extend previous research in applied social psychology. It is even the case that some health, social and community psychological researchers have also made similar claims that environments should not be viewed simply as 'backdrops to social processes' (Hodgetts et al., 2010a: 287). Quite rightly, those writers state that such a focus takes us away from the located-ness of place, how people derive meaning from being in different places, both on their own and with others, and in terms of preventing consideration of what social processes may keep people together or apart. That work foregrounds the importance of place-identity and associated processes of social change. The link between place identity and social change is key here and is echoed not only in the work of Dixon and Durrheim (2004), Dixon et al. (2008) but also Proshansky et al. (1983). With the arguments made here in terms of moving beyond the a-contextualised study of individuals and social processes, we now turn to research on segregation and intergroup conflict.

Allport (1954) argued that increased contact between groups would reduce conflict and prejudice. He developed what is known as the contact hypothesis. His work laid the foundations for other psychologists to consider how to reduce conflict and to increase harmony between groups. In more recent research, social psychologists such as Dixon and Durrheim (2004) have considered the spatial relations of segregation in relation to Black and White South African communities at a beach resort in KwaZulu Natal called 'Sunshine Coast'. They argued that desegregation changes the relations between individuals and others and to specific places. They also indicated that dominant groups often resist processes of change in their communities. In contrast, other writers have argued that if people feel a positive affiliation with place then they are more likely to get involved with actions which would be for the good of the community (Nowell et al., 2006). The aims of intergroup conflict research, as well as place identity research and work on activity settings, are of paramount importance in reducing conflict between people in society. However, a case can be made here for focusing out from conflict between groups in context to consider how the wider context itself can cause conflict. Here the focus is on neoliberalism and of everyday life as being increasingly commodified, which we now turn to discuss.

Keith and Pile (1993) argued that the academic study of place identity must be related to relations of power and to the study of ideology. Importantly, in other critical research on place identity, Dixon and Durrheim (2004) also make the case for studying landscapes of meaning and for studying relations of power and power struggles between people in places. Merrifield (1993: 522) discusses capitalist spaces and explains how 'place is where everyday life is situated'. He also argues that place should not be simply seen as a blank slate onto which meanings can be written but rather that contemporary places are written on via processes of capitalism and commerce and this, in turn, shapes peoples' subjective experiences of places (Merrifield, 1993). Lefebvre (1976) discusses how capitalism is a geographical endeavour:

> What has happened is that capitalism has found itself able to attenuate (if not resolve) its internal contradictions for a century, and consequently, in the hundred years since the writing of *Capital*, it has succeeded in achieving 'growth'. We cannot calculate at what price, but we do know the means: *by occupying space, by producing a space*. (Lefebvre, 1976: 21; original emphasis)

Lefebvre argues that it is necessary to understand, read and consider what spaces may mean (1976). Examples of how everyday social spaces can be read via social psychological methods can be exemplified in relation to work by Hodgetts et al. (2010b). In their book, titled *Social Psychology and Everyday Life*, they draw on the motif of everyday life to consider topics such as place, health and the media. Miles (2010: 8) indicates that consumerism is such a 'thoroughly cultural phenomenon that serves to legitimate capitalism on an everyday basis'.

Here then can be seen an interface between psychology and place which could be termed as psychogeography. However, the term psychogeography, and what that may mean in the domain of applied social psychology, needs unpicking and explaining. Early signs of reference to 'psychogeography' can be evidenced in psychology journals such as the *Journal of Environmental Psychology*, where writers such as Wood (1987) refer to the relation of psychology to geography and to key political issues of the time. However, the reference to psychogeography within the arena of Environmental Psychology is very different to that which has been considered by others. Definitions of psychogeography previously provided by social psychologists have tended to focus on the causal impact of environments on peoples' attitudes and behaviours.

This then brings us to the work of the situationists as it is important to consider the extent to which their work can contribute to a workable psychogeographical approach for social psychologists. The situationists were deeply concerned with capitalist gentrification and they envisioned a world beyond the capitalist order of things. The aims of experimental social psychologists tend not to be focused on political concerns but rather their aims are generally to understand social processes and individual behaviour. In contrast to experimental social psychologists, the situationists' focus on place was on intervening and creating situations to lead to 'permanent change' (Khatib, 1958: para. 2). Those ideas underpinned both their written work and their practical actions in urban contexts. The aims of the situationists are thus quite different to social psychologists and their more moderate intentions to study the internal workings of the mind and why people behave in the ways that they do based on social context and casual factors.

The situationists created the group name of the 'Situationist International', which comprised intellectuals, artists and activists who were committed to the cause of revolutionary social change and to the overthrow of consumer capitalism. They were not actually academics and they opposed the institutionalisation of their ideas and practices and would have been against the world of academia. During the late 1950s and early 1960s, Paris was undergoing tremendous gentrification of the inner-city districts and whole areas were being destroyed and rebuilt. It was noted by the situationists that many working-class areas were also being demolished and they were both dismayed and upset at what was happening to the everyday spaces and places in which they lived, worked and partook in leisure activities (Chtcheglov, 1958; Khatib, 1958).

The situationists' approach to their work was a critique of everyday life in relation to the capitalist formation of the built environments in which they lived, worked and played. They believed they had planted the seeds of revolt in those people who had engaged in rioting during May 1968. In the late 1950s and early 1960s, the situationists coined the term psychogeography to explore and critique the rapidly changing towns and cities under consumer capitalist social conditions (Debord, 1958). Sadler, a historian on the situationist movement, explained that psychogeography could be viewed as a self 'therapy' and as a way of 'exciting the senses and the body' to 'rescue drifters from the clutches of functionalism' (Sadler, 1999: 80). Such concerns are not the focus of social psychologists operating within a mainstream experimental focus on studying behavioural variables and situational contexts, though arguably the psychogeographical approach could produce potentially interesting and illuminating findings and implications.

The situationists conducted many psychogeographical walks around Paris and other towns and cities to critique the changing form of such places and spaces (Khatib, 1958). They referred to psychogeographical walks as dérives or drifts which were meant to have a dream-like quality (Wollen, 2001) and which aimed to deliberately disorientate people. The aims of such walks were meant to break from the usual habitual patterns of movement across spaces and places (Debord, 1958; Kotanyi and Vaneigem, 1961). Readers should note here that this doesn't mean that the walks were pointless and aimless, but rather that the certain 'unplanned and unstructured' element to such actions (Jenks and Neves, 2000: 7) was meant to lead to chance encounters, insights and observations. Indeed, spontaneity was central to the process of doing dérives; as Wollen rightly points out, 'Debord's basic idea is that this project of wandering through the city should be determined not by any preconceived plan, but by the attractions or discouraging counter-attractions of the city itself'. The concept of the dérive can be described as:

> Dérives involve playful constructive behaviour and awareness of psychogeographical effects, and are thus quite different from the classic notions of journey or stroll. In a dérive, one or more persons during a certain period drop their relations, their work and leisure activities and all other motives for movement and action, and let themselves be drawn by the attractions of the terrain and the encounters they find there. Chance is a less important factor in this activity than one might think: from a dérive point of view, cities have psychogeographical contours, with constant currents, fixed points and vortexes that strongly encourage and discourage entry into or exit from certain zones. (Debord, 1958: n.p.)

Debord (1958: n.p.) defined psychogeography as 'the study of the precise laws and specific effects of the geographical environment, consciously organised or not, on the emotions and behaviours of individuals'. Such a definition does not look dissimilar to arguments provided by environmental psychologists and social psychologists interested in the psychological study of spaces (Moser and Uzzell, 2003), the impact of context upon peoples' behaviour and the relations between individuals and social processes (Gifford, 2014). However, as has already been discussed, there are indeed clear differences in the use and application of that term in relation to experimental social psychologists and situationists. It has been argued that experimental social psychological research has reinforced Euro-American notions of individualism and capitalist achievement (Corral-Verdugo and Pinheiro, 2009). This is a problem because other writers have argued that peoples' experiences need to be located in specific social contexts and that those accounts are underpinned via discourses of 'capitalism, rationalism, modernisation, the Puritan work ethic and spectacle' (Sader, 1999: 96). Such concerns with capitalism and the spectacle are not considered within experimental social psychological research. Therefore, what is needed in applied social psychology are methods and approaches which are sensitive to such focus. It is necessary here to consider arguments by Parker (2007: 136) to thread through a rationale for why a psychogeographical approach is needed:

> Now it is necessary to find a way to open up new ways of thinking about the domain of the 'psychological' – perhaps by refocusing on such things as 'experience', 'subjectivity' or 'interaction' – so that the methodologies we develop follow from the research question.

Some of the current methods of research in applied social psychology research can be sedentary (Sheller and Urry, 2000), and there is not much work that documents how walking can be used to document peoples' experiences (Sheller and Urry, 2006). An argument can therefore be made for mobile methods of research in applied social psychology and to consider work by Anderson (2004) on bimbling, photo methods of elicitation by Hodgetts et al. (2010a), go-along methods by Kusenbach (2003), walking methods research by Radley et al. (2010) and psychogeographical walking (Bridger, 2014). Other writers in neighbouring disciplines, such as Cultural, Urban and Visual Studies, have also called for a 'new mobilities paradigm' (Sheller and Urry, 2006) with Brown and Durrheim in Social Psychology (2009: 916) explaining that knowledge is always 'constructed in and through mobile interactivity'. However, such a plan is not simply to generate new methods for social psychologists to use but rather to produce new methodological approaches to consider the commodification of places and why a political analysis of places is important via the approach of psychogeography.

PROJECT EXEMPLAR – PSYCHOGEOGRAPHICAL COMMUNITY WORK AT A LOCAL ARTS AND HEALTH CENTRE

In the section that now follows, one main project exemplar, involving academic colleagues Sophia Emmanouil from the Architecture Division at the University of Huddersfield and Professor Rebecca Lawthom from the Psychology Division at Manchester Metropolitan University, will be discussed. This is part of a more recent phase in the past two years of work with colleagues which has involved considering how psychogeographical work can be applied in, and beyond, an academic arena. It involved using psychogeography techniques and concepts in relation to doing community group work with members of an arts and health organisation. In formulating an applied way of doing psychogeographical work, it has been useful to make links with others doing similar applied and community based research in areas including community psychology, health and social psychological research (Hodgetts et al., 2010b; Radley et al., 2010). That work has been most useful in terms of considering a social psychological study of place and in conceptualising psychogeographical community group work. The project involved members of an arts and health organisation with the aims being: to do community group work in order to create contributions both inside and outside academia, to use a psychogeographical approach to playfully challenge everyday life in a consumer capitalist world and to consider the conditions of possibility for personal and social changes. The project idea came about via discussions between Emmanouil and Bridger who were seeking to do psychogeographical work in a non-University educational setting.

The project took place at the Hoot community centre in Huddersfield, which is run in association with an organisation called Out of the Blue (OOB). The Hoot centre is a community organisation which is run for the public as well as for adults with mental health needs and involves sessional activities, consultancy and training programmes (http://www.hootcreativearts.co.uk). Hoot and OOB focus on arts, music and other creative means by which to facilitate individuals to enhance their mental health and well-being. Such activities at the Hoot centre include yoga, dance workshops, photography and music production. Emmanouil contacted the management team at Hoot and OOB and obtained ethical clearances from that centre as well as from the University of Huddersfield ethics committee. Necessary risk assessment documentation was also completed along with plans for the activities that were submitted to the management team at Hoot. All the materials were approved by the relevant authorities and the activities took place over a period of three months. It is essential before any activities take place at Hoot that all organisers of activities undergo Criminal Records Bureau checks as well as gain approval for the work they plan to do on site.

Emmanouil and Bridger designed the psychogeographical activities to take place at the Hoot centre, and it was a central premise that such activities would be differentiated from sessional activities at Hoot because they would be underpinned by the approach of psychogeography and the focus on the exploration of peoples' reflective responses to place. The proposed outcomes were to produce an archive of work which would be exhibited at the Huddersfield Art Gallery as well as to produce a paper to discuss the work and represent the Hoot centre. Five psychogeographical workshops were planned, to take place once every two weeks for two months and included: the spirit of place, sculpting paths, dice walk, scavenger hunting and map making. In this chapter, the focus will be on explanation of the scavenger hunting and map making workshops. For readers that are interested in finding out more about the specific methodological aspects of the project, as well as the other workshop sessions, they can refer to the paper by Bridger et al. (2017). This chapter focuses in a specifically different manner on the social psychological aspects of that project and the psychogeographical turn in doing such social psychological community group work.

The scavenger hunt workshop began with going for a walk outside the Hoot centre to collect items which would be exhibited in a cabinet. Items that participants collected included stamps, driftwood, leaves and buttons. Once we had returned to the Hoot centre, we then put the items into jars, labelled the jars and wrote narrative accounts about our walks and why we had chosen those items. The idea for the scavenger hunt workshop had evolved from inspiring work by Smith (2008), who had used the process of scavenger hunting to explore his local environment to break out of habitual patterns of behaviour in the everyday places which he encountered. Such principles connect with the ideas of situationist psychogeography. The process of collecting items for the scavenger hunt and then creating a piece of artwork for the exhibition could be viewed as a form of 'participatory creativity', as evidenced in Figures 25.1 and 25.2.

The scavenger hunt workshop was then followed two weeks later by a 'do it yourself' map making workshop. Most participants returned for that final workshop and got to work in collating materials from all the workshops to create artistic maps. Suggestions were provided by Emmanouil and Bridger on how participants could create artistic maps, and they were provided with maps of Huddersfield and situationist quotes which could be used to produce art. The point of the final session was to reflect on all the psychogeographical workshops and to put into practice some of the concepts used by the situationists in relation to their practice of psychogeography.

Figure 25.1 Materials for the scavenger hunt workshop

Figure 25.2 Terry Barnes and Dave Jordan at the scavenger hunt workshop

Figure 25.3 Exhibition cabinet – The Scavenger Hunt

In order that the activities we had planned would be different to any other community activities at the centre, we ensured that there was always a distinctive theoretical underpinning to what we did. To underpin the activities at the centre, we drew on four key tenets of situationist theory to underpin the work, which were: psychogeography, participatory creativity, detournement and provocation. These tenets come from Barbrook's (2014) book, where the four concepts are used to critique consumer capitalism and to begin to think about a world beyond the current capitalist order of things. However, readers should be alerted here that these tenets are not strictly methodological rules but are rather playful strategies to consider and critique everyday life under consumer capitalist conditions. The first tenet on psychogeography has already been covered in this paper and refers to the overarching framework through which the activities at Hoot had been designed. The second tenet here is participatory creativity and refers to how we, as facilitators in the project, wanted to enable participation and creativity in relation to the workshop activities which will henceforth be discussed. The third tenet is detournement, which refers to a process whereby elements of texts are reused in new and different ways as a way to question the dominant order of things with a view to creating new and subversive ideas and practices (International, 1958), which can be evidenced via the construction of artistic maps, as will be explained later on in this chapter. The fourth and last tenet here is referred to as provocation and relates to ultra-left ideas on political agitation with one example being sloganeering on the streets of Paris in the 1950s and 1960s, 'Be realistic! Demand the impossible!' The extent to which provocation could be enabled through the psychogeographical activities at Hoot will be evidenced later in this chapter in relation to a short talk at the launch night for the exhibition, by one of the participants, Terry Barnes.

The work at the Hoot centre produced numerous outcomes and a plethora of reflective, ethical and political issues. In this section of the chapter, we will discuss some of the key threads from that work. It is important to begin with the notion of subject positions in that project in relation to researcher roles as 'scholar-activists' wishing to do community based research. It is important to draw affiliation with other scholar-activists, such as Kagan et al. (2011) as well as with Parker (2007, 2015). It was not an aim to simply jet into that community context and conduct research as 'experts' as it was important to establish social relationships, both with users of the centre as well as with the general staff and management team. The relational aspect of working with participants at Hoot was important and we wanted to present ourselves as working alongside, rather than on, the group.

The second core theme is related to the idea of working ethically, sustainably and with moral principles. Arguably these are threads that underpin all social psychology research, particularly that of the applied variety. In working with people with mental health needs (Bridger et al., 2017) and with homeless people (Radley et al., 2010), it is clearly important to address issues of ethics and morals. In our study, we endeavoured to create a safe and comfortable environment for our participants. Emmanouil worked with the group at the Hoot centre for several months before introducing the idea for a psychogeography community project. During the psychogeographical activities at the Hoot centre, participants took a range of photographs of places to document the walks and activities conducted. Ethics were clearly important, as some participants wished to remain anonymous, and so we did not make use of all the photographs produced. The use of the photographs in the map making and story workshops was useful to form bonds between participants and researchers and, again, is something which other researchers have also indicated (Hodgetts et al., 2007; 2011).

A third core theme relates to the question of intellectual theory and accessibility. Often it is the case that the use of unfamiliar terminology and language can alienate other people, so it was important for us, as researchers in the project, to explain things in ways that would make sense to them. We aimed to do the work tactfully and sensitively and would hope that our roles as teachers would give us the means to do that for a wide range of people.

Next, the outcome of these workshop activities at Hoot was important, and so it was necessary to discuss the exhibition of participants' work at the local Huddersfield Art Gallery. Sophia Emmanouil was involved in planning the exhibition at the gallery and ensured that everyone's work would be presented at that place. Emmanouil sought consent from the participants to showcase their work at the gallery and gained approval from the management team at Hoot and OOB. The launch of the exhibition (http://transdisciplinarydialogueanddebate.com) was not attended by many of the participants, but one participant, Terry Barnes, delivered a short speech discussing the elitism and non-accessibility of art in relation to everyday people and explained that certain voices are not always represented in places such as art galleries. His talk could be considered as a situationist political intervention in an art space. Figure 25.3 represents a section of the exhibition cabinet at the Huddersfield art gallery, where Emmanouil collected and arranged participants' work in relation to the scavenger hunt activity.

Figure 25.4 depicts the exhibition at the Huddersfield art gallery with video footage, textual accounts of participants' work and an exhibition cabinet.

During and after the process of the workshops at Hoot, Emmanouil and I gained feedback from the participants about the psychogeographical workshops. We were

Figure 25.4 Psychogeography exhibition at the Huddersfield Art Gallery

pleasantly surprised with how they found the workshops 'playful and interesting' and 'nothing similar to what they had done before'. Another participant indicated that using dice methods in the walking workshop had enabled him to think about different perspectives of the social world. One participant stated that they found the relaxation practices 'highly enjoyable and set them in the mood for creating', whilst another person indicated that he had gained 'tools and skills to work with in future projects'. Another person said that 'from the moment we stepped out, our mind was collecting ideas, we had a collective mind and awareness was increased. We felt we were leaving our mark. We felt like we were pushing our boundaries, creating events within events within events. We had a trigger to be creative and have fun'. Emmanouil and Bridger did indeed design the activities in a way that would be straightforward to pick up and do for those involved. The feedback from most of the participants was overwhelmingly positive. Emmanouil also spoke with the management team at Hoot to see what their views were on the psychogeographical project and they were also pleased with what we had organised. In fact, the Hoot management team asked if further similar activities could be organised and Emmanouil duly did so over the following summer period.

As part of researcher reflections on that project work, Emmanouil and Bridger arranged to do a 'go-along' interview (Kusenbach, 2003) to talk about the work we had conducted at Hoot as well as to discuss the participants' feedback and the Hoot management team feedback. That type of interview approach fitted with what we wanted to do because we wished to trace the routes that we had wandered through during the psychogeographical workshops in and around the Hoot centre. We discussed key topics and themes, such as our academic standpoints, the legacy of the project and feedback from the participants. At that point, we had also just received additional feedback from some participants about the activities where they had indicated that the activities had 'changed their perspective on things' and that it had 'changed the way they look at the town, Huddersfield town'. It would appear then that the psychogeographical activities had been not only interesting and thought provoking but also perspective changing. As to whether the activities have created longer lasting changes would need to be discerned with follow up work, which Emmanouil and Bridger plan in the future. Furthermore, the management team at Hoot were also pleased about the exhibition at the Huddersfield Art Gallery in relation to a published paper about the project by Bridger et al. (2017). The management team at Hoot indicated that it had put the Hoot centre more firmly 'on the map' and the sorts of activities that take place at that site.

CONCLUSIONS, REFLECTIONS AND IMPLICATIONS

The following questions and themes, informed by Khatib's work (1958: n.p.), are arguably of relevance to doing psychogeographical research in applied social psychology in terms of: how environments make us feel and what the effects are of particular places, consideration of the extent to which psychogeographical work can facilitate changes in terms of methodological innovation and subsequent research 'findings', what particular personal and political changes are possible through doing such work and imaginative consideration of what future environments look like. The psychogeographical 'turn' is deployed to critique the consumer capitalist landscape and to build reflective awareness in communities about how neoliberal commodification impacts on our everyday lives. The point of such work is to produce collective routes for action to take place in order to change situations.

Arguably, there are no fixed answers to the themes and questions above as they are dependent on those that carry out the work and what their aims and objectives may be. The situationists were not concerned with producing answers as they argued that people could collectively consider, plan and put into practice the sort of future societies that they wished to live in. However, in working with what may arguably be marginalised communities (i.e. people facing mental health issues, poverty and other hardship), we do have a duty of care as social psychologists to act ethically and to protect the welfare of others according to the code of conduct and ethical guidelines set out by the British Psychological Society (2009). Individuals who may struggle to fight for better living and working conditions should be supported to do so by social psychologists, other professionals, the public, families and friends. We should use our knowledge and working practices as social psychologists to support those that experience distress in all forms. Whilst people experiencing distress, poverty and discrimination may not be focused on the overthrow of capitalism, it is still possible to at least draw on the playful elements of psychogeography to consider day to day life under consumer capitalist conditions and to think about the impacts of neoliberalism and consumer spaces upon our everyday lives. A situationist psychogeographical approach in applied social psychology can be focused on a political analysis of environments and can be used to consider the extent to which social change is possible. The question of what change research can enable is important to address, and the authors of this paper do not proclaim to be able to make those changes ourselves. If one is serious about doing applied social psychological research, then it is important to create and maintain relations with a range of communities to consider what environments we want and to do so as part of a process of considering peoples' well-being and health in sociopolitical contexts.

It is important to do critical and community based research that connects with people from all walks of life. There are other social psychologists on the Left who are also concerned with doing psychology differently and with engaging in action based research and with various forms of social action and political alliances with Mad Pride, Asylum, Left Unity and the Stop the War Coalition. Parker (2007) argues for the importance of working in, against and beyond institutions, social systems and structures and that it is a necessary part of striving for social change in society. This then brings us to a very different consideration of what the term 'applied' should mean in the context of applied social psychology. It is important to hold to account and reflect on the work that we do in the discipline. It would be a great shame to only produce papers on psychogeography for an academic audience. For such work to have proper value, and to be applied, and of relevance, to communities beyond academia, it is therefore necessary to work in and beyond academia. One way to do this is to organise events for both academic and non-academic audiences, as has been done with recent conferences and festivals, including the World Congress of Psychogeography hosted at the Heritage Quays Archive space in Huddersfield (http://4wcop.org), the Loiterers Resistance Festival hosted at the Peoples' History Museum in Manchester (http://aboutmanchester.co.uk/loitering-with-intent-at-the-peoples-history-museum/) and Territories Reimagined: International Perspectives Conference (https://trip2008.wordpress.com) hosted at Manchester Metropolitan University and also at the Green Room, the Zion Centre and the Urbis Museum in Manchester. Collaboration is key here in terms of constructing solidarity with those outside of academia, in order that we 'use our own academic position to transform the cultural practices that we participate in' (Parker, 2015: 7), so that we can start to create new connections of work with political practice. In alliance with Hodgetts et al. (2014: 164), 'We need to embrace the long history in psychology of working in partnership with communities to challenge inequitable social structures and to affect change'. The question then is not simply to consider which methods to use in social psychological research about place and context, but rather to draw on whatever approach and associated methods will best enable us to tackle issues such as social inequalities in place and to consider the consumer capitalist landscape.

The aims of such work should be to draw together ideas and practices from situationist psychogeography in relation to working with people in, and beyond, academia. This work does not necessarily create social change, but it can shift the ways that we, as researchers and participants, think about everyday life and can enable us to reconsider and think about what future conditions of possibility could be. Plant (1992: 76) raises the problematic issue of appearing to do 'revolutionary critique' whilst at the same time 'reproducing the specialisation of knowledge and the lucrative elitism' of such 'roles'. Debord, a leading member of the Situationist International, wanted to avoid the institutionalisation of situationism into academia. His fear was that radical ideas could become 'watered down' and devoid of the potential to effect changes in capitalist society. Any critical academic work is, to some extent, recuperated into the dominant sphere, though the challenge is to continue to do work that detourns, subverts and calls into question the capitalist order of things. One should take seriously the argument made by Vaneigem (1967: 186–99), where he argues that group activities can enable the 'self-realisation' of each person and that such realisations can lead to wider social changes in society. Parker (2007) has also argued for working in, against and beyond capitalist social systems and institutions. Hopefully this chapter has laid the foundations for future development and innovation in the use of psychogeography as a social psychological approach to critique the consumer capitalist landscape and to open up and enable avenues for collection action and social change.

REFERENCES

Allport, G. W. (1954). *The nature of prejudice*. Reading, MA: Addison-Wesley.

Altman, I. (1993). Challenges and opportunities of a transactional world view: Case study of contemporary Mormon polygamous families. *American Journal of Community Psychology, 21*, 135–163.

Anderson, J. (2004). Talking whilst walking: A geographical archaeology of knowledge. *Area 36*(3), 254–261.

Barbrook, R. (2014). *Class wargames: Ludic subversion against spectacular capitalism*. New York: Minor Compositions.

Billig, M., Condor, S., Edwards, D., Ganr, M., Middleton, D., & Radley, Al. (1988). *Ideological dilemmas: A social psychology of everyday thinking*. London: Sage.

Bridger, A. J. (2014). Visualising Manchester: Exploring new ways to study urban environments with reference to situationist theory, the dérive and qualitative research. *Qualitative Research in Psychology, 11*(1), 78–97.

Bridger, A. J., Emmanouil, S., & Lawthom, R. (2017). trace.space: a psychogeographical community project with members of an arts and health organisation. *Qualitative Research in Psychology, 14*(1), 42–61.

British Psychological Society. (2009). *Code of ethics and conduct: Guidance published by the Ethics Committee of the British Psychological Society*. The British Psychological Society: Leicester.

Brown, L., & Durrheim, K. (2009). Different kinds of knowing: Generating interview data through mobile interviewing. *Qualitative Inquiry, 15*(5), 911–930.

Chtcheglov, I. (1958). Formulary for a new urbanism. *Situationist International*. Retrieved from http://www.cddc.vt.edu/sionline/presitu/formulary.html

Corral-Verdugo, V., & Pinheiro, J. Q. (2009). Environmental psychology with a Latin American taste. *Journal of Environmental Psychology, 29*, 366–374.

Cuba, L., & Hummon, D. M. (1993). A place to call home: Identification with dwelling, community and region. *The Sociological Quarterly, 34*, 111–131.

Debord, G. (1958). Theory of the dérive. *Situationist International*. Retrieved from http://www.cddc.vt.edu/sionline/si/theory.html

Dixon, J., & Durrheim, K. (2004). Dislocating identity: Desegregation and the transformation of place. *Journal of Environmental Psychology, 24*, 455–473.

Dixon, J., Tredoux, C., Durrheim, K., Finchilescu, G., & Clack, B. (2008). 'The inner citadels of the color line': Mapping the micro-ecology of racial segregation in everyday life spaces. *Social and Personality Psychology Compass, 2*(4), 1574–1569.

Gifford, R. (2014). Environmental psychology matters. *Annual Review of Psychology, 65*, 541–579.

Hodgetts, D., Chamberlain, K., & Groot, S. (2011). Reflections on the visual in community research and action. In P. Reavey (Ed.), *Visual methods in psychology: Using and interpreting images in qualitative research*. London: Routledge.

Hodgetts, D., Chamberlain, K., & Radley, A. (2007). Considering photographs never taken during a photo-production project. *Qualitative Research in Psychology, 4*(4), 263–280.

Hodgetts, D., Stolte, O., Chamberlain, K., Radley, A., Groot, S., & Waimarie Nikora, L. (2010a). The mobile hermit and the city: Considering links between places, objects and identities in social psychological research on homelessness. *British Journal of Social Psychology, 49*, 285–303.

Hodgetts, D., Drew, N., Sonn, C., Stolte, O., Nikora, L. W., & Curtis, C. (2010b). *Social psychology and everyday life*. Palgrave MacMillan: Basingstoke.

Hodgetts, D., Stolte, O., & Groot, S. (2014). Towards a relationally and action-orientated applied social psychology of homelessness. *Social and Personality Psychology Compass, 8*(4), 156–164.

International, S. (1958). Preliminary problems in constructing a situation. *Nothingness: The library*. [Electronic Version]. Retrieved from http://library.nothingness.org/articles/SI/en/display/313

Jenks, C., & Neves, T. (2000). A walk on the wild side: Urban ethnography meets the flâneur. *Journal for Cultural Research*, *4*(1), 1–17.

Kagan, C., Burton, M., Duckett, P. S., Lawthom, R., & Siddiqque, A. (2011). *Critical community psychology*. Oxford: Wiley-Blackwell.

Keith, M., & Pile, S. (Eds.) (1993). *Place and the politics of identity*. New York: Routledge.

Khatib, A. (1958). Attempt at a psychogeographical description of Les Halles. *Situationist International*. Retrieved from http://www.cddc.vt.edu/sionline/si/leshalles.html

Kotanyi, A., & Vaneigem, R. (1961). Basic programme of the bureau of unitary urbanism. *Situationist International*. Retrieved from http://www.cddc.vt.edu/sionline/si/bureau.html

Kusenbach, M. (2003). Street phenomenology: The go-along as ethnographic research tool. *Ethnography*, *4*(3), 455–485.

Lefebvre, H. (1976). *The survival of capitalism*. London: Allison and Busby.

Manzo, L. C. (2003). Beyond house and haven: Toward a revisioning of emotional relationships with places. *Journal of Environmental Psychology*, *23*, 47–61.

McKenzie, J. (2008). Queing and intervention. In *Territories Reimagined: International Perspectives*, Manchester Metropolitan University, Manchester, 19–21 June 2008.

Merrifield, A. (1993). Place and space: A Lefebvrian reconciliation. *Transactions of the British Institute of Geographers*, *18*, 516–531.

Miles, S. (2010). *Spaces for consumption*. London: Sage.

Moser, G., & Uzzell, D. (2003). Environmental psychology. In I. B. Weiner (Series Ed.), Th. Milon, & M. J. Lerner (Vol. Ed.), *Handbook of psychology: Vol 5. Personality and social psychology* (pp. 419–445). New York: Wiley.

Nowell, B. L., Berkowitz, S. L., Deacon, Z., & Foster-Fishman, P. (2006). Revealing the cues with community places: Stories of identity, history and possibility. *American Journal of Community Psychology*, *37*, 29–46.

Parker, I. (2007). *Revolution in psychology: From alienation to emancipation*. London: Pluto Press.

Parker, I. (2015). *Psychology after discourse analysis: Concepts, methods, critique*. London: Routledge.

Plant, S. (1992). *The most radical gesture: The situationist international in a postmodern age*. London: Routledge.

Proshansky, H., Fabian, A. K., & Kaminoff, R. (1983). Place-identity: Physical world socialization of the self. *Journal of Environmental Psychology*, *3*, 57–83.

Radley, A., Chamberlain, K., Hodgetts, D., Stotle, O., & Groot, S. (2010). From means to occasion: Walking in the life of homeless people. *Visual Studies*, *25*(1), 36–45.

Sadler, S. (1999). *The situationist city*. London: MIT Press.

Said, E. (1993). *Culture and imperialism*. New York: Knopf.

Sheller, J., & Urry, J. (2000). The city and the car. *International Journal of Urban and Regional Research*, *24*, 737–757.

Sheller, M., & Urry, J. (2006). The new mobilities paradigm. *Environment and Planning A*, 28, 207–226.

Smith, S. (2008). *How to be an explorer of the world*. New York: Penguin Group Inc.

Twigger-Ross, C. L., & Uzzell, D. L. (1996). Place and identity processes. *Journal of Environmental Psychology*, *16*, 205–220.

Vaneigem, R. (1967). The revolution of everyday life. *Nothingness: The library*. [Electronic Version] Retrieved from http://library.nothingness.org/articles/SI/en/pub_contents/5

Wollen, P. (2001). Situationists and architecture. *New Left Review*, *8*(1), 123–139.

Wood, D. (1987). I don't feel that about environmental psychology today. But I want to. *Journal of Environmental Psychology*, *7*, 417–424.

26

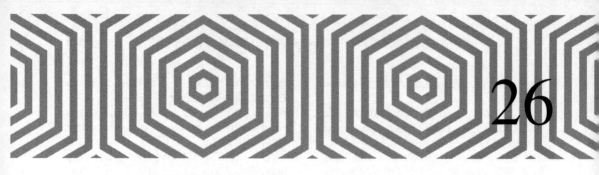

Community and Participatory Approaches to the Environment

Bianca Dreyer and Manuel Riemer

INTRODUCTION

Environmental dilemmas are of increasing psychological relevance. Global climate change is not only threatening our physical environment, but also human wellbeing and communities. Likewise, human existence continues to shape the magnitude and presence of environmental dilemmas. While it is certainly integral to advance the physical sciences related to the mitigation of the effects of climate change, it is perhaps of equal importance to advance the social sciences of climate change. This importance was articulated as part of the key conclusions of the 2007 Intergovernmental Panel on Climate Change: 'Preventing global climate change and establishing *more sustainable development practices* for ecological conservation and *social integration* are important challenges [emphases added], if not the key challenges of current and future generations'. It is well-established that climate change and other environmental challenges result from a combination of exponential population growth, technological developments, unsustainable consumption of renewable and non-renewable resources, and production of significant waste and pollution, especially greenhouse gases (GHGs) (Wackernagel and Rees, 1998). To halt the current path toward ecological destruction, these are the things that need to change. Those who express doubts, such as major stakeholders in the fossil fuel industry and the politicians they financially support, tend to be those who personally gain from the status quo (Korten, 1995). These financial interests are supported by laws that require publicly traded corporations to be driven by a single motivation, to maximize value for stakeholders and to continue to make as much money as possible (Leonard, 2007a). These forces, to say the least, are powerful.

Thus, changes cannot be achieved by simple, disconnected, or localized solutions. Rather, in order to enact meaningful change, we must carefully consider issues of power, capitalism, and consumerism. In the face of global climate change, fundamental societal transformation toward sustainability is both a necessity and inevitability. Core to this transformation is a fundamental reorientation of the complex dynamic between human beings, their social structures, and their physical environment. Finding the right path forward is challenging; there is critical need for applied social psychological research to contribute to actionable knowledge in addressing these increasingly global challenges. As scientists, we cannot shy away from social problems, especially problems that are as complex as global climate change. While research is a necessary, but insufficient, condition for scientific progress, it is more necessary for progress related to widespread social transformation (Heller and Monahan, 1977). Social movements and community reform efforts are short-lived unless they have empirically demonstrated practical impact (Heller and Monahan, 1977). Likewise, applied social scientists and change agents need to build on good theory in their attempts to work toward social transformation. As Lewin (1951: 169) said, broad scale transformations can 'only be accomplished […] if the theorist does not look toward applied problems with highbrow aversion or with a fear of social problems and if the applied psychologists realize that there is nothing so practical as good theory'.

Initial efforts to establish an applied psychology focused on environmental issues came from the desire of social psychologists to move beyond laboratory-based, experimental designs that tend to produce findings that tend to be a 'failure in the real world' (Proshansky, 1978). Many social issues identified by social psychologists, such as the effects of noise (e.g., Glass and Singer, 1972) and overcrowding (e.g., Galle et al., 1972), are specific to particular places and, therefore, they argued, call for location-specific fieldwork (Proshansky et al., 1983). These early applications, in which behavior–environment interactions are related to community-problem solving, have mostly focused on specific settings and groups. They are not adequately implemented in an integrative fashion across multiple environments and populations (Stokols et al., 2009). Thus, there is a need for a community-based psychology that addresses the interdependencies of multiple settings, multiple social and global locations, identities, and social issues (Gardner and Stern, 2002). A pioneering example is the work of Niki Harré (e.g., 2011) that builds on applied social psychology to advance knowledge and community action on sustainability.

In the following chapter, we examine how applications of psychology have made, or have the potential to make, significant contributions to further the transformative change needed to effectively mitigate climate change, loss of biodiversity, desertification, fresh water scarcity, and other looming catastrophes. We discuss the relevance of a form of applied social psychology that utilizes community and participatory approaches to the environment. We explore the connections between practices of sustainability as they relate to action, research, and theoretical perspectives within this field. We will illustrate how the knowledge accumulated and experience gained in this field have great relevance to many topics related to the environment. To begin, we will introduce a key concept that defines community-based work – upstreaming. We will then provide a brief overview of the current crisis and its root causes. Next, we will focus on gaps and opportunities in the field of psychology and sustainability before we move on to describe upstream solutions, as identified by community and participatory frameworks. We will then outline common frameworks and approaches for researchers interested in community and participatory approaches to the environment. Lastly, we provide some practical examples of action-research that applies these frameworks before we conclude the chapter.

Upstream Versus Downstream Solutions

'Sustainability' is a term used to describe the movement toward a world in which the previous environmental problems are mostly overcome and people have fulfilling lives without destroying the natural resources needed to provide for current and future generations (Riemer and Harré, 2017). There is widespread agreement among sustainability scientists and authors that a movement in that direction requires pragmatic idealism, an appreciation of complexity, ecological thinking, cross-sectorial collaboration, and citizen participation (Thiele, 2016). Community and participatory approaches to the environment consider these aspects. Thus, there are several theories and approaches that can supplement existing theories from applied social psychology. A popular parable told in prevention-oriented fields, such as community-based psychology, describes a group of villagers who discover a person floating downstream in the local river. A member of the village rushes out to rescue the person; however, over the next several days, more people are found floating downstream. Before long there is a flow of people floating downstream. The villagers do all they can to rescue as many people as possible and take care of them. Eventually, after some arguments about the right approach, one of the villagers decides to go upstream to figure out how all these people have ended up in the river in the first place. As it turns out, there are several bridges *that are weak and debilitated, with missing boards or flimsy railings, which cause all these people to fall into the river.*

Psychological approaches to dealing with our environmental crises, such as global climate change, often feel like fishing out the people floating downstream. Psychologists tend to target individuals in order to change one environmentally impactful behavior. This approach of addressing individual problems one at a time, without much consideration of the possible upstream causes, can be rather ineffective; if one considers all the behaviors involved in producing our individual unsustainable ecological footprints, this approach is simply insufficient for societal change. Yet, this is still one of the most common approaches to promoting sustainability: psychologists might look at one behavior (e.g., turning off lights), examine how one might go about changing that behavior (e.g., prompts, cues, etc.), then implement the strategy and repeat for each behavior and each individual. Considering the sheer number of environmentally impactful behaviors and all the different behavior change strategies one would have to develop, we would quickly run out of both financial resources to support these campaigns and time necessary to address these issues. Given the urgency of the climate change crisis, we need 'upstream solutions'; we need to find the bridges that are broken and understand the causes of their deterioration in the first place. Only by way of an understanding of their underlying cause could we then mobilize the necessary resources to repair those bridges and advocate for the changes necessary to maintain these bridges in the long term. In essence, this is what most community-based approaches to sustainability are about – eschewing psychological manipulations to get individuals to adopt or change a particular behavior in favor of community-based approaches focused at the root causes of global climate change and other anthropogenic environmental degradation. Community-based approaches are oriented toward engaging people in co-creating the more fundamental political and cultural changes needed to sustain our species and fellow species on this planet now and into the future.

The Crisis We Are Facing

> The environmental crisis is an outward manifestation of a crisis of mind and spirit. There could be no greater misconception of its meaning than to believe it is concerned only with endangered wildlife, human-made ugliness, and pollution.

These are parts of it, but more importantly, the crisis is concerned with the kind of creatures we are and what we must become in order to survive. (Lynton K. Caldwell, quoted by Koger and DuNann Winter, 2010: 1)

Since the industrial revolution, human activities have changed our biosphere more rapidly and extensively than in any comparable period of history (IPCC, 2007; MEA, 2005). This has led scientists and historians to suggest that we have entered a new epoch, the Anthropocene, a geological age during which human activity has been the dominant influence on climate and the environment (Smith and Zeder, 2013). This rapid change is resulting in significant environmental and human consequences. Significant environmental degradation is felt in the extreme drought in the Horn of Africa, devastating storms in Southeast Asia, and melting ice in the Arctic Circle. However, we also pay a human cost. 'Conflict, sex trafficking, suicide, infectious disease, economic inequality – these are among the harsh new realities of living on a planet in peril' (Miley, 2017).[1]

These changes are occurring at such a fast rate that it is becoming increasingly doubtful that the human species (and many other species) will be able to adapt to their changing environment in time to avoid significant catastrophes. Those countries and individuals already vulnerable because of their disadvantaged economic and societal positions will be the first and hardest hit by these negative consequences of anthropogenic environmental degradation (Agyeman, 2005). As increasingly difficult agricultural conditions and increasing oil prices force food prices to go up, millions of people living close to, or below, the poverty line will no longer be able to afford basic staples such as rice and flour (Godfray et al., 2010). Thus, there is a clear link between our actions as individuals, institutions, and governments and the current and future suffering of billions of people. As humans, we have a moral obligation to create rapid and significant transformational changes. This type of change requires us to go upstream and understand how we got into this trouble in the first place.

Going Upstream: Understanding the Root Causes

To begin to examine the needed changes requires a deep understanding of the dominant social paradigm (DSP) that is driving our decisions and actions so that this paradigm can be changed. According to psychologists Koger and DuNann Winter (2010), the DSP is the dominant Western worldview and its 'accompanying beliefs that encourage the use and abuse of nature' (Koger and DuNann Winter, 2010: 6). They describe how specific historical developments and shifts in philosophical beliefs, especially during the enlightenment period, have shifted the dominant worldview from one that considered nature as a spiritual interconnected living system to one that has the following four key tenants: (1) nature is composed of inert, physical elements, (2) which can, and should, be controlled (3) by individual human beings seeking private economic gain (4) whose work results in progress (mostly economic development). This 'worldview has fostered an ideology of limitless economic growth that, in the last century, has been fueled and exacerbated by the dominance of capitalism, globalization, and more recently, the neoliberal policies of deregulation, privatization, and individualization of risk' (Riemer and Van Voorhees, 2014: 50). The problem with progress and growth as a 'goal' is that the scale we use to measure progress, the Gross Domestic Product (GDP), does not distinguish between growth that improves people's lives and growth that impedes it. Robert F. Kennedy (1968, March 18) remarked that the GDP counts 'air pollution, the destruction of the redwoods and the loss of our natural wonder in chaotic sprawl. It counts napalm, and it counts nuclear warheads, and armored cars for the police to fight the riots in our cities'. However, it does allow for the 'health of our children, the quality of their education, [...] the intelligence of our public debate or the integrity of our public officials'. Yet, there is a 'big difference between more kids in school and more kids in jail. More windmills or more coal fired power plants. More super-efficient public trains or more gas wasted in traffic jams' (Leonard, 2007b). However, all of these forms of growth contribute to increasing this number we use as a measure of national success, the GDP.

Further, our materials economy is based on a linear way of thinking which disrupts the cyclical process of nature. To some extent, all human societies are processing natural resources in a linear direction, transforming valuable resources into useless garbage (Robert, 1991), although many Indigenous communities do so significantly less than the mass of the majority world. As Koger and DuNann Winter (2010) articulate, this linear notion of progress requires empty space. Yet, on a finite planet, we are running out of spaces to acquire new resources or leave our waste; which the majority world has primarily done in the minority world. Thus, it is time to question the very assumption of our worldview, the goodness of consumption, and the individual freedom to live without responsibility for the natural environment.

Taking responsibility of the environment urges us to re-examine how sources of problems were sought out and addressed in the past; this is upstream work. Sustainability scientists and advocates for example point to a lack of system thinking – that is, considering systems as interconnected – in the way we have approached past challenges (Smith, 2011). Challenges, such as high levels of poverty, were approached separately from other challenges, such as environmental degradation, often with unintended negative consequences in other parts of the natural and/or human system. Rachel Carson in her influential book *Silent Spring* (1962), for example, highlighted the unintended consequences of the then widespread use of dichlorodiphenyltrichloroethane (DDT), an organochlorine popular for its insecticidal properties. As an insecticide, DDT played an important role in the so-called 'green revolution', a series of technology transfer initiatives (e.g., the distribution of hybridized seeds, synthetic fertilizers, and pesticides) that contributed to a worldwide increase in agricultural production, especially in minority world countries, saving millions of people from starvation. Unfortunately, it also had significant negative impacts on the food chain within the ecosystem, resulting in the extinction of several species, especially birds, which eventually led to its ban in most countries or significant reductions in its use (Carson, 1962; Mrak, 1969; Ribicoff, 1966). System thinking is a form of analysis and practice that places emphasis on how a problem (e.g., the reduction of poverty through increased agricultural production) interacts in complex ways with other parts of the system, including those in which it was created (e.g., economic, policy, and cultural conditions; Arnold and Wade, 2015).

Finally, it is important to highlight the multi-faceted and global nature of our current environmental challenges. Environmental issues are multi-faceted because they are closely related to other important issues; for example, a public health crisis due to malnutrition after droughts, cancer due to toxin exposure, or disease (infectious, cardiorespiratory, diarrheal) due to creating better conditions for disease transmitting mosquitos, as in the case of Zika, malaria, and dengue fever. Environmental challenges are also global because they will impact ecosystems and affect human societies worldwide, both directly and indirectly, via flooding, droughts, wildfires, insect proliferation, changes in land use, fragmentation of natural systems, and extreme weather events (Webster et al., 2005). Thus, only by considering our current environmental issues within systems, recognizing the multi-faceted nature, and working at a global scale can we begin to tackle the broken bridges and keep them stable.

Gaps and Opportunities: Moving From Downstream to Upstream

However, it is difficult to ignore the people who have fallen into the river while searching for upstream solutions. Thus, often solutions proposed first will be focused on downstream solutions – pulling people out of the water – rather than upstream solutions. In the 1960s and 1970s, the coalescence of theoretical and empirical research programs under the umbrella of environmental psychology spurred considerable enthusiasm and collaboration (Stokols, 1995). Proshansky, Rivlin, and Ittleson played key roles in the new field and founded environmental psychology's first academic program at The Graduate Center of the City University of New York. During the beginning phases, hundreds of journal articles were written (Stokols, 1995), journals were published (e.g., *Environment and Behavior*, *Population & Environment*, and *Journal of Environmental Psychology*), and new professional associations were started (e.g., Division 34 of the American Psychological Association, the Environmental Psychology section of the International Association of Applied Psychology). A field of environmental psychology developed that focuses largely on studying specific types of behaviors, such as car use or composting, and finding effective ways of changing these behaviors, getting at downstream solutions (e.g., Theory of Planned Behavior, Value-Beliefs-Norm Theory).

The use of this approach has expanded since its early inception because results and successes can be readily observed, its logic appears self-evident, and study-design can be simple. However, issues of sustainability are complex, 'wicked problems' (Rittel and Webber, 1973); that is, these problems are hard to define and are influenced by multiple dynamic political and social systems (Kreuter et al., 2004). Further, these problems also influence multiple systems in return. Physical upheavals of climate and weather, for instance, will directly affect social systems and community well-being. For example, heatwaves significantly impact daily life, such as water quality, power consumption, pollution, and physical and mental health (Zuo et al., 2015), particularly for vulnerable sections of the community such as children, seniors, people experiencing homelessness, and socially disadvantaged individuals (Peng et al., 2011; Vandentorren et al., 2006; Vaneckova et al., 2010; Wilson et al., 2011). Thus, no simple solution can tackle these wicked problems.

Heatwaves are but one occurrence increasing with the changing climate. Other issues are increases in infectious diseases, malnutrition, etc. 'The anatomy of a silent crisis' by the Global Humanitarian Forum (2009), led by former UN Secretary General Kofi Annan, estimated that, every year, climate change leaves over 300,000 people dead, 325 million people seriously affected, and economic losses of US$125 billion. Thus, global climate change is not just an issue of individual and community wellbeing but also one of social justice (Hossay, 2006). For example, overfishing is not just an environmental issue, but it also threatens the livelihood of fishers. Yet, they are often the ones who engage in overfishing (referred to as the 'tragedy of the commons' borrowing from Hardin's 1969 article with the same title). Successful models of dealing with these complex issues require collaborative work focused on finding an agreement where everyone respects the limits of the natural environment but also where the social sustainability of people relying on natural resources is secured. This is the balance that community-based scholars are trying to strike. This work can only be successfully done through inter- and transdisciplinary research collaborations (Hunecke, 2003; Mieg, 2003; Rambow, 2003) and, more importantly, by developing community-based collaborations (Gray, 1989; Israel et al., 2005; Kegler et al., 2010) and engaging in collaborative research (Minkler and Wallerstein, 2008; Trickett, 2009), as such research provides partners with actionable knowledge

(Münger and Riemer, 2012). In one research project studying the cultural impacts of climate change in Tuvalu, a minority world nation in the South Pacific, for example, the researcher noted that 'projects that are not based within the community and do not engage the collectivist nature of Tuvalu's cultures tend not to succeed' (Corlew and Johnson-Hakim, 2013).

Psychological work in community-based environmental scholarship is not focused on any particular methodology; rather it shares a common understanding of values, engagement in action-oriented research, and focus on social justice. People working from this approach are often motivated by values such as social justice, respect for diversity, and self-determination and how to engage people in working towards these values. While there is significant overlap between community-based approaches and cognitive or critical approaches in terms of focus on applied topics, critical engagement, values, and focus on social justice, it is the action-research component that mostly distinguishes it. Action-research, as defined by Reason and Bradbury (2001: 1), is:

> a participatory, democratic process concerned with developing practical knowing in the pursuit of worthwhile human purposes, grounded in a participatory worldview [...].
>
> It seeks to bring together action and reflection, theory and practice, in participation with others, in the pursuit of practical solutions to issues of pressing concern to people, and more generally the flourishing of individual persons and their communities.

While the focus on action-research is what differentiates community-based psychological approaches to sustainability from mainstream environmental psychology, it is an approach that emerged in many academic disciplines (Brydon-Miller et al., 2003). Scholars in fields such as environment and development studies (Scott and Oelefse, 2005), legal studies (Scott, 2016), politics (Dobson, 1998), and many more conduct community-based environmental action-research, although they may not frame it in a psychological lens.

In the past, action-research-oriented psychological research on environmental issues, as described above, has been very limited. A major sub-discipline of applied psychology that generally has focused on action-research – community psychology – only relatively recently started to pay attention to environmental issues, first after the Love Canal toxic waste scandal. This environmental disaster in New York State was the result of a chemical dumpsite with improper management and regulation. Hazardous waste from this site started seeping up into backyards, playgroups, public schools, and swimming pools of the surrounding community, leading to birth defects, increased cancer rates, and eventually resulting in the evacuation of all families living in the area (Beck, 1979). Lois Gibbs, the leader of the citizen movement in the context of the Love Canal toxic waste scandal, gave the keynote address during the second biennial convention of the Society for Community Research and Action (SCRA; Division 27 of the American Psychological Association). However, it was not until more recently, in 2009, that the SCRA Environment & Justice Interest Group was founded, which publishes a quarterly column in *The Community Psychologist* (Riemer and Van Voorhees, 2009). Roundtable discussions focused on global climate change and community psychology were organized at the last four SCRA biennial conferences. In 2011, the *American Journal of Community Psychology* published a special section on 'Community Psychology and Global Climate Change' (Riemer and Reich, 2011) and recently there has been an increased representation of environmentally-focused posters and presentations at community-based psychology conferences, such as a keynote at the 2013 SCRA Biennial by Niki Harré (Harré, 2013). Further, there is increased representation of environmental content in textbooks such as *Community Psychology: In pursuit of liberation and well-being* by Nelson and Prilleltensky (2010), the *APA Handbook of Community Psychology* (Bond et al., 2016), and now this Handbook has a chapter on community approaches to the environment as well.

These developments are promising given the urgency of addressing the causes and impacts of global climate change and other environmental problems and the potential for applied social psychology to make significant contributions toward a more sustainable world. There are gaps in current approaches to environmental issues that cannot be addressed without considering collaborative, community-based approaches. Finding upstream solutions requires different forms of knowledge production that encourage more rapid knowledge dissemination and uptake (Münger and Riemer, 2012). In the comprehensive report on global climate change published by the American Psychological Association (APA) in 2009, Janet Swim and her colleagues conclude that 'psychologists can be dramatically more effective if they connect psychological work to concepts developed in the broader climate research community and collaborate with scientists from other fields' (Swim et al., 2009: 160). Finding multi-faceted and multi-level solutions necessitates support from diverse stakeholders from multiple sectors of society (such as government, non-governmental organizations (NGOs), and corporations). As academic researchers involved in sustainability work, it becomes crucial to engage in interdisciplinary, multi-sectorial, participatory action research. Doing community-based work means that one is more likely to do field research in real-world contexts. Naturally, field research also requires flexibility to using multiple research methods (see Riemer and Schweizer-Ries, 2012, for an overview). It is impossible and unproductive to single out one behavior to focus on as the core problem in sustainability. To side-step the complexity of sustainability and reduce it to a single behavior or factor leads to theories based on artificial scenarios which often have little to do with community needs or the issues one faces in real-world settings. A skill essential to community-based work is the ability to work with, instead of around, complexity. The challenge is to find the relevant issues in complex and messy data in order to make sense of the research. The researcher is a detective; community-based research means to consciously decide against the easy way out. It means walking upstream and figuring out why people fall into the water in the first place.

Community-based and participatory approaches were thus born out of an understanding of the complexity of environmental issues and the desire to work toward finding upstream solutions; something that can only happen as a community where multiple sectors of society collaboratively solve the problems we are facing today. Psychological knowledge needed for this, then, is how to develop effective collaborations, how to bring different sectors and disciplines together, and how to engage communities in having important conversations about our core values and to what degree our institutions, policies and regulations, resource use and allocation, leadership, and our individual actions and practices reflect those values.

Building Bridges, and Keeping Them. What Are Upstream Solutions?

With the development of community-based and participatory approaches to the environment, a shift started to happen not just in the methodological practices and approaches to research (e.g., action-research) but also in identifying and working towards upstream solutions. Broadly speaking, global climate change is the *problem* that got us thinking about sustainability in a more fundamental way. Sustainability is the transformation (*solution*) that needs to happen to create the kind of society that we need to be to live beyond the next 100 years.

As societies develop, they must develop in ways likely to sustain themselves into the next century, which means they have to take climate changes into account. There are different aspects of this transformation that are discussed and much disagreement about how to foster the needed changes (Dryzek, 2005). Some believe that we can retain the current capitalist, corporation-run system, largely unchanged and unchallenged. These people advocate for adjustments to the existing system primarily through technological changes and individual behavior changes. In reference to our earlier river parable, these could be considered downstream solutions. The 'technological change' focuses on more sustainable technologies, such as electric cars. However, these advances are not sufficient as technical efficiency gains resulting from, for example, energy-efficient appliances, home insulation, and water-saving devices tend to be overtaken by consumption growth (Midden et al., 2007). Moreover, technological innovations require the proper use and engagement of individuals who use and interact with them. The 'personal change' focuses on our individual practices and behaviors, such as reducing meat consumption or car usage. However, there are environmentalists such as George Monbiot who believe changes to our individual behaviors make no difference and who see changes in legislation as the only solution (Monbiot, 2009). On the other hand, proponents of behavior change point toward the fact that most instances of deteriorating environmental conditions are caused by human behavior and that 'conservation is a goal that can *only* be achieved by changing behavior' [emphasis added] (Schultz, 2011: 1080). Apparent in these debates is the consideration of 'what kind of problem' sustainability is, as this will ultimately determine the (only) possible solution to addressing it (Harré, 2011). In the end, if the focus is on sustainability as a kind of *problem*, we will be vulnerable to arguments that suggest that *any* of the solutions we propose are not good enough. Thus, there is a third kind of transformation people propose, which is less concerned about solving a problem and instead focuses on creating a more radical cultural shift, 'one which represents fundamental rethinking of most patterns of human activity, which integrates ecological sustainability with social justice, and which sees sustainability as a promising metaphor for a historic and necessary structural *and* personal transformation' (Sterling 1996: 18–19). These would be the upstream solutions getting at the root causes.

As highlighted by Sterling (1996) this shift happens at two levels. There is the societal structural transformation but then there is also the personal transformation. It is difficult to imagine one happening without the other, similar to the chicken and egg problem. We need to be transformed as people but we also want to see our society transformed. If society gets transformed, then that has an impact on the individual but we will not see a lot of transformation at the societal level if individuals are not pushing for it. Thus, instead of focusing on solving a problem, as a sustainability advocate you are focusing on creating an alternative way of life (Harré, 2011), a shift toward a culture of sustainability. The transformation that we believe sustainability entails won't happen if one individual starts recycling. If the structures that maintain certain behaviors don't change, as an individual there are only so many changes one can make. Consider public transportation as an example. If there is no bus where you live, you cannot make the choice to use public transportation. To conceptualize these issues as a community or city means to focus on how public transportation options are made available and how other options might be dis-incentivized, for example, by decreasing parking or charging a fee for driving in city centers. Thus, to address issues of transportation, collaboration between stakeholders such as city planners, politicians, business owners, and residents are required.

This cultural shift is not just focused on the natural environment but also on the social and economic environment. One of the reasons we focus on sustainability is because of the opportunity to transform society in a more fundamental way. 'Sustainability' contains as its word stem the word 'sustain'. That is somewhat of a misnomer, however, because a transformation toward sustainability does not mean maintenance of the current status quo. As humans, we want to sustain our ability to continue living as a species. However, as sustainability advocates we *don't* want to maintain the current levels of inequality and poverty. Prillentensky (2003; 2008) articulates the need for increased psycho-political validity of psychological theories, maximizing the extent to which theories address power issues and encourage positive structural changes in communities. These power issues are reflected in differential access of affluent and impoverished communities to clean water, food, impact of global climate change, energy resources, exposure to toxic pollutants, etc. That is why the conversation about sustainability needs to go beyond environmental issues and needs to transform into a bigger conversation about the kind of society that we want to be. A lot of the issues societies and communities are dealing with today have common root causes. A conversation about sustainability provides us with a useful platform to have the more fundamental conversations because everybody will feel the effects of global climate change. An important focus for sustainability scientists working with participatory and community approaches, then, needs to be about envisioning a better society together.

Approaches and Frameworks: Some Questions for Consideration

When working with communities to create transformative change, there are some key questions to consider while conducting action-research. In the following, we discuss specific concepts that have been used within community-based and participatory research. These concepts are particularly useful for supporting applied social psychological work related to sustainability. We introduce these concepts as guiding questions that researchers interested in participatory and community-based approaches seriously consider before engaging in research. These example questions are illustrative rather than exhaustive; through the research process, other questions will also become relevant, depending on the scope and nature of the project.

ECOLOGICAL FRAMEWORK AND SYSTEMS THINKING: HAVE WE SUFFICIENTLY CONSIDERED THE INTERCONNECTEDNESS OF THE ISSUE WE ARE ADDRESSING?

Given the complexities of sustainability issues, one needs to work within theoretical frameworks that highlight the interconnections among individual cognitions, emotions, and actions. These interconnections are important to consider in relation to micro- and macro-level factors characteristic of an economic system focused on unsustainable growth and profit maximization. Doing so will allow us to conceptualize our current crises in a more complex way, which will help us to find innovative and sustainable alternatives to current ways of living. As Albert Einstein observed, the world we have created today as a result of our thinking thus far has problems that cannot be solved by thinking the way we thought when we created them (Calaprice, 2005). One theoretical model that allows for thinking differently about complexity is the ecological model (Bronfenbrenner, 1994).

As illustrated in Figure 26.1, the ecological model exemplifies the network of interactions among multiple levels of the ecological system, such as individual (*demo*), relational (*micro*), organizational (*meso*), community (*exo*), socio-cultural levels (*macro*), and the geosphere (*geo*) (Moskell et al., 2011).

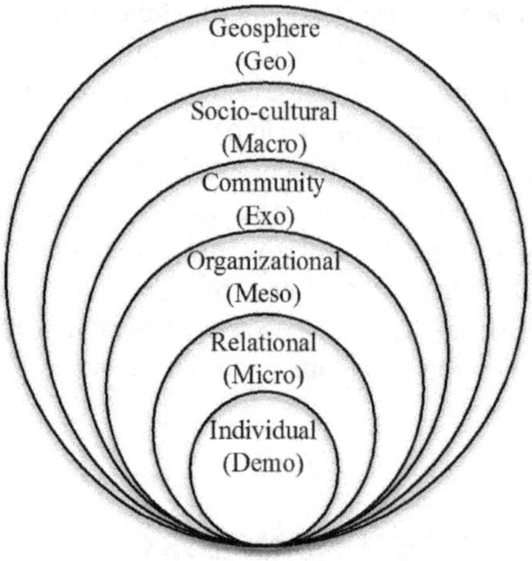

Figure 26.1 Illustration of the ecological model

Source: Adapted from Moskell and Allred (2013)

Developments in the original ecological model (Neal and Neal, 2013) emphasize the social relationships that connect actors of different ecological levels to each other and in doing so create networked structures. Environmental issues and their actors (such as individuals and institutions) permeate each of these levels, making it crucial to work simultaneously at multiple levels. A practical use of this model is as a tool to consider unanticipated consequences of our actions and technological inventions at different levels of a given system. For instance, in researching issues related to overfishing, one needs to consider both technological advances in the fishing industry with the financial pressures of fishers themselves, which include community structures that provide little alternative employment and socio-cultural factors such as population growth, which can exacerbate or alleviate these other factors. The same ecological model can be used to identify upstream solutions when addressing environmental issues. The visual representation of multiple ecological levels can facilitate peoples' understanding of the complexity of primary and secondary causes of global climate change. This increased understanding allows for greater consideration of the kinds of strategies necessary to address these causes (Dittmer and Riemer, 2013). For example, consider the issue of recyclable waste. Using the various levels of the ecological model, one can investigate how recycling is influenced by family members, neighbors, city regulations, and services such as curbside recycling, business practices, cultural values, etc. (Dittmer and Riemer, 2013). Being able to map these multiple influences on a visual model can make the complexity of this activity less overwhelming and allows researchers to investigate at which level solutions should be targeted within the system. Keeping with the example of recycling, researchers have found that the best strategy to get people to recycle is to provide curbside pickup (Oskamp, 1995). Implementing curbside recycling is a municipal decision; no individual alone can make this choice. When individuals recognize how outside layers (e.g., exo, macro) affect individuals, the conversation related to environmental issues changes toward a more careful examination of the structural forces that shape these behaviors. The ecological model is thus used as a tool to guide research questions and to facilitate the potential outcomes of community interventions targeted at various levels.

ENGAGEMENT: HAVE WE IDENTIFIED AND ENGAGED STAKEHOLDERS?

In order to engage in this work at these multiple levels, it is critical that decision makers, citizens, and other stakeholders are involved with the research at the macro, micro, and individual levels. Community participation in research provides important insight into the interconnections between the different levels. While conventional research tends to generate 'knowledge for understanding' or 'knowledge for knowledge's sake', which needs not be linked to its practical application, most action research focuses on 'knowledge for action' (Cornwall and Jewkes, 1995).

While these collaborative approaches are increasingly popular in many fields and have even garnered their own sources of funding (e.g., Cornwall and Jewkes, 1995; El. Ansari, 2005; Flicker, 2008; Israel et al., 1998; Minkler, 2004; 2005; Mosavel et al., 2005; Viswanathan et al., 2004), developing and maintaining effective collaboration is a difficult task. Collaborative efforts, particularly between universities and communities, face numerous challenges. Ambiguous objectives and roles, as well as difficult group dynamics, such as power imbalances and negative relationships, are typical barriers to successful collaborative work between communities and universities (Münger and Riemer, 2012). Despite these challenges, collaborative approaches that aim to bring together the technical skills of researchers and the practical experience and community knowledge of practitioners create a more unified research process. By acknowledging and integrating the experience of community members, this research also aims to produce research that is more relevant, has greater quality, validity, and practicality to real-world issues (Israel et al., 2003). The engagement of community members often occurs around issues of relevance to the community, local or regional (such as water pollution), with the aim of advancing the community's goals and development strategies (Israel et al., 2003). Research approaches, such as participatory action-research (PAR) or community-based research (CBR), have been used successfully to advance communities' change agendas. These approaches, as a group, are typically referred to as community-based participatory research, or CBPR (Minkler and Wallerstein, 2011). The three interconnected elements of CBPR are: participation, research, and action. CBPR is described as supporting 'collaborative, equitable partnerships in all phases of the research process', which will promote 'co-learning and capacity building among all partners', 'disseminate findings and knowledge gained to all partners and involve all partners in the dissemination process' (Israel et al., 2003). Engaging in this process will ensure the utilization of research findings toward the anticipated transformative changes.

ENVIRONMENTAL ACTION: HAVE WE CONSIDERED CITIZEN PARTICIPATION?

As illustrated from our analysis of recycling, while personal practices are an important consideration for sustainability, they are not sufficient in and of themselves: we also need to work collaboratively with others to change the conditions that limit sustainability. Necessary cultural transformation requires fundamental political and institutional change. One approach toward these changes is to engage citizens in environmental actions. Environmental actions are defined as 'intentional and conscious civic behaviors that are focused on systemic causes of environmental problems and the promotion of environmental sustainability through collective efforts' (Alisat and Riemer, 2015). They can range from participatory actions, such as signing a petition, to collective actions such as attending protests or joining an environmental group, or even leadership actions such as organizing a boycott or protest (Alisat and Riemer, 2015). These actions typically require significant effort and sustained personal commitment and are distinct from personal practices or behaviors, which are focused on changing one's private and personal environmental impact, for example by reducing energy consumption in the home. Environmental actions are targeted at transformative change at a systems level and therefore aim to influence the behavior and actions of many individuals or the policy system as a whole (Stern et al., 1999). Encouraging environmental action includes three important elements: raising consciousness, building action competence, and fostering engagement.

Raising Consciousness

Consciousness raising is about more than just providing people with knowledge. This concept refers to understanding, at a deeper level, why we should even care about issues of sustainability and how these issues are related to other forms of societal action, such as participation in democracy, poverty, etc. (i.e., going upstream). Some have argued traditional behavior change strategies treat people as passive objects, to be manipulated (Kenis and Mathijs, 2012), rather than agents of change (e.g., Fox and Prilleltensky, 1997). Community-based and participatory approaches aim to provide a comprehensive understanding of the nature of a problem, its effects, and root causes. This kind of causal understanding leads naturally to collective empowerment and increases the likelihood people will engage in transformative action (Clover, 2002; Dittmer and Riemer, 2013; Montada and Kals, 2000).

Action Competence

While working with people in community-based and participatory research there is an exchange of skills and the development of community capacity. Capacity, or action competence, refers to the knowledge and skills necessary to act on sustainability, not just in terms of changing personal behaviors but also to work politically towards civic objectives. This includes skills such as writing an effective letter to a local representative, making your voice heard in public, knowing who to call to express opinion or grievances about specific issues or concerns, etc. Yet, while these skills are part of a basic skill set and necessary to affect meaningful change in a democracy, many people lack competency and confidence in this area. Lack of competence is a significant deterrent to action, even if these actions are considered necessary for change (Jensen and Schnack, 2006). Political decision makers and members of parliament need people calling them, writing them, or otherwise pointing them to issues of importance to their constituents. Building capacity to act civically is an important component of fostering environmental action.

Engagement

Lastly, individuals need to have the motivation to act in the first place. Different internal and external motivators can be invoked to foster sustainability. In many cases, motivational strategies for fostering sustainable behaviors rely on the individual's self-interest (e.g., saving money; Dobson, 2007). Financial incentives, however, only work if they are continuously reinforced (Dobson, 2007). For example, between 2007 and 2014, people in the United States were discouraged from buying large cars that were inefficient as a result of high gas prices. However, when the gas prices in the United States dropped again in 2014, people starting buying large cars as they did before (Gross, 2015). If, on the other hand, the motivational strategy to buy more efficient cars had focused on reducing their environmental impact and the consequences for people suffering and dying as a result of climate change and pollution, there would have been less of a dependency on the fluctuation in gas prices for changing behavior. Another focus of motivation for pro-environmental behavior change is related to health and wellbeing (Nisbet and Gick, 2008). For example, choosing to ride a bike, reducing pollution, or reducing meat consumption is often framed in terms of benefit to one's personal health. Yet, even this approach is still ultimately grounded in an appeal to self-interest; these types of motivations often insufficient for change beyond modifications to personal behaviors.

In 1999, Chawla identified two distinct paths that tend to motivate individuals to go beyond personal practices: a concern for the environment and a concern for social justice. The latter includes the realization that a healthy environment is an essential component of social justice. Hickman (2012) showed that a group of university students in India were more willing to engage in environmental action after they had learned about the negative impacts of global climate change on people from a small nearby village. Other studies have confirmed that people are motivated to act because of their concern for fairness, reduction of harm, and social justice (Dittmer and Riemer, 2013; Stovold, 2014). Furthermore, people who are politically progressive are more likely to favor stronger responses to climate change and engage in collective environmental action compared to people whose environmental behaviors are mostly driven by self-interest (Dawson and Tysen, 2012; Kenis and Mathijs, 2012; see also Koger and DuNann Winter, 2010). Together, consciousness, action competence, and engagement can facilitate both the personal and societal transformation we are looking to achieve. Alisat and Riemer (2015) have developed a psychometrically sound environmental action scale that can assess the degree to which individuals engage in environmental actions and how engagement changes over time. This scale can serve as a tool for those interested in studying environmental action by providing a reliable assessment tool of this construct.

ENVIRONMENTAL JUSTICE: HOW DOES THIS WORK IMPACT MARGINALIZED AND VULNERABLE COMMUNITIES?

When Bianca (one of the authors of this chapter), asked Manuel (the other author) why he became involved in sustainability, he responded that it was while watching the film *An Inconvenient Truth* (2007), which features the former US Vice President Al Gore. He realized the extent to which the negative consequences of global climate change affect those who are already among the most vulnerable and least able to protect themselves. These include those living in poverty, people experiencing homelessness, people living in economically deprived regions of the world, socially isolated seniors, etc. Through climate change and other environmental degradation, existing inequalities widen further, making establishing climate change a social justice issue. The strong connection between environmental issues and social justice is captured by the concept of *environmental justice*. Environmental justice is defined by the US Environmental Protection Agency (2007: 1) as: 'fair treatment for people of all races, cultures, and incomes, regarding the development of environmental laws, regulations, and policies'. The environmental justice movement integrates mainstream environmental concerns (e.g., natural resource conservation) with related issues for people of color and those in poverty (e.g., health, local economy, education, housing, and urban land use) to form a more comprehensive vision of the shared human environment (Camacho, 1998). This concern for environmental justice is something shared by many of those who apply community-based approaches to sustainability. It links directly to ecological and system thinking. If unchecked, the changes to our global climate will dramatically exacerbate existing inequality. James Gustave Speth, former Environment Adviser to the White House, succinctly summarized this: 'today's environmental reality is linked powerfully with other realities, including growing social inequality and neglect and the erosion of democratic governance and popular control' (Speth, 2008: xi). To try to disentangle these topics from one-another is impossible as they are borne of the same roots. The challenge for applied psychology will be to recognize the connections between all realities mentioned by Speth (i.e., those of poverty and social injustice) and to find approaches that are able to meaningfully recognize these complex interactions (Riemer and

Schweizer-Ries, 2012). As it currently stands, discussions of environmental justice are largely absent from the psychological literature (for a review, see Riemer and Van Voorhees, 2014).

Applications in Research and Action

In order to address the root causes of our current crises we need to apply the principles of the ecological model, engagement, environmental action and justice in the work we do. In the following section, we examine how community-based and participatory approaches to the environment have used these frameworks to inform their work as well as to challenge the status quo and to work towards transformative social change. This section will also give specific considerations to the realities of applied scholars through a reflection of our own research practices.

ECOLOGICAL MODEL

Learning and applying theoretical models, such as the ecological model, to practical initiatives can significantly change the focus of change initiatives and how they frame the issues being addressed. *Reduce the Juice*, for example, an environmental organization in Waterloo, Canada, trained local youth to engage residents in conversation about global climate change and ask them to publically commit to reducing their own ecological footprint (e.g., by taking public transportation). After Manuel and his student conducted a workshop teaching the ecological model to youth members of *Reduce the Juice*, the youth leading the campaign altered their strategies: rather than simply talking to local residents, these youths decided to take action towards community change (Dittmer and Riemer, 2013). Prior to the workshop, the youth focused primarily on personal practices because they were less knowledgeable about how to affect change at other ecological levels (e.g., exo, or community level) and how to build action competence. After the workshop, however, when residents referred to lack of access to public transportation as a barrier to changing their behaviors, the youth responded by working with residents to devise a strategy by which they would call the local representative to advocate for getting a bus stop installed. Thus, this research by Dittmer and Riemer (2013) highlighted how knowledge of the different levels of change influenced practitioners' (in this case, the youth's) approach to community interventions.

Focusing on systems also helps identify the best leverage points for creating meaningful change in a given system. Knowing these leverage points is important as it pools resources toward action that has the most impact. In order to challenge the status quo, one has to collaborate with both marginalized and vulnerable communities as well as those best suited to affect change toward greater sustainability. Currently, we (the two authors, Manuel and Bianca) are engaged in a large-scale research project focused on developing office buildings that have a positive environmental impact and also foster human wellbeing. Buildings are a key target for strategies aimed at minimizing environmental impact, as they account for 40% of global energy use and 38% of global GHG emissions (UNEP, 2012). And yet, buildings designed for high-performance still consistently fail to deliver the reduction targets they promise (Fedoruk et al., 2015). The performance gap is largely attributed to the behavior and decision making of those who occupy, manage, and maintain high-performance buildings (Janda, 2011; Wilson and Dowlatabadi, 2007). To close this performance gap, a better understanding of how to engage building citizens at emotional, cognitive, behavioral, and collective levels is necessary. To do this, a lasting culture of sustainability (COS) is needed. A COS is characterized by shared values, norms, language, and practices focused on making individual and societal choices that foster social, economic, and environmental sustainability (Riemer et al., 2014). Currently, psychological research regarding occupant interventions in commercial buildings is very limited and there is a notable lack of evidence-based approaches that sustainability scholars and building industry practitioners can use in creating a COS (Carrico and Riemer, 2011; Lopes et al., 2012). Traditional behavior change models applied to these few interventions tend to be individualistic, overly focused on employees as fully-autonomous agents, targeted to a single personal behavior, and lacking overall attention to the organizational and institutional context of these buildings (Manika et al., 2015; Unsworth et al., 2013). In essence, the complexity of the system is not accounted for, resulting in limited applied utility. What is needed are evidence-based engagement strategies that foster a systems-level culture which is focused on the promotion of both environmental sustainability and the wellbeing of the building citizens. Important interconnections are ignored when interventions fail to consider the building within its existing system (Foster-Fishman et al., 2007). This leads to the endurance of the performance gap in today's high-performance office buildings.

ENGAGEMENT

Enabling meaningful change in the context of climate change mitigation and adaption also requires the development of truly democratic participatory processes. Unfortunately, engagement can also result in the maintenance of the status quo if participants are not empowered to overcome internalized or external oppression. For example, analyses from public debates in two different nuclear host communities (Culley and Angelique, 2011) highlight the challenges of participatory approaches to environmental debates. Culley and Angelique (2011) discuss how participation in federally mandated processes is shaped by existing power relations. Under restrictive conditions, it is possible that local communities will make choices that are not necessarily in the best interests of future generations and the environment, such as investments in nuclear power. This is an important issue that needs to be discussed when engaging with citizens in the process of empowering them to take environmental action. Public participation may be impacted by several dimensions of social power, such as control of resources, barriers to participation, agenda setting, and shaping conceptions about what participation is necessary or possible (Culley and Hughey, 2008).

An example of how empowerment and social justice in the engagement process can be considered within the context of climate change adaptation can be seen in a recent community-based project conducted in Waterloo, Ontario (Klein and Riemer, 2011; Wandel et al., 2010). The community and university partners were interested in exploring the vulnerability of people in urban centers to global climate change. The team decided to focus on one of the most vulnerable populations: people experiencing homelessness. As a first step in this research project, the research team engaged potential stakeholders, which included individuals with lived experience of homelessness but also agencies involved in providing services and support to these citizens, such as community health centers, local shelters, and the city's public health and social service departments. These agencies are important stakeholders as they are the decision makers who can affect issues of vulnerability (barriers to coping strategies, lack of services, etc.) identified by the research. The ability to effectively engage these different stakeholders is a skill that a community-based scholar must bring to the research table. In this case, the main approach to engagement focused on being present, having conversations, and aligning interests as a researcher with those of the various stakeholders. As the research began, the team had a general idea about what topic they wanted to study but, in true collaborative form, they were open about the research process, methods, and how they intended to frame the research questions. Some of the key stakeholders contributed to how it was ultimately decided to approach the project and who to talk to during the course of the research process. Another important component was the inclusion and engagement of peer researchers (for other examples and empirical evidence of this approach, see Price and Hawkins, 2002; Shah et al., 1999), who were paid research assistants with lived experiences of homelessness. People with lived experiences were also part of the advisory committee, among representatives of other stakeholder groups. When bringing together individuals with differing power status like this, considerations of power dynamics are paramount. In order to attempt to decrease power differentials between executive members of government and vulnerable members of the group, the team had a pre-meeting with people who had lived experiences. During this pre-meeting, the research team talked about what would be addressed during the main meeting and encouraged participation and assured them that their voice was valued. Even just having people with lived experiences in the room when the meeting began changed the power dynamics of the group.

This study is a good example in that it highlights how collaborative approaches require more than a symbolic attempt at participation. Intentional considerations of issues of power are important because, otherwise, participation can very easily turn into tokenism (Arnstein, 1969). Genuine engagement requires a specific appreciation of social justice when making project-related decisions. During this particular project, for example, there were issues related to the timing of the advisory group meetings that needed to be resolved. While regular work hours were convenient for those in government, this time was difficult for people with lived experiences who could not take time off work. Furthermore, considerations of childcare are important (Reason, 2005). In this case, the research team paid for childcare during the meetings.

ENVIRONMENTAL ACTION

Fostering environmental action leads to transformations of individuals that have broad effects on a range of decisions and actions, some of which may lead individuals to become leaders of transformative social change in their own communities. An example of the effects of studying environmental action is the Youth Leading Environmental Change (YLEC) project. The YLEC project challenged participating youth to develop a broad consciousness about global climate change, its root causes, and its unequal impacts. In doing so, the project sought to foster a sense of responsibility that encouraged them to consider their decisions and actions in the context of sustainability. As a consequence of this project, youths did not alter just a single behavior, they changed a whole set of behaviors related to sustainable living and ethical consumption; they decided to begin recycling, eat more locally, to use a bike more regularly, and even to contact their city to advocate for more bus routes, etc., because they wanted to promote sustainability in their local communities.

This project was a collaborative environmental change program grounded in environmental and social justice (Hickman et al., 2016) and was initially implemented in six countries (Bangladesh, Canada, Germany, India, Uganda, and the United States). This initiative was motivated by the idea that engaged and critically aware youth often become change agents for social movements. Instead of focusing on mass marketing campaigns to change single behaviors, focus was placed on an educational workshop. The vision was that these youths would then influence members of their social networks to rethink their sustainable behaviors and take actions locally (Dittmer and Riemer, 2013). The community partner for the YLEC project in Uganda, for example, was teaching youth participants how to create more efficient wood-fired ovens and how to convey that knowledge to local villagers in their community. Traditional ovens contribute significantly to the GHG effect. The action project focused on teaching villagers how to make their ovens more efficient in a way that was affordable and used materials that were readily available in the village. While the project costs for the Uganda project were just slightly over $3,000 CAD, the students were able to have an impact on hundreds of villagers, resulting in significant reduction of GHGs. Similar amounts spent on informational behavior change campaigns in North America would have resulted in significantly less impact, due to the cost of these. This is a good example of how global climate justice can be considered and acted upon in a specific local context.

The greatest success of the YLEC study was not specific behavior changes in the youth or any specific actions with which they engaged but the more enduring personal transformation the program participants experienced across six countries (Riemer et al., 2016). During their three-month follow-up interviews, the youth commented that, after participating in the YLEC workshop series, they now related to environmental issues in whole new ways. They also saw themselves as people who should, and can, act on/with the environment. The concept that best captures this transformation is *environmental citizenship* (Dobson, 2007). To feel like an environmental citizen means to feel responsibility towards the environment, other humans, and fellow species. This feeling of citizenship in turn prompts one to figure out how to act in ways consistent with that sense of responsibility. For example, in the YLEC study, the project fostered student exchanges with students from Bangladesh and the United States. During these exchanges, the students from Bangladesh described their direct experiences of the impacts of global climate change and, thus, provided a concrete and real connection to climate change for students from the United States, who appeared to be somewhat uninformed about the issues Bangladeshi people face. This exchange invoked empathy among the US students as a motivator to engage in environmental action (Sayal et al., 2016). While it is important to foster empathy toward other humans, it is equally crucial to expand the definition of environmental justice to include the fair treatment of the natural environment and develop strategies that cultivate this expanded empathy (Harré, 2016).

Other examples of transformative sustainability education programs include the Make-a-Difference (MAD) environmental leadership program in New Zealand (Blythe and Harré, 2012). MAD nourishes future eco-leaders through immersion in the values and practices of a sustainable way of living; transforming the leaders involved in the program and the people they interact with to commit to sustainability rather than to simply change their personal behaviors (Bourassa et al., forthcoming).

ENVIRONMENTAL JUSTICE

Lastly, an important difference we see between community-based and critical approaches compared to other approaches to sustainability in psychology is in the perceived need to act in a way that would be considered political. Sustainability, with its impetus for transformative change and social justice, is inherently political (Riemer and Schweizer-Ries, 2012). It is not surprising, for example, that political affiliation is among the strongest predictors of environmental attitudes (Koger and DuNann Winter, 2010).

Recent conservative governments in Canada (Harper from 2006 to 2015) and the United States (Trump starting in 2017) actively suppressed scientific evidence of climate change to avoid having to acknowledge or take any meaningful action related to it (Delvin, 2017). Thus, as a community-based scholar working on sustainability, it is important to be comfortable with being political; we cannot hide behind the illusion of objectivity. Paradoxically, psychologists who invoke objectivity (or its concomitant virtues of disinterestedness and neutrality) sometimes undermine the very social relevance of their science, thus weakening the authority they have seek to rescue by way of relevance to everyday life.

This balance of science and political action, however, can be a threat to a scientist's perceived credibility. Manuel experienced this during a court case in which he was invited as an expert witness. This case was about a potentially harm-causing decision made by an environmental director of a provincial government in Canada and involved two residents of a local Indigenous reserve and a large international oil company. The reserve is surrounded by over a dozen petrochemical plants, creating one of the most polluted areas in North America ('Chemical Valley') with significant negative impacts on the physical and psychological wellbeing of its Indigenous residents. The two Indigenous environmental activists received legal support from an environmental justice organization, which recruited Manuel as an expert witness to inform the court about the psychological impacts of living in a polluted area. During the cross-examination, Manuel was questioned about his commitment to environmental justice and his close relationships with various environmental organizations. The purpose of this was to bring into question his credibility as an objective scientist (and his testimony as such). He had to push back and explain that sustainability is inherently linked to environmental justice and that, as a community-engaged sustainability scientist, one works very closely with different community organizations and government agencies as well as industry.

As illustrated above, sustainability itself is inherently political; whether you are a scientist or an activist (or both), it is a political issue. Due to its precarious scientific status as both social and natural science, Psychology has a historically been defensive of its position among the more 'hard sciences'. Mainstream psychologists are thus less comfortable with this inherent political orientation of environmental action and tend to be suspicious of upstream interventions; being non-political, however, is inadequate for this kind of research and, thus, will do little to transform the status quo.

CONCLUSION

As the environmentalist Patrick Hossay (2006: 220) stated, 'this system was built by human beings […]. If enough human beings want change, then we will have it. A global transformation is more than possible, it is necessary, and, if we are to survive as a species, it is inevitable'. In order to contribute to this change, psychologists will have to leave their comfort zone of the controlled environments and engage with the complex and messy political reality that sustainability research presents and necessitates. While developing downstream solutions is an important contribution, it is not sufficient for actually mitigating climate change and to move towards a truly sustainable society. Community-based approaches, as we have described them in this chapter, try to use theories and approaches to research and action that contribute to upstream solutions and are matched to the complexity and community-based nature of sustainability itself.

It is important to note, however, that the distinctions between different applied psychological approaches to sustainability are somewhat artificial; they are, in many cases, more fluid and situational, reflecting the inherent subjectivity and variability of human experience. In community-based approaches, for example, we have applied knowledge and strategies developed first in other fields of applied social psychology, such as action-research and the ecological model. In addition, as evident from other chapters in this Handbook, there is a great variety of community-based approaches. Within applied social psychology, this area is nascent and only recently emerging. Thus, in order to illuminate some key features, we had to create a somewhat idealized version of the approaches we were asked to describe in this chapter.

Our hope is that this chapter provides food for thought regarding the ways psychologists can move beyond fostering changes related to specific individual behaviors and contribute to transformative change toward a culture of sustainability through theory, research, and most of all, action.

Note

1 For more information about these topics and more, see the special report 'Living Proof' by the GroundTruth Project: http://thegroundtruthproject.org/projects/climate-change-living-proof/

REFERENCES

Agyeman, J. (2005). *Sustainable communities and the challenge of environmental justice*. New York, NY: New York University Press.

Alisat, S., & Riemer, M. (2015). The environmental action scale: Development and psychometric evaluation. *Journal of Environmental Psychology*, *43*, 13–23.

Arnold, R. D., & Wade, J. P. (2015). A definition of systems thinking: A systems approach. *Procedia Computer Science*, *44*, 669–678.

Arnstein, S. R. (1969). A ladder of citizen participation. *Journal of the American Institute of Planners*, *35*(4), 216–224.

Beck, E. C. (1979, January). *The Love Canal Tradegy*. Retrieved from https://archive.epa.gov/epa/aboutepa/love-canal-tragedy.html

Blythe, C., & Harré, N. (2012). Inspiring youth sustainability leadership: Six elements of a transformative youth eco-retreat. *Ecopsychology*, *4*(4), 336–344.

Bond, M. A., Keys, C., & Serrano-García, I. (2016). *APA handbook of community psychology: Vol 2. Methods for community research and action for diverse groups and issues*. Washington, DC: American Psychological Association.

Bourassa, L., Riemer, M., & Dreyer, B. C. (forthcoming). The ripple effect: Young leaders motivating environmental action in the community (Unpublished Master's thesis). Wilfrid Laurier University, Waterloo.

Bronfenbrenner, U. (1994). Ecological models of human development. *Readings on the Development of Children*, *2*(1), 37–43.

Brydon-Miller, M., Greenwood, D., & Maguire, P. (2003). Why action research? *Action Research*, *1*(1), 9–28.

Calaprice, A. (Ed.) (2005). *The new quotable Einstein*. Princeton, NJ: Princeton University Press.

Camacho, D. E. (1998). The environmental justice movement: A political framework. In D. E. Camacho (Ed.), *Environmental injustices, political struggles: Race, class, and the environment* (pp. 11–30). Durham, NC: Duke University Press.

Carrico, A. R., & Riemer, M. (2011). Motivating energy conservation in the workplace: An evaluation of the use of group-level feedback and peer education. *Journal of Environmental Psychology*, *31*(1), 1–13.

Carson, R. (1962). *Silent spring*. New York, NY: Houghton Mifflin Harcourt.

Chawla, L. (1999). Life paths into effective environmental action. *Journal of Environmental Education*, *31*(1), 15–26.

Clover, D. (2002). Traversing the gap: Concientización, educative-activism in environmental adult education. *Environmental Education Research*, *8*(3), 315–323.

Corlew, L. K., & Johnson-Hakim, S. M. (2013). Community and cultural responsivity: Climate change research in Tuvalu. *Global Journal of Community Psychology*, *4*(3).

Retrieved from http://www.gjcpp.org/en/resource.php?issue=15&resource=177

Cornwall, A., & Jewkes, R. (1995). What is participatory research? *Social Science & Medicine*, *41*(12), 1667–1676.

Culley, M. R., & Angelique, H. L. (2011). Social power and the role of community psychology in environmental disputes: A tale of two nuclear cities. *American Journal of Community Psychology*, *47*, 410–426.

Culley, M. R., & Hughey, J. (2008). Power and public participation in a hazardous waste dispute: A community case study. *American Journal of Community Psychology*, *41*, 99–114.

Dawson, S. L., & Tyson, G. A. (2012). Will morality or political ideology determine attitudes to climate change? *Australian Community Psychologist*, *24*(2), 8–25.

Delvin, H. (2017, February 15). Trump's likely science adviser calls climate scientists 'glassy-eyed cult'. *The Guardian*. Retrieved from https://www.theguardian.com/us-news/2017/feb/15/trump-science-adviser-william-happer-climate-change-cult

Dittmer, L. D., & Riemer, M. (2013). Fostering critical thinking about climate change: Applying community psychology to an environmental education project with youth. *Global Journal of Community Psychology Practice*, *4*(1), 1–12.

Dobson, A. (1998). *Justice and the environment: Conceptions of environmental sustainability and theories of distributive justice*. New York, NY: Oxford University Press.

Dobson, A. (2007). Environmental citizenship: towards sustainable development. *Sustainable Development*, *15*(5), 276–285.

Dryzek, J. S. (2005). Designs for environmental discourse revisited: A greener administrative state. *Managing Leviathan: Environmental politics and the administrative state* (2nd edn., pp. 81–96). Plymouth, UK: Broadview.

El. Ansari, W. (2005). Collaborative research partnership with disadvantaged communities: Challenges and potential solutions. *Public Health*, *119*, 785–770.

Fedoruk, L. E., Cole, R. J., Robinson, J. B., & Cayuela, A. (2015). Learning from failure: Understanding the anticipated–achieved building energy performance gap. *Building Research & Information*, *43*(6), 750–763.

Flicker, S. (2008). Who benefits from community-based participatory research? A case study of the positive youth project. *Health Education & Behavior*, *35*(1), 70–86.

Foster-Fishman, P. G., Nowell, B., & Yang, H. (2007). Putting the system back into systems change: A framework for understanding and changing organizational and community systems. *American Journal of Community Psychology*, *39*(3–4), 197–215.

Fox, D., & Prilleltensky, I. (1997). *Critical psychology: An introduction*. London, UK: Sage.

Galle, O. R., Gove, W. R., & McPherson, J. M. (1972). Population density and pathology: What are the relations for man? *Science*, *176*(4030), 23–30.

Gardner, G. T., & Stern, P. C. (2002). *Environmental problems and human behavior* (2nd edn.). Boston, MA: Pearson Custom.

Glass, D. C., & Singer, J. E. (1972). *Urban stress*. New York, NY: Academic Press.

Global Humanitarian Forum. (2009). *Human impact report: Climate change – The anatomy of a silent crisis.* Global Humanitarian Forum, Geneva. Retrieved from http://www.phaa.net.au/documents/humanimpactreport.pdf

Godfray, H. C. J., Beddington, J. R., Crute, I. R., Haddad, L., Lawrence, D., Muir, J. F., Pretty, J., Robinson, S., Thomas, S. M., & Toulmin, C. (2010). Food security: The challenge of feeding 9 billion people. *Science*, *327*(5967), 812–818.

Gore, A., Guggenheim, D., David, L., Bender, L., Burns, S. Z.. (2007). *An inconvenient truth*. Viking.

Gray, B. (1989). *Collaborating: Finding common ground for multiparty problems.* San Francisco, CA: Jossey-Bass.

Gross, D. (2015, October 12) Yes, gas is cheap. You should still buy a hybrid. *Slate.* Retrieved from http://www.slate.com/articles/business/the_juice/2015/10/gas_is_cheap_and_americans_are_buying_less_efficient_cars_horrible_idea.html

Hardin, G. (1969). The tragedy of the commons. *Journal of Natural Resources Policy Research*, *1*(3), 243–253.

Harré, N. (2011). *Psychology for a better world.* Auckland, New Zealand: Department of Psychology, University of Auckland.

Harré, N. (2013, August 5). *Psychology and the infinite game: Keynote address at the 2013 SCRA Biennial, University of Miami*. Retrieved from https://youtu.be/HdP9_wmvkBc

Harré, N. (2016). Commentary of the special issue: Youth leading environmental change. *Ecopsychology*, *8*(3), 202–205.

Heller, K., & Monahan, J. (1977). *Psychology and community change*. Oxford, UK: Dorsey.

Hickman, G. M. (2012). Producing ecological citizens, not just green consumers: Engaging youth in environmental action (Unpublished Master's thesis). Department of Psychology, Wilfrid Laurier University, Waterloo, Canada.

Hickman, G., & Riemer, M. (2016). A theory of engagement for fostering collective action in Youth Leading Environmental Change. *Ecopsychology*, *8*(3), 167–173.

Hickman, G., & Riemer, M., & the YLEC Collaborative (2016). A theory of engagement for fostering collective action in Youth Leading Environmental Change. *Ecopsychology*, *8*, 167–173.

Hossay, P. (2006). *Unsustainable: A primer for global environmental and social justice*. London: Zed Books Ltd.

Hunecke, M. (2003). Umweltpsychologie und Sozial-Oekologie: Impulse fuer ein transdisziplinaeres Forschungsprogram. *Umweltpsychologie*, *7*(2), 10–31.

Intergovernmental Panel on Climate Change [IPCC]. (2007). Summary for policymakers. In S. Solomon, D. Qin, M. Manning, Z. Chen, M. Marquis, K. B. Averyt, M. Tignor, & H. L. Miller (Eds.), *Climate change 2007: The physical science basis. Contribution of Working Group I to the Fourth Assessment Report of the Intergovernmental Panel on Climate Change*. New York, NY: Cambridge University Press.

International Organization for Migration: IOM. (2008). *Migration and global climate change*. Retrieved from http://www.migrationdrc.org/publications/resource_guides/Migration_and_Climate_Change/MRS-31.pdf

Israel, B. A., Eng, E., Schulz, A., & Parker, A. E. (Eds.) (2005). *Methods in community-based participatory research for health*. San Francisco, CA: Jossey-Bass.

Israel, B. A., Schulz, A. J., Parker, E. A., & Becker, A. B. (1998). Review of community-based research: Assessing partnership approaches to improve public health. *Annual Review of Public Health*, *19*(1), 173–202.

Israel, B. A., Schulz, A. J., Parker, E. A., Becker, A. B., Allen, A. J., & Guzman, J. R. (2003). Critical issues in developing and following community based participatory research principles. *Community-based Participatory Research for Health*, *1*, 53–76.

Janda, K. B. (2011). Buildings don't use energy: People do. *Architectural Science Review*, *54*(1), 15–22.

Jensen, B. B., & Schnack, K. (2006). The action competence approach in environmental education. *Environmental Education Research*, *12*(3–4), 471–486. [Reprinted from *Environmental Education Research* (1997) *3*(2), 163–178.

Kegler, M. C., Rigler, J., & Ravani, M. K. (2010). Using network analysis to assess the evolution of organizational collaboration in response to a major environmental health threat. *Health Education Research*, *25*(3), 413–424.

Kenis, A., & Mathijs, E. (2012). Beyond individual behaviour change: The role of power, knowledge and strategy in tackling climate change. *Environmental Education Research*, *18*(1), 45–65.

Kennedy, R. F. (1968, March 18). *Remarks at the University of Kansas, March 18, 1968*. Retrieved from https://www.jfklibrary.org/Research/Research-Aids/Ready-Reference/RFK-Speeches/Remarks-of-Robert-F-Kennedy-at-the-University-of-Kansas-March-18-1968.aspx

Klein, K., & Riemer, M. (2011). Experiences of environmental justice and injustice in communities of people experiencing homelessness. *Ecopsychology*, *3*(3), 195–204.

Korten, D. C. (1995). *When corporations rule the world*. Connecticut: Kumarian Press.

Koger, S. M., & DuNann Winter, D. (2010). *The psychology of environmental problems: Psychology for sustainability*. Hove, UK: Psychology Press.

Kreuter, M. W., De Rosa, C., Howze, E. H., & Baldwin, G. T. (2004). Understanding wicked problems: A key to advancing environmental health promotion. *Health Education & Behavior*, *31*(4), 441–454.

Leonard, A. (2007a). *Story of citizens united vs. FEC, referenced and annotated script*.

Retrieved from https://storyofstuff.org/wp-content/uploads/movies/scripts/SoCitizensUnitedvFEC_Annotated_Script.pdf

Leonard, A. (2007b). *Story of solutions, referenced and annotated script*. Retrieved from https://storyofstuff.org/wp-content/uploads/movies/scripts/SoSolutions_Annotated_Script.pdf

Lewin, K. (1951). *Field theory in social science: Selected theoretical papers*. D. Cartwright (Ed.). New York, NY: Harper & Row.

Lopes, M.A.R., Antunis, C.H., & Martins, N. (2012). Energy behaviours as promoters of energy efficiency: A 21st century review. *Renewable and Sustainable Energy Reviews*, *16*(6), 4095–4104.

Manika, D., Wells, V., Gregory-Smith., & Gentry, M. (2015). The impact of individual attitudinal and organisational variables on workplace environmentally friendly behaviours. *Journal of Business Ethics*, *126*(4), 663–684.

Midden, C. J., Kaiser, F. G., & Teddy McCalley, L. (2007). Technology's four roles in understanding individuals' conservation of natural resources. *Journal of Social Issues*, *63*(1), 155–174.

Mieg, H. A. (2003). Interdisziplinaritaet braucht Organisation: Erfahrungen eines Psychologen im Umweltbereich. *Umweltpsychologie*, *7*(2), 32–52.

Miley, M. (2017). *Living proof: The human toll of climate change*. Retrieved from http://thegroundtruthproject.org/projects/climate-change-living-proof/

Millennium Ecosystems Assessment [MEA]. (2005). *Ecosystems and human well-being: Current state and trends: Findings of the condition and trends working group of the millennium ecosystem assessment* (Vol. 2). Washington, DC: Island Press.

Minkler, M. (2004). Ethical challenges for the 'outside' researcher in community based participatory research. *Health Education & Behavior*, *3*(6), 684–697.

Minkler, M. (2005). Community based research partnerships: Challenges and opportunities. *Journal of Urban Health: Bulletin of the New York Academy of Medicine*, *82*(2), ii3–ii11.

Minkler, M., & Wallerstein, N. (2008). *Community-based participatory research: from process to outcomes*. San Francisco, CA: Jossey-Bess.

Minkler, M., & Wallerstein, N. (Eds.) (2011). *Community-based participatory research for health: From process to outcomes*. San Francisco, CA: John Wiley & Sons.

Monbiot, G. (2009, November 6). We cannot change the world by changing our buying habits. *The Guardian*, Retrieved from https://www.theguardian.com/environment/georgemonbiot/2009/nov/06/green-consumerism

Montada, L., & Kals, E. (2000). Political implications of psychological research on ecological justice and proenvironmental behaviour. *International Journal of Psychology*, *35*(2), 168–176.

Mosavel, M., Simon, C., Stade, D., & Buchbinder, M. (2005) Community based participatory research in South Africa: Engaging multiple constituents to shape the research question, *Social Science and Medicine*, *61*, 2577–2578.

Moskell, C., & Allred, S. B. (2013). Integrating human and natural systems in community psychology: An ecological model of stewardship behavior. *American Journal of Community Psychology*, *51*(1–2), 1–14.

Moskell, C., Broussard Allred, S., & Ferenz, G. (2011). Examining volunteer motivations and recruitment strategies for engagement in urban forestry. *Cities and the Environment (CATE)*, *3*(1), 9.

Mrak, E. M. (1969). *Report of the Secretary's Commission on pesticides and their relationship to environmental health*. Washington, DC: Department of Health, Education and Welfare Publication, Food and Drug Administration.

Münger, F., & Riemer, M. (2012). Introducing a process model for research collaborations and its application in environmental and sustainability fields. *Umweltpsychologie*, *16*(1), 112–142.

Neal, J. W., & Neal, Z. P. (2013). Nested or networked? Future directions for Ecological Systems Theory. *Social Development*, *22*(4), 722–737.

Nelson, G., & Prilleltensky, I. (Eds.) (2010). *Community psychology: In pursuit of liberation and well-being*. London: Palgrave Macmillan.

Nisbet, E. K., & Gick, M. L. (2008). Can health psychology help the planet? Applying theory and models of health behaviour to environmental actions. *Canadian Psychology/ Psychologie Canadienne*, *49*(4), 296.

Oskamp, S. (1995). Resource conservation and recycling: Behavior and policy. *Journal of Social Issues*, *51*(4), 157–177.

Peng, R. D., Bobb, J. F., Tebaldi, C., McDaniel, L., Bell, M. L., & Dominici, F. (2011). Toward a quantitative estimate of future heat wave mortality under global climate change. *Environmental Health Perspectives*, *119*(5), 701.

Price, N., & Hawkins, K. (2002). Researching sexual and reproductive behaviour: A peer ethnographic approach. *Social Science & Medicine*, *55*(8), 1325–1336.

Prilleltensky, I. (2003). Understanding, resisting, and overcoming oppression: Toward psychopolitical validity. *American Journal of Community Psychology*, *31*, 195–201.

Prilleltensky, I. (2008). The role of power in wellness, oppression, and liberation: The promise of psychopolitical validity. *Journal of Community Psychology*, *36*, 116–136.

Proshansky, H. M. (1978). The city and self-identity. *Environment and Behavior*, *10*, 147–169.

Proshansky, H. M., Fabian, A. K., & Kaminoff, R. (1983). Place identity: Physical world socialization of the self. *Journal of Environmental Psychology*, *3*, 57–83.

Quaghebeur, K., Masschelein, J., & Nguyen, H. H. (2004). Paradox of participation: Giving or taking part? *Journal of Community & Applied Social Psychology*, *14*(3), 154–165.

Quimby, C. C., & Angelique, H. (2011). Identifying barriers and catalysts to fostering pro-environmental behavior: Opportunities and challenges for community psychology. *American Journal of Community Psychology*, *47*(3–4), 388–396.

Rambow, R. (2003). Zur Rolle der Psychologie fuer Architektur und Stadtplanung: Didaktische und konzeptionelle Ueberlegungen. *Umweltpsychologie*, *7*(1), 54–68.

Reason, P. (2005). Living as part of the whole: The implications of participation. *Journal of Curriculum and Pedagogy*, *2*(2), 35–41.

Reason, P., & Bradbury, H. (Eds.) (2001). *Handbook of action research: Participative inquiry and practice*. London: Sage.

Ribicoff, A. (1966). *Pesticides and public policy* (Report of the Committee on Government Operations, US Senate, 89th Congress, 2nd session, report 1379). Washington, DC: US Government Printing Office.

Rich, R. C., Edelstein, M., Hallman, W. K., & Wandersman, A. H. (1995). Citizen participation and empowerment: The case of local environmental hazards. *American Journal of Community Psychology*, *23*, 657–676.

Riemer, M. (2010). Community psychology, the natural environment, and global climate change. In G. Nelson, & I. Prilleltensky (Eds.), *Community psychology: In pursuit of liberation and well-being* (2nd edn.). New York, NY: Palgrave.

Riemer, M., & Harré, N. (2016). Environmental degradation and sustainability: A community psychology perspective. In M. A. Bond, I. Serrano-García, C. B. Keys, & M. Shinn (Eds.), *APA handbook of community psychology: Methods for community research and action for diverse groups and issues* (Vol. 2, pp. 441–455). Washington, DC, USA: American Psychological Association.

Riemer, M., & Reich, S. M. (2011). Community psychology and global climate change: Introduction to the special section. *American Journal of Community Psychology*, *47*(3–4), 349–353.

Riemer, M., & Schweizer-Ries, P. (2012). Psychology and sustainability science: Complexity, normativity, and transdisciplinarity in meeting sustainability challenges. *Umweltpsychologie*, *16*(1), 143–165.

Riemer, M., & Van Voorhees, C. W. (2009). Environment, justice, and community. *The Community Psychologist*, *42*(2), 36–39.

Riemer, M., & Van Voorhees, C. W. (2014). Sustainability and social justice. In C. Johnson, H. Friedman, J. Diaz, B. Nastasi, & Z. Franco (Eds.), *Praeger handbook of social justice and psychology* (pp. 49–66). Westport, CT: Praeger Publishers.

Riemer, M., Lynes, J., & Hickman, G. (2014). A model for developing and assessing youth-based environmental engagement programmes. *Journal of Environmental Education Research*, *20*(4), 552–574.

Riemer, M., Voorhees, C., Dittmer, L., Alisat, S., Alam, N., Sayal, R., … & Mugagga, F. (2016). The Youth Leading Environmental Change project: A mixed-method longitudinal study across six countries. *Ecopsychology*, *8*(3), 174–187.

Rittel, H. W., & Webber, M. M. (1973). Dilemmas in a general theory of planning. *Policy Sciences*, *4*(2), 155–169.

Robert, K. (1991, Spring). Educating a nation: The Natural step. *In Context*, *28*, 11.

Sayal, R., Bidisha, S. H., Lynes, J., Riemer, M., Jasani, J., Monteiro, E., Hey, B., De Souza, A., Wicks, S., & Eady, A. (2016). Fostering systems thinking for Youth Leading Environmental Change: A multinational exploration. *Ecopsychology*, *8*(3), 188–201.

Schultz, P. (2011). Conservation means behavior. *Conservation Biology*, *25*(6), 1080–1083.

Scott, D. N. (2016). 'We are the monitors now': Experiential knowledge, transcorporeality and environmental justice. *Social & Legal Studies*, *25*(3), 261–287.

Scott, D., & Oelofse, C. (2005). Social and environmental justice in South African cities: including 'invisible stakeholders' in environmental assessment procedures. *Journal of Environmental Planning and Management*, *48*(3), 445–467.

Shah, M. K., Zambezi, R., & Simasiku, M. (1999). *Listening to young voices: Facilitating participatory appraisals on reproductive health with adolescents.* Retrieved from https://www.iywg.org/sites/iywg/files/focus_listening-to-young-voices.pdf

Shapin, S. (2010). *Never pure: Historical studies of science as if it was produced by people with bodies, situated in time, space, culture, and society, and struggling for credibility and authority*. Baltimore, OH: JHU Press.

Shippee, G. E., & Gregory, W. L. (1982). Public commitment and energy conservation. *American Journal of Community Psychology*, *10*, 81–93.

Smith, T. (2011). Using critical systems thinking to foster an integrated approach to sustainability: A proposal for development practitioners. *Environment, development and sustainability*, *13*(1), 1–17.

Smith, B. D., & Zeder, M. A. (2013). The onset of the Anthropocene. *Anthropocene*, *4*, 8–13.

Speth, J. G. (2008). *The bridge at the edge of the world: Capitalism, the environment, and crossing from crisis to sustainability*. New Haven, CT: Yale University Press.

Sterling, S. (1996). Education in change. In J. Huckle, & S. Sterling (Eds.), *Education for sustainability* (pp. 18–39). London, UK: Earthscan.

Stern, P. C., Dietz, T., Abel, T., Guagnano, G. A., & Kalot, L. (1999). A value-belief-norm theory of support for social movements: The case of environmentalism. *Research in Human Ecology*, *6*(*2*), 81–97.

Stokols, D. (1995). The paradox of environmental psychology. *American Psychologist*, *50*(10), 821.

Stokols, D., Misra, S., Runnerstrom, M. G., & Hipp, J. A. (2009). Psychology in an age of ecological crisis: From personal angst to collective action. *American Psychologist*, *64*(3), 181.

Stovold, A. L. (2014). *Youth's comprehension of environmental justice across multiple countries*. Retrieved from Wilfrid Laurier University Theses and Dissertations (Comprehensive). (1690)

Swim, J., Clayton, S., Doherty, T., Gifford, R., Howard, G., Reser, J., Stern, P., & Weber, E. (2009). Psychology and global climate change: Addressing a multi-faceted phenomenon and set of challenges. A report by the American Psychological Association's task force on the interface between psychology and global climate change. *American Psychological Association*, *Washington*.

Thiele, L. P. (2016). *Sustainability* (2nd edn.). Cambridge, UK: Polity Press.

Trickett, E. J. (2009). Multilevel community-based culturally situated interventions and community impact: An ecological perspective. *American Journal of Community Psychology*, *43*(3–4), 257–266.

UNEP. (2012, June). *Building design and construction: Forging resource efficiency and sustainable development.* Sustainable Buildings and Climate Initiative. Retrieved from https://www.usgbc.org/Docs/Archive/General/Docs19073.pdf

United States Environmental Protection Agency. (2007). *Definition of environmental justice*. Retrieved from https://www.epa.gov/environmentaljustice/learn-about-environmental-justice

Unsworth, K.L., Dmitrieva, A., & Adriasola, E. (2013). Changing behaviour: Increasing the effectiveness of workplace interventions in creating pro-environmental behaviour change. *Journal of Organizational Behaviour, 34*, 211–229.

Vandentorren, S., Bretin, P., Zeghnoun, A., Mandereau-Bruno, L., Croisier, A., Cochet, C., Riberon, J., Siberan, I., Declercq, B., & Ledrans, M. (2006). August 2003 heat wave in France: Risk factors for death of elderly people living at home. *The European Journal of Public Health, 16*(6), 583–591.

Vaneckova, P., Beggs, P. J., & Jacobson, C. R. (2010). Spatial analysis of heat-related mortality among the elderly between 1993 and 2004 in Sydney, Australia. *Social Science & Medicine, 70*(2), 293–304.

Viswanathan, M., Ammerman, A., Eng, E., Garlehner, G., Lohr, K. N., Griffith, D., Rhodes, S., Samuel-Hodge, C., Maty, S., Lux, L., Webb, L., Sutton, S. F., Swinson, T., Jackman, A., & Whitener, L. (2004). *Community-based participatory research: Assessing the evidence: Summary, Evidence Report/Technology Assessment: Number 99*. AHRQ Publication Number 04-E022-1, August 2004. Rockville, MD: Agency for Healthcare Research and Quality. Retrieved from: http://www.ahrq.gov/clinic/epcsums/cbprsum.htm

Voorhees, C. C., Vick, J., & Perkins, D. D. (2007). 'Came hell and high water': The intersection of Hurricane Katrina, the news media, race and poverty. *Journal of Community & Applied Social Psychology, 17*(6), 415–429.

Wackernagel, M., & Rees, W. (1998). *Our ecological footprint: Reducing human impact on the earth* (No. 9). Gabriola Island, Canada: New Society Publishers.

Wandel, J., Riemer, M., de Gómez, W., Klein, K., de Schutter, J., Randall, L., Morrison, M., Poirier, S., & Singleton, C. (2010). *Homelessness and Global Climate Change: Are we ready? A report from the study on the vulnerability to global climate change of people experiencing homelessness in Waterloo Region*. Available from: https://www.researchgate.net/publication/269689517_A_Report_from_the_Study_on_the_Vulnerability_to_Global_Climate_Change_of_People_Experiencing_Homelessness_in_Waterloo_Region [accessed July 20 2018].

Webster, P. J., Holland, G. J., Curry, J. A., & Chang, H. R. (2005). Changes in tropical cyclone number, duration, and intensity in a warming environment. *Science, 309*(5742), 1844–1846.

William, L. (1999). Participatory research, knowledge, and community-based change: Experience, epistemology, and empowerment. *Research in Community Sociology, 9*, 3–40.

Wilson, C., & Dowlatabadi, H. (2007). Models of decision making and residential energy use. *Annual Review of Environment and Resources, 32*(1), 169.

Wilson, L., Black, D., & Veitch, C. (2011). Heatwaves and the elderly: The role of the GP in reducing morbidity. *Australian Family Physician, 40*(8), 637.

Zuo, J., Pullen, S., Palmer, J., Bennetts, H., Chileshe, N., & Ma, T. (2015). Impacts of heat waves and corresponding measures: A review. *Journal of Cleaner Production, 92*, 1–12.

PART X

Criminal Justice, Law and Crime

27

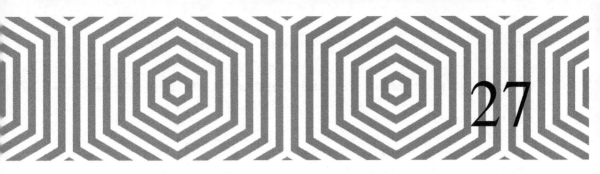

Social Psychology and Law

Fabiana Alceste, Aria Amrom,
Johanna Hellgren and Saul M. Kassin

In December of 2015, Netflix aired a documentary series, written and directed by Laura Ricciardi and Moira Demos, entitled *Making a Murderer.* This ten-part series told the story of Steven Avery, from Manitowoc County, Wisconsin, who was convicted of rape for which he spent 18 years in prison. At trial, Avery had presented 16 alibi witnesses who vouched for his presence 40 miles away at the time of the assault. Yet the jury convicted him after only four hours of deliberation – based solely on a mistaken eyewitness identification. In 2003, he was exonerated by DNA, which also identified the actual rapist – Gregory Allen, a convicted felon who bore a striking resemblance to Avery.

Two years after Avery's release, while he was suing Manitowoc County for 36 million dollars, Avery was arrested by local police for the murder of photographer Teresa Halbach. He insisted he was innocent. In 2007, however, he was tried by jury and convicted on the basis of controversial forensic blood evidence, which his attorneys claimed had been planted, as well as a confession taken from his 16-year-old nephew, Brendan Dassey. Is it possible that Avery had been wrongfully convicted yet again? To this day, this question lingers as a source of controversy.

The Dassey story, in particular, enraged millions of viewers. Dassey, who had an IQ of 73, was interrogated four times, called a liar, and misled into thinking there was evidence against him. Eventually, he succumbed to the pressure and confessed to involvement in the murder. Moments later, in a jaw-dropping exchange that put on display how little grasp Dassey had of his own perilous situation, he asked if he would get back to school in time for a project he had to present.

As we write this chapter, Steven Avery remains in prison. In 2016, a federal judge overturned Dassey's conviction on the grounds that his confession was coerced. But then, in 2017, the US Seventh Circuit Court of Appeals reversed this decision and reinstated Dassey's conviction. In 2018, the US Supreme Court declined to examine the case, so Dassey will likely remain incarcerated until 2048. In October of 2018, a follow-up Part II was released.

This story illustrates many of the research issues that consume social psychologists interested in law and justice. In contrast to forensic clinical psychologists, who might ask about why people in general commit crimes, what types of individuals are more disposed than others, or whether aspects of a crime can be used to identify the culprit's profile or predict future offenses, social psychologists focus on social factors that influence decision-making throughout the criminal justice system – from the crime scene into the police station, courtroom, and system as a whole.

Reflecting much of this work, this chapter overviews three sets of topics. First, we explore the social psychology of evidence, as seen in work on eyewitness perceptions, memory, identifications, and testimony; alibi witnesses who vouch for a defendant's whereabouts at a specific point in time; and police interviews, interrogations, and confessions. Next, we examine the adjudication of guilt and innocence, both in jury trials – which involve the processes of jury selection, deliberation, and decision-making – and in plea bargaining, where most defendants plead guilty as part of an agreement struck with prosecutors. Lastly, we examine people's perceptions of justice, apart from outcomes and what constitutes a process that is seen as fair and an authority that is seen as legitimate.

At the outset, we think it is important to note that, while legal systems vary in different parts of the world, the underlying social psychologies of perception, memory, influence, and decision-making are generally applicable. Hence, the research cited in this chapter was conducted in various parts of the world – including the United States, Canada, the UK, Sweden, Spain, Germany, the Netherlands, New Zealand, Australia, and Israel.

THE SOCIAL PSYCHOLOGY OF EVIDENCE

Whenever a crime is committed and reported, a police investigation is set into motion. Forensic (CSI) examiners are called in to collect fingerprints, shoe prints, hairs, fibers, blood stains, and other forms of physical evidence. At the same time, police will interview eyewitnesses, victims, and others who might have information about the culprit and his or her possible motive and opportunity. At some point, police might also identify a suspect to be interviewed; if they determine during the course of that interview that this suspect is not being truthful, they may conduct an accusatory interrogation aimed at getting that suspect to confess. In all of these phases of evidence gathering, research shows that social psychological factors are at work, which may impact upon accuracy, error, and the possibility of bias. In this chapter, we examine the psychology of eyewitness identifications, alibis, confessions, jury decision-making, plea bargaining, and perceptions of justice.

Eyewitness Testimony

Like Steven Avery, approximately 75% of DNA exonerees in the United States were convicted at least partly because of one or more mistaken eyewitness identifications (www.innocenceproject.org; also see Brewer and Wells, 2011; Cutler, 2013). For this reason, researchers in this field have extensively studied the factors that influence eyewitness perceptions, identifications, and testimony. This research has shown that eyewitness accounts are not as reliable as police or laypeople tend to assume. Sometimes the problem is that eyewitnesses are distracted, focused elsewhere, or otherwise not paying attention to the crime as it occurs (Erickson et al., 2014; Chabris and Simons, 2009). At other times, the problem is that human memory is fallible over time – not like a video camera that can be played back at will (Loftus, 1996).

The key evidence in Steven Avery's initial wrongful rape conviction was an incorrect identification made by the victim who picked him from a photo lineup and again later from a live lineup (Demos and Ricciardi, 2015). Police said that the victim's initial description of her attacker was generally consistent with Avery, though her initial report described a man of a different height, weight, and eye color. The Chief Deputy then proceeded to create a composite sketch of the perpetrator based not on the victim's description but on a previous mugshot of Avery. The victim was shown this sketch before choosing that very mugshot out of a photo lineup and identifying Avery in a live lineup.

How could an eyewitness identify someone from a lineup whose physical appearance did not match her own description? This discrepancy in the Avery case reflects the operation of a classic *misinformation effect*, a phenomenon that describes how memory for an initial event, or person, can be altered by exposure to incorrect post-event information (Loftus, 2005). A typical misinformation effect experiment consists of three parts in which a participant: (1) witnesses a staged crime-like event, (2) receives misleading suggestions about that event, and (3) gets tested for recall of the original event. Consistently, research has shown that mock witnesses will often incorporate the misinformation into their memory for the original event (Hirst et al., 2015; Loftus, 2005; Loftus and Hoffman, 1989; Wright et al., 2009) – and that they are particularly vulnerable when under intense stress (Morgan et al., 2013) or are not alert, as when sleep deprived (Frenda et al., 2011). Only when witnesses are warned in advance or told afterward that specific misinformation had been presented can the effects on memory be prevented (Higham et al., 2017).

Misinformation can be delivered in many ways. For example, eyewitness memories can be distorted by conversations with other witnesses. Gabbert et al. (2004) conducted a laboratory study in which participants watched a video of a crime after which they were exposed to misinformation, either socially through a conversation with a confederate or within the body of a written report. Those exposed to misinformation, regardless of presentation medium, were generally less accurate in their memory of the event than control participants who did not receive misinformation. Interestingly, participants remembered more misinformation details when presented within the context of a conversation than in a written report. This co-witness contamination demonstrates the extent to which social influences can corrupt eyewitness memory (for a review, see Wright et al., 2009).

In 1978, Gary Wells introduced an important distinction that helped guide eyewitness research. Specifically, he distinguished between (1) estimator variables that affect identification accuracy in ways that can only be estimated after the fact, not systematically controlled (e.g., lighting and distance, the witness's vision and level of stress, and race of the perpetrator), and (2) system variables affecting accuracy that can be controlled by police to improve versus impair eyewitness performance (e.g., whether a lineup is fair or suggestive, how the witness is instructed).

Research has identified a number of *estimator variables* that affect eyewitness performance. For example, identification accuracy is diminished when witnesses have quick, limited exposure to the perpetrator's face (Bornstein et al., 2012; Memon et al., 2003), when they are under intense levels of stress (Deffenbacher et al., 2004; Morgan et al., 2004), when they observe an event in which a weapon is visible, which draws their attention away from the face (this is referred to as the 'weapon focus effect'; see Fawcett et al., 2013; Loftus et al., 1987), when the perpetrator is a member of a racial group other than their own (this is referred to as the cross-race bias; see Meissner and Brigham, 2001; Wilson et al., 2013), and when a significant period of time intervenes between the event and memory retrieval – which can cause forgetting (Schacter, 1999).

Once police have identified a suspect, they often call on their witnesses to view a live or photographic lineup that contains the suspect and five to seven other individuals known to be innocent, often referred to as 'fillers' or 'foils'. This procedure may take place within hours or days of the crime or months later. It is this lineup procedure that often yields tragic results.

Based on decades of research on *system variables* on lineups involving mock witness experiments and field studies of real witnesses, researchers have made a number of specific recommendations for how to conduct lineups in a manner that improves eyewitness performance (National Research Council, 2014; Wells et al., 1998; 2000). Some key guidelines and their empirical basis are briefly summarized in this section.

Double-blind lineups

In many cases involving eyewitness mistakes that led to wrongful convictions, police who assembled a lineup containing a suspect and innocent foils inadvertently steered the witness toward their suspect – who was not the actual culprit. In the same way that psychology researchers try to guard against experimenter bias (Rosenthal, 1966), social psychologists have argued for a 'double-blind administration' procedure in which not only the witness is 'blind' as to who the suspect is but so is the officer who administers the lineup.

In a study that demonstrates the risk, Greathouse and Kovera (2009) paired student 'witnesses' to a staged theft with student 'police' who were trained to administer a lineup in which the actual culprit was present or absent. Half the administrators were informed of who the police suspect was in the lineup; the other half were blind as to the suspect's identity. The results showed that witnesses made more suspect identifications overall – even when the suspect was innocent – when the administrator was informed rather than blind. Videotapes of the sessions showed that the informed administrators unwittingly increased identification rates by telling witnesses to look carefully, or to look again, and in some cases by letting on that they knew who the suspect was. Other studies have shown that gestures, words, and facial expressions made by an informed lineup administrator may also suggest to the eyewitness which lineup choice is desired (Austin et al., 2013). This research strongly supports an important point of reform: Use of a double-blind procedure in which neither the witness nor the police administrator know who the suspect is within the lineup (for a review, see Kovera and Evelo, 2017).

Unbiased lineup instructions

How a witness is instructed before a lineup can also influence lineup identification decisions. In a study by Roy Malpass and Patricia Devine (1981), students saw a staged act of vandalism, after which they saw a lineup. Half of the students received a 'biased' instruction which stated that the culprit was in the lineup. The others were given an 'unbiased' instruction that the culprit might or might not be present. Lineups were then presented either with, or without, the culprit. Results showed that when witnesses received biased instructions, they felt compelled to identify *someone* and often picked an innocent person. Additional studies have both confirmed and qualified this basic result: When the police suspect is the culprit, biased instructions are not problematic. When the suspect is not the culprit, however, biased instructions substantially increase both the rate at which witnesses select someone from the lineup and mistaken identifications (Steblay, 1997).

Witness confidence ratings

In determining if a witness's identification is accurate, juries are highly influenced by a witness's stated level of confidence

(Wells et al., 1979). Yet confident does not necessarily mean accurate. Summarizing many years of research casting doubt as to the value of a witness's confidence, Wixted and Wells (2017) have concluded eyewitness confidence can reliably signal accuracy when the lineup is fairly conducted and the witness's confidence is taken right away – but not when a lineup is biased or other influences have had a chance to intervene.

For this reason, it is important that a witness's confidence level is assessed immediately upon identification and not tainted by *post-identification feedback* by police or others. In the first study to demonstrate the importance of this point, Wells and Bradfield (1998) found that eyewitnesses who made incorrect identifications and then received positive feedback from the experimenter ('Oh good, you identified our suspect') went on not to become more confident but to reconstruct their entire account of the eye-witnessing experience, 'recalling' that they had paid more attention, had a better view, and found it easier to make the identification. Numerous studies involving 20,000 mock witnesses have consistently shown that positive feedback can inflate a witness's level of confidence (Steblay et al., 2014).

Additional research has shown that witnesses who receive post-identification feedback before stating their confidence, relative to those who did not, are later more difficult for juries to evaluate for accuracy. Indeed, the problem is that even inaccurate witnesses express high levels of confidence after confirming feedback (Smalarz and Wells, 2014). The indisputable practical implication is clear: Police should record a witness's statement of confidence immediately after he or she has made an identification decision – without confirming or disconfirming feedback.

Sequential lineup formats

Many psychologists who have studied eyewitness identifications have suggested that lineups and photo arrays be administered sequentially, as opposed to simultaneously (Lindsay and Wells, 1985). In the conventional lineup procedure, the suspect and foils stand alongside each other or appear together in a one-page array of photographs. Either way, this *simultaneous lineup* procedure presents all faces at once, a process that may encourage witnesses to make a relative judgment, comparing faces and selecting the one that best fits their memory. In contrast, a *sequential lineup* involves showing each face to the witness one-by-one, each followed by an absolute yes or no decision.

Over the years, numerous studies have been conducted to determine which procedure produces the best results, as measured by the number of accurate versus false identification decisions that are produced. Overall, results show that the sequential lineup yields slightly fewer culprit identifications than a simultaneous lineup – but significantly fewer false identifications (Steblay et al., 2001; 2011). In a recent field experiment in which actual witnesses were randomly assigned to one of the two procedures, sequential lineups had no effect on identification of police suspects (whose actual guilt is unknown) but they did decrease identifications of non-suspect foils (which are known errors) compared to simultaneous lineups (Wells et al., 2015).

Eyewitnesses in court

Part of the problem with eyewitnesses is that often they make mistaken identifications. Another part of the problem is that their accuracy is not easy for a judge and jury to evaluate. By the time an eyewitness testifies in court, he or she has likely made an identification on one or more occasions and has received positive feedback from police regarding that decision. Can a jury observing witnesses being questioned detect the inaccurate identification? Research suggests the answer is no. As noted earlier, people tend to trust eyewitnesses who express high levels of confidence, yet there are times when confidence is a misleading predictor of accuracy (Cutler and Penrod, 1989; Penrod and Cutler, 1995; Wells et al., 1979; Wixted and Wells, 2017).

One possible way to improve the jury's ability to evaluate eyewitnesses is through psychological expert testimony designed to educate jurors about the relevant scientific research. However, while eyewitness experts tend to agree on the reliability of many findings as to what tends to increase or impair accuracy (Kassin et al., 2001), the effect of expert testimony on juries is less clear (Cutler et al., 1989; Jones et al., 2017; Leippe, 1995).

Alibis: Eyewitnesses to Innocence

An alibi is a form of evidence that places a suspect in another place while a crime was committed, making it impossible for him or her to be the perpetrator. A defendant's alibi may consist of physical evidence (e.g., surveillance camera footage, cell phone records, store receipts) or person evidence (e.g., sworn testimony from friends, family members, strangers, or acquaintances). What makes alibis a vital means of defense is that they can contradict the prosecutor's evidence, thereby creating a reasonable doubt as to the defendant's guilt (Gooderson, 1977; Nolan, 1990).

As seen in numerous wrongful conviction cases in which alibis had been offered, alibi testimony is not as persuasive as one might think (Kassin, 2012; Wells et al., 1998). Even when an alibi witness corroborates a defendant's story, placing the defendant away from the crime scene, observers are often skeptical (Culhane and Hosch, 2004; Dysart and Strange, 2012; Hosch et al., 2011; Olson and Wells, 2004). The initial wrongful conviction of Steven Avery is a case in point. At Avery's first trial, he presented 16 alibi witnesses – including a store clerk and a time-stamped receipt – as proof of his whereabouts 40 miles from the assault when it occurred. Nevertheless, he was found guilty and spent 18 years in prison before being exonerated (www.innocenceproject.org).

Why are alibis, an important form of exculpatory evidence, often undervalued or disregarded? The study of alibis has focused on two sets of questions: (1) How do suspects generate alibi stories, and (2) once they do, how are these stories evaluated with regard to their implications for guilt and innocence? In this section the term *alibi provider* refers to the suspect or defendant; *alibi witness* or *corroborator* refers to those asked to confirm the alibi provider's statement.

Generating the alibi

Asked for their whereabouts during the time a crime was committed, suspects often accompany their denials with an alibi story. The utility of this story as a defense rests on the assumption that an innocent suspect is able to provide an accurate accounting of his or her whereabouts at a particular moment in time (Olson and Charman, 2012). Yet even an innocent alibi provider may be unable, or his or her recollection may be incorrect, or the alibi provided may be weak and uncorroborated. In a laboratory experiment involving student participants, Olson and Charman (2012) found that, within a sample of innocent alibi providers, 36% were mistaken and the majority provided weak supportive evidence. Similarly, Strange et al. (2014) found that 50% of innocent alibi providers exhibited inconsistencies in their story when re-questioned one week later. It appears that convincing alibis are difficult to generate, even for those who are innocent. Strange et al. (2014) noted that inconsistencies in alibi statements, even from truth-tellers, are 'a normal byproduct of an imperfect [autobiographical] memory system' (Smith et al., 2014: 82). Indeed, routine and insignificant events are especially unlikely to be recalled correctly (Leins and Charman, 2016).

During the validation phase, an effort is made to corroborate the suspect's statement through physical and/or person evidence. Police officers are typically the first to gather and evaluate corroborating evidence. In a survey designed to assess their beliefs, Dysart and Strange (2012) found that police are generally distrustful of alibi statements; that, while they see physical evidence as crucial to validation, only 20% of alibis contain this type of proof; and that they see most alibi witnesses not as objective but as motivated parties – such as family members, significant others, and friends.

To further complicate matters, research shows that alibi corroborators may not be as accurate as one would think. In a novel experiment, Charman and others (2017) had 60 college students ('innocent suspects' who might later need an alibi) each interact casually with one of 60 workers on campus ('alibi corroborators'). After 24 hours, however, and even though the students believed they would be recognized, most workers were unable to identify their student from a photograph. This result suggests that innocent suspects who rely on strangers to corroborate their alibis may be putting themselves at risk.

Alibi witnesses can also be misled by extrinsic evidence, causing them to lose confidence in their memories and recant even an accurate corroboration of the suspect's story. In a laboratory experiment that demonstrates this risk, Marion et al. (2016) brought individual participants and a confederate together to complete a series of problem-solving tasks. The confederate was subsequently accused of stealing money from an adjacent office during the study session. After initially corroborating the innocent confederate's alibi that she never left the testing room, only 45% of participants maintained their support of that alibi after being led to believe that the confederate had confessed (versus 95% when participants were told that the confederate had denied involvement).

Are alibis believable?

Once a suspect generates an alibi story, is that story seen as credible? It depends. People who are accused of a crime, but are innocent, often have alibis that can be corroborated by either physical evidence or person evidence. Research shows that certain types of corroboration are perceived as more credible than others – in particular, physical evidence over witness evidence; and strangers and mere acquaintances over family members and friends (Hosch et al., 2011; Olson and Wells, 2004). Mock jury studies have shown that an alibi witness having a prior relationship with the alibi provider is seen as less persuasive than one who does not (Culhane and Hosch, 2004; Lindsay et al., 1986); alibi witnesses are less persuasive if they are biologically related or romantically connected to the defendant than if they have a mere social relationship (Culhane and Hosch, 2004; Hosch et al., 2011).

Ultimately, the strength or weakness of alibi evidence can have a significant impact on whether a defendant is found guilty. Verdicts of guilt are correlated with negative views of the alibi provider and witness (Jung et al., 2013). Paralleling research on perceptions of eyewitness identifications, mock jurors are more likely to vote for acquittal when the alibi witness corroborated the defendant's story at a high versus low level of confidence (Culhane and Hosch, 2004; Hosch et al., 2011).

Confessions

As seen in *Making A Murderer*, the video camera in Brendan Dassey's interrogation room captured the moment that he morphed from Steven Avery's alibi witness to his accomplice and co-defendant. The video footage of Dassey's interrogations and confession also expose certain police tactics found in numerous false confession cases.

Confession evidence is common, persuasive, and highly incriminating. Yet history indicates that confessions are fallible. Over the years, countless numbers of innocent people have been wrongfully convicted because they confessed, or were alleged to have confessed, to crimes they did not commit. In the United States, even today, false confessions are a contributing factor in nearly 30% of wrongful convictions overturned by DNA exonerations (www.innocenceproject.org). It is important to note that this population represents a mere fraction of all wrongful convictions. Confessions have been proved false in other ways too – as when it is discovered that the confessed crime was never committed, when new evidence shows it was physically impossible for the confessor to have committed the crime, when the real perpetrator is identified, and when other non-DNA evidence establishes the confessor's innocence (Drizin and Leo, 2004; also see the National Registry of Exonerations (www.law.umich.edu/special/exoneration/Pages/about.aspx).

Over the years, social psychologists have used a variety of research methods to understand why innocent people confess to crimes they did not commit and the effect these false confessions have on the judicial process. Generally speaking, this research shows that there are both dispositional and situational risk factors which precipitate one of three types of false confessions (Kassin and Wrightsman, 1985): *Voluntary*, in which an individual who is innocent of a crime confesses at his or her own initiative, without pressure from police; *coerced-compliant*, in which a suspect agrees to confess as an act of compliance in order to escape the stress of the interrogation and/or in response to promises of leniency and threats of punishment; and *coerced-internalized*, in which a suspect, because of misinformation communicated during interrogation, comes to believe that he or she committed the crime.

Social influence processes of police interrogation

In *Criminal Interrogations and Confessions*, a classic manual on interrogation first published by Inbau and Reid (1962; for the most recent edition, see Inbau et al., 2013), police are trained in a two-step process by which a neutral information-gathering *interview* is conducted to determine if the suspect is truthful or lying, followed by a multistep *interrogation* that is accusatory and designed to elicit a confession. Named after its architect, police polygrapher John Reid, this approach is known as the Reid technique and is used in many parts of the world.

The pre-interrogation interview

During the course of investigating a crime, police may identify one or more suspects for interrogation. Sometimes this identification is based on witnesses, informants, or tangible evidence. Often, however, it is based on nothing more than a personal impression that police form during a pre-interrogation interview. To assess whether a suspect is telling the truth or lying, investigators are trained to conduct a preliminary interview in which they ask non-accusatory questions and observe the suspect's behavior, attending to cues such as eye contact, pauses, changes in posture, and fidgeting. According to Inbau et al. (2013), interrogators can be trained in these ways to make judgments of truth and deception at high levels of accuracy.

Despite the claims, research conducted in social psychology laboratories all over the world has shown that people, on average, are not adept at distinguishing between truth and deception; that eye contact, posture, and other behavioral cues touted by the Reid technique are not diagnostic; that training does not consistently improve performance; and that police and other so-called experts perform only slightly better, if at all (Bond and DePaulo, 2006; DePaulo et al., 2003; Granhag and Strömwall, 2004; Vrij, 2008).

In two illustrative studies aimed at evaluating this process, the results were not encouraging. In one study, Vrij et al. (2006a) had some participants, but not others, commit a mock crime they were incentivized to deny. All participants were then interviewed using questions promoted by the Reid technique.

The results showed that responses did not significantly distinguish between truth-tellers and liars in the predicted manner.

There is also no evidence to indicate that the behavioral cues police are trained to observe are indicative of deception. Kassin and Fong (1999) trained some college students, but not others, in the use of 'behavioral symptoms' cited by the Reid technique. Then they showed students videotaped interviews of mock suspects, some of whom committed a mock crime; others of whom did not. All denied involvement. Consistent with past research on deception detection, participants could not reliably differentiate between true and false denials. In fact, those who underwent training were significantly less accurate, more confident, and more prone to see deception. Using these same interviews, Meissner and Kassin (2002) tested experienced police detectives and found that they too exhibited low rates of accuracy – accompanied by high levels of confidence and a tendency to see deception. In additional research, Jaume Masip and others (2012) also found that police tend to make prejudgments of guilt, with confidence, that are frequently in error. This bias is not harmless; it means that the post-interview interrogation is, by definition, a guilt-presumptive process aimed squarely at eliciting a confession (Kassin et al., 2003).

It is important to note that the search for valid methods of deception detection has a long history dating as far back as medieval times. Research aimed at improving people's ability to distinguish truths and lies is important not only in criminal justice but in business, politics, national security, and international relations. Is there a better way? The most common supplement to human judgment for this purpose is the polygraph – an instrument that records multiple channels of physiological arousal, such as respiration, pulse rate, and sweat-gland activity. Use of the polygraph is based on the assumption that, when people lie, they become anxious – and that this anxiety can be measured via physiological arousal. Over the years, research on use of the polygraph in lie detection has yielded mixed and controversial results. Specifically, although properly administered tests may be more accurate than humans alone under controlled laboratory conditions, polygraph results are subject to examiner bias in many real-world settings (Raskin et al., 2014).

Human lie detection is an important, and yet highly flawed, enterprise. Through a meta-analysis, Bond and DePaulo (2006) found that there were no consistent and reliable cues, that the accuracy rate among both lay people and experts was, on average, 54%, and that individuals harbor many misconceptions regarding the typical behavior of liars. In a cross-national study involving 2,320 participants from 58 countries, for example, the Global Deception Research Team (2006) found that 64% erroneously cited gaze aversion as indicative of deception. In light of such misconceptions, Anders Granhag, Aldert Vrij, and others have recently sought to improve lie detection accuracy by developing interviewing strategies aimed at 'outsmarting liars' (Granhag et al., 2015; Vrij et al., 2010a).

Two lines of research in particular have proved promising in this regard. One approach is based on the fact that lying requires more effort than telling the truth. Vrij et al. (2006) thus theorized that interviewers should tax a suspect's cognitive load and attend to cues that betray effort. In one study, interviewers had truth tellers and liars recount their stories in reverse chronological order and found that observers became more accurate in their ability to distinguish between the truthful and deceptive accounts (Vrij et al., 2008). In a second study, researchers found that forcing suspects to maintain eye contact during the interview, which proved distracting, likewise impaired liars more than truth tellers and increased observers' accuracy (Vrij et al., 2010b).

The second promising technique involves the 'strategic use of evidence' (SUE). This approach is based on the fact that, if police present their evidence at the outset, the suspect will know how to avoid contradicting the investigator's case-specific knowledge and evade detection. When the investigator refrains from disclosing the evidence, the guilty suspect will risk making statements that are inconsistent, thereby getting trapped in a discernible lie (e.g., claiming never to have visited a location at which his or her fingerprints were found). In the first SUE study, Hartwig et al. (2005) had participants commit a mock theft or a non-criminal act and were then interviewed about the event. The interviewers conducted either a standard interview in which evidence against the 'suspect' was disclosed at the outset or they withheld disclosure until later in the interview. Results showed that observers were later more accurate in distinguishing truth and deception when they saw SUE interviews than standard early disclosure interviews (61.7% versus 42.9%). Additional research has produced similar results (Hartwig et al., 2006; Tekin et al., 2015).

The interrogation

Over the years, police would sometimes use 'third degree' methods of interrogation – inflicting physical pain and discomfort in suspects to extract confessions. Among the commonly used coercive methods are prolonged confinement and isolation; explicit threats of harm or punishment; deprivations of sleep, food, and other needs; extreme sensory discomfort; and assorted forms of physical violence (e.g., shining a bright, blinding strobe light on a suspect's face, forcing suspects to stand for hours at a time, or beating them with a rubber hose, which seldom left visible marks).

As a result of a number of Supreme Court rulings – most notably *Brown v. Mississippi* (1936) – in which confessions extracted by physical coercion were ruled inadmissible, psychological approaches to interrogation in the United States were developed that rely heavily on trickery and deception (for an historical overview, see Leo, 2008). Thirty years later, in *Miranda v. Arizona* (1966), the Court ruled that police must inform suspects of their rights to silence and an attorney and obtain a 'knowing, intelligent, and voluntary' waiver of those rights in order for statements taken to be ruled admissible as evidence (for an overview, see Smalarz et al., 2016). Since that time, numerous countries have implemented Miranda-like protections. Interestingly, it appears, while these rules have been weakened in the United States, they have been more forcefully implemented elsewhere, leading one legal scholar to comment that perhaps Miranda has 'moved to Europe, where it is living under an assumed name' (Weisselberg, 2017: 1291).

The psychological approach to interrogation is exemplified by the Reid technique noted earlier. In *Criminal Interrogation and Confessions*, Inbau et al. (2013) advise police, once they have identified a suspect, to isolate that suspect in a small, bare, soundproof room, with no friends or family present, to arouse feelings of discomfort. Once a suspect is isolated, they recommend a multistep procedure reducible to an interplay of two processes (Kassin, 1997; Kassin and Gudjonsson, 2004): One process is to confront the suspect with an accusation and express certainty in his or her guilt and even, at times, claim falsely to have damaging evidence such as fingerprints or an eyewitness. In this way, the accused is led to believe that it is futile to continue in his or her denials. The second process is to befriend the suspect, offer sympathy and friendly advice, and 'minimize' the offense by offering face-saving excuses or blaming the victim. Under stress, feeling trapped, lulled into a false sense of security, and led to expect leniency, many suspects agree to give a confession. Collectively, these processes are designed to increase the anxiety associated with denial and reduce the anxiety associated with making an admission (for social-psychological perspectives, see Davis and O'Donahue, 2004; Kassin, 2015; Vrij et al., 2017).

Why innocent people confess

Through archival analyses of actual cases, basic principles of psychology, and empirical research, researchers have identified both dispositional and situational risk factors that increase the risk of a false confession (for a multi-authored White Paper on risk factors and recommendations for reform, see Kassin et al., 2010; for a recent survey of experts' opinions from all over the world, see Kassin et al., 2018).

As in other domains of social influence, some people are more compliant, and others more resistant, when confronted by figures of authority pressing for a confession. In particular, three sources of vulnerability have been identified: Youth, intellectual disability, and various psychological disorders – including autism and attention-deficit/hyperactivity disorder (for an overview of individual differences, see Gudjonsson, 2018).

Children and adolescents are particularly vulnerable as suspects (Kassin et al., 2010; for a review, see Owen-Kostelnik et al., 2006). Archival records show that juveniles overall are far more likely than adults to be wrongfully convicted on the basis of a false confession (Drizin and Leo, 2004; Gross et al., 2005). These statistics are supported by other types of research. Redlich and Goodman (2003) examined variation in the age of participants using a popular laboratory paradigm in which innocent participants are urged to confess to causing a computer crash. False confession rates varied as a function of age: 78% among 12- and 13-year-olds compared to 72% among 15- and 16-year-olds and 59% of young adults. On the basis of self-report measures, other researchers have observed high false confession rates among juveniles in Europe (Gudjonsson et al., 2009) and in the United States (Malloy et al., 2014).

This vulnerability is consistent with basic research which shows that the adolescent brain is not fully developed, which may be why they exhibit 'immature judgment', as seen in their excessive focus on short-term rewards and punishments rather than long-term consequences (Cauffman and Steinberg, 2000; Steinberg and Cauffman, 1996). Relative to adults, they also have difficulty comprehending and knowing how to apply their *Miranda* rights compared to adults (Grisso, 1998; Goldstein et al., 2003). These vulnerabilities were on display in the interrogation of Brendan Dassey who was visibly confused, under stress, and had no grasp of the consequences of the confession he was urged to give (Crane et al., 2016).

Turning from personal characteristics of vulnerable suspects to situational factors that increase coercion, research has shown that the length of an interrogation can pose a risk to the innocent suspect. Observational studies in the United States have consistently shown that most interrogations last from 30 minutes up to two hours (Feld, 2013; Leo, 1996; Wald et al., 1967). In a survey, 631 North American police investigators estimated that the mean length of interrogation is 1.60 hours and that their longest interrogations lasted an average of 4.21 hours (Kassin et al., 2007). Yet cases involving false confessions contrast sharply with these norms. Examining 125 proven false confessions, Drizin and Leo (2004) found, in cases in which interrogation time was recorded, the mean length was 16.3 hours.

Certain interrogation tactics may also increase the risk of a false confession. Two in particular have been identified in research. The first concerns the presentation of false evidence. In confronting suspects with accusations, American police are permitted to lie about the presence of incriminating evidence (e.g., a fingerprint, hair sample, eyewitness identification, or failed polygraph) – even if there is no such evidence. This tactic can be traced to numerous cases involving proven false confessions. Empirical research also points to the risk. In the first such study, Kassin and Kiechel (1996) accused participants of hitting a forbidden key during a computer-typing task and disabling a computer. Some participants, but not others, were confronted by a confederate who claimed to have witnessed the participant hit the key.

Despite their innocence and initial denials, participants were then asked to sign a confession and later questioned to determine if they also had internalized a belief in their culpability. Results showed that the presentation of false evidence nearly doubled the number of those who signed a confession and internalized the belief in their guilt. Follow-up studies involving other independent variables as well have replicated these basic effects (e.g., Horselenberg et al., 2003; Nash and Wade, 2009; Perillo and Kassin, 2011; Wright et al., 2013).

The second concerning tactic is *minimization*, a tactic by which the interrogator minimizes the criminal act by providing a moral justification and face-saving excuses, suggesting to suspects that their actions were unplanned, accidental, provoked, or otherwise precipitated by external factors. Actual false confession cases and empirical research confirm that these tactics are frequently used (Kassin et al., 2007; King and Snook, 2009; Leo, 1996). Moreover, controlled laboratory experiments have demonstrated that, by downplaying the seriousness of an offense, minimizing remarks communicate by implication or innuendo a promise of leniency in exchange for confession (Kassin and McNall, 1991). In one study, for example, Russano et al. (2005) had a confederate coax some participants, but not others, into giving help on a problem, thereby violating the experimenter's protocol calling for working individually. The experimenter later separated the two, accused the participant of cheating, and tried to get the participant to sign a confession by either making an explicit promise of leniency, making minimizing remarks, using both tactics, or using none at all. Overall, the confession rate was higher among guilty participants than innocents, when leniency was promised than when it was not, and when minimization was used than when it was not. Confirming concerns stemming from actual cases, minimizing remarks increased the rate of false confessions among innocent participants in the same way that promises of leniency had done.

Investigative interviewing: alternative to interrogation

To address the fact that some individuals are vulnerable and that certain interrogation tactics put innocent people at risk, some researchers have advocated for various reforms that would protect certain types of suspects (i.e., juveniles, people with intellectual impairments or mental health problems) and limit or prohibit use of the most perilous interrogation practices (i.e., presentations of false evidence, minimization tactics that imply leniency).

At a macro level, another approach is to fully reconceptualize the process of interrogation. The recent history in Great Britain is instructive in this regard. In the 1980s, after a series of high-profile false confession cases, British police transitioned from a Reid-style confrontational approach to 'investigative interviewing', in which the primary objective is to gather information, not necessarily get confessions. In 1993, British police adopted a five-part approach called PEACE, a mnemonic for *Preparation and Planning* (organizing the evidence and planning the interview), *Engage and Explain* (establishing a rapport and communicating the purpose of the interview to the suspect), *Account* (conducting a 'Cognitive Interview' to get the compliant suspect to speak freely and 'conversation management' to open up the non-compliant suspect), *Closure* (addressing discrepancies that may appear in the suspect's narrative account), and *Evaluation* (comparing the suspect's final statement to evidence, trying to resolve inconsistencies, and drawing conclusions). Within PEACE, lying to suspects is not permitted; interviewers seek to establish rapport with the suspect and listen, not interrupt; and all sessions should be recorded (Clarke and Milne, 2001; for a proposal to use PEACE in Canada, see Snook et al., 2010). This model has served as a precursor to 'investigative interviewing' – a popular cognitive approach, found more and more in Europe, that focuses more on information gathering than on confession taking (see Bull, 2014; Shepherd and Griffiths, 2013; Williamson, 2006).

The British experience suggests that investigative interviewing more generally provides an effective and less perilous alternative to the Reid technique. In a comparison of the two approaches, Meissner et al. (2014) conducted a meta-analysis, statistically combining the results of twelve laboratory experiments in which guilty and/or innocent subjects were questioned using accusatorial and/or information gathering methods. As measured by outcomes, the results showed that, while the accusatorial approach increased both true and false confession rates, information gathering produced more diagnostic outcomes, increasing the rate of true confessions without also yielding false confessions. While more comparative research is needed, it appears that investigative interviewing using PEACE and other similar approaches can be used to solve crimes without high risk to innocent suspects.

ADJUDICATING GUILT AND INNOCENCE

Once evidence is gathered and analyzed from the crime scene, as well as from witnesses and suspects, a prosecutor must determine whether there is sufficient evidence to try a defendant. If so, there are two mechanisms for achieving an outcome: A trial in court before a judge and/or jury, or a plea agreement by which the defendant pleads guilty in exchange for reduced charges or sentencing. Social psychologists have examined both of these processes.

Jury Decision-Making

The jury system that evolved in England plays an important role in the criminal justice systems of more than 50 countries and territories around the world. In countries that aspire to be more democratic, as well as those with a longstanding tradition, it is now common to recruit ordinary citizens to decide cases (Vidmar, 2000).

Within criminal justice systems, and in civil justice systems involving lawsuits, the evidence gathered may culminate in a courtroom trial, an infrequent but highly dramatic event. In some countries, the decision-maker is a lay jury. In other countries, verdicts are rendered by professional judges or mixed groups of judges and laypersons. Whatever the model, it is the threat of trial that motivates parties to gather evidence and negotiate an agreement. Over the years, many American social psychologists, in particular, have examined three stages of a trial: The selection of individual jurors, the presentation of evidence and arguments in court, and the processes by which juries deliberate as a group to reach a verdict. We briefly overview the research in each of these domains.

Jury selection

Jury selection is a three-stage process. First, the court compiles a master list of eligible citizens from the community. Second, a small number of people from the list are randomly drawn and summoned for duty, at which point they are questioned under oath by the judge and lawyers seeking signs of bias. Third, lawyers are permitted to challenge a limited number of prospective jurors who exhibit no clear signs of bias. These are called peremptory challenges. The reasons why lawyers would use peremptory challenges to accept some jurors and reject others – typically on the basis of implicit personality theories and stereotypes – have proved particularly interesting to social psychologists (Vidmar and Hans, 2007).

This process can have two troubling effects. First, if lawyers approach a prospective juror with a set of expectations, say based on stereotypes, they are likely to ask questions designed to confirm their beliefs and thereby increase the likelihood of doing so.

In a mock trial study, practicing attorneys who were asked to prepare questions on the basis of juror profiles asked questions consistent with those profiles and ultimately formed conclusions that were biased by the questions they asked (Otis et al., 2014).

A second problem with this aspect of jury selection is that it opens the door for lawyers to disproportionately remove women, or men, or members of specific racial and ethnic groups, thereby stripping the jury of its diversity. To prevent this, the US Supreme Court limited the use of these challenges by requiring lawyers suspected of discriminating to explain the basis of their challenges (*Batson v. Kentucky,* 1986). Unfortunately, research has shown (1) that the influence of conscious and unconscious racial stereotypes on social perceptions is prevalent and likely to influence lawyers in the courtroom; and (2) that these racial biases are difficult to identify in specific instances because lawyers, like people in general, typically do not acknowledge having been influenced by their stereotypes (Sommers and Norton, 2008).

The courtroom trial

Once an American jury is selected, the trial officially begins and the evidence is presented through the testimony of witnesses. The trial is a highly orchestrated event. Lawyers for both sides make opening statements. Witnesses then answer questions under oath. Lawyers make closing arguments. The judge instructs the jury. Yet there are many problems in this all-too-human enterprise: The evidence is often not accurate or reliable, jurors may harbor bias from extraneous factors, and the process of deliberation may cause some jurors to vote for a verdict that contradicts their beliefs. Researchers have studied jury decision-making for many years (Bornstein and Greene, 2017; Kovera, 2017; Vidmar and Hans, 2007).

In *The American Jury,* Henry Kalven and Hans Zeisel (1966) surveyed 550 judges who had presided over 3,576 criminal jury trials nationwide. While each jury was deliberating, judges were asked to indicate what their verdict would be. A comparison of their responses to the actual jury verdicts revealed that judges and juries agreed on a verdict in 78% of all cases. Among the 22% of cases in which there was a disagreement, the jury voted to acquit a defendant that judges perceived to be guilty. This result suggests that juries are more lenient than judges. Since that initial study, hundreds of mock jury experiments have been conducted to examine the determinants of jury verdicts. Generally speaking, this research has shown that juries are sound decision-makers whose verdicts are based largely on the strength of the evidence presented at trial (Diamond and Rose, 2005; Eisenberg et al., 2005; Hans et al., 2011).

Despite this assuring conclusion that juries tend to follow the evidence, their verdicts can be tainted in two ways. First, we saw earlier that juries tend to accept eyewitness identifications and confessions, often without sufficient scrutiny or understanding of the underlying psychology. For example, despite the large body of evidence that eyewitness identifications are unreliable, eyewitnesses exert a powerful influence on jurors who are insensitive to factors that influence identification accuracy (Cutler et al., 1989; Devenport et al., 2002). Similarly, confessions increase conviction rates significantly, even when it is not logically appropriate – as when the confession is indisputably coerced (Kassin and Sukel, 1997), reported by a motivated informant (Neuschatz et al., 2008), or contradicted by DNA testing (Appleby and Kassin, 2016).

The second problem with juries stems from their exposure to non-evidentiary information. Juries are supposed to base their verdicts solely on courtroom testimony – not on internet rumors, news stories, a defendant's physical appearance, and other information. Yet mock jury experiments have shown that juries can be biased by exposure to extraneous information such as prejudicial pretrial publicity that might be reported in a newspaper (e.g., Daftary-Kapur et al., 2014; Kramer et al., 1990). Pretrial publicity is potentially dangerous because it often divulges information that is not later allowed into the trial record and because it often precedes the actual trial. Indeed, analyses of secretly recorded mock jury deliberations showed that exposure to pretrial publicity was openly discussed and completely tainted their discussions of the defendant and evidence – despite the judge's warning to disregard that information (Ruva and Guenther, 2015; Ruva and LeVasseur, 2012).

Jury deliberations

It is often said that the unique power of the jury stems from the wisdom that emerges when individuals come together privately as one *group.* Is this assumption justified? By interviewing jurors after trials and by recruiting people to participate on mock juries and recording their deliberations, researchers have learned a great deal about how juries come together to reach a verdict.

Research shows that the jury decision-making process typically passes through three stages (Hastie et al., 1983; Stasser et al., 1982). Like other problem-solving groups, they begin with an *orientation* period during which they set an agenda, talk in general terms, raise questions, and explore the facts. Then, once differences of opinion are revealed, during and after the first vote is taken, factions develop and the group shifts abruptly into a period of *open conflict.* At that point, discussion takes on a more focused, argumentative tone. Together, jurors scrutinize the evidence, construct stories to account for that evidence, and discuss the judge's instructions (Pennington and Hastie, 1992). If all jurors agree, they return a verdict. If not, the majority tries to achieve a consensus by converting the holdouts through informational and social pressure. If unanimity is achieved, the group enters a period of *reconciliation,* during which the members try to smooth over conflicts and affirm their satisfaction with the verdict (if the holdouts continue to disagree, the judge may declare the deadlocked group a hung jury).

When it comes to decision-making *outcomes,* deliberations follow a predictable course first discovered by Kalven and Zeisel (1966). By interviewing the members of 225 juries, they were able to reconstruct how these juries split on their very first vote. Out of 215 that had opened with an initial majority, 209 reached a final verdict consistent with that first vote. This simple finding – which was later corroborated by mock jury studies (Kerr, 1981; Stasser and Davis, 1981) – led Kalven and Zeisel (1966: 489) to conclude that 'the deliberation process might well be likened to what the developer does for an exposed film; it brings out the picture, but the outcome is predetermined'. There is one interesting exception to the majority-wins rule: In criminal trials, the process of deliberation tends to produce a leniency bias that favors the defendant. All other factors being equal, individual jurors are more likely to vote guilty on their own than in a group; and they are also more prone to convict before deliberations than afterward (Kerr and MacCoun, 2012; MacCoun and Kerr, 1988).

Guilty Pleas: The Common Alternative to Trial

In many countries, defendants often make a special form of confession outside the police station with the prosecutor and often the defense lawyer present. That confession involves pleading guilty, typically in exchange for lesser charges and a more lenient sentence. Every day, thousands of defendants decide to plead guilty. In fact, an estimated 97% of convicted defendants in the US federal criminal justice system resolve their cases in this way. For legal systems all over the world, this process represents a quick alternative to trial that results in enormous savings of time, money, and other resources (Rauxloh, 2010).

People are far more likely to plead guilty if they have committed the crime for which they are charged than if they have not. Still, with so many cases getting resolved in a plea agreement between a prosecutor and defendant, it is natural to wonder how often innocent people who fear conviction at trial and a harsh sentence plead guilty 'in the shadow of trial' (Bibas, 2004). In an article entitled 'Understanding guilty pleas through the lens of social science', Redlich and colleagues (2017) described how an innocent person might make a rational decision to plead guilty, in the same way that an innocent person might confess to police, after considering the crime that is charged, the strength of the evidence, the punishment alternatives, and the pressures that are brought to bear on the process. To the extent that these decisions are further 'informed' by pressure from the prosecutor – a figure of authority in a position to elicit obedience – the decision to plead guilty is often made in the presence of powerful social influences (Bordens and Bassett, 1985).

The actual incidence of false guilty pleas is not known (Tor et al., 2010). Laboratory experiments that have involved role-playing in response to hypothetical scenarios, or in which participants make decisions that they believe will have a real consequence, have shown that many innocent people will accept a false guilty plea at surprisingly high rates (e.g., Dervan and Edkins, 2012). This finding extends beyond the laboratory. Approximately 10% of innocent people who were wrongfully convicted in the United States had pled guilty rather than risk conviction on more serious charges (www.innocenceproject.org).

Pleading takes place 'in the shadow of trial' based on the expected outcome and sentencing at trial. Consistent with this model, simulation studies involving practicing attorneys have shown that plea recommendations were predictably influenced by how strong the evidence was against the defendant (Kramer et al., 2007; Pezdek and O'Brien, 2014). In some ways, however, this model does not fully account for psychological factors that affect the plea decision. In one simulation study, for example, practicing defense attorneys recommended harsher plea agreements for black defendants than for white defendants – even when the crime and evidence were the same (Edkins, 2011). Other studies too suggest that some defendants are more 'at risk' than others. For example, the rate of self-reported false guilty pleas, although they cannot be corroborated, is particularly high among juvenile detainees – 18% (Malloy et al., 2014) and defendants with mental illness – 37% (Redlich et al., 2010).

To sum up, plea bargaining in countries all over the world offers a cost-efficient way to resolve criminal cases without trial. This alternative does not come without risk, however. At present, social psychologists are examining the process and whether it produces outcomes that are accurate, fair, and just for everyone.

PERCEPTIONS OF JUSTICE

Netflix's *Making a Murderer* captured attention worldwide and an impressive 19.3 million viewers in just one month. Many of those who watched reacted with 'near-universal outrage' – angered not only by the convictions of Avery and Dassey but by the perception of procedural injustices occurring throughout the proceedings, from the gathering of physical evidence to the Dassey interrogation, to the conduct of the trials (Schulz, 2016).

How do people determine whether a dispute, legal or otherwise, has been decided fairly? In an early book entitled *Procedural Justice* (1978), Thibaut and Walker proposed that our satisfaction with the way legal and other disputes are resolved depends not only on outcomes but also on the procedures used to achieve those outcomes. In matters of law, the effectiveness of any judicial system rests on the willingness of citizens to adhere to laws and decisions that may deviate from their own self-interests (Tyler, 2000).

Thibaut and Walker (1978) theorized that satisfaction with a decision-maker's judgment is not merely a function of distributive outcomes but the process by which that resolution is reached. Thibaut and Walker distinguished between *decision control* – whether a procedure affords the involved parties the power to accept, reject, or otherwise influence the final decision – and *process control* – whether a procedure offers the parties an opportunity to present their case to a third-party decision maker. In a courtroom, the disputants have limited decision control; hence, their sense of justice depends on whether they feel that they had a chance to express their views. Both laboratory and field research have demonstrated that this 'voice effect' strengthens people's judgments of procedural justice. Having a voice and the opportunity to present one's case during the decision-making process thus plays an important role in people's perceptions of fairness – regardless of the ultimate outcome (Lind et al., 1980; 1983; Tyler et al., 1985). This aspect of the legal system is important because it makes the system appear fair and legitimate and fosters cooperation – which is why many social psychologists study people's perceptions of justice (Törnblom and Vermunt, 2007; Tyler, 2011).

In addition to voice and the ability to participate in proceedings, other factors contribute to the perception that decision-makers are objective and that litigants are treated respectfully and impartially. For example, Leventhal (1980) identified consistency, bias suppression, accuracy, correctability, representativeness, and ethicality as core principles of procedural justice. Subsequent research suggests that these factors are important (Tyler, 1988). To ensure that legal judgments are respected and accepted by litigants and the public, the decision-making process and the ultimate verdict must be perceived as fair. Procedural justice thus enables the public's obedience to rules and laws, cooperation with police and other authorities, and acceptance of verdicts and other legal findings (Tyler, 2006; Tyler et al., 2015).

SUMMARY AND CONCLUSIONS

For decades, cases like that depicted in *Making A Murderer* have inspired the study of social perceptions and influences on decision-making in the legal system. In this chapter, we have described current research on (1) the social psychology of evidence, as seen in research on eyewitness identifications, alibis, police interviews, interrogations, and confessions; (2) the processes by which guilt and innocence are adjudicated, accurately and in error, both in jury trials and in plea bargaining; and (3) laypeople's perceptions of justice, which form the basis for citizen cooperation with legitimate authority. With all the research conducted thus far, far more is needed in an effort both to identify ways to enhance the administration of justice and to raise public awareness on these matters.

REFERENCES

Appleby, S. C., & Kassin, S. M. (2016). When self-report trumps science: Effects of confessions, DNA, and prosecutorial theories on perceptions of guilt. *Psychology, Public Policy, and Law, 22*(2), 127.

Austin, J. L., Zimmerman, D. M., Rhead, L., & Kovera, M. B. (2013). Double-blind lineup administration: Effects of administrator knowledge on eyewitness decisions. In B. L. Cutler (Eds.), *Reform of eyewitness identification procedures* (pp. 139–160). Washington, DC: American Psychological Association.

Bibas, S. (2004). Plea bargaining outside the shadow of trial. *Harvard Law Review, 117*, 2463–2547.

Bond, Jr., C. F., & DePaulo, B. M. (2006). Accuracy of deception judgments. *Personality and Social Psychology Review*, *10*(3), 214–234.

Bordens, K. S., & Bassett, J. (1985). The plea bargaining process from the defendant's perspective: A field investigation. *Basic and Applied Social Psychology*, *6*(2), 93–110.

Bornstein, B. H., Deffenbacher, K. A., Penrod, S. D., & McGorty, E. K. (2012). Effects of exposure time and cognitive operations on facial identification accuracy: a meta-analysis of two variables associated with initial memory strength. *Psychology, Crime & Law*, *18*(5), 473–490.

Bornstein, B. H., & Greene, E. (2017). *American Psychology-Law Society series. The jury under fire: Myth, controversy, and reform.* New York: Oxford University Press.

Brewer, N., & Wells, G. L. (2011). Eyewitness identification. *Current Directions in Psychological Science*, *20*(1), 24–27.

Brown v. *Mississippi*, 297 US 278 (Supreme Court 1936).

Bull, R. (2014). When in interviews to disclose information to suspects and to challenge them? In R. Bull (Ed.), *Investigative interviewing.* New York: Springer.

Cauffman, E., & Steinberg, L. (2000). (Im)maturity of judgment in adolescence: Why adolescents may be less culpable than adults. *Behavioral Sciences & the Law*, *18*(6), 741–760.

Chabris, C. F., & Simons, D. J. (2009). *The Invisible gorilla: How our intuitions deceive us.* New York: Crown Books.

Charman, S. D., Reyes, A., Villalba, D. K., & Evans, J. R. (2017). The (un)reliability of alibi corroborators: Failure to recognize faces of briefly encountered strangers puts innocent suspects at risk. *Behavioral Sciences & the Law*, *35*, 18–36.

Clarke, C., & Milne, R. (2001). *A national evaluation of the PEACE Investigative Interviewing Course*. London: Home Office.

Crane, M., Nirider, L., & Drizin, S. A. (2016). The truth about juvenile false confessions. *Insights on Law & Society*, *16*(2), 10–15.

Culhane, S. E., & Hosch, H. M. (2004). An alibi witness' influence on mock jurors' verdicts. *Journal of Applied Social Psychology*, *34*(8), 1604–1616.

Cutler, B. L. (2013). *Reform of eyewitness identification procedures* (Vol. ix). Washington, DC: American Psychological Association.

Cutler, B. L., & Penrod, S. D. (1989). Forensically relevant moderators of the relation between eyewitness identification accuracy and confidence. *Journal of Applied Psychology*, *74*(4), 650–652.

Cutler, B. L., Penrod, S. D., & Dexter, H. R. (1989). The eyewitness, the expert psychologist, and the jury. *Law and Human Behavior*, *13*(3), 311–332.

Daftary-Kapur, T., Penrod, S. D., O'Connor, M., & Wallace, B. (2014). Examining pretrial publicity in a shadow jury paradigm: Issues of slant, quantity, persistence and generalizability. *Law and Human Behavior*, *38*(5), 462–477.

Davis, D., & O'Donohue, W. (2004). The road to perdition: Extreme influence tactics in the interrogation room. In W. O'Donohue, & E. Levensky (Eds.), *Handbook of forensic psychology* (pp. 897–996). California: Elsevier, Inc.

Deffenbacher, K. A., Bornstein, B. H., Penrod, S. D., & McGorty, E. K. (2004). A meta-analytic review of the effects of high stress on eyewitness memory. *Law and Human Behavior*, *28*(6), 687–706.

Demos, M., & Ricciardi, L. (2015). *Making a murderer*. In Synthesis Films. Manitowoc, Wisconsin: Netflix.

DePaulo, B. M., Lindsay, J. J., Malone, B. E., Muhlenbruck, L., Charlton, K., & Cooper, H. (2003). Cues to deception. *Psychological Bulletin*, *129*(1), 74–118.

Dervan, L., & Edkins, V. A. (2012). The innocent defendant's dilemma: An innovative empirical study of plea bargaining's innocence problem. *Journal of Criminal Law and Criminology*, *103*, 1–48.

Devenport, J. L., Stinson, V., Cutler, B. L., & Kravitz, D. A. (2002). How effective are the cross-examination and expert testimony safeguards? Jurors' perceptions of the suggestiveness and fairness of biased lineup procedures. *Journal of Applied Psychology*, *87*(6), 1042–1054.

Diamond, S. D., & Rose, M. R.. (2005). Real Juries. *Annual Review of Law and Social Science*, *1*, 255–284.

Drizin, S. A., & Leo, R. A. (2004). The problem of false confessions in the post-DNA world. *North Carolina Law Review*, *82*, 891–1008.

Dysart, J. E., & Strange, D. (2012). Beliefs about alibis and alibi investigations: A survey of law enforcement. *Psychology, Crime, & Law, 18*(1), 11–25.

Edkins, V. A. (2011). Defense attorney plea recommendations and client race: does zealous representation apply equally to all? *Law and Human Behavior, 35*(5), 413–425.

Eisenberg, T., et al. (2005). Judge-jury agreement in criminal cases: A partial replication of Kalven and Zeisel's The American Jury, *Journal of Empirical Legal Studies, 2*, 171–206.

Erickson, W. B., Lampinen, J. M., & Leding, J. K. (2014). The weapon focus effect in target-present and target-absent line-ups: The roles of threat, novelty, and timing. *Applied Cognitive Psychology, 28*(3), 349–359.

Fawcett, J. M., Russell, E. J., Peace, K. A., & Christie, J. (2013). Of guns and geese: a meta-analytic review of the 'weapon focus' literature. *Psychology, Crime & Law, 19*(1), 35–66.

Feld, B. C. (2013). Real interrogation: What actually happens when cops question kids. *Law & Society Review, 47*(1), 1–36.

Frenda, S. J., Nichols, R. M., & Loftus, E. F. (2011). Current issues and advances in misinformation research. *Current Directions in Psychological Science, 20*(1), 20–23.

Gabbert, F., Memon, A., Allan, K., & Wright, D. B. (2004). Say it to my face: Examining the effects of socially encountered misinformation. *Legal and Criminological Psychology, 9*(2), 215–227.

Global Deception Research Team. (2006). A world of lies. *Journal of Cross-Cultural Psychology, 37*, 60–74.

Goldstein, N. E. S., Condie, L. O., Kalbeitzer, R., Osman, D., & Geier, J. L. (2003). Juvenile offenders' Miranda rights comprehension and self-reported likelihood of offering false confessions. *Assessment, 10*(4), 359–369.

Gooderson, R. N. (1977). *Alibi*. London, England: Heinemann Educational.

Granhag, P. A., & Strömwall, L. A. (2004). *The detection of deception in forensic contexts.* Cambridge, UK: Cambridge University Press.

Granhag, P. A., Vrij, A., & Verschuere, B. (2015). *Detecting deception: current challenges and cognitive approaches.* Hoboken, NJ: John Wiley & Sons.

Greathouse, S. M., & Kovera, M. B. (2009). Instruction bias and lineup presentation moderate the effects of administrator knowledge on eyewitness identification. *Law and Human Behavior, 33*(1), 70–82.

Grisso, T. (1998). *Forensic evaluation of juveniles.* Sarasota, FL: Professional Resource Press.

Gross, S. R., Jacoby, K., Matheson, D. J., Montgomery, N., & Patil, S. (2005). Exonerations in the United States 1989 through 2003. *The Journal of Criminal Law and Criminology (1973-), 95*(2), 523–560.

Gudjonsson, G. H. (2018). *The psychology of false confessions: Forty years of science and practice.* Chichester, UK: John Wiley & Sons Ltd.

Gudjonsson, G. H., Sigurdsson, J. F., & Sigfusdottir, I. D. (2009). Interrogation and false confessions among adolescents in seven European countries. What background and psychological variables best discriminate between false confessors and non-false confessors? *Psychology, Crime & Law, 15*(8), 711–728.

Hans, V. P., Kaye, D. H., Dann, B. M., Farley, E. J., & Albertson, S. (2011). Science in the jury box: Jurors' comprehension of mitochondrial DNA evidence. *Law and Human Behavior, 35*(1), 60–71.

Hartwig, M., Granhag, P. A., Strömwall, L. A., & Kronkvist, O. (2006). Strategic use of evidence during police interviews: When training to detect deception works. *Law and Human Behavior, 30*(5), 603–619.

Hartwig, M., Granhag, P. A., Strömwall, L. A., & Vrij, A. (2005). Detecting deception via strategic disclosure of evidence. *Law and Human Behavior, 29*(4), 469–484.

Hastie, R., Penrod, S. D., & Pennington, N. (1983). *Inside the jury.* Clark, NJ: The Lawbook Exchange, Ltd.

Higham, P. A., Blank, H., & Luna, K. (2017). Effects of postwarning specificity on memory performance and confidence in the eyewitness misinformation paradigm. *Journal of Experimental Psychology: Applied, 23*, 417–432.

Hirst, W., Phelps, E. A., Meksin, R., Vaidya, C. J., Johnson, M. K., Mitchell, K. J., & Olsson, A. (2015). A ten-year follow-up of a study of memory for the attack of September 11, 2001: Flashbulb memories and memories for flashbulb events. *Journal of Experimental Psychology: General, 144*(3), 604–623.

Horselenberg, R., Merckelbach, H., & Josephs, S. (2003). Individual differences and false confessions: A conceptual replication of Kassin and Kiechel (1996). *Psychology, Crime & Law*, *9*(1), 1–8.

Hosch, H. M., Culhane, S. E., Jolly, K. W., Chavez, R. M., & Shaw, L. H. (2011). Effects of an alibi witness's relationship to the defendant on mock jurors' judgments. *Law and Human Behavior*, *35*(2), 127–142.

Inbau, F. E., & Reid, J. E. (1962). *Criminal interrogation and confessions* (1st edn.). Baltimore: Williams and Wilkins.

Inbau, F. E., Reid, J. E., Buckley, J. P., & Jayne, B. C. (2013). *Criminal interrogation and confessions* (5th edn.). Burlington, MA: Jones & Bartlett Learning.

Jones, A. M., Bergold, A. N., Dillon, M., & Penrod, S. D. (2017). Comparing the effectiveness of Henderson instructions and expert testimony: Which safeguard improves jurors' evaluations of eyewitness evidence? *Journal of Experimental Criminology*, *13*, 29–52.

Jung, S., Allison, M., & Bohn, L. (2013). Legal decision-making on crimes involving an alibi. *Applied Psychology in Criminal Justice*, *9*(1), 45–58.

Kalven, H., & Zeisel, H. (1966). The American jury and the death penalty. *The University of Chicago Law Review*, *33*(4), 769–781.

Kassin, S. M. (1997). The psychology of confession evidence. *American Psychologist*, *52*(3), 221–233.

Kassin, S. M. (2012). Why confessions trump innocence. *American Psychologist*, *67*(6), 431–445.

Kassin, S. M. (2015). The social psychology of false confessions. *Social Issues and Policy Review*, *9*(1), 25–51.

Kassin, S. M., & Fong, C. T. (1999). 'I'm innocent!': Effects of training on judgments of truth and deception in the interrogation room. *Law and Human Behavior*, *23*(5), 499–516.

Kassin, S. M., & Gudjonsson, G. H. (2004). The psychology of confessions: A review of the literature and issues. *Psychological Science in the Public Interest*, *5*(2), 33–67.

Kassin, S. M., & Kiechel, K. L. (1996). The social psychology of false confessions: Compliance, internalization, and confabulation. *Psychological Science*, *7*(3), 125–128.

Kassin, S. M., & McNall, K. (1991). Police interrogations and confessions: Communicating promises and threats by pragmatic implication. *Law and Human Behavior*, *15*(3), 233–251.

Kassin, S. M., & Sukel, H. (1997). Coerced confessions and the jury: An experimental test of the 'harmless error' rule. *Law and Human Behavior*, *21*(1), 27–46.

Kassin, S. M., & Wrightsman, L. S. (1985). Confession evidence. In S. M. Kassin, & L. S. Wrightsman (Eds.), *The psychology of evidence and trial procedure* (3rd edn., pp. 67–94). Beverly Hills, CA: Sage.

Kassin, S. M., Drizin, S. A., Grisso, T., Gudjonsson, G. H., Leo, R. A., & Redlich, A. D. (2010). Police-induced confessions: Risk factors and recommendations. *Law and Human Behavior*, *34*(1), 3–38.

Kassin, S. M., Goldstein, C. C., & Savitsky, K. (2003). Behavioral confirmation in the interrogation room: On the dangers of presuming guilt. *Law and Human Behavior*, *27*(2), 187–203.

Kassin, S. M., Leo, R. A., Meissner, C. A., Richman, K. D., Colwell, L. H., Leach, A.-M., & Fon, D. L. (2007). Police interviewing and interrogation: A self-report survey of police practices and beliefs. *Law and Human Behavior*, *31*(4), 381–400.

Kassin, S. M., Redlich, A. D., Alceste, F., & Luke, T. J. (2018). On the general acceptance of confessions research: Opinions of the scientific community. *American Psychologist*, *73*, 63–80.

Kassin, S. M., Tubb, V. A., Hosch, H. M., & Memon, A. (2001). On the 'general acceptance' of eyewitness testimony research: A new survey of the experts. *American Psychologist*, *56*(5), 405–416.

Kerr, N. L. (1981). Social transition schemes: Charting the group's road to agreement. *Journal of Personality and Social Psychology*, *41*(4), 684–702.

Kerr, N. L., & MacCoun, R. J. (2012). Is the leniency asymmetry really dead? Misinterpreting asymmetry effects in criminal jury deliberation. *Group Processes & Intergroup Relations*, *15*(5), 585–602.

King, L., & Snook, B. (2009). Peering inside a Canadian interrogation room: An examination of the Reid model of interrogation, influence tactics, and coercive strategies. *Criminal Justice and Behavior*, *36*(7), 674–694.

Kovera, M. B. (Ed.) (2017). *The psychology of juries*. Washington, DC: American Psychological Association.

Kovera, M. B., & Evelo, A. J. (2017). The case for double-blind lineup administration. *Psychology, Public Policy, and Law, 23*, 421–437.

Kramer, G. P., Kerr, N. L., & Carroll, J. S. (1990). Pretrial publicity, judicial remedies, and jury bias. *Law and Human Behavior, 14*(5), 409.

Kramer, G. M., Wolbransky, M., & Heilbrun, K. (2007). Plea bargaining recommendations by criminal defense attorneys: Evidence strength, potential sentence, and defendant preference. *Behavioral Sciences & the Law, 25*(4), 573–585.

Leins, D. A., & Charman, S. D. (2016). Schema reliance and innocent alibi generation. *Legal and Criminological Psychology, 21*(1), 111–126.

Leippe, M. R. (1995). The case for expert testimony about eyewitness memory. *Psychology, Public Policy, and Law, 1*, 909–959.

Leo, R. A. (1996). Inside the interrogation room. *The Journal of Criminal Law and Criminology (1973-), 86*(2),

Leo, R. A. (2008). *Police interrogation and American justice*. Cambridge, MA: Harvard University Press.

Leventhal, G. S. (1980). What should be done with equity theory? New approaches to the study of fairness in social relationships. In K. Gergen, M. Greenberg, & R. Willis (Eds.), *Social exchange* (pp. 27–55). New York, NY: Plenum.

Lind, E. A., Kurtz, S., Musante, L., Walker, L., & Thibaut, J. W. (1980). Procedure and outcome effects on reactions to adjudicated resolution of conflicts of interests. *Journal of Personality and Social Psychology, 39*(4), 643–653.

Lind, E. A., Lissak, R. I., & Conlon, D. E. (1983). Decision control and process control effects on procedural fairness judgments. *Journal of Applied Social Psychology, 13*(4), 338–350.

Lindsay, R. C. L., Lim, R., Marando, L., & Cully, D. (1986). Mock-juror evaluations of eyewitness testimony: A test of metamemory hypotheses. *Journal of Applied Social Psychology, 16*(5), 447–459.

Lindsay, R. C. L., & Wells, G. L. (1985). Improving eyewitness identification from lineups: Simultaneous versus sequential lineup presentations. *Journal of Applied Psychology, 70*, 556–564.

Loftus, E. F. (1996). *Eyewitness testimony*. Cambridge, MA: Harvard University Press.

Loftus, E. F. (2005). Planting misinformation in the human mind: A 30-year investigation of the malleability of memory. *Learning & Memory, 12*(4), 361–366.

Loftus, E. F., & Hoffman, H. G. (1989). Misinformation and memory: The creation of new memories. *Journal of Experimental Psychology: General, 118*(1), 100–104.

Loftus, E. F., Loftus, G. R., & Messo, J. (1987). Some facts about 'weapon focus.' *Law and Human Behavior, 11*(1), 55–62.

MacCoun, R. J., & Kerr, N. L. (1988). Asymmetric influence in mock jury deliberation: Jurors' bias for leniency. *Journal of Personality and Social Psychology, 54*(1), 21.

Malloy, L. C., Shulman, E. P., & Cauffman, E. (2014). Interrogations, confessions, and guilty pleas among serious adolescent offenders. *Law and Human Behavior, 38*(2), 181–193.

Malpass, R. S., & Devine, P. G. (1981). Eyewitness identification: Lineup instructions and the absence of the offender. *Journal of Applied Psychology, 66*(4), 482–489.

Marion, S. B., Kukucka, J., Collins, C., Kassin, S. M., & Burke, T. M. (2016). Lost proof of innocence: The impact of confessions on alibi witnesses. *Law and Human Behavior, 40*(1), 65–71.

Masip, J., Barba, A., & Herrero, C. (2012). Behaviour analysis interview and common sense: A study with novice and experienced officers. *Psychiatry, Psychology & Law, 19*(1), 21–34.

Meissner, C. A., & Brigham, J. C. (2001). Thirty years of investigating the own-race bias in memory for faces: A meta-analytic review. *Psychology, Public Policy, and Law, 7*(1), 3–35.

Meissner, C. A., & Kassin, S. M. (2002). 'He's guilty!': Investigator bias in judgments of truth and deception. *Law and Human Behavior, 26*(5), 469–480.

Meissner, C. A., Redlich, A. D., Michael, S. W., Evans, J. R., Camilletti, C. R., Bhatt, S., & Brandon, S. (2014). Accusatorial and information-gathering interrogation methods and their effects on true and false confessions: A meta-analytic review. *Journal of Experimental Criminology, 10*(4), 459–486.

Memon, A., Hope, L., & Bull, R. (2003). Exposure duration: Effects on eyewitness accuracy and confidence. *British Journal of Psychology*, *94*(3), 339–354.

Miranda v. *Arizona*, 384 US 436 (Supreme Court 1966).

Morgan, C. A., Hazlett, G., Doran, A., Garrett, S., Hoyt, G., Thomas, P., Baransoki, M., & Southwick, S. M. (2004). Accuracy of eyewitness memory for persons encountered during exposure to highly intense stress. *International Journal of Law and Psychiatry*, *27*, 265–279.

Morgan, C. A., Southwick, S., Steffian, G., Hazlett, G. A., & Loftus, E. F. (2013). Misinformation can influence memory for recently experienced, highly stressful events. *International Journal of Law and Psychiatry*, *36*(1), 11–17.

Nash, R. A., & Wade, K. A. (2009). Innocent but proven guilty: Eliciting internalized false confessions using doctored-video evidence. *Applied Cognitive Psychology*, *23*(5), 624–637.

National Research Council. (2014). *Identifying the culprit: Assessing eyewitness identification*. Washington, DC: The National Academies Press.

Neuschatz, J. S., Lawson, D. S., Swanner, J. K., Meissner, C. A., & Neuschatz, J. S. (2008). The effects of accomplice witnesses and jailhouse informants on jury decision making. *Law and Human Behavior*, *32*(2), 137–149.

Nolan, J. R. (1990). *Black's law dictionary* (6th edn.). St. Paul, MN: West Publishing.

Olson, E. A., & Charman, S. D. (2012). 'But can you prove it?'– examining the quality of innocent suspects' alibis. *Psychology, Crime & Law*, *18*(5), 453–471.

Olson, E. A., & Wells, G. L. (2004). What makes a good alibi? A proposed taxonomy. *Law and Human Behavior*, *28*(2), 157–176.

Otis, C. C., Greathouse, S. M., Kennard, J. B., & Kovera, M. B. (2014). Hypothesis testing in attorney-conducted voir dire. *Law and Human Behavior*, *38*(4), 392–404.

Owen-Kostelnik, J., Dickon, N., & Meyer, J. R. (2006). Testimony and interrogation of minors: Assumptions about maturity and morality. *American Psychologist*, *61*(4), 286–304.

Pennington, N., & Hastie, R. (1992). Explaining the evidence: Tests of the Story Model for juror decision making. *Journal of Personality and Social Psychology*, *62*(2), 189.

Penrod, S., & Cutler, B. (1995). Witness confidence and witness accuracy: Assessing their forensic relation. *Psychology, Public Policy, and Law*, *1*(4), 817–845.

Perillo, J. T., & Kassin, S. M. (2011). Inside interrogation: The lie, the bluff, and false confessions. *Law and Human Behavior*, *35*(4), 327–337.

Pezdek, K., & O'Brien, M. (2014). Plea bargaining and appraisals of eyewitness evidence by prosecutors and defense attorneys. *Psychology, Crime & Law*, *20*, 222–241.

Raskin, D. C., Honts, C. R., & Kircher, J. C. (2014). *Credibility assessment: Scientific research and applications: First Edition*. Cambridge, MA: Academic Press.

Rauxloh, R. E. (2010). Negotiated history: The historical record in international criminal law and plea bargaining. *International Criminal Law Review*, *10*(5), 739–770.

Redlich, A. D., & Goodman, G. S. (2003). Taking responsibility for an act not committed: The influence of age and suggestibility. *Law and Human Behavior*, *27*(2), 141–156.

Redlich, A. D., Summers, A., & Hoover, S. (2010). Self-reported false confessions and false guilty pleas among offenders with mental illness. *Law and Human Behavior*, *34*, 70–90.

Redlich, A. D., Wilford, M. M., & Bushway, S. (2017). Understanding guilty pleas through the lens of social science. *Psychology, Public Policy, and Law*, *23*, 458–471.

Rosenthal, R. (1966). *Experimenter effects in behavioral research* (Vol. xiii). East Norwalk, CT: Appleton-Century-Crofts.

Russano, M. B., Meissner, C. A., Narchet, F. M., & Kassin, S. M. (2005). Investigating true and false confessions within a novel experimental paradigm. *Psychological Science*, *16*(6), 481–486.

Ruva, C. L., & Guenther, C. C. (2015). From the shadows into the light: How pretrial publicity and deliberation affect mock jurors' decisions, impressions, and memory. *Law and Human Behavior*, *39*(3), 294.

Ruva, C. L., & LeVasseur, M. A. (2012). Behind closed doors: The effect of pretrial publicity on jury deliberations. *Psychology, Crime & Law*, *18*(5), 431–452.

Schacter, D. L. (1999). The seven sins of memory: Insights from psychology and cognitive neuroscience. *American Psychologist*, *54*(3), 182–203.

Schulz, K. (2016, January 25). Dead certainty: How 'Making a Murderer' goes wrong. *The New Yorker.* Retrieved from http://www.newyorker.com/magazine/2016/01/25/dead-certainty

Shepherd, E., & Griffiths, A. (2013). *Investigative interviewing: The conversation management approach* (2nd edn.). Oxford, UK: Oxford University Press.

Smalarz, L., & Wells, G. L. (2014). Post-identification feedback to eyewitnesses impairs evaluators' abilities to discriminate between accurate and mistaken testimony. *Law and Human Behavior*, *38*(2), 194–202.

Smalarz, L., Scherr, K. C., & Kassin, S. M. (2016). Miranda at 50. *Current Directions in Psychological Science*, *25*(6), 455–460.

Snook, B., Eastwood, J., Stinson, M., Tedeschini, J., & House, J. C. (2010). Reforming investigative interviewing in Canada. *Canadian Journal of Criminology and Criminal Justice*, *52*(2), 215–229.

Sommers, S. R., & Norton, M. I. (2008). Race and jury selection: Psychological perspectives on the peremptory challenge debate. *American Psychologist*, *63*(6), 527–539.

Stasser, G., & Davis, J. H. (1981). Group decision making and social influence: A social interaction sequence model. *Psychological Review*, *88*(6), 523.

Stasser, G., Kerr, N. L., & Bray, R (1982) The social psychology of jury deliberations: Structure, process, and product. In N. L. Kerr, & R. Bray (Eds.), *The psychology of the courtroom*. New York, NY: Academic Press.

Steblay, N. M. (1997). Social influence in eyewitness recall: A meta-analytic review of lineup instruction effects. *Law and Human Behavior*, *21*(3), 283–297.

Steblay, N., Dysart, J., Fulero, S., & Lindsay, R. C. L. (2001). Eyewitness accuracy rates in sequential and simultaneous lineup presentations: A meta-analytic comparison. *Law and Human Behavior*, *25*(5), 459–473.

Steblay, N. K., Dysart, J. E., & Wells, G. L. (2011). Seventy-two tests of the sequential lineup superiority effect: A meta-analysis and policy discussion. *Psychology, Public Policy, and Law*, *17*(1), 99–139.

Steblay, N. K., Wells, G. L., & Douglass, A. B. (2014). The eyewitness post identification feedback effect 15 years later: Theoretical and policy implications. *Psychology, Public Policy, and Law*, *20*(1), 1–18.

Steinberg, L., & Cauffman, E. (1996). Maturity of judgment in adolescence: Psychosocial factors in adolescent decision making. *Law and Human Behavior*, *20*(3), 249–272.

Strange, D., Dysart, J., & Loftus, E. F. (2014). Why errors in alibis are not necessarily evidence of guilt. *Zeitschrift für Psychologie*, *222*, 82–89.

Tekin, S., Granhag, P. A., Strömwall, L., Giolla, E. M., Vrij, A., & Hartwig, M. (2015). Interviewing strategically to elicit admissions from guilty suspects. *Law and Human Behavior*, *39(3)*, 244–252.

Thibaut, J., & Walker, L. (1978). *Procedural justice: A psychological analysis*. Hillsdale, NJ: Erlbaum.

Tor, A., Gazal-Ayal, O., & Garcia, S. M. (2010). Fairness and the willingness to accept plea bargain offers. *Journal of Empirical Legal Studies*, *7*(1), 97–116.

Törnblom, K., & Vermunt, R. (Eds.) (2007). *Distributive and procedural justice: Research and social applications*. Ashgate Publishing, Ltd.

Tyler, T. R. (1988). What is procedural justice? Criteria used by citizens to assess the fairness of legal procedures. *Law and Society Review*, *22*(1), 103–136.

Tyler, T. R. (2000). Social justice: Outcome and procedure. *International Journal of Psychology*, *35*(2), 117–125.

Tyler, T. R. (2006). *Why people obey the law*. Princeton, NJ: Princeton University Press.

Tyler, T. R. (2011). *Why people cooperate: The role of social motivations*. Princeton, NJ: Princeton University Press.

Tyler, T. R., Goff, P. A., & MacCoun, R. J. (2015). The impact of psychological science on policing in the United States: Procedural justice, legitimacy, and effective law enforcement. *Psychological Science in the Public Interest*, *16*(3), 75–109.

Tyler, T. R., Rasinski, K. A., & Spodick, N. (1985). Influence of voice on satisfaction with leaders: Exploring the meaning of process control. *Journal of Personality and Social Psychology*, *48*(1), 72–81.

Vidmar, N. (Ed.) (2000). *World jury systems.* Oxford, England: Oxford University Press.

Vidmar, N., & Hans, V. P. (2007). *American juries: The verdict*. Amherst, NY: Prometheus Books.

Vrij, A. (2008). *Detecting lies and deceit: Pitfalls and opportunities* (2nd edn.). Chicester, UK: John Wiley.

Vrij, A., Fisher, R., Mann, S., & Leal, S. (2006). Detecting deception by manipulating cognitive load. *Trends in cognitive sciences, 10*(4), 141–142.

Vrij, A., Granhag, P. A., & Porter, S. (2010). Pitfalls and opportunities in nonverbal and verbal lie detection. *Psychological Science in the Public Interest, 11*(3), 89–121.

Vrij, A., Mann, S., & Fisher, R. P. (2006). An empirical test of the behaviour analysis interview. *Law and Human Behavior, 30*(3), 329–345.

Vrij, A., Mann, S. A., Fisher, R. P., Leal, S., Milne, R., & Bull, R. (2008). Increasing cognitive load to facilitate lie detection: The benefit of recalling an event in reverse order. *Law And Human Behavior, 32*(3), 253–265.

Vrij, A., Mann, S., Leal, S., & Fisher, R. (2010b). 'Look into my eyes': Can an instruction to maintain eye contact facilitate lie detection? *Psychology, Crime & Law, 16*(4), 327–348.

Vrij, A., Meissner, C. A., Fisher, R. P., Kassin, S. M., Morgan, C. A., & Kleinman, S.M. (2017). Psychological perspectives on interrogation. *Perspectives on Psychological Science, 12*, 927–955.

Wald, M. S., Ayres, R., Hess, R., Schantz, M., & Whitebread, C. (1967). Interrogations in New Haven: The impact of Miranda. *The Yale Law Journal, 76*(8), 1519–1648.

Weisselberg, C. D. (2017). Exporting and importing Miranda. *Boston University Law Review, 97*, 1235–1291.

Wells, G. L. (1978). Applied eyewitness-testimony research: System variables and estimator variables. *Journal of Personality and Social Psychology, 36*(12), 1546–1557.

Wells, G. L., & Bradfield, A. L. (1998). 'Good, you identified the suspect': Feedback to eyewitnesses distorts their reports of the witnessing experience. *Journal of Applied Psychology, 83*(3), 360–376.

Wells, G. L., Lindsay, R. C., & Ferguson, T. J. (1979). Accuracy, confidence, and juror perceptions in eyewitness identification. *Journal of Applied Psychology, 64*(4), 440–448.

Wells, G. L., Malpass, R. S., L, R. C., Fisher, R. P., Turtle, J. W., & Fulero, S. M. (2000). From the lab to the police station: A successful application of eyewitness research. *American Psychologist, 55*(6), 581–598.

Wells, G. L., Small, M., Penrod, S., Malpass, R. S., Fulero, S. M., & Brimacombe, E, C. A. (1998). Eyewitness identification procedures: Recommendations for lineups and photospreads. *Law and Human Behavior, 22*(6), 603–647.

Wells, G. L., Steblay, N. K., & Dysart, J. E. (2015). Double-blind photo lineups using actual eyewitnesses: An experimental test of a sequential versus simultaneous lineup procedure. *Law and Human Behavior, 39*(1), 1–14.

Williamson, T. (Ed.) (2006). *Investigative interviewing: Rights, research, regulation*. Portland, OR: Willan Publishing.

Wilson, J. P., Hugenberg, K., & Bernstein, M. J. (2013). The cross-race effect and eyewitness identification: How to improve recognition and reduce decision errors in eyewitness situations. *Social Issues and Policy Review, 7*(1), 83–113.

Wixted, J. T., & Wells, G. L. (2017). The relationship between eyewitness confidence and identification accuracy: A new synthesis. *Psychological Science in the Public Interest, 18*, 10–65.

Wright, D. B., Memon, A., Skagerberg, E. M., & Gabbert, F. (2009). When eyewitnesses talk. *Current Directions in Psychological Science, 18*(3), 174–178.

Wright, D. S., Wade, K. A., & Watson, D. G. (2013). Delay and déjà vu: Timing and repetition increase the power of false evidence. *Psychonomic Bulletin & Review, 20*(4), 812–818.

28

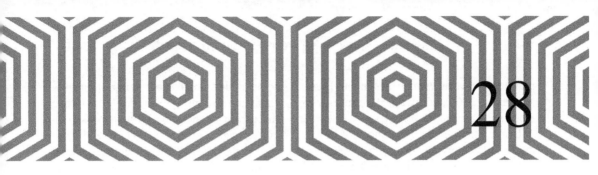

Critical Social Psychology and Victims of Crime: Gendering Violence, Risk and Dangerousness in the Society of Captives

Mandy Morgan, Leigh Coombes, Stephanie Denne and Melissa Rangiwananga

Critical social psychology is a burgeoning field of theory and research applicable to social problems, like those of domestic violence, poverty or political instability. Such problems are recognised as global issues and interlinked with each other in complex relationships even though they manifest differently in different locations. Critical psychology is a difficult field to define, since it is informed by multiple theories that are often ignored in mainstream psychology and concern social phenomena such as class, gender, race and social injustice (Gough et al., 2013). The field has formed over the past five decades in relation to a broader movement critiquing mainstream psychology's focus on the individual and neglect of social context (Parker, 2015). For critical psychologists, social context is neither an external variable nor a concept distinct from our subjective experiences: 'individual subjectivity is embedded in social, cultural and historical contexts' (Teo, 2015: 245). Social power relations are crucial to the social and political changes necessary to address injustices that are central concerns in applying critical theory and research. Our chapter is principally concerned with a critical psychological approach to the injustices of criminal victimisation. Both the concepts of crime and experiences of victimisation occur in historically specific socio-political contexts that shape our understanding of the people and events involved.

We illustrate our approach to criminal victimisation through the exemplary case of domestic violence. Widely acknowledged as a gendered social problem, domestic violence has only been specifically criminalised in most jurisdictions since the late twentieth century. Where individuals are prosecuted for physical assault of an intimate partner, questions remain as to how well the criminal justice system can deal with the complexities of intimate violence or redress the injustices of gendered violence. Globally, violence against an intimate partner is recognised as a form of gendered violence involving unequal power relations between women and men (Russo and Pirlott, 2006), where not all forms of violence are criminalised.

Bearing in mind the importance of history and social context for critical social psychology, we begin our chapter with a discussion of the classic case of Kitty Genovese, a woman who was raped and murdered in the United States in 1964. Although Genovese was victimised by someone she didn't know, rather than an intimate partner, her case blatantly involves gendered violence and provokes social psychology's interest in criminal victimisation. The story of Genovese's assault and the social context in which it occurs begins a tradition of research on social processes that affect witnesses of victimisation. Social psychology's interest in Genovese's case sets the scene for our chapter by illustrating how researchers in the mid-twentieth century responded to a real-world situation of gendered violence and how critical psychology critiques mainstream approaches.

Social psychological responses to the Genovese case focused attention on the dangers of crime for individuals, without attending to the social context in which victimisation is criminalised or risks of dangerousness are understood. Neither was the social context of the researchers' interest in witnesses of Genovese's victimisation taken into account. Once social context becomes a consideration, the limitations of mainstream responses to Genovese's rape and murder are clearer. We are also able to explicitly connect them with the notion of the risk society: a concept that allows us to critically reflect on the ways we imagine the dangerousness of crimes and the vulnerabilities of individual victims. After discussing Genovese's case and its consequences, we turn our attention to the recognition of domestic violence as social problem, considering how this also coincided with the emergence of the risk society and came to involve the criminal justice system. Criminalising domestic violence is complicated by the history, knowledge and technologies of the system itself, as well as social understandings of victimisation within intimate relationships. To enable a thorough discussion of the ways in which historical, cultural and social contexts are implicated in understanding domestic violence victimisation, we introduce the Society of Captives thesis (Arrigo, 2013). This theory provides the critical concepts for analysing how social norms are implicated in the power relations that individualise the risks and dangerousness of domestic violence.

RISK, DANGER AND THE BYSTANDER EFFECT

> Walking home on March 13, 1964, Catherine 'Kitty' Genovese reached her apartment in Questions, New York at 3:30 A.M. Suddenly, a man approached her with a knife, stabbing her repeatedly, and then raped her. Kitty screamed, into the early morning stillness, 'Oh my God, he stabbed me! Please help me!' Lights went on and windows opened in nearby buildings. Seeing the lights, the attacker fled. When he saw no one come to the victim's aid, he returned to stab her eight more times and rape her again. (Geller, 2016: 55)

Geller provides us with a commonly told story of Kitty Genovese's sexual assault and murder, emphasising that her cries for help were heard but no-one responded. For Geller, as for others (e.g. Burr, 2005; van Heugten, 2011; Van Bommell et al., 2016), the case was a catalyst for social psychological research on the behaviour of bystanders who witness emergencies. Especially significant is social psychology's challenge to the concept of bystander apathy; the idea that no-one came to Genovese's aid because densely urbanised spaces alienated people from each other and led them to be disinterested in one another. In the wake of this common sense understanding, propagated by the media at the time, city-life became associated with high risks of criminal victimisation (Lurigio, 2015). Decades of mainstream social psychological research were dedicated to explaining the circumstances in which bystanders do, or do not, intervene when others are experiencing emergencies, whether crimes or injuries, with little concern for the social justice issues implicated in their studies.

Programmatic experimental research from the late 1960s to the early 1980s, conducted primarily in the United States, established the bystander effect as a significant and robust social psychological phenomenon. The concept refers to an individual's diminishing likelihood of helping in a critical situation when they are in the company of other uninvolved bystanders (Fischer et al., 2011). Repeatedly, experimental findings established that bystanders took less personal responsibility for intervening in an emergency when they were among greater numbers of bystanders. At its most extreme, the bystander effect means that no-one intervenes because each member of the bystander group believes that other members of the group do not regard the situation as an actual emergency. In retrospect, we might ask how social psychologists overlooked the real-life situation that provoked investigation of the bystander effect. How could rape and murder not be regarded as 'an actual emergency'? Instead, between the 1980s and 2010, social psychologists studying the bystander effect experimentally turned their attention to investigating how the phenomenon was moderated. In relation to the dangerousness of the emergency, the smaller bystander effect is attributed to dangerous situations being less ambiguous to bystanders, so it is more obvious that intervention is needed and could be resolved by co-operative action. In terms of the competency of bystanders, Fischer et al. (2011) draw attention to the findings that show bystander groups comprised only of men increase the likelihood of intervention in comparison to groups involving women. The competency of men is attributed to their perceived strength as a resource for intervention. While the more recent findings identify important features of situations where bystanders are not apathetic to, or so alienated from, each other that they ignore the plight of victims, traditional social psychology remains uncertain as to the psychological processes involved with these findings (Fischer et al., 2011). Such uncertainty poses challenges for understanding the processes we need to apply to real-life situations where witnesses are reluctant to intervene in cases of intimate violence. However, we also notice that the programmatic investigation of the bystander effect for more than half a century is dominated by experimental research in the United States and emphasises the individual as the traditionally proper object of social psychological inquiry.

Rather than continuing to explore the traditional individualised approach, we pick up two threads of critique associated with the Genovese case and social psychology's response: The status of the initial account of her murder that provoked studies of bystander apathy, and ways that both the account and the programmatic research excluded considerations of gender and sexuality involved in her rape. Along both threads, the consequences of ignoring social context in conceptualising and investigating the bystander effect in relation to the victimisation of women are critically important.

PARABLE, GENDER AND RISK

Geller's (2016) retelling of the Kitty Genovese case is one of many in social psychology textbooks, and it is not uncommon for specific details to be repeated: There were 38 witnesses who watched the attack from their apartment windows and took no action (Griggs, 2015). The story has also been retold in journalism, real crime drama, film, television programmes and a novel: Kitty Genovese has become one of the most well-known crime victims in the United States (Lurigio, 2015).

However, it was not until the mid-1990s that social psychology recognised a crucial exclusion in the story's most popular versions: The failure to mention that Genovese's victimisation took place in a social context where non-intervention into women's victimisation by men was commonplace (Cherry, 1995). At the time, it was assumed that violence against women was a crime committed by strangers; men who were pathologically motivated to injure women. Domestic violence was also understood as psychopathological and there was little recognition of its widespread prevalence. Legally, rape within marriage was not a crime, and although wives could provide evidence of physical violence as grounds for divorce, it was rare for non-lethal assault by a husband to result in criminal prosecution. However, there is one unusual study from the mid-1970s that did conceptualise the crime against Genovese as gendered violence and investigated how bystanders would respond in conditions that varied according to whether they believed the victim and perpetrator were strangers or a couple. Perhaps unsurprisingly from our contemporary perspective, 65% of bystanders in that experiment intervened when they believed the perpetrator was a stranger, but only 19% did so when they believed he was the victim's husband or were unsure about their relationship. The researchers concluded that domestic assault was not taken seriously by society but that, if neighbours knew each other better and could correctly distinguish between stranger and intimate assault, communities would exercise social sanctions for men's violence against women they did not know (Cherry, 1995). As attention was drawn to the way social psychology's bystander research had ignored the social context of gendered violence in Genovese's case, so too did the complex intersections of sexuality, race and class become increasingly recognised as crucial dimensions. Disregarded in the commonly told story of Genovese's victimisation was her life as a lesbian woman, her status as a financially independent white woman living in a middle-class suburb, the racial tensions that fuelled outrage about bystanders' non-intervention when a black man assaulted her, and movements of people that fractured and divided communities along ethnic, racial and class lines (Gallo, 2014).

Importantly too, the versions of the Genovese case that focused on witness inaction have been challenged as misrepresentations of the bystanders' apparent apathy. On the basis of evidence presented in the trial of the man convicted of Genovese's victimisation and the work of attorney and historian, Joseph De May Jn., an alternative account emerges. According to this evidence, the attack on Genovese was only visible to a few witnesses for a matter of moments and they did call the police, who arrived before Genovese died (Gallo, 2014; Manning et al., 2007). Despite this evidence, the repeated retelling of the story as a representation of apathy has given it the status of a parable: a moral tale of the dangerousness of modern urban life. Within social psychology, Manning et al. argue that the story 'served to curtail the imaginative space of helping research in social psychology… [causing] psychologists to be slow to look for the ways in which the power of groups can be harnessed to promote intervention' (2007: 556). Socially, the parable has transformed Genovese's victimisation from one of many sexually motivated murders to a 'signal crime', constructed as a warning of risks that crystallised a sensibility of the time and place (Innes, 2003; 2004; Manning et al., 2007). It is an example of the way that retelling stories attribute their events with truth status (Chamberlain and Hodgetts, 2008). Thus signal crimes function to focus 'a number of previously inchoate and nebulous fears and concerns about social life and the potential dangers that assail us' (Innes, 2003: 64) into a problem with crime and criminality. As a shared understanding of the dangerousness of mid-twentieth century US social conditions, the parable of the

38 witnesses to Genovese's victimisation marked the emergence of a social milieu theorised as the risk society and characterised by fear of crime and risk of criminal victimisation.

At the intersection of the parable as a moral tale and analysis of the risk society is the notion that both are constructions; inaccessible to empirical inquiry as matters of social fact. Risks are constituted through 'the application of technologies... the making of sense and the technological sensibility of a potential harm, danger or threat' (Adam and van Loon, 2000: 2). It is crucial to recognise that risk is not a matter of events that happen but of a social imagination focused on potential events articulated through language that fails to differentiate threats along social dimensions such as gender, sexuality, race and class. Homogeneous constructions of risk draw attention to insecurity, ignoring inequitable social power relations, so they are incompatible with a politics of social justice (Adam and van Loon, 2000). Rather than attending to the uneven distribution of suffering in specific social contexts, a risk society imagines dangerousness and threat without regard for our socially constituted relationships with each other (Coombes et al., 2016). In this social context, where risk is imagined and constructed through our language, knowledges and technologies, the question that guides our analysis of women's victimisation in intimate relationships asks: How do we open up new imaginative spaces that reflexively critique our contributions to reproducing the risk society and simultaneously challenge the erasure of heterogeneous differences and social injustices from our knowledge production and practice?

To begin addressing our question, we discuss how domestic violence emerges as a social problem of gendered violence against women during the same historic period that research on the 'bystander effect' contributed to imagining the risk society in the nations of the global North.

COINCIDENTAL EMERGENCE: THE DOMESTIC VIOLENCE EPIDEMIC IN THE RISK SOCIETY

As is evident in the public and social psychological responses to the Genovese case, domestic violence was primarily regarded as a rare form of violence against women until the latter part of the twentieth century. More commonly, abuse and violence occurring in intimate relationships was understood as a private matter of interpersonal conflict rather than a gendered social issue (Westmarland and Kelly, 2016). Across much of the global North, advocacy from the refuge movement throughout the 1970s and 1980s increased public attention to women's victimisation in cases of domestic violence. Networks of safe houses were established, leading to co-ordinated community responses and expanded community services aiming to improve women and children's safety and hold men accountable for violence in the home. Now globally recognised as a social problem of epidemic proportions, affecting around 30% of women at some time in their lives (World Health Organization, 2013), the problem of domestic violence has generated multiple approaches to intervention as well as disagreement and debate over how it is to be understood (DeKeseredy and Schwartz, 2010). Issues of the meaning of domestic violence are exemplified clearly in the shift from community led responses emphasising women's and children's safety to the involvement of criminal justice systems and campaigns to use the law to address the social problem of domestic violence (Westmarland and Kelly, 2016).

In an historical context where social problems were increasingly understood as matters of crime and criminality, advocates for criminalising domestic violence called on substantive issues of the risks and dangers women faced in their homes. They also drew attention to the symbolic implications of the way that women's victimisation had traditionally been trivialised by the law: the assumption that physical and sexual assaults were 'interpersonal conflicts'; policing practices that focused on calming 'the situation' and mediating 'disputes'; and such widespread tolerance of violence against women that, even in cases of lethal violence, it was not uncommon for murder charges to be reduced to manslaughter on the grounds of provocation. When it came to women victims of partner violence, crimes were treated differently. From this perspective, it is logical to advocate for domestic violence to be criminalised (Westmarland and Kelly, 2016) on the same basis that Genovese's rape and murder was a crime.

By the mid-1990s, legal jurisdictions in Aotearoa New Zealand, the United States, UK, Australia and Canada had introduced legislation that defined domestic violence as a pattern of abuse involving psychological, emotional, physical and sexual harm. For example, the Domestic Violence Act (1995) in Aotearoa New Zealand conceptualises domestic violence as a pattern of abuse and includes recognition that victimisation occurs 'even though some or all of the acts, when viewed in isolation, may appear to be minor or trivial' (Domestic Violence Act, 1995; 15). However, located in family law and providing the grounds for protective orders that are intended to support victim safety, this definition does not criminalise the patterns of abusive acts that are defined as violence. In relation to the criminal justice system, the focus remains on discrete incidents for which physical evidence can be presented to court (Hester, 2013; Westmarland and Kelly, 2016). With some exceptions, such as threatening to kill, theft and damage to property, incidents of emotional, psychological, financial and spiritual abuse are not criminal acts, even when they form a pattern that is consistent with the definition of domestic violence in family law.

The distinction between discrete criminal acts of violence and ongoing patterns of abuse in relation to domestic violence has wider social meanings and is implicated in disagreements among researchers and practitioners over the conceptualisation of the issues to be addressed, as well as the formulation of appropriate interventions. It is common for domestic violence to be represented as 'battering': frequent, serious and potentially lethal physical attacks. The term 'wife battering' was one of the earliest names given to women's victimisation by intimate partners, and it has significant implications for the way that legal interventions, expert knowledge and social understandings of the problem assess the seriousness of instances of victimisation. Thus understood, domestic violence involves one or more incidents of physical assault, while domestic abuse involves the less tangible forms of emotional, psychological, financial and spiritual assault, which are calibrated as less serious forms of harm (Bettinson and Bishop, 2015; Stark, 2007). While this distinction follows the logic of scaling acts of violence from the most evidently lethal to the more indiscernibly hurtful, it also prioritises discrete incidents over the complexities of intimate gendered violence.

Almost two decades into the twenty-first century, diverse forms of legal changes to recognise domestic violence as a crime have occurred globally. In many jurisdictions, physical abuse perpetrated by intimate partners is more frequently treated as a crime; some have introduced new offences, others have developed specialist domestic violence courts, sentencing, prosecution or policing procedures. In civil or family law, it is more common for protective orders to be accessible for victims of domestic violence, although evaluative studies document the complexities of their implementation (e.g. Kelly et al., 2013; Robertson et al., 2007). Despite an increased rate of arrest for physical domestic assaults, conviction rates remain low and sentencing sanctions rarely involve incarceration (Stark, 2007; Westmarland and Kelly, 2016). Perpetrators are likely to be held legally accountable through referrals to programmes: stopping violence or anger management programmes, counselling or cognitive behaviour therapy (Phillips et al., 2013), sometimes in combination with other sanctions such as fines or community service orders. Many of the sanctions and the goals of protection orders presume that they will provide the opportunities for perpetrators and their victims to exercise a self-interested choice to end either the abuse or their relationship (Stark, 2007). In this instance too, evaluative research has failed to demonstrate consistent desistance (Kelly and Westmarland, 2015) and domestic violence does not necessarily cease when women separate from perpetrators (Holt, 2015; Laing, 2017; Zeoli et al., 2013).

It is credible to argue that the difficulties of conceptualising domestic violence for the purpose of an effective legal or criminal justice response are themselves evidence that domestic violence, after all, 'is not a crime like any other' (Westmarland and Kelly, 2016: 34). Yet the implications of the definitional difficulties exceed the boundaries of legislative and criminal justice responses. For instance, unless they are the victims of direct assaults or psychological harms themselves, children are characterised as passive witnesses of violence perpetrated against their mother. They are then accorded the status of '"collateral damage" in families affected by domestic violence' (Callaghan et al., 2018: 1555). Social understanding and support of children's proactive meaning-making and resistance in their experiences of violence in their homes is rarely recognised. For women who have been victimised, the historic and legislative emphasis on physical violence and the image of victimisation as 'battering' contributes to how they recognise their experiences in the absence of serious or frequent assaults (Bettinson and Bishop, 2015; Callaghan et al., 2018; Morgan and Coombes, 2016).

The turn from community advocacy and activism towards legal and criminal justice responses to domestic violence connects with the emergence of the risk society through a focus on crime and the criminal justice system as the mechanism for addressing the risks and dangerousness of social problems. Yet, in the case of domestic violence, the criminal justice system's history of trivialising violence against women, gender neutral language, conceptualisation of crime as a discrete event and requirements for physical evidence, exemplifies the inadequacies of criminalisation as a language, knowledge and technique for intervening to address a gendered social problem. Legislation, government policy, statutory, community and psychological interventions are embedded in historical and cultural contexts where gendered power relations are implicated in who we are as persons and how we understand each other.

In the following section, we introduce the Society of Captives thesis (Arrigo, 2013) to open up an imaginative space which theorises how the actions of government, legal systems, expert knowledges and their implementations may be understood as bound to, and by, the historical and cultural conditions through which the risk society emerged. We also discuss theories of gender that enable critical consideration of the tensions and implications of contemporary knowledges and interventions for domestic violence.

THE SOCIETY OF CAPTIVES THESIS

As critique, the Society of Captives thesis (Arrigo, 2013) shares the understanding that the risk society is constructed through our language, knowledges and technologies. The thesis envisions risk society as imprisoning social subjects with hypervigilant fears. Drawing on Foucaultian theories of social power relations (Foucault, 1980; 1982), the Society of Captives attends to the ways in which we are constrained by contemporary social and cultural conditions and incarcerated in social hierarchies that specify how our subjectivities are formed in relation to our bodies and our actions.

As a metaphor to explain how modern forces of power operate through individuals' self-surveillance and discipline of their own bodies, rather than as 'top down' repression or oppression exercised by a social elite such as a ruling class, Foucault (1977) drew on the Panopticon model for an ideal prison. Developed in the late eighteenth century by Jeremy Bentham, the Panopticon is designed as physical structure that would enable both control of those imprisoned and an environment that fostered reform. Total surveillance and control of prisoners in separate cells is assured by a central guard tower. However, prisoners are unable to see whether guards are present in the tower or not. Each prisoner needs to be conscious of their visibility from the guard tower and responsible for surveillance of their own actions. They must discipline themselves to demonstrate that they are not deserving of any further punishment.

The kind of power that Foucault imagines through the metaphor of the Panopticon is intimately connected with discourse and knowledge. Discourse references language and social practice in the sense that meanings are constituted systematically through statements that coherently construct an object, concept, process or type of person (Gavey, 1989; Hook, 2001; Parker, 1990). For instance, in our exemplary case of domestic violence, there are ways of making sense of physical violence that cohere around the concept of battering and involve valuing physical violence as more serious than other forms of violence. Battering also implicates a perpetrator and a victim who are understood to be individual subjects, the former often characterised as the 'type' of man who would use assault to gain instrumental control over his partner or as a means of expressing his frustrations or anger. Social practices involved in constructing domestic violence as battering include criminalising discrete instances of physical violence against women through specific offences; for example, the charge of 'male assaults female' that is available in Aotearoa New Zealand law. They also involve forms of expert knowledge of domestic violence that legitimate some ways of conceptualising the problem and exclude other possibilities.

Power operates productively through discourses and knowledges, not only enabling understandings and social practices but also enabling subjectivities. The concept of subjectivity concerns the way in which self-surveillance and disciplinary power work through discourse on our actions and bodies. We are subjects of discourse in two ways: We are subjected to the coherent meanings of personhood that discourse constructs; and we are subjects of discourse since those coherent meanings refer to us (Burman, 2016). Discourses are historically, culturally and socially specific; they are multiple and complex in their relationships with each other; they may co-articulate easily or contradict each other. Thus, our ways of being, acting, thinking, feeling and identifying ourselves in relation to others also shift and change over time and in different locations. We are embedded in our historical and social contexts through the productive relationship between discourse and power.

In relation to the particular form of contemporary risk society, the Society of Captives thesis draws attention to the constraints of hegemonic social power relations that homogenise subjectivities. Individualism and normalisation are processes through which our subjectivities are constrained by Eurocentric knowledge systems, like psychology, and are discursively constituted through dominant political ideologies, particularly neoliberalism. In our contemporary social contexts, individualism is intensified by neoliberalism and globalisation. Neoliberalism refers to a widespread political–economic ideology practiced by governments of the global North, which prioritises the participation of citizens in a capitalist market-place where they appear to be offered freedom of choice among commodities and opportunities. At the same time, they are personally responsible for their individual wellbeing and their ability to proactively participate as citizens (Coombes and Morgan, 2015). Neoliberalism is associated with the demise of welfare state policies, exemplified by welfare-to-work programmes (e.g. Dostal, 2008; Hamnet, 2014) where it is assumed that paid employment is a benefit for individual wellbeing as well as a necessity for productive citizenship. Class domination is restored by neoliberalism through remaking social relations to affirm individuality rather than collective or social connectedness and belonging (Tsianos et al., 2012). It is also intertwined with the expansion of global capital that establishes hierarchies of economic development among nations. The traditional modes of social psychological inquiry privileging individualism contribute Eurocentric forms of psychological expertise and knowledge production into the processes that unevenly form neoliberal subjects. Simultaneously, globalisation carries Western modes of technologised, economic ideology well beyond the borders of wealthy nation-states. Individualism is recognisably a contemporary, social and culturally specific form of discursively producing subjectivities. Processes of normalisation are intertwined with modern disciplinary power exercised through self-surveillance.

Of particular relevance to domestic violence are the norms of gender and the individualisation of crime and victimisation that are implicated in the social meanings and conceptual disagreements that inform contemporary intervention strategies. Within the theoretical context of the Society of Captives, gender norms regulate the production of masculine and feminine subjects in a complex relationship with sexed bodies. The historically Western and predominant psychological conceptualisation of an essential biological link between masculinity and male bodies, femininity and female bodies is undone (Risman and Davis, 2013). Gender is understood as a manifestation of normative discourses enacted through our bodies rather than as individualised substantiation of the sexed bodies we are born within. Social, cultural and temporal expectations of being men or being women are enacted through self-surveillance and disciplining our bodies to produce our gender identities (Butler, 1990). In this sense, gender is performative: an enacting of norms that is repetitive and involves multiple sites (Butler, 1993; 1997a; 2009). For instance, our dress, movement, shape, use of cosmetics, romantic gestures, sexual availability or manners of speech are all enactments contained by normative gendered discourse (Bartky, 1998). Gender norms are intertwined with other norms, such as those of sexuality and romance. They are differently meaningful depending on how particular sexed bodies are located in the intersections of Eurocentric social hierarchies privileging white, middle-class, educated, urban, youthful and able-bodied. In this sense, gender is uncertain and potentially unstable since gendered performativity varies depending on cultural values and social expectations of acceptable gendered performances. Russo and Pirlott provide this example of such variation in their discussion of gender norms and gendered violence:

> ... in some contexts, being a good mother who devotes herself to her children is the role expectation for being a wife, and the roles are highly compatible. In contrast, in another context being a good wife may mean serving as a trophy for your husband's success and sending children off to boarding school so that you can make your husband's needs the priority in your life. (Russo and Pirlott, 2006: 180)

Yet the uncertain instability of gender operates to affirm rather than transform normativity, since the possibility of transgressing norms institutes and maintains the rewards and sanctions that hold them in place.

Repetitive iterations of gendered norms form regimes of intelligibility through which we are 'subjected' in order to become a subject who is included within the predominant norms of our time and location (Butler, 1997b). These regimes of sense making are discursive and enable us to form our gendered identities. They are also policed through various institutional powers such as the family, heterosexuality, coupledom, monogamy, so that gender normativity is reproduced through social sanctions and rewards (e.g. Farvid and Braun, 2013; Lynch and Maree, 2013). In socio-temporal locations that privilege Eurocentric ideals of masculinity and femininity, and constitute neoliberal individuals as autonomous subjects, it becomes our responsibility to act in ways that socially converge with, and reproduce, our gendered identity. If our bodily conduct fails to accord with our assigned gender, we are held responsible for that failing and face social consequences (Butler, 1993; 1997a; 2009). For instance, men might avoid being perceived as emotional, weak or vulnerable, and women may take care not to be seen as too independent or too aggressive. Likewise, where iterative repetitions of intelligible gendered enactments are enabled, they feel more comfortable, more 'natural' and easier. Some men may not consciously avoid housework or childcare because it is historically associated with women's work but simply because they feel more comfortable taking care of outside chores and playing with the children in their spare time. Some women might not consciously 'dress up' to attract men's sexual attention but because they enjoy feeling sexy. The ability to 'claim' an authentic gendered identity, and the rewards of comfort, safety and normality that are associated with such identities, are at risk of being revoked or denied. Our social relationships manifest the threat of such social sanctions and reprimands, so we act and react in ways that establish our gendered identity while also protecting and defending our claim to such an identity as authentic.

Within the context of the Society of Captives thesis, gender norms operate through discourse and knowledge as technologies of power. They work through dominant social meanings that hold us captive to self-surveillance and disciplining our bodies, so as to produce ourselves as intelligible individual subjects (Riggs and Augoustinos, 2005). The norms through which we understand and enact ourselves precede us in the sense that we are born into the social and cultural conditions that specify how gender is to be enacted and how bodies are implicated in keeping social hierarchies in place (Butler, 2004). Crucially, how we are enabled and constrained in our gender performativity depends on how our bodies are made meaningful in the specific social conditions of our time. In contemporary neoliberal societies, the intersections of historical oppressions involving sexed and racialised bodies are particularly significant in the socially productive construction of risks (Arrigo, 2010; 2013).

GENDER CAPTIVITY: BEARERS OF RISK AND TARGETS OF INTERVENTION

Risks of social sanctions for violating gender norms are central to conceptualising gender performativity. The Society of Captives thesis argues that, in social conditions of neoliberalism, such risks reify and individualise differences from Eurocentric norms. For example, men who perpetrate violence against their women partners are treated differently according to their embodied locations in social hierarchies. In the United States, Black men, men of colour and poor men are more likely to be seen as perpetrators and criminalised than wealthier, middle-class white men (Flood, 2015). In Aotearoa New Zealand, statistical estimates of intimate partner violence identify more victimisation among indigenous and immigrant women, yet do not take account of the ways in which such measurement ignores the social consequences of colonisation and privileges Eurocentric concepts of violence and measurement of incidents (e.g. Ministry of Justice, 2014). Here too, indigenous and immigrant men of colour are disproportionately subjected to police and criminal justice intervention for domestic violence (Paulin and Edgar, 2013). Beyond the specific case of domestic violence, contemporary risk societies disproportionately criminalise and imprison men whose racialised bodies and impoverished class identities differ from white, middle-class normativity (Davis, 1997; 2013). The relationship among positions in social hierarchies organised through Eurocentric norms produce systematic deficit representations of 'others' (Coombes et al., 2016). Difference constitutes deficit; yet, as in the case of Genovese's difference from heterosexual normativity, it is discursively erased through disciplinary techniques of individualism that inscribe the risk of difference on particular 'othered' bodies.

The Society of Captives thesis argues that the social context of neoliberalism produces a preoccupation with managing and containing risky individuals. Risk management and containment operate through the invisibility of normative social power relations. In relation to domestic violence, perpetrators are represented as individualised violent men, largely without regard for masculine norms that enable manhood to be intelligible. Where research has correlated individual men's endorsement of traditional masculinity with their willingness to physically assault their partner (Reidy et al., 2014), the focus has remained on identifying and managing individual 'risky' men. Critical analysis of the relationship between gender norms of masculinity and assumptions about men draws attention to the conflation of the terms 'men' and 'masculinity' that represents men as a homogeneous category and inhibits strategies for addressing intersections of gender, race, class and sexuality (Jewkes et al., 2015). Simultaneously, the construction of 'traditional' or 'hegemonic' masculinity as strongly associated with men's violence against their partners enables an individualised distinction between 'men of conscience' who do not act violently towards their partners and 'other men' who do. The construction of a morally admirable 'us' and category of 'others' who are the perpetrators reproduces a simplistic binary. As a consequence, the ways in which 'men of conscience' enact masculinities of privilege and may also enact traditional masculine positions as protectors and defenders of women and children is ignored (Flood, 2015: S167). Categorisations of men and masculinity that are organised through binary terms enable normative gender performativity to remain invisible. Even so, they actively organise the axes for self-surveillance through which disciplined gender performances separate intelligibly responsible 'non-violent' men from recognisable different 'others' who bear the risks that require management.

Binary categorisations of women and femininity are also complicit in the identification of individual victims at risk of men's violence. Alongside essentialist divisions between women and men, linked to femininity and masculinity, two crucial distinctions in the domestic violence field separate women into categories: The difference between agents and victims and the difference between survivors and victims (Campbell and Mannell, 2016).

Agency for women in Eurocentric, neoliberal social contexts is fraught with tensions and contradictions in relation to traditional gender norms. Norms of femininity traditionally involve disciplines of subordination to masculine norms (Budgeon, 2013): passivity, nurturance, emotional dependence and sexual loyalty in deference to activity, dominance, independence and sexual prowess. The postfeminist sensibility of contemporary neoliberal societies ostensibly accords women individualised rights to choice, autonomy and independence (Gill and Donaghue, 2013), although these rights are enacted through more intensive and extensive 'forms of surveillance, monitoring and disciplining of women's bodies' (Gill, 2016: 613). Within these social conditions, women's gender performativity necessitates complex self-surveillance in relation to contradictory social sanctions and rewards for too overtly transgressing feminine norms. For instance, in the

UK, young professional women are rewarded with peer support for binge drinking that demonstrates their strength and daring, transgressing feminine norms of weakness. Simultaneously, they experienced shame and social stigma for excessive alcohol consumption and 'out of control' public behaviour that transgress feminine norms of modesty (Watts et al., 2015). This example speaks to a social context that expects individual women to take responsibility for their equality with men by demonstrating their agency while accentuating self-surveillance to manage the social risks of conforming to, and transgressing, feminine norms.

In the context of domestic violence, the binary categorisation of agency and victimisation individualises the distinction between women who choose non-violent partners from those who chose to partner with men who abuse them. The survivor and victim binary distinguishes women who choose to leave violent partners from women who choose to stay with their partner, despite abuse. Women's agency is implicated in both sets of binary categorisations. Yet they ignore the social conditions that constrain women's relationship choices, including financial dependence, commitments to maintaining their family, lack of social and familial support for separation, stigma and shame associated with failed relationships or victimisation, and fear of escalating violence should they attempt to leave. The organisation of women into categories of agents/survivors and victims, ignores women's complex and diverse responses to violence in contexts of multiple inequalities (Campbell and Mannell, 2016) and the uneven distribution of rewards and sanctions for gender normativity along social intersections of race, class, ethnicity, poverty and sexuality (Hayes and Jeffries, 2013).

Social psychology construes agency as precisely the kind of individualised choice that categorises some women as survivors of domestic violence and others as victims: Agency involves intentional acts resulting from assessments of different options that are responsive to social demands beyond the immediate situation (Campbell and Mannell, 2016). By imagining the agent as a responsible neoliberal individual, this account ignores the complexities of contemporary gender normativity. Likewise, the structural inequalities of social relations remain invisible and the historical oppressions which precede and inform them, including colonialism, racism and masculine dominance, seem irrelevant. Psychology has also participated in the typographical categorisation of perpetrators, victims and violent relationships (e.g. Gadd and Corr, 2017), individualising and reifying differences to locate risk within the individual in need of treatment and management. The discipline participates in the Society of Captives at the interface of social and political management of risk, commodifying knowledge and practices that produce technologies to define, categorise, treat and manage perpetrators and victims (Coombes et al., 2016).

Across the sectors involved with addressing domestic violence, the significance of risk management has intensified as expert technologies are developing for identifying individual bearers of risk. Cross-sector, multi-agency risk management frameworks have been established in the UK, Australia and elsewhere across the Western world (Herbert and Mckenzie, 2014). Risk management is a broader concept than risk assessment and it involves domestic violence responders in assessing and communicating risk, deciding on appropriate actions for intervention and implementing and evaluating intervention strategies. None-the-less, technologies for identifying 'risky' individuals are usually incorporated into risk management frameworks (Gulliver and Fanslow, 2015). Risk assessment tools vary in relation to whether they focus on offenders or victims, predictions of recidivism or re-victimisation. Within the context of risk management, their purpose concerns the potential danger of violence, enabling 'risky' individuals to be categorised on continuums from 'low' to 'high' risk (Northcott, 2014). For instance, a Lethality Screen forms part of a protocol for first responders in many jurisdictions, to target high risk victims for a combined response from social services and the criminal justice system (Messing et al., 2017). From early reliance on the experiential expertise of responders for assessing risk, there is now an array of scientific instruments, often developed in forensic mental health fields with psychological measurement expertise (Northcott, 2014).

At the interface of psychological assessments of individualised risk and legal interventions into domestic violence, we return to the problematic definition of domestic violence as battering and its implications for managing individualised 'risky' subjects. Earlier, we argued that the focus on physical assault in relation to legal interventions into domestic violence understood the pattern of psychological, emotional, financial, spiritual, sexual and physical violence defining domestic violence as discrete incidents, following a logic that scales incidents from the most serious to the least harmful. Since discrete incidents are emphasised over complex patterns of abuse, women misrecognise victimisation when their partners do not physically assault them frequently or seriously. Risk management frameworks that involve assessing individual risk of lethality or dangerousness reproduce risks in the sense that focusing on physical violence limits understandings of women's and children's safety (Jenney et al., 2014) As a consequence, government policies and statutory interventions focus primarily on identifying women who are 'high risk' on the basis of frequent physical assault and whose victimisation has come to the attention of police or social services (Westmarland and Kelly, 2016), without regard for the social conditions of their victimisation. These practices also replicate normative understandings of violence as physical assault, reiterating the conditions that enable misrecognition of abuse.

GENDER CAPTIVITY: REGULATING INDIVIDUALISED RISK AND DANGEROUSNESS

The Society of Captives thesis argues that the law and government policies, as well as the social service sectors, including non-government agencies bound to government by financial dependence and accountabilities for policy implementation, surveys and regulates the population through the same Eurocentric norms that form individual subjects through self-surveillance and disciplinary power. For example, the legal system, including juridical principles, court protocols and practices, standards of evidence, attention to risk and dangerousness, is formed through ubiquitous adherence to traditional masculine gender norms: logical, rational, adversarial, ordered. Legal discourse reproduces the gendered inequities of Eurocentric normativity, disregarding other ways of experiencing, knowing and understanding, including women's understandings of their experiences (Arrigo, 2010). Neglect of social inequities and non-normative ways of being, precarity and structural violence constitute 'a gross absence of concern for widespread and pervasive suffering' (Williams, 2008: 6). Such neglect and disregard within the legal system reproduces masculinist Eurocentrism as institutionalised, material and symbolic forms of structural violence.

Structurally, the law, legal systems, government policies and the organisations responsible for their implementation become regulators of the institutionalised forms of violence that perpetuate our socially imagined constructions of risk and the individualised subjects who bear the risks and become the targets of intervention. Where social problems like domestic violence are increasingly conceptualised as matters of crime and criminality, structural violence perpetuates constricted understandings of the risks and dangers that women experience in their homes. For instance, through regulating institutions that prioritise physical violence in assessments of high risk, in social contexts where women's agency distinguishes victims from survivors, women who experience ongoing patterns of multiple abuses become targets of repeated interventions aiming to empower them to separate from their partner (Campbell and Mannell, 2016). Yet they are frequently stigmatised by service providers who understand their persistent need for help as an inability to make properly autonomous decisions for their safety. Individualising risk, and narrowly construing women's experiences of victimisation in a regulatory context where inequitable gender norms are invisible, produces interpretations of high risk 'repeat' victims as suffering individual deficits of character, exaggerating the dangerousness they face, or afflicted by mental disorders and categorising them as a 'type' of woman who will inevitably be abused (Bettinson and Bishop, 2015). In situations where women do separate from their partners, invoking orders of protection or seeking support for resolving issues of child custody through family or civil court systems, professional assessments of the risks they face and judicial decisions on custody and access fail to account for the ways in which perpetrators continue abuse after separation, even escalating threats and extending abusive tactics to include post-separation legal contests (Elizabeth, 2015; Elizabeth et al., 2012; Fleury-Steiner et al., 2014; Jeffries, 2016). For mothers, separation from violent partners enacts compliance with gendered norms and social expectations that they will protect their children. Yet women who proactively seek protection by challenging their ex-partner's custody or access to their children encounter the court system's regulation of their help seeking as pathologising them and trivialising their reports of victimisation (Davis et al., 2010; Rivera et al., 2012). Thus, in various institutional contexts where women individually bear the risk of their victimisation, normative expectations of agency reconstitute victims as the site of the problem of their victimisation.

In relation to perpetrators, interventions focusing on criminalisation and delimited by prioritising discrete incidents of physical assault, requiring standards of evidence that exclusively focus on signs of physical harm or medical symptoms of psychological injury (Bettinson and Bishop, 2015), reduce risks of dangerousness to exceptional episodes. These episodes are disconnected from both the specific context of ongoing patterns of abuse (Westmarland and Kelly, 2012) and the gendered norms through which masculine performativity distinguishes among types of men. The regulatory institutions that perpetuate structural violence against women through marginalising their experiences, individualising their risk and burdening them with responsibility for ending their victimisation through exercising their agency, collude with more personal, intimate violence perpetuated by their partners.

Perpetrator programmes for stopping violence, initially grounded in anger management and psycho-educational programmes aimed at changing men's attitudes to partner violence, have diversified. Yet they still focus on individual men, usually those who are mandated by regulatory systems, although some include a minority of ostensibly voluntary attendees. While evidence has been found for programme success in attitude change, they are not necessarily related to changes in perpetrating violence or abuse (Flood, 2015). In most cases, preferred measures of 'successful' programmes are lower rates of repeat offending, which reproduces priorities on physical violence, narrow understandings of women's safety and accountability to regulatory systems rather than the women and children who bear the risk of victimisation (e.g. Kelly and Westmarland, 2014; Wojnicka et al., 2016). While various studies have demonstrated that perpetrator programmes reduce physical violence, they are less effective in addressing patterns of psychological, emotional, financial and spiritual abuses (Kelly and Westmarland, 2015). Women's experiences of re-victimisation are more rarely taken into account; however, their reporting to authorities is crucial to recidivism measures. The complexities of reporting are over-simplified by standard measurement. Re-victimisation reports depend on women's previous experiences of reporting, the outcomes of their involvement with justice and social service interventions (Kelly and Westmarland, 2015) as well as their experiences of continuing victimisation.

The Society of Captives thesis allows us to reflect on the ways in which neoliberal risk societies intensify the criminalisation of social problems, ignore social inequalities and individualise risk and dangerousness. Structural violence is held in place through regulatory systems that homogenise difference and exclude ways of knowing and being that do not reproduce dominant gendered norms. In relation to domestic violence, regulatory systems are so bound by Eurocentric masculinism that it has proved impossible to incorporate definitions of domestic violence as an 'ongoing pattern' of abuse within criminal justice responses, even where such definitions are written into family law or non-statutory government policies (Bettinson and Bishop, 2015). The criminal justice system has failed to understand and respond to women's experiences of violence and abuse. Critics of the exclusions and contradictions of contemporary justice system interventions have increasingly called for reconceptualising domestic violence as coercive control: A manifestation of gendered social power inequities (e.g. Hayes and Jeffries, 2013).

ENTRAPMENT: COERCIVE CONTROL

The theory of domestic violence as coercive control involves conceptualising the patterns of abuse defined in legislation like the Aotearoa New Zealand Domestic Violence Act (1995) as involving distinctive forms of tactical entrapment. While emotional and psychological abuses are usually coextensive with physical and sexual violence, the concept of coercive control specifies particular domains of abuse that include multiple tactics of intimidation, isolation and control of minutiae in women's lives. Intimidation, for example, includes sexual degradation of various types as well as more commonly understood acts of threat and belittlement. Isolation involves tactics as obvious as preventing a woman from leaving the house and prohibiting contact with friends and family to monitoring communication with others, insisting on accompanying her or deliberately embarrassing her socially. Control, too, involves various tactics from granting or denying access to material resources, sleep or movement to embedding everyday activities within imposed rules (Stark, 2007; 2010; 2013). The tactics overlap and form a systematic micro-regulation of women's lives that benefit men incrementally with 'resources garnered, personal service, sexual exclusivity and subjective reinforcement of gender identity' (Stark, 2010: 207). This understanding of domestic violence is explicitly linked to gender norms through connection with the way that men utilise gender inequalities to assert dominance and accrue benefits, while targeting traditionally normative gendered expectations of women for micro-regulation.

The concept of coercive control makes gender normativity visible in relation to domestic violence. It explains women's entrapment as a process of internalising controlling rules imposed by her partner under threat of violence to ensure her compliance (Dutton and Goodman, 2005). Coercive control attributes a victim's apparent transgression of agency, observed from regulatory and social positions outside the context of her intimate relationship, to the imperceptible operations of her partner's coercive threats. It provides an account of the regulatory limitations that emerge from prioritising physical assault, since the scaling of harms from most to least serious according to evidence of injury does not correspond to the tactical intricacy of coercive control. Of critical importance is the inclusion of women's experiences of victimisation in the way coercive control is understood, so that differences among women and the interplay of structural inequalities and entrapment may also be taken into account (Family Violence Death Review Committee, 2016). For example, men's intentional limitations of women's space for action can be enhanced by the intersectional social locations that women inhabit, as when disclosing victimisation has particular consequences for immigrant women (Kelly, 2016).

Explicitly connecting coercive control with gender normativity also enables the structural violence of institutional, regulatory interventions and service provision to be visible in relation to men's systematic microregulation of women's lives. For instance, the intervention or service provider who has regulatory authority to assess and manage a woman's risk of harm necessarily misunderstands her decision to return to a relationship in which she has been physically assaulted if they interpret her as an autonomous individual agent who is freely choosing to live with her partner (Bettinson and Bishop, 2015). This is not to say that such misunderstanding is without compassion. Compassionate intentions to respect a woman victim's motives as emotional or financial dependence, mental disorder or fear of social stigma may simply reiterate her positioning as an agent, yet as one who is disempowered. The questionable decisions, inappropriate interventions, unreasonable expectations and failed responses of regulatory systems reproduce structural violence that depends on the invisibility of inequitable social power relations of gender, race, class and so on.

Recent changes to legislation in the UK have attempted to incorporate coercive control within criminal justice jurisdictions. However, the practical implications for the criminal justice system have been called into question given the system's focus on evidence of specific incidents, privileging physical violence (Bettinson and Bishop, 2015). The historical and contemporary context of the legal systems' masculinist Eurocentrism also deserves consideration. Attempts to criminalise coercive control are themselves among the ample evidence that Western legal systems have failed to address women's experiences of victimisation by their intimate partners. Where the law fails in the sense that it is unable to exercise state sovereignty to sanction offences against citizen-subjects, then sovereignty is returned to the dominant social power relations that entrap us in social inequities. In the specific case of women's victimisation, normative gender performativity that privileges masculinity emerges as the ruling social system.

The Society of Captives thesis enables us to imagine how we are implicated in the enactment of gendered norms that manifest in coercive control. As domestic violence sector workers engaged in service provision, expert producers of knowledge or intervention practitioners, we are also disciplinary subjects of self-surveillance who enact social sanctions and rewards for the gendered performativity of others as we live our everyday social lives. Making visible the entrapment of regulators, victims and perpetrators within predominantly neoliberal gender normativity makes it possible to imagine that targeting individual bearers of risk for interventions has little potential to disrupt the social power relations or transform the entrapment of women coercively controlled by their intimate partners.

CONCLUSION: TRANSFORMATIVE ACTION AND COMMUNITY

Imagining that social power relations cannot be disrupted or transformed through targeting individuals does not mean that individuals are not held responsible for their acts of violence: They are not 'absolved' of their actions through appeals to wider social, cultural and historical processes of subjectification and structural inequalities. Instead, we are able to imagine that individuals are not a 'sole cause' for the conditions of violence and therefore not *the only* site for discipline, regulation and intervention to reduce or eliminate domestic violence in our communities. This is an approach that is able to hold individuals responsible for their actions and place their actions in context. It opens possibilities for more meaningful engagement with the network of systemic and structural conditions that enable such actions to emerge (Butler, 2006). Far from providing absolution for the offender, or denying harm for the victim, the Society of Captives thesis enables analysis of the complex interplay between notions of the individual subject and subjectification embedded in, and emerging from, specific socio-cultural and temporal contexts. If we begin to think about the conditions, not causes, of intricate, multiply located tactics of coercive control, then we can open spaces for investigating the conditions of gendered violence and formulate responses to those conditions.

We began with social psychology's interest in the signal crime of Kitty Genovese's murder. One of the limitations of the parable of the 38 witnesses to Genovese's death is a constraint on social psychology's imaginative space for helping research in psychology. In a similar fashion one of the constraints of emphasising legal interventions, criminalisation and 'risky' individuals as sites for intervention into domestic violence is overlooking the transformative potentials of mobilising communities to change violence in our homes. Despite a long history of activist and community involvement bringing the issue of domestic violence to public attention, establishing services and lobbying for legislative change, community mobilisation has only recently entered the literature as a systematic approach to addressing violence in our homes (Hann and Trewartha, 2015). Recognising that social norms may be understood as 'risk or protective factors' for victimisation, the approach involves long-term, complex engagement in fostering community activism that is iterative, community led and emerging specifically from the conditions of particular communities. Focused primarily on prevention through changing norms that support women's victimisation by their partners, community mobilisation is inclusive of phases where interventions are developed for crisis situations, desistence and longer term recovery. Activities are multiple and dependent on particular communities' capacity and engagement. Examples may include such diverse strategies as networking, social marketing, involving sports teams, churches or local businesses, community conversations, art and music projects (Hann and Trewartha, 2015).

The Society of Captives thesis would remind us, though, that some communities may be excluded from actively engaging in activism for change since they are already positioned as communities of 'risky' individuals, marked by their differences from normative social expectations. The visibility of gender, race, ethnicity, age and ability norms is critically important to the process of mobilising communities in processes of social change activism. For example, in a recent stocktake of men's involvement in prevention strategies addressing violence against women, Flood (2015) found evidence of increasing participation from men in both community activist and national violence prevention campaigns. Nonetheless, he identifies several domains in which a critically informed approach to men's participation is necessary: Potential conflict with victim organisations over resources or leadership sharing; women being left to organise campaigns and events ostensibly led by men; men dominating conversations, laying claim to 'unearned expertise' or responding defensively to other men's transgression of masculine norms. Intersectional issues are also raised. Economically privileged, educated, white men may find that violence prevention activism is more readily accessible to them. Heterosexism may exclude gay men's participation and homogenise the diversity of sexual practices among men. In each of these examples, Flood draws attention to the ways in which gender norms and intersecting social inequalities could entrap community mobilisations within processes that reproduce, rather than transform, the social and historical conditions that enable coercive control that victimises women.

Community mobilisation holds promise for preventing domestic violence through shifting away from a predominant focus on identifying and disciplining risky individuals towards increasing activism for transforming social inequities. Through the Society of Captives thesis, we are able to understand that recognising and undoing our entrapment at multiple intersections of dominant norms is complex. As critical social psychologists, whether engaged in knowledge production or interventions in our communities, it is vital for us to rethink the very idea of individuals – the concept on which mainstream approaches to crime, or criminal victimisation or even 'bystander' intervention into criminal victimisation depend. Acknowledging that we are all implicated in the iterative processes through which we reproduce or change the conditions of possibility for women's victimisation opens new possibilities for engaging together to transform the structural violence that enables and supports more intimate victimisation.

REFERENCES

Adam, B., & van Loon, J. (2000). Introduction: Repositioning risk: the challenge for social theory. In B. Adam, U. Beck, & J. Van Loon (Eds.), *The risk society and beyond: Critical issues for social theory* (pp. 1–32). London: Sage.

Arrigo, B. A. (2010). De/reconstructing critical psychological jurisprudence: Strategies of resistance and struggles for justice, *International Journal of Law in Context*, 6, 363–396.

Arrigo, B. A. (2013). Managing risk and marginalizing identities on the society-of-captives thesis and the harm of social disease, *International Journal of Offender Therapy and Comparative Criminology*, 57, 672–693.

Bartky, S. L. (1998). Foucault, femininity, and the modernization of patriarchal power. In R. Weitz (Ed.), *The politics of women's bodies: Sexuality, appearance and behaviour* (pp. 25–45). Oxford: Oxford University Press.

Bettinson, V., & Bishop, C. (2015). Is the creation of a discrete offence of coercive control necessary to combat domestic violence? *Northern Ireland Legal Quarterly*, 66, 179–197.

Budgeon, S. (2013). The dynamics of gender hegemony: Femininities, masculinities and social change, *Sociology*, 48, 317–334.

Burman, E. (2016). Knowing Foucault, knowing you: 'Raced'/classed and gendered subjectivities in the pedagogical state, *Pedagogy, Culture and Society*, 24, 1–25.

Burr, V. (2005). Bystander intervention. In W. Hollway, H. Lucey, A. Phoenix, & G. Lewis (Eds.), *Critical readings in social psychology* (pp. 164–188), Milton Keynes: The Open University.

Butler, J. (1990). *Gender trouble: Feminism and the subversion of identity*. New York, NY: Routledge.

Butler, J. (1993). *Bodies that matter: On the discursive limits of sex*. London: Routledge.

Butler, J. (1997a). *Excitable speech: A politics of the performative*. London: Routledge.

Butler, J. (1997b). *The psychic life of power: Theories in subjection*. Stanford, CA: Stanford University Press.

Butler, J. (2004). Bodies and power revisited. In D. Taylor, & K. Vintges (Eds.), *Feminism and the final Foucault* (pp. 183–194). Chicago: University of Illinois Press.

Butler, J. (2006). *Precarious life: The powers of mourning and violence*. London & New York: Verso.

Butler, J. (2009). Performativity, precarity and sexual politics, *AIBR-Revista de Antropologia Iberoamericana*, 4, i–xiii.

Callaghan, J. E., Alexander, J. H., Sixsmith, J., & Fellin, L. C. (2018). Beyond 'Witnessing': Children's experiences of coercive control in domestic violence and abuse, *Journal of Interpersonal Violence*, *33*(10), 1551–1581.

Campbell, C., & Mannell, J. (2016). Conceptualising the agency of highly marginalised women: Intimate partner violence in extreme settings, *Global Public Health*, *11*, 1–16.

Chamberlain, K., & Hodgetts, D. (2008). Social psychology and media: Critical considerations. *Social and Personality Psychology Compass*, *2*(3), 1109–1125.

Cherry, F. (1995). *The stubborn particulars of social psychology: Essays on the research process*. London: Routledge.

Coombes, L., & Morgan, M. (2015). South Pacific: Tensions of space in our place. In I. Parker (Ed.), *Handbook of critical psychology* (pp. 444–453). London & New York: Routledge.

Coombes, L., Denne, S., & Rangiwananga, M. (2016). Social justice and community change. In W. W. Waikaremoana, J. S. Feather, N. R. Robertson, & J. J. Rucklidge. *Professional practice of psychology in Aotearoa New Zealand* (3rd edn., pp. 437–449). Wellington: The New Zealand Psychological Society.

Davis, A. (1997). Race and criminalization: Black Americans and the punishment industry. In W. Lubiano (Ed.), *The house that race built* (pp. 264–279). New York: Vintage Books.

Davis, A. (2013). *The meaning of freedom: And other difficult dialogues*. San Francisco: City Lights Books.

Davis, M. S., O'Sullivan, C. S., Susser, K., & Fields, M. D. (2010). Custody evaluations when there are allegations of domestic violence: Practices, beliefs and recommendations of professional evaluators. Retrieved from https://www.ncjrs.gov/App/Publications/abstract.aspx?ID=256422%20

DeKeseredy, W. S., & Schwartz, M. D. (2010). Theoretical and definitional issues in violence against women. In C. M. Renzetti, J. L. Edleson, & R. K. Bergen (Eds.), *Sourcebook on violence against women* (3rd edn., pp. 3–22). California & London: Sage Publications. (1st edn. 2000).

Domestic Violence Act. (1995). Public Act 1995 No 86. Reprint, 1 October, 2014. Retrieved from http://www.legislation.govt.nz/act/public/1995/0086/latest/DLM371926.html

Dostal, J. M. (2008). The workfare illusion: Re-examining the concept and the 'British case', *Social Policy & Administration*, *42*, 19–42.

Dutton, M. A., & Goodman, L. A. (2005). Coercion in intimate partner violence: Toward a new conceptualization, *Sex Roles*, *52*, 743–756.

Elizabeth, V. (2015). From domestic violence to coercive control: Towards the recognition of oppressive intimacy in the Family Court, *New Zealand Sociology*, *30*(2), 26–43.

Elizabeth, V., Gavey, G., & Tolmie, J. (2012). 'He's just swapped his fists for the system.' The governance of gender through custody law, *Gender & Society*, *26*, 239–260.

Family Violence Death Review Committee. (2016). *Fifth Annual Report: January 2015–December 2015*. Wellington: Family Violence Death Review Committee.

Farvid, P., & Braun, V. (2013). Casual sex as 'not a natural act' and other regimes of truth about heterosexuality, *Feminism and Psychology*, *23*, 359–378.

Fischer, P., Krueger, J. I., Greitemeyer, T., Vogrincic, C., Kastenmüller, A., Frey, D., Moritz, H., Wicher, M., & Kainbacher, M. (2011). The bystander-effect: A meta-analytic review on bystander intervention in dangerous and non-dangerous emergencies, *Psychological Bulletin*, *137*, 517–537.

Fleury-Steiner, R. E., Miller, S. L., Maloney, S., & Postel, E. B. (2014). 'No contact, except...' Visitation decisions in protection orders for intimate partner abuse, *Feminist Criminology*, *11*, 3–22.

Flood, M. (2015). Work with men to end violence against women: A critical stocktake, *Culture, Health & Sexuality*, *17*, 159–176.

Foucault, M. (1977). *Discipline and punish: The birth of the prison* (trans. A. Sheridan). London: Penguin.

Foucault, M. (1980). *Power/knowledge: Selected interviews and other writings*, 1972–1977. London: Harvester.

Foucault, M. (1982). The subject and power. In H. L. Dreyfus, & P. Rabinow (Eds.), *Michel Foucault: Beyond structuralism and hermeneutics*. Brighton, MA: The Harvester Press.

Gadd, D., & Corr, M. L. (2017). Beyond typologies: Foregrounding meaning and motive in domestic violence perpetration, *Deviant Behavior*, *38*(7), 781–791.

Gallo, M. M. (2014). The parable of Kitty Genovese, the *New York Times*, and the erasure of lesbianism, *Journal of the History of Sexuality*, *23*, 273–294.

Gavey, N. (1989). Feminist poststructuralism and discourse analysis: Contributions to feminist psychology, *Psychology of Women Quarterly*, *13*, 459–475.

Geller, E. S. (2016). The psychology of AC4P behaviour. In E. S. Geller (Ed.), *Applied psychology: Actively caring for people* (pp. 45–82). Cambridge: Cambridge University Press.

Gill, R. (2016). Post-postfeminism? New feminist visibilities in postfeminist times, *Feminist Media Studies*, *16*, 610–630.

Gill, R., & Donaghue, N. (2013). As if Postfeminism had come true: The turn to agency in cultural studies of 'sexualisation'. In S. Madhok, A. Phillips, & K. Wilson (Eds.), *Gender, agency, and coercion* (pp. 240–258). London: Palgrave Macmillan.

Gough, B., McFadden, M., & McDonald, M. (2013). *Critical social psychology: An introduction*. London: Palgrave Macmillan.

Griggs, R. A. (2015). The Kitty Genovese Story in introductory Psychology textbooks fifty years later, *Teaching of Psychology*, *42*, 149–152.

Gulliver, P., & Fanslow, J. (2015). *Risk assessment: What is it and how can it be applied in family violence?* Auckland, NZ: New Zealand Family Violence Clearinghouse, University of Auckland.

Hamnet, C. (2014). Shrinking the welfare state: The structure, geography and impact of British government benefit cuts, *Transactions of the Institute of British Geographers*, *39*, 490–503.

Hann, S., & Trewartha, C. (2015). *Creating change: Mobilising New Zealand communities to prevent family violence*. Auckland, NZ: New Zealand Family Violence Clearinghouse, University of Auckland.

Hayes, S., & Jeffries, S. (2013). Why do they keep going back? Exploring women's discursive experiences of intimate partner abuse, *International Journal of Criminology and Sociology*, *2*, 57–71.

Herbert, R., & Mackenzie, D. (2014). *The way forward: An integrated system of intimate partner violence and child abuse and neglect in New Zealand*. Wellington: The Impact Collective.

Hester, M. (2013) Who does what to whom? Gender and domestic violence perpetrators in English police records, *European Journal of Criminology*, *10*, 623–637.

Holt, S. (2015). Post-separation fathering and domestic abuse: Challenges and contradictions, *Child Abuse Review*, *24*, 210–222.

Hook, D. (2001) The 'disorders of discourse', *Theoria: A Journal of Social and Political Theory*, *97*, 41–68.

Innes, M. (2003). 'Signal crimes': Detective work, mass media and constructing collective memory. In P. Mason (Ed.), *Criminal visions. Media representations of crime and justice* (pp. 49–69). London & New York: Routledge.

Innes, M. (2004). Signal crimes and signal disorders: Notes on deviance as communicative action, *The British Journal of Sociology*, *55*, 335–355.

Jeffries, S. (2016). In the best interests of the abuser: Coercive control, child custody proceedings and the 'expert' assessments that guide judicial determinations, *Laws*, *5*, 14–31.

Jenney, A., Mishna, F., Alaggia, R., & Scott, K. (2014). Doing the right thing? (Re) Considering risk assessment and safety planning in child protection work with domestic violence cases, *Children and Youth Services Review*, *47*, 92–101.

Jewkes, R., Flood, M., & Lang, J. (2015). From work with men and boys to changes of social norms and reduction of inequities in gender relations: A conceptual shift in prevention of violence against women and girls, *The Lancet*, *385*, 1580–1589.

Kelly, L. (2016). Moving in the shadows: Introduction. In Y. Rehman, L. Kelly, & H. Siddiqui (Eds.), *Moving in the Shadows: Violence in Black, Minority Ethnic and Refugee families* (pp. 1–11). London & New York: Routledge.

Kelly, L., Adler, J. R., Horvath, M. A. H., Lovett, J., Coulson, M., Kernohan, D., & Gray, M. (2013) *Evaluation of the pilot of domestic violence protection orders. Research Report (76)*. London: Home Office. Retrieved from https://www.gov.uk/government/uploads/system/uploads/attachment_data/file/260897/horr76.pdf

Kelly, L., & Westmarland, N. (2014). New approaches to assessing effectiveness and outcomes of domestic violence perpetrator programs. In H. Johnson, B. S. Fisher, & V. Jaquier (Eds.), *Critical issues on violence against women: International perspectives and promising strategies* (pp. 183–198). London & New York: Routledge.

Kelly, L., & Westmarland, N. (2015). *Domestic violence perpetrator programmes: Steps towards change. Project Mirabel Final Report*. London & Durham: London Metropolitan University and Durham University. Retrieved from https://www.dur.ac.uk/resources/criva/ProjectMirabalfinalreport.pdf

Laing, L. (2017). Secondary victimization: Domestic violence survivors navigating the family law system, *Violence Against Women*, *23*(11), 1314–1335.

Lurigio, A. J. (2015). Crime narratives, dramatizations, and the legacy of the Kitty Genovese murder. A half century of half truths, *Criminal Justice and Behavior*, *42*, 782–789.

Lynch, I., & Maree, D. J. F. (2013). Negotiating heteronormativity: Exploring South African bisexual women's constructions of marriage and family, *Feminism & Psychology*, *23*, 459–477.

Manning, R., Levine, M., & Collins, A. (2007). The Kitty Genovese murder and the social psychology of helping: The parable of the 38 witnesses, *American Psychologist*, *62*: 555–562.

Messing, J. T., Campbell, J., Wilson, J. S., Brown, S., & Patchell, B. (2017). The Lethality Screen: The predictive validity of an intimate partner violence risk assessment for use by first responders, *Journal of Interpersonal Violence*, *32*(2), 205–226.

Ministry of Justice (2014). *New Zealand crime and safety survey. Main findings*. Wellington, NZ: Ministry of Justice. Retrieved from http://www.justice.govt.nz/assets/Documents/Publications/NZCASS-201602-Main-Findings-Report-Updated.pdf

Morgan, M., & Coombes, L. (2016). Protective mothers: Women's understandings of protecting children in the context of legal interventions into intimate partner violence, *The Australian Community Psychologist*, *28*, 55–74.

Northcott, M. (2014). *Intimate partner violence risk assessment tools: A review*. Canada: Department of Justice. Ministère de la Justice.

Parker, I. (1990). Discourse: Definitions and contradictions, *Philosophical Psychology*, *3*, 187–204.

Parker, I. (2015). Introduction. Principles and positions. In I. Parker (Ed.), *Handbook of critical psychology* (pp. 1–9). London and New York: Routledge.

Paulin, J., & Edgar, N. (2013). *Towards freedom from violence: New Zealand family violence statistics disaggregated by ethnicity*. Wellington NZ: Office of Ethnic Affairs. Te Tari Matāwaka.

Phillips, R., Kelly, L., & Westmarland, N. (2013). Domestic violence perpetrator programmes: an historical overview, London & Durham: London Metropolitan University and Durham University. Retrieved from http://dro.dur.ac.uk/11512/1/11512.pdf

Reidy, D. E., Berke, D. S., Gentile, B., & Zeichner, A. (2014). Man enough? Masculine discrepancy stress and intimate partner violence, *Personality and Individual Differences*, *68*, 160–164.

Riggs, D. W., & Augoustinos, M. (2005). The psychic life of colonial power: Racialised subjectivities, bodies and methods, *Journal of Community & Applied Social Psychology*, *15*, 461–477.

Risman, B. J., & Davis, G. (2013). From sex roles to gender structure, *Current Sociology Review*, *61*, 733–755.

Rivera, E. A., Sullivan, C. M., & Zeoli, A. M. (2012). Secondary victimization of abused mothers by family court mediators, *Feminist Criminology*, *7*, 234–252.

Robertson, N., Busch, R., D'Souza, R., Lam Sheung, F., Anand, R., Balzer, R., Simpson, A., & Paina, D. (2007). *Living at the cutting edge: Women's experiences of protection orders. Volume 2: What's to be done? A critical analysis of statutory and practice approaches to domestic violence*. Hamilton, NZ: University of Waikato.

Russo, N. F., & Pirlott, A. (2006). Gender-based violence, *Annals of the New York Academy of Sciences*, *1087*(1), 178–205.

Stark, E. (2007). *Coercive control: The entrapment of women in personal life*. Oxford & New York: Oxford University Press.

Stark, E. (2010). Do violent acts equal abuse? Resolving the gender parity/asymmetry dilemma, *Sex Roles*, *62*, 201–211.

Stark, E. (2013). Coercive control. In N. Lombard, & L. McMillan (Eds.), *Violence against women: Current theory and practice in domestic abuse, sexual violence and exploitation* (pp. 17–33). London and Philadelphia: Jessica Kingsley Publishers.

Teo, T. (2015) Critical psychology: A geography of intellectual engagement and resistance, *American Psychologist*, *70*, 243–254.

Tsianos, V., Papadopoulos, D., & Stephenson, N. (2012). This is class war from above and they are winning it: What is to be done? *Rethinking Marxism: A Journal of Economics, Culture & Society*, *24*, 448–457.

Van Bommel, M., Van Prooijen, J. W., Elffers, H., & Van Lange, P. A. (2016). Booze, bars, and bystander behavior: People who consumed alcohol help faster in the presence of others, *Frontiers in Psychology*, *7*, Article 128: 1–7.

Van Heugten, K. (2011). Theorizing active bystanders as change agents in workplace bullying of social workers, *Families in Society: The Journal of Contemporary Social Services*, *92*, 219–224.

Watts, R., Linke, S., Murray, E., & Barker, C. (2015). Calling the shots: Young professional women's relationship with alcohol, *Feminism & Psychology*, *25*, 219–234.

Westmarland, N., & Kelly, L. (2012). Why extending measurements of 'success' in domestic violence perpetrator programmes matters for social work, *British Journal of Social Work*, *43*, 1092–1110.

Westmarland, N., & Kelly, L. (2016). Domestic violence: The increasing tensions between experience, theory, research, policy and practice. In R. Matthews (Ed.), *What is to be done about Crime and Punishment?* (pp. 31–55). London: Palgrave Macmillan.

Williams, C. R. (2008). Compassion, suffering and the self: A moral psychology of social justice, *Current Sociology*, *56*, 5–24.

Wojnicka, K., Scambor, C., & Kraus, H. (2016). New pathways in the evaluation of programmes for men who perpetrate violence against their female partners, *Evaluation and Program Planning*, *57*, 39–47.

World Health Organization. (2013). *Global and regional estimates of violence against women: Prevalence and health effects of intimate partner violence and non-partner sexual violence*. Geneva: WHO.

Zeoli, A. M., Rivera, E. A., Sullivan, C. M., & Kubiak, S. (2013). Post-separation abuse of women and their children: Boundary-setting and family court utilization among victimized mothers, *Journal of Family Violence*, *28*, 547–560.

Index

Page numbers in **bold** indicate tables and in *italic* indicate figures.